Frommer's®

ITALY 2020
14th Edition

By Stephen Brewer, Elizabeth Heath, Stephen Keeling, Michelle Schoenung, Donald Strachan

D0032910

FrommerMedia LLC

Published by
Frommer Media LLC

Frommer's Complete Guide to Italy 2020, 14th Edition
ISBN 978-1-62887-474-7 (paper), 978-1-62887-475-4 (e-book)

Editorial Director: Pauline Frommer
Editor: Holly Hughes
Production Editor: Lindsay Conner
Cartographer: Liz Puhl
Photo Editor: Meghan Lamb
Assistant Photo Editor: Phil Vinke

For information on our other products or services, see www.frommers.com.

Frommer Media LLC also publishes its books in a variety of electronic formats. Some content that appears in print may not be available in electronic formats.

Manufactured in China

5 4 3 2 1

HOW TO CONTACT US

In researching this book, we discovered many wonderful places—hotels, restaurants, shops, and more. We're sure you'll find others. Please tell us about them, so we can share the information with your fellow travelers in upcoming editions. If you were disappointed with a recommendation, we'd love to know that, too. Please write to: Support@FrommerMedia.com

FROMMER'S STAR RATINGS SYSTEM

Every hotel, restaurant and attraction listed in this guide has been ranked for quality and value. Here's what the stars mean:

★ Recommended
★★ Highly Recommended
★★★ A must! Don't miss!

AN IMPORTANT NOTE

The world is a dynamic place. Hotels change ownership, restaurants hike their prices, museums alter their opening hours, and buses and trains change their routings. And all of this can occur in the several months after our authors have visited, inspected, and written about these hotels, restaurants, museums, and transportation services. Though we have made valiant efforts to keep all our information fresh and up-to-date, some few changes can inevitably occur in the periods before a revised edition of this guidebook is published. So please bear with us if a tiny number of the details in this book have changed. Please also note that we have no responsibility or liability for any inaccuracy or errors or omissions, or for inconvenience, loss, damage, or expenses suffered by anyone as a result of assertions in this guide.

CONTENTS

LIST OF MAPS

ABOUT THE AUTHORS

Stephen Brewer is an editor and writer with a focus on European coverage. In addition to magazine articles, he has been writing travel guides for three decades, including several for Frommer's. Stephen divides his time between Manhattan and Italy.

Elizabeth Heath, a long-time contributor to Frommer's, is a writer and editor based in Umbria, central Italy, from where she writes about travel and culinary adventures in Italy, Europe, and farther afield. Her work has appeared in HuffPost, The Telegraph, Cara, and other outlets. Her first edition guidebook on the architecture of Rome debuts in 2019. Read more of her work at www.elizabethfheath.com.

Stephen Keeling has been traveling to Italy since 1985 and covering his favorite nation for Frommer's since 2007. He has written for *The Independent, Daily Telegraph*, various travel magazines, and numerous travel guides as well as the award-winning *Frommer's Florence, Tuscany & Umbria*. Stephen resides in New York City.

Michelle Schoenung is an American journalist and translator in Milan who relocated to the Belpaese in 2000 for what was to be a yearlong adventure. Almost 2 decades later, she is pleased that Milan has evolved into a much more international and cosmopolitan city and has shed its image of merely being a foggy northern Italian business hub. Her writings and translations have appeared in magazines and books in the United States and Italy. In her free time, she likes to read, run, travel, and explore the city with her two rambunctious Italian-American bambini.

Donald Strachan is a travel journalist who has written about Italy for publications worldwide, including *National Geographic Traveler, The Guardian, Sunday Telegraph*, CNN.com, and many others. He has also written several Italy guidebooks for Frommer's, including *Frommer's EasyGuide to Rome, Florence, and Venice*. He lives in London, England. For more, see www.donaldstrachan.com.

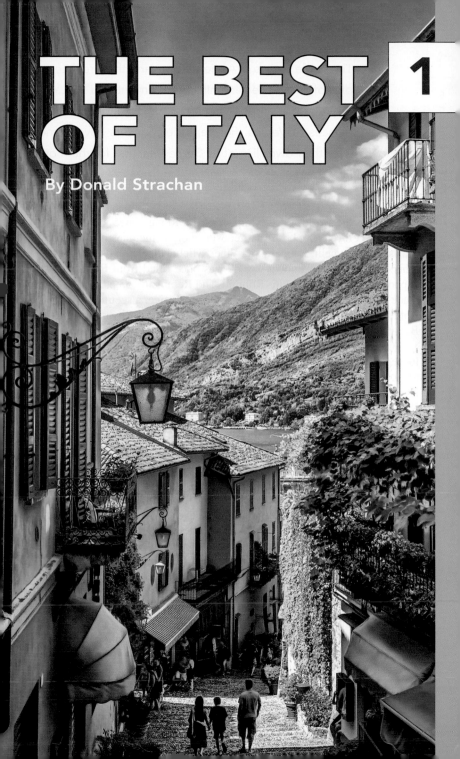

THE BEST OF ITALY

1

By Donald Strachan

Just think the word "Italy" and you can already see it. The noble stones of Ancient Rome and the Greek temples of Sicily. The wine hills of Piedmont and Tuscany, the ruins of Pompeii, the secret canals and crumbling palaces of Venice. For centuries, visitors have come here looking for their own slice of *La Dolce Vita*, and for the most part, they have found it.

Nowhere in the world felt the impact of the Renaissance more than its birthplace, **Florence,** whose vast repository of art includes works left by Masaccio, Botticelli, Leonardo da Vinci, Michelangelo, and many, many others. Much of the "known world" was once ruled from **Rome,** a city supposedly founded by twins Romulus and Remus in 753 B.C. There's no place with more artistic treasures—not even **Venice,** a seemingly impossible floating city whose beauty and history were shaped by trade with the Byzantine and Islamic worlds to the east.

Of course, there's more. Long before Italy was a country, it was a loose collection of city-states. Centuries of alliance and rivalry left a legacy of art and architecture in **Verona,** with its Shakespearean romance and intact Roman Arena; and in **Mantua,** which blossomed during the Renaissance under the Gonzaga dynasty. **Padua** and its sublime Giotto frescoes are within easy reach of Venice, too. In **Siena,** ethereal art and Gothic palaces survive, barely altered since their 1300s heyday.

A millennium earlier, the eruption of Vesuvius in A.D. 79 preserved **Pompeii** and **Herculaneum** under volcanic ash. They remain the best places to get close-up with everyday life in the Roman era. The buildings of Ancient Greece still stand at **Paestum,** in Campania, and at sites on **Sicily,** the Mediterranean's largest island. Cave dwellings, frescoed rupestrian churches, and even a rock cathedral honeycomb the rocks of **Matera,** in the unspoiled Basilicata region.

The corrugated, vine-clad hills of the **Chianti** and the cypress-studded, emerald-green expanses of the **Val d'Orcia** serve up iconic images of **Tuscany.** Adventurous walkers of all ages can hike between the coastal villages of the **Cinque Terre,** where you can roam untroubled by the 21st century. Whether it's seafood along the Sicilian coast, pizza in **Naples,** pasta in **Bologna,** pesto in **Genoa,** or the red Barolo and Barbaresco wines of **Piedmont,** your taste buds are in for their own adventure. For shoppers, **Milan** and Florence are centers of world fashion. Welcome to *La Bella Italia.*

PREVIOUS PAGE: **Bellagio, one of several beautiful resort towns on Lake Como.**

Exploring a tiny harbor in Riomaggiore, one of the Cinque Terre towns.

ITALY'S best AUTHENTIC EXPERIENCES

o **Dining Italian style:** There is no pastime here more cherished than eating—even better, eating outdoors with a view of a medieval church or a vineyard. There's no such thing as a single "Italian" cuisine: You'll discover each region and city has its own beloved recipes, handed down over generations. *Buon appetito!*

o **Exploring Rome's Mercato di Testaccio:** The opening of a modern version of Testaccio's historic market signaled a rebirth of this gritty, genuine neighborhood south of the Aventine. The bustling market is a culinary and cultural treat, where local chefs jostle elbow-to-elbow with feisty *signore,* clamoring for the best *pomodori, mozzarella di bufala,* and *trippa* (tripe). Sustain yourself with street food as you soak up this slice of real Rome. See p. 157.

o **Cicchetti and a spritz in Venice:** *Cicchetti*—tapas-like small servings, usually eaten while standing at a bar—are a Venetian tradition. To make the experience complete, accompany them with a spritz made with Aperol and sparkling Prosecco wine from the Veneto hills. Find many of the best spots on the San Polo side of the Rialto Bridge. See p. 441.

o **Catching an opera at Verona's Arena:** In summer, Italians enjoy opera under the stars. The setting for Italy's largest and most famous outdoor festival is the ancient Arena di Verona, a site grand enough to

Shopping in Testaccio Market offers a slice of the real Rome.

accommodate as many elephants as might be needed for "Aïda." See p. 458.

o **Feeling the modern pulse of historic Bologna:** The youthful exuberance of Bologna, Europe's oldest university town, reveals itself amid medieval palaces; rowdy, renowned food markets; and 25 miles of portico-sheltered sidewalks. See chapter 8.

o **Slowing down to Italy pace:** Nothing happens quickly here: Linger over a glass of wine from the Tuscan hills, slurp a gelato made with seasonal fruit, enjoy the evening *passeggiata* (ritual walk) just like the locals. They call it Slow Food for a good reason.

ITALY'S most memorable RESTAURANTS

o **Ottava Nota** (Palermo): Palermo's old Arab quarter, the Kalsa buzzes these days, especially at this sleek restaurant with its creative spin on Sicilian cuisine. Ingredients come straight from the city's famous produce markets. See p. 758.

o **Osteria dell'Enoteca** (Florence): When successful wine-bar owners open a restaurant, you know the *vino* will be first rate. Osteria dell'Enoteca doesn't disappoint, but also serves food, which unites the best of Tuscany's traditional ingredients and a light, contemporary cooking style. Their stone-and-slate dining room is an atmospheric spot for a special occasion. See p. 220.

- **Taverna San Giuseppe** (Siena): A brick-vaulted room from the 12th century is a characterful setting for hand-rolled *pici* with a *ragù* of *cinghiale* (wild boar), ricotta-filled *gnudi*, and other expert takes on Tuscan comfort food. It's a place travelers long remember. See p. 246.

- **Ai Artisti** (Venice): Venice's culinary rep is founded on the quality of the catch from its famous fish market. At Ai Artisti, both *primi* and *secondi* feature the freshest fish from the lagoon and farther afield. See p. 444.

ITALY'S most charming HOTELS

- **Villa Spalletti Trivelli** (Rome): Recent upgrades have only enhanced the unique experience of staying in a neoclassical mansion in the middle of the capital. Opulence plus impeccable, understated service comes at a price, of course. When our lottery numbers come up, we will be booking a stay here—a long one. See p. 134.

- **Santa Caterina** (Amalfi): Set in fragrant citrus groves above the sea, Santa Caterina is not outrageously posh, just magically transporting. Ceramic tiles, a smattering of antiques, sea-view terraces, a garden path leading to a private beach—it's worth the splurge. Shoulder season rates and special offers bring prices out of the stratosphere. See p. 665.

- **Palazzo Tolomei** (Florence): A palace where Raphael once stayed—perhaps even giving its owners a painting to pay his rent—sounds grand indeed, and you won't be disappointed. The Renaissance layout and a baroque redecoration from the 1600s are intact. See p. 210.

- **Frances' Lodge Relais** (Siena): Nestled on a sunny hillside, this family olive estate has many quiet corners, a pool in the garden, richly hued rooms, and suites accented with family heirlooms. The towers of Siena beckon in the near distance. See p. 242.

- **Fra I Sassi Residence** (Matera): Staying in a cave is an experience in itself, especially when accommodations are as stylish and comfortable as these. All open onto a meandering, sunny terrace with a front-row seat on a sculpted cluster of cave dwellings that tumble down surrounding cliffs. See p. 711.

- **Hotel Mediterraneo** (Rome): Upscale Art Deco Hotel Mediterraneo is the flagship of a trio of hotels near Termini Station run by the Bettoja family. Others are even more budget-friendly, but all offer vintage charm, old-school comforts, and warm service from a loyal, longtime staff. They don't make 'em like this anymore. See p 137.

ITALY'S best FOR FAMILIES

o **Climbing Pisa's wonky tower** (Tuscany): Are we walking up or down? Pleasantly disoriented kids are bound to ask as you spiral your way to the rooftop-viewing balcony atop one of the world's most famous pieces of botched engineering. It's an easy day trip from Florence; 8 is the minimum age for climbing. See p. 300.

o **Visiting the Acquario di Genova** (Liguria): Genoa's star attraction may not be as large as some North American super-aquariums, but it is beautifully designed (by architect Renzo Piano) and houses sharks, seals, and much weird and wonderful sea life, on a harborfront of family-friendly attractions. See p. 553.

o **Exploring underground Naples:** There's more to Naples than you can see at eye level. Head below its maze of streets to walk the remains of ancient Greek and Roman cities—not just your typical agora and forum, but creepy catacombs used for centuries to bury the Christian dead and tunnels that sheltered refugees from an 1884 cholera epidemic and the bombs of World War II. See p. 603.

o **Enjoying a trip to an artisan gelateria:** When it comes to Italian ice cream, choose carefully—Smurf-blue or bubblegum-pink flavors are a sure sign of color enhancers, and beware of ice crystals and fluffy heaps that betray additives and pumped-in air. Authentic *gelaterie* produce good stuff from scratch daily, with fresh seasonal produce; look for a short, all-natural ingredient list posted proudly for all to see. Check "Where to Eat" and "Gelato" sections in individual chapters.

Bottlenose dolphins swim in Genoa's Acquario di Genova.

Rome (p. 144) and Florence (p. 220) have several genuine gelato artisans. Believe us when we say: You will taste the difference.

o **Discovering an untrammeled beach in Puglia:** Some of Italy's best beaches are in the southeast, often an easy hike through forests on well-marked paths. The best white sands include Torre Guaceto, north of Brindisi; Porto Selvaggio, north of Gallipoli; and Punta della Suina, in a turquoise bay south of Gallipoli. See chapter 14.

ITALY'S most OVERRATED

o **Circus Maximus** (Rome): Visitors with Hollywood visions of Ben Hur racing his chariot around a majestic arena are in for a major let-down: Pillaged of its marble and stone over the centuries, the circus today is little more than a big dusty oval field beside a Metro station. A recently opened archaeological exhibit cranks up the interest a little. But still, don't place this high on your must-see list. See p. 91.

o **Ponte Vecchio** (Florence): Sorry, lovers, this isn't even the prettiest bridge in Florence, let alone one of the world's great spots for romantics. It's packed at all hours, and hemmed in by shops that cater mostly to tourism. For a special moment with a loved one—perhaps even to "pop the question"—head downstream one bridge to the Ponte Santa Trínita. Built in the 1560s by Bartolomeo Ammanati, its triple-ellipse design is pure elegance in stone. At dusk, it is also one of Florence's best spots to photograph the Ponte Vecchio . . . if you must. See p. 189.

o **Capri** (Campania): Capri can be enchanting, but the island falls victim to its own popularity. Arrive in midsummer on a day excursion, and you'll corral through the gardens of Augustus, crowd into a boat to the Blue Grotto, and shell out 5€ for a bottle of water. Solution: Spend the night here, to properly enjoy the scenery and sparkling-white towns after day trippers leave, or to walk scented flower paths early on a spring morning. See p. 679.

ITALY'S best MUSEUMS

o **Vatican Museums** (Rome): The 100 galleries of the Musei Vaticani are loaded with papal treasures accumulated over the centuries. Musts include the Sistine Chapel, such ancient Greek and Roman sculptures as "Laocoön" and "Belvedere Apollo," room after room of Raphael's frescoes (among them his "School of Athens"), and endless collections of Greco-Roman antiquities and European Renaissance art. See p. 82.

o **Galleria degli Uffizi** (Florence): This U-shaped High Renaissance building designed by Giorgio Vasari was the administrative headquarters, or *uffizi* (offices), for the dukes of Tuscany when the Medici called the shots in Florence. It's now the crown jewel of Europe's fine-art museums, housing the world's greatest collection of Renaissance

Michelangelo's Sistine Chapel, Vatican Museums.

paintings, including iconic works in revamped rooms dedicated to Botticelli, Leonardo da Vinci, and Michelangelo. See p. 181.

o **Accademia** (Venice): One of Europe's great museums houses an unequaled array of Venetian paintings, exhibited chronologically from the 13th to the 18th century. Walls are hung with works by Bellini, Carpaccio, Giorgione, Titian, and Tintoretto. See p. 416.

o **Museo Archeologico Nazionale** (Naples): Come here to see mosaics and frescoes from Pompeii and Herculaneum—the original of a much-reproduced "Cave Canem" ("Beware of the Dog") mosaic, the Villa of the Papyri frescoes—and much else, including the "Farnese Bull," which once decorated Rome's Terme di Caracalla, and some of the finest statuary to survive from ancient Europe. See p. 600.

o **Museo Egizio** (Turin): With a dazzling refit, Turin's Egyptology museum has doubled in size, with more space than ever for displaying the finest collection of Egyptian artifacts outside Cairo. See p. 552.

o **Santa Maria della Scala** (Siena): The building is as much the star as the collections—the frescoed wards, ancient chapels, sacristy, and labyrinthine basement of a medieval hospital that was still housing patients until the 1990s. See p. 241.

ITALY'S best FREE THINGS TO DO

o **Watching the sun rise over the Roman Forum:** A short stroll from the Capitoline Hill down Via del Campidoglio to Via di Monte Tarpeo brings you to a perfect outlook: The terrace behind the Michelangelo-designed square, an ideal photo op when the sun rises behind the Temple of Saturn, illuminating the archaeological complex below in pink-orange light. Early risers can reward themselves with breakfast from bakeries in the nearby Jewish Ghetto. See p. 93.

o **Basking in the Lights of the Renaissance:** At dusk, make the steep climb up to the ancient church of San Miniato al Monte, Florence. Sit down on the steps and watch the city begin its evening twinkle. See p. 202.

o **Discovering you're hopelessly lost in Venice:** You haven't experienced Venice until you have turned a corner, convinced you're on the way to somewhere, only to find yourself smack against a canal with no bridge. All you can do is shrug, smile, and give the city's maze of narrow streets another try, because getting lost in Venice is a pleasure. See chapter 9.

o **Driving the Amalfi Coast:** The SS163, "road of 1,000 bends," hugs vertical cliffs and deep gorges, cutting through olive groves, lemon terraces, and whitewashed villages—against a background of the bluest ocean you can picture. One of the world's classic drives, it provokes fear, nausea, and wonder in equal doses. The secret is to make sure someone else is at the wheel. Someone you trust. See p. 638.

o **Surrendering to the madness of a Palermo market:** In Sicily's capital—a crossroads between East and West for some 2,000 years—the chaotic, colorful street theater is a vignette of a culture that often

The Pantheon, Rome's best-preserved ancient building.

feels more Middle Eastern than European. The Vucciria isn't what it was, however: Focus on the Capo and Ballarò markets. See p. 760.

ITALY'S best ARCHITECTURAL LANDMARKS

o **Brunelleschi's dome** (Florence): It took the genius of Filippo Brunelleschi to raise a vast dome over the huge hole in Florence's cathedral roof. Though rejected for a commission to cast the Baptistery doors, Filippo didn't sulk. He went away and became the city's greatest architect, and creator of one of Europe's most recognizable landmarks. See p. 182.

o **The Gothic center of Siena** (Tuscany): The shell-shaped Piazza del Campo stands at the heart of one of Europe's best-preserved medieval cities. Steep canyonlike streets, icons of Gothic architecture like the Palazzo Pubblico, and Madonnas painted on gilded altarpieces transport you back to a time before the Renaissance. See p. 235.

Detail of a preserved ancient fresco from Pompeii.

o **Pompeii** (Campania): When Mt. Vesuvius blew its top in A.D. 79, it buried Pompeii under molten lava and ash, ending the lives of perhaps 35,000 citizens and suspending the city in a time capsule. Today, still in the menacing shadow of the volcano, this poignant ghost town can be coaxed into life with little imagination. See p. 624.

o **Valley of the Temples, Agrigento** (Sicily): Seven Greek temples overlooking the sea were built to impress, and their honey-colored columns and pediments still do. Seeing these romantic ruins—some, like the Temple of Concordia, beautifully preserved; others like the Temple of Juno, timeworn but still proud—is an experience of a lifetime. See p. 793.

o **Beehive towns of the southeast** (Puglia): In the hinterlands of the Adriatic coast, storybook *trulli* dwellings enchant travelers to Alberobello and the Valle d'Itria. And once you're here, a bonus: The mazelike "white cities" of Ostuni, Martina Franca, Locorotondo, and Cisternino. See chapter 14.

best UNDISCOVERED ITALY

o **Drinking your coffee al banco:** Italians—especially city dwellers—don't often linger in a piazza sipping their morning cappuccino. For them, a *caffè* is a pit stop: They stand at the counter *(al banco),* throw back the bitter elixir, and continue on their way, reinforced by a hit of caffeine. You will also save a chunk of change drinking Italian style, at least 50 percent less than the sit-down price, even in the grand baroque surrounds of Turin's Piazza San Carlo. See p. 159.

o **Genoa's UNESCO center:** Don't be fooled by a rough, industrial exterior: Genoa has Italy's largest *centro storico,* with architecture to rival Venice. A restored old port, the Palazzo Reale, and the *palazzi* of Strada Nuova are just a few highlights of a trading city that got rich from the sea. See chapter 11.

o **The art at Padua's Cappella degli Scrovegni:** Step aside, Sistine Chapel. Art lovers armed with binoculars behold this scene in awe, a cycle of frescoes by Giotto that revolutionized 14th-century painting; it's the most important work of art leading up to the Renaissance, and visiting is an unforgettable, intimate experience. See p. 455.

o **The canals of Treviso:** Venice's near-neighbor has canals of its own, and much thinner crowds, even in peak season. Visit its atmospheric old fish market and city churches adorned with artworks by Tommaso da Modena. See p. 460.

o **The view from T Fondaco dei Tedeschi:** This Venice department store—renovated by stellar architect Rem Koolhas, no less—was once an elegant *palazzo* beside the Grand Canal. Views from its free rooftop deck are even more spectacular than the opulent goods inside. See p. 413.

ITALY'S best ACTIVE ADVENTURES

o **Seeing Ferrara on two wheels:** Join bike-mad *Ferraresi* as they zip along narrow, cycle-friendly lanes that snake through the old center, past the Castello Estense and the Renaissance elegance of Palazzo Schifanoia. You can also bike a circuit atop the city's medieval walls. See p. 368.

o **Kayaking or paddle-boarding around Venice:** Why let the gondoliers have all fun? Piloting a rented kayak or stand-up paddleboard gives you a different angle on the noble palaces and quiet canalside corners of Italy's fairytale floating city. See p. 428.

o **Riding the Monte Bianco Skyway, Valle d'Aosta:** In Italy's far northwestern corner, you can ride a revolving cable car high on Europe's tallest mountain, departing from the hiking, biking, and skiing resort of Courmayeur. Standing 4,810m (15,780 ft.) tall on the

Paddleboarding on the canals of Venice.

border between France and Italy, Monte Bianco ("Mont Blanc" to the French) is flanked by perilous glaciers and jagged granite peaks. The cableways are pricey, but unforgettable. See p. 542.

o **Walking the Cinque Terre** (Liguria): For sheer beauty, we love the 3-mile path from Corniglia to Vernazza and a 2-mile section from Vernazza to Monterosso, but the entire Cinque Terre area is rewarding: Narrow paths skirt past terraced vineyards; olive and lemon groves hover over the sapphire Mediterranean. This coastal path is best tackled in early morning, before the crowds. Out of season, you might have it to yourself. See p. 575.

ITALY'S best NEIGHBORHOODS

o **Monti, Rome:** Between Termini Station and the Forum, the area now called Monti was once known as *Suburra*—the source of our word "suburbs." A slum and red-light district during the Roman Empire, today it's a colorful, authentic neighborhood that retains working-class roots, with a lively dining and nightlife scene and shops offering antiques, bijou jewelry, and one-of-a-kind gifts. See chapter 4.

o **San Frediano, Florence:** Most Florentines have abandoned their *centro storico* to the visitors, but the Arno's Left Bank in San Frediano has plenty of local action after dark. Dine at **iO** (p. 219), slurp a gelato by the river at **La Carraia** (p. 221), then sip cocktails during an acoustic gig at **Libreria-Café La Cité** (p. 224).

o **Cannaregio, Venice:** This residential neighborhood has silent canals, elegantly faded mansions, and hidden churches graced by Tiepolo paintings. Here, too, is the old Ghetto Nuovo, a historic area of Jewish bakeries, restaurants, and synagogues. It's all a great escape from the chaos of San Marco. See chapter 9.

o **Navigli, Milan:** The city is still riding high on a post-Expo wave, and nowhere exudes Milanese confidence more than the Navigli neighborhood, around the Darsena, once Milan's canal port. It's now a market, shops, and bars; locals come here after dark for summer concerts, Christmas markets, or to watch a game on the big screen. See chapter 10.

o **Spaccanapoli, Naples:** It's sometimes said Naples is Italy on overdrive, and the city goes up another gear in the narrow, crowded, laundry-strung lanes of its *centro storico*. Gird your loins, watch your wallet, and forget about a map—just plunge into the grid and enjoy. Shops sell everything from *limoncello* and carved nativity scenes to fried snacks and the world's best pizza. It's a European *souk*. See chapter 12.

o **La Kalsa, Palermo:** Arabs first settled this seaside quarter a thousand years ago, and its narrow lanes and palm-shaded squares still feel beyond Europe. Old palaces house fine hotels and restaurants, plus the Galleria Regionale della Sicilia and more excellent museums. See chapter 15.

o **Sasso Barisano and Sasso Caveoso, Matera:** Inhabited for more than 3,000 years, clusters of cave dwellings carved into limestone cliffs create one of Italy's weirdest spectacles. The primitive, earth-hued assemblage of homes, churches, and monasteries pile one atop the other along a jumble of twisting stepped streets. They now house unique restaurants and hotels, too. See p. 708.

Shopping for antiques on Via San Gregorio in Spaccanapoli, Naples.

2

ITALY IN CONTEXT

By Donald Strachan

Many stereotypes you have heard about this extraordinary country are accurate. Children are fussed over wherever they go; food and soccer are a religion; the north–south divide is alive and well; and (alas) bureaucracy is a frustrating feature of daily life for families and businesses. Some stereotypes, however, are wide of the mark: Not every Italian you meet will be open and effusive. Every now and then—but rarely in the South—they do taciturn pretty well, too. This chapter provides a little historic and cultural background to help you understand what makes Italy tick.

One important fact to remember is that, for a land so steeped in history—three millennia and counting—Italy has only a short history *as a country*. In 2021 it will celebrate its 160th birthday. Prior to 1861, the map of the peninsula was in constant flux. War, alliance, invasion, and disputed noble successions caused that map to change color as often as a chameleon crossing a field of wildflowers. Republics, mini-monarchies, client states, Papal states, and city-states, as well as Islamic emirates, colonies, dukedoms, and Christian theocracies, roll on and off the pages of Italian history with regularity. In some regions, you'll hear languages and dialects other than Italian. It all combines to form an identity that's often more regional than national.

This confusing history explains why your Italian experience will differ wildly if you visit, say, Turin rather than Matera. (And why you should visit both, if you can.) The architecture is different; the food is different; the legends and important historical figures are different, as are the issues of the day. And the people are different: While the north–south schism is most often written about, cities as close together as Florence and Siena can feel very dissimilar. Milan to Naples is just over 4 hours by train, but the experience is like two different worlds. This chapter will help you understand why.

ITALY TODAY

As in many Western democracies, politics in Italy is experiencing a period of turbulence. (For the cynics out there: When is Italian politics ever anything *but* turbulent?) Populism has swapped the online fringe for the mainstream. A left-leaning, "anti-establishment" party formed by activist

FACING PAGE: The basilica of Santa Maria della Salute overlooks Venice's Grand Canal.

15

WHAT DID YOU MISS? 5 TIMES ITALY made the news SINCE OUR PREVIOUS EDITION

Straight up: The Leaning Tower of Pisa leans a half-degree less than everyone thought. www.theguardian.com/world/italy

Straight shot: You can now make a direct rail connection between Rome's main international airport and Florence or Venice, without changing trains in the Eternal City. www.thelocal.it

Explosive error: Vesuvius's eruption date has been set in stone for centuries: August 24, A.D. 79. But an inscription dating to early October of the same year has been uncovered in Pompeii. www. bbc.com/news

500th birthday: It is now 5 centuries since the death of Leonardo da Vinci. The one-off celebrations finished in 2019, but you can admire his masterpieces in a new permanent Leonardo room at Florence's Uffizi. www.theflorentine.net

Coffee controversy: Starbucks finally opened in the country that inspired its founder, with a lavish, industrial-chic branch in Milan (and 15 more following close behind). forbes.com

comedian Beppe Grillo—the *MoVimento 5 Stelle* (Five Star Movement, or M5S)—polled around a third of the vote in the 2018 election and leads a governing coalition with the provocative, anti-immigrant *Lega* (League), whose origins are as a separatist movement for Italy's richer North. If that sounds complicated and somewhat uneasy, that's because it is. The center-left Democratic Party—led by former Florence mayor and former prime minister, Matteo Renzi—came third. At 39, Renzi himself had been Italy's youngest prime minister but resigned in 2016 after defeat in a referendum on wide-ranging electoral reform. Opinion polling suggests support for traditional, "free market" center-right parties is collapsing.

The government has a formidable task. Recovery from the global financial crisis has been painfully slow. The *Crisi* had a disastrous effect on Italy's economy, causing the deepest recession since World War II. Public debt grew to alarming levels—as high as 1,900 trillion€—and is still around 130 percent of GDP. Italy only just survived a European banking crisis which almost brought down the euro currency, and discontent over unemployment, wages, and pensions is widespread. Italy has, in effect, experienced almost no GDP growth in well over a decade.

Immigration is another persistent national issue, and there is impatience with the European Union over a collective inability to control illegal immigration on Europe's southern (mostly sea) borders. Italy's population is aging and the youth vacuum is being filled by immigrants, especially those from Eastern Europe, notably Romania and Albania. The plight of migrant refugees from Syria through 2019 added yet another layer of complexity to Italy's relationship with *stranieri* (foreigners). Italy had scant colonial experience, and does not have a "melting pot" history. Tensions were inevitable, and discrimination is a daily fact of life for

Italian cities like Milan still bustle, but lingering economic woes and political instability continue to undermine the national confidence.

many minorities (though you are very unlikely to experience it as a visitor). Change is coming: In 2013, Cécile Kyenge became Italy's first government minister of African descent. But it is coming too slowly for many.

While others arrive, a "brain drain" continues to push young Italians abroad to seek opportunity. The problem is especially ingrained in rural communities and on the islands, where the old maxim, "it's not what you know, it's who you know," applies more strongly than ever.

M5S and its young leader, Luigi Di Maio, had been on a roll. Yet, as Rome's first female mayor, M5S's Virginia Raggi discovered: Winning power can be easier than wielding it. She has said she will not run for reelection in 2021. Di Maio's popularity is waning. Prospects for everyone will improve if and when Italy puts its economic turmoil behind it. From top to toe, highlands to islands, fingers are firmly crossed that the good times are coming around again. What happens next? It's impossible to say. This is Italy, after all.

THE MAKING OF ITALY
Prehistory to the Rise of Rome

Of all the early inhabitants of Italy, the **Etruscans** left the most extensive legacy. Archaeologists debate exactly where they came from, and the inscriptions they left behind (often on graves in *necropoli*) are too bland to be of much help. Whatever their origins, within 2 centuries of appearing on the peninsula around 800 B.C., they had subjugated the lands now

Italians know how to cook—just ask one. But be sure to leave plenty of time: Once Italians start talking food, they do not pause for breath. Yet Italy doesn't have one national "Italian" cuisine; it's more a loose grouping of regional cuisines that share a few staples, notably pasta, bread, tomatoes, and pig meat cured in many ways. On a **Rome** visit, you'll encounter authentic local specialties such as *saltimbocca alla romana* (literally "jump-in-the-mouth"—thin slices of veal with sage, cured ham, and cheese)—and *carciofi alla romana* (artichokes cooked with herbs, such as mint and garlic), plus a dish that's become ubiquitous, *spaghetti alla carbonara*—pasta coated in a silky sauce made with egg, *pecorino romano* (ewe's milk cheese), and cured pork (*guanciale*, or cheek, if it's authentic). For reasons of historical migration, a strong current of Jewish cuisine also runs through Roman cooking.

To the north, in **Florence** and **Tuscany,** you'll find seasonal ingredients served simply; it's the antithesis of "French" cooking, with its multiple processes. The main ingredient for almost any savory dish is the local olive oil, prized for low acidity. The typical Tuscan pasta is wide, flat *pappardelle,* generally tossed with a game sauce such as *lepre* (hare) or *cinghiale* (boar). Tuscans are fond of their own strong ewe's milk pecorino cheese, made most famously around the Val d'Orcia town of Pienza. Meat is usually the centerpiece of any *secondo:* A *bistecca alla fiorentina* is the classic main dish, a T-bone-like cut of meat. An authentic *fiorentina* should come only from the white Chianina breed of cattle. Sweet treats are also good here, particularly Siena's *panforte* (a dense sticky cake); *biscotti di Prato* (hard almond-flour biscuits for dipping in dessert wine, also known as *cantuccini*); and the *miele* (honey) of Montalcino.

Emilia-Romagna is the country's gastronomic center. Rich in produce, its school of cooking first created many pastas now common around Italy: tagliatelle, tortellini, and cappelletti (made in the shape of "little hats"). Pig also comes several ways, including in Bologna's mortadella (rolled, ground pork) and *prosciutto di Parma* (cured ham). Served in paper-thin slices, it's deliciously sweet. The distinctive cheese Parmigiano–Reggiano is made by hundreds of small producers in the provinces of Parma and Reggio Emilia.

known as Tuscany (so named to reflect that heritage), northern Lazio, and Campania, along with the so-called **"Villanovan"** tribes that lived there.

The **Latins,** who were based at Rome, were eventually conquered by the Etruscans around 600 B.C. Their new overlords introduced gold tableware and jewelry, bronze urns and terra-cotta statuary, and the art and culture of Greece and Asia Minor; they also made Rome the government seat of Latium. "Roma" is an Etruscan name, and the early, perhaps mythical kings of Rome had Etruscan names: Numa, Ancus, even Romulus.

Etruscan rule began to end with the **Roman Revolt** around 510 B.C.: by 250 B.C. Romans and their allies had vanquished or assimilated the Etruscans, wiping out their language and religion. However, many of the former rulers' manners and beliefs remained and became integral to what we now understand as "Roman culture."

Probably the most famous dish of **Lombardy** is *cotoletta alla milanese* (veal cutlet dipped in egg and bread-crumbs and fried in olive oil)—German-speakers call it *Wienerschnitzel. Osso buco* is another Lombard classic: shin of veal cooked in a ragout sauce. **Piedmont** and Turin's iconic dish is *bagna càuda*—literally "hot bath" in the Piedmontese language, a sauce made with olive oil, garlic, butter, and anchovies, into which you dip raw vegetables. Piedmont is also the spiritual home of *risotto*, particularly the town of Vercelli, which is surrounded by rice paddies.

Venice is rarely celebrated for its cuisine, but fresh seafood is usually excellent, and figures heavily in the Venetian diet. Grilled fish is often served with red radicchio, a bitter leaf that grows best around nearby **Treviso.** Two more classic Venetian dishes are *fegato alla veneziana* (liver and onions) and *risi e bisi* (rice and peas) **Liguria** also turns toward the sea for its inspiration, as reflected by its version of bouillabaisse, *burrida.* The region's most famous food is pesto *alla genovese,* a sauce made with fresh basil, hard cheese, olive oil, and crushed pine nuts, which is used to dress pasta, fish, and many more local dishes.

So many Neapolitans moved to the New World that the cookery of **Campania**—including pizza and spaghetti with clam sauce—is familiar to North Americans. Mozzarella is the local cheese, the best of it *mozzarella di bufala,* made with milk from water buffalo (first introduced to Campania from Asia in the Middle Ages). Mixed fish fries (a *fritto misto*) are a staple of many a lunch table, and genuine Neapolitan pizza is in a class of its own. The cuisine of **Basilicata** and **Puglia** is founded on peasant simplicity: pasta, often made without egg, tossed with oil and seasonal vegetables such as broccoli rabe (*cime di rapa*) or garbanzo beans. The region is known for its sweet, piquant Senise peppers and spicy or fennel-spiked Lucanica sausage.

Sicily's distinctive cuisine features strong flavors and aromatic sauces influenced by North Africa. One staple is *pasta con le sarde* (with pine nuts, wild fennel, spices, chopped sardines, and olive oil). Fish is good and fresh almost everywhere (local swordfish is excellent). Classic desserts include *cannoli,* cylindrical pastry cases filled with ricotta and candied fruit or chocolate. Sicilian *gelato* and homemade pastries are among the best in Italy.

Meanwhile, the **Greeks**—who predated both the Etruscans and the Romans—had built powerful colonial outposts in the south, notably in Naples, founded as Greek "Neapolis." Remains of the *Àgora,* or market square, survive below **San Lorenzo Maggiore** (p. 601), in the old center of the city. The Greeks left stone monuments above ground too, including at the **Valley of the Temples,** Agrigento, Sicily (p. 793).

To see remnants of Etruscan civilization, Rome's **Museo Nazionale Etrusco** (p. 114) and the Etruscan collection in Rome's **Vatican Museums** (p. 82) are a logical starting point. Florence's **Museo Archeologico** (p. 196) houses one of the greatest Etruscan bronzes yet unearthed, the "Arezzo Chimera." Further fine Etruscan collections are in **Volterra,** Tuscany (p. 280) and **Orvieto,** Umbria (p. 337). Tombs are scattered around

At Florence's Museo Archeologico, the Arezzo Chimera is possibly the most famous artwork surviving from the Etruscan period.

the countryside of southern Tuscany and northern Lazio. Mary Beard's excellent book "SPQR" is packed with insight on the rise of Ancient Rome.

The Roman Republic: ca. 510–27 B.C.

After the Roman Republic was established around 510 B.C.—precision is impossible—the Romans continued to increase their power by conquering neighboring communities in the highlands and forming alliances with other Latins in the lowlands. They began to give to their allies, and then to conquered peoples, partial or complete Roman citizenship, with a corresponding obligation of military service. This further increased Rome's power and reach. Citizen colonies were set up as settlements of Roman farmers or military veterans, including both **Florence** and **Siena.**

The stern culture of the Roman Republic was characterized by belief in the gods, the necessity of learning from the past, the strength of the family, education through reading and performing public service, and most importantly, obedience. The all-powerful Senate presided as Rome defeated rival powers one after another and came to rule the Mediterranean. The Punic Wars with **Carthage** (in modern-day Tunisia) in the 3rd century B.C. were a temporary stumbling block, as Carthaginian general **Hannibal** (247–182 B.C.) conducted a devastating campaign across the Italian peninsula, crossing the Alps with elephants and winning bloody battles by the shore of **Lago Trasimeno,** in Umbria, and at Cannae, in Puglia. In the end, however, Rome prevailed.

No figure was more towering during the late Republic, or more instrumental in its transformation into the Empire (see below), than **Julius Caesar,** the charismatic conqueror of Gaul—"the wife of every husband and the husband of every wife," according to scurrilous rumors reported by 1st-century historian Suetonius. After defeating the last resistance of the Pompeians in 45 B.C., he came to Rome and was made dictator and consul for 10 years. Conspirators, led by Marcus Junius Brutus, stabbed him to death at the Theater of Pompey on March 15, 44 B.C., the "Ides of March." The site, now Largo di Torre Argentina, is an Instagrammers' hotspot these days. (Not for the history; it is home to a photogenic feral cat colony.)

The conspirators' motivation was to restore the power of the Republic and topple dictatorship. But they failed: **Mark Antony,** a Roman general, assumed control. He made peace with Caesar's willed successor, **Octavian,** and after the Treaty of Brundisium dissolved the Republic, found himself married to Octavian's sister, Octavia. This marriage, however, didn't prevent him from also marrying Cleopatra in 36 B.C. A furious Octavian gathered the legions and defeated Antony at the **Battle of Actium** on September 2, 31 B.C. Cleopatra fled to Egypt, followed by Antony, who committed suicide in disgrace a year later. Cleopatra, unable to seduce his successor and retain her rule of Egypt, followed suit with the help of an asp. The permanent end of the Republic was nigh.

Many standing buildings around ancient Rome date to periods after the Republic, but parts of the **Roman Forum** (p. 93) were built during the Republic, including the **Temple of Saturn.** The adjacent **Capitoline Hill**

A statue of Julius Caesar, the charismatic leader of the Roman Republic.

and **Palatine Hill** have been sacred religious and civic places since the earliest days of Rome. Rome's best artifacts from the Republic are inside the **Musei Capitolini** (p. 90).

The Roman Empire in Its Pomp: 27 B.C.–A.D. 395

Born Gaius Octavius in 63 B.C., and later known as Octavian, **Augustus** became the first Roman emperor in 27 B.C. and reigned until A.D. 14. His autocratic rule ushered in the *Pax Romana,* 2 centuries of peace. In Rome you can still see the remains of the **Forum of Augustus** (p. 92) and admire his statue in the **Vatican Museums** (p. 82).

By now, Rome ruled the entire Mediterranean world, either directly or indirectly. All political, commercial, and cultural pathways led straight to Rome, a sprawling city set on seven hills: the Capitoline, Palatine, Aventine, Caelian, Esquiline, Quirinal, and Viminal. It was in this period that **Virgil** wrote his epic poem, "The Aeneid," which supplied a grandiose founding myth for the great city and its empire; in this era **Ovid** also composed his erotic poetry and **Horace** wrote his "Odes."

Emperors brought Rome to new heights. Yet without the checks and balances once provided by the Senate and legislatures, success led to corruption. These centuries witnessed a steady decay in ideals and traditions on which the Empire was founded. The army became a fifth column of unruly mercenaries, and for every good emperor (Augustus, Claudius, Trajan, Vespasian, and Hadrian, to name a few) there were several cruel, debased, or incompetent tyrants (Caligula, Nero, Caracalla, and many others).

EARLY ROMAN emperors

Caligula (r. A.D. 37–41): Young emperor whose reign of cruelty and terror ended when he was assassinated by his Praetorian guard

Nero (r. A.D. 54–68): The last emperor of the Julio-Claudian dynasty and another cruel megalomaniac. He killed his own mother and was blamed—probably unjustly—for starting the Great Fire of Rome (A.D. 64)

Vespasian (r. A.D. 69–79): First emperor of the Flavian dynasty, who built the Colosseum (p. 91) and lived as husband-and-wife with a freed slave, Caenis

Domitian (r. A.D. 81–96): Increasingly paranoid authoritarian and populist who became fixated on the idea he would be assassinated—and was proven right

Trajan (r. A.D. 98–117): Virtuous soldier-ruler who presided over the moment Rome was at its geographically grandest scale, and also rebuilt much of the city

Hadrian (r. A.D. 117–138): Humanist, general, and builder who redesigned the Pantheon (p. 104) and added the Temple of Venus and Roma to the Forum

Marcus Aurelius (r. A.D. 161–180): Philosopher-king, and the last of the so-called "Five Good Emperors," whose statue is exhibited in the Musei Capitolini (p. 90)

After Augustus died (by poison, perhaps), his widow, **Livia**—a shrewd operator who had divorced her first husband to marry Augustus— set up her son, **Tiberius,** as ruler through intrigues and poisonings. A series of murders and purges ensued, and Tiberius, who ruled during Pontius Pilate's trial and crucifixion of Christ, was eventually murdered in his late '70s. Top-level murders were common; a short time later, **Domitian** (ruled A.D. 81–96) became so obsessed with the possibility of assassination that he had his palace walls covered in reflective mica to see behind his back at all times. (He was killed anyway.)

Excesses ruled the day—at least, if you believe tracts written by biased contemporary chroniclers: **Caligula** supposedly committed incest with his sister, Drusilla, appointed his horse to the Senate, lavished money on egotistical projects, and proclaimed himself a god. Caligula's successor, his uncle **Claudius,** was poisoned by his final wife—his niece Agrippina the Younger—to secure the succession of **Nero,** her son by a previous marriage. Nero's thanks were to later murder not only his mother but also his wife (Claudius's daughter) and his rival, Claudius's 13-year-old son, Britannicus. An enthusiastic persecutor of Christians, Nero committed suicide with the cry, "What an artist I destroy!"

By the 3rd century, rivalry and corruption had become so prevalent that 23 emperors ruled in 73 years. Few, however, were as twisted as **Caracalla** who, to secure control, had his brother Geta slashed to pieces while Geta was in the arms of his mother, former empress Julia Domna.

Constantine the Great, who became emperor in A.D. 306, made Constantinople (or Byzantium) the new capital of the Empire in 330, moving administrative functions away from Rome altogether, partly because of the growing menace of barbarian attacks. Constantine was the first Christian emperor, allegedly converting after he saw the "True Cross" in a dream, accompanied by the words, "in this sign shall you conquer." He defeated rival emperor Maxentius and his followers at the **Battle of the Milivan Bridge** (A.D. 312), a victory that's remembered by Rome's triumphal **Arco di Costantino** (p. 88). Constantine formally ended the persecution of Christians with the **Edict of Milan** (A.D. 313).

It was during the Imperial period that Rome flourished in architecture, advancing in size and majesty far beyond earlier cities built by the Greeks. **Classical orders** were simplified into forms of column capital: **Doric** (a plain capital), **Ionic** (a capital with a scroll), and **Corinthian** (a capital with flowering acanthus). Much of this advance was due to the discovery of a form of concrete and the fine-tuning of the arch, used with a logic, rhythm, and ease never before seen. Many of these monumental buildings still stand in Rome, notably **Trajan's Column** (p. 93), the **Colosseum** (p. 91), and Hadrian's **Pantheon** (p. 104). Elsewhere in Italy, Verona's **Arena** (p. 458) bears witness to the crowds the brutal sport of gladiatorial combat could draw. Three **Roman cities** have been preserved, with street plans and in some cases, even buildings intact: doomed

Pompeii (p. 629) and its neighbor **Herculaneum** (p. 625), both buried by Vesuvius's massive A.D. 79 eruption, and Rome's ancient seaport, **Ostia Antica** (p. 162). At Herculaneum, one of Rome's greatest writers perished, **Pliny the Elder** (A.D. 23–79). It's thanks to him, his nephew, **Pliny the Younger,** historians **Tacitus, Suetonius, Cassius Dio,** and **Livy,** and satirist **Juvenal,** that much knowledge of ancient Roman life and history was not lost.

Surviving Roman **art** had a major influence on the painters and sculptors of the Renaissance (see p. 29). In Rome itself, look for the marble bas-reliefs (sculptures that project slightly from a flat surface)

Trajan's Column.

on the **Arco di Costantino** (p. 88), the sculpture and mosaic collections at the **Palazzo Massimo alle Terme** (p. 116), and the gilded equestrian statue of Marcus Aurelius at the **Musei Capitolini** (p. 90). In Florence, the **Uffizi** (p. 181) displays the Medici rulers' vast collection of Roman statuary. Naples's **Museo Archeologico Nazionale** (p. 600) houses the world's most extraordinary collection of Roman art, preserved for centuries under the lava at Pompeii.

The Fall of the Empire through the "Dark Ages"

The Eastern and Western sections of the Roman Empire split in A.D. 395, leaving the Italian peninsula without the support it once received from east of the Adriatic. When the **Goths** moved toward Rome in the early 5th century, citizens in the provinces, who had grown to hate the bureaucracy set up by **Emperor Diocletian,** initially welcomed the invaders. And then the pillage began.

Rome was first sacked by **Alaric I,** king of the Visigoths, in A.D. 410. The populace made no attempt to defend their city, other than trying in vain to buy him off (a tactic that worked 3 years earlier); most people fled to the hills. The feeble Western emperor **Honorius** hid out in **Ravenna** the entire time, which from A.D. 402 he had made the new capital of the Western Roman Empire.

More than 40 troubled years passed. Then **Attila the Hun** invaded Italy to besiege Rome. While Attila was dissuaded from attacking, thanks largely to a peace mission headed by Pope Leo I in A.D. 452, relief was short-lived: In A.D. 455, **Gaiseric,** king of the **Vandals,** carried out a

ALL ABOUT vino

Italy is the largest **wine**-producing country in the world; as far back as 800 B.C. the Etruscans were vintners. However, only in 1965 were laws enacted to guarantee consistency in winemaking. Quality wines are labeled **"DOC"** (Denominazione di Origine Controllata). If you see **"DOCG"** on a label (the "G" means *garantita*), this denotes an even higher quality wine region (at least, in theory). **"IGT"** (Indicazione Geografica Tipica) indicates a more general wine zone—for example, "Umbria"—but still with mandatory quality control.

Tuscany: Tuscan red wines rank with some of the finest in the world. **Sangiovese** is the prince of grapes here, and **Chianti** from the hills south of Florence is the most widely known sangiovese wine. The premium zone is **Chianti Classico,** where lively ruby-red wine has a bouquet of violets. The Tuscan south houses two even finer DOCGs: mighty, robust **Brunello di Montalcino,** a garnet-red ideal for roasts and game; and almost purple **Vino Nobile di Montepulciano,** which has a rich, velvet body. End a meal with the Tuscan dessert wine called **vin santo,** which is often accompanied by hard *biscotti* to dunk into your glass.

Veneto and Lombardy: Reds around Venice and the Lakes vary from light and lunchtime-friendly **Bardolino** to **Valpolicella,** which can be particularly intense if its grapes are partly dried before fermentation to make an **Amarone.** White, garganega-based **Soave** has a pale amber color and a velvety flavor; **Lugana** at its best has a sparkle of gold and a rich, dry structure. **Prosecco** is the classic Italian sparkling white, and the base for both a Bellini and a Spritz (joints that use Champagne are doing it wrong!).

Piedmont: The finest reds in Italy may hail from the vineclad slopes of Piedmont, particularly those from the late-ripening **Nebbiolo** grape in the Langhe hills south of Alba. The big names—with big flavors and big price tags—are **Barbaresco** (brilliant ruby red with a delicate flavor) and **Barolo** (also brilliant ruby red, gaining finesse when it mellows into a velvety old age).

The South and Sicily: From the volcanic soil around Vesuvius, the wines of **Campania** have been admired for centuries: Homer praised **Falerno,** straw yellow in color. The key DOCG wines from Campania these days are **Greco di Tufo** (a mouth-filling, full white) and **Fiano di Avellino** (subtler and more floral). The wines of **Sicily**—once called a "paradise of the grape"—were also extolled by the ancients, and even table wines here are improving lately. Sicily is the home of **Marsala,** a fortified wine often served with desserts; it also makes a great sauce for cooking veal.

2-week sack unparalleled in its savagery. The empire of the West lasted for only another 20 years; finally, in A.D. 476, the sacks and chaos ended the once-mighty city, and Rome itself was left to the popes, though it was ruled nominally from Ravenna by an Exarch from Byzantium (aka Constantinople).

Although little detailed history of Italy in the immediate post-Roman period is known—and few buildings survive—it's certain the gradual spread of **Christianity** was creating a new society. The religion was probably founded in Rome about a decade after the death of Jesus, and gained strength despite early (and enthusiastic) persecution by the Romans. The

A Growing Taste for Beer

Italy will always be known, and adored, for its wine. But one gastronomic trend to watch for as you travel is the growth in popularity of artisanal beer, especially among the young. Although supermarket shelves are stacked with mainstream brands like Peroni and Moretti, smaller stores and bars increasingly offer craft microbrews (known as *birre artigianali*).

Italy had fewer than 50 breweries in 2000. It was over 1,000 by 2018. Craft-beer consumption has more than tripled since 2012, according to brewers' association Unionbirrai. Look for Unionbirrai's official seal on the label of genuine craft brewery products. You'll even find these beers on the hallowed shelves of some wine vendors.

best way today to relive the early Christian era is to walk along the **Via Appia Antica** (p. 122), just outside Rome's ancient walls. A church on the Appian Way marks the spot where the disciple Peter, fleeing Roman persecution, is said to have had a pivotal vision of Christ; nearby the **Catacombs** (p. 123), the first cemeteries of the Christian community of Rome, house the remains of early popes and martyrs.

We have Christianity, along with the influence of Byzantium, to thank for Italy's next great artistic style: the **Byzantine.** Painting and mosaic work in this era was very stylized and static, but also ornate and ethereal. The most accomplished examples of Byzantine art are found in the churches of **Ravenna** (p. 376). Later buildings in the Byzantine style include Venice's **Basilica di San Marco** (p. 405).

The Middle Ages: 9th Century to the 14th Century

A ravaged Rome entered the Middle Ages, its population scattered. A modest number of residents continued to live in the swamps of the **Campus Martius.** The seven hills—now without water because the aqueducts were cut—stood abandoned and crumbling.

The Pope turned toward Europe, where he found a powerful ally in **Charlemagne,** king of the Franks. In A.D. 800, Pope Leo III crowned him emperor. That didn't mean Rome was back in the big time, however: Charlemagne ruled his empire from Aachen, in what's now northwest Germany. And although Charlemagne pledged allegiance to the church and made the pope the final arbiter in most religious and cultural matters, he also set Western Europe on a course of bitter opposition to papal meddling in affairs of state.

The successor to Charlemagne's empire was a political entity known as the **Holy Roman Empire** (A.D. 962–1806). The new Empire defined the end of the Dark Ages but ushered in a long period of bloody warfare. Magyars from Hungary invaded northeastern Lombardy and, in turn, were defeated by increasingly powerful **Venice,** which, having defeated its naval rival **Genoa** in the 1380 Battle of Chioggia, reigned over most of the eastern Mediterranean. Venetian merchants ruled a republic that lasted a millennium, and built a city full of imposing architecture like the **Doge's Palace** (p. 410). The Lion of St. Mark—symbol of the city's dominion—appears as far away as **Bergamo** (p. 491), close to Milan.

Meanwhile, **Rome** during the Middle Ages was a quaint backwater. Narrow lanes with overhanging buildings filled areas that had once been showcases for imperial power. The forums, mercantile exchanges, temples, and theaters of the Imperial era slowly disintegrated. It remained the seat of the Roman Catholic Church, and its state was almost completely controlled by priests, who aggressively expanded church influence and acquisitions. An endless series of power struggles ensued. Between 1378 and 1417, competing popes—one in Rome, another **"antipope"** in Avignon—made simultaneous claims to St. Peter's legacy.

Down in **Sicily,** Normans gained military control from the Arabs in the 11th century, dividing the island from the rest of Italy and altering forever its ethnic makeup. The reign of **Roger II of Sicily** (ruled A.D. 1130–54) was notable for his religious tolerance, the multiracial nature of his court, and distinctive architecture. The **Palazzo dei Normanni** (p. 752), in Palermo, and nearby **Monreale** (p. 761), are just two of many great projects from Sicily's Norman era.

In the mid–14th century, the **Black Death** ravaged Europe, killing perhaps a third of Italy's population; the unique preservation of Tuscan towns like **San Gimignano** (p. 275) and **Siena** (p. 232) owes much to the fact they never fully recovered after the devastations of the 1348–49 plague. Despite such setbacks, Italian **city-states** grew wealthy from Crusades booty, trade, and banking. The **Florin,** a gold coin minted in Florence, became the first truly international currency for centuries, and dominated trade all over the European continent.

The medieval period marks the beginning of building in stone on a mass scale. Flourishing from A.D. 800 to 1300, **Romanesque** architecture took its inspiration and rounded arches from Ancient Rome. Architects built large churches with wide aisles to accommodate the masses. Pisa's **Campo dei Miracoli** (1153–1360s; p. 297) is typical of the Pisan-Romanesque style, with stacked arcades of mismatched columns on the cathedral's facade (and wrapped around the **Leaning Tower of Pisa**), and blind arcading set with diamond-shaped lozenges. The influence of Arab architecture is obvious; Pisa was a city of seafaring merchants.

Romanesque **sculpture** was fluid but still far from naturalistic. Often wonderfully childlike in its narrative simplicity, works frequently mix biblical scenes with the myths and motifs of local pagan traditions that were incorporated into medieval Christianity. Among Italy's greatest surviving examples of Romanesque sculpture are 48 relief panels on the bronze doors of the **Basilica di San Zeno Maggiore** in Verona (p. 458). The exterior of Parma's **Baptistery** (p. 386) has Romanesque friezes by Benedetto Antelami (1150–1230).

As the appeal of Romanesque and Byzantine faded, the **Gothic** style flourished from the 13th to the 15th centuries. In architecture, Gothic was characterized by flying buttresses, pointed arches, and delicate stained-glass windows. These engineering developments freed architecture from the heavy, thick walls of the Romanesque and allowed ceilings to soar, walls to thin, and windows to proliferate.

Although the Gothic age continued to be religious, many secular buildings arose, including palaces designed to show off the prestige of various ruling families. Siena's civic **Palazzo Pubblico** (p. 238) and many great buildings in **Venice** (see chapter 9) date from this period. **San Gimignano** (p. 275), in Tuscany, has a preserved Gothic center. Milan's **Duomo** (p. 472) is one of Europe's supreme Gothic cathedrals.

Painters such as **Cimabue** (1251–1302) and **Giotto** (1266–1337) in Florence, **Pietro Cavallini** (1259–ca. 1330) in Rome, and **Duccio di Buoninsegna** (ca. 1255–1319) in Siena, began to lift art from Byzantine rigidity and set it on the road to realism. Giotto's finest work is his fresco cycle at Padua's **Cappella degli Scrovegni** (p. 455); he was the harbinger of the oncoming Renaissance, which would forever change art and architecture. Duccio's 1311 "Maestà," now in Siena's **Museo dell'Opera Metropolitana** (p. 240), influenced Sienese painters for centuries. Ambrogio Lorenzetti painted the greatest civic frescoes of the Middle Ages—his "Allegories of Good and Bad Government" in Siena's **Palazzo Pubblico** (p. 238)—before he succumbed to the Black Death, along with almost every significant Sienese artist of his generation.

The medieval period also saw the birth of literature in the Italian language, a written version of the **Tuscan dialect**—primarily because the great writers of the age were Tuscans. Florentine **Dante Alighieri** wrote his "Divine Comedy" in the 1310s, and Boccaccio's "Decameron"—a kind of Florentine "Canterbury Tales"—appeared in the 1350s.

On Siena's Piazza del Campo, the Palazzo Pubblico is a grand example of secular Gothic architecture.

Renaissance & Baroque Italy

The story of Italy from the dawn of the Renaissance in the early 15th century to the "Age of Enlightenment" in the 17th and 18th centuries is as fascinating and complicated as that of the rise and fall of the Roman Empire.

During this period, **Rome** underwent major physical changes. The old centers of culture reverted to pastures and fields, and great churches and palaces were built with the stones of Ancient Rome. Cows grazed on the crumbling Roman Forum. The city's construction boom did more damage to the ancient temples than any barbarian sack had ever done. Rare marbles were stripped from Imperial baths and used as altarpieces or sent to lime kilns for "recycling." So enthusiastic was the popes' destruction of Imperial Rome, it's a genuine miracle that anything is left.

Milan was a glorious Renaissance capital, particularly under the Sforza dynasty and Ludovico "Il Moro" (1452–1508), patron of Leonardo da Vinci. Smaller but still significant centers of power included the Gonzaga family's **Mantua** (p. 495) and the Este clan's **Ferrara** (p. 368).

This era is best remembered because of its art, and around 1400 the most significant power in Italy was the city where the Renaissance began: **Florence** (see chapter 5). Slowly but surely, the **Medici** family rose to become the most powerful of the city's ruling oligarchy, gradually usurping the powers of the guilds and the republicans. They reformed law and commerce, expanded the city's power by taking control of neighbors such as **Pisa,** and sparked a "renaissance," or rebirth, in painting, sculpture, and architecture. Christopher Hibbert's "The Rise and Fall of the House of Medici" is the most readable detailed account of the era. Netflix's "Medici: Masters of Florence" serves up a sensationalized, fictionalized, but fun "history" of power plays in the Renaissance city.

Under the patronage of the Medici (as well as other powerful Florentine families), innovative young painters and sculptors pursued more expressiveness and naturalism. **Donatello** (1386–1466) cast the first freestanding nude since antiquity (a bronze now in Florence's **Museo Nazionale del Bargello,** p. 185). **Lorenzo Ghiberti** (1378–1455) labored for more than 50 years on two sets of doors for Florence's **Baptistery** (p. 176), the most famous of which were dubbed the "Gates of Paradise." **Masaccio** (1401–28) produced the first painting that realistically portrayed linear perspective, on the nave wall of **Santa Maria Novella** (p. 172).

Next followed a brief period known as the **High Renaissance.** The epitome of the Renaissance man, Florentine **Leonardo da Vinci** (1452–1519), painted his "Last Supper," now in Milan's **Santa Maria delle Grazie** (p. 479), and an "Annunciation" (1481), now hanging in Florence's **Uffizi** (p. 181) alongside countless Renaissance masterpieces from such iconic painters as Paolo Uccello, Sandro Botticelli, Piero della Francesca, and others. **Raphael** (1483–1520) produced a sublime body of work in his

37 years. Skilled in sculpture, painting, and architecture, **Michelangelo** (1475–1564) and his career marked the apogee of the Renaissance: His giant "David" at the **Galleria dell'Accademia** (p. 195) in Florence is the world's most famous statue, and his **Sistine Chapel** frescoes lure millions to the **Vatican Museums** (p. 82) in Rome. The father of the Venetian High Renaissance was **Titian** (1485–1576), known for his mastery of color and tone. Venice (see chapter 9) offers a rich trove of Titian's work, along with works by earlier Venetian masters such as **Gentile Bellini** (1429–1507), **Giorgione** (1477–1510), and **Vittore Carpaccio** (1465–1525).

As in painting, Renaissance **architecture** stressed proportion, order, classical inspiration, and mathematical precision. **Filippo Brunelleschi** (1377–1446), in the early 1400s, grasped the concept of "perspective" and provided artists with ground rules for creating the illusion of 3-D on a flat surface. (Read Ross King's "Brunelleschi's Dome" for the story of his greatest achievement, the crowning of Florence's cathedral with its massive terra-cotta dome.) Even **Michelangelo** took up architecture late in life, designing the Laurentian Library (1524) and New Sacristy (1524–34) at Florence's **Medici Chapel** (p. 191), then moving south to complete his crowning glory, the soaring dome of Rome's **St. Peter's Basilica** (p. 79). The third great Renaissance architect—and most influential of them all— **Andrea Palladio** (1508–80) worked in a classical mode of columns, porticoes, pediments, and other ancient-temple-inspired features. His masterpieces include fine churches in Venice. (The "Palladian" style of many U.S. capitol buildings is named for him.)

In time, the High Renaissance gradually evolved into the **baroque.** Stuccoes, sculptures, and paintings were carefully designed to complement each other—and the space itself—to create a unified whole. The baroque movement's spiritual home was Rome, and its towering figure was **Gian Lorenzo Bernini** (1598–1680), the greatest baroque sculptor, an accomplished architect, and a more-than-decent painter as well. Among many fine, flowing sculptures, you'll find his best in Rome's **Galleria Borghese** (p. 112) and **Santa Maria della Vittoria** (p. 116). Baroque architecture is especially prominent in the South: in the churches and devotional architecture of **Naples** (p. 586) and in **Siracusa** (p. 776), Sicily. **Turin** (p. 516) under the Savoys was remodeled by the baroque architecture of **Guarino Guarini** (1624–83) and **Filippo Juvarra** (1678–1736). In music, the most famous of the baroque composers is Venetian **Antonio Vivaldi** (1678–1741), whose "Four Seasons" is among the most performed classical compositions of all time.

In painting, many baroque artists mixed a kind of super-realism based on using everyday people as models and an exaggerated use of light and dark—a technique called *chiaroscuro*—with compositional complexity and explosions of dynamic fury, movement, and color. The period produced many fine painters, notably **Caravaggio** (1571–1610). Among his masterpieces are a "St. Matthew" (1599) cycle in Rome's **San Luigi dei**

A flamboyant fresco by Giambattista Tiepolo, perhaps Italy's finest rococo painter, in Milan's Palazzo Clerici.

Francesi (p. 102) and "The Acts of Mercy" in **Pio Monte della Misericordia** (p. 598), Naples. The baroque era also had an outstanding female painter in **Artemisia Gentileschi** (1593–1652): Her brutal "Judith Slaying Holofernes" (1620) hangs in Florence's **Uffizi** (p. 181).

Frothy and ornate, **rococo** art was the baroque taken to flamboyant extremes, and had few serious proponents in Italy. **Giambattista Tiepolo** (1696–1770), arguably the best of the rococo painters, specialized in ceiling frescoes and canvases with cloud-filled heavens of light. He worked extensively in Venice and the northeast. For rococo building—more a decorative than an architectural movement—look no further than Rome's **Spanish Steps** (p. 110) or the **Trevi Fountain** (p. 111).

At Last, a United Italy: The 1800s

By the 1800s, the glories of the Renaissance were a fading memory. From Turin to Naples, chunks of Italy had changed hands many, many times— between the Austrians, the Spanish, and the French, among autocratic thugs and enlightened princes, between the noble and the merchant classes. The 19th century witnessed the final collapse of many Renaissance city-states. The last of the Medici, Gian Gastone, had died in 1737, leaving Tuscany in the hands of foreign Lorraine and Habsburg princes.

French emperor **Napoleon** brought an end to a millennium of republican government in **Venice** in 1797, and installed puppet or client rulers across the Italian peninsula. During the **Congress of Vienna** (1814–15), which followed Napoleon's defeat by an alliance of the British, Prussians, and Dutch, Italy was once again divided.

Political unrest became a fact of Italian life, some of it spurred by the industrialization of the north and some by the encouragement of insurrectionaries like **Giuseppe Mazzini** (1805–72). Europe's year of revolutions, **1848,** rocked Italy, too, with violent uprisings in Lombardy and Sicily. After decades of political machinations, nationalism, and intrigue, and thanks to the efforts of statesman **Camillo Cavour** (1810–61) and rebel general **Giuseppe Garibaldi** (1807–82), the Kingdom of Italy was proclaimed in 1861 and **Victor Emmanuel (Vittorio Emanuele) II** of Savoy became its first monarch. The kingdom's first capital was **Turin** (1861–65), seat of the victorious Piedmontese, followed by **Florence** (1865–71).

The establishment of the kingdom, however, didn't signal a complete unification of Italy because Latium (including Rome) was still under papal control and Venetia was held by Austria. This was partially resolved in 1866, when Venetia joined the rest of Italy after the **Seven Weeks' War** between Austria and Prussia. In 1871, Rome became the capital of the newly formed country, after the city was retaken on September 20, 1870. Present-day **Via XX Settembre** is the very street up which patriots advanced after breaching the city gates. The **Risorgimento**—the "resurgence," Italian unification—was complete.

Political heights in Italy seemed to correspond to historic depths in art and architecture. Among the few notable practitioners of this era, the most well-known is probably Venetian **Antonio Canova** (1757–1822), Italy's major neoclassical sculptor, who became notorious for portraying both Napoleon and his sister Pauline as mythical nudes. His best work is in Rome's **Galleria Borghese** (p. 112). Tuscany also bred a late–19th-century precursor to French Impressionism, the **Macchiaioli** movement; see their works in the "modern art" galleries at Florence's **Palazzo Pitti** (p. 201).

THE A-LIST OF italian novels AVAILABLE IN ENGLISH

- Alessandro Manzoni, "The Betrothed" (1827)
- Alberto Moravia, "The Conformist" (1951)
- Giuseppe Tomasi di Lampedusa, "The Leopard" (1958)
- Elsa Morante, "History: A Novel" (1974)
- Italo Calvino, "If on a Winter's Night a Traveler" (1979)
- Umberto Eco, "Foucault's Pendulum" (1988)
- Niccolo Ammaniti, "I'm Not Scared" (2001)
- Elena Ferrante, "Neapolitan Novels" (2012–15)

Via dei Fori Imperiali, built in 1932 on the orders of Benito Mussolini, sliced through areas of classical monuments.

If art was hitting an all-time low, **music** was experiencing its Italian golden age. It's **opera** for which the 19th century is largely remembered. *Bel canto* composer **Gioachino Rossini** (1792–1868) was born in Pesaro, in the Marches, and found fame in 1816 with "The Barber of Seville." The fame of **Gaetano Donizetti** (1797–1848), a prolific native of Bergamo, was assured when his "Anna Bolena" premiered in 1830. Both were perhaps later overshadowed by **Giuseppe Verdi** (1813–1901), whose arias from such operas as "Rigoletto" and "La Traviata" took on profound national symbolism, and have since become some of the most whistled tunes on the planet. At the turn of the century, however, the Romantic movement that had dominated music gave way to the *verismo* ("realism") of composer **Giacomo Puccini** (1858–1924), whose operas "La Bohème" (1896), "Tosca" (1900), "Madama Butterfly" (1904), and the unfinished "Turandot" (1924) still pack houses worldwide. He's celebrated with a museum and opera festival in **Lucca,** Tuscany (p. 286).

The 20th Century: Two World Wars & One Duce

In 1915, Italy entered **World War I** on the side of the Allies. Italy joined Britain, Russia, and France to help defeat Germany and the traditional enemy to the north—now known as the Austro-Hungarian Empire—and so to "reclaim" Trentino and Trieste. (Mark Thompson's "The White War" tells the story of Italy's catastrophic campaign.) In the aftermath of wartime carnage, Italians suffered further with rising unemployment and horrendous inflation. As in Germany, a deep political crisis led to the emergence of a dictator.

On October 28, 1922, **Benito Mussolini,** who started his Fascist Party in 1919, knew the country was ripe for change. He gathered 30,000 Black Shirts for his **March on Rome.** Inflation was soaring and workers had called a general strike, so rather than recognize a state under siege, **King Victor Emmanuel III** (1900–46) proclaimed Mussolini as the new leader. In 1929, Il Duce—a moniker Mussolini began using from 1925—defined the divisions between the Italian government and the Pope by signing the Lateran Treaty, which granted political, territorial, and fiscal autonomy to the microstate of **Vatican City.** During the Spanish Civil War (1936–39), Mussolini's support for General Franco's Fascists, who had staged a coup against the elected government of Spain, helped seal the Axis alliance between Italy and Nazi Germany. Italy was inexorably and disastrously sucked into **World War II.**

Deeply unpleasant though their politics were, the Fascist regime did sponsor some remarkable **rationalist architecture,** at its best in Rome's planned satellite community, **EUR** (p. 121). In a city famed for Renaissance works, Florence's **Santa Maria Novella station** (1934) is another masterpiece of modernism. (Today a plaque at the station remembers Jews who were sent from this terminus to their death in Nazi Germany.)

After defeat in World War II, Italy's people voted for the establishment of the First Republic—overwhelmingly so in northern and central Italy, which outvoted a southern majority that wanted to keep the monarchy. Italy quickly succeeded in rebuilding its economy, in part because of U.S. aid under the **Marshall Plan** (1948–52). By the 1960s, as a member of the European Economic Community (founded by the **Treaty of Rome** in 1957), Italy had become one of the world's leading industrialized nations, and prominent in the manufacture of automobiles and office equipment. Fiat (from Turin), Ferrari (from Emilia-Romagna), and Olivetti (from northern Piedmont) were known around the world.

The postwar Italian **film industry** became celebrated for innovative directors. **Federico Fellini** (1920–93) burst onto the scene with his highly individual style, beginning with "La Strada" (1954) and later such classics as "The City of Women" (1980). His "La Dolce Vita" (1961) seems to define an era in Rome. The gritty "neorealism" of controversial **Pier Paolo Pasolini** (1922–75) is conveyed most vividly in "Accattone" (1961), which he wrote and directed.

The country was plagued, however, by economic inequality, including between the industrially prosperous North and the depressed South. During the late 1970s and early 1980s, it was also rocked by domestic terrorism: These were the so-called **Anni di Piombo** (Years of Lead), during which extremists of the left and right bombed and assassinated with impunity. Conspiracy theories became an Italian staple diet; everyone from a shadow state to Masonic lodges to the CIA was accused of involvement in what became, in effect, an undeclared civil war. The most notorious incidents were the kidnap and murder of Prime Minister **Aldo Moro** in 1978 and the **Bologna station bombing,** which killed 85 in 1980. You'll find a succinct account of these murky years in Tobias Jones's "The Dark Heart of Italy."

In the early 1990s, many of the country's leading politicians were accused of corruption. These scandals uncovered during the judiciary's

Mani Pulite (Clean Hands) investigations—often dubbed **Tangentopoli**

("Bribesville")—provoked a constitutional crisis, ushering in the **Second Republic** in 1992.

Resonant events in recent Italian history have also centered on religion. As much of the world watched and prayed, Pope John Paul II died in April 2005, at the age of 84, ending a reign of 26 years. A doctrinal hardliner next took the papal throne as Pope Benedict XVI. He was succeeded by the surprisingly liberal Pope Francis in 2013, after Benedict became the first pope since the 1400s to resign the office.

WHEN TO GO

The best months for traveling in much of Italy are from **April to June** and **mid-September to October:** Temperatures are usually comfortable, rural colors are rich, and the crowds aren't too intense (except around Easter). Easter, May, and June usually usher in the highest hotel prices in Rome and Florence. From July through early September the country's holiday spots teem with visitors. **August,** however, is the worst month in many places: Not only does it get uncomfortably hot and muggy, but seemingly the entire country goes on vacation for at least 2 weeks (many Italians take off the entire month). Plenty of family-run restaurants and shops are closed, except at the spas, beaches, and islands, where most Italians head. Paradoxically, you will have many urban places almost to yourself if you visit in August—Turin and Milan in particular can seem ghost towns, and even excellent hotels there are heavily discounted. (Florence and Rome are no longer as quiet as they once were.) Be aware that many fashionable restaurants and nightspots are closed for the whole month.

From late October to Easter, many attractions operate on shorter winter hours, and some hotels are closed for renovation or redecoration, although inconvenience is much less likely if you visit a city. Between November and February, beach resorts become padlocked ghost towns, and many family-run restaurants take a week or two off.

Weather

It's warm all over Italy in **summer;** it can be very hot in the south, and almost anywhere inland. Landlocked cities in Tuscany and Umbria, and on the plains of Veneto, Lombardy, and Emilia-Romagna, feel stifling during a July or August hot spell. The higher temperatures (measured in Italy in degrees Celsius) usually begin everywhere in May, often lasting until sometime in October. **Winters** in the north of Italy are cold, with rain and snow. A biting wind whistles over the mountains into Milan, Turin, Venice, and sometimes even Florence. In Rome and the south the weather is warm (or at least, warm-ish) almost all year, averaging 10°C (50°F) in winter. But even here chilly snaps are possible, even occasional freezing temperatures and heavy snow.

The rainiest months pretty much everywhere are usually October and November.

Italy's Average Daily High Temperature & Monthly Rainfall

ROME

	JAN	FEB	MAR	APR	MAY	JUNE	JULY	AUG	SEPT	OCT	NOV	DEC
TEMP. (°F)	55	56	59	63	71	77	83	83	79	71	62	57
TEMP. (°C)	12	13	15	17	21	25	28	28	26	21	16	13
RAINFALL (IN.)	3.2	2.8	2.7	2.6	2	1.3	.6	1	2.7	4.5	4.4	3.8

FLORENCE

	JAN	FEB	MAR	APR	MAY	JUNE	JULY	AUG	SEPT	OCT	NOV	DEC
TEMP. (°F)	49	53	60	68	75	84	89	88	81	69	58	50
TEMP. (°C)	9	11	15	20	23	28	31	31	27	20	14	10
RAINFALL (IN.)	1.9	2.1	2.7	2.9	3	2.7	1.5	1.9	3.3	4	3.9	2.8

VENICE

	JAN	FEB	MAR	APR	MAY	JUNE	JULY	AUG	SEPT	OCT	NOV	DEC
TEMP. (°F)	42	47	54	61	70	77	81	81	75	65	53	44
TEMP. (°C)	6	8	12	16	21	25	27	27	24	18	11	7
RAINFALL (IN.)	2.3	2.1	2.2	2.5	2.7	3	2.5	3.3	2.6	2.7	3.4	2.1

Public Holidays

Offices, government buildings (but usually not tourist offices), and shops in Italy are generally closed on: January 1 (*Capodanno,* or New Year); January 6 (*La Befana,* or Epiphany); Easter Sunday *(Pasqua);* Easter Monday *(Pasquetta);* April 25 (Liberation Day); May 1 (*Festa del Lavoro,* or Labor Day); June 2 (*Festa della Repubblica,* or Republic Day); August 15 (*Ferragosto,* or the Assumption of the Virgin); November 1 (All Saints'

Historic gondolas open Venice's Regata Storica.

Day); December 8 (*L'Immacolata*, or the Immaculate Conception); December 25 (*Natale*, Christmas Day); and December 26 (*Santo Stefano*, or St. Stephen's Day). You'll often find businesses closed for the annual daylong celebration dedicated to a local patron saint (for example, on January 31 in San Gimignano, Tuscany).

Italy Calendar of Events

JANUARY

Festa di Sant'Agnese, Sant'Agnese Fuori le Mura, Rome. In this ancient ceremony, two lambs are blessed and shorn; their wool is used later for *palliums* (Roman Catholic vestments). www.santagnese. com. Jan 21.

FEBRUARY

Carnevale, Venice. At this riotous time, theatrical presentations and masked balls take place across Venice and on islands in its lagoon. The balls are by invitation only (except the Doge's Ball), but street events and fireworks are open to everyone. www.carnevale.venezia.it. 2 weeks before Ash Wednesday, the beginning of Lent.

Festival della Canzone Italiana (Festival of Italian Popular Song), San Remo, Liguria. At this 6-day competition, major artists perform previously unreleased Italian songs. www.rai.it/programmi/ sanremo. Late Feb.

MARCH

Festa di San Giuseppe, the Trionfale Quarter, Rome. A decorated statue of St. Joseph is brought out at a fair with food stalls, concerts, and sporting events. Usually Mar 19.

APRIL

Holy Week, nationwide. Processions and age-old ceremonies, some from pagan days, others from the Middle Ages. The most notable procession is led by the Pope, passing the Colosseum and Roman Forum; a torch-lit parade caps the observance. Beginning a week before Easter; late Mar or early Apr.

Easter Sunday (Pasqua), Piazza San Pietro, Rome. In an event broadcast around the world, the Pope gives his blessing from the balcony of St. Peter's.

Scoppio del Carro (Explosion of the Cart), Florence. At this ancient observance, a cart laden with flowers and fireworks is drawn by 3 white oxen to the Duomo. At the 11am Mass, a mechanical dove detonates it. Easter Sunday.

MAY

Maggio Musicale Fiorentino (Florentine Musical May), Florence. Italy's oldest and most prestigious music festival emphasizes music from the 14th to the 20th centuries, including ballet and opera. www.maggiofiorentino.it. Late Apr to end of June.

Giro d'Italia, nationwide. One of Europe's three great cycling endurance races, this month-long event has been staged for more than a century. www.giroditalia.it.

Mille Miglia, Brescia, Lombardy. Vintage and classic cars depart Brescia and spend 4 days parading around the towns and cities of northern and central Italy as part of the annual "1000 Miles." www.1000miglia.it. Mid-May.

Concorso Ippico Internazionale (International Horse Show), Piazza di Siena, Rome. Top-flight international equestrian show in the Villa Borghese. www.piazza-disiena.it. Late May.

JUNE

Festa di San Ranieri, Pisa, Tuscany. The city honors its patron saint with candlelit parades, followed the next day by eight-rower teams competing in 16th-century costumes. June 16 and 17.

Calcio Storico (Historic Football), Florence. A revival of a raucous 15th-century form of football, pitting four teams in medieval costumes against one another. The matches usually culminate on June 24, the feast day of St. John the Baptist. www.calciostoricofiorentino.it. Late June.

Gioco del Ponte, Pisa, Tuscany. Teams in Renaissance costume take part in a long-contested "push-of-war" on the Ponte di Mezzo, which spans the River Arno. www.giocodelpontedipisa.it. Last weekend in June.

Arena di Verona Opera Festival, Verona, Veneto. Verona's 20,000-seat Roman-era amphitheater hosts Italy's most famous outdoor opera season, now over 100 years old. www.arena.it. Late June–late Aug.

Biennale Arte, Venice. One of the most famous recurring art events in the world takes place every 2 years (odd-numbered years). Even-numbered years see related events, including Biennale Architettura. www.labiennale.org. June–Nov.

JULY

Il Palio, Piazza del Campo, Siena, Tuscany. Palio fever grips this Tuscan hill town for a wild and exciting horse race dating from the Middle Ages, with pageantry, costumes, and the celebrations of the victorious *contrada* (neighborhood social club). July 2.

Umbria Jazz, Perugia, Umbria. One of Europe's top jazz festivals always attracts top-class artists. www.umbriajazz.com. July.

Puccini Festival, Torre del Lago, Tuscany. At an outdoor lakeside venue, the Tuscan maestro's blockbuster operas are celebrated. www.puccinifestival.it. Mid-July–late Aug.

Festa del Redentore (Feast of the Redeemer), Venice. This festival marks the lifting of a plague in 1576, with fireworks, pilgrimages, and boating. www.redentorevenezia.it. 3rd Sat & Sun of July.

AUGUST

Il Palio, Piazza del Campo, Siena, Tuscany. See July (above). This second annual race is dedicated to the Assumption of the Virgin Mary. Aug 16.

Venice International Film Festival, Venice. Second only to Cannes, this festival brings stars, directors, producers, and filmmakers from all over the world to the Palazzo del Cinema on the Lido. While many seats are reserved for jury members, the public can attend, too. www.labiennale.org/en/cinema. Late Aug–early Sept.

SEPTEMBER

Regata Storica, Grand Canal, Venice. A maritime spectacular. Many gondolas participate in the canal procession, though gondolas don't race in the regatta itself. www.regatastoricavenezia.it. 1st Sun in Sept.

Festa di San Gennaro, Naples, Campania. The cathedral is the focal point for a celebration in honor of the city's patron saint. A solemn procession is followed by the miraculous "liquefaction" of the holy blood. Sept 19.

Palio di Asti, Asti, Piedmont. Riders race for Italy's "second" Palio around this Piedmont town's central square. Expect medieval pageantry and daring horsemanship. www.astiturismo.it. 1st Sun in Sept.

DECEMBER

La Scala Opera Season Opening, Teatro alla Scala, Milan. At the most famous house of them all, the season begins each December 7, the feast day of Milan's patron, St. Ambrose Even though opening-night tickets are almost impossible to find, it is worth a try. www.teatroallascala.org. Dec–Jul (also Sept–mid-Nov).

Christmas Blessing of the Pope, Piazza San Pietro, Rome. Delivered at noon from the balcony of St. Peter's Basilica, the Pope's words are broadcast to the faithful around the globe. Dec 25.

3

SUGGESTED ITALY ITINERARIES

By Donald Strachan

taly is so vast and treasure-filled, it's hard to resist the temptation to pack too much into too little time. This is a dauntingly diverse destination, and you can't even skim the surface in 1 or 2 weeks—so relax, and don't try. If you're a first-time visitor with little touring time on your hands, we suggest you zero in on the classic cities: Rome, Florence, and Venice could be packed into 1 very busy week, better yet in 2.

How can you accomplish that? Well, for starters, Italy has well-maintained highways (called *autostrade*). You'll pay a toll to drive on them (p. 815), but it's much quicker to use them than to trust your limited time to the minor roads, which can be *much* slower going.

The country also has one of the most efficient high-speed rail networks in Europe. Rome, Bologna, and Milan are the key hubs of this 21st-century transportation empire—for example, from Rome's Termini station, Florence can be reached in only 95 minutes. If you're city-hopping between Rome, Florence, and Venice, you need never rent a car, because all the key routes are served by comfortable, quick trains. You'll only require a rental car for rural detours.

The itineraries that follow introduce some of our favorite places. The pace may occasionally be a bit breathless for some visitors, so consider skipping a stop to take some chill-out time—after all, you're on vacation. Of course, you can also use any itinerary as a jumping-off point to develop your own custom-made adventure. *Buon viaggio!*

ITALY'S REGIONS IN BRIEF

Although bordered on the northwest by France, on the north by Switzerland and Austria, and on the northeast by Slovenia, Italy is mostly surrounded by the sea. It isn't enormous; the peninsula's slender boot shape gives the impression of a much larger area. Here's a brief rundown of the cities and regions covered in this guide. See the inside front cover for a map of Italy by region.

ROME & LATIUM   The region of **Latium** ("Lazio" in Italian) is dominated by **Rome,** capital of both the ancient empire and modern Italy. Much of the "civilized world" was once ruled from here, starting from when Romulus and Remus are said to have founded Rome, in 753 B.C. No place has more artistic monuments, or a bigger buzz.

FLORENCE, TUSCANY & UMBRIA   **Tuscany** is one of Italy's most culturally and politically influential provinces. The development of Italy without Tuscany is simply unthinkable; in fact, today's Italian language is

The baroque Trevi Fountain, a tourist gathering spot in Rome.

essentially an update of the medieval Florentine dialect. Nowhere in the world is the impact of the Renaissance still felt more fully than in **Florence,** the repository of artistic works by Masaccio, Leonardo da Vinci, Michelangelo, and many others. The main Tuscan destinations beyond Florence are the smaller cities of **Lucca, Pisa,** and especially **Siena,** Florence's great historical rival, as well as the **Chianti** winelands. Neighboring **Umbria** is a land of rolling green hills and olive groves, where the pace of life is sedate. It has outstanding art sights in **Perugia** and the former Etruscan capital of **Orvieto.**

BOLOGNA & EMILIA-ROMAGNA   Italians don't agree on much, but one national consensus is that food in **Emilia-Romagna** is the best in Italy. The regional capital, **Bologna,** also has museums, churches, and a fine university born in the Middle Ages. Among the region's other cities, none is nobler than Byzantine **Ravenna,** with mosaics dating to a time when it was capital of a Western Roman Empire in decline.

VENICE & THE VENETO   Northeastern Italy is one of Europe's treasure troves, encompassing **Venice** (certainly the world's most unusual city) and the surrounding **Veneto** region. Aging, decaying, and sinking into the sea, Venice is so alluring we're tempted to say: Visit even if you have to skip Rome and Florence. Also recommended are the art cities of the Venetian Arc: **Verona,** with its Shakespearean romance and intact Roman amphitheater hosting a famous summer opera festival; and **Padua,** with its Giotto frescoes on the walls of the Cappella degli Scrovegni.

LOMBARDY, PIEDMONT & THE LAKES   Flat, fertile, and prosperous, **Lombardy** is dominated by **Milan,** with Leonardo's "Last Supper," the La Scala opera house, shopping, and some major museums. You'll also find charm in the nearby cities of **Bergamo** and **Mantua,** as well as the photogenic lakes of **Como** and **Garda.** In Piedmont's largest city, **Turin**— home of the Fiat empire—the best-known sight is the Sacra Sindone (Holy Shroud), which some Christians believe is the cloth in which Christ's crucified body was wrapped.

LIGURIA   Comprising most of the **Italian Riviera,** the region of **Liguria** incorporates the major historical seaport of **Genoa,** charming upscale resorts such as the harbor at **Portofino,** and Italy's best coastal hiking, among the traditional villages of the **Cinque Terre.**

CAMPANIA, PUGLIA & BASILICATA **Campania** encompasses both the fascinating anarchy of **Naples** and the elegant beauty of **Capri** and the **Amalfi Coast.** The region also has some of the world's most renowned ruins, at **Pompeii** and **Herculaneum.** Cave dwellings pepper **Matera,** in **Basilicata**—the *Sassi*—inhabited almost continuously since the Paleolithic Era. **Puglia** (sometimes called "Apulia" in English) is home to the conical *trulli* houses of **Alberobello** and the Valle d'Itria, and the baroque architecture of **Lecce**—sometimes nicknamed (ambitiously) "the Florence of the South."

SICILY The largest island in the Mediterranean Sea, **Sicily** has a unique mix of bloodlines and architecture from medieval Normandy, Aragónese Spain, Moorish North Africa, Ancient Greece, Phoenicia, and Rome. Cars, street markets, and fashionable people clog the lanes of its capital, **Palermo.** Areas of ravishing beauty and eerie historical interest include the coastal towns of **Syracuse** (Siracusa in Italian) and **Taormina,** and the ruins at **Agrigento** and **Selinunte.**

THE BEST OF ITALY IN 1 WEEK: ROME, FLORENCE & VENICE

Let's be realistic: It's impossible to see this storied country properly in a week. However, a fast, efficient rail network along the Rome–Florence–Venice line makes it surprisingly easy to see a handful of the best these 3 elegant, art-stuffed cities have to offer. This weeklong itinerary treads the familiar highlights, but there's a reason why they are the country's most visited sights: They're sure to provide memories that last a lifetime.

DAYS 1, 2 & 3: Rome: Capital, Ancient & Modern ★★★

You could spend forever in the Eternal City, but 3 days is enough to catch a flavor. There are two essential areas to focus on in a short visit. The first is the legacy of Imperial Rome, with the **Forum, Campidoglio,** and **Colosseum** (p. 91). Bookend **DAY 1** with the Forum and Colosseum (one first, the other last) to avoid the busiest crowds; the same ticket is good for both. On **DAY 2,** tackle **St. Peter's Basilica** and the **Vatican Museums** (p. 82), with a collection unlike any other in the world (including, of course, Michelangelo's **Sistine Chapel**). On **DAY 3,** it's a toss-up: Choose between the underground catacombs of the **Via Appia Antica** (p. 122); or spend the day wandering the **Centro Storico** (p. 101) and the **Tridente** (p. 107), on the busy streets connecting Piazza Navona, the Pantheon, the Spanish Steps, the Trevi Fountain, and more. Spend your evenings in the bars of **Campo de' Fiori** or **Monti** (p. 160) and the restaurants of **Trastevere** (p. 149) or **Testaccio** (p. 152). Toward the end of your third day, catch a late train to Florence. *Tip:* Make sure you've booked tickets in advance: Walk-up fares are much more expensive than advanced tickets on the high-speed rail network.

DAYS 4 & 5: Florence: Cradle of the Renaissance ★★★

You have 2 whole days to explore the city of Giotto, Leonardo, Botticelli, and Michelangelo. Start with their masterpieces at the **Uffizi** (p. 181; definitely pre-book tickets, months ahead if possible), followed by the **Duomo** complex (p. 180): Scale Brunelleschi's ochre dome, and follow up with a visit to the nearby **Battistero di San Giovanni** (p. 176), the revamped **Museo dell'Opera del Duomo** (p. 181), and **Campanile di Giotto** (p. 180). Start **DAY 5** with "David" at the **Accademia** (p. 195). For the rest of your time, get to know the intimate murals of **San Marco** (p. 197), paintings hanging at the **Palazzo Pitti** (p. 201), and Masaccio's revolutionary frescoes

Piazza San Marco in Venice.

in the **Cappella Brancacci** (p. 203). In the evenings, head south of the Arno, in San Frediano or San Niccolò, for lively wine bars and more creative restaurants than you generally find in the historic center. Leave on an early train on the morning of **DAY 6.**

DAYS 6 & 7: Venice: City that Defies the Sea ★★★

Ride into the heart of Venice on a *vaporetto* (water bus), taking in the **Grand Canal,** the world's greatest thoroughfare. Begin the sightseeing at **Piazza San Marco** (p. 400). The **Basilica di San Marco** is right there, and after exploring it, visit the nearby **Palazzo Ducale (Doge's Palace;** p. 410) before walking over the **Bridge of Sighs.** Begin your evening with the classic Venetian *aperitivo,* an Aperol spritz, followed by *cicchetti* (Venetian tapas) before a late dinner. Make **DAY 7** all about the city's unique art: the **Gallerie dell'Accademia** (p. 416), the modern **Peggy Guggenheim Collection** (p. 418), and **San Rocco** (p. 422). Catch a late train back to Rome. Or add another night . . . You can never stay too long in Venice.

THE BEST OF ITALY IN 2 WEEKS

It's still difficult to see the top sights of Italy—and to see them properly—in just 2 weeks. But in this itinerary, we show you some of the best of them. We go beyond the well-trodden (and spectacular) Rome–Florence–Venice trail to include the southern region of Campania, specifically Pompeii, which has Europe's most precious Roman ruins. Additional stops in the center and north are Pisa (for the Leaning Tower and more) and Verona (the city of lovers since "Romeo and Juliet").

DAYS 1, 2 & 3: Rome ★★★

Follow the itinerary suggested in "The Best of Italy in 1 Week," above. On your third day take a late afternoon train to Naples, where you'll be based for the next 2 nights.

DAY 4: Naples ★★

Spend a full day taking in the major attractions of urban Naples, the historic "capital" of southern Italy. Pore over the unparalleled collection of ancient artifacts at the **Museo Archeologico Nazionale** (p. 600), then see Titians and Caravaggios at the **Museo e Gallerie Nazionale di Capodimonte** (p. 603). After dark, wander **Spaccanapoli**—the old center's main east–west thoroughfare—then make a date with a **pizzeria:** Neapolitans claim pizza was invented here. After dinner, stroll the **Mergellina** boardwalk to enjoy sea breezes and views across the Bay of Naples.

DAY 5: Pompeii ★★ & Sorrento ★

Take the Circumvesuviana train from Porta Nolana Station 24km (15 miles) south of Naples to spend a day wandering Europe's best-preserved Roman ruins at **Pompeii** (p. 629). Pack water and lunch, because onsite services aren't great. Buried for almost 2,000 years, after nearby Vesuvius erupted in A.D. 79, Pompeii exhibits some of the great archaeological treasures of Italy, including the patrician **Casa dei Vettii** and the frescoed **Villa dei Misteri.** Continue by local train to the pretty seaside town of **Sorrento,** where you will lodge for 2 nights (you may leave luggage at Pompeii Station while you tour the ruins).

DAY 6: The Amalfi Coast ★★

On the morning of **DAY 6,** take a bus along the **Amalfi Drive,** of which Andre Gide said: "[There is] nothing more beautiful on this earth." The drive winds around the twisting, steep coastline to the southern resorts of **Positano** and **Amalfi,** either of which would make an idyllic stopover to extend your stay. Allow at least 4 hours for a roundtrip back to Sorrento, because it can be slow-moving and you will want to linger. (You can also rent a car to do the Amalfi Coast drive solo, but it's a fairly hair-raising route. Only for the bold.)

Terraced towns climb up coastal hillsides along the scenic Amalfi Coast.

DAYS 7 & 8: Florence ★★★

Connect from Sorrento by rail to Napoli Garibaldi (1 hr.) then onward via an early high-speed train from Naples Centrale to Florence (journey time: 3 hrs.). Follow the itinerary suggested in "The Best of Italy in 1 Week," above. You'll be staying in Florence for the next 4 nights.

DAY 9: Siena ★★★

It's just over an hour to Siena on the *rapida* bus from Florence's bus station (p. 174). Leave early and set out immediately on arrival for **Piazza del Campo,** the shell-shaped main square, including its art-filled **Museo Civico** (inside the **Palazzo Pubblico;** p. 238). Squeeze in a look at the **Duomo** (p. 237) and **Museo dell'Opera Metropolitana,** where you'll find Sienese master Duccio's giant "Maestà" painting. Stop on the Campo for an early evening drink and then head to a restaurant in Siena's atmospheric back streets. Reserve an early table: The last bus back to Florence departs around 8:45pm (Sun 7:10pm).

DAY 10: Pisa ★★

Most trains between Florence and Pisa take around an hour. On arrival, hop aboard the LAM Rossa bus outside Pisa Centrale Station, heading to the **Campo dei Miracoli** ("Field of Miracles"). The set-piece piazza here is one of the most photographed slices of real estate on the planet—and home to the **Leaning Tower** (p. 300). Visit the **Duomo,** with its Arab-influenced Pisan-Romanesque façade; the **Battistero** with its carved pulpit and crazy acoustics; and the rest of the piazza's monuments and museums on the same combination ticket. Book a slot ahead of time if you want to climb the Leaning Tower, however. For dining *alla pisana,* head away from the touristy piazza to the warren of streets around the market square, **Piazza delle Vettovaglie.** Finish your visit with a stroll along the handsome promenade beside the **River Arno.** The last train back to Florence usually leaves at 10:30pm (though the 9:30pm train is 20 mins. quicker).

DAYS 11 & 12: Venice ★★★

Set your alarm clock for an early start: It takes around 2 hours to reach Venice from Florence aboard the high-speed train. Follow the itinerary suggested in "The Best of Italy in 1 Week," p. 42. You'll be staying in Venice for 3 nights.

DAY 13: Verona ★★★

Tip: Book round-trip tickets ahead of time for a high-speed Frecciarossa or Frecciabianca train between Venice and Verona—the journey is just 1 hour, 10 minutes, compared with around 2 hours for local train service. Although he likely never set foot in the place, Shakespeare placed the world's most famous love story, "Romeo and Juliet," here. Wander **Piazza dei Signori** and take in another square, **Piazza delle Erbe,** before descending on the **Arena di Verona**

Italy in Two Weeks

0   100 mi
0   100 km

- **1-3** Rome
- **4** Naples
- **5** Pompeii & Sorrento
- **6** The Amalfi Coast
- **7** & **8** Florence
- **9** Siena
- **10** Pisa
- **11** & **12** Venice
- **13** Verona
- **14** Milan

(p. 458): The world's best-preserved gladiatorial arena, it's packed for monumental open-air opera performances in summer. Head back to Venice for the night.

DAY 14: Milan ★★

Pre-book a fast train connection between Venice and Milan, a journey of between 2¼ and 2½ hours. The most bustling city in Italy isn't only about industry and commerce. Milan has one of Europe's finest Gothic cathedrals, the **Duomo** (p. 472). Its **Biblioteca-Pinacoteca Ambrosiana** houses one of Italy's great art collections. The city of St. Ambrose also hosts the **Pinacoteca di Brera** (p. 478), a treasure trove of painting, laden with masterpieces from the likes of Mantegna and

Piero della Francesca. Book ahead, too, to view Leonardo's fading but still magnificent **"Last Supper"** (p. 479). Stay overnight here if you are flying home or onward: It is one of Europe's major airline hubs.

ITALY FOR FAMILIES

Italy is probably the friendliest family vacation destination in all Europe. Practically, it presents few challenges. If you're traveling by rental car with young children, be sure to request safety car seats ahead of time. Let the rental company know the age of your child and they will arrange for a seat to comply with E.U. regulations. Rail travelers should remember reduced-price family fares are available on much of the high-speed network; ask when you buy your tickets or use a booking agent.

As you tour, don't go hunting for "child-friendly" restaurants or special kids' menus. There is always plenty available for little ones anywhere you dine, even dishes that aren't offered to grown-up patrons. Never be afraid to ask if you have a fussy eater in the family. Pretty much any request is met with a smile.

Perhaps the main issue for travelers with children is spacing your museum visits so you get to see the masterpieces without having young kids suffer a meltdown after one saint painting too many. Remember to punctuate every day with a **gelato** stop. Italy has the world's best ice cream, and you will find soya milk flavors for anyone with an intolerance. We also suggest limiting long, tiring day trips out of town, especially by public transportation. And end your trip in Venice, which for most kids is every bit as magical as a Disney theme park.

DAY 1: Rome's Ancient Ruins ★★★

History is on your side here: The wonders of **Ancient Rome** (p. 88) should appeal as much to kids (of almost any age) as to adults. There are gory tales to tell at the **Colosseum** (p. 91), where the bookshop has a good selection of city guides aimed at kids. After that, they can let off steam wandering the **Roman Forum** and the **Palatine Hill.** (The roadside ruins of the **Imperial Forums** can be viewed at any time.) Cap the afternoon by exploring the **Villa Borghese** (p. 112), a large park in the heart of Rome where you can rent bikes. For dinner, head for some crispy crusts at an authentic Roman **pizzeria.**

DAY 2: Rome: Living History ★★★

Head early to **St. Peter's Basilica** (p. 79). The kids will find it spooky wandering the Vatican grottoes, and few can resist climbing up to Michelangelo's dome at 114m (375 ft.). After time out for lunch, begin your assault on the **Vatican Museums** and the **Sistine Chapel.** Even if your kids don't like art museums, they are sure to gawp at the grandeur. Later in the day head for the **Spanish Steps** (a good spot for upscale souvenir shopping; see p. 154) before wandering over to

Italy for Families

1. Rome's Ancient Ruins
2. Rome: Living History
3. Rome: Underground
4. & 5. Florence
6. Pisa
7. & 8. Genoa & the Riviera di Levante
9. & 10. Lake Garda
11-13. Venice

the **Trevi Fountain.** Let them toss coins into the fountain, which is said to ensure a return to Rome—perhaps when they are older and can fully appreciate the city's many more artistic attractions.

DAY 3: Rome: Underground ★★★

There are, literally, layers of history below the city streets, and kids will love exploring the catacombs of the **Via Appia Antica** (p. 68), the first cemetery of Rome's Christian community, where the devout practiced their faith in secret during periods of persecution. **Context Travel** (p. 125) runs an excellent 2-hour family tour of the city's subterranean layers, which takes in **San Clemente** (p. 97) and **Santi Giovanni e Paolo.** It costs 325€ per party. Eat more **pizza** before you leave; Rome's pizzerias are matched only by those in Naples, to the south, and our next recommended stops all lie to the north. Leave on a late afternoon train to Florence.

DAYS 4 & 5: Florence ★★★

Florence is usually thought of as a grown-up city, but there's enough to fill two family days. A bonus: Much of the center is traffic-free these days. With multiple nights here, renting an apartment will give you space to spread out—see p. 207 for apartment rental suggestions. Close to the Duomo, **Residence Hilda** (p. 214) is a family-friendly hotel with large, apartment-style rooms and kitchenettes.

Begin with the city's monumental main square, **Piazza della Signoria,** now an open-air museum of statues. The **Palazzo Vecchio** (p. 188) dominates one side; you can all tour it with special family-friendly guides, including a docent dressed as Cosimo de' Medici. Turn a visit to the famed **Uffizi Gallery** into a treasure trail by first visiting the shop to select postcards of key artworks to hunt down. On the second morning, kids will delight in climbing to the top of Brunelleschi's dome on the **Duomo** for a classic panorama. Get there early—queues lengthen through the day. If kids and adults have still more energy to burn, climb the 414 steps up to the **Campanile di Giotto,** run around in the **Giardino di Boboli,** and cross the **Ponte Vecchio** at dusk. With older, fit children, you could add another day here, to allow time to see the Chianti hills on two wheels (see p. 206 for bike-tour info).

DAY 6: Pisa ★★

If your kids are age 7 or under, consider skipping **Pisa** (p. 295): Eight is the minimum age for the iconic ascent up the bell tower of Pisa's cathedral, a.k.a. the **Leaning Tower.** Older kids will enjoy the hyper-real monuments of the **Campo dei Miracoli** and learning about the city's Galileo links: The scientist was born here, and supposedly discovered his law of pendulum motion while watching a swinging lamp inside the **Duomo.** Take the kids to taste a local specialty, *cecina,* a pizzalike garbanzo-bean flatbread served warm. Your daylong visit complete, whiz up the coast on the fast train to Genoa. There is a luggage storage facility *(deposito bagagli)* at Pisa Centrale station.

DAYS 7 & 8: Genoa & the Riviera di Levante ★★

The industrial city-seaport of Genoa is home to one of Italy's most popular family attractions: The **Acquario di Genova** (p. 553), Europe's largest aquarium, where you can all enjoy a trip around the world's oceans. It requires a half-day to see properly, so get in early, and then head out to the **Riviera di Levante** (p. 563), a coastline of pretty ports and rocky coves east of the city. Our favorite base around here is romantic **Portofino,** where you can easily kill your second day in Liguria beside the azure sea. **Santa Margherita Ligure** is a budget-friendlier alternative, with an easy rail link, a fine promenade, and a laid-back vibe.

DAYS 9 & 10: Lake Garda ★★

Slow down for a couple of days by Italy's biggest inland lake, perhaps basing yourself at photogenic **Sirmione** (p. 513). Take a ferry trip, hire a pedal boat or kayak, eat simple grilled lake fish, and ease into lakeside life. In Sirmione you can scramble on the ramparts of the **Castello Scaligero,** then ride the little train out to Roman ruins at the **Grotte di Catullo,** a villa supposedly once inhabited by the poet Catullus (ca. 84 B.C.–ca. 54 B.C.). For active families with more time to spend, **Riva del Garda** (p. 514), close to the lake's northernmost point, is one of Europe's major windsurfing/sailboarding centers.

DAYS 11, 12 & 13: Venice ★★★

In Venice, the fun begins the moment you arrive and take a *vaporetto* ride along the **Grand Canal.** Head straight for **Piazza San Marco** (p. 429), where children will delight in feeding the pigeons and riding the elevator up the great **Campanile.** Catch the mosaics inside the **Basilica di San Marco,** which dominates the square. At the **Palazzo Ducale** cross the infamous **Bridge of Sighs.** As in Florence, make time for some art: Visit the **Gallerie dell'Accademia** (p. 416) and **San Rocco,** where kids view the episodic Tintoretto paintings like a picture book or graphic novel. If it's summer, save time for the beach at **Lido** (p. 427) and perhaps for getting a different angle on Venice's canals, from the seat of a **gondola** (p. 403).

On Lake Garda, windsurfing and sailboarding attract sports-minded families.

A WHISTLESTOP WEEK-OR-SO FOR FOOD & WINE LOVERS

Italy has one of Europe's great cuisines—or rather, make that *several* of Europe's great cuisines (some claim that Italy has as many as 50 distinct culinary traditions). The nation's history as a collection of independent city-states and noble fiefdoms has left a diverse legacy in food. Each regional cuisine is committed to its own local produce and artisanal specialties, with treasured recipes handed down through generations.

Italy is also the world's biggest wine producer. Although much of the output is undistinguished (if perfectly drinkable) table wine, many icons of world wine also hail from here. Our itinerary takes in three of the great Italian red wine zones: **Montepulciano,** whose noble wine was known to the Etruscans; **Chianti,** the first legally defined wine zone in the world; and **Piedmont,** whose robust reds Barolo and Barbaresco command top prices at restaurants around the globe.

DAYS 1 & 2: Rome ★★★

Italy's capital is packed with restaurants serving cuisine from pretty much everywhere on the Italian peninsula. The **Trastevere, Monti,** and **Testaccio** neighborhoods are great for dining and drinks after dark. While here, sample traditional Roman dishes like pasta with *cacio e pepe* (sheep's milk cheese and black pepper); *spaghetti alla carbonara* (similar but enriched with egg yolk plus added *guanciale,* cured pork cheek) or *alla gricia* (also with *guanciale* and *pecorino* cheese, but no egg); *saltimbocca alla romana*—literally, "jump in the mouth," a veal cutlet with prosciutto and sage; and *coda alla vaccinara* (stewed oxtail with tomatoes and celery). **Gelato** is either Florentine or Sicilian in origin, depending on who you ask, but in Rome you'll find lots of the country's tastiest (see p. 144). The city also has some of Italy's best craft beer bars (see p. 160). You'll need a rental car for your next leg. Collect it on your second afternoon and head north to Tuscany, to leave yourself a full day at your next stop.

DAY 3: Montepulciano ★★

Begin with a walk up the handsome, steep Corso from the town gate to **Piazza Grande,** monumental heart of the *comune.* Here you'll find the **Palazzo Comunale** (climb it for a panorama of the surrounding winelands) and **Cattedrale.** Oenophiles should head to the **Consorzio del Vino Nobile di Montepulciano** enoteca, where you can taste vintages from small producers and seek advice for nearby wineries to visit. Our favorite cellar in the center is **Gattavecchi.** End the evening at **Acquacheta** (p. 255), where the menu's all about beef— *"bistecca numero uno,"* is how Contucci winemaker Adamo once described it to us. Other local delicacies include sheep's milk cheese, *pecorino di Pienza.*

1 & **2** Rome
3 Montepulciano
4 & **5** The Chianti
6 & **7** Bologna
8 & **9** Turin

DAYS 4 & 5: The Chianti ★★★

Pick a base close to **Greve in Chianti** (p. 249) to lodge right at the heart of Tuscany's largest quality wine region. Sangiovese-based Chianti is a diverse wine: Chianti Classico denotes grapes from the original (and best) growing zone, and tasting opportunities abound at cellars such as **Villa Vignamaggio** and **Castello di Volpaia.** Book ahead if you require a tour anywhere. They are widely offered. The Chianti is also famed for its butchers, where you can buy everything from cuts of fresh beef (ideal if you're staying in a villa) to salami made from a local breed of pig, the *Cinta Senese.* **Falorni,** in Greve, is outshone perhaps only by **Dario Cecchini,** in nearby Panzano. Also look for Tuscan extra virgin olive oil. Obtained from the first pressing of olives harvested in November, this local elixir is famed for its low acidity. It is among Italy's best.

DAYS 6 & 7: Bologna ★★

You have arrived in Italy's gastronomic capital. Leave the rental car here; it's easy to continue onward by train. The agricultural plains of Emilia-Romagna are Italy's breadbasket. So much of the produce we think of as typical "Italian food" hails from here: cured prosciutto and

Vineyards in Tuscany.

Parmigiano-Reggiano cheese from Parma and Reggio nell'Emilia; the finest balsamic vinegar from Modena; mortadella and tortellini (filled pasta) from Bologna itself. Foodies should browse Bologna's markets, the **Mercato delle Erbe** and the **Quadrilatero,** a warren of lanes with enticing food shops. Make a dinner reservation at a restaurant specializing in classic Bolognese cooking; see p. 362 for our picks.

DAYS 8 & 9: Turin ★

Snowcapped alpine peaks dot the horizon north and west of the Piedmontese capital, and the cooking in Italy's northwest reflects the heartier and hardier mountain folk that live on the city's doorstep. Nearby **Vercelli** is Italy's rice capital—this town is surrounded by paddy fields—and *risotto* is at its creamy best here. There's also a noticeable Ligurian current in Torinese food: Basil-based pesto is superb and the favorite slice-on-the-go isn't pizza but *farinata,* chickpea-flour flatbread dusted with rosemary or pepper. The **Langhe Hills** (p. 537), south of the city, are famed for blockbuster red wines and white truffles. Sweet vermouth was also invented in Turin; the classic local labels are slightly bitter Punt e Mes ("point and a half" in Piedmontese) and vanilla-rich Carpano Antica Formula.

HISTORIC CITIES OF THE NORTH

Often overshadowed by blockbusters like Rome and Florence, the cities of northern Italy make an excellent itinerary for return visitors. Each city on our tour has a center with refined architecture, and a history of independence—as well as struggle with and eventual subjection to the great regional powers, often Venice. The logical starting point is Milan, gateway to Italy for flights from across the globe. Spend a day there, collect your rental car or rail tickets—all train connections on this tour are easy—and set off early. The endpoint is Venice, where we recommend you extend your stay by as many days as you can; see chapter 9 for full coverage of the city.

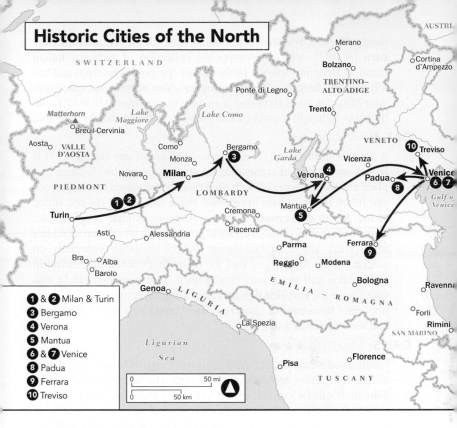

Historic Cities of the North

SWITZERLAND

AUSTRI

Merano

Bolzano

Cortina
d'Ampezzo

Ponte di Legno

TRENTINO–
ALTO ADIGE

Trento

Matterhorn
Breuil-Cervinia

Lake
Maggiore

Lake Como

VENETO

Treviso **10**

Aosta
VALLE
D'AOSTA

Como

Monza

Bergamo
3

Lake
Garda

Vicenza

Venice

Novara

Milan

Verona **4**

Padua

6 7

PIEDMONT

LOMBARDY

8

Gulf o
Venice

Turin

1 2

Cremona

Mantua

5

Asti

Alessandria

Piacenza

Bra
Alba

Barolo

Genoa

LIGURIA

Parma

Reggio Modena

Ferrara
9

Bologna

Ravenna

EMILIA – ROMAGNA

Forlì

La Spezia

Rimini

SAN MARINO

Ligurian
Sea

Pisa

Florence

TUSCANY

0 ____ 50 mi
0 ____ 50 km

1 & **2** Milan & Turin
3 Bergamo
4 Verona
5 Mantua
6 & **7** Venice
8 Padua
9 Ferrara
10 Treviso

DAYS 1 & 2: Milan ★★ & Turin ★★

See Milan under "The Best of Italy in 2 Weeks," above. Spend **DAY 2** taking a day trip by train to **Turin** (p. 516). The city of Fiat and football (meaning soccer) has a handsome baroque center, the finest Egyptian collection outside of Cairo at the **Museo Egizio** (p. 552), and views of the Alps from the top of the **Mole Antonelliana** tower (p. 520). It also has a food culture every bit as refined as Bologna's; Turin is the city of vermouth and on the doorstep of the Piedmont wine-growing region, so you need not go thirsty. You can complete the rail journey between the cities in as little as 45 minutes: There's no need to relocate your base from Milan, if you prefer to minimize changes of lodging.

DAY 3: Bergamo ★★

Whether you arrive by train or car, alight in the **Lower Town** (Città Bassa) and ascend to the **Upper Town** (Città Alta) in style, on the town's century-old funicular railway. **Piazza Vecchia** (p. 494) is the architectural heart of the Upper Town. Beyond its arcades you'll find the Romanesque **Basilica di Santa Maria Maggiore** and the Renaissance **Cappella Colleoni,** with a frescoed ceiling by Venetian rococo

55

painter Tiepolo. You should also make time for the **Accademia Carrara** (p. 492), with its exceptional collection of northern Italian painting. Bergamo was the birthplace of composer Donizetti and has a lively arts (largely operatic) program. You needn't relocate from your Milanese base: Bergamo is an easy daytrip from Milan (50 min. by train), although it makes a delightfully serene overnight stop, too.

DAY 4: Verona ★★

A visit to northern Italy's most renowned small city (see p. 457) is less about ticking off sights than about soaking up the elegance of a place eternally associated with Shakespeare's doomed lovers, Romeo and Juliet. If you're here in summer, make straight for the box office at the **Arena di Verona;** Italy's most intact Roman amphitheater hosts monumental outdoor operatic productions, which you shouldn't miss. There are often last-minute tickets available, especially on weekdays; see *Aïda* if you can, the opera that opened the festival in 1913 and is still most associated with it. Your roaming should also take you to the **Basilica di San Zeno Maggiore,** one of Italy's most important Romanesque churches. Use Verona as a base for 2 nights and see Mantua as a day visit.

DAY 5: Mantua ★★★

Landlocked it may be, but the Renaissance city of Mantua (p. 495) is almost completely, romantically surrounded by lakes fed by the River Mincio. It's just 45 minutes from Verona by train, and owes its grandeur to the Gonzaga family, who built piazzas and palaces and filled them with art by the greatest masters of the period, such as Mantegna. One day is just enough to visit architect L. B. Alberti's **Basilica di Sant'Andrea,** the frescoed **Palazzo Ducale,** and the Room of Giants inside **Palazzo Te.**

Juliet's Balcony in Verona.

DAYS 6 & 7: Venice ★★★

Follow the itinerary suggested in "The Best of Italy in 1 Week," p. 42. Use Venice as a base for your last 4 nights, seeing Padua and Ferrara on day-trip excursions.

DAY 8: Padua ★★

Stop first at the tourist office to buy a PadovaCard, a discount ticket that buys entrance to almost everything in town plus free public transportation or parking. Then head for the most historically significant paintings in northern Italy, Giotto's frescoes in the **Cappella degli Scrovegni** (p. 455). Also stop by the **Basilica di Sant'Antonio,** the final resting place of St. Anthony of Padua, the second-most eminent Franciscan saint after St. Francis himself.

DAY 9: Ferrara ★★

Like nearby Mantua, this small, stately city owes its grandeur to one despotic family—in this case, the Este dukes, who held sway from the 1200s to the 1500s, ruling the city from the **Castello Estense** (p. 370). Elsewhere in the center, check out the facade of the Gothic-Romanesque **Duomo** and the **Palazzo dei Diamanti,** another Este creation, named for the 9,000 diamond-shaped stones adorning its facade. Ferrara is under an hour by high-speed train from Venice.

DAY 10: Treviso ★★

It's not far (a half-hour by train) from Venice to its small northern neighbor, which the powerful Venetians dominated for over 450 years from the 14th century. They left a rich architectural legacy—plus canals, of course. The pace here is sedate. You'll have ample time to survey the greatest hits of painter **Tomaso da Modena,** at the churches of **Santa Lucia** and **San Nicoló** and the **Museo di Santa Caterina** (p. 461), before repairing to **Piazza dei Signori,** the medieval city's pretty heart, to enjoy a glass of local Prosecco sparkling wine.

ITALY'S ANCIENT RUINS

Italy itself isn't old—as a unified country, it only recently passed the 150-year mark. But the peninsula is rightly considered a cradle of European civilization. Michelangelo and the Renaissance, Gothic architecture, even the Byzantine mosaics of Ravenna: These are relatively recent moments in Italian time. Even the Romans were not the first civilization to leave a mark here. Several ancient buildings still standing owe their construction to expatriates from classical Greece.

DAYS 1, 2, 3 & 4: Sicily ★★★

As Greek Syracuse, modern-day **Siracusa** (p. 776) was one of the cultural hotspots of the ancient Mediterranean: Dramatist Aeschylus was a visitor, and lyric poet Sappho was exiled here toward the end of the 7th century B.C. A ruined Doric **Temple of Apollo** stands in town, and the **Parco Archeologico della Neapolis** (p. 781) has a Greek theater still used to stage drama each summer. Our suggestion: Fly into Catania, 67km (41 miles) north of Siracusa, which is well connected by air with Rome (1 hr., 15 min. flight), then rent a car and make your

Ruins of the Temple of Apollo in Syracuse, Sicily.

base in Sicily's southwest for at least half your time on the island, to tour coastal **Selinunte** (p. 806), **Segesta** (p. 765), the Valley of the Temples at **Agrigento** (p. 793), and the mosaics of the **Villa Romana del Casale** in Piazza Armerina (p. 791). Return to Siracusa and fly back from Catania to Rome.

DAYS 5, 6 & 7: Rome ★★★

Rome is to archaeology as Coke is to fizzy brown liquids: This is the brand that counts when it comes to ancient ruins. Rome was the epicenter of a republic and empire which for centuries ruled most of Europe and Asia Minor, as well as much of North Africa and the Middle East. Spend **DAY 5** walking ancient Rome's civic and spiritual heart, the **Forum** (p. 93). The same ticket gets you into the **Colosseum** (p. 91). Between visits to those two, it makes sense to see the **Imperial Forums, Trajan's Markets,** and the city's best artifact collection, at the **Musei Capitolini** (p. 90). Rome's museums display an array of relics dug up over the centuries: Add the ancient collections of the **Vatican Museums** (p. 82) and the busts and Roman art at **Palazzo Massimo alle Terme** (p. 116) to your to-do list for **DAY 6**. The ruins of Rome's former seaport, **Ostia Antica** (p. 162), stand a short train journey from the city—a comfortable half-day roundtrip for **DAY 7**. On the way back into the city, jump off at the Circo Massimo Metro stop to visit the **Terme di Caracalla** (p. 88) baths complex, and to admire for one last time the view of the **Palatine Hill** from the Circus Maximus. You could probably spend a month here just looking at the remnants of Ancient Rome.

DAYS 8, 9 & 10: Naples & Campania ★★

Ancient Naples—established as the fishing port of Parthenope, then refounded as Neapolis in the 6th century B.C.—was a key settlement in Magna Graecia, or "Greater Greece." Remnants of the ancient world remain in Naples's *centro storico:* In the excavations below

San Lorenzo Maggiore (p. 601), you can walk around remains of the Greek *Ágora* (market) and a later Roman Forum. Day trips to the Roman towns of **Pompeii** and **Herculaneum** (p. 624) reveal haunting artifacts preserved for centuries under ash and lava after Vesuvius's cataclysmic eruption in A.D. 79; visit Naples's **Museo Archeologico Nazionale** (p. 600) to see wall art from Pompeii and Roman statuary, including the "Farnese Bull." Another day trip heads west of Naples to the amphitheater at **Pozzuoli** (p. 616), the third-largest in the Roman world. Leave Naples on the high-speed Frecciarossa or Italo service late on **DAY 10** to get to Florence, just under 3 hours by rail.

DAYS 11 & 12: Florence ★★

Florence's Renaissance heyday, in the 1400s and 1500s, dominates much of the center's art and architecture. However, the **Museo Archeologico** (p. 196) displays relics from a civilization that pre-dated the Romans: the Etruscans. While other visitors zero in on Michelangelo & co., you may have the "Arezzo Chimera" and other precious Etruscan objects to yourself. You can also visit parts of a Roman theater uncovered below the **Palazzo Vecchio** (p. 188), and

59

a 20-minute bus journey from Florence gets you to **Fiesole** (p. 204), a now-overgrown village with a preserved Roman theater, a stretch of Etruscan wall, and an archaeological area where visitors can roam among the stones.

DAY 13: Verona ★★

It seems harsh to label the **Arena di Verona** (p. 458) "a ruin." This city's enormous amphitheater is the best preserved in Italy. Come in summer—and book ahead—to experience one of Europe's most atmospheric outdoor opera festivals.

ROME

By Elizabeth Heath

4

Once it ruled the Western World, and even the partial, scattered ruins of that awesome empire—of which Rome was the capital—are today among the most overpowering sights on earth. To walk the Roman Forum, to view the Colosseum, the Pantheon, and the Appian Way: These are among the most memorable, instructive, and illuminating experiences in all of travel. To see evidence of a once-great civilization that no longer exists is a humbling experience that everyone should have.

As a visitor to Rome, you will be constantly reminded of this city's extraordinary history. Take the time to get away from the crowds to explore the intimate piazzas and lesser basilicas in the back streets of Trastevere and the *centro storico*. Indulge in eno-gastronomic pursuits at coffee bars, trattorias, enotecas and gelaterias. Have a picnic in Villa Borghese or climb to the top of the Gianicolo for million-dollar views. Rome is so compact that without planning too much, you'll end up stumbling across its monuments and its simpler pleasures.

Walk the streets of Rome, and the city will be yours.

DON'T LEAVE ROME WITHOUT . . .

Exploring The World's Smallest Country: Vatican City is just .2 square miles, but what riches this tiny nation holds! From one of the finest museums on the planet, to its largest Catholic church, to the architectural masterwork that is St. Peter's Square, your trip isn't complete without at least a day spent here. See p. 76.

Gazing Over The Roman Forum And Palatine From Capitoline Hill Terraces At Night. Yes, explore the ruins by day too, but after dark—as spotlights cast dramatic glows over solitary columns and crumbling arches—the view is truly, disarmingly spectacular. See p. 158

Spending Hours Over Dinner. Take time to unwind at a typical Roman trattoria, with a steady and wonderfully affordable flow of wine and delicious food. See p. 139

Seeing How The Other Half Once Lived In Palazzo Valentini. Rome's newest archaeological attraction is also one of its best. An exceedingly well-conceived installation brings the stones of these once-posh ancient Roman homes to life like nowhere else in the city. See p. 99

Mixing With Locals At The Lively Mercato Di Testaccio. No other market in the city has such a strong sense of community, coupled with the chance to sample real Roman street food. See p. 157.

ESSENTIALS

Arriving

BY PLANE   Most flights arrive at Rome's **Leonardo da Vinci International Airport** (www.adr.it; ✆ **06-65951**), popularly known as **Fiumicino,** 30km (19 miles) from the city center. (If you're arriving from other European cities, you might land at Ciampino Airport, discussed below). After you leave passport control, you'll see a **tourist information desk,** staffed Monday through Saturday from 8:15am to 7pm. A *cambio* (money exchange) operates daily from 7:30am to 11pm, but it's just as easy, and less expensive, to withdraw cash from an ATM *(bancomat)* in the airport. See p. 821 for tips on using Italian ATMs.

Follow signs marked treni to find the **airport train station,** about a 10-minute walk from the arrivals area. From there, catch the delightfully named **Leonardo Express** for a 31-minute shuttle ride to Rome's main station, **Stazione Termini.** The shuttle runs every 15 minutes (every 30 minutes at off-peak hours) from 6:08am to 11:23pm for 14€ one-way (free kids 12 and under). On the way to the train, you'll pass a yellow machine dispensing tickets (cash or credit), or you can buy them at the Trenitalia window near the tracks. You can also buy e-tickets at www.trenitalia.com or use the Trenitalia mobile app.

A **taxi** from da Vinci airport to the city costs a flat-rate 48€ for the 45-minute to 1-hour trip, depending on traffic (hotels charge 50€–60€ for pickup service). Note that the flat rate is applicable from the airport to central Rome (and vice-versa) only if your Rome location is inside the Aurelian Walls (most hotels are). Otherwise, standard metered rates can bump the fare to 75€ or higher. There are also surcharges for large luggage, Sunday and holiday rides, and more than 4 passengers.

Train or Taxi?

Whether to take the airport shuttle train or a taxi into Rome from FCO depends on your budget and your tolerance for schlepping. If you're traveling solo and/or traveling light, the train is the most economical option for getting into the city, and takes about the same time as a taxi. If you've got a lot of bags, however, bear in mind that the train is a long walk from the arrivals terminal—and that, once your train arrives at Termini station, you'll still have to walk, or take Metro, bus, or taxi, to your final destination. (See p. 69 for more on Termini station options.) Bottom line? If there are 3 or more in your party or you're carrying lots of luggage, go for a taxi.

If you arrive at **Ciampino Airport** (www.adr.it/ciampino; ✆ **06-65951**), you can take a Terravision bus (www.terravision.eu; ✆ **06-4880086;** first bus 8:15am, last bus 11:40pm) to Stazione Termini. This takes about 45 minutes and costs 5€. A **taxi** from Ciampino costs a flat rate of 30€ if you're going to a destination within the Aurelian Walls.

From either airport, ride-sharing service **Uber** is available—sort of. Because of licensing laws (and strong resistance from Rome's taxi drivers), only Uber Black or Uber Van service is offered, and it's much more expensive than a taxi. If you want Uber-like convenience and in-app payments, consider the **MyTaxi** app, available for iPhones or Androids.

BY TRAIN OR BUS   Trains and buses (including trains from the airport) arrive in the center of old Rome at **Stazione Termini**, Piazza dei Cinquecento. This is the train, bus, and transportation hub for all of Rome, and it is surrounded by many hotels, especially budget ones.

The station is filled with services. A money exchange window is located close to the end of platform 14, and an ATM is at the end of platform 24. **Informazioni Ferroviarie** (in the outer hall) dispenses info on rail travel to other parts of Italy. There is also a **tourist information booth,** plus baggage services, newsstands, clean public toilets (1€), and snack bars. *Tip:* Be wary of young men/women lingering around ticket machines offering to help you. They will expect a tip, or at worst will be distracting you so that an accomplice can pick your pocket.

To get from Termini to your final destination in Rome, you have several options. If you're taking the **Metropolitana** (subway), follow the illuminated red-and-white M signs; to catch a city bus, go straight through the outer hall to the sprawling bus lot of **Piazza dei Cinquecento.** (See p. 69 for information about getting around Rome by public transport.) You will also find a line of **taxis** parked out front. Note that taxis now charge a 2€ supplement for any fares originating at Termini, plus 1€ for each bag in the trunk. Use the official taxi queue right in front of the station; don't go with a driver who approaches you or get into any cab where the meter is "broken."

BY CAR   From the north or south, the main access route is the **Autostrada A1** highway, running from Milan to Naples via Bologna, Florence, and Rome. At 754km (469 miles), it is the spinal cord of Italy's road network. All the autostrade join with the **Grande Raccordo Anulare** (GRA), a ring road encircling Rome, channeling traffic into the congested city. *Tip:* Long before you reach the GRA, study your route carefully to see what part of Rome you plan to enter. Route signs along the ring road tend to be confusing.

If you must drive a car into Rome, return your rental car immediately on arrival, or at least get yourself to your hotel, park your car, and leave it there until you leave the city. Seriously **think twice before driving in Rome**—the traffic and the parking options are nightmarish. Most of

Essentials

ROME

Roma & OMNIA **PASSES**

If you plan to do serious sightseeing in Rome (and why else would you be here?), the **Roma Pass** (www.romapass.it) is worth considering. For 38.50€ per card, valid for 3 days, you get free entry to the first two museums or archaeological sites you visit; "express" entry to the Colosseum; discounted entry to all other museums and sites; free use of the city's public transport network (bus, Metro, tram, and railway lines; airport transfers not included); a free map; and free access to a special smartphone app with audioguides and interactive maps. If your stay in Rome is shorter, you may want to opt for the **Roma Pass 48 Hours** (28€), which offers the same benefits as the 3-day pass, except that only the first museum you visit is free and the ticket is valid for just 48 hours.

The free transportation perk with the Roma Pass is not insignificant, if only because it saves you the hassle of buying paper tickets. In any case, do some quick math; one major museum or attraction entrance is 12€–15€, and each ride on public transportation is 1.50€. Discounts to other sites range from 20–50%. If you plan to visit a lot of sites and dash around the city on public transport, it's probably worth the money. You can buy Roma passes online (www.romapass.it) and pick them up at one of the city's Tourist Information Points (INFOPOINTS); you can also order in advance by phone, with a credit card, at ✆ **06-060608.** Roma Passes are also sold directly at Tourist Information Point offices (see below) or at participating museums and ATAC subway ticket offices.

A glaring disadvantage of the Roma Pass is that it does not include access to the Vatican Museums or the paid areas of St. Peter's. That's where the **OMNIA Card** comes to the rescue. This 72-hour card combines all the benefits of the Roma Pass with skip-the-line entry to the Vatican Museums, an audioguide to St. Peter's, a hop-on-hop-off bus pass, and admission to other Vatican properties. At 113€ it's an investment, but worth it if you want to take in all the heavy hitters of Rome and the Vatican. The pass can be purchased online at www.omniakit. org/en and picked up at Largo Argentina, St Peter's Square, or the Basilica of Saint John Lateran.

Finally, note that the Colosseum, Roman Forum, and Palatine Hill are included under one ticket for 12€, good for 2 days and available for purchase online (plus small fee) or at the sites. For more on ticket options for these 3 sites, see p. 91 and 93.

central Rome is a **ZTL** (Zona Traffico Limitato), off-limits to nonresidents and rigorously enforced by cameras. You will almost certainly be fined; the ticket might arrive at your home address months after your trip.

Visitor Information

Information, maps, and the Roma Pass (see below) are available at 11 Tourist Information Points around the city maintained by **Roma Capitale** (www.turismoroma.it). Bizzarely, each kiosk keeps its own hours and none are exactly the same. You can reliably find them open after 9:30am and before 6pm (though some stay open later). The one at Termini (daily 8am–6:45pm), located in Building F next to platform 24, often has a long line; if you're staying near other offices listed here, skip it. See the Turismo Roma website (link above) for additional information points.

City Layout

The bulk of what you'll want to visit—ancient, Renaissance, and baroque Rome—lies on the east side of the **Tiber River** (Fiume Tevere), which curls through the city. However, several important landmarks are on the other side: **St. Peter's Basilica** and the **Vatican, Castel Sant'Angelo,** and the colorful **Trastevere** neighborhood. Even with those slightly-farther-afield sights, Rome has one of Europe's most compact and walkable city centers. That doesn't mean you won't get lost from time to time (most newcomers do). Arm yourself with a detailed street map of Rome, or a smartphone with a hefty data plan. Most hotels hand out a pretty good version of a city map.

Rome's Neighborhoods in Brief

Much of the historic core of Rome does not fall under easy or distinct neighborhood classifications. Instead, when describing a location, the frame of reference is the name of the nearest large monument or square, like St. Peter's or Piazza di Spagna. Street numbers usually run consecutively, odd numbers on one side of the street, evens on the other. However, in centro, the numbers sometimes run up one side and then run back down on the other side (so #50 could be potentially opposite #308).

VATICAN CITY & PRATI   **Vatican City** is technically a sovereign state, although in practice it is just another part of Rome. The **Vatican Museums, St. Peter's,** and the **Vatican Gardens** take up most of the land area; the popes have lived here for 7 centuries. Close to Vatican City sights, **Prati,** a middle-class neighborhood, has a smattering of affordable hotels and shopping streets, as well as some excellent places to eat.

CENTRO STORICO & THE PANTHEON   One of the most desirable (and busiest) areas of Rome, the **Centro Storico** (historic center) is a maze of narrow streets and cobbled alleys dating from the Middle Ages and filled with Renaissance and baroque churches and palaces, as well as countless hotels and Airbnb rentals. Its heart is elegant **Piazza Navona,** bustling with overpriced sidewalk cafes and restaurants, street artists, musicians, and milling crowds. Nearby, the area around the ancient Roman **Pantheon** is abuzz with crowds, a cafe scene, and nightlife. South of Corso Vittorio Emanuele. the lively square of **Campo de' Fiori** is home to the famous produce market. West of Via Arenula lies the old Jewish **Ghetto,** where restaurants far outnumber hotels.

ANCIENT ROME, MONTI & CELIO   Although no longer the heart of the city, this is where Rome began, with the **Colosseum, Palatine Hill, Roman Forum, Imperial Forums,** and **Circus Maximus.** This area offers only a few hotels—and, in **Monti** (Rome's oldest *rione,* or quarter, north of the Colosseum), a handful of very good restaurants and lots of nightlife. Restaurants closer to the Colosseum are often tour-bus traps. Just beyond the Circus Maximus, the **Aventine Hill** is now a posh residential quarter with great city views. For more of a neighborhood feel, stay in Monti or **Celio,** south of the Colosseum.

TRIDENTE & THE SPANISH STEPS   Full of expensive hotels, designer boutiques, and chic restaurants, the area north of Rome's center is often called the Tridente, because Via di Ripetta, Via del Corso, and Via del Babuino form a trident leading down from **Piazza del Popolo.** The star here is unquestionably **Piazza di Spagna,** which attracts Romans and tourists alike (though mostly the latter) to linger at its celebrated **Spanish Steps** (just don't eat lunch on the steps! See p. 110). Some of Rome's most high-end shopping streets fan out from here, including **Via Condotti.**

VIA VENETO & PIAZZA BARBERINI   In the 1950s and early 1960s, the tree-lined boulevard **Via Veneto** was the swinging place to be, the haunt of la Dolce Vita celebrities and paraparazzi. Luxury hotels, cafes, and restaurants still cluster here, although the restaurants are mostly overpriced tourist traps. To the south, Via Veneto ends at **Piazza Barberini** and the

to Centrale is a handy food stop in Termini Station

magnificent **Palazzo Barberini,** begun in 1623 by Carlo Maderno and later completed by Bernini and Borromini.

VILLA BORGHESE & PARIOLI   **Parioli** is Rome's most elegant residential section, a setting for excellent restaurants, hotels, museums, and public parks. Bordered by the green spaces of the **Villa Borghese** to the south and the **Villa Glori** and **Villa Ada** to the north, Parioli (and just to its south, Pinciano) is one of the city's safest districts, but it's not exactly central. It's not the best base if you plan to depend on public transportation.

AROUND STAZIONE TERMINI   For many visitors, their first glimpse of Rome is the main train station and adjoining **Piazza della Repubblica.** There are a lot of affordable hotels in this area; while they may lack charm, the location is convenient, near the city's transportation hub and not far from ancient Rome. Hotels on the Via Marsala side often occupy floors of a *palazzo* (palace), with clean and decent, sometimes even charming, rooms. Traffic and noise are worse on the streets to the left of the station. The once-seedy neighborhoods on either side of Termini (Esquilino and Tiburtino) have slowly been cleaning up, but caution is always advisable.

TRASTEVERE   Based on the Latin *Trans Tiber,* Trastevere means "across the Tiber." Since the 1970s, when expats and other bohemians discovered it, this once-medieval working-class district has been gentrified and is now most definitely on the tourist map. Yet Trastevere retains its colorful appeal, with dance clubs, offbeat shops, pubs, and little *trattorie* and wine bars. Trastavere has places to stay—mostly rather quaint rentals and Airbnb's—and excellent restaurants and bars, too. The area centers on the ancient churches of **Santa Cecilia** and **Santa Maria in Trastevere.**

TESTACCIO & SOUTHERN ROME   Once home to slaughterhouses and Rome's port on the Tiber, the working-class neighborhood of **Testaccio** was built around one strange feature: A huge compacted mound of broken amphorae and terracotta roof tiles began under Emperor Nero in A.D. 55 and added to over the centuries. Houses were built around the mound; caves were dug into its mass to store wine and foodstuffs. Now known for its authentic Roman restaurants, Testaccio is also one of Rome's liveliest areas after dark. Stay here if you want a taste of a real Roman neighborhood, but bear in mind that you're a bus, tram or subway ride from most touristic sights.

THE APPIAN WAY   Farther south and east, the 2,300-year-old **Via Appia Antica** road once extended from Rome to Brindisi on the southeast coast. This is one of the most historically rich areas of Rome, great for a day trip, but not a convenient place to stay. Its most famous sights are the **Catacombs,** the graveyards of early Christians and patrician families.

Getting Around Rome

Central Rome is perfect for exploring on foot, with sites of interest often clustered together. Much of the inner core is traffic-free, so you will need to walk whether you like it or not. *Tip:* Plan ahead and wear sturdy, comfortable walking shoes. In the most tourist-trod parts of the city, walking can be challenging, due to crowds, uneven cobblestones, heavy traffic, and narrow (if any) sidewalks.

BY SUBWAY   The **Metropolitana (Metro)** (www.romametropolitane.it; © 06-454640100) operates daily from 5:30am to 11:30pm (until 12:30am on Saturday). A big red **m** indicates the entrance to the subway. If your destination is close to a Metro stop, hop on, as your journey will be much faster than by taking surface transportation. There are currently three lines: **Line A** (orange) runs southeast to northwest via Termini, Barberini, Spagna, and several stations in Prati near the Vatican; **Line B** (blue) runs north to south via Termini and stops in Ancient Rome; **Line C** (green), to be completed by 2022, will run from Monte Compatri in the southeast to Clodio/Mazzini (just beyond the Ottaviano stop on Line A). The portion from Piazza Lodi to San Giovanni opened in May 2018. Metro tickets are 1.50€ and are available from *tabacchi* (tobacco shops), many newsstands, and vending machines at all stations. Booklets of tickets are available at newsstands, *tabacchi,* and in some terminals. You can also buy a **pass** on either a daily or a weekly basis. To open the subway barrier, insert your ticket. If you have a **Roma Pass** (p. 65), touch it against the yellow dot and the gates will open. See Metro map on the book's pullout.

BY BUS & TRAM   Roman buses and trams are operated by **ATAC** (Agenzia del Trasporto Autoferrotranviario del Comune di Roma; www.atac.roma.it; © **06-57003**). For 1.50€ you can ride to most parts of Rome on buses or trams, although it can be slow going in all that traffic, and the buses are often very crowded. A ticket is valid for 100 minutes, so you can get on many buses and trams (plus one journey on the Metro) during that time by using the same ticket. Tickets are sold in *tabacchi,* at newsstands,

---

Walk or Ride?

Rome is a walkable city, one where getting there (on foot) is half the fun, and public transportation doesn't necessarily save that much time. (For example, walking from Piazza Venezia to Piazza di Santa Maria in Trastevere takes about 25 minutes at a leisurely pace; it takes 12 minutes via bus and tram, but that doesn't include potential time spent waiting for the bus or tram to show up.) My take? On a nice day and for relatively short distances, enjoy the stroll. On the other hand, if you want to save your steps (maybe for a marathon tour of the Vatican Museums), then head to the nearest Metro, tram, or bus stop.

and at bus stops; there are seldom ticket-issuing machines on the vehicles themselves. Note that if you switch from a bus or tram to Metro within your 100-minute ticket time, you must revalidate your ticket before boarding the subway.

Special **timed passes** include a 24-hour (ROMA 24H) ticket (7€); a 48-hour ticket (12.50€); a 72-hour ticket (18€); and a 7-day ticket (24€). If you plan to ride public transportation a lot—and if you are skipping between the *centro storico,* Roman ruins, and Vatican, as you likely will—these passes save time and hassle over buying a new ticket every time you ride. Purchase the appropriate pass for your length of stay in Rome. All the passes allow you to ride on the ATAC network and on the Metro (subway). On the first bus you board, place your ticket in a small (typically yellow) machine, which prints the day and hour you boarded, and then withdraw it. The machine will also print your ticket's time of expiration (*"scad."*—short for scadenza). One-day and weekly tickets are available at *tabacchi,* many newsstands, and at vending machines at all stations. If you plan to do a lot of sightseeing, however, the **Roma Pass** (p. 65) is a smarter choice.

Buses and trams stop at areas marked *fermata.* Signs will display the numbers of the buses that stop there and a list of all the stops along each bus's route, making it easier to scope out your destination. Digital displays at most stops show how soon the next bus or tram will arrive. Generally, buses run daily from 5am to midnight. From midnight until dawn, you can ride on special night buses (look for the "n" in front of the bus number), which run only on main routes. It's best to take a taxi in the wee hours—if you can find one. Call for one (see p. 71) in a pinch. **Bus**

Rome's Key Bus Routes

First, know that any map of the Roman bus system will likely be outdated before it's printed. There's always talk of renumbering the whole system; the route numbers we've listed might have changed by the time you travel. Second, take extreme caution when riding Rome's overcrowded buses—pickpockets abound! This is particularly true on bus no. 64, a visitor favorite because of its route through the historic districts, and thus also a favorite of Rome's pickpocketing community. This bus has earned various nicknames, including the "Pickpocket Express" and "Wallet Eater."

Although routes may change, a few reliable bus routes have remained valid for years in Rome:

o **40 (Express):** Stazione Termini to the Vatican via Via Nazionale, Piazza Venezia and Piazza Pia, by the Castel Sant'Angelo

o **64:** The "tourist route" from Termini, along Via Nazionale and through Piazza Venezia and along Via Argentina to Piazza San Pietro in the Vatican

o **75:** Stazione Termini to the Colosseum

o **H:** Stazione Termini via Piazza Venezia and the Ghetto to Trastevere via Ponte Garibaldi

information booths at Piazza dei Cinquecento, in front of Stazione Termini, offer advice on routes.

BY TAXI   If you've reached your walking limit, don't feel like waiting for a bus, or need to get someplace in a hurry, taking a taxi in Rome is reasonably affordable compared to other major world cities. Just don't count on hailing a taxi on the street. Instead, have your hotel call one, or if you're at a restaurant, ask the waiter or cashier to dial for you. If you want to phone for yourself, try the **city taxi service** at ☏ **06-0609** (Italian only), or one of these **radio taxi numbers**, which may or may not have English-speaking operators on duty: ☏ **06-6645,** 06-3570, or 06-4994. You can also text a taxi at ☏ **366-6730000** by typing the message "Roma [address]" (assuming you know the address in Italian). Taxis on call incur a surcharge of 3.50€. Larger taxi stands are at Piazza Venezia (east side), Piazza di Spagna (Spanish Steps), the Colosseum, Corso Rinascimento (Piazza Navona), Largo Argentina, the Pantheon, Piazza del Popolo, Piazza Risorgimento (near St. Peter's), and Piazza Belli (Trastevere).

Many taxis accept credit cards, but it's best to check before getting in. Between 6am and 10pm, the meter begins at 3€ (4.50€ Saturday–Sunday) for the first 3km (1¼ miles) and then rises 1.10€ per kilometer. From 10pm to 6am every day, the meter starts at 6.50€. Trips from Termini incur a 2€ surcharge. The first suitcase is free; every additional piece of luggage costs 1€. *Note:* Italians don't tip taxi drivers like Americans do and, at most, will simply round up to the nearest euro. If the driver is really friendly or helpful, a tip of 1€ to 2€ is sufficient.

As in the rest of the world, taxi apps have caught on in Rome. The main app for official city taxis is **it Taxi** (www.ittaxi.it), run by Rome's largest taxi company, **3570** (www.3570.it). It allows users to pay directly from the app using a credit card or PayPal. Popular throughout Europe, the **MyTaxi** app offers Uber-like convenience for ordering and prepaying a cab. **Uber** is currently available in Rome in a limited capacity only.

BY CAR   All roads might lead to Rome, but you probably won't want to drive once you get here. If you do drive into the city, call or email ahead to your hotel to find out the best route into Rome from wherever you are starting out. You will want to get rid of your rental car as soon as possible, or park it in a garage and leave it there until you depart Rome.

If you want to rent a car to explore the countryside around Rome or drive to another city, you'll save money if you reserve before leaving home (see p. 814 in chapter 16). If you decide to book a car here, most major car rental companies have desks inside Stazione Termini.

Note that rental cars in Italy may be smaller than what you are used to, including in terms of trunk space. Make sure you consider both luggage size and the number of people when booking your vehicle.

4

ROME | Essentials

[FastFACTS] ROME

Business hours In general, banks are open Monday–Friday 8:30am–1:30pm and 2:30 or 2:45–4pm. (Note that few banks offer currency exchange.) Most Roman shops open at 10am and close at 7pm Monday–Saturday. Smaller shops close for 1 or 2 hours at lunch, and may remain closed Monday morning and Saturday afternoon. Most restaurants are closed for *riposo* (rest) 1 day per week, usually Sunday or Monday.

Dentists **American Dental Arts Rome,** Via del Governo Vecchio 73 (near Piazza Navona; www.adadentists rome.com; ✆ **06-6832613**), uses the latest technology.

Doctors Call the U.S. Embassy at ✆ **06-46741** for a list of English-speaking doctors. You'll find English-speaking doctors at the privately run **Salvator Mundi International Hospital,** Viale delle Mura Gianicolensi 67 (in the Gianicolo neighborhood; www.salvator mundi.it; ✆ **06-588961**); or at the **Rome American Hospital,** Via Emilio Longoni 69 (www.hcitalia.it/rome americanhospital; ✆ **06-22551**), located well east of central Rome. The **International Medical Center** is on 24-hour duty at Via Firenze 47 (near Piazza della Repubblica; www.imc84.com; ✆ **06-4882371**). **Medi-Call Italia,** Via Cremera 8 (www.medi-call.it; ✆ **06-8840113**) can arrange for a doctor to make a house call at your hotel or anywhere in Rome.

Emergencies To call the police, dial ✆ **113;** for an ambulance ✆ **118;** for a fire ✆ **115.**

Newspapers & Magazines The bi-weekly English-language expat magazine *Wanted in Rome* (www.wantedinrome.com) lists current events and shows. *Time Out* has a Rome edition (www.timeout. com/rome).

Pharmacies *Farmacie,* recognizable by their neon green or red cross signs, are generally open 8:30am–1pm and 4–7:30pm, though some stay open later. **Farmacia Piram** at Via Nazionale 228 is open 24 hours. All closed pharmacies have signs in their windows indicating any open pharmacies nearby.

Police Dial ✆ **113.**

Safety Violent crime is virtually nonexistent in Rome's touristed areas, though pickpocketing is common. Purse snatching happens on occasion, by young men speeding by on scooters; keep your purse on the wall side of your body with the strap across your chest. Some pickpockets dress like businesspeople, so always be suspicious of anyone who tries to "befriend" you in a tourist area. Walking alone at night is usually fine anywhere in the *centro storico.*

EXPLORING ROME

Rome's ancient monuments are a constant reminder that this was one of the greatest centers of Western civilization. In the heyday of the Empire, all roads led to Rome, with good reason. It was one of the first cosmopolitan cities, importing food, textiles, slaves, gladiators, great art, and even citizens from the far corners of the world. Despite its brutality and corruption, Rome left a legacy of law, a heritage of art, architecture, and engineering, and a canny lesson in how to conquer enemies by absorbing their cultures.

But ancient Rome is only part of the spectacle. The Vatican has had a tremendous influence on making the city a tourism center. Although Vatican architects stripped down much of the city's ancient glory during the

St. Peter's Basilica and the Vatican, viewed from the Tiber River.

Renaissance, looting ruins (the Forum especially) for their precious marble, they created more treasures and occasionally incorporated the old into the new—as Michelangelo did when turning Diocletian's Baths complex into a church. And in the years that followed, Bernini adorned the city with baroque wonders, especially his glorious fountains.

Welcome to Rome (Corso Vittorio Emanuele II, 203, www.welcometo-rome.it/en; © **06-879 11 691**) takes visitors on a 30-minute multimedia and 3-D journey through the city's evolution from a farming village to the greatest power in the Western world. Whether this is your first or fiftieth trip to Rome, the context provided through vivid projections, holograms, and lively narration will help make sense of the Eternal City's complicated history. Shows run continuously on the half hour, Monday through Thursday 9am to 7pm, Friday to Sunday 10am to 9pm. Tickets are 12€ adults 12€; family discounts are available.

Bypassing the Lines

If you don't plan ahead, you'll be dealing with interminable lines at three big attractions: the Colosseum, the Vatican Museums, and St. Peter's Basilica. Reservation services can help you avoid the wait, at least for two

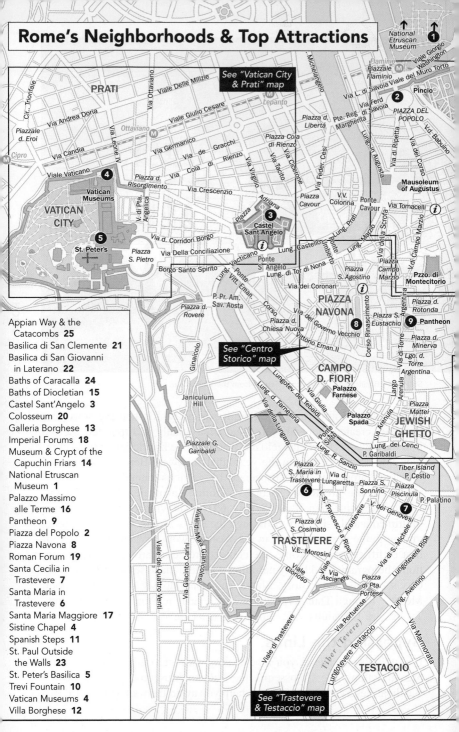

Rome's Neighborhoods & Top Attractions

National Etruscan Museum

PRATI

VATICAN CITY

Vatican Museums **4**

St. Peter's **5**

Castel Sant'Angelo **3**

Mausoleum of Augustus

PIAZZA DEL POPOLO

Pincio

Piazza del Popolo **2**

See "Vatican City & Prati" map

See "Centro Storico" map

See "Trastevere & Testaccio" map

PIAZZA NAVONA

Piazza Navona **8**

Pantheon **9**

CAMPO D. FIORI

Palazzo Farnese

Palazzo Spada

JEWISH GHETTO

Tiber Island

TRASTEVERE

Santa Maria in Trastevere **6**

Santa Cecilia in Trastevere **7**

TESTACCIO

Janiculum Hill

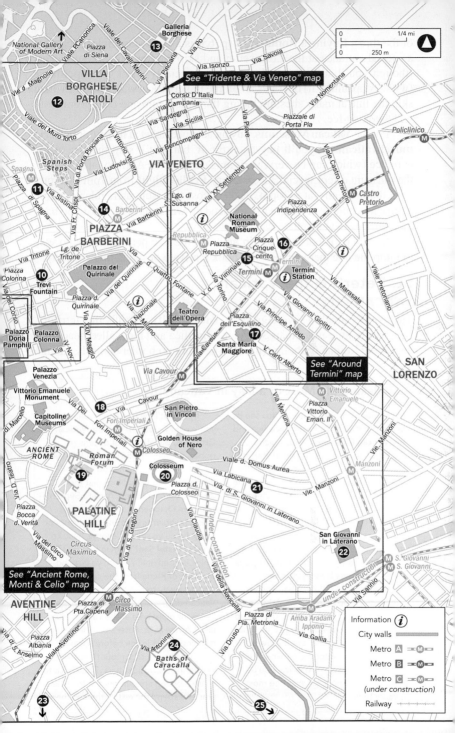

National Gallery of Modern Art

VILLA BORGHESE / PARIOLI

Galleria Borghese **13**

Piazza di Siena

See "Tridente & Via Veneto" map

12

Corso D'Italia

Piazzale di Porta Pia

Policlinico

VIA VENETO

Spanish Steps

Spagna

Piazza di Spagna **11**

14 Barberini

PIAZZA BARBERINI

Lgo. di S. Susanna

National Roman Museum

Piazza Indipendenza

Castro Pretorio

Lg. de Tritone

Repubblica

Piazza Repubblica

Piazza Cinquecento **16**

Piazza Colonna **10** Trevi Fountain

Palazzo del Quirinale

15 Termini

Termini

Termini Station

Piazza d. Quirinale

Palazzo Doria Pamphilj

Palazzo Colonna

Teatro dell'Opera

Piazza dell'Esquilino **17**

SAN LORENZO

Palazzo Venezia

Santa Maria Maggiore

See "Around Termini" map

Vittorio Emanuele Monument

Capitoline Museums

Via Cavour

San Pietro in Vincoli

Vittorio Emanuele

Piazza Vittorio Eman. II

ANCIENT ROME

18

Roman Forum

Golden House of Nero

Manzoni

19

Colosseo

Viale d. Domus Aurea

Piazza Bocca d. Verità

Colosseum **20**

Via Labicana

21

Piazza d. Colosseo

Via di S. Giovanni in Laterano

PALATINE HILL

Circus Maximus

San Giovanni in Laterano **22**

See "Ancient Rome, Monti & Celio" map

S. Giovanni

S. Giovanni

AVENTINE HILL

Piazza di Pta.Capena

Circo Massimo

Piazza di Pla. Metronia

Amba Aradam Ipponio

Via Gallia

Piazza Albania

24

Baths of Caracalla

Information (i)

City walls

Metro A

Metro B

Metro C (under construction)

Railway

23

25

0   1/4 mi
0   250 m

75

of the three. Buying a **Roma Pass** (p. 65) is a good start; holders can use a special entrance at the Colosseum and skip the long line to buy tickets (though you'll still have to line up for a security check). **Coopculture** (www.coopculture.it) operates an online ticket office, which allows you to skip the line at many sites, including the Colosseum and the Forum, with a 2€ booking fee.

For the **Vatican Museums,** buy an advance ticket at **http://biglietteria musei.vatican.va**; you'll pay an extra 4€ but you'll skip the line at the entrance (which can be very, very long). From late April to late October, the museum offers special access every **Friday night** from 7pm to 11pm, with the last entry at 9:30pm. Tickets cost the same as regular daytime admission, but given the greatly reduced crowds, you'll feel like you have the galleries to yourself.

St. Peter's is not included in any skip the line perk: There is no way to jump the line there, unless you book a private or group tour (p. 125).

St. Peter's & the Vatican
VATICAN CITY

The world's smallest sovereign state, **Vatican City** is a truly tiny territory, comprising little more than St. Peter's Basilica and the walled headquarters of the Roman Catholic Church. There are no border controls, though

---

Making the Most of a Day in Vatican City

Most Vatican visitors allot a day to see its two major sights, **St. Peter's Basilica** and the **Vatican Museums** (including the Sistine Chapel). We recommend starting with the museums. **Pre-order** tickets for the earliest time slot (from 9am) available the day you wish to visit. Plan to devote several hours to see the highlights of the museum collections (see p. 82).

After viewing the museums, grab a quick lunch, either in the museum cafeteria or at a nearby sandwich shop or pizza joint. The streets leading from the museum exit to St. Peter's Basilica are lined with cheap eateries—mostly mediocre, but they'll do in a pinch. Then head for **St. Peter's Square,** going to the back of the line (always long, but it moves fairly quickly) to enter the basilica. From the time you enter the basilica, you'll need at least 1 hour for even the most cursory tour.

By now it'll be late afternoon, and you've got 2 options: Visit the **Vatican Grottoes,** burial place of dozens of popes, or climb the 551 steps (320 if you take the elevator) to the top of the **dome of St. Peter's.** Note that the dome is open until 6pm April to September, 5pm October to March. The grottoes stay open to 7pm and 6pm, respectively. If you've still got energy, head to nearby **Castel Sant'Angelo** (see p. 87), which is open until 7:30pm year-round—the view of Rome from the castle's roof is a perfect way to cap off your marathon Vatican day.

Want more time at the Vatican Museums? Arrive at St. Peter's early in the morning to get in line before it opens at 7am; that way you can tour the basilica before the crowds get thick. Then head to a late morning appointment at the museums and spend the rest of the day there.

Vatican City & Prati

Lepanto Ⓜ

Mercato
Rionale

PRATI

VATICAN CITY

Castel
Sant'Angelo

St. Peter's

Piazza di
San Pietro

Piazza
Pio XII

Via della Conciliazione

Borgo Santo Spirito

Piazza di
Ponte
Sant'Angelo

| 0 | 200 y |
| 0 | 200 m |

Metro Ⓐ ⨯Ⓜ⨯

ATTRACTIONS	**RESTAURANTS**	**HOTELS**
Castel Sant'Angelo **10**	Bonci Pizzarium **1**	QuodLibet **2**
St. Peter's Basilica **6**	Duecento Gradi **4**	Residenza Paolo VI **8**
St. Peter's Square	Old Bridge	Rome Armony Suites **11**
(Piazza San Pietro) **7**	Gelateria **3**	Villa Laetitia **12**
Vatican Museums &	Taverna Angelica **9**	
the Sistine Chapel **5**		

the city-state's 800 inhabitants (essentially clergymen and Swiss Guards) have their own radio station, daily newspaper, tax-free pharmacy and petrol pumps, postal service, and head of state—the Pope. The Pope had always exercised a high degree of political independence from the rest of Italy, formalized by the 1929 Lateran Treaty between Pope Pius XI and the Italian government to create the Vatican. The city is still protected by the flamboyantly uniformed (allegedly designed by Michelangelo) Swiss Guards, a tradition dating from when the Swiss, known as brave soldiers, were often hired out as mercenaries for foreign armies. Today the Vatican remains the center of the Roman Catholic world, the home of the

Pope—and the resting place of St. Peter. **St. Peter's Basilica** is obviously one of the highlights, but the only part of the Apostolic Palace itself that you can visit independently is the **Vatican Museums,** the world's biggest and richest museum complex.

On the left side of Piazza San Pietro, the **Vatican Tourist Office** (www.vatican.va; ✆ **06-69882019;** Monday–Saturday 8:30am–7:30pm) sells maps and guides that will help you make sense of the treasures in the museums; it also accepts reservations for tours of the Vatican Gardens. Adjacent to the information office, the **Vatican Post Office** sells special Vatican postage stamps (open Monday–Friday 8:30am–7pm, Saturday 8:30am–6pm).

The only entrance to St. Peter's for tourists is through one of the glories of the Western world: Bernini's 17th-century **St. Peter's Square (Piazza San Pietro).** As you stand in the huge piazza, you are in the arms of an ellipse partly enclosed by a majestic **Doric-pillared colonnade.** Stand in the marked marble discs embedded in the pavement near the fountains to see all the columns lined up in a striking optical/geometrical play. Straight ahead is the facade of St. Peter's itself, and to the right, above the colonnade, are the dark brown buildings of the **papal**

The grand interior of St. Peter's Basilica.

apartments and the Vatican Museums. In the center of the square stands a 4,000-year-old **Egyptian obelisk,** created in the ancient city of Heliopolis on the Nile delta and appropriated by the Romans under Emperor Augustus. Flanking the obelisk are two 17th-century **fountains.** The one on the right (facing the basilica), by Carlo Maderno, who designed the facade of St. Peter's, was placed here by Bernini himself; the other is by Carlo Fontana.

St. Peter's Basilica ★★★ CHURCH   The Basilica di San Pietro, or simply **St. Peter's,** is the holiest shrine of the Catholic Church, built on the site of St. Peter's tomb by the greatest Italian artists of the 16th and 17th centuries. The line to enter the basilica forms on the right side of the piazza. Once inside, look for entrances to the treasury and underground grottoes. To climb the dome, head to the courtyard to the right of the Holy Door, past the security checkpoint but outside the basilica proper. To enter any of these areas, you must be **properly dressed**—a rule that is very strictly enforced.

In Roman times, the Circus of Nero, where Peter is said to have been crucified, was just to the left of where the basilica is today. He was allegedly buried here in A.D. 64, and in A.D. 324 Emperor Constantine commissioned a church to be built over Peter's tomb. That structure stood for more than 1,000 years. The present basilica, mostly completed in the 1500s and 1600s, is predominantly High Renaissance and baroque. Inside, the massive scale is almost too much to absorb, showcasing some of Italy's greatest artists: Bramante, Raphael and Michelangelo. In a church of such grandeur—overwhelming in its detail of gilt, marble, and mosaic—you can't expect much subtlety. It is meant to be overpowering.

Going straight into the basilica, the first thing you see on the right side of the nave—the longest nave in the world, as clearly marked in the floor along with other cathedral measurements—is the chapel containing Michelangelo's graceful **"Pietà" ★★★.** Created in the 1490s when the master was still in his 20s, it clearly shows his genius for capturing the human form. (The sculpture has been kept behind reinforced glass since an act of vandalism in the 1970s.) Note the lifelike folds of Mary's robes

papal AUDIENCES

When the pope is in Rome, he gives a public audience every Wednesday beginning at 10:30am (sometimes 10am in summer). If you want to get a good seat near the front, arrive early and prepare to wait—security begins to let people in between 8 and 8:30am but the line starts much earlier. Audiences take place in the Paul VI Hall of Audiences, although sometimes St. Peter's Basilica and St. Peter's Square are used to accommodate a large attendance in the summer. You can check on Pope Francis's appearances and the ceremonies he presides over, including celebrations of Mass, on the Vatican website (www.vatican.va). Anyone is welcome, but you must first obtain a **free ticket;** without a reservation you can try the Swiss Guards by the Bronze Doors located just after security at St. Peter's (8am–8pm in summer and 8am–7pm in winter). You can pick up tickets here up to 3 days in advance, subject to availability.

If you prefer to reserve a place in advance, visit www.vatican.va/various/prefettura/index_en.html to download a request form, which must be submitted via fax (yes, really) to the **Prefecture of the Papal Household** at ℭ **06-69885863.** Tickets can be picked up at the office located just inside the Bronze Doors from 3 to 7pm on the preceding day or on the morning of the audience from 7 to 10am.

At noon on Sundays, the Pope speaks briefly from his study window and gives his blessing to the visitors and pilgrims gathered in St. Peter's Square (no tickets are required for this). From about mid-July to mid-September, the Angelus and blessing historically takes place at the Pope's summer residence at **Castel Gandolfo,** some 26km (16 miles) out of Rome. Under Pope Francis, the residence, gardens, and villas of the castle have been opened to visitors as a museum, accessible via Metro and bus as well as a new train service that leaves from the Roma San Pietro station. Visit biglietteriamusei.vatican.va for information on seeing Castel Gandolfo by train.

and her youthful features; although she would've been middle-aged at the time of the Crucifixion, Michelangelo portrayed her as a young woman to convey her purity.

Further inside the nave, Michelangelo's dome is a mesmerizing space, rising high above the supposed site of St. Peter's tomb. With a diameter of 41.5m (136 ft.), the dome is Rome's largest, supported by four bulky piers decorated with reliefs depicting the basilica's key holy relics: St. Veronica's handkerchief (used to wipe the face of Christ); the lance of St. Longinus, which pierced Christ's side; and a piece of the True Cross.

Under the dome is the twisty-columned **baldacchino ★★**, by Bernini, sheltering the papal altar. The ornate 29m-high (96-ft.) canopy was created in part, so it is said, from bronze stripped from the Pantheon. Bernini sculpted the face of a woman on the base of each pillar; starting with the face on the left pillar (with your back to the entrance), circle the entire altar to see the progress of expressions from the agony of childbirth through to the fourth pillar, where the woman's face is replaced with that of her newborn baby.

Just before reaching the dome, on the right, the devout stop to kiss the foot of the 13th-century **bronze of St. Peter ★**, attributed to Arnolfo di Cambio. Elsewhere the church is decorated by more of Bernini's lavish sculptures, including his monument to Pope Alexander VII in the south transept, its winged skeleton writhing under the heavy marble drapes.

An entrance off the nave leads to the Sacristy and the **Historical Museum (Museo Storico)** or **treasury ★**, which is chock-full of richly jeweled chalices, reliquaries, and copes, as well as the late-15th-century bronze tomb of Pope Sixtus IV by Pollaiuolo.

An entrance to the left of the baldacchino leads down to the **Vatican grottoes ★★**, with their tombs of the popes, both ancient and modern. **Pope John Paul II** was once interred here in an austere tomb, but after his 2011 beatification, his remains were moved to a more prominent chapel in St. Peter's. Behind a wall of glass is what is considered to be the tomb of St. Peter.

After you leave the grottoes, you find yourself in a courtyard and ticket line for the grandest sight in the basilica: the climb to **Michelangelo's dome ★★★**, about 114m (375 ft.) high. You can walk all the way up or take the elevator as far as it goes. The elevator saves you 171 steps, but you *still* have 320 to go after getting off. After you've made it to the top, you'll have a scintillating view over the rooftops of Rome and even the Vatican Gardens and papal apartments. The elevator back down drops you back in the basilica interior, near the front entrance, or you can descend via a spiral ramp, the walls of which are lined with inscriptions recalling famous visitors to the dome.

An Unofficial Assist

Though it's not an official portal for Vatican City, the independent website **www.stpetersbasilica.info** offers a wealth of current detailed and helpful information for navigating your way through St. Peter's and its associated components.

Visits to the **Necropolis Vaticana ★★** and St. Peter's tomb itself are restricted to 250 persons per day on guided 90-minute tours. You must send a fax or e-mail 3 weeks beforehand, or apply in advance in person at the Ufficio Scavi (℗/fax **06-69873017;** e-mail: scavi@fsp.va; Monday–Friday 9am–6pm, Saturday 9am–5pm), located through the arch to the left of the stairs up from the basilica. For details, check **www.vatican.va**. Children aged 14 and under are not admitted to the Necropolis.

Piazza San Pietro. www.vatican.va. ℗ **06-69881662.** Basilica (including grottoes) free. Necropolis Vaticana (St. Peter's tomb) 13€. Stairs to the dome 8€; elevator (partway) to the dome 10€; sacristy (with Historical Museum) 5€ adults, 3€ 12 and under. **Basilica** Oct–Mar daily 7am–6:30pm, Apr–Sept 7am–7pm. **Dome** Oct–Mar daily 7:30am–5pm, Apr–Sept 7:30am–6pm. **Sacristry/museum** Oct–Mar 9am–5:15pm, Apr–Sept 9am–6:15pm. **Grottoes** Oct–Mar 7am–5pm, Apr–Sept 7am–6pm. Metro: Ottaviano/San Pietro, then a 10-min walk; or take bus 40, 46, or 62 to Piazza Pia/Traspontina, then about a 10-min walk.

Fontana Della Pigna in the courtyard of the Vatican Museum

Vatican Museums & the Sistine Chapel ★★★ MUSEUM   Nothing else in Rome quite lives up to the awe-inspiring collections of the **Vatican Museums,** a 15-minute walk from St. Peter's out the north side of Piazza San Pietro. It's a vast treasure store of art from antiquity and the Renaissance gathered by the Roman Catholic Church through the centuries, filling a series of ornate Papal palaces, apartments, and galleries leading to one of the world's most beautiful interiors, the justly celebrated **Sistine Chapel.**

Note that the Vatican dress code also applies to its museums (no sleeveless blouses, no miniskirts, no shorts, no hats allowed), though it tends to be less rigorously enforced than at St. Peter's.

Obviously, one trip will not be enough to see everything here. Below are previews of the main highlights, showstoppers, and masterpieces on display (in alphabetical order).

APPARTAMENTO BORGIA (BORGIA APARTMENTS) ★   Created for Pope Alexander VI (the infamous Borgia pope) between 1492 and 1494, these rooms were frescoed with biblical and allegorical scenes by Umbrian painter Pinturicchio and his assistants. Look for what is thought to be the earliest European depiction of Native Americans, painted little more than a year after Columbus returned from the New World.

COLLEZIONE D'ARTE CONTEMPORANEA (COLLECTION OF MODERN RELIGIOUS ART) ★   Spanning 55 rooms of almost 800 works, these galleries contain the Vatican's concession to modern art. There are some big names here and the quality is high. Themes usually have a spiritual and religious component: Van Gogh's "Pietà, after Delacroix" is here, along with Francis Bacon's eerie "Study for a Pope II." You will also see works by Paul Klee ("City with Gothic Cathedral"), Siqueiros ("Mutilated Christ No. 467"), Otto Dix ("Road to Calvary"), Gauguin ("Religious Panel"), Chagall ("Red Pietà"), and a whole room dedicated to Georges Rouault.

MUSEI DI ANTICHITÀ CLASSICHE (CLASSICAL ANTIQUITIES MUSEUMS) ★★★   The Vatican maintains four classical antiquities museums, the most important being the **Museo Pio Clementino** ★★★, crammed with Greek and Roman sculptures in the small Belvedere Palace of Innocent VIII. At the heart of the complex lies the Octagonal Court, where highlights include the sculpture of the Trojan priest **"Laocoön"** ★★★ and his two sons locked in a struggle with sea serpents, dating from around 40 B.C., and the exceptional **"Belvedere Apollo"** ★★★ (a 2nd-century Roman reproduction of an authentic Greek work from the 4th century B.C.), the symbol of classic male beauty and a possible inspiration for Michelangelo's "David." Look also for the impressive gilded bronze statue of **"Hercules"** in the Rotonda, from the late 2nd century A.D., and the **Hall of the Chariot,** containing a magnificent sculpture of a chariot combining Roman originals and 18th-century work by Antonio Franzoni.

The **Museo Chiaramonti** ★ occupies the long loggia that links the Belvedere Palace to the main Vatican palaces, jam-packed on both sides with more than 800 Greco-Roman works, including statues, reliefs, and sarcophagi. In the **Braccio Nuovo** ★ ("New Wing"), a handsome Neoclassical extension of the Chiaramonti sumptuously lined with colored marble, lies the colossal statue of the **"Nile"** ★, the ancient river portrayed as an old man with his 16 children, most likely a reproduction of a long-lost Alexandrian Greek original. The **Museo Gregoriano Profano** ★★, built in 1970, houses more Greek sculptures looted by the Romans (some from the Parthenon), mostly funerary steles and votive reliefs, as well as some choice Roman pieces, notably the restored mosaics from the floors of the public libraries in the **Baths of Caracalla** (p. 88).

MUSEO ETNOLOGICO (ETHNOLOGICAL MUSEUM) ★★   Founded in 1926, this astounding assemblage of artifacts and artwork is from cultures around the world, from ancient Chinese coins and notes, to plaster sculptures of Native Americans and ceremonial art from Papua New Guinea.

MUSEO GREGORIANO EGIZIO ★★   Nine rooms are packed with plunder from Ancient Egypt, including sarcophagi, mummies, pharaonic statuary, votive bronzes, jewelry, cuneiform tablets from Mesopotamia, inscriptions from Assyrian palaces, and Egyptian hieroglyphics.

Strategies for Visiting the Vatican Museums

The sheer size of the collections and vast crowds mean that seeing one of the greatest museums of art in the world isn't a leisurely, or even pleasant, experience. Visitors tend to get herded through room after room of galleries as they make their way to the Sistine Chapel, and lack of descriptive labels means they often don't know what they're looking at. Here are some tips to make sense of it all:

o Book **"skip the line"** tickets in advance through the Vatican Museums website. Once you see the entrance line stretching around the walls of Vatican City, the €4 booking feel will feel like money well-spent.

o Buy the **Guide to the Vatican Museums and City** book (14€) sold at the Vatican Tourist Office, on the left side of Piazza San Pietro (also, at a higher price, on Amazon.com).

o Once you're in the museum, take a few minutes to review the galleries map and decide which collections or works of art are a priority.

o If your priority is to see the Sistine Chapel, follow signs for the "Percorso Breve" (short route) to the Cappella Sistina.

To shake the daily herd of visitors and have a deeper experience, consider a breakfast or after-hours visit (p. 86), or springing for a private tour of the collections. These are a great way to get the most out of a visit, especially if you have limited time. They're also the only way to visit the **Vatican Gardens.** Booking online is mandatory; visit **https://biglietteria musei.vatican.va/musei/tickets** for information. See Organized Tours (p. 125) for info on private companies offering Vatican tours.

MUSEO GREGORIANO ETRUSCO ★★ The core of this collection is a cache of rare Etruscan art treasures dug up in the 19th century, dating from between the 9th and the 1st centuries B.C. The Romans learned a lot from the Etruscans, as the highly crafted ceramics, bronzes, silver, and gold on display attest. Don't miss the **Regolini-Galassi tomb** (7th century B.C.), unearthed at Cerveteri. The museum is housed within the *palazzettos* of Innocent VIII (reigned 1484–92) and Pius IV (reigned 1559–65), the latter adorned with frescoes by Federico Barocci and Federico Zuccari.

PINACOTECA (ART GALLERY) ★★★ The great painting collections of the Popes are displayed in the Pinacoteca, including work from all the big names in Italian art, from Giotto and Fra' Angelico to Perugino, Raphael, Veronese, and Crespi. Early medieval work occupies Room 1, with the most intriguing piece a keyhole-shaped wood panel of the "Last Judgment" by Nicolò e Giovanni, dated to the late 12th century. **Giotto** takes center stage in Room 2, with the "Stefaneschi Triptych" (six panels) painted for the old St. Peter's basilica between 1315 and 1320. **Fra' Angelico** dominates Room 3, his "Stories of St. Nicholas of Bari" and "Virgin with Child" justly praised (check out the Virgin's microscopic eyes in the latter piece). Carlo Crivelli features in Room 6, while decent works by Perugino and Pinturicchio grace Room 7, though most visitors press on to the **Raphael salon** ★★★ (Room 8), where you can view five paintings by the Renaissance master. The best are the "Coronation of the Virgin," the "Madonna of Foligno," and the vast "Transfiguration" (completed shortly before his death). Room 9 boasts Leonardo da Vinci's **"St. Jerome with the Lion"** ★★, as well as Giovanni Bellini's "Pietà." Room 10 is dedicated to Renaissance Venice, with Titian's "Madonna of St. Nicholas of the Frari" and Veronese's "Vision of St. Helen" being paramount. Don't skip the remaining galleries: Room 11 contains Barocci's "Annunciation," while Room 12 is really all about one of the masterpieces of the baroque, Caravaggio's **"Deposition from the Cross"** ★★.

STANZE DI RAFFAELLO (RAPHAEL ROOMS) ★★★   In the early 16th century, Pope Julius II hired the young Raphael and his workshop to decorate his personal apartments, on the second floor of the Pontifical Palace. Completed between 1508 and 1524, the **Raphael Rooms** now represent one of the great artistic spectacles inside the Vatican.

The **Stanza dell'Incendio** served as the Pope's high court room and later, under Leo X, a dining room. Most of its lavish frescoes have been attributed to Raphael's pupils. Leo X commissioned much of the work here, which explains the themes (past Popes with the name Leo). Note the intricate ceiling, painted by Umbrian maestro Perugino, who was Raphael's first teacher.

Raphael is the main focus in the **Stanza della Segnatura,** originally used as a Papal library and private office. It's home to the awe-inspiring **"School of Athens"** ★★★ fresco, depicting primarily Greek classical philosophers such as Aristotle, Plato, and Socrates. Many of the figures are thought to be based on portraits of Renaissance artists, including Bramante (on the right as Euclid, drawing on a chalkboard), Leonardo da Vinci (as Plato, the bearded man in the center), and even Raphael himself (in the lower-right corner with a black hat). On the wall opposite stands the equally magnificent "Disputa del Sacramento," where Raphael used a similar technique; Dante Alighieri stands behind the pontiff on the right, and Fra' Angelico poses as a monk (which in fact, he was) on the far left.

Immediately after he did the Segnatura, Raphael painted the **Stanza d'Eliodoro,** a room used by the Pope for private audiences. His aim here was to flatter his papal patron, Julius II: The depiction of the pope driving Attila from Rome was meant to symbolize the contemporary mission of Julius II to drive the French out of Italy. Finally, the **Sala di Costantino,** used for Papal receptions and official ceremonies, was completed by Raphael's students after the master's death, but based on his designs and drawings. It's a jaw-dropping space, commemorating four major episodes in the life of Emperor Constantine.

4

ROME | Exploring Rome

SISTINE CHAPEL ★★★ This important chapel, where the Papal Conclave still meets to elect new popes, is the Vatican Museum's artistic showstopper. Commissioned by Pope Julius II, Michelangelo labored for 4 years (1508–12) to paint the ceiling of the Sistine Chapel; it is said he spent the entire time on his feet, paint dripping into his eyes. But what a result! Thanks to a massive restoration effort in the 1990s, the world's most famous fresco is today as vibrantly colorful and filled with roiling life as it was in 1512. The "Creation of Adam," at the center of the ceiling, is one of the best known and most reproduced images in history, the outstretched hands of God and Adam—not quite touching—an iconic symbol of not just the Renaissance but the Enlightenment that followed. (It is somewhat ironic that this is Michelangelo's best-known work: The artist always regarded himself as a sculptor first and foremost.)

The ceiling frescoes primarily depict nine scenes from the Book of Genesis (including the famed "Creation of Adam"), from the "Separation of Light and Darkness" at the altar end to the "Great Flood" and "Drunkenness of Noah." Surrounding these main frescoes are paintings of 12 people who prophesied the coming of Christ, from Jonah and Isaiah to the Delphic Sibyl. *Tip:* Staring at the ceiling frescoes tends to take a heavy toll on the neck. To relieve your neck (and your tired feet), make your way to one of the benches that line both long sides of the gallery. As soon as someone gets up, grab a seat so you can gaze upward in relative comfort.

Once you have admired the ceiling, turn your attention to the altar wall. At the age of 60, Michelangelo was summoned to finish the chapel décor, 23 years after he finished the ceiling work. Apparently saddened by leaving Florence, and depressed by the morally bankrupt state of Rome at that time, he painted these dark moods into his "Last Judgment," where he included his own self-portrait on a sagging human hide held by St. Bartholomew (who was martyred by being flayed alive).

Seeing the Vatican at Night . . . or for Breakfast

Vatican Museum visitors now have an extraordinary opportunity to stroll through the galleries after sunset, at least on Friday nights from 7pm to 11pm (last entrance at 9:30) during the high tourist season, from the last Friday in April through July and the first Friday in September through the end of October. These **twilight visits** allow access to important collections, including the Pio-Clementine Museum, the Egyptian Museum, the Upper Galleries (candelabra, tapestries and maps), the Raphael Rooms, the Borgia Apartments, the Collection of Modern Religious Art, and the Sistine Chapel. Tickets are 21€.

Early birds should consider a **breakfast tour** of the museums. Starting at 7:15am (before the official opening time), breakfast visits cost 68€, including a buffet breakfast and access to all galleries. It's a far more tranquil visitor experience that daytime visits.

For either of these visits, book online at https://biglietteriamusei.vatican.va.

The Sistine Chapel isn't all Michelangelo, however. The south wall is covered by a series of astonishing paintings completed in the 1480s: "Moses Leaving to Egypt" by Perugino, the "Trials of Moses" by Botticelli, "The Crossing of the Red Sea" by Cosimo Rosselli (or Domenico Ghirlandaio), "Descent from Mount Sinai" by Cosimo Rosselli (or Piero di Cosimo), Botticelli's "Punishment of the Rebels," and Signorelli's "Testament and Death of Moses." On the right-hand north wall are Perugino's "The Baptism of Christ," Botticelli's "The Temptations of Christ," Ghirlandaio's "Vocation of the Apostles," Perugino's "Delivery of the Keys," Cosimo Rosselli's "The Sermon on the Mount" and "Last Supper." On the east wall, originals by Ghirlandaio and Signorelli were painted over in the 1570s by Hendrik van den Broeck's "The Resurrection" and Matteo da Lecce's "Disputation over Moses."

Vatican City, Viale Vaticano (a long walk around the Vatican walls from St. Peter's Sq.). www.museivaticani.va. *(C)* **06-69884676.** 17€ adults, 8€ children 6–13, free for ages 5 and under; 2-hr. tours of Vatican Gardens 33€ (no tours Wed or Sun). Mon–Sat 9am–6pm (ticket office closes 4pm). Also open last Sun of every month 9am–2pm (free admission). For early morning and Fri evening visits, see box p. 86. Closed Jan 1 and 6, Feb 11, Mar 19, Easter, May 1, June 29, Aug 14–15, Nov 1, and Dec 25–26. Advance tickets (reservation fee 4€) and guided tours (33€ per person) through https://biglietteriamusei.vatican.va. Metro: Ottaviano or Cipro–Musei Vaticani; bus 46 stops in front of the entrance.

Castel Sant'Angelo ★★ CASTLE/PALACE Over the years, this bulky cylindrical fortress on the Vatican side of the Tiber has had many lives: As the mausoleum tomb of Emperor Hadrian in A.D. 138; as a papal residence in the 14th century; as a castle, where in 1527 Pope Clement VII hid from the looting troops of Charles V; and as a military prison from the 17th century on. Consider renting an audio guide at the entrance to fully appreciate its various manifestations.

From the entrance a stone ramp *(rampa elicoidale)* winds to the upper terraces, where you can see amazing views of the city and enjoy a coffee at the outdoor cafe. The sixth floor features the **Terrazza dell'Angelo,** crowned by a florid 18th-century statue of the Archangel Michael. It's famous to opera fans—the last act of Puccini's "Tosca" is set here.

From here you can walk back down through five floors. On levels 3 to 5 you'll see the Renaissance apartments used by some of Rome's most infamous Popes, including Alexander VI, the Borgia pope. The art collection displayed throughout is fairly mediocre by Rome standards, although there are a few works by Carlo Crivelli and Luca Signorelli, notably a "Madonna and Child with Saints" from Signorelli. Below the apartments are the grisly dungeons **("Le Prigioni")** used as torture chambers in the medieval period (Cesare Borgia made great use of them). The castle is connected to St. Peter's Basilica by **Il Passetto di Borgo,** a walled passage built in 1277 by Pope Nicholas III, used by popes who needed to make a quick escape to the fortress in times of danger.

Note that the dungeons, Il Passetto, and the apartments of Clement VII are usually open by guided tour only (English tours Tuesday–Sunday at 10am and 4pm, 5€), with occasional late-night openings in the summer. Classical music and jazz concerts are also held in and around the castle in summertime.

Lungotevere Castello 50. www.castelsantangelo.com. ☏ **06-6819111.** 11€. Tues–Sun 9am–7:30pm. Bus: 23, 40, 62, 271, 280, 982 (to Piazza Pia).

The Colosseum, Forum & Ancient Rome
THE MAJOR SIGHTS OF ANCIENT ROME

Your sightseeing experience will be enhanced if you know a little about the history and rulers of Ancient Rome: See p. 17 for a brief rundown.

Arch of Constantine (Arco di Costantino) ★★ MONUMENT

The photogenic triumphal arch next to the Colosseum was erected by the Senate in A.D. 315 to honor Emperor Constantine's defeat of the pagan Maxentius at the Battle of the Milvian Bridge (A.D. 312). Many of the reliefs have nothing whatsoever to do with Constantine or his works, but they tell of the victories of earlier Antonine rulers (lifted from other, long-forgotten memorials).

The arch marks a period of great change in the history of Rome. Converted to Christianity by a vision on the eve of battle, Constantine ended the centuries-long persecution of the Christians, during which many followers of the new religion had been put to death in a gruesome manner. Although Constantine didn't ban paganism (which survived officially for another half century or so), he espoused Christianity himself and began the process that ended in the conquest of Rome by the Christian religion.

Btw. Colosseum and Palatine Hill. Metro: Colosseo.

Baths of Caracalla (Terme di Caracalla) ★★ RUINS

Named for Emperor Caracalla, a particularly unpleasant individual, the baths were completed in A.D. 217 after his death. The richness of decoration has faded, but the massive brick ruins and the mosaic fragments that remain give modern visitors an idea of the complex's scale and grandeur. In their heyday, the baths sprawled across 11 hectares (27 acres) and included hot, cold, and tepid pools, as well as a *palestra* (gym) and changing rooms. A museum in the tunnels below the complex—built over an even more ancient *mithraem,* a worship site of an eastern cult—explores the hydraulic and heating systems (and slave power) needed to serve 8,000 Romans per day. Summer operatic performances here are an ethereal treat (see p. 159).

Via delle Terme di Caracalla 52. www.coopculture.it/en. ☏ **06-39967700.** 8€. For combined ticket with Tomb of Caecilia Metella see p. 122. Late Oct–late Mar Mon 9am–2pm, Tues–Sun 9am–dusk; late Mar–late Sept Mon 9am–2pm, Tues–Sun 9am–7pm. Last entry 1 hr. before closing. Bus: 118 or 628.

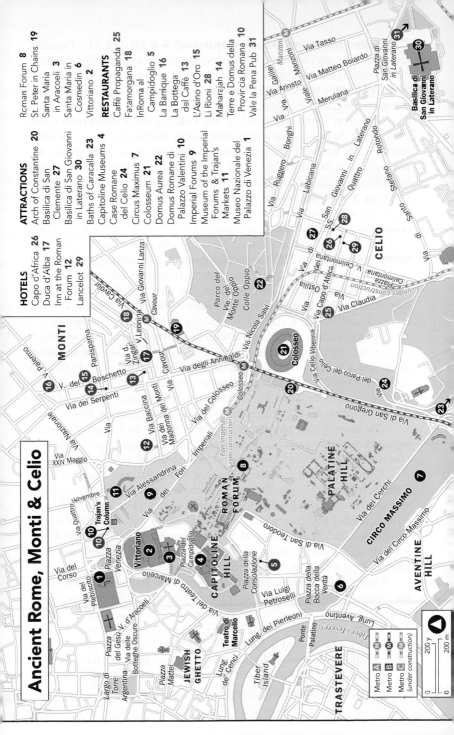

Ancient Rome, Monti & Celio

HOTELS
Capo d'Africa **26**
Duca d'Alba **17**
Inn at the Roman Forum **12**
Lancelot **29**

ATTRACTIONS
Arch of Constantine **20**
Basilica di San Clemente **27**
Basilica di San Giovanni in Laterano **30**
Baths of Caracalla **23**
Capitoline Museums **4**
Case Romane del Celio **24**
Circus Maximus **7**
Colosseum **21**
Domus Aurea **22**
Domus Romane di Palazzo Valentini **10**
Imperial Forums **9**
Museum of the Imperial Forums & Trajan's Markets **11**
Museo Nazionale del Palazzo di Venezia **1**
Roman Forum **8**
St. Peter in Chains **19**
Santa Maria in Aracoeli **3**
Santa Maria in Cosmedin **6**
Vittoriano **2**

RESTAURANTS
Caffè Propaganda **25**
Fatamorgana **18**
InRoma al Campidoglio **5**
La Barrique **16**
La Bottega del Caffè **13**
L'Asino d'Oro **15**
Li Rioni **28**
Maharajah **14**
Terre e Domus della Provincia Romana **10**
Vale la Pena Pub **31**

Capitoline Museums (Musei Capitolini) ★★ MUSEUM   The masterpieces here are considered Rome's most valuable (recall that the Vatican Museums are *not* technically in Rome). They certainly were collected early: This is the oldest public museum *in the world.* So try and schedule adequate time, as there's much to see.

First stop is the courtyard of the **Palazzo dei Conservatori** (the building on the right of the piazza designed by Michelangelo, as you enter from Piazza Venezia), scattered with gargantuan stone body parts—the remnants of a massive 12m (39-ft.) statue of the emperor Constantine, including his colossal head, hand, and foot. It's nearly impossible to resist snapping a selfie next to the giant finger. On the palazzo's ground floor, the unmissable works are in the first series of rooms: "Lo Spinario" (Room III), a lifelike bronze of a young boy digging a splinter out of his foot that was widely copied during the Renaissance; and the **"Lupa Capitolina"** (Room IV), a 500 B.C. bronze statue of the famous she-wolf that suckled Romulus and Remus, the mythical founders of Rome. The twins were not on the original Etruscan statue, but were added in the 15th century. Room V has Bernini's famously pained portrait of **"Medusa,"** even more compelling when you see its writhing serpent hairdo in person.

Before heading upstairs, go toward the newer wing at the rear, which houses the original equestrian **statue of Marcus Aurelius** ★★★, dating to around A.D. 180—the piazza outside, where it stood from 1538 until 2005, now has a copy. There's a giant bronze head from a statue of Constantine (ca. A.D. 337) and the foundations of the original Temple of Jupiter that stood on the Capitoline Hill since its inauguration in 509 B.C.

The second-floor **picture gallery** ★ is strong on baroque oil paintings. Masterpieces include Caravaggio's "John the Baptist" and "The Fortune Teller" (1595) and Guido Reni's "St. Sebastian" (1615).

A tunnel takes you under the piazza to the Palazzo Nuovo, via the **Tabularium** ★★, built in 78 B.C. to house ancient Rome's city records; it was later used as a salt mine and then as a prison. Here, the moody *galleria lapidaria* houses a well-executed exhibit of ancient portrait tombstones and sarcophagi, many of their poignant epitaphs translated into English, and provides access to one of the best balcony **views** ★★★ in Rome: along the length of the Forum toward the Palatine Hill.

Much of the **Palazzo Nuovo** is dedicated to statues excavated from the forums below and brought in from outlying areas like Hadrian's Villa in Tivoli (p. 164). If you're running short on time, head straight for the 1st-century **"Capitoline Venus"** ★★, in Room III—a modest girl covering up after a bath—and in Rooms IV and V, a chronologically arranged row of expressive busts of Roman emperors and their families. Another favorite is the beyond-handsome **"Dying Gaul"** ★★, a Roman copy of a lost ancient Greek work. Lord Byron considered the statue so lifelike and moving that he mentioned it in his poem "Childe Harold's Pilgrimage."

Piazza del Campidoglio 1. www.museicapitolini.org. © **060608**. 11.50€ (more during special exhibits), 12.50€ for a 7-day ticket that includes the Centrale Montemartini (see p. 120). Daily 9:30am–7:30pm. Last entry 1 hr. before closing. Bus: 40, 44, 60, 63, 64, 70, 118, 160, 170, 628, 716, or any bus that stops at Piazza Venezia.

Circus Maximus (Circo Massimo) ★ RUIN   Today mostly an oval-shaped field, the once-grand circus was pilfered by medieval and Renaissance builders in search of marble and stone—it's a far cry from its *Ben-Hur*-esque heyday. What the Romans called a "circus" was a large arena ringed by tiers of seats and used for sports or spectacles. At one time, 300,000 Romans could assemble here, while the emperor observed the games from his box high on the Palatine Hill.

The last games were held in A.D. 549 on the orders of Totilla the Goth, who had seized Rome (twice). Afterward, the Circus Maximus was never used again, and the demand for building materials reduced it, like so much of Rome, to a great dusty field, now used mostly for big-name rock concerts. An archaeological area at its eastern end (closest to the Metro station) offers insights into how the space once functioned. *Tip:* If you're crunched for time, bypass the Circus Maximus and instead take in the emperor's-eye views of the arena from atop the Palatine Hill.

Btw. Via dei Cerchi and Via del Circo Massimo. http://mobile.060608.it/en. © **060608**. Archaeological area, 5€. Sat–Sun 10am–4pm, or by guided tour only Tues–Fri. Metro: Circo Massimo. Bus: 81, 118, 160.

Colosseum (Colosseo) ★★★ ICON   No matter how many pictures you've seen, your first view of the Flavian Amphitheater (the Colosseum's original name) is likely to amaze you with its sheer size and ruined grandeur. While you're still outside its massive walls, it's important to walk completely around its 500m (1,640-ft.) circumference. It doesn't matter where you start, but do the circle. Look at the various stages of ruin; note the different column styles on each level. Mere photos could never convey its physical impact.

Vespasian ordered the construction of the elliptical bowl in A.D. 72; it was inaugurated by Titus in A.D. 80. Built for gladiator contests and wild animal fights, the stadium could hold as many as 87,000 spectators by some counts; seats were sectioned on three levels, dividing the people by social rank and gender. Some 80 entrances allowed the massive crowds to be seated and dispersed within a few minutes. When the Roman Empire fell, however, the abandoned arena was eventually overgrown. Much of the travertine that once sheathed its outside was scavenged for palaces like the nearby Palazzo Venezia and Palazzo Cancelleria.

An ongoing conservation effort, funded by the Italian design house Tod's, cleared nearly 2,000 years of soot from the monument's exterior;

4

ROME | Exploring Rome

restoration efforts have now shifted to its underground vaults and passage-ways. Access to the **Colosseum Underground** and **Belvedere** (upper tier) is by guided tour only, ticketed separately from admission to the Colosseum (and *not* included with the RomaPass). The process for purchasing tickets online can be baffling, but essentially you can reserve a tour of the underground OR the belvedere OR both areas, up to one month in advance. These tours sell out very quickly. A combined tour costs 15€, in addition to the 12€ admission fee. Remember that the same ticket you buy for the Colosseum includes admission to the Forum and Palatine Hill, and is valid for 2 days. A prepurchased Colosseum ticket (or RomaPass) allows you to skip the long line to enter, but you still must go through security screening, which can take up to an hour on busy days. As of 2019, **RomaPass holders** must reserve a time to enter the Colosseum, either online or by calling ☏ **06-39967575** *or* by appearing at one of the Forum/Palatine ticket offices the day you wish to enter. There's a 2€ per person service charge to reserve a time.

Piazzale del Colosseo. www.coopculture.it/en/colosseo-e-shop.cfm. ☏ **06-39967700.** 12€; 14€ online (recommended), includes Roman Forum & Palatine Hill. Guided tours of Underground and Belvedere 15€ (in addition to full entry fee). Opening hours 8:30am–dusk (as early as 4:30pm in winter, 7:15pm summer). Last entry 1 hr. before closing. Metro: Colosseo. Bus: 51, 75, 85, 87, 118. Tram: 3, 8.

Imperial Forums (Fori Imperiali) ★ RUINS   Begun by Julius Caesar to relieve overcrowding in Rome's older forums, the Imperial Forums were, at the time of their construction, flashier, bolder, and more impressive than anything that had come before them in Rome. They conveyed the unquestioned authority of the emperors at the height of their power. Alas, Mussolini felt his regime was more important than the ancient one, and issued controversial orders to cut through centuries of debris and buildings to carve out Via dei Fori Imperiali, linking the Colosseum to the 19th-century monuments of Piazza Venezia. Excavations under his Fascist regime uncovered countless archaeological treasures: Most ruins more recent than imperial Rome were destroyed.

The best view of the Forums is from the railings on the north side of Via dei Fori Imperiali; begin where Via Cavour joins the boulevard. (Visitors are not permitted down into the ruins.) Closest to the junction are the remains of the **Forum of Nerva,** built by the emperor whose 2-year reign (A.D. 96–98) followed the assassination of the paranoid Domitian. Notice how much the ground level has risen in 19 centuries. The only really recognizable remnant is a wall of the Temple of Minerva with two fine Corinthian columns. Next along is the **Forum of Augustus ★★**, built to commemorate Emperor Augustus's victory over Julius Caesar's assassins, Cassius and Brutus, in the Battle of Philippi (42 B.C.). Continuing along the railing, you'll see the vast multilevel semicircle of **Trajan's Markets ★★**, essentially an ancient shopping mall whose arcades were once stocked with merchandise from the far corners of the Roman world. One part has been transformed into the **Museo dei Fori Imperiali & Mercati di Traiano** (see p. 97). In front of the markets, the **Forum of Trajan** ★★, built between A.D. 107 and 113, was designed by Greek architect Apollodorus of Damascus (who also laid out the adjoining market building). Many statue fragments and pedestals bear still-legible inscriptions, but more interesting is the great Basilica Ulpia, whose gray marble columns rise roofless into the sky. This forum was once regarded as one of the architectural wonders of the world. Beyond the Basilica Ulpia is **Trajan's Column** ★★★, in magnificent condition, with an intricate bas-relief sculpture depicting Trajan's victorious campaign. The **Forum of Julius Caesar** ★★, the first of the Imperial Forums to be built, lies on the opposite side of Via dei Fori Imperiali, adjacent to the Roman Forum. This was the site of the stock exchange as well as the Temple of Venus.

Along Via dei Fori Imperiali. Metro: Colosseo. Bus: 51, 75, 85, 87, 118.

Roman Forum (Foro Romano) & Palatine Hill (Palatino) ★★★

RUINS   Traversed by the **Via Sacra (Sacred Way)** ★, the main thoroughfare of ancient Rome, the Roman Forum flourished as the center of

THREE free views TO SAVOR FOR A LIFETIME

The Forum from the Campidoglio   Standing on Piazza del Campidoglio, outside the Musei Capitolini (p. 90), walk around the right or left side of the Palazzo Senatorio to terraces overlooking the best panoramas of the Roman Forum, with the Palatine Hill and Colosseum as a backdrop. At night, the ruins look even more haunting when the Forum is dramatically floodlit.

The Whole City from the Janiculum Hill   From many vantage points in the Eternal City, the views are panoramic. But one of the best spots for a memorable vista is the Janiculum Hill *(Gianicolo)*, above Trastevere. Laid out before you are Rome's rooftops, peppered with domes ancient and modern. From up here, you will understand why Romans complain about the materials used to build the 19th-century Vittoriano (p. 100)—it's a white shock in a sea of rose- and honey-colored stone. Walk 50 yards north of the famous balcony (favored by tour buses) for a slightly better angle, from the Belvedere 9 Febbraio 1849. Views from the

1612 Fontana dell'Acqua Paola are also splendid, especially at night.

The Aventine Hill & the Priori dei Cavalieri di Malta   The mythical site of Remus's original settlement, the Aventine *(Aventino)* is now a leafy, upscale residential neighborhood—but also blessed with some magical views. From Via del Circo Massimo walk through the gardens along Via di Valle Murcia, and keep walking in a straight line. Along your right side, gardens offer views over the dome of St. Peter's. When you reach Piazza dei Cavalieri di Malta, look through the keyhole of the Priory gate (on the right) for a "secret" view of the Vatican.

Ruins of the Temple of the Dioscuri in the Roman Forum.

religious, social, and commercial life in the days of the Republic, before it gradually lost prestige (but never spiritual draw) to the Imperial Forums (see p. 92). You'll see ruins and fragments, some partially intact columns, and an arch or two, but you can still feel the rush of history here. That any semblance of the Forum remains today is miraculous: Used for years as a quarry (as was the Colosseum), it eventually reverted to a *campo vaccino* (cow pasture). Excavations in the 19th century and later in the 1930s began to bring to light one of the world's most historic spots.

You can spend at least a morning wandering the ruins of the Forum. Enter via the gate on Via dei Fori Imperiali, at Via della Salara Vecchia. Turn right at the bottom of the entrance slope to walk west along the old Via Sacra toward the arch. Just before it on your right is the large brick **Curia ★★**, the main seat of the Roman Senate, built by Julius Caesar, rebuilt by Diocletian, and consecrated as a church in A.D. 630. The triumphal **Arch of Septimius Severus ★★** (A.D. 203), the next important sight, displays time-bitten reliefs of the emperor's victories in what are now Iran and Iraq. During the Middle Ages, when Rome was a provincial backwater and frequent flooding of the Tiber buried most of the Forum, some bits still stuck out aboveground, including the top half of this arch, which was used to shelter a barbershop!

Just to the left of the arch, you can make out the remains of a cylindrical lump of rock with some marble steps curving off it. That round stone was the **Umbilicus Urbus,** considered the center of Rome and of the entire Roman Empire; the curving steps are those of the **Imperial Rostra ★,** where great orators and legislators stood to speak and the people gathered to listen. Nearby, a much-photographed trio of fluted columns with Corinthian capitals supports a bit of architrave from the corner of the **Temple of Vespasian and Titus ★★** (emperors were routinely turned into gods upon dying).

Start heading to your left toward the eight Ionic columns marking the front of the **Temple of Saturn ★★** (rebuilt in 42 B.C.), which housed the first treasury of Republican Rome. It was also the site of one of the Roman year's biggest annual blowout festivals, the December 17 feast of Saturnalia, which, after a bit of tweaking, Christians now celebrate as Christmas. Turn left to start heading back east, past the worn steps and stumps of brick pillars outlining the enormous **Basilica Julia ★★,** built by Julius Caesar. Farther along, on the right, the three Corinthian columns of the **Temple of the Dioscuri ★★★** are dedicated to the Gemini twins, Castor and Pollux. Forming one of the most photogenic sights of the Roman Forum, a trio of columns supports an architrave fragment. The founding of this temple dates from the 5th century B.C.

Beyond the bit of curving wall that marks the site of the little round **Temple of Vesta** (rebuilt several times after fires started by the sacred flame within), you'll find the reconstructed **House of the Vestal Virgins** (A.D. 3rd–4th c.). The temple was the home of the consecrated young women who tended the sacred flame in the Temple of Vesta. Vestals were girls chosen from patrician families to serve a 30-year-long priesthood. During their tenure, they were among Rome's most venerated citizens, with unique powers such as the ability to pardon condemned criminals. The cult was quite serious about the "virgin" part of the job description— if one of Vesta's earthly servants was found to have "misplaced" her virginity, the miscreant Vestal was buried alive, because it was forbidden to shed a Vestal's blood. (Her amorous accomplice was merely flogged to death.) The overgrown rectangle of their gardens is lined with broken, heavily worn statues of senior Vestals on pedestals.

The path dovetails back to Via Sacra. Turn right, walk past the so-called Temple of Romulus, and then left to enter the massive brick remains of the 4th-century **Basilica of Constantine and Maxentius ★★** (Basilica di Massenzio), Rome's public law courts. Its architectural style was adopted by early Christians for their houses of worship—which is why so many ancient churches are called "basilicas."

Return to the path and continue toward the Colosseum. Veer right to the Forum's second great triumphal arch, the extensively rebuilt **Arch of Titus ★★** (A.D. 81), on which one relief depicts the carrying off of treasures from Jerusalem's temple. Look closely and you'll see a menorah among the booty. The war that this arch glorifies ended with the expulsion of Jews from colonized Judea, signaling the beginning of the Jewish Diaspora throughout Europe. You can exit behind the Arch to continue on to the Colosseum, or head up to the Palatine Hill.

Access the **Palatine Hill** ★★ (Palatino)—where Romulus, after eliminating his twin brother Remus, founded Rome around 753 B.C.—via the **Imperial Ramp,** a secret passageway built by Emperor Domitian in the 1st century A.D. The 11m- (36 ft.) tall switchback ramp allowed the assassination-paranoid ruler to go back and forth undetected between his palace and the forum below. (He was murdered in the passageway anyway.) Later, emperors and other ancient bigwigs built their palaces and private entertainment facilities up here. Upon exiting at the top of the ramp, visitors are presented with a sprawling, mostly crowd-free archaeological garden, with some shady spots for cooling off in summer.

The Palatine was where the first settlers built their huts under the direction of Romulus. In later years, the hill became a patrician residential district that attracted such citizens as Cicero. In time, however, the area was gobbled up by imperial palaces and drew an infamous roster of tenants. The elaborately decorated **houses of Livia and Augustus** ★★ are open to S.U.P.E.R. ticket holders (see box below). Other sites include the houses of Tiberius, Caligula (murdered here by members of his Praetorian Guard), Nero, and Domitian. A museum houses some of the most important finds from hill excavations.

Only the ruins of the Palatine's grandeur remain today, but it's worth the climb for the panoramic views of both the Roman and the Imperial Forums, as well as the Capitoline Hill, the Colosseum, and Circus Maximus. You can also enter from here, and do the entire tour in reverse.

Forum entrance at Via della Salara Vecchia 5/6, Palatine Hill entrance at Via di San Gregorio 30 (south of the Colosseum). www.coopculture.it/en/heritage.cfm?id=4. ✆ **06-39967700.** 12€ (includes Colosseum),14€ prepurchased. See box below for information on S.U.P.E.R tickets. Open 8:30am–dusk. Last entry 1 hr. before closing. Metro: Colosseo. Bus: 51, 75, 85, 87, 118. Tram: 3, 8.

S.U.P.E.R. tickets for archaeology lovers

A new ticket option allows Palatine Hill visitors to access archaeological sites which normally have limited hours or are closed to the public entirely. The **S.U.P.E.R. ticket** (Seven Unique Places to Explore in Rome), available in lieu of a normal Colosseum/Forum/Palatine ticket, includes access to the Houses of Livia and Augustus, the Neronion Crytpoporticus, the Palatine Museum, the Temple of Romulus, the Loggia Mattei (part of a Renaissance palace) and, at the foot of the Palatine, the paleochristian church of Santa Maria Antiqua. The 20€ ticket, for those who want a deep dive into the Palatine's layers of history, can be ordered at www.coopculture.it. Note that RomaPass holders must buy a separate S.U.P.E.R. ticket to enter the limited-access Palatine areas.

Museum of the Imperial Forums & Trajan's Markets (Museo dei Fori Imperiali & Mercati di Traiano) ★★ RUINS/MUSEUM

Built on three levels, Emperor Trajan's Market housed 150 shops and commercial offices—think of it as the world's first shopping mall. Grooves still evident in the thresholds allowed merchants to slide doors shut and lock up for the night. You're likely to have the covered, tunnel-like market halls mostly to yourself—making the ancient past feel all the more present in this overlooked site. Occupying a converted section of the market, the Museum of the Imperial Forums has excellent visual displays that help you imagine what these grand public squares and temples used to look like. All in all, it's home to 172 marble fragments from the Fori Imperiali; here are also original remnants from the Forum of Augustus and Forum of Nerva.

Avoid Ancient Overload

Even though they're all included in the same admission fee, the ruins of the Colosseum, Roman Forum, and Palatine Hill are quite a lot to take in on a single day, particularly in the heat of Roman summer. We recommend that you take advantage of the 2-day window your ticket allows. See the Forum and Palatine on your first day, then hit the Colosseum on day 2, going first thing in the morning before the crowds pile in.

Via IV Novembre 94. www.mercatiditraiano.it. © **060608.** 12.50€. Daily 9:30am–7:30pm. Last admission 1 hr. before closing. Bus: 40, 60, 64, 70, 170.

OTHER ATTRACTIONS NEAR ANCIENT ROME

Basilica di San Clemente ★★ CHURCH   A perfect example of how layers of history overlap in Rome, this 12-century Norman church, full of beautiful Byzantine mosaics, hides much more. Down in its eerie grottos you'll find frescoes and mosaic floors from its previous incarnations as a 4th-century Christian church and a temple dedicated to the pagan deity Mithras—and below that, the foundations of a Roman house from the 1st century A.D., where early Christians worshipped in secret.

Via San Giovanni in Laterano (at Piazza San Clemente). www.basilicasanclemente.com. © **06-7740021.** Basilica free; excavations 10€. Mon–Sat 9am–12:30pm and 3–6pm; Sun 12:15–6pm. Last entry 30 min before closing. Metro: Colosseo. Bus: 51, 85, 87, 117. Tram: 3.

Basilica di San Giovanni in Laterano ★ CHURCH   This church, not St. Peter's, is officially the cathedral of the diocese of Rome; the Pope celebrates Mass here on certain holidays. Though it was built in A.D. 314 by Constantine, only parts of the original baptistery remain; what you see today is an 18th-century facade by Alessandro Galilei (note signs of damage from a 1993 terrorist bomb) and an interior by Borromini, built for Pope Innocent X. In a misguided redecoration long ago, frescoes by Giotto were apparently destroyed; remains attributed to Giotto, discovered in 1952, are displayed against the first inner column on the right.

NERO'S golden HOUSE ★★★

After the Great Fire of A.D. 64, charismatic despot Emperor Nero staged a land grab to facilitate construction of his *Domus Aurea*, or Golden House, a massive gilded villa complex covering all or parts of the Palatine, Esquiline, and Caelian hills, displaying a level of ostentation and excessiveness unheard of even among past emperors. After his death by noble suicide in A.D. 68, a campaign to erase all traces of Nero from the imperial city ensured that the palace was stripped of its gold, marble, jewels, mosaics, and statuary, then intentionally buried under millions of tons of rubble. It remained buried until the Renaissance, when young artists, including Raphael, descended into its "grottos" (actually the vaulted ceilings) to study the fanciful frescoes. Later excavations, both haphazard and scientific, revealed the scale and richness of the villa, but also subjected it to catastrophic moisture damage. After a years-long closure for restoration and restabilization, the Domus Aurea is once again open for tours—but only if you time your trip well and plan ahead. Guided tours (16€; www.coopculture.it/en) of the scaffolded underground site (hardhats required) are offered on **Saturdays and Sundays only,** and with advance reservations. The tour includes a spectacular virtual reality experience that in itself is worth the visit.

Underground tour of Nero's Domus Aurea.

Across the street, the **Santuario della Scala Santa (Palace of the Holy Steps),** Piazza San Giovanni in Laterano 14 (𝄐 **06-7726641**) is a set of 28 marble steps supposedly brought from Jerusalem by Constantine's mother, Helen. Though some historians say the stairs might date only from the 4th century, legend claims these were the stairs Christ climbed at Pontius Pilate's villa the day he was sentenced to death. Today pilgrims from all over the world come here to climb the steps on their knees.

Piazza San Giovanni in Laterano 4. 𝄐 **06-69886433.** Free. Daily 7am–6:30pm. Metro: San Giovanni.

Case Romane del Celio ★ RUINS Beneath the 5th-century Basilica of SS. Giovanni e Paolo lies a fascinating archaeological site: A complex of Roman houses of different periods—a wealthy family's townhouse from the 2nd century A.D. and a 3rd-century-A.D. apartment building for artisans. According to tradition, the latter was the home of two Roman officers, John and Paul (not the Apostles), who were beheaded during the reign of Julian the Apostate (361–63) for refusing to serve in a military campaign. They were later made saints, and their bones were said to have been buried here. The two-story construction also contains a small museum with finds from the site and fragmentary 12th-century frescoes.

Piazza Santi Giovanni e Paolo 13 (entrance on Clivo di Scauro). www.caseromane.it. ℂ 06-70454544. 8€ adults, 6€ ages 12–18. Thurs–Mon 10am–1pm and 3–6pm. Metro: Colosseo or Circo Massimo. Bus: 75, 81, 118. Tram: 3.

Domus Romane di Palazzo Valentini ★★★ RUINS/EXHIBIT   All too often in Italy, archaeological sites are presented with little context, and it's difficult for untrained eyes to really understand what they're seeing. Not so at Palazzo Valentini, possibly Rome's best-presented ancient site. Visitors descend underneath a Renaissance palazzo and peer through a glass floor into the remains of several upscale Roman homes. With innovative use of 3-D projections, the walls, ceilings, floors, and fountains of these once-grand houses spring to life, offering a captivating look at lifestyles of the ancient rich and possibly famous. A scale model shows the surrounding area (adjacent to Trajan's Column) as it looked around the time of its completion (113 A.D.).

Via Foro Traiano 85 (near Trajan's Column). www.palazzovalentini.it. ℂ 06-22761280. 13.50€. Wed-Mon 9:30am–6:30pm. Timed entrance, with guided tours in English several times daily; reservations suggested. Metro: Colosseo. Bus: 40, 63, 70, 81, 83, 87, or any bus to Piazza Venezia. Tram: 8.

Museo Nazionale del Palazzo di Venezia ★ MUSEUM   Best remembered today as Mussolini's Fascist headquarters in Rome, the palace was built in the 1450s as the Rome outpost of the Republic of Venice, hence the name. Today, it houses an eclectic mix of European paintings and decorative and religious objects spanning the centuries; highlights include Giorgione's enigmatic "Double Portrait" and some early Tuscan altarpieces.

Via del Plebiscito 118. www.museopalazzovenezia.beniculturali.it. ℂ 06-6780131. 10€. Tues–Sun 8:30am–7:30pm. Bus: 30, 40, 46, 62, 64, 70, 87, or any bus to Piazza Venezia. Tram: 8.

St. Peter in Chains (San Pietro in Vincoli) ★ CHURCH   Founded in the 5th century to house the chains that supposedly bound St. Peter in Jerusalem (preserved under glass below the main altar), this lovely church is mainly worth visiting to see one of the world's most famous sculptures: **Michelangelo's "Moses" ★★**, carved for the tomb of Pope Julius II. Michelangelo never completed the 44 magnificent figures planned for the tomb, but this "minor" figure he did complete now numbers among his masterpieces.

Piazza San Pietro in Vincoli 4A. ℂ 06-97844952. Free. Spring–summer daily 8:30am–12:30pm and 3:30–7pm (fall–winter to 6pm). Metro: Colosseo or Cavour. Bus: 75.

Santa Maria in Aracoeli ★ CHURCH According to legend, Augustus once ordered a temple erected on this spot, on the Capitoline Hill, where a sibyl foretold the coming of Christ. The current church, built for the Franciscans in the 13th century, boasts a coffered Renaissance ceiling and the tomb of Giovanni Crivelli (1432) carved by the great Renaissance sculptor Donatello. The **Cappella Bufalini ★** (first chapel on the right) was frescoed by Pinturicchio with scenes of the life and death of St. Bernardino of Siena. A chapel behind the altar contains the **Santo Bambino,** a devotional wooden figure of the Baby Jesus, which is venerated annually on Christmas Eve. The long flight of stairs leading up to the church was built in 1348 to celebrate the end of the Black Plague.

Scala dell'Arcicapitolina 12. ℂ **06-69763838.** Free. Daily 9am–6:30pm (fall–winter to 5:30pm). Bus: 30, 40, 46, 62, 64, 70, 87, or any bus to Piazza Venezia.

Santa Maria in Cosmedin ★ CHURCH People line up outside this ancient church with a Romanesque bell tower not for great art treasures, but to see the **"Mouth of Truth,"** a large disk on the wall of the portico. As Gregory Peck demonstrated to Audrey Hepburn in the film *Roman Holiday,* the mouth is supposed to chomp down on the hands of liars. It may have been an ancient drain cover, though one hypothesis says it was a so-called "talking statue," where anonymous notes were left to betray wrongdoers. Our take? Save this hokey photo op until you've seen everything else you want to see in Rome.

Piazza della Bocca della Verità 18. ℂ **06-6787759.** Free. Daily 9:30am–5:50pm; closes 4:50pm in winter. Bus: 23, 81, 118, 160, 280, 715.

Vittoriano (Altare della Patria) ★ MONUMENT It's impossible to miss the white marble Vittorio Emanuele monument dominating Piazza Venezia. Built in the late 1800s to honor the first king of a united Italy, this flamboyant (and widely disliked) landmark has been compared to everything from a wedding cake to a Victorian typewriter, its harsh white color glaring in a city of honey-gold tones. An eternal flame burns at the Tomb of the Unknown Soldier. For a panoramic city view, take a glass elevator to the **Terrazza delle Quadrighe (Terrace of the Chariots) ★.**

Piazza Venezia. ℂ **06-6780664.** Elevator 7€. Daily 9:30am–7:30pm (last entry 6:45pm). Bus: 30, 40, 46, 62, 64, 70, 87, or any bus to Piazza Venezia.

All Roads Lead to . . . Piazza Venezia

Love it or loathe it, the massive Vittoriano monument at Piazza Venezia is a helpful landmark for visitors to get their bearings, and almost every bus line convenient to tourists stops here. Streets fanning out from the piazza lead to Termini Station, the Colosseum, the Trevi Fountain, and across the Tiber to the Vatican.

Centro Storico & the Pantheon
CENTRO STORICO

Just across the Tiber from the Vatican and Castel Sant'Angelo lies the true heart of Rome, the **Centro Storico,** or "historic center," the triangular wedge of land that bulges into a bend of the river. Although the area lay outside the Roman city, it came into its own during the Renaissance, and today its streets and alleys are crammed with piazzas, elegant churches, and lavish fountains, all buzzing with scooters and people. It's a wonderful area in which to wander and get lost.

PIAZZA NAVONA & NEARBY ATTRACTIONS

Rome's most famous square, **Piazza Navona ★★★**, is a gorgeous baroque gem, lined with cafes and restaurants and often crammed with tourists, street artists, and pigeons. Its long, oval shape follows the contours of the old ruined Roman Stadium of Domitian, where chariot races once took place, made over in the mid-17th century by Pope Innocent X. On the piazza's western side, the twin-towered facade of 17th-century **Sant'Agnese in Agone** sits opposite the **Fontana dei Quattro Fiumi (Fountain of the Four Rivers) ★★★**, one of three great fountains in the square. It's a typically exuberant creation by Bernini, topped with an Egyptian obelisk, with four stone figures personifying the world's greatest rivers: the Ganges, Danube, de la Plata, and Nile. It's fun to try to figure out which is which. (***Hint:*** The figure with the shroud on its head is the Nile, so represented because the river's source was unknown at the time.) At the south end are Bernini's **Fontana del Moro (Fountain of the Moor)** and the 19th-century **Fontana di Nettuno (Fountain of Neptune).**

Fountain of the Four Rivers in Piazza Navona

Art lovers should make the short walk from the piazza to **Santa Maria della Pace ★★** on Arco della Pace, a 15th-century church given the usual baroque makeover by Pietro da Cortona in the 1660s. The real gems are inside, beginning with Raphael's **"Four Sibyls"** ★★ fresco, above the arch of the Capella Chigi, and the **Chiostro del Bramante (Bramante cloister)** ★, built between 1500 and 1504 and the Renaissance master's first work in the city. The church is normally open on Monday, Wednesday, and Saturday 9am to noon, while the cloister opens daily 10am to 8pm (to 9pm Sat and Sun). Admission to the church and cloister is free (www.chiostrodelbramante.it).

Tip: Waiters from Piazza Navona's overpriced restaurants lie in wait, hoping to woo tourists. Buyer beware: while the setting is unmatchable, you'll have a far better meal on any of the sidestreets off the piazza.

Palazzo Altemps ★★ MUSEUM   Inside this 15th-century *palazzo,* today a branch of the National Museum of Rome, is one of Rome's most charming museums. It's rarely crowded yet houses some of Rome's most famous private and public art collections. Much of it was once part of the famed Boncompagni Ludovisi Collection, created by Cardinal Ludovico Ludovisi (1595–1632). Among the highlights is the **"Ludovisi Ares"** ★★, a handsome 2nd-century copy of an earlier Greek statue of Mars (Ares to the Greeks). Equally renowned is the **"Ludovisi Gaul"** ★, a marble depiction of a Gaulish warrior plunging a sword into his chest (rather than become a slave of Rome), looking backwards defiantly as he supports a dying woman with his left arm. Also worth a look is the **"Ludovisi Throne,"** a sculpted block of white marble, thought to date from the 5th century B.C., depicting Aphrodite rising from the sea.

Piazza di Sant'Apollinare 46. www.museonazionaleromano.beniculturali.it. (C) **06-39967700.** 12€ (15€ during special exhibits), valid for 3 days; also includes Palazzo Massimo, Baths of Diocletian, Crypta Balbi. 17 and under free. Tues–Sun 9am–7:45pm. Last entry 1 hr. before closing. Bus: C3, 70, 81, 87, 492, 628.

San Luigi dei Francesi ★★ CHURCH   For a painter of such stratospheric standards as Caravaggio, it's impossible to definitively name his "masterpiece." However, the **"Calling of St. Matthew"** ★★, in the far-left chapel of Rome's French church, must be a candidate. In Caravaggio's distinct *chiaroscuro* (extreme light and shade) style, the panel dramatizes the moment Jesus and Peter "called" the customs officer Matthew to join them. Around the same time (1599–1602) Caravaggio also painted two other St. Matthew panels in the church's Capella Contarelli—including one depicting the saint's martyrdom. Other highlights include Domenichino's masterful "Histories of Saint Cecilia" fresco cycle.

Via di Santa Giovanna d'Arco 5. www.saintlouis-rome.net. (C) **06-688271.** Free. Mon–Fri 9:30am–12:45pm; Sat 9:30am–12:15pm; Sun 11:30–12:45pm, plus daily 2:30–6:30pm. Bus: C3, 70, 81, 87, 492, 628.

THE PANTHEON & NEARBY ATTRACTIONS

The Pantheon stands on **Piazza della Rotonda,** a lively square with cafes, vendors, and great people-watching.

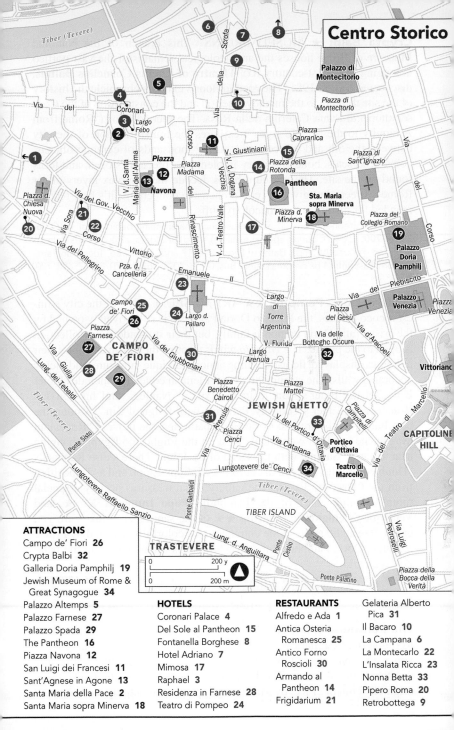

Centro Storico

Palazzo di
Montecitorio

Piazza di
Montecltorlo

Piazza
Capranica

Piazza di
Sant'Ignazio

Tiber (Tevere)

Via del Coronari

Largo Febo

Piazza
Navona

Piazza
Madama

Piazza della
Rotonda

Pantheon

Sta. Maria
sopra Minerva

Piazza d.
Chiesa
Nuova

Via d.Santa Maria dell'Anima

V. d. Dogana Vecchia

V. Giustiniani

Piazza del
Collegio Romano

Piazza d.
Minerva

Via del Gov. Vecchio

Via Sora

Corso

Via del Pellegrino

Vittorio

Rinascimento

V. d. Teatro Valle

Palazzo
Doria
Pamphilj

Pza. d.
Cancelleria

Emanuele

II

Largo
di
Torre
Argentina

Plebiscito

Palazzo
Venezia

Piazza
Venezia

Campo
de' Fiori

Largo d.
Pallaro

V. Florida

Piazza
del Gesù

Via delle
Bottcghc Oscure

Vittorianc

Piazza
Farnese

CAMPO
DE' FIORI

Via dei Giubbonari

Largo
Arenula

Via Giulia

Lung. dei Tebaldi

Tiber (Tevere)

Piazza
Benedetto
Cairoli

Piazza
Mattei

JEWISH GHETTO

Piazza di
Campitelli

CAPITOLINE
HILL

Arenula

Piazza
Cenci

V. del Portico d'Ottavia

Via Catalana

Portico
d'Ottavia

Teatro di
Marcello

Via del Teatro di Marcello

Ponte Sisto

Lungotevere Raffaello Sanzio

Lungotevere de' Cenci

Ponte Garibaldi

Tiber (Tevere)

TIBER ISLAND

TRASTEVERE

Lung. d. Anguillara

Ponte Cestio

Ponte Palatino

Via Luigi Petroselli

Piazza della
Bocca della
Verità

0   200 y
0   200 m

103

Crypta Balbi ★ MUSEUM/RUINS This branch of the National Museum of Rome houses the archaeological remains of the vast portico belonging to the 1st-century-B.C. **Theatre of Lucius Cornelius Balbus,** discovered here in 1981. The ground floor's exhibits chronicle the history of the site through to the medieval period and the construction of the Conservatorio di Santa Caterina della Rosa. The second floor ("Rome from Antiquity to the Middle Ages") explores the transformation of the city between the 5th and 9th centuries, using thousands of ceramic objects, coins, lead seals, bone and ivory implements, precious stones, and tools found on the site. The museum helps decode the complex layers under Rome's streets, but given its comprehensive collections, it's best recommended for history and archaeology buffs.

Via delle Botteghe Oscure 31. www.museonazionaleromano.beniculturali.it. ℂ **06-39967700.** 12€ (15€ during special exhibits), valid for 3 days; also includes Palazzo Massimo, Palazzo Altemps, Baths of Diocletian. 17 and under free. Tues–Sun 9am–7:45pm. Last entry 1 hr. before closing. Bus: C3, H, 40, 46, 62, 64, 70, 81, 87, 492, 780. Tram: 8.

Galleria Doria Pamphilj ★★ ART MUSEUM One of the city's finest rococo palaces, the Palazzo Doria Pamphilj is still privately owned by the aristocratic Doria Pamphilj family, but their stupendous art collection is open to the public. The *galleria* winds through the old apartments, their paintings displayed floor-to-ceiling among antique furniture and richly decorated walls. The strong Dutch and Flemish collection includes Pieter Brueghel the Elder's "Battle in the Port of Naples," and his son Jan Brueghel the Elder's "Earthly Paradise with Original Sin." Among the best Italian works are two Caravaggio paintings, the moving "Repentant Magdalene" and his wonderful "Rest on the Flight into Egypt," hanging near Titian's "Salome with the Head of St. John." There's also Raphael's "Double Portrait," an "Annunciation" by Filippo Lippi, and a "Deposition from the Cross" by Vasari. The gallery's real treasures occupy a special room: Bernini's bust of the Pamphilj **"Pope Innocent X"** ★, and **Velázquez's enigmatic painting** ★★ of the same man. Make sure you grab a free audio guide at the entrance—it's colorfully narrated by Prince Jonathan Doria Pamphilj himself, who recalls roller-skating in the palazzo as a child.

Via del Corso 305 (just N of Piazza Venezia). www.doriapamphilj.it. ℂ **06-6797323.** 12€ adults, 8€ students. Daily 9am–7pm, last entry 6pm. Bus: 64 or any to Piazza Venezia.

The Pantheon ★★★ HISTORIC SITE Stumbling onto Piazza della Rotunda from the dark warren of streets surrounding it will likely leave you agape, marveling at one of ancient Rome's great buildings—the only one that remains intact. The Pantheon ("Temple to All the Gods") was originally built in 27 B.C. by Marcus Agrippa but was entirely reconstructed by Hadrian in the early 2nd century A.D. This remarkable building, 43m (142 ft.) wide and 43m (142 ft.) high (a perfect sphere resting in a cylinder) is among the architectural wonders of the world, even today. Hadrian himself is credited with the basic plan. There are no visible arches or vaults holding up the dome; instead they're sunk into the concrete of the building's walls. The ribbed dome outside is a series of almost weightless cantilevered bricks. Animals were once sacrificed and burned in the center, with the smoke escaping through the only means of light, the oculus, an opening at the top 5.5m (18 ft.) in diameter. The interior was richly decorated, with white marble statues in niches ringing the central space. Nowadays, apart from the jaw-dropping size of the space, the main items of interest are the tombs of two Italian kings (Vittorio Emanuele II and his successor, Umberto I) and artist **Raphael** (fans still bring him flowers), with its poignant epitaph. Since the 7th century, the Pantheon has been a Catholic church, **Santa Maria ad Martyres,** informally known as Santa Maria della Rotonda. A newly launched mobile app, A Bit of Pantheon, offers helpful context for before or during your visit.

Piazza della Rotonda. www.pantheonroma.com/en. ℰ **06-68300230.** Free. Mon–Sat 9am–7:15pm; Sun 9am–5:45pm. Bus: 40, 46, 62, 64, 70, 81, 87, 492, 628 to Largo di Torre Argentina.

Santa Maria sopra Minerva ★★ CHURCH   Just one block behind the Pantheon, Santa Maria sopra Minerva is Rome's most significant Dominican church and the only major Gothic church downtown. The church was begun in 1280 but worked on until 1725; the facade is in Renaissance style, but the arched vaulting inside is pure Gothic. The main art treasures here are the "Statua del Redentore" (1521), a statue of Christ by **Michelangelo** (just to the left of the altar), and a wonderful fresco cycle in the **Cappella Carafa** (on the right before the altar), created by Filippino Lippi between 1488 and 1493 to honor St. Thomas Aquinas. Devout Catholics flock to the tomb of **Saint Catherine of Siena** under the high altar—the room where she died in 1380 was reconstructed by Antonio Barberini in 1637 (far left corner of the church). **Fra' Angelico,** the Dominican friar and painter, also rests here, in the Cappella Frangipane e Maddaleni-Capiferro. A delightful elephant statue by **Bernini** holds up a small obelisk in the piazza in front of the church.

Piazza della Minerva 42. www.basilicaminerva.it. ℰ **06-69920384.** Free. Mon–Fri 6:55am–7pm; Sat 10am–12:30pm and 3:30–7pm; Sun 8:10am–12:30pm and 3:30pm–7pm.

CAMPO DE' FIORI

The southern section of the Centro Storico, **Campo de' Fiori** is another neighborhood of narrow streets, small piazzas, and ancient churches. Its main focus remains the piazza of **Campo de' Fiori ★★** itself, where a touristy but delightful open-air market runs Monday through Saturday from early in the morning until midday, selling a dizzyingly colorful array of fruits, vegetables, and spices as well as cheap T-shirts and handbags. (Keep an eye on your valuables here.) From the center of the piazza rises a statue of the severe-looking monk **Giordano Bruno,** a reminder that heretics were occasionally burned at the stake here: Bruno was executed by the Inquisition in 1600. Curiously this is the only piazza in Rome that doesn't have a church in its perimeter.

Built from 1514 to 1589, the **Palazzo Farnese ★,** on Piazza Farnese just to the south of the Campo, was designed by Sangallo and Michelangelo, among others, and was an astronomically expensive project for the time. Its famous residents have included a 16th-century member of the Farnese family, plus Pope Paul III, Cardinal Richelieu, and the former Queen Christina of Sweden, who moved to Rome after abdicating. During the 1630s, when the heirs couldn't afford to maintain the *palazzo,* it was inherited by the Bourbon kings of Naples and was purchased by the French government in 1874; the French Embassy is still located here. While the building is closed to the general public, small group tours are offered on Monday, Wednesday, and Friday (9 €; www.inventerrome. com).

Palazzo Spada/Galleria Spada ★ MUSEUM   Built around 1540 for Cardinal Gerolamo Capo di Ferro, Palazzo Spada was purchased by the eponymous Cardinal Spada in 1632, who then hired Borromini to restore it—most of what you see today dates from that period. Its richly ornate facade, covered in high-relief stucco decorations in the Mannerist style, is the finest of any building from 16th-century Rome. The State Rooms are closed (the Italian Council of State still meets here), but the richly decorated courtyard and corridor, Borromini's masterful illusion of perspective *(la prospettiva di Borromini),* and the four rooms of the **Galleria Spada** are open to the public. Inside you will find some absorbing paintings, such as the "Portrait of Cardinale Bernardino Spada" by Guido Reni, and Titian's "Portrait of a Violinist," plus minor works from Caravaggio, Parmigianino, Pietro Testa, and Giambattista Gaulli.

Piazza Capo di Ferro 13. www.galleriaspada.beniculturali.it. © **06-6874893.** 5€. Mon–Sun 8:30am–7:30pm. Bus: H, 23, 63, 280, 780. Tram: 8.

THE JEWISH GHETTO

Across Via Arenula, Campo de' Fiori merges into the old **Jewish Ghetto ★★,** established near the River Tiber by a Papal Bull in 1555, which required that all the Jews in Rome live in one area. Walled in, overcrowded, prone to floods and epidemics, and on some of the worst land in the city, it was an extremely grim place to live. After the Ghetto was abolished in 1882, its walls were finally torn down and the area largely reconstructed. In the waning years of WWII, Nazis sent more than 1,000 Roman Jews to concentration camps; only a handful returned. Today, the **Via**

Portico d'Ottavia forms the heart of a flourishing Jewish Quarter, with Romans and tourists flocking here to sample the Roman-Jewish and Middle Eastern food for which the area is known.

Museo Ebraico di Roma (Jewish Museum of Rome) & Great Synagogue ★ MUSEUM   On the premises of the Great Synagogue of Rome, this museum chronicles the history of not only Roman Jews but Jews from all over Italy. There are displays of works of 17th- and 18th-century Roman silversmiths, precious textiles from all over Europe, and a number of parchments and marble carvings that were saved when the Ghetto's original synagogues were demolished. Admission to the museum includes a guided English-language tour of the **Great Synagogue of Rome** (Tempio Maggiore), built from 1901 to 1904 in an eclectic style evoking Babylonian and Persian temples. Attacked by terrorists in 1982, the synagogue is now guarded by Italian *carabinieri* with machine guns.

Via Catalana. www.museoebraico.roma.it. ✆ **06-6840061.** 11€ adults, 5€ students, free for children 10 and under. Apr–Sept Sun–Thurs 10am–6pm and Fri 10am–4pm; Oct–Mar Sun–Thurs 10am–5pm and Fri 9am–2pm. Closed Jewish holidays.

The Tridente & the Spanish Steps

The northern half of central Rome is known as the **Tridente,** thanks to the trident shape formed by three roads—Via di Ripetta, Via del Corso, and Via del Babuino—leading down from **Piazza del Popolo.** The area around **Piazza di Spagna** and the **Spanish Steps** was once the artistic quarter of the city, attracting English poets Keats and Shelley, German author Goethe, and film director Federico Fellini (who lived on Via Margutta). Institutions such as Antico Caffè Greco and Babington's Tea Rooms are still here (see p. 146), but between the high rents and the throngs of tourists and shoppers, you're unlikely to see many artists left.

PIAZZA DEL POPOLO

Elegant **Piazza del Popolo** ★★ is haunted with memories. Legend has it that the ashes of Nero were enshrined here, until 11th-century

Tourists gather on the Spanish Steps.

residents began complaining to the pope about his imperial ghost. The **Egyptian obelisk** dates from the 13th century B.C.; it was moved from Heliopolis to Rome during Augustus's reign (it once stood at the Circus Maximus).

The current piazza was designed in the early 19th century by Valadier, Napoleon's architect. Standing astride the three roads that form the "trident" are almost-twin baroque churches, **Santa Maria dei Miracoli** (1681) and **Santa Maria di Montesanto** (1679). The stand-out church, however, is at the piazza's northern curve: the 15th-century **Santa Maria del Popolo ★★**, with its splendid baroque facade modified by Bernini between 1655 and 1660. Inside, look for Raphael's mosaic series the "Creation of the World" adorning the interior dome of the **Capella Chigi** (the second chapel on the left). Pinturicchio decorated the main choir vault with frescoes such as the "Coronation of the Virgin." The **Capella Cerasi** (to the left of the high altar) contains gorgeous examples of baroque art: an altarpiece painting of "The Assumption of Mary" by Carracci, and on either side two great works by Caravaggio, "Conversion on the Road to Damascus" and "The Crucifixion of Saint Peter."

MAXXI (National Museum of the XXI Century Arts) ★

MUSEUM   Ten minutes north of Piazza del Popolo by tram, leave the Renaissance far behind at MAXXI, a masterpiece of contemporary architecture with bending and overlapping oblong tubes designed by the late Zaha Hadid. The museum is divided into two sections, MAXXI art and MAXXI architecture, primarily serving as a venue for temporary exhibitions of contemporary work in both fields (although it does have a small permanent collection). The building is worth a visit in its own right.

Via Guido Reni 4a. www.fondazionemaxxi.it. ✆ **06-3201954.** 12€ adults, 9€ ages 25 and under, 9€ students, free children 13 and under. Tues–Fri and Sun 11am–7pm; Sat 11am–10pm. Metro: Flaminio, then tram 2.

Museo dell'Ara Pacis ★★ MUSEUM

Set in a stunning ultra-modern building designed by American architect Richard Meier, the temple-like marble "Altar of Peace" was erected in 9 B.C. to honor soon-to-be-Emperor Augustus's success in subduing tribes north of the Alps. For centuries the monument was lost to memory; signs of its existence surfaced in the 16th century, but it wasn't until the 1930s that it was fully excavated, and even so it lay virtually abandoned after World War II, until a true restoration began in the 1980s. The exhibit complex provides context, with interactive displays in English. From here you get great views of the huge, overgrown ruin of **Augustus's Mausoleum (Mausoleo di Augusto),** built in the 1st century B.C., where the ashes of emperors Augustus, Caligula, Claudius, Nerva, and Tiberius once rested. Long closed to the public, the tomb is now being restored, with plans to reopen in 2020. Most Friday and Saturday evenings (nightly in high season), the immersive

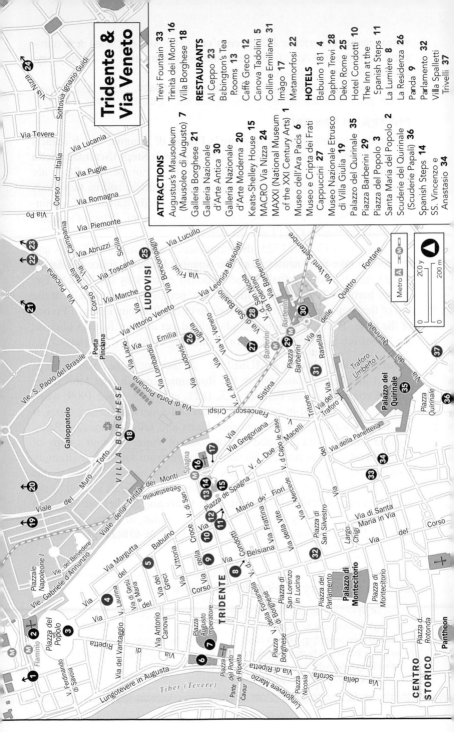

Tridente & Via Veneto

ATTRACTIONS
Augustus's Mausoleum (Mausoleo di Augusto) 7
Galleria Borghese 21
Galleria Nazionale d'Arte Antica 30
Galleria Nazionale d'Arte Moderna 20
Keats-Shelley House 15
MACRO Via Nizza 24
MAXXI (National Museum of the XXI Century Arts) 1
Museo dell'Ara Pacis 6
Museo e Cripta dei Frati Cappuccini 27
Museo Nazionale Etrusco di Villa Giulia 19
Palazzo del Quirinale 35
Piazza Barberini 29
Piazza del Popolo 3
Santa Maria del Popolo 2
Scuderie del Quirinale (Scuderie Papali) 36
Spanish Steps 14
SS. Vincenzo e Anastasio 34
Trevi Fountain 33
Trinità dei Monti 16
Villa Borghese 18

RESTAURANTS
Al Ceppo 23
Babington's Tea Rooms 13
Caffè Greco 12
Canova Tadolini 5
Colline Emiliane 31
Imàgo 17
Metamorfosi 22

HOTELS
Babuino 181 4
Daphne Trevi 28
Deko Rome 25
Hotel Condotti 10
The Inn at the Spanish Steps 11
La Lumière 8
La Residenza 26
Panda 9
Parlamento 32
Villa Spalletti Trivelli 37

virtual reality experience **L'Ara com'era** (The Ara as it was) ★★ transports visitors to the Ara and its surroundings during their 1st-century heyday (adults 12€, no children under 13).

Lungotevere in Augusta. www.arapacis.it/en. © **06-060608.** 10.50€. Daily 9:30am–7:30pm (last entry 6:30pm). Metro: Spagna. Bus: C3, 70, 81, 87, 280, 492, 628, 913.

PIAZZA DI SPAGNA

The undoubted highlight of Tridente is **Piazza di Spagna,** which attracts hordes of tourists to admire its celebrated **Spanish Steps (Scalinata della Trinità dei Monti)** ★★, the widest stairway in Europe. The Steps are especially enchanting in early spring, when they are framed by thousands of blooming azaleas. At their foot lies "Fontana della Barcaccia," a fountain shaped like an old boat, the work of Pietro Bernini, father of sculptor and fountain-master Gian Lorenzo Bernini.

Built from 1723 to 1725, the monumental stairway of 135 steps and the square take their names from the Spanish Embassy (once headquartered here), but were actually funded almost entirely by the French: The stately baroque **Trinità dei Monti** church, perched photogenically at the top of the Steps, was under the patronage of the Bourbon kings of France at the time. Trinità dei Monti stands behind yet another Roman obelisk, the "Obelisco Sallustiano." It's worth climbing up just for the views.

Keats-Shelley House ★ MUSEUM   At the foot of the Spanish Steps is the 18th-century house where the Romantic English poet John Keats died of consumption on February 23, 1821, at age 25. Since 1909, when it was bought by well-intentioned English and American literary types, it has been a working library honoring Keats and fellow Romantic Percy Bysshe Shelley, who drowned off the coast of Viareggio with a copy of Keats' works in his pocket. Mementos range from kitsch to extremely moving. The apartment where Keats spent his last months, tended by his close friend Joseph Severn, shelters a death mask of Keats as well as the "deadly sweat" drawing by Severn. Both Keats and Shelley are buried in the Protestant cemetery near the Pyramid of Cestius, in Testaccio (p. 68).

Piazza di Spagna 26. www.keats-shelley-house.org. © **06-6784235.** 6€. Mon–Sat 10am–1pm and 2–6pm. Metro: Spagna.

No swimming or picnicking allowed

In an effort to keep tourists from littering the city's monuments, or soaking their feet and even swimming (yes, it's happened) in its famous fountains, visitors are no longer permitted to picnic (or even eat a gelato) on the Spanish Steps, or sit on the edge of the Trevi and other landmark fountains. You can stop long enough for a photo or coin toss, but don't plan on getting comfortable (or taking a dip).

Palazzo del Quirinale ★★ HISTORIC SITE   Until the end of World War II, this palace was home to the king of Italy; before that, it was the summer residence of the pope. Since 1946 the palace has been the official residence of the President of Italy, but parts of it are open to the public. There's little art or furniture in the rooms, but the palace's baroque and neoclassical walls and ceilings are quite a spectacle. Highlights include the richly decorated 17th-century **Salone dei Corazzieri,** the **Sala d'Ercole** (once the apartments of Umberto I but completely rebuilt in 1940), and the tapestry-covered 17th-century **Sala dello Zodiaco.** The piazza outside crowns the highest of the seven ancient hills of Rome, with a sweeping view of the city. Colossal statues of the "Dioscuri," Castor and Pollux, were found in the nearby Baths of Constantine and now form part of the fountain in the piazza; in 1793 Pius VI had an ancient Egyptian obelisk moved here from the Mausoleum of Augustus.

Piazza del Quirinale. palazzo.quirinale.it/palazzo.html. ✆ **06-39-96-7557.** 1.50€ for basic tour; 10€ for extended tour including gardens, carriages, and special collections. Reservations required at least 5 days prior to visit. Tues–Wed and Fri–Sun 9:30am–4pm. Closed Aug. Metro: Barberini. Bus: C3, 40, 60, 62-64, 70, 71, 80, 83, 85, 492.

Trevi Fountain (Fontana di Trevi) ★★ MONUMENT   As you elbow your way through the summertime crowds around the **Trevi Fountain,** it's hard to believe that this little piazza was usually deserted before 1950,

The Trevi Fountain.

when it began starring in films: *Roman Holiday* (1953), *Three Coins in the Fountain* (1954), and Fellini's 1960 masterpiece *La Dolce Vita*. To this day, thousands of euros worth of coins are tossed into the fountain daily. The area is always jam-packed with tourists and selfie-stick hawkers, so keep your eye (and your hands) on your belongings. Completed in 1762, this glorious baroque fountain centers on the triumphant figure of Neptune, standing on a shell chariot drawn by winged steeds. Allegorical figures in the side niches represent good health and fertility. On the southwestern corner of the piazza, the church of **SS. Vincenzo e Anastasio** has a strange claim to fame: Within it are the relics (hearts and intestines) of several popes.

> ### Coin Toss: A Guaranteed Return to Rome?
>
> The custom of tossing a coin into the Trevi Fountain to ensure your return to Rome apparently only works if you use correct form: With your back to the fountain, toss a coin with your right hand over your left shoulder. Works for me every time!

Piazza di Trevi. Metro: Barberini. Bus: C3, 51, 53, 62, 63, 71, 80, 83, 85, 160, 492.

Villa Borghese & Parioli

Villa Borghese ★★, just northeast of the Tridente, is not actually a villa but one of Europe's most elegant large parks, 6km (3¾ miles) in circumference. Cardinal Scipione Borghese created the park in the 1600s; Umberto I, king of Italy, acquired it in 1902 and presented it to the city of Rome. The greenbelt is crisscrossed by roads, but you can escape from the traffic and seek a shaded area under a tree to enjoy its landscaped vistas. On a sunny weekend, it's a pleasure to stroll here and see Romans at play, relaxing or inline skating. The park has a few casual cafes and food vendors; you can also rent bikes or Segways here. In the northeast part of the park you'll find a **zoo** and the **Galleria Borghese** (see below). The neighborhoods to the north, Parioli and Pinciano, are elegant enclaves for those wishing to stay outside the crowded city center.

Galleria Borghese ★★★ ART MUSEUM   On the far northeastern edge of the Villa Borghese, the Galleria Borghese occupies the former

> ### Art in the Pope's Stables
>
> Across from the Palazzo del Quirinale, the **Scuderie del Quirinale** or **Scuderie Papali**, Via XXIV Maggio 16 (www.scuderiequirinale.it; ✆ **06-39967500**), originally 18th-century stables for the pope's horses, now function as remarkably atmospheric art galleries hosting temporary exhibitions ranging from the likes of Picasso and Leonardo to Japanese prints to Islamic art. The galleries are open Sunday to Thursday 10am to 8pm and Friday and Saturday 10am to 10:30pm. Admission is 15€, free for those 17 and under.

Lake at Villa Borghese.

Villa Borghese Pinciana, built between 1609 and 1613 for Cardinal Scipione Borghese, an early patron of Bernini and an astute collector of work by Caravaggio. Today the gallery displays much of his collection and a lot more besides, making this one of Rome's great art treasures. It's also one of Rome's most pleasant sights to tour, thanks to the curators' mandate that only a limited number of people be allowed in at a time. The ground floor is a **sculpture gallery** par extraordinaire, housing Canova's famously risqué statue of Paolina Borghese, sister of Napoleon and wife of the reigning Prince Camillo Borghese (when asked if she was uncomfortable posing nude, she reportedly replied, "No, the studio was heated."). The genius of Bernini reigns supreme in the following rooms, with his "David" (the face of which is thought to be a self-portrait) and **"Apollo and Daphne"** ★★, both seminal works of baroque sculpture. Look also for Bernini's Mannerist sculpture next door, "The Rape of Persephone." Caravaggio is represented by the "Madonna of the Grooms," the shadowy "St. Jerome," and the frightening **"David Holding the Head of Goliath"** ★★. Upstairs lies a rich collection of paintings, including Raphael's graceful "Deposition" and his sinuous "Lady with a Unicorn." There's also a series of self-portraits by Bernini, and his lifelike busts of Cardinal Scipione and Pope

Paul V. One of Titian's best, **"Sacred and Profane Love"** ★, lies in one of the final rooms.

Essential tip: No more than 360 visitors at a time are allowed on the ground floor, and no more than 90 are allowed on the upper floor, during set 2-hour windows. **Reservations are essential,** so call ✆ **06-32810** (Monday–Friday 9am–6pm; Saturday 9am–1pm). You can also make reservations by visiting **www.tosc.it**, or stop by in person to reserve tickets for a later date. English labeling in the museum is minimal. Guided tours of the galleries in English cost 6.50€; failing that, opt for an audio guide.

Piazzale del Museo Borghese 5 (off Via Pinciana). www.galleriaborghese.it. ✆ **06-32810.** 15€; 18 and under 2€. Audio guides 5€. Tues–Sun 9am–7pm. Bus: C3, 53, 61, 89, 160, 490, 495, 590, 910.

MACRO Via Nizza ★ MUSEUM   Rome's contemporary art museum was recently expanded to occupy an entire block of early-1900s industrial buildings, formerly the Peroni beer factory, located near the Porta Pia gate of the Aurelian walls. Designed by French architect Odile Decq, the museum hosts contemporary art exhibits with edgy installations, visuals, and multimedia events. Another branch of the museum is housed in a converted slaughterhouse in Testaccio (p. 121).

Via Nizza 138. www.museomacro.org. ✆ **06-696271.** Free (special exhibits may be ticketed). Tues–Sun 10am–8pm (Sat until 10pm). Last entry 7pm. Bus: 38, 60, 62, 66, 80, 82, 88-90. Tram: 3, 19.

Museo Nazionale Etrusco di Villa Giulia (National Etruscan Museum) ★★★ MUSEUM   The great Etruscan civilization was one of Italy's most advanced, although it remains relatively mysterious, in part because of its centuries-long rivalry with Rome. Rome definitively conquered the Etruscans by the 3rd century B.C., and though they adopted certain aspects of Etruscan culture, including religious practices, engineering innovations, and gladiatorial combat, gradual Romanization eclipsed virtually all the Etruscans' achievements. This museum, housed in the handsome Renaissance Villa Giulia, built by Pope Julius III between 1550 and 1555, is the best place in Italy to learn about the Etruscans, thanks to a cache of precious artifacts, sculptures, vases, monuments, tools, weapons, and jewels, the vast majority of it from tombs. Fans of ancient history could spend several hours here, but for those with less time, the most striking attraction is the **Sarcofago degli Sposi (Sarcophagus of the Spouses)** ★★, a late 6th-century-B.C. terracotta funerary monument featuring a life-size bride and groom, supposedly lounging at a banquet in the afterlife (Paris's Louvre has a similar monument). Equally fascinating are the **Pyrgi Tablets,** gold-leaf inscriptions in both Etruscan and Phoenician from the 5th century B.C., and the **Apollo of Veii,** a huge painted terracotta statue of Apollo dating to the 6th century B.C.

Piazzale di Villa Giulia 9. www.villagiulia.beniculturali.it. ✆ **06-3226571.** 8€. Tues–Sun 9am–8pm. Bus: C3, 982. Tram: 2, 3, 19.

Galleria Nazionale d'Arte Moderna (National Gallery of Modern Art) ★ ART MUSEUM   Housed in the monumental Bazzani Building constructed in 1911, this "modern" art collection ranges from unfashionable neoclassical and Romantic paintings and sculpture to 20th-century works. Quality varies, but fans should seek out van Gogh's "Gardener" and "Portrait of Madame Ginoux" in Room 15, a handful of Impressionists in Room 14 (Cézanne, Degas, Monet, and Rodin), and Klimt's harrowing "Three Ages" in Room 16. Surrealist and Expressionist works by Miró, Kandinsky, and Mondrian appear in Room 22, and Pollock's "Undulating Paths" and Calder's "Mobile" reign in Room 27. One of Warhol's "Hammer and Sickle" series is tucked away in Room 30. Viale delle Belle Arti 131. www.gnam.beniculturali.it. © **06-322981.** 10€; ages 17 and under free. Tues–Sun 8:30am–7:30pm. Bus: 61, 160, 490, 495. Tram: 3, 19.

Via Veneto & Piazza Barberini

Piazza Barberini lies at the foot of several streets, among them Via Barberini, Via Sistina, and Via Vittorio Veneto. It would be a far more pleasant spot were it not for the traffic swarming around its principal feature, Bernini's **Fontana del Tritone** (Fountain of the Triton) ★. For almost 4 centuries, the figure sitting in a vast open clam has been blowing water from his triton. To one side of the piazza is the aristocratic facade of the **Palazzo Barberini,** named for one of Rome's powerful families; inside is the **Galleria Nazionale d'Arte Antica** (see p. 116). The Barberini reached their peak when a son was elected pope as Urban VIII; he encouraged Bernini and gave him patronage.

As you walk up **Via Vittorio Veneto,** look for the small fountain on the right corner of Piazza Barberini—it's another Bernini, the **Fountain of the Bees** (Fontana delle Api). At first they look more like flies, but they're the bees of the Barberini, the crest of that powerful family complete with the crossed keys of St. Peter above them. (Keys were always added to a family crest when a son was elected pope.)

Museo e Cripta dei Frati Cappuccini (Museum and Crypt of the Capuchin Friars) ★★ RELIGIOUS SITE/MUSEUM   One of the most macabre sights in all Christendom, this otherwise restrained museum dedicated to the Capuchin order ends with a series of six chapels in the crypt, adorned with the skulls and bones of more than 3,700 Capuchin brothers, woven into mosaic "works of art." Some of the skeletons are intact, draped with Franciscan habits; others form lamps and ceiling friezes. The tradition of the friars dates to a period when Christians had a richly creative cult of the dead and great spiritual masters meditated and preached with a skull in hand; the experience is a mix of spooky and meditative. The entrance is halfway up the first staircase on the right of the church of the Convento dei Frati Cappuccini, completed in 1630 and

rebuilt in the early 1930s. *Note:* This site is located within a church, so it maintains a strict dress code—no short pants or skirts and no bare arms.

Beside the Convento dei Frati Cappuccini, Via Vittorio Veneto 27. www.cappuccini viaveneto.it. © **06-88803695.** 8.50€, 5€ ages 17 and under. Daily 9am–7pm, last entry 6:30pm. Metro: Barberini. Bus: 52, 53, 61, 63, 80, 160.

Galleria Nazionale d'Arte Antica (National Gallery of Ancient Art) ★★ ART MUSEUM   On the southern side of Piazza Barberini, the grand **Palazzo Barberini** houses the Galleria Nazionale d'Arte Antica, which despite the "ancient" in its title is a trove of Italian art mostly from the early Renaissance to late baroque periods. Some of the art on display is wonderful, but the building itself is the main attraction, a baroque masterpiece begun by Carlo Maderno in 1627 and completed in 1633 by Bernini, with additional work by Borromini (notably a whimsical spiral staircase). The **Salone di Pietro da Cortona** in the center is the most captivating space, with a trompe l'oeil ceiling frescoed by da Cortona, a depiction of "The Triumph of Divine Providence." The museum's works include Raphael's "La Fornarina," a baker's daughter thought to have been the artist's lover (look for Raphael's name on her bracelet); paintings by Tintoretto and Titian (Room 15); a Holbein portrait of English King Henry VIII (Room 16); and a couple of unsettling El Grecos in Room 17. Caravaggio dominates room 20 with the justly celebrated **"Judith and Holofernes"** ★★★ and **"Narcissus"** ★★.

Via delle Quattro Fontane 13. www.barberinicorsini.org. © **06-4814591.** 12€, valid for 10 days, also includes Palazzo Corsini; 17 and under free. Tues–Sun 8:30am–7pm; last entry 6pm. Metro: Barberini. Bus: 53, 61–63, 80, 81, 83, 160, 492, 590.

Around Stazione Termini

Palazzo Massimo alle Terme ★★ MUSEUM   A third of Rome's ancient art can be found at this branch of the Museo Nazionale Romano; among its treasures are a major coin collection, extensive maps of trade routes (with audio and visual exhibits on the network of traders over the centuries), and a vast sculpture collection that includes portrait busts of emperors and their families, as well as mythical figures like the Minotaur and Athena. The real draw is on the second floor, where you can see some of Rome's oldest **frescoes** ★★; they depict an entire garden, complete with plants and birds, from the Villa di Livia a Prima Porta. (Livia, the wife of Emperor Augustus, was deified after her death in A.D. 29.)

Largo di Villa Peretti. www.museonazionaleromano.beniculturali.it. © **06-39967700.** 12€ (15€ during special exhibits), valid for 3 days, also includes Palazzo Altemps, Baths of Diocleziano, Crypta Balbi. 17 and under free. Tues–Sun 9am–7:45pm. Last entry 1 hr. before closing. Metro: Termini or Repubblica. Bus: 40, 64, or any bus that stops at Termini.

Santa Maria della Vittoria ★ CHURCH   A visit to this pretty little baroque church is all about one artwork: Gian Lorenzo Bernini's **"Ecstasy**

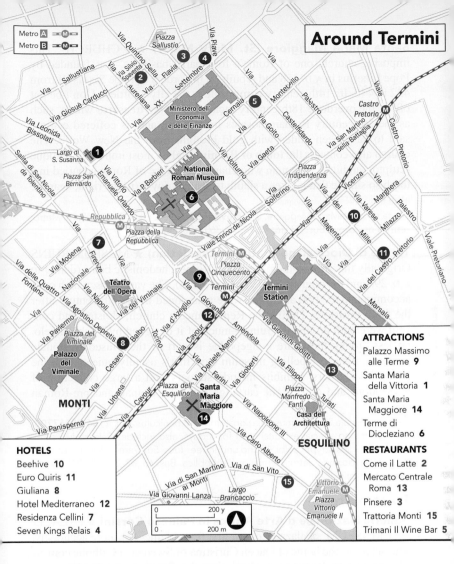

Metro A ◻ 🄼 ◻
Metro B ◻ 🄼 ◻

Around Termini

Piazza Sallustio

Via Plave

Via Quintino Sella

Via Silvio Spaventa

Via Flavia

Settembre

Via Sallustiana

Via Aureliana XX

Via Montecello

Palestro

Viale Castro Pretorio

Via Giosuè Carducci

Ministero dell' Economia e delle Finanze

Cernaia

Via Goito

Castelfidardo

Via San Martino della Battaglia

Castro Pretorio

Via Leonida Bissolati

Via

Via Gaeta

Largo di S. Susanna ✦🖼 **1**

Via Vittorio Emanuele Orlando

National Roman Museum

Via Volturno

Piazza Indipendenza

Vicenza

Via Marghera

Palestro

Salita di San Nicola da Tolentino

Piazza San Bernardo

Via P.Barberini

6

Via Solferino

Via Varese

Milazzo

Viale Pretoriano

Republica

Viale Enrico de Nicola

Via dei

Via Magenta

10

Via delle Quattro Fontane

Via Modena

Firenze

Piazza della Repubblica

7

Via Nazionale

Termini 🄼

Piazza Cinquecento

Via Mille

Via del Castro Pretorio

11

Via delle Quattro Fontane

Via Napoli

Via del Viminale

Teatro dell'Opera

9

Termini 🄼

Termini Station

Marsala

Via Palermo

Via Agostino Depretis

Via d'Azeglio

Giovanni

12

Via Giovanni Giolitti

Piazza del Viminale

8

Cesare

Torino

Via Cavour

Amendola

13

Palazzo del Viminale

Via Urbana

Cavour

Via Daniele Manin

Via Farini

Via Gioberti

Via Filippo

Piazza Manfredo Fanti

Turati

MONTI

Piazza dell' Esquilino

Santa Maria Maggiore

Via Napoleone III

Casa dell' Architettura

Via Panisperna

14

Via Carlo Alberto

ESQUILINO

Via di San Martino ai Monti

Via di San Vito

Via Giovanni Lanza

Largo Brancaccio

15

Vittorio Emanuele 🄼

Piazza Vittorio Emanuele II

0 ——— 200 y
0 ——— 200 m

of St. Teresa" ★★★. Crafted from marble between 1644 and 1647, it shows the Spanish saint at the moment of her ecstatic encounter with an angel (the so-called "Transverberation"), who gleefully pierces her with a spear. Bernini's depiction is deliciously erotic. Look for the Cornaro family, who sponsored the chapel's construction, watching the saint's ecstasy from their voyeuristic perch on the right.

Via XX Settembre 17 (at Largo S. Susanna). www.chiesasantamariavittoriaroma.it. ✆ **06-42740571.** Free. Mon–Sat 8:30am–noon and 3:30–6pm; Sun 3:30–6pm. Metro: Repubblica. Bus: 60 62, 66, 82, 85, 492, 590, 910.

Santa Maria Maggiore (St. Mary Major) ★★ CHURCH   This imposing church, one of Rome's four papal basilicas, was founded by Pope Liberius in A.D. 358 and rebuilt on the orders of Pope Sixtus III from 432 to 440. Its 14th-century **campanile** is the city's loftiest. Don't be put off by the overdone 18th-century façade; there are treasures within, such as the 5th-century Roman mosaics in its nave, and its coffered ceiling, said to have been gilded with gold brought from the New World. The church also contains the **tomb of Bernini,** Italy's most important baroque sculptor–architect. The man who changed the face of Rome is buried in a tomb so simple that it takes a sleuth to track it down (to the right, near the altar).

Piazza di Santa Maria Maggiore. ℂ **06-69886800.** Free. Daily 7am–6:45pm. Metro: Termini or Cavour. Bus: C3, 16, 70, 71, 75, 360, 590, 649, 714.

Terme di Diocleziano (Baths of Diocletian) ★ MUSEUM/RUINS   Originally this spot held the largest of Rome's hedonistic baths (dating to A.D. 298 and the reign of Emperor Diocletian). The vast baths, which once accommodated 3,000 at a time, were abandoned in the 6th century after the Goth invasions. During the Renaissance a church, cloister, and convent were built around the ruins—much of it designed by Michelangelo, no less. Today the entire hodgepodge is part of the Museo Nazionale Romano; it's a compelling museum stop that's usually quieter than the city's blockbusters. Exhibits include statuary and a large collection of inscriptions and other stone carvings from the Roman and pre-Roman eras.

Viale E. di Nicola 78. www.museonazionaleromano.beniculturali.it. ℂ **06-39967700.** 12€ (15€ during special exhibits) valid for 3 days, also includes Palazzo Massimo, Palazzo Altemps, Crypta Balbi. 17 and under free. Tues–Sun 9am–7:30pm. Last entry 1 hr. before closing. Metro: Termini or Repubblica. Bus: 66, 82, 85, 590, 910, or any bus to Termini.

Trastevere

Galleria Nazionale d'Arte Antica in Palazzo Corsini ★ PALACE/ ART MUSEUM   Palazzo Corsini first found fame—or more accurately, notoriety—as the home of Queen Christina of Sweden, a Catholic convert who moved to Rome after abdicating the Swedish throne. (She was famously described as "Queen without a realm, Christian without a faith, and a woman without shame," referring to her open bisexuality.) Several other big names stayed in this beautiful palace, from Michelangelo to Napoleon's mother, Letizia. Today one wing houses a moderately interesting museum, with a lot of the runoff from Italy's national art collection. Worth a look is Caravaggio's "St. John the Baptist" (1606) and panels by Luca Giordano, Fra' Angelico, and Poussin; otherwise the palace history is more interesting than the museum itself.

Via della Lungara 10. www.barberinicorsini.org. ℂ **06-68802323.** 12€, valid for 10 days, also includes Palazzo Barberini; ages 17 and under free. Wed–Mon 8:30am– 7pm. Bus: 23 or 280.

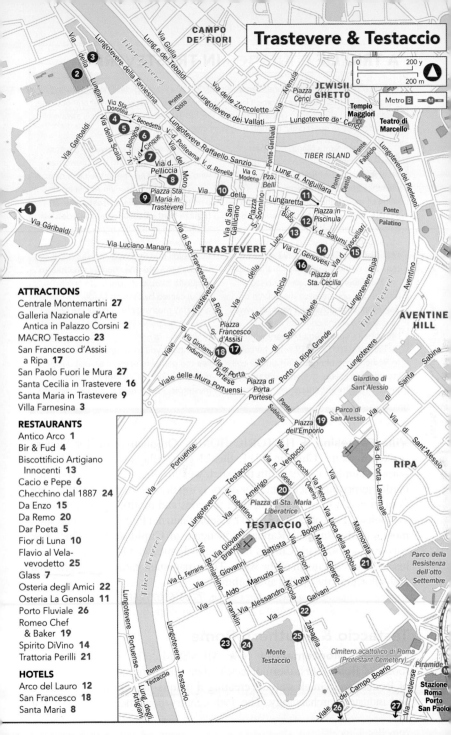

Trastevere & Testaccio

CAMPO DE' FIORI

JEWISH GHETTO

Tempio Maggiori

Teatro di Marcello

TIBER ISLAND

TRASTEVERE

AVENTINE HILL

Piazza S. Francesco d'Assisi

Piazza di Porta Portese

Giardino di Sant'Alessio

Parco di San Alessio

RIPA

Piazza dell'Emporio

Piazza di Sta. Maria Liberatrice

TESTACCIO

Monte Testaccio

Cimitero acattolico di Roma (Protestant Cemetery)

Parco della Resistenza dell'otto Settembre

Stazione Roma Porto San Paolo

Piramide

A TRIO OF churches IN TRASTEVERE

Before Trastevere became bohemian and cool, it was a working-class neighborhood, separated by the Tiber from Rome's bustle. Step into the shadowy calm of any of these neighborhood churches to get a glimpse of the old Trastevere. Admission is always free, and they're open daily, though they may close at lunchtime.

On Piazza Santa Maria, the heart of Trastevere, ornate Santa Maria in Trastevere ★★ is one of Rome's oldest churches, founded around A.D. 350. The pride of the neighborhood, it's spectacular inside and out, with a Romanesque brick bell tower, colorful frescoes, mosaics, and loads of recycled ancient marbles. Look for Cavallini's 1293 mosaics of the "Life of the Virgin Mary" in the apse.

From there, Via di San Francisco a Ripa angles southeast to the church of **San Francesco d'Assisi a Ripa ★** (www.sanfrancescoinripa.com), so named because it's built over a convent where St. Francis stayed in 1219 when he came to Rome to see the pope (his simple cell is preserved inside). A Bernini treasure is tucked into the last chapel on the left:

the "Tomb of Beata Ludovica Albertoni" (1675), commemorating a noblewoman who dedicated her life to the city's poor.

From there, follow Via Anicia northeast to **Santa Cecilia in Trastevere ★ (Piazza Santa Cecilia;** www.benedettine-santacecilia.it), a still-functioning convent with a peaceful courtyard garden. Tradition holds that St. Cecilia herself once lived on this site; the church's altar has an exquisite marble sculpture of her (ca. 1600) carved by Stefano Maderno. On weekday mornings for a small fee (2.50€) you can go under the church to see a set of Roman-era ruins, and then a nun will accompany you to an upstairs room to see the partial remains of a "Last Judgment," by Pietro Cavallini (ca. 1293), a masterpiece of Roman medieval painting.

Villa Farnesina ★ HISTORIC HOME   Originally built for Sienese banker Agostino Chigi in 1511, this elegant villa was acquired by the Farnese family in 1579. With two such wealthy Renaissance patrons, it's hardly surprising that the interior decor is top drawer. Architect Baldassare Peruzzi began the decoration, with frescoes and motifs rich in myth and symbolism. He was later assisted by Sebastiano del Piombo, Sodoma, and, most notably, Raphael. Raphael's **"Loggia of Cupid and Psyche" ★★** was frescoed to mark Chigi's marriage to Francesca Ordeaschi—though his assistants did much of the work. The ornamental gardens are perfumed and colorful in the spring and summer.

Via della Lungara 230. www.villafarnesina.it. ✆ **06-68077268.** 5€, 10€ with audio-guide. Mon–Sat 9am–2pm; 2nd Sun of month 9am–5pm. Bus: 23, 280.

Testaccio & Southern Rome

Centrale Montemartini ★★ MUSEUM   The renovated boiler rooms of Rome's first thermoelectric plant now house a grand collection of Roman and Greek statues, creating a unique juxtaposition of classic and industrial archaeology. The 19th-century powerhouse was the first public plant to produce electricity for the city. Striking installation spaces include the vast boiler hall, a 1,000-square-meter (10,764-sq-ft.) room where classical statues share space with a complex web of pipes, masonry, and metal walkways. Equally striking is the Hall of Machines, where two towering turbines stand opposite the reconstructed pediment of the Temple of Apollo Sosiano, which illustrates a famous Greek battle. Unless you run across a school group, this place is never crowded, and it provides an intimate look at the ancient world, despite the cavernous setting.

Via Ostiense 106. www.centralemontemartini.org. $\mathcal{C}$ **06-0608**. 7.50€, or 12.50€ for a 7-day ticket that includes the Capitoline Museums. Tues–Sun 9am–7pm. Last entry 30 min before closing. Metro: Garbatella. Bus: 23 or 792.

MACRO Testaccio ★ MUSEUM   The Testaccio outpost of Rome's contemporary art museum is housed—appropriately for this former meat-packing neighborhood—in a converted slaughterhouse. The edgy programs and exhibits are a mix of installations, visuals, events, and special viewings. Opening times are made for night owls: Make a late visit before going on to Testaccio's bars and restaurants.

Piazza Orazio Guistiniani 4. www.mattatoioroma.it. $\mathcal{C}$ **06-671070400**. Free, 6€ for special exhibits. Tues–Sun 2–8pm. Last entry 30 min before closing. Metro: Piramide. Bus: 23, 75, 83, 170, 280, 719. Tram: 3, 8.

San Paolo Fuori le Mura (St. Paul Outside the Walls) ★★ CHURCH   The giant Basilica of St. Paul, whose origins date from the time of Constantine, is Rome's fourth great patriarchal church. It was erected over the tomb of St. Paul and is the second-largest church in Rome after St. Peter's. The basilica fell victim to fire in 1823 and was subsequently rebuilt—hence the relatively modern look. Inside, translucent alabaster windows illuminate a forest of single-file columns and mosaic medallions (portraits of the various popes). Its most important treasure is a 12th-century marble candelabrum by Vassalletto, who's also responsible for the remarkable cloisters containing twisted pairs of columns enclosing

Mussolini's City of the Future

South of the city center, the outlying **EUR suburb** ★ (the acronym stands for *Esposizione Universale Romana*) was designed and purpose-built by Mussolini in the Fascist era to stage the planned World Fair of 1942—canceled, thanks to World War II. Today, EUR's mix of rationalist and classical-inspired elements will enthuse anyone with a serious interest in architecture. Perfect symmetry and sleek marble-lined avenues house a number of museums, corporate headquarters, and office agglomerates, easily connected to the *centro* by Metro (Line B). The **Museum of Roman Civilization** (www.museociviltaromana.it; closed for renovation well into 2019) features a huge scale model of Rome at the time of Emperor Constantine.

a rose garden. Miraculously, the baldacchino by Arnolfo di Cambio (1285) wasn't damaged in the fire; it now shelters the tomb of St. Paul the Apostle.

Via Ostiense 190 (at Piazzale San Paolo). www.basilicasanpaolo.org. ℂ**06-69880800.** Basilica free; cloisters 4€. Basilica daily 7am–6:30pm. Cloisters daily 8:30am–6pm. Metro: Basilica di San Paolo. Bus: 23.

The Via Appia (Appian Way) & the Catacombs

Of all the roads that led to Rome, **Via Appia Antica** (begun in 312 B.C.) was the most famous. It stretched all the way to the seaport of Brindisi, through which trade with Greece and the East was funneled. (According to Christian tradition, it was along the Appian Way that an escaping Peter encountered the vision of Christ, causing him to go back into the city to face martyrdom.) The road's initial stretch in Rome is lined with the monuments and ancient tombs of patrician Roman families—burials were forbidden within the city walls as early as the 5th century B.C.—and, below ground, miles of tunnels hewn out of the soft *tufa* stone that hardens on exposure to the air.

These tunnels, or catacombs, were where early Christians buried their dead. A few are open to the public, so you can wander through musty-smelling tunnels whose walls are gouged out with tens of thousands of now mostly empty burial niches, including small niches made for children. Early Christians referred to each chamber as a *dormitorio*—they believed the bodies were only sleeping, awaiting resurrection (which is why they could not observe the traditional Roman practice of cremation). In some you can still discover the remains of early Christian art. The obligatory guided tours feature occasionally biased history, plus a dash of sermonizing, but the guides are very knowledgeable.

The Appia Antica park is a popular Sunday picnic site for Roman families, following the half-forgotten pagan tradition of dining in the

---

A Noble Survivor

Of all the monuments on the Appian Way itself, the most impressive is the **Tomb of Cecilia Metella ★**, within walking distance of the catacombs. The cylindrical tomb, clad in travertine and topped with a marble frieze, honors the wife of one of Julius Caesar's military commanders from the republican era. Why such an elaborate tomb for a figure of relatively minor historical importance? Other mausoleums may have been even more elaborate, but Cecilia Metella's earned enduring fame simply because her tomb has remained while the others have decayed. Part of the reason is its symbiotic relationship with the early-14th-century **Castle Caetani** attached to the rear. For centuries, the tomb survived being plundered for building materials because of the castle, which was built to guard the road and collect tolls; in later eras, the castle was spared because it was attached to the romantic ruin of the tomb. Admission to the tomb is 5€.

Almost half a million early Christians are entombed in the Catacombe di San Callisto.

presence of one's ancestors on holy days. The Via Appia Antica is closed to cars on Sundays, left for the picnickers, walkers and bicyclists. See **www.parcoappiaantica.it** for more, including downloadable maps.

To reach the catacombs area, take bus no. 218 from the San Giovanni Metro stop or the 118 from Colosseo or Circus Maximus. *Tip:* The 118 runs more frequently than the 218 and deposits you closer to the catacombs, but there's no service on Sundays. If you are in a hurry to accommodate your visit to the catacombs, take a cab (p. 71).

Catacombe di Domitilla ★★★ RELIGIOUS SITE/TOUR   The oldest of the catacombs is the hands-down winner for most enjoyable experience. Groups are relatively small (in part because the site is not directly on the Appian Way), and guides are entertaining and personable. The catacombs—Rome's longest at 17km (11 miles)—were built below land donated by Domitilla, a noblewoman of the Flavian dynasty who was exiled from Rome for practicing Christianity. They were rediscovered in 1593, after a church abandoned in the 9th century collapsed. The visit begins in the sunken church founded in A.D. 380, the year Christianity became Rome's state religion.

There are fewer "sights" here than in the other catacombs, but this is the only catacomb where you'll still see bones; the rest have emptied their tombs to rebury the remains in inaccessible lower levels. Elsewhere in the tunnels, 4th-century frescoes contain some of the earliest representations of Saints Peter and Paul. Notice the absence of crosses: It was only later that Christians replaced the traditional fish symbol with the cross. During this period, Christ's crucifixion was a source of shame to the community: He had been killed like a common criminal.

Via delle Sette Chiese 282. www.domitilla.info. © 06-5110342. 8€ adults, 5€ children ages 6–14. Wed–Mon 9am–noon and 2–5pm. Closed mid-Dec to mid-Jan. Bus: 714 or 30 (to Piazza dei Navigatori) or 218.

Catacombe di San Callisto (Catacombs of St. Callixtus) ★★

RELIGIOUS SITE/TOUR   "The most venerable and most renowned of Rome," said Pope John XXIII of these funerary tunnels. These catacombs are often packed with tour-bus groups, but the tunnels are phenomenal. They're the first cemetery of Christian Rome, burial place of 16 popes in the 3rd century. They bear the name of the deacon St. Callixtus, who served as pope from A.D. 217–22. The network of galleries is on four levels and reaches a depth of about 20m (65 ft.), the deepest in the area. There are many sepulchral chambers and almost half a million tombs of early Christians.

Entering the catacombs, you see the most important crypt, that of nine popes. Some of the original marble tablets of their tombs are preserved. Also commemorated is St. Cecilia, patron of sacred music (her relics were moved to her church in Trastevere during the 9th century; see p. 120). Farther on are the Cubicles of the Sacraments, with 3rd-century frescoes.

Via Appia Antica 110–26. www.catacombe.roma.it. © **06-5130151.** 8€ adults, 5€ children ages 7–15. Thurs–Tues 9am–noon and 2–5pm. Closed late Jan to late Feb. Bus: 118 or 218.

Catacombe di San Sebastiano (Catacombs of St. Sebastian) ★

RELIGIOUS SITE/TOUR   Today the tomb and relics of St. Sebastian are in the ground-level basilica, but his original resting place was in the catacombs beneath it. Sebastian was a senior Milanese soldier in the Roman army who converted to Christianity and was martyred during Emperor Diocletian's persecutions, which were especially brutal in the first decade of the 4th century. From the reign of Valerian to that of Constantine, the bodies of Saints Peter and Paul were also hidden in the catacombs, which were dug from the soft volcanic rock *(tufa)*. The church was built in the 4th century and remodeled in the 17th century. In the tunnels and mausoleums are mosaics and graffiti, along with many other pagan and Christian objects, as well as four Roman tombs with their frescoes and stucco fairly intact, found in 1922 after being buried for almost 2,000 years.

Via Appia Antica 136. www.catacombe.org. © **06-7850350.** 8€ adults, 5€ children 6–15. Mon–Sat 10am–4:30pm. Closed Dec. Bus: 118, 218, or 660.

organized TOURS

Forget the flag-waving guides leading a herd of dazed travelers around monuments. A better class of professionally guided tours delivers insider expertise, focused themes, and personal attention, plus perks such as skipping entry lines and visiting after hours.

One of the leading tour operators in Rome, **Context Travel** ★ (www.context travel.com; ✆ **800/691-6036** in the U.S., or 06-96727371) uses local scholars—historians, art historians, archaeologists—to lead small-group walking tours around Rome's monuments, museums, and historic piazzas, as well as culinary walks and excellent family programs. Custom-designed tours are also available. Tour prices are high, beginning at about 80€ per person for 2 hours, but most participants consider them a highlight of their trip.

The affable team at **The Tour Guy,** formerly The Roman Guy (thetourguy. com, ✆ **06-342-8761859**) provides knowledgeable guides who explain thousands of years of history in an engaging, informal way. They offer small-group (most about 15 people) tours of the Colosseum (including dungeons), Vatican Museums, Catacombs, and food tours of Trastevere, among other options. Prices run from 60€ per person to much more for exclusive VIP access and/or private excursions.

Eating Europe (www.eatingeurope. com) offers in-depth small-group food and wine tours in Rome, particularly of Testaccio and Trastevere. Guides connect Rome's culinary culture to the city's history and traditions, and guests leave with their curiosity (and hunger) sated. Tours from 79€.

Walks of Italy (www.walksofitaly. com; ✆ **06-95583331**) also runs excellent guided tours of Rome starting from 34€; more in-depth explorations of the Colosseum, Vatican Museums, and Forum go for 55€ to 125€.

Enjoy Rome (www.enjoyrome.com; ✆ **06-4451843**), offers a number of "greatest hits" walking tours, plus an early-evening tour of the Jewish Ghetto and Trastevere; their bus excursion to the Catacombs and Appian Way visits an ancient aqueduct that most Romans, let alone tourists, never see. Tours cost 30€ to 90€ per person; entrance fees are included with some, but not all tours.

The team at **Through Eternity** (www. througheternity.com; ✆ **06-7009336**) are art historians and architects; what sets them apart is their theatrical delivery, helped along by the dramatic scripts that many of the guides follow. It can be a lot of fun, but it's not for everyone. A 3½-hour tour of the Vatican is 64€; most other tours range from 39€ to 90€.

In addition to small group tours of the Vatican and Forum sights, **Roma Experience** (www.romaexperience.com) has some more unusual offerings, such as a private Caravaggio that includes a visit to an art restoration lab, or a tongue-in-cheek "Insta-Boyfriend" tour with a private driver and personal photographer to capture guests' most Instagrammable moments. Tours cost from 59€ to way, way up.

For something completely different, artist Kelly Medford runs **Sketching Rome Tours** (www.sketchingrometours. com), 3-hour small group drawing and painting lessons in some of Rome's prettiest corners. Supplies are provided and no artistic talent is required (95€ per person).

Especially for Kids

There's a real Jekyll and Hyde quality to exploring Rome with kids. On the one hand, it's a capital city, big, busy, and hot, and with sometimes dodgy public transportation. On the other, the very best parts of the city for kids—Roman ruins, subterranean worlds, and *gelato*—are aspects you'd want to explore anyway. Seeing Rome with kids doesn't demand an itinerary redesign. And despite what you have heard about its famous seven hills, much of the center is mercifully flat, and pedestrian-friendly.

Food is pretty easy too: Roman **pizzas** are some of the best in the world—see "Where to Eat" (p. 139) for our favorites. Ditto the ice cream, or *gelato* (p. 144). Kids are welcomed virtually everywhere, including late in the evening.

Rome is shorter on green spaces than many European cities, but the landscaped gardens of the **Villa Borghese** have plenty of space for kids to let off steam. Pack a picnic or rent some bikes. The **Parco Appia Antica** (www.parcoappiaantica.it) is another favorite, especially on a Sunday or holiday when the old cobbled road is closed to traffic. The park's **Catacombs** (p. 122) are eerie enough to satisfy young minds, but also fascinating Christian and historical sites in their own right.

Museums are trickier. Make the bookshop at the **Colosseum** (p. 91) an early stop; it has a good selection of guides aimed at under-12s, themed on gladiators and featuring funny cartoonish material. The **Musei Capitolini** (p. 90) invites kids to hunt down the collection's treasures highlighted on a free leaflet—it'll buy you a couple of hours to admire the exhibits and perhaps see them from a new and unexpected angle. The multiple levels below **San Clemente** (p. 97) and the **Case Romane del Celio** (p. 98) are another draw for small visitors. Aspiring young gladiators may want to spend 2 hours at the **Scuola Gladiatori Roma** (**Rome Gladiator School,** www.gruppostoricoromano.it/en), where they can prepare for a duel in a reasonably authentic way.

Kids will also likely enjoy some of the cheesier city sights, good to share on Facebook or Instagram. Build in some time to place your hands in the Bocca della Verità, at **Santa Maria in Cosmedin** (p. 100), to throw a coin in the **Trevi Fountain** (p. 111).

If you want to delve deeper into the city as a family, check out the tours on **Context Travel**'s family program (see Organized Tours, p. 125). The 2- to 3-hour tours are pricey (350€–450€ per family) but first-rate, and you will have the docent all to yourselves.

WHERE TO STAY IN ROME

Hotels in Rome's *centro storico* are notoriously overpriced, and all too often the grand exteriors and lobbies of historic buildings give way to bland modern rooms. Our selections here made the cut because they offer unique experiences, highly personalized service, or extreme value—and in many cases all of the above.

Room rates vary wildly depending on the season, and last-minute deals are common. For example, a room at a hotel we classify as "expensive" might be had for as low as 99€ if said hotel has empty beds to fill. Always book directly with the hotel—you'll usually get a better rate and the chance to build some rapport with reception staff.

Breakfast in all but the highest echelon of hotels is often a buffet with coffee, fruit, rolls, and cheese. It's not always included in the rate, so check the reservation options carefully. If you are budgeting and breakfast is a payable extra, skip it and go to a nearby cafe-bar, where a caffè and *cornetto* (espresso and croissant) will likely be much cheaper.

Most hotels are heated in the winter, but not all are air-conditioned in summer, which can be vitally important during a stifling July or August. Be sure to check before you book if it's important to you.

SELF-CATERING APARTMENTS

Rental apartments have some great virtues: They're often cheaper than standard facilities, and they let you save money by preparing at least some of your own meals.

Nearly every vacation rental in Rome—and there are tens of thousands of them—is owned and maintained by a third party (that is, not the rental agency). That means that the decor and flavor of the apartments, even in the same price range and neighborhood, can vary widely. Every reputable agency, however, puts multiple photos of each property they handle on its website, so you'll have a sense of what you're getting into. The photos should be accompanied by a list of amenities. Goliath booking sites **Airbnb.com**, **Homeaway.com**, and **vrbo.com**, platforms that allow individuals to rent their own apartments to guests, have thousands of listings in Rome. These will often be cheaper than apartments rented through local agencies, but they won't be vetted, and sometimes you're on your own if something goes wrong.

If you decide to rent through one of the agencies below, know that its standard practice for them to collect 30 percent of the total rental amount upfront to secure a booking. When you get to Rome and check in, the balance of your rental fee is often payable in cash only. Upon booking, the agency should provide you with detailed check-in procedures. *Tip:* Make sure you ask for a few numbers to call in case of emergency. Most apartments come with information sheets that list neighborhood shops and services.

RECOMMENDED AGENCIES **Cross Pollinate** (www.cross-pollinate. com; ✆ **06-99369799**), a multi-destination agency with a roster of apartments and B&Bs in Rome, was created by the American owners of the Beehive Hotel in Rome (see p. 137). Each property is inspected before it gets listed. **GowithOh** (www.gowithoh.com; ✆ **800/567-2927** in the U.S.) is a hip rental agency that covers 12 European cities, Rome among them. **Eats & Sheets** (www.eatsandsheets.com; ✆ **06-83515971**) is a small boutique collective comprising a B&B and a handful of beautiful apartments near the tourist center. The plain-dealing staff of **Cities**

Reference (www.citiesreference.com/en/rome; © **06-48903612**) offers no-surprises property descriptions (with helpful and diplomatic tags like "better for young people") and even includes the "eco-footprint" for each apartment. **Rental in Rome** (www.rentalinrome.com; © **06-3220068**) has an alluring website—with video clips of the apartments—and the widest selection of midrange and luxury apartments in the *centro storico* zone (there are less expensive ones, too).

MONASTERIES & CONVENTS

Staying in a convent or a monastery can be a great bargain. But remember, these are religious houses, which means the decor is most often stark and the rules inflexible. Cohabitating is almost always frowned upon—though marriage licenses are rarely required—and unruly behavior is not tolerated (so, no staggering in after too much *limoncello* at dinner). Plus, there's usually a curfew. Most rooms in convents and monasteries do not have private bathrooms, but ask when making your reservation in case some are available. However, if you're planning a mellow, "contemplative" trip to Rome, and you can live with these parameters, convents and monasteries are an affordable and fascinating option. The place to start is **www.monasterystays.com**, which lays out all your monastic options for the Eternal City.

> ### A Note on a *Notte* in Rome
>
> The Rome City Council applies a sojourn tax of 3€ to 7€ (depending on hotel class) per person, per night. Many hotels will request this fee in cash upon check-in or check-out; this is perfectly normal. Children ages 10 and under are exempt.

Around Vatican City & Prati

For many, this is a rather dull area to be based in. It's well removed from the ancient sites, and though Prati has some good restaurants, the area overall is not geared to nightlife. But if the main purpose of your visit centers on the Vatican, you'll be fine here, and you will be joined by thousands of other pilgrims, nuns, and priests (see map p. 77).

EXPENSIVE

Residenza Paolo VI ★★   Literally across the street from Vatican City limits, Residenza Paolo can legitimately claim it's "steps from St. Peter's." Taking breakfast on the rooftop terrace is a special treat, as this narrow strip overlooks St. Peter's Square—if your timing's right, you'll see the Pope blessing crowds on Sunday. (There's bar service on the terrace from 4pm onwards.) Old-worldy rooms feature tile or hardwood floors, heavy drapes, Oriental rugs, and quality beds, though standard guest rooms can be a bit cozy.

Via Paolo VI 29. www.residenzapaolovi.com. © **06-684870.** 35 units. 125€–400€ double. Some rates include breakfast. Metro: Ottaviano. Bus: 64. **Amenities:** Bar; room service; free Wi-Fi.

Villa Laetitia ★★★   This elegant hotel overlooking the River Tiber is the work of Anna Fendi of the Roman fashion dynasty. Thanks to her design aesthetic, the rooms are anything but traditional, despite the 1911 villa setting surrounded by tranquil gardens. The decor features bold patterns on the beds and floors and modern art on the walls. Splurge for the black-and-white Giulio Cesare suite, with a round leather bed and blissful garden views. Standard rooms are on the snug side, but most have kitchenettes. Look for great last-minute rates on the hotel website. **Note:** It's a 20-minute walk to centro and thus maybe not the best choice for first-timers to Rome. **Enoteca la Torre** is the villa's Michelin-starred restaurant.

Lungotevere delle Armi 22–23. www.villalaetitia.com. ✆ **06-3226776.** 20 units. 139€–340€ double. Rates include breakfast. Metro: Lepanto. **Amenities:** Restaurant; bar; babysitting; bike rentals; fitness room; room service; free Wi-Fi.

MODERATE

QuodLibet ★★★   The name is Latin for "what pleases," and we'll be frank: Everything pleases us here. This upscale B&B boasts spacious, colorful rooms, gorgeous artwork and furnishings, and generous breakfasts (served on the roof terrace, which offers evening bar service). All the rooms are set on the fourth floor of an elegant building (with elevator and A/C), so it's quieter than many places. It's located just a 10-minute walk from the Vatican Museums, and a block from the Metro. Charming, conscientious hosts possess a deep knowledge of Rome and what will interest visitors. A top pick!

Via Barletta 29. www.quodlibetroma.com. ✆ **06-1222642.** 4 units. 100€–250€ double. Rates include breakfast. Metro: Ottaviano. **Amenities:** Free Wi-Fi.

INEXPENSIVE

Rome Armony Suites ★★★   A warning: Rome Armony Suites is almost always booked up months in advance, so if you're interested, book early. Why so popular? The answer starts with service; owner Luca is a charming, sensitive host, especially helpful with first-time visitors to Rome. Rooms are big, clean, and modern, with minimalist decor, tea and coffee facilities, and a fridge in each unit. Final, major perk: free loaner smartphones loaded with maps and tourist info, to help guests get the most out of their visit; calls to the U.S. and Canada included, too.

Via Orazio 3. www.romearmonysuites.com. ✆ **348-3305419.** 6 units. 65€–150€ double. Rates include breakfast. Metro: Ottaviano. **Amenities:** Free Wi-Fi.

Ancient Rome, Monti & Celio

There aren't many hotel rooms on earth with a view of a 2,000-year-old amphitheater, so there's a definite "only in Rome" feeling to lodging on the edge of the ancient city (see map p. 89). The negative to staying in this area—and it's a big minus—is that the streets adjacent to those ancient monuments have little life outside tourism.

EXPENSIVE

Capo d'Africa ★★   Twin palm trees guard the entrance to this elegant boutique hotel, located in the heart of Imperial Rome and set in an early-20th-century *palazzo*. Guests are welcomed as if they were in a relaxed and unpretentious Roman home, albeit one with chic design, sweeping vistas from the manicured roof terrace (where you eat breakfast), and an upscale vibe. Light-filled rooms are spacious, smart, and modern, with cherrywood furniture, touches of glass and chrome, incredibly comfy beds, marble bathrooms, and lots of cupboard space. For a truly unforgettable stay, book a studio suite, which comes with a welcome bottle of wine and a private terrace with ethereal views of the Colosseum.

Via Capo d'Africa 54. www.hotelcapodafrica.com. ℂ **06-772801.** 65 units. 155€–325€ double. Rates include breakfast. Bus: 53, 85, 87. Tram: 3. **Amenities:** Restaurant; bar; exercise room; loaner bikes; room service; free Wi-Fi in common areas.

The Inn at the Roman Forum ★★★   This small hotel is tucked down a medieval lane, on the edge of Monti, with the forums of several Roman emperors as neighbors. Rooms are tastefully luxurious, with colorful silks, soothing tones, and spacious bathrooms. The posh fifth-floor Master Garden Rooms have private patios surrounded by flowers and greenery, ochre walls, and busts of emperors, and a plush apartment with a kitchen sleeps up to six people. The hotel's **roof lounge** has views of the Campidoglio, and for archaeology buffs there's an ancient Roman *cryptoporticus* behind the lobby. The inn isn't cheap, but the views alone more than make up for it.

Via degli Ibernesi 30. www.theinnattheromanforum.com. ℂ **06-69190970.** 20 units. 160€–790€ double. Rates include breakfast. Metro: Cavour. **Amenities:** 2 bars; concierge; room service; free Wi-Fi.

MODERATE

Duca d'Alba ★★   Located on one of the main drags of hip Monti, with all the nightlife and authentic dining you'll need, Duca d'Alba strikes a fine balance between old-world gentility and 21st-century amenities. Rooms in the main building are snug and contemporary, with modern furniture and gadgetry but tiny bathrooms. If you want to spring for slightly higher rates, the spacious annex rooms next door have a *palazzo* character, with terracotta floors, oak and cherry furniture, and soundproofed street-facing rooms. Second-floor rooms are the brightest.

Via Leonina 14. www.hotelducadalba.com. ℂ **06-484471.** 31 units. 73€–205€ double. Some rates include breakfast. Metro: Cavour. **Amenities:** Bar; bike rentals; free Wi-Fi.

Lancelot ★   Expect warmth and hospitality from the minute you walk in the door. The staff, all of whom have been here for years, are the heart and soul of Lancelot, and the reason why the hotel has so many repeat guests. The room decor is simple, and most of the units are spacious, immaculately kept, and light-filled, thanks to large windows. Sixth-floor rooms have private terraces overlooking Ancient Rome—well worth springing for. What makes this place truly remarkable are the genteel, chandelier-lit common areas for meeting other travelers, *Room With A View*-style. Unusual for Rome, Lancelot also has private parking, for which you'll need to book ahead.

Via Capo d'Africa 47. www.lancelothotel.com. ℰ **06-70450615.** 60 units. 140€–200€ double; 280€–330€ suite. Rates include breakfast. Bus: 53, 85, 87. Tram: 3. **Amenities:** Restaurant; bar; free Wi-Fi.

The Centro Storico & Pantheon

There's nothing like an immersion in the atmosphere of Rome's lively Renaissance heart, though you'll pay for *location, location, location.* Since many of Centro's characteristic streets are pedestrian only, expect to do a lot of walking, but that's a reason many visitors come here in the first place—to wander and discover the glory that was and is Rome. Many restaurants and cafes are an easy walk from the hotels here.

EXPENSIVE

Del Sole al Pantheon ★   For history and atmosphere, it's hard to beat a place that's been hosting wayfarers since 1467, with past guests including Jean-Paul Sartre and Simone de Beauvoir, as well as at least one Hapsburg king. Rooms are decorated in a lavish period decor, with lots of brocade drapery, fine fabrics, and classic furniture. Each room comes equipped with air-conditioning and satellite TV, and some feature views of the Pantheon. Suites offer separate bedrooms and Jacuzzi tubs.

Piazza della Rotonda 63. www.hotelsolealpantheon.com. ℰ **06-6780441.** 32 units. 160€–350€ double. Rates include breakfast. **Amenities:** Bar; bike rentals; concierge; garden; free Wi-Fi.

Raphael ★★★   Planning on proposing? This ivy-covered palace, just off Piazza Navona, is an ideal choice for a special-occasion stay, with luxurious rooms, enthusiastic staff, and a roof terrace with spectacular views across Rome. It's a gorgeous hotel, highlighted by 20th-century artwork inside, including Picasso ceramics and paintings by Miró, Morandi, and De Chirico scattered across the property. The standard rooms are all decorated in Victorian style, with antique furnishings and hardwood floors. Some prefer staying in the Richard Meier–designed executive suites, which blend modern and Asian design and feature oak paneling, contemporary art, and Carrara marble. A haute organic, vegetarian restaurant will leave even diehard carnivores sated.

Largo Febo 2, Piazza Navona. www.raphaelhotel.com. ℰ **06-682831.** 51 units. 220€–510€ double. Rates include breakfast. **Amenities:** Restaurant; bar; babysitting; concierge; room service; free Wi-Fi.

MODERATE

Fontanella Borghese ★   Occupying two floors of a palazzo that once belonged to the Borghese family, this is a noble address (equidistant from the Pantheon, Spanish Steps, and Piazza del Popolo) at sort-of plebeian prices. It's not a fancy place, but the classically decorated, family-friendly rooms are bright and spacious, with high ceilings, parquet or marble inlaid floors, and well-organized, if unremarkable, bathrooms.

Largo Fontanella Borghese 84. www.fontanellaborghese.com. ℂ **06-68809504.** 29 units. 99€–250€ double. Rates include breakfast. Metro: Spagna. **Amenities:** Free Wi-Fi.

Hotel Adriano ★★★   Just 5 minutes from the Pantheon, this stylish retreat occupies an elegant 17th-century *palazzo*. Rooms boast a chic and modern vibe, though standard rooms can be a tad utilitarian. A few deluxe rooms and suites have terraces with views of the Roman rooftops. In a crowded hotel market, Adriano stands out for its plush, well-designed common areas, including **The Gin Corner,** a trendy cocktail bar specializing in . . . you guessed it. Rooms in the nearby "Domus Adriani" are more akin to self-catering apartments. *Tip:* E-mail the hotel directly for the lowest rates.

Via di Pallacorda 2. www.hoteladriano.com. ℂ **06-68802451.** 80 units. 100€–300€ double. Rates include breakfast. Bus: C3, 70, 81, 87. **Amenities:** Bar; babysitting; bikes; concierge; gym; free Wi-Fi.

Coronari Palace ★   Once a cozy little 10-room guesthouse with classic décor, Coronari Palace has recently been redone and now sings a modern tune. Its 16 rooms feature modular furnishings and wood laminate floors; three junior suites have terraces. While some bathrooms are on the snug side, they're sleek and well-designed, most with enough counter/sink space for a toiletry bag. The communal roof terrace invites guests to BYOB and enjoy a pleasant evening looking out on the terra-cotta rooftops of Rome. There are no surprises here, just clean, up-to-date facilities, good prices, and amiable staff.

Via del Coronari 231. www.coronaripalace.com. ℂ **06-68309541.** 16 units. 100€–350€ doubles. Rates include breakfast. **Amenities:** Roof terrace, Wi-Fi (free).

Residenza in Farnese ★★   This little gem is tucked away in a 15th-century mansion across the street from the Palazzo Farnese, within stumbling distance of Campo de' Fiori but still reasonably quiet. Most rooms are spacious and artsy, with tiled floors and a vaguely Renaissance theme. Standard rooms are on the small side but come with free minibars, and prices are usually on the low end of the range shown here. The complimentary breakfast spread is downright generous. *Tip:* Last-minute rates are often much lower than those shown below.

Via del Mascherone 59. www.residenzafarneseroma.it. ℂ **06-68210980.** 31 units. 140€–240€ double. Rates include breakfast. **Amenities:** Airport transfer (free with min. 4-night stay); bar; concierge; room service; free Wi-Fi.

Teatro di Pompeo ★★ History buffs will appreciate this small hotel, built atop the ruins of the 1st-century Theatre of Pompey, where on the Ides of March Julius Caesar was stabbed to death (p. 21). The atmospheric breakfast area is actually part of the old theater's arcades, with original Roman walls. The large, simple rooms have an authentic feel, with wood beam ceilings, cherrywood furniture, and terra-cotta-tiled floors. Some rooms overlook the internal courtyard, others face the small square; all are quiet, despite the Campo de' Fiori crowds right behind the hotel. Staff members are extremely helpful. *Tip:* Avoid the Trattoria Der Pallaro restaurant next door; it's a tourist trap.

Largo del Pallaro 8. www.hotelteatrodipompeo.it. ℂ **06-68300170.** 13 units. 115€–220€ double. Rates include breakfast. **Amenities:** Bar; room service; free Wi-Fi.

INEXPENSIVE

Mimosa ★ This budget stalwart in the heart of the *centro storico* enjoys great word of mouth, so book early. Decor is hodgepodge at best, but the straightforward modern rooms are bright and air-conditioned (*not* a given at this price point); larger units are suitable for families with small children. A location this close to the Pantheon at these prices is hard to beat. Mention Frommer's for a 10-percent discount.

Via di Santa Chiara 61. www.hotelmimosa.net. ℂ **06-68801753.** 11 units. 89€–150€ double. Rates include breakfast. **Amenities:** Free Wi-Fi.

Tridente, the Spanish Steps & Via Veneto

The heart of the city is a great place to stay if you're a serious shopper or enjoy the romantic, somewhat nostalgic locales of the Spanish Steps and Trevi Fountain. But expect to part with a lot of extra euro for the privilege. This is one of the most elegant areas in Rome (see map p. 109), but we've found you a few bargains (and some worthy splurges).

EXPENSIVE

Babuino 181 ★★ Leave Renaissance and baroque Italy far behind at this sleek, contemporary hotel, with relatively spacious rooms and apartment-size suites outfitted with Frette linens, iPod docks, and Nespresso machines. Bathrooms are heavy on the marble and mosaics, and shuttered windows with hefty curtains provide a quiet and perfectly blacked-out environment for light sleepers. A surcharged breakfast buffet is served on the rooftop terrace, which doubles as a cocktail bar at night. An affiliated restaurant, **Assaggia,** serves small plates of modern Roman fare in a similarly chic atmosphere.

Via del Babuino 181. www.romeluxurysuites.com/babuino. ℂ **06-32295295.** 24 units. 180€–380€ double. Metro: Flaminio or Spagna. **Amenities:** Bar; babysitting; concierge; restaurant; room service; free Wi-Fi.

The Inn at the Spanish Steps ★★★ Set in one of Rome's most desirable locations on the famed Via dei Condotti shopping street, this

A balcony view from the Inn at the Spanish Steps.

hotel is the epitome of luxe. Rooms are fantasias of design and comfort, some with parquet floors and cherubim frescoes on the ceiling, others decked out with wispy fabrics draping canopied beds; upgraded units have swoon-worthy views of Piazza di Spagna. Swank standard perks include iPod docks, Jacuzzi tubs, double marble sinks, pet amenities, and so forth. Rooms located in the annex tend to be larger than those in the main building. The perfectly manicured rooftop garden provides beautiful views, to be enjoyed at breakfast—with its generous buffet spread—or at sunset, with complimentary happy-hour snacks.

Via dei Condotti 85. www.atspanishsteps.com. ⓒ **06-69925657.** 24 units. 170€–490€ double. Rates include breakfast. Metro: Spagna. **Amenities:** Bar; babysitting; concierge; room service; free Wi-Fi.

Villa Spalletti Trivelli ★★★ This really is an experience rather than a hotel, an early-20th-century neoclassical villa remodeled into an exclusive 14-room guesthouse, where lodgers mingle in the gardens or the great hall, as if invited by an Italian noble for the weekend. There is no key for the entrance door; ring a bell and a staff member will open it for you, often offering you a glass of Prosecco as a welcome. Onsite is a Turkish bath, a sizeable and modern oasis for those who want extra pampering, while rooms feature elegant antiques and Fiandra damask linen sheets, with sitting areas or separate lounges. And the minibar? All free, all day. A rooftop lounge boasts Jacuzzis and a bar serving light fare.

Via Piacenza 4. www.villaspalletti.it. © **06-48907934.** 14 units. 325€–695€ double. Rates include breakfast. Metro: Barberini. **Amenities:** Restaurant; bar; concierge; exercise room; roof terrace; room service; Jacuzzis; sauna; free Wi-Fi.

MODERATE

Daphne Trevi ★★ In a neighborhood with a lot of overpriced hotels, this boutique option, in an 18th-century building minutes from Trevi Fountain, is a good value even in the summer. What rooms lack in size they make up for with sleek modern design and spotless bathrooms with mosaic tiles (two rooms share a bathroom). A 5th-floor covered terrace is the setting for an ample breakfast buffet with lots of home-baked goodies, as well as evening cocktails and occasional happy hours.

Via di San Basilio 55. www.daphne-rome.com. © **06-87450086.** 10 units. 120€–220€ double. Rates include breakfast. Metro: Barberini. **Amenities:** Concierge; free Wi-Fi.

Deko Rome ★★ Exceptionally warm and welcoming, this boutique hotel (just six rooms) occupies the second floor of an early-20th-century *palazzo.* The chic interior blends antiques, vintage '60s pieces, and modern design in a way that's happily retro and quite comfortable; each room comes with an iPad and flatscreen TV. Add the friendly, fun owners (Marco and Serena) and excellent location near Via Veneto, and Deko is understandably hugely popular. Reserve months in advance, though you can find the occasional last-minute bargain.

Via Toscana 1. www.dekorome.com. © **06-42020032.** 6 units. 99€–230€. Rates include breakfast. Metro: Barberini. Bus: 910 (from Termini). **Amenities:** Bar; babysitting; free Wi-Fi.

Hotel Condotti ★ This cozy hotel can be a tremendously good deal depending on when you stay and how far out you book. For your money you'll get a clean, unpretentious room, though the common areas aim higher, with marble floors, antiques, tapestries, and a Venetian-glass chandelier. Standard rooms are tight; you'll get a bit more space and modernity in the nearby annex rooms. Overall it's worth considering for its proximity to the Spanish Steps. *Tip:* The type of breakfast included depends on which rate and room you select. If you want a big breakfast, read the fine print when reserving.

Via Mario de' Fiori 37. www.hotelcondotti.com. © **06-6794661.** 16 units. 70€–210€. Rates include breakfast. Metro: Spagna. **Amenities:** Bar; babysitting; bikes; room service; free Wi-Fi.

La Lumière ★ You won't be checking in for chic design or innovation—this traditional hotel just off Via dei Condotti smacks of middle-class comforts, from rooms with matchy-matchy color schemes, wood floors, and warm lighting to the glassed-in roof terrace or open-air patio where breakfast and evening aperitivo is served. But for all but highest season and holidays, it's a winner on the price/location ratio.

Via Belsiana 72. www.lalumieredipiazzadispagna.com. ℅ **06-69380806.** 10 units. 120€–350€ double. Rates include breakfast. Metro: Spagna. **Amenities:** Bar; free Wi-Fi.

La Residenza ★ Considering its location just off Via Veneto, this hotel—hosting guests since 1936—is a smart deal. Renovated, modern rooms retain a touch of Art Deco appeal, and are all relatively spacious, with a couple of easy chairs or a small couch in addition to a desk. Families with children are especially catered to, with quad rooms and junior suites on the top floor featuring a separate kids' alcove with two sofa beds, and an outdoor terrace with patio furniture. The excellent breakfast buffet includes quality charcuterie and cheeses, homemade breads, and pastries.

Via Emilia 22–24. www.hotel-la-residenza.com. ℅ **06-4880789.** 29 units. 125€–250€ double. Rates include breakfast. Metro: Barberini. **Amenities:** Bar; babysitting; café; room service; free Wi-Fi.

INEXPENSIVE

Panda ★ Panda has long been popular among budget travelers, so it books up quickly. Rooms are spare, but not without some old-fashioned charm, like characteristic Roman *cotto* (terra-cotta) floor tiles, and the odd frescoed ceiling or exposed beams. Most rooms are a bit cramped, but for these prices in this neighborhood they remain a very, very good deal. Outside your doorstep are several great cafes and wine bars where you can start the day with espresso and end it with a nightcap. *Tip:* With its budget single rooms with shared baths, Panda is a good pick for solo travelers.

Via della Croce 35. www.hotelpanda.it. ℅ **06-6780179.** 28 units (8 with shared bath). 85€–130€ double with bath. Metro: Spagna. **Amenities:** Free Wi-Fi.

Parlamento ★ Set on the top floors of a 17th-century *palazzo,* this is one of the best budget deals in the area. All 10 rooms are freshly renovated and equipped with satellite TVs, desks, wood floors, and subdued color schemes. Breakfast is served on the rooftop terrace—you can also chill up there with a glass of wine in the evening. Trevi Fountain, Spanish Steps, and the Pantheon are all within a 5- to 10-minute walk.

Via delle Convertite 5 (at Via del Corso). www.hotelparlamento.it. ℅ **06-69921000.** 21 units. 130€–218€ double. Rates include breakfast. Metro: Spagna. **Amenities:** Bar; concierge; room service; free Wi-Fi.

Around Termini

Known for its concentration of cheap hotels, the Termini area (see map p. 117) is about the only part of the center where you can score a high-season double for under 100€. The area has some upscale hotels, though admittedly, streets close to the train station are hardly picturesque, and parts of the neighborhood are downright seedy. Still, it's very convenient to most of Rome's top sights, and a hub for Metro lines, buses, and trams. Following are some of our favorites near Termini.

MODERATE

Hotel Mediterraneo ★★★ Within sight of Termini station, this suprisingly luxurious hotel offers vintage art deco style, along with a team of long-time employees who warmly evoke the spirit of a bygone era of class and service. Rooms are large and well-equipped, with bathrooms of grand proportions; suites are downright palatial, and 7 top-floor units have terraces with sweeping views. Read about the hotel's interesting WWII-era history as you linger over cocktails in its old-school bar. Sister properties **Atlantico** and **Massimo D'Azeglio,** located next door and across the street, respectively, offer lower room prices and share amenities with Mediterraneo. *Tip:* Check online for off-season or last-minute deals on those top-floor suites.

Via Cavour 15. www.romehotelmediterraneo.it. © **06-4884051.** 245 units. 124€– 250€ double. Rates include breakfast. Metro: Termini. **Amenities:** Babysitting; bar; concierge; gym; restaurant; roof terrace; room service; free Wi-Fi.

Residenza Cellini ★★ For every rule, there's an exception, and in this case, spending a little more near Termini pays off at Cellini. The feeling of refinement begins the second you walk through the door to find a vase of fresh lilies in the elegant, high-ceilinged hall. Antique-styled rooms are proudly 19th century, with thick walls (so no noise from your neighbors), solid furnishings, and handsome parquet floors, yet also offer modern comforts like memory-foam mattresses and A/C. Bathrooms come with Jacuzzi tubs or jetted showers. Service is topnotch and wonderfully personal.

Via Modena 5. www.residenzacellini.it. © **06-47825204.** 18 units. 89€–209€ double. Metro: Repubblica. **Amenities:** Concierge; room service; free Wi-Fi.

Seven Kings Relais ★★ This unfussy hotel has a slightly retro feel, kitted out with dark wooden furniture, chocolate-brown bedspreads, and modern tiled floors. Despite its location right on one of Rome's busiest thoroughfares, street noise is minimal—an external courtyard and modern soundproofing see to that. Breakfast is a 24-hour self-service bar with tea, coffee, and packaged cookies, but the area has plenty of inexpensive dining options. Management has several other nearby properties as well, run through **Roma Termini Suites** (www.romaterminisuites.com).

Via XX Settembre 58A. www.sevenkingsrelais.com. © **06-42917784.** 11 units. 60€– 120€ double. Metro: Repubblica. **Amenities:** Free Wi-Fi.

INEXPENSIVE

Beehive ★★★ Conceived as part hostel and part hotel, the Beehive is an utterly cheerful lodging experience, run by eco-minded American owners and offering rooms for a variety of budgets. Some have private bathrooms, others have shared facilities or are six-bed dorms—but all are decorated with flair, adorned with artwork or flea-market treasures. A garden offers trees and secluded reading/relaxing space; a buzzy cafe offers breakfast a la carte, as well as budget-friendly vegan/vegetarian meals. The Beehive's "Other Honey"—Clover and Cacaia guesthouses—are a smart option for groups of traveling friends, offering private rooms and shared bathrooms; they're a 10-minute walk from the original B&B.

Via Marghera 8. www.the-beehive.com. ℂ 06-44704553. 20 units. 60€–100€ double; 20€–35€ dorm beds. Metro: Termini or Castro Pretorio. **Amenities:** Café; garden; lounge; free Wi-Fi.

Euro Quiris ★   There's not a frill in sight at this one-star a couple of blocks north of the station. Rooms are on the 5th floor and simply decorated with functional furniture, but they are spotless, and mattresses are a lot more comfortable than you should expect in this price bracket. Bathrooms are en suite, too. The friendly reception staff dispenses sound local knowledge, including tips on where to have breakfast in cafes nearby. No credit cards are accepted, and you'll pay extra for A/C.

Via dei Mille 64. www.euroquirishotel.com. ℂ 06-491279. 9 units. 40€–80€ double. Metro: Termini. **Amenities:** Free Wi-Fi.

Giuliana ★★   The Santacroce family and their staff bend over backwards to make guests feel welcome at this moderate-priced inn near the station and Santa Maria Maggiore. Basic but comfy rooms, most done up in crimson and buttercream, come with surprisingly large bathrooms. Breakfast is a simple affair, but all in all, this is a good value for this side of the (train) tracks.

Via Agostino Depretis 70. www.hotelgiuliana.com. ℂ 06-4880795. 11 units. 50€–160€ double, includes breakfast (with most rates). Metro: Termini or Repubblica. **Amenities:** Bike rentals; concierge; free Wi-Fi.

Trastevere

This was once an "undiscovered" neighborhood—but no longer. Being based here does give some degree of escape from the busy *centro storico*, though Trastevere's narrow streets can be packed to the gills in the evenings, as there are bars, shops, and restaurants galore in this boho section of Rome (see map p. 119). The panorama from the **Gianicolo** (p. 93) is also walkable from pretty much everywhere in Trastevere.

MODERATE

Santa Maria ★★   Hidden behind an ivy-covered wall, the lovely Santa Maria is built around a 16th-century cloister, now a relaxing courtyard fragrant with orange trees. Cheerful rooms, some with exposed brick walls and beamed ceilings, are mostly on the ground floor. Free breakfast and loaner bikes, a roof garden, and a cocktail bar all make this charmer a stand-out in hotel-deprived Trastevere. *Tip:* Several spacious, multi-bed rooms make this a fine option for families.

Vicolo del Piede 2. www.htlsantamaria.com. ℰ **06-5894626.** 20 units. 89€–227€ double. Rates include breakfast. Tram: 8. Bus: 23, 280, 780 or H. **Amenities:** Bar; loaner bikes; free Wi-Fi.

INEXPENSIVE

Arco del Lauro ★★　Hidden in Trastevere's snaking alleyways, this serene little B&B occupies the ground floor of a shuttered pink *palazzo*. Bright rooms have wood floors, plush beds, and simple decor, with a mix of modern and period furnishings. Rooms can't be defined as large, but they all feel spacious thanks to lofty wood ceilings. Breakfast is taken at a nearby café (5€ surcharge), while coffee and snacks are laid out around the clock. No credit cards.

Via Arco de' Tolomei 29. www.arcodellauro.it. ℰ **06-97840350.** 6 units. 105€–145€ double. Bus: 23, 280, 780, or H. Tram: 8. **Amenities:** Free Wi-Fi.

Hotel San Francesco ★★　Lying at the edge of Trastevere, close to the Porta Portese gate in an area that hasn't (yet) been gentrified, this hotel still has a local feel that has disappeared from much of the neighborhood. All rooms are bright, with color-washed walls and modern tiling. Doubles are fairly small, but the bathrooms are palatial. The grand piano in the lobby adds a touch of old-time charm; a top-floor garden with a cocktail bar overlooks terra-cotta rooftops and pealing church bell towers. *Tip:* Book a "charity room," and the hotel will match your 2€ donation to help Rome's shelter dogs.

Via Jacopa de' Settesoli 7. www.hotelsanfrancesco.net. ℰ **06-48300051.** 24 units. 96€–199€ double. Bus: H, 44, 75. Tram: 3 or 8. **Amenities:** Bar; free Wi-Fi.

WHERE TO EAT IN ROME

Rome remains a top destination for food lovers and today offers more dining diversity than ever. Though many of its *trattorie* haven't changed their menus in a quarter of a century (for better or worse), the city has an increasing number of creative spots with chefs willing to revisit tradition.

Restaurants generally serve lunch between 12:30 and 2:30pm, and dinner between 7:30 and 10:30pm. At all other times, most restaurants are closed—though a new generation is moving toward all-day dining, with a limited service at the "in-between" time of mid-afternoon.

If you have your heart set on any of these places below, we seriously recommend *reserving ahead of arrival.* Hot tables go quickly, especially on high-season weekends—often twice: once for the early-dining tourists, and then again by locals, who dine later, typically around 9pm.

A *servizio* (tip or service charge) is almost always added to your bill or included in the price. Sometimes it is marked on the menu as *coperto e servizio* or *pane e coperto* (bread, cover charge, and service). You can leave extra if you wish—a couple of euros as a token—but in general, big

Delectable cannoli pastries round off a culinary tour of Testaccio.

tipping is not the norm here. If you have any questions about an item on your bill, don't hesitate to ask for an explanation.

Near Vatican City

For restaurant locations, see map p. 77. If you just want a quick, tasty sandwich before or after your Vatican safari, **Duecento Gradi** ★★ is a topnotch panino joint with lots of yummy choices, right across from the Vatican walls at Piazza Risorgimento 3 (www.duecentogradi.it; ✆ **06-39754239;** Sun–Thurs 10am–2am; Fri–Sat 11am–5am).

EXPENSIVE

Taverna Angelica ★★ MODERN ITALIAN/SEAFOOD   In a sea of overpriced, touristy restaurants near St. Peter's, Angelica serves up surprisingly good and fairly priced (though not cheap) fare. Specialties include handmade pasta with crunchy bacon and leeks, a divine lime risotto with artichokes and parmesan, or grilled octopus, stuffed calamari, or duck breast in a port-wine reduction. Save room for the delicious, non-run-of-the-mill dessert options. Reservations are required.

Piazza A. Capponi 6. www.tavernaangelica.it. ✆ **06-6874514.** Entrees 16€–22€; tasting menus 45€. Mon–Thurs 11:30pm–4pm, Sun 11:30pm–3:30pm, dinner daily 6pm–midnight. Closed 10 days in Aug. Metro: Ottaviano.

MODERATE

Bonci Pizzarium ★★★ PIZZA   Celebrity chef Gabriele Bonci has always had a cult following in the Eternal City. And since he's been featured on TV shows overseas and written up by influential bloggers, you can expect long lines at his pizzeria. No matter—it's worth waiting (and walking 10 minutes west of the Vatican Museums) for some of the best pizza you'll ever taste, sold by the slice or by weight. His ingredients are fresh and organic, the crust is perfect, and the toppings often experimental (try the mortadella and crumbled pistachio). There's also a good choice of Italian craft IPAs and wheat beers, and wines by the glass. There are only a handful of stand-up tables inside and benches outside for seating, and reservations aren't taken. Bonci also has a counter at Termini's Mercato Centrale (see p. 149).

Via della Meloria 43. www.bonci.it. © **06-39745416.** Pizza 12€–40€ per kilo, depending on toppings. Mon–Sat 11am–10pm; Sundays noon–4pm and 6–10pm. Metro: Cipro.

Ancient Rome, Monti & Celio

For restaurant locations, see map p. 89. For a cappuccino, a quick bite, or aperitivo snacking, head to the epicenter of Monti, **La Bottega del Caffè** ★★ (© **06-4741578**) on lively Piazza Madonna dei Monti, open from 8am to the wee hours. When we hanker for something other than Italian food, we head to **Maharajah** ★★, an elegant Northern Indian eatery at Via dei Serpenti 124 (www.maharajah.it; © **06-4747144**).

EXPENSIVE

L'Asino d'Oro ★★ CONTEMPORARY UMBRIAN/ROMAN   This isn't your typical Roman eatery. Helmed by Lucio Sforza, a renowned chef from Orvieto, L'Asino d'Oro offers a seriously refined take on the flavors of central Italy without a checked tablecloth in sight; the setting is contemporary with a Scandinavian feel, thanks to the light-wood interior. The food is marked by creativity and flair, in both flavor and presentation. Expect highly polished takes on hearty Umbrian standards, such as *baccala* (salted cod) with onions, raisins, and chestnut cream, or a super-savory handmade fettuccine with black truffles, anchovies, and porcini mushrooms.

Via del Boschetto 73. © **06-48913832.** Entrees 15€–18€. Tues–Sat 12:30–2:30pm, 7:30–11pm. Closed last 2 wks Aug. Metro: Cavour.

MODERATE

Caffè Propaganda ★ MODERN ITALIAN   This stylish eatery— part lively Parisian bistro, part cocktail bar—is your best bet for scoring a good meal within eyeshot of the Colosseum. Diners lounge on caramel-colored leather banquettes and choose from a diverse menu that mixes Roman classics such as *carbonara* (pasta with cured pork, egg, and cheese) with inventive Continental fare or more familiar dishes—like an 18€ hamburger. Desserts are Instagram-worthy affairs. After dark, confident bartenders shake up Propaganda's signature cocktails. Service is relaxed by North American standards, so only eat here if you have time to linger.

Via Claudia 15. www.caffepropaganda.it. ✆ **06-94534255.** Entrees 14€–22€. Tues–Sun 8:30am–2am. Metro: Colosseo. Bus: C3, 75, 81, 118. Tram: 3 or 8.

InRoma al Campidoglio ★ ITALIAN   Once a club for Rome's film industry, InRoma sits on a cobbled lane opposite the Palatine Hill. Though the place rests heavily on its cinematic laurels, it still serves up authentic Roman and regional cuisine. Meals might start with *caprese di bufala affumicata* (salad of tomatoes and smoked buffalo mozzarella) followed by classic Roman pastas like *all'amatriciana* (cured pork, tomato, and pecorino) or a main course of *tagliata* (beef strip steak) with a red wine reduction. The ambience inside is fairly generic; we recommend the terrace for a table to remember.

Via dei Fienili 56. www.inroma.eu. ✆ **06-69191024.** Entrees 10€–20€. Daily noon–3:30pm and 7–11pm. Bus: C3, H, 81, 83, 160, 170, 628.

La Barrique ★★ MODERN ROMAN   This cozy, contemporary *enoteca* (wine bar with food) has a kitchen that knocks out fresh farm-to-table fare that complements the well-chosen wine list. The atmosphere is lively and informal, with rustic place settings and friendly service—as any proper *enoteca* should be. The menu offers creative takes on familiar Italian dishes, such as ricotta-stuffed ravioli with lemon, roe, and celery, or grilled octopus served over a cream of chick peas and sesame paste.

Via del Boschetto 41B. ✆ **06-47825953.** Entrees 9€–16€. Mon–Fri 1–3pm and 7–11:30pm, Sat 7–11:30pm. Metro: Cavour.

INEXPENSIVE

Li Rioni ★★ PIZZA   This fab neighborhood pizzeria is close enough to the Colosseum to be convenient, but just distant enough to avoid the dreaded "touristy" label that applies to so much dining in this part of town. Roman-style pizzas baked in the wood-stoked oven are among the best in town, with perfect crisp crusts. There's also a bruschetta list (from around 4€) and a range of salads. Outside tables can be cramped, but there's plenty of room inside. If you want to eat late, booking is essential or you'll be fighting with hungry locals for a table. *Tip:* After visiting the Colosseum or the Basilica of San Clemente, stop for an aperitivo, then head here at 7 for an early (and cheap) pizza dinner.

Via SS. Quattro 24. www.lirioni.it. ✆ **06-70450605.** Pizzas 6€–9€. Wed–Mon 7pm–midnight. Closed most of Aug. Metro: Colosseo. Bus: C3, 51, 85, 87. Tram: 3 or 8.

Centro Storico & the Pantheon

For restaurant locations, see map p. 103. Vegetarians looking for massive salads (or anyone who just wants a break from all those heavy meats and

Dine & drink for a good cause

It's always nice when you can combine a great meal or night out with a dose of community support. At both Terre e Domus della Provincia Romana ★★ and Vale la Pena Pub & Shop ★, inmates from Rome's Rebibbia prison engage in work release programs that combat recidivism and help them develop employable skills for after they complete their sentences. Terre e Domus is set in the stunning Palazzo Valentini (see p. 99), just opposite Trajan's Column, and offers a menu showcasing the best in local wines and foods, using produce grown at the prison. (Foro di Traiano 82–84, www.palazzovalentini.it, ☎ **06-69940273,** main courses 10€–15€, daily 7:30am–12:30am). **Vale la Pena** features pub fare and craft beers from its own microbrewery, and is out in the working-class Tuscolano district. It's a worthwhile stop after touring **Basilica di San Giovanni in Laterano** (p. 97), just a few Metro stops away. (Via Eurialo 22, www.valelapena.it, ☎ **06 8760 6875,** most menu items under 10€, Tues–Sun 6pm–late night.)

starches) can find great food at the neighborhood branch of **L'Insalata Ricca,** Largo dei Chiavari 85 (www.linsalataricca.it; ☎ **06-68803656;** daily noon–midnight).

EXPENSIVE

Pipero Roma ★★ MODERN ITALIAN   Whether you're accustomed to dining in Michelin-starred temples or it's a once-in-a-lifetime event, consider adding Pipero to your bucket list. This long-established foodie haven has moved to chic new digs opposite the Chiesa Nuova, in a setting that's as sophisticated as the plates paraded forth from the kitchen. Start with a risotto of mussels, lemon, and ficoide (a trendy, edible succulent), followed by an artful arrangement of duck breast, reinforcement salad (a traditional pickled salad from Naples), and salmon roe. Everything is expensive here and the small, precious servings will either dazzle you or drive you nuts with their pretension—it's better to make that decision beforehand.

Corso Vittorio Emanuele II 250. www.piperoroma.it. ☎ **06-68139022.** Entrees 35€–45€. Tasting menus 130€–150€. Mon–Sat 12:30–2:30pm, 7–10:30pm. Bus: 40, 46, 62, 64, 916.

MODERATE

Antica Hostaria Romanesca ★ ROMAN   It's very easy to eat badly on Campo de'Fiori, which makes this authentic spot with ringside seats on the piazza such a pleasant surprise. Romanesca does dependable, old-school Roman fare at fair prices, including a gloriously juicy *pollo e pep-eroni* (stewed chicken with peppers) and *abbacchio scottadito,* lamb chops hot off the grill. Locals snatch up the tables after 9pm, so a reservation is advised.

Campo de' Fiori 40 (east side of square). ☎ **06-6864024.** Entrees 9€–15€. Daily noon–3pm and 6:30–11pm. Bus: 30, 40, 46, 62, 64, 70, 81, 87, 492. Tram: 8.

GETTING YOUR FILL OF gelato

Don't leave town without trying one (or several) of Rome's outstanding **ice-cream parlors.** However, choose your gelato carefully: Don't buy close to the tourist-packed piazzas, and don't be dazzled by vats of brightly (and artificially) colored, air-pumped gelato. The best gelato is made only from natural ingredients, which impart a natural color—if the pistachio gelato is bright green, move on. Take your cone (cono) or small cup (coppetta) and stroll as you eat—sitting down on the premises is usually more expensive. The recommended spots below are generally open mid-morning to late, sometimes after midnight on summer weekends. Cones and small cups cost between 2.50€ and 5€.

Near Campo de' Fiori, one of Rome's oldest artisan gelato makers, **Gelateria Alberto Pica ★★★** (Via della Seggiola 12; © **06-6868405;** bus H, 63 or 780; tram 8) produces top-quality gelato churned with local ingredients, including wild strawberries grown on the family's country estate. In Monti, fabulous (and gluten-free) **Fatamorgana ★★★** (Piazza degli Zingari 5; www.gelateriafatamorgana.it; © **06-86391589;** metro Cavour) is the place to try inventive flavors like delicate lavender and chamomile, or zingy avocado, lime, and white wine.

Two exceptions to the rule about avoiding gelato in touristy areas: venerable **Old Bridge Gelateria ★** (Viale Bastioni di Michelangelo; © **328-411-9478**; gelateriaoldbridge.com), which delights customers lined up for the Vatican Museums; and, near Piazza Navona, **Frigidarium ★★★** (Via del Governo Vecchio 112; www.frigidarium-gelateria.com; © **334-995-1184**), whose intense and creamy flavors will make you weep with joy. Have a copetta of mango and coconut for me.

In the Termini area, tiny but sleek **Come il Latte ★★★** (Via Silvio Spaventa 24; www.comeillatte.it; © **06-42903882;** metro Repubblica or Castro Pretorio) turns out artisan gelatos in flavors ranging from salted caramel (yes please!), to mascarpone and crumbled cookies; fruit flavors change according to season.

Trastevere's best artisan gelato, **Fior di Luna ★★★** (Via della Lungaretta 96; www.fiordiluna.com; © **06-64561314;** bus H or 780; tram 8), is made with natural and fair-trade produce. Star flavors are the incredibly rich chocolates, spiked with fig or orange, and an absolutely perfect pistachio.

Armando al Pantheon ★★ ROMAN/VEGETARIAN You know you're sure of your place in the Roman culinary pantheon (sorry, couldn't resist) when you opt to take Saturday nights and Sundays off. Despite the odd hours and a location just a few steps from the *actual* Pantheon, this family-run trattoria serves as many locals as tourists. Chef Armando Gargioli took over the place in 1961, and his sons now run the business. Roman favorites to look out for include *cacio e pepe*, marinated artichokes, and the Jewish-influenced *aliciotti all'indivia* (endive and roasted anchovies; Tuesday and Friday only). A Roman rarity: Vegetarians get their own, fairly extensive, menu. Advance reservations are a must.
Salita dei Crescenzi 31. www.armandoalpantheon.it. © **06-68803034.** Entrees 10€–25€. Mon–Fri 12:30–3pm and 7–11pm; Sat 12:30–3pm. Closed Sat night, Sun, all of Aug. Bus: 30, 70, 81, 87, 492, 628. Tram: 8.

Il Bacaro ★ MODERN ITALIAN   Romantic and low-key, Il Bacaro's setting on a hidden backstreet near the Pantheon offers respite from the traffic and tourist crush. Insanely delicious *primi* and *secondi* (like rich *panzerotti* pasta with chestnuts and red wine sauce, or beef filet with gorgonzola and walnuts) are a welcome departure from the usual Roman fare. Desserts revolve around mousses paired with Bavarian chocolate, hazelnuts, caramel, and pistachio. The 600-label wine list features well-priced varietals from all over Italy. Try to get a prized sidewalk table on a balmy summer evening.

Via degli Spagnoli 27 (near Piazza delle Coppelle). No website. ☎ **06-6872554.** Entrees 14€–26€. Daily noon–midnight. Bus: 30, 70, 81, 87, 492, 628.

La Campana ★★ ROMAN/TRADITIONAL ITALIAN   Family atmosphere and a classic Roman elegance permeate the spacious, well-lit rooms of this venerable address, Rome's oldest restaurant (feeding guests since 1518!). The atmosphere is convivial yet refined, with a lovely mixture of regulars and locals. The broad selection of *antipasti* is displayed on a long table at the entrance, and the daily menu features authentic *cucina romana* that is heavy on offal—if you're not a fan, be sure to bring your Italian/English dictionary. You'll also find classics like *cacio e pepe*, plus myriad vegetarian choices. The wine list includes interesting local labels, and the staff and service are impeccable.

Vicolo della Campana 18. www.ristorantelacampana.com. ☎ **06-6875273.** Entrees 10€–22€. Tues–Sun 12:30–3pm and 7:30–11pm. Metro: Spagna. Bus: 70, 81, 87, 280, 492, 628.

Nonna Betta ★★ ROMAN/JEWISH   Though not strictly kosher, this is the only restaurant in Rome's old Jewish quarter historically owned and managed by Roman Jews. Traditional dishes include delicious *carciofi alla giudia:* deep-fried artichokes served with small morsels like battered cod filet, stuffed and fried zucchini flowers, carrot sticks, and whatever vegetable is in season. Don't forego the *baccalà* with onions and tomato or the tagliolini with chicory and mullet roe. Middle Eastern specialties such as falafel and couscous are on the menu, and all desserts are homemade, including a stellar cake with pine nuts.

Via del Portico d'Ottavia 16. www.nonnabetta.it. ☎ **06-68806263.** Entrees 10€–20€. Wed–Mon 11am–5pm and 6–11pm. Bus: H, 23, 63, 280, 780. Tram 8.

Retrobottega ★★ ROMAN   Fresh, modern, and progressive, the somewhat misnamed Retrobottega is a nice contrast to the well-worn streets of the touristy heart of town. This culinary laboratory, founded by four young, accomplished chefs, is an intimate but convivial choice. Most seats surround the open kitchen and customers interact directly with the chefs—there is no waitstaff. The day's offerings focus on local, seasonal, responsibly sourced ingredients and unexpected pairings, like artichokes with mint and pecorino, or tortelli with anchovies and broccoli Romanesco.

Via della Stelletta 4. www.retro-bottega.com. ☎ **06-68136310.** Entrees 15€–28€. Tues–Sun noon–11:30pm, Sat 7–11:30pm. Bus: 30, 70, 81, 87, 492, 628.

INEXPENSIVE

Alfredo e Ada ★★ ROMAN   No menus here, just the waiter—and it's usually owner Sergio—explaining, in Italian, what the kitchen is preparing that day. Look for classic trattoria comfort food, like eggplant parmigiana, artichoke lasagna, excellent carbonara, or tripe. The whole place oozes character, with shared tables, scribbled walls, and the house wine poured into carafes from a tap in the wall. There are only five tables, so it's best to make a reservation or get here early. This sort of place is becoming rare in Rome—enjoy it while you can.
Via dei Banchi Nuovi 14. ℂ **06-6878842.** Entrees 8€–12€. Tues–Sat noon–3pm and 7–10:30pm. Closed Aug. Bus: 40, 46, 62, 64, 916.

Antico Forno Roscioli ★★ BAKERY   The Rosciolis have been running this celebrated bakery for three generations since the 1970s, though bread has been made here since at least 1824. Today it's the home of the finest crusty sourdough in Rome, assorted cakes, and addictive pastries and biscotti, as well as exceptional Roman-style *pizza bianca* and *pizza rossa* sold by weight. This is largely a takeout joint, with limited seating—and the wider range of pizza toppings is only available from noon to 2:30pm. Around the corner is the wonderful **Roscioli restaurant and** *salumeria* **deli** at Via dei Giubbonari 21 and, at Via Cairoli 16, **Roscioli Caffè,** the latest outpost of the family empire, which offers breakfast treats, cappuccini, and palate-pleasing panini.
Via dei Chiavari 34. www.anticofornoroscioli.it. ℂ **06-6864045.** Pizza from 5€ (sold by weight). Mon–Sat 7am–8pm, Sun 8:30am–7pm. Tram: 8.

La Montecarlo ★★ PIZZA   Dirt-cheap and immensely popular with locals, Montecarlo feels like a big party: Efficient, flirtatious servers sling piping-hot, thin-crusted pies, and the wine and beer flow freely. Sure, they serve other fare, but seriously, come for the pizza. Montecarlo's longtime rival, the equally recommendable **Baffetto** ★★ (www.pizzeriabaffetto. it), is just around the corner on Via del Governo Vecchio. Lines at both joints are long, but move quickly. Cash only.
Vicolo Savelli 11 (at Corso Vittorio Emanuele II). www.lamontecarlo.it. ℂ **06-6861877.** Pizzas 6€–10€. Tues–Sun noon–1am. Bus: 40, 46, 62, 64, 916.

Tridente, the Spanish Steps & Via Veneto

For restaurant locations, see map p. 109. The historic cafes near the Spanish Steps are saturated with history but, sadly, tend to be overpriced tourist traps, where mediocre slices of cake or even a cup of coffee or tea will cost 5€. Nevertheless, you may want to pop inside the two most celebrated institutions: **Babington's Tea Rooms** (www.babingtons.com; ℂ **06-6786027;** daily 10am–9:30pm), established in 1893 at the foot of the Spanish Steps by a couple of English *signore,* and **Caffè Greco,** Via dei Condotti 86 (ℂ **06-6791700;** daily 9am–9pm), Rome's oldest bar, which opened in 1760 and has hosted Keats, Ibsen, Goethe, and many other historical *cognoscenti*.

EXPENSIVE

Al Ceppo ★★ MARCHIGIANA/ROMAN   The setting of this Parioli dining institution is an elegant 19th-century parlor, with dark wood furnishings, chandeliers, fresh flowers, family portraits on the walls, and an open kitchen with a wood-stoked hearth. The menu features regional dishes from the owners' home, the Le Marche region northeast of Rome: *marchigiana*-style rabbit, fish stews, fresh seafood, and grilled meats, all artfully prepared and presented, along with pastas both hearty and delicate. It's reason enough to head north to explore Parioli's many charms.

Via Panama 2 (near Piazza Ungheria). www.ristorantealceppo.it. ℂ **06-8419696.** Entrees 17€–30€. Tues–Sun 12:30–3pm and 7:30–11pm. Mon 7:30pm–11pm. Closed last 2 wks in Aug. Bus: 52, 53, 223, 910. Tram: 3 or 19.

Imàgo ★★★ INTERNATIONAL   The views of Rome from this 6th-floor hotel restaurant are jaw-dropping, the old city laid out before you, glowing pink as the sun goes down. The food is equally special, as chef Francesco Apreda reinterprets Italian cuisine, borrowing heavily from Indian and Japanese culinary traditions. The Michelin-star menu changes seasonally, but may include buffalo mozzarella with bitter puntarelle, fettucini with quali ragu and caviar, or grilled pigeon with mango and lentils. Reservations are essential; jackets required for the gentlemen.

In Hotel Hassler, Piazza della Trinità dei Monti 6. www.imagorestaurant.com. ℂ **06-69934726.** Entrees 33€–56€; tasting menus 130€–170€. Daily 7–10:30pm. Closed most of Jan. Metro: Spagna.

Metamorfosi ★★★ MODERN ITALIAN   For our money, this is the place to have your blow-the-vacation-budget meal in Rome. This prestigious Michelin-starred restaurant is a feast for the eyes and the taste buds, with minimalistic decor and astonishingly inventive cooking. Chef Roy Caceres, a native of Colombia, likes to tell a story with each beautifully crafted dish, from exquisite risotto and pasta preparations to elegant meat and fish interpretations. Be prepared for memorable items like fish soup ravioli, "encased" risotto with mushrooms and hazelnut, or lamb with red mole sauce and chia seeds. Tasting menus are full of delightful surprises, and the artistry of the presentations is jaw-dropping.

Via Giovanni Antonelli 30/32. www.metamorfosiroma.it. ℂ **06-8076839.** Entrees 29€–45€, tasting menus 110€–150€. Mon–Fri 12:30–2:30pm and 8–10:30pm; Sat 8–10:30pm. Bus: 52, 168, 910.

MODERATE

Canova Tadolini ★★ ROMAN   Few restaurants are as steeped in history as this place. Antonio Canova's sculpture studio was kept as a workshop by the descendants of his pupil Adamo Tadolini until 1967, and even today it's littered with tools and sculptures in bronze, plaster, and marble. The whole thing really does seem like a museum, with tables squeezed between models, casts, drapes, and bas-reliefs. The pasta menu features interesting riffs on gnocchi and traditional *alla carbonara,* while entrees might include sea bass with a salt crust or steak salad with arugula and cherry tomatoes.

Via del Babuino 150A–B. www.canovatadolini.com. ℂ **06-32110702.** Entrees 14€– 30€. Daily noon–11pm (bar/cafe from 8am). Metro: Spagna.

Colline Emiliane ★★ EMILIANA-ROMAGNOLA This family-owned restaurant tucked in an alley beside the Trevi Fountain has been serving traditional dishes from Emilia-Romagna since 1931. Service is excellent and so is the food: Classics include *tortelli di zucca* (pumpkin ravioli in butter sauce) and magnificent *tagliatelle alla Bolognese,* the mother of all Italian comfort foods. A menu of *secondi* is heavy on beef. Save room for the walnut-and-caramel cake or lemon meringue pie. Reservations are essential.

Via degli Avignonesi 22 (off Piazza Barberini). www.collineemiliane.com. ℂ **06-4817538.** Entrees 14€–22€. Tues–Sun 12:45–2:45pm; Tues–Sat 7:30–10:45pm. Closed Aug. Metro: Barberini.

Around Termini

For restaurant locations, see map p. 117. Mostly catering to dazed travelers toting wheeled suitcases and crumpled maps, restaurants around Termini don't have to be good in order to bring in business. The following are some of our favorite exceptions to that norm.

MODERATE

Trattoria Monti ★★ REGIONAL/MARCHE Word is definitely out on this cozy, plain-Jane trattoria near Termini station. But that just means you need to reserve in advance to sample outstanding, hearty pastas and meat and game dishes from the Marche region. You will remember the *tortello al rosso d'uovo*—a large, delicate ravioli filled with spinach, ricotta, and egg yolk—for the rest of your life. You also may discover a few new favorites among the territory's underappreciated wines. Vegetarians take heart: There are always 4 or 5 non-meat entrees available.

Via di San Vito 13A (at Via Merulana). ℂ **06-4466573.** Entrees 12€–22€. Tues–Sat 1–2:30pm and 8–10:30pm; Sun 1–2:30pm. Metro: Cavour or Vittorio Emanuele. Bus: 50, 71, 105, 360, 590, 649. Tram: 5 or 14.

Trimani Il Wine Bar ★ MODERN ITALIAN This small bistro and well-stocked wine bar (with a 20-page wine list!) attracts white collars and wine lovers in a modern, relaxed ambience, accompanied by smooth jazz. The refined entrees might include rabbit stuffed with asparagus or Luganega sausage with a zucchini puree. The wines-by-the-glass list changes daily. If you just want a snack to accompany your vino, cheese and salami platters range from 9€ to 14€. The selection at Trimani's vast wine shop next door boggles the oenophilic mind.

Via Cernaia 37B. www.trimani.com. ✆ **06-4469630**. Entrees 12€–21€. Mon–Sat 11:30am–3pm and 5:30pm–midnight. Closed 2 wks mid-Aug. Metro: Repubblica or Castro Pretorio.

INEXPENSIVE

Mercato Centrale Roma ★★ GOURMET MARKET   This ambitious three-story gourmet dining hall and street food hub is the best place to dine in Termini Station, with top-notch purveyors of everything from gourmet pizza to chocolate to truffles, plus a wine bar and a high-end restaurant. The space is inviting, if a little chaotic. Even if you don't have a train to catch, it's worth having lunch or a quick snack here. *Tip:* Walk through the hall and check out all the offerings, then snag a table and have members of your party take turns going to order their food.

Via Giovanni Giolitti 36 (in Termini Station). www.mercatocentrale.it/roma; ✆ **06-46202900**. Daily 8am–midnight. Metro: Termini.

Pinsere ★★ PIZZA   *Pinsa* is an ancient Roman preparation: an oval focaccia made with a blend of four organic flours and olive oil that's left to rise for 2 to 3 days. The result is a crispy yet feather-light single-portion snack perfect for a light lunch. This friendly, small bakery always has an assortment of pies ready to pop in the oven. Favorites come with pureed pumpkin, smoked cheese, and pancetta; classic tomato, basil, and *bufala;* or the surprising combo of ricotta, fresh figs, raisins, pine nuts, and honey. Food to go only, or to eat standing up at one of the few small inside or outside counters. *Note:* Closed Saturday and Sunday.

Via Flavia 98. ✆ **06-42020924**. Pinsa 3.50€–5.50€. Mon–Fri 9am–9pm. Metro: Castro Pretorio. Bus: 60-62, 66, 82, 492, 590, 910.

Trastevere

For restaurant locations, see map p. 119. Popular craft-beer bar **Bir and Fud ★** (p. 160) also serves pizzas and traditional snacks like *supplì* (fried, stuffed rice croquettes) to hungry drinkers. It serves dinner daily and lunch Thursday through Sunday. Hearts and taste buds soar at **Biscottificio Artigiano Innocenti ★★** (Via della Luce 21; ✆ **06-5803926**), where Stefania and her family have been turning out delicate handmade cookies and cakes since the 1920s.

EXPENSIVE

Antico Arco ★★★ CREATIVE ITALIAN   This well-known address for new Italian cuisine consistently delivers exquisite dishes made with the finest local and seasonal ingredients—like wild game-stuffed tortelli with blueberries and sautéed cabbage, or duck breast with wild carrots,

Al fresco dining in Trastevere

ginger, and plum chutney, accompanied by excellent wine and topnotch service. A full meal here makes for a special night out (reservations are essential), but you can also just come to the restaurant's wine bar for vino and some finger food—it pairs nicely with the rapturous *centro storico* views from the nearby terraces of the Janiculum Hill. *Tip:* It's a 15-minute walk uphill from Trastevere, but the climb is gradual and pleasant.

Piazzale Aurelio 7 (at Via San Pancrazio). www.anticoarco.it. *©* **06-5815274.** Entrees 16€–30€, tasting menus 78€. Daily noon–midnight. Bus: 115, 710, 870.

Glass ★★ CONTEMPORARY ROMAN   In an industrial-chic setting of exposed brick, stark white walls, and polished floors, Michelin-starred chef Cristina Bowerman and partner Fabio Spada serve refined food using high-quality ingredients. The menu changes seasonally, but expect carefully prepared shellfish, inventive dishes such as gnocchi with sea urchin and salted lemon, or beef filet with chocolate, mushrooms, and aged foie gras. A vegetarian menu is available. Glass remains one of Rome's hottest tables—reservations are essential.

Vicolo del Cinque 58. www.glass-restaurant.it. *©* **06-58335903.** Entrees 25€–55€; fixed-price menus 90€–150€. Tues–Sun 7:30–11pm. Closed 2 wks Jan, 2 wks July. Bus: 23 or 280.

Spirito DiVino ★★ ROMAN/SLOW FOOD In a medieval synagogue on a 2nd-century street (which you can visit on a cellar tour), the Catalani family does exceptional modern plates (like an appetizer salad of spinach, pine nuts, pomegranate, and gorgonzola) as well as ancient Roman cuisine (like *maiale alla mazio*, a favorite pork dish of Julius Caesar's), food as warm and comforting as the ambience. Finish with the delicately perfumed lavender panna cotta, a cream-based dessert.

Via dei Genovesi 31 (at Vicolo dell'Atleta). www.ristorantespiritodivino.com. ⓒ **6-5896689**. Entrees 14€–26€. Mon–Sat 7–11:30pm. Bus: H, 23, 44, 280. Tram: 8.

MODERATE

Cacio e Pepe ★ ROMAN This ultra-traditional trattoria, complete with paper tablecloths, a TV showing the game, the owner chatting up the ladies, and a bustling crowd of patrons waiting to be seated, is a Trastevere neighborhood stalwart. Start with cheapo plates of fried tidbits, from rice *suppli* to cod to vegetables, then move on to the namesake pasta *cacio e pepe* or other classic Roman pasta dishes—and be ready for hearty portions. For *secondo*—if you have room left—consider *polpette* (stewed meatballs), *saltimbocca alla romana* (veal cutlets with sage and ham), or grilled meats, all sold reasonably priced. They even have pizza for the kids.

Vicolo del Cinque 15. www.osteriacacioepepe.it. ⓒ **06-89572853**. Main courses 9€–19€. Mon–Fri 6:30pm–midnight; Sat–Sun 1pm–midnight. Bus: 23, 280. Tram: 8.

Da Enzo ★★ ROMAN For traditional Roman cuisine, try this down-homey, non-touristy, family-run trattoria. *Cucina romana,* including classic carbonara, *amatriciana,* and *cacio e pepe,* win the gold, as do meat-heavy *secondi* like stewed tripe, or meatballs braised in tomato sauce. Local wines can be ordered by the jug or glass, and desserts (try the mascarpone with wild strawberries) come served in either full or half portions (a good thing, considering Enzo's hefty servings). A few outdoor tables look out on some of Trastevere's characteristic alleyways.

Via dei Vascellari 29. www.daenzoal29.com. ⓒ **06-5812260**. Entrees 9€–15€. Mon–Sat 12:30–3pm and 7:30–11pm. Bus: 23, 44, 280. Tram: 8.

Osteria La Gensola ★★★ SEAFOOD/ROMAN Considered one of the best seafood destinations in Rome, this warm and welcoming family-run restaurant feels like a true Trastevere home; the decor is cozy, with soft lighting and a life-size wood-carved tree in the middle of the main dining room. Fish-lovers come for heavenly spaghetti with fresh clams, *polpettine* (meatballs) made with tuna, and other traditional Roman cuisine with a marine twist. The grill churns out succulent beefsteaks, among non-fish dishes. Reservations are a must on weekends.

Piazza della Gensola 15. www.osterialagensola.it. ⓒ **06-58332758**. Entrees 15–20€. Daily 12:30–3pm and 7:30–11:30pm. Bus: H, 23, 280, 780. Tram: 8.

4

ROME

Where to Eat in Rome

INEXPENSIVE

Dar Poeta ★ PIZZA   Ranking among the best pizzerias in Rome, "the poet" is a fine place to enjoy a classic Roman pizza margherita (tomato sauce, mozzarella, and fresh basil) or a more creative combo like the *patataccia* (potatoes, creamed zucchini, and *speck* [a smoked prosciutto]). The lines are long to eat in, but you can also order takeout. The decadent dessert calzone is filled with fresh ricotta and Nutella.

Vicolo del Bologna 45. www.darpoeta.com. ✆ **06-5880516.** Pizzas 5€–9€. Daily noon–midnight. Bus: 23, 280.

Testaccio

The slaughterhouses of Rome's old meatpacking district (see map p. 68) have been transformed into art venues, markets, and the museum **MACRO** (p. 128), but restaurants here still specialize in (though are not limited to) meats from the *quinto quarto* (the "fifth quarter")—the leftover parts of an animal after slaughter, typically offal like sweetbreads, tripe, tails, and other goodies you won't find on most American menus. This is an area to eat *cucina romana*—either in the restaurants below or from street-food stalls in the **Nuovo Mercato di Testaccio** (p. 157). Food-themed tours of Rome invariably end up here.

EXPENSIVE

Checchino dal 1887 ★★ ROMAN   Often mischaracterized as an offal-only joint, this establishment, opened in 1887 across from Rome's now-defunct abattoir, is a special-night-out type of place, serving wonderful *bucatini all'amatriciana* and veal saltimbocca—as well as hearty plates of spleens, lungs, and livers. Checchino is a pricier choice than most of the other restaurants in this area, but Romans from all over the city keep coming back when they want the real thing. Despite its meat-centric leanings, Checchino also has a decent vegetarian menu. They will also make gluten-free pasta.

Via di Monte Testaccio 30 (at Via Galvani). www.checchino-dal-1887.com. ✆ **06-5746316.** Main course 12€–27€. Tasting menus 40€–65€. Tues–Sat 12:30–3pm and 8–11:45pm, Sun 12:30–3pm. Closed Aug and part of Dec–Jan. Metro: Piramide. Bus: 83, 673, 719. Tram: 3.

MODERATE

Flavio al Velavevodetto ★ ROMAN   Flavio's plain dining room is burrowed out of the side of Rome's most unusual "hill": a large mound made from amphorae discarded during the Roman era (see p. 68). Food-lovers, however, come here for classic Roman pastas like *cacio e pepe* and *amatriciana*, plus *quinto quarto* (nose-to-tail) entrees at fair prices. Hearty dishes like *polpette al sugo* (meatballs in red sauce), *coda alla vaccinara* (oxtail), and *involtini* (stuffed rolled veal) are good for sharing. *Note:*

Maybe it was just an off day, but on our last trip to Flavio our meal was just okay—hence we dinged them a star.

Via di Monte Testaccio 97–99. www.ristorantevelavevodetto.it. ℰ **06-5744194.** Entrees 9€–20€. Daily 12:30–3pm and 7:30–11pm. Metro: Piramide. Bus: 83, 673, 719. Tram: 3.

Osteria degli Amici ★★ MODERN ROMAN   On the corner of nightclub central and the hill of broken amphorae, this intimate and friendly *osteria* serves both traditional Roman classics and creative iterations thereof. Claudio and Alessandro base their menu on produce from the nearby market and their combined experience in famous kitchens around the world. Signature musts include fish- and seafood-based pastas and mains, golden-fried mozzarella *in carrozza,* and a range of pastas from classic *carbonara* to *paccheri* tubes with shrimp, mint, and zucchini. Leave room for the apple tartlet with cinnamon gelato.

Via Nicola Zabaglia 25. www.osteriadegliamiciroma.it. ℰ **06-5781466.** Entrees 11€–20€. Wed–Mon 12:30–3pm and 8pm–midnight. Metro: Piramide. Bus: 83, 673, 719. Tram: 3.

Porto Fluviale ★ MODERN ITALIAN   This multifunctional restaurant—part trattoria, part street-food stall, part pizzeria—can accommodate pretty much whatever you fancy. The decor is vaguely industrial, with a daytime clientele made up of families and white collars—the vibe gets younger after dark. From the various menus, best bets are the 30 or so *cicchetti,* small plates that allow you to taste the kitchen's range. Both the locale and the menus are highly kid-friendly.

Via del Porto Fluviale 22. www.portofluviale.com. ℰ **06-5743199.** Cicchetti (tapas) 3€–5€, entrees 7€–19€. Sun–Thurs 10:30am–2am, Fri–Sat 10:30am–3am. Metro: Piramide. Bus: 23, 673, 715, 716.

Romeo Chef & Baker ★★ MODERN ITALIAN/PIZZA   In a cavernous former car showroom at the foot of the Avetine Hill, this ambitious venture from dynamic duo Cristina Bowerman and Fabio Spada of **Glass** (p. 150) marries French bistro, street food, craft cocktail, old-school pizzeria, and gourmet gelateria. The ultramodern space has seating for 500 (!), plus standing noshing/cocktail space for hundreds more. It's a real experience, offering the chance to sample Bowerman's creations—she's a Michelin-starred chef—at everyday prices.

Piazza dell'Emporio 28. www.romeo.roma.it. ℰ **06-32110120.** Entrees 15€–20€. Metro: Piramide. Bus: 23, 75, 280, 716. Tram: 3.

Trattoria Perilli ★★ ROMAN   Dine elbow-to-elbow with locals and enjoy the old-school atmosphere at this beloved institution of Roman *ristorazione.* With zero pretense, Perilli's formally attired waitstaff serve unadulterated renditions of Roman classics. The dishes are reliable, from pasta standbys like *carbonara* and *cacio e pepe* to grilled meats to that most English of Italian desserts, *zuppa inglese* (literally "English soup," or trifle). It's a fun and reasonably affordable place to go for a real four-course meal of *antipasto, primo, secondo,* and *dolce.* Reservations recommended.

Via Marmorata 39 (at Via Galvani). No website. ℰ **06-5742415.** Entrees 11€–18€. Thurs–Tues 12:30–3pm and 7:30–11pm. Metro: Piramide. Bus: 23, 75, 280, 716. Tram: 3.

INEXPENSIVE

Da Remo ★★ PIZZA   Mentioning "Testaccio" and "pizza" in the same sentence elicits one typical response from locals: Da Remo, a Roman institution. In the summer especially, come early or be prepared to wait for a table. Every crisp-crusted, perfectly foldable pizza is made for all to see behind open counters. The most basic ones (margherita and marinara) start at around 7€. If it's too crowded on a summer evening, order your pizza for takeout and eat it in the park across the street.

Piazza Santa Maria Liberatrice 44. No website. ℰ **06-5746270.** Most pizzas 6€–8€. Mon–Sat 7pm–1am. Bus: 83, 673, 719.

ROME SHOPPING

While Rome's status as a shopping capital is somewhat eclipsed by fashion mecca Milan (see p. 489), it's still a magnet for high-end shoppers, foodies, and lovers of antiques. In our limited space below we've summarized streets and areas known for their shops. Keep in mind that the monthly rent on the famous streets is very high, and those costs are passed on to you. Note that **sales** usually run twice a year, starting in January and July.

The Top Shopping Streets & Areas

AROUND PIAZZA DI SPAGNA   Most of Rome's haute couture and seriously upscale shopping fans out from the bottom of the Spanish Steps. **Via Condotti** is probably Rome's poshest shopping street, where you'll find Prada, Gucci, Bulgari, and the like. A few more down-to-earth stores have opened, but it's still largely a playground for the super-rich. Neighboring **Via Borgognona** is another street where the merchandise is chic and ultra-expensive, but thanks to its pedestrian-only access and handsome baroque and neoclassical facades, it offers a nicer window-browsing experience. Shops are more densely concentrated on **Via Frattina,** the third member of this trio of upscale streets. Chic boutiques for adults and kids rub shoulders with ready-to-wear fashions, high-end chains, and a few tourist tat vendors. It's usually crowded with shoppers who appreciate the lack of motor traffic.

VIA COLA DI RIENZO   The commercial heart of the Prati neighborhood, this long, straight street runs from the Tiber to Piazza Risorgimento and is known for stores selling a variety of merchandise at reasonable prices—from jewelry to fashionable clothing, bags, and shoes. Among the most prestigious is the historic Roman perfume store (with products for men and women), **Bertozzini Profumeria dal 1913,** at no. 192 (www.bertozzinidal1913.it). The department store **Coin** is at no. 173 (with a large supermarket in the basement), the largest branch of venerable gourmet food store **Castroni** at no. 196 (www.castroni.it), and the smaller, more selective gourmet grocery **Franchi** at no. 200 (www.franchi.it).

VIA DEL CORSO　With less of a glamour quotient (and less stratospheric prices) than Via Condotti or Via Borgognona, Via del Corso boasts affordable styles aimed at younger consumers. Occasional gems are scattered amid international shops selling jeans and sports equipment. The most interesting stores are toward the Piazza del Popolo end of the street (**Via del Babuino** here has a similar profile). The farther south you walk (towards the Vittoriano monument), the more narrow the sidewalks—and generally, the more tacky the stores. *Tip:* If you are shopping with young children, it's useful to know that the upper part of Via del Corso (from Piazza Colonna to Piazza del Popolo) is largely car-free, save for taxis and the occasional bus.

VIA DEI CORONARI　An antique-lover's souk. If you're shopping, or just window-shopping for antiques, art, or vintage-style souvenir prints, then spend an hour walking the length of this pretty, pedestrian-only street.

CAMPO DE'FIORI　Though the campo itself is now chockablock with restaurants, the streets leading up to it, notably **Via dei Giubbonari** and **Via Dei Baullari,** offer edgy and often one-of-a-kind fashions. Boutiques go in and out of business with dizzying frequency, but something interesting is always popping up.

VIA DEL GOVERNO VECCHIO　It's Vintage Valhalla on this pretty street that winds parallel to Corso Vittorio Emanuele II. Lined with tiny resale shops that are stuffed to the gills with merchandise, Via del Governo Vecchio also has great places to eat and drink, particularly on the end closest to Piazza di San Pantaleo. Poke into vintage treasure trove **Dafano Omero** (at no. 110) or **Ciznia** (no. 45) before taking a restorative gelato break at **Frigidarium** (p. 144).

VIA MARGUTTA　This beautiful, tranquil street is home to numerous art stalls and artists' studios—Federico Fellini used to live here—although these days all the stores tend to offer the same sort of antiques and mediocre paintings. You have to shop hard to find real quality. Highlights include **Bottega del Marmoraro** (at no. 53b) and **Saddlers Union** (at no. 11; www.saddlersunion.com) for exquisite (and exquisitely priced) handmade leather items.

MONTI　Rome's most fashion-conscious central neighborhood has a pleasing mix of artisan retailers, vintage boutiques, and honest, everyday

Upscale shopping on Via Condotti.

stores frequented by locals, with not a brand name in sight. Roam the length of **Via del Boschetto** for one-off fashions, designer ateliers, and unique homewares. In fact, you can roam in every direction from the spot where Via del Boschetto meets **Via Panisperna.** Turn on nearby **Via Urbana** or **Via Leonina,** where boutiques jostle for space with cafes that are ideal for a break or light lunch. Via Urbana also hosts the weekend **Mercatomonti** (see "Rome's Best Markets," below).

Rome's Best Markets

Campo de' Fiori ★   Central Rome's food market has been running since at least the 1800s. It's no longer the place to find a produce bargain (though the fruit and veg displays are dazzling and colorful) and it tends to attract more tourists than locals, but it's still a genuine slice of Roman life in one of its most attractive squares. The market runs Monday through Saturday 7am to 1 or 2pm. Campo de' Fiori. No phone. Bus: H, 40, 46, 62-64, 280, 780. Tram: 8.

Eataly ★   Remember how cool the Hard Rock Café was when there was just *one* of them? Now that branches of Eataly, the mega-grocery store devoted to Italian food, have opened around the world, some of the novelty has been lost. For lovers of the brand, this four-floor homage to all things Italiano is a must-see, must-shop experience. Still, for foodie souvenirs to carry home, we prefer to buy from small local shops. *Tip:* Eataly is great for filling a gourmet picnic basket on your way out to Ostia Antica or Tivoli (see p. 162 and 164). Piazzale XII Ottobre 1492 (at Ostiense train station). www.roma.eataly.it. © 06-90279201. Metro: Piramide.

Mercatomonti ★★ Everything from contemporary glass jewelry to vintage cameras, handmade clothes for kids and adults, and one-off designs are sold here in the heart of trendy Monti. The indoor market runs Saturdays and Sundays September to June, from 10am to 8pm. Via Leonina 46. www.mercatomonti.com. No phone. Metro: Cavour.

Nuovo Mercato di Testaccio (New Testaccio Market) ★★★ Traditional food and produce stalls meet street food central in this modernist, sustainably powered market building. It's not just the best place to go produce shopping, but a terrific stop for a lunch of *suppli* (fried rice balls) and craft beer (at **Food Box** ★★, Box 66), meat and sauce-stuffed panini (at **Mordi e Vai** ★★, Box 15, www.mordievai.it), or an espresso and something sweet from **Chicchi e Lettere** ★ (Box 43). There are also clothes and kitchenware stalls, but the food is the star. The market runs Monday through Saturday 7am to 3:30pm. Btw. Via Luigi Galvani and Via Aldo Manuzio (at Via Benjamin Franklin). www.mercatoditestaccio.it. No phone. Metro: Piramide. Bus: 83, 673, 719.

Porta Portese ★ Trastevere's vast weekly flea market stretches all the way from the Porta Portese gate along Via di Porta Portese to Viale di Trastevere. You have to wade through a lot of junk (and a sea of humanity—hold tight to your belongings), but there are good stalls for vintage housewares, clothing, and collectibles. It runs Sundays from dawn until midafternoon. Via di Porta Portese. No phone. Tram: 8.

ENTERTAINMENT & NIGHTLIFE

Several English-language outlets offer current information about nightlife and cultural events in the Eternal City. *Wanted in Rome* (www.wantedinrome.com) has listings of opera, rock, English-language cinema showings, and such and gives an insider look at expat Rome. **Un Ospite a Roma** (www.unospitearoma.it) offers comprehensive details on cultural events and kid-friendly pursuits. *Romeing* (www.romeing.it) is worth consulting, especially for contemporary arts and culture.

Unless you're dead set on making the Roman nightclub circuit, try what might be a far livelier and less expensive option—sitting late into the evening on **Piazza della Rotonda** (the Pantheon), **Piazza del Popolo,** or one of Rome's other piazzas, all for the (admittedly inflated) cost of an espresso or a Campari and soda. If you're a clubber who likes it loud and

Rome, Illuminated

When the sun goes down, Rome's palaces, ruins, fountains, and monuments are bathed in a theatrical white light. During your stay in Rome, be sure to make time for a memorable evening stroll past the solemn pillars of old temples or the cascading torrents of Renaissance fountains glowing under the blue-black sky.

The **Fountain of the Naiads** ("Fontana delle Naiadi") on Piazza della Repubblica, the **Fountain of the Tortoises** ("Fontana della Tartarughe") on Piazza Mattei, the **Fountain of Acqua Paola** ("Fontanone") at the top of the Janiculum Hill, and the **Trevi Fountain** (p. 111) are particularly beautiful at night. The **Capitoline Hill** (or Campidoglio) is magnificently lit after dark, with its Renaissance facades glowing like jewel boxes. The view of the Roman Forum seen from the rear of Piazza del Campidoglio is perhaps the grandest in Rome (see "Three Free Views to Remember for a Lifetime" box, p. 93). If you're across the Tiber, the Vatican's **Piazza San Pietro** (p. 78) is impressive at night without the crowds. The combination of illuminated architecture, baroque fountains, and sidewalk shows makes **Piazza Navona** (p. 101) even more delightful at night.

late, jump in a cab to **Monte Testaccio** or **Via del Pigneto** and bar-hop wherever your fancy takes you. In Trastevere, there's always a bit of life on **Via del Politeama** where it meets **Piazza Trilussa.** In the *centro storico,* a nice *aperitivo-cena* scene unfolds along **Via del Governo Vecchio.**

Performing Arts & Live Music

Rome's music scene doesn't have the same vibrancy as Florence's (p. 224), nor the high-quality opera of Milan's **La Scala** (p. 491) or **La Fenice** in Venice (p. 413). Still, classical music fans are well catered to here. In addition to the major venues featured below, be on the lookout for concerts and one-off events in churches and salons around the city. Check **www.operainroma.com** for a calendar of opera and ballet staged by the Opera in Roma association at enchanting venues across the city. The **Pontificio Instituto di Musica Sacra,** Piazza Sant'Agostino 20A (www.musicasacra.va; *✆* **06-6638792**), and **All Saints' Anglican Church,** Via del Babuino 153 (www.accademiadoperaitaliana.it; *✆* **06-7842702**), both regularly run classical music and operatic evenings.

Alexanderplatz Jazz Club ★ Alexanderplatz has been the home of Rome's jazz scene since the early 1980s. If there's a good act in the city, you'll find it here. After closing down in 2018, the club is back in business, with live music 7 nights a week. Via Ostia 9. www.alexanderplatzjazzclub.com. *✆* **06-39742171.** Cover usually 10€. Metro: Ottaviano. Bus: 23, 70, 492, 913, 990.

Auditorium–Parco della Musica ★★ This exciting multipurpose center for the arts, designed by Renzo Piano, brings a refreshing breath of modernity to Rome. The schedule features lots of aging rockers and eclectic singer-songwriter acts, as well as traditional orchestras. Great cafes and a bookstore on-site, too. Viale Pietro de Coubertin 30. www.auditorium. com. © **06-80241281.** Bus: 53, 168, 910, 982. Tram: 2.

Teatro dell'Opera di Roma ★★ Here you'll find marquee operas such as *La Traviata, Carmen,* and *Tosca;* classical concerts from top-rank orchestras; and such ballets as *Giselle, Swan Lake,* and *The Nutcracker.* In summer the action moves outdoors for unforgettable open-air operatic performances at the ruined **Baths of Caracalla** (p. 88). Piazza Beniamino Gigli 1 (at Via del Viminale). www.operaroma.it. © **06-4817003** (box office). Tickets 25€–150€. Metro: Repubblica.

Cafes

Remember: In Rome and everywhere else in Italy, if you just want to drink a quick coffee and bolt, walk up to *il banco* (the bar), order *"un caffè, per favore"* or *"un cappuccino,"* and stay at the bar. They will make it for you to drink on the spot. It will usually cost more (at least double) to sit down to drink it (if you're in touristy areas—which you'll most likely be!), and outdoor table service is the most expensive way to go. Even in the heart of the city center, a short coffee *al banco* should cost no more than 1€; add around .30€ for a *cappuccino.* Expect to pay up to five times that price if you sit outdoors on a marquee piazza. Most cafes in Rome serve a decent cup of coffee, but here's a small selection of places worth hunting down.

Outdoor cafes dot the streets of Rome

With its shabby-chic interior and namesake fig tree backdrop to charming outdoor seating, **Bar del Fico ★** (Piazza del Fico 26; www.bardelfico.com; © **06 6880 8413**) is one of Rome's most beloved aperitivo spots and a coveted see-and-be-seen nightlife destination. **Sant'Eustachio il Caffè ★★** (Piazza Sant'Eustachio 82; www.santeustachioilcaffe.it; © **06-68802048**) roasts its own fair-trade Arabica beans and draws a friendly crowd a few deep at the bar. (Unless you ask, the coffee comes with sugar.) Debate still rages among Romans as to whether the city's best cup of coffee is served at Sant'Eustachio or **Tazza d'Oro** ★, near the Pantheon (Via degli Orfani 84; www.tazzadoro coffeeshop.com; ✆ **06-6789792**). Jacketed baristas work at 100mph at **Spinelli** ★ (Via dei Mille 60; ✆ **06-31055552**), a no-nonsense locals' café near Termini station.

Wine Bars, Cocktail Bars & Craft Beer Bars

The mass social phenomenon of the *aperitivo* (happy hour) provides great insight into the particular ways of real Romans. It started in hard-working northern cities like Milan, where you'd go to a bar after leaving the office and, for the price of one drink, get access to an unlimited buffet of high-quality food—often with cheese, cured meats, bruschetta, and pasta salad. Luckily for Rome, the custom trickled down here, and now the city is filled with casual little places to drop in for a drink (from 6 or 7pm onward) and eat to your heart's content. Apertivo spreads vary in quantity and quality, but generally you'll pay less than 10€ per person for a drink and buffet. All the places listed here are fine for families, too—Italian kids love *aperitivo* (minus the alcohol)! Look for signs in the window and follow your nose. The **Monti** neighborhood is a good place to begin. The **Terre e Domus della Provincia di Roma** (see p. 143) also does good *aperitivo*.

Ai Tre Scalini ★   This little *bottiglieria* (wine bar) is the soul of Monti. There's a traditional menu, as well as a wine list sourced from across Italy. Arrive early or call for a table: This place is usually jammed. Via Panisperna 251. www.aitrescalini.org. ✆ **06-48907495.** Metro: Cavour.

Barnum Café ★★   An honest-to-goodness cocktail bar (with wine and craft beers to boot), Barnum draws a grown-up crowd getting mellowly buzzed—making it a nice alternative to the nighttime antics at Campo de'Fiori. It's also a good morning stop for caffe and cornetti. Via del Pellegrino 87. www.barnumcafe.com. ✆ **06-64760483.** Bus: 40, 46, 62, 64, 916.

Bir and Fud ★   Around 15 beers are on tap (most of them Italian craft brews, some as strong as 9%) at this Trastevere hub, perfect for washing down carb-heavy snacks like pizza and *supplì* (fried rice balls). It's 5€ for a small beer. Via Benedetta 23. www.birandfud.it. ✆ **06-5894016.** Bus: 23, 280.

Cavour 313 ★★   This traditional wine bar is as genuine as you will find this close to the ancient ruins. It serves over 30 wines by the glass (from 3.50€) as well as cold cuts, cheese, and vegetable platters, or excellent carpaccio. Closed Sunday in summer. Via Cavour 313. www.cavour313.it. ✆ **06-6785496.** Metro: Colosseo and Cavour.

Ex Circus ★   This convivial hub for digital nomads, hungry tourists on a budget, and aperitivo drinkers seeking an ample spread is just a few blocks from Piazza Navona. They also do great salads, smoothies, and Sunday brunch. Via della Vetrina 15. ex-circus.business.site. ℂ **06-97619258.** Bus: 30, 70, 81, 87, 492, 628.

Freni e Frizioni ★★   Trastevere's "Brakes and Clutches" is a former mechanics garage turned nighttime hot spot, with an ethnic-inflected *aperitivo* spread (think curried risotto). On the adjacent square, an effervescent crowd lounges against stone walls and parked *motorini*. Via del Politeama 4–6 (near Piazza Trilussa). www.freniefrizioni.com. ℂ **06-45497499.** Bus: 23, 280, or H. Tram: 8.

La Bottega del Caffè ★   Beers, wine, cocktails, *aperitivo*—there's a little of everything at one of Monti's busiest neighborhood bars. Piazza Madonna dei Monti 5. ℂ **06-64741578.** Metro: Cavour.

Litro ★★   This wine bar in Monteverde Vecchio (a residential area above Trastevere) serves natural wines, cocktails, and snacks sourced from Lazio-based purveyors of cured meats and cheeses, plus bruschetta and stellar alcoholic sorbets. An entire menu is devoted to mezcal, tequila's smoky cousin. Via Fratelli Bonnet 5. ℂ **06-45447639.** Bus: 75 or 982.

Open Baladin ★★   If anyone ever tells you "Italians don't do good beer," send them to this bar near the Ghetto. A 40-long row of taps lines the bar, with beers from their own Piedmont brewery and across Italy. Via degli Specchi 5–6. open-baladin-roma.business.site. ℂ **06-6838989.** Tram: 8.

Salotto42 ★★   It's all fancy cocktails and well-chosen wines at this über-hip "bookbar" set opposite the columned facade of 2nd-century Hadrian's Temple (near the Pantheon). This makes for a classy after-dinner stop. It also does shared plates, fresh juices, smoothies, and infused teas. Piazza di Pietra 42 (off Via del Corso). www.salotto42.it. ℂ **06-6785804.** Bus: 51, 62, 63, 80, 83, 85, 117, 160, 492, 628.

Stravinskij Bar ★   An evening at this award-winning cocktail bar inside one of Rome's most famous grand hotels is always a regal affair. Mixology, ingredients, and canapés are all topnotch. Inside Hotel de Russie, Via del Babuino 9. ℂ **06-32888874.** Metro: Spagna.

Vale la Pena Pub ★   This casual, tongue-in-cheek brewpub with a social mission (see p. 143) offers beer from its own microbrewery, served by inmates from Rome's Rebibbia prison. It fits like a glove in the working-class Tuscolano district. Via Eurialo 22. www.valelapena.it. ℂ **06-87606875.** Metro: Furio Camillo.

SIDE TRIPS FROM ROME
Ostia Antica ★★

24km (15 miles) SW of Rome

The ruins of Rome's ancient port are a must-see for anyone who can't make it to Pompeii. It's an easier day trip than Pompeii, on a similar theme: the chance to wander around the preserved ruins of an ancient Roman settlement that has been barely touched since its abandonment.

Ostia, at the mouth of the Tiber, was the port of Rome, serving as the gateway for riches from the far corners of the Empire. Founded in the 4th century B.C., it became a major port and naval base under two later emperors, Claudius and Trajan. A prosperous city developed, full of temples, baths, theaters, and patrician homes.

Ostia flourished between the 1st and 3rd centuries and survived until around the 9th century before it was abandoned. It became little more than a malaria bed, a buried ghost city fading into history. A papal-sponsored commission launched a series of digs in the 19th century; however, the major work of unearthing was carried out under Mussolini's orders from 1938 to 1942. The city is only partially dug out today, but it's believed that all the chief monuments have been uncovered. It has quite a few impressive ruins—this is no dusty field like the Circus Maximus.

Note: Ostia is a mostly flat site, but the Roman streets underfoot are all clad in giant basalt cobblestones—wear comfortable walking shoes.

ESSENTIALS

ARRIVING   Take the Metro to Piramide, changing lines there for the Lido train to Ostia Antica. Departures to Ostia run every half-hour; the trip is 25 minutes and included in the price of a Metro single-journey ticket or **Roma Pass** (see p. 65). It's just a 5-minute walk to the excavations from the Metro stop: Exit the station, walk over the footbridge, and continue straight until you reach the car park. The ticket booth is to the left.

VISITOR INFORMATION   The site opens daily at 8:30am. Closing time is at dusk, so it ranges seasonally, from 7:15pm in spring/summer (Apr–Aug) to 4:30pm fall/winter (Nov–Feb 15); check at **www.ostiaantica. beniculturali.it** or call ℂ **06-56350215.** The ticket office closes 1 hour before the ruins close. Admission costs 10€, free for ages 17 and under and 65 and over. The inexpensive map on sale at the ticket booth is a wise investment.

PARKING   The car park, on Viale dei Romagnoli, costs a few euro per day, but it is fairly small. Arrive early if you're driving.

EXPLORING OSTIA ANTICA

The principal monuments are all labeled. On arrival, visitors first pass the *necropoli* (burial grounds, always outside the city gates in Roman towns

Around Rome

493 Lago di Bracciano

Bracciano

Anguillara

Monti Sabatini

Campagnano di Roma

A1

Tiber

Monterotondo

Mentana

4

Monti Sabini

E80

Villa Gregoriana

Cerveteri

E80

A12

Vatican City

ROME

Tivoli

Villa Adriana

A24

Villa d'Este

Palestrina

Fregene

Tiber

Rome Ciampino Airport

7

Frascati

Marino

CASTELLI ROMANI

A1

Rome Fiumicino Airport

Fiumicino

Lido di Ostia

Ostia Antica

Castel Gandolfo

Albano

Ariccia

Genzano

Rocca di Papa

Nemi

Velletri

Tyrrhenian Sea

601

Pomezia

Ardea

148

Aprília

Cisterna di Latina

0   100 mi
0   100 km

207

To Naples & Pompeii ↘

156

and cities). The main route follows the giant cobblestones of the **Decumanus ★** (the main street) into the heart of Ostia. The **Piazzale delle Corporazioni ★★** is like an early version of Wall Street: This square contained nearly 75 corporations, the nature of their businesses identified by the patterns of preserved mosaics. Nearby, Greek dramas were performed at the **Teatro,** built in the early days of the Empire. The theater as it looks today is the result of much rebuilding. Every town the size of Ostia had a **Forum ★**, and the layout is still intact: A well-preserved **Capitolium** (once the largest temple in Ostia) faces the remains of the 1st-century-A.D. **Temple of Roma and Augustus.**

Elsewhere in the grid of streets are the ruins of the **Thermopolium ★★**, which was a bar; its name means "sale of hot drinks." **Casa Diana ★,** an *insula* (a Roman block of apartments), remains, its rooms arranged around an inner courtyard. The **Terme di Nettuno ★** was a vast baths complex; climb the building at its entrance for an aerial view of its well-preserved mosaics.

WHERE TO EAT IN OSTIA ANTICA

There is no real need to eat by the ruins—a half-day here should suffice, and Ostia is within easy reach of Rome's city center. The obvious alternative is a picnic; the well-stocked food emporium **Eataly** (see p. 156) is just a couple of minutes from the Lido platform at Piramide Metro station, making it easy to grab provisions when you change trains. There are perfect picnic spots beside fallen columns or old temple walls. If you crave a sit-down meal, trattoria **Allo Sbarco di Enea,** Viale dei Romagnoli 675 (www.allosbarcodienea.it, © 06-5650034) is right outside the archaeological park. There's also a snack and coffee bar at the site.

Tivoli & the Villas ★★

32km (20 miles) E of Rome

Perched high on a hill east of Rome, ancient Tivoli has always been a place of retreat from the city. In Roman times it was known as Tibur, a retirement town for the wealthy; during the Renaissance it again became the playground of the rich, who built their country villas here. You need a full day to do justice to the gardens and villas that remain—especially if the Villa Adriana is on your list, as indeed it should be—so set out early.

ESSENTIALS

ARRIVING   Tivoli is 32km (20 miles) east of Rome on Via Tiburtina, about an hour's drive with traffic (the Rome–L'Aquila *autostrada,* A24, is usually faster). If you don't have a car, take Metro Line B to Ponte Mammolo. After exiting the station, transfer to a Cotral bus for Tivoli (www.cotralspa.it). Cotral buses depart every 15 to 30 minutes during the day. Villa d'Este is in Tivoli itself, close to the bus stop; to get to Villa Adriana you need to catch a regional bus from town.

EXPLORING TIVOLI AND THE VILLAS

Villa Adriana (Hadrian's Villa) ★★★ HISTORIC SITE/RUINS Globe-trotting Emperor Hadrian spent the last 3 years of his life in grand style. Less than 6km (3¾ miles) from Tivoli, between A.D. 118 and 134 he built one of the greatest estates ever conceived, filling acre upon acre with architectural wonders he'd seen in his travels. Hadrian erected theaters, baths, temples, fountains, gardens, and canals, filling palaces and temples with sculpture, some of which now rest in the museums of Rome. In later centuries, barbarians, popes, and cardinals, as well as anyone who needed a slab of marble, carted off much that made the villa so spectacular. But enough of the fragmented ruins remain to inspire a real sense of awe.

The most outstanding remnant is the **Canopo ★★★,** a re-creation of the Egyptian town of Canopus with its famous Temple of the Serapis. The ruins of a rectangular area, **Piazza d'Oro,** are still surrounded by a double portico. Likewise, the **Edificio con Pilastri Dorici (Doric Pillared Hall)** remains, with its pilasters with bases and capitals holding up a Doric architrave. The apse and the ruins of some magnificent vaulting are found at the **Grandi Terme (Great Baths),** while only the north wall remains of the **Pecile ★,** otherwise known as the *Stoà Poikile di Atene* or "Painted

Porch," which Hadrian discovered in Athens and had reproduced here. The best is saved for last—the **Teatro Marittimo** ★★★, a circular theater in ruins, with its central building enveloped by a canal spanned by small swing bridges.

Largo Marguerite Yourcenar 1, Tivoli. www.villaadriana.beniculturali.it. © **0774-312070**. 10€. Daily 8:30am–sunset. Bus: 4 from Tivoli.

Villa d'Este ★★ PARK/GARDEN   Like Hadrian centuries before, Cardinal Ippolito d'Este of Ferrara in the mid-16th century ordered this villa built on a Tivoli hillside. The dank Renaissance structure, with its second-rate paintings, is not that interesting; the big draw for visitors is the **spectacular gardens** ★★★, designed by Pirro Ligorio. As you descend the cypress-studded garden slope you're rewarded with everything from lilies to gargoyles spouting water, torrential streams, and waterfalls. The loveliest fountain is the **Fontana dell Ovato** ★★, by Ligorio. Nearby is the most spectacular engineering achievement: the **Fontana dell'Organo Idraulico (Fountain of the Hydraulic Organ)** ★★, dazzling with music and water jets in front of a baroque chapel (the fountain "plays" every 2 hours from 10:30am). The moss-covered **Fontana dei Draghi (Fountain of the Dragons)**, also by Ligorio, and the so-called **Fontana di Vetro (Fountain of Glass)**, by Bernini, are also worth seeking out, as is the main promenade, lined with 100 spraying fountains. The garden is worth hours of exploration, but it involves a lot of walking, with some steep climbs.

The musical Fountain of the Hydraulic Organ and fishpond, Villa d'Este.

Piazza Trento 5, Tivoli. www.villadeste tivoli.info. © **0774-312070**. 10€. Tues–Sun 8:30am to 1 hr. before sunset; Mon from 2pm. Bus: Cotral service from Ponte Mammolo (Roma–Tivoli); the bus stops near the entrance.

Villa Gregoriana ★ PARK/GARDEN   Villa d'Este dazzles with artificial glamour, but the Villa Gregoriana relies more on nature. Originally laid out by Pope Gregory XVI in the 1830s, its main highlight is the panoramic waterfall of Aniene, with the trek to the bottom studded with grottoes and balconies that open onto the chasm. The only problem is that if you do make the full descent, you might need a helicopter to pull you up again (the climb back up is fierce). From one of the belvederes, there's a view of the **Temple of Vesta** on the hill.

Largo Sant'Angelo, Tivoli. www.visitfai.it/parcovillagregoriana. ℭ **0774-332650.** 8€. Daily Mar–Oct, 10am–dusk. Closed Nov–Feb. Bus: Cotral service from Ponte Mammolo (Roma–Tivoli); the bus stops near the entrance.

WHERE TO EAT IN TIVOLI

Tivoli's gardens make for a pleasant picnic place (see **Eataly,** p. 156), but if you crave a sit-down meal, **Antica Trattoria del Falcone,** Via del Trevio 34 (ℭ **0774-312358**), is a dependable option in Tivoli. Just off Largo Garibaldi, it's been open since 1918 and specializes in excellent pizza, Roman pastas, and roast meats. It's open daily lunch and dinner.

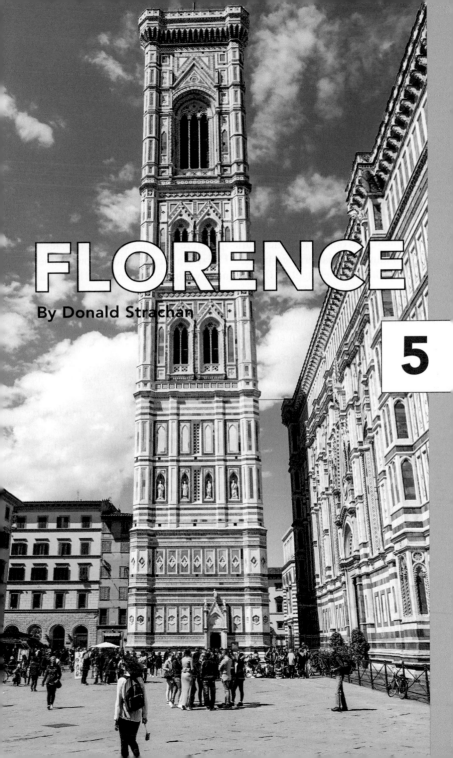

FLORENCE

By Donald Strachan

5

F lorence may be small, but over the centuries it has packed a major punch in European history. Its center—which you can easily cross on foot—evokes this illustrious past, packed as it is with monuments from the city's golden age. In the 15th and 16th centuries, Florence's achievements in art and architecture, science, literature, and even banking, were unmatched—and the rest of Europe knew it.

This was the center of the Renaissance movement and the hometown of its leading lights: Michelangelo, Brunelleschi, Leonardo da Vinci, Giotto, Galileo, and others. Florence built up a store of riches that still dazzles—including the masterpiece-packed **Uffizi Gallery,** the ingenious domed Cathedral, Michelangelo's *David,* and any number of decorated halls, palaces, and chapels. These treasures are still representative of the best humankind can achieve, and because of this, Florence remains a must-visit for every first-time traveler to Italy, and a must-return destination for anyone who cares about art and architecture.

DON'T LEAVE FLORENCE WITHOUT . . .

Seeing Michelangelo's *David*. Rarely does an icon of art live up to its reputation as this one does. See p. 195.

Touring the Uffizi. Yes, everyone does it, but for good reason: the Uffizi has the best Renaissance art collection on earth. See p. 181.

Getting into Leather. A mecca for leather goods, Florence attracts hundreds of jacket-, boot-, and bag-makers. Browse the street stalls of San Lorenzo Market (p. 223) for a deal, or the higher-end offerings at Santa Croce's leather school (p. 223) for exquisite craftsmanship.

Roaming the Dome. Allot plenty of time to explore Piazza del Duomo, Florence's cathedral square dominated by Brunelleschi's ingenious dome—which you can experience from the inside, the outside, and up on top. See p. 188.

Feasting on Bistecca alla Fiorentina. Thick, juicy steak prepared over a wood-burning grill—the city's succulent signature dish makes carnivores very happy indeed.

Shopping and Dining on the Left Bank. Observe fifth-generation artisans in family workshops around the Oltrarno neighborhood, then hit the restaurants and lively bars of San Frediano.

ESSENTIALS
Arriving

BY PLANE   Most international travelers will reach Florence via the airports in Rome (see p. 63) or Milan (see p. 465), proceeding on to Florence via train (see below). There are also direct international flights into Pisa's **Galileo Galilei Airport** (see p. 296), 97km (60 miles) west of Florence; several budget airlines fly here from other European cities. Around 15 daily **Autostradale** buses (www.airportbusexpress.it; ℂ 02/3008-9000) connect downtown Florence with Pisa Airport in just over 1 hour (14€ adults; 7€ children 2–12). **Sky Bus Lines** (www.caronnatour.com) runs the same route, with the same prices, 5 to 8 times daily.

A few European airlines, including British Airways and Vueling, also serve Florence's **Amerigo Vespucci Airport** (www.aeroporto.firenze.it/en; ℂ 055/306-15), sometimes called **Peretola,** just 5km (3 miles) northwest of town. Opened in 2019, the new **tram line (T2)** is the most cost-efficient way to reach the center from there (1.50€ each way). Trams depart every 4 to 9 minutes from 5am to midnight. Journey time to Florence's rail station is 20 minutes. **Taxis** line up outside the arrivals terminal: Exit and turn immediately to the right to find the rank. They charge a regulated flat rate of 22€ for the 15-minute journey to the city center (24€ on holidays, 25.30€ after 10pm; additional 1€ per bag).

Florence is also connected with Bologna Airport, by the **Appennino Shuttle** (www.appenninoshuttle.it; ℂ 055/5001-302), which runs 10 times each day and takes between 80 and 90 minutes; tickets cost 20€, 8€ ages 5 to 10, free ages 4 and under (25€/10€ if you pay on board, cash only). Buses arrive at and depart from Piazzale Montelungo, between Florence's Santa Maria Novella rail station and the Fortezza da Basso.

BY TRAIN   Most travelers arrive in Florence by train. Luckily, Florence is Tuscany's rail hub, with regular connections to all Italy's major cities. To get here from Rome, take a high-speed **Frecciarossa** or **Frecciargento** train (1½ hr.; www.trenitalia.com) or rival high-speed trains operated by **Italo** (www.italotreno.it). High-speed trains run from Venice (2 hr.) via Padua and Bologna and also direct from Rome's Fiumicino Airport.

Most Florence-bound trains roll into **Stazione Santa Maria Novella,** Piazza della Stazione (www.firenzesantamarianovella.it), which you'll see abbreviated as **S.M.N.** The station is an architectural masterpiece, albeit one dating to Italy's Fascist period, rather than the Renaissance. It lies on the northwestern edge of the city's compact historic center, a 10-minute walk from the Duomo and a brisk 15-minute walk from Piazza della Signoria and the Uffizi.

BY CAR   The **A1 autostrada** runs north from Rome past Arezzo to Florence and continues to Bologna, and **unnumbered superhighways** run to and from Siena (the *SI-FI raccordo*) and Pisa (the so-called *FI-PI-LI*). To reach Florence from Venice, take the A13 southbound then switch to the A1 at Bologna.

Driving *to* Florence is easy; the problems begin once you arrive. Almost all cars are banned from the historic center for much of the time; only residents or merchants with special permits are allowed into this clearly marked, camera-patrolled *zona a trafico limitato* (ZTL). You can enter the ZTL to drop off baggage at your hotel or go direct to a pre-booked parking garage (either can organize a temporary ZTL permit when provided with your license plate). Usual ZTL hours are Monday to Friday 7:30am to 8pm, Saturday 7:30am to 4pm. Evenings Thursday through Saturday the ZTL also operates until 3am the following morning. It's a real hassle, so only rent a car if you're leaving town to visit somewhere off the rail network.

If you do drive here, your best bet for overnight or longer-term parking is one of the city-run garages. The best deal—better than most hotels' garage rates—is at the **Parterre parking lot** under Piazza Libertà at Via del Ponte Rosso 4 (℡ **055/5030-2209**). Open around the clock, it costs 2€ per hour, or 10€ for the first 24 hours, 15€ for the second, then 20€ per day; it's 70€ for up to a week's parking. Find more info on parking at **www.fipark.com**.

Don't park your car overnight on the streets in Florence without local knowledge; if you're towed and ticketed, it will set you back substantially, and the headaches to retrieve your car are beyond description. If this happens to you, start by calling the vehicle removal department (**Recupero Veicoli Rimossi**) at ℡ **055/422-4142**. One more reason **you should not drive in Florence.**

Visitor Information

TOURIST OFFICES The most convenient tourist office is under the Loggia del Bigallo on the corner of Piazza San Giovanni and Via dei Calzaiuoli (℡ 055/288-496). It's open Monday through Saturday from 9am to 7pm and Sunday to 2pm. Its free map is adequate for finding the key sights; there's no need to upgrade to a paid map, especially if you'll also be navigating with your smartphone.

The train station's nearest tourist office (℡ **055/212-245**) is opposite the terminus at Piazza della Stazione 4. With your back to the tracks, take the left exit and then bear right—it's across the tram tracks and road junction ahead. It is usually open Monday through Saturday 9am to 7pm, Sunday 9am to 2pm. This office gets crowded; unless you're really lost, go to the Bigallo office (see above).

Another helpful office is at Via Cavour 1R (℡ **055-290-832**), 2 blocks north of the Duomo. The office is open only Monday through Friday from 9am to 1pm. There's also a central **phone number for tourist assistance:** ℡ **055/000** (daily 9am–7pm).

Advance Reservations for the Uffizi, Accademia & More

As soon as you decide to visit Florence, consider making advance reservations for the **Uffizi** and the **Accademia** museums—it's the best way to avoid spending hours in line. (Buying a cumulative ticket—see "Discount Tickets for Florence," p. 177—is your other smart strategy for joining the express queue.) Contact **Firenze Musei** at **www.firenze musei.it**. There's a 4€ fee; you can pay by credit card. Reservations are also possible, but usually not necessary, for the Galleria Palatina in the Pitti Palace, the Bargello, and several others. If you arrive in Florence without reservations, you can also reserve in person at a kiosk in the facade of Orsanmichele, on Via dei Calzaiuoli (Monday–Saturday); or at a desk inside the bookshop **Libreria My Accademia,** Via Ricasoli 105R (© **055/288-310**), almost opposite the Accademia (open Tuesday–Sunday).

WEBSITES The official Florence tourism website, **www.firenzeturismo.it**, contains a wealth of reasonably up-to-date information. At the "Tools" section of the site, you can download the latest opening hours for city sights, as well as themed apps, maps, and a monthly events calendar. For one-off exhibitions and culture, **Art Trav** (www.arttrav.com) is an essential bookmark, and written in English. The city itself maintains a more detailed local events portal: Visit **http://eventi.comune.fi.it**. For more Florence info, go to **www.frommers.com/destinations/florence**.

City Layout

Florence is a smallish city, sitting on the Arno River and petering out rather quickly to olive-planted hills to the north and south, but extending farther west and east along the Arno valley with suburbs and light industry. It has a compact center and is best negotiated on foot. No two major sights are more than a 25-minute walk apart, and most of the hotels and restaurants in this chapter are in the relatively small *centro storico* **(historic center),** a compact tangle of medieval streets and *piazze* (squares) where visitors spend most of their time. The bulk of Florence, including the majority of sights, is north of the river, with the **Oltrarno,** an old working artisans' neighborhood, hemmed in between the Arno and hills on the south side.

Florence Neighborhoods in Brief

THE DUOMO The area surrounding Florence's gargantuan cathedral is as central as you can get. The Duomo itself is halfway between the two monastic churches of Santa Maria Novella and Santa Croce, as well as at the midpoint between the Uffizi Gallery and the Ponte Vecchio to the south and San Marco and the Accademia (home of Michelangelo's "David") to the north. A medieval tangle of streets south of the Duomo head toward **Piazza della Signoria** (see below). Southwest of the Duomo,

Piazza della Repubblica lies in an even older part of town, still laid out in its Roman-era grid, though the square itself was "modernized" in the 19th century and chafes architecturally with the rest of the center. The Duomo neighborhood is one of the most hotel-heavy parts of town, offering a range from luxury inns to student dives, but beware: Many hotels and restaurants here rely on location, rather than quality, for success.

PIAZZA DELLA SIGNORIA The city's civic heart is also prime territory for museum hounds—the Uffizi Gallery, Palazzo Vecchio, Bargello sculpture collection, and **Ponte Vecchio** are all nearby. A few blocks just north of the Ponte Vecchio have good shopping, but unappealing modern buildings, due to post-WWII reconstruction. The neighborhood is stiflingly crowded in peak season—**Via Por Santa Maria** is one street to avoid—but in rare moments when it's empty of tour groups, its narrow medieval lanes remain the romantic heart of pre-Renaissance Florence. As in the Duomo neighborhood, be *very* choosy when picking a restaurant (or even an ice cream shop!) around here.

SAN LORENZO & THE MERCATO CENTRALE Centered on the Medici's family church of **San Lorenzo,** this wedge of streets between the train station and the Duomo is market territory. The vast indoor **Mercato Centrale** food market is here, along with the **San Lorenzo street market,** full of stalls hawking leather and other souvenirs. It's a colorful but rarely quiet area, with many budget hotels and some very good, affordable dining.

PIAZZA SANTA TRÍNITA This piazza is just north of the river at the south end of Florence's high-end shopping mecca, **Via de' Tornabuoni.** It's a quaint, well-to-do, and still medieval neighborhood—and if you're an upscale shopping fiend, there's no better place to be.

SANTA MARIA NOVELLA Bounding the western edge of the *centro storico,* this neighborhood has two characters: a bland zone around the train station, and a nicer area south of it. In general, the rail-station area is noisy and lacks medieval atmosphere, but it does have more budget hotel options than any other quarter, especially along **Via Faenza** and its tributaries. Try to avoid staying on traffic-heavy **Via Nazionale.** The situation improves dramatically as you head south toward the river, where **Piazza Santa Maria Novella** and its tributary streets have several stylish hotels.

SAN MARCO & SANTISSIMA ANNUNZIATA   On the northern edge of the *centro storico,* you'll find **Piazza San Marco**, a busy transport hub, and **Piazza Santissima Annunziata,** the most architecturally unified square in the city. The neighborhood is home to Florence's university, the **Accademia,** the San Marco paintings of Fra' Angelico, and quiet streets with some hotel gems. It's not a bad walk from the heart of the action, but just far enough to escape tourist crowds.

SANTA CROCE   Few tourists roam east beyond **Piazza Santa Croce,** so if you want to feel like a local, head here. The streets around the **Mercato di Sant'Ambrogio** have an appealing feel, and they get lively after dark, especially **Via Pietrapiana** and the northern end of **Via de' Macci.** Some of the city's best restaurants and bars are in this area; *aperitivo* time is vibrant along **Via de' Benci.**

THE OLTRARNO, SAN NICCOLÒ & SAN FREDIANO   "Across the Arno" is the artisans' neighborhood, still dotted with workshops. It began as a working-class neighborhood to catch overflow from the expanding medieval city, and later became a chic area for aristocrats to build palaces with country views. The largest of these, the **Pitti Palace,** today houses a set of paintings second only to the Uffizi in scope. The Oltrarno's lively tree-shaded center, **Piazza Santo Spirito,** is lined with bars and close to great restaurants and nightlife. West of here, the neighborhood of **San Frediano** is ever more fashionable, and **San Niccolò** at the foot of Florence's

Market stalls crowd the lively streets of the San Lorenzo neighborhood.

southern hills has popular bars. Oltrano's hotel range isn't great, but here you can eat and drink better, at better prices, than in the *centro storico*.

Getting Around Florence

Florence is a **walking** city. You can stroll between the two top sights, Piazza del Duomo and the Uffizi, in 5 minutes or so. The hike from the most northerly major sights, San Marco and the Accademia, to the most southerly, the Pitti Palace across the Arno, will take no more than 30 minutes for most. From Santa Maria Novella eastward to Santa Croce is a flat 20- to 30-minute walk. But beware: **Flagstones,** some of them uneven, are everywhere. Wear sensible shoes with good padding and foot support.

BY BUS & TRAM   You'll rarely need Florence's efficient **ATAF bus system** (www.ataf.net; ✆ **800/424-500** in Italy) since the city is so compact. Bus tickets cost 1.20€ (2.50€ on board) and are good for 90 minutes, irrespective of how many changes you make (even if you switch to a tram). Tickets are sold at *tabacchi* (tobacconists), automatic machines, some bars, and most newsstands. *Note:* Once on board, validate a paper ticket in the box to avoid a steep fine. Since traffic is restricted in most of the center, buses make runs on principal streets only, except for four tiny electric bus lines (*bussini* services C1–44) that trundle about the *centro storico*. The most useful routes to outlying areas are no. 7 (for Fiesole) and nos. 12 and 13 (for Piazzale Michelangiolo). Buses run from 7am until 9 or 9:30pm daily, with a limited night service on a few key routes.

   Tram lines (www.gestramvia.com) run until after midnight. Route T1 connects Santa Maria Novella station with the Opera di Firenze, Cascine Park, and Florence's southwestern suburbs. Finally opened in 2019, lines T2 and the T1 extension head northward from the station: T2 to the airport and T1 to Careggi via the Fortezza.

BY TAXI   Taxis aren't cheap, and with the city so small and the one-way system forcing drivers to take convoluted routes, they aren't an economical way to get about. They're most useful to get you and your bags between the train station and a hotel. It's 3.30€ to start the meter (which rises to 5.30€ on Sunday, or to 6.60€ 10pm–6am), plus 1€ per bag or for a fourth passenger in the cab. There are taxi stands outside the train station, on Borgo San Jacopo, and in Piazza Santa Croce; otherwise, call **Radio Taxi SOCOTA** at ✆ **055/4242** or **Radio Taxi COTAFI** at ✆ **055/4390.** For the latest tariff information, see **www.4242.it**.

BY BICYCLE & SCOOTER   Many of the bike-rental shops in town are located between San Lorenzo and San Marco. They include **Alinari,** Via San Zanobi 38R (www.alinarirental.com; ✆ **055/280-500**), which rents city bikes (2.50€ per hour; 12€ per day) and mountain bikes (3€ per hour; 18€ per day). It also hires out 125cc scooters (15€ per hour; 55€ per day). Another renter with similar prices is **Florence by Bike,** Via San Zanobi

54R (www.florencebybike.it; ✆ 055/488-992). Make sure to use a lock (one will be provided with your rental): Bike theft is common. Global app-powered **bike-sharing** scheme **Mobike** (www.mobike.com) also operates in Florence. When you've downloaded the app, registered, and paid a 1€ deposit, you're free to rent in periods of up to 30 minutes (.50€). All payments are handled inside the app.

BY CAR   Trying to drive in the *centro storico* is a frustrating, useless exercise, and moreover, for most of the time unauthorized cars will be fined if they enter the limited traffic zone (ZTL). You need a permit to do anything beyond dropping off and picking up bags at your hotel. Park your vehicle in one of the underground lots on the center's periphery and pound the sidewalk. (See "By Car" under "Arriving," p. 169.)

[Fast FACTS] FLORENCE

Business Hours   Hours mainly follow the Italian norm (see p. 821), although many larger and more central shops stay open through the midday *riposo* or nap (note the sign *orario nonstop*).

Doctors & Dentists
Tourist-oriented **Medical Service Firenze,** at Via Roma 4 (www.medical service.firenze.it; ✆ **055/ 475-411**) is open for walk-ins Mon–Fri 11am–noon, 1–3pm, and 5–6pm; Sat 11am–noon and 1–3pm. **Dr. Stephen Kerr** has an office at Piazza Mercato Nuovo 1 (www.dr-kerr.com; ✆ **335/ 836-1682** or 055/288-055), open Mon–Fri 3–5pm without an appointment (appointments are available 9am–3pm). His consultation fee is 70€, or 49€ if you show a student ID card. Prices are similar for the **Medico Subito** service (www.retepas.com/medico subito; ✆ **055/711-111;** Mon–Fri 10am–1pm and

3–6pm), which connects you with an English-speaking doctor to deal with minor injuries or dental pain.

Hospitals   The most central hospital is **Santa Maria Nuova,** a block northeast of the Duomo on Piazza Santa Maria Nuova (www.usl centro.toscana.it; ✆ **055/69- 381**), with an emergency room (*pronto soccorso*) open 24 hours.

Left Luggage   At Santa Maria Novella Station, you can leave luggage at **KiPoint** (www.kipoint.it), open daily 6am–11pm; the cost is 6€ per item for the first 5 hours, 1€ per hour thereafter. Even cheaper (1€/hr.; 6€/ day) is **Left Luggage Florence,** Via de' Boni 5R (www. leftluggageflorence.com).

Mail   Florence's **main post office** (✆ **055/273-6481**) is at Via Pellicceria 3, off the southwest corner of Piazza della Repubblica. It's open Mon–Fri 8:20am–1:35pm, Sat 8:20am–12:35pm.

Pharmacies   There is a 24-hour pharmacy (also open Sun and state holidays) in **Stazione Santa Maria Novella** (✆ **055/216-761;** ring the bell across from the taxi rank 11pm–7am). On holidays and at night, look for the sign in any pharmacy window telling you which ones are open locally.

Police   To report a crime or passport problems, call the *questura* (police headquarters) at ✆ **055/49-771.** Lost property might find its way to the *Ufficio oggetti ritrovati:* ✆ **055/334-802.**

Safety   As in any city, pickpockets are a risk in Florence, often light-fingered youngsters (especially around the train station) Otherwise it's a fairly safe city, but steer clear of the Cascine Park anytime after dark, and in the wee hours when nightlife is finished, avoid the area around Piazza Santo Spirito and the back-streets behind Santa Croce.

EXPLORING FLORENCE

Many small museums in Florence still accept only cash at the door. **Precise opening times can change** without notice, especially at city churches (for example, the Baptistery sometimes remains open until 11pm in summer). The tourist office maintains an up-to-date list of hours, also available for download from www.firenzeturismo.it. Note, too, the **last admission** to the museums and monuments listed is usually between 30 and 45 minutes before the final closing time.

Piazza del Duomo

The cathedral square is always crowded—filled with tourists and caricature artists during the day, strolling crowds in the early evening, and students strumming guitars on the Duomo's steps at night. The piazza's vivacity amid the glittering facades of the cathedral and the Baptistery doors keeps this an eternal Florentine sight.

Battistero (Baptistery) ★★★ CHURCH   In choosing a date to mark the beginning of the Renaissance, art historians often seize on 1401, the year Florence's powerful wool merchants' guild held a contest for the commission to design the **North Doors** ★★ of the Baptistery to match its Gothic **South Doors,** cast 65 years earlier by Andrea Pisano. The era's foremost Tuscan sculptors each cast a bas-relief bronze panel depicting their vision of the "Sacrifice of Isaac." Twenty-two-year-old Lorenzo Ghiberti, competing against Donatello, Jacopo della Quercia, and Filippo Brunelleschi, won. He spent the next 21 years casting 28 bronze panels and building his doors. The restored originals are inside the **Museo dell'Opera del Duomo** (see p. 181).

The result so impressed the merchants' guild—not to mention the public and Ghiberti's fellow artists—that they asked him in 1425 to do the **East Doors** ★★★, facing the Duomo, this time giving him artistic freedom to realize his Renaissance ambitions. Twenty-seven years later, just before his death, Ghiberti finished 10 dramatic Old Testament scenes in gilded bronze, each a masterpiece of Renaissance sculpture and some of the finest examples of low-relief perspective in Italian art. Each illustrates episodes in the stories of Noah (second down on left), Moses (second up on left), Solomon (bottom right), and others. The panels mounted here are also copies, created using historically accurate techniques, with the originals displayed in the Museo dell'Opera del Duomo. Years later, Michelangelo was standing before these doors and someone asked his opinion. His response sums up Ghiberti's accomplishment as no art historian could: "They are so beautiful that they would grace the entrance to Paradise." They've been nicknamed the Gates of Paradise ever since.

The octagonal building itself is ancient, first mentioned in city records in the 9th century but probably 300 years old by then. Its exterior is clad in gleaming white Carrara and green Prato marble. Even the roof is marble, making this the world's only building completely covered in marble.

discount TICKETS FOR FLORENCE

It may seem a little odd to label the **Firenze Card ★★** (www.firenzecard.it) a "discount" ticket, since it costs a substantial 85€. Is it a good buy? If you are planning a busy, museum-packed break here, the Firenze Card is a good value. If you only expect to see a few highlights, skip it.

The details: the card (valid for 72 hr.) allows one-time entrance to 60-plus sites, including some that are free anyway, but also the Uffizi, Accademia, Cappella Brancacci, Palazzo Pitti, Brunelleschi's dome, San Marco, and many more. In fact, *everything* we recommend in this chapter is included with the card, even sites in **Fiesole** (p. 204). It gets you into much shorter lines, and takes ticket pre-booking hassles out of the equation—another saving of 3€ to 4€ for busy museums, above all the Uffizi and Accademia. If you buy a **digital FirenzeCard** (an app) you are entitled to an extra 48 hours' validity anytime within 12 months. The **FirenzeCard+** add-on (7€) includes up to 3 days' bus travel (which you likely won't use).

Don't buy a Firenze Card for anyone ages 17 and under: With a full-priced card you can take immediate family members ages 17 and under for free. Any companions under 18 can join the express queue with you and pay only the "reservation fee" at state-owned museums (it's 4€ at the Uffizi, for example).

Those under 17 gain free admission to civic museums (such as the Palazzo Vecchio) anyway. Private museums and sights have their own payment rules, but it will not add up to 72€ per child.

If you don't spring for the Firenze card, you'll need to buy the **Grande Museo del Duomo ★★★** ticket to visit any of the sites on the cathedral square. The joint ticket, which costs 18€ (3€ for ages 6 to 11) and is valid for 72 hours, covers Brunelleschi's dome (including the now **obligatory** booking of a time slot), the Baptistery, Campanile di Giotto, the revamped Museo dell'Opera, and crypt excavations of Santa Reparata (inside the cathedral). In Florence, buy it at the ticket office across from the Baptistery, on the north side of Piazza San Giovanni, or inside the Museo dell'Opera. See **www.ilgrande museodelduomo.it** for more details, to buy online ahead of arrival, and to book a time slot for the dome. **Do not buy "skip the line" or other tickets for Brunelleschi's dome on the street.** These are not valid and you will be turned away.

The interior is ringed with columns pilfered from ancient Roman buildings, with a riot of mosaic-work above and below. The floor was inlaid in 1209, and between 1225 and the early 1300s the ceiling was covered with glittering **mosaics ★★**, most crafted by Venetian or Byzantine-style workshops working off designs by the era's best artists. Coppo di Marcovaldo drew sketches for a 7.8m-high (26-ft.) "Christ in Judgment" and a "Last Judgment" that fills over a third of the ceiling. Four separate, concentric registers tell stories from the Old and New Testaments. Bring binoculars for a closer look. Until the 1700s, this was the only place in Florence you could be baptized.

Piazza San Giovanni. www.ilgrandemuseodelduomo.it. ✆ **055/230-2885.** 18€ Grande Museo del Duomo ticket. Mon–Sat 8:15–10:15am and 11:15am–7:30pm; Sun (and 1st Sat of month) 8:30am–1:30pm. Bus: C2.

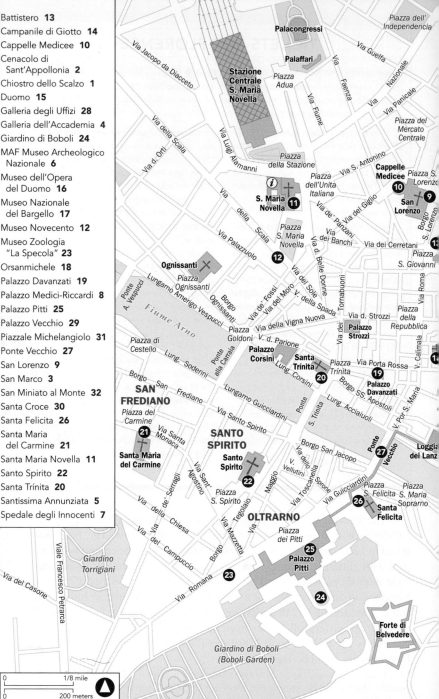

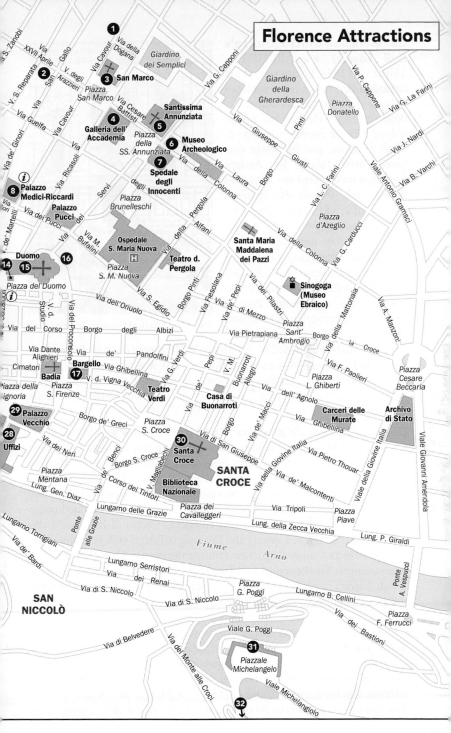

Florence Attractions

① Via della Dogana

Giardino dei Semplici

③ San Marco

Piazza San Marco

② ·

Via Cavour
Via XXVII Aprile
Via Gallo
Via v. degli Arazzieri
Via S. Reparata
S. Zanobi
Via degli

Giardino della Gherardesca

Piazza Donatello

Via Cesare Battisti

⑤ Santissima Annunziata

Via G. Capponi

Via P. Cappone

Via G. La Farini

④ Galleria dell' Accademia

Piazza della SS. Annunziata

⑥ Museo Archeologico

⑦ Spedale degli Innocenti

Via Guelfa
Via Cavour
Via Ricasoli

Piazza Brunelleschi

Via Giuseppe

Pinti

Giusti

Via J. Nardi

Via B. Varchi

Viale Antonio Gramsci

ⓘ

⑧ Palazzo Medici-Riccardi

Palazzo Pucci

Via de' Ginori
Via de' Martelli
Via on
Via de' Pucci
Via dei

Via M. Bufalini

Ospedale S. Maria Nuova

Piazza S. M. Nuova

⑭ ⑮ ✠ ⑯ Duomo

Piazza del Duomo

ⓘ

Via Servi degli
Via della Pergola
Via della Colonna
Via della Laura
Borgo Pinti

Teatro d. Pergola

Santa Maria Maddalena dei Pazzi

Via della Colonna

Piazza d'Azeglio

Via G. Carducci

Via della Mattonaia

Via A. Manzoni

✡ Sinagoga (Museo Ebraico)

Via dell'Oriuolo

Via d. Studio

Via del Corso
Borgo degli Albizi

Borgo Pinti
Via Fiesolana
Via de' Pepi
Via di Mezzo
Via dei Pilastri

Piazza Sant' Ambrogio

Borgo la Croce

Piazza Cesare Beccaria

Via Dante Alighieri
Cimatori
Piazza della ignoria

✠ Badia

⑰ Bargello

V. d. Vigna Vecchia
Via Ghibellina

Teatro Verdi

Casa di Buonarroti

Via G. Verdi
Via de' Pepi
V. M.
Via Buonarroti
Via Macci
Via dell'Agnolo

Piazza L. Ghiberti

Via F. Paolieri

Piazza Cesare Beccaria

⑨ Palazzo Vecchio

⑧ Uffizi

Via dei Neri
Piazza Mentana
Lung. Gen. Diaz

Piazza S. Firenze
Borgo de' Greci

Piazza S. Croce

Via de' Benci
Borgo S. Croce
Via de' Magliabechi
Via de' Corso dei Tintori

㉚ ✠ Santa Croce

Biblioteca Nazionale

Via di San Giuseppe

SANTA CROCE

Carceri delle Murate

Via Ghibellina

Via Pietro Thouar

Via della Giovine Italia

Archivio di Stato

Viale Giovanni Amendola

Lungarno Torrigiani
Via de' Bardi

Ponte alle Grazie

Lungarno delle Grazie

Piazza dei Cavalleggeri

Via Tripoli

Lung. della Zecca Vecchia

Piazza Piave

Lung. P. Giraldi

SAN NICCOLÒ

Fiume Arno

Lungarno Serristori
Via dei Renai
Via di S. Niccolò

Piazza G. Poggi

Lungarno B. Cellini

Ponte A. Vespucci

Piazza F. Ferrucci

Via di Belvedere
Via del Monte alle Croci

Viale G. Poggi

Via dei Bastioni

㉛ Piazzale Michelangelo

Viale Michelangiolo

㉜ ↓

Campanile di Giotto (Giotto's Bell Tower) ★★ ARCHITECTURE

In 1334, Giotto started the cathedral bell tower but completed only the first two levels before his death in 1337. He was out of his league with the engineering aspects of architecture, and the tower was saved from falling by Andrea Pisano, who doubled the thickness of the walls. Pisano also changed the design to add statue niches—he even carved a few of the statues himself—before quitting the project in 1348. Francesco Talenti finished the job between 1350 and 1359. The **reliefs** and **statues** in the lower levels—by Andrea Pisano, Donatello, Luca della Robbia, and others—are all copies; the weather-

The ornate facade of Florence's Duomo.

worn originals are housed in the Museo dell'Opera (p. 181). We recommend climbing the 414 steps to the top; the **view** ★★ is memorable as you ascend, and offers one of the city's best close-ups of Brunelleschi's dome.

Piazza del Duomo. www.ilgrandemuseodelduomo.it. ✆ **055/230-2885.** 18€ Grande Museo del Duomo ticket. Daily 8:30am–7pm. Bus: C2, 14, 23.

Duomo (Cattedrale di Santa Maria del Fiore) ★★ CATHEDRAL

By the late 13th century, Florence was feeling peevish. Archrivals Siena and Pisa had flamboyant new cathedrals while it was saddled with the tiny 5th- or 6th-century cathedral of Santa Reparata. So, in 1296, the city hired Arnolfo di Cambio to design a new Duomo, and he raised the facade and the first few bays before his death (around 1310). Work continued under the auspices of the Wool Guild and architects Giotto di Bondone (who concentrated on the bell tower) and Francesco Talenti (who expanded the planned size and finished up to the drum of the dome). Over the centuries, many designs for the unfinished façade were offered and rejected. One lavish Medici wedding even saw a temporary façade built in papier-mâché. The permanent one is a neo-Gothic design by Emilio de Fabris, built from 1871 to 1887.

The Duomo's most distinctive feature, however, is its enormous **dome** ★★★ (or *cupola*), which dominates the skyline and has become the symbol of Florence itself. The raising of this dome, the largest in the world in its time, was no mean architectural feat, tackled by Filippo Brunelleschi between 1420 and 1436 (see "A Man & His Dome," p. 181). You can climb up between its two shells for one of the classic panoramas

A MAN & HIS dome

Filippo Brunelleschi, a diminutive man whose ego was as big as his talent, managed in his arrogant, quixotic, and brilliant way to invent Renaissance architecture. Having been beaten by Lorenzo Ghiberti in the contest to cast the **Baptistery** doors (see p. 176), Brunelleschi decided he would rather be Florence's top architect than the second-best sculptor and took off for Rome to study the buildings of the ancients. On returning to his home city, he combined subdued gray *pietra serena* stone with smooth white plaster to create airy arches, vaults, and arcades of perfect classical proportions, in his own variant on the ancient Roman orders of architecture. He designed **Santo Spirito** (p. 204), the elegant **Spedale degli Innocenti** (p. 198), a chapel at **Santa Croce** (p. 199), and a new sacristy for **San Lorenzo** (p. 193), but his greatest achievement was erecting the dome over Florence's cathedral.

The Duomo—at that time the world's largest church—had already been built, but nobody had figured out how to cover the daunting space over its center without spending a fortune. No one was even sure they could create a dome that would hold up under its own weight. Brunelleschi insisted he knew how, and once granted the commission, revealed his ingenious plan, probably inspired by close study of Rome's **Pantheon** (p. 104). He built the dome in two shells, the inner one thicker than the outer, both shells thinning as they neared the top, thus leaving the center hollow and removing a good deal of the weight. He also planned to construct the dome from giant vaults with ribs crossing them, and dovetailed the stones making up the actual fabric of the dome. In this way, the walls of the dome would support themselves as they were erected. In the process of building, Brunelleschi found himself as much an engineer as an architect, constantly designing winches and hoists to carry the materials (plus food and drink) faster and more efficiently up to the level of the workmen. Reputedly, only one person died during construction—a drunken worker who fell.

His finished work speaks for itself, 45m (148 ft.) wide at the base and 90m (295 ft.) high. The marble lantern—which Brunelleschi did not live to see dropped into place in 1446—serves as the structure's keystone. For his achievement, Brunelleschi was accorded the honor of a burial inside Florence's cathedral.

across the city—something that is not recommended for claustrophobes or anyone with no head for heights. Booking a time slot to climb the dome is now **compulsory, even if you hold a FirenzeCard.** Queues can be long, but your best shot at a short wait comes with the first or last slots of the day.

The cathedral is rather spartan inside, though check out the optical-illusion equestrian "statue" of English mercenary soldier Sir John Hawkwood on the north wall, painted in 1436 by Paolo Uccello. The remains of old **Santa Reparata ★** are in the crypt, with mosaic floors revamped in 2018.

Piazza del Duomo. www.ilgrandemuseodelduomo.it. ✆ **055/230-2885.** Church free; Santa Reparata and cupola with 18€ Grande Museo del Duomo ticket. Church Mon–Fri 10am–4:30pm; Sat 10am–4:45pm; Sun 1:30–4:30pm. Cupola Mon–Fri 8:30am–7pm; Sat 8:30am–5pm; Sun 1–4pm. Bus: C1 or C2.

Museo dell'Opera del Duomo (Cathedral Museum) ★★★
MUSEUM   Florence's Cathedral Museum reopened to huge acclaim in 2015, a major overhaul doubling the space to show off Italy's second-largest collection of devotional art after the Vatican Museums (p. 82). The site is significant, as it was once the workshop where Michelangelo sculpted his statue of "David." Today the museum's prize exhibits are the original **Gates of Paradise** ★★★ cast by Lorenzo Ghiberti in the early 1400s (see "Baptistery," p. 176), displayed as the centerpiece of an extraordinary, lifesized re-creation of the early 1400s piazza, complete with a re-imagined version of what the cathedral's Gothic-era façade looked like. Ghiberti's Baptistery **North Doors** ★★ have also been moved inside, scrubbed to reveal the rose gold below years of soot and dirt (and joined in 2019 by Pisano's **South Doors**).

Also on the ground floor is a Michelangelo **"Pietà"** ★★ that nearly wasn't. Early in the process he had told students that he wanted this "Pietà" to stand at his tomb, but when he found an imperfection in the marble, he began attacking it with a hammer (look at Christ's left arm). The master never returned to the work, but his students later repaired the damage. The figure of Nicodemus was untouched—legend has it, because it was a self-portrait of the artist—a Michelangelo myth that, for once, is probably true. Elsewhere are works by Donatello—including his restored **"Magdalen"** ★—Andrea del Verrocchio, and Luca della Robbia, plus multimedia displays explaining in incredible detail the engineering process behind Brunelleschi's dome. A restored early Giotto **"Madonna"** ★ still shows damage from the 1993 Uffizi car bomb.

Piazza del Duomo 9 (behind cathedral). www.ilgrandemuseodelduomo.it. © **055/230-2885.** 18€ Grande Museo del Duomo ticket. Daily 9am–7pm. Closed 1st Tues of month. Bus: C1.

Around Piazza della Signoria & Santa Trínita

Galleria degli Uffizi (Uffizi Gallery) ★★★ MUSEUM   There is no collection of Renaissance art on the planet that can match the Uffizi. For all its crowds and other inconveniences, the Uffizi remains a must-see. And what will you see? Some 60-plus rooms and marble corridors—built in the 16th century as the Medici's private offices, or *uffici*—all packed with famous paintings, among them Botticelli's "Birth of Venus," Leonardo da Vinci's "Annunciation," Michelangelo's "Holy Family," and many, many more.

Start with **Room 2** for a look at the pre-Renaissance, Gothic style of painting born in the Middle Ages. Compare Cimabue's "Santa Trínita Maestà," painted around 1280, with his student Giotto's **"Ognissanti Madonna"** ★★★, done in 1310. Both paintings have a similar subject and setting but Giotto transformed Cimabue's iconlike Byzantine style into something more human. Giotto's Madonna looks like she's sitting on a throne, her clothes emphasizing the curves of her body, whereas Cimabue's Madonna and angels float in space, like portraits on coins, with stiff

The Uffizi Gallery displays an incredible collection of Renaissance art.

positioning. Also worth a look: Duccio's **"Rucellai Madonna"** ★ (1285), a founding, ethereal work for the Sienese School of painters.

Room 3 showcases the Sienese School at its peak, with Simone Martini's dazzling **"Annunciation"** ★★ (1333) slathered in gold leaf and Ambrogio Lorenzetti's "Presentation at the Temple" (1342). Tragically, the Black Death of 1348 wiped out this entire generation of Sienese painters (and most of Siena's population along with them). **Rooms 5–6** show Florentine painting at its most decorative, in a style now termed International Gothic. The iconic work, Gentile da Fabriano's **"Procession of the Magi"** ★★★ (1423), depicts the line to see newborn Jesus as full of decorative and comic elements (it's even longer than the line waiting outside the Uffizi).

The unflattering profiles of the Duke Federico da Montefeltro of Urbino and his duchess, painted in oil by **Piero della Francesca** around 1465, are the centerpiece of **Room 8.** The subjects are portrayed in a starkly realistic way—the duke exposes his warts and his crooked nose, which was broken in a tournament. This focus on earthly, rather than Christian, elements recalls the secular teachings of Greek and Roman times and is made more vivid by a depiction (on the back) of the couple riding chariots driven by the humanistic virtues of faith, charity, hope, and modesty (for her) and prudence, temperance, fortitude, and justice (for him). The same room displays works by **Filippo Lippi** from the mid–15th century. The best backstory belongs to his **"Madonna and Child with Two Angels"** ★★, from around 1465. The work was a celebrity scandal.

The woman who modeled for Mary was said to be Filippo's lover—would-be nun Lucrezia Buti, whom he spirited away from a convent before she took vows—and the child looking toward the viewer the product of their union. (That son, Filippino Lippi, would also become a painter of note.) Note the background, with distant mountains on one side and water on the other framing the portrait of a woman's face; Leonardo da Vinci shamelessly stole it 40 years later for his "Mona Lisa."

Rooms 10 to 14 (two separate spaces, despite the numbering) are devoted to the works of Filippo's student (and later Filippino's teacher) Sandro Filipepi, better known by his nickname "Little Barrels," or Botticelli, one of the most famous artists of the 15th century. Botticelli's 1485 **"Birth of Venus"** ★★ hangs like a billboard you have seen a thousand times. Venus's pose is taken from classical statues, while the winds Zephyr and Aura blowing her to shore, and the muse welcoming her, are from Ovid's "Metamorphosis." Botticelli's 1478 **"Primavera"** ★★★, its dark, bold colors a stark contrast to filmy, pastel "Venus," defies definitive interpretation. But again it features Venus (center), alongside Mercury, with the winged boots, the Three Graces, and the goddess Flora. In **Room 15** a monumental "Adoration of the Shepherds" by Flemish painter Hugo Van Der Groes is almost contemporaneous (ca. 1475).

To cross to the Uffizi's west wing, you pass picture windows with views of the Arno River to one side and the perfect Renaissance perspective of the Uffizi piazza to the other—plus an often-overlooked Roman sculpture gallery most museums would kill for.

Following years of itinerant existence, the Uffizi unveiled in 2018 permanent homes for two true Renaissance heavyweights. **Room 35** displays Leonardo da Vinci's magnificent, unfinished **"Adoration of the Magi"** ★★★ and **"Annunciation"** ★★. In the latter, completed in the early 1470s while Leonardo was still a student in Verrocchio's workshop, da Vinci's ability to orchestrate the viewer's focus is already masterful: The line down the middle of the brick corner of the house draws your glance to Mary's delicate fingers, which themselves point along the top of a stone wall to the angel's two raised fingers. Those, in turn, draw attention to the mountain between the two parallel trees dividing Mary from the angel, representing the gulf between the worldly and the spiritual. Its unusual perspective was painted to be viewed from the lower right.

In **Room 41** is Michelangelo's 1505–08 **"Holy Family"** ★. The twisting shapes of Mary, Joseph, and Jesus recall those in the Sistine Chapel for their sculpted nature and bright colors. The Uffizi has several Raphaels; this room displays his often-copied **"Madonna of the Goldfinch"** ★★, with a background landscape lifted from Leonardo and Botticelli.

The torsion and tensions of Michelangelo's painting and sculpture inspired the next generation of Florentine painters, known as the **Mannerists.** Andrea Del Sarto, Rosso Fiorentino, and Pontormo are all represented in the **Sale Rosse (Red Rooms, 57–61)** downstairs. A few rooms farther on, you'll find Titian's reclining nude **"Venus of Urbino"** ★★ (Room 83). It's no coincidence that the edge of the curtain, the angle of her hand and leg, and the line splitting floor and bed all intersect at the forbidden part of her body.

The nearby **Sale Seicento (1600s Rooms)** showcase paintings by Caravaggio, notably his crazed **"Medusa"** ★ self-portrait and an enigmatic **"Bacchus"** ★. These rooms also explore the 17th-century artists who aped his *chiaroscuro* (bright light and dark shadows) style. Greatest among them was Artemisia Gentileschi, a rare female painter from this period. Her **"Judith Slaying Holofernes"** ★ (ca. 1612), is one of the bloodiest paintings in the gallery.

If you find yourself flagging at any point (it happens to us all), there is a **coffee shop** at the far end of the west wing. Prices are in line with the piazza below, plus you get a great close-up of the Palazzo Vecchio's facade from the terrace. Fully refreshed, you can return to discover works by the many great artists we haven't space to cover here: Cranach and Dürer; Velazquez, El Greco, and Goya; Giorgione, Bellini, and Mantegna; and Uccello, Masaccio, Bronzino, and Veronese. There are original Greek and Roman friezes, too, notably in a room dedicated to the Medici garden at San Marco. In short, there is nowhere like the Uffizi anywhere—in Italy or the world.

Piazzale degli Uffizi 6 (off Piazza della Signoria). www.uffizi.it. (Reserve tickets at www.firenzemusei.it or ℂ **055/294-883.**) Mar–Oct 20€, Nov–Feb 12€. Tues–Sun 8:15am–6:50pm. Bus: C1 or C2.

Museo Nazionale del Bargello (Bargello Museum) ★★ MUSEUM

This is the most important museum anywhere for Renaissance **sculpture**—yet it's often inexplicably quieter than other museums in the city. Originally the city's prison, torture chamber, and execution site, the Bargello now stands as a three-story art museum containing some of the best of Michelangelo, Donatello, and Ghiberti, as well as of their most successful Mannerist successor, Giambologna.

In the ground-level Michelangelo room, you'll witness the variety of his craft, from a whimsical 1497 **"Bacchus"** ★★ to a severe, unfinished "Brutus" of 1539. "Bacchus," created when Michelangelo was just 22, genuinely looks drunk, leaning back a little too far, his head off kilter, with a cupid about to bump him over. Nearby is Giambologna's twisting **"Mercury"** ★, about to take off, propelled by the breath of Zephyr.

Upstairs an enormous vaulted hall is filled with some of Donatello's most accomplished sculptures, including his original "Marzocco" (from outside the Palazzo Vecchio; p. 188), and **"St. George"** ★, from a niche on the outside of Orsanmichele (p. 187). Notable among them is his bronze **"David"** ★★ (which some think might actually be the god Mercury), done in 1440, the first freestanding nude sculpture since Roman times. The classical detail of these sculptures, as well as their naturalistic poses and reflective mood, is the essence of the Renaissance style.

PIAZZA DELLA signoria

When the medieval Guelph party came out on top after a long political struggle with the Ghibellines, they razed part of Florence's old city center to build a new palace for civic government. It's reputed that the Guelphs ordered architect Arnolfo di Cambio to build what we now call the **Palazzo Vecchio** (p. 188) in the corner of this space to make sure not an inch of it would sit on Ghibelline land. (This odd legend was probably fabricated to explain Arnolfo's off-center architecture.) At any rate, the L-shaped space around the *palazzo* became the new civic center of town, **Piazza della Signoria ★★**, named after the medieval city's oligarchic ruling body (the "Signoria"). Today, it's an outdoor sculpture gallery, teeming with tourists, postcard stands, horses and buggies, and outdoor cafes. If you want to catch the square at its serene best, arrive by 8am.

The statuary on the piazza is particularly beautiful, starting on the far left (as you face the Palazzo Vecchio) with Giambologna's 1594 equestrian statue of Grand Duke Cosimo I. To its right is one of Florence's favorite sculptures to hate, the **Fontana del Nettuno** (Neptune Fountain; 1560–75), created by Bartolomeo Ammannati as a tribute to Cosimo I's naval ambitions. (Florentines have dubbed it "Il Biancone," or "Big Whitey.") A **porphyry plaque** in the ground in front of the fountain marks the site where puritanical monk Savonarola held the Bonfire of the Vanities. With fiery apocalyptic preaching, he whipped Florentines into a frenzy, and hundreds filed into this piazza, arms loaded with their "decadent" possessions to throw it all on the flames.

To the right of Neptune, a long-raised platform fronting the Palazzo Vecchio was known as the *arringheria*, from which soapbox speakers would lecture to crowds (from which we get our word "harangue"). On its far-left corner is a copy (original in the Bargello) of Donatello's "Marzocco," symbol of the city, with a Florentine lion resting his raised paw on a shield emblazoned with the city's

emblem, the *giglio* (lily). To its right is another Donatello replica, "Judith Beheading Holofernes." Farther down is a man who needs little introduction, Michelangelo's **"David,"** a 19th-century copy of the original now in the Accademia (p. 195). Near enough to David to look truly ugly in comparison is Baccio Bandinelli's lumpy "Hercules and Cacus" (1534).

At the piazza's south end, the airy **Loggia dei Lanzi ★★** (1376–82) is named after the Swiss guard of lancers (*lanzi*) whom Cosimo de' Medici stationed here. (It's also called the Loggia della Signoria or the Loggia di Orcagna, after its designer Andrea Orcagna.) At front left stands Benvenuto Cellini's masterpiece in bronze, **"Perseus" ★★★** (1545), holding up the severed head of Medusa. On the far right is Giambologna's **"Rape of the Sabines" ★★**, one of the most successful Mannerist sculptures in existence. You must walk all the way around to appreciate it, catching the action and artistry of its spiral design from different angles. Talk continues about moving it indoors, safe from the elements . . . but for now, it's still here.

Side by side on the back wall are the contest entries submitted by Ghiberti and Brunelleschi for the commission to do the Baptistery doors in 1401. With the "Sacrifice of Isaac" as their biblical theme, both displayed innovative use of perspective. Ghiberti won the contest, perhaps because his scene is more thematically unified. Brunelleschi could have ended up a footnote in art history, but instead he gave up the chisel and turned his attentions to architecture instead (see "A Man & His Dome," p. 181).

Via del Proconsolo 4. www.bargellomusei.beniculturali.it. © **055/064-9440.** 8€ (9€ during temporary exhibitions; free 1st Sun of month). Daily 8.15am–2pm. Closed 1st, 3rd, and 5th Mon, and 2nd and 4th Sun of each month. Bus: C1 or C2.

Orsanmichele ★★ CHURCH   This bulky structure halfway down Via dei Calzaiuoli looks more like a Gothic warehouse than a church—which is exactly what it was, built as a granary and grain market in 1337. After a miraculous image of the Madonna appeared on a column inside, the lower level was turned into a shrine and chapel. The city's merchant guilds each undertook the task of decorating a Gothic tabernacle around the lower level with a statue of their guild's patron saint. Masters such as Ghiberti, Donatello, Verrocchio, and Giambologna all cast or carved masterpieces to set here (those remaining are mostly copies, including Donatello's "St. George"). In the dark interior, an elaborate Gothic stone **Tabernacle** ★ (1349–59) by Andrea Orcagna protects a luminous 1348 "Madonna and Child" painted by Giotto's student Bernardo Daddi, to which miracles were ascribed during the Black Death of 1348–50. *Tip:* On Mondays (10am–4:50pm) and Saturdays (10am–12:30pm) only, you can also access the upper floors, which house many of the original sculptures that once adorned Orsanmichele's exterior niches. Among the treasures of this so-called **Museo di Orsanmichele** ★ you'll see a trio of bronzes: Ghiberti's "St. John the Baptist" (1412–16), the first life-size bronze of the

Miracles have been attributed to Bernardo Daddi's "Madonna and Child" icon in Orsanmichele church.

Renaissance; Verrocchio's "Incredulity of St. Thomas" (1483); and Giambologna's "St. Luke" (1602). Climb up one floor further, to the top, for an unforgettable 360° panorama ★★ of the city.

Via Arte della Lana 1. ℂ **055/238-8610.** Free, donations accepted. Daily 10am–5pm. Bus: C2.

Palazzo Davanzati ★★ PALACE/MUSEUM   One of the best-preserved 14th-century palaces in the city offers a glimpse of domestic life during the medieval and Renaissance period. It was originally built for the Davizzi family in the mid-1300s, then bought by the Davanzati clan; the latter's family tree, dating back to the 1100s, is emblazoned on the ground-floor courtyard walls. The palace's painted wooden ceilings and murals have aged well (even surviving World War II damage), but the emphasis here is not on decor, but on providing insights into the medieval life of a noble Florentine family—feasts and festivities in the **Sala Madornale;** a private internal well to secure water supply when things in Florence got sticky; and magnificent 14th-century bedchamber frescoes that recount, comic-strip style, "The Chatelaine of Vergy," a medieval morality tale. Interesting footnote: In 1916, a New York auction of furnishings from this palace launched a "Florentine style" trend in U.S. interior design circles.

Via Porta Rossa 13. ℂ **055/064-9460.** 6€. Mon–Fri 8:15am–2pm, Sat–Sun 1:15–7pm. Closed 2nd and 4th Sun, and 1st, 3rd, and 5th Mon of each month. Bus: C2.

Palazzo Vecchio ★★ PALACE   The core of Florence's fortress-like town hall was built from 1299 to 1302 to the designs of Arnolfo di Cambio, Gothic master builder. Home to various Florentine governments, the palace remains home today to the city government. When Duke Cosimo I and his Medici family moved to the *palazzo* in 1540, they redecorated. Michelozzo's 1453 **courtyard** ★ was left architecturally intact but frescoed by Vasari with scenes of Austrian cities, to celebrate the 1565 marriage of Francesco I de' Medici and Joanna of Austria. A grand staircase leads up to the **Sala dei Cinquecento** ★, named for the 500-man assembly that met here in the pre-Medici days of the Florentine Republic. It's also the site of the greatest fresco cycle that ever wasn't: Leonardo da Vinci was commissioned in 1503–05 to paint one long wall with a battle scene celebrating Florence's victory at the 1440 Battle of Anghiari. Always trying new methods and materials, he decided to mix wax into his pigments. Leonardo had finished painting part of the wall, but it wasn't drying fast enough, so he brought in braziers stoked with hot coals to try to hurry the process. As onlookers watched in horror, the wax in the fresco melted under the heat and colors ran to a puddle on the floor. The search for what remains of his work continues; some hope was provided in 2012 with the discovery of pigments similar to those used by Leonardo in a cavity behind the current wall. Michelangelo was also supposed to paint a fresco on the opposite wall, but he never got past preparatory drawings before Pope Julius II called him to Rome to paint the Sistine Chapel. Vasari and his assistants covered the bare walls from 1563 to 1565, with subservient frescoes exalting Cosimo I and the military victories of his regime, against Pisa (on the near wall) and Siena (far wall). Opposite the door you enter is Michelangelo's statue of **"Victory"** ★, carved from 1533 to 1534 for Pope Julius II's tomb but later donated to the Medici.

The first series of rooms on the upper floor is the **Quartiere degli Elementi,** frescoed with allegories and mythological characters, again by Vasari. Crossing the balcony overlooking the Sala dei Cinquecento, you enter the **Apartments of Eleonora di Toledo** ★, decorated for Cosimo's Spanish wife. Her **private chapel** ★★★ is a masterpiece of mid–16th-century fresco painting by Bronzino. Under the coffered ceiling of the **Sala dei Gigli** is Ghirlandaio's fresco of "St. Zenobius Enthroned," with figures from Republican and Imperial Rome, and Donatello's original **"Judith and Holofernes"** ★ bronze (1455), one of his last works. In the palace basement are the **Scavi del Teatro Romano** ★, remnants of Roman Florentia's theater, upon which the medieval palace was built, with walls and an intact paved street.

Visitors can also climb the **Torre di Arnolfo** ★★, the palace's crenelated tower. If you can bear small spaces and 218 steps, the views from the top of this medieval skyscraper are sublime. The 95m (312-ft.) Torre is closed during bad weather. The minimum age to climb it is 6, and children ages 17 and under must be accompanied by an adult.

Piazza della Signoria. www.museicivicifiorentini.comune.fi.it. © **055/276-8325.** Palazzo 12.50€; Torre 12.50€; Palazzo plus Torre 17.50€; Palazzo plus Scavi 16€; admission to all 19.50€. Palazzo/Scavi: Fri–Wed 9am–7pm (Apr–Sept until 11pm); Thurs 9am–2pm. Torre: Fri–Wed 10am–5pm (Apr–Sept 9am–9pm); Thurs 9am–2pm. Bus: C1 or C2.

Ponte Vecchio ★ ARCHITECTURE   The oldest and most famous bridge across the Arno, the Ponte Vecchio was built in 1345–50 by Taddeo Gaddi to replace an earlier version. Overhanging shops have lined a bridge here since at least the 12th century. In the 16th century, it was home to butchers, until Duke Ferdinand I moved into the Palazzo Pitti across the river. He couldn't stand the stench, so he evicted the meat cutters and moved in goldsmiths, silversmiths, and jewelers, who occupy it to this day.

Vasari's Corridor

The enclosed passageway that runs along the top of the Ponte Vecchio is part of the **Corridoio Vasariano (Vasari Corridor)** ★, a private elevated link between the Palazzo Vecchio and Palazzo Pitti, in which hangs the world's best collection of artists' self-portraits. Duke Cosimo I found the idea of mixing with the hoi polloi on his way to work distressing—and assassination was a real danger—so he commissioned Vasari to design his V.I.P. route in 1565. At time of writing, the corridor is closed. It is scheduled to open for wider public access in 2021. Dates for the Corridor have a habit of changing on a regular basis: Inquire at the tourist office for the latest news.

The Ponte Vecchio spans the River Arno.

The Ponte Vecchio's fame saved it in 1944 from the Nazis, who had orders to blow up all the bridges before retreating out of Florence as Allied forces advanced. They couldn't bring themselves to reduce this span to rubble, so they blew up the ancient buildings on either end instead to block it off. Not so discriminating was the **Great Arno Flood** of 1966, which severely damaged the shops. A private night watchman saw waters rising alarmingly and called many of the goldsmiths at home. They rushed to remove valuable stock before it was washed away.

Via Por Santa Maria/Via Guicciardini. Bus: C3 or C4.

Santa Trínita ★★ CHURCH   Beyond Bernardo Buontalenti's late-16th-century facade lies a dark church, rebuilt in the 14th century but founded by the Vallombrosan order before 1177. The third chapel on the right has remains of ancient frescoes by Spinello Aretino, found beneath Lorenzo Monaco's 1424 "Scenes from the Life of the Virgin" frescoes in the next chapel along. In the right transept, Ghirlandaio frescoed the **Cappella Sassetti ★** in 1483 with a cycle on the "Life of St. Francis," setting all the scenes against Florentine backdrops peopled with portraits of contemporary notables. His "Francis Receiving the Order from Pope Honorius" (in the lunette) takes place under an arcade on the north side of Piazza della Signoria; you'll recognize the Loggia dei Lanzi in the middle, and on the left, the Palazzo Vecchio (the Uffizi hadn't yet been built between them). *Tip:* The south end of the piazza leads to the **Ponte Santa Trínita ★★,** Florence's most graceful bridge. In 1567, Ammannati built this span, set with four 16th-century statues of the seasons, for the wedding of Cosimo

II. After the Nazis blew up the bridge in 1944, it was rebuilt, and all was set into place—save the head on the statue of Spring, which remained lost until a team dredging the river in 1961 found it by accident. If you want to photograph the Ponte Vecchio, head here at dusk.

Piazza Santa Trínita. © **055/216-912.** Free. Mon–Sat 8:30am–noon and 4–6pm; Sun 8:30–10:45am and 4–6pm. Bus: C3, C4, 6, 11.

Around San Lorenzo & the Mercato Centrale

Until the market's controversial—and *perhaps* temporary—move in 2014, the church of San Lorenzo was lost behind the leather stalls and souvenir carts of Florence's vast **San Lorenzo street market** (see p. 223). A bustle of commerce characterizes this whole neighborhood, centered on both the tourist market and the nearby **Mercato Centrale**, whose upper floor is a showcase for Italian street food (see p. 218).

Cappelle Medicee (Medici Chapels) ★ MONUMENT When Michelangelo built the New Sacristy between 1520 and 1533 (finished by Vasari in 1556), it was to be a tasteful monument to Lorenzo the Magnificent and his generation of relatively pleasant Medici. When work got underway in 1604 on the adjacent **Cappella dei Principi** (Chapel of the Princes), it was to become one of Italy's most god-awful and arrogant memorials, dedicated to the grand dukes, whose ranks include some of Florence's most decrepit tyrants. The Cappella dei Principi is an exercise in bad taste, a mountain of cut marbles and semiprecious stones—jasper, alabaster, mother-of-pearl, agate, and the like—slathered onto the walls and ceiling with no regard for composition and still less for chromatic unity. The pouring of ducal funds into this monstrosity lasted until Gian Gastone de' Medici drank himself to death in 1737, without an heir. Teams kept doggedly at the thing, and they were still finishing the floor in 1962. Judge for yourself.

Michelangelo's **Sagrestia Nuova (New Sacristy)** ★★, built to jibe with Brunelleschi's Old Sacristy in San Lorenzo proper (see p. 193), is much calmer. (An architectural note: The windows in the dome taper as they get near the top to fool you into thinking the dome is higher.) Michelangelo was supposed to produce three tombs here (perhaps four) but ironically got only the two less important ones done. So, Lorenzo de' Medici

---

Catch an Exhibition at the Strozzi

The Renaissance **Palazzo Strozzi** ★★, Piazza Strozzi (www.palazzostrozzi.org; © 055/264-5155) is Florence's major space for temporary and contemporary art shows, and has been experiencing a 21st-century renaissance of its own. Hit shows in recent years include Bill Viola's "Electronic Renaissance" in 2017 and Marina Abramović in 2019. There's always plenty going on, including talks, evening events, late opening (usually Thursdays), and discovery packs for kids of different ages. Check the website for the latest exhibition news.

("the Magnificent")—wise ruler of his city, poet of note, grand patron of the arts, and moneybags behind much of the Renaissance—ended up with a mere inscription of his name next to his brother Giuliano's on a plain marble slab against the entrance wall. They did get one Michelangelo sculpture to decorate their slab, an unfinished **"Madonna and Child"** ★. On the left wall of the sacristy, Michelangelo's **"Tomb of Lorenzo"** ★ commemorates the duke of Urbino (Lorenzo the Magnificent's grandson), whose seated statue symbolizes the contemplative life. Below him on the curves of the tomb stretch a pair of sculptures, "Dawn" (female) and "Dusk" (male). Observing them, one might wonder if Michelangelo perhaps hadn't seen many naked women.

Piazza Madonna degli Aldobrandini (behind San Lorenzo, where Via Faenza and Via del Giglio meet). © **055/238-8602.** 8€ (free 1st Sun of month). Daily 8:15am–5pm. Closed 1st, 3rd, and 5th Mon, and 2nd and 4th Sun of each month. Bus: C1, C2, 22.

Palazzo Medici-Riccardi ★ PALACE   Built by Michelozzo in 1444 for Medici "godfather" Cosimo il Vecchio, this is the prototype Florentine *palazzo,* on which the more overbearing Strozzi and Pitti palaces were later modeled. It remained the Medici private home until Cosimo I officially declared his power as duke by moving to the Palazzo Vecchio, the city's civic nerve center. A door off the courtyard leads up a staircase to the **Cappella dei Magi,** the oldest chapel to survive from a private Florentine palace; its walls are covered with dense and colorful Benozzo Gozzoli **frescoes** ★★ (1459–63), classics of the International Gothic style.

Courtyard of the Medici-Riccardi palace, the model for many a Florentine *palazzo.*

The walls depict an extended "Journey of the Magi" to see the Christ child, who's being adored by Mary in the altarpiece.

Via Cavour 3. www.palazzomediciriccardi.it. © **055/276-8224.** 7€ (10€ during temporary exhibitions). Thurs–Tues 9am–7pm. Bus: C1, 14, 23.

San Lorenzo ★ CHURCH   A rough brick anti-facade fronts what is most likely the oldest church in Florence, founded in A.D. 393. It was later the Medici family's parish church, and Cosimo il Vecchio, whose wise behind-the-scenes rule made him popular with Florentines, is buried in front of the high altar. The plaque marking the spot is inscribed pater patriae, "Father of the Homeland." Off the left transept, the **Sagrestia Vecchia (Old Sacristy)** ★ is one of Brunelleschi's purest pieces of early Renaissance architecture. The focal sarcophagus contains Cosimo il Vecchio's parents, Giovanni di Bicci de' Medici and his wife, Piccarda Bueri. A side chapel is decorated with a star map showing the night sky above the city in the 1440s—a scene that also features, precisely, in Brunelleschi's Pazzi Chapel in Santa Croce; see p. 400. On the wall of the left aisle is Bronzino's huge fresco of the **"Martyrdom of San Lorenzo"** ★, showing the poor saint being roasted on a grill in Rome.

Piazza San Lorenzo. www.operamedicealaurenziana.org. © **055/214-042.** 6€. Mon–Sat 10am–5pm. Bus: C1.

Near Piazza Santa Maria Novella

The two squat obelisks in **Piazza Santa Maria Novella** ★, resting on Giambologna tortoises, once served as turning posts for "chariot" races held here from the 16th to the mid–19th century. Once down-at-heel, this part of the center now has some of Florence's priciest hotels.

Museo Novecento ★ MUSEUM   This 21st-century museum covers 20th-century Italian art in a multitude of media. Crowds are often sparse—let's face it, you're in Florence to experience the 1400s, not the 1900s. But that is no reflection on the collection's quality, which spans 100 years of visual arts. Exhibits include works by major names such as De Chirico and Futurist Gino Severini, and close examinations of Florence's role in fashion and Italy's relationship with European avant-garde art. In a tiny top-floor room, a 20-minute movie-clip montage shows Florence through the lens of the century's filmmakers, from Arnaldo Ginna's 1916 "Vita Futurista" to such recent hits as "Room with a View" and "Tea with Mussolini."

Piazza Santa Maria Novella 10. www.museonovecento.it/en. © **055/286-132.** 9.50€. Apr–Sept daily 11am–8pm (closes 2pm Thurs, 11pm Fri); Oct–Mar daily 11am–7pm (closes 2pm Thurs). Bus: 6 or 11.

Santa Maria Novella ★★ CHURCH   Of all Florence's major churches, the home of the Dominicans is the only one with an original **facade** ★★ from the era of its greatest importance. The lower Romanesque half was started in the 1300s by architect Fra' Jacopo Talenti. Renaissance architect Leon Battista Alberti finished the facade, adding a classically inspired

A set of 14th-century frescoes in Santa Maria Novella's Spanish Chapel.

top that not only went seamlessly with the lower half but also created a Cartesian plane of perfect geometry. Inside, Masaccio's **"Trinità"** ★★★ (ca. 1425) is the first painting ever to use linear mathematical perspective. Florentine citizens and artists flooded in to see the fresco's unveiling, many remarking in awe that it seemed to punch a hole into space, creating a chapel out of a flat wall. Frescoed chapels by Filippino Lippi and others fill the **transept.** The **Sanctuary** ★ behind the main altar was frescoed after 1485 by Ghirlandaio with the help of his assistants and apprentices, probably including a young Michelangelo. The left wall is covered with a cycle on the "Life of the Virgin," and the right has a "Life of St. John the Baptist," works that are also snapshots of the era's fashions, stuffed with portraits of the Tornabuoni family who commissioned them.

For many years the church's frescoed cloisters were treated as a separate site. The church and cloisters are now accessible on one admission ticket (although, confusingly, there are two separate entrances: through the church's garden and via the tourist office at the rear, on Piazza della Stazione.) The **Chiostro Verde (Green Cloister)** ★★ was partly frescoed between 1431 and 1446 by Paolo Uccello, a Florentine painter who became increasingly obsessed with the mathematics behind perspective. His Old Testament scenes include a "Universal Deluge," which ironically was badly damaged by the Great Arno Flood of 1966. Off the cloister, the **Spanish Chapel** ★ is a complex piece of Dominican propaganda, frescoed in the 1360s by Andrea di Bonaiuto. The **Chiostro dei Morti (Cloister of the Dead)** ★, one of the oldest parts of the convent, was also badly damaged in 1966. Its low-slung vaults were decorated by Andrea Orcagna and others. Visitors can also access the **Chiostro Grande** (Florence's largest cloister) and papal apartments frescoed by Florentine Mannerist Pontormo. Allow at least 90 minutes to explore the complex.

Piazza Santa Maria Novella/Piazza della Stazione 4. www.smn.it. © **055/219-257.** 7.50€. Mon–Thurs 9am–5:30pm (Apr–Sept until 7pm); Fri 11am–5:30pm (Apr–Sept until 7pm); Sat 9am–5:30pm (July–Aug until 6:30pm); Sun 1–5:30pm (July–Aug noon–6:30pm; Sept noon–5:30pm). Bus: C2, 6, 11, 22.

Near San Marco & Santissima Annunziata

Cenacolo di Sant'Apollonia ★ MUSEUM   Andrea del Castagno (1421–57) learned his trade painting portraits of condemned men in city prisons, and it's easy to see the influence of this apprenticeship on the faces of the disciples in his version of **"The Last Supper,"** the first of many painted in Florence during the Renaissance. This giant fresco, completed around 1447, covers an entire wall at one end of the former convent refectory. Judas is banished to the far side of a communal table. Castagno's "Crucifixion," "Deposition," and "Entombment" complete the sequence.

Via XXVII Aprile 1. © **055/238-8608.** Free. Daily 8:15am–1:50pm. Closed 1st, 3rd, and 5th Sat and Sun of each month. Bus: 1, 6, 11, 14, 17, 23.

Chiostro dello Scalzo ★ ARCHITECTURE   You need luck or great timing to catch this place open, but it is well worth the short detour from San Marco. Between 1509 and 1526 Mannerist painter Andrea del Sarto frescoed a cloister belonging to a religious fraternity dedicated to St. John the Baptist, who is the theme of an unusual monochrome *(grisaille)* fresco cycle. The cloister is usually blissfully empty, too.

Via Cavour 69. © **055/238-8604.** Free. Mon and Thurs 8:15am–1:50pm; also open (same hours) 1st, 3rd, and 5th Sat, and 2nd and 4th Sun of each month. Bus: 1 or 17.

Galleria dell'Accademia ★★ MUSEUM   **"David"** ★★★—"Il Gigante"—is much larger than most people imagine, looming 4.8m (16 ft.) on top of a 1.8m (6-ft.) pedestal. He hasn't faded with time, either; the marble still gleams as if it were unveiling day in 1504. Viewing the statue is a pleasure in the bright and spacious room custom-designed for him after his move to the Accademia in 1873, following 300 years of pigeons perching on his head in Piazza della Signoria. (Replicas now take the abuse there, and at Piazzale Michelangiolo; the spot high on the northern flank of the Duomo, for which he was originally commissioned, stands empty.) But the Accademia is not only about "David"; you will be delighted to discover he is surrounded by an entire museum of

Seeing 'David' Without a Reservation

The wait to get in to see "David" can be an hour or more if you don't **reserve ahead** or buy a Firenze Card (p. 177). Try getting there before the museum opens in the morning or an hour before closing time. During high summer late-night openings at the Accademia (Tuesdays and Thursdays), you should also try during dinner time.

Renaissance works. Michelangelo's unfinished **"Prisoners"** ★★ statues are a contrast to "David," their rough forms struggling to emerge from the raw stone. Michelangelo famously said that he tried to free the sculpture from within every block, and you can see this technique here. Rooms showcase paintings by Perugino, Filippino Lippi, Giotto, Giovanna da Milano, Andrea Orcagna, and others.

Via Ricasoli 60. © **055/238-8609.** (Pre-book tickets at www.firenzemusei.it or © 055/294-883.) 12€. Tues–Sun 8:15am–6:50pm (Jun–Sept, Tues and Thurs until 10pm). Bus: C1, 1, 6, 14, 19, 23, 31, 32.

MAF Museo Archeologico Nazionale (Archaeological Museum) ★
MUSEUM   If you can force yourselves away from the Renaissance, rewind a millennium or two at one of the most important archaeological collections in central Italy, which has a particular emphasis on the Etruscan period. You'll need a little patience, however. The collection inside 17th-century Palazzo della Crocetta is not easy to navigate, though you will easily find the **"Arezzo Chimera"** ★★, a bronze figure of a mythical lion–goat–serpent dating to the 4th century B.C., perhaps the most important bronze sculpture to survive from the Etruscan era. It's displayed alongside the "Arringatore," a life-sized bronze of an orator dating to the 1st century, just as Etruscan culture was being subsumed by Ancient Rome. On the top floor is the **"Idolino"** ★, an exquisite and slightly mysterious, lithe bronze. The collection is also strong on Etruscan-era *bucchero* pottery and funerary urns, and Egyptian relics including several sarcophagi displayed in a series of eerie galleries. In late 2018, the museum inaugurated a section dedicated to the vast collection of gems,

Florence's archaeological museum is rich in Etruscan artifacts, including the famous bronze figure known as the Arezzo Chimera.

cameos, and intaglio gathered by generations of Medici and Lorraine dukes. Some pieces date back many centuries B.C. With other travelers so focused on medieval and Renaissance sights in the city, you may have this museum almost to yourself.

Piazza Santissma Annunziata 9b. ℭ **055/23-575.** 4€ (free 1st Sun of month and anytime with Uffizi ticket). Tues–Fri 8:30am–7pm; Sat–Mon 8:30am–2pm. Closed 2nd, 4th, and 5th Sun of each month. Bus: 6, 19, 31, 32.

San Marco ★★★ MUSEUM   We have never understood why this place is not mobbed. Showcasing the work of Fra' Angelico, Dominican monk and Florentine painter in the International Gothic style, it is the most important collection in the world of his altarpieces and painted panels, residing in a deconsecrated 13th-century convent the artist-monk once called home. Seeing it all in one place allows you to appreciate how his decorative impulses and the sinuous lines of his figures place his work right on the cusp of the Renaissance. The most moving and unusual is his **"Annunciation"** ★★★, but a close second are the intimate frescoes of the life of Jesus—painted not on one giant wall, but scene by scene on the individual walls of small monks' cells that honeycomb the upper floor. The idea was that these scenes, painted by both Fra' Angelico and his assistants, would aid in the monks' prayer and contemplation. The final cell on the left corridor belonged to the firebrand preacher Savonarola, who briefly incited the populace of the most art-filled city in the world to burn their "decadent" paintings, illuminated manuscripts, and anything else he felt was a worldly betrayal of Jesus's ideals. (Ultimately, he ran afoul of the pope.) You'll see his notebooks, rosary, and what's left of the clothes he wore in his cell, as well as an anonymous panel painted to show the day in 1498 when he was burned at the stake in Piazza della Signoria. There's much more Fra' Angelico secreted around the cloisters, including a **"Crucifixion"** ★ in the Chapter House. The former Hospice is now a gallery dedicated to Fra' Angelico and his contemporaries; look especially for his **"Tabernacolo dei Linaioli"** ★★ and a seemingly weightless **"Deposition"** ★★.

Piazza San Marco 3. ℭ **055/238-8608.** 4€. Mon–Fri 8:15am–1:50pm; Sat–Sun 8:15am–4:50pm. Closed 1st, 3rd, and 5th Sun and 2nd and 4th Mon of month. Bus: C1, 1, 6, 7, 10, 11, 14, 17, 19, 20, 23, 25, 31, 32.

Santissima Annunziata ★★ CHURCH   This church's story begins humbly, in 1233, when seven Florentine nobles had a spiritual crisis, gave away their possessions, and retired to the forest to contemplate divinity. In 1250, they returned to what were then fields outside the city walls and founded a small oratory, proclaiming themselves Servants of Mary (the "Servite Order"). Over the years, however, thanks to a miraculous painting (more on that later), the oratory grew into a grand basilica, enlarged by Michelozzo (1444–81) and later redecorated in unrestrained baroque style.

Visitors enter through the **Chiostro dei Voti (Votive Cloister),** which is today the church's main art draw, decorated with some of the city's finest **Mannerist frescoes** ★★ (1465–1515). A 5-year restoration reinstated their original vibrancy. Rosso Fiorentino provided an "Assumption" (1513) and Pontormo a "Visitation" (1515) just to the right of the door. Their master, Andrea del Sarto, contributed a "Birth of the Virgin" (1513), in the far-right corner, one of his finest works. To the right of the door into the church is a damaged but still fascinating "Procession of the Magi" (1514) by del Sarto, who included a self-portrait at the far right, looking out at us from under his blue hat.

The church's interior is a flamboyant affair, smothered in multicolored marble and topped with a gilded coffered ceiling. In a side chapel to the left of the entrance, look for the ornate tabernacle housing a small 14th-century painting of the "Annunciation." Why such a grandiose setting? Well, according to legend, the friar who was painting the picture became vexed that he couldn't paint the Madonna's face as beautifully as she should be, and went to take a nap. When he awoke, he found an angel had completed the face for him. The miraculous painting became an object of cult worship, and a once-humble church was changed forever.

On **Piazza Santissima Annunziata** ★★ outside, flanked by elegant Brunelleschi porticos, an equestrian statue of Grand Duke Ferdinand I was Giambologna's last work, cast in 1608 after his death by his student Pietro Tacca, who also did the two fountains of fantastical mermonkey-monsters. *Tip:* You can stay right on this spectacular piazza, at one of our favorite Florence hotels, the **Loggiato dei Serviti** ★★ (p. 213).

Piazza Santissima Annunziata. ℂ **055/266-181.** Free. Cloister: daily 7:30am–12:30pm and 4–6:30pm. Church: daily 4–5:15pm. Bus: 6, 19, 31, 32.

Spedale degli Innocenti ★★ MUSEUM/ARCHITECTURE Originally funded by the silk guild, the "Nocenti" opened in 1419, and ever since has been one of the world's most famous childcare institutions. (The Institute still works with UNICEF and others.) Their landmark building was designed by Brunelleschi himself, with elegant Renaissance loggias on the façade and surrounding its interior "Women's" and "Men's" **courtyards.** Inside, a three-floor museum has multimedia exhibits tracing the history of the place and the personal stories of many who benefited from its care. The Institute also has a fine **art collection,** including Renaissance works by Botticelli and Ghirlandaio displayed in a top-floor gallery alongside the original painted ceramic roundels by Della Robbia which elegantly completed Brunelleschi's façade. As you leave, notice the little grated window on the far north wall of the main loggia, where for centuries babies were delivered anonymously to the care of the orphanage.

Piazza Santissima Annunziata. www.museodeglinnocenti.it. ℂ **055/203-7308.** 7€; 10€ family. Daily 10am–7pm. Bus: 6, 19, 31, 32.

Around Piazza Santa Croce

Piazza Santa Croce is pretty much like any grand Florentine square—an open space ringed with souvenir and leather shops and thronged with tourists. Once a year (during late June) it's covered with dirt as violent Renaissance-style soccer is played on the piazza in the tournament known as **Calcio Storico Fiorentino.**

Santa Croce ★★ CHURCH   The center of Florence's Franciscan universe was begun in 1294 by Gothic master Arnolfo di Cambio to rival the church of Santa Maria Novella being raised by the Dominicans across the city. The church wasn't consecrated until 1442, and even then, it remained faceless until the neo-Gothic **facade** was added in 1857. This art-stuffed complex demands 2 hours of your time to see properly.

The Gothic **interior** is vast, and populated with the tombs of famous Florentines. Starting from the front door, immediately on the right is the tomb of the most venerated Renaissance master, **Michelangelo Buonarroti,** who died in Rome in 1564 at the ripe age of 89. The pope wanted him buried in the Eternal City, but Florentines managed to sneak his body back to Florence. Two berths along from Michelangelo's monument is a pompous 19th-century cenotaph to **Dante Alighieri,** one of history's great poets, whose "Divine Comedy" laid the basis for the modern Italian language. (Exiled from Florence, Dante is buried in Ravenna—see p. 381.) Elsewhere are monuments to philosopher **Niccolò Machiavelli,** composer **Gioacchino Rossini,** sculptor **Lorenzo Ghiberti,** and scientist **Galileo Galilei.**

The church's right transept is richly decorated with **frescoes.** The **Cappella Castellani** was frescoed with stories of saints' lives by Agnolo Gaddi. His father, Taddeo Gaddi—one of Giotto's closest followers—painted the **Cappella Baroncelli ★** (1328–38) at the transept's end. The frescoes depict scenes from the "Life of the Virgin," and include an "Annunciation to the Shepherds," the first night scene in Italian fresco. Giotto himself frescoed the two chapels to the right of the high altar. Whitewashed over

Michelangelo's tomb in the church of Santa Croce.

in the 17th century, they were uncovered in the 1800s and inexpertly restored. The **Cappella Peruzzi** ★ is a late work with many references to antiquity, reflecting Giotto's trip to Rome's ruins. The more famous **Cappella Bardi** ★★ appeared in the movie "A Room with a View". Key panels, featuring episodes in the life of St. Francis, include the "Trial by Fire Before the Sultan of Egypt" on the right wall; and, one of Giotto's best-known works, the "Death of St. Francis," in which monks weep and wail with convincing pathos.

Outside in the cloister is the **Cappella Pazzi** ★, one of Filippo Brunelleschi's architectural masterpieces (faithfully finished after his death in 1446). Giuliano da Maiano probably designed the porch that now fronts the chapel, set with glazed terracottas by Luca della Robbia. The chapel is one of Brunelleschi's signature pieces, decorated with his trademark *pietra serena* gray stone. It is the defining example of early Renaissance architecture. Note that the ceiling of the smaller dome depicts the same night sky as his Old Sacristy in San Lorenzo (p. 193). In the church **Sacristy** is a Cimabue **"Crucifix"** ★ that was almost destroyed by the Arno Flood of 1966. It became an international symbol of the ruination wreaked that November day.

Piazza Santa Croce. www.santacroceopera.it. ℂ **055/246-6105.** 8€ (children 17 and under free admission with parent or guardian). Mon–Sat 9:30am–5pm; Sun 2–5pm. Bus: C1, C2, C3.

The Oltrarno, San Niccolò & San Frediano

Giardino di Boboli (Boboli Garden) ★★ PARK/GARDEN   The statue-filled park behind the Pitti Palace is one of the earliest and finest Renaissance gardens, laid out mostly between 1549 and 1656 with box hedges in geometric patterns, groves of ilex (holm oak), dozens of statues, and rows of cypress. Just above the entrance through the courtyard of the Palazzo Pitti is an oblong **amphitheater** modeled on Roman circuses, with a **granite basin** from Rome's Baths of Caracalla and an **Egyptian obelisk** of Ramses II. In 1589 this was the setting for the wedding reception of Ferdinand de' Medici and Christine of Lorraine. For the occasion, the family commissioned entertainment from Jacopo Peri and Ottavio Rinuccini, who decided to set a classical story entirely to music and called it "Dafne"—the world's first opera. (Later, they wrote a follow-up hit, "Erudice," performed here in 1600; this is the first opera whose score

The Boboli Garden is a welcome stretch of greenery, just across the Arno river.

survives.) At the south end of the park, the **Isolotto** ★ is a dreamy island in a pond full of huge goldfish, with Giambologna's "L'Oceano" sculptural composition at its center. At the north end, around the end of the Pitti Palace, are fake caverns filled with statuary, attempting to invoke a classical sacred grotto. The most famous, the **Grotta Grande,** was designed by Giorgio Vasari, Bartolomeo Ammannati, and Bernardo Buontalenti between 1557 and 1593. Dripping with phony stalactites, it's set with replicas of Michelangelo's unfinished "Prisoners" statues. You can usually get inside on the hour (but not every hour) for 15 minutes.

Entrance via Palazzo Pitti. © **055/238-8791.** Mar–Oct 10€, Nov–Feb 6€; includes Giardino Bardini. Nov–Feb daily 8:15am–4:30pm; Mar and Oct daily 8:15am–5:30pm; Apr–May and Sept daily to 6:30pm; June–Aug daily to 7:30pm. Closed 1st and last Mon of month. Bus: C3, C4, 11, 36, 37.

Museo Zoologia "La Specola" ★ MUSEUM   This may be the only museum in Florence where kids eagerly drag parents from room to room. Creepy collections of threadbare stuffed-animal specimens transition into rooms filled with wax anatomical models—lifelike human bodies that appear flayed, dismembered, and eviscerated. These models served as anatomical illustrations for medical students studying at this scientific institute from the 1770s. (You must be accompanied to see many of them; no pre-booking required.) Grisly plague dioramas were also created from wax in the early 1700s to satisfy the lurid tastes of Duke Cosimo III.

Via Romana 17. www.msn.unifi.it. © **055/275-6444.** 6€ adults, 3€ ages 6–14 and seniors 65 and over; additional 3€ to see waxworks. Tues–Sun 9am–5pm (Jul–Aug Fri–Sun closes 1pm). Guided 30-min visits to waxworks Tues–Fri 11:30am, noon, 3pm, 3:30pm; Sat–Sun 11:30am, noon, 12:30pm, 1pm, 3pm, 3:30pm. Bus: 11, 36, 37.

Palazzo Pitti (Pitti Palace) ★★ MUSEUM/PALACE   Although built by and named after a rival of the Medici—the merchant Luca Pitti—in the 1450s, this gigantic *palazzo* soon came into Medici hands. It was the Medici family's principal home from the 1540s, and continued to house Florence's rulers until 1919. The Pitti contains five museums, including one of the world's best collections of canvases by Raphael. Out back are elegant Renaissance gardens, the **Boboli** (see p. 200).

In the art-crammed rooms of the Pitti's **Galleria Palatina** ★★, paintings are displayed like cars in a parking garage, stacked on walls above each other following the "Enlightenment" method of exhibition. Rooms are alternately dimly lit, or garishly bright; this is how many of the world's great art treasures were seen and enjoyed by their original commissioners. You will find important historical treasures amid the Palatina's vast and haphazard collection; some of the best efforts of Titian, Raphael, and Rubens line the walls. Botticelli and Filippo Lippi's **"Madonna and Child"** ★ (1452) provide the key works in the **Sala di Prometeo** (Prometheus Room). Two giant versions of the "Assumption of the Virgin," both by Mannerist painter Andrea del Sarto, dominate the **Sala dell'Iliade** (Iliad Room). Here you will also find another Biblical woman painted by Artemisia Gentileschi, "Judith." The **Sala di Saturno** (Saturn Room) ★ is stuffed with Raphaels; in the **Sala di Giove** (Jupiter Room) is his sublime, naturalistic portrait of **"La Velata"** ★★, as well as **"The Ages of Man"** ★. The current attribution of the latter painting is awarded to Venetian Giorgione, though that has been disputed.

At the **Appartamenti Reali** (Royal Apartments) you get a feeling for the conspicuous consumption of the Medici Grand Dukes, and their Austrian and Belgian Lorraine successors—and see some notable paintings in their original, ostentatious setting. Italy's first king lived here for several years during Italy's 19th-century unification process—when Florence was the second national capital, after Turin—until Rome was finally conquered and the court moved there. Much of the stucco, fabrics, furnishings, and general decoration is in thunderously poor taste, but you should look for Caravaggio's subtle canvas **"Knight of Malta"** ★.

The Pitti's "modern" gallery, the **Galleria d'Arte Moderna** ★, has a good collection of 19th-century Italian paintings with a focus on Romanticism, Neoclassical works, and the **Macchiaioli,** a school of Italian painters who worked in an "impressionistic style" before the French Impressionists. If you have limited time, head straight for major works of the latter, in Sala 18 through 20, where Maremma landscapes by **Giovanni Fattori** ★ (1825–1908) hang. The Pitti's two lesser museums—the **Galleria del Costume** (Costume Gallery) and **Museo degli Argenti** (Museum of Silverware)—combine to show that wealth and taste do not always go hand in hand. One thing you will notice in the Costume Gallery is how much smaller locals were just a few centuries ago.

Piazza Pitti. www.uffizi.it. Mar–Oct 16€, Nov–Feb 10€; half-price admission before 9am. Tues–Sun 8:15am–6:50pm. Bus: C3, C4, 11, 36, 37.

Piazzale Michelangiolo (Michelangelo) ★★ SQUARE   This pedestrianized, panoramic piazza is on the itinerary of every tour bus. The balustraded terrace was laid out in 1869 to give a sweeping **vista** ★★ of the Renaissance city, spread out in the valley below and backed by the green hills of Fiesole beyond. A bronze replica of "David" here points directly at his original home, outside the Palazzo Vecchio.

Viale Michelangelo. Bus: 12 or 13.

San Miniato al Monte ★★ CHURCH   High atop a hill, its gleaming white-and-green marble facade visible from the city below, San Miniato is one of the few ancient churches of Florence to survive the centuries virtually intact. The current building took shape in 1013, under the auspices of the powerful Arte di Calimala guild, whose symbol, a bronze eagle clutching a bale of wool, perches on the **facade** ★★. Above the central window is a 13th-century mosaic of "Christ Between the Madonna and St. Minias" (a theme repeated in the apse). The interior has a few Renaissance additions, but they blend well with the overall medieval aspect—an airy, stony space with a raised choir at one end, painted wooden trusses on the ceiling, and tombs interspersed with inlaid marble symbols of the zodiac paving the floor. Below the choir is an 11th-century **crypt** with remains of frescoes by Taddeo Gaddi. Off to the right of the raised choir is the sacristy, which Spinello Aretino covered in 1387 with elaborate frescoes depicting the **"Life of St. Benedict"** ★. Off the left of the nave is the 15th-century **Cappella del Cardinale del Portogallo ★★**, a collaborative effort by Renaissance artists to honor the Portuguese humanist Cardinal Jacopo di Lusitania. It's worth timing your visit to come here when the Benedictine monks are celebrating mass in Gregorian chant (usually 5:30pm). Around the back of the church is San Miniato's monumental **cemetery ★**, whose streets are lined with tombs and mausoleums built in elaborate pastiches of every generation of Florentine architecture. It's a peaceful spot, accompanied only by birdsong and the occasional tolling of the church bells.

Via Monte alle Croci/Viale Galileo Galilei (behind Piazzale Michelangiolo). ℂ **055/ 234-2731.** Free. Mon–Sat 9:30am–1pm and 3pm until dusk; Sun 1pm until dusk. Bus: 12 or 13.

Santa Felicita ★ CHURCH   Greek sailors who lived in this neighborhood in the 2nd century brought Christianity to Florence, and this little church was probably the second to be established in the city, the first version of it rising in the late 4th century. The current church was thoroughly remodeled in the 1730s. The star works are in the first chapel on the right, the Brunelleschi-designed **Cappella Barbadori-Capponi,** with paintings by Mannerist master Pontormo (1525–27). His **"Deposition" ★★** and frescoed "Annunciation" are rife with his garish color palette of oranges, pinks, golds, lime greens, and sky blues, and exhibit his trademark surreal sense of figure.

Piazza Santa Felicita (on left off Via Guicciardini across the Ponte Vecchio). ℂ **055/213-018.** Free (1€ to illuminate chapel lights). Mon–Sat 9:30am–12:30pm and 3:30–5:30pm. Bus: C3 or C4.

Santa Maria del Carmine ★★★ CHURCH   Following a 1771 fire that destroyed everything but the transept chapels and sacristy, this Carmelite church was almost entirely reconstructed in high baroque style. To see the **Cappella Brancacci ★★★** in the right transept, you have to enter through the cloisters and pay admission. The frescoes here were commissioned by an enemy of the Medici, Felice Brancacci, who in 1424 hired Masolino and his student Masaccio to decorate it with the "Life of St. Peter." Masolino probably worked out the cycle's scheme and painted a few scenes along with his pupil before taking off for 3 years to serve as court painter in Budapest, while Masaccio kept painting, quietly creating the early Renaissance's greatest frescoes. Masaccio eventually left for Rome in 1428, where he died at age 27; the cycle was completed between 1480 and 1485 by Filippino Lippi. Masolino painted "St. Peter Preaching," the upper panel to the left of the altar, and the two top scenes on the right wall, which shows his fastidious, decorative style in a long panel of "St. Peter Healing the Cripple" and "Raising Tabitha," and his "Adam and Eve." Contrast this first man and woman, about to take the bait offered by the snake, with Masaccio's **"Expulsion from the Garden" ★★★**, opposite it. Masolino's figures are highly posed, expressionless models, while Masaccio's Adam and Eve burst with intense emotion. The top scene on the left wall, Masaccio's **"Tribute Money"** ★★, showcases his use of linear perspective. The scenes to the right of the altar are Masaccio's as well; the **"Baptism of the Neophytes"** ★★ is among his masterpieces.

Piazza del Carmine. www.museicivicifiorentini.comune.fi.it. ☎ **055/276-8224.** Church free; Cappella Brancacci 8€ (10€ Sat–Mon). Mon and Wed–Sat 10am–5pm; Sun 1–5pm. Bus: C4.

Santo Spirito ★ CHURCH   One of Filippo Brunelleschi's masterpieces of architecture, this 15th-century church doesn't look much from the outside (no proper facade was ever built). But the **interior** ★ is a marvelous High Renaissance space—an expansive landscape of proportion and mathematics in classic Brunelleschi style, with coffered ceiling, lean columns with Corinthian capitals, and the stacked perspective of arched arcading. Late Renaissance and baroque paintings are scattered throughout, but the best stuff lies in the transepts, especially the **Cappella Nerli** ★, with a panel by Filippino Lippi (right transept). The church's extravagant baroque altar has a ciborium inlaid in *pietre dure* around 1607—and frankly, looks a bit silly against the restrained elegance of Brunelleschi's architecture. A separate entrance (with a 3€ admission fee) gets you into the **Sacristy**—to see a wooden "Crucifix" which has, controversially, been attributed to Michelangelo—as well as Santo Spirito's 17th-century cloister and refectory. *Tip:* Tree-shaded Piazza Santo Spirito ★ is one of the focal points of the Oltrarno, lined with cafes that see action late into the evening. Sometimes a few farmers sell their fruit and vegetables on the piazza.

Piazza Santo Spirito. www.basilicasantospirito.it. ☎ **055/210-030.** Free (3€ sacristy & cloister). Mon–Tues and Thurs–Sat 10am–12:30pm and 4–6pm; Sun 11:30am–1:30pm and 4–6pm. Bus: C3, C4, 11, 36, 37.

A Side Trip to Fiesole

Although it's only a short distance from Florence, **Fiesole** ★ has a proud status as an independent municipality. In fact, this hilltop village high above Florence predates its big neighbor in the valley by centuries.

Etruscans from Arezzo probably founded a town here in the 6th century B.C., on the site of a Bronze Age settlement. *Faesulae* became the most important Etruscan center in the region, and although it eventually became a Roman town—conquered in 90 B.C., its inhabitants built a theater and adopted Roman customs—it always retained a bit of otherness. Following the barbarian invasions, it became part of Florence's administrative district in the 9th century, yet continued to struggle for self-government. Medieval Florence settled things in 1125 by attacking and razing the entire settlement, save the cathedral and bishop's palace.

An oasis of cultivated greenery still separates Fiesole from Florence. Even with the big city so close, Fiesole preserves the character of a Tuscan small town, which makes it a perfect escape from peak season crowds. It stays relatively cool in summer, and while you sit at a cafe on Piazza

Mino, sipping an iced cappuccino, the lines at the Uffizi and throng around the Duomo seem very distant indeed.

San Francesco ★ MONASTERY/MUSEUM   The ancient high-point of the Etruscan and Roman town is now occupied by a tiny church and monastery. The 14th-century church has been largely overhauled, but at the end of a small nave hung with devotional works—Piero di Cosimo and Cenni di Francesco are both represented—is a fine "Crucifixion and Saints" altarpiece by Neri di Bicci. Off the cloisters is a quirky little **Ethnographic Museum,** stuffed with objects picked up by Franciscan missionaries, including an Egyptian mummy and Chinese jade and ceramics. Entrance to the church's painted, vaulted **crypt** is through the museum. To reach San Francesco, you will climb a sharp hill. Pause close to the top, where a little balcony provides perhaps the best **view** ★★★ of Florence, and the wine hills of the Chianti beyond.

Via San Francesco 13. www.fratifiesole.it. *C* **055/59-175.** Free. Tues–Sun 9:30am–noon and 2:30–5pm (6pm in summer). Bus: 7.

Teatro Romano (Roman Theater) ★ RUINS   Fiesole's archaeological area is romantically overgrown and scattered with sections of columns, broken friezes, and other remnants of the ancient world. It is also dramatically sited, terraced into a hill with views over the olive groves and forests north of Florence. Beyond the **Roman Theater** ★ (which seated 1,500 in its day), three rebuilt arches mark the remains of 1st-century-A.D. **baths.** Near the arches, a cement balcony over the far edge of the archaeological park gives a good view of the best remaining stretch of Fiesole's 4th-century-B.C. **Etruscan walls.** At the other end of the park from the baths, the floor and steps of a 1st-century-B.C. **Roman Temple** were built on top of a 4th-century-B.C. Etruscan one dedicated to Minerva. To the left are oblong **Lombard tombs** from the 7th century A.D., when this part of Fiesole was a necropolis.

Via Portigiani 1. *C* **055/596-1293.** For admission and hours, see "Fiesole Essentials," above. Bus: 7.

Organized Tours

To really get under Florence's surface, book an insightful culture tour with **Context Travel** ★★ (www.contexttravel.com; ✆ **800/691-6036** in the U.S. or 06/96727371 in Italy). Led by academics and other experts in their field on a variety of themes, from the gastronomic to the archaeological and artistic, these tours are limited to six people and generally cost around 95€ per person. The quality of Context's walks is unmatched, and well worth the above-average cost.

Offerings from **CAF Tours** (www.caftours.com; ✆ **055/283-200**) include several themed walks and cooking classes costing from 19€ to over 100€. **I Just Drive** (www.ijustdrive.us; ✆ **055/093-5928**) offers fully equipped cars (Wi-Fi, complimentary bottle of Prosecco) plus an English-speaking driver for various themed visits; for example, you can book a ride in a luxury Bentley or Mercedes up to San Miniato al Monte at dusk (1½ hr.; 129€). They also operate full-day and half-day private and group food and wine tours into the Chianti hills. For other options, surf to **Viator.com**, a marketplace site that lists a wide range locally organized tours and activities, reviewed by travelers.

Especially for Kids

You have to put in a bit of work to reach some of Florence's best views—and the climbs, up claustrophobic medieval staircases, are a favorite with many kids. The cupola of **Santa Maria del Fiore** (p. 180), the **Palazzo Vecchio**'s (p. 188) Torre di Arnolfo, and the **Campanile di Giotto** (p. 180) are perfect for any youngster with a head for heights.

The best activities with an educational component are run by **Mus.e** ★★ (www.musefirenze.it; ✆ **055/276-8224**), a program that offers child's-eye tours in English around the Palazzo Vecchio, led by guides in period costumes. Lively, affordable activities focus on life at the ducal court—pitched at children ages 4–7 ("The Turtle and the Snail") or 10-plus ("At Court with Donna Isabella" and "Secret Passages")—or take kids into the workshop to learn fresco painting (ages 8-plus). Programs cost 5€ per person; book online or at the desk next to the Palazzo Vecchio ticket booth.

When youngsters just need a crowd-free timeout space, head for the **Biblioteca delle Oblate,** Via dell'Oriuolo 24 (www.biblioteche.comune.fi.it; ✆ 055/261-6526), where you'll find a library with books for little ones (including in English), as well as space to spread out, color, or draw. It's free and open 9am to 6:45pm, except for Monday morning and all day Sunday (closed 1 week mid-Aug). *Tip:* The Oblate's **cafe** (p. 225) is an excellent place to kick back, and has a great view of Brunelleschi's dome which few visitors see.

Cycling is a pleasure in the riverside Parco delle Cascine: See p. 174 for bike rental advice. And remember you are in the **gelato** capital of the world. At least one multi-scoop gelato per day is the minimum recommended dose; see p. 220. Better still, plan to be in town during the **Gelato Festival** (www.gelatofestival.it) in late April.

WHERE TO STAY IN FLORENCE

Thanks to a rapidly growing stock of hotel beds, lodging prices in Florence have not increased in recent years, although that does not mean they're exactly cheap. It is hard to find a high-season double you'd want to stay in for much less than 100€, and once-attractive August deals have mostly dried up. Florence no longer seems to get much quieter in its hottest month.

On top of that, Florence's government levies an extra .80€ to 2€ **per person per night per government-rated hotel star,** for the first 10 nights of any stay. It is payable on departure, and is not usually included in quoted rates. Children below age 12 are exempt from the tax. Airbnb and other holiday rentals are **not** exempt.

Peak hotel season is Easter through early July, September through early November, and Christmas through January 6. May, June, and September are very popular; January and February are the months to grab a bargain—never be shy to haggle if you're coming then. **Booking direct** via phone, e-mail, or the hotel's own website, is often key to unlocking the lowest rates or complimentary extras.

To help you decide in which area you'd like to base yourself, consult "Florence Neighborhoods in Brief," p. 171. Note that we have included parking information only for those places that offer it. As indicated below, many hotels offer babysitting services; however, these are almost always "on request." At least a couple days' notice is advisable.

APARTMENT RENTALS & ALTERNATIVE ACCOMMODATIONS

It's the way of the modern world: Global players in apartment rentals have overtaken most of the local specialists in Florence. **HomeAway.com,** TripAdvisor–owned **HolidayLettings.co.uk, Airbnb,** and others are well stocked with central and suburban apartments. Online agency **Cross Pollinate** ★ (www.cross-pollinate.com; ✆ **800/270-1190** in U.S., 06/9936-9799 in Italy) has built a Florence apartment portfolio over 2 decades. Apartments are all handpicked and service is personal from the Rome-based team. The budget range is especially good.

An alternative budget option (offering a unique perspective) is to stay in a **religious house** ★. A few monasteries and convents in the center receive guests for a modest fee. Our favorites are the **Suore di Santa Elisabetta,** Viale Michelangiolo 46 (near Piazza Ferrucci; ✆ **055/681-1884**), in a colonial villa just south of the Ponte San Niccolò; and close to Santa Croce, the **Istituto Oblate dell'Assunzione,** Borgo Pinti 15 (✆ **055/2480-582**), which has simple, peaceful rooms in a Medici-era building ranged around a courtyard garden. The easiest way to build a monastery and convent itinerary in Florence and beyond is via agent **MonasteryStays.com** ★. Remember that most religious houses have a curfew, generally 11pm or midnight.

Tip: For basic grocery shopping in the center, try **Conad City,** Via dei Servi 56R (✆ **055/280-110**), or any central branch of **Carrefour**

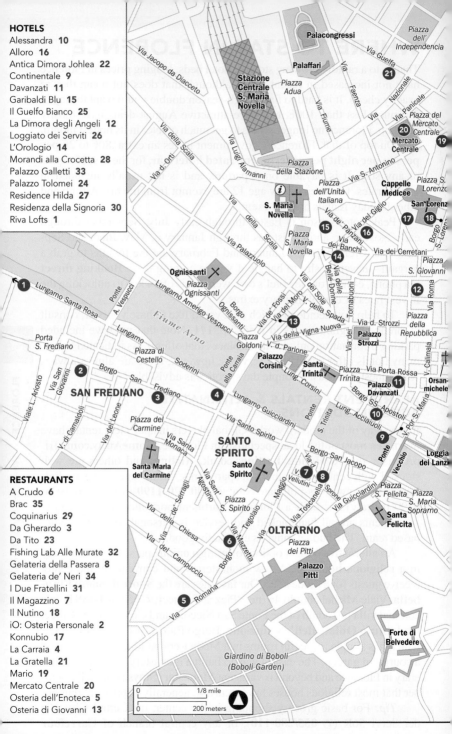

HOTELS
Alessandra **10**
Alloro **16**
Antica Dimora Johlea **22**
Continentale **9**
Davanzati **11**
Garibaldi Blu **15**
Il Guelfo Bianco **25**
La Dimora degli Angeli **12**
Loggiato dei Serviti **26**
L'Orologio **14**
Morandi alla Crocetta **28**
Palazzo Galletti **33**
Palazzo Tolomei **24**
Residence Hilda **27**
Residenza della Signoria **30**
Riva Lofts **1**

RESTAURANTS
A Crudo **6**
Brac **35**
Coquinarius **29**
Da Gherardo **3**
Da Tito **23**
Fishing Lab Alle Murate **32**
Gelateria della Passera **8**
Gelateria de' Neri **34**
I Due Fratellini **31**
Il Magazzino **7**
Il Nutino **18**
iO: Osteria Personale **2**
Konnubio **17**
La Carraia **4**
La Gratella **21**
Mario **19**
Mercato Centrale **20**
Osteria dell'Enoteca **5**
Osteria di Giovanni **13**

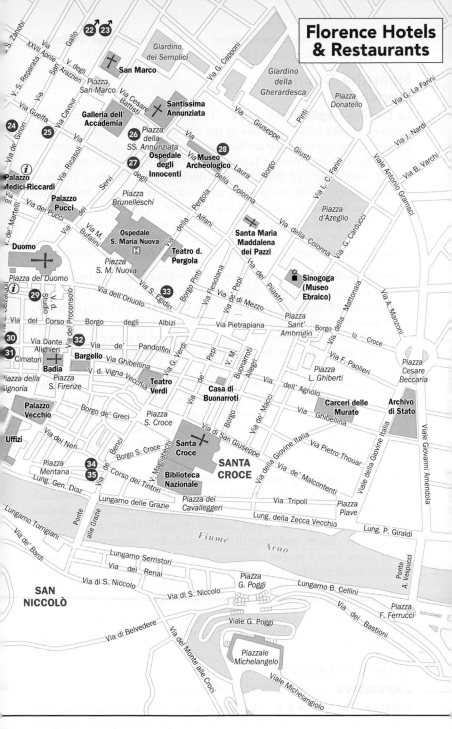

Express. Both the **Mercato Centrale** and **Mercato di Sant'Ambrogio** sell farm-fresh produce (see "Florence's Best Markets," p. 223).

Near the Duomo
MODERATE

La Dimora degli Angeli ★★★   This B&B occupies two levels of a grand apartment building in one of the city's busiest shopping districts. Rooms on the original floor are for romantics; bright wallpaper contrasts pleasingly with iron-framed beds and classic furniture. (Beatrice is the largest, with a view of Brunelleschi's dome—just.) The floor below is totally different, with sharp lines and leather or wooden headboards throughout. Breakfast is available at a local café, or if you prefer, you can grab a coffee in the B&B and use your token for a light lunch instead.

Via Brunelleschi 4. www.dimoredeicherubini.it. 🕐 **055/288-478.** 12 units. 58€–198€ double. Breakfast (at café) 7€–12€. Parking 26€. Bus: C2. **Amenities:** Wi-Fi (free).

Palazzo Galletti ★★   Not many hotels within a sensible budget give you the chance to live like a Florentine noble. Rooms here have towering ceilings and an uncluttered arrangement of carefully chosen antiques; most have frescoed or painted-wood showpiece ceilings. Bathrooms, in contrast, have a contemporary design, decked out in travertine and marble. Aside from two street-facing suites, every room has a small balcony, ideal for a pre-dinner glass of wine. If you're here for a once-in-a-lifetime trip, spring for the large suites "Giove" or (especially) "Cerere"; the latter has walls covered in frescoes from the 1800s. Snag a free bottle of their organic estate wine when you book direct and show this Frommer's guide.

Via Sant'Egidio 12. www.palazzogalletti.it. 🕐 **055/390-5750.** 11 units. 100€–170€ double; 170€–240€ suite. Rates include breakfast. Parking 30€–35€. Bus: C1, C2, 14, 23. **Amenities:** Babysitting; Wi-Fi (free).

Residenza della Signoria ★   Location and value take center-stage at this small inn on the fourth floor of an old palace. It's right on Florence's main drag, but thanks to modern soundproofing you'd never know. Rooms are spacious with antique-styled furnishings and ceilings, parquet flooring, luscious drapes, and king-size beds with firm mattresses. Only the junior suites have a proper panorama of Brunelleschi's cathedral dome, but for a smaller outlay, room 6 has a view from its bathroom window. A simple but tasty Continental breakfast is served next door at one of our favorite Florence café-bars, **Cantinetta dei Verrazzano** (p. 225).

Via dei Tavolini 8. www.residenzadellasignoria.com. 🕐 **055/264-5990.** 7 units. 89€–159€ double. Some rates include breakfast in café (otherwise 3.50€). Bus: C2. **Amenities:** Wi-Fi (free).

Near San Lorenzo
EXPENSIVE

Palazzo Tolomei ★★★   In its heyday, this palace was at the heart of Medici power. In 1505 it even welcomed the painter Raphael as a guest (probably in two rooms at the front, now Barocco 1 and 2). Guest rooms are all large, with Renaissance wooden ceilings and terracotta floors. Modern fittings—leather sofas, soft mattresses, and florid crystal chandeliers—chime perfectly with a 17th-century baroque redecoration, complete with ceiling frescoes by Alessandro Gherardini. The lower floor is given over to opulent public rooms, just like when it was the *piano nobile* of the family palazzo. These days you'll find a music room, art books, a welcoming host, and probably an open bottle of Tuscan red wine. Book direct for deals—perhaps free nightly aperitivo, free late checkout, or a discounted room rate.

Via de' Ginori 19. www.palazzotolomei.it. © **055/292-887.** 8 units. 120€–378€ double. Rates include breakfast (in nearby cafe). Bus: C1. **Amenities:** Concierge; Wi-Fi (free).

MODERATE

Il Guelfo Bianco ★★   Decor in this former noble Florentine home retains its authentic palazzo feel, though carpets have been added for comfort and warmth and there's full hotel service. No two rooms are the same—stone walls this thick cannot be knocked through—and several have antiques integrated into their individual schemes. Grand rooms at the front (especially 101, 118, and 228) have Renaissance coffered ceilings and masses of space. Sleep at the back and you'll wake to an unusual sound in Florence: birdsong. Under the same ownership, adjacent "farm-to-table" **Il Desco Bistrot** (www.ildescofirenze.it; © **055/288-330**) serves seasonal dishes made with organic ingredients. It's open to guests and non-guests alike.

Via Cavour 29 (near corner of Via Guelfa). www.ilguelfobianco.it. © **055/288-330.** 40 units. 90€–280€ double. Rates include breakfast. Parking 27€–33€. Bus: C1, 14, 23. **Amenities:** Restaurant; bar; babysitting; room service; Wi-Fi (free).

INEXPENSIVE

Alloro ★★   Officially a "bed-and-breakfast," this feels more like a small hotel, whose modern rooms inside a Renaissance palace overlook a silent inner courtyard—neatly soundproofing them against a noisy neighborhood. Rooms offer an excellent value for the price and location, with high ceilings, color-washed walls, and air-conditioning. Breakfast is a traditional spread of fresh fruit and pastries. A friendly ghost from the Renaissance era reputedly roams part of the palace; you're unlikely to get a discount if you spot him, but there's no harm in asking.

Via del Giglio 8. www.allorobb.it. © **055/211-685.** 5 units. 62€–183€ double. Rates include breakfast. Bus: C1. **Amenities:** Concierge; Wi-Fi (free).

Near the Ponte Vecchio
EXPENSIVE

Continentale ★★★   Everything about the Continentale is cool, and the effect is achieved without even a hint of frostiness. Rooms are uncompromisingly modern, decorated in bright white and bathed in natural light. Deluxe units, which are built into a medieval riverside tower, have mighty walls and medieval-sized windows (that is, small). Standard rooms are large (for Florence), and there's a retro-1950s feel to the overall styling.

Communal areas are a major hit, too: A relaxation room has a glass wall with a front-row view of the Ponte Vecchio. Top-floor **La Terrazza** (p. 225) is our favorite rooftop cocktail bar.

Vicolo dell'Oro 6R. www.lungarnocollection.com. ℂ **055/27-262.** 43 units. 230€–750€ double. Parking 35€. Bus: C3 or C4. **Amenities:** Bar; concierge; spa; Wi-Fi (free).

MODERATE

Alessandra ★   This typical Florentine *pensione* transports you back to the age of the gentleman and lady traveler. Decor has grown organically since it opened as a hotel in 1950; Alessandra is a place for evolution, not revolution. A pleasing mix of styles is the result—some rooms with carved headboards, gilt frames, and gold damask; others with eclectic postwar furniture, like a mid-century period movie set. A couple have views of the Arno, while front-side rooms overlook Borgo SS. Apostoli, one of the center's most atmospheric streets. Five additional rooms with all-out contemporary decor—including, across the street, two mezzanine mini-apartments with kitchenettes—have a separate website, **www.residenzaalessandra.com.**

Borgo SS. Apostoli 17. www.hotelalessandra.com. ℂ **055/283-438.** 27 units. 160€–180€ double. Rates include breakfast. Parking 25€. Bus: C3, C4, 6, 11, 36, 37. Closed a few days around Christmas. **Amenities:** Wi-Fi (free).

Davanzati ★★   Although installed inside a historic building, the Davanzati never rests on its medieval laurels: There is a laptop and an iPad with cellular data in every room for free guest use around the city, and movies to stream to your TV. Rooms are simply decorated in the Tuscan style, with color-washed walls and half-canopies over the beds. Room 100 is probably the best family hotel room in Florence, full of nooks, crannies, and split-levels that give the adults and the kids some private space. A free *aperitivo* for guests is part of the Davanzati's family welcome.

Via Porta Rossa 5 (on Piazza Davanzati). www.hoteldavanzati.it. ℂ **055/286-666.** 27 units. 99€–216€ double. Rates include breakfast. Parking 26€. Bus: C2. **Amenities:** Bar; babysitting; concierge; use of nearby gym; Wi-Fi (free).

Near Santa Maria Novella
MODERATE

Garibaldi Blu ★★   The hotels of Piazza Santa Maria Novella are frequented by fashion models, rock stars, and blue-chip business folk. You can get a taste of that, for a fraction of the price, at this boutique hotel with attitude. Each of the mostly midsize rooms is immaculate, and reflects the

---

The Untouchables

With a list finalized in 2019, Florence's government gives the ultimate protection to buildings and businesses interwoven with the city's historical fabric. At 150 locations, neither name nor trade can change—no matter who owns the business. These "untouchables" include some of our longtime favorite places to **stay** (Loggiato dei Serviti, p. 213; Morandi alla Crocetta, p. 213), or just have a **coffee** (Procacci, p. 225).

"warm denim" palette, with retro 1970s furniture, parquet floors, and marble bathrooms. It's well worth paying 30€ extra for a deluxe room at the front: These have much more space and a view over Florence's prettiest church facade, Santa Maria Novella. Dotted around the hotel, life-sized models of superheroes like Captain America add a fun surreal touch.

Piazza Santa Maria Novella 21. www.hotelgaribaldiblu.com. © **055/277-300.** 21 units. 130€–350€ double. Rates include breakfast. Parking 35€–48€. Bus: C2, 6, 11, 22. **Amenities:** Bar; babysitting (pre-booking essential); concierge; Wi-Fi (free).

L'Orologio ★   As the name suggests, this hotel is an homage to the clock, with historic timepiece designs scattered artfully about. The color palette is rich, with mahogany wood and natural leather everywhere. The cheapest rooms ("superior") are not large, but their marble bathrooms are, and library-like wood-paneled common areas are spacious and comfortable. Staff is superb. L'Orologio is atmospheric and close to the train station; the view from its top-floor breakfast room is a showstopper.

Piazza Santa Maria Novella 24. www.hotelorologioflorence.com. © **055/277-380.** 55 units. 95€–350€ double. Rates include breakfast. Parking 35€–48€. Bus: C2, 6, 11, 22. **Amenities:** Bar; babysitting; concierge; gym; sauna; Wi-Fi (free).

Near San Marco & Santissima Annunziata
MODERATE
Loggiato dei Serviti ★★   Stay here to experience Florence as the gentleman and lady visitors of the Grand Tour did. For starters, the building is a genuine Renaissance landmark, built by Sangallo the Elder in the 1520s. There is a sense of faded grandeur and unconventional luxury throughout—no gadgetry or chromatherapy showers, but you will find rooms with writing desks and lots of vintage ambience. No unit is small, but standard rooms lack a view of either Brunelleschi's dome or the perfect piazza outside. Air-conditioning is pretty much the only concession to the 21st century—and you will love it that way. Book direct for the best deals.

Piazza Santissima Annunziata 3. www.loggiatodeiservitihotel.it. © **055/289-592.** 37 units. 120€–330€ double. Rates include breakfast. Valet parking 22€. Bus: C1, 6, 14, 19, 23, 31, 32. **Amenities:** Babysitting; concierge; Wi-Fi (free).

Morandi alla Crocetta ★★   Like many in Florence, Morandi alla Crocetta was built in the shell of a former convent, and it has retained the original convent layout, meaning some rooms are snug. But what you lose in size, you more than gain in character: Every single one oozes *tipico fiorentino*—even the "new" breakfast room feels like you're on the Grand Tour. Rooms have parquet floors, throw rugs, and antique wood furniture. Original 1744 Zocchi prints of Florence are scattered around the place. Superior rooms have more space and either a private courtyard terrace or, in one, original frescoes decorating an entrance to the former convent chapel (the chapel itself is sealed off). The hotel is set on a quiet street.

Via Laura 50. www.hotelmorandi.it. © **055/234-4747.** 12 units. 90€–177€ double. Rates include breakfast. Parking 25€. Bus: 6, 19, 31, 32. **Amenities:** Bar; babysitting; concierge; Wi-Fi (free).

Residence Hilda ★★   With no hint of the Renaissance, these luxe mini-apartments are all bright-white decor and designer furnishings, with natural wood flooring, hypoallergenic mattresses, Starck chairs, and modern gadgetry. Each is spacious, cool in summer, and soundproofed against Florence's perma-noise. Every unit has a mini-kitchen, equipped for preparing a simple meal, ideal if you have kids in tow. The top-floor Executive unit has a Nespresso machine, yoga mat, and an exercise bike. Unusual for apartments, all are bookable by the single night.

Via dei Servi 40. www.residencehilda.com. ✆ **055/288-021.** 12 units. 90€–400€ for 2–4-person apartments. Parking 31€. Bus: C1. **Amenities:** Airport transfer; babysitting; concierge; room service; Wi-Fi (free).

West of the Center
MODERATE

Riva Lofts ★★   The traditional Florentine alarm call—a morning mix of traffic and tourism—is replaced by birdsong when you awake in one of these stylish rooms on the banks of the River Arno. A former artisan workshop, Riva had a refit to earn its "loft" label: mellow color schemes, laminate flooring, floating staircases, marble bathrooms with rainfall showers, and clever integration of natural materials such as original wooden workshop ceilings. Noon checkouts are standard—a traveler-friendly touch. The center is a 30-minute walk, or hop on one of Riva's vintage-style bikes and cycle to the Uffizi along the river. Another standout feature in this price bracket is the shaded garden with outdoor plunge pool.

Via Baccio Bandinelli 98. www.rivalofts.com. ✆ **055/713-0272.** 10 units. 145€–335€ double. Rates include breakfast. Parking 20€. Bus: 6. Tram: T1 (3 stops from central station). **Amenities:** Bar; bike rental (free); outdoor pool; Wi-Fi (free).

North of the Center
MODERATE

Antica Dimora Johlea ★   There's a real neighborhood feel to the streets around this *dimora* (traditional Florentine home) guesthouse, which means evenings are lively and Sundays are quiet (although it's less than a 10-minute walk to San Lorenzo). Standard-size rooms are snug; upgrade to a deluxe if you need more space, but there is no difference in the standard of decor, a mix of Florentine and earthy boho. Help yourself to coffee, a soft drink, or a glass of wine from the honesty bar and head up to a roof terrace for knockout views over the terra-cotta rooftops to the center and hills beyond. It is pure magic at dusk. No credit cards.

Via San Gallo 80. www.antichedimorefiorentine.it. ✆ **055/463-3292.** 6 units. 90€–220€ double. Rates include breakfast. Parking 25€. Bus: C1, 1, 6, 11, 14, 17, 23. **Amenities:** Bar; Wi-Fi (free).

WHERE TO EAT IN FLORENCE

Florence is well supplied with restaurants, though in the most touristy areas (around the Duomo, Piazza della Signoria, Piazza della Repubblica,

Coquinarius is known for its rustic Tuscan fare.

and the Ponte Vecchio), you must choose carefully—many eateries are of below-average quality or charge high prices, sometimes both. The highest concentrations of excellent *ristoranti* and *trattorie* are around **Santa Croce** and across the river in the **Oltrarno** and **San Frediano.** There's also an increasing buzz around **San Lorenzo,** including the top floor of the Mercato Centrale (p. 218) where a wealth of counters sell delicious street food. Bear in mind that menus at restaurants can change weekly or even daily. The city has also become much more **gluten-savvy.** If you have any sort of food intolerance, don't be afraid to ask.

Reservations are strongly recommended if you have your heart set on eating anywhere in particular, especially at dinner on weekends. *Tip:* You can book at many Florence restaurants, including several of our favorites below, using **The Fork** (www.thefork.it) or **Quandoo** (www. quandoo.it) restaurant reservation services.

Near the Duomo
MODERATE
Coquinarius ★★ TUSCAN   There is a regular menu here of pasta, main courses such as beef cheeks with red wine and caramelized onions, and traditional desserts. But it's equally pleasurable just tucking into a couple of sharing plates and quaffing from the excellent wine list. Go for something from an extensive carpaccio list (beef, boar, octopus, swordfish) and maybe pair a *misto di salumi e formaggi* (mixed Tuscan salami and cheeses) with a full-bodied red wine, to cut through the strong flavors of the deliciously fatty, salty pork and Tuscan sheep's milk cheese, pecorino. Via delle Oche 11R. www.coquinarius.it. © **055/230-2153.** Entrees 15€–20€. Daily 12:30–3pm and 6:30–10:30pm. Bus: C1 or C2.

Fishing Lab Alle Murate ★★ SEAFOOD   This contemporary-styled temple to seafood serves fish any way you like (almost). The range is safe—shrimp, tuna, bream, bass, and salmon dominate—but fish are carefully sourced and preparation is modern. Tartare and carpaccio are both super-fresh and dressed delicately with citrus fruit. Hot main courses include grilled fillets, fishy pastas, and *fritto misto* (a mixed fry of baby squid, shrimp, and sardines served in a skillet). Both clientele and staff are young and lively, matching the decor of urban furniture amid frescoes. Service is brisk. Half-portions are available at lunch; they also do takeout (even fish and chips). Reservations highly recommended.

Via del Proconsolo 16R. www.fishinglab.it. *C* **055/240-618.** Entrees 12€–14€. Daily 11am–11pm. Bus: C1 or C2.

INEXPENSIVE

I Due Fratellini ★ SANDWICHES   This hole-in-the-wall has been serving food to go since 1875. The drill is simple: Choose a filling, pick a drink, then eat your fast-filled roll on the curb opposite or find a nearby piazza to perch. There are around 30 fillings to choose from, including the usual Tuscan meats and cheeses—salami, pecorino, cured ham—and more flamboyant combos such as goat cheese and Calabrian spicy salami or *bresaola* (air-dried beef) and wild arugula. A glass of wine to wash it down costs from 2€. No credit cards. Lunchtime lines can be long.

Via dei Cimatori 38R (at corner of Via Calzaiuoli). www.iduefratellini.it. *C* **055/239-6096.** Sandwiches 4€. Daily 10am–7pm. Bus: C2.

Near Santa Trinita

MODERATE

Osteria di Giovanni ★★ MODERN TUSCAN   If only every Tuscan restaurant in town was this good. Family-run Osteria di Giovanni is a standout in this category and therefore always buzzing: You should reserve even in low season. Meat is a specialty, both traditional (the *bistecca alla fiorentina* is legendary) and modern interpretations like *faraona all'arancia* (guinea hen stewed in slightly sweet orange). Only the very brave should attempt a *primo/secondo/dolce* route, since portions are large. A seemingly steep cover charge (4€) is actually a good deal, because it includes a couple of tasty snacks and all the mineral water you can drink.

Via del Moro 22. www.osteriadigiovanni.com. *C* **055/284-897.** Entrees 18€–28€. Daily 7–10:30pm; Sat–Sun also 12:30–2:30pm. Bus: 6, 11.

Near San Lorenzo

Florence's best sandwich bar, **Sandwichic** ★★, Via San Gallo 3R (www.sandwichic.it; *C* **055/281-157**), keeps things simple, with freshly baked bread and expertly sourced ingredients including Tuscan-cured meats and savory preserves. Try the likes of *finocchiona* (salami spiked with fennel), pecorino cheese, and *crema di porri* (a creamy leek relish). Sandwiches cost around 4.50€. It's open daily 11am to 5:45pm.

MODERATE

Konnubio ★ CREATIVE TUSCAN/VEGAN   There's a warm glow (candles and low-watt lighting) about this place; it makes you instantly happy, and the cooking keeps you there. Ingredients are largely Tuscan, but combined creatively, such as in warm guinea hen salad with cream of roasted tomatoes, or a risotto of pumpkin, gorgonzola cheese, and almond. There's an extensive vegan menu, too, like curried cream of yellow squash with crispy tofu and mango. Under brick vaults and a covered courtyard, it could work for a romantic dinner; but you won't be out of place in a family group either. Dishes are simpler at lunch.

Via dei Conti 8R. www.konnubio.com/it. ℰ **055-238-1189.** Entrees 18€–28€; tasting menus 45€–85€. Daily noon–3pm and 7–10:30pm. Bus: C1.

Il Nutino ★★ TUSCAN   This tiny, traditional joint has been in business since the 1950s. It's become our go-to for sublime *bistecca alla fiorentina,* in both classic and marbled styles. Whichever you choose, it spends a short time on the grill and is best served simply with roasted potatoes and *fagioli al fiasco* (beans stewed in olive oil). There's also a full Tuscan menu of fresh pasta, *crostini,* soups and the like. Service is attentive and knowledgeable, especially when it comes to selecting a wine to wash down the red meat (Chianti Rufina Nipozzano is our choice). The location is one of Florence's most heavily touristed areas, but with over 6 decades behind them, they are doing things the right way.

Borgo San Lorenzo 39R. ℰ **349/453-6035.** Entrees 12€–22€. Daily 10am–11pm. Bus: C1.

La Gratella ★★ FLORENTINE/GRILL   It doesn't look much—a workers' canteen on a nondescript side street—but looks don't matter much when you can source and cook meat like they do here. Star of the show is the *fiorentina* steak, a large T-bone-like cut grilled on the bone and brought to the table over coals. It is sold by weight and made for sharing; expect to pay about 50€. Pair this or any market-fresh meat on the menu with simple Tuscan sides like beans stewed in olive oil. They cater to celiacs, too.

Via Guelfa 81R. www.lagratella.it. ℰ **055/211-292.** Entrees 10€–20€. Daily noon–3pm and 7–11pm. Bus: 1, 6, 11, 14, 17, 23.

INEXPENSIVE

Mario ★ TRADITIONAL FLORENTINE   There is no doubt that this market workers' trattoria is firmly on the tourist trail. But Mario's clings to the traditions and ethos it adopted when it first fired up the burners 60 years ago. Food is simple, hearty, and served at communal tables—"check in" on arrival and you will be offered seats together wherever they come free. Think *passato di fagioli* (bean puree soup) followed by traditional Tuscan beef stew, *peposo,* or *coniglio arrosto* (roast rabbit). No reservations or credit cards.

Via Rosina 2R (north corner of Piazza Mercato Centrale). www.trattoriamario.com. ℰ **055/218-550.** Entrees 8.50€–14€. Mon–Sat noon–3:30pm. Closed Aug. Bus: C1.

Mercato Centrale ★★ MODERN ITALIAN   The upper floor of Florence's produce market is a bustling shrine to modern street food. Counters sell dishes from all over Italy: pasta, vegetarian and vegan fare, authentic Neapolitan pizza, meats and cheeses, fresh fish, Chianina burgers, Florentine boiled beef dripping in its own juices, and much more. It works perfectly for families who can't agree on a dinner choice, or just stop by for a drink and soak up the buzz: There's a beer bar and a superb enoteca where you can buy by the glass or bottle, plus soccer matches on a big screen.
Piazza Mercato Centrale. www.mercatocentrale.it. ℂ**055/239-9798.** Dishes 5€–20€. Daily 10am–midnight. Bus: C1.

Near San Marco

San Marco is the place to head for *schiacciata,* olive-oil flatbread loaded with savory toppings. You will find some of the best at **Pugi ★**, Piazza San Marco 9B (www.fornopugi.it; ℂ **055/280-981**), open Monday to Saturday 7:30am to 8pm, but closed most of August.

MODERATE

Da Tito ★★ TUSCAN/FLORENTINE   Every night feels like party night at one of central Florence's rare genuine neighborhood trattorias. (For that reason, it's usually packed. Book ahead.) The dishes are classic Florentine, with a few modern Italian curveballs: Start, perhaps, with the *risotto con piselli e guanciale* (rice with fresh peas and cured pork cheek) before going on to a traditional grill such as *lombatina di vitella* (veal chop steak). The neighborhood location, a 10-minute walk north of San Lorenzo, and a mixed clientele keep quality very consistent.
Via San Gallo 112R. www.trattoriadatito.it. ℂ **055/472-475.** Entrees 10€–18€. Mon–Sat 12:30–3pm and 7–11pm. Bus: C1, 1, 7, 20, 25.

Near Santa Croce
MODERATE
Brac ★★ VEGETARIAN/VEGAN   An artsy cafe-bookshop for most of the day, at lunch and dinner this place turns into one of Florence's best spots for vegetarian and vegan food. There are seasonal salads and

creative pasta dishes, but a *piatto unico* works out best for hungry diners: one combo plate loaded with three different dishes from the menu, perhaps pear carpaccio with Grana Padano cheese and a balsamic reduction; *tagliatelle* with broccoli, pecorino, and lemon; plus a *pane carasau* (Sardinian flatbread) with eggplant and buffalo mozzarella. The courtyard atmosphere is intimate and romantic, yet singletons won't feel out of place eating at the counter out front. Booking at dinner is a must.

Via dei Vagellai 18R. www.libreriabrac.net. ✆ **055/094-4877.** Entrees 10€–15€. Daily noon–midnight. Bus: C1, C3, 23.

In the Oltrarno & San Frediano
EXPENSIVE

iO: Osteria Personale ★★★ CONTEMPORARY TUSCAN There's a definite hipster atmosphere here, with the whitewashed brick and young staff, but a fine dining ethos is ingrained, too. Ingredients are familiar to Tuscan cooking, but combined in a way you may not have seen before. The menu always has a range of seafood, meat, and vegetarian dishes—think tempura artichoke flowers stuffed with taleggio cheese and marjoram, followed by smoked chestnut ravioli with wild fennel, then roasted octopus with celeriac, green apple, and cardamom. Reservations are advised. This place's reputation has only grown in the years since we first recommended it.

Borgo San Frediano 167R. www.io-osteriapersonale.it. ✆ **055/933-1341.** Entrees 21€–24€; tasting menus 40€–57€. Mon–Sat 7:30–10pm. Closed 10 days in Jan and all of Aug. Bus: D or 6.

MODERATE

A Crudo ★ CONTEMPORARY ITALIAN/RAW FOOD The name means "raw," which provides a clue to the strengths of this inventive spot. A short carpaccio list might include the likes of venison with bitter citrus and pink peppercorn vinaigrette. But the real star is the meat tartare, done in traditional style as well as in such creative combos as Kathmandù (with lime and avocado) and Marinata (with gin and parsley). There's also vegetarian raw food tartare. A Crudo is a perfect example of modern Florence doing what it does best: tapping into food traditions and letting them breathe some 21st-century air.

Via Mazzetta 5R. ✆ **055/265-7483.** Entrees 10€–20€. Daily 12:30–3pm and 7pm–midnight. Bus: C3, 11, 36, 37.

Il Magazzino ★ FLORENTINE A traditional *osteria* that specializes in the flavors of old Florence, it looks the part, too, with its terracotta tiled floor and barrel vault, chunky wooden furniture, and hanging lamps. If you dare, this is a place to try tripe or *lampredotto* (intestines), the traditional food of working Florentines, prepared expertly in ravioli or meatballs, boiled, or *alla fiorentina* (stewed with tomatoes and garlic). The rest of the menu is carnivore-friendly too. Follow *tagliatelle al ragù bianco* (pasta ribbons with a "white" meat sauce made with a little milk instead of tomatoes) with *guancia di vitello in agrodolce* (veal cheek stewed with baby onions in a sticky-sweet sauce).

Piazza della Passera 3. ✆ **055/215-969.** Entrees 10€–20€. Daily noon–3pm and 7:30–11pm. Bus: C3 or C4.

Osteria dell'Enoteca ★★★ MODERN TUSCAN Opened in 2017 by experienced wine bar owners, this place majors in reasonably priced, refined dining. Traditional flavors dominate, although combinations are just as often modern, in such dishes as a poached egg "affogato," floating in a pecorino cheese cream with wild mushrooms. Portions are not large, so cut loose and order three courses. There's also no wine list; an English-speaking waiter leads you to a chiller stocked with boutique labels—strong on Tuscan as well as Langhe/Piedmont reds. The dining room itself is elegant and refined, with slate floor, stripped brick, and soft jazz; this is the place for a special occasion or romantic meal that won't bust your budget.

Via Romana 70R. ✆ **055/228-6018.** Entrees 12€–18€. Wed–Mon noon–2:30pm and 7–10:30pm. Bus: 11, 36, 37.

INEXPENSIVE

Da Gherardo ★★ PIZZA This informal, cave-like restaurant is packed tight with tables for a reason: It's always busy. Pizzas arrive quickly from a wood-fired oven, in Naples style. Toppings go well beyond Neapolitan tradition, however—with *'nduja* (soft, spicy salami), *provola* cheese, and basil on the menu—but the marinara (tomato, garlic, oregano, basil) is hard to beat. Reservations are strongly advised, but if you forget, they do takeout, which you can munch around the corner in Piazza del Carmine.

Borgo San Frediano 57R. ✆ **055/205-2888.** Pizzas 5€–12€. Daily 7:30pm–1am. Bus: C4 or 6.

Gelato

Florence has a fair claim to being the birthplace of gelato, and has some of the world's best *gelaterie*—but many poor imitations, too. Steer clear of spots around major attractions with air-fluffed mountains of ice cream and flavors so full of artificial colors they glow in the dark. If you can see the Ponte Vecchio or Piazza della Signoria from the front door of the gelateria, you may want to move on. Walk a block, or duck down a side street, to find a genuine gelato artisan. Trust us, you'll taste the difference. Opening hours tend to be discretionary; when it's warm, many places stay open beyond 11pm.

Florence's gelato is considered by many to be Italy's—and therefore the world's—best.

Gelateria della Passera ★★ Milk-free water ices here are among the most intensely flavored in the city, and relatively low in sugary sweetness. Try the likes of pink grapefruit or jasmine tea gelato. Via Toscanella 15R (at Piazza della Passera). www.gelaterialapassera.wordpress.com. (✆) **055/291-002.** Cone from 2€. Bus: C3 or C4.

Gelateria de' Neri ★ There's a large range of fruit, white, and chocolate flavors here, but nothing over-elaborate. If the ricotta and fig flavor is offered, you are in luck. There's also a restroom. Via dei Neri 9R. (✆) **055/210-034.** Cone from 1.80€. Bus: C1, C3, 23.

La Carraia ★★ It's packed with locals late into the evening on summer weekends—for good reason. The range is vast, the quality high. Piazza N. Sauro 25R. www.lacarraiagroup.eu. (✆) **055/280-695.** Cone from 2€. Bus: C3, C4, 6, 11, 36, 37. Closed Jan. Also at: Via de' Benci 24R ((✆) 329/363-0069).

FLORENCE SHOPPING

After Milan, Florence is **Italy's top shopping city**—beating even Rome. Here's what to buy: leather, designer fashion, shoes, marbleized paper, hand-embroidered linens, ceramics, Tuscan wines, handmade jewelry, *pietre dure* (known also as "Florentine mosaic," inlaid semiprecious stones), and antiques. *Note:* It is illegal to knowingly buy fake goods anywhere in the city (and yes, a "Louis Vuitton" bag at 10€ counts as *knowingly*). You may be served a hefty on-the-spot fine if caught.

Traditionally, Florentine **shopping hours** are Monday through Saturday from 9:30am to noon or 1pm and 3 or 3:30 to 7:30pm. Increasingly, larger shops and those in tourist areas stay open on Sunday and through the midafternoon *riposo,* or "nap." Some small or family-run places close Monday mornings instead of Sundays.

Top Shopping Streets & Areas

AROUND SANTA TRÍNITA The cream of the crop of Florentine shopping lines both sides of elegant **Via de' Tornabuoni,** with an extension along **Via della Vigna Nuova** and other surrounding streets. Here you'll find the big Italian fashion names like **Gucci** ★ (at no. 73R; www.gucci.com; (✆) **055/264-011**), **Pucci** ★ (at no. 22R; www.emilio pucci.com; (✆) **055/265-8082**), and **Ferragamo** ★ (at no. 5R; www. ferragamo.com; (✆) **055/292-123**), ensconced in old palaces or minimalist boutiques; couture meets

Florence is known for its beautiful hand-tooled leather goods.

streetwear at concept sneaker store **SOTF** ★ (at no. 17R; www.sotf.com; ✆ **055/588-302**). Florence-headquartered **Benheart** ★★ (Via della Vigna Nuova 97R; www.benheart.it; ✆ **055/239-9483**) sells up-to-the-minute Italian leather clothing, footwear and accessories. Stricter traffic control has made shopping on Via de' Tornabuoni a more sedate experience, though somewhat at the expense of surrounding streets.

AROUND VIA ROMA & VIA DEI CALZAIUOLI These are some of Florence's busiest streets, packed with storefronts offering mainstream shopping. Here you'll find the city's major department stores, **Coin,** Via dei Calzaiuoli 56R (www.coin.it; ✆ **055/280-531**), and **La Rinascente,** Piazza della Repubblica (www.rinascente.it; ✆ **055/219-113**), alongside quality clothing chains such as Geox and Zara. **La Feltrinelli RED,** Piazza delle Repubblica 26 (www.lafeltrinelli.it; ✆ **199/151-173**), is the center's best bookstore. A three-floor branch of upscale food-market mini-chain **Eataly** lies just north of the Baptistery at Via de' Martelli 22 (www.eataly.net; ✆ **055/015-3601**). Online couture sales sensation **Luisa Via Roma** ★ (www.luisaviaroma.com) also has its flagship physical store here, at Via Roma 21R.

AROUND SANTA CROCE The eastern part of the center has seen a flourishing of one-of-a-kind stores, with an emphasis on young, independent fashions. **Borgo degli Albizi** and its tributary streets are worth roaming— **Sabatini** ★ (at no. 75R; www.sabatiniscarpe.it; ✆ **055/234-0240**) is a well-established go-to for affordable casual footwear.

Crafts & Artisans

Florence has a longstanding reputation for its craftsmanship. Although storefront display windows along touristed streets are often stuffed with cheap imports and mass-produced goods, if you search around you can still find handmade, top-quality items.

Madova ★★ For a century, this has been the best city retailer for handmade leather gloves, lined with silk, cashmere, or lambs' wool. You'll pay between 50€ and 90€ for a pair. Madova is the real deal, even this close to the Ponte Vecchio. Closed Sundays. Via Guicciardini 1R. www.madova.com. ✆ **055/239-6526.** Bus: C3 or D.

Marioluca Giusti ★★ The boutique of this renowned Florentine designer sells only his trademark synthetic acrylic crystal. The range includes colorful reinventions of cocktail and wine glasses, jugs, and tumblers—every piece both tough and chic. Via della Spada 20R. www.mariolucagiusti.it. ✆ **055/214-583.** Bus: 6 or 11. Also at: Via della Vigna Nuova 88R; Via Por S. Maria 16R.

Officina Profumo-Farmaceutica di Santa Maria Novella ★★★
A shrine to scents and skin care, this is Florence's historic herbal pharmacy, with roots in the 17th century, when it was founded by Dominicans from the adjacent convent of Santa Maria Novella. Nothing is cheap, but

the perfumes, cosmetics, moisturizers, and other products are handmade from the finest natural ingredients and packaged exquisitely. Via della Scala 16. www.smnovella.com. ✆ **055/216-276.** Bus: C2.

Parione ★   This traditional Florentine stationer stocks notebooks, marbleized paper, fine pens, and souvenirs like handmade wooden music boxes and playing cards with 17th-century Florentine designs. Via dello Studio 11R. www.parione.it. ✆ **055/215-684.** Bus: C1 or C2.

Scuola del Cuoio ★★   Florence's leading leather school is also open house for visitors. You can watch trainee leatherworkers and gilders at work (Monday–Friday), then visit the small store to buy the best soft leather. Portable items like wallets, belts, and bags are a good buy. Closed Sundays in low season. Via San Giuseppe 5R (or enter through Santa Croce, via right transept). www.scuoladelcuoio.com. ✆ **055/244-534.** Bus: C3.

Florence's Best Markets

Mercato Centrale ★★   The center's main market stocks the usual fresh produce, but you can also browse (and taste) cheeses, salamis and cured hams, Tuscan wines, takeout food, and more. This is picnic-packing heaven. It runs Monday to Saturday until 2pm (until 5pm Sat for most of the year). Upstairs is street-food nirvana, all day, every day; see p. 218. Btw. Piazza del Mercato Centrale and Via dell'Ariento. No phone. Bus: C1.

Mercato di San Lorenzo ★ The city's tourist street market is a fun place to pick up T-shirts, marbleized paper, a leather-bound notebook, or some other city souvenir. Leather wallets, purses, bags, and jackets are popular with international visitors—be sure to assess the workmanship, which can be variable, and haggle shamelessly. This busy market runs daily; watch for pickpockets. Via dell'Ariento and Via Rosina. No phone. Bus: C1.

Food stall in the Mercado Centrale.

ENTERTAINMENT & NIGHTLIFE

Florence has excellent, mostly free listings publications. At the tourist offices, pick up the free monthly *Informacittà* (www.informacitta.net), which is strong on theater, concerts, and other arts events, as well as one-off markets. Younger and hipper *Zero* (www.zero.eu/firenze), available free from trendy cafe-bars and shops, is hot on the latest eating, drinking, and edgy nightlife. *Firenze Spettacolo,* a 2€ Italian-language monthly sold at newsstands, is the most detailed and up-to-date listing of nightlife, arts, and entertainment. English-language magazine "The Florentine" publishes weekly events and listings at **www.theflr.net/weekly**.

If you just want to wander and see what grabs you, you will find plenty of tourist-oriented action in bars around the city's main squares. For something a little livelier—with a more local focus—visit **Borgo San Frediano, Piazza Santo Spirito,** or the northern end of **Via de' Macci,** close to where it meets Via Pietrapiana. **Via de' Benci** is usually buzzing around *aperitivo* time, and is popular with an expat crowd. **Via de' Renai** and the bars of San Niccolò around the **Porta San Miniato** are often lively too, with a mixed crowd of tourists and locals.

Arts & Live Music

Florence does not have the musical cachet of Milan, Venice, Naples, or Rome, but there are two symphony orchestras and a fine music school in Fiesole, as well as a modern opera house (see p. 224). The city's theaters are respectable, and most major touring companies stop in town. Get tickets to all cultural events online, or buy in person at **Box Office,** Via delle Vecchie Carceri 1 (www.boxofficetoscana.it; ℭ **055/210-804**).

Many classical chamber music performances are sponsored by the **Amici della Musica** (www.amicimusicafirenze.it; ℭ **055/607-440**), so check their website to see what's on while you are here. The venue is often the historic **Teatro della Pergola;** prices range 15€ to 28€. The restored Art Deco **Odeon Firenze ★** (Piazza Strozzi; www.odeonfirenze.com; ℭ 055/214-068) theater shows the latest movies in their original language (8.50€).

Libreria-Café La Cité ★   A relaxed café-bookshop by day, after dark this place becomes a bar and small-scale live music venue. The lineup is eclectic, with often offbeat or world music. One night, it's forrò or swing, the next Italian folk or chanteuse. Check their Facebook page to see what's on. Borgo San Frediano 20R. ℭ **055/210-387.** Bus: C3, C4, 6, 11, 36, 37.

Opera di Firenze ★★   This vast new concert hall and arts complex seats up to 1,800 in daring modernist surrounds on the edge of the Cascine Park. Its program incorporates opera, ballet, and orchestral music. In May and June, the same venue hosts the **Maggio Musicale Fiorentino,** one of Italy's most prestigious music festivals. Piazzale Vittorio Gui. www.operadifirenze.it. ℭ **055/277-9350.** Tickets 10€–120€. Tram: T1.

St. Mark's ★   Operatic duets and budget full-scale operas in costume are the lure here. The program sticks to crowd-pleasers like "The Barber of Seville," "La Traviata," and "La Bohème" and runs most nights of the week all year (fewer January–February). Via Maggio 18. www.concertoclassico.info. ℭ **340/811-9192.** Tickets 15€–35€. Bus: D, 11, 36, 37.

Volume ★   By day, it's a laid-back cafe and art space selling coffee, books, and crepes. By night, it serves *aperitivo* from 6:30pm then becomes a buzzing cocktail bar with live acoustic sets. Piazza Santo Spirito 5R. www.volumefirenze.com. ℭ **055/238-1460.** Bus: C3, 11, 36, 37.

Cafes

Florence no longer has a glitterati or intellectuals' cafe scene, and when it did—from the 19th-century Risorgimento era through 1950s *Dolce Vita*—it was basically copying the idea from Paris. Although they're often overpriced tourist spots today—especially around **Piazza della Repubblica**—Florence's high-toned cafes are fine if you want pastries served to you while you sit and people-watch.

Caffetteria delle Oblate ★   This relaxing terrace is popular with local families and students, well away from the tourist crush (and prices). As a bonus, it has a unique view of Brunelleschi's dome, and serves light lunch and *aperitivo*. Closed Monday morning. Top floor of Biblioteca dell'Oblate, Via del Oriuolo 24. www.caffetteriadelleoblate.it. ℂ **055/263-9685.** Bus: C1 or C2.

Cantinetta dei Verrazzano ★★
One of the coziest little café-bars in the center is decked out with antique wooden wine cabinets, in genuine *enoteca* style. Wines come from the first-rate Verrazzano estate, in Chianti (see p. 249). Light breakfast and morning cappuccino is a delight. Closed evenings and all day Sunday. Via dei Tavolini 18R. www.verrazzano. com. ℂ **055/268-590.** Bus: C2.

La Terrazza ★   The prices, like the perch, are a little elevated (3€– 5€ for a coffee). But you get to enjoy your drink on a hidden terrace in the sky, with just the rooftops,

Cantinetta dei Verrazzano.

towers, and Brunelleschi's dome for company. Top floor of La Rinascente, Piazza della Repubblica. www.larinascente.it. ℂ **055/219-113.** Bus: C2.

Procacci ★   The second you walk through the door, you're hit with the perfume of Procacci's specialty: *panini tartufati,* brioche rolls spread with truffle butter. Via Tornabuoni 64R. www.procacci1885.it. ℂ **055/211-656.** Bus: C3.

Rivoire ★   If you want to pick one overpriced sidewalk cafe in Florence, make it this one. The steep prices (6€ a cappuccino, 4.50€ for a small mineral water) help pay the rent of one of the prettiest slices of real estate on the planet. Piazza della Signoria (at Via Vaccherreccia). www.rivoire.it. ℂ **055/214-412.** Bus: C2.

Wine Bars, Cocktail Bars & Craft Beer Bars

To party into the wee hours, you will likely find Italian **nightclubs** rather cliquey. People usually go in groups to hang out and dance only with one another. There's plenty of flesh showing, but no meat market. Out in the 'burbs, **Tenax,** Via Pratese 46 (www.tenax.org; ℭ 335/523-5922), is a nightlife icon and attracts big-name DJs on Friday and Saturday nights.

Beer House Club ★   Artisan beers from Tuscany, Italy, and farther afield are poured: between 5 and 8pm, house beers are 5€ a pint instead of 6€. Corso Tintori 34R. www.beerhouseclub.eu. ℭ **055/247-6763.** Bus: C1, C3, 23.

Bitter Bar ★★   New-breed craft cocktails and twisted classics are served in a speakeasy-style bar with low lighting and moody, midcentury modern décor. Mixology is first rate. Reserve a table on weekends. Via di Mezzo 28R. www.bitterbarfirenze.it. ℭ **340/549-9258.** Bus: C2 or C3.

Fermento ★   Right opposite the Medici Chapels, this tiny bar serves Italian and Belgian craft beers in every style from IPA to stout, and carb-rich food to soak it up. Via Canto dei Nelli 38R. http://fermentofirenze.com. ℭ **055/267-5817.** Bus: C1.

Mayday ★   A Florence original, this laidback bar offers virgin and eccentric signature cocktails commemorating famous Tuscans and events in 20th-century history. Decked out like a mismatched junk store, there's a randomness that's genuinely effective—everything from old school desks to low-watt lamps hang from the ceiling. Via Dante Alighieri 16R. www.maydayclub.it. ℭ **055/238-1290.** Bus: C2.

Mostodolce ★   Burgers, pizza, snacks, Wi-Fi, and sports on the screen—so far, so good. And Mostodolce also has its own artisan beers on tap, brewed just outside Florence at Prato (some are very strong). Happy hour is 3:30 to 7:30pm, when it is 4€ a pint. Via Nazionale 114R. ℭ **055/230-2928.** Bus: 1, 6, 11, 14, 17, 23.

O' Café ★   At this elegant, minimalist *aperitivo* spot, you'll pay 10€ to 14€ for a cocktail or glass of sparkling wine and help yourself to the buffet between 6:30 and 9pm every night. Live jazz plays from 8:30pm 3 nights a week (usually Monday & Friday–Saturday) in the adjoining Golden View Open Bar (essentially the same place). Via dei Bardi 56R. www.goldenviewopenbar.com. ℭ **055/214-502.** Bus: C3.

Sant'Ambrogio ★   This wine and cocktail bar is in a lively part of the center, northeast of Santa Croce. It is popular with locals without being too achingly hip. In summer, everyone spills out onto the little piazza and church steps outside. Piazza Sant'Ambrogio 7R. No phone. Bus: C2 or C3.

Santino ★★   This snug wine bar stocks niche labels from across Italy and serves exquisite "Florentine tapas" (5€–9€) to munch while you sip. Via Santo Spirito 60R. ℭ **055/230-2820.** Bus: C4, 11, 36, 37.

Terrazza Lounge at the Continentale ★★   There are few surprises on the list here—a well-made Negroni, Moscow Mule, Bellini, and the like—and prices are a little steep at 19€ to 20€ a cocktail. But the setting, on a rooftop right by the Ponte Vecchio, makes them practically a steal. Arrive at sundown to see the city start to twinkle. Closed in bad weather. Continentale Hotel, Vicolo dell'Oro 6R. ✆ **055/2726-5806.** Bus: C3.

Spectator Sports

There's only one game in town when it comes to spectator sports: *calcio.* To Italians, soccer/football is akin to a second religion, and an afternoon at the stadium can offer you more insight into local culture than a lifetime in the Uffizi. Florence's team, **Fiorentina ★** (nicknamed *i viola,* "the purples"), is often among the best in Italy's top league, *Serie A.* You can usually catch them alternate Sundays from September through May at the **Stadio Comunale Artemio Franchi,** Via Manfredo Fanti 4 (www.viola channel.tv). Book tickets online or head for an official ticket office on arrival (you **must** have a photo I.D.): There is a sales desk on the Mercato Centrale's upper floor (p. 218) and at Via dei Sette Santi 28R, open from 10am on match days. With kids, get seats in a Tribuna (stand) rather than a Curva, where the fanatical fans sit. To reach the stadium, take match-day-only bus no. 52 or no. 17 from Santa Maria Novella. You can get kitted out in home colors at **Alè Viola,** Via del Corso 58R (✆ **055/295-306**), or at stalls around the ground on match day.

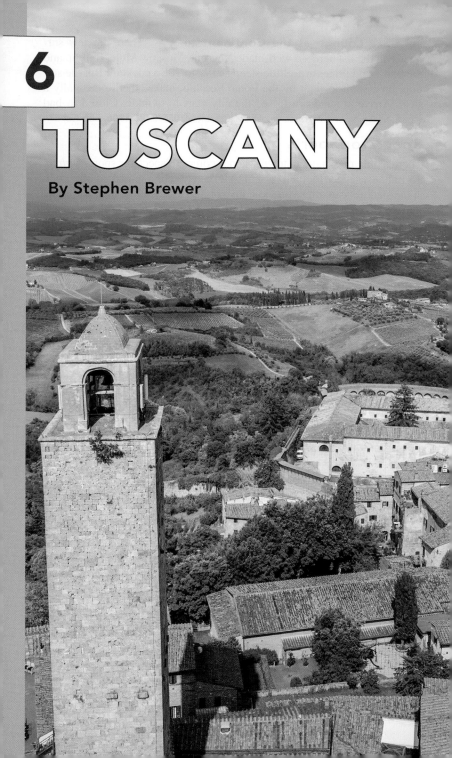

TUSCANY

By Stephen Brewer

T ravelers have been descending upon Italy's most popular region for centuries—and little wonder why. Even for Italians from other parts of the peninsula, Tuscany is the epitome of everything that's good about their country: Beguiling landscapes carpeted with cypresses and vineyards, delicious food and wine, evocative medieval churches and castles, and some of the greatest art and architecture of the Renaissance—the Leaning Tower of Pisa, Piero della Francesca's frescoes in Arezzo, Ambrogio Lorenzetti's "Allegories" in Siena's Palazzo Pubblico. Even a short visit inundates a traveler with an embarrassment of riches.

Soaking up culture is certainly part of the allure, and the pleasures of the palate are just as noted. Even a simple meal can seem like a work of art in places as bountiful as the Val di Chiana and Val d'Orcia. Somehow it only makes sense that full-bodied red wines should come from towns as appealing as Montepulciano and Montalcino, and character-filled whites from proud little San Gimignano. Then there's all that iconic scenery, in landscapes like the rolling fields and pointy cypresses in the Crete Sienese or the vineyards of Chianti. Art, scenery, food, wine—you may come to agree that all the good things in life come together in Tuscany.

DON'T LEAVE TUSCANY WITHOUT . . .

Getting Into Hill Town Life. Panoramic views, cobblestone squares, friendly cafes—these are the charms of everyday life in a Tuscan hill town, ready to be savored in Cortona, Montepulicano, Volterra, San Gimignano, and Montalcino.

Fresco Gazing In Siena. Two medieval masterworks bring the past to life in Siena: Ambrogio Lorenzetti's "Allegory of Good and Bad Government," in the Palazzo Pubblico, and depictions of the healing arts by Domenico di Bartolo and others in the former hospital Santa Maria della Scala.

Basking In Some Of The World's Most Beautiful Landscapes. Open your senses to the beauties of the Tuscan countryside as you drive through the famous Chianti vineyards between Siena and Florence, or along the meandering roads of the Val d'Orcia between Pienza and Montalcino.

Enjoying Fine Wines. You've seen the vines; now sample the wines. Tuscany's bounty, of course, includes famous Chianti, Brunello di Montalcino, and Vino Nobile di Montepulciano, but don't stop there—almost

FACING PAGE: **A tower in San Gimignano overlooks the fertile Tuscan countryside.**

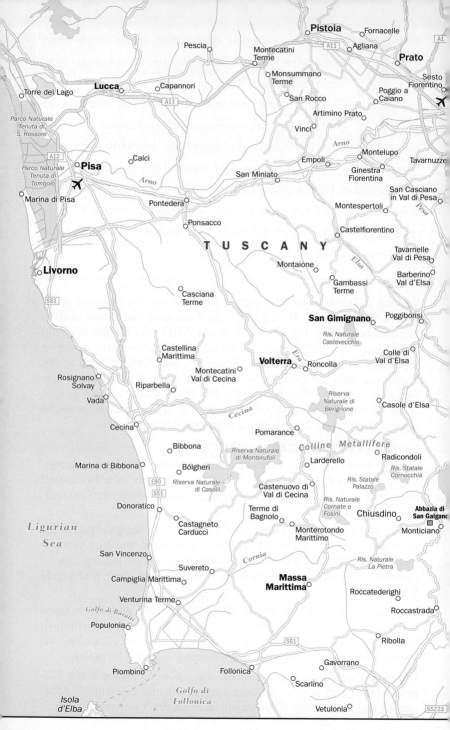

Tuscany

every town has its own trademark vintages, from San Gimignano's Vernaccia to Cortona's Syrah.

SIENA ★★★

70km (43 miles) S of Florence, 232km (144 miles) N of Rome

Florence's longtime rival, this medieval city of rose-colored brick seems to have come out on top in terms of grace and elegance. With steep, twisting stone alleys and proud churches, palaces, and crenellated public buildings draped across its gentle hillsides, Siena is for many admirers the most beautiful town in Italy. At its heart is a ravishing piazza, and from its heights rises a magnificent duomo of striped marble.

The city trumpets the she-wolf as its emblem, a holdover from its days as Saena Julia, the Roman colony founded by Augustus about 2,000 years ago (though the official Sienese myth has the town founded by the sons of Remus, younger brother of Rome's legendary forefather). Civic projects and artistic prowess reached their greatest heights in the 13th and 14th centuries, when artists invented a distinctive Sienese style as banking and a booming wool industry made Siena one of the richest Italian republics. Then, in 1348, the Black Death killed more than half of the population, decimating the social fabric and devastating the economy. Siena never recovered, and much of the city has barely changed since, inviting you to slip into the rhythms and atmosphere of the Middle Ages.

Essentials

ARRIVING

BY TRAIN Siena's **train station** is at Piazza Roselli, about 3km (1¾ miles) north and far below the city center. Trains connect Siena with **Florence** (usually 90 min.), with a change in Empoli; trains to and from Rome (3 to 4 hr.) require a change in Chiusi. To get into town, take the **no. 3, 8, or 10 bus** to Piazza Gramsci (buy your ticket, 1.20€, at the newsstand in the station). Don't take the buses that stop in front of the station, but go into the big brick shopping center across the street and take the escalator to the underground bus stop. Be sure to say *"Gramsci"* when you board, or you can end up in a far-flung district. You can also take a series of escalators up toward town from the top floor of the shopping center—these too are poorly marked, but as long as you're going up you're moving in the right direction. You will be deposited onto Via Vittorio Emanule II; turn left to reach the Porta Camollia, then follow Via Camollia into the city center. It becomes Via Montanini, then Via Banchi di Sopra as it heads down to the Piazza del Campo. *Note:* Siena's train station does not have a baggage storage office, though there is one at the bus station on Piazza Gramsci (see below).

BY BUS It's often easier and faster to travel between Siena and Florence and other towns by **bus** than it is by train. Buses let you off right in town at Piazza Gramsci, at the edge of the historic center: Tiemme

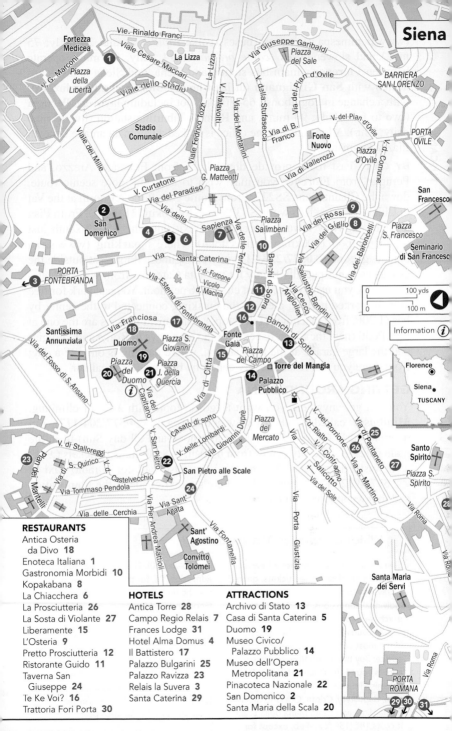

Siena

RESTAURANTS
Antica Osteria
da Divo **18**
Enoteca Italiana **1**
Gastronomia Morbidi **10**
Kopakabana **8**
La Chiacchera **6**
La Prosciutteria **26**
La Sosta di Violante **27**
Liberamente **15**
L'Osteria **9**
Pretto Prosciutteria **12**
Ristorante Guido **11**
Taverna San
Giuseppe **24**
Te Ke Voi? **16**
Trattoria Fori Porta **30**

HOTELS
Antica Torre **28**
Campo Regio Relais **7**
Frances Lodge **31**
Hotel Alma Domus **4**
Il Battistero **17**
Palazzo Bulgarini **25**
Palazzo Ravizza **23**
Relais la Suvera **3**
Santa Caterina **29**

ATTRACTIONS
Archivio di Stato **13**
Casa di Santa Caterina **5**
Duomo **19**
Museo Civico/
Palazzo Pubblico **14**
Museo dell'Opera
Metropolitana **21**
Pinacoteca Nazionale **22**
San Domenico **2**
Santa Maria della Scala **20**

(www.tiemmespa.it) express buses (*corse rapide;* around 25 daily; 75 min.) and slower buses (*corse ordinarie;* 14 daily; 95 min.) operate between **Florence**'s main bus station and Siena, and Siena is also connected with **San Gimignano** (at least hourly Mon–Sat, either direct or with a change in Poggibonsi; 65–80 min. not including layover), **Perugia** (two to four daily; 90 min.), and **Rome**'s Tiburtina station (five to nine daily; 3 hr.). A luggage storage office is tucked away in an arcade beneath Piazza Gramsci.

BY CAR   Fast roads provide direct links from Florence, Arezzo, and Perugia; from **Florence** you may wish to take the more scenic route, down the Chiantigiana SS222. From **Rome** get off the A1 north at the Val di Chiana exit and follow the SS326 west for 50km (31 miles). From **Pisa** take the highway toward Florence and exit onto the SS429 south just before Empoli (100km/62 miles total). There's **parking** (www.siena parcheggi.com; ✆ **0577/228-711**) in well-signposted lots just outside the city gates. An especially handy lot is Santa Caterina, from which escalators whisk you up to town. Most charge 2€ per hour. You can park for free at well-marked parking areas in the outskirts, connected to the center by bus (1.20€, from machines at the stops); convenient choices are the one at Due Ponti (near the Siena Est exit for the highways to Rome and Perugia) and the large garage at the train station, where parking is only 2€ a day; from there you can reach the city center by bus, taxi, or escalator.

GETTING AROUND SIENA

You can get anywhere you want to go on foot, with a bit of climbing. **Minibuses,** called *pollicini* (www.tiemmespa.it; ✆ **0577/204-117**), run quarter-hourly (every half-hour Sat afternoon and all day Sun) from the main gates into the city center from 6:30am to 8:30pm. Buy tickets (.95€) at newsstands or tabacchi-bars. You can also call for a radio **taxi** at ✆ **0577/49222** (7am–9pm only); there's a taxi queue at the train station and in town at Piazza Matteotti.

Which Cumulative Tickets to Buy?

Siena's main attractions offer a bewildering selection of combined tickets, geared to saving you money over the cost of individual admissions. Which ones to purchase depends on what you want to see, of course, but to see the main sights in the most cost-effective way, here's our advice: Buy the **Acropoli pass,** which admits you to the Duomo, Libreria Piccolomini, Museo dell'Opera Metropolitana, Baptistery, Cripta, Oratorio di San Bernardino, and Santa Maria della Scala. It costs 18€ (13€ Nov–Feb, except for Dec 26–Jan 10). Then, pay the individual admission, 9€, for the Museo Civico, to see the remarkable fresco "Allegory of Good and Bad Government and Their Effects on the Town and Countryside." You can pay another 10€ to climb the Torre del Mangia, but you'll get the same sweeping views of the city and countryside from the Facciatone, a walkway atop of the Museo dell'Opera Metropolitana, and admission to that viewpoint is included with the Acropoli pass.

VISITOR INFORMATION

The **tourist office,** where you can get a fairly useless free map or pay .50€ for a detailed one, is in the Santa Maria della Scala complex at Piazza Duomo 1 (www.terresiena.it; © **0577/280-551**). It's open Monday to Friday 10am to 6:30pm and weekends 10:30am to 6:30pm. Here you can purchase the Acropli and Opa Si passes (see box p. 234).

Exploring Siena

At the heart of Siena is a serious contender for the most beautiful square in Italy—the sloping, scallop-shell-shaped **Piazza del Campo (Il Campo)**. Laid out in the 1100s on the site of the Roman forum, the welcoming expanse is a testament to the city's civic achievements; it's anchored by a crenellated town hall, the **Palazzo Pubblico** (1297–1310), and the herringbone brick pavement is divided by white marble lines into nine sections representing the city's medieval ruling body, the Council of Nine. A 19th-century replica of Jacopo della Quercia's 14th-century fountain, the **Fonte Gaia,** is on one side of the square (some of the restored, but badly eroded, original panels are in Santa Maria della Scala, see p. 241). The dominant public monument is the slender 100m-tall (328-ft.) brick **Torre del Mangia** (1338–48), named for a slothful bell ringer nicknamed Mangiaguadagni, or "profit eater." (There's an armless statue of him in the courtyard.) From the platform atop the tower's 503 steps, the undulating Tuscan hills seem to rise and fall to the ends of the earth (admission to tower 10€, mid-Oct to Feb 10am–4pm, Mar to mid-Oct 10am–7pm).

Palio delle Contrade Race in the Piazza del Campo in Siena.

Siena's main streets run toward the Campo from seven gates in the old city walls. Enter through **Porta Camollia,** where the phrase cor magis tibi sena pandit ("Siena opens her heart to you") is carved over the arch. Medieval pilgrims stopped in Siena while walking the Via Francigena holy road between Canterbury and Rome; as you walk down narrow Via Camollia, note the simple-fronted church of **San Pietro alla Magione,** once a pilgrim's hospice. Farther down the street (now called Via Montanini) you'll pass the imposing Gothic **Palazzo Salimbeni,** the fortress-home of a wealthy banker-merchant clan and, since 1472, headquarters of the Monte die Paschi, one of the oldest banks in the world. On up the street (now called Banca di Sopra) is **Palazzo Tolomei,** home of the Salimbenis' bitterest banking rivals—the competition took a bloody turn when the Salimbenis stabbed 18 Tolomeis to death with roasting spits. Via di Citta flows to the right off Banca di Sopra and skirts the **Campo,** then rises toward the **Duomo,** passing the elegant arcaded **Palazzo Chigi Saracini** (Via di Citta 89). In September 1260, during the Battle of Montaperti—the bloodiest European skirmish of the Middle Ages—as the Sienese successfully fought Florentine forces on a ridge outside the city walls, a drummer in the palace tower tapped out ongoing reports to citizens inside the walls.

A DAY AT THE races

Siena lets its guard down every year, on the evenings of July 2 and August 16, when the **Palio delle Contrade** transforms the Piazza del Campo into a racetrack, with hordes of spectators squeezing through the city's narrow alleyways to watch. This aggressive bareback horse race around the Campo involves 10 of Siena's 17 contrade (districts), chosen by lot to participate, and is preceded by a showy flag-waving ceremony and parade. The race itself is over in just 2 minutes. Frenzied celebrations greet the winning rider, and the day is rounded off with communal feasts in each district.

To witness the event from the cordoned-off public view section in the middle of the Campo, you'll end up standing for hours in the sun—you'll need to arrive at least 5 hours before racetime and, while vendors are on hand with refreshments, there are no toilet facilities. To view the Palio in relative comfort, reserve a spot in the temporary stands, operated by the bars and shops in front of which they're erected. Getting a seat on one of these stands, for at least 200€, involves making arrangements with an establishment or a travel agent as long as a year in advance. Another option is to share a terrace or even a window with one of the aristocratic occupants of the apartments overlooking the campo—for one of these perches, expect to pay at least 400€ and as much as 700€ a person. Among the travel agents handling such arrangements is **2Be Travel Designers** (www.paliotickets.com) or self-proclaimed Palio expert **Jacopo della Torre** (www.jacopodellatorre.com).

Otherwise, you may want to settle for the trial races, also held in the Campo (starting June 29 and Aug 13). There's a crowd, but it's smaller and tamer. Trial races aren't as fast and furious as the real thing, but they're just as photogenic and fun to watch. There are usually six in the mornings (9am) and evenings (7:45pm June, 7:15pm Aug).

Archivio di Stato ★ MUSEUM   Tucked into the 1469 Florentine Renaissance-style Palazzo Piccolomini off the southeast corner of the Campo, this state archive displays such historic documents as Boccaccio's will and Jacopo della Quercia's contract for designing the Fonte Gaia fountain. The intriguing "Tavolette di Biccherna" is a remarkable set of wooden covers made in 1258 for the city's account books; they're painted with religious scenes, vignettes of daily working life, and important events in Siena's history. Note the Piccolomini family coat of arms above the palace entrance; the papal tiara in the crest refers to the family's most illustrious member, Pope Pius II, who served from 1458 to 1464. You'll see portraits of him in the Duomo's Libreria Piccolomini; he was also known for designing the town of Pienza (see p. 256), the first planned city in Europe.

Palazzo Piccolomini, Via Banchi di Sotto 52. ✆ **0577/247-145.** Free. Mon–Sat hourly viewings at 9:30, 10:30, and 11:30am

Duomo ★★★ CATHEDRAL   Much of the artistic greatness of Siena comes together in this black-and-white-marble cathedral, a magnificent showcase of Italian Gothic architecture begun in the 12th century and completed in the 13th century. You're likely to come away with a great appreciation for the Pisanos, father and son. Nicola was the principal architect of the church, until he fell out of favor with the group overseeing construction; young Giovanni did much of the carving on the facade, where an army of prophets and apostles appears around three portals (most of the originals are now in the Museo dell'Opera Metropolitana; see p. 240). Both worked on the pulpit, with sumptuously sculpted scenes of the life of Christ and the prophets and evangelists.

Beneath the pulpit spreads a flooring mosaic of 59 etched and inlaid marble panels (1372–1547), a showpiece for 40 of Siena's medieval and Renaissance artistic luminaries. Most prolific among them was Domenico Beccafumi, born into a local peasant family and adopted by his lord, who saw the boy's talent for drawing. Beccafumi studied in Rome but returned to Siena and spent much of his career designing 35 scenes for the flooring (from 1517–47); his richly patterned images are a repository of Old Testament figures. Matteo di Giovanni, another Sienese, did a gruesome Slaughter of the Innocents—a favorite theme of the artist, whose fresco of the same scene is in Santa Maria della Scala (see p. 241). Many of the panels are protected by cardboard overlays and uncovered only from mid-August to early October in honor of the Palio.

Umbrian Renaissance master Bernardino di Betto (better known as Pinturicchio, or Little Painter, because of his stature) is the star in the **Libreria Piccolomini,** entered off the left aisle. Cardinal Francesco Piccolomini built the library in 1487 to house the illuminated manuscripts of his famous uncle, a popular Sienese bishop who later became Pope Pius II. (Cardinal Piccolomini himself later became Pope Pius III—for a mere 18 days, before dying in office.) Pinturicchio's frescoes depict 10 scenes

Something New Under the Duomo

Siena's "newest" work of art is a cycle of frescoes painted between 1270 and 1275, discovered during excavation work in 1999. The colorful works are on view in a subterranean room called the **Cripta,** though the space was never used as a burial crypt. Most likely the room was a lower porch for the Duomo (staircases lead to the nave), but it became a storeroom when the choir area above was expanded. What remains are fascinating fragments of scenes from the New Testament, full of emotion and painted in vibrant colors. Scholars are still trying to determine who painted what in the room. Admission is 8€; the Cripta is also included in the Acropoli and Opa Si passes.

from Pope Pius II's life, including an especially dramatic departure for the Council of Basel as a storm rages in the background.

In the **Baptistery** (not a separate building but beneath the choir), the great early Renaissance trio of Sienese and Florentine sculptors—Jacopo della Quercia, Lorenzo Ghiberti, and Donatello—crafted the gilded bronze panels of the baptismal font. Donatello wrought the dancing figure of Salome in the "Feast of Herod," and della Quercia did the statue of St. John that stands high above the marble basin.

Piazza del Duomo. www.operaduomo.siena.it. ✆ **0577/283-048.** Acropoli pass 18€ (13€ Nov–Feb except Dec 26–Jan 10) includes Duomo, Libreria Piccolomini, and Baptistery, as does the Opa Si pass (15€ Jul–Oct, 13€ Mar–June and holiday periods, 8€ Nov–Feb). Duomo only 4€, except when floor uncovered 7€. Libreria Piccolomini only 2€. Baptistery only 4€. Mar–Oct Mon–Sat 10:30am–7pm, Sun 1:30–6pm; Nov–Feb Mon–Sat 10:30am–5:30pm, Sun 1:30–5:30pm.

Museo Civico/Palazzo Pubblico ★★★ MUSEUM   Presiding over the Piazza del Campo, this great Gothic-style town hall houses some of the city's finest artistic treasures. Siena's medieval governors, the Council of Nine, met in the **Sala della Pace,** and to help ensure they bore their duties responsibly, Ambrogio Lorenzetti frescoed the walls with what has become the most important piece of secular art to survive from medieval Europe. His 1338 "Allegory of Good and Bad Government and Their Effects on the Town and Countryside" provides not only a moral lesson but also a remarkable visual record of Siena and the nearby countryside as it appeared in the 14th century. Probably not by accident, the good-government frescoes are nicely illuminated by natural light, while scenes of bad government are cast in shadow (and have deteriorated over the years). In a panorama on the good side of the room, the towers, domes, and rooftops of Siena appear much as they do today, with horsemen, workers, and townsfolk going about their daily affairs; in the countryside, genteel lords on horseback overlook bountiful fields. On the bad-government side, streets are full of rubble, houses are collapsing, and soldiers pillage; beyond the walls, fields are barren and villages are ablaze.

Among other frescoes in these rooms is Sienese painter Simone Martini's greatest work, and his first, a "Maestà" (or Majesty), finished in

The Duomo of Siena.

1315 (he went over it again in 1321), in the **Sala del Mappamondo.** He shows the Virgin Mary as a medieval queen beneath a royal canopy, surrounded by a retinue of saints, apostles, and angels. The work not only introduces a secular element to a holy scene but also adds a sense of three-dimensional depth and perspective that later came to the fore in Renaissance painting. Mary's presence here in the halls of civil power reinforces the idea of good government, with the Virgin presiding as a protector of the city. Just opposite is another great Martini work (though the attribution has been called into question), the "Equestrian Portrait of Guidoriccio da Fogliano." The depiction of a proud mercenary riding past a castle he has just conquered was part of a long lost "castelli," or "castles," fresco cycle that showed off Sienese conquests.

Palazzo Pubblico, Piazza del Campo. © **0577/292-226.** Museo Civico 9€ adults (8€ with reservation), 4.50€ students (4€ with reservation); ages 11 and under free. Cumulative ticket with Santa Maria della Scala 13€; with Torre del Mangia and Santa Maria della Scala 20€. Daily 10am–7pm (Nov–mid-Mar closes 6pm). Bus: A (pink), B.

Museo dell'Opera Metropolitana ★★ MUSEUM   In 1339, Siena decided to show off its political, artistic, and spiritual prominence by expanding the Duomo. Work had just begun when the Black Death killed more than half the city's inhabitants in 1348, and the project ground to halt, never to be resumed—partly because it was later discovered that the foundations could not support the massive structure. The aborted nave of the so-called "New Duomo" has now been repurposed to house many of the church's treasures. Here you can see the glorious-if-worse-for-wear statues by Giovanni Pisano that once adorned the facade, as well as a 30-sq-m (323-sq-ft) stained-glass window made for the apse in the late

SIENA'S saintly SCHOLAR

Catherine Benincasa (1347–1380), one of 25 children of a wealthy Sienese cloth dyer, had her first vision of Christ when she was 5 or 6 and vowed to devote her life to God. She took a nun's veil but not the vows when a teenager, was wed "mystically" to Christ when she was 21, and became known for helping the poor and infirm. She founded a woman's monastery outside Siena, and traveled throughout central Italy promoting "the total love for God" and a stronger church. Frequent fasting eventually took such a toll on her health that she died at age 33. She was canonized as St. Catherine of Siena in 1461 by Pope Pius II—himself a native of Siena.

The stark, cavernous church of **San Domenico** in Piazza San Domenico (free admission, 9am–6:30pm daily) houses Catherine's venerated head, preserved in a gold reliquary, and her thumb. Her family home, the **Casa di Santa Caterina,** Costa di Sant'Antonio (✆ **0577/44177;** free admission, 9am–6pm daily), has been preserved as a religious sanctuary; the former kitchen is now an oratory with a spectacular 16th-century majolica-tiled floor.

1280s, with nine colorful panels—beautifully illuminated to full effect in these new surroundings—depicting the Virgin Mary, Siena's four patron saints, and the four Biblical Evangelists.

Upstairs is the "Maestà" by Duccio di Buoninsenga, an altarpiece that was declared a masterpiece when it was unveiled in 1311, carried in a procession from the painter's workshop to the Duomo's altar. As a contemporary wrote, "all honorable citizens of Siena surrounded said panel with candles held in their hands, and women and children followed humbly behind." The front depicts the Madonna and Child surrounded by saints and angels, while the back once displayed 46 scenes from the lives of Mary and Christ. In 1711 the altarpiece was dismantled, and pieces are now in collections around the world. What remains here shows the genius of Duccio, who slowly broke away from a one-dimensional Byzantine style to imbue his characters with nuance, roundness, and emotion.

The **Facciatone,** a walkway atop the would-be facade of the "New Duomo," is the city's second most popular viewpoint, with a stunning perspective of the cathedral across the piazza and sweeping views over the city's rooftops to Siena's favorite height, the Torre del Mangia towering over the Campo.

Piazza del Duomo 8. www.operaduomo.siena.it. ✆ **0577/283-048.** Acropoli pass 18€ (13€ Nov–Feb except Dec 26–Jan 10) includes Museo dell'Opera Metropolitana. Opa Si Pass (15€ Jul–Oct, 13€ Mar–June and holiday periods, 8€ Nov–Feb) includes Museo dell'Opera Metropolitana. Museum only 7€. Mar–Oct Mon–Sat 10:30am–7pm, Sun 1:30–6pm; Nov–Feb Mon–Sat 10:30am–5:30pm, Sun 1:30–5:30pm.

Pinacoteca Nazionale ★ ART MUSEUM   While the greatest works of Sienese art have long since been dispersed to museums around the world, these adjoining palaces provide an overview of the city's major artists, especially those of the 12th through the 16th centuries. What you'll notice is that while the Renaissance was flourishing in Florence, Siena held to its old ways—these works are rich in Byzantine gold and Eastern styling. Duccio (of the famous "Maestà" in the Museo dell'Opera, p. 240) is represented by "Madonna and Child with Saints," in which a placid, otherworldly looking Mary holds a very wise-looking infant Jesus. Simone Martini (painter of Siena's other great "Maestà," in the Museo Civico, p. 260) did the wonderful "Agostino Novello" altarpiece, in which St. Augustine is shown performing all sorts of heroic deeds, such as flying over boulders to save a monk trapped in a ravine. There are some charming landscapes by Ambrogio Lorenzetti (artist of the "Allegory of Good and Bad Government" in the Palazzo Pubblico, p. 238), including the almost surreal "Castle on the Lake," an architectural fantasy reminiscent of the 20th-century works of Giorgio di Chirico. His brother Pietro's "Madonna of the Carmelites," an altarpiece created for the Carmelite church in Siena, shows the Virgin and Child in a distinctly medieval setting, in a Sienese landscape complete with horsemen and planted hillsides. Domenico Beccafumi's sketches for his Duomo floor panels are on the first floor.

Via San Pietro 29. ✆ **0577/286-143.** 4€. Sun–Mon 9am–1pm; Tues–Sat 8:15am–7:15pm.

Santa Maria della Scala ★★★ MUSEUM   One of Europe's first hospitals, probably founded around 1090, raised abandoned children, took care of the infirm, fed the poor, and lodged pilgrims who stopped in Siena on their way to and from Rome. These activities are recorded in scenes in the **Sala del Pellegrinaio** (Pilgrims' Hall), where colorful depictions of patients and healers from the Middle Ages looked down upon rows of hospital beds as recently as the 1990s. These are some of the finest secular works of the Middle Ages, color-rich 15th-century frescoes by Domenico di Bartolo and others, showing such scenes as surgeons dressing a leg wound or holding a flask of urine to the light, or caregivers offering fresh clothing to an indigent young man. One of Bartolo's panels encapsulates an orphan's lifetime experience at the hospital, as he pictures infants being weaned, youngsters being taught by a stern-looking schoolmistress, and a young couple being wed (young women raised in the hospital were given dowries). As these activities transpire, a dog and cat scuffle, foundlings climb ladders toward the Virgin Mary, and wealthy benefactors stand on Oriental carpets.

You'll also see other frescoes and altarpieces commissioned by the hospital as it acquired considerable wealth over the centuries. One gallery houses some original panels from Jacopo della Quercia's 14th-century fountain in the Piazza del Campo, the Fonte Gaia. In the cellars is the dark and eerie **Oratorio di Santa Caterina della Notte,** where St. Catherine (see p. 263) allegedly passed her nights in prayer.

Piazza del Duomo 2. www.santamariadellascala.com. ✆ **0577/534-571.** Acropoli pass 18€ (13€ Nov–Feb except Dec 26–Jan 10) includes Santa Maria della Scala. Cumulative ticket with Museo Civico 13€, with Museo Civico and Torre del Mangia 20€. Museum only 9€ adults, 8€ students. Mon and Wed–Fri 10:30am–4:30pm; Sat–Sun 10:30am–6:30pm.

Where to Stay in Siena

Many hotels have discount arrangements with garages in the city center; around 15€ to 25€ per day is standard. When making parking arrangements with a hotel, though, check carefully to make sure the garage is not in a restricted zone, in which you are only allowed to drive once a day—meaning you can take the car out for a day trip but can't bring it back into the city later that day without incurring a fine.

EXPENSIVE

Relais la Suerva ★★ One of the world's most distinctive country-house hotels was once the country palace of Pope Julius II (the same pope who commissioned the Sistine Chapel), lavishly adorned with loggias, Italian gardens, a private church, and refined salons. The current owner, the Marquis Ricci, has added his own touches in elaborately decorated suites and rooms in the papal palace and an adjoining farm building, furnished with family antiques, rich fabrics, decadently huge bathrooms, and centuries' worth of bibelots. The overall effect is design-magazine-worthy yet surprisingly welcoming and comfortable. You probably won't want to slouch around in your bathing suit in the swanky lounges (lined with 19th-century finery and other collectibles), but the hotel also has a delightful pool and many relaxing corners. Siena and other Tuscan towns are within easy reach.

Via della Suvera 70, Pievescola Casole d'Elsa (28km/16 miles west of Sienna). www.lasuvera.it. ℂ **0577/960-300.** 36 units. From 350€ double. Closed Nov–mid-Apr. **Amenities:** Restaurant; bar; pool; spa; Wi-Fi (free).

MODERATE

Campo Regio Relais ★★★ A "Room with a View" ambience pervades this stylish old house a 10-minute walk from the Campo. Two of the beautifully appointed rooms have spectacular views up a hillside crowned with the Duomo, one from its own sun-filled terrace, and all guests enjoy the same vista from an inviting sitting room/bar/breakfast room that also opens to a terrace. The old-fashioned *pensione* atmosphere is enhanced with modern updates that include lush fabrics and elegant furnishings, chic rather than staid. Amenities include an honesty bar, a library, attentive service, and excellent breakfast.

Via della Sapienza 25. www.camporegio.com. ℂ **0577/222-073.** 6 units. 150€–450€ double. Rates include breakfast. Usually closed Jan–mid-Mar. **Amenities:** Library; Wi-Fi (free).

Frances' Lodge Relais ★★★ With the towers of Siena beckoning in the near distance, a pool glimmering in the garden, and lots of quiet corners nestled on a hillside planted with olive trees, this beautiful estate seems like a slice of heaven. Hosts Franco and Franca (Frances) Mugnai created this earthly paradise out of their ancestral home; the richly hued rooms and suites are accented with family pieces and decorated with quirky charm—Moroccan fabrics in one, a rose theme in another, all tucked away in old stone farm buildings. A hearty made-to-order breakfast is served in the garden; in bad weather the day begins in a lounge fashioned out of the old *limonaia* (lemon house), filled with kilims and vibrant art. There's a 2-night minimum stay, and guests must be at least 18 years old. Strada di Valdipugna 2. www.franceslodge.it. © **0577/42379**. 6 units. Doubles from 200€. Rates include breakfast. Closed mid-Nov to late Mar. **Amenities:** Bar; pool; Wi-Fi (free).

Il Battisero ★★★   Only a brief stroll from the Campo, this character-filled small palazzo, once home to a pope, adds quiet sophistication to Siena's medieval charm, blending old tile work and rough-hewn beams with contemporary furnishings and modern art. Individually designed rooms and suites—some with terraces—overlook the baptistery or across rooftops to San Domenico. As sophisticated as the surroundings are, the hospitality is warm, with a welcoming guest lounge/library, a wine shop at one end of the reception hall, and an atmospheric tasting cellar below. Piazza San Giovanni 12. www.battisterosiena.com. © **057/288-921.** 7 units. Doubles from 150€. Rates include breakfast. **Amenities**: Wi-Fi (free).

Palazzo Ravizza ★★   Generations of travelers have fallen under the spell of this 17th-century Renaissance *palazzo,* where high ceilings, oil paintings, highly polished antiques, and the gentle patina of age all suggest an era of grand travel. A large garden in the rear stretches towards green hills and can tempt anyone to give up sightseeing for a few hours and just relax; it's a popular cocktail spot for guests and Sienese alike. All the rooms are different, though most have wood beams and a surfeit of period detail, including some frescoes and coffered ceilings; furnishings throughout are comfortable and traditionally stylish. While this wonderful old place has the aura of a country hideaway, it's right in the city center, just a few streets below the Piazza del Campo—yet has its own private parking lot, easily reached from Porta San Marco. Pian dei Mantellini 34 (near Piazza San Marco). www.palazzoravizza.it. © **0577/280-462.** 35 units. 105€–180€ double. Rates include breakfast. Free parking. Closed early Jan–early Feb. Bus: A (green, yellow). **Amenities:** Bar; babysitting; concierge; room service; Wi-Fi (free).

Santa Caterina ★★   Just outside the Siena walls—literally so, as this is the first house after Porta Romana—this homey old inn feels as if it's in the countryside, yet it's only a 10-minute walk from Piazza del Campo. There's a large, shady garden where you can have breakfast or a drink under the trees in good weather; for indoor lounging, there's a snug little bar, a well-upholstered lounge, and a glass-enclosed breakfast room. Most of the cozy rooms, with wood-beamed ceilings, simple wood furnishings, and old prints on the walls, face the back, where wide-sweeping views of the green Val d'Orcia seem to go on forever. One choice room has a little balcony; a few others are bi-level, with bedrooms tucked beneath the eaves. Ask for a rear-facing room or you'll miss that wonderful view.

Via Enea Silvio Piccolomini 7. www.hscsiena.it. © **0577/221-105.** 22 units. 75€–130€ double. Rates include breakfast. Bus: A (red) or 2. **Amenities:** Babysitting; bikes; concierge; Wi-Fi (free).

INEXPENSIVE

Antica Torre ★ A 16th-century tower house dishes up no end of medieval atmosphere, with eight smallish rooms tucked onto four floors. If you don't mind the climb, the two on the top floor come with the advantage of views across the tile rooftops, and just treading on the old stone staircase is a pleasure. The rooms have plenty of character—with marble floors, brick and timbered ceilings, and handsome iron bedsteads—which for some guests may compensate for the fairly cramped quarters, small bathrooms, and lack of many hotel services. Continental breakfast (5€ extra) can get the day off to a rocky start, literally, as it's served downstairs in a rough-hewn stone vault.

Via di Fiera Vecchia 7. www.anticatorresiena.it. © **0577/222-255.** 8 units. 70€–105€ double. **Amenities:** Wi-Fi (free).

Hotel Alma Domus ★ This modern redo of the former drying rooms of a medieval wool works is run by the nuns of St. Catherine, who provide homey and spotless lodgings with a slightly contemporary flair. Set into the hillside below San Domenico church, near the Fontebranda (the oldest and most picturesque of the city's fountains), the place has the quiet air of a retreat—or a meditative, monastic calm, if you choose to see it that way—along with a great perk: city-view balconies in the more expensive rooms. Less expensive rooms do not come with views or air-conditioning. Breakfast is included, but it's a bit basic; you may prefer to walk up the hill and enjoy a cappuccino in the Campo.

Via Camporegio 37. www.hotelalmadomus.it. © **0577/44177.** 28 units. 85€–120€ double. Rates include breakfast. Bus: A (red). **Amenities:** Wi-Fi (free).

Palazzo Bulgarini ★★ The converted *piano nobile* salons of an old palace aren't as opulent as they once were—furnishings are dated, and some better lighting would be welcome—but enough of the grandeur remains to elicit a gasp or two as you enter one of the six enormous guest rooms embellished with marble fireplaces and ceiling frescoes. Unchanged over the centuries are the stunning views from the rear rooms over the Val d'Orcia, a surprise given the city-center location. Prices are very reasonable, especially for accommodations so genuinely palatial.

Via Pantaneto. www.bbpalazzobulgarini.com. © **0577/152-4466.** 6 units. 70€–120€ double. Rates include breakfast. Bus: A (pink). **Amenities:** Wi-Fi (free).

Where to Eat in Siena

While a drink or meal on the Campo can be an expensive and less-than-satisfying experience, a pleasant exception is friendly **Liberamente,** Piazza del Campo 7 (www.liberamenteosteria.it; © **0577/274-733**), where drinks are well-priced and usually come with generous nibbles. Siena's favorite fast-food stop, **Te Ke Voi?** (℃ **0577/40139**)—translates as Whaddaya Want?—is a pleasant, bustling room on Vicolo San Pietro, one of the narrow, sloping alleyways leading into the Campo; pasta, pizza, and burgers are dispensed from a self-service counter, along with wine and beer. For a quick meal, step into bright little **Pretto Prosciutteria** for sandwiches, delicious bruschetta, and generous platters of hams and cheeses, near the Campo at Via dei Termini 4 (www.prettoprosciutteria.it; ℃ **0577/289-089**), or **La Prosciutteria,** on the corner of Via Magialotti and Via Pantaneto (www.laprosciutteria.com; ℃ **0577/42026**), where you can quite literally pig out on a platter of Tuscan hams or a *porchetta* sandwich, served on tables out front or in a medieval cellar. At **Gastronomia Morbidi,** Via Banca di Sopra 75, the city's busiest deli and gourmet shop, you can stock up on cheeses, hams, and pastries, enjoy a glass of wine or a cocktail, or partake of the buffet (www.morbidi.com; ℃ **0577/280-268**).

The **Enoteca Italiana** (www.enoteca-italiana.it; ℃ **0577/228843**; Mon noon–8pm; Tues–Sat noon–1am) in the 16th-century Fortezza Medicea di Santa Barbara is the only state-sponsored wine bar in Italy, in vaults that were built for Cosimo de' Medici in 1560. You can sample a choice selection of Italian wines by the glass and accompany your choices with small plates of meats and cheeses.

Every Italian city has a favorite *gelateria,* and Siena's is **Kopakabana,** at Via de' Rossi 52–54 (www.gelateriakopakabana.it; ℃ **0577/284-124;** mid-Feb to mid-Nov noon–8pm, later in warm weather), with flavors that include *panpepato,* based on the peppery Sienese cake.

EXPENSIVE

Antica Osteria da Divo ★★ CONTEMPORARY SIENESE   It's hard to know what cuisine would best suit this almost-eerie setting of brick vaulting, exposed timbers, walls of bare rock, and even some Etruscan tombs—either some sort of medieval gruel or else something innovatively refined, which luckily is the direction this menu goes. Many of the offerings are uniquely Sienese, as in *pici alla lepre* (thick spaghetti in hare sauce), *sella di cinghiale* (saddle of wild boar braised in Chianti), or a breast of guinea fowl *(faraona)* roasted with balsamic vinegar. Such meals are well paired with vegetables, often caramelized onions or crisp roasted potatoes with herbs. Service is outstanding, and the intimate spaces are beautifully candlelit at night.

Via Franciosa 25–29. www.osteriadadivo.it. ℃ **0577/284-381.** Entrees 20€–24€. Wed–Mon noon–2:30pm and 7–10:30pm. Closed 2 wks Jan–Feb. Bus: A (green, yellow).

MODERATE

La Sosta di Violante ★★ SIENESE   This warm, friendly, rose-hued room is only a 5-minute walk from Piazza del Campo but far enough off the beaten track to seem like a getaway (*sosta* means rest or break, as in "take a break"). The surroundings attract a mostly neighborhood crowd that has come to count on the kitchen for excellent preparations of *papardelle, pici,* and other Tuscan pastas in rich sauces. Grilled Florentine steaks are another specialty, but so are many vegetarian choices, including delicious *fritelle di pecorino* (pecorino cheese fritters) and a cauliflower *(cavolfiore)* soufflé. The restaurant's name refers to Violante, the Bavarian-born 18th-century duchess who, after her Medici husband died from syphilis, became a beneficent governor of Siena; she was the one who divided the city into its famous present-day *contrade* (districts).

Via di Pantaneta 115. www.lasostadiviolante.it. ℭ **0577/43774.** Entrees 10€–17€. Mon–Sat 12:30–2:30pm and 7:30–10:30pm. Bus: A (pink).

Ristorante da Guido ★★ SIENESE   Italian celebs whose photos hang among etchings and paintings are among generations of diners who have enjoyed this wonderfully old-world place. Ristorante Guido seems to radiate hospitality from every brick in the cavernous, vaulted dining room. Waiters in crisp jackets and ties make a special occasion of meals that might include one of the housemade pastas—*pici fatti al cacio e pepe* (with cheese and pepper) is a house classic—and one of several variations of grilled Tuscan beef.

Vicolo Beato Pier Pettinaio 7. www.ristoranteguido.com. ℭ **0577/280-042.** Entrees 12€–22€. Daily 12:30–2:30pm and 7:30–10:30pm.

Taverna San Giuseppe ★★★ TUSCAN/GRILL   A long, brick vaulted room from the 12th century is the setting for meals many travelers long remember as among the best they've had in Italy. It's a testament to the warmth of the staff that, despite the popularity (reserve for dinner) and reputation among even the discerning Sienese, they work so hard to make diners feel at home; they are justly proud of the Tuscan classics they bring out of the kitchen. *Pici,* the thick local pasta, with a ragu of *cinghiale* (wild boar), is surprisingly delicate, while ricotta-filled *gnudi* almost floats off the plate. Meals often begin with a complimentary glass of Prosecco and might end with a dessert on the house, bookends to an experience that in its entirety seems like a treat.

Via G. Dupré 132. www.tavernasangiuseppe.it. ℭ **0577/42286.** Entrees 10€–21€. Mon–Sat noon–2:30pm and 7–10pm. Bus: A (red).

Trattoria Fori Porta ★★ TUSCAN/GRILL   Just outside of *(fori)* the gate *(porta)* Porta Romana, this chicly comfortable spot is slightly out of the center of things, a 15-minute walk from the Campo. The location makes a meal here feel all the more authentic, served in two intimate dining rooms where plain wood tables on white-tile floors are offset by contemporary paintings and heavy beams. The Tuscan menu leans toward grilled steaks, with some innovative accompaniments, including a memorable trio of small onions stuffed with sausage, or the house version of a homey classic, braised cabbage rolls stuffed with pork.

Via Claudio Tomei 1. www.foriportasiena.it. ℭ **0577/222-1000.** Entrees 11€–20€. Tues–Sun 7:30–10pm. Bus: A (red) or 2.

INEXPENSIVE

La Chiacchera ★★ SIENESE   A hole in the wall is an apt description for this tiny, rustically decorated room tucked halfway along a steep alleyway. The climb can help work up an appetite for large portions of *ribollita* (hearty bread and vegetable soup), *salsicce e fagioli* (sausage and white beans); or *tegamata di maiale* (a Sienese pork casserole). Good weather provides a unique dining experience on the street out front, where the legs of tables and chairs have been cut to accommodate the steep slope.
Costa di Sant'Antonio 4 (near San Domenico). www.osterialachiacchera.it. © **0577/ 280-631.** Entrees 7€–9€. Wed–Mon noon–3pm and 6:30pm–10:30pm. Bus: A (red).

L'Osteria ★★ TUSCAN/GRILL   One of Siena's culinary treasures is this simple tile-floored, wood-beamed room where straightforward local cuisine is expertly prepared and served at extremely reasonable prices. Truffles occasionally appear in some special preparations, but for most of the year the short menu sticks to the classics—*pici al cinghiale* (pasta with wild boar sauce), tripe *(trippa)* stew, and thick steaks, accompanied by *fagioli bianchi* (white beans) and *patate fritte* (fried potatoes). Service can be brusque, but that's because nightly crowds keep the waiters hopping.
Via de' Rossi 79–81. © **0577/287-592.** Entrees 8€–17€. Mon–Sat 12:30–2:30pm and 7:30–10:30pm, Sun 12:30–3pm. Bus: A (red).

Siena Shopping

Siena is famous for its *panforte,* a sweet, dense cake created by city bakers in the Middle Ages and sold in shops all over town. Made from candied fruit and nuts glued together with honey, it resembles a gloopy fruit cake. Each shop has its own recipe, with the most popular varieties being sweet Panforte Margherita and bitter Panforte Nero. Try a slice at **Drogheria Manganelli,** Via di Città 71–73 (© **0577/280-002**), which has made its own *panforte* and soft *ricciarelli* almond cookies since the 19th century. Some Sienese would send you just as enthusiastically to the delectable and venerable **Nannini,** just off the Campo at Via Banchi di Sopra 24 (© **0577/303-080**). The **Consorzio Agrario Siena,** Via Pianigiani 9 (www.capsi.it; © **0577/2301**), showcases local wines, cheeses, pasta, even pastry, all from small Tuscan producers.

Authentic Sienese ceramics feature only three colors: black, white, and the reddish-brown "burnt sienna," or *terra di Siena.* **Ceramiche Artistiche Santa Caterina,** at Via di Città 74–76 (© **0577/283-098**), sells high-quality pieces, courtesy of Maestro Marcello Neri, who trained at Siena's premier art and ceramics institutions, and his son, Fabio.

A Side Trip into the Chianti

For many visitors to Italy, heaven on earth is the 167 sq. km (64 sq. miles) of land between Florence and Siena, known as the Chianti. Traversing the gentle hillsides on the SR222, a twisting, picturesque route known as the Chiantigiana, is a classic drive, especially the stretch between Castellina

Tuscan vineyards.

in Chianti and Greve. Landscapes are smothered in vineyards and olive groves, punctuated by woodland and peppered with *case coloniche*—stone farmsteads with trademark square dovecotes protruding from the roofs. You'll need a car to get the most out of the route, but from Siena's train station you can get as far as Radda by twice-daily bus service, for a quick taste of the countryside; the trip takes an hour, and round-trip fare is about 10€; you'll find schedules at www.tiemmespa.it.

First stop for wine lovers is **Radda in Chianti,** 36km (22 miles) north of Siena; the turnoff is just north of Castellina. This important wine center retains its medieval street plan and a bit of its walls. The center of town is the 15th-century **Palazzo del Podestà,** studded with the mayoral coats of arms of past *podestà.* **Porciatti** will give you a taste of traditional salami and cheeses at their *alimentari* on Piazza IV Novembre 1 at the gate into town (www.casaporciatti.it; ✆ **0577/738-055**).

Seven kilometers (4⅓ miles) north of Radda on a secondary road is the **Castello di Volpaia ★★** (www.volpaia.com; ✆ **0577/738-066**), a Florentine holding that was buffeted by Sienese attacks from the 10th to 16th centuries. The still-impressive central keep is all that remains, but it's surrounded by a 13th-century *borgo* (village) containing the Renaissance La Commenda church. The central tower has an enoteca for tastings and sales, plus award-winning olive oils and farm-produced vinegars.

Back on the Chiantigiana (SR222), the next town is **Panzano in Chianti,** 12km (7 miles) north of Radda, known for its embroidery and a celebrity butcher, Dario Cecchini. At his shop **Antica Macelleria Cecchini,** Via XX Luglio 11 (www.dariocecchini.com; ✆ **055/852-020**), the flamboyant Cecchini entertains visitors with classical music, product samples, sometimes even poetry recitations.

Just north of Panzano, the SR222 takes you past the turnoff for Lamole. Along that road you'll find **Villa Vignamaggio** ★★ (www. vignamaggio.com; ✆ 055/854-661), a russet-orange villa surrounded by elegant gardens where Lisa Gherardini, who grew up to pose for da Vinci's "Mona Lisa," was born in 1479. In 1404 the estate's wine was the first red wine to be referred to as "chianti." Book ahead at least a week to tour the cellar and gardens, sample the wines, or even stay overnight in atmosphere-laden rooms (from 180€ for a double).

Greve in Chianti, 8km (5 miles) north of Panzano on the SR222, is the center of the wine trade and the unofficial capital of Chianti. The central **Piazza Matteotti** is a rough triangle surrounded by a mismatched patchwork arcade—each merchant had to build the stretch in front of his own shop. Greve is the host of Chianti's annual September wine fair, and there are, naturally, dozens of wine shops in town. The best is the **Enoteca del Chianti Classico,** Piazzetta Santa Croce 8 (✆ 055/853-297). At Piazza Matteotti 69–71 is another famous butcher, **Macelleria Falorni** (www.falorni.it; ✆ 055/854-363), established in 1700, containing a cornucopia of hanging *prosciutti* and dozens of other cured meats.

The **Castello di Verrazzano** (www.verrazzano.com; ✆ 055/854-243 or 055/290684), 6km (4 miles) northwest of Greve, is a significant stop for Americans: the ancestral home of the Verrazzano family, birthplace in 1485 of Giovanni Verrazzano, who discovered New York. The estate has been making wine since at least 1170; free tastings are offered daily at the roadside shop. Their "jewel" is a 100 percent sangiovese called Sasello, while the Bottiglia Particolare (Particular [Special] Bottle) is a Super Tuscan wine, at 70 percent sangiovese and 30 percent cab. Tours of the gardens and cellars run Monday through Friday (prebooking essential), and a rustic farmhouse inn, Foresteria Casanova, offers rooms from 95€ double.

From here it's 29km (17 miles) to Florence, or 50km (30 miles) back to Siena—allow a little over an hour without stops for the return trip.

WHERE TO STAY IN THE CHIANTI REGION

Castello Vicchiomaggio ★★ A 700-year-old storybook castle, complete with a crennellated tower, has hosted Renaissance nobles, such luminaries as Leonardo da Vinci and the poet-biologist Francesco Redi, and modern-day visitors who enjoy a stay on a working wine estate set amid world-acclaimed vineyards. Large, character-filled apartments in the castle are tucked into turrets and medieval salons along twisting staircases and corridors, each filled with old-fashioned furnishings that are more homey than grand. An adjacent priory has been converted into six comfortable suites that surround a communal lounge. All share a shady formal garden and a swimming pool that hangs over the vineyards.

Via Vicchiomaggio, Greve in Chianti. www.vicchiomaggio.it. ✆ **055/854079.** 12 units. 150€–205€ double. Rates include breakfast. **Amenities:** Restaurant; pool; Wi-Fi (free).

Palazzo Leopoldo ★★ One of the grandest palaces in Radda in Chianti dates to the 15th century and was redone as a noble residence in the

FEEL THE magic AROUND SIENA

If the Disney empire were to set up shop in Tuscany, it would have some ready-made stage sets near Siena. **Monteriggioni,** 14km (8 1/2 miles) northwest of Siena along the SS2, is one of the most perfectly preserved fortified villages in all of Italy. The town was once a Sienese outpost, where soldiers were posted in towers to keep an eye out for Florentine troops—an image that Dante once likened to the circle of Titans guarding the lowest level of Hell. All 14 towers have survived, and you can climb up for a view (admission 3.50€, open Apr–Sept daily 9:30am–1:30pm and 2–7:30pm). A walk from one end of Monteriggioni to the other takes about 5 minutes—as you pass, note the garden plots tucked against the walls, which once kept townsfolk nourished during times of siege. The **tourist office** is at Piazza Roma 23, 53035 Monteriggioni (www.monteriggioniturismo.it; © **0577/304810**). Siena city buses 130A and 130R run out to Monteriggioni every hour.

The enchanting **Abbey of San Galgano,** in a grassy meadow on the banks of the River Merse, has a great "Sword in the Stone"–like back story. Galgano, born in Siena in 1148, was pursuing his career as a knight when he had a vision of the archangel Michael, who led him to a circular temple outside the village of Montesiepi, where he met the 12 apostles. Moved by the vision, Galgano went off to Montesiepi, drove his sword into a stone to renounce his knighthood, and built a round stone hermitage. After his death in 1182, his simple dwelling was expanded into a spectacular rotunda, which became the center of a community of Cistercian monks. Great church builders, they designed the cathedral in Siena as well as a Gothic abbey down the hill, now an evocative ruin—you can prowl around it, admiring its high arches, carved capitals, and stone settings for long-vanished stained-glass windows. The saint's tomb is up the hill in the hermitage; though his body long ago went missing, his sword remains in the stone, with only its handle protruding. The abbey and hermitage (www.prolocochiusdino.it; © **055/756700;** admission 3€, open daily) are outside the village of Chiusdino about 40km (25 miles) southwest of Siena via S73.

18th century. Not much has changed since then. Guest rooms open off vaulted salons and have chunky beams, colorful frescoes, and comfy traditional furnishings to offer a satisfyingly historic, slightly regal ambience. Breakfast is served in the 18th-century kitchens, while a sunny terrace overlooks the nearby hills. A hedonistic **spa** is tucked beneath pleasant but slightly less atmospheric lodgings in an adjoining house.

Via Roma 33, Radda in Chianti. www.palazzoleopoldo.it. © **0577/735605.** 22 units. 110€–150€ double. Rates include breakfast. **Amenities:** Restaurant; bar; pool; spa; Wi-Fi (free).

MONTEPULCIANO ★★

67km (41 miles) SE of Siena, 124km (77 miles) SE of Florence, 186km (116 miles) N of Rome

Sipping a delicious ruby wine in a friendly hill town is a good reason to trek across the beautiful Tuscan countryside. There are few better places to aim

Wine barrels in a Montepulciano cellar.

for than Montepulciano, with its medieval alleyways, Renaissance palaces, and famous violet-scented, orange-speckled Vino Nobile di Montepulciano. You'll earn your libation with some serious exercise, because Montepulicano's steep streets gives new meaning to the notion of a "hill town."

Montepulciano is also a good base for exploring other hill towns, especially nearby Pienza (see p. 256) and Montalcino (p. 259), and for excursions into the enchantingly beautiful Val d'Orcia region (p. 263).

Essentials

ARRIVING   Driving is the best method: From Siena, the most scenic route is south through the Val d'Orcia on the SS2 to San Quirico d'Orcia, where you get the SS146 east through Pienza to Montepulciano. A dozen or so well-marked parking lots surround the town. Convenient lots are P8, at the top of the town next to the fortress, and P1, at the bottom of town just outside Porta al Prato. Rates are about 1.20€ an hour.

Six Tiemme **buses** (www.tiemmespa.it; ✆ **0577/204-111**) run daily from Siena (1½ hr.). Montepulciano is served by train, with frequent service from Siena, but the station is about 15km (9 miles) outside of town, with few bus connections; a taxi into town will cost about 25€.

GETTING AROUND   Montepulciano's Corso is very steep, but for those not up to the climb, little orange *pollicini* buses connect the junction just below the Porta al Prato and Piazza Grande in about 8 minutes. The official point of origin is "the fifth tree on the right above the junction." Tickets cost 1€ each way (buy them on the bus) and run every 20 minutes.

VISITOR INFORMATION   Montepulciano's **tourist office** is in the P1 parking lot just below Porta al Prato at Piazza Don Mizzoni 1 (www.proloco montepulciano.it; ✆ **0578/757-341**). It's open Monday through Saturday, usually with a lunchtime closure from 1pm to 3pm; from April through

October it's also open on Sundays from 9am to 1pm, and in August it stays open all day until 8pm (Sunday 9am–1pm and 3–6:30pm). Another office, at Piazza Grande 7 (www.stradavinonobile.it; © **0578/717-484**) represents the so-called **Strada del Vino Nobile di Montepulciano e dei Sapori della Valdichiana Senese**—that is, vineyards and other sights in the countryside around Montepulciano, so it's a good place to learn about wine touring and smaller towns in the region. The office is open Monday to Friday 9:30am to 1:30pm and 2:30 to 6pm, Saturday 10am to 1pm and 2 to 5pm, and Sunday 10am to 1pm (except in November, January, and February, when it's only open Monday to Friday).

Exploring Montepulciano

It's all uphill from **Porta al Prato,** where the Medici crest (five balls) above the gate hint at Montepulciano's long association with Florence. It's a steep climb up the Corso (the street name changes several times), but along the way you can see some impressive palaces—at no. 91, the massive **Palazzo Avignonesi,** with grinning lions' heads; across the street, the **Palazzo Tarugi** (no. 82); and at no. 73, the **Palazzo Bucelli,** its facade embedded with a patchwork of Etruscan reliefs and funerary urns, placed there by an 18th-century resident, antiquarian scholar Pietro Bucelli. About halfway up the street, in Piazza Micelozzo, is a light-hearted diversion: a playful puppet character atop the Torre del Pulcinella rings out the hour.

At the highest point in a very high town is **Piazza Grande.** You might recognize the 14th-century **Palazzo Comunale** from the movie *Twilight: New Moon*—it was filmed here, though the story was supposedly set in Volterra (see p. 280). One side of the piazza is taken up by the facade of the never-completed **Cattedrale di Santa Maria Assunta.**

A short walk north along Via Ricci brings you to **Piazza San Francesco,** where views extend south across the Valdichiana to Lago Trasimeno in Umbria and northeast across the hilly Val d'Orcia toward Siena.

Cattedrale di Santa Maria Assunta ★ CATHEDRAL   Montepulciano's homely, bare-brick cathedral was erected in 1680 on the site of a much earlier church (only a relatively new 15th-century bell tower was left in place). The plan was to build a landmark worthy of its noble neighbors on Piazza Grande, but the city ran out of funds, and the exterior was never sheathed in marble as planned. Inside is Montepulciano's great work of art, a 1401 gold-hued altarpiece by Taddeo di Bartolo (1363–1422) of "The Assumption of the Virgin with Saints." This is one of the greatest works by Bartolo, one of Siena's post-Black-Death generation of artists. You can't get too close to the massive triptych soaring above the high altar, which is a shame, because the charm lies in the detail of the many various panels. The main sections show the death of the Virgin, with the apostles by her bedside; her ascension into Heaven, as the apostles survey her empty tomb; and the Virgin's coronation in heaven. The remnants of a marble sculptural group by Florentine architect and sculptor

Montepulciano

0 — 100 yds
0 — 100 m

Michelozzo (1396–1472) were crafted for the tomb of papal secretary Bartolomeo Aragazzi. The tomb was disassembled in the 17th century (some pieces ended up in the Victoria and Albert Museum in London), but a few figures remain here—a reclining, hooded statue of Aragazzi himself, to the right of the central entrance door; figures of fortitude and justice on either side of the high altar; and, leaning against a nearby pillar, St. Bartholomew, Aragazzi's namesake.

Piazza Grande. No phone. Free. Daily 9am–12:30pm and 3:15–7pm.

Pinacoteca Crociani ★   A few years ago this unassuming little collection found itself in possible possession of a blockbuster masterpiece, when it was suggested that its painting "Portrait of a Gentleman" was done by Caravaggio, the wildly popular art star of the late 16th and early 17th centuries. Many art historians remain skeptical, though a nifty digital display next to the painting makes a compelling case for the provenance. The museum's other showpiece is a transcendently glowing portrait of Montepulciano's patron saint, St. Agnes, by Domenico Beccafumi, who did much of the flooring in Siena's Duomo (see p. 237).

Via Ricci 10. www.museociviomontepulciano.it. © **0578/717-300**. 5€. Wed–Mon 10:30am–6:30pm.

Wine Tasting in Montepulciano

The cellars of the **Gattavecchi** *cantine* (wineries), Via di Collazzi 74 (www.gattavecchi.it; ✆ **0578/757-110**), have been in use since before 1200, originally by the friars of the adjacent church Santa Maria del Servi. Older still is the tiny room at the bottom, probably an Etruscan tomb. Gattavecchi's Vino Nobile is top-notch, as is the 100% Sangiovese Parceto. Tasting is free. Cavernous cellars at **Cantina Ricci**, Via di Collazzi 7 (www.cantinadericci.it; ✆ **0578/757166**), seem to spread beneath half of Montepulciano, with the main cellar, soaring 60 feet high, filled with centuries-old oak barrels. The cantina is open daily, with tastings (glasses from 2€, at the end of the tour. **Contucci** (www.contucci.it;

✆ **0578/757-006**), in the 11th-century cellars of a historic palace in Piazza Grande, has a fine range of Vino Nobile wines; it's open for free tastings every day of the year. Opposite the cathedral, the **Palazzo del Capitano del Popolo** is another stop for wine buffs, with the **Consorzio del Vino Nobile di Montepulciano** (www.consorziovinonobile.it; ✆ **0578/757-812**; Easter–Oct Mon–Fri 11:30am–1:30pm and 2–6pm, Sat 2–6pm) offering a rotating menu of tastings for a small fee. If you're heading into the country for some wine touring, staff here can provide maps. Across the corridor, the **Strada del Vino Nobile** office (www.stradavinonobile.it; ✆ **0578/717-484**) can help you arrange a wine itinerary.

Tempio di San Biagio ★ CHURCH   This lovely church just outside the town walls, completed in 1534, is the masterwork of Antonio da Sangallo the Elder. Best known for fortresses and other military defenses, here Sangallo broke out of the mold to create a beautiful travertine church on the plan of a Greek cross, with the four arms of equal length radiating from a central dome. Since the church is in the countryside with no other buildings nearby, it's easy to admire its classical unity. The interior is as refined as the exterior, but a bit dull at close inspection.

Via di San Biagio. No phone. Free. Daily 9am–12:30pm and 3:30–7:30pm.

Where to Stay in Montepulciano

Meublé il Riccio ★★   This atmospheric 800-year-old palazzo near Piazza Grande, passed down through the innkeeper's family, lays on the charm—in the arcaded, mosaic-tiled courtyard, the antiques-and-art-filled salon and breakfast room, the comfy lounge, and the rooftop terrace overlooking the landscapes of the Valdichiana far below. Some suites do justice to the surroundings with palatial expanses and terraces of their own, while other rooms are simpler and viewless but not without character. Carved wooden *ricci,* hedgehogs, which once emblazoned the 13th-century façade, make an appearance in all rooms. Ivana and Giorgio Caroti are on hand to dispense advice and make restaurant reservations, serving up delicious homemade pastries at breakfast and drinks throughout the day.

Via di Tolosa 21. www.ilriccio.net. ✆ **0578/757-713**. 10 units. 100€–110€ double. Rates includes breakfast. **Amenities:** Bar; Wi-Fi (free).

Osteria del Borgo ★   Wood beams and exposed brickwork supply these bright, good-size rooms and apartments with rustic charm, while comfortably stylish furnishings and modern baths lend them a chic flair. The hilltop perch is just off Piazza Grande, so views from some rooms and the shared courtyard are expansive. A homey restaurant downstairs serves Tuscan specialties and spills out to a nice terrace in good weather.
Via Ricci. www.osteriadelborgo.it. ℃ **0578/716-799.** 5 units. 90€–120€ double. Rates include breakfast and parking. **Amenities:** Restaurant; Wi-Fi (free).

Vicolo dell'Oste ★★   Tuscan chic prevails in this house on a narrow lane off the Corso, just below Piazza Grande. Wood-beamed ceilings set off streamlined modern furnishings, while deluxe touches such as large Jacuzzis are tucked into the corners of some rooms. Practical amenities include simple kitchens in several rooms. While there are no communal spaces, breakfast is served in a nearby cafe, and innkeepers Giuseppe and Luisa seem to always be near at hand to take care of your needs.
Via delle Oste. www.vicolodelloste.it. ℃ **0578/758-393.** 5 units. 95€–110€ double. Rates include breakfast. **Amenities:** Wi-Fi (free).

Where to Eat in Montepulciano

With a local wine that pairs especially well with hearty sauces and red meat, it's no accident that food in Montepulciano is typically Tuscan, relying heavily on game, beef from the Valdichiana, and thick pastas like hand-rolled *pici* topped with rich sauces. Aside from the town's many tasting rooms, you can also quaff the wine and taste local salamis and cheeses in an atmospheric old cafe, the late-19th-century **Poliziano,** on the Corso (number 27; ℃ **0578/758-615**).

Acquacheta ★★★ SOUTHERN TUSCAN/GRILL   If you're craving steak, head for this cellar eatery, where the emphasis is on local products. In a rustic dining room, long and narrow, seating is at shared tables, and meat is sold by weight and brought to your table by a cleaver-wielding chef for your approval before it goes onto the grill. A choice of pastas and sauces (mix and match as you please) are also available, as are hearty salads. Please don't ask for a separate wine glass—drinking water and wine from the same glass is an age-old tradition in simple eateries in these parts.
Via del Teatro 22. www.acquacheta.eu. ℃ **0578/717-086.** Entrees 7€–18€. Wed–Mon noon–3pm and 7:30–10:30pm. Closed mid-Jan–mid-Mar.

La Bottega del Nobile ★ TUSCAN   It's a challenge to walk up the Corso without stopping at one of the many shops for a sip or two of wine, and this appealing tasting room and restaurant satisfies that temptation and much more, serving food and drink throughout the day. The upper floor is part cafe and part wine shop, representing the region's best producers. Snug, brick-walled cellars below are filled with tables where an affable young staff serves thick Tuscan steaks and hearty ragouts, and eagerly pairs just the right wine to complement each dish.
Corso 95. ℃ **0578/757-016.** Entrees 8€–16€. Daily 9am–9pm.

Osteria del Conte ★ SOUTHERN TUSCAN   A trek to the top of town is rewarded with a delicious meal in this simple room off Piazza Grande, overseen by a mother-and-son team who are devoted to home cooking and warm hospitality. Put yourself in their hands with one of the set menus, which include several local specialties and wine, or choose from a nice a la carte selection—the *pici all'aglione* (handmade spaghetti with garlic sauce) is a memorable first course, and most of the meats are grilled to order.

Via di San Donato 19. www.osteriadelconte.it. ✆ **0578/756-062.** Entrees 9€–14€; set menus 25€ and 30€. Tues–Sun 12:30–2:30pm and 7:30–11:30pm.

Montepulciano Shopping

You may leave town with more than some wine in your shopping bags. The Mazzetti family has been crafting copper in Montepulciano since the end of the 19th century, and Cesare and his craftspeople display their pots, pans, and other beautiful wares in the **Bottega del Rame** at Via dell'Opio nel Corso 64 (✆ **0578/758-753**); an adjacent museum shows off some of the family's prized pieces.

Side Trips from Montepulciano

Montepulciano, Montalcino, and Pienza are in the Crete Siense, literally the "Sienese Clay Hills," a terrain of lone farmhouses and pointy cypress trees in a stark landscape of golden rolling hills, planted with wheat, fava beans, and sunflowers. You'll get a nice sense of the Crete Siense on the drive between the three towns on SP 146. This is another face of Tuscany, quite different from the vineyard-clad hills of Chianti country; at times the countryside seems forsaken, almost like the surface of the moon.

PIENZA ★★
14km (9 miles) W of Montepulciano, 55km (34 miles) SE of Siena

A 20-minute drive west of Montepulciano on the SS146, this lovely hill-town sits perched above the Val d'Orcia, with glorious landscapes of vine-yards and wheat fields rising and falling in every direction. Narrow side

The Valdichiana: The Big Valley

Montepulciano, Cortona, and Arezzo nestle on the flanks of the Valdichiana (or Val di Chiana), a wide swath of farmland running north–south for some 100km (62 miles) through central Italy. Etruscans settled the valley 2,500 years ago, leaving behind remnants of their sophisticated civilization in Cortona, Chiusi, and other centers of their 12-city confederation. These days the valley supplies some of Italy's most prized beef, *bistecca alla fiorentina*, from Chianina cattle, along with stunning views from Cortona and the other hill towns that overlook the green and golden landscape. You can shoot through the valley on the A1 *autostrada* or on fast trains between Rome and Florence, but for a nice close-up look, opt for the scenic 33-km (20-mile) drive between Cortona and Montepulciano.

A tranquil courtyard in Pienza, designed to be the ideal Renaissance city.

streets are lined with shops selling the town's famous pecorino (sheep's milk cheeses) and honey, but Pienza has a unique noble heritage, dating to the mid-15th century, when it was rebuilt by humanist Pope Pius II and architect Bernardo Rossellino to be the ideal Renaissance town. Piazzas and palaces, spaces and perspectives, were to be designed to reflect Renaissance ideals of rationality and humanism, and to instill the populace with notions of peace and harmony. Rossellino's budget was 10,000 florins and he spent 50,000, but Pius was so pleased with the transformation of his birthplace that he scrapped the old name of Corsignano and named the town after himself. Sadly, Pius died soon thereafter, and most of his plans for palaces, churches, piazzas and well-ordered streets were never realized.

Park in one of the well-marked paid lots outside the town walls (1.25€ first hour, 1€ each following hour) and follow the main street, **Corso Rossellino,** through to the center of the little town: the splendid **Piazza Pio II,** the focal point of Pius's town-planning dream and a Renaissance stage set of architectural perfection. Here you'll find the two main buildings of Pius's ambitious dream: A church (the **Duomo**) and the pope's own residence (**Palazzo Piccolomini**). Pienza's **tourist office** is also here, inside the Palazzo Vescovile on Piazza Pio II, Corso Rossellino 30, 53026 Pienza (www.ufficioturisticodipienza.it; © **0578/749-071;** open daily 9:30am–1pm and 3–6:30pm.

Duomo ★ CATHEDRAL   This light-drenched *domus vitrea* (literally "a house of glass") fulfilled Pius's notion that the church should symbolize enlightenment. The exterior represents Renaissance ideals of unity with a facade of three blind arches, atop which the pope immodestly placed his coat of arms. The interior was in part inspired by his travels in Germany, where he admired the local style of church architecture, hall churches lit by tall windows. For all of its perfection, the structure showed a serious flaw almost as soon as it was completed—the hillside on which it is built is unstable, and the foundations are slowly shifting (as you walk toward the rear, you'll notice the floor slightly slopes).

Piazza Pio II. © **0578/749-059.** Free. Daily 7am–1pm and 2:30–7pm.

Palazzo Piccolomini ★ HISTORIC SITE   Pope Pius had to have a residence worthy of his lofty status, of course, and his dining room, bedroom, library, and other chambers are appropriately regal, and rather stuffy. The pope's descendants lived here until 1968, and nothing in the cavernous salons is very exciting (the dry-as-dust free audio guide doesn't help, either). The bright spot is the palazzo's hanging garden and triple-decked loggia, reached through the painted courtyard; you can linger a while to take in the incredible views south over the Val d'Orcia. With a setting like this it's easy to see why Pius II, born Silvio Piccolomini into an impoverished branch of a noble Sienese family, wanted to return to this humble town of his birth after an event-filled life as a humanist scholar, itinerant diplomat, and pope from 1458 to 1464.

Piazza Pio II. www.palazzopiccolominipienza.it. © **0578/74-392.** 7€ adults, 5€ students and children 6–17, children under 5 free. Mid-Mar–mid-Oct Tues–Sun 10am–6:30pm; mid-Oct–mid-Mar Tues–Sun 10am–4:30pm.

Where to Stay & Eat in Pienza

Fonte Berusi ★★★   Rural Tuscany doesn't get much more welcoming than it does at this enchanting olive estate just outside Pienza, where old farm buildings have been redone as eight gracious apartments. Color-rich, character-filled living and sleeping spaces open to vine-draped terraces and sunny patios. Guests share extensive grounds and a pool, along with a book-lined living room filled with artworks by Eduardo and Andrea, father and son artists who, along with daughter-in-law Manuela, are the attentive resident proprietors.

Podere Fonte Bertusi. www.fontebertusi.it. © **0578/748-077.** 8 units. Doubles from 130€. Rates include breakfast. **Amenities:** Pool; Wi-Fi (free).

La Bandita Townhouse ★★   Just as Pope Pius introduced the latest in Renaissance fashion to little Pienza, this stylish guesthouse does the same with 21st-century decor. Huge, loftlike guest quarters seem better suited to New York or Berlin (the elevator is the only one for miles around), but they certainly prove that contemporary chic can be comfortable. Amid design-magazine staples like steel frame beds, distressed leather armchairs, and slinky divans, you can enjoy luxuries you might not have at home, such as slipping effortlessly from a supremely comfortable mattress into a deep tub perched right alongside. Timeless pleasures include honey-colored stone walls and garden views over the surrounding countryside. The dining room, decked out with retrofitted furnishings from a 1950s-era Florence school, sticks to straightforward takes on local cuisine, with innovations that include hamburgers made from the best Val-dichiana beef.

Corso il Rossellino. www.la-bandita.com. © **0578/749-005.** 12 units. 250€–495€ double. Rates include breakfast. **Amenities:** Restaurant; bar; Wi-Fi (free).

La Casa di Adelina ★★★ Montichiello, a little walled village 10km (6 miles) east of Pienza, is an enchanting warren of piazzas and stone towers, and adding to the charm are these three rooms and three apartments (rooms and one attic apartment are in a grand old house on a central square, one apartment is in a nearby house, and another is in a medieval tower). All are full of antiques, family heirlooms, and tasteful vintage-modern and contemporary pieces. Guests share a large beamed lounge where a fire burns in the stove on chilly evenings and a breakfast with homemade pastries is served by affable host Francesco. With a couple of shops and places to eat, the village is a good base for exploring the Val d'Orcia and some of Tuscany's most enticing towns.

Piazza San Martina 3, Montichiello. www.lacasadiadelina.eu. © **0578/755-167.** 6 units. 90€–140€ double. Rates include breakfast. Usually closed 2 wks. in Feb. **Amenities:** Lounge; Wi-Fi (free).

Trattoria da Fiorella ★★ TUSCAN An old stable is now an unusual and inviting dining room, with just eight or so tables on the main floor and a few on a balcony above. The setting seems almost theatrical, and the two friendly proprietor-brothers give the town's famous pecorino cheese the star treatment: *crespelle al forno ripiene con zucchini e pecorino fresco,* baked crêpes filled with zucchini and young pecorino cheese; *verdure grigliata con pecorino,* a nice assortment of vegetables topped with shaved cheese; and mixed pecorinos with honey and walnuts. Several hearty homemade pastas, some with sauces of *cinghiale* (wild boar), and grilled steak and pork also show off the local bounty.

Via Condotti 11. www.trattoriadafiorella.it. © **0578/749-045.** Entrees 8€–15€. Thurs–Tues noon–2:30pm and 7–9:30pm.

Trattoria Latte di Luna ★ TUSCAN Home-cooked meals are prepared by mom in the kitchen and served by dad and daughter in the yellow stucco dining room, off a little square at one end of the town's main street. *Pici all'aglione* (with spicy tomato-and-garlic sauce) or *zuppa di pane* (a local variant on *ribollita,* with more cabbage) are stellar starters, followed by wild boar or suckling pig in season or grilled steaks any time. The dessert of choice is the house-made *semifreddo* flavored with walnuts and seasonal fruits and berries.

Corso Rossellino, next to Porta al Ciglio. © **0578/748-606.** Entrees 7€–16€. Wed–Mon 12:15–2:15pm and 7:15–9:15pm.

MONTALCINO ★★

23km (14 miles) W of Pienza; 28km (17 miles) W of Montepulicano; 40km (25 miles) S of Siena

Montalcino presents a warm welcome on the approach from the Ombrone River valley below, its medieval houses clinging higglety-pigglety to precipitous alleys beneath prickly towers. Of course, if you know wine, you're aware that scenery is not the town's real calling card—that's Brunello di Montalcino, one of the world's most acclaimed reds, of which the town produces more than 3.5 million bottles a year, along with 3 million of its lighter-weight cousin, Rosso di Montalcino.

Montalcino was known as the "Republic of Siena at Montalcino" for housing Sienese refugees after Florence conquered Siena in 1555 (see **La Fortezza,** below); after Montalcino fell to Florence in 1559, it more or less languished until the 1960s, when the world began waking up to the fact that the local sangiovese grosso grapes—known as "Brunello" to the locals—yielded a wine to be reckoned with.

The **tourist office** is at Costa del Municipio 1 (✆ **0577/849-331;** daily 10am–1pm and 2–5:40pm, closed Mon Nov–Mar).

La Fortezza ★ HISTORIC SITE   Built in 1361, this castle's moment arrived when the Sienese holed up here for 4 years after their city's final defeat by Florence in 1555 (ironically, the fortress had only recently been expanded and strengthened by Florence's Medici dukes). You can wander round the pentagonal walls and scale a ladder to the highest turret for a view across hills and dales all the way to Siena—but do so before you sample wine in the on-premise enoteca, perhaps the only tasting room in the world with ramparts.

Piazzale Fortezza. www.enotecalafortezza.it. ✆ **0577/849-211.** 4€, 2€ children 6–17, includes Museo di Montalcino. Tastings from 15€. Daily 9am–8pm.

Museo Civico e Diocesano d'Arte Sacra ★ ART MUSEUM   Coming upon this small collection is a bit of a treat, as the cloisters of the church of Sant'Agostino house a trove of masterpieces you wouldn't expect to find in such a small town. The painting galleries are devoted largely to Sienese artists, who despite their static Byzantine influences were bold innovators of their times. The Virgin Mary, the favorite subject of early Renaissance painters, shows up in works of Bartolo di Fredi and

---

Sampling the Vino

Brunello di Montalcino is one of Italy's mightiest reds, a brawny wine that can hold its own with the rarest *bistecca alla fiorentina*. It's also the perfect accompaniment to game, pungent mushroom sauces, and aged cheeses. Brunello exudes the smell of mossy, damp earth and musky berries; it tastes of dark, sweet fruits and dry vanilla, and as the deep ruby liquid mellows to garnet, the wine takes on its characteristic complex and slightly tannic aspect. Although Montalcino has produced wine for centuries, its flagship Brunello is a recent development, born from late-19th-century sangiovese experiments. Most Brunellos are drinkable after about 4 to 5

years in the bottle; the complex ones are best after 10 years or so (few last beyond 30 years). Staff members at Montalcino's wine consortium **Consorzio del Vino Brunello di Montalcino** (www.consorziobrunellodimontalcino.it; ✆ **0577/848-246**), Piazza Cavour 8, can provide info on local wines and steer you to vineyards that are open to the public. **Poggio Antico** (www.poggioantico.com; ✆ **0577/84804;** daily 10am–6pm), 4.5km (3 mi) south of Montalcino off SP14 toward Grosetto, gives free, informative tours in English that provide an excellent introduction to Brunello and other wines of the region. Tastings begin at 2€ a glass.

Luca Tomme; Fredi's multi-panel painting of "The Coronation of Mary" is considered to be his masterpiece. The "Madonna dell'Unita (Madonna of Humility)," by Sano di Pietro (1406–1481), was quite radical in its time, showing Mary kneeling on a cushion rather than seated on her traditional throne. Andrea della Robbia's terra-cotta statue of a refreshingly boyish St. Sebastian brings the collection into the full flowering of the Renaissance.

Via Ricasoli 31. www.comunedimontalcino.it. © **0577/846-014.** 4.50€, children 3€. Jan–Mar Tues–Sun 10am–1pm and 2–6pm; Apr–Dec, Tues–Sun 10am–6pm.

Near Montalcino
Abbazia di Monte Oliveto Maggiore ★★★ RELIGIOUS SITE
The most famous of Tuscany's rural monasteries is set in the scarred hills of the Crete Senesi, 22km (13 miles) northeast of Montalcino. Founded in 1313 by a group of wealthy Sienese businessmen who wanted to devote themselves to the contemplative life, the Olivetan order built this redbrick monastic complex in the early 15th century. What draws most visitors today is one of the masterpieces of High Renaissance narrative painting: a 36-scene fresco cycle by Luca Signorelli and Sodoma illustrating the Life of St. Benedict. Signorelli started the job in 1497, before skipping town to work on Orvieto's Duomo, where he created his masterpiece, a "Last Judgment" (see p. 261). Antonio Bazzi, who arrived in 1505 and finished the cycle by 1508, is better known as "Il Sodoma" (probably a reference to his predilection for young men, although he was married at least three times and had as many as 30 children). Look for his self-portrait in scene 3—he's the richly dressed fellow with flowing black hair, accompanied by two pet badgers, a chicken, and a raven. To follow the cycle's narrative, start in the back left-hand corner, with a scene of the young Benedict, astride a spirited white horse, leaving his parents' home to study in Rome. The scenes are especially appealing because of their precise details of medieval life: Check out the construction crews in scene 11, or the harlots smuggled into the monastery in scene 19 (allegedly, the abbot made Sodoma add clothing to the nudes he'd first painted). Also inside the church are gorgeous choir stalls crafted in intarsia in 1505 by the monk Giovanni da Verona, showing city scenes with remarkably detailed perspective.

SP 451, Strada di Monte Oliveto, Asciano. www.monteolivetomaggiore.it. From Montalcino, follow SP14 north to Buonconvento, then head NE on SP451 to the abbey. © **0577/707-611.** Free. Daily 9:15am–noon and 3–6pm (closes at 5pm in winter).

Abbazia di Sant'Antimo ★★★ RELIGIOUS SITE
This exquisite Romanesque abbey of pale yellow stone nestles serenely in a valley amid vines and olive groves at the foot of the village of Castelnuovo dell'Abate, 9km (6 miles) south of Montalcino on SP55. Legend has it that the first stone here was laid on the order of Charlemagne in A.D. 781, after an angel cured his plague-stricken entourage on a journey from Rome. While that story is debatable, the monastery does date to the 8th century and may

Abbazia di Sant'Antimo.

have once housed the relics of namesake Saint Anthimus, an early Christian priest. Near the entrance is a charming medieval relief of the Madonna and Child, and carvings of mythological animals and geometric designs surround the doors. Inside the columned interior, the carving continues; look on the right side for an intricate depiction of Daniel in the lion's den. In the chapel, 15th-century frescoes by Giovanni di Asciano show scenes from the Life of St. Benedict, rich in earthy detail (one scene features two blatantly amorous pigs). A well-marked cross-country hiking trail from Montalcino to the monastery takes about 2 hours. For a quicker return, ask for a bus timetable at Montalcino's tourist office.

Via Della Badia di Sant'Antimo, Castelnuovo dell'Abate. www.antimo.it. ⌀ **0577/835-659.** Free; video guides 3€ and 6€. Daily 10am–7pm (closed at 5pm Nov–Mar).

Where to Stay & Eat in Montalcino

Castello Banfi ★★ WINERY   One of Tuscany's leading wine producers houses guests in stylish luxury, in a repurposed little *borgo* pressed against the castle walls. What were once peasant cottages are now extraordinarily luxurious suites and rooms fitted with stylish traditional furnishings, sumptuous fabrics, and rare antiques, plus the latest tech gadgetry. Aside from the polished and attentive service, guests enjoy such amenities as a swimming pool, a secluded rose garden, and two excellent restaurants. Also on the estate is a farmhouse where five large apartments provide a much more informal experience; furnishings are comfortably rustic, wide terraces overlook miles of vineyards, and the kitchens are well stocked with estate wines and provisions for a satisfying breakfast.

Castello di Poggio alle Mura, Montalcino. www.castellobanfi.com. ⌀ **0577/877-505.** 14 borgo units, 5 farmhouse apartments. Borgo units from 350€, apartments from 150€. Rates include breakfast. **Amenities:** 2 restaurants; bar; pool (borgo suites only); Wi-Fi (free).

Fiaschetteria Italiana ★★ WINE BAR Montalcino's most popular drinking spot, in the center of town on Piazza del Popolo, was founded in 1888 by Ferrucci Biondi Santi, a pioneer in the development of Brunello wine. He modeled his establishment on Caffe Florian in Venice, which is why locals refer to the Art Deco establishment with red velvet sofas and marble-top tables as "The Florian." The square out front may not be as grand as the Piazza San Marco but it's certainly picturesque. Prince Charles is among the famous patrons who have quaffed the excellent Brunellos and other wines offered here. Snacks and light meals are available, and the coffee, almost as treasured as the wines, is hands-down the best for miles around.

Piazza del Popolo 6. www.caffefiaschetteriaitaliana.com. ✆ **0577/849-043.** Entrees 8€–12€. Daily 7:30am–11pm, closed Thurs Nov–Mar.

HOT SPOT: THE val d'orcia

If you're driving from Montalcino to Pienza, an easy side trip takes you to the rippling golden hills of the Val d'Orcia. First stop is San Quirico d'Orcia, about 15km (9 miles) east of Montalcino on SR2, where the honey-colored **Collegiata dei Santi Quirico e Giulitta** assaults you with a wealth of carved stone: capitals composed of animal heads, friezes of dueling fantasy creatures, and columns rising from the backs of stone lions. The church was once a popular stop for pilgrims on the Francigena road from Canterbury to Rome. Its namesake saints were a mother and son: 3-year-old Quirico, who inadvertently scratched the face of the pagan governor of Taurus and was thrown down a flight of stairs, and his mother Giulitta, whose calm acceptance of her son's martyrdom so angered the governor, he had her ripped apart with hooks and beheaded. Just down the block in the main square, Piazza della Libertà, you'll find **Horti Leonini,** a Renaissance Italianate garden (1580) with geometric box-hedge designs and shady holm oaks, originally a resting spot for pilgrims, open daily sunrise to sunset. The town's tourist office is inside the Palazzo Chigi, Via Dante Alighieri (✆ **0577/897211,** open Apr–Oct Thurs–Tues 10am–1pm and 3:30–6:30pm).

Five kilometers (3 miles) south and well signposted off the SS2 is **Bagno Vignoni,** little more than a group of houses surrounding one of the most memorable *piazze* in Tuscany. Instead of paving stones you'll find a steaming pool of mineral water, created when the Medici harnessed the hot sulfur springs percolating from the ground. Even St. Catherine of Siena (see p. 240) relaxed here with a sulfur cure. To see the springs in their more natural state, as Roman legionnaires did, take the second turnoff on the curving road into town and pull over after about a km (half a mile), where on your right you see a tiny sulfurous

mountain where the waters bubble up in dozens of tiny rivulets. You can also look down on the spectacle from the Parco di Mulino at the edge of town. From both vantage points, there's a fairy-tale view of the **Rocca d'Orcia,** the 11th-century stronghold of the Aldobrandeschi clan, formidable toll collectors along the Francigena pilgrim road. Should you wish to partake of the waters, head to **Antiche Terme di Bagno Vignoni,** Piazza del Moretto 12 (www.termedibagnovignoni. it; ✆ **0577/887-635**), or **Piscina Val di Sole,** at the Hotel Posta Marcucci (www. piscinavaldisole.it; ✆ **0577/887112**), to soak away your cares.

AREZZO ★

53km (32 miles) NE of Montepulicano

This lively little city on the eastern flanks of the Valdichiana is not as often visited as its more famous Tuscan neighbors, but get past that fairly unremarkable 20th-century perimeter—much of it built atop the rubble left by Allied bombings in World War II—and you'll find an enticing medieval city of cobbled streets. Arezzo's rich cultural life has left it with a number of art-filled churches. Famous natives of Arezzo include not only Giorgio

Antiques fair in the Tournament Square in Arezzo.

Vasari (author of the gossipy *Lives of the Artists*) but also painter Piero della Francesca, from nearby Sansepolcro, the poet Petrarch (1304–74), and actor and director Roberto Benigni, who filmed parts of his 1999 Oscar-winning *La Vita è Bella (Life Is Beautiful)* here.

Essentials

ARRIVING Arezzo is just off the A1 autostrada, putting it within fairly easy reach of Florence and most Tuscan towns by car; there's also bus service (**Tiemme:** www.tiemmespa.it; ✆ **0575/39881**) from Siena. Arezzo is on a main north-south train line, with frequent service to and from Florence and Rome. Two easy-to-reach underground parking garages near the historic center are **Parcheggio Piazzza del Popolo,** at Piazza del Popolo 1, 2€ an hour, and **Parcheggio Piazza della Misericordia,** at Via Garibaldi 143, 1.50€ an hour (www.arezzoparcheggi.it; ✆ **393/921-3276**).

VISITOR INFORMATION The **tourist information office** (www.arezzo turismo.it; ✆ **0575/182-2770**) at Emiciclo Papa Giovanni Paolo II 1 is open daily 9am to 7pm.

Treasure Hunters and Knights

Arezzo's famous **antiques fair** takes over the Piazza Grande and adjoining streets the first Sunday of each month and the preceding Saturday. More than 500 vendors come from around Italy to sell an appealing array of old furniture, silver, oil paintings, and other wares, at very good prices.

The **Giostra del Saracino,** a jousting contest between the four districts of the

town, turns the clock back to medieval times twice a year in June and September. A lively procession through the streets to the accompaniment of trumpets and drums ends in Piazza Grande, where jousters on colorfully bedecked horses wield their lances against armor-plated dummies.

Exploring Arezzo

Arezzo's medieval core centers on the charmingly lopsided **Piazza Grande.** An elegant loggia by Giorgio Vasari anchors one side of the piazza, while the rest of the space drapes rather casually across the slope, with slanting cobblestones and an irregular shape. The Duomo crowns the hilltop, while next it to the green expanse of the Parco del Prato, with airy views of the countryside, surrounds a ruined 16th-century fortress.

Basilica di San Francesco ★★★ CHURCH   The timed-entry admission only lets you spend about 30 minutes in front of Piero della Francesca's "Legend of the True Cross," but that is reason enough to come to Arezzo. One of the greatest artists of the Renaissance painted one of the world's greatest fresco cycles, in a league with the Sistine Chapel, between 1452 and 1466. The 10 panels are remarkable for their grace, narrative detail, compositional precision, perfect perspective, depth of humanity, and dramatic light effects—"the most perfect morning light in all Renaissance painting," wrote art historian Kenneth Clark. The full religious significance of the story may escape you, but with stalwart knights and fair ladies, the scenes seem like a medieval romance. The beauty is in the details: heaving bosoms, pouty lips, and dreamy eyes, along with some wonderful ancient and medieval finery. You may have seen these frescoes in the film *The English Patient,* when Kip hoists Hana up to the frescoes by means of ropes and pulleys; we see her expressions of delight and wonder as she comes face to face with Piero's colorful ladies and gents. You'll feel the same, even when earthbound and jostling for a good look with your co-viewers.

Piazza San Francesco. www.museistataliarezzo.it. $\mathbb{C}$ **0575/352-727.** Church free: Mon–Fri 9am–7pm (closes 6pm Nov–mid-Mar), Sat 9am–5:30pm, Sun 1–6pm (closes 5:30 Nov–mid-Mar). Della Francesca cycle 8€, 5€ students and ages 16 and under: timed-entry tickets (30 min) only; reservations required by phone, website, or in person; Mon–Fri 9am–7pm, Sat 9am–6pm, Sun 1–6pm.

Casa di Vasari (House of Vasari) ★★ HISTORIC HOUSE   Giorgio Vasari was born in Arezzo in 1511, just as the Renaissance was flowering all around him. Though he never achieved the greatness of many of the other artists working around him, Vasari helped define the period— and may have even coined the term "Renaissance" for the creative period that led Europe out of the Dark Ages. An architect as well an artist—he designed the Galleria degli Uffizi in Florence (see p. 181)—Vasari is best known for *Lives of the Most Excellent Painters, Sculptors and Architects,* a rather juicy account of the great masters, many of whom Vasari knew personally. He settled down here in his hometown in 1540 and set about frescoing the walls and ceilings of his gracious house with classical themes and portraits. Check out his playful fresco "Virtue, Envy, and Fortune" in which each of the three competing figures appears most prominent depending on where you're standing. In the Room of Celebrities, Vasari painted portraits of Michelangelo, Andrea del Sarto, and other

LEGEND OF THE true cross

Piero della Francesca based his great Arezzo frescoes on a story from Jacopo da Varazze's 1260 *Golden Legend,* a compilation of saintly lore that was a wildly popular medieval bestseller. As the story goes, Seth, son of Adam, planted on his father's grave the seeds from the apple tree that had led to his parents' fall from Eden; timbers from the tree were eventually made into a bridge. Many years later, the much-mythologized Queen of Sheba recognized while crossing the bridge that its wood had special significance. She predicted to Solomon, king of Israel, that a savior would one day be hung from the timbers and cause the downfall of the Jewish nation. Solomon prudently had the wood buried—but, you guessed it, Romans inevitably discovered the beams and used them to crucify Christ.

Two centuries later, Roman emperor Constantine the Great saw the cross in a vision, emblazoned the image on his army's shields, defeated his co-emperor Maxentius, and converted to Christianity. His mother, Helen, went in search of the true cross in Jerusalem (her methods included torturing Jews to reveal the cross's whereabouts). Fragments of the Cross became popular medieval religious relics. It's a far-fetched story indeed, but in the hands of Piero della Francesca, its twists and turns become riveting.

notable contemporaries, surrounding himself with the cultural greats of his day. Vasari's copious correspondence, including 17 letters from Michelangelo, is sometimes on view. While the original furnishings are no longer in place, part of the beautiful garden remains, and like the rest of the house provides a glimpse of a cultured Renaissance lifestyle.
Via XX Settembre 55. ℰ **0575/409-040.** 4€, 2€ students and children under 17. Mon–Sat 8:30am–7pm, Sun 8:30–1pm.

Cattedrale di Arezzo ★ CATHEDRAL   This big and austere Gothic barn, at the highest point in town, reveals some nice surprises once you step inside the coldly stark interior. First to catch your eye will be the stained-glass windows by Guillaume de Marcillat (1470–1529), a French master summoned to Rome to work for the popes, who spent the last 10 years of his life in Arezzo creating these seven magnificent windows. His colorful scenes include the Calling of St. Matthew, the Baptism of Christ, the Expulsion of Merchants from the Temple, the Adulteress, and the Raising of Lazarus along the right wall; and Saints Silvester and Lucy in the chapel to the left of the apse. (Lucy has a amazingly serene face, considering that she's about to have her eyes gouged out.) Beneath these colorful tableaux are some other fine works: a robust Mary Magdalene portrayed in a fresco by Piero Della Francesca in an arch near the sacristy door; the stone-carved battle scenes on the tomb of Guido Tarlati, an Aretine bishop who died in 1327; and in the chapel on the left near the entrance, a series of terra-cottas by della Robbia showing the Assumption, the Crucifixion, and a Madonna and Child.
Piazza del Duomo. ℰ **0575/23991.** Free. Daily 7am–12:30pm and 3–6:30pm.

Santa Maria della Pieve ★★ CHURCH   Most great churches are intended to draw the eye heavenward, but few achieve the effect quite as dramatically as this 12th-century arched facade. Three stacked arcades of beige stone subtly narrow as they rise above a five-arched lower floor and the street below; above it all rises a bell tower with five rows of windows. The effect is all the more powerful since the church sits on a slope. Inside is an altarpiece by Pietro Lorenzetti, a Sienese artist who eventually perished when the Black Death devastated the city in 1348. Like the church's facade, his work here is multitiered, with figures getting smaller on each successive layer. The paintings are unusually vivacious for the austere Sienese school. Remains of the town's patron saint, Donato—a 4th-century bishop of Arezzo—are here, too, in a beautiful gold reliquary.

Corso Italia 7. ℰ **0575/377-678**. Free. Daily May–Sept 8am–7pm, Oct–Apr 8am–noon and 3–6pm.

Where to Stay in Arezzo

Antiche Mura ★   Tucked into the town walls just a few steps below the Duomo, this tall, narrow house dates from the 1200s. Rock outcroppings, stone walls, glass walkways over ancient foundations, and an old olive press celebrate the heritage, while sleekly simple furnishings, bright white walls, and splashes of color add a distinctly contemporary flair. Each room is named and styled after a famous woman in literature or the movies, from Madame Bovary's period decor to the sensual reds used in the Marilyn Monroe room.

Piaggia di Murello 35. www.antichemura.info. ℰ **0575/20410**. 6 units. 65€–95€ double. Rates include breakfast. Free parking nearby. **Amenities:** Wi-Fi (free).

Graziella Patio Hotel ★★   Decor in this old palace a stone's throw from the church of San Francesco is based on the travel essays of the late Bruce Chatwin. The gimmick actually works, adding romance and drama without sacrificing comfort, along with flourishes like huge bathtubs in the sitting/sleeping areas and a pleasantly contemporary lounge and breakfast room. The Colonial India room, with bright yellow walls and a four-poster bed, seems especially well-suited to the palatial surroundings, and the Moroccan room, with beautiful glazed-tile walls, is as colorful as the town's famous frescoes. Three especially extravagant rooms are on a lower floor that opens to a hidden garden. One is equipped with a hot tub the size of a small swimming pool, and another has a huge sunken bathtub reached by a dramatic staircase behind the bed. Guests have use of a Mac-Book for the duration of their stay, and spa services are available.

Via Cavour 23. www.hotelpatio.it. ℰ **0575/401-962**. 10 units. 135€–200€ double. Rates include breakfast. **Amenities:** Spa services; Wi-Fi (free).

Vogue Hotel ★★   With a name like this a hotel had better be stylish, and these good-size and gracious rooms deliver on the promise, bringing comfortable flair to centuries-old surroundings. Stone walls and beams accent rooms where huge soaking tubs are tucked behind glass headboards, enormous showers have windows, and sitting areas are set into alcoves. Traditional comforts include rich fabrics, fine carpets, and handsome wood furnishings. Some rooms also provide a timeless view of the town's towers and rooftops, and all the sights are just steps away.

Via Guido Monaco 54. www.voguehotel.it. © **0575/24361.** 26 units. 120€–220€ double. Rates include breakfast. **Amenities:** Bar; Wi-Fi (free).

Where to Eat in Arezzo

In all but the worst weather, Aretines turn out for the evening *passeggiata.* Two prime spots to sit on a terrace and enjoy a pre-dinner glass of wine or aperitif while watching the comings and goings are **Caffe dei Costanti** in Piazza San Francesco (© **0575/182-4075**) and **Caffe Vasari** (© **0575/21945**) under the Loggia overlooking Piazza Grande, a good place to perch even in the rain. The most popular place in town for a quick bite is **Dal Moro,** Via Cavour 68 (© **0575/043-208**), with creative sandwiches and a huge selection of local cheeses and cold cuts. **Cremì,** Corso Italia 100 (© **333/976-6336**) dishes up the best artisan gelato in town, along with crepes with a choice of sweet fillings.

Antica Osteria l'Agania ★★★ TUSCAN   On any given night, half the town seems to be packed into these two floors of plain, brightly lit dining rooms, yet the waitstaff never seems daunted by the din or the crowds. Pastas are homemade from organic ingredients, produce is market fresh, and the meat is from local farms. Daily specials include such local favorites as *trippa* (tripe) and *grifi e polenta* (chunks of veal stomach in polenta), but lighter fare is usually available, too, and specials often include eggs topped with fresh asparagus or *tartufo* (dried truffles), especially tasty when accompanied with a Pinot Grigio. The house wine is excellent, and the house grappa puts the perfect finish on a meal.

Via Mazzini 10. www.agania.com. © **0575/295-381.** Entrees 7€–9€. Tues–Sun 12:30–2:30pm and 7:30–10:30pm.

PAY HOMAGE TO piero

Piero della Francesco, whose Legend of the True Cross graces Arezzo's basilica di San Franceso, was a visionary whose figures appear as vivid, thriving beings even 500 years after he committed them to canvas. The master's "Madonna del Prato" hangs in the little museum in **Monterchi,** 28km (16 mi) east of Arezzo on SS73. The painting is rare in Italian art in that it depicts a heavily pregnant Virgin Mary—she holds her hand against her side to support her belly, and if you happen to be in the same condition, the 6.50€ admission fee is waived (www.madonnadelparto.it; © 0575/70713; daily 9am–1pm and 2–7pm, slightly shorter hours mid-Oct–mid-Mar). **Sansepolcro,** 15km (9 mi) farther north on SS73, houses another of Piero's great works, a 1468 "Resurrection of Christ" that British writer Aldous Huxley called "the greatest picture." In World War II a British officer demanded that shelling of the town cease lest the painting be damaged, and the transcendent work remains in the Museo Civico (www.museocivicosansepolcro.it; © 1991/51121; admission 11€; daily 10am–1:30pm and 2:30–7pm, slightly shorter hours in winter).

La Torre di Gnicche ★★ WINE BAR   The emphasis here is on wine, with more than 30 choices available by the glass and hundreds by the bottle, and it's accompanied by a tempting choice of small plates and meals. A huge selection of local cheeses and salamis is available, as are many local favorites, such as *baccalà in umido* (salt-cod stew) and, in summer, *pappa al pomodoro* (a thick bread and tomato soup served at room temperature). The cluttered, bottle-lined room just off Piazza Grande is a nice hideaway on a chilly evening, and a few tables in the narrow lane outside are much in demand in warm weather.

Piaggia San Martino 8. www.latorredignicche.it. ℂ **0575/352-035.** Entrees 7€–11€. Thurs–Tues noon–3pm and 6pm–1am. Closed 2 weeks in Jan.

CORTONA ★★

34km (22 miles) S of Arezzo; 31km (19 miles) NE of Montepulciano

Draped across a green mountain-side above terraced olive groves, austere-looking Cortona is a steep medieval city, where cut-stone staircases take the place of many streets. In recent years, the book and film *Under the Tuscan Sun* have brought waves of appreciative fans to town, but Cortona has survived the onslaught. The somber streets and stage-set piazzas are a bit more crowded in summer than they once were, but the town's

Palazzo Comunale in Cortona.

appeal is as strong as ever and includes some significant art treasures and romantic misty views over the wide Valdichiana.

Essentials

ARRIVING   Cortona is on **rail** lines that run between Florence to the north and Perugia and Chiusi (with easy connections to Rome) to the south. The Camucia/Cortona train station (ℂ **0575/603-018**) is 5km (3 miles) below Cortona in the workaday town of Camucia, where many services are located as well. **Buses** run from here to Cortona, but not as frequently as you'd wish—only once an hour at some periods during the day. Tickets are sold on the bus (1.60€).

VISITOR INFORMATION   In historic Cortona, you'll find a **tourist office** at Piazza Signorelli 9, in the courtyard beyond the Museo dell'Accademia Etrusca ticket office (www.cortonaweb.net; ℂ **0575/637-223**). Several paid-parking areas are located just outside the city walls, including large ones at Piazzale del Mercato and Porta Colonia, where you'll pay about 1€ an hour.

Exploring Cortona

Via Nazionale, known as the **Rugapiana** ("flat street," since it's the only one in town that even comes close to fitting that description), runs east-west through the medieval town to **Piazza della Repubblica,** presided over by a stern city hall loaded with towers, a stone staircase, and wooden balconies. On the northern corner the square opens into **Piazza Signorelli,** a lovely expanse named for the town's famous Renaissance artist, Luca Signorelli (1445–1523). This piazza was once the headquarters of Cortona's Florentine governors, whose coats of arms adorn the **Casali Palace** (now home to the excellent Etruscan museum, see p. 114). From here, streets lead down to the **Piazza del Duomo** and a treasure trove of art in the **Museo Diosceano** (p. 272). Other streets climb steeply uphill from Piazza Signorelli to the **Basilica di Santa Margherita** and, even higher, to the hilltop **Fortezza di Girifalco** (p. 271). You can, however, stay on level ground and walk east along Via Nazionale to airy **Piazza Garibaldi,** which opens into public gardens with views south to Lago Trasimeno in Umbria and west across the Valdichiana to Montepulciano.

Basilica di Santa Margherita ★

CHURCH   High above the town, this 19th-century church with a red-and-white-striped interior would be quite forgettable if it were not for the intriguing story of its patron, Margaret of Cortona (1247–1297), a follower of St. Francis. In her late twenties, Margaret—the former mistress of a lord from Montepulciano—devoted her life to caring for the sick and poor, establishing a hospital and order of nursing sisters. The 13th-century crucifix through which she carried on a prayer dialogue with God hangs in the church, and her embalmed body—to which the centuries have not been terribly kind—lies in full view in a lavish 14th-century tomb above the main altar.

Basilica di Santa Margherita in Cortona.

Piazza Santa Margherita. © **0575/605-064.** Free admission. Apr–Oct daily 8am–noon and 3–7pm; Nov–Mar 9–noon and 3–6pm.

Church of San Francesco ★ CHURCH

This rather simple Romanesque church with its wood-raftered ceiling is the second Franciscan church ever built (the first, in St. Francis' home town of Assisi, was begun around 1228, while this one dates to 1245). This church contains the tomb of Brother Elias of Cortona, who administered the Franciscan Order after

Francis's death in 1226. It also houses three precious relics of St. Francis himself—his tunic, his manuscript of the New Testament, and a cushion he often used. On the high altar is the Reliquary of the Holy Cross, an ornate 10th-century ivory tablet containing a fragment of Christ's cross, presented to Elias by the Byzantine Emperor in 1244. The artist Luca Signorelli, who died in Cortona in 1523, is believed to be buried in the crypt.

Via Berrettini. ℂ **0575/603-205.** Free admission. Daily 9am–5:30pm.

Eremo le Celle ★★★ RELIGIOUS SITE   St. Francis passed through Cortona in 1240, on his way to a mountainside hermitage 3km (2 miles) outside of town. Francis' companion Brother Elias then took up residence in one of the caves and redid the place into a bona fide monastery, which it remains to this day, home to a small community of monks and a place of solitary retreat for the religious. The honey-colored stone dwellings, forest paths, bubbling streams, and simple, rock-hewn chapels are lovely and humbling, and the walk out from town is a delight. From Piazza Mazzini, outside Porta Colonia, walk northeast (to the right as you leave the gate) for about 500 feet to a gravel road on the left that skirts olive groves high above the baroque church of Santa Maria Nuova. At the entrance to a villa garden you will come to a fork; follow the road on the right to the Celle.

Localita Cappuccini 1. ℂ **0575/603-362.** Donations welcome. Daily 7am–7pm.

Fortezza di Girifalco ★ HISTORIC SITE   It's all uphill to Cortona's rugged defenses, built in 1556 on the orders of Duke Cosimo di Medici (Cortona was a prosperous city under Medici rule). The torturous stepped ascent is enlivened by 15 modern mosaics depicting the Stations of the Cross, by the Futurist artist Gino Severini (1883–1966), a Cortona native. By the second time Christ falls, you'll feel like doing the same, though you can pause for a restorative drink at the bar by the Basilica Santa Margherita. Views from the four surviving bastions reward the climb, across the Valdichiana to Montepulciano, south toward Lago Trasimeno, and north toward Arezzo and the colossal Monte Amiata.

Viale Raimondo Bistacci. ℂ **0575/637-235.** 5€. Hours vary; usually daily 10am–7pm.

Museo dell'Accademia Etrusca ★ MUSEUM   In pre-Roman Italy, Cortona was one of the 12 cities of the Etruscan confederation. So many artifacts from that era were discovered nearby that an Etruscan Academy was founded in 1727, a collection still housed in the Palazzo Casali, a 13th-century mansion built for the city's governors. The lower galleries tackle the Etruscan and Roman history of Cortona, with lots of gold from excavated tombs and the enigmatic Cortona Tablet, a 200-word document inscribed in bronze. On the sprawling upper floors, the most intriguing object is a one-of-a-kind oil lamp from the late 4th century B.C., decorated with human heads, allegorical figures, and a few virile Pans playing their pipes, all surrounding a leering Gorgon's head on the bottom.

Piazza Signorelli 9. www.cortonamaec.org. ℂ **0575/637-235.** 10€, 7€ children under 17, 3€ students. Apr–Oct daily 10am–7pm, Nov–Mar Tues–Sun 10am–5pm.

Museo Dioscoceano ★★ MUSEUM Almost every work in this small collection in the former Gesu church is a masterpiece. Pride of place, however, belongs to Fra Angelico and Luca Signorelli. The Fra Angelico gem is a splendid 1436 altarpiece of "The Annunciation," graced by his mastery of perspective and command of detail—notice the angel's precious garment embroidered in gold, the Virgin's elaborate robes, and the carpet of wildflowers (the new Eden) on which her house sits. Luca Signorelli, who was born in Cortona around 1450, is represented by a vividly detailed "Deposition" originally painted for Cortona's cathedral in 1502. The painter instilled his figure of Christ with so much realism and passion that legend claims he modeled it on his own son, who'd died of the plague that same year. Signorelli's "Communion of the Apostles" (1512) in the same room shows the artist's strong sense of architectural space. Notice Judas in the foreground, hiding the communion host in his purse—ashamed of his imminent betrayal, he can't swallow it.

Via Mura del Duomo. ℭ **0575/877-3610.** 5€. Apr–Oct daily 10am–7pm; Nov–Mar Tues–Sun 10am–5pm.

Where to Stay in Cortona

Some of Cortona's most reasonably priced accommodations are in two convents just outside the city walls, **Casa Betania,** Via Gino Severini 50 (www.casaperferiebetania.com; ℭ **0575/630-423**), and **Instituto Santa Margherita,** Viale Cesare Battisti 17 (www.santamargherita.smr.it; ℭ **0575/178-7203**). Just a few minutes' walk from the town center, spartan but pleasant doubles at both begin at about 60€.

Casa Zeni ★★★ You'll take to hill town life easily in one of these charming, stone-walled apartments in a meticulously restored medieval house in the center of town. Apartments sleep from 3 to 6 guests in great style, with contemporary furniture that blends well with rustic tile floors and wood-beamed ceilings. Amenities include kitchens, washers/dryers, superb beds, and beautifully equipped bathrooms. Hosts Silvia and Cristian provide caring hospitality and a wealth of handy advice.

Via Maccari 21. ℭ **338/830-7737.** www.casazeni.com. 3 units. Apartments from 80€. 2-night min. stay; discounts for stays of 1 week or longer. Rates include breakfast at nearby cafe. **Amenities:** Wi-Fi (free).

Hotel Italia ★ This 15th-century palace is not as grand as the neighboring San Michele (see below), but the hospitality hits the same high notes, Piazza Signorelli is just steps away, and the relaxed ambience suits Cortona's small-town pace. Spacious rooms are plain but atmospheric, with tasteful rustic wood furnishings, beamed ceilings, and other architectural flourishes. Only a few have views, but all guests can enjoy those in the panoramic top-floor breakfast room or on the roof terrace.

Via Ghibellina 5–7. www.hotelitaliacortona.com. ℭ **0575/630-254.** 17 units. 65€–150€ double. Rates include breakfast. **Amenities:** Wi-Fi (free).

Hotel San Michele ★★   In this 15th-century palazzo in the center of town, the salons and high-ceilinged guest rooms, a few frescoed and paneled, are reminders of Cortona's prosperous and noble past. Tile-floored rooms are appealingly furnished in what might be described as "fading grandeur" style. Some have views over the valley below, while a choice few, including tower suites, have their own terraces. A roof terrace with the same vistas is open to all guests, as is a decidedly medieval-looking courtyard. The San Michele also operates **Residence Borgo San Pietro** (www.borgosanpietro.com; ℂ **0575/612-402**), 4km (2½ miles) outside town in San Pietro a Cegliolo, with a countrified take on grand living—14 rooms and 5 apartments set amid 7 acres of olive trees and lavender, with a swimming pool.
Via Guelfa 15. www.hotelsanmichele.net. ℂ **0575/604-348.** 42 units. 125€–145€ double. Rates include breakfast. Closed Nov–mid-Mar. **Amenities:** Bar; Wi-Fi (free).

Relais Il Falconiere ★★   When Riccardo Baracchi inherited a farm from his grandmother, he and his wife, Sylvia, created a stylish and sophisticated retreat, with antiques-filled rooms scattered among a villa and stone farmhouses. Beamed ceilings and terra-cotta floors accompany the rural setting, with a pool and gardens amid 20 acres of olive groves and vineyards. A luxurious spa with a walled garden enhances the sense of relaxation. Sylvia oversees one of the best restaurants in the area, serving refined Tuscan food in the refitted lemon house.
San Martino (3km/2 mi N of Cortona). www.ilfalconiere.it. ℂ **0575/612-616.** 15 units. Doubles from 250€. Rates include breakfast. Closed Nov–Mar. **Amenities:** Restaurant; bar; 2 swimming pools; spa; free Wi-Fi in public areas.

Relais la Corte dei Papi ★★   The hospitable David Papi has converted his family's country house, dating from 1770, into a quiet and luxurious retreat in the valley just below Cortona. The farm shows few traces of its humble rustic origins and instead is geared to a luxurious romantic getaway, as many of the enormous suites are set up as spas, with sumptuous handcrafted furnishings surrounding pool-size soaking tubs and hydromassage showers that double as steam rooms. Surrounding the handsome stone buildings are lawns and flower gardens tended by David's lovely mom, Gabriella, among them two outbuildings set up as guest cottages. A well-regarded restaurant overlooks the swimming pool and its surrounding terraces.
Via la Dogana 12. www.lacortedeipapi.com. ℂ **0575/614-109.** 15 units. Doubles from 240€. Rates include breakfast. **Amenities:** Restaurant; bar; swimming pool; Wi-Fi (free).

Where to Eat in Cortona

A walk through town usually includes a stop at **Molesini,** Piazza della Repubblica 3, a local institution that will pour you a glass of wine and offer a big selection of cheese, olive oil, and other local products. The shop's selection features Cortona vineyards, where Syrah grapes are producing increasingly sophisticated yields. A standout is Usciòlo, from Cantina Doveri, just outside of town. **Caffe Tuscher,** Via Nazionale 43 (www.caffetuschercortona.com; © **0575/62053**), is the most elegant spot in town for a cocktail, served in a welcoming two-story space, along with snacks and light meals throughout the day. **Enoteca Enotria,** Via Nazionale 81, sells wine by the glass and sandwiches, making the rustic room a popular hangout well into the late evening.

Osteria al Teatro ★★★ TUSCAN   Chef Emiliano Rossi lays on the theatrics in three character-filled, candlelit rooms filled with antiques and old prints. All the good things of the palate come together in these amiable surroundings—excellent wines from a vast cellar, including many Cortona vintages; a thoughtful and innovative menu, on which beef from the Valdichiana is presented many different ways (look for truffle pairings in season); and to end the meal, a carving board of house-made chocolate.
Via Maffei 2. www.osteria-del-teatro.it. © **0575/630-556.** Entrees 10€–18€. Thurs–Tues 12:30–2:30pm and 7–10pm.

Ristorante la Loggetta ★★★ TUSCAN/GRILL   You would probably be happy eating canned spaghetti while savoring the view over the Piazza della Repubblica from this restaurant's namesake loggia—or for that matter, dining under the enchanting stone-and-brick vaults inside. It's a moot point, however: The food here is very well done, and nicely, if rather stiffly, served. The kitchen is acclaimed for its preparations of beef from the Valdichiana, often served with a rich red-wine reduction.
Piazza di Pescheria. www.laloggetta.com. © **0575/630-575.** Entrees 9€–28€. Thurs–Tues 12:15–2:30pm and 7:15–9:30pm.

Trattoria Dardano ★ TUSCAN/GRILL   Cortonans come to this simple, brightly lit room for meat—roasted here over a charcoal fire, with the emphasis on *bistecca alla fiorentina* from cattle raised in the valley below town (generally considered to be the best beef in Italy). *Pollo* (chicken), *anatra* (duck), *miale* (pork) and *faraona* (guinea hen) also go onto the flames. The heaping platters are usually preceded by *crostini neri* (little black toasts), with chicken liver, some local salamis, and often *ribollita*, the thick Tuscan soup, all accompanied by local wine.
Via Dardano 24. www.trattoriadardano.com. © **0575/601944.** Entrees 8€–13€. Daily noon–3pm and 6:30–11pm.

Trattoria la Grotta ★ TUSCAN   For many regulars, any meal in this medieval, brick-vaulted dining room or in the tiny courtyard just off Piazza della Repubblica must include the light-as-a-feather house gnocchi. All the pastas are housemade, and topped with rich, sweet sauces, while fresh locally grown zucchini and artichokes are a light antidote for the deftly grilled steaks. The house wine is delicious and reasonably priced.
Piazza Baldelli 3. trattorialagrotta.it. © **0575/630-271.** Entrees 8€–18€. Wed–Mon noon–2:30pm and 7–9:30pm.

Cortona Shopping

Cortona produces its own distinctive ceramics, in warm creamy yellows and pleasant greens. You'll find handsome wares in pleasant surroundings at **Terraburga,** Via Nazionale 54 (www.terrabruga.com; ✆ **0575/605-099,** which ships its finely crafted tableware anywhere. **Il Pozzo** ("the Old Well") is a treasure trove of well-curated photography and art by local artists, alongside leather goods, handcrafted paper, and much more, shown off in historic surroundings at Via Nazionale 10/12 (www.cortona giftshop.com; ✆ **0575/603-730**).

SAN GIMIGNANO ★★

42km (26 miles) NW of Siena, 52km (32 miles) SW of Florence

Let's just get the clichés out of the way, shall we?—"Manhattan of the Middle Ages" and "City of Beautiful Towers." As every brochure will tell you, in the 12th and 13th centuries more than 70 towers rose above the tile roofs of San Gimignano, built partly to defend against outside invaders but mostly as command centers and status symbols for San Gimignano's powerful families. A dozen towers remain, and as you approach across the rolling countryside, they do indeed appear like skyscrapers, giving the town the look of a fantasy kingdom. Once inside the gates, the Manhattan reference seems all too apt, with visitors shoulder-to-shoulder in its narrow lanes, obliterating the medieval aura you've come to savor. Almost everyone traveling the hilltown circuit makes a stop here, while bus tours pour in from Siena and Florence, and Italians arrive on weekend outings. If you want to be swept back to the Middle Ages, you're best visiting mid-week in off-season, or late on weekday afternoons after the buses have headed home.

Essentials

ARRIVING Approximately 30 daily **trains** run between **Siena** and **Poggibonsi** (one about every half hour, trip time: 25–40 min.), from where more than 30 buses make the 25-minute run to San Gimignano Monday through Saturday; only six buses run on Sunday.

   Tiemme buses (www.tiemmespa.it; ✆ **199/161-182**) run hourly (fewer on Sun) for most of the day from both **Florence** (50 min) and **Siena** (45 min) to Poggibonsi. Many of those buses immediately connect with buses to San Gimignano (a further 20–25 min). From **Siena** there are also 10 direct buses (a 1¼ hr. journey) Monday through Saturday.

   Arriving by **car,** take the Poggibonsi Nord exit off the **Florence-Siena** highway or the SS2. San Gimignano is 12km (7½ miles) from Poggibonsi. Parking is tight, and the *centro storico* is off-limits to most vehicles (including those of visitors). Read signs carefully, since many spots are reserved for residents, and at some parking is allowed for only 1 hour. The most convenient parking is at **Parcheggio Montemaggio,** outside the Porta San Giovanni (2€ an hour, 20€ a day). You can easily walk into town from here, but shuttle buses also take you up to Piazza della Cisterna (1€, tickets sold from parking-ticket machines).

VISITOR INFORMATION The **tourist office** at Piazza Duomo 1 (www.sangimignano.com; © **0577/940-008**) is open daily March–October 10am–1pm and 3–7pm, November–February 10am–1pm and 2–6pm.

Exploring San Gimignano

You'll see the town at its lively best if you come on a Thursday or Saturday morning, when the interlocking **Piazza della Cisterna** and **Piazza del Duomo** fill with market stalls. Piazza della Cisterna is named for the well at its center, a fairly ingenious device that for centuries was a repository for rainwater channeled from rooftops—a reliable and safe source of water that could not be tampered with or contaminated by events occurring outside the city walls. For a refreshing break from the crowds, head up from the Duomo to the well-marked **Rocca e Parco di Montestaffoli.**

Piazza della Cisterna in San Gimignano.

Filling the shell of the town's 14th-century fortress, this park provides greenery, quiet, and views over the town and countryside, all the better from the little tower in the far corner. Another refreshing vantage point, with views for miles across the rolling countryside, is a circuit around the top of the **town walls,** about 1½ miles in its entirety and accessed from any of the four gates; **Porta delle Fonti,** at the east end of town, is an especially scenic entrypoint, as just outside the portal are romantically arched medieval fountains.

Basilica di Santa Maria Assunta (Il Duomo/Collegiata) ★★

CHURCH San Gimignano's main church is awash in frescoes. Around the main door, a gruesome "Last Judgment" by Sienese artist Taddeo di Bartolo (1410) shows mean-looking little devils taunting tortured souls (Bartolo allegedly modeled some of the characters after townsfolk who rubbed him the wrong way). Much of the nave is covered in flat, two-dimensional frescoes of the Sienese school—a comic-strip-like Poor Man's Bible, illustrating familiar stories for the illiterate faithful. The left wall is frescoed with scenes from the Old Testament (look for the panel showing the Pharaoh and his army being swallowed by the Red Sea), and the right wall features the New Testament (a very shifty-looking Judas receives his 30 pieces of silver for betraying Christ). The best frescoes in the church are in the tiny **Cappella di Santa Fina,** where Domenico Ghirlandaio decorated the walls with airy scenes of the life of Fina—a local girl who, though never officially canonized, is one of San Gimignano's patron saints. Little Fina was so devout that when she fell ill with paralysis, she refused a bed and lay instead on a board, never complaining even when worms and rats fed off her decaying flesh. As you'll see in one of the panels, St. Gregory foretold the exact day (his feast day, March 12) when Fina would die. She expired right on schedule and began working miracles immediately—all the bells in town rang spontaneously at the moment of her death.

Piazza del Duomo. ℂ **0577/286-300.** 4€ adults, 2€ ages 6–18. Mon–Fri 10am– 7:30pm, Sat 10am–5:30pm, Sun 12:30–7:30pm (Nov–Mar closes 5pm); closed 2nd half of Nov and Jan.

Palazzo Comunale & Torre Grossa ★★ MUSEUM   The late-13th-century home of the city government, also known as Palazzo del Popolo, is topped with San Gimignano's tallest tower, the aptly named Torre Grossa (Big Tower), finished in 1311. Your reward for a climb to the top will be views of the cityscape and rolling countryside of the Val d'Elsa. (*Tip:* Save your knees and enjoy the same outlook for free by making the gentler 5-minute climb uphill from Piazza del Duomo to the ruined Rocca.) Inside the palazzo's **Camera del Podestà** (Room of the Mayor) are San Gimignano's most famous frescoes, Memmo di Filippuccio's "Scenes of Married Life." In one scene, a couple takes a bath together, and in the other, the scantily-clad fellow climbs into bed beside his naked wife. In the adjoining painting gallery, look for the "Coppo di Marcovaldo Crucifix," an astonishingly touching work in which a vulnerably human figure of Christ is surrounded by six intricate little scenes of the Crucifixion. The artist Coppo, a Florentine soldier, was captured by the Sienese, who soon realized what a treasure they had in him; his masterpieces show a transition from flat Byzantine style to more varied texture and three-dimensionality. The head of St. Fina (see the Collegiata, p. 277) is kept in the **Tabernacle of Santa Fina** (1402), painted with scenes of the teenage saint's miracles. Taddeo di Bartolo (see his terrifying "Last Judgment" in the Collegiata, p. 276) painted the "Life of St. Gimignano" for this room. St. Gimignano was a 5th-century bishop of Modena who saved his people from an attack by Attila the Hun by conjuring up a dense fog. Residents of the little town then known as Silvia prayed to Gimignano to spare them from the barbarians; the saint obliged and the grateful citizenry changed their town's name to San Gimignano. The saint is depicted cradling his namesake town in his lap, towers and all.

Piazza del Duomo. www.sangimignanomusei.it. ℂ **0577/286-300.** 9€. Cumulative ticket (also includes Santa Maria Assunta, church of San Lorenzo in Ponte, and other sights) 13€ adults, 10€ ages 6–17. Apr–Sept daily 10am–7:30pm; Oct–Mar daily 11am–5:30pm.

Civic Art

Towers and medieval ambience aside, you'll also discover that San Gimignano is full of frescoes and other art—in churches, public buildings, and even outdoors. In **Piazza Pecori,** reached through the archway to the left of the Collegiata's facade, is a fresco of the "Annunciation," possibly painted in 1482 by the Florentine Domenico Ghirlandaio. The door to the right of the tourist office leads into a courtyard of the **Palazzo del Commune,** where Taddeo di Bartolo's 14th-century "Madonna and Child" is flanked by two works on the theme of justice by Sodoma. The simple 13th-century **church of San Lorenzo in Ponte** (Via Santo Stefano 8) features several frescoes depicting the life of St. Benedict (look for the scene where he almost gives into temptation and accepts a loaf of poisoned bread); entry to this church is included in the cumulative ticket that also includes Santa Maria Assunta, the Museo Civico, and other sights; see p. 234. **Galleria Continua** (Via Del Castello 11, galleriacontinua.com, ☏ **0577/943-134,** open daily 10am to 1pm and 2 to 7pm) introduces contemporary art to the town's medieval ambiance, showcasing well-known and emerging artists in a former cinema, a tower, a cellar, and an old apartment.

Sant'Agostino ★ CHURCH   An especially appropriate presence in this 13th-century church at the north end of town is St. Sebastian, the "saint who was martyred twice." As a stop on trade and pilgrimage routes, San Gimignano was decimated by the plague time and again; this gave them a special fondness for the 3rd-century saint Sebastian, who also was prone to repeated bad fortune. In 1464, after surviving yet another plague, the town hired Florentine painter Benozzo Gozzoli to paint a thankful scene. As the fresco shows, when Sebastian first proclaimed his faith, the emperor Diocletian ordered that he be taken to a field and shot full of arrows. Sebastian miraculously survived and was nursed back to health, but he tempted fate again by haranguing Diocletian as he passed in royal procession; the emperor had him bludgeoned to death on the spot. Gozzoli also frescoed the choir behind the main altar with scenes from the life of St. Augustine, a worldly scholar who, faced with the decision to give up his concubine, famously prayed, "Grant me continence and chastity but not yet." The scenes are rich in landscape and architectural detail.

Piazza Sant'Agostino. ☏ **0577/907-012.** Free. Daily 10am–noon and 3–7pm (closes 6pm Nov–Dec).

Where to Stay & Eat in San Gimignano

San Gimignano's slightly peppery, dry white wine, **Vernaccia di San Gimignano,** is the only DOCG white wine in Tuscany, and it has quite a provenance, too: It's cited in Dante's *Divine Comedy.* A relaxing place to sip a glass or two is **diVinorum,** former stables with a small terrace at Via degli Innocenti 5 (www.divinorumwinebar.com; ☏ **0577/907-192**). At the famous **Gelateria Dondoli,** Piazza della Cisterna 4 (www.gelateriadi piazza.com; ☏ **0577/942-244**), master gelato maker Sergio offers creative combinations like refreshing Champelmo, with sparkling wine and pink grapefruit, and *crema di Santa Fina,* made with saffron and pine nuts.

Chiribiri ★ ITALIAN   This tiny vaulted cellar almost next to the walls seems more serious about what it sends out of the kitchen than do many pricier spots in the center of town. Ravioli with pumpkin, white beans, and sage, beef in Chianti, wild boar stew, and other Tuscan classics are done well and served without fuss. *Note:* They don't take credit cards.

Piazzetta della Madonna 1. © **0577/941-948.** Entrees 8€–12€. Daily 11am–11pm.

Dorandò ★★ TUSCAN   Three stone-walled rooms with brick-vaulted ceilings are the setting for San Gimignano's most elegant and best dining, though there's nothing fussy about the cooking. Ingredients and recipes are decidedly local—beef is done in a sauce of Chianti classic, local pork comes with an apple puree, and *cibrèo,* a rich ragout, comes with chicken livers and giblets scented with ginger and lemon. If you want to dine here during your trip, you'll need a reservation.

Vicolo dell'Oro 2. www.ristorantedorando.it. © **0577/941-862.** Entrees 20€–24€. Tues–Sun noon–2:30pm and 7–9:30pm (daily Easter–Sept). Closed Dec 10–Jan 31.

Hotel l'Antico Pozzo ★★★   When this 15th-century palazzo was a convent, the namesake "ancient well" served a grim purpose—young novices were dangled over the depths when they resisted *droit de seigneur,* the feudal rights of noblemen to have their way with young women living on their lands. Thankfully, the present incarnation is far more enlightened, being all about taste, elegance, and comfort. Reached by a broad stone staircase (or an elevator if you choose), rooms are filled with character, some beamed and frescoed, others with nice views of the town and Rocca. All are good-size and beautifully decorated, with classic furnishings that sometimes include canopied beds, along with fine prints and other appointments. A grassy garden in the rear is a welcome escape from the daytime crowds.

Via San Matteo 87. www.anticopozzo.com. © **0577/942-014.** 18 units. 100€–170€ double. Rates include breakfast. Closed part of Feb. **Amenities:** Bar; Wi-Fi (free).

La Cisterna ★   Behind the ivy-clad entrance on the town square, you'll find rooms that vary considerably in size and outlook—some of the smaller ones overlook a quaint courtyard, while larger rooms and suites may have balconies and views that extend for miles. Furnishings are simply and unobtrusively traditional Tuscan, with wrought-iron bedsteads and flourishes like arches, tile floors, and stone walls, although the surroundings—and the service, too—can seem a bit impersonal. The restaurant and terrace, along with a view-filled, glassed-in dining room upstairs, serve Tuscan food that's a lot better than you'd expect, given the presence of large tour groups that often pile in for lunch.

Piazza della Cisterna 24. www.hotelcisterna.it. © **0577/940-328.** 48 units. 100€–145€ double. Rates include breakfast. Closed Jan–Mar. **Amenities:** Restaurant, bar, Wi-Fi (free).

VOLTERRA ★★

29km (18 miles) SW of San Gimignano, 50km (31 miles) W of Siena

Volterra, in the words of British novelist D.H. Lawrence, perches "on a towering great bluff that gets all the winds and sees all the world." Volterra seems higher than any other Tuscan town, rising 540m (1,772 ft.) above the valley below. (You'll see the town long before you arrive.) Lawrence came here to study relics of the Etruscans—in the 4th century B.C., Volterra, then known as Velathri, was one of the largest cities in the Etruscan confederation. While some visitors come here to see Etruscan bronzes and alabaster urns, if you're a fan of Stephanie Meyer's teen vampire trilogy *Twilight,* you've probably come to see the hometown of the Volturi vampire coven. Whatever brings you to Volterra, you'll soon find it's a pleasant place, more focused on day-to-day life than on plying the tourist trade (unlike some of its Tuscan neighbors!).

Essentials

ARRIVING Driving is the easiest way to get here: Volterra is on the SS68 about 30km (19 miles) from the Colle di Val d'Elsa exit on the Florence-Siena highway. From San Gimignano, head southwest on the road to Castel di San Gimignano, where you can pick up the SS68. You can park for free in a large lot below Porta Fiorentina, but you will pay a price—a climb up 350 steps to town.

A classic car race in the hilltown of Volterra.

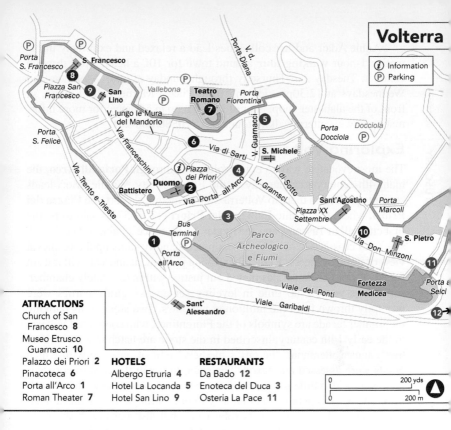

Volterra

(i) Information
(P) Parking

ATTRACTIONS
Church of San
  Francesco **8**
Museo Etrusco
  Guarnacci **10**
Palazzo dei Priori **2**
Pinacoteca **6**
Porta all'Arco **1**
Roman Theater **7**

HOTELS
Albergo Etruria **4**
Hotel La Locanda **5**
Hotel San Lino **9**

RESTAURANTS
Da Bado **12**
Enoteca del Duca **3**
Osteria La Pace **11**

From **Siena,** some 16 daily **Tiemme buses** (www.tiemmespa.it) make the 20- to 30-minute trip to **Colle di Val d'Elsa,** from which there are four daily buses to Volterra (50 min.). From **San Gimignano,** first take a bus to Poggibonsi (20 min.) then link up with those Colle di Val d'Elsa buses to Volterra. From **Florence,** take one of five daily buses (three on Sunday) to Colle di Val d'Elsa and transfer there (2½–3 hr. total). Six to 10 **CPT buses** (www.cpt.pisa.it) run to Volterra Monday through Saturday from **Pisa** (change in Pontedera; 2–2½ hr. total).

VISITOR INFORMATION   Volterra's helpful **tourist office,** Piazza dei Priori 19–20 (www.volterratur.it; © **0588/87257**), offers both tourist information and free hotel reservations. It's open daily 9:30am to 1pm and 2 to 6pm. The office rents an audio guide (5€ for a handset) for an hour-long walk around town, providing some good tidbits about churches, palaces, and Etruscan and Roman remains along the way. You can also purchase a Volterra Card, worth the 16€ even if you're planning to see only the Etruscan museum and Pinacoteca, both of which are included; you can step into the Roman Theater and some other sights with it as well.

Annie Adair and her colleagues lead a relaxed and extremely informative 1-hour **walking tour** around town for 10€ a head, April through October, Tuesday and Thursday through Sunday at 6pm, Mondays and Wednesdays at 12:30pm, leaving from Piazza Martiri della Libertà, in front of the alabaster shop. No need to sign up in advance; for more information, www.volterrawalkingtour.com; ✆ **0588/086-201.**

Exploring Volterra

The most evocative way to enter Volterra is through **Porta all'Arco,** the main 4th-century-B.C. gateway to the Etruscan city. Via die Priori leads steeply uphill from there to Volterra's stony medieval heart, the **Piazza dei Priori,** where the Gothic **Palazzo dei Priori** (1208–57) is said to be the first city hall in Tuscany, and the model for Florence's Palazzo Vecchio. A skull and crossbones outside the main hall handily sums up the medieval view of righteousness: "Remember divine judgement and you will not sin for all eternity." Magistrates meted out justice within the stately chamber, sometimes wasting no time in leveling sentences—guilty parties were promptly thrown from the mullioned windows. Two stone lions flanking the somber facade are symbols of the Florentines, who conquered Volterra in the early 14th century; inscribed in the stone are hatch marks marking the "canna votleranna," the city's medieval unit of measure with which goods were assessed and taxed. The squat tower in the eastern corner is festooned with a little pig *(porcellino),* hence its name, **Torre del Porcellino.** The beast is actually a boar, a symbol of strength for medieval residents—not only because of its robust heft but also because boars were plentiful in the surrounding woods and the mainstay of their diet (pasta with *ragù di cinghiale* and grilled boar are still menu favorites). Inside the modest-looking **Duomo** around the corner is a life-size "Deposition from the Cross," carved in wood around 1228 by anonymous Pisan masters and painted in bright colors. With their fluidity and emotional expressiveness, the figures look surprisingly contemporary.

Church of San Francesco ★ CHURCH   Volterra's 13th-century Franciscan church, just inside the Porta San Francesco, has one overwhelming reason to visit: Halfway up the right aisle is the **Cappella Croce del Giorno,** frescoed with the "Legend of the True Cross" in medieval Technicolor by Cenni di Francesco in 1410. While not nearly as beautifully executed as Piero della Francesca's telling of the same story in in Arezzo (see p. 266), Cenni's version of this popular medieval tale is quite compelling, especially with his knack for reproducing the dress and architecture of his era. Though the artist worked for some of Florence's most important families, this is his only remaining signed work. It shows a unique style: golden backgrounds, flattened space, and elongated figures with elegant features.

Piazza San Francesco. No phone. Free. Daily 8:30am–6:30pm.

Museo Etrusco Guarnacci ★★ MUSEUM   Volterra's remarkable collection of Etruscan artifacts is dusty, poorly lit, and devoid of a lot of English labeling. It is nonetheless a joyful celebration of the farmers, seafarers, and miners who flourished between the Tiber and Arno rivers from about 800 B.C. until their assimilation by Rome in the 1st century A.D. (the name "Tuscany" is derived from "Etruscan"). The bulk of the holdings are on the ground floor, with row after row of **Etruscan funerary urns,** most from the 3rd century B.C., but some from as early as the 7th century B.C. Ashes were placed in these urns, which were topped with elaborately carved lids—finely dressed characters lounging with wine cups to offer to the gods, or horse and carriage rides into the underworld. One of the finest, the **Urna degli Sposi,** is a striking portrait of a husband and wife, somewhat dour-faced and full of wrinkles, together in death as in life. The Etruscans also crafted bronze sculptures, and one of the finest is a lanky young man with a beguiling smile known as the "Ombra della Sera (Shadow of the Evening)"—so called because the elongated shape looks like a shadow stretched in evening light.

Via Don Minzoni 15. www.comune.volterra.pi.it. *©* **0588/86347.** 8€, or with 16€ Volterra Card. Mid-Mar–Oct, daily 9am–7pm; Nov–mid-Mar, daily 10am–4:30pm.

Pinacoteca ★ MUSEUM   While much of Volterra preserves the Etruscan, Roman, and medieval past, the town's worthy painting gallery transports you to the Renaissance. Room 4 has a remarkably intact 1411 polyptych of the "Madonna with Saints" signed by Taddeo di Bartolo. (The fellow in the red cape and beard in the tiny left tondo is the original Santa Claus, St. Nicholas of Bari.) In room 11 is "Christ in Glory with Saints" (1492), the last great work of Florentine master Domenico Ghirlandaio. If you look hard, you can spot a giraffe being led along the road—an exotic animal that had only recently been acquired by the Medici for their menagerie. In Room 12 hangs a remarkably colored "Annunciation" (1491) by Luca Signorelli—note the great rush of feeling as the archangel bursts through the doorway to announce the news to Mary. In the same room is a "Deposition" (1521) by 26-year-old Rosso Fiorentino, a redheaded (and reportedly hot-headed) Florentine painter, who ended up going to France to work at the Chateau Fontainebleau. Painted in his odd color palette of flat grays and reds, it unusually portrays this solemn scene of Christ being taken off the cross as a frantic swirl of action, with sashes flapping in the wind and workers scurrying up and down ladders.

Via del Sarti 1. www.comune.volterra.pi.it. *©* **0588/87580.** 8€, or with 16€ Volterra Card. Mid-Mar–Oct daily 9am–7pm; Dec daily 9am–6pm; Nov and Jan–mid-Mar daily 10am–4:30pm.

Porta all'Arco ★★ HISTORIC GATE   Volterra's greatest landmark is this huge, magnificent gate built by the Etruscans as early as the 3rd century B.C. in their 7km (4 mi) of city walls. The round arch contains a keystone that the Romans later incorporated into so much of their architecture. On the outside are mounted three basalt heads—features worn away by well over 2,000 years of wind and rain—said possibly to represent the Etruscan gods Tinia (Jupiter), Uni (Juno), and Menrva (Minerva). The gateway almost didn't survive World War II, when retreating German troops decided to blow it up to block the Allied advance through the city. Volterrans dug up the surrounding paving stones and temporarily plugged the opening, convincing the Germans not to destroy a gate that no one could pass through anyway.

Porta all'Arco. No phone. Free.

Roman Theater ★ ARCHAEOLOGICAL SITE   Take a stroll along Via Lungo le Mure, a walkway atop the medieval ramparts, to overlook the impressive remains of Volterra's Roman theater and baths, some of the best-preserved Roman remains in Tuscany. The theater dates back to the 1st century B.C., though parts of it were torn up for building materials during the construction of the medieval walls. The view from up here is the best way to see it all, and for free, but if you do want to wander among the stones, there's an entrance down on Viale Francesco Ferrucci.

Viale Francesco Ferrucci. © **0588/86050.** 4€, or with 16€ Volterra Card. Mid-Mar–Oct and Dec daily 10:30am–5:30pm; Nov and Jan–mid-Mar Sat–Sun 10am–4:30pm.

Where to Stay in Volterra

Staying within Volterra's city walls can be a transporting experience, especially in the evening when residents regain their historic town. Choices are fairly limited, so book ahead if you're planning a visit in the busy period of May through September.

Albergo Etruria ★★   The lounge and guest kitchen are homey touches, but the real attraction of this cozy lodging is the roof garden, a leafy retreat where the greenery is backed by the town's brick towers and tile rooftops. Parts of an Etruscan wall enhance the historic character of the old house, but rooms are charmingly up-to-date, filled with comfortable, attractive furniture handpicked by the friendly owners. The Piazza dei Priori is only a few steps from this stylish haven.

Via Matteotti 32. www.albergoetruria.it. © **0588/87377.** 18 units. 70–100€ double. Rates include breakfast. **Amenities:** Wi-Fi (free).

Hotel La Locanda ★★   A location just inside the town walls makes this converted convent a good choice if traveling by car, since parking is just steps away. High-ceilinged rooms are done in soothing pastels, a few have massage showers and whirlpool tubs, and most pay homage to Volterra's medieval ambience with a patch or two of exposed stone and timber. The piazza and other sights are an easy walk away, and a quiet terrace tucked in the back offers a breath of fresh air.

Via Guarnacci 24. www.hotel-lalocanda.com. © **0588/81547.** 18 units. 70€–110€ double. Rates include breakfast. **Amenities:** Restaurant; bar; Wi-Fi (free).

Hotel San Lino ★ There's a slightly utilitarian ring to the hallways and some of the guest rooms here, probably because for many centuries the 13th-century palazzo served as a cloistered convent. The enclosed gardens are still in place, and a little terrace looks across miles of countryside. There's also a small pool, the only one inside the city walls and reason enough to stay here in the summer. Some rooms are merely functional, while others are nicely turned out with a mix of modern and traditional furnishings. The best rooms overlook the gardens and sweeping landscapes beyond.

Via San Lino 6 (near Porta San Francesco). www.hotelsanlino.net. © **0588/85250.** 44 units. 90€–130€ double. Rates include breakfast. **Amenities:** Restaurant; bar; pool; Wi-Fi (free).

Where to Eat in Volterra

Da Bado ★★ TUSCAN Owner Giacomo's mom, Lucia, is in the kitchen of this favorite in the San Lazzero neighborhood, just outside the

---

crafty **VOLTERRANS**

The Etruscans made good use of the easily mined local stone, a translucent calcium sulfate known as **alabaster**—witness the hundreds of alabaster sarcophagi in the Guarnacci museum (see p. 283). Alabaster became a major industry in Volterra again at the end of the 19th century, when the material was much in demand for lampshades, with the rise of electric lighting. Today local artisans work alabaster into a mind-boggling array of objects, from fine art pieces to some remarkable kitsch.

Plaques around town denote the workshops of some of the best traditional artisans, where you will find only hand-worked items. Via Porta all'Arco has several fine shops, including internationally known **Paolo Sabatini**, at no. 45 (www.paolosabatini.com; © **0588/87594**), whose alabaster sculptural pieces often combine wood and stone. The large **Rossi Alabastri** (www.rossialabastri.com; © **0588/86133**) shop at Piazzetta della Pescheria shows off some especially distinctive lighting pieces, as well as alabaster bowls, fruits, and all sorts of other easily portable items. At **alab'Arte**, Via Orti S. Agostino 28 (www.alabarte.com; © **0588/87-968**), near the Guarnacci museum, Roberto Cini and Giorgio Finazzo create sculptural pieces of museum quality—in fact, they are often called upon to help restore sculpture in churches and museums around Italy.

You'll find the work of many local artisans at the **Società Cooperativa Artieri Alabastro,** Piazza dei Priori 4/5 (© **0588/87590**), a sales showroom for smaller workshops. To learn more about the town's alabaster industry, visit the **Ecomuseo dell'Alabastro,** Piazzetta Minucci (© **0588/87580;** admission 8€ or with 16€ Volterra Card; daily 9:30am–7:30pm in summer, 10:30am–4:30pm in winter).

Alabaster isn't the only craft in town. **Fabula Etrusca,** Via Lungo le Mura del Mandorlo 10 (www.fabulaetrusca.it; © **0588/87401**), sells intricate handmade jewelry based on original Etruscan designs. For prints created from hand-engraved zinc plates—another local specialty—visit **L'Istrice,** Via Porta all'Arco 23 (© **0588/85422**).

walls. She prepares a few daily choices that often include *zuppa volter-rana* (bread and vegetable soup) and *baccalà rifatto* (pan-fried salted cod-fish stewed with tomatoes), along with *pappardelle alla lepre* (wide fettuccine with rabbit sauce) and other hearty pastas well suited to the homey, stone arched surroundings. Lucia also makes the jams that fill her delicious homemade tortes (cakes). A cafe in front serves coffee and pastries all day.

Da Bado. Borgo San Lazzero 9. ✆ **0588/80402.** Entrees 8€–13€. Thurs–Tues 12:30–2:30pm and 7:30–10:30pm.

Enoteca del Duca ★★ MODERN TUSCAN   At Volterra's best restaurant, you'll have a choice of surroundings: the elegant, high-ceilinged dining room, a bottle-lined enoteca, or a pretty patio out back. Wherever you choose to enjoy them, the offerings are innovative and refined takes on Tuscan classics. All the salamis and cheeses are from local producers, *lavagnette* (homemade egg pasta) comes with a sauce of celery and pecorino pesto, and local beef is grilled to perfection. Some of the wines come from the owners' vineyards.

Via di Castello 2. www.enoteca-delduca-ristorante.it. ✆ **0588/81510.** Entrees 15€–25€. Wed–Mon 12:30–3pm and 7:30–10pm (also Tues dinner in summer).

Osteria La Pace ★ VOLTERRAN/TUSCAN   No restaurant in Volterra can boast of such a long provenance, serving since 1600 and in the hands of the same family since 1939. The old brick walls and vaults look just as they must have 400 years ago, and the kitchen follows suit with perfectly prepared versions of such Volterra classics as tagliatelle with chestnuts and mushrooms and a hearty stew of wild boar.

Via Don Giovanni Minzoni 29. www.osteria-lapace.com. ✆ **0588/86511.** Entrees 7€–11€. Daily 10am–4pm and 6:30–11pm.

LUCCA ★★

72km (45 miles) W of Florence

Lucca is the forgotten Tuscan town, just far enough off the beaten track to be left out of package tours. But travelers have been waxing poetic about the place for a long time. In the 19th century, novelist Henry James called Lucca "a charming mixture of antique character and modern inconsequence"—the "inconsequence" bit meaning that Lucca, beautifully preserved within 16th- and 17th-century walls (designed in part, allegedly, by Leonardo da Vinci), is much more a remnant of the past than a part of the modern world. The Etruscans were here as early as 700 B.C., and the Romans after them; the city flourished as a silk center in the Middle Ages. No doubt such a long and colorful history inspired the romantic operas of Lucca's native son Giacomo Puccini (1858–1924), composer of *Tosca, Madame Butterfly,* and *La Bohème.* Lucca can seem like a stage set, and

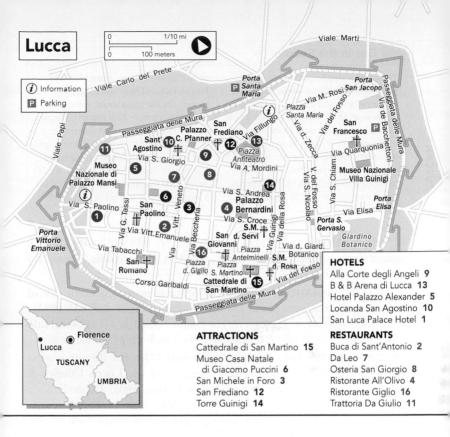

Lucca

Information

Parking

HOTELS
Alla Corte degli Angeli **9**
B & B Arena di Lucca **13**
Hotel Palazzo Alexander **5**
Locanda San Agostino **10**
San Luca Palace Hotel **1**

ATTRACTIONS
Cattedrale di San Martino **15**
Museo Casa Natale
  di Giacomo Puccini **6**
San Michele in Foro **3**
San Frediano **12**
Torre Guinigi **14**

RESTAURANTS
Buca di Sant'Antonio **2**
Da Leo **7**
Osteria San Giorgio **8**
Ristorante All'Olivo **4**
Ristorante Giglio **16**
Trattoria Da Giulio **11**

it's easy to look at the tiered facade of the church of San Michele and hear the strains of Puccini's aria "O Mio Bambino Caro."

Essentials

ARRIVING Lucca is on the Florence-Viareggio **train** line, with about 30 trains daily (fewer on Sunday) connecting with **Florence** (75–90 min.). A similar number of trains make the short hop to/from **Pisa** (30 min.). The **station** is a short walk south of Porta San Pietro.

By **car,** the A11 runs from Florence past Prato, Pistoia, and Montecatini before hitting Lucca. Inside the walls, you'll usually find a pay-parking space underground at **Mazzini** (enter from the east, through the Porta Elisa, and take an immediate right); aboveground parking areas surround the other gates as well, with rates from 1€ an hr.

A **VaiBus** (www.vaibus.it) service runs hourly from Florence (70 min.) and from Pisa (50 min.) to Lucca's Piazzale Verdi.

GETTING AROUND A set of *navette* (electric **minibuses**) whiz down the city's peripheral streets, but the flat center is easily traversed on foot. Taxis line up at the train station (*©* **0583/494-989**), Piazzale Verdi

Get in the Saddle

The popular way to get around Lucca, you'll soon learn, is on a bike. Enjoy the medieval lanes and squares on foot, but equip yourself with two wheels for a ride on the Passeggiata della Mura, atop the medieval walls. You can do so in style on one of the neon-green or Barbie-pink models from **Antonio Poli**, near the tourist office at Piazza Santa Maria 42 (www.biciclettepoli.com; ℗ 0583/493-787;

daily 8:30am–7:30pm, closed Sun mid-Nov to Feb and Mon mornings year-round). On the same street, bikes are also available from **Cicli Bizzarri**, Piazza Santa Maria 32 (www.ciclibizzarri.net; ℗ 0583/496-682; Mon–Sat 8:30am–1pm and 2:30–7:30pm, plus Sun same hours Mar to mid-Sept). The going rates are 3€ an hour for a regular bike, 4€ to 4.50€ for a mountain bike, and 6.50€ for a tandem.

(℗ 0583/581305), and Piazza Napoleone (℗ 0583/491-646). To get around like a Lucchese, rent a bike—see "Get in the Saddle," above, for rental information.

VISITOR INFORMATION   The **tourist office** is inside the north side of the walls at Piazza Santa Maria 35 (www.luccaturismo.it; ℗ 0583/919931; daily 9am–7pm, later in summer). The *comune* also has a small **local info office** on Piazzale Verdi (℗ 0583/538-150), which keeps similar hours.

SPECIAL EVENTS   For a few days at the end of October, the city is over-run with several hundred thousand attendees of the **Lucca Comics & Games** convention (www.luccacomicsandgames.com). Depending on whether you want to share the streets and squares with a multitude of cos-tumed Darth Vaders and other fantasy figures, you might want to stay away from Lucca then.

Exploring Lucca

Lucca has many remarkable architectural landmarks, but the first you'll notice are its incredibly intact city walls—more than 4km (2½ miles) of them, with 11 bastions and six gates; some stretches are 18m (59 ft.) wide. Topping the walls, the tree-shaded **Passeggiata delle Mura** can be cir-cumnavigated on foot or by bike (see "Get in the Saddle," p. 288), as you peer across Lucca's rooftops toward the hazy mountains.

The most curious feature of Lucca's street plan is **Piazza Anfiteatro**, near the north end of Via Fillungo, the main shopping street. This semi-circle of handsome medieval houses stands atop what were once the grandstands of a 1st- or 2nd-century-A.D. Roman amphitheater, and some of the little alleys leading into the square from surrounding, elliptical Via dell'Anfiteatro are the original entrances to the theater, with portions of their marble archways still visible. Nearby, **Torre Guinigi** rises from the 14th-century palace of Lucca's iron-fisted rulers; notice that the tower is topped with a little grove of 7 holm oaks, one of many such gardens that once flourished atop hundreds of similar tower houses around the city.

Piazza Anfiteatro in Lucca.

Climb the 230 steps for a spectacular view of Lucca's skyline, the snow-capped Apuan Alps, and the rolling green valley of the River Serchio (3.50€ adults, 2.50€ children 6–12 and seniors 65 and older; open daily Apr–May 9am–7:30pm, June–Sept 9am–6:30pm, Oct and Mar 9:30am–5:30pm, Nov–Feb 9:30am–4:30pm).

The facade of **San Frediano,** Piazza San Frediano (© **0583/493-627**), glitters with a two-story-tall 13th-century mosaic that depicts the Apostles watching Christ's ascent to heaven. San Fernando faces east, so the facade is a glittering spectacle when the mosaics catch the morning sun. As you stroll around town, especially along the main shopping street, **Via Fillungo,** notice how many shopfronts display Art Nouveau signs etched in glass, adding a modern grace note to the city's medieval atmosphere. A splendid exception is the Renaissance cabinetry of fine wood and glass in front of **Carli,** at number 95, a gold and silver shop founded in 1651.

Cattedrale di San Martino ★★ CATHEDRAL   Completed in 1070 to house one of the most renowned artifacts in Christendom, the Volto Santo (more on that below), Lucca's ornate Duomo does justice to its prized procession. On the facade, three arches open to a deep portico sheathed in marble; above it rise three tiers of arcaded loggias supported by dozens of little columns, each different. Legend has it that the Lucchese commissioned many artists to carve the columns, with the promise of hiring the best to do them all; they used all the entries and never paid anyone. A pair of binoculars will help you pick out the elaborate details of figures, animals, vines, and patterns in the loggias and on the portico. St. Martin, the former Roman soldier to whom the cathedral is dedicated, figures prominently—look for the statue of him ripping his cloak to give half to a beggar. A labyrinth is carved into the wall of the right side of the portico, for the faithful to make a figurative pilgrimage to the center of the maze, as if to Jerusalem, before entering the church. A Latin inscription reads, "This is the labyrinth built by Daedalus of Crete; all who entered therein were lost, save Theseus, thanks to Ariadne's thread."

Inside, the handsome sweep of inlaid pavement and the high altar are the work of 15th-century Lucca native Matteo Civitali. He also designed the **Tempietto,** an octagonal, freestanding chapel of white and red marble in the left nave, where the famous **Volto Santo** is kept—a venerable crucifix said to have been carved by Nicodemus, the man who helped remove Christ's body from the cross. (See "A Crucifix With a Mind of Its Own," below). The cathedral's other great treasure is the **Tomb of Ilaria Carretto Guinigi,** the young wife of Lucca ruler Paolo Guinigi, who died in 1405 at the age of 26; she lives on, accompanied by a little dog (a sign of her faithfulness) in a beautiful image carved by Jacopo della Quercia, the Sienese sculptor whose work heavily influenced Michelangelo. An unseen presence is that of the great composer Giacomo Puccini, who was born nearby in 1858 and sang in the church choir.

Piazza San Martino. ℂ **0583/957-068.** 3€ adults, 2€ ages 6–14. Summer daily 7am–7pm, winter daily 7am–5pm.

A crucifix WITH A MIND OF ITS OWN

Throughout the medieval era, the legends of the Volto Santo attracted pilgrims to Lucca from throughout Europe. Tradition claimed that when Nicodemus was carving this crucifix, he did not complete the face, fearing he could not do the holy visage justice. He fell asleep—and when he awoke, a beautiful face had miraculously been carved on the crucifix. St. Nicodemus stashed the Volto Santo crucifix in a cave for safekeeping; centuries later, an 8th-century Italian bishop on pilgrimage to the Holy Land discovered it (apparently the location had come to him in a dream). The bishop put the crucifix adrift in a boat, which magically washed up on the shores of northern Italy; the relic somehow got into a driverless wagon pulled by two oxen, and all by itself it arrived in Lucca. It was first placed in the church of San Frediano, but the crucifix clearly had other ideas and transported itself to the cathedral. On May 3 and September 13 to 14, the Lucchese walk in a candlelit procession from San Frediano to the cathedral, where the famous statue awaits them, dressed in gold and wearing a gold crown.

Museo Casa Natale di Giacomo Puccini ★ MUSEUM Walking around Lucca, a Puccini aria could pop into your head at any moment—but the maestro comes most vividly to life in **Piazza Cittadella,** where the composer, in the guise of a bronze statue, sits, legs crossed, in an armchair. Puccini was born around the corner at 9 Corte San Lorenzo, and lived there until he left for Milan in his early 20s. The modest-yet-comfortable rooms display some of his scores, some random pieces of heavy furniture, and, most notably, the piano on which he often composed.

9 Corte San Lorenzo. www.puccinimuseum.org. ℭ **0583/584-028.** 7€. May–Sept daily 10am–7pm, Mar–Apr and Oct daily 10am–6pm, Nov–Feb Wed–Mon 10am–1pm and 3–5pm.

San Michele in Foro ★ CHURCH The magnificent facade of the Cattedrale di San Martino is matched, maybe even outdone, by the delicately stacked arches and arcades of this 12th-century church, which rises above the site of Lucca's Roman forum. The show begins just above the main portal, where St. Michael slays a dragon; above that two lions flank a rose window. Then begin four soaring tiers of little columns, inlaid with intricate carvings and topped with human heads, flowers, and animals; above each row is a frieze on which carved animals jump and run. The two narrow top tiers are capped by a bronze-winged statue of **St. Michael the Archangel,** flanked by two trumpeting cohorts. Lucchese claim to see a distinct glow emanating at sunset from St. Michael's right hand, created by a sapphire that, only according to legend, he wears on his finger. The interior is rather dull by comparison, although in the right transept it does have a fine painting of "Sts. Roch, Sebastian, Jerome, and Helen" by Filippino Lippi. Born of a notorious relationship between the painter Fra Filippo Lippi and a young nun, Lucrezia Buti, Filippino became one of the most accomplished painters of the late 15th century; his work shows the influence of his father as well as his teacher, Sandro Botticelli.

Piazza San Michele. ℭ **0583/48459.** Free. Daily 7:30am–noon and 3–6pm.

Where to Stay in Lucca

Lucca has many B&B–style inns. For a complete listing, ask the tourist board for the handy booklet "Extra Alberghiero."

Alla Corte degli Angeli ★★ Some of the most charming accommodations in Lucca flow across four floors of this beautifully restored pink *palazzo* just off Via Fillungo, the main shopping street. It's hard not to fall for the gimmicky decor, which provides just the right touch of playful ambience in the smallish but extremely tasteful rooms. In each, colorful murals incorporate a flower, and rich draperies and upholstered headboards pick up the theme; a scattering of antique pieces and excellent lighting enhance the stylish comfort. Some of the good-size bathrooms have both showers and hydromassage tubs. A room on an upper floor ensures an extra amount of sunlight—third-floor Paolina, with two exposures, is an especially good choice.

Via degli Angeli 23 (off Via Fillungo). www.allacortedegliangeli.com. ✆ **0583/469-204.** 21 units. 120€–210€ double. Rates include breakfast. Closed 2 weeks in Jan. **Amenities:** Bikes; concierge; Wi-Fi (free).

B & B Arena di Lucca ★★★ It's a stroke of good fortune that this parcel of prime real estate, an old apartment overlooking the Arena, welcomes guests, surrounding them with sublime views. Terra-cotta floors, oil paintings, and comfy sofas and chairs fill the shared lounge, while two high-ceilinged rooms also face the lively scene below from small balconies; two other rooms look onto the atmospheric Via del Anfiteatro. Hosts Alex and Livia treat guests as if they have come for a stay in a family home, serving a large breakfast by the kitchen hearth.

Via dell'Anfiteatro 16. www.bbarenalucca.com. ✆ **0339/678-6299.** 4 units. 100€–130€ double. Rates include breakfast. **Amenities:** Wi-Fi (free).

Bertolli Villas ★★★ Two beautiful villas tucked away on an olive estate in the hills surrounding Lucca are all about relaxing in comfortable and gracious style: Warmly decorated living rooms and bedrooms (each with private bath) are full of cushy armchairs, polished antiques, and colorful art. Olive groves and the mist-hung valley stretch beyond the large windows and terraces, and gardens surround sparkling pools. The villas can be rented in their entirety, as they often are during the summer; at other times bedrooms in each are available for 2-night minimum stays, with guests sharing living areas and kitchens. An attentive staff prepares meals on request and goes out of the way to treat their guests like visiting friends.

Via della Chiesa 13, San Colombano Alto (11km/7 mi N of Lucca). www.bertollivillas. com. ✆ **335/776-7610.** 2 villas or 6 individual units. Villas from 1,200€ a week depending on season; rooms 120€ double. Rates include breakfast. **Amenities:** Kitchens; meals on request; pools; Wi-Fi (free).

Hotel Palazzo Alexander ★ Stepping into this 12th-century palace tucked into medieval streets feels a bit like walking onto an operatic stage set, and the feeling certainly doesn't let up as you settle in amid gilded and polished wood, reproduction antiques, old prints, and plush fabrics. You might have *putti* (cherubs) grinning down on you from the frescoed ceiling, while at the same time marble baths, Jacuzzi tubs in some rooms, excellent beds and fine linens, and other amenities are thoroughly up to date. Rooms are named after Puccini operas, and some of the especially charming suites have vaulted and beamed ceilings reminiscent of Rodolfo's *La Bohème* garret—that is, if the young poet had lived very, very well. Service is as memorable as the surroundings.

Via Santa Giustina 28. www.hotelpalazzoalexander.it. ✆ **0583/47615.** 9 units. Doubles from 110€. Rates include breakfast. **Amenities:** Bar; Wi-Fi (free).

Locanda San Agostino ★★   Three large, stylish, and atmospheric guest rooms are tucked away in a moody old palace. Four-poster beds, polished antiques, old oil paintings, and elegant wall coverings provide a character-filled and fairly luxurious ambience, as does the wisteria-shaded terrace and the raised hearth in the attractive lounge/breakfast room. The aptly named Teatro room comes with a big bonus: a private balcony with views over the ruins of a Roman theater.

Piazza San Agostino 3. www.locandasantagostino.it. ✆ **0583/467-884.** 3 units. 100€–200€ double. Rates include breakfast. **Amenities:** Wi-Fi (free).

San Luca Palace Hotel ★★   A sense of tasteful, old-world comfort begins in the downstairs hall and sitting room and continues into the large guest rooms, nicely done up with parquet floors and well-coordinated fabrics and draperies. Among the many inviting flourishes are table-and-chair arrangements in all rooms and small "reading" alcoves with day beds in many. This old palace just inside the walls also has plenty of practical conveniences, including an easy-to-reach location (parking is adjacent) just a short stroll from the sights and train station. There's no in-house restaurant, but an extremely pleasant bar off the lobby serves light snacks.

Via San Paolino 103 (off Piazza Napoleone). www.sanlucapalace.com. ✆ **0583/317-446.** 26 units. Doubles from 85€. Rates include breakfast. **Amenities:** Bar; Wi-Fi (free).

Where to Eat in Lucca

Lucca's extra-virgin olive oil appears on every restaurant table. An atmospheric 19th-century pastry shop, **Taddeucci,** Piazza San Michele 34 (www.buccellatotaddeucci.com; ✆ **0583/494-933**), is famous for *buccellato,* a Lucca specialty—a ring-shaped sweet bread flavored with raisins and fennel seeds. For a fortifying (and addictive) snack, stop by **Amedo Giusti,** Via Santa Lucia 18 (✆ **0583/496-285**), where focaccia with many different toppings emerges piping hot from the oven. Sample Lucca's excellent DOC wines at **Enoteca Vanni,** Piazza San Salvatore 7 (www.enotecavanni.com; ✆ **0583/491-902**). The atmospheric **Antica Bottega di Prospero,** Via Santa Lucia 13, will instill a deep appreciation of Lucca's sophisticated palate—it's stocked with local olive oils, vegetables, and an amazing array of dried beans and grains.

Buca di Sant'Antonio ★ LUCCHESE   At least 3 centuries old, Lucca's most venerable dining room coasts a bit on its reputation these days, but sitting in the handsome surroundings amid copper pots and brass instruments is still a terribly pleasant experience—and usually requires a dinnertime reservation. Quietly formal service, with waiters in bow ties, and a welcoming glass of Prosecco nicely accent a meal of traditional Lucchese dishes. The menu changes regularly, but usually includes such specialties as *farro alla garfagnana* (spelt, or barley, soup) and *coniglio in umido* (rabbit stew). A house dessert is *buccellato,* a ring-shaped confection named for the bread that sustained Roman legionnaires.

Via della Cervia 3 (just west of Piazza San Michele). www.bucadisantantonio.com. *©* **0583/55881.** Entrees 15€. Tues–Sat 12:30–3pm and 7:30–10:30pm; Sun 12:30–3pm.

Da Leo ★★ LUCCHESE/TUSCAN   It's a good sign when you have to veer off the beaten path to find a place, even better when everyone you ask along the way knows how to get there. The pleasantly old-fashioned room with plastic-draped tablecloths has been serving local classics for 50 years, and the *arrosto di maialino con patate* (roast piglet and potatoes), *coniglio* (rabbit), and other authentic Lucchese fare remain as good as ever. This is the place to try the typically Luccan *zuppa di farro,* a soup made with spelt, a barleylike grain cooked al dente.

Via Tegrimi 1 (just north of Piazza San Salvatore). www.trattoriadaleo.it. *©* **0583/492-236.** Entrees 9€–16€. Cash only. Daily noon–3pm and 7:30–10:30pm.

Osteria San Giorgio ★ LUCCHESE/TUSCAN   On a quiet street near the Piazza Anfiteatro, this local favorite has a courtyard out front and comfortably informal rooms decorated with old photos. The menu is geared to neighbors looking for a home-cooked meal: hearty *farro alla luchesse* (beans and barley) soup, *coniglio stufato con olive taggiasche e uva* (rabbit stew with olives and grapes), and a local seafood favorite, *baccalà alla griglia con ceci* (grilled cod with chickpeas).

Via San Giorgio 26. www.osteriasangiorgiolucca.it. *©* **0583/953-233.** Entrees 8€–13€. Daily noon–3pm and 7–10:30pm.

Ristorante All'Olivo ★ LUCCHESE/SEAFOOD   This is where the Lucchese come when they're in the mood for fish. Taking a seat in one of its four comfortable and elegant little rooms—one with a fireplace, another like a covered garden—definitely elevates a meal to a special occasion. Seafood is brought in daily from the nearby Tuscan port of Viareggio and appears in a bounty of pastas, grilled platters, a nice choice of *antipasti di mare,* and a simply prepared catch of the day. Meat lovers will not be disappointed with the hearty roasts and grilled Tuscan steaks.

Piazza San Quirico 1. www.ristoranteolivo.it. *©* **0583/496-264.** Entrees 12€–20€. Daily noon–3:30pm and 7–10:30pm.

Ristorante Giglio ★★ LUCHESE   White tablecloths, fine china, and marble mantelpieces do justice to the setting in the 18th-century Palazzo Arnolfini, and the well-laid tables on the terrace add a splash of elegance to quietly refined Piazza Giglio out front. The food is reassuringly Old World and traditionally Tuscan. Many Lucchese regulars would not think of dining anywhere else, or wavering from a meal of the house specials: tagliatelle topped with shaved white truffles, perfectly grilled beef tenderloin with porcini mushrooms, and for dessert, Lucchese *buccellato* (sweet bread) filled with ice cream and berries.

Piazza del Giglio. ristorantegiglio.com. ℭ **0583/494-058.** Entrees 9€–20€. Wed–Mon 12:15–2:45pm and 7:30–10:30pm.

Trattoria Da Giulio ★★ LUCCHESE/TUSCAN   You may have to go out of your way to find this local favorite, tucked away on back streets near the northwest corner of the city walls. Once there, it seems like everyone in town is on a first-name basis with the busy staff that dashes between the tables in the three brightly lit rooms. A long menu of local classics includes *salsicce con fagioli all'ucelletto,* sausage with beans in tomato sauce and sage; *tagliatelle alla contadina,* with fresh tomatoes, basil and oregano; and a few variations of *cavallo* (horsemeat, served raw, *tartara,* and otherwise). Excellent house wines are available by the pitcher.

Via delle Conce 25. ℭ **0583/55948.** Entrees 8€–13€. Mon–Sat noon–2:30pm and 6:30–10:30pm.

Lucca Entertainment & Nightlife

Every evening at 7pm from April through October, the church of San Giovanni (Piazza di San Giovanni) hosts an opera recital or orchestral concert dedicated to hometown composer Giacomo Puccini, in a series called **Puccini e la sua Lucca (Puccini and His Lucca;** www.pucciniela-sualucca.com). Tickets are 17€ (13€ for those 22 and under) and can be purchased all day inside San Giovanni. Just try listening to "Nessun Dorma" in this lovely church in the composer's hometown without chills running up your spine. Nearby Lago di Massaciuccoli is the backdrop for the summer **Puccini Festival** ★ (www.puccinifestival.it; ℭ **0584/359-322**), the biggest date in a local opera lover's calendar. Buy tickets at the seasonal ticket office at Viale Puccini 257a, in Torre del Lago, or online (35€–125€).

PISA ★★

85km (53 miles) south of Lucca, 76km (47 miles) W of Florence

It's ironic that one of the most famous landmarks in a country that has given Western civilization much of its greatest art and architecture is in fact an engineering failure. Built on sandy soil too unstable to support so much heavy marble, Pisa's famous tower began to lean even while it was still under construction. Eight centuries later, however, the Leaning Tower puts Pisa on the map. Seeing it, maybe climbing it, and touring other landmarks on the Piazza del Duomo is probably why you come to this city near Tuscany's northwestern coast.

Pisa began as a seaside settlement around 1000 B.C. and was expanded into a naval trading port by the Romans in the 2nd century B.C. By the 11th century, the city had grown into one of the peninsula's most powerful maritime republics. In 1284, however, Pisa's battle fleet was destroyed by Genoa at Meloria (off Livorno), forcing Pisa's long slide into twilight. Florence took control in 1406 and, despite a few small rebellions, stayed in charge until Italian unification in the 1860s.

Today Pisa is lively and cosmopolitan, home to a university founded in 1343, one of Europe's oldest. Once away from the Piazza del Duomo, however, there's not a whole lot to do but soak in the medieval and Renaissance ambience of this pleasant city, so you may want to join the ranks of day-trippers who visit from Florence or nearby Lucca.

Essentials

ARRIVING Around 25 trains run between **Lucca** and Pisa every day (25–35 min.); from **Florence,** 50 daily trains make the trip (60–90 min.). On the Lucca line, day-trippers should get off at **San Rossore station,** a few blocks west of Piazza del Duomo and the Leaning Tower. All other trains pull into **Pisa Centrale** station (eventually the Lucca one will too). The **baggage deposit** office (Deposito Bagali) is open daily 6am to 9pm, and the cost per bag is 4€ for 12 hours, 6€ for 24 hours. This is handy if you want to stop in Pisa on your way to somewhere else—if you're on the way from Genoa to Florence, for instance.

There's a Florence-Pisa fast **highway** along the Arno valley. Take the SS12 or SS12r from Lucca. Parking anywhere near the Duomo is not easy. Best bet is the Pietrasantina lot, in the northwest corner of the city and well-marked as you exit the autostrada at Pisa Nord; it's free, within walking distance of the Duomo, and also connected by frequent shuttle-bus service (1€ on the bus or at the cafe in the lot). For details on parking locations and charges, see **www.pisamo.it**.

Tuscany's main international airport, **Galileo Galilei** (www.pisa-airport.com), is just 3km (2 miles) south of the center and is served by many European carriers, with service to and from London, Paris, Amsterdam, Frankfurt, and other international hubs. The so-called **PisaMover** is an automated tram that runs every 5 to 8 minutes between the airport terminal and Pisa Centrale station (2.70€). A metered taxi ride to the station or Campo dei Miracoli costs 10€ to 15€ (drivers accept credit cards).

GETTING AROUND CPT (www.cpt.pisa.it; © **800/570-530** in Italy) runs the city's **buses.** Bus no. 4 and the LAM Rossa bus run from Pisa Central station to the Piazza del Duomo. The fare is 1.50€ and you can buy tickets at newsstands and tobacco shops. It's also an easy and pleasant 20-minute walk from the station to the Duomo on a route that will take you through the heart of the medieval city. Head north from the station on Corso Italia toward the river, and from the other bank, Via Santa Maria into the Duomo.

Taxis can be found on Piazza della Stazione and Piazza del Duomo. Call a radio taxi at © **050/541600.**

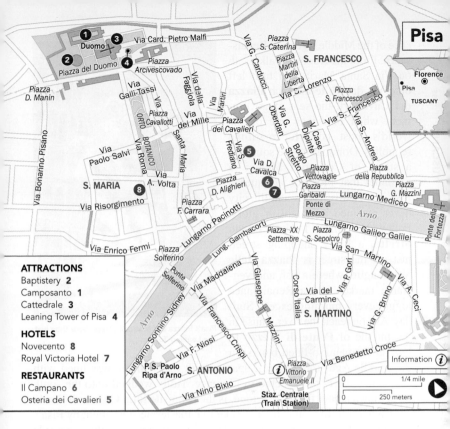

Florence
● Pisa
TUSCANY

ATTRACTIONS
Baptistery **2**
Camposanto **1**
Cattedrale **3**
Leaning Tower of Pisa **4**

HOTELS
Novecento **8**
Royal Victoria Hotel **7**

RESTAURANTS
Il Campano **6**
Osteria dei Cavalieri **5**

Information ⓘ

0 ——— 1/4 mile
0 ——— 250 meters

VISITOR INFORMATION   The main **tourist office** is at Piazza Vittorio Emanuele II 16 (www.pisaunicaterra.it; ℂ **050/42291;** daily 10am–1pm and 2–4pm). There's also an office near the Leaning Tower on Piazza del Duomo (℃ **050/42291;** daily 9:30am–5:30pm). Both offer a basically worthless map (with no street names) for free and sell a decent one for 3€.

Exploring Pisa

On a grassy lawn wedged into the northwest corner of the city walls, medieval Pisans created one of the most dramatic squares in the world. Often dubbed **Piazza dei Miracoli** (Piazza of Miracles) or **Campo dei Miracoli** (Field of Miracles), Piazza del Duomo's elegant buildings epito-mize the Pisan-Romanesque style. A subtle part of its appeal, aside from the beauty of the white marble-sheathed buildings, is its spatial geometry. If you were to look at an aerial photo of the square and draw connect-the-dot lines between the doors and other focal points, you'd come up with all sorts of perfect triangles and tangential lines.

Aside from immersing yourself in this spectacle, take a little time to see the rest of the city, where much of the historic center is a well-preserved slice of the Middle Ages and Renaissance. From the Duomo, walk south on Via Santa Maria and turn left onto Via dei Mille to reach **Piazza dei Cavalieri,** the seat of government when Pisa was one of the world's most powerful maritime republics. Dominating the square is a statue of Cosimo I Medici, a reminder that Florence conquered Pisa in the early 1500s and the city never regained its might or glory. Follow Via Ulisse Dini to **Borgo Stretto,** a lively shopping street; just off the street is **Piazza delle Vettovaglie,** where a fish and vegetable market fills a Renaissance loggia every morning except Sunday. As you reach the river, pause in the middle of **Ponte di Mezzo** to look at the palazzo-lined banks; in

Pisa's Piazza dei Miracoli offers more than just the Leaning Tower.

the Middle Ages this graceful span, rebuilt many times, was lined with shops, like the Ponte Vecchio in Florence. Tidily wedged onto the south bank, downstream from the bridge, is the exquisite little **Chiesa di Santa Maria della Spina,** an extravagant Gothic masterpiece wrought by Pisa's leading Gothic sculptors, including Giovanni Pisano. From the south side of the bridge, shop-lined **Corso Italia** passes a graceful Florentine loggia and continues to the central train station. At Corso Vittorio Emanuele II, a slight detour to the west brings you to Via Zandonai and an unexpected sight: shortly before his death in 1990, New York street artist Keith Haring painted the giant **Tuttomondo** mural on the theme of "peace and harmony," filling it with his trademark Pop Art figures.

Baptistery ★★ CHURCH   Italy's largest baptistery (104m/341 ft. in circumference), begun in 1153 and capped with a Gothic dome in the

---

Visiting the Campo dei Miracoli

Admission charges for the monuments and museums of the Campo are tied together. There a separate 18€ admission to the main attraction, the **Leaning Tower,** and the **cathedral** is free. For the Campo's other sights (the **Baptistery,** **Camposanto,** or the **Museo delle Sinopie**) it costs 5€ to enter one sight; any two sights cost 7€; and three cost 8€. For more information, visit **www.opapisa.it.**

1300s, is built on the same unstable soil as the Leaning Tower—the first thing you will notice is a decided tilt towards the cathedral. But it's the Baptistery's unadorned interior that is of greatest interest: Art historians considered this to be where the Renaissance, with its emphasis on classical style, first began to flower, in the pulpit created by sculptor Nicola Pisano (1255–60). Pisano had studied ancient Roman works that the Pisan navy brought back from Rome as booty, and the classical influence on his work is obvious—note the nude Roman god Hercules taking his place next to statues of St. Michael and St. John the Baptist (who is bathed in ethereal light on June 24, when the sun shines through a strategically placed opening in the walls to illuminate the saint on the feast of his nativity). In scenes of the life of Christ, figures wear tunics and Mary wears the headdress of a Roman matron. Roughly once an hour or so, one of the guards will stand near the middle of the structure and sing, and the sound will reverberate melodically (the performer deserves a small tip). These acoustics are no accident—studies show that the baptistery was designed in such a way to amplify sounds to mimic a perfectly tuned pipe organ.

Piazza del Duomo. www.opapisa.it. © **050/835-011.** For prices, see box p. 298. Open daily, Apr–Sept 8am–8pm; Oct 9am–7pm; Nov–Feb 10am–5pm; Mar 9am–6pm.

Camposanto ★ CEMETERY   Pisa's cemetery, where the city's aristocracy was buried until the 1800s, was begun in 1278, when Crusaders began shipping back dirt from Golgotha (the mount where Christ was crucified). Giovanni di Simone (architect of the Leaning Tower) enclosed the field in a marble cloister, and the walls were covered by magnificent 14th- and 15th-century frescoes. Unfortunately, these were mostly destroyed by Allied bombings in World War II, but you can see renderings of them in the Museo delle Sinopie across the square. Roman sarcophagi, used as funerary monuments, fared better (84 of these survive), as did the huge chains that medieval Pisans used to protect their harbor, which now hang on the cemetery walls.

Piazza del Duomo. www.opapisa.it. © **050/835-011.** For prices, see box p. 298. Open daily, Apr–Sept 8am–8pm; Oct 9am–7pm; Nov–Feb 10am–5pm; Mar 9am–6pm.

Cattedrale ★★ CATHEDRAL   Pisa's magnificent white marble cathedral will forever be associated with Galileo Galilei (1564–1642), a native son and founder of modern physics. Bored during church services, he discovered the law of perpetual motion (a pendulum's swings always take the same amount of time) by watching the swing of a bronze chandelier now known as the "Lamp of Galileo." (It's also said that Galileo dropped two wooden balls of differing sizes from the Leaning Tower; they hit the ground at the same time, thus proving that gravity exerts the same force on objects no matter what they weigh.) The exuberant cathedral, with its intricate tiers of arches and columns, is quite remarkable in its own right as a prime example of Pisan Romanesque architecture, which was heavily

Streets leading up to the Piazza dei Miracoli are lined with craft and souvenir sellers.

influenced by Pisa's trading contact with the Arab world. Giovanni Pisano, whose father, Nicola, sculpted the pulpit in the Baptistery, created the pulpit here (1302–11), covering it with scenes from the New Testament. They're now considered a masterpiece of Gothic sculpture, but 16th-century restorers deemed them too old-fashioned and packed them away in crates; they were reassembled, rather clumsily, in 1926.

Piazza del Duomo. www.opapisa.it. ℂ **050/835-011.** For prices, see box p. 298. Open daily, Apr–Sept 8am–8pm; Oct 9am–7pm; Nov–Feb 10am–5pm; Mar 9am–6pm.

Leaning Tower of Pisa ★★★ ICON   Construction began on the bell tower of Pisa Cathedral in 1173. Three stories into the job, it became apparent the structure was leaning distinctly, whereupon architects Guglielmo and Bonnano Pisano called off the work. A century later, Giovanni di Simone resumed the job, having quite literally gone back to the drawing board—he tried to compensate for the tilt by making successive layers taller on one side than the other, thus giving the tower a slight banana-like curve. Over the centuries engineers have poured concrete into the foundations and tried other solutions, all in vain. By the late 20th century the tower was in such serious danger of collapse, it was closed and braced with cables. Crews removed more than 70 tons of earth from beneath the structure, allowing it to slightly right itself as it settled. With a lean of only 4m (13 ft.), compared to a precarious 4.6m (15 ft.) before the fix, the tower has been deemed stable for now and safe to climb once again. But before you do, take time to notice just how lovely the multicolor marble tower is, with eight arcaded stories that provide a mesmerizing sense of harmony as you look up its height.

The only way to climb the tower is to book a visit in the office on the north side of the piazza—or, for peak season, book online well in advance. Visits are limited to 30 minutes, and you must be punctual for your slot or you'll lose your chance to climb the 293 steps. Children under 8 are not permitted to climb the tower, and those 8 to 18 need to be accompanied by an adult (8 to 12s must hold an adult's hand at all times).

Piazza del Duomo. www.opapisa.it. © **050/835-011.** 18€. Open daily, Apr–Sept 8am–8pm; Oct 9am–7pm; Nov–Feb 10am–5pm; Mar 9am–6pm.

Where to Stay & Eat in Pisa

Most visitors come to Pisa on a day trip, usually from Florence, which helps keep hotel prices down but also limits quality options. The low season for most hotels in Pisa is August. Any visit should include a stop for a coffee and pastry at **Caffè dell'Ussero,** one of Italy's oldest literary cafe-bars, doing a brisk business since 1775 from the ground floor of riverside Palazzo Agostini, Lungarno Pacinotti 27 (© **050/581-100**). For pizza or *cecina* (a flatbread made of garbanzo-bean flour and served warm), stop in at **Il Montino,** in the historic center a block or so west of Borgo Stretto at Vicolo del Monte (© **050/598-695**). At the end of Borgo Stretto, at number 11 in the riverside Piazza Garibaldi, is Pisa's best gelato shop, **Bottega del Gelato** (© 050/575-467).

Il Campano ★★ PISAN   A meal in the simply furnished brick-and-stone rooms of an 18th-century tower house can be an evening-long event, as the kitchen makes everything to order. The *pappardelle alla lepre* (homemade pasta with hare sauce), *tagliata di scamerita di maiale* (grilled pork chops), the Florentine steaks, and everything else on the menu is well worth waiting for. It's an inviting place to spend a couple of hours or more.

Via Cavalca 19. www.ilcampano.com. © **050/580-585.** Entrees 10€–24€. Mon–Fri 7:30–11pm, Sat–Sun 12:30–3pm and 7:30–11pm.

Osteria dei Cavalieri ★ PISAN   The "Restaurant of the Knights" operates out of stone rooms that date to the 12th century; the cooking is traditionally Tuscan but founded on the Slow Food principles of fresh and local. Being Pisa, this means seafood, including *tagliolini* with razor clams and a classic *baccala,* dried cod lightly battered and fried; some hearty meat choices, such as *pappardelle* with rabbit sauce, grilled steaks, and robust vegetable soups. You can get away with a one-dish meal here—in fact, it's encouraged at lunchtime, when local office workers pack in.

Via San Frediano 16. www.osteriacavalieri.pisa.it. © **050/580-858.** Entrees 10€–18€. Mon–Fri 12:30–2:30pm and 7:45–10pm, Sat 7:45–10pm.

Novecento ★ These small and simple rooms set around a courtyard in an old villa are strictly contemporary, not an antique armoire in sight. Instead, Philippe Starck chairs and upholstered headboards are set against colored accent walls. A lush garden is filled with lounge chairs; off to one side is the best room in the house, a self-contained, cottage-like unit. Pisa's Botanical Garden is just up the street and the Duomo is a 10-minute walk.

Via Roma 37. www.hotelnovecento.pisa.it. © **050/500-323.** 14 units. 80€–100€ double. Rates include breakfast. **Amenities:** Wi-Fi (free.

Royal Victoria Hotel ★★★ The gracious Piegaga family has been hosting travelers since the days of the 19th-century Grand Tour, and their high-ceilinged guest rooms and fern-filled parlors ooze old-world charm. Not too much has changed since Charles Dickens and legions of other Victorians stayed here, so guests looking for spas, high-tech gadgetry and chic designer style should bed down elsewhere. The rest of us will delight in the views of the Arno from the front rooms, an airy upper floor terrace for cocktails, and all the art deco tile work, marble mantelpieces, frescoes, and other old-fashioned trappings that only get better with age.

Lungarno Pacinotti 12. www.royalvictoria.it. © **050/940-111.** From 65€ double. **Amenities:** Bar; Wi-Fi (free).

UMBRIA & THE MARCHES

By Stephen Brewer

7

t's easy to write off Umbria as second to Tuscany, its more-visited neighbor to the north, but that's a good thing—being slightly out of the limelight is one of the region's great assets. Perugia, Spoleto, Gubbio, and dozens of other noble hill towns are a little quieter than their Tuscan neighbors—a bit easier to enjoy, yet still filled with rival-worthy art treasures, from Giotto's famous fresco cycle in Assisi to Signorelli's horrifying view of Judgment Day in Orvieto. Even less visited are the rugged valleys of the Marches to the east, where charming towns like Urbino cling to hillsides in relative isolation.

Umbrian landscapes are most memorably green, a picturesque mix of vineyards and olive groves, fertile valleys, and unspoiled forests, edged by the western Apennine mountains. All this mellow scenery befits a region often called *la terra dei santi* (land of the saints), in homage to St. Francis of Assisi and his followers, reminders of whom are everywhere

DON'T LEAVE UMBRIA WITHOUT . . .

Taking an Evening Passeggiata on Corso Vannuci in Perugia. Stop to admire the Fontana Maggiore and other landmarks, then wander up and down enticing medieval lanes that traverse the city's many hills.

Communing with the Spirit of St. Francis. The kindly saint is still a presence in medieval Assisi and Gubbio, where he lived and performed miracles, as well as in the region's forested hills and mist-shrouded valleys.

Getting Vertigo While Crossing Spoleto's Ponte Delle Torre. High above the Tessino river gorge, this majestic medieval span leads off a scenic 4-mile walk through Umbrian forests and olive groves.

Scenting a Whiff of Brimstone in Orvieto. Luca Signorelli's masterpiece, his Last Judgment fresco cycle in the Duomo, delivers all the spine-tingling thrill of a horror movie—it may literally "put the fear of God in you!"

Finding Your Inner Renaissance Courtier in Urbino. As you stroll through the palace of the Duke da Montefeltro—model for Castiglione's 1507 bestseller Book of the Courtier—the ghosts of the Renaissance's highest ideals of art and thought still seem very much present.

Umbria

0   10 mi
0   10 km

Urbino
Ponte di Trajano
Fermignano
Urbania
Mercatello sul Metauro
Pieve Santo Stefano
Caprese Michelangelo
Piobbico
Pergola
Cagli
Arcevia
Sansepolcro
Anghiari
San Giustino
Selci Lama
Cantiano
Sassoferrato
Monterchi
Città di Castello
Pietralunga
Scheggia
Morra
Montone
Fabriano
Trestine
Gubbio
Osteria del Gatto
Umbertide
Monte Urbino
Gualdo Tadino

TUSCANY
Cortona
SS71
Terontola
Passignano sul Trasimeno
Monte Tezio
UMBRIA
MARCHE
Monte Pennino
Camerino
Magione
Corciano
Valfabbrica
Serravalle di Chienti
Lago Trasimeno
San Feliciano
PERUGIA
Petrignano
Nocera Umbra
Castiglione del Lago
Lago di Chiusi
Assisi
Monte Subasio
Visso
Bastia Umbra
Torgiano
Rivotorto
Chiusi
Panicale
Deruta
Cannara
Spello
Città della Pieve
Tavernelle
Foligno
Piegaro
Gualdo Cattaneo
Bevagna
Marsciano
Montefalco
Fabro
Montegabbiano
Collazzone
Trevi
Ficulle
San Venanzo
Bastardo
Campello sul Clitunno
Monte Castello di Vibio
Castel Ritaldi
Norcia
Monte Peglia
Ponterio
Todi
Massa Martana
Madonna di Lugo
Castel Viscardo
Fontanelle di Bardano
Spoleto
Càscia
Orvieto
Lago di Corbara
Acquasparta
Baschi
Castel Giorgio
Guardea
Castell dell'Aquila
Ferentillo
Bolsena
Bagnoregio
San Gemini
Montefranco
Leonessa
Lago di Bolsena
Lugnano in Teverina
Terni
Torreorsina
Piediluco
Posta
SS2
Amelia
Montefiascone
Giove
Narni
Lago di Piediluco
Marta
SS571
Antroloco
Orte
Calvi dell'Umbria
Rieti
Viterbo
Monti Sabini
LAZIO
Magliano Sabina
Vetralla
Lago di Vico
Civita Castellana
Tiber

305

PERUGIA ★★

164km (102 miles) SE of Florence, 176km (109 miles) N of Rome

Perugia is Umbria's capital, but at its heart it's still a charming medieval hill town. Ancient alleys drop precipitously off **Corso Vannucci,** the cosmopolitan shopping promenade, and Gothic palaces rise above stony piazzas. The city produced and trained some of Umbria's finest artists, whose works fill the excellent art gallery. Thousands of students from Perugia's two universities impart a youthful energy, and Perugia's most famous product, chocolate, adds a sweet note to the town's appeal.

Essentials

ARRIVING   Two **rail** lines serve Perugia. The state railway connects with **Rome** (2–3 hr.; most trains require a change at Foligno) and **Florence** (2¼ hr.; most trains require a change at Terontola) every couple of hours. There are also hourly trains to **Assisi** (20–30 min.) and **Spoleto** (1¼ hr.). Limited high-speed Frecciarossa service connects Perugia with Florence (about 1 ½ hrs.) and Milan (about 3 hrs.) with a daily round trip departing Perugia at 5:13am and departing Milan at 6:45pm, with a return to Perugia at 10:20pm. The station is a few kilometers southwest of the center at Piazza Vittorio Veneto (✆ **147/888088**) but well connected with buses

Corso Vannucci, Perugia's main artery.

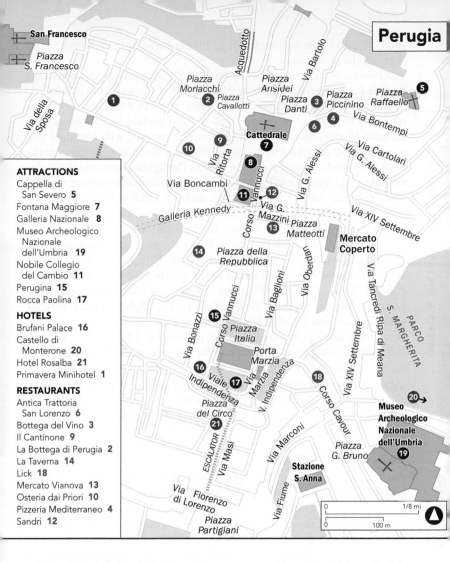

Perugia

San Francesco

Piazza S. Francesco

Acquedotto

Via Bartolo

Piazza Morlacchi **2**

Piazza Cavallotti

Piazza Ansidei

Piazza Danti **3**

Piazza Piccinino

Piazza Raffaello **5**

Via della Sposa

1

Via Bontempi

6

4

Via Cartolari

Via G. Alessi

Via G. Alessi

Cattedrale **7**

9

10

Via Ritorta

8

Via Vannucci

Via Boncambi

11

12

Via G. Mazzini

Piazza Matteotti

Via XIV Settembre

Galleria Kennedy

Corso Vannucci

13

14

Piazza della Repubblica

Mercato Coperto

Via Oberdan

Via Baglioni

Via Tancredi Ripa di Meana

S. MARGHERITA

PARCO

Via Bonazzi

15

Corso Vannucci

Piazza Italia

Porta Marzia

Via XIV Settembre

16

Viale Indipendenza

17

Via Marzia

V. Indipendenza

18

Corso Cavour

20

Museo Archeologico Nazionale dell'Umbria

19

Piazza del Circo

ESCALATOR

Via Masi

21

Via Marconi

Piazza G. Bruno

Stazione S. Anna

Via Fiume

Via Florenzo di Lorenzo

Piazza Partigiani

0   1/8 mi
0   100 m

ATTRACTIONS

Cappella di San Severo **5**
Fontana Maggiore **7**
Galleria Nazionale **8**
Museo Archeologico Nazionale dell'Umbria **19**
Nobile Collegio del Cambio **11**
Perugia **15**
Rocca Paolina **17**

HOTELS

Brufani Palace **16**
Castello di Monterone **20**
Hotel Rosalba **21**
Primavera Minihotel **1**

RESTAURANTS

Antica Trattoria San Lorenzo **6**
Bottega del Vino **3**
Il Cantinone **9**
La Bottega di Perugia **2**
La Taverna **14**
Lick **18**
Mercato Vianova **13**
Osteria dai Priori **10**
Pizzeria Mediterraneo **4**
Sandri **12**

to/from Piazza Italia (1€). Perugia's seven-stop, 3km (2-mile) long "mini-metro" also makes the run from the station up to stops in the town center (1.50€, buy tickets in machines). Stazione Sant'Anna, for the **Umbria Mobilità–operated regional railway** (☏ **800/512141**), is in Piazzale Bellucci (near the bus station). These tiny trains run to neighboring hill towns—Assisi, Spello, Spoleto, Todi, Orvieto—every couple of hours.

SULGA lines (www.sulga.it; ☏ **075/500-9641**) operates 4 to 5 buses a day to and from Rome (2½ hr.), stopping at Florence's Fiumicino airport; some also stop at Assisi, Deruta, and Todi. **BusItalia Nord buses** (www.fsbusitalia.it; ☏ **075/963-7001**) also connect Perugia with Assisi (6 buses daily, 50 min.), Gubbio (6 buses daily, 70 min.), and Todi (6 buses daily, 75 min.). The bus station is in Piazza Partigiani and connected to Piazza Italia by escalator.

Perugia is well connected by **road** to Siena (a little over an hour on the free Raccordo), Rome (about 2 hrs. via the A1 autostrada), and Assisi, Spoleto, and other Umbrian towns. While much of the *centro storico* is off-limits to nonresident drivers, well-marked parking lots are situated at the base of the hills over which old Perugia sprawls, with elevators and escalators to take you up to the center. Some of the most convenient parking is at the underground pay lot at **Piazza Partigiani,** from which escalators take you up to Piazza Italia (with some amazing underground scenery along the route; see box p. 311). Rates are from 1.10€ to 1.50€ for the first hour, 1.50€ to 1.90€ for each successive hour, and 17€ daily. Some hotels issue a card that allows you to park for 5€ a day, leaving and entering as you wish. For more about parking in Perugia, visit **www.sipaonline.it**.

While most visitors arrive by train or car, Perugia does have a small airport, **Aeroporto Internazionale dell'Umbria** (www.airport.umbria.it; ✆ **075/592141**), 10km (6 miles) east of the city, which serves some inter-European flights. **Ryanair** (www.ryanair.com) flights connect Perugia with Brussels and London Stansted. Buses connect the airport with the Perugia bus station (30–40 min.; 2.50€ in terminal, 3.50€ on bus), but service is infrequent; check airport website for schedules. Taxis to or from the airport cost around 25€.

VISITOR INFORMATION   The **tourist office** at Piazza Matteotti 18 (turismo.comune.perugia.it; ✆ **075/573-6458**) is open daily 8:30am to 6:30pm. They provide a fairly useless free map and charge 1€ for a good one.

Exploring Perugia

Perugia's main public square, **Piazza Italia,** hangs like a balcony over the hillside at one end of the old town. Among the somber, formidable banks and government buildings fronting the piazza you'll see the imposing porticoes of the Provincia d'Umbria, the provincial offices, to your left as you face the airy, view-filled end of the square. A favorite game in town is to stand in a corner of one of the huge arches, place a companion in the corner diagonally across, and whisper—even the softest murmur travels as if transmitted over a phone. From Piazza Italia the sophisticated **Corso Vannucci** flows north to **Piazza IV Novembre,** presided over by the massive Palazzo dei Priori (p. 282) (home of the Galleria Nazionale delle'Umbria), and the city's cathedral. The

---

The Perugia Card

Many attractions in Perugia—including the four top sights we cover in this book—are included on the **Perugia City Museum Card.** You can buy it at any participating museum; it costs 14€ for one adult and one child under 18, and is valid for 48 hours. Combined admission for just these four sights would be 21.50€ without the card—the savings can be significant.

Piazza IV Novembre.

square's focal point is the elaborate **Fontana Maggiore,** with its carved panels and figures depicting saints, prophets, ancient Roman figures, and biblical scenes (look for the temptation of Adam and Eve), crafted by Nicola Pisano and his son Giovanni between 1275 and 1278.

It's especially entertaining to stroll up the Corso in the early evening, when the wide stretch of pavement becomes the stage set for one of Italy's most lively and decorous evening *passeggiate.* Anywhere you walk in Perugia, however, an upward glance reveals a tower, an arch, or a Renaissance facade decorated with marble figures. An especially scenic walk is along **Via dell'Acquedotto,** north of Piazza IV Novembre, following the 13th-century aqueduct constructed to bring water into the city to the Fontana Maggiore. As the narrow way crosses a ravine, an airy panorama of the old city and green hills unfolds.

Cappella di San Severo ★ CHURCH   Don't be fooled by the modest 18th-century exterior; the 14th-century chapel inside contains a real treasure. Before young Raphael Sanzio made a name for himself in Florence and Rome, he settled briefly in Perugia, where in 1504 he painted the first of the many frescoes that would make him famous in his own lifetime (not to mention vaulting him into the triumvirate of great Renaissance masters, with Da Vinci and Michelangelo). Unfortunately only the upper half of his "Holy Trinity" remains here, and that is damaged. The work seems touchingly modest compared to the complex "School of Athens" and other works he later did for the Vatican. As energetic in life as he was in his work, Raphael ran a huge workshop, had dozens of patrons, was in line to be a cardinal, and died on his 37th birthday, allegedly after a lustful session with his mistress. After Raphael's death, his then-septuagenarian teacher, Perugino, painted the six saints along the bottom of the fresco.

Piazza Raffaello. www.perugiacittamuseo.it. ℂ **075/573/947-1766.** 4€ adults, 1€ ages 7–14, free for children 6 and under. Included on the Perugia City Museum Card. Apr daily 10am–1:30pm and 2:30–6pm; May, Sept–Oct Tues–Sun 10am–1:30pm and 2:30–6pm; June–July Tues–Sun 10am–6pm; Aug daily 10am–6pm; Nov–Mar Tues–Sun 11am–1:30pm and 2:30–5pm.

Galleria Nazionale dell'Umbria ★★★ MUSEUM   Seven or so centuries of Umbrian art are housed in the crenellated Palazzo dei Priori, where a ruling council of powerful merchants and guilds met in medieval times. It's only fitting that the star of the museum is native son Perugino, who was born nearby in Città della Pieve and spent much of his career working in Perugia (he also studied alongside Leonardo da Vinci in Florence and executed frescoes in the Sistine Chapel in Rome). Perugino's altarpieces in Rooms 22–26 are full of delicate landscapes, sweet Madonnas, and grinning Christ Childs that reveal his spare, precise style. Their divine beauty seems ironic, given that Perugino was openly anti-religion and had a fairly turbulent life—he was arrested in Florence for assault and battery and barely escaped

Galleria Nazionale in the Palazzo dei Priori, Perugia.

exile; sued Michelangelo for defamation of character; and more than once was censored for reusing images. He persevered, however, and worked prodigiously until his death at age 73, leaving a considerable fortune.

The museum's other showpiece is Piero della Francesca's "Polyptych of Perugia," painted for the city's church of Sant'Antonio in 1470. The symmetry and realistic dimensions reflect the artist's other occupation as a mathematician; at the same time, his figures are robustly human. Della Francesca works sheer magic at the top of the piece, in a scene of the Annunciation, where an angel appears to Mary to tell her she will be the mother of the son of God. She's standing in a brightly lit cloister, and the illusion of pillars leading off into the distance is regarded as one of the greatest examples of perspective in Renaissance art.

Perugia's Medieval Pompeii

Beneath Piazza Italia is some remarkable underground scenery. Around 1530 the Perugians rebelled against Pope Paul III over a tax on salt (to this day, Perugian bread is salt-free). In retribution, the Pope demolished more than a quarter of the city, building his **Rocca Paolina** atop the ruins. After Italian unification in 1860, locals ripped the castle to pieces and built Piazza Italia on top of that. Today, however, the vaults of the Pope's fort and the even older remains of medieval dwellings and streets are in full view beneath the piazza. You can clamber through doorless entrances, climb the remains of stairways, walk through empty rooms, and wander at will through the brick maze. Enter the underground city (free; open daily 6:15am–1:45am) from the escalators that connect Piazza Italia to the lower town's Piazza Partigiani, with its car park and bus station.

Palazzo dei Priori, Corso Vannucci 19. gallerianazionaledellumbria.it. ℂ **075/574-1247.** 8€ adults, free for ages 17 and under. Included on the Perugia City Museum Card. Tues–Sun 8:30am–7:30pm; Apr–Oct also open Mon noon–7:30pm.

Museo Archeologico Nazionale dell'Umbria (National Archeological Museum of Umbria) ★ MUSEUM

Etruscans stand out as the stars of the show among these ancient artifacts displayed in the former church, convent, and cloisters of San Domenico. Most riveting are the large tombs, brought from around the Tuscan/Umbrian region that 2,500 years ago was the heartland of an Etruscan 12-city confederation. To best appreciate the artistry of ancient masters, just wander along the porticos of the vast cloisters and enjoy the stories of everyday life that emerge in stone on the tombs that line the walls. A man with scales in hand, perhaps an architect, stands in front of a town gate; a young couple kisses; workers harvest grapes. One of the most fascinating pieces is the Sarcophagus dello Sperandio, from the tomb of a warrior. When discovered in 1843, it was surrounded by iron weapons. On one side, three men recline on a divan, enjoying a banquet as a slave serves them; in another long relief, men, women, and animals (including heavily laden pack animals and collared dogs) follow one another in a procession, possibly a ceremonial parade or migration. It's believed the sarcophagus was fashioned in Chiusi and brought to Perugia in heavy wagons along a rough ancient track. The Cipo di Perugia, from the 3rd century B.C., is the longest piece of Etruscan script ever found: It's a land contract between two families, proof that real estate has always been a sound investment.

Piazza Giordano Bruno 10. polomusealeumbria.beniculturali.it. ℂ **075/572-7141.** 5€ adults. Included on the Perugia City Museum Card. Daily 8:30am–7:30pm.

Nobile Collegio del Cambio ★★ MUSEUM

The cubicles and fluorescent lighting of modern office life will seem even more banal after you visit the frescoed meeting rooms of Perugia's Moneychanger's Guild, one of the best-preserved "office suites" of the Renaissance. Perugino was hired in 1496 to fresco the Sala dell' Udienza (Hearing Room), perhaps with the help of his young student Raphael. The images merge religion (scenes of the Nativity and Transfiguration) with classical references (female representations of the virtues) and, most riveting of all, glimpses of 15th-century secular life.

Palazzo dei Priori, Corso Vannucci 25. www.collegiodelcambio.it. © **075/572-8599.** 4.50€ adults, free for ages 12 and under. Included on the Perugia City Museum Card. Mon–Sat 9am–12:30pm and 2:30–5:30pm.

Where to Stay in Perugia

Most Perugia hotels are flexible about rates, which often dive 40 to 50 percent below posted prices in the off-season.

Brufani Palace ★★   Perugia's bastion of luxury commands one side of Piazza Italia, looming proudly over the valley below. Built in 1883 to host English travelers on the Grand Tour, the premises have not changed too much in the intervening years, except that the large, traditionally furnished rooms are now equipped with lavish marble bathrooms and lots of other amenities, including comfortable lounge chairs and sofas. Despite the grand surroundings, the real pleasures here are in the details: fires burn in big stone hearths in the dining room and lounges; a swimming pool has been carved out of subterranean brick vaults, with see-through panels exposing Etruscan ruins beneath; and a large rooftop terrace is a perfect spot for a glass of wine at sunset.

Piazza Italia 12. www.sinahotels.com. © **075/573-2541.** 94 units. Doubles from 135€. Rates include breakfast. **Amenities:** Restaurant/bar; babysitting; concierge; small exercise room; indoor pool; room service; Wi-Fi (free).

GO jump IN THE LAKE

Lago Trasimeno, Italy's fourth-largest lake, washes up against the Tuscany–Umbria border between Cortona and Perugia. The shallow waters aren't quite a match for the beauty of Como and the other lakes up north, but Trasimeno is nonetheless a refreshing splash of blue amid olive groves and sunflower fields. **Passignano,** on the northern shore 30km (18 miles) northwest of Perugia, is the liveliest lakeshore town, with a shoreline promenade and a good stop for a gelato or a sunset aperitivo at Bar del Sole, Via Aganor Pompili. At **Castiglione del Lago,** on the western shore 50km (30 miles) west of Perugia, you can swim from a pebbly beach or cycle on shoreline paths; rent bikes for 8€ half a day, 10€ a day at **Cicli Valentini,** Via Firenze 68/B (ciclivalentini. it; © **333/9678327;** open Sat–Sun 9am–1pm and 3:30–8pm).

From either town, 30-minute ferry trips run hourly across the lake to picturesque **Isola Maggiore,** an especially nice place to take a dip in the cool waters, or to buy lace from the few local women who carry on the longstanding tradition. Stepping ashore on Isola Maggiore, you'll be following in the footsteps of St. Francis, who spent Lent of 1213 here. Allegedly, the saint even charmed the local fish—when Francis threw a pike given to him by a fisherman back into the lake, the creature swam alongside his savior until the saint gave him a special blessing.

Castello di Monterone ★★★　It's surprising just how inviting a medieval castle can be. That's partly because in the 19th century the Piceller family of musicians, artists, and archaeologists made this 13th-century stronghold their home, creating lounges surrounding massive fireplaces and a beautiful cloister garden dotted with ancient artifacts. These days the many nooks and crannies have been converted to utterly charming guest rooms embellished with wide beams, stone walls, and handcrafted iron and wood furniture, and equipped with large marble bathrooms. Adding to the ambience is a library tucked away on a landing, a cozy lounge bar in the old hall, a swimming pool surrounded by lawns, and a roof terrace on the old battlements. Though the castle is nestled on a rural hillside, the center of Perugia is only 10 minutes away on a road used by the Etruscans and Romans.

Strada Monteville 3. www.castellomonterone.it. ✆ **075/572-4214.** 14 units. 150€– 250€. Rates include breakfast. **Amenities:** Restaurant; bar; pool; Wi-Fi (free).

Hotel Rosalba ★　You'll enjoy a quirky ride into the center of town from this hillside villa—via escalators through the Rocca Paolina up to Piazza Grande and Corso Vannucci. The location ensures valley views from rear rooms and one on the top floor with a large terrace. All are modestly furnished in functional style that doesn't do justice to the airy spaces and Art Nouveau styling, but they're attractive and comfortable. If you're arriving by car, ask for directions in navigating Perugia's devilish traffic system and where to park.

Piazza del Circo. www.hotelrosalba.com. ✆ **075/572-8285.** 11 units. From 80€ double. Rates include breakfast in adjacent bar. **Amenities:** Wi-Fi (free).

Primavera Minihotel ★★　It's well worth the climb up the three flights of stairs to this aerie-like retreat, just down some twisty streets from Piazza della Repubblica. The high locale means that all the tall windows frame views of rooftops and the green valleys below. Rooms surround a welcoming lounge/breakfast room (breakfast costs extra), except for the best room in the house—a large rooftop double with a terrace. Some are furnished with Art Nouveau pieces, others with traditionally rustic furnishing and Deruta pottery, and all have hardwood floors and lots of timber, stone, and other architectural details.

Via Vincioli 8. www.primaveraminihotel.it. ✆ **075/572-1657.** 8 units. 65€–90€ double. **Amenities:** Wi-Fi (free).

Where to Eat in Perugia

Perugia's youthful student population seems to subsist on pizza and *panini* (sandwiches), good news for the rest of us looking for a snack or light meal. Most popular among plenty of cheap *pizzerie* is **Mediterranea,** at Piazza Piccinino 11 (✆ **075/572-4021**). Pizzas cost 6€ to 8€, and it's open daily (Mon–Fri noon–2:30pm and 7–11pm; weekends 7–11pm). Top choice for a *panino* is **La Bottega di Perugia,** Piazza Francesco

Morlacchi 4 (www.labottegadiperugia.it; *℗* **075/573–2965**), whose young proprietors pride themselves on using only local Umbrian hams, greens, and other ingredients; *panini* cost about 4€ and can be washed down with wine or beer (Mon–Sat 10:30am–12:30am). Far more elegant is the venerable **Sandri,** Perugia's oldest (opened in 1860) and most esteemed *pasticceria,* serving coffee, pastry, and light meals in Art Deco surroundings at Corso Vannucci 32 (*℗* **075/572-4112;** Sun–Thurs 7:30am–9pm; Fri 7:30am–11pm; Sat 7:30am–midnight). For stylish cocktails, try the popular **Mercato Vianova,** Via Giuseppe Mazzini 15 (www.mercatovianova. it; *℗* **075/573-04450**). The name says it all at **Lick,** Corso Cavour 40 (*℗* **075/572-6917**), which dishes up gelato in such unusual (and delicious!) variations as gorgonzola cheese and basil with Prosecco.

Antica Trattoria San Lorenzo ★★ MODERN ITALIAN   Everything here is local, right down to the Perugia-made pottery on the candlelit tables. Chef/owner Simone Ciccotti sources his ingredients from producers in the nearby countryside, then creates inventive dishes that emphasize those flavors, such as a "muffin" of caramelized onions and foie gras, or a *millefeuille* of grilled vegetables with smoked mozzarella. The restaurant's namesake, San Lorenzo, is a patron saint of Perugia—and also the patron saint of chefs.

Piazza Danti 19a. www.anticatrattoriasanlorenzo.com. *℗* **075/527-1956.** Entrees 10€–18€. Daily 12:30–2pm and 7:30–10pm.

Bottega del Vino ★ UMBRIAN   A snug, vintage-photo-lined room right off Piazza IV Novembre serves wines by the glass along with a nice assortment of Umbrian hams and cheeses, perfect for an evening *aperitivo* as all of Perugia promenades by the tables out front. The small lunch and dinner menus include salads and a couple of pastas, as well as a dish or two of the day—a steak, say, or roasted leg of lamb. Live jazz often plays into the wee hours, making this a popular after-dinner spot.

Via del Sole 1. www.labottegadelvino.net. *℗* **075/571-6181.** Entrees 13€. Tues–Sun noon–3pm and 7pm–midnight. Closed Jan.

The City of *Cioccolato* and Jazz

Perugia is a chocoholic's paradise. **Perugina,** with a sweet-scented shop at Corso Vannucci 101 (*℗* **075/573-4760**), has been making candy here since 1907 and now pumps out 120 tons a day of the sweet stuff, including 1½ million Baci (kisses), its gianduja-and-hazelnut bestseller. Every year Perugia hosts a weeklong **Eurochocolate Festival** (www.eurochocolate.com) from mid- to late October. The highlight: a chocolate-carving contest, when the scraps of 1,000kg (455-lb.) blocks are handed out for sampling. **Umbria Jazz** (www.umbria jazz.com), one of Europe's top jazz festivals, draws big international names to town for 2 weeks in mid-July.

Il Cantinone ★★ UMBRIAN/PIZZA   Even a pizza seems like a meal fit for a medieval courtier in this softly lit, stone-walled, and brick-vaulted 14th-century cantina in a hidden courtyard around the corner from Piazza Maggiore. The excellent Umbrian fare befits the distinctively Old Perugia surroundings, with such hearty choices as homemade tagliatelle with duck ragù or wild boar sauce and locally sourced beef from the Val di Chiana topped with black truffles. And yes, they do serve pizzas, making this the most elegant pizzeria in town.

Via Ritorta. ristoranteilcantinoneperugia.com. ℂ **075/573-4430.** Entrees 8€–15€. Wed–Mon 12:30–2:30pm and 7:30–10:30pm.

La Taverna ★★ UMBRIAN   For many Perugians, a tiny courtyard down a flight of steps from Corso Vannucci is the epicenter of good dining. In warm weather, tables fill the courtyard; inside, barrel-vaulted ceilings shimmer with candlelight in evening, and the service and the cooking are similarly warm and down-to-earth. Everything, from bread to pasta to desserts, is made in-house and typically Umbrian: Pappardelle is sauced with a hearty ragù, *caramelle rosse al gorgonzola* (beet ravioli with gorgonzola) is made with local beets, and meats are seasoned with fresh herbs from the surroundings hillsides. Chef Claudio will make his way to your table at some point to ensure that everything is *tutto bene.*

Via delle Streghe 8 (near Piazza Repubblica). www.ristorantelataverna.com. ℂ **075/572-4128.** Entrees 9€–16€. Daily 12:30–2:30pm and 7:30–11pm.

Osteria dai Priori ★★★ UMBRIAN   You'll pass through a wine shop and climb a flight of stairs to reach this welcoming brick-vaulted room with contemporary wood furnishings, where the emphasis is on age-old Umbrian recipes. A portion of slowly cooked beans *(fagiolina)* is paired with eggs and onions and bread salad; *gnocconi* (large potato dumplings) are stuffed with fresh ricotta; slow-roasted pork shank *(stinco di mialale)* is served with crisp potatoes. The staff will eagerly walk you through the ever-changing menu and pair wines with each course.

Via dei Priori 39. www.osteriaapriori.it. ℂ **075/572-7098.** Entrees 9€–12€. Mon–Sat 12:30–2:30pm and 7:30–10pm.

Perugia Shopping

At **Museo Atelier Giuditta Brozzetti,** in a former church at Via Tiberio Berardi 5/6 (www.brozzetti.com; ℂ **075/402-360**), Marta Cucchia oversees a centuries-old family weaving workshop, based on ages-old techniques. The atmospheric studio/shop is open Monday to Friday, 9am to 6pm; pillows, runners, and other textiles are available for sale or to custom-order. For authentic ceramics, visit **Deruta,** a little hill town 20km (12 miles) south of Perugia via SS3bis. Known for its ceramics since the Middle Ages, Deruta today has some 300 studios making and selling ceramics. The tourist office in Perugia can give you a list of shops.

GUBBIO ★★

39 km (24 miles) northeast of Perugia

Hands-down the most medieval-looking town in Umbria, Gubbio presents itself to the world with a crenellated skyline backed by forest-covered mountains. At this old hill town's stony heart, the rather severe red-brick expanse of Piazza Grande dramatically drops away on its south side to soul-soothing views of misty hills and a sweeping valley.

When it comes to St. Francis lore, proud and beautiful Gubbio gets overshadowed by Assisi (see p. 321), yet it was here that the saint performed one of his most popular miracles, taming a wolf that was terrorizing the town (see Taverna del Lupo, p. 319), and it was here that the wealthy young Francis first cast off his finery and put on a rough monk's habit, forsaking his worldly goods. Gubbio is also associated with another holy presence, Don Matteo, the priest detective of a wildly popular Italian TV series that was filmed in the town. The setting has since moved to Spoleto (see p. 330), but don't mention this to anyone in Gubbio, lest someone drops one of the geranium-filled pots adorning the stone balconies on your head.

Essentials

ARRIVING   By **car,** the SS298 branches north from Perugia, off the E45, through rugged scenery. Faster but less scenic is the new four-lane SS318, connecting Perugia and Gubbio in about half an hour—making it all the easier to include this rewarding stop on an Umbrian itinerary. Gubbio is not served directly by **train,** though Fossato di Vico, 18km (11 miles) south, is on the Rome–Ancona line, with trains arriving about every 2 hours. Buses run from that station to Gubbio about every hour. Eight or nine daily **BusItalia Nord buses** (www.fsbusitalia.it; ✆ **075/963-7001**) run between Gubbio and Perugia (70 min.); they arrive at Piazza 40 Martiri, named for citizens killed by the Nazis for aiding partisans during World War II. This is also a good place to park, in **Parcheggio Via della Repubblica** (www.gubbioculturamultiservizi.it; ✆ **075/922-2027**), where you'll pay about 1.10€ an hour between 8am and 8pm. From here it's an easy level walk to an elevator that will take you up to Piazza Grande.

VISITOR INFORMATION   The **tourist office,** Via della Repubblica 15 (www.comune.gubbio.pg.it; ✆ **075/922-0693** or 075/922-0790), is open daily (Mon–Fri 8:30am–1:45pm and 3:30–6:30pm, Sat 9am–1pm and 3:30–6:30pm, Sun 9:30am–1pm and 3–6pm; Oct–Mar afternoon hours are 3–6pm). Staff hand out maps and, for 1€, sell a brief but handy walking guide to the town.

SPECIAL EVENTS   Aside from the springtime Corso dei Ceri (see Monte Igino, p. 318), Gubbio's biggest event is lighting the **world's largest Christmas tree** on the slopes in December. Lights are laid out to form a shape 2,130 feet high and 1,100 feet wide at the base. The pope often does the honors of lighting the tree, using a computer in the Vatican palace. The town seems especially medieval the **last weekend in May,** when Eugubian *balestrieri,* or crossbow competitors, line up in Piazza Grande to face off with competitors from Sansepolcro, Tuscany.

Exploring Gubbio

Start your explorations on hillside **Piazza Grande** (to avoid the climb, take the free elevator at the junction of Via Repubblica and Via Baldassini, which runs daily 7:45am–7pm). After marveling at the airy view over the valley below, turn around to admire the rambling **Palazzo Ranghiasci** behind you, on the north side. That the facade resembles an 18th-century neoclassical British country house is no accident: A nobleman of the time married an English lady and brought her back to Gubbio, where she languished in homesickness before fleeing. To lure his wife back, the heartbroken duke commissioned an architect to rebuild the front of his palace in the latest British fashion, but to no avail—his bride never returned. Note that one of the Greek-style columns has been clumsily replaced with bricks—it needed patching after the Allies lobbed a shell into the piazza to dislodge Nazi occupiers at the end of World War II. Next head for the **Fountain of the Madmen** in Largo Bargello, a short walk west of the piazza along Via Consoli, but approach with care—it's said that if you circle the monument three times you are sure to go mad.

Steep, narrow lanes switchback up the hill to Gubbio's sturdy **Duomo** and fortresslike **Palazzo Ducale** at the top of the town, where church and

Festa dei Ceri celebrations outside the Palazzo dei Consoli in Gubbio.

state could keep an eye on the citizens below (you may also reach the Duomo and palazzo on another elevator off the east side of Piazza Grande). In 1472 Duke Frederico da Montefeltro commissioned for his palace the Gubbio Studiolo, a glorious room decorated with wood inlay; to see this treasure nowadays, however, you'd have to go to the Metropolitan Museum of Art in New York City.) What remains in the formal, painting-hung salons is less inspiring, though the classically proportioned Renaissance courtyard is beautiful (open Tuesday through Sunday, 8:30am to 7:30pm, 5€). As you approach the palace on Via Federico da Montefeltro, through a gate you'll see the **Botte dei Canonici** (Canon's Barrel), a humongous vessel capable of holding more than 5,000 gallons of wine. Monks in the monastery above, or so the story goes, could serve themselves by dipping a ladle through a trapdoor in the ceiling.

Museo del Palazzo dei Consoli ★★ MUSEUM   The former home of the town government is a solidly Gothic-looking palace, with crenellations, a tower, and an imposing stone staircase that seems to demand you climb up from Piazza Grande. The main hall, where the medieval commune met, houses the sleep-inducing town museum, where one prize stands out amid the old coins and bits of pottery: the seven **Eugubine Tables,** inscribed on bronze from 200 to 70 B.C., which provide the only existing record of the Umbri language transposed in Etruscan and Latin letters—in other words, ancient Umbria's Rosetta Stone. A local farmer turned up the tablets while plowing his fields in 1444, and city officials convinced him to sell them for 2 years' worth of grazing rights. Be sure to find the secret corridor that leads from the back of the ceramics room to the Pinacoteca upstairs, via the medieval toilets.

Piazza Grande. ☏ **075/927-4298.** 10€ adults, 8.50€ over 65, 5€ ages 7–25, free for 6 and under. Mon–Fri 10am–1pm and 3–6pm, Sat–Sun 10am–1:30pm and 2:30–6pm; closes at 5:30pm Nov–Mar.

Monte Igino ★ PARK/GARDEN   An open-air funicular, **Funivia Colle Eletto** (www.funiviagubbio.it; ☏ **075-927-3881**), whisks you in about 6 minutes to the top of this 908m (2,980-ft.) summit for yet more stupendous Umbrian views. On the ascent you can be glad you're not taking part in the May 15 **Corso dei Ceri,** when teams race up the mountainside carrying 15-foot-long wooden battering-rams called *ceri,* or "candles." The race is part of festivities honoring St. Ubaldo, the bishop who allegedly smooth-talked Frederick Barbarossa out of sacking the town in the 1150s. Ubaldo's corpse is up here, too, in a glass casket at the Basilica di Sant'Ubaldo, a 5-minute walk from the funicular stop.

Funicular leaves from Via San Girolamo. Round trip 5€ adults, 4€ ages 4–13. June daily 9:30am–1:15pm and 2:30–7pm; July and Aug daily 9am–8pm; early Sept daily 9:30am–7pm; late Sept Mon–Sat 9:30am–1:15pm and 2:30–7pm, Sun 9am–7pm; Oct daily 10am–1:15pm and 2:30–6pm; Nov–Feb Thurs–Tues 10am–1:15pm and 2:30–5pm; Mar daily 10am–1:15pm and 2:30–5:30pm (until 6pm Sun); Apr–May daily 10am–1:15pm and 2:30–6:30pm (until 7pm Sun).

Where to Stay & Eat in Gubbio

Grotta dell'Angelo ★ ITALIAN/UMBRIAN   A barrel-vaulted dining room where locals have been gathering for the past 700 years or so is the place to sit in winter, while warm-weather dining is on a vine-shaded terrace. Wherever you eat, enjoy homemade gnocchi and other pastas, followed by sausages and other meats roasted over the open fire—the whole roast chicken stuffed with fennel is especially delicious.
Via Gioia 47. www.grottadellangelo.it. © **075/927-1747.** Entrees 9€–14€. Wed–Mon 12:30–2:30pm and 7:30–11pm. Closed Jan 7–Feb 7.

Hotel Relais Ducale ★★★   Just off the Piazza Grande, this hotel is set in palace annexes of the Montefalco dukes, those great Umbrian Renaissance power-brokers. Extremely comfortable guest rooms are scattered over several levels, with highly polished floors and well-tended traditional furnishings that befit the royal surroundings. Some have barrel vaulting and a few open to terraces, though are all within easy reach of delightful patios and shady nooks. Proprietors Daniela and Sean offer lots of personal attention; they'll even pick you up at the train station in Fossato di Vico.
Via Galeotti 19. www.relaisducale.com. © **075/922-0157.** 30 units. 80€–140€. Rates include breakfast. **Amenities:** Bar; room service; Wi-Fi (free).

Taverna del Lupo ★★ UMBRIAN   Around 1220, or so the story goes, a ferocious wolf *(lupo)* was menacing the good people of Gubbio, devouring them the moment they stepped outside the town gates. St. Francis, then living a monkish life of contemplation in Gubbio, went to the beast's lair, tamed him, and led him back into the marketplace, where townsfolk agreed to feed him in return for good behavior. A charming fresco depicting Francis and the wolf is one of many artworks on the stone walls of these former cellars, where legend says the animal often popped in to eat. These days diners count on the refined surroundings for specialties like homemade tagliatelle with truffles or the kitchen's famous *faraona al ginepro,* guinea hen roasted with juniper berries.
Via Ansidei 21. www.tavernadellupo.it. © **075/927-4368.** Entrees 10€–18€. Daily noon–3pm and 7–10pm. Closed Jan 7–Feb 7.

A Side Trip to Urbino ★

One of the steepest hill towns in Italy, Urbino is a time-capsule of the Renaissance, a storybook compilation of towers, domes, and red-tile roofs. Though the glory days wound down about 500 years ago, this remote hill town is still prosperous and lively; you'll share the streets with students at Urbino's prestigious university. The only easy way to get here from Gubbio is by car, 66km (40 miles) northeast through mountainous terrain on the SP3. The trip takes a slow hour, but the landscape en route puts on quite a show, its rippling hills carpeted with fields and forests and topped with the occasional walled village. Stash your car in the large parking lot at Borgo del Mercatale (1.20€ per hr.), and then attack the steep cobblestone streets on foot.

Aside from the scenic hills, Urbino's main draws are all about art: It's the birthplace of Raphael, Renaissance painter of glorious frescos, and home to the outstanding art collection of Duke Frederico da Montefeltro.

Galleria Nazionale delle Marche Palazzo Ducale di Urbino ★★

MUSEUM   Wise and worldly Duke Federico da Montefeltro (1422–82) paced the halls of this palace and contemplated his vast holdings from the study window, all the while dreaming up some of the most enlightened ideals of the Renaissance. One of the palace's most enchanting rooms is that study, beautifully paneled with intarsia depicting classical and humanistic writers as well as great religious thinkers. The duke famously came up with the concept of *sprezzatura,* the ideal of maintaining grace under pressure. Duke Federico and his son, Guidobaldo, oversaw a court so enlightened that Baldassare Castiglione set his 1507 bestseller, *Book of the Courtier,* in the palace's Hall of Vigils. Father and son were also patrons of some of the great artists of their day, whose works now hang in the salons and staterooms. "Ideal City," attributed to Piero della Francesca, perfectly evokes the dukes' enlightened ideas; della Francesca's "Flagellation," another of the palace's treasures, is one of the Renaissance's finest accomplishments in perspective. Also look for Paolo Uccello's similarly masterful work of perspective, "The Profanation of the Host," a striking bit of 15th-century anti-Semitic propaganda depicting a Jewish pawnbroker attempting to cook the sacred communion wafer (believed to transform into the body of Christ during the Eucharist), as blood seeping under his door attracts bailiffs.

Piazza Duca Federico. www.gallerianazionalemarche.it. © **0722/322-625.** 8€. Mon 8:30am–2pm; Tues–Sun 8:30am–7:15pm.

Raphael's Birthplace ★ MUSEUM

One of the great artists of the High Renaissance (you can see his work at Cappella di San Severo in Perugia, p. 310, and his best efforts at the Vatican, p. 82) was born here in 1483. His earliest known work, a modest boyhood fresco, "Madonna and Child," is on one of the walls here in his childhood home. Compare this modest effort to his "Portrait of a Young Woman," in the nearby Palazzo Ducale (see above), which shows the genius of his mature style. The museum also holds works by Raphael's lesser-known father, Giovanni Santi, a court painter to the duke.

Via Rafaello 57. www.casaraffaello.com. 3€. Mar–Oct Mon–Sat 9am–1pm and 3–7pm, Sun 10am–1pm; Nov–Feb Mon–Sat 9am–2pm, Sun 10am–1pm.

WHERE TO EAT IN URBINO

Taverna degli Artisti ★ ITALIAN   These vaulted underground rooms, one with colorful frescoes, are the place to try *Strozzapretti con salmone, asparagi, funghi,* thick elongated pasta (the name means "priest choker") with a creamy sauce of salmon, asparagus, and mushrooms. It's an Urbino favorite that even locals claim is expertly done here. The other pastas and pizzas are excellent, too.

Via Bramante 52. ℂ **0722/2676.** Entrees 10€–15€. Daily 12:30–2:30pm and 7:30–10pm.

ASSISI ★★★

27km (17 miles) E of Perugia

St. Francis is still working miracles: His birthplace remains a lovely Umbrian hill town, despite a steady onslaught of visitors. Many pilgrims come to pay homage to Francis at the Basilica di San Francisco, and almost as many are drawn by Giotto's frescoes celebrating the life of the saint. You'll find a blend of romance and magic in Assisi's honey-colored stone, the quiet lanes, and the mists that rise and fall over the Val di Spoleto below town. With this saintly presence and so much pleasing ambience, Assisi is an essential stop on any Umbrian tour.

Essentials

ARRIVING   About 20 trains run daily from **Perugia** (25–30 min.). From **Florence** (2–3 hr.), trains run every 2 hours or so, though some require a transfer at Terontola. Trains arrive in the modern valley town of Santa Maria degli Angeli, about 5km (3 miles) from Assisi, with bus connections to Assisi every 20 minutes (1€); **taxis** are available for about 15€ to 20€.

The Basilica di San Francesco, resting place of St. Francis of Assisi.

The World's Favorite Saint

For Christian pilgrims, the magic of Assisi is all about St. Francis, one of the patron saints of Italy (along with Catherine of Siena, see p. 263). Founder of one of the world's largest monastic orders, Francis is generally considered to be just about the holiest person to walk the earth since Jesus.

Born to a wealthy merchant, Francis was a spoiled young man of his time, until he did an about-turn in his early 20s and dedicated himself to a life of poverty. His humility, love of animals, and invention of the Christmastime crèche scenes have all helped ensure his legend. Francis traveled as far as Egypt (in an unsuccessful attempt to convert the sultan and put an end to the Crusades), but he is most associated with the gentle countryside around Assisi, where he spent months praying and fasting in lonely hermitages.

By **car,** Assisi is 18km (11 miles) east of Perugia, off the SS75bis. The center's steep streets are off-limits to non-resident drivers. The best strategy is to **park** in Piazza Matteotti (1.15€ per hour), keep walking west, and finish at the basilica; it's all downhill. A dependable alternative is the Mojano multi-story garage (1.05€ first 2 hrs.; 1.45€/hr. thereafter) halfway up the hill from Piazza Giovanni Paolo II to Porta Nuova. Escalators whisk you into the center of town.

At least six **BusItalia Nord buses** (www.fsbusitalia.it; © 075/963-7001) connect Perugia with Assisi (50 min.) and five buses a day run between Assisi and **Gubbio** (1¾ hr.). **SULGA** (www.sulga.it; © 075/500-9641) runs at least two buses daily from **Rome** (3 hrs.), from Tiburtina train station and Fuimicino airport.

VISITOR INFORMATION The **tourist office** (www.comune.assisi.pg.it; © 075/812534) is in the Palazzo die Priori on Piazza del Comune. It's open daily in summer (8am–6:30pm) and winter (Mon–Sat 8am–2pm and 3–6pm; Sunday 9am–1pm). On Saturdays, the office leads a 2-hour tour around town for a look at Roman remains that include the Tempio di Minverva, an amphitheater, and a couple of lavish residences (book at the office and ask if the guide speaks English; 10€. The private websites **www.assisionline.com** and **www.assisiweb.com** also have good info. A good place to stock up on maps and guidebooks about Assisi (and anywhere else on earth) is the vintage shop **Zubboli** at Piazza del Comune 5 (© 075/812381; daily 8am–8pm), which also sells beautiful stationery and leather-bound journals.

Exploring Assisi

Assisi's geographical and civic heart is **Piazza del Comune,** with its 13th-century Palazzo del Capitano and the stately Corinthian columns of the Roman Tempio di Minerva guarding its northern fringe. The most atmospheric route to the basilica goes downhill from here along medieval Via Portica, which becomes Via Fortini and Via San Francesco before arriving at the main event. Some pilgrims like to end a visit with a walk or

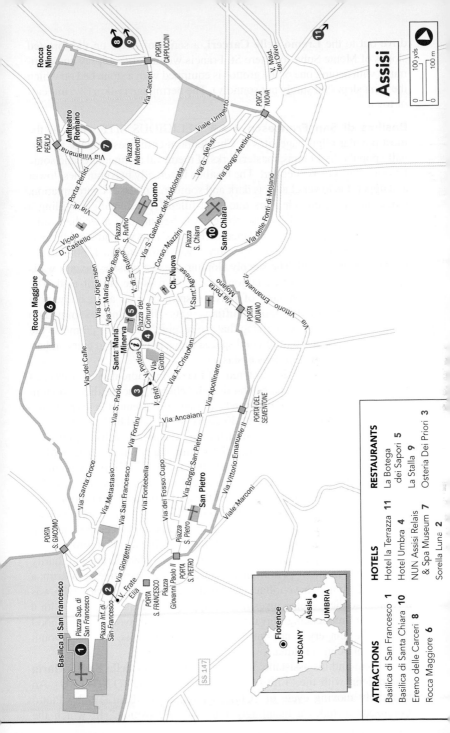

Assisi

ATTRACTIONS
Basilica di San Francesco **1**
Basilica di Santa Chiara **10**
Eremo delle Carceri **8**
Rocca Maggiore **6**

HOTELS
Hotel la Terrazza **11**
Hotel Umbra **4**
NUN Assisi Relais
& Spa Museum **7**
Sorella Luna **2**

RESTAURANTS
La Botega
dei Sapori **5**
La Stalla **9**
Osteria Dei Priori **3**

0   100 yds
0   100 m

drive out to the **Eremo delle Carceri,** a series of caves on the forested slopes of Monte Subasio where St. Francis would retire to pray and commune with nature; one of the grottos is equipped with a stone bed on which the saint slept (but surely not soundly). The hermitage is 4km (2½ mi) east of town

Basilica di San Francesco ★★★ RELIGIOUS SITE   One of the most popular pilgrimage sites in Christendom combines homage to eternally popular St. Francis, masterworks of medieval architecture, and some favorite works of Western art. The basilica is actually two churches, lower and upper; the lower church is dark and somber, a place of contemplation, while the upper church soars into light-filled Gothic vaults, instilling a sense of celebration. This assemblage was begun soon after the saint's death in 1226, under the guidance of Francis's savvy and worldly colleague, Brother Elias. The lower church was completed in 1230, and the upper church in 1280. The steeply sloping site just outside the city walls was previously used for executions and known as the Hill of Hell. The presence of the patron saint of Italy, in spirit as well as in body, now makes this one of Italy's most uplifting sights. His kindness, summed up in his saying, "For it is in giving that we receive," seems to permeate the soft gray stones, and the frescoed spaces move the devout to tears and art lovers to fits of near-religious ecstasy.

   The Lower Church   Entered off Piazza Inferiore di San Francesco (the lower of the two squares abutting the church), the basilica's bottom half is a cryptlike church that is indeed, first and foremost, a crypt, housing the stone **sarcophagus of St. Francis,** surrounded by four of his disciples. An almost steady stream of the faithful files past the monument, many on their knees. Inside is the saint's remarkably intact skeleton. Most saints of the Middle Ages fell victim to the purveyors of relics, who made enormous profit dispensing bones, a finger here, a toe there. It's said that Brother Elias had the foresight to seal the coffin in stone, and it remained undetected until 1818. The dimly lit atmosphere is greatly enlivened by the presence of many rich frescoes, including Simone Martini's action-packed "Life of St. Martin" in the **Cappella di San Martino** (1322–1326). Martini displays his flair for boldly patterned fabrics and familiarity with detailed manuscript illumination. Martini was also, like St. Martin, a knight, which may have influenced his depictions of the saint—who was a Roman soldier—being investitured, ripping his cloak to share it with a beggar, and renouncing chivalry and weaponry in favor of doing good deeds. The imagery is not out of keeping with Francis, who as a youth dreamed of being a soldier.

   Giotto and his assistants frescoed the **Cappella della Santa Maria Maddalena** with the "Life of St. Mary Magdalene" (1303–1309). An incredibly moving cycle of "Christ's Passion" (1316–1319) by Pietro Lorenzetti includes a hauntingly humane "Deposition," in which the young Sienese artist depicts a gaunt Christ and sorrowful Mary, displaying a naturalism and emotion not before seen in painting.

The Upper Church   Entering the light-filled interior of the Upper Church, you'll first encounter **scenes of the New Testament** by Cimabue, the last great painter of the Byzantine style; some critics say only the faded and vaguely surreal "Crucifixion" (1277) is his, and the rest are by his assistants. In any case, it's rather ironic he's here at all. The artist was infamous for his stubbornness and difficult character (in the *Divine Comedy*, Dante places him in Purgatory among the proud, adding that "Cimabue thought to hold the field of painting, and now Giotto hath the cry.") It's Giotto who famously holds court in this church, with his 28-part fresco cycle on **"The Life of St. Francis,"** completed in the 1290s. Even nonreligious viewers love the scenes of the saint removing his clothing to renounce material processions, marrying poverty (symbolized by a woman in rags), and preaching to the birds (the subject of ubiquitous postcards for sale). Assisi itself is the star in the panel in which a humble man spreads his cloak before Francis, with the sturdy, easily recognizable palaces of Piazza del Comune as a backdrop.

Piazza Superiore di San Francesco. www.sanfrancescoassisi.org. ⓒ **075/819001.** Free. Lower Church daily 6am–6:50pm; Upper Church daily 8:30am–6:50pm (churches close at 6pm Mar–Oct).

Basilica di Santa Chiara ★ CHURCH   One of the first followers of St. Francis was a young woman, Chiara (Clare, in English), daughter of a count and countess, who was so swept away by the teachings of the zealot that she allowed him to cut her hair and dress her in sackcloth. She founded the order of the Poor Dames (now known as Poor Clares), whose members continue to renounce material possessions, and her remains lie in this vast, stark church on full view, her face covered in wax. Also in this church, the **Oratorio del Crocifisso** houses the venerated 12th-century crucifix from which the figure of Christ allegedly spoke to St. Francis and asked him to rebuild his church (the institution had by then become mired in corruption and warfare). As Clare lay ill on Christmas Eve 1252, she allegedly voiced regrets that she would not be able to attend services in the new Basilica di San Francisco. Suddenly, in a vision, she saw and heard the Mass clear as a bell and in color, a miracle for which in 1958 she was named the patron saint of television.

> **Dress Appropriately**
>
> San Francesco and Santa Chiara have a strict dress code. Entrance is *forbidden* to those wearing shorts or miniskirts or showing bare shoulders. You also must remain silent and cannot take photographs in the Upper Church of San Francesco.

Piazza Santa Chiara. www.assisisantachiara.it. ⓒ **075/812282.** Free. Daily 6:30am–noon and 2–7pm (6pm in winter).

Rocca Maggiore ★★ CASTLE This civic show of might built of bleached yellow stone perches atop a steep hillside very high above Assisi. Some claim that a sharp-eyed observer can see all the way to the Mediterranean on a clear day, but that's probably a delusion induced by the climb through narrow medieval lanes. Hyperbole aside, views across the Umbrian plain below are wonderful—much more exhilarating than the dull displays of costumes and weapons in the restored keep and soldiers' quarters. Skip going inside; enjoy the views, and spend the admission fee on a glass of wine when you get back down.

Piazzale delle Libertà Comunali, at the ends of Via della Rocca, Via del Colle, and Vicolo San Lorenzo off Via Porta Perlici. ☏ **075/8138680.** 6€ adults; 4€ students, ages 8–18; free for ages 7 and under. Daily June–Aug 10am–8pm; Sept 10am–7:30; Apr–May and Oct 10am–7pm; Nov–Feb 10am–4:30pm; Mar 10am–5:30pm.

Where to Stay in Assisi

Especially from Easter to fall, never show up in Assisi without a hotel reservation. Don't even *think* of showing up without a reservation on pilgrim-thronged **church holidays** or the **Calendimaggio,** a spring celebration the first weekend (starting Thursday) after May 1, with processions, medieval contests of strength and skill, and late-night partying—all in 14th-century costume, of course. At these times you may wind up stuck overnight in one of the bus-pilgrimage facilities 4km (2½ miles) away in Santa Maria degli Angeli.

Hotel la Terrazza ★★ The best of two worlds come together here in the countryside just outside the town walls—the basilica and other sights are a 20-minute walk away, while a pool, garden, and green surrounds provide a break from Assisi's stony streets and squares. The nicest rooms are in a low-slung outbuilding facing lawns on one side and balcony views of the valley on the other, but those in a hotel section also open to gardens or balconies. Room decor is functionally comfortable, enlivened with colorful reproductions of Giotto's basilica murals over the beds, no doubt instilling dreams of doing saintly deeds.

Via Fratelli Canonichetti 1. www.laterrazzahotel.it. ☏ **075/812368.** 41 units. 80€–120€ double. Rates include breakfast. **Amenities:** Restaurant; bar; pool; spa; Wi-Fi (free).

Hotel Umbra ★ Assisi lodgings just don't get any homier than the Laudenzi family's traditional little inn, down a tiny alley from Piazza del Comune. A gate opens into a shady patio, and beyond are comfortable, if a bit outdated, guest rooms with vaulted ceilings, fresco fragments, and other historic remnants here and there, all nicely furnished with old-fashioned armoires and dressers. Views over rooftops to the valley below unfold through the tall windows, from the private terraces off a few choice rooms and the rooftop terrace. The dining room is one of the most pleasant places to eat in town and extends into a lovely garden.

Via Delgli Archi 6 (off west end of Piazza del Comune). www.hotelumbra.it. ☏ **075/812240.** 24 units. 85€–115€ double. Rates include breakfast. Closed mid-Jan–Easter. **Amenities:** Restaurant; bar; babysitting; concierge; room service; Wi-Fi (free).

NUN Assisi Relais & Spa Museum ★★   Here's a dramatic change of pace from Assisi's heavily medieval aura: A contemporary redo of a centuries-old convent, offering handsome guest quarters with all-white surfaces and bursts of color, accented with stone walls and arches and boldly turned out with Eames chairs, laminate tables, and high-tech lighting. A two-level suite with a hanging sleeping loft is focused on a massive 13th-century fresco of saints in the wilderness, bound to instill nighttime visions. A breakfast buffet and other meals are served in the refectory, and downstairs are pleasures the former tenants could never have dreamed of: two pools, saunas and steam rooms, and a state-of-the-art spa.

Eremo delle Carceri 1A. www.nunassisi.com. ℰ **075/815-5150.** 18 units. Doubles from 320€. Rates include breakfast. **Amenities:** Restaurant; bar; concierge; indoor pools; room service; sauna; steam room; spa; Wi-Fi (free).

Sorella Luna ★   Recent renovations have given this 15th-century palace a contemporary slant, with a flower-filled terraced garden and glassed-in atriums. In the bright guest rooms, stone walls and wood beams offset the modern furnishings and tiled baths. The name refers to Clare (Sorella Luna), the follower of St. Francis whose church is on the other end of town. The Basilica di San Francisco is just down the street.

Via Frate Ella 5. www.hotelsorellaluna.it. ℰ **075/816194.** 13 units. From 95€ double. Rates include breakfast. **Amenities:** Wi-Fi (free).

Villa Zuccari ★★★   If you have a car, consider visiting Assisi from smaller nearby towns, like the appealing wine village of Montefalco (see "High and Low, p. 330), about 20 minutes south. This old estate, in the Zuccari family since the 16th century, will make you feel like a guest in a gracious Italian home and is a nice place to relax while touring the region—you'll also be within easy reach of Spello, Perugia, Trevi, Spoleto, Todi, and other Umbrian towns. Airy, light-filled bedrooms are large and comfortably equipped with armchairs, king-size beds, nice antiques, and big marble-sheathed bathrooms. Palm-shaded gardens surround the pool, and welcoming lounges are filled with books and pottery. Dinners are served in a vaulted room glistening with terracotta tiles.

Locanda San Luca (just east of Montefalco). www.villazuccari.com. ℰ **0742/399-402.** 34 units. Doubles from 120€. Rates include breakfast. **Amenities:** Restaurant; bar; pool; Wi-Fi (free).

Where to Eat in Assisi

Several of Assisi's restaurants and bars serve a local flatbread called *torta al testa,* often split and stuffed with cheeses, sausages, and vegetables (spinach is popular). It's a meal in itself and a fast and cheap lunch. **La Botega dei Sapori,** a wine and food shop right on Piazza del Commune (no. 34) (ℰ **075/812204**), serves platters of local meats and cheese and a delicious porchetta sandwich, accompanied by one of the excellent wines and served in a cozy tasting room or at a table on the piazza; seating is limited, but if you wish, they'll fix a snack plate for you to take back to your hotel. They also ship wines.

La Stalla ★★ GRILL/UMBRIAN   The term "old barn" isn't often associated with good dining, but a meal in these rustic and rather raucous converted livestock stalls, with stone walls and low ceilings, can be the highlight of a trip to Assisi (even the servers seem to be having a good time). The pleasant, 15-minute walk out here will work up an appetite, so begin with the *assaggini di torta al testo,* samplers of Assisian flatbread stuffed with cheese, meat, and vegetables, then move through the selection of pastas to the simple servings of steak, pork and sausage skewers, chicken, and even potatoes that come off the grill. House wines complement the meals, and you can dine on a terrace in good weather.
Santuario della Carceri 24, 1½km (less than 1 mi) from center, direction Eremo. www. fontemaggio.it. ℭ **075/812317.** Entrees 8€–13€. Thurs–Tues 12:30–2:30pm and 7:30–10pm.

Osteria Dei Priori ★★★ UMBRIAN   With cool jazz playing softly in the background and warm-hued brick vaults soaring above a red accent wall, it doesn't take long to feel at home at this appealing spot below Piazza Communale. The small, daily changing menu is just as enticing, with an emphasis on Umbrian classics made with the freshest local ingredients. Garden-grown eggplant appears in a delicious flan with *scamorza* (cow's milk cheese), and homemade *maccheroni* is served *alla Norcia,* with sausage and a light cream sauce. This welcoming place stays open through the winter, when many other Assisi restaurants close.
Via Giotto 4. ℭ **0329/612-1742.** Entrees 8€–15€. Wed–Mon 12:30–3pm and 7–11pm.

A Side Trip to Spello ★

14km (9 miles) S of Assisi

There are a couple of couple of compelling reasons to make the short trip down SS75 from Assisi to this little hill town of pink and honey-colored stone, lying on the flanks of Monte Subasio. For one thing, it's beguilingly pretty, unspoiled, and relatively undiscovered, with none of the crowds that descend upon its more famous neighbor. Then there's Pinturicchio, or "The Little Painter," who created one of Umbria's great masterpieces, color-saturated frescoes of the life of Christ tucked away in the Cappello Baglioni (see below). The **tourist office** in Piazza Matteotti (www. comune.spello.pg.it; ℭ **0742/301-009**) is open daily 9:30am–12:30pm and 3:30–5:30pm.

Cappella Baglioni ★★ CHURCH/MUSEUM   Spello's powerful Baglioni family decided to use this side chapel in the Santa Maria Maggiore church to generate some good press, and maybe some goodwill with the Almighty. After the Red Wedding in June 1500—when one branch of the family turned against the other in a murderous bloodbath—survivor

The flower-lined streets of Spello.

Troilio Bagnoli commissioned Pinturrichio to paint scenes from the boyhood of Christ. The color-filled frescoes are enchanting, filled with rich architectural detail and Umbrian landscapes, with some sly cynical commentaries on medieval life (notice the church treasurer with the bursting money bags witnessing the Annunciation). Pinturrichio himself appears in a portrait in the Annunciation scene, and Troilo Baglioni, looking unscathed, shows up in the Disputation in the Temple. The chapel has been closed during restoration of the church of Santa Maria Maggiore but is scheduled to be open in 2020.

Piazza Matteotti. Free. Daily 8:30am–noon and 3–7pm.

WHERE TO STAY & EAT IN SPELLO

Hotel Palazzo Bocci ★★   If rooms at the inns in Assisi are full, settle into Spello in style at the palace of a 15th-century merchant, converted in the 18th and 19th centuries to its fairly splendid current state. The vaulted salons are suitably regal, filled with antiques and trompe l'oeil detailing, while guest rooms retain all the character you'd expect from historic surroundings in which frescoes and marble mantelpieces are standard issue. Views from rooms in the rear are especially refreshing, overlooking a large garden and terrace to the valley below.

Via Cavour 17. www.palazzobocci.com. ℂ **0742/301-021.** 130€–160€ double. Rates include breakfast. **Amenities:** Restaurant; bar; Wi-Fi (free).

high AND LOW

For sheer picturesqueness, few hill towns in Umbria can match proud **Todi,** 45km (28 mi) northwest of Spello. At the top of the town is the finest square in Umbria, an assemblage of 12th- to 14th-century palaces and the Duomo, with belvederes that provide soaring views of the rolling Umbrian countryside and the Tiber Valley below.

Montefalco, 19km (11 mi) southwest of Spello on SR316, tops a hill above the Valle Umbra, with the five-sided Piazza del Commune at the highest point in town. Surrounding vineyards yield Sagrantino reds; the **Strada del Sagrantino** wine trail office, Piazza del Comune 17 (www.montefalcodoc.it; ✆ **0742/ 378490**) can set you up with maps and winery tour info. Art lovers come here for a charming mid-15th-century fresco cycle of the life of St. Francis by Florentine master Benozzo Gozzoli, in the **Museo di San Francesco,** Via Ringhiera Umbra 6 (www.museodimontefalco.it; ✆ **0742/ 379598;** 7€; Apr–Oct daily 10:30am– 6pm [to 7pm Aug]; Nov–Mar Wed–Sun 10:30am–1pm and 2:30–5pm).

Rather than clinging to a hillside, **Bevagna,** 8km (5 mi) north of Montefalco on SP443, nestles on the floor of the Valle Umbra beside the River Teverone. Inside sturdy gates, Bevagna seems firmly locked into the Middle Ages, with the simply ornamented churches of **San Michele Arcangelo** and **San Silvestro** facing each other across Piazza Silvestri (both usually open 9am–1pm and 4–7pm). The mosaic floor of a ruined bath complex on Via Terme Romana, with a swirl of octopi and other sea creatures, is a reminder of the town's prosperity as a Roman outpost on the Via Flaminia; the ruins are part of the **Museo Civico,** Corso Giacomo Matteotti 70 (www.sistemamuseo.it, ✆ **0742/360081;** 7€; Apr–Sept Fri–Sun 10:30am–1pm and 3–6pm, Oct–Mar Fri–Sun 10:30am–1pm and 2:30–5pm).

Il Molino ★★ UMBRIAN   A 13th-century olive mill has been bringing gourmands to Spello since the 1960s and still delights with its inspired use of local ingredients. Beef and lamb from the valley below is grilled over the fireplace, while ham from Norcia, asparagus and herbs from the mountains, and even beans from nearby farms show up in such pastas as cappelletti with beans and onion sauce and *zuppa di faro macinato,* soup with barley, beans, and cabbage. It's hard to pass up the chance to enjoy a meal in the series of arched, low-ceilinged rooms inside, though a seat on the terrace comes with a view of small-town life.
Piazza Matteotti. ✆ **0742/651-305.** Entrees 10€–24€. Daily 12:30–2:45pm and 7:30–10pm.

SPOLETO ★★

63km (39 miles) SE of Perugia

Spoleto feels like the center of the cultured world in June, when the **Festival dei Due Mondi** (a.k.a. **Spoleto Festival**) draws performers and

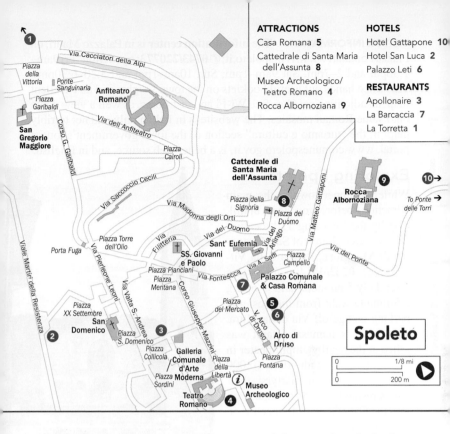

ATTRACTIONS
Casa Romana **5**
Cattedrale di Santa Maria
  dell'Assunta **8**
Museo Archeologico/
  Teatro Romano **4**
Rocca Albornoziana **9**

HOTELS
Hotel Gattapone **10**
Hotel San Luca **2**
Palazzo Leti **6**

RESTAURANTS
Apollonaire **3**
La Barcaccia **7**
La Torretta **1**

audiences from all over the world. For most of the year, though, Spoleto is just another lovely Umbrian hill town, a pleasant warren of steep streets and airy piazzas lined with artifacts from the Roman past and prosperous Middle Ages, including one of Italy's most beautifully situated cathedrals.

Essentials

ARRIVING   Spoleto is a main **rail** station on the Rome-Ancona line, and 16 daily trains from **Rome** stop here (about 1½ hr.). From **Perugia,** take one of the 20 daily trains to Foligno (25 min.) to transfer to this line for the final 20-minute leg. From outside the station, you can take bus A, B, or C to Piazza Carducci on the edge of the old town, but it's an easy 10-minute walk.

By **car,** approach town on the old Roman Via Flaminia, now the SS3. Three lots/garages are at the base of the hill: Spoletosfera, Posterna, and Ponzianina are all connected to sights in the old town above via escalators, moving sidewalks, and elevators. Parking is about 1€ per hour; take a ticket upon entering and pay in a machine upon leaving. Hotels will help you arrange long-term parking.

VISITOR INFORMATION The **information center** is in Palazzo Mauri, on Piazza Fontana (www.visitspoleto.it; © **0743/220773;** open Mon–Fri 9am–1:30pm and 2–7pm; Sat 9am–1pm; Sun 10am–1pm and 3:30–6:30pm). The office hands out useful booklets on the town's sights and an excellent map; an adjoining café has free Wi-Fi and restrooms, as well a view down onto some Roman mosaics. The website is in Italian only and not terribly helpful; the "turismo e cultura" section of the town government's tourist portal, www.comunespoleto.gov.it, is a better web source, and in English.

Exploring Spoleto

While the upper town is the main attraction, before you head uphill, stop by the imposing 11th-century Romanesque church of **San Gregorio di Maggiore,** Piazza della Vittoria (© **0743/44140;** admission free; daily 8am–noon and 4–6pm), a 5-minute walk from the Posterna parking garage off Via della Mura. The church's namesake saint was killed at the nearby amphitheater in A.D. 304, along with some 10,000 other lesser-known martyrs; their bones reside beneath the altar. Pop into the Capella degli Innocenti, on the left side of the portico, to see a fresco depicting Spoleto as it looked in the 16th century (little has changed since then). Across the piazza, a gated staircase, open most mornings, leads down to a platform where you can view **Ponte Sanguinario,** a massive 1st-century travertine bridge 24 meters (79 feet) long,

Cattedrale di Santa Maria Assunta in Spoleto.

and 4.5 meters (15 feet) wide, which over the centuries was buried in sediment from the stream it once crossed.

Just to the south, off the busy SS3 toward Terni and a 10-minute walk from the Spoletosfera parking garage, is the remarkable 12th-century church of **San Pietro ex Moenia,** set atop a monumental stone staircase. There's no need to go inside, but you can easily spend half an hour contemplating New Testament scenes and a complex catechism of Christian symbols on the church's remarkable Romanesque façade—Christ washing the feet of his disciples, deer and snakes, foxes and crows, holy men in little boats, all charmingly rendered by medieval sculptors.

Return to Posterna and get on the handy **moving walkway** (Percorso Meccanizzato) that runs deep beneath the historic center. Its upper terminus, at **Piazza Campello,** is near the Duomo and the Rocca; other exits along the way connect via elevator to most of the important sights in town. A similar system of escalators runs up the hill from the Ponzianina parking lot to the Rocca, with exits at the Duomo and other sights. **Piazza del Mercato,** the probable site of the old Roman forum, is a bustling spot in the Upper Town lined with grocers and fruit vendors' shops.

Casa Romana ★ HISTORIC HOME   As a stop on the busy Via Flaminia route and an important wine supplier, Spoletium was fairly prosperous in the Roman world. Enough of this patrician's home remains, including frescoes and mosaics, to give an idea of what the good life was like for a Roman occupant in the 1st century A.D. The resident was obviously well-to-do, though there's no proof for the claim that it was Vespasia Polla, the mother of the Emperor Vespasian.

Via di Visiale. (C) **0743/40255.** 3€ adults, 2€ ages 15–25 and 65 and over, 1€ children 7–14, free for children 6 and under. Wed–Mon 10:30am–1:30pm and 2–5:30pm.

Cattedrale di Santa Maria dell'Assunta ★★ CATHEDRAL   Spoleto's almost playfully picturesque cathedral was consecrated in 1098, barely 40 years after Frederick Barbarossa, Holy Roman Emperor, razed the entire town in retaliation for the citizens' lack of support in his ongoing wars against the papacy. The church seems to defy the brutality of that catastrophe, set in a broad piazza at the bottom of a long leisurely cascade of steps. White marble and golden mosaics on the dazzling facade are framed against a gentle backdrop of a forested hill. Inside, the apse is graced with frescoes of the "Life of the Virgin," largely from the brush of Filippo Lippi, one of the more colorful characters of his time. An ordained priest, Filippo shirked his duties and was eventually given permission to paint full-time. Though he worked frequently and was a favorite of the Medicis, he was chronically impoverished, supposedly because he spent so much money on women. The commission to come to Spoleto must have been a plum for the artist, then close to 60. His engaging scenes of the Virgin being visited by the Archangel and holding her sweet-looking infant betray nothing of the turbulence in his life—he was fighting to get dispensation to marry a young nun, Lucrezia Buti, who had borne his son, Filippino Lippi (who would soon match his father's greatness as a painter). Both Lippis appear in the Dormition of the Virgin scene, Filippo wearing a white habit with young Filippino, as an angel, in front of him. Fillippo died before he completed the frescoes; his assistants finished the task. The cause of his death was suspected to be poison, perhaps administered by Lucrezia's family or yet another paramour. He is buried beneath a monument on the right side of the transept, which his son Filippino designed. The Cappella delle Reliquie (Reliquary Chapel), on the left aisle, holds a rare treasure—a letter written and signed by St. Francis. (Assisi has his only other bona fide signature.)

Piazza del Duomo. © **0743/218620.** Free. Daily 8:30am–7pm (until 6pm Nov–Mar).

Museo Archeologico/Teatro Romano ★ MUSEUM/RUINS

Spoleto had the good fortune to flourish through the Dark Ages and the Middle Ages—which meant that most of the Roman city was quarried or built over. In 1891 it was discovered that the monastery of St. Agata had been built atop this splendid ancient theater. Thoroughly restored in the 1950s, the theater is an evocative performance venue, often used during the Spoleto Festival. Much of the original orchestra flooring is intact, as is an elaborate drainage system (installed for flushing out the blood of slain animals and martyrs). Busts and statuary that once adorned the theater are on display in the adjoining Museo Archeologico. *Tip:* You can view the theater for free from the east end of Piazza della Libertà.

Via di Sant'Agata 18A. © **0743/223277.** 4€ adults, 2€ ages 18–25, free for ages 17 and under. Daily 8:30am–7:30pm.

Rocca Albornoziana ★★ CASTLE

Cardinal Albornoz, a power-hungry zealot tasked with rebuilding and strengthening the papal states, arrived in Spoleto in the mid-14th century and commissioned the Umbrian architect Matteo Gattapone to build a fortress. The site was perfect—atop a high hill above the town and, as history would prove, virtually impregnable. The walled-and-moated castle became famous in the 20th century as one of Italy's most secure prisons, where members of the Red Brigades terrorist organization were routinely incarcerated. (The fortunate ones might have had a view through their cell windows of the majestic **Ponte delle Torri**—see "Getting Outdoors," p. 336). The current occupant of the fortress is the **Museo Nazionale del Ducato di Spoleto** (© **0743/223055**), a collection of sarcophagi, mosaics, and statuary so numbing that you needn't feel guilty about missing it and saving the entrance fee. (There's also a highly reputed school here that trains students in the craft of restoring books and manuscripts, but that's off-limits to the public.) You can walk around the Rocca grounds, no admission fee required, to enjoy spectacular views of the town and Umbrian countryside—and it's an easy trip up to these heights, via a series of escalators and elevators.

> ### Spoleto's Big Bash
>
> Spoleto's be-all and end-all annual event bridges the end of June and early July. The **Spoleto Festival** (www.festivaldispoleto.it) offers 3 weeks of world-class drama, music, and dance held in evocative spaces like an open-air restored Roman theater and the piazza fronting the Duomo. A secondary **Spoleto Estate** season runs from just after the festival through September.

Piazza Campello. © **0743/224952.** 7.50€ adults, 3.75€ ages 15–25, free for ages 17 and under. Tues–Sun 9:30am–6pm (Apr–Oct, also Mon 9:30am–1:30pm).

Where to Stay in Spoleto

Accommodations are tight during the Spoleto Festival; reserve by March if you want to find a good, central room.

Hotel Gattapone ★ From the street, this hideaway beneath the Rocca Albornozina looks like a relatively modest 19th-century villa. But step inside and all is polished wood, free-floating staircases, and leather couches, with windows overlooking the Ponte delle Torre and green Monteluco hillsides. There's a 1960s Antonioni-film feel to the place. Guest rooms have slightly dated but well-maintained contemporary furnishings mixed with traditional pieces, and huge bay windows. Some guests comment that the air-conditioning is vintage, too. Anyone with mobility issues should know there's no elevator, and rooms and lounges are set on several levels.

Via del Ponte 6. www.hotelgattapone.it. ✆ **0743/223-447.** 15 units. Doubles from 90€. Rates include breakfast. **Amenities:** Bar; Wi-Fi (free).

Hotel San Luca ★★ A 19th-century tannery at the far edge of the city next to the Roman walls lends itself well to its current incarnation. A book-lined lounge, where canaries chirp in an antique cage and a fire crackles in cold months, faces a large courtyard, and so do many rooms; others overlook a rose garden to the side. The unusually large quarters are all different, a mix of traditional and contemporary pieces with a smattering of antiques, plus extremely large and well-equipped marble bathrooms. Sights and restaurants are about a 5-minute walk away, and the attentive staff will map out a route that involves the least amount of climbing. The easy-to-reach in-house garage is a real rarity in Spoleto.

Via Interna delle Mura 21. www.hotelsanluca.com. ✆ **0743/223-399.** 35 units. 100€–150€ double. Rates include breakfast. **Amenities:** Bar; babysitting; bikes; concierge; room service; Wi-Fi (fee).

Palazzo Leti ★★ An entrance through a Renaissance garden that opens to the Tessino gorge announces that this beautifully restored 13th-century palace of the Leti family is a pretty special place. Views of the gorge and green Monteluco hills are the focal point of most rooms, though a few overlook a medieval alley that has its own charm; all have period furniture and rich fabrics, plus couches and armchairs in the larger rooms and wood beams, granite hearths, and vaulted ceilings throughout. Anna Laura and Giampolo, who restored the palace from a dilapidated pile, are a friendly presence and provide all sorts of helpful advice.

Via degli Eremiti 10. www.palazzoleti.com. ✆ **0743/224930.** 12 units. 120€–200€ double. Rates include breakfast. **Amenities:** Bar; bikes; spa; Wi-Fi (free).

Where to Eat in Spoleto

For some gastro-shopping, visit **Bartolomei Orvieto** at 97 Corso Cavour (www.oleificiobartolomei.it; ✆ **0743/344550**), where you can sample the products before buying. **Colder Gelateria** (✆ **0743/235015;** daily

12:30pm–midnight) serves some of the best gelato (notably the "bread and chocolate" flavor) in Umbria, created by local artisans Crispini.

Apollonaire ★ UMBRIAN   The low wood ceilings, stone walls, and beams are traditional holdovers from a 12th-century Franciscan monastery, but the menu is innovative and adventurous. Dishes rely on fresh local ingredients and traditional recipes but have that extra twist: *Strangozzi* (the local long, rectangular wheat pasta) is topped with a pungent sauce of cherry tomatoes and mint; herb-roasted rabbit is served with black olive sauce; and pork filet mignon is topped with a sauce of pecorino cheese and pears soaked in Rosso di Montefalco.

Via Sant'Agata 14 (near Piazza della Libertà). www.ristoranteapollinare.it. ☏ **0743/223256.** Entrees 12€–24€. Wed–Mon 12:30–3pm and 7:30–10:30pm. Closed Feb.

La Barcaccia ★ UMBRIAN   Despite the name (the "Old Boat"), these brightly lit rooms are set on dry land near the top of the town—and, except for some Adriatic fish choices, the menu is firmly landlocked in Umbrian classics. This is the place to strangle the priest, that is, enjoy the *strangozzi alla spoletina* (with peppery tomato sauce), named for rebellious clergy who broke with the papacy in the 14th century. A good choice of vegetarian dishes includes *scamorza,* a cow's milk cheese similar to mozzarella, baked with radicchio.

Piazza Fratelli Bandiera 4. www.ristorantelabarcaccia.it. ☏ **0743/225082.** Entrees 9€–16€. Wed–Mon 12:30–2:30pm and 7–10:30pm.

La Torretta ★★ UMBRIAN   In two welcoming rooms in a medieval tower, brothers Stefano and Elio Salvucci extend a genuine welcome and a nice selection of Umbrian dishes. The *tris di antipasti al tartufo estivo* (trio of truffle-based appetizers) is a memorable way to work up to beautifully seasoned pork or beef grilled over a wood fire. The kitchen also makes a light-as-air truffle omelet, a memorable break from heavier *secondi.*

Via Filitteria 43. www.trattorialatorretta.com. ☏ **0743/44954.** Entrees 9€–16€. Mon, Wed–Sat 12:30–2:30pm and 7:15–10pm, Sun noon–3pm.

Hiking Around Spoleto

Climbing Spoleto's steep streets is exercise in itself, but if you want to stretch your legs a bit more, try the well-marked 6km (4-mile) scenic walk along the **Giro dei Condotti.** The route begins just below the **Rocca** (p. 326) and starts out with a bang—a vertigo-inducing crossing of the **Ponte delle Torri,** a 232m- (760 ft.) long aqueduct built in the 13th century on Roman foundations. Its arches span a deep, verdant gorge, 90m (295 ft.) down to the Tessino river. From there the trail crosses a forested hillside, then descends through olive groves into the valley. The only gear you'll need for the fairly easy trek are comfortable walking shoes and a camera.

ORVIETO ★★

87km (54 miles) W of Spoleto, 86km (53 miles) SW of Perugia

Walking through the streets of Orvieto, you might be pleased to discover that nothing much has changed in the past 500 years. Adding to the magic is what might be Italy's most beautiful cathedral, covered in dazzling mosaics and statuary and rising above an airy piazza. The final coup de grace is the fact that the entire town is set atop a volcanic outcropping some 315m (1,033 ft.) above the green countryside. This impenetrable perch ensured that Etruscan "Velzna" was among the most powerful members of the *dodecapoli* (Etruscan confederation of 12 cities). The lofty setting continues to make Orvieto seem a world apart.

Exploring Orvieto's narrow cobbled lanes.

Essentials

ARRIVING Fourteen **trains** on the main **Rome-Florence** line stop at Orvieto daily (1 hr., 45 min. from Florence; 1 hr., 20 min. from Rome). From **Perugia,** take the train to Terontola (16 trains daily) to transfer to this line heading south toward Rome (1¼ hr. total train time). Orvieto makes a convenient stopover on a train trip between Rome and Florence; you can store bags at the Welcome Center (www.orvieto viva.com; ✆ **0763/300-480**) behind the train station in the Piazza della Pace (3€ per large bag for 4 hours, 15€ for 24 hours, open 9am to 6pm). Orvieto's **station** is in the valley, in Orvieto Scalo, but right across the street from the station, there's a **funicular** (www.atcterni.it; 1.30€, ascending every 10 min. (8am–8:30pm) to hilltop Orvieto. It's an easy, level 10-minute walk from the upper terminus to the Duomo and other sights in the historic center, and a free shuttle bus runs to and from Piazza Duomo.

Orvieto is easy to reach by **car:** It's right by the A1. The main link to the rest of Umbria is the SS448 to Todi (40 min.). There's a large free parking lot behind the train station off Piazza della Pace, so you can drop off your car and take the funicular up to town; if you want to get a bit closer, there's a garage at Campo della Fiera, just outside the Porta Romana, which is connected by an elevator/escalator system up to Piazza San Giovanni or Piazza Ranieri. Parking lots on the perimeter of the upper town charge about 1.50€ an hour.

VISITOR INFORMATION   The **tourist office** is opposite the Duomo at Piazza Duomo 24 (www.comune.orvieto.tr.it; © **0763/341772**). It's open Monday to Friday 8am to 2pm and 4 to 7pm, Saturday and Sunday 10am to 1pm and 3:30 to 6pm.

Exploring Orvieto

Life in Orvieto transpires along the animated **Corso Cavour,** cutting through the center of town. If you take the funicular up from the lower town, you'll begin your walk through Orvieto at the eastern end of the street. In the very center of town rises the **Torre del Moro,** a 13th-century show of civic might that provides views across all the territory the medieval city controlled, stretching east to the Apennines and west to the Mediterranean. To enjoy those views today, you'll take an elevator and then climb up 171 steps (3€; open daily, May–Aug 10am–8pm, Mar–Apr and Sept–Oct 10am–7pm; Nov–Feb 10:30am–1pm). The tower's bell is a familiar sound to locals—it has rung every 15 minutes for the past 700 years. Just to the north is **Piazza del Popolo,** where the Capitano del Popolo (Captain of the People) ruled from the formidable, crenellated Palazzo del Popolo. The square is filled with market stalls on Thursday and Saturday mornings. **Via del Duomo** leads south from the tower to Orvieto's masterwork, one of the most celebrated cathedrals in Italy.

Orvieto's other great wonder is the volcanic plug upon which it sits. To look at the city's tufa foundations, take a hike along the *rupe,* a path that encircles the base of the cliff. (The tourist office can supply a map.) A landmark along the path is the **Necropoli Etrusca di Crocifisso del Tufo** (Etruscan Necropolis), where ancient Etruscan tombs lie in a gridlike pattern in subterranean caverns (3€; daily 8:30am–5:30pm). You can also stroll along the high ramparts that fringe the edges of town. Some of the most accessible are on the west side, just past Sant'Agostino church.

Duomo ★★ CATHEDRAL   Orvieto's pièce de résistance is a mesmerizing assemblage of spikes and spires, mosaics and marble statuary—and that's just the facade. The rest of the bulky-yet-elegant church is banded in black and white stone and seems to perch miraculously on the edge of the cliffs that surround the town. The church is wider at the front than at the back, designed to create the optical illusion upon entering that it is longer than it actually is. The facade has been compared to a medieval altarpiece, and it reads like an illustrated Catechism. On the four broad marble panels that divide the surface, Sienese sculptor and architect Lorenzo Maitani (who more or less designed the church) and others carved scenes from the Old and New Testament. On the far left is the story

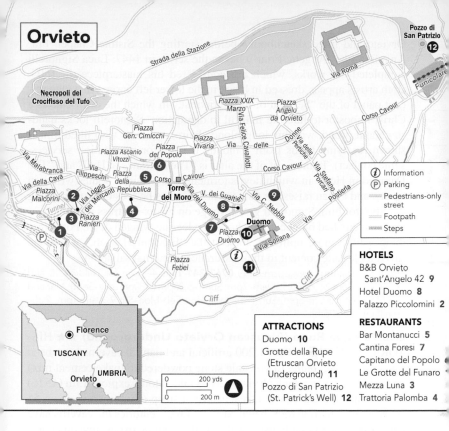

of creation, with Eve making an appearance from Adam's rib; on the far right, Christ presides over the Last Judgment, as the dead shuffle out of their sarcophagi to await his verdict. Prophets and the Apostles surround a huge rose window, and Mary appears in lush mosaics inlaid in fields of gold.

Capella del Corporale In 1263, a Bohemian priest, Peter of Prague, found himself doubting transubstantiation, the sacrament in which the communion bread, or host, is transformed into the body of Christ during mass. He went to Rome to pray on St. Peter's tomb that his faith be strengthened and, stopping in Bolsena, just below Orvieto, was saying Mass when the host began to bleed, dampening the corporal, or altar cloth. Pope Urban IV had the cloth brought to him in Orvieto, and a few decades later, Pope Nicholas IV ordered the cathedral built to house the relic. Frescoes in the chapel tell the story of the miracle, and the exquisite enamel reliquary that once held the cloth remains in place.

Cappella San Brizio The cathedral's other treasure is one of the Renaissance's greatest fresco cycles. Its themes are lofty—temptation, salvation, damnation, resurrection—yet the scenes are rich in everyday humanity. These frescoes allegedly inspired Michelangelo, who came to

Orvieto and filled sketchbooks before starting the Sistine Chapel. Fra' Angelico (the "Angelic Friar") began the series in 1447; Luca Signorelli completed the works, which are considered his masterpiece, in 1504. Both artists appear, dressed in black in the lower left corner, in a magnificent panel of the "Sermon of the Antichrist," in which the devil coaxes a Christ impostor to lure the faithful to damnation. Signorelli looks handsome and proud, with his long blonde hair; a mistress who jilted him is shown receiving funds from a money lender (for prostitution services, some conject). To the right of the altar is "The Entrance to Hell" and "The Damned in Hell," in which devils torment their victims, bodies writhe in agony, and a man raises his fists to curse God as he sees Charon crossing the Styx for him. Signorelli gets revenge on his ex-mistress again here—she's the terrified blonde on the back of a leering winged devil. For something a little more uplifting, look at the "Elect in Heaven," where the saved look quite content in their assurance of eternal salvation.

Piazza del Duomo. www.opsm.it. *(C)* **0763/341-167.** 4€, free for children 10 and under. Apr–Sept Mon–Sat 9:30am–7pm, Sun 1–5:30pm (6:30pm July–Sept); Mar and Oct Mon–Sat 9:30am–6pm, Sun 1–5:30pm; Nov–Feb Mon–Sat 9:30am–1pm, 2:30–5pm (Sun to 4:30pm).

Grotte della Rupe (Etruscan Orvieto Underground) ★★ HISTORIC SITE   More than 1,200 artificial and natural caverns have been found in the *pozzolana* (a volcanic stone powdered to make cement mix) and *tufa* rock upon which Orvieto rests. Guided tours explore 15m (45 ft.) below Santa Chiara convent, reached by a steep climb up and down 55 steps, along a narrow rock-hewn passage. Over centuries the caverns have been used as Etruscan houses, water wells, ceramic ovens, pigeon coops, and cold storage (the temperature is a constant 14°C/58°F). Medieval citizens considered the tunnels safe refuges in times of siege, and residents took shelter in them during World War II Allied bombings, but most unwisely—a direct hit would have annihilated the soft rock.

Piazza Duomo 23. www.orvietounderground.it. *(C)* **0763/344-891.** Guided tours only, 6€ adults, 5€ students and seniors. Tours (45 min–1 hr) daily 11am and 12:15, 3, 4, and 5:15pm; only Sat–Sun in Feb. Tours at 12:15 and 5:15pm usually in English.

Pozzo di San Patrizio (St. Patrick's Well) ★ HISTORIC SITE Orvieto's position atop a rocky outcropping made it a perfect redoubt in time of siege, easy to defend but with one big drawback—a lack of water. When Pope Clement VII decided to hole up in Orvieto in 1527 to avoid turbulence in Rome, he hired Antonio Sangallo the Younger to dig a new well. Sangallo's design was unique: He dug a shaft 53m (175-ft.) deep and 14m (45-ft.) wide, accessible via a pair of wide spiral staircases that form a double helix, lit by 72 internal windows. Mule-drawn carts could descend on one ramp and come back up the other. You can climb down, too, though it's a 496-step trek down and back up, and there's nothing to see at the bottom but, well, a well. A few steps up and down is all you need

St. Patrick's Well in Orvieto.

to get the idea. The name refers to St. Patrick's Purgatory, a pilgrimage site in Ireland where Christ allegedly showed St. Patrick a cave and told him it was an entrance to hell.

Viale San Gallo (near the funicular stop on Piazza Cahen). www.inorvieto.it. ℗ **0763/ 343768.** 5€ adults, 3.50€ over 65, under 18, and students. May–Aug daily 9am–8pm; Mar–Apr and Sept–Oct daily 9am–7pm; Nov–Feb daily 10am–5pm.

Where to Stay in Orvieto

The upper town has few places to stay, so book ahead—especially on weekends, when Romans flock to Orvieto for a small-town getaway.

B&B Orvieto Sant'Angelo 42 ★★★   From the moment you step into the stone-floored foyer you'll feel right at home in Giulia Donato's pretty house on a narrow street off the Corso. In a lounge/breakfast room, a couch and chairs surround a huge hearth, and up a stone staircase are high-ceilinged guest rooms, two large doubles and a suite-size triple. Bathrooms are large (with deep tubs in the larger rooms), beds are luxurious, and handsome traditional pieces complement highly polished floors and mellow old beams and stones. Top-floor rooms come with a perk: little step-out balconies looking across rooftops to the distant hills.

Via Sant'Angelo 42. www.bborvieto.com. ℗ **0763/341-959.** 3 units. 95€–110€ double. **Amenities:** Lounge; Wi-Fi (free).

Hotel Duomo ★★ These snug quarters just a few steps from the Duomo (viewable from some rooms with a lean out the window) are not only extremely comfortable—with lots of modern built-in wood furnishings and excellent lighting—but also quirky. A local artist, Livio Orazio Valentini, did the decor and hung his surrealistic paintings in the hallways, lounges, and rooms, complementing them with colorful upholstery and carpets. (He also created the sculptural light fixtures hanging over many of the desks.) The bohemian and yet homey ambience is topped off nicely with a pleasant garden to one side of the hotel.

Vicolo dei Maurizio 7. www.orvietohotelduomo.com. ✆ **0763/341-887.** 18 units. 80€–130€ double. Rates include breakfast. **Amenities:** Wi-Fi (free).

Palazzo Piccolomini ★★ Orvieto's most luxurious and character-filled rooms are in a 16th-century *palazzo*, resurrected from a dilapidated wreck 30 years ago. The stone and vaulted subterranean breakfast room and a couple of frescoed salons whisk you into the past, but most of the guest rooms are done in contemporary Umbrian chic: wood and tile floors, dark furnishings, and crisp white walls with soothing neutral-tone accents. Some rooms have sitting areas or open to terraces, or are two-level; rooms on the upper floors even have a countryside view.

Piazza Ranieri 36 (2 blocks from Piazza della Repubblica). www.palazzopiccolomini.it. ✆ **0763/341-743.** 32 units. Doubles from 130€. Rates include breakfast. **Amenities:** Restaurant; babysitting; concierge; room service; Wi-Fi (free in public areas).

Where to Eat in Orvieto

Orvieto's favorite pasta is *umbrichelli*, simple flour-and-water spaghetti rolled out unevenly by hand and somewhat chewy—similar to the *pici* of southern Tuscany, but not as thick. To sample a glass (or buy a bottle) of Orvieto Classico (accompanied by a *panino*), drop by the **Cantina Foresi,** Piazza Duomo 2 (✆ **0763/341-611**). Ask to see the small, moldy cellar carved directly into the *tufa*. **Bar Montanucci** is a popular spot for snacks and drinks at Corso Cavour 23 (www.bar montanucci.com; ✆ **0763/341-262**), with playful wooden sculptures, a large rear terrace, and a huge selection of chocolates, some house-made. **Gastronomia Aronne** (✆ **0763/340-014**) elevates a snack or light meal into a gourmet indulgence, with excellent meat and cheese platters, sandwiches, pastas, and other beautifully prepared fare served in a light-filled shop/dining room at Via Cavour 101.

> ### Orvieto's Liquid Gold
>
> The plains and low hills around Orvieto grow the grapes—verdello, grechetto, and Tuscan varietals trebbiano and malvasia—that go into one of Italy's great wines, a pale straw-colored DOC white called simply **Orvieto Classico.** A well-rounded and fragrant white (often with a hint of crushed almonds), it goes great with lunch. Most Orvieto Classico you run across is *secco* (dry), but you can also find bottles of the more traditional *abboccato* (semidry/semisweet), *amabile* (medium sweet), and *dolce* (sweet) varieties. To visit a vineyard, pick up a copy of the "Strada dei Vini" brochure at the tourist office; it lists the wineries along with the hours.

Capitano del Popolo ★★★ UMBRIAN   Chef/proprietor Valentina Santanicchio grew up on a farm just outside of Orvieto, and she brings together her passion for cooking, commitment to locally grown ingredients, and flair for presentation in a former bakery on the town's market square. Leather couches and upholstered chairs are scattered around an all-day cafe up front, while in back, the dining room has vintage '50s cabinets and tables topped with crisp linens and fresh flowers. Valentina prides herself on a *carbonara* that rivals the best in Rome, along with spicy boar ragùs, roast duck, and other Umbrian classics, including sweetbreads.

Piazza del Popolo 7–9. www.capitanodelpopolo.com. ✆ **320/928-7474.** Entrees 8€–12€. Daily 8:30am–11pm (opens at 9am Tues).

Le Grotte del Funaro ★ UMBRIAN   A *funaro* (ropemaker) had his workshop in these grottoes carved into the cliff's *tufa* a thousand years ago, and you can almost see him at work in the shadowy recesses of the cave-like rooms. You can sit outside in good weather or better yet—so you don't miss the atmosphere inside—ask for one of the few window seats. You'll dine simply and well on grilled meats, the house specialty (including a *grigliata mista* of suckling pig, lamb, sausage, and yellow peppers), as well as excellent pizzas.

Via Ripa Serancia 41 (near Porta Maggiore). www.grottedelfunaro.it. ✆ **0763/343-276.** Entrees 10€–13€; pizza 5.50€–8.50€. Tues–Sun noon–3pm and 7pm–midnight. Closed 1 wk in July.

La Mezza Luna ★★ UMBRIAN   When booking your Orvieto hotel room, do yourself a favor and ask them to reserve a table for you at this little vaulted room behind a vine-covered entrance on a side street. Reserving well in advance is the only way you're likely to eat here. Don't expect gracious service or even a smile from grumpy proprietor Averino. Still, for more than 40 years he's been serving what many diners claim is the best carbonara they've ever eaten—and that's enough to attract customers by the busload from the ends of the earth. The kitchen also prepares other pastas and grills meat, but you're only here for the standout attraction.

Via Ripa Serancia 5. ✆ **0763/341-234.** Entrees 7€–10€. Daily 12:30–2pm and 7:30–9pm.

Trattoria Palomba ★★ UMBRIAN   This is the kind of place you'll want to linger, for a long lunch after a morning of sightseeing or a comfy evening dinner, because a meal here deserves leisurely appreciation. Black Umbrian truffles top many of the homemade pastas, most notably *umbrichelli al tartufo,* tossed with egg yolk and parmigiano. The signature dish, *palomba* (wild dove), is roasted in a delicious sauce of capers, rosemary, olives, and a hint of anchovies. Any of the meat dishes, including beef in a red wine sauce, are similarly satisfying. It's best to reserve, especially on weekends.

Via Cipirano Menente 16. ✆ **0763/343-395.** Entrees 10€–16€. Thurs–Tues 12:30–2:30pm and 7:30–10:30pm.

Orvieto Shopping

With its stream of visitors, Orvieto supports a tempting shopping scene. **Orogami** (Via del Duomo 14/16, www.orogami.com; ✆ **0763/344206**) sells a distinctive line of gold jewelry, including playful pieces like a medallion mimicking the Duomo's rose window. The showroom of internationally acclaimed ceramicist **Marino Moretti** at Via del Duomo 55 (www.marinomoretti.it; ✆ **0763/361663**) sells tiles, dinnerware, and other modern takes on traditional designs. Gifted young shoemaker **Federico Badia** hand-fashions made-to-order shoes, purses, bags, and belts in his workshop at Via Garibaldi 27 (federicobadiashoes.com).

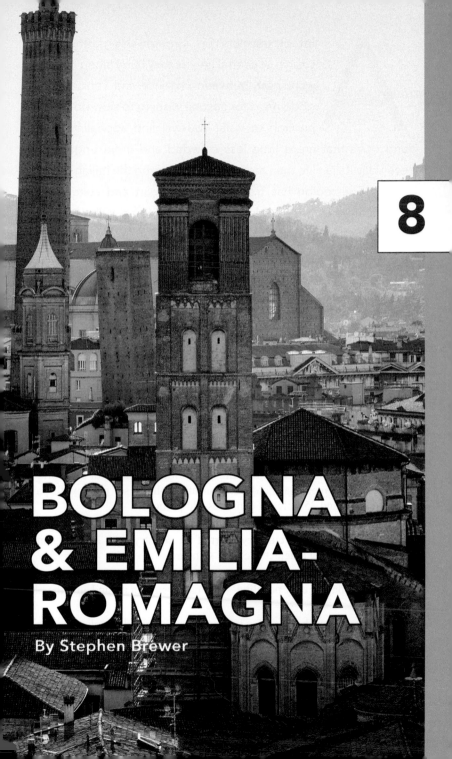

BOLOGNA & EMILIA-ROMAGNA

By Stephen Brewer

A lot of travelers zip through this northernmost stretch of central Italy as they hurry along the well-worn path between Florence and Venice. That's good news for anyone wishing to slow down long enough to visit—you will find appealing towns and cities that are a little less crowded and more engaged in everyday Italian life than more popular stops on the Italian tourism circuit. The region has treasure troves of art and culture, and there's another bright side to its personality as well: an almost hedonistic devotion to fine food.

Each of the region's main towns has its own distinct character and appeal. Bologna is one of Europe's largest remaining medieval enclaves, its old palaces are filled with art, and its stony piazzas host an animated street life revved up by students at Europe's oldest university. Ferrara is a time capsule of the Renaissance, and Ravenna seems to be entirely covered in glittering Byzantine mosaics. Parma proudly shows off its famous hams and cheeses, its musical traditions, and its art.

It's easy to get from one place to the other by train—Bologna makes a handy base for exploring the entire region—and once you reach these old cities, the preferred ways to get around are walking and biking.

DON'T LEAVE BOLOGNA & EMILIA-ROMAGNA WITHOUT . . .

Immersing Yourself in the Middle Ages. Bologna is one of the world's best-preserved medieval holdovers, an atmospheric set piece with palaces, towers, and 25 miles of centuries-old porticos.

Enjoying Some of the Best Food in Italy. Even other Italians agree: Emilia-Romagna is the culinary heart of the country, with Parma's hams and cheeses setting a delectable gold standard.

Biking Around Ferrara. The city's palace- and convent-lined streets are delightfully flat for easy pedaling—you can even spin around atop the old city walls!

Be Bedazzled by the Mosaics in Ravenna. Saturated in color, the intricate mosaics blanketing Ravenna's churches and mausoleums have awed travelers since the city's fifth-century heyday.

BOLOGNA ★★

It's easy to love a city so enamored of food that it's nicknamed *La Grassa* (the Fat); so devoted to scholarship (home of Europe's oldest university, founded in 1088) that it's called *La Dotta* (the Learned); and so noted for its fiery liberal politics that it's known as *La Rossa* (the Red). There are plenty of other reasons to like Bologna. The lively city of more than a million residents is built around one of the Europe's largest and best-preserved medieval cores, an attractive swath of palaces and towers, grand piazzas, and narrow lanes all easily traversed on foot. Quirky museums and art-filled churches seem all the more appealing amid the animated street life of the Quadrilatero, the medieval town center where shop windows brim with the region's famous hams and cheeses. You don't even have to carry an umbrella in Bologna, because 25 miles of sidewalks are covered with handsome loggias.

Essentials

ARRIVING

BY PLANE The international **Aeroporto Guglielmo Marconi** (www.bologna-airport.it; *C* **051/647-9615**) is 6km (3¾ miles) north of the city

The Quadrilatero, Bologna's medieval heart.

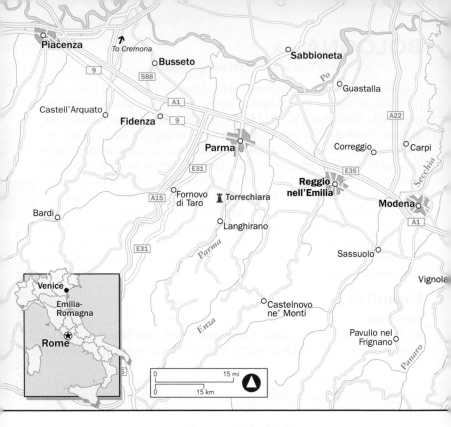

center and served by such domestic carriers as Alitalia and Air Italy; all the main European airlines also fly to this airport, including Ryanair (London-Stansted), EasyJet, and British Airways (both London-Gatwick). The airport does not accommodate transatlantic flights, so travelers from the U.S. will make connections in London or another European hub. A **bus** (marked aerobus; aerobus.bo.it) runs daily (5:30am–12:15am) every 11 to 15 minutes from the airport to Bologna's rail station (Stazione Centrale). A one-way ticket costs 6€ (buy from machines in the airport and the train station); the trip usually takes 20 minutes. A taxi from the airport into the city center costs about 16€.

BY TRAIN   Bologna's **Stazione Centrale** is at Piazza Medaglie d'Oro 2 (© **892-021**). High-speed trains arrive hourly from Florence (trip time: about 30 min.) and Milan (about 1 hr.). Most service between Bologna and Florence and Milan is now via high-speed train; only a few slower and less expensive trains run on these routes. Bologna is well connected to nearby cities by train, making it easy to explore a lot of the region without a car. The station has a well-marked, staffed luggage storage facility

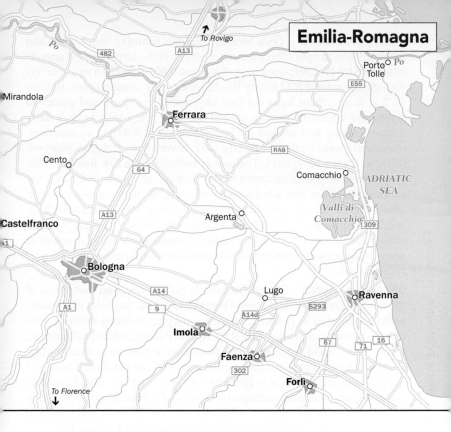

on the ground floor, open daily 6am to midnight, where you can store baggage for 5€ for each piece for the first 5 hours, 1€ an hour after that, with lower rates for multi-day storage. This makes it easy to stash your bags, then make day trips to Ferrara, Ravenna, or Parma.

Bus nos. A, 25, and 30 run between the station and the historic core of Bologna, Piazza Maggiore; taxi trips into the center cost around 6€. However, it's an easy 15-minute walk from the station to Piazza Maggiore down Via dell'Indipendenza, most of the way under covered loggias.

BY CAR If you are driving in from Florence, continue north along A1 until reaching the outskirts of Bologna, where signs direct you to the city center. From Milan, take A1 southeast along the Apennines. From Venice or Ferrara, follow A13 southwest. From Rimini, Ravenna, and the towns along the Adriatic, cut west on A14. See the note on p. 359 about driving and parking in Bologna; if you have a choice, it's much easier to arrive in Bologna without a car.

VISITOR INFORMATION The Bologna Welcome **tourist office** (www. bolognawelcome.com; *©* **051/658-3111**), at Piazza Maggiore in the

Palazzo del Podestà, is open Monday through Saturday 9am to 7pm and Sunday 10am to 5pm. There are other offices at the airport, in the arrivals hall (© **051/647-2201;** open Mon–Sat 9am–7:30pm and Sun and holidays 9am–5pm) and at FICO Eataly World (open daily 10am–10pm). Helpful staff at these offices hand out free city maps, bus maps, and guides to sights and what's happening around the city. The office leads a daily 2-hour walking tour around the historic center at 4:45pm, an excellent, informative introduction to the city (15€; leaves from Bologna Welcome office in Piazza Maggiore). The tour is included on a 25€ Bologna Welcome Card—a good investment if you plan on taking the tour, since the card also provides free admission to other sights including 4 must-sees: Museo Medievale, Museo Morandi, the church of Santa Maria della Vita, and the Pinacoteca Nazionale; individual admissions to these 4 sights alone adds up to 21€. You can also find 6 audio-guide walking routes at www.bolognawelcome.com/en/home/discover/itineraries/culture/audio-guides.

GETTING AROUND   Central Bologna is easy to cover **on foot;** most of the major sights are in and around Piazza Maggiore, and most of the sidewalks are covered by porticos, a handy convenience during the rainy winters. **City buses,** operated by **TPER** (Trasporto Passeggeri Emilia-Romagna; www.tper.it), leave for most points from Piazza Nettuno or Piazza Maggiore in the city center and the train station. You can buy tickets at one of many booths and *tabacchi* in Bologna for 1.30€; they are valid for 1 hour. A **day ticket** valid until midnight on the day of validation costs 5€; a **city pass**—a single ticket that allows 10 rides—costs 12€. Once on board, you must validate your ticket or you'll be fined up to 150€; many buses are equipped with machines from which you may buy a ticket for 1.50€, exact change required. A TPER office, with English-speaking staff dispensing info and selling tickets, is just outside the entrance to the train station in Piazza Medaglie d'Oro (open Mon–Sat 6am–7pm and Sun 7am–7pm).

Taxis are on 24-hour radio call at © **051/372-727** (Cooperativa Taxisti Bolognesiare; www.cotabo.it) or © **051/4590** (Consorzio Autonomo Taxisti; www.taxibologna.it). The meter starts at 4€ and goes up 1.08€ per kilometer.

Exploring Bologna

A huge statue of a virile Neptune presides over the center of Bologna, the sweeping expanse of **Piazza Maggiore.** On one end looms the enormous, though never completed, **Basilica di San Petronio;** crenellated 12th- and 13th-century *palazzi* occupy the other sides, including, on the northeast, the **Palazzo di Rei Enzo.** In the long-running feud between the Ghibellines (who supported the Holy Roman Empire) and the Guelphs (supporters of the Pope), Enzo—the illegitimate son of German Emperor Frederick

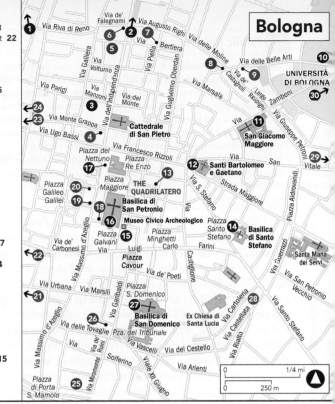

Bologna

II, and king of Sardinia—sided with the Ghibellines at the wrong time. He was imprisoned in this grim-looking palace for 23 years until his death, though he didn't exactly languish in a dungeon—he was known for his lavish feasts and romantic conquests, and almost escaped once (his blond hair, protruding from a basket, gave him away).

Most of the city's sights are within an easy walk from the piazza. Just to the east of the square rise the **Due Torri,** Bologna's iconic leaning towers, presiding over the atmospheric **Piazza della Mercanzia,** a marketplace from Roman times through the Middle Ages. The poet Dante, exiled from his native Florence, sat in cafés on the piazza and watched beautiful women stroll by—still a popular pastime. From the square, little lanes dive southwest into the **Quadrilatero,** the old quarter of food shops (see p. 362); Via San Stefano leads south to the basilicas of **San Stefano** and **San Domenico;** and Via Zamboni heads northeast into the **university district.**

Basilica di San Domenico ★★ CHURCH   Spanish-born St. Dominic, founder of the Dominican order and patron saint of astronomers, lived

351

Public Indecency

Bologna's famous **Fontana di Nettuno** (Neptune Fountain) was designed in 1566 by a Belgian named Giambologna (the Italians altered his name), who gave the naked sea god many rippling muscles and surrounded him with erotic cherubs and sirens spouting water from their breasts. When the papal legate who occupied the Palazzo d'Accursio opposite protested that the spectacle was indecent, Giambologna got his revenge: If you approach the statue from its rear right side, you'll notice that the left arm is positioned in such a way to suggest an indecently large . . . well, walk around the statue and see for yourself.

only 3 years in Bologna, but he rests forever here in a shrine designed by the 13th century's greatest sculptor, Nicola Pisano. Raised in wealth, Dominic aligned himself with the poor as a young student. To feed the starving, he sold his belongings, including his manuscripts, saying, "Would you have me study off these dead skins, when men are dying of hunger?" In Bologna he encouraged his followers "to have charity, to guard their humility, and to make their treasure out of poverty." The saint traveled from one end of Europe to the other before dying in 1221 on a bed of sackcloth; now he lies beneath elaborate carvings depicting his colorful life, the work of Arnolfo di Cambio. In the 15th century Nicolo di Bari added a canopy, carved with images of saints and evangelists, and was so proud of his work that he changed his name to Nicolo di Arca. A young Michelangelo, arriving in Bologna in 1495 when his patrons, the Medici, were expelled from Florence, added transcendent renderings of two other Bologna saints, Petronius and Proculus (who appears to be the prototype for his "David"). Bologna-born Guido Reni topped off the shrine in 1615 with a ceiling fresco depicting Dominic entering heaven. Piazza San Domenico 13. ℰ **051/640-0411.** Free. Mon–Sat 9am–noon and 3:30–6pm; Sun 3:30–5pm. Bus: A, 16, 30, 38, 39, 59.

Basilica di San Petronio ★ CHURCH   The massive church honoring Bologna's patron, the 5th-century bishop Petronio, was begun in 1390, designed to be larger than St. Peter's in Rome. Papal powers cut off funding and the basilica remains unfinished—the formidable brick walls were never sheathed in marble as intended and transepts are severely truncated (look down either side of the church to see where extensions end abruptly in the surrounding streets). Among the few flourishes are a magnificent central doorway surrounded by Old Testament figures rendered in marble by Jacopo della Quercia of Siena (where he designed the Fonte Gaia for the Campo; see p. 235). He was a well-regarded artist in his 50s when he came to Bologna in 1425 to undertake the commission; he finished just before his death in 1438. Michelangelo claimed that della Quercia's rendering of the Creation of Adam here inspired his Genesis in the Sistine Chapel. In the **Cappella Bolognini** (also known as **Capella dei Magi**),

A stained-glass window depicting St. Paul in the Basilica di San Petronio.

the fourth on the left as you enter, Giovanni da Modena's fresco cycle, painted between 1408 and 1420, depicts the life of Petronio. Scenes of Hell from Dante's Inferno include a startling image of Satan eating and excreting doomed souls and Mohammed being devoured by devils (Al-Qaida operatives and other terrorists in recent years have tried to blow up the church in retaliation). If you visit the church around noon, look for a shadow falling on a meridian line in the left aisle, indicating the day of the year; it's the world's longest sundial, 70m (231 ft.) long, designed by Bologna's famed 17th-century astronomer Giovanni Domenico Cassini. Piazza Maggiore. www.basilicadisan petronio.it. © **051/225-442.** Free; 3€ for Cappella dei Magi. Basilica: Mon–Thurs 7:45am–1:30pm and 2:30–6pm, Fri–Sun 7:45am–6:30pm. Capella dei Magi: daily 10am–6pm. Bus: A, 11, 13, 14, 17, 18, 19, 20, 25.

Basilica di Santo Stefano ★★★ CHURCH Bologna's most storied religious site is actually seven churches (and hence also known as Sette Chiese), a stone maze of medieval apses, romantic porticos, and courtyards awash in legend. Petronio, the 5th-century bishop of Bologna, allegedly founded the church on the remains of a Roman temple to the earth goddess Isis. He was originally laid to rest here in the **Church of the Sepulcher,** where pregnant Bolognese women would circle his tomb 33 times—once for every year of Christ's life—stopping at every turn to crawl through a low door to say a prayer before the saint's remains (his body has been since been reunited with his head in the Basilica di San Petronio). The mothers-to-be moved on to the **Church of the Trinity** to pray before a fresco depicting a very pregnant Madonna stroking her belly. The **Church of Vitale and Agricola** is devoted to two other popular Bolognese saints and the city's first Christian martyrs, the 4th-century nobleman Agricola and his devoted slave; a cross near the tomb is said to be the one Agricola was holding when he was crucified, though it dates from much later. Similarly, a marble basin in the **Cortile di Pilato** (Courtyard of Pilate), alleged to be the one in which Pontius Pilate washed his hands after condemning Christ to death, actually dates to the 8th century; a statue atop a nearby column pays homage to the rooster who crowed three times when Peter denied knowing Jesus. It's said that Dante used to sit in the Romanesque **cloister** and reflect during his exile in Bologna. Look at the carved capitals atop the pillars, with their grotesque imagery of swiveling heads and men crushed beneath boulders—perhaps Dante found inspiration here for the hellish scenes of the *Divine Comedy*.

Via Santo Stefano 24. ☏ **051/223-256.** Free. Daily 9:15am–6pm (until 7:15pm in summer). Bus: 11, 13, 90, 96.

FICO Eataly World ★ THEME PARK The purveyor of upscale food markets around the world has outdone itself in Bologna, opening a 25-acre food-oriented theme park with educational "rides," dozens of outlets for cheeses, prosciutto, olive oil, and other Italian fare, and 44 restaurants and fast-food kiosks (head for Osteria il Frito, with Neapolitan street food, and Nave Erante, for seafood snacks). Barnyard animals graze next to vineyards and olive groves, while workshops demonstrate pasta- and gelato-making, flour-grinding, and other fundamentals of Italian cuisine. Three-wheeled bikes with roomy shopping baskets are a sporting way to explore the premises. Even with all the gimmicks, however, a day here doesn't match the pleasure of a stroll through the Quadrilatero (see p. 362), where Eataly has another trademark food boutique.

Via Paolo Canali 8 (5 mi NE of city center). www.eatalyworld.it. ☏ **051/002-9001.** Free. Sun–Fri 10am–11pm, Sat 10am–midnight. Shuttle bus from Via de' Carracci, across from train station, 7€ round trip; buy tickets from TPER office outside station entrance.

Le Due Torri ★★ MONUMENT It's been estimated that in the 12th and 13th centuries as many as 180 stone towers rose above the rooftops of Bologna, reaching heights of up to 100m (330 ft.). Probably built as places of refuge in times of war, they were proof of a family's wealth—it took enormous expense to erect such towers, carefully crafted with successively thinner layers of masonry on the upper levels. Some 22 towers remain; the most famous are these two slender medieval skyscrapers that lean tipsily but poetically just east of Piazza Maggiore. The **Garisenda**

Le Due Torri, near Piazza Maggiore.

Sidewalk Porticos: Staying Dry in Bologna

Almost 40km (25 miles) of porticos cover the sidewalks of Bologna, providing the Bolognese with a venue to stroll and strut during the evening *passeggiata*, no matter how inclement the weather. Most are high enough to accommodate a man on horseback, as mandated by a 14th-century city ordinance. It's said they were originally modeled after the porticos of the ancient Greek academies, giving students a place to walk and ponder; they also allowed residents to extend the upper stories of their homes over the sidewalks, helping ease a medieval housing crunch. Showiest is the 3.5km (2 mi.) stretch of porticos that climb a green hillside to the **Santuario della Madonna di San Luca** (www.santuariobeatavergine sanluca.com). As you tackle the seemingly endless steps, note that the arcades are supported by 666 arches, a number associated with the devil—and you might believe there's a diabolical presence afoot as you huff and puff your way toward your reward, heavenly views of the city and countryside from the church's front steps. You can save yourself the climb (though that defeats the purpose of a pilgrimage, doesn't it?) by hopping aboard the **San Luca Express** (cityredbus.com), a tourist train that operates from Piazza Maggiore daily from March through Dec, with 5 trips a day Tues–Thurs and 10 trips Fri–Mon; round-trip fare is 10€, 5€ children 6–10, and 3€ 5 and under. Check the website for hours of operation in January and February.

rises 49m (162 ft.) and leans about 3m (10 ft.) from perpendicular; the **Asinelli** stands 102m (334 ft.) tall and inclines almost 2.5m (8 ft.). Garisenda is off limits, but a climb up Asinelli's 500 steps reveals Bologna's finest aerial panorama, a sea of red-tile roofs and the green hills beyond.

Piazza di Porta Ravegnana. www.duetorribologna.com. Buy tickets at tourist office or online: 5€ adults, 3€ under 12 and over 65. Daily Mar–Nov 5 9:30am–7:30pm; Nov 6–Feb 9:30am–5:30pm. Entry at 45-min intervals. Bus: 11, 13, 14, 19, 25, 27.

Museo Civico Medievale ★★ MUSEUM   Displayed in the salons of the magnificently medieval Palazzo Ghisilardi, the treasures in this museum bring the Bologna of the Middle Ages to life. You'll find rare illuminated manuscripts and artifacts of everyday life, such as a courtesan's dainty shoes. There's a bronze statue of Pope Boniface VIII, crafted by Manno Bandini da Siena in 1302 on behalf of the city of Bologna, to thank the pontiff for stepping in to resolve some particularly nasty local disputes. Other statues show off the haircuts and clunky headgear of the times, while ordinary funeral slabs provide such telling glimpses as a relief of a supine professor with his hands resting on a book, as if he has fallen asleep while reading.

Via Manzoni 4. www.museibologna.it/arteanticaen. ℭ **051/219-3930.** 5€ adults, under 18 free. Tues–Sun10am–6:30pm. Bus: A, 11, 20, 27, 28.

Museo d'Arte Moderna di Bologna (MAMbo) ★★ MUSEUM
This is the city's showcase for the avant-garde, with an emphasis on post–World War II art. The standout is a museum within a museum, the **Museo**

Morandi ★★★, exhibiting a collection of works by Bolognese artist Giorgio Morandi (1890–1964). The painter and printmaker once said, "What interests me most is expressing what's in nature, in the visible world"—an understatement given his deceptively straightforward still lifes, which seem almost abstract in their minimalism. Morandi's studio has been reconstructed here, and you can also visit his apartment at Via Fondazza 36 (✆ **051/649-6653;** by appointment; free admission), converted to stark galleries where his personal effects and the vases, utensils, and other objects he painted are on view. In the larger museum, one standout piece is Renato Guttuso's "I Funerali di Togliatti" (1972), awash in red flags, which depicts the funeral of the leader of the communist party, surrounded by images of left-wing luminaries.

Via Don Minzoni 14. www.mambo-bologna.org. ✆ **051/649-6611.** 6€ adults, 4€ students and ages 6–17, free for children 5 and under. Tues, Wed, and Fri–Sun 10am–6:30pm; Thurs 10am–8pm. Bus: A, 11, 20, 27, 28.

Museo per la Memoria di Uscita ★★ MUSEUM   In this haunting installation, artist Christian Boltanski commemorates the crash of a Bologna–Palermo flight off the eponymous Sicilian island on June 27, 1980, with wreckage of the DC-9 and lighting and sound effects. Victims are represented by 81 lights blinking off and on against the black ceiling while from 81 speakers come snippets of ordinary conversation. Most effective of all is the shattered aircraft, allegedly shot down by an Italian military missile when it was mistaken for a Libyan spy plane. The incident was the subject of an extensive cover-up and investigation.

Via di Saliceto 3/22. www.museomemoriaustica.it. ✆ **051/377-680.** Free. Thurs–Fri 9am–1pm, Sat–Sun 10am–6:30pm.

Palazzo dell'Archiginnasio ★★ HISTORIC SITE   It's no accident that one of the grander buildings of Bologna University, completed in 1563, is adjacent to the basilica of San Petronio. Pope Pius IV ordered this central hall for the university faculties to be built here for a reason: to prevent the basilica from expanding and surpassing in size St. Peter's in Rome. Corridors and staircases decorated with family crests lead to the **Teatro Anatomico,** a handsome spruce-paneled lecture hall with tiers of wood benches surrounding a marble slab. Apollo, god of medicine, gazes down from the ceiling, and statues of Hippocrates and other august physicians line the walls; the doctor holding a nose is Gaspare Tagliacozzi, a pioneer of rhinoplasty (aka "nose job"), a procedure much in demand in an era when noses were routinely cut off for punishment. Look for the secret panel, where a church inquisitor spied on classes to make sure dissections followed church protocol—dissections had to take place in one continuous session (often 2 full days), in cold weather to preserve the bodies, and all organs had to remain *in situ* and intact, ready for Judgment Day.

Piazza Galvani. www.archiginnasio.it. ✆ **051/276-811.** 3€. Mon–Fri 10am–6pm; Sat 10am–7pm; Sun 10am–2pm. Bus: A or 29B.

Pinacoteca Nazionale di Bologna ★★ MUSEUM   Beginning in the late 18th century, the former St. Ignatius monastery began to house altar pieces and other works gathered from religious institutions throughout Bologna. The collection grew considerably after 1815 when many works the French had carted off to the Louvre were returned to Bologna after the fall of Napoleon. Among the great works is Raphael's "St. Cecilia in Ecstasy" (Gallery 15), in which the saint, patron of music, is portrayed holding a lute, rapturously listening to a heavenly choir. Guido Reni (1575–1642), born and buried in Bologna, dominates Gallery 24 with his "Massacre of the Innocents," in which two muscular, knife-wielding soldiers set upon a group of screaming women and children. Gallery 23 features Bologna's Carracci family—brothers Agostino and Annibale and their cousin Lodovico—who opened a famous academy in Bologna in the 1580s. Agostino's masterpiece is "The Communion of St. Jerome," but the work for which he became best known was "I Modi" (The Way), a highly erotic series of engravings. Annibale was the greater and more passionate painter, known for his realistic renderings of human features, as you'll see in his darkly moving "Mocking of Christ." Annibale was famous for his photographic memory: When still a child, he and his father were set upon by robbers, and young Annibale could draw the thieves with such precision that they were soon apprehended and the Carraccis' money returned.

Via delle Belle Arti 56. www.pinacotecabologna.beniculturali.it. ☏ **051/420-9411.** 6€ adults, 2€ ages 18–25, free for children 17 and under. Tues–Sun 8:30am–7:30pm. Bus: 20, 28, 36, 37, 89, 93, 94, 99 (to Porta San Donato).

BEYOND THE greatest hits

The Carraccis are the stars of the Pinacoteca Nazionale (p. 357), but their masterpiece is the *Founding of Rome* fresco cycle in the **Palazzo Magnani-Salem,** Via Zamboni 20 (quadreriapalazzomagnani.it, ☏ **051/296-2503;** free; hours vary but usually Wed 10am–1:30pm and 2:30–6pm and second Sat of month). The Carraccis also decorated the first floor of **Palazzo Fava,** Via Manzoni 2 (genusbononiae.it; ☏ **051/1993-6305;** 6€; usually Tues–Sun 10am–7pm), with colorful renditions of Jason and the Argonauts and other mythical scenes. A gentle portrait of Medea bathing next to a stream is considered to be the first female nude since classical times.

Aside from his carvings on the tomb of St. Dominic (p. 351) Niccolo dell'Arca's other great work in Bologna is "Compianto sul Cristo Mortois" in the **Church of Santa Maria della Vita** (Via Clavature 8; 4€; Tues–Sun 10:30am–6:30pm). These life-size terracotta figures depicting Christ being taken from the cross are some of the most humane and moving religious images you'll ever see, the expressions on the faces of the lamenters etched in grief—even though they're clumsily shored up with wood to prevent earthquake damage.

THE WAY OF ALL flesh

Life was precarious in the Middle Ages, and the medieval mindset—which you'll encounter often in Bologna—never forgot that we are, in the end, just flesh and blood. For a grisly reminder of this, head to **Chiesa della Santa,** Tagliapietre 19, where the body of St. Catherine—a 15th-century nun who's the city patron and protector of artists—sits on a golden throne in a side chapel. The faithful claim Catherine has remained miraculously intact since her death; the blackened, leathery flesh stretched over skeletal features suggests otherwise. To join the faithful in the little sanctuary, adorned with the saint's violin and other relics, ring the bell next to a wooden door on the left in the church vestibule (Tues–Thurs and Sat–Sun 9:30–11:30am and 4–5:45pm). There's a similarly creepy vibe at the University of Bologna's **Museo di Palazzo Poggi,** Via Zamboni 33, a wonderful 16th-century cabinet of curiosities founded to assemble all the living organisms on earth. Along with fossils and an (alleged) unicorn tusk, you'll see anatomically correct wax models in various states of flaying, as well as remarkably lifelike models of infants in the womb. Gruesome, yes, but remember that these helped medieval physicians advance medicine from folk practice to science (www.sma.unibo.it, ✆ **051/20-99610,** 5€; Mon–Fri 10am–4pm, Sat–Sun 10am–6pm).

On a lighter note, the frescoed salons of the Palazzo Sanguinetti, Strada Maggiore 34, are home to the **Museo Internazionale e Biblioteca della Musica** and filled with scores, libretti, and musical instruments from the 16th century on, including an utterly charming re-creation of a lute-maker's studio (www. museibologna.it/musica, ✆ **051/275-711,** 5€; Tues–Sun 10am–6:30pm). Harpsichords, pianos, and some 70 other early instruments fill the beautiful former church of St. Columbano, Via Parigi 5, all part of the **Collezione Tagliavani** (genus bononiae.it; ✆ **051/1993-6366,** 7€, Tues–Sun 11am–7pm).

San Giacomo Maggiore (Church of St. James) ★ CHURCH This Romanesque church in its present form was largely funded by Bologna's most powerful 15th-century family, the Bentivoglio clan, who were constantly plotting and being plotted against. Many are laid to rest in the **Cappella Bentivoglio,** decorated in vivid frescoes by Lorenzo Costa, who came to Bologna in the 1480s before moving on to great fame in Mantua (see p. 495). In "Madonna Enthroned," you'll see Giovanni II Bentiviglio—who was eventually excommunicated and imprisoned in Rome—kneeling with his wife next to the Madonna, as his family gives thanks for the unmasking of a conspiracy against them. Anton Galeazzo Bentivoglio, who fell out of favor with the papacy and was beheaded in 1435, lies in a tomb designed by Jacopo della Quercia. For an eerie thrill, follow the left-side chapels about halfway down until you come to a terrifyingly realistic effigy of the corpse of Christ, complete with lash marks, oozing wounds, and plenty of blood.

Piazza Rossini, Via Zamboni. ✆ **051/225-970.** Free. Mon–Fri 7:30am–12:30pm and 3:30–6:30pm, Sat–Sun 8:30am–12:30pm and 3–6:30pm. Bus: C.

Where to Stay In Bologna

Bologna hosts four to six major trade fairs a year, during which times hotel room rates rise dramatically. You'll save a lot of money if you choose another time to visit (you'll find a calendar of fairs at www.bolognafiere. it). Bologna has a booming bed-and-breakfast scene, as well as many short-term rental apartments. Good places to browse offerings include **Airbnb.com** and **HomeAway.com**. The most unique rental in town is **Torre Prendiparte,** a 12th-century tower—guests get the entire 11-story structure with roof terrace all to themselves, so along with plenty of medieval atmosphere and great views from the top comes some stair-climbing exercise to get from one level to the next (Piazzetta Prendiparte 5, prendiparte.it, 𝒞 **335-561-6858;** from 500€ a night).

An important note on driving and parking: Parts of central Bologna (Via Ugo Bassi, Via Rizzoli, and Via Indipendenza) are closed to cars almost entirely, and large parts of the central city are entirely off-limits to traffic on Sundays, when you will have to park outside the center. Other areas are closed to cars without special permits from 7am to 8pm daily (including Sun and holidays). If your hotel is in a limited traffic zone, you will be allowed to drive in to unload your bags and park, but only if you've first registered with the police. When booking a room, present your car registration number, which the hotel will then provide to the police to ensure that you are not fined for driving in a restricted area. If you're planning to drive into Bologna, ask about these restrictions when booking, and also ask where to find nearby parking facilities. Best yet, come to this easily walkable city without a car.

EXPENSIVE

Art Hotel Commercianti ★★   You can't stay any closer to San Petronio than this atmosphere-rich *palazzo*—in the best rooms and suites you can lie in bed, sit on a leafy terrace, or even soak in a deep tub while admiring the church's exquisite brickwork and statuary. Exposed timbers and fresco fragments lend a medieval aura to the decor, though many of the furnishings are plush and contemporary, with armchairs and couches that invite you to relax after forays to the surrounding sights. In the lower-level breakfast room, a morning buffet is served beneath vaulted arches that show off the hotel's 13th-century origins.

Via de' Pignattari 11. www.art-hotel-commercianti.it. 𝒞 **051/745-7511.** 34 units. 150€–200€ double. Rates include breakfast. Parking 28€ per day. Bus: 11, 13, 20, 30. **Amenities:** Bar; babysitting; bikes; room service; Wi-Fi (free).

Art Hotel Orlogio ★★   This tall, narrow old house has been an inn for a couple of centuries and takes its name from the adjoining clock tower. The comfy surroundings have more nooks and crannies than the surface of Mars, and no two of the traditionally furnished guest rooms are the same. Most rooms are done in soothing, deep-hued wall coverings, and many have nice touches like little writing nooks. The higher you get, the more likely your room or suite has a glimpse of nearby Piazza Maggiore, or at least a tower and dome or two. Most of the sights and the lively market streets of the Quadrilatero (see p. 362) are just steps away.

Via 4 Novembre 10. www.art-hotel-orologio.it. © **051/745-7411.** 33 units. 150€–180€ double. Rates include breakfast. Parking 28€ per day. Bus: 11, 13, 20, 30. **Amenities:** Bar; room service; Wi-Fi (free).

MODERATE

Hotel Metropolitan ★★★ This stylish haven is just a few steps off Via Indipendenza but a world removed, an oasis of calm and comfort. Soothing whites and neutral shades offset Indonesian antiques and other Asian pieces. All rooms have large mosaic-tiled bathrooms, many have small sitting rooms, and several have terraces. In addition to a rooftop terrace, five airy, two-room suites open off a leafy roof garden planted with olive trees; they're some of the most restful accommodations in the city center. Piazza Maggiore and most city sights are an easy walk away. The hotel also rents out modern and well-equipped apartments nearby; rates range from 100€ to 400€ per day.

Via Dell'Orso 6. www.hotelmetropolitan.com. © **051/229-393.** 50 units. 120€–170€ double. Rates include breakfast. Parking 20€ a day. Bus: A, 11, 20, 27, 28. **Amenities:** Restaurant; bar; babysitting; room service; Wi-Fi (free).

Hotel Porta San Mamolo ★★ Most of these rather romantic rooms surround a leafy courtyard, bringing the sense of a country retreat to the heart of Bologna—Piazza Maggiore is only a 15-minute walk away. Nice-sized, tile-floored rooms are done in soothing creams and warm golds and reds, with furnishings that are vaguely Florentine in style and offset with exposed beams, vaulted ceilings, and other architectural details. A few rooms have large terraces; others open directly into the garden. Breakfast is served in an airy, greenhouse-like pavilion that seems summery even during the gray Bolognese winter.

Vicolo del Falconi 6–8. www.hotel-portasanmamolo.it. © **051/583-056.** 43 units. 120€–150€ double. Rates include breakfast. Parking 20€ per day. Bus: 29B or 52. **Amenities:** Bikes; room service; Wi-Fi (free).

Hotel Roma ★★ What this old Bologna fixture lacks in chic style it makes up for with plenty of old-school charm and hospitality and a wonderful location just off Piazza Maggiore. Downstairs lounges and a small bar are gracious and welcoming, and the no-nonsense guest rooms upstairs are large and pleasantly done with brass beds and gleaming wooden floors; many open to small terraces overlooking the surrounding streets, and many of the large tiled bathrooms are windowed. The excellent in-house restaurant, **C'era Una Volta**—which translates as "Once Upon a Time"—offers Bolognese classics served by crisply uniformed waiters.

Via Massimo d'Azeglio 64. www.hotelroma.biz. © **051/226-322.** 86 units. Doubles from 120€. Rates include breakfast. Parking 20€ per day. Bus: 11, 13, 20, 30. **Amenities:** Restaurant; bar; bikes; room service; Wi-Fi (free).

Hotel Touring ★★ A rooftop terrace overlooking tile roofs and domes to the hills that surround Bologna is perfect for a few hours of quiet relaxation, an *aperitivo*, or even a soak in the hot tub. Guest rooms are all geared to quiet comfort, too, done in soothing cream colors and functional furnishings, and those on the third and fourth floors have a great amenity: city-view terraces or balconies. A ground-floor reading room warmed by a fireplace is a perfect hideout in cooler weather.

Via De' Mattuiani 1/2. www.hoteltouring.it. ℂ **051/584-305.** Doubles from 100€. Rates include breakfast. Parking 25€. **Amenities:** Bar; Wi-Fi (free).

INEXPENSIVE

Albergo delle Drapperie ★ This centuries-old guesthouse is smack in the middle of the bustling market streets and steps from Piazza Maggiore. Top-floor rooms, the largest and best, have vaulted ceilings, wooden beams, gables, window seats that double as extra beds, and other touches. Lower-floor rooms are smaller and furnished with not much more than beds, though they're enlivened with homey iron bedsteads and the occasional fresco or coffered ceiling. You'll have to do some climbing to reach any of these rooms, as well as the lobby and breakfast room. The Drapperie also rents out apartments in a nearby building.

Via Drapperie 5. www.albergodrapperie.com. ℂ **051/223-955.** 21 units. 95€–120€ double. Rates include breakfast. Bus: A, 11, 20, 27, 28. **Amenities:** Wi-Fi (free).

Alberta D Bed and Breakfast ★★★ Some of the homiest lodgings in Bologna are scattered across two floors of this sophisticated, rambling home in a former medieval hospital. Character-filled units face gardens and a tranquil inner courtyard, set up for warm-weather lounging; a large well-equipped and nicely furnished apartment stretches across an upper floor. Much of the furniture is antique or vintage, accented by chic accessories, and Alberta is a welcoming and gracious host. A filling breakfast includes Alberta's home-baked breads and cakes, homemade jams, fresh juices, and fine hams and cheeses.

Via Sant'Isaia 58. www.albertadbedandbreakfast.com. ℂ **051/333-479.** 6 units. Doubles from 85€. Rates include breakfast. Bus: 21. **Amenities:** Sauna; Wi-Fi (free).

Hotel Accademia ★ The neighborhood is a bit scruffy, but one of the few hotels in the university district is surrounded by lively clubs, bars, and affordable student-oriented *osterie*. Large guest rooms have high ceilings and are spiffily up to date, with polished wooden floors, blond furniture, muted colors, and shiny bathrooms—many with that ever-so-rare fixture in less-expensive Italian hotels, a bathtub. The colorful street life can be a late-night curse—ask for a room facing the quiet courtyard.

Via delle Belle Arte 6. www.hotelaccademia.com. ℂ **051/232-318.** 28 units. 100€– 120€ double. Rates include breakfast. Parking 15€ per day. Bus: A, 11, 20, 27, 28. **Amenities:** Bikes; Wi-Fi (free).

A moveable feast IN THE QUADRILATERO

On a warren of medieval lanes behind Piazza Maggiore, the **Quadrilatero** is the gastronome epicenter of Bologna, full of venerable gourmet shops. At **Tamburini,** one of Italy's most lavish food shops, Via Caprarie 1 (tamburini.com; ℂ 051/232-226), a selection of pastas, meats and fish, soups and salads, vegetables, and sweets is sold to be taken away or enjoyed in-house, accompanied by 200 wines by the glass. **La Baita,** Via Pescherie Vecchie 3A (ℂ **051/223-940**), lets you choose from a dizzying selection of hams and cheeses and enjoy them in a busy mezzanine dining room. While FICO Eataly World (see p. 354) Disney-fies the gourmet experience, foodies still flock to **Bologna Eataly** (Via degli Orefici 19; www.eataly.it; ℂ **051/095-2820**), which sells cookbooks, cheese, hams, and other products, as well as prepared foods and wine that can be consumed picnic-style at indoor and outdoor tables. The covered marketplace across the way has been converted into the **Mercato di Mezzo** (Via Clavature; ℂ **051/232919**), a food hall housing small bars and food stands; in the evenings many offer free snacks to accompany drinks.

Osteria del Sole, Vicolo Ranocchi 1D (osteriadelsole.it; ℂ **348/225-6887;** closed Sun), is an invitingly rundown room with a novel twist on the bring-your-own policy—you bring the food, they supply the wine for 2€ a glass. Good places to shop for your DIY meal are **Salumeria Simoni,** Via Drapperie 5/2A (www.salumeriasimoni.it; ℂ **051/231880**), and **Enoteca Italiana,** Via Marsala 2/B (www.enotecaitaliana.it; ℂ **051/235-989**)—at both you can take a seat to dine well on cheese and meat platters, sandwiches, and other dishes. You might want to throw in a pastry from **Atti,** Via Caprarie 7 (www.paoloatti.com; ℂ **051/220-425**).

Venture a few blocks west of the Quadrilatero to find Bologna's central food market, **Mercato delle Erbe,** at Via Ugo Bassi 25 (www.mercatodelleerbe.eu; Mon–Thurs 7am–midnight, Fri–Sat 7am–2pm). Aside from produce, fish, and other food vendors, the hall has fast-food outlets with a couple of clamorous dining areas.

Local appetizers at a market in Bologna.

Where to Eat in Bologna

As capital of Italy's most productive agricultural region, Bologna has been a food center for centuries. Specialties include locally raised beef, exquisitely cured meats (especially prosciutto and salami), fresh pastas, truffles, and hearty sauces—far more than just the rich meat sauce or the

Americanized sandwich meat that was named after the city. See p. 362 for details on the food shops of the **Quadrilatero** neighborhood. For an inexpensive meal, head to **Via del Pratello,** west of Piazza Maggiore near the basilica of San Francesco; the narrow street is lined with low-cost osterias, bars, and no-frills take-out shops. **Capra e Cavoli,** at number 58c (*℃* **342/775-7553**), and **Pasta Fresca Naldi,** at number 69 (*℃* **051/523288**), prepare delicious pastas, including *tortellini alla panna,* to match those from the finest kitchens in town. **MozzaBella-Pratello,** at number 65 (*℃* **051/550-506**), transforms pizza slices into gourmet concoctions.

If you've got room left after a meal, a favorite Bologna post-prandial attraction is **Gelatauro,** Via San Vitale 98 (www.gelatauro.com; *℃* **051/230-049;** Mon 9am–8pm, Tues–Thurs 8:30am–11pm, Fri–Sat 8:30am–midnight, Sun 9:30am–11pm), run by three brothers and known for its organic gelato, including a divine concoction made from Sicilian oranges.

EXPENSIVE

Caminetto d'Oro ★★ BOLOGNESE/ITALIAN   Despite the sleekly contemporary appearance of the formal dining room and a more casual bistro to one side, the Carrati family has been feeding Bologna for 80 years, from premises that were once a bakery. A decades-old oven is still used to bake their own delicious breads, which are all made, along with the pasta, using wheat flour from a mill near Modena. The *tagliatelle al ragu* here is renowned—and a favorite of many performers and theatergoers from nearby Arena del Sole. This is also the best place in town for a steak; T-bones from local Romagnola cattle are seared on soapstone.

Via de'Falegnami 4. www.caminettodoro.it. *℃* **051/263-494.** Entrees 10€–22€. Mon–Sat 12:30–2:30pm and 7:30–10:30pm. Bus: C.

Ristorante da Nello al Montegrappa ★★ BOLOGNESE   This Bologna institution occupies several cozily paneled subterranean rooms just off Piazza Maggiore. Crisply uniformed waiters who seem to have been here since the place began serving in 1948 will lead you through the specialties, which include the house signature dish, *tortellini Montegrappa,* served in a cream-and-meat sauce. *Funghi porcini* and truffles appear in many of the classics, including a fragrant veal scallopine in truffle sauce. The kitchen also prepares daily specials with some surprising variations of Bolognese standards, such as spinach tortellini with chicken filling. Meals should begin with a platter of buttery prosciutto and end with a selection of cheeses, all washed down with one of the fine wines from local vineyards. To ensure a table in the cheerful rooms downstairs, reserve for dinner.

Via Montegrappa 2. www.ristorantedanello.com. *℃* **051/236-331.** Entrees 10€–17€. Tues–Sun noon–3pm and 7–11:30pm. Closed 1 wk in Jan/Feb and all of Aug. Bus: A, 11, 20, 27, 28.

Casa Monica ★★ BOLOGNESE/VEGETARIAN   Tucked away in what looks like a converted garage at the western edge of the historic center is this pleasant, low-key dining room, an oasis of calm and refinement. Deep rose hues and warm lamplight give the contemporary surroundings a welcoming glow, and the cuisine might be a welcome break from heavier Bolognese fare. Many choices are vegetarian, including creamy risottos and an airy flan *di zucca* (squash), and several main courses are fish. Even the desserts are deceptively light. This transporting spot is only a 15-minute walk or a short cab or bus ride away from Piazza Maggiore.

Via San Rocco 16. www.casamonica.it. ⟲ **051/522-522.** Entrees 10€–18€. Daily 7:30–11pm. Bus: 13 or 96.

Drogheria della Rosa ★★★ BOLOGNESE/ITALIAN   This former apothecary looks much as it always has, except that now wine bottles are mixed in among the old-fashioned jars on the wooden shelves. Just as the premises once dispensed medicines, chef/owner Emanuele Addone dishes out down-to-earth Bolognese cooking, with an emphasis on market-fresh ingredients. There's no menu, but a waiter, often Emanuele himself, will guide you through the daily offerings and suggest wines to match. A meal usually begins with a plate of prosciutto and a glass of Prosecco. Tortellini are stuffed with zucchini blossoms or eggplant puree. Filet mignon is roasted to perfection and drizzled with balsamic vinegar from Modena; guinea fowl is done beautifully with a honey sauce. Desserts, including a mascarpone with chocolate shavings, are sumptuous, but leave a bit of room—some of the best gelato in Bologna is dispensed around the corner at **La Sorbetteria Castiglione,** at Via Castiglione 44.

Via Cartoleria 10. www.drogheriadellarosa.it. ⟲ **051/222-529.** Entrees 10€–18€. Daily 12:30–3pm and 8–11:45pm. Closed Aug 10–27 and 1st wk of Jan. Bus: C, 11, 13.

Il Rovescio ★ BOLOGNESE/VEGETARIAN   The name of this rustic-looking little room just off bar- and *osterie*-lined Via Pratello translates roughly as "upside down" or "backwards"—a clue that you're likely to find some unusual takes on traditional Bolognese cuisine. All the food is locally sourced; the menu changes frequently to reflect what's in season, and—a rarity in Bologna—includes many vegetarian choices, like grilled radicchio on a bed of polenta, or crepes filled with caramelized squash. Meat presentations, such as little ginger-laced meatballs on a bed of pureed peas, can be surprising. Rovescio operates an evenings-only **bio-pizzeria** next door, where only organically grown ingredients are used.

Via Pietralata 28. www.rovescio.it. ⟲ **051/523-545.** Entrees 10€–18€. Daily 12:30–3pm and 7pm–10:30pm. Bus: C, 11, 13.

Trattoria dal Biassanot ★★★ EMILIAN   The wood beams, lace tablecloths, warm service, and other grace notes of this welcoming bistro (the name roughly means "night owl") do justice to the expertly prepared Bolognese classics that emerge from the kitchen. Light-as-a-feather *tagliatelle* with Bolognese sauce has a reputation as one of the best in a city that's famous for the dish, but all of the handmade pastas and succulent sauces are excellent; even the bread is house-made and delicious. Put yourself in the hands of the kitchen and opt for the very reasonably priced tasting menu, wine included.

Via Piella 16a. www.dalbiassanot.it. 𝄇 **051/230-644.** Entrees 8€–15€; fixed-price menu 25€. Daily noon–2:30pm and 7–10:30pm. Closed Aug. Bus: 19, 27, 94.

INEXPENSIVE

All'Osteria Bottega ★★★ BOLOGNESE/ITALIAN   In this unassuming storefront, the simple tables are covered with butcher paper, and pride of place belongs to the bright red meat slicer and the meats and cheeses on display. These find their way into *affetati misti* and delicious pastas, followed by roast rabbit and other hearty main courses. Owner Danielle Minarelli is on hand to enthuse about the daily offerings and will guide you through one of your most memorable meals in Italy. Reservations are recommended, especially for dinner.

Via Santa Caterina 51. 𝄇 **051/585-111.** Entrees 8€–14€. Tues–Sat 12:30–2:30pm and 8–10:30pm. Bus: 11 or 13.

Trattoria Anna Maria ★ BOLOGNESE   Photographs of Sophia Loren, Marcello Mastroianni, and legions of other celebrities line the walls of these high-ceilinged, welcoming rooms, but everyone in Bologna knows that the real star is Anna Maria, who has been serving her freshly made pasta for 30 years. *Tortellini in brodo,* parcels of pasta filled with minced pork and floating in chicken broth, and *taglietelle* with a hearty Bolognese sauce are her signature dishes, but the lasagnas are memorable, too. Anna Maria will probably find her way to your table at some point during your meal to make sure you've eaten every bite, but that won't be an issue.

Via Bella Arti 17/A. www.trattoriannamaria.com. 𝄇 **051/266-894.** Entrees 10€–18€. Tues–Sun 12:30–3pm and 7:30–11pm. Bus: 11, 13, 20, 29B, 30, 38, 39.

8

BOLOGNA & EMILIA-ROMAGNA

Bologna

Shopping

Shopping in Bologna often revolves around food; see p. 362 above for some recommended gourmet stops. U.S. travelers should keep in mind that you are allowed to bring Parmigiano and other hard cheese home with you, as long as it's wrapped and labeled from the shop, but not prosciutto or most other meats. Olive oil and vinegar are okay, too, but any container over 3.5 ounces will have to go into your checked luggage. See p. 821 for more info.

Maybe it's not unexpected that Bologna has many famous chocolatiers. **Majani,** Via de' Carbonesi 5 (© 051/234-302), claims to be Italy's oldest sweets shop, making confections since 1796. **Roccati,** Via Clavature 17A (www.roccaticioccolato.com; © 051/261-964), is run by a husband-and-wife team that makes the *gianduja* (hazelnut and cognac-filled chocolate) their ancestors once concocted for the princes of Savoy.

It also only stands to reason that this youth-oriented city is awash in bohemian chic, and the place to seek out some stylish vintage fashion is **La Leonarda**, Via San Leonarda 2/2A (© 340-936-8884), with a well-chosen, ever-changing selection of stylish second-hand fashions; proceeds go to an organization that aids the homeless.

Entertainment & Nightlife

Bologna's large student population keeps late hours in bars, clubs, and *osterie,* many clustered near the university on Via Zamboni and Via delle Belle Arti. Bolognese of all stripes, even those who plan to turn in early, stop at bars all over town for an *aperitivo,* when a glass of wine or a cocktail comes with snacks, usually served "all you can eat" buffet style.

Camera a Sud ★   Three shabby-chic rooms in the Jewish ghetto are part coffeehouse, part wine bar and late-night hangout, and popular any time of the day. Via Valdonica 5. www.cameraasud.net. © 051/095-1448. Mon–Sat noon–1am, Sun 5pm–1am.

Cantina Bentivoglio ★★   You'll hear some of the best jazz in Bologna in the cellars of this 16th-century *palazzo* near the university. Select from one of more than 500 labels that fill the wine racks. Via Mascarella 4B. www.cantinabentivoglio.it. © 051/265-416. Daily 8pm–2am. Lunch Mon–Fri 12:15–2:45pm.

Le Stanze ★   Cocktails are accompanied by a lavish buffet (it comes with the cost of a drink plus 1€), but the real feast here is visual—the atmospheric premises occupy the heavily frescoed salons and 17th-century chapel of an aristocratic palace. Via del Borgo di San Pietro www.lestanze cafe.it. © 051/228-767. Mon–Sat 11am–1am.

Nu Lounge Bar ★★   Hip young professionals check out each other (and themselves in the huge mirrors) while enjoying martinis under the porticos in the Quadrilatero. Via dei Musei 6. www.nuloungebar.com. ✆ **051/ 222-532.** Daily noon–2:30am.

Osteria de Poeti ★   Bologna's oldest *osteria*, feeding students since around 1600, not only dishes up cheap pastas and hearty *secondi* but live jazz and folk music as well, set against a mellow background of brick arches. Via De' Poeti 1. www.osteriadepoeti.com. ✆ **051/236-166.** Tues–Fri 12:30–2:30pm and 7:30pm–2:30am, Sat–Sun 7:30pm–2:30am.

Side Trip to Modena
45km (28 miles) northwest of Bologna

By all appearances, residents of this elegant little city, only a half-hour train ride from Bologna, excel at whatever pursuit they undertake. The city is famous for cars (see box below); for hams and cheeses, like its

PULLING INTO THE fast lane

Prosperous **Modena**, 40km (25 miles) northwest of Bologna, lies in the center of what's known as La Terra dei Motori, the "Land of Motors." A car enthusiast who's been patiently traipsing through museums and churches might be delighted to learn that all of Italy's famed sports-car manufacturers are located here—and open to the public. **Maserati,** founded in Bologna in 1914, is now based in Modena, and 20 vintage models are parked permanently at the **Museo Panini** (www.paninimotormuseum.it; visits by written request only [use form on website]; free; Mar–July and Sept–Oct Mon–Fri 9am–12:30pm and 2:30–6pm, Sat 9am–12:30pm), in the Modena suburb of Cittanova (on the SS9). Highlights include a rare Maserati Tipo 6CM from the 1930s and a Maserati A6G/54 from the 1950s.

In Maranello, 18km/11 miles from central Modena, **Museo Ferrari,** Via Dino Ferrari 43 pays homage to the magnificent cars that Enzo Ferrari began turning out in 1929; vintage and current models are on display. Tours run at 12:30pm and 1:30pm; buy tickets in advance on the website. More Ferraris, and the engines that power them, are on display at the **Museo Enzo Ferrari,** Via Paolo Ferrari 85, Modena. Both museums have the same website and phone (musei.ferrari.com; ✆ **0536/943-204**); Museo Ferrari charges 17€ admission, while Museo Enzo Ferrari charges 16€; a combined ticket costs 27€, over 65 and students 23€. Both are open daily 9:30am–7pm (closing 6pm Nov–Mar). A shuttle bus (6€) links the two museums and both with the Modena train station.

A visit to the **Museo Lamborghini,** in the company's hometown of Sant' Agata Bolognese, between Bologna and Modena (Via Modena 12, www. lamborghini.com; ✆ **051/681-7611;** 15€; Apr–Oct daily 9:30am–7pm, Nov–Mar daily 9:30am–6pm), can include a tour of the factory for 75€.

It's possible to make the pilgrimage by public transport, but not easily, and you certainly couldn't do the whole circuit in a day. Besides, a car buff will probably want to rent a car anyway, right? As an alternative, **Motorstars** (motorstars tour.com; ✆ **059/921-667**) provides a full day of touring, with transport from Bologna and lunch, from 300€.

neighbors in Emilia-Romagna; and for balsamic vinegar, *aceto balsemico,* made from grape must. You will taste the dark, intense elixir at just about any meal around town, and sample a wide variety at such specialty shops as **La Consertia 1066,** Piazza Giuseppe Mazzini 9 (*©* **393/802-7841**) or on a walk through **Mercato Albinelli,** the covered market at Via Albinelli 13.

At the city center is the showiest creation of all, the 12th-century **Duomo,** probably the finest creation of Romanesque architecture, above which towers a slightly leaning bell tower, the Ghirlandina (Duomo, www. visitmodena.it, *©* **059/216078;** free admission, Tues–Sun 7am–7pm, Mon 7am–12:30 and 3:30–7pm). The sculptor Wigilemo surrounded the main Duomo entrance with a fearsome medieval bestiary of monsters and beasts, depicting the temptation-ridden perils of our mortal journey, offset with poignant scenes of Adam and Eve, Noah's Ark, and other scenes from the Old Testament to suggest the path to redemption. On the northern side, the Porta della Pescheria (Fish Market doorway) is framed with an utterly charming assemblage of scenes of the 12 months (an old crone huddles in front of a fire in February) and knights-on-steeds tales from Arthurian legend.

A treasure trove of Italian painting (including a transcendent Madonna and Child by Botticelli), the legacy of the Este dukes who ruled the city from the 14th through 18th centuries, is in the **Galleria Estense,** Largo Porta Sant'Agostino 337 (www.gallerie-estensi.beniculturali.it; *©* **059/439-5711;** Tues–Sat 8:30am–7:30pm, Sun 2–7:30pm; 6€).

FERRARA ★★

52km (32 miles) N of Bologna, 100km (62 miles) SW of Venice

It's not that quiet, elegant Ferrara hasn't had some big moments. The powerful Este family controlled the city on the Po River for almost 4 centuries. Painters, composers, and poets came to town under their patronage and made Ferrara one of Europe's great capitals of culture. Lucrezia Borgia, notorious femme fatale of the Renaissance, arrived by ceremonial barge in 1502 to marry Prince Alfonso Este. They and the other Estes built pleasure pavilions and gardens and expanded their holdings into the Addizione, a model city of the Renaissance crisscrossed

Ferrara by Bike

Ferrara is known in Italy as a *città della bicicletta,* because just about everyone in town, regardless of age, gets around on two wheels. The flat streets and squares lend themselves to easy pedaling, and the medieval walls are topped with trees, lawns, and a wide path that's ideal for cycling. Views of the city and surrounding farmlands are terrific, and if you want to go farther afield, well-marked bike paths lead into the Po Delta. Many hotels offer guests free use of bikes, or you can rent them from the lot outside the train station (2.50€ an hour, 10€ a day).

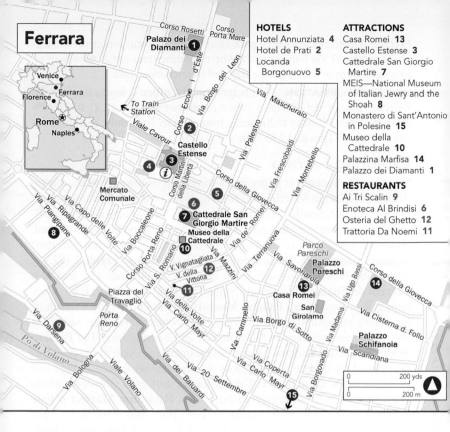

Ferrara

Venice
Florence · Ferrara
Rome ⊛
Naples

← To Train
Station

Corso Rosetti   Corso
Porta Mare

Palazo dei
Diamanti ❶

Via Borgo del Leon

Corso Ercole I d'Este

Via Mascheraio

Viale Cavour

❷

Castello
Estense

❹ ❸
ⓘ

Via Palestro

Via Frescobaldi

Via Montebello

Corso Martiri
della Libertà

Corso della Giovecca

❺

Mercato
Comunale

Via Capo delle Volte

Via Ripagrande

Via Piangipane

Via Boccaleone

❽

❻

❼ Cattedrale San
Giorgio Martire

Museo della
Cattedrale

❿

Corso Porta Reno

Via S. Romano

V. Vignatagliata

V. della
Vittoria

⓬

Via Mazzini

Via de' Romei

Via Terranuova

Via Savonarola

Parco
Pareschi

Palazzo
Pareschi

⓭

Casa Romei

San
Girolamo

Corso della Giovecca

Via Madama

Via Ugo Bassi

⓮

Via Cisterna d. Follo

⓫

Piazza del
Travaglio

Porta
Reno

Via delle Volte

Via Carlo Mayr

Via Cammello

Via Borgo di Sotto

Via Darsena

❾

Po di Volano

Via Bologna

Viale Volano

Via dei Baluardi

Via 20 Settembre

Via Carlo Mayr

Via Coperta

Via Borgovado

Via Scandiana

Palazzo
Schifanoia

⓯

0   200 yds
0   200 m

HOTELS
Hotel Annunziata **4**
Hotel de Prati **2**
Locanda
  Borgonuovo **5**

ATTRACTIONS
Casa Romei **13**
Castello Estense **3**
Cattedrale San Giorgio
  Martire **7**
MEIS—National Museum
  of Italian Jewry and the
  Shoah **8**
Monastero di Sant'Antonio
  in Polesine **15**
Museo della
  Cattedrale **10**
Palazzina Marfisa **14**
Palazzo dei Diamanti **1**

RESTAURANTS
Ai Tri Scalin **9**
Enoteca Al Brindisi **6**
Osteria del Ghetto **12**
Trattoria Da Noemi **11**

---

with straight, palace-lined avenues. By the end of the 16th century, how-ever, the Estes were gone—and Ferrara has looked pretty much the same ever since. That, of course, is the appeal. In what's essentially a time cap-sule, the Estes' castle and palaces and encircling walls, and proud old convents and churches are the backdrop for everyday life in an attractive provincial city.

Essentials

ARRIVING   Ferrara is on the main **train** line between Bologna and Ven-ice, with service to and from both cities twice an hour (30–45 min. from Bologna; 1–1½ hrs. from Venice). Ravenna is an hour away, with hourly departures all day. From the train station it's an easy 20-minute walk to the Duomo, but you can also take the frequent no. 1 or 9 bus to Piazza Travaglio (1.30€; buy your ticket at the bus office inside the train station or at a tobacco shop; www.tper.it). You may also rent a **bike** at the station and get around the way most locals do (see "Ferrara By Bike," p. 368).

　　If you have a **car** and are coming from Bologna, take A13 north. From Venice, take A4 southwest to Padua and continue on A13 south to

Ferrara. A convenient spot to park close to the historic center is Parcheggio Darsena, 47 Via Nino Bonnet, where daytime rates are .80€ an hour up to a maximum of 3.20€ for the day and free for overnight.

VISITOR INFORMATION   The helpful **tourist office** is inside the Castello Estense, Piazza del Castello (www.ferraraterraeacqua.it; ℘ **0532/299-303**). It's open Monday to Saturday from 9am to 1pm and 2 to 6pm, Sunday 9:30am to 1pm and 2 to 5pm.

Exploring Ferrara

The **Castello Estense** is pretty much the center of town, with the **Cattedrale San Giorgio Martire** and twisting lanes of the medieval town just to the southeast. South of Castello lies the city's most atmospheric medieval lane, narrow cobblestoned **Via delle Volte,** darkened with arched, upper-story passageways that once linked merchants' houses with their riverside warehouses. North from the Castello, **Corso Ercole I d'Este,** flanked by beautiful *palazzi,* leads into the Renaissance city and past **Palazzo dei Diamanti** to the city walls. Turn right onto Corso Porto Mare to pass Renaissance-era **Palazzo Massari** (Corso Porto Mare 9), with its marvelous collections of 19th-century and contemporary art; sadly, it's still closed for renovations following the 2012 earthquake. The **Palazzo Schifanoia,** Via Scandiana 23, with its mesmerizing cycle of frescoes, has also closed for structural renovations with no date set for reopening.

East of the Castello, Via Cavour turns into Corso Giovecca, where you can visit the well-preserved brick villa **Palazzina Marfisa d'Este** (Corso Giovecca 170, ℘ **0532/244-949;** 4€; Tues–Sun 9:30am–12:30pm and 3–6pm), whose 16th-century resident Marfisa d'Este was a granddaughter of Lucrezia Borgia. Marfisa allegedly used to ride through these streets on moonlit nights in a carriage pulled by wolves; she is said to have enjoyed entertaining young men in her elegant salons before murdering them.

Casa Romei ★★ PALACE   Ambitious 15th-century financier Giovanni Romei worked his way up in the Este administration, capping off his rise by marrying the daughter of an Este duke. He built this palatial townhouse between 1440 and 1450, commissioning lavish frescoes for salons surrounding a vast interior courtyard. Though the Estes carted off most of the furnishings when they left Ferrara in 1598, the Sala delle Sibille, with its original terracotta fireplace, coffered wooden ceiling, and images of the sibyls (classical Greek prophetesses), provides an idea of the comfortable lifestyle the occupants enjoyed. Scattered about the place are frescoes and sculptures from churches and chapels around the city.

Via Savonarola 30. www.ferraraterraeacqua.it. ℘ **0532/234-130.** 3€. Sun–Wed 8:30am–2pm; Thurs–Sat 2–7:30pm. Bus: 11.

Castello Estense ★★ CASTLE   With its moat, hefty brick walls, drawbridges, heavy gates, and four sturdy towers, the domain of the Este

Cyclists on Via Giuseppe Mazzini in Ferrara.

family still suggests power and might. Niccolò II d'Este ordered the castle built in 1385 as a place of refuge when his subjects, becoming restless after a series of tax increases, quite literally tore one of his officials to pieces. A long elevated gallery links the castle to the family's onetime residence, now the Palazzo Municipale, next door (wander into the double courtyard for a look at the monumental staircase). Duke Niccolò d'Este III forever made the castle a place of infamy when, in 1425, he used a contrivance of mirrors to catch his 20-year-old wife, Parisina d'Este, *in flagrante delicto* with his illegitimate son, Ugolino. He promptly had the pair taken to the dungeons and beheaded; Robert Browning tells the story in his poem "My Last Duchess." (Ironically, Niccolò himself boasted of sleeping with 800 women; a popular rhyme of the time was "left and right of the river Po, everywhere there are children by Niccolò.") Young Lucrezia Borgia, with her reputation for adultery, incest, and poisoning, arrived in 1502 as the wife of Duke Alfonso d'Este, who kept his half-brother, Giulio, in the dungeons for 53 years for plotting to overthrow him; the old boy allegedly created quite a stir when he re-emerged onto the streets in half-century-old finery. For all their perfidy, the Estes hosted one of the finest courts in Europe and cultivated Renaissance arts and humanities. Their refined tastes come to the fore in the frescoed **Salone dell'Aurora** (the Salon of Dawn) and **Salone dei Giochi** (the Salon of Games), and an *orangerie* that continues to flourish on terraces high above the city. Take a walk up the innovative ramplike spiral staircase ascending from the court-yard that allowed the dukes to ride their horses right up to their quarters. Largo Castello. www.castelloestense.it. ☏ **0532/299-233.** 8€ adults, 6€ ages 11–18, free for children 10 and under. Mar–Sept daily 9:30am–5:30pm; Oct–Feb Tues–Sun 9:30am–5:30pm. Bus: 1, 7, 9, 11, 21.

Cattedrale San Giorgio Martire ★ CATHEDRAL

The faithful did not even have to step beyond the magnificent 12th-century porch of Ferrara's cathedral to understand that salvation was a pretty dicey affair. In exquisite carvings above the entryway, the dead creep out of their tombs as an angel weighs sins and good deeds on a scale; as if to prove that the odds are against salvation, a devil mischievously tugs on the evil side so it skews toward sin. The saved, gloriously crowned and robed, proceed toward Heaven, where they are welcomed into the lap of Abraham; the naked damned slouch down to Hell to be tormented by sneering devils. In the vast interior—redone in dark baroque style after an 18th-century fire—look for a fresco by Guercino ("the squinter") portraying the martyrdom of St. Lawrence. When Roman authorities demanded that Lawrence, an early church deacon, turn over ecclesiastic treasures, he brought them the poor, saying "Behold in these poor persons the treasures which I promised to show you." As punishment Lawrence was tied to a spit and burned over a roaring fire. After the good-natured saint roasted for a time, he allegedly said, "I'm well done, turn me over," a wisecrack that has earned him a place as patron of chefs and cooks. The **cathedral museum,** housed in the former San Romano church and monastery opposite the church, is well stocked with works by Ferrara's leading 15th-century painter of the Este court, Cosmé Tura.

Piazza della Cattedrale. www.ferraraterraeacqua.it. ☏ **0532/207-449.** Church free. Mon–Fri 7:30–11am and 4–7pm; Sat 7:30am–noon and 3–7pm; Sun 7:30am–1pm and 3:30–8pm. Church free. Museum: 6€ adults, 3€ for students, ages 17 and under free. Tues–Sun 9:30am–1pm and 3–6pm. Bus: 11.

Monastero di Sant'Antonio in Polesine ★★ CHURCH

The Estes weren't all about worldly goods and power. In the early 13th century the aristocratic lady who would become Saint Beatrice d'Este entered this tranquil convent near the city walls when her groom-to-be died of battle wounds just before their wedding day. Over the years Este money paid for improvements that included a colorful fresco cycle by the school of Giotto in the nun's chapel; their charming images include an exuberant Christ climbing a ladder onto the cross, where two spike-wielding tormentors await, and a gentle-looking Virgin fluttering her hands to ascend to Heaven. Ring the bell to enter, and a nun will emerge to show off the frescoes (in Italian). She'll also invite you to return for 5pm vespers, where you'll hear the cloistered order sing Gregorian chants from behind a grill.

Vicolo del Gambone. www.ferraraterraeacqua.it. ☏ **0532/64068.** Free (donations welcome). Mon–Fri 9:30–11:30am and 3:15–5pm, Sat 9:30–11:30am and 3:15–4:30pm. Bus 2 to XX Settembre Ghisiglieri stop.

The Jews of Ferrara

Ferrara's Jewish heritage dates to the Middle Ages—a Jewish community flourished here when the Este family controlled the city. The sad fate of Ferrara's socially prominent 20th-century Jews is the subject of Giorgio Bassani's novel *The Garden of the Finzi-Contini,* brought evocatively to the screen in director Vittorio de Sica's 1970 film. Ferrara's excellent **Jewish Museum,** encompassing two synagogues in an old palazzo at Via Mazzini 95, was severely damaged in the 2012 earthquakes and its reopening date is still to be determined. However, Ferrara is also the home of **MEIS—National Museum of Italian Jewry and the Shoah,** which is opening in stages and scheduled for completion in 2021

(Via Piangipane 81; www.meisweb.it; ✆ **0532/769-137**). Already on view in the complex, a former prison, are manuscripts and other artifacts, as well as video and multimedia exhibits on the Jewish-Italian experience from the Roman era through the rise of Christianity; on Jews in the Renaissance; and on the holocaust experience in Italy. Among special exhibitions is "The Garden that Doesn't Exist," conceptual artist Dani Karavan's model and schematics for a planned installation depicting the fictional garden of the novel and film *Garden of the Finzi-Contini* as an homage to the Jews of Ferrara murdered in World War II (Tues–Sun 10am–6pm, 8€).

Palazzo dei Diamanti ★ MUSEUM   The facade of the Estes' most remarkable residence—8,500 spiky diamond-shaped white marble blocks—creates an architectural spectacle, shimmering in the light and seemingly constantly in movement. The *palazzo* stands at the intersection of two monumental avenues that were the main thoroughfares of the Addizione that Ercole d'Este laid out in the late 15th century, doubling the size of Ferrara and making the city a Renaissance showplace. On the first floor of the *palazzo,* the **Pinacoteca Nazionale** provides a handy overview of the School of Ferrara, especially the trio of old masters who flourished under the Estes—Cosmé Tura, Francesco del Cossa, and Ercole de' Roberti. Pride of place belongs to Tura's "Martyrdom of St. Maurelius," in which the saint, an early bishop of Ferrara, calmly kneels as his executioner swings a sword above his neck and some nattily attired, cheerful-looking soldiers look on.

Corso Ercole d'Este 21. www.gallerie-estensi.beniculturali.it ✆ **0532/205-844** or 0532/244-949. Pinacoteca 6€ adults, free for ages 17 and under. Daily 10am–5:30pm. Bus: 3C or 4C.

Where to Stay in Ferrara

Hotel Annunziata ★★   The setting, across from Castello Estense, is medieval, and Casanova spent the night here when the place was a simple inn. But once inside the doors, you'll feel like you've been transported from old Ferrara into a Milanese showroom for contemporary style. The white color scheme strays into grays and beige here and there, even the occasional burst of red or orange, but for the most part this place is all about sleek lines, soothing neutrals, and minimalist calm. In the large and bright guest rooms, the best with castle views, high-tech lighting and snowy linens contrast with wood floors and the occasional timbered ceiling, and bathrooms are luxurious. Six stylish apartments with kitchenettes are located in a 14th-century annex.

Piazza Repubblica 5. www.annunziata.it. © **0532/201-111.** 27 units. 70€–140€ double. Rates include breakfast. Bus: 1, 7, 9, 11, 21. **Amenities:** Restaurant; bar; babysitting; bikes; room service; Wi-Fi (free).

Hotel de Prati ★★   This welcoming inn is nicely appointed with polished antiques and wrought-iron bedsteads in bright, quiet rooms enlivened with colorful paintings by local artists. Timbered beams and old archways show off the house's centuries-old origins. The refined old-world air extends to the gracious service provided by the de Prati family, who have been running the place for three generations.

Via Padiglioni 5. www.hoteldeprati.com. © **0532/241-905.** 28 units. 75€–120€ double. Rates include breakfast. Bus: Bus: 3C or 4C. **Amenities:** Bikes; Wi-Fi (free).

Locanda Borgonuovo ★★★   This lovely old house, converted from a 17th-century convent and just down a cobblestone street from the *castello,* could set the gold standard for B&Bs everywhere. The four rooms are furnished with family pieces, including some serious antiques, and share a flowery courtyard; one especially large double has an extra bed and a kitchenette. An excellent breakfast is served in the family living room, and the gracious hosts lend bikes and dispense advice about the best ways to enjoy their beloved Ferrara. They also rent a few one- and two-bedroom apartments in an adjoining building.

Via Cairoli 21. www.borgonuovo.com. © **0532/211-100.** 75€–100€ double. Rates include breakfast. Bus: 4C or 7. **Amenities:** Bikes; Wi-Fi (free).

Where to Eat in Ferrara

You'll get a good intro to Ferrara's gastronomic pleasures on a stroll down Via Cortevecchia, a narrow brick lane near the cathedral where traditional *salumerias* such as Marchetti at no. 35 (© **0532/204-800**) sell the city's famous *salama da suga,* handmade sausages. The food stalls of the **Mercato Comunale,** at the corner of Via Santo Stefano and Via del Mercato, are also good grazing grounds. Look for *coppia Ferrarese,* sourdough bread stretched into intertwining rolls that resemble two sets of legs (hence the name, "the couple"). In restaurants, the pasta to try is *cappellacci di zucca*—round pasta stuffed with squash, served *al burro e salvia* (with butter and sage sauce) or *al ragu* (with meat sauce).

Ai Tri Scalin ★ FERRARESE   Locals pack into this simple, half-paneled room near the city walls at mealtimes (best to reserve for dinner) to enjoy the ages-old dishes their grandmothers used to make. Grilled *salami da suga,* the city's famed sausages, are the preferred starters, followed by *maccheroni alla ferrarese,* a concoction of pasta, béchamel sauce, truffles, and ground beef baked in a pie crust. By now you may have figured

Ferrara's Piazza Trento Trieste.

out that the Ferrarese are shameless carnivores: *Cotechino,* boiled sausage, is served with a rich salami sauce, and lamb chops or steaks are seasoned with green peppercorns and grilled to perfection. The dessert of choice is *tenerina,* the city's own version of chocolate cake, with a crunchy crust and creamy interior.

Via Darsena 50. ℭ **0532/760-331.** Entrees 7€–14€. Sun–Mon 12:30–3pm; Tues–Sat 12:30–3pm and 7:30–10pm. Bus: 2.

Enoteca Al Brindisi ★ FERRARESE   It would be easy for this atmospheric little place—probably the oldest wine bar in the world, dating from 1435—to rest on its laurels. Titian was a regular, Copernicus is said to have lived upstairs while studying for his degree in 1503, and it looks like some of the dusty bottles stacked above the cramped tables have been around ever since. Locals (some of whom look like they've been around awhile, too) still pack the place, and waiters take earnest pride in recommending Italian wines, accompanied by a short menu of *cappellacci di zucca* (squash ravioli) and a few other local specialties.

Via Adelardi 11. www.albrindisi.net. ℭ **0532/473-744.** Entrees 7€–12€. Daily 11am–1am. Bus: 11.

Osteria del Ghetto ★ FERRARESE/SEAFOOD   From a simple storefront on the narrow cobblestone lanes of Ferrara's centuries-old

Lucrezia Borgia, A Woman Misjudged?

Five hundred years after their Renaissance heyday, the Borgias are still one of history's most dysfunctional families. Lucrezia, born into the clan in 1480, was the illegitimate daughter of Cardinal Rodrigo Borgia (soon to be Pope Alexander VI). By the time she was 20, she had a child, allegedly fathered by her brother Cesare, and had been married twice—one husband fled for his life when the Pope decided Lucrezia needed a more politically useful alliance, another was strangled as he lay recovering from knife wounds (both attacks arranged by Cesare). No wonder Lucrezia got a chilly reception when she arrived in Ferrara in 1500 as the new bride of Duke Alfonso d'Este. However, she proved herself a brilliant conversationalist and patron of the arts; while she is said to have carried on a passionate affair with the poet Pietro Bembo, she was also a loving wife and attentive mother, dying just before her 39th birthday after giving birth to her fifth child.

Jewish ghetto, a staircase leads to two homey upstairs rooms enlivened with colorful murals. A small selection of pasta and meat dishes is available, but clearly the kitchen's passion is for fish—a fresh catch is usually on the menu, as is fried calamari and shrimp, rich fish soup, *spaghetti alle vongole,* seafood salads, and other choices to tempt you away from the region's meat-heavy staples.

Via Vittoria 26/28. www.osteriadelghetto.it. ✆ **0532/764-936.** Entrees 8€–16€. Tues–Sun noon–2:30pm and 7:30–10:30pm. Bus: 2.

Trattoria Da Noemi ★★ FERRARESE   The surroundings date to 1400, with a pleasant old-world decor that befits the provenance and gracious service. The menu leans to Ferrarese classics—some residents say no one does them better. This is the place to become acquainted with *cappellacci di zucca,* the city's signature dish, little pockets of light egg pasta stuffed with roasted butternut squash with hints of nutmeg and parmigiano. Much of the meat-heavy *secondi* features local beef grilled over a wood fire. The house *semifreddo,* a delicious half-frozen custard with pistachio and walnuts or mint, is the perfect finish.

Via Ragno 31. www.trattoriadanoemi.it. ✆ **0532/769-070.** Entrees 8€–24€. Wed–Mon 12:30–2:30pm and 7:30–10:30pm. Bus: 2 or 11.

RAVENNA ★★

74km (46 miles) E of Bologna, 145km (90 miles) S of Venice, 130km (81 miles) NE of Florence

It's hard to believe that Ravenna was the epicenter of the Western World for a brief spell, when it was the capital of the Western Roman Empire from A.D. 402 to A.D. 476. Those rulers and the fathers of the early Christian church, and then the Goths and Byzantines who followed them, blanketed Ravenna's churches and monuments in glittering mosaics to create

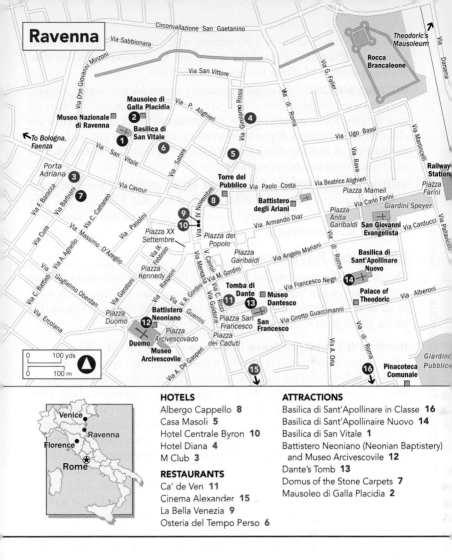

Ravenna

Circonvallazione San Gaetanino

Via Sabbionara

Via San Vittore

Theodoric's Mausoleum

Rocca Brancaleone

Via G. Falier

Via Don Giovanni Minzoni

Via P. Alighieri

Via Girolamo Rossi

Via di Roma

Mausoleo di Galla Placidia **2**

Museo Nazionale di Ravenna **1**

Basilica di San Vitale **6**

Via Ugo Bassi

Via Maroncelli

To Bologna, Faenza

Via San Vitale

Via Salara

5

Via Rava

Railway Station

Porta Adriana

Via Cavour

3

7

Via F. Baracca

Via Barbiani

Via C. Cattaneo

Via Pasolini

Via Massimo D'Azeglio

Torre del Pubblico **8**

Via Paolo Costa

Via Beatrice Alighieri

Piazza Mameli

Piazza Farini

Giardini Speyer

Via IV Novembre

Battistero degli Ariani **9** **10**

Via Armando Diaz

Piazza Anita Garibaldi

San Giovanni Evangelista

Via Carlo Farini

Via Carducci

Via Pellaincini

Piazza XX Settembre

Via IX Febbraio

Piazza del Popolo

Piazza Garibaldi

Via Angelo Mariani

Basilica di Sant'Apollinare Nuovo

Via A. Agnello

Via Garatoni

Via Guerrini

V. Cairoli

Via M. Gordini

Piazza Garibaldi

Via di Roma

14

Via C. Battisti

Guglielmo Oberdan

Piazza Kennedy

Via R. Gordini

Via C. Ricci

Via Guidarei

Tomba di Dante **11**

Museo Dantesco **13**

Via Francesco Negri

Palace of Theodoric

Via Alberoni

Via Ercolana

Piazza Duomo

Battistero Neoniano **12**

Piazza Arcivescovado

Piazza San Francesco

San Francesco

Via Girotto Guaccimanni

Via di Roma

Via A. Oria

Duomo

Museo Arcivescovile

Piazza dei Caduti

Via A. De Gasperi

15

Giardino Pubblico

Pinacoteca Comunale **16**

0   100 yds
0   100 m

Venice

Ravenna

Florence

Rome

HOTELS
Albergo Cappello **8**
Casa Masoli **5**
Hotel Centrale Byron **10**
Hotel Diana **4**
M Club **3**

RESTAURANTS
Ca' de Ven **11**
Cinema Alexander **15**
La Bella Venezia **9**
Osteria del Tempo Perso **6**

ATTRACTIONS
Basilica di Sant'Apollinare in Classe **16**
Basilica di Sant'Apollinaire Nuovo **14**
Basilica di San Vitale **1**
Battistero Neoniano (Neonian Baptistery) and Museo Arcivescovile **12**
Dante's Tomb **13**
Domus of the Stone Carpets **7**
Mausoleo di Galla Placidia **2**

an artistic legacy that rivals the splendors of Venice and Istanbul. (The poet Dante, who's buried here, described Ravenna's mosaics as "the sweet color of Oriental sapphires.") Set amid the marshy landscapes of Emilia-Romagna's coastal plain, this once glamorous and powerful city is a bit off the beaten path but well worth the effort to reach.

Essentials

ARRIVING   With hourly **trains** that take only 1 hour, 20 minutes from Bologna, Ravenna can easily be visited on a day trip. There's also frequent service from Ferrara (1 hr., 15 min.), which has connections to

Venice. The train station is a 10-minute walk from the center at Piazza Fernini (© **892-021**). If you have a **car** and are coming from Bologna, head east along A14. From Ferrara, take the S16.

GETTING AROUND   Ravenna operates a useful bicycle rental system; keys provided by the tourist office give you unlimited access to bikes all over the city. Rates are 10€ per day for adults and 9€ for students (free for children 10 and under). If you need to take a local **bus** (as you will to visit the Basilica di Sant'Apollinare in Classe; see below), buy tickets (1.30€) in advance from any bar or *tabacchi*.

VISITOR INFORMATION   The **tourist office** at Piazza San Francesco (www.turismo.ravenna.it; © **0544-35755;** Mon–Sat 8:30am–6pm, Sun 10am–4pm) offers a good map, bike rentals, and attraction tickets. They also book accommodations.

Exploring Ravenna

The elegant, Venetian-looking **Piazza del Popolo** was laid out in the late 15th century, when Venice ruled the city. From here you can easily walk to all of the sights, with the exception of Sant'Apollinare in Classe, for which you'll want to take a bus or drive.

Basilica di Sant'Apollinare in Classe ★★ CHURCH   What is now a landlocked suburb was at one time the seaport of the capital of the Western Roman Empire. This huge 6th-century church—dedicated to St. Apollinare, the first bishop of Ravenna—befits the city's importance back then. Apollinare allegedly landed in Ravenna sometime in the 2nd century and converted the locals; look for the dazzling mosaic that shows him in prayer, surrounded by lambs (his flock) against a background of rocks, birds, and plants, including the pines that still grow outside the church. (Lord Byron used to ride here with his Ravennese mistress, Teresa Guiccioli.) Above Apollinare is a scene of the Transfiguration, when Christ became radiant with light; he is represented as a golden cross on a starry blue background, while Peter, James, and John, the three disciples who witnessed the event, are shown as lambs. Some especially touching mosaics on the right of the church shows three Old Testament figures who

---

Ravenna Combo Tickets

Admission to just about all of the sights we recommend in this book is covered by one tourist card, valid for 7 days, that costs 9.50€ (8.50€ for students). You need this card to get into any of these sites; you can buy it at any of them (www.ravennamosaici.it) and it's valid for 7 days, with one entry per monument. The one big exception is the Basilica di Sant'Apollinare in Classe, which costs 5€. Put them together and you can see the major sights in Ravenna for just 14.50€— how's that for a good deal?

Ravenna's Piazza del Popolo with Orologio tower and Palazzo del Governo.

made sacrifices to God: Abel, Melchizedek, and Abraham. The church is in the town of Classe, about 6km (3¾ miles) south of Ravenna.

Via Romea Sud 224, Classe. © **0544/473-569.** 5€ adults, 2.50€ ages 18–25, free for children 17 and under. Mon–Sat 8:30am–7:30pm, Sun 1–7:30pm. Bus: 4 from rail station or Piazza Caduti.

Basilica di Sant'Apollinare Nuovo ★★ CHURCH   The church that Emperor Theodoric built in the first part of the 6th century for followers of Arianism, a Christian sect, seems to be in perpetual motion. On the left side of the nave, reserved for women, 22 female saints and martyrs approach Mary and the Christ child as they receive gifts from the three magi. On the right side, 26 male martyrs led by St. Martin approach a bearded Christ. Above these processions are 26 charmingly rendered scenes from the life of Christ, including one of Christ standing on the shore and calling to Peter and Andrew in their small fishing boat, asking them to be his disciples. Mosaics near the door provide a picture-postcard view of the old city, including Theodoric's palace and the port city of Classe. Look for the detached hand and forearm wrapped around a column of Theodoric's palace—it was once part of a portrait of Theodoric's court that was removed when the church became a Catholic basilica.

Via di Roma. www.ravennamosaici.it. © **0544/541-688.** Cumulative ticket 9.50€ adults, 8.50€ students, free for children 10 and under. Mar–Oct daily 9am–7pm; Nov–Feb daily 10am–5pm.

Basilica di San Vitale ★★★ CHURCH The emperor Justinian (who never visited Ravenna and ruled instead from Constantinople) completed this octagonal church—richly ornamented with intensely green, blue, and gold mosaics—in 540 as a symbol of his power. Endowed with a halo to indicate his role as head of church and state, Justinian stands next to a clean-shaven Christ, perched atop the world, flanked by saints and angels. Looking on are Justinian's two most important adjuncts, his empress, Theodora, and a bald Maximianus, bishop of Ravenna. Theodora's presence suggests her immense influence and rapacious rise to power. Born into the circus, she became a famous actress and courtesan known for her beauty. As Justinian's wife, she wielded such power that in 532, not long before this church was completed, she ordered that 30,000 insurgents be gathered up, brought to the Hippodrome in Constantinople, and slaughtered.

Via San Vitale 17. www.ravennamosaici.it. © **0544/215-193.** Cumulative ticket 9.50€ adults, 8.50€ students, free for children 10 and under. Mar–Oct daily 9am–7pm; Nov–Feb daily 10am–5pm.

Battistero Neoniano (Neonian Baptistery) and Museo Arcivescovile ★ CHURCH/MUSEUM Ravenna's oldest monument was erected by Bishop Ursus around 400, to accompany a basilica (long since destroyed) on the site of an ancient Roman bath. The eight sides of this octagonal structure represent the 7 days of the week, as set out in Genesis, plus the day of the Resurrection, when Christ gave mankind eternal life. Bishop Neon embellished the structure at the end of the 5th century, adding the intensely colored blue, green, and gold mosaics that spread over the dome, showing John the Baptist baptizing Christ in the River Jordan, surrounded by the 12 Apostles carrying crowns as a sign of celestial glory. Many of the marble panels in the walls were taken from the Roman bathhouse. Note that the baptistery was originally at street level, which has risen more than 3m (10 ft.) over the intervening centuries. Adjacent is the Museo Arcivescovile, set in what was the private oratory of the 5th-century bishops of Ravenna. A mosaic in its chapel portrays Christ in a way he

Mosaics in the Neonian Baptistery in Ravenna.

In 1993, archeologists found a small Roman palace beneath the church of Sant'Eufemia—14 rooms and 3 courtyards carpeted in colorful mosaics, with scenes of dancers, lute players, and frolicking forest animals. The so-called **Domus of the Stone Carpets** (Via Barbiani 16, www.domusdeitappetidipietra.it, ✆ **0544/32512**) evokes a lavish lifestyle at the very end of the Roman empires. The mosaics are on view year-round (Mar–Sept daily 10am–6:30pm, Oct–Dec Mon–Fri 10am–5pm, Sat–Sun 10am–6pm; and Jan–Feb Sat–Sun 10am–6pm); admission is 4€, or 3€ for students. And in the **Basilica of San Francesco** (Piazza San Francesco; free; daily 8am–1pm and 4–7pm), go down into the 5th-century crypt for an eerie sight: floodwaters have seeped into the crypt, and mosaics on the submerged floor can be seen shimmering in the light.

is rarely seen elsewhere—as a victorious warrior in battle garb standing on a snake. The museum is a warren of cramped little galleries, but make sure you find one item in particular: A 6th-century bishops' throne that just may be the finest bit of ivory work in the world.

Piazza del Duomo. www.ravennamosaici.it. ✆ **0544/215-201.** Cumulative ticket 9.50€ adults, 8.50€ students, free for children 10 and under. Mar–Oct daily 9am–7pm; Nov–Feb daily 10am–5pm.

Mausoleo di Galla Placidia ★★ MONUMENT   One of the most powerful women of the Byzantine world, Galla Placida was the daughter and granddaughter of Roman emperors, sister of one ruler of the Western Roman Empire, and widow of another. Captured by the Visigoths during the sack of Rome in 410, she married King Athaulf, moved with his barbarian hordes to Barcelona, was traded back to the Romans for grain when Athaulf was murdered, and then married co-emperor Constantius, with whom she had a son, Valentinian III. When Constantius died and Valentinian became emperor at the age of 6, Galla acted as regent, ruling the Western world for 12 years. Though she's most likely buried in Rome, her mausoleum here is spectacular, crowned with a dome decorated with mosaics in vivid hues of peacock blue, moss green, Roman gold, eggplant purple, and burnt orange. Their simple spirituality is striking—doves drink from fountains, as the devout are nourished by God; a purple-robed Christ is surrounded by lambs, as the Heavenly king is surrounded by the faithful; and 570 tiny gold stars, suggesting life eternal, twinkle in the cupola. Soft light filtered by alabaster infuses everything with otherworldly luminosity.

Via Fiandrini Benedetto. www.ravennamosaici.it. ✆ **0544/541-688.** Cumulative ticket 9.50€ adults, 8.50€ students, free for children 10 and under. Mar–Oct daily 9am–7pm; Nov–Feb daily 10am–5pm.

Tomba di Dante (Dante's Tomb) ★ MONUMENT   The author of the *Divine Comedy* settled in Ravenna in 1318, having traveled restlessly throughout Italy after he was exiled from his native Florence in 1302, when he fell out of political favor. He died of marsh fever here on September 14, 1321. This simple marble tomb, erected in 1780, is inscribed with a harsh reprimand to the Florentines, who are still clamoring for the body's return: "Here in this corner lies Dante, exiled from his native land, born to Florence, an unloving mother."

Via Dante Alighieri. ✆ **0544/33662.** Free. Daily 10am–6:30pm (Oct–Mar closes 4pm).

Where to Stay in Ravenna

Ravenna's hotels do a slow business off-season (anytime outside of summer); rates come down accordingly and are usually open to some negotiation.

Albergo Cappello ★★ An old palace in the center of town retains enough damask, Murano chandeliers, stone fireplaces, and impressive old furnishings to make any guest feel like an aristocrat. (One former highborn inhabitant was Francesca da Polenta, whose story Dante told in his *Divine Comedy*—her husband caught her with her lover and strangled them both.) Most of the seven large, high-ceilinged rooms are suites that open off salons on the *piano nobile,* while a few less grand but similarly character-filled quarters are tucked into a wing in the rear. Breakfast is served in a morning room downstairs amid a charming bestiary of forest creatures; a handsome wood-beamed wine bar serves well into the evening.

Via IV Novembre 41. www.albergocappello.it. ✆ **0544/212-114.** 7 units. 140€–170€ double. Rates include breakfast. **Amenities:** Bar; restaurant; Wi-Fi (free).

Casa Masoli ★★★ An 18th-century *palazzo* near the city center exudes a familial and slightly bohemian ambience, like the home of your favorite aunt and uncle, the arty ones. Two splendid suites at the front of the house are especially grand and cavernous—one retains the original brick vaulting, another frescoes and a marble tub—but high ceilings, tall windows, and wood-veneered bathrooms lend all the rooms a big dose of grandeur; those in the back face a surprisingly verdant garden. Scattered antiques, comfy lounge chairs and couches, and framed lithographs are friendly touches, as is the generous breakfast buffet with lots of homemade fare served in a frescoed salon.

Via Girolamo Rossi 22. www.casamasoli.it. ✆ **0544/217-682.** 7 units. 70€–130€ double. Rates include breakfast. **Amenities:** Wi-Fi (free).

Hotel Centrale Byron ★ From 1819 to 1821 Lord Byron shared a nearby palace with his lover, Contessa Teresa Guiccioli, a husband who was 40 years her senior, and a bestiary of pets that included peacocks and ducks, and Ravenna has been milking the menage ever since. This hotel—one of several establishments in town named for the Romantic poet—is a lot less evocative than its name suggests, but it is wonderfully located a stone's throw from most of the sights, a few steps from Piazza del Popolo, and an easy stroll from the train station. Constant updating has given the rooms a contemporary patina more geared toward comfort than character, with welcome touches such as soundproofing and excellent lighting.

Via IV Novembre 14. www.hotelsravenna.it. © **0544/212-225.** 54 units. 75€–110€ double. Most rates include breakfast. **Amenities:** Bar; room service; Wi-Fi (free).

Hotel Diana ★ Tucked away slightly off the beaten path at the edge of the city center, but within an easy stroll to the sights, these large, bright, and simply furnished rooms are enlivened with bright colors and attractive prints (and many have extremely large windowed bathrooms). Downstairs, an English-speaking staff dispenses recommendations with genuine enthusiasm, and a generous buffet breakfast is served on a large, glass-enclosed patio. This is a handy base for motorists, with several easy-to-reach garages nearby.

Via Girolamo Rossi 47. www.hoteldiana.ra.it. © **0544/39164.** 33 units. 50€–95€ double. Rates include breakfast. **Amenities:** Bikes; Wi-Fi (free).

M Club ★★★ Keeping in step with the quiet elegance of old Ravenna, these bright quarters at the edge of the historic center are stylish and welcoming, crisscrossed with heavy beams and filled with a tasteful mix of antiques, oil paintings, French and Italian prints, and family memorabilia. Large windows open to Hadrian's Gate across the square out front or a quiet garden in back. While the six distinctively decorated rooms are set up for relaxing in private (the suite has a monastery table long enough to host a banquet), lounges are inviting as well.

Via Baracca. www.m-club.it. © **333/955-6466.** 5 units. 90€–130€ double. Rates include breakfast. **Amenities:** Bikes; Wi-Fi (free).

Where to Eat in Ravenna

Ravenna's **Mercato Coperto** (near the center of town on Piazza Andrea Costa), once an attraction in itself, has been closed for renovation for years and after much delay is slated to reopen as a food hall, with shops, bars, and restaurants, by mid-2020. **Gastronomia Marchesini,** an elegant food store at Via Mazzini 2 (© **0544/212309**), is a good place to load up on regional hams and cheeses; it operates a reasonably priced self-service restaurant upstairs and a full-service restaurant above that. **Profumo di Piadina,** 24 Via Cairoli, tops warm-from-the oven *piadina* (flatbread) with prosciutto, creamy *squacquerone* (cheese), and other locally produced ingredients that you can eat on the go or enjoy at one of the few tables.

Ca' de Ven ★★ ROMAGNOLA A 16th-century guesthouse and former spice warehouse with frescoed ceilings and lots of paneling and exposed timbers makes a character-filled stop for lunch or a light dinner.

Heavier fare is offered, but the emphasis here is on *piadina,* the local flat-bread, and that's the way to go. It's served with a dozen or so fillings or, even better, by itself warm from the oven with a selection of cured meats and *squaquerone,* a delicate soft cheese. There's also a huge selection of wine by the glass. At lunch and in early evening you'll rub elbows at communal tables with what seems like half the population of Ravenna, so enjoy the atmosphere and ignore the often-brusque service.

Via Corrado Ricci 24. www.cadeven.it. © **0544/30163.** *Piadine* about 4€; entrees 11€–15€. Tues–Sun 11am–2:30pm, 6:30–11pm.

La Bella Venezia ★ ROMAGNOLA   The name suggests a certain airy elegance, and the cream-colored walls and light, starched tablecloths in this small room off the Piazza della Popolo deliver on the promise. Despite the name, don't expect Venetian specialties: This restaurant's menu is typically and deliciously Romagnolese. The kitchen is much respected for its *cappelletti alla romagnola* (cap-shaped pasta stuffed with ricotta, roasted pork loin, chicken breast, and nutmeg, and served with meat sauce) and other homemade pastas, including simple ravioli with butter and sage, and risotto with fresh seasonal vegetables. Everything on the small menu is prepared with finesse and served with the kind of old-world flair that keeps a local clientele coming back.

Via IV Novembre 16. www.bellavenezia.it. © **0544/212-746.** Entrees 10€–15€. Mon–Fri 12:15–2:30pm and 7:30–10pm, Sat 7:30–10pm.

Osteria del Tempo Perso ★★ SEAFOOD/ROMAGNOLA   Ravenna is no longer a port, but the sea is close enough to supply fresh seafood for an innovative menu, accompanied by soft jazz in warm-hued rooms lined with books and wine bottles. It would be a shame not to indulge in at least one seafood course, maybe the *spaghetti con bocconcini di spade,* with savory chunks of swordfish, or a hefty *fritto misto,* though *tortelloni di zucca,* pumpkin-filled pasta, and other regional land-based favorites are expertly done, too.

Via Gamba 12. www.osteriadeltempoperso.it. © **0544/215-393.** Entrees 12€–16€. Mon–Fri 7:30–11pm, Sat–Sun 12:30–2:30pm and 7:30–11pm.

Ristorante Alexander ★ ITALIAN/SEAFOOD   In this former church later converted to a movie house, vintage movie posters hang beneath ancient beams in a vast, double-height hall—a blend of sacred and profane that makes a sophisticated setting for refined cooking. Ravenna's proximity to the sea comes to the fore in beautifully sauced fresh fish, and in nice combinations like fusilli with tuna and pork or calamari couscous; meat dishes lean toward roasted game birds and some unusual local preparations, such as veal cheeks with potato and lemon puree. Service is friendly and attentive, as soft jazz and mellow renditions of movie themes float through the space.

Via Bassa del Pignataro 8. www.ristorantealexander.it. © **0544/212-967.** Entrees 15€–28€. Tues–Sun 12:30–2:30pm and 7:30–11:30pm (closed Sun in summer).

PARMA ★

457km (283 miles) NW of Rome, 97km (60 miles) NW of Bologna, 121km (75 miles) SE of Milan

This prosperous little city on the Roman Via Emilia, about an hour north of Bologna, delivers a slice of the good life. Residents are surrounded by art-filled palaces and churches bestowed upon them by the Renaissance Farnese family and later Marie-Louise, wife of Napoleon. They enjoy the music of their own Giuseppe Verdi in a grand opera house, and when it comes to food, elegant Parma has given the world some of the finest hams and cheeses ever. You can easily fill a very satisfying day or two here, enjoying beautiful monuments, listening to music, stepping in and out of tempting food shops, and sitting down to some memorable meals.

Essentials

ARRIVING   Parma is served by the Milan-Bologna **rail** line, with hourly trains arriving from Milan (trip time: 1 hr. on frequent fast trains, 1½ hr. on less expensive slower trains). From Bologna, trains depart for Parma every 30 minutes or so (a little under an hour). There are a few direct trains a day from Florence (2 hr.); most journeys will require a change in Bologna. For information and schedules, go to www.trenitalia.com. The station doesn't have baggage-storage facilities, but you can stash your bags for 5€ at the Hotel Century, just outside the main entrance at Piazzale Carlo Alberto dalla Chiesa 5/A, hotelcenturyparma.it; ✆ **0521/039-800.**

If you have a **car** and are coming from Bologna, drive northwest along A1. Note that driving in the historic center is restricted—from October through March it's off-limits to cars entirely on Thursdays and cars are not allowed within the ring roads on the first Sunday of the month, December excluded. Don't drive into the old city without first contacting your hotel—without a special pass you'll be fined 90€. Outside the restricted area, you can park on the street wherever you see blue lines (not blue-and- white lines; purchase a ticket from the curbside machines), or aim for the official parking lots: Goito, Toschi, Duc, Dus, and Via Abbeveratoia (around 1€–1.70€ per hour), with free shuttle service to the city center.

GETTING AROUND   Parma is bike friendly, with rentals available from the large stand outside the train station in Piazzale Carlo Alberto dalla Chiesa (www.infomobility.pr.it; ✆ **0521/281-979**). Rates are 1.50€ an hour, 12€ per day. Bus number 15 (1.30€, buy ticket at newsstands) makes a handy run from the train station to Teatro Reggio and the historic center, though the walk is only about 10 minutes.

VISITOR INFORMATION   The **tourist office** at Piazza Garibaldi 1 (www.turismo.comune.parma.it; ✆ **0521/218-889**) is open daily 9am to 7pm.

Exploring Parma

It's easy to explore Parma on foot, since most of the sights surround Piazza del Duomo and Palazzo della Pilotta and are within easy walking distance of the train station.

Battistero (Baptistery) and Duomo ★★★ CATHEDRAL   The moment you walk into the Piazza del Duomo, you're in for a wallop of delightful visual storytelling. To one side rises the elegant **baptistery,** primarily the work of Italy's great Romanesque master Benedetto Antelami and begun in 1196. Octagonal in shape, it has four open loggias and tiers of 16 slender columns—all playing off the number eight, the sign of the Resurrection. Alternating bands of white and pink marble represent purity and the blood of Christ; carvings above the entrance are scripture in stone (look for the sequence depicting King Herod pulling his beard in rage, Salome dancing, and St. John losing his head). Inside, colorful 13th-century frescoes depict the zodiac, the months and seasons, and the life of Christ with a wealthy of medieval iconography.

Two stone lions guard the entrance to the adjacent **Duomo,** one crushing a serpent (the devil), the other a lamb (symbol of sacrifice) under their paws. Inside are two of Parma's greatest treasures. Correggio, the master of light and color, spent 8 years painting the cupola; after finishing in 1530, he took his payment in a sack full of small change, went home, and died of fever at the age of 40. His "Assumption of the Virgin" is a sea of free-floating angels and billowing clouds; a leggy Christ tumbles out of the celestial light to meet the outstretched arms of his ascending mother. A contemporary compared the effect to a "hash of frogs' legs," and Charles Dickens commented that this was a scene that "no operative surgeon gone mad could imagine in his wildest delirium." Church authorities supposedly approached Titian to redo the dome; he replied that the work was so masterful, they should have filled the structure with gold and presented it to Correggio. The other highlight is in the transept to the right: a somber bas-relief of "The Deposition from the Cross" by Antelami, creator of the baptistery next door. A melancholy Christ stretches his elongated arms over two groups—Mary and pious converts to one side, the unenlightened on the other, including a group of Roman soldiers playing cards.

Piazza del Duomo 1. www.cattedrale.parma.it. ⓒ **0521/235-886.** Free. Daily 10am–6:30pm. Battistero: 8€ with Museo Diocesano, 6€ students and over 65, 2€ under 18. Daily 10am–6pm.

Camera di San Paolo ★★ CONVENT   San Paolo was one of many well-endowed convents where wealthy women who did not marry could spend their lives in relative comfort. When, around 1519, the cultured abbess Giovanna di Piacenza wanted to fresco her private dining room, she had the means to hire Correggio, who created vivid mythological

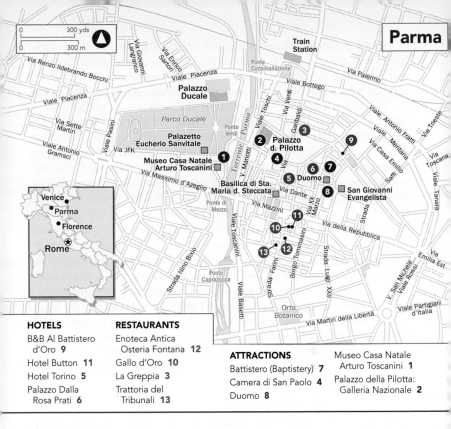

Parma

0 ——— 300 yds
0 ——— 300 m

HOTELS	RESTAURANTS
B&B Al Battistero d'Oro **9**	Enoteca Antica Osteria Fontana **12**
Hotel Button **11**	Gallo d'Oro **10**
Hotel Torino **5**	La Greppia **3**
Palazzo Dalla Rosa Prati **6**	Trattoria del Tribunali **13**

ATTRACTIONS

Battistero (Baptistery) **7**
Camera di San Paolo **4**
Duomo **8**
Museo Casa Natale Arturo Toscanini **1**
Palazzo della Pilotta: Galleria Nazionale **2**

scenes, cherubs, astrological references, and an image of Diana, goddess of the hunt. The frescoes may have sparked conversation for the intellectuals who frequently gathered at the abbess's table, though the significance of the images remains a mystery. Church authorities later sealed off the chamber—with no religious subjects and so many bare-bottomed *putti*, it was deemed profane.

Via Melloni 3 (off Strada Garibaldi). © **0521/533-221.** 6€ adults, 2€ ages 18–25, children 17 and under free (automated ticket machine accepts coins and credit cards). Mon–Sat 1:10–6:50pm.

Palazzo della Pilotta: Galleria Nazionale ★★ MUSEUM   Like many Italian cities, Parma became a great center of the Renaissance under one ruling family—in this case, the Farneses, whose members included popes, cardinals, and the dukes of Parma. They began their fortresslike Palazzo della Pilotta in the 1580s and remained there until the last heiress, Elisabetta, married King Philip of Spain and decamped for Madrid in 1714. The Hapsburg princess Marie-Louise (1791–1847)—Napoleon's second wife and a great-niece of Marie Antoinette—was awarded the duchy a century later, and she set about gathering art treasures from the city in the palace the Farneses had left empty; she also collected works from villas and churches throughout Italy, confiscated when her husband marched down the peninsula. Badly bomb-damaged in World War II, the restored palace now houses the Galleria Nazionale. It's not surprising that the Vienna-born duchess's collection would include such northern artists as Hans Holbein, Brueghel, and Van Dyck, but Parma artists steal the show. Correggio's "Madonna della Scodella (With a Bowl)" portrays Joseph as an elderly man and Mary as a young woman gazing adoringly at her infant son; his "St. Jerome with the Madonna and Child" also represents age, youth, and love—a gentle ode to tenderness. (Napoleon supposedly wanted to cart these off to the Louvre, but Marie-Louise insisted they remain in Parma.) The alluring "Turkish Slave," by the city's own Parmigiano, portrays a well-kept young woman dressed in gold-threaded finery; everything about her—turban, cheeks, eyes, breasts—is beautifully rounded. "La Scapigliata" (aka the "Female Head") is one of the most celebrated works by Italian master Leonardo da Vinci. The palace's other treasure is the **Teatro Farnese,** a wooden theater the Farneses had built, along the lines of Palladio's theater at Vicenza, to impress the Medicis. It's been used only a few times, including an inaugural event in 1639 when the section in front was flooded for mock naval battles.

Piazzale della Pilotta 15. pilotta.beniculturali.it. © **0521/233-309.** 10€ adults, 5€ ages 18–25, free for children 17 and under; includes Teatro Farnese. Tues–Sat 8:30am–7pm, Sun 1–7pm.

Where to Stay in Parma

B&B Al Battistero d'Oro ★★★   It's easy to slip into the Parma good life in this elegant 19th-century house just behind the Duomo, where Patrizia Valenti's sprawling and tasteful apartment surrounds a courtyard. The hostess puts up her guests in a delightful ground-floor room with a private entrance and another large bedroom off a back corridor, welcoming them also into her bright and handsomely furnished living room and polished dining room, where she serves a delicious breakfast. She also offers a modern studio apartment in a nearby house. All rooms are beautifully equipped with fine linens and handy amenities (fridges in the rooms and a kitchenette in the apartment), and Patrizia is on hand to dispense advice on getting the most out of her native Parma.

Strada Sant'anna 22. www.albattisterodoro.com. © **338/490-4697.** 3 units. 100€–140€ double. Rates include breakfast. **Amenities:** Wi-Fi (free).

Hotel Button ★★   The Cortesa family has been welcoming guests to this 17th-century *palazzo* for more than 40 years, providing lots of advice and dispensing excellent coffee from the small lobby bar. The premises have long ago been stripped of any of their historic provenance, and the current reincarnation, with floral wallpaper and dark furnishings, seems like a relic from the mid-20th century. You might be charmed by the extra-large rooms and old-fashioned ambience (as we are) or find the place to be a bit stuffy and out of date, but you can't quibble with the excellent location in the heart of old Parma just off Piazza Garibaldi.

Borgo delle Salina 7. www.hotelbutton.it. © **0521/208-039.** 40 units. 65€–105€. double. Rates include breakfast. **Amenities:** Babysitting; bar; Wi-Fi (free).

Hotel Torino ★ A couple of handsome lounges off the lobby and a sprightly, patio-like breakfast room do justice to one of Parma's best lodging locations, just down the street from Piazza del Duomo. Guest rooms are a bit more banal, though the muted tones and neutral furnishings are soothing; the small spaces are streamlined with lots of handy built-ins for stashing gear (some of the singles feel like ship cabins). Parking in a small garage beneath the hotel is 15€ a night.

Borgo Angelo Massa. www.hotel-torino.it. © **0521/281046.** 39 units. 65€–100€ double. Rates include breakfast. **Amenities:** Bar; Wi-Fi (free).

Palazzo Dalla Rosa Prati ★★★ You really will be living like royalty in this magnificent *palazzo* on a corner of the Piazza del Duomo, sharing the premises with the Marquis Dalla Rosa Prati and his family. They have converted one wing of the palace to seven sprawling, handsomely furnished suites, all with kitchenettes, and another section to 10 large apartments. In the suites, huge wooden bedsteads, massive armoires, and other polished antiques complement the largely 18th-century surroundings. Apartments are tasteful but functional, with one or two bedrooms and generous space to spread out. Suites are accessible by elevator; the apartments require a climb up a grand staircase.

Strada al Duomo 7. www.palazzodallarosaprati.com. © **0521/386-429.** 17 units. 90€–160€ double. Rates include breakfast. **Amenities:** Bar; cafe; Wi-Fi (free).

Where to Eat in Parma

Topping the tasting list in Parma is *parmigiano* cheese, made from the milk of cows raised just outside town and aged for at least 12 months. A meal often begins and ends with a small wedge, and it's grated over pastas and fresh vegetables, used as a filling in crepes, and generally makes its way into almost every course. Then there's ham. Parma gourmands do not settle for any old *prosciutto*. The antipasto of choice is *culatello,* cut from the right hind leg (if you observe a pig sitting down, you'll see this part usually carries less weight, and hence is less sinewy). You can purchase ham and cheese all over town, but if you're thinking of bringing some of these products home with you, remember that Americans are allowed to bring cheese but not meat into the country. An especially attractive and aromatic shop is **Salumeria Garibaldi,** Via Garibaldi 42 (www.special itadiparma.it; © **0521/235-606;** Mon–Sat 8am–8pm). You might also want to visit the cheese production operations at **Consorzio del Parmigiano Reggiano** (www.parmigianoreggiano.com; © **0521/292-7000**), at Via Gramsci 26; call or e-mail to make an appointment.

Enoteca Antica Osteria Fontana ★ PARMIGIANA   Cheap nibbles and a huge selection of wine by the glass draw a local crowd to this plain room with a long bar and battered wooden tables. Grilled *panini* are on offer, but the real treats are the morsels of *parmigiano* dribbled with balsamic vinegar from Modena, slices of prosciutto, and *crostini,* pieces of bread topped with everything from pesto to chicken livers.
Via Farini 24. ✆ **0521/286-037.** Sandwiches and snacks from 4€. Tues–Sat noon–2:30pm and 8–10:30pm.

Gallo d'Oro ★ PARMIGIANA   Parma's formidable food scene becomes decidedly more relaxed at this bric-a-brac-filled trattoria just off Piazza Garibaldi. A young crowd seems to appreciate the old local traditions: Lambrusco, a slightly sparkling red, is the wine of choice, and *cavallo* (horse) and *coniglio* (rabbit) are served a few different ways. Less adventurous eaters can work their way through *tortelli ripieni* (pasta stuffed with cheese and vegetables), *ravioli alla zucca* (pumpkin), and a long list of other delicious local pastas, all homemade.
Borgo della Salina 3. www.gallodororistorante.it. ✆ **0521/208-846.** Entrees 9€–11€. Daily noon–2:30pm and 7:30–11pm.

La Greppia ★★ PARMIGIANA/ITALIAN   Looking toward the window at one end of the simple dining room, you'll see into the kitchen and notice that the kitchen crew is mostly female. In the hands of *le donne* you'll be treated to exquisite dishes, some of which you've probably never encountered before—pears poached in red wine with a dense cream sauce is the house antipasto, the pastas are all homemade and often filled with the freshest local vegetables, and the secondi menu is heavy with slow-cooked goat, *trippa alla parmigiana* (tripe), and other regional favorites. The homemade *tortas,* filled with marmalade and a miraculous mélange of other ingredients, are irresistible. Service does the cuisine justice.
Via Garibaldi 39. ✆ **0521/233-686.** Entrees 18€–28€. Sun–Thurs noon–2:30pm and 7:30–10:30pm, Fri–Sat noon–2:30pm and 7–10:30pm.

Trattoria del Tribunali ★★★ PARMIGIANA/ITALIAN   Two floors of dining rooms stretch beyond counters hung with hams, and they're often filled to bursting. Locals rely on the kitchen for such staples as huge platters of prosciutto and some distinctly local fare, such as horsemeat hash. More familiar choices range from delicious pastas, such as *tortelli* (pasta pockets) stuffed with pumpkin or ricotta, to steaks with Barolo and veal stuffed with *parmigiano.* A veteran staff never seems too flustered to be friendly, even during lunchtime and evening rushes. It's a good idea to reserve, especially on weekend nights.
Vicolo Politi 5. www.trattoriadeltribunale.it. ✆ **0521/285-527.** Entrees 8€–12€. Daily noon–3pm and 7–11pm.

HITTING THE high NOTES

Besides collecting art in the Palazzo della Pilotta (see p. 387), Duchess Marie-Louise also enriched Parma's cultural life in 1829 by building the **Teatro Reggio,** Via Garibaldi 16, near Piazza della Pace (www.teatroregioparma.it; ℰ **0521/203-911**). Still considered one of the world's finest music theaters, it hosts an opera season that rivals Milan's. Particularly favored are the operas of **Giuseppe Verdi,** composer of "Il Trovatore" and "Aïda," who was born outside Parma in 1813 and later lived with his mistress, soprano Giuseppina Strepponi, in nearby Busseto. **Villa Verdi** shows off their personal effects, pianos, portraits, and the bed upon which the maestro died in Milan in 1901 (www.villaverdi.org; ℰ **0523/830-210;** 9€; Tues–Sun 9:30–11:45am and 2:30–6:15pm [closes 4:30pm Nov–Mar]). Each October, Parma celebrates the **Verdi Festival,** with concerts and performances in the Teatro Reggio and other venues.

Parma's other musical genius, **Arturo Toscanini,** the great 20th-century orchestral conductor, was born in Parma in 1867. His birthplace, **Museo Casa Natale Arturo Toscanini,** Via Rodolfo Tanzi 13, now displays his scores, photos, and other personal effects (www.museo toscanini.it; ℰ **0521/031-769;** 2€; Tues 9am–1pm, Wed–Sat 9am–1pm and 2–6pm; Sun 10am–6pm)

NEARBY

Hostaria d'Ivan ★★★ EMILIA-ROMAGNAN   A trip out to this welcoming inn, in a farming hamlet near the banks of the River Po, is an immersion course in all that's good about the region's cooking. *Culatello,* the choicest cut of prosciutto, and *parmigiano,* aged for several years, are produced on nearby farms; the duck, roasted with herbs, comes from marshes along the river banks. On request, you can experience the "salametherapy room," where you'll dine on cured meats hanging from the ceiling, but a convivial meal in the simply furnished dining room, overlooking a small garden, is just as memorable. Four cozy bedrooms are tucked under the eaves at the top of the house, a good reason to let a meal last all evening.

Via Villa 24, Fontanelle di Roccabianca (25km/15 mi NW of Parma via SP10). www.hostariadaivan.it. ℰ **0521/870-113.** Entrees 10€–18€. Wed–Fri noon–11pm, Sat–Sun noon–11:30pm.

9

VENICE

By Stephen Keeling

N o other place in the world looks quite like Venice. This vast, floating city of grand *palazzi*, elegant bridges, gondolas, and canals is a magnificent spectacle, truly magical when approached by sea for the first time, when its golden domes and soaring bell towers seem to rise straight from the sea. While it can sometimes appear that Venice is little more than an open-air museum where tourists always outnumber locals—by a large margin—it is still surprisingly easy to lose the crowds. Indeed, the best way to enjoy Venice is to simply get lost in its labyrinth of narrow, enchanting streets, stumbling upon a quiet *campo* (square), market stall, or cafe far off the beaten track, where even the humblest medieval church might contain masterful work by Tiepolo, Titian, or Tintoretto.

The origins of Venice—known as "La Serenissima" for centuries—are as muddy as parts of the lagoon it now occupies, but most histories begin with the arrival of refugees from Attila the Hun's invasion of Italy in the mid-5th century (though the official foundation date is 421 A.D.) The mudflats were gradually built over and linked together, channels and streams eventually becoming canals. By the 11th century, Venice had emerged as a major independent trading city, and by the 13th century its seaborne empire (which included Crete, Corfu, and Cyprus) was held together by a huge navy and commercial fleet. Despite being embroiled with wars against rival Italian city Genoa and the Turks, the next few centuries were golden years for Venice, when booming trade with the Far East funded much of its grand architecture and art. Although it remained an outwardly rich city, by the 1700s the good times were over, and in 1797 Napoleon dissolved the Venetian Republic without a shot (handing it over to the Austrians shortly afterwards). You'll gain a sense of some of this history touring **Piazza San Marco** and **St. Mark's Basilica,** or by visiting the **Accademia,** one of Italy's great art galleries. But only when you wander the back *calli* (streets) will you encounter the true, living, breathing side of Venice, still redolent of those glory days.

DON'T LEAVE VENICE WITHOUT . . .

Getting Lost. So sublime is the city's lineup of architectural eye-candy that Venice simply invites aimless wandering. If you stick to the areas

FACING PAGE: **Getting lost along Venice's picturesque side canals is one of the city's greatest pleasures.**

congested with tourists (which are surprisingly small), you'll never discover the real Venice.

Cruising the Waters of The Grand Canal. Hop aboard a gondola or *vaporetto* no. 1 (see p. 403) for a complete lap of Venice's primary marine highway, adorned with views of the city's most jewel-like *palazzi.*

Exploring St. Mark's Basilica. This Byzantine gem may be one of the city's busiest tourist attractions, but that doesn't make it any less wondrous (see p. 405).

Snacking on *Cicchetti* (Appetizers) at a *Bàcaro*. Eating tapas-style with an *ombra* (glass of local Veneto wine) in age-old *bàcari*, the small bars where locals mingle, is an essential Venice experience.

Experiencing Art, Art, and More Art. The Accademia Gallery (p. 416) has the greatest collection of classic Venetian art on earth, while the nearby Peggy Guggenheim Collection (see p. 418) displays some of the best of Western Modernism. All around the city are churches and *scuole* (schools) stuffed with compelling masterpieces.

ESSENTIALS

Arriving

BY PLANE From North America, the cheapest flights to Venice tend to route through Rome or Milan via **Alitalia**, though **Swissair** (via Zurich), **Lufthansa** (via Frankfurt), **KLM** (via Amsterdam) and **Air France** (via Paris) usually offer cheap fares in low season (code-sharing with US carriers). If traveling in the peak spring and summer seasons however, it's worth considering far more convenient seasonal non-stop flights, which are often priced competitively (assuming you buy far enough in advance). **Delta Airlines** (www.delta.com) flies from Atlanta (late June–Aug only) and New York-JFK (Apr–Sept only), **United Airlines** (www.united.com) from Newark (June–late Sept), and **American Airlines** (www.aa.com) from Chicago and Philadelphia (May–Oct). For those already in Europe, numerous budget airlines serve Venice, offering rock-bottom prices. No-frills **easyJet** (www.easyjet.com) flies from Amsterdam, Berlin, London-Gatwick, Manchester, Paris, and Zurich, while **Ryanair** (www.ryanair. com) flies from Bristol, Barcelona, and London, with many more of its flights routed through nearby **Treviso** (a 1-hr. bus ride to Venice).

Flights land at the **Aeroporto di Venezia Marco Polo,** 7km (4¼ miles) north of the city on the mainland (www.veniceairport.it; ✆ **041/ 2609260**). There are several alternatives for getting into town. The **cheapest** is by **bus,** though this is not recommended if you have heavy luggage; buses can't drive into Venice itself, so you'll have to walk to or from the final stop, Piazzale Roma, to the nearby *vaporetto* (water bus) stop for the final connection to your hotel. (See *vaporetto* advice under "By Train,"

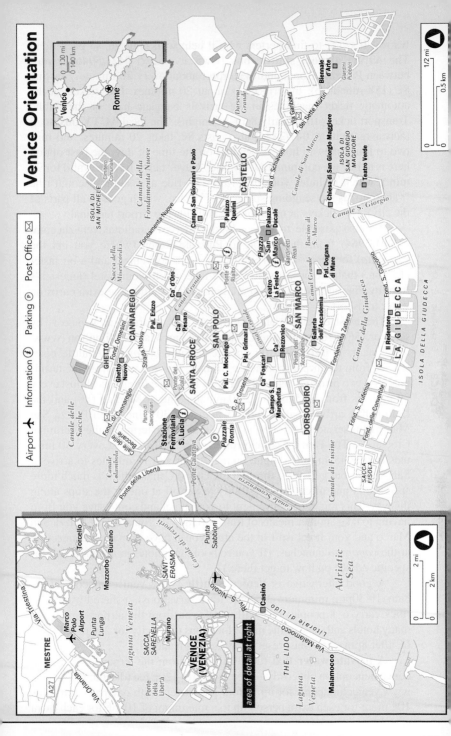

Venice Orientation

Airport ✈ Information ⓘ Parking ⓟ Post Office ⊠

0   1/2 mi

0   0.5 km

0   130 mi
0   190 km

Venice ●
Rome ★

ISOLA DI
SAN MICHELE

Cimitero
Comunale

Canale delle
Sacche

Canale delle
Fondamenta Nuove

Sacca della
Misericordia

Fondamenta Nuove

GHETTO

Fond. Ormesini

CANNAREGIO

Ghetto
Nuovo

Strada Nuova

Pal. Erizo

Ca' d'Oro

Ca'
Pesaro

Canal Grande

Campo San Giovanni e Paolo

Palazzo
Querini

CASTELLO

Riva d. Schiavoni

Canale di San Marco

BIENALE
d'Arte

Giardini
Pubblici

Darsena
Grande

Via Garibaldi

R. dei Sette Martiri

Fond. di Cannaregio

Parco di
Savorgnan

Ponte dei
Scalzi

SANTA CROCE

Ponte del
Rialto

SAN POLO

Pal. C. Mocenigo

Pal. Grimani

C. P. Crosera

Ca' Foscari

Campo S.
Margherita

DORSODURO

Ca'
Rezzonico

Ponte dell'
Accademia

Galleria
dell'Accademia

Fondamenta Zattere

SAN MARCO

Teatro
La Fenice

Piazza
San
Marco ⓘ

Palazzo
Ducale

Gardinetti
Reali

Pal. Dogana
di Mare

Bacino di
S. Marco

Canal Grande

Canale della Giudecca

Il Redentore

Fond. S. Eufemia

Fond. delle Convertite

LA GIUDECCA

ISOLA DELLA GIUDECCA

Fond. S. Giacomo

Canale S. Giorgio

ISOLA DI
SAN GIORGIO
MAGGIORE

Chiesa di San Giorgio Maggiore

Teatro Verde

Canale di Fusine

SACCA
FISOLA

Stazione
Ferroviaria
S. Lucia ⓘ

Calle delle
Beccarie

Piazzale
Roma ⓟ

Ponte Calatrava

Ponte della Libertà

Canale
Colambola

Canale Scomenzera

MESTRE

Marco
Polo
Airport ✈

Via Triestina

Punta
Lunga

A27

Via Orlanda

Ponte
della
Libertà

SACCA
SARENELLA

Murano

Laguna Veneta

Mazzorbo Burano

Torcello

SANT'
ERASMO

Canale di Treporti

Punta
Sabbioni

VENICE
(VENEZIA)

area of detail at right

Casinó

Riv. S. Nicolò ✈

THE LIDO

Via Malamocco

Litorale di Lido

Malamocco

Laguna
Veneta

Adriatic
Sea

0   2 mi
0   2 km

below.) It's rare to find porters who'll help with luggage, so pack light. The **ATVO airport shuttle bus** (www.atvo.it; ℂ 0421/594672) runs between Piazzale Roma and the airport about every 20 minutes, costing 8€ (15€ roundtrip); the trip takes about 20 minutes. Buy tickets at the automatic ticket machines in the arrivals baggage hall, or the Public Transport ticket office (daily 8am–midnight). The local **ACTV bus no. 5** (actv.avmspa.it; ℂ 041/2424) also costs 8€, takes 20 minutes, and runs two to four times an hour depending on the time of day; the best option here is to buy the combined ACTV and "Nave" ticket for 14€ (valid for 90 min.), which includes your first *vaporetto* ride at a slight discount (the "vaporetto" is the seagoing streetcar of Venice, which goes to all parts of the city). Buy tickets at machines just outside the airport terminal.

It's also possible to take a **land taxi** (www.radiotaxivenezia.com; ℂ 041/5964) from the airport to Piazzale Roma (where you get the *vaporetto*) for about 40€. While this is more convenient and a bit faster (15 min.) than the bus, it still doesn't take you to your hotel (unless it's right by Piazzale Roma)—you are better off spending the extra euros on water transport.

The most evocative and traditional way to arrive in Venice is by sea. For 15€ (14€ online), the **Cooperative San Marco/Alilaguna** (www.alilaguna.it; ℂ 041/2401701) operates a large *motoscafo* (shuttle boat) service from the airport boathouse (a short, covered walk from the terminal) with two primary routes. The **Linea Blu** (blue line) runs almost every 30 minutes from 6:15am to 12:30am, stopping at Murano (8€) and the Lido before arriving, after about 1 hour and 30 minutes, in Piazza San Marco (this service continues on to the cruise ship terminal, the "Terminal Crociere"). The **Linea Arancio** (orange line) runs almost every 30 minutes from 7:45am to midnight, taking 1 hour and 15 minutes to arrive at San Marco, but gets there through the Grand Canal, which is much more spectacular and offers the possibility to get off at one of the stops along the way. This might be convenient to your hotel and could save you from having to take another means of transportation. If you arrive at Piazza San Marco and your hotel isn't in the area, you'll have to make a connection at the *vaporetto* launches. (If you're booking a hotel in advance, ask for specific advice on how to get there.)

A good alternative is **Venice Shuttle** (www.venicelink.com; daily 8am–10:30pm; minimum 2 people for reservations), a shared water taxi (they carry 6–8 people) that will whisk you from the airport directly to many hotels and most of the major locations in the city for 25€ to 32€ (add 6€ after 8pm). You must reserve online in advance.

A **private water taxi** (20–30 min. to/from the airport) is the most convenient option but costly—there is a 110–120€ fee (discounted rates at www.venicelink.com) for up to four passengers with one bag each (plus 10€ more for each extra person up to a maximum of 10, 5€ for each extra suitcase, and another 20€ for 10pm–7am arrivals). It's worth considering if you're pressed for time, have an early flight (taxis run 24 hrs.), are carrying a lot of luggage (a Venice no-no), or can split the cost with a friend or two. The taxi may be able to drop you off at the front (or side) door of your hotel, or as close as it can maneuver given your hotel's location (check with the hotel before arriving). Your taxi captain should be able to tell you before boarding just how close you can get. Try **Corsorzio Motoscafi Venezia** (www.motoscafivenezia.it; ✆ **041/5222303**) or **Venezia Taxi** (www.veneziataxi.it; ✆ **041/723112**).

BY TRAIN   Trains from Rome (3¾ hr.), Milan (2½ hr.), Florence (2 hr.), and all over Europe arrive at the **Stazione Venezia Santa Lucia.** To get there, all must pass through a station marked Venezia-Mestre. Don't be confused: Mestre is a charmless industrial city that's the last major stop on the mainland (some trains also stop at the next station, Venezia Porto Marghera, before continuing to Venice proper). Occasionally trains end in Mestre, in which case you have to catch one of the frequent 10-minute shuttles connecting with Venice; it's inconvenient, so when you book your ticket, confirm that the final destination is Venezia Santa Lucia.

The Vaporetto Lowdown

Whether you're arriving by train, bus, or car, your first challenge upon arriving in Venice will be to take a vaporetto (water bus) on to your final destination in the city. Here's how to do it right.

Finding the right boat is a little easier if you're arriving by bus or car, because you'll be in Piazzale Roma, the route **no. 1** vaporetto terminus, and all these boats will be going the right direction. (See "Getting Around Venice," p. 401, for information on tickets). Exiting the train station, however, you'll find the Grand Canal immediately in front of you, with the docks for a number of vaporetti lines to your left and right. Head to the booths to your left, near the bridge, to buy tickets, then head for the docks farther to your right.

The most useful routes are the two lines plying the Grand Canal: the **no. 2 express** (from bay "D"), which stops only at the San Marcuola, Rialto Bridge, San Tomà, San Samuele, and Accademia before hitting San Marco (30 min. total); and the slower **no. 1** (from bay "E"),

which makes 13 stops before arriving at San Marco (a 36-min. trip). Both leave every 10 minutes or so, but before 9am and after 8pm, the no. 2 sometimes stops short at Rialto, meaning you'll have to disembark and hop on the next no. 1 or 2 that comes along to continue to San Marco.

Word to the wise: The vaporetti go in two directions from the train station. Those heading left go down the Grand Canal toward San Marco—which is the (relatively) fast and scenic way. The no. 2 route heading right also eventually gets you to San Marco (at the San Zaccaria stop), but takes more than twice as long because it goes the long way around Dorsoduro (this line serves mainly commuters). As for the no. 1 line going to the right from the train station, it will go only one more stop before it hits its terminus at Piazzale Roma. **Make sure the vaporetto you get on is heading to the left.** Departing from **Piazzale Roma, make sure no. 2 is going to the right** (no.1 will only go right).

BY BUS　Although rail travel is more convenient and commonplace, Venice is serviced by long-distance buses from all over mainland Italy and some international cities. The final destination is Piazzale Roma, where you'll need to pick up *vaporetto* no. 1 or no. 2 (see box p. 397) to connect you with stops in the heart of Venice and along the Grand Canal. Eurolines (www.eurolines.eu) buses drop off on the adjacent island of **Tronchetto,** which is a much longer walk from the action. Buses stop at the Tronchetto **People Mover** station where a light railway takes you to Piazzale Roma in just 3 min. (1.50€ one-way), though you will most likely need onward transportation from there. *Vaporetto* line 2 does stop at Tronchetto: facing the water, boats depart left to the train station and Grand Canal, right to San Marco.

BY CAR　The only wheels you'll see in Venice are those attached to luggage. **No cars are allowed,** or more to the point, no cars could drive through the narrow streets and over the footbridges—even the police, fire department, and ambulance services use boats. You can drive across the Ponte della Libertà from Mestre (on the mainland) to Venice, but you can go no farther than Piazzale Roma at the Venice end, where many garages eagerly await your euros (and in high season are often full). The **Autorimessa Comunale garage** (www.avm.avmspa.it; © **041/2727301**) charges 26€ for a 24-hour period (23.40€ on-line), while **Garage San Marco**

Vaporetti (water buses) ply Venice's main canals.

(www.garagesanmarco.it; ℭ **041/5232213**) costs 32€ for 24 hours. From Piazzale Roma, you can catch *vaporetti* lines 1 and 2 (see box p. 397), which go down the Grand Canal to the train station and, eventually, Piazza San Marco. Cheaper (and in some cases free) parking is available on the adjacent island of Tronchetto (see "By bus", above), first right as you cross the Ponte della Libertà.

Visitor Information

TOURIST OFFICES The most central **Venezia Unica information office** lies in the arcade at the western end of Piazza San Marco (Calle Larga de l'Ascensione 71F), near Museo Correr (daily 9am–7pm; ℭ **041/2424**). There are also offices at Piazzale Roma (kiosk near Ponte della Costituzione; daily 7am–8pm), the train station (opposite platforms 2 and 3; daily 7am–9pm), and in the arrivals hall at Marco Polo Airport (daily 8:30am–7pm). See also **www.veneziaunica.it**.

The monthly magazine *Un Ospite di Venezia* (www.unospitedivenezia.it) is a useful source of information (published in Italian and English); most hotels have free copies. Also very useful is *VeNews* (www.venezianews.it), published monthly and sold at newsstands all over the city (also in English and Italian).

City Layout

Even armed with the best map or a hefty smartphone data plan, expect to get a little bit lost in Venice, at least some of the time (GPS directions are notoriously unreliable here). View it as an opportunity to stumble upon Venice's most intriguing corners. Keep in mind as you wander hopelessly among the *calli* (streets) and *campi* (squares) that Venice wasn't built to make sense to those on foot, but rather to those plying its canals.

Venice lies 4km (2½ miles) from terra firma, connected to the mainland at Mestre by the Ponte della Libertà, which leads to Piazzale Roma. Snaking through the city like an inverted *S* is the **Grand Canal,** the wide main artery. Central Venice refers to the built-up block of islands in the lagoon's center, the six main *sestieri* (districts) that make up the bulk of the tourist city. Greater Venice includes all the inhabited islands of the lagoon—central Venice plus Murano, Burano, Torcello, and the Lido.

9

VENICE

Essentials

399

Venice Neighborhoods in Brief

SAN MARCO   The most visited, and most central, *sestiere* is anchored by the magnificent Piazza San Marco and St. Mark's Basilica to the south and the Rialto Bridge to the north. This has been the commercial, religious, and political heart of the city for more than a millennium. Unfortunately, ever-rising rents have persuaded most locals to look for housing in other neighborhoods, but the area is laced with first-class hotels—see p. 430 for suggestions on where to stay in the heart of Venice without going broke.

CASTELLO   Just east of Piazza San Marco, Castello's tony waterside esplanade Riva degli Schiavoni follows the Bacino di San Marco (St. Mark's Basin), skirting Venice's most congested area to the north and east. Riva degli Schiavoni is often thronged, but if you head farther east in the direction of the Arsenale or inland away from the *bacino,* the crowds thin out. Here you'll find such major sights as Campo SS. Giovanni e Paolo and the Scuola di San Giorgio.

DORSODURO   Residential Dorsoduro, the largest of the *sestieri,* lies across the Accademia Bridge from San Marco. Home to the Accademia and Peggy Guggenheim museums, it was known as an artists' haven until rising rents forced many residents to relocate. Come here for good neighborhood restaurants, a charming gondola boatyard, lively Campo Santa Margherita, and the sunny canalside quay of le Zattere.

SAN POLO   This mixed bag of residential corners and tourist sights stretches northwest of the Rialto Bridge to the church of Santa Maria dei Frari. At the foot of the bridge, you'll find the bustling Rialto Market. Some of the city's best restaurants flourish here alongside some of its worst tourist traps. Spacious Campo San Polo is the main piazza.

SANTA CROCE   North and northwest of the San Polo district and across the Grand Canal from the train station, Santa Croce stretches all the way to Piazzale Roma. Less lively than San Polo but just as authentic, it feels light-years away from San Marco; its little-visited eastern section is a great place for curious visitors to explore. Quiet, lovely Campo San Giacomo dell'Orio is its heart.

Night market in Venice's Cannaregio neighborhood.

CANNAREGIO On the same side of the Grand Canal as San Marco and Castello, Cannaregio stretches north and east from the train station to include the old Jewish Ghetto. One-quarter of Venice's ever-shrinking population of 55,000 lives here. Many one-star hotels are clustered about the train station—not a dangerous neighborhood but not known for its charm, either. Strada Nova is Cannaregio's main thoroughfare, leading to the Rialto bridge.

LA GIUDECCA Across the Giudecca Canal from Piazza San Marco and Dorsoduro, tranquil La Giudecca is a residential island where you'll find a youth hostel and a few hotels (including the deluxe Cipriani, see p. 427).

LIDO DI VENEZIA This slim, 11km-long (6¾-mile) island, the only spot in the Venetian lagoon where cars circulate, is the city's beach, fronting the open sea. It's also the home of the annual Venice Film Festival.

Getting Around Venice

Aside from traveling by boat, the only way to explore Venice is by walking—and by getting lost repeatedly. You'll navigate many twisting streets whose names change constantly and don't appear on any map, and streets that may very well simply end in a blind alley or spill abruptly into a canal. You'll also cross dozens of footbridges. Treat getting bewilderingly lost in Venice as part of the fun, and budget more time than you'd think necessary to get wherever you're going.

STREET MAPS & SIGNAGE   The map sold by the tourist office (3€) and free maps provided by most hotels don't always show—much less name or index—all the *calli* (streets) and pathways of Venice. Pick up a more detailed map (ask for a *pianta della città* at news kiosks—especially those at the train station and around San Marco or most bookstores). The best is the highly detailed **Touring Club Italiano map,** available in a variety of forms (folding from 8.50€) and scales. If using your phone, note that GPS directions are often unreliable in Venice, though Google Maps has definitely improved in recent years (and has added its "streetview" option to the city).

Still, Venice's confusing layout confounds even the best navigators. You're better off just stopping every couple of blocks and asking a local to point you in the right direction (always know the name of the *campo/* square or major sight closest to the address you're looking for, and ask for that).

As you wander, look for the yellow signs (well, *usually* yellow) whose destinations and arrows direct you toward five major landmarks:

Getting away from the tourist center is one of the best ways to get to know Venice—but you'll definitely need a good map.

CRUISING THE canals

A leisurely cruise along the **Grand Canal ★★★** (p. 410) from Piazza San Marco to the train station (Ferrovia)—or the reverse—is one of Venice's must-dos. It's the world's most unusual Main Street, a watery boulevard whose *palazzi* have been converted into condos. Lower water-lapped floors are now deserted, but the higher floors are still coveted by the city's titled families, who have inhabited these glorious residences for centuries; others have become the dream homes of privileged expats, drawn as irresistibly as the romantic Venetians-by-adoption who preceded them—Richard Wagner, Henry James, Robert Browning, and Lord Byron among them.

As much a symbol of Venice as the winged lion, the **gondola ★★★** is one of Europe's great traditions, incredibly expensive but truly as romantic as it looks (detractors who write it off as too touristy have most likely never tried it). The official, fixed rate is 80€ for a 30-minute gondola tour for up to six passengers. The rate bumps up to 100€ from 7pm to 8am (for 35 minutes), and it's 40€ for every additional 20 minutes (50€ at night). That's not a typo: 150€ for a 1-hour evening cruise. *Tip:* Although the price is fixed by the city, a good negotiator at the right time of day (when business is slow) can sometimes grab a small discount for a shorter ride. And at these ridiculously inflated prices, there is no need to tip the gondolier. You might also find **discounts online.**

Aim for late afternoon before sundown, when the light does its magic on the canal reflections (and bring a bottle of Prosecco and glasses). If the price is too high, ask visitors at your hotel or others lingering about at the gondola stations if they'd like to share it. Though the price is "fixed," before setting off establish with the gondolier the cost,

time, and route (back canals are preferable to the trafficked and often choppy Grand Canal). They're regulated by the **Ente Gondola** (www.gondolavenezia.it; ✆ **041/5285075**); call if you have questions or complaints.

And what of the **serenading gondolier** immortalized in film? Frankly, you're better off without, but if warbling is de rigueur for you, here's the scoop: An ensemble of accordion player and tenor is so expensive that it's shared among several gondolas traveling together. A number of tour operators (and online brokers such as www.viator.com) book evening serenades for around 50€ per person.

Venice has 12 gondola stations, including Piazzale Roma, the train station, the Rialto Bridge, and Piazza San Marco. There are also a number of smaller stations, with *gondolieri* in striped shirts standing alongside their sleek 11m (36-ft.) black wonders looking for passengers. They all speak enough English to communicate the necessary details. Remember, if you just want a quick taste of being in a gondola, you can take a cheap *traghetto* across the Grand Canal.

Ferrovia (the train station), **Piazzale Roma** (the parking garage), **Rialto** (one of four bridges over the Grand Canal), **San Marco** (the city's main square), and the **Accademia** (the southernmost Grand Canal bridge).

BY VAPORETTO The various *sestieri* are linked by a comprehensive *vaporetto* (water bus/ferry) system of about a dozen lines operated by the **Azienda del Consorzio Trasporti Veneziano** (ACTV; actv.avmspa.it; ✆ **041/5287886**). Transit maps are available at the tourist office and most

ACTV ticket offices. It's easier to get around the center on foot; the *vaporetti* mostly serve the Grand Canal, outskirts, and outer islands. The crisscross network of small canals is the province of delivery vessels, gondolas, and private boats.

A ticket for 75 minutes of travel (after validation) on a *vaporetto* is a steep 7.50€, while the 24-hour ticket is 20€. Most lines run every 10 to 15 minutes from 7am to midnight, and then hourly until morning. Most *vaporetto* docks have timetables posted. You can buy tickets at Venezia Unica offices, authorized retailers that display the ACTV/Venezia Unica sticker in town, and usually at the dock itself, though not all of these have machines or kiosks that sell tickets. If you haven't bought a pass (p. 414) or tickets beforehand, you'll have to settle up with the conductors onboard (look for them immediately on boarding—they won't come looking for you) or risk a stiff fine of at least 60€ (plus ticket price and administrative fees). No excuses accepted. Also available are 48-hour tickets (30€), 72-hour tickets (40€) and 1-week tickets (60€). If you're planning to stay in Venice for a week or more and intend to use the *vaporetto* service a lot, it makes sense to pick up a **Venezia Unica city pass** (see "Venice Discounts," p. 414), with which you can buy *vaporetto* tickets for just 1.50€. You **must validate** (stamp) all tickets in the yellow machines at the docks before getting aboard.

BY TRAGHETTO Just four bridges span the Grand Canal, and to fill in the gaps, *traghetti* skiffs (oversize gondolas rowed by two standing *gondolieri*) cross the Grand Canal at several intermediate points. Stations were traditionally located at the end of streets named Calle del Traghetto, and indicated by a yellow sign with the black gondola symbol. These days only a handful operate regularly, primarily at San Tomà, Santa Maria del Giglio, and Santa Sofia (check with a local if in doubt). The fare is 2€ (locals pay just 0.70€), which you hand to the gondolier when boarding. Most Venetians cross standing up. Try the Santa Sofia crossing (Apr–Sep Mon–Sat 7:30am–7pm, Sun 9am–7pm; Oct–Mar Mon–Sat 7:30am–6:30pm, Sun 9am–6.30pm), which connects the Ca' d'Oro and the Pescheria fish market, on the Grand Canal just north of the Rialto Bridge—the gondoliers expertly dodge water traffic at this point of the canal, where it's the busiest and most heart-stopping.

BY WATER TAXI *Taxi acquei* (water taxis) charge high prices and aren't for visitors watching their euros. Trips in town are likely to cost at least 50€ to 90€, depending on distance, time of day, and whether you've booked in advance or just hired on the spot. Each trip includes allowance for up to four to five pieces of luggage—beyond that there's a surcharge of 3€ to 5€ per piece (rates differ slightly according to company and how you reserve your trip). Plus there's a 20€ supplement for service from 10pm to 7am, and a 5€ charge for taxis on-call. Those rates cover up to four people; if any more squeeze in, it's another 5€ to 10€ per extra passenger (maximum 10 people). Taking a water taxi from the train station to Piazza San Marco or any area hotels costs around 90€ (the Lido is around 100€), while fixed fees to the airport range 112–120€ (for up to four people). Taxis to Burano or Torcello will be at least 140€. Note that only taxi boats with a yellow strip are the official operators sanctioned by the city. You can book trips with **Consorzio Moscafi Venezia** online at **www.motoscafivenezia.it** or call ✆ **041/5222303.**

Six water-taxi stations serve key points in the city: the Ferrovia, Piazzale Roma, the Rialto Bridge, Piazza San Marco, the Lido, and Marco Polo Airport.

[Fast FACTS] VENICE

Doctors & Hospitals The **Ospedale Civile Santi Giovanni e Paolo** (✆ 041/ **5294111**), on Campo Santi Giovanni e Paolo in Castello, has English-speaking staff and provides 24/7 emergency service (*vaporetto:* Ospedale).

Emergencies To call the police, dial ✆ **113;** for an ambulance, ✆ **118;** for a fire ✆ **115.**

Internet Access Venice offers citywide Wi-Fi through the **Wi-Fi Venezia** (www.veneziaunica.it) network of 200 hotspots. Buy

packages online (5€/24 hr., 15€/3 days, or 20€/7 days); access codes are then sent via e-mail.

Mail The most convenient post offices are: **Venezia Centro** at Calle de la Acque, San Marco (✆ **041/ 2404149;** Mon–Fri 8:25am– 7:10pm and Sat 8:25am– 12:35pm); **Venezia 4** at Calle de l'Ascension 1241, off the west side of Piazza San Marco (✆ **041/ 2446711;** Tues–Fri 8:25am– 1:35pm and Sat 8:25am– 12:35pm); and **Venezia 3** at Campo San Polo 2012

(✆ **041/5200315;** same hours as Venezia 4).

Police Dial ✆ **113.**

Safety Generally speaking, Venice is one of Italy's safest cities. Be aware of petty crime like pickpocketing on the crowded *vaporetti,* particularly the tourist routes, where passengers are more intent on the passing scenery than on watching their bags. Venice's often deserted back streets are virtually crime-free, though occasional tales of theft have circulated.

EXPLORING VENICE

Venice is notorious for changing and extending the opening hours of its museums and, to a lesser degree, its churches (often due to special events). Before you begin your exploration of Venice's sights, check online or ask at the tourist office for the season's list of museum and church hours.

San Marco

Basilica di San Marco (St. Mark's) ★★★ CATHEDRAL   One of the grandest, and certainly the most exotic of all cathedrals in Europe, **Basilica di San Marco** is a treasure heap of Venetian art and all sorts of booty garnered from the eastern Mediterranean. Legend has it that **St. Mark,** on his way to Rome in the 1st century a.d, was told by an angel his

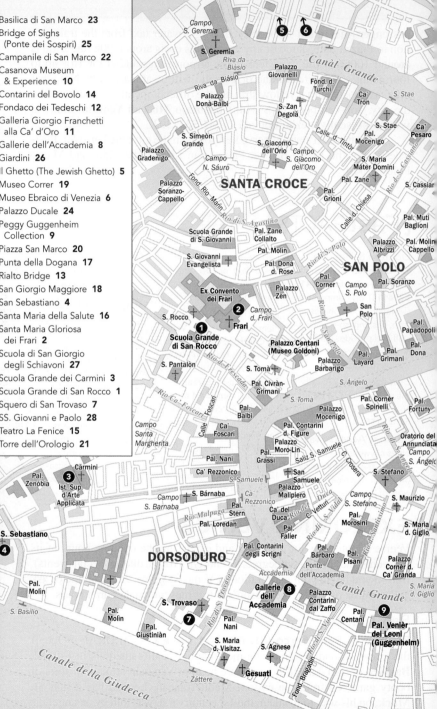

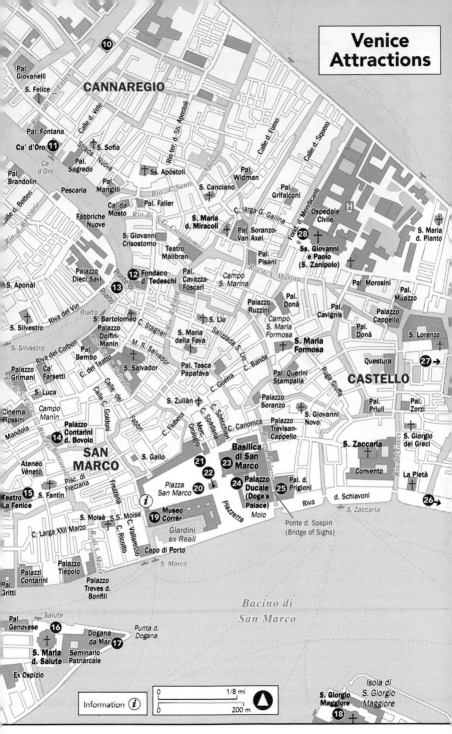

Venice Attractions

CANNAREGIO

Pal. Giovanelli
S. Felice
Pal. Fontana
Ca' d'Oro
Ca d'Oro
Pal. Sagredo
S. Sofia
Pal. Brandolin
Pescaria
Pal. Mangilli
Ss. Apóstoli
Pal. Widman
Fábbriche Nuove
Ca' da Mosto
Pal. Falier
S. Canciano
Pal. Grifalconi
Palazzo Dieci Savi
S. Giovanni Crisostomo
S. Maria d. Miracoli
Pal. Soranzo-Van Axel
C. larga G. Gallina
Ospedale Civile
S. Maria d. Pianto
S. Aponàl
Teatro Málibran
Fondaco d. Tedeschi
Pal. Cavazza-Foscari
Pal. Pisani
Ss. Giovanni e Paolo (S. Zanipolo)
Rialto
Campo S. Marina
Pal. Donà
Pal. Morosini
Pal. Muazzo
S. Silvestro
S. Bartolomeo
C. Stagneri
S. Lio
Palazzo Ruzzini
Campo S. Maria Formosa
Pal. Cavignis
Palazzo Cappello
S. Silvestro
Palazzo Dolfin-Manin
M. S. Salvador
S. Maria della Fava
Salizzada S. Lio
S. Maria Formosa
Pal. Donà
S. Lorenzo
Riva del Carbon
Pal. Bembo
S. Salvador
Pal. Tasca Papafáva
C. Bande
Pal. Querini Stampalia
Questura
Ruga Giuffa
Palazzo Grimani
Ca' Farsetti
C. del Teatro
C. Guerra
Palazzo Soranzo
CASTELLO
S. Luca
Campo Manìn
Cinema Rossini
Mandola
Palazzo Contarini d. Bovolo
S. Zulián
C. Spadaria
Merc. Orologio
C. Canonica
Palazzo Trevisan-Cappello
S. Giovanni Novo
Pal. Priuli
Pal. Zorzi
Ateneo Véneto
SAN MARCO
C. Fiubera
S. Gallo
Basílica di San Marco
S. Zaccaria
S. Giorgio dei Greci
Teatro La Fenice
S. Fantin
Pisc. di Frezzaria
Piazza San Marco
Palazzo Ducale (Doge's Palace)
Pal. d. Prigioni
Convento
La Pietà
C. Larga XXII Marzo
S. Moisè
S.S. Moisè
Museo Corrèr
Piazzetta
Molo
S. Zaccaria
d. Schiavoni
C. Vallaresso
C. Ricotto
Giardini ex Reali
Ponte d. Sospiri (Bridge of Sighs)
Riva
Capo di Porto
S. Marco
Palazzi Tiépolo
Palazzo Treves d. Bonflli
Pal. Contarini
Pal. Gritti
Bacino di San Marco
Salute
Pal. Genovese
Dogana da Mar
Punta d. Dogana
S. Maria d. Salute
Seminario Patriarcale
Ex Ospizio
Isola di S. Giorgio Maggiore
S. Giorgio Maggiore

Information (i)

0 ——— 1/8 mi
0 ——— 200 m

Byzantine mosaics adorn the Basilica di San Marco.

body would rest near the lagoon that would one today become Venice. Hundreds of years later, the city fathers were looking to replace their original patron St. Theodore with a saint of high stature, someone more in keeping with their lofty aspirations. In 828 the prophecy was fulfilled when Venetian merchants stole the remains of St. Mark from Alexandria in Egypt (supposedly the body was packed in pickled pork to avoid the attention of the Muslim guards). Today the high altar's green marble canopy on alabaster columns is believed to cover the remains of St Mark (despite a devastating fire in 976), and continues to be the focus of the basilica, at least for the faithful.

Modeled on Constantinople's Church of the Twelve Apostles, the original shrine of St. Mark was consecrated in 832, but in 976 the church burned down. The present incarnation was completed in 1094, then extended and embellished over the years; it served as the doge's personal church. Today, San Marco looks more Orthodox cathedral than Roman Catholic church, with a cavernous interior gilded with Byzantine mosaics added over 7 centuries, covering every inch of ceiling and pavement.

For a closer look at the most remarkable ceiling mosaics and a better view of the Oriental carpet-like patterns of the pavement mosaics, it's worth it to pay the admission to go upstairs to the **Museo di San Marco** (enter in the atrium at the principal entrance); this was originally the women's gallery, or *matroneum,* and includes access to the outdoor **Loggia dei Cavalli.** Here you can admire a panoramic view of the piazza below and replicas of the celebrated *Triumphal Quadriga,* four gilded bronze horses dating from the 2nd or 3rd century A.D.; the Roman originals were moved inside in the 1980s for preservation. (The word *quadriga* actually refers to a car or chariot pulled by four horses, though in this case there are only the horses.) The horses were transported to Venice from Constantinople in 1204, along with lots of other loot from the Fourth Crusade.

The basilica's greatest treasure is the altarpiece known as the **Pala d'Oro (Golden Altarpiece),** a Gothic masterpiece encrusted with over 2,000 precious gems and 83 enameled panels. It was created in 10th-century Constantinople and embellished by Venetian and Byzantine artisans between the 12th and 14th centuries. Second to the Pala d'Oro in importance is the 10th-century **"Madonna di Nicopeia,"** a bejeweled icon also purloined from Constantinople and exhibited in its own chapel. Also worth a visit is the **Tesoro (Treasury),** a collection of crusaders' plunder from Constantinople and other relics amassed over the years. Much of the loot has been incorporated into the interior and exterior of the basilica in the form of marble, columns, capitals, and statuary.

Between April and October, it's worth taking one of the informative 1-hour tours Monday to Saturday (at least one daily, from noon; guides speak English). Book tours (25€–27€) online at www.venetoinside.com. The church also organizes free tours, but these run for limited periods (mostly late July)—see the website for details.

Piazza San Marco. www.basilicasanmarco.it. (C) **041/2708311.** Basilica free; Museo di San Marco (includes Loggia dei Cavalli) 5€, Pala d'Oro 2€, Tesoro (Treasury) 3€. Basilica Mon–Sat 9:30am–5pm, Sun 2–4:30pm (Jun–Nov opens 9:45am Mon–Sat; closes Sun 5pm). Tesoro and Pala d'Oro Mon–Sat 9:45am–4:45pm, Sun 2–4:30pm (Jun–Nov closes 5pm daily). Museo di San Marco daily 9:45am–4:45pm. *Vaporetto:* San Marco.

Know Before You Go

Lines can be long at the basilica (average 45 min), but you can avoid waiting by **reserving access in advance** online (www.venetoinside.com; 3€), up to 10 minutes before your chosen entry time. This service is only available April through October; at other times try to arrive 30 minutes before opening time to avoid the worst of the crush (and skip holidays altogether). You can also use the same website to skip the line at the Campanile di San Marco (p. 410). The guards at St. Mark's entrance are serious about forbidding entry to anyone in **inappropriate attire**—shorts, sleeveless shirts, cropped tops, and skirts above the knee. Note also that you cannot enter the basilica with luggage, and that photos and filming inside are forbidden. Although the basilica is open Sunday morning for anyone wishing to attend Mass, non-worshippers cannot enter merely to tour the site.

Campanile di San Marco (Bell Tower) ★★★ ICON   An elevator whisks you to the top of this 97m (318-ft.) brown brick bell tower where you get awe-inspiring views of St. Mark's cupolas. With a gilded angel atop its spire, it is the highest structure in the city, offering a pigeon's-eye panorama that includes the lagoon, neighboring islands, and the red rooftops and church domes of Venice. Originally built in the 9th century, the bell tower was reconstructed in the 12th, 14th, and 16th centuries, when the pretty marble loggia at its base was added by Jacopo Sansovino. It collapsed unexpectedly in 1902, miraculously hurting no one except a cat. Nine years later it was rebuilt exactly as before, using most of the same materials—even one of the five historical bells that it still uses today.

Piazza San Marco. www.basilicasanmarco.it. ℂ **041/2708311.** 8€ (13€ for skip-the-line). Daily: Apr 1–mid-Apr 9am–5:30pm; mid-April to Sept 8:30am–9pm; Oct 9:30am–6pm; Nov–Mar 9:30am–4:45pm (often closes Jan for maintenance). *Vaporetto:* San Marco.

Canal Grande (Grand Canal) ★★★ NATURAL ATTRACTION   A leisurely cruise along the "Canalazzo" from Piazza San Marco to the Ferrovia (train station), or the reverse, is one of Venice's (and life's) must-do experiences (see box, p. 403). Hop on the **no. 1 *vaporetto*** in the late afternoon (try to get one of the coveted outdoor seats in the prow), when the weather-worn colors of the former homes of Venice's merchant elite are warmed by the soft light and reflected in the canal's rippling waters, and the busy traffic of delivery boats, *vaporetti,* and gondolas that fills the city's main thoroughfare has eased somewhat.

Best stations to start/end a Grand Canal tour: Ferrovia (train station) or Piazzale Roma on northwest side of canal; Piazza San Marco in southeast. Tickets 7.50€.

Palazzo Ducale and Ponte dei Sospiri (Doge's Palace and Bridge of Sighs) ★★★ PALACE   The pink-and-white marble Gothic-Renaissance **Palazzo Ducale,** residence of the doges who ruled Venice for more than 1,000 years, stands between the Basilica di San Marco and the sea. A symbol of prosperity and power, the original was destroyed by a succession of fires, with the current building started in 1340, extended in the 1420s, and redesigned again after a fire in 1483. If you want to understand something of this magnificent place, the history of the 1,000-year-old maritime republic, and the intrigue of the government that ruled it, take the **Secret Itineraries tour** ★★★ (see "Secrets of the Palazzo Ducale," p. 412). Failing that, at least download the free iPhone/Android app (see the website) or shell out for the audio-guide tour (available at entrance, 5€) to help make sense of it all. Unless you can tag along with an English-speaking tour group, you may otherwise miss out on the importance of much of what you're seeing.

The 15th-century **Porta della Carta (Paper Gate)** opens onto a splendid inner courtyard with a double row of Renaissance arches (today visitors enter through a doorway on the lagoon side of the palace). The self-guided route through the palace begins on the main courtyard, where the **Museo dell'Opera** contains assorted bits of masonry preserved from the palazzo's exterior. Beyond here, the first major room you'll come to is the spacious **Sala delle Quattro Porte (Hall of the Four Doors),** with a worn ceiling by Tintoretto. The **Sala dell'Anticollegio,** where foreign ambassadors waited to be received by the doge and his council, is covered in four works by Tintoretto, including "Mercury & the Three Graces" and **"Bacchus and Ariadne"** ★★, the latter deemed one of his best by some critics. The Tintorettos are outshone, however, by Veronese's **"Rape of Europa"** ★★, considered one of the palazzo's finest. The highlight of the adjacent **Sala del Collegio** (the Council Chamber itself) is the spectacular cycle of **ceiling paintings** ★★ by Veronese, completed between 1575 and 1578 and one of his masterpieces. Next door lies the most impressive of the interior rooms, the richly adorned **Sala del Senato (Senate Chamber),** with Tintoretto's ceiling painting "The Triumph of Venice." After passing again through the Sala delle Quattro Porte, you'll come to the Veronese-decorated **Stanza del Consiglio dei Dieci (Room of the Council of Ten)**, where justice was dispensed and decapitations ordered by the Republic's dreaded security police. Formed in the 14th century to deal with emergency situations, the Ten were considered more powerful than the Senate and feared by all. In the **Sala della Bussola (the Compass Chamber),** notice the **Bocca dei Leoni (Lion's Mouth),** a slit in the wall into which secret denunciations and accusations of enemies of the state were placed for quick action by the much-feared Council.

The main sight on the next level down—indeed, the main sight in the entire palace—is the **Sala del Maggior Consiglio (Great Council Hall).** This enormous space is animated by Tintoretto's huge **"Paradiso"** ★ at the far end of the hall above the doge's seat. Measuring 7×23m (23×75 ft.), it is said to be the world's largest oil painting; together with Veronese's gorgeous **"Il Trionfo di Venezia" ("The Triumph of Venice")** ★★ in the oval panel on the ceiling, it affirms the power emanating from the council sessions held here. Tintoretto also did the portraits of the 76 doges encircling the top of this chamber; note that the picture of the Doge Marin Falier, who was convicted of treason and beheaded in 1355, has been

secrets OF THE PALAZZO DUCALE

The **Itinerari Segreti (Secret Itineraries)** ★★★ guided tours of the Palazzo Ducale are a must-see for any visit to Venice of more than 1 day. The tours offer an unparalleled look into the world of Venetian politics over the centuries and are the only way to access the otherwise restricted quarters and hidden passageways of this enormous palace, such as the doges' private chambers and the torture chambers where prisoners were interrogated. The tour must be reserved in advance online (www.vivaticket.it), by phone (© **041/4273-0892**), or in person at the ticket desk. Tours often sell out at least a few days ahead, especially from spring through fall. Tours in English are daily at 9:55am, 10:45am and 11:35am, and cost 20€ for adults, 14€ for children ages 6 to 14 and students ages 15 to 25. There are also tours in Italian at 9:30am and 11:10am, and French at 10:20am and noon. The tour lasts about 75 minutes.

blacked out—Venice has never forgiven him. Tours culminate at the enclosed **Ponte dei Sospiri (Bridge of Sighs),** built in 1600, which connects the Ducal Palace with the grim **Palazzo delle Prigioni (Prison).** The bridge took its current name in the 19th century—Lord Byron popularized it in his epic poem *Childe Harold's Pilgrimage* (1812–1818), romantically imagining the prisoners' final breath of resignation upon viewing the outside world one last time. Some of the cells still have the original graffiti of past prisoners, many of them locked up interminably for petty crimes.

San Marco, Piazza San Marco. www.palazzoducale.visitmuve.it. © **041/2715911.** Admission only with Museum Pass (20€; see "Venice Discounts," p. 414). For an Itinerari Segreti (Secret Itineraries) guided tour in English, see "Secrets of the Palazzo Ducale," p. 412. Daily 8:30am–7pm (Nov–Mar until 5:30pm). *Vaporetto:* San Marco.

Rialto Bridge ★★ ICON   This graceful arch over the Grand Canal, linking the San Marco and San Polo districts, teems with tourists and overpriced boutiques. Until the 1800s, it was the only bridge across the Grand Canal, originally built as a pontoon bridge at the canal's narrowest point. The 1444 incarnation was the first to include shops, interrupted by a drawbridge in the center. In 1592, the current graceful stone span was finished to the designs of Antonio da Ponte, who beat out Sansovino, Palladio, and Michelangelo with plans that called for a single, vast, 28m-wide (92-ft.) arch in the center to allow trading ships to pass.

Ponte del Rialto. *Vaporetto:* Rialto.

Scala Contarini del Bovolo ★★ VIEW   Part of a palazzo built in the late 15th century, this multi-arch spiral staircase was artfully restored in 2016, featuring a belvedere with fabulous views of Venice. Halfway up, the **Sala del Tintoretto (Tintoretto Room)** contains the rare portrait of Lazzaro Zen, an African who converted to Christianity in Venice in 1770, as well as a preparatory painting by Tintoretto of his monumental "Paradise" (the final version is in the Palazzo Ducale). You can buy **timed entry tickets** in advance at www.ticketlandia.com (advisable in peak season).

Corte Contarini del Bovolo 4299, San Marco. www.gioiellinascostidivenezia.it. © **041/309-6605.** Admission 7€; audio guide 1€. Daily 10am 6pm. Vaporetto: Rialto.

Teatro La Fenice ★★★ One of Italy's most famous opera houses (it ranks third after La Scala in Milan and San Carlo in Naples), La Fenice was originally completed in 1792 but has been rebuilt twice after devastating fires in 1837 and in 2004. Self-guided tours take in the opulent main theater, ornate side rooms, the gilded "royal box," and a small exhibit dedicated to soprano Maria Callas. For seeing a show at La Fenice, see p. 452.

Campo San Fantin 1965, San Marco. www.teatrolafenice.it. © **041/2424.** Admission 11€. Daily 9:30am–6pm.Vaporetto: Giglio.

T Fondaco dei Tedeschi ★★ This 16th-century palazzo was converted into a posh department store in 2016, centered on an elegant courtyard and the **Rooftop Terrace,** with quite possibly Venice's greatest view—the Rialto, Grand Canal, and all the city's bell towers laid out before you. It's worth making reservations for the terrace in advance in peak season, either on the store website or via iPads on the 4th and the 5th floors.

Calle de Fontego dei Tedeschi, Ponte di Rialto, San Marco. www.dfs.com/en/venice. © **041/3142000.** Daily 10am–8pm (roof deck free; visits limited to 15 min). Vaporetto: Rialto.

The colorful Renaissance Torre dell'Orologio on Piazza San Marco still keeps perfect time.

Torre dell'Orologio (Clock Tower) ★ MONUMENT As you enter the magnificent **Piazza San Marco,** it's one of the first things you see, standing on the north side, the centerpiece of the stately white **Procuratie Vecchie** (the ancient administration buildings for the Republic). The Renaissance clock tower, with its distinctive blue face ringed by astrological symbols, was built between 1496 and 1506, and the clock mechanism still keeps perfect time. On the top, two bronze figures, known as "Moors" because of the dark color of the bronze, pivot to strike the hour. Visits inside are by guided tour only (included in the price of admission), but unless

VENICE discounts

Venice offers a somewhat bewildering range of passes and discount cards. For short stays, we recommend buying an **ACTV travel card** and combining that with one of the first two passes listed below. The more complex Venezia Unica card scheme is convenient once you've worked out what you want online, and is recommended if you intend to stay up to 7 days and do a lot of sightseeing. The Venezia Unica website (www.veneziaunica.it) is a one-stop shop for all the passes listed below.

The **Museum Pass** (MUVE) grants admission to all the city-run museums over a 6-month period. It also lets you skip any ticketing lines, a useful perk in high season. The pass includes the museums of St. Mark's Square (Palazzo Ducale, Museo Correr, Museo Archeologico Nazionale, and the Biblioteca Nazionale Marciana) as well as the Museo di Palazzo Mocenigo (Costume Museum), the Ca' Rezzonico, the Ca' Pesaro, the Museo del Vetro (Glass Museum) on Murano, and the Museo del Merletto (Lace Museum) on Burano. The Museum Pass is available online (for an extra 0.50€), or at any of the participating museums and costs 24€ for adults, 18€ for students under 26, kids aged 6–14, and seniors over 65. It's a good deal, as the Doge's Palace alone will set you back 20€ (13€ reduced); visit one more major museum (the Ca' Rezzonico and Ca' Pesaro are both 10€ each) and you've made a decent savings.

If churches are your interest, consider the **Chorus Pass** (www.chorusvenezia. org), which grants admission to almost every major church in Venice, 18 in all, for 12€ (8€ for students under 30), for up to 1 year. For 24€, the **Chorus Pass Family** gives you the same perks for two adults and their children up to 18 years old. Most churches charge 3€ admission, which means you'll need to visit more than four to make this pass worthwhile.

The **Venezia Unica card** (www. veneziaunica.it) combines the above passes, transport, discounts, and even Internet access on one card via a "made-to-order" online system, where you choose the services you want. The most useful options are the **Silver, Gold,** and **Platinum** passes. The **Platinum Pass** (from 125.90€) is the best option if you plan to spend a week of heavy sightseeing in Venice. Valid for 7 days, it includes the Museum Pass, the Chorus Pass, the Jewish Museum, Scala Contarini del Bovolo, Teatro La Fenice tours, a lagoon boat tour, free Wi-Fi access all week, a 7-day travelcard and a host of other discounts. You can also buy various transportation packages and just Wi-Fi access (from 5€ for 24 hr.) from Venezia Unica. Once you've paid, you'll be able to simply print out a voucher to use at museums and sights in Venice; to use public transport you must collect tickets by entering your booking code at one of the ACTV automatic ticket machines or by visiting one of the official Points of Sale in in the city (there's one in the train station open 7am to 9pm).

For visitors between the ages of 6 and 29, the **Rolling Venice** card (also available at www.veneziaunica.it) is valid until the end of the year in which you buy it, costs just 6€, and entitles the bearer to significant (20%–30%) discounts at participating restaurants (but only applies to cardholder's meal) and a similar discount on ACTV travel cards (22€ for 3 days). Holders of the Rolling Venice card also get discounts in museums, stores, hotels, and bars across the city (it comes with a thick booklet listing everywhere you're entitled to get discounts).

you are interested in the clock's history, these are easily skipped, especially if you've already been up the Campanile di San Marco.

Piazza San Marco. www.torreorologio.visitmuve.it. © **848/082000** or 041-42730892. 12€, 7€ for ages 6–14 and students 15–25; ticket also good for Museo Correr, Museo Archeologico Nazionale, and Biblioteca Nazionale Marciana (but not Palazzo Ducale). Tours (1hr) in English Mon–Wed 11am and noon, Thurs–Sun 2pm and 3pm (must be reserved in advance online); tours start at Museo Correr ticket office. There are also tours in Italian and French. *Vaporetto:* San Marco.

Castello

Basilica SS. Giovanni e Paolo ★ CHURCH   This massive Gothic church was built by the Dominican order from the 13th to the 15th century and, together with the Frari Church in San Polo, is second in size only to the Basilica di San Marco. An unofficial Pantheon where 25 doges are buried (a number of tombs are part of the unfinished facade), the church, commonly known as Zanipolo in Venetian dialect, is also home to many artistic treasures. The brilliantly colored **"Polyptych of St. Vincent Ferrer"** (ca. 1465), attributed to a young Giovanni Bellini, is in the right aisle. You'll also see the mummified foot of St. Catherine of Siena—considered a holy relic—encased in glass near here. Visit the **Cappella del Rosario ★**, through a glass door off the left transept, to see three restored ceiling canvases and one oil painting by Paolo Veronese, particularly "The Assumption of the Madonna."

Anchoring the large and impressive *campo* outside the church, a popular crossroads for this area of Castello, is the **statue of Bartolomeo Colleoni ★★**, the Renaissance *condottiere* (mercenary) who defended Venice's interests at the height of its power until his death in 1475. The 15th-century sculpture by the Florentine **Andrea Verrocchio** is considered one of the world's great equestrian monuments.

Campo Santi Giovanni e Paolo 6363. www.basilicasantigiovanniepaolo.it. © **041/ 5235913**. 3.50€. Daily 7:30am–7pm (open to tourists Mon–Sat 9am–6pm and Sun noon–6pm). *Vaporetto:* Rialto.

Scuola di San Giorgio degli Schiavoni ★★ MUSEUM   One of the most mesmerizing spaces in Europe, the tiny main hall of this *scuola* once served as a meeting house for Venice's Dalmatian community (Dalmatia is a region of Croatia—*schiavoni* means "Slavs"). Venetian *scuole,* or schools, were guilds that brought together merchants and craftspeople from certain trades or similar religious devotions. Built beside its sister church, San Giovanni di Malta, in the early 16th century, the scuola is most famous for the awe-inspiring painting cycle on its walls, created by Renaissance master **Vittore Carpaccio** between 1502 and 1509. The paintings depict the lives of the Dalmatian patron saints George (of

COME HELL OR high water

During the tidal *acqua alta* (high water) floods, Venice's lagoon rises until it engulfs the city, leaving up to 1.5 to 1.8m (5–6 ft.) of water in the lowest-lying streets. Piazza San Marco, as the lowest point in the city, goes first. As many as 50 floods a year have been recorded since they first started keeping track in the late 1700s. One of the most devastating was in 1966, though the 4th highest ever recorded occurred as recently as November 2018.

Significant *acqua alta* can begin as early as late September or October, but usually takes place November to March (there is no way to predict them in advance). Remember, though, the waters usually recede after just a few hours—there is no need to get wet and the city doesn't shut down. Walkways are set up along the main routes, but if you intend to wander around, do as the locals do and buy rubber wading boots, available from most stores from 20€ (souvenir shops and stands in Piazza San Marco also sell disposable knee-high plastic waterproof slippers for about 10€, good for a couple of days). A complex system of hydraulic gates—the Modulo Sperimentale Elettromeccanico or just **"MOSE"**—is being built out in the lagoon to cut off the highest of these high tides (controversial because of its environmental impact and the seemingly endless delays that have plagued construction); it is expected to be operational sometime in 2022.

dragon-slaying fame), Tryphon, and Jerome; in the upper hall (Sala dell'Albergo) is Carpaccio's masterful "Vision of St. Augustine."
Calle dei Furlani 3259A. ✆ **041/5228828.** 5€. Mon 1:30–5:30pm, Tues–Sat 9:30am–5:30pm, Sun 9:30am–1:30pm. *Vaporetto:* Rialto.

Dorsoduro

Gallerie dell'Accademia (Academy Gallery) ★★★ MUSEUM Along with San Marco and the Palazzo Ducale, the Accademia is one of the city's highlights, a magnificent collection of European art and Venetian painting from the 14th to the 18th centuries. Visitors are currently limited to 300 at one time, so lines can be long in high season—advance reservations are essential (these are timed entry, so you can skip the line). In general, the least crowded times tend to be at opening in the morning and around 2 hours before closing.

There's a lot to take in here, so buy a catalog in the store, as these contain detailed descriptions of the core paintings and plenty of context—the audio guides are a little muddled and not worth 6€. Note also that Da Vinci's iconic **Vitruvian Man** ★★★ (*L'Uomo Vitruviano*), one of the museum's prize holdings, is an extremely fragile ink drawing and rarely displayed in public; check the website before you visit, as exhibitions featuring the painting are rare but well publicized.

Rooms are laid out in rough chronological order, though renovations and closures mean some rooms may be off-limits when you visit (call ahead to check on specific paintings; the website is updated monthly). Work began on the second-floor galleries in 2018—rooms 6 to 13, plus 15, each are likely to be closed at some point over the next 3 years. The following artworks should be on display somewhere in the museum, though locations will change (check the website for the latest.)

Visits normally begin upstairs on the second floor, where room 1 (the grand meeting room of the Scuola Grande di Santa Maria) displays a beautifully presented collection of lavish medieval and early Renaissance art, primarily religious images and altarpieces dating from 1300 to 1450. The giant canvases in room 2 include Carpaccio's "Presentation of Jesus in the Temple," and works by Giovanni Bellini (one of Bellini's images of St. Peter lies in room 3). Rooms 6 to 8 feature Venetian heavyweights Tintoretto, Titian, Veronese, and Lorenzo Lotto, while Room 10 is dominated by Paolo Veronese's mammoth **"Feast in the House of Levi" ★★**. Vast Tintoretto canvases make up the rest of the room. Opposite is Titian's last painting, a "Pietà" intended for his own tomb. Room 11 contains work by Tiepolo, the master of 18th-century Venetian painting, and several paintings by Tintoretto.

Room 19 has traditionally contained the monumental cycle of nine paintings by Carpaccio illustrating the **Story of St. Ursula ★★**; most of these continue to undergo restoration, with "Arrival in Cologne" the only one likely to be displayed for some time. Room 20 is filled by Gentile Bellini's cycle of **"The Miracles of the Relic of the Cross" ★**, painted around 1500. While renovations are ongoing, room 23 will contain some of the museum's most famous paintings—check before you visit with the museum information desk (or on-line) if there's a particular work you would like to see. Finally, room 24 is adorned with Titian's "Presentation of the Virgin," actually created to hang in this space between 1534 and 1538.

Downstairs, the renovated ground-floor galleries cover the late 18th to 19th centuries, a far more mediocre collection of baroque and romantic works, though delicate paintings by Tiepolo share space with his large tondo "Feast of the Cross" in gallery 2, along with Veronese's "Venice

The Biennale

Venice hosts the latest in contemporary art and sculpture from dozens of countries during the prestigious **Biennale d'Arte ★★★** (www.labiennale.org; ☎ 041/5218711), one of the world's top international art shows. It fills the pavilions of the **Giardini** (public gardens) at the east end of **Castello** and at the **Arsenale,** as well as in other spaces around the city from May to November every odd-numbered year (in 2021, 2023, and so on; usually open Tues–Sun 10am–6pm). Tickets cost around 25€, 20€ for those 65 and over, and 15€ for students and ages 26 and under.

The sculpture garden at the Peggy Guggenheim Collection.

Receives Homage from Hercules and Ceres." Sculpture galleries (featuring the work of Canova) should also be open on this level.

Campo della Carità 1050, at foot of Ponte dell'Accademia. www.gallerieaccademia. it. ℂ **041/5200345.** Admission 15€ adults, 2€ ages 18–25, children17 and under free (price may change during temporary exhibitions); free 1st Sun of month (check in advance). 1.50€ charge for reservations by phone or online. Daily 8:15am–6:15pm (Mon until 1pm). *Vaporetto:* Accademia.

Peggy Guggenheim Collection ★★ MUSEUM   It's one of the best museums in Italy covering American and European art of the 20th century, but you might find the experience a little jarring, given its location in a city so heavily associated with the High Renaissance and the baroque. Nevertheless, art aficionados will find some fascinating work here, and the main galleries occupy Peggy Guggenheim's wonderful former home, the 18th-century "unfinished" Palazzo Venier dei Leoni, right on the Grand Canal (you can access the waterfront from the main building). Guggenheim purchased the mansion in 1949 and lived here, on and off, until her death in 1979 (the history of this once derelict palace is wonderfully brought to life in Judith Mackrell's *The Unfinished Palazzo*). Today the entire villa has been converted into galleries. Highlights include Picasso's extremely abstract "Poet," and his more gentle "On the Beach," several works by Kandinsky ("Landscape with Red Spots No. 2" and "White Cross"), Miró's expressionistic "Seated Woman II," Klee's mystical "Magic Garden," and some unsettling works by Max Ernst ("The Kiss," "Attirement of the Bride"), who was briefly married to Guggenheim in the 1940s. Also look for Magritte's "Empire of Light," Dalí's "Birth of Liquid Desires," and a couple of gems from Pollock (who was especially championed by Guggenheim): his early "Moon Woman," which recalls Picasso, and "Alchemy," a more typical "poured" painting. The Italian Futurists are also well represented here, with a rare portrait from Modigliani ("Portrait of the Painter Frank Haviland"). Adjacent buildings have since been added to the complex (serving as temporary exhibition space, a café and shop), connected to the main building by the pleasantly shady Nasher Sculpture Garden (Guggenheim is buried in the corner, marked by a simple headstone). *Tip:* It's not a good idea to visit the Guggenheim and St. Mark's on the same day—it's a fairly long walk between the two. We also don't advise seeing it on the same day as the Accademia, even though they're only 10 minutes apart; the artistic overload is likely to prove too much for even the most avid art aficionado.

Fondamenta Venier dai Leon 704. www.guggenheim-venice.it. ✆ **041/2405411.** Admission 15€ adults, 13€ 65 and over, and those who present an Alitalia ticket to or from Venice dated no more than 7 days previous; 9€ students 26 and under and ages 10–18. Printed guide 5€; audioguide 7€. Wed–Mon 10am–6pm. *Vaporetto:* Accademia (walk around left side of Accademia, take 1st left, and follow signs).

San Sebastiano ★★ CHURCH   Lose the crowds as you make a pilgrimage to the parish church of **Paolo Veronese,** home to some of his finest work. Veronese painted the coffered nave ceiling with the florid "Scenes from the Life of St. Esther." In the 1560s he also decorated the organ shutters and panels in the chancel with scenes from the life of St. Sebastian. Although Veronese is the main event here, don't miss Titian's sensitive "St. Nicholas" (just inside the church on the right). Veronese's sepulchral monument (with bust by Mattia Carneri) is to the left of the altar. The real highlight is the sacristy (go through the door under the organ), a tiny jewel box of a room adorned with more wonderful Veronese paintings of the "Coronation of the Virgin" and the "Four Evangelists."

Campo San Sebastiano. ✆ **041/2750462.** 3€. Mon–Sat 10:30am–4:30pm. *Vaporetto:* San Basilio.

Santa Maria della Salute (Church of the Virgin Mary of Good Health) ★ CHURCH   Known as "La Salute," this jewel of baroque architecture proudly reigns at a commercially and aesthetically important point, almost directly across from the Piazza San Marco, where the Grand Canal empties into the lagoon. The first stone was laid in 1631 after the Senate decided to honor the Virgin Mary for delivering Venice from a plague that had killed around 95,000 people. It was built from the revolutionary plans of a young, relatively unknown architect, Baldassare Longhena, who dedicated the next 50 years of his life to overseeing its progress

Entrance to Santa Maria della Salute church.

(he would die 5 years before its completion). Today the dome of the church is an iconic presence on the Venice skyline, recognized for its exuberant exterior of volutes, scrolls, and more than 125 statues. The most revered image inside is the **Madonna della Salute,** a rare black-faced sculpture of Mary brought back from Candia in Crete in 1670 as war booty. The otherwise sober interior is enlivened by the **sacristy** (4€ entry), with a number of important ceiling paintings and portraits by **Titian.** On the right wall of the sacristy is Tintoretto's **"Marriage at Cana"** ★, considered one of his best paintings.

Campo della Salute 1. www.basilicasalutevenezia.it. ℂ **041/5225558.** Church free; sacristy 4€. Daily 9:30am–noon and 3–5:30pm. *Vaporetto:* Salute.

Scuola Grande dei Carmini ★★ CHURCH   The former Venetian base of the Carmelites, finished in the 18th century, is now a shrine of sorts to **Giambattista Tiepolo,** who painted the ceiling of the upstairs hall between 1739 and 1744. It's a magnificent sight. Tiepolo's elaborate rococo interpretation of "Simon Stock Receiving the Scapular" is now fully restored, along with various panels throughout the building.

Campo San Margherita 2617. www.scuolagrandecarmini.it. ℂ **041/5289420.** 7€. Daily 11am–5pm. *Vaporetto:* San Basilio.

Squero di San Trovaso ★★ HISTORIC SITE   One of the most intriguing sights in Venice is this small *squero* (boatyard), which first opened in the 17th century. Just north of the Zattere (the wide, sunny walkway that runs alongside the Giudecca Canal in Dorsoduro), the boatyard lies next to the Church of San Trovaso on the narrow Rio San Trovaso (not far from the Accademia Bridge). It is surrounded by Tyrolean-looking wooden structures (a rarity in this city of stone) that are home to the multigenerational owners and original workshops for traditional Venetian boats. Aware that they themselves have become a tourist sight, the gondoliers don't mind if you watch them at work from across the narrow Rio di San Trovaso, but don't try to invite yourself in.

Gondolas are built and repaired at the Squero di San Trovaso boatyard in Dorsoduro.

Dorsoduro 1097 (on the Rio San Trovaso). *Vaporetto:* Zattere.

San Polo & Santa Croce

Santa Maria Gloriosa dei Frari ★★ CHURCH   Known simply as "i Frari," this immense 14th-century Gothic basilica built by the Franciscans is the largest church in Venice after San Marco. It houses a number of important artworks, including two Titian masterpieces: the **"Assumption of the Virgin"** ★★ over the main altar, painted when the artist was in his late 20s, and "Virgin of the Pesaro Family" in the left nave, for which Titian's wife posed for the figure of Mary (she died soon afterward in childbirth). Don't miss Giovanni Bellini's **"Madonna & Child"** ★★ over the altar in the sacristy, of which novelist Henry James wrote, "It is as solemn as it is gorgeous." The grand **mausoleum of Titian** is on the right as you enter the church, opposite an incongruous pyramid-shaped 18th-century monument to sculptor **Antonio Canova**—designed by Canova himself, this was originally supposed to be Titian's tomb.

Campo dei Frari 3072. 🕻 **041/2728611.** 3€, audio guide 2€. Mon–Sat 9am–6pm; Sun 1–6pm. *Vaporetto:* San Tomà (walk straight on Calle del Traghetto, turn right and immediately left across Campo San Tomà; walk straight ahead on Ramo Mandoler then Calle Larga Prima, turn right when you reach beginning of Salizada San Rocco).

Scuola Grande di San Rocco (Confraternity of St. Roch) ★★★
MUSEUM   Like many medieval saints, French-born San Rocco (St. Roch) died young, but thanks to his work healing the sick in the 14th century, his cult became associated with the power to cure the plague and other serious illnesses. When his body was brought to Venice in 1485, this *scuola* began to reap the benefits, and by 1560, the current complex was completed. Work soon began on more than 50 paintings by **Tintoretto,** and today the *scuola* is primarily a shrine to the masterful Venetian artist. You enter at the **Sala Terrena** (Ground Floor Hall), where the paintings were created between 1583 and 1587, led by one of the most frenzied "Annunciations" ever made. The "Flight into Egypt" here is undeniably one of Tintoretto's greatest works. Upstairs is the **Sala Superiore** (Great Upper Hall), where Old Testament scenes cover the ceiling. The paintings around the walls, based on the New Testament, are generally regarded as a master class of perspective, shadow, and color. In the **Sala dell'Albergo,** an entire wall is adorned by Tintoretto's mind-blowing "Crucifixion" (as well as his "Glorification of St. Roch," on the ceiling, the painting that actually won him the contract to paint the *scuola*). Way up in the loft, the **Tesoro** (Treasury) is a tiny space dedicated primarily to gold reliquaries containing venerated relics such as the fingers of St. Peter and St. Andrew, and one of the thorns that crowned Christ during the crucifixion.

Campo San Rocco 3052, adjacent to Campo dei Frari. www.scuolagrandesanrocco. org. ✆ **041/5234864.** 10€ adults (includes audio guide); 8€ ages 18–26; 18 and under free. Daily 9:30am–5:30pm. *Vaporetto:* San Tomà (walk straight on Calle del Traghetto, turn right and immediately left across Campo San Tomà; walk straight ahead on Ramo Mandoler, Calle Larga Prima, and Salizada San Rocco, which leads into the *campo* of the same name—look for crimson sign behind Frari Church).

Cannaregio

Casanova Museum & Experience ★★ MUSEUM   One of the city's newest attractions pays homage to one of its most famous sons, **Giacomo Casanova** (1725–1798). The absorbing, interactive exhibition features information boards and multimedia installations, set in the otherwise bare rooms of the Palazzo Pesaro Papafava (you're given a headset that wirelessly translates the audio in each room as you enter). The first section covers aspects of Casanova's exceptional life as adventurer, writer, diplomat, and spy, though his more infamous role as seducer and libertine gets most attention. In one segment you even don headgear for a virtual reality jaunt through 18th-century Venice. Other rooms add context to the fashions and popular parlor games of the time (Casanova claimed to have mastered at least 22).

Calle de la Racheta 3764. www.casanovamuseum.com. ✆ **041/237-9736.** 13€. Daily 10am–8pm. *Vaporetto:* Ca' d'Oro (follow Calle d'Oro, turn left onto Calle del Pistor, right onto Calle Pruili, after crossing canal it becomes Calle de la Racheta, museum is on left).

Galleria Giorgio Franchetti alla Ca' d'Oro ★★ MUSEUM   This magnificent palazzo overlooking the Grand Canal, the "golden house" was built between 1428 and 1430 for the noble Contarini family. Baron Giorgio Franchetti bought the place in 1894, and it now serves as an atmospheric gallery for his exceptional art collection (mostly early Renaissance Italian and Flemish). The highlight is Paduan artist Andrea Mantegna's **"St. Sebastian"** ★★, displayed in its own marble side chapel. Mantegna's third and final painting of the saint, created around 1490, it's quite different from the other two (in Vienna and Paris); it's a bold, deeply pessimistic work, with none of Mantegna's usual background details to detract from the saint's suffering. Don't miss also the three panels from Carpaccio's "Stories of the Virgin" series on the second floor.
Strada Nuova 3932. www.cadoro.org. ☎ **041/520-0345.** 11€ (when 3rd floor closed 7€), plus 1.50€ reservation fee. 2nd floor: Mon 8:15am–2pm; Tues–Sun 8:15am–7:15pm; 3rd floor: Mon 10am–2pm; Tues–Sun 10am–6pm. *Vaporetto:* Ca' d'Oro.

Museo Ebraico di Venezia (Jewish Museum of Venice) ★ MUSEUM/SYNAGOGUE   In the heart of the Ghetto Nuovo, the Jewish Museum contains a small but precious collection of artifacts related to the long history of the Jews in Venice, beginning with an exhibition on Jewish festivities in the first room: chandeliers, goblets, and spice holders used to celebrate Shabbat, Shofàrs (ram's horns), and a Séfer Torà (Scroll of Divine Law). The second room contains a rich collection of historic textiles and a rare marriage contract from 1792. A newer area explores the

IL GHETTO AND THE jews OF VENICE

Jews began settling in Venice in great numbers in the 15th century, and the Republic soon came to value their services as moneylenders, physicians, and traders. In 1516, however, fearing their growing influence, the Venetians forced the Jewish population to live on an island with an abandoned foundry (*ghetto* is old Venetian dialect for "foundry"), and drawbridges were raised to enforce a nighttime curfew. By the end of the 17th century, as many as 5,000 Jews lived in the Ghetto's cramped confines. Napoleon tore down the Ghetto gates in 1797, but it wasn't until the unification of Italy in 1866 that Jews achieved equal status. Il Ghetto remains the spiritual center for Venice's ever-diminishing community of Jewish families, with two synagogues and a Chabad House; it's said that anywhere from 500 to 2,000 Jews live in all of Venice and Mestre, though very few now live in the Ghetto. Aside from its historic interest, this is also one of the less touristy neighborhoods in Venice (although it has become something of a nightspot) and makes for a pleasant and scenic place to stroll. Venice's first kosher restaurant, **Gam Gam,** opened here in 1996, at 1122 Ghetto Vecchi on the canal (www.gamgamkosher.com; ☎ **366/2504505**), close to the Guglie *vaporetto* stop. Owned and run by Orthodox Jews, it is open Sunday to Thursday noon to 10pm, Friday noon to 2 hours before Shabbat (sunset), and Saturday from 1 hour after Shabbat until 11pm (excluding summer).

immigration patterns of Jews to Venice, and their experiences once here. But for many, the real highlight is the chance to tour three of the area's five historic synagogues: **German** (Scuola Grande Tedesca), founded in 1528; **Italian** (Scuola Italiana), founded in 1575; **Sephardic** (Scuola Levantina), founded in 1541 but rebuilt in the 17th century; **Spanish** (Scuola Spagnola), rebuilt in the first half of the 17th century; and the baroque-style **Ashkenazi** (Scuola Canton), largely rebuilt in the 18th century. The ones you visit depends on which synagogues are being used; the Levantina and the Spanish are the most lavishly decorated, with one usually included on the tour. Ladies must have shoulders covered and men must have heads covered; no photos.

Cannaregio 2902B (on Campo del Ghetto Nuovo). www.museoebraico.it. 🕽 **041/ 715359.** Museum 8€ adults, 6€ children and students ages 6–26; museum and synagogue tour 12€ adults, 10€ children and students ages 6–26. Museum Sun–Fri 10am–7pm (Oct–May until 5:30pm); synagogue guided tours in English hourly 10:30am–5:30pm (Oct–May last tour 4:30pm). Closed on Jewish holidays. *Vaporetto:* Guglie.

Giudecca & San Giorgio

Il Redentore ★★ CHURCH   Perhaps the greatest masterpiece of Andrea Palladio, the great Renaissance architect from nearby Padua, Il Redentore was commissioned by Venice to give thanks for being delivered from the great plague (1575–77), which claimed over a quarter of the population (some 46,000 people). The doge established a tradition of visiting this church by crossing a long pontoon bridge made up of boats from the Dorsoduro's Zattere on the third Sunday of each July, a tradition that survived the demise of the doges and remains one of Venice's most popular festivals ("Festa del Redentore," see p. 38). The interior is done in austere but elegant Palladian style. Artworks tend to be workshop pieces (from the studios or schools of Tintoretto and Veronese), but a fine "Baptism of Christ" by Veronese himself is in the sacristy (accessed through a door in the last chapel on the right).

Campo del Redentore 195, La Giudecca. 🕽 **041/523-1415.** 3€. Mon–Sat 10:30am– 4:30pm. *Vaporetto:* Redentore.

San Giorgio Maggiore ★★ CHURCH   Sitting on the little island of San Giorgio Maggiore across from Piazza San Marco, this church is another Palladio masterpiece. Most known for his country villas built for Venice's wealthy merchant families, Palladio designed this church in 1565 and it was completed in 1610. To impose a classical front on the traditional church structure, Palladio designed two interlocking facades, with repeating triangles, rectangles, and columns that are harmoniously proportioned. Founded as early as the 10th century, the church had its interior reinterpreted by Palladio with whitewashed stucco surfaces, an unadorned but harmonious space. The main altar is flanked by two epic paintings by Tintoretto, "The Fall of Manna," to the left, and the more noteworthy **"The Last Supper"** ★★ to the right, famous for its chiaroscuro. Accessed by free guided tour only (usually Apr–Oct only, times vary), the adjacent **Cappella dei Morti** (Chapel of the Dead) contains Tintoretto's "Deposition," and the upper chapel contains Carpaccio's St. George Killing the Dragon." To the left of the choir is an elevator that you can take to the top of the 1791 campanile—for a charge of 6€—to experience an unforgettable view of the island, the lagoon, and the Palazzo Ducale and Piazza San Marco across the way.

San Giorgio Maggiore. ℰ **041/5227827.** Free. Daily Apr–Oct 9am–7pm, Nov–Mar 8:30am–6pm. *Vaporetto:* Take Giudecca-bound *vaporetto* no. 2 on Riva degli Schiavoni (San Marco/San Zaccaria) and get off at 1st stop, San Giorgio Maggiore.

Exploring Venice's Islands

Venice shares its lagoon with four other principal islands: **Murano, Burano, Torcello,** and the **Lido.** Guided tours of the first three are available (25€–40€ for 3–4 hours), but while these can be informative, unless you are very short of time you'll enjoy exploring the islands in far more leisurely fashion on your own, easily done using the *vaporetti.* Line nos. 4.1 and 4.2 make the journey to **Murano** from Fondamente Nove (north side of Castello). For **Murano, Burano,** and **Torcello,** Line no. 12 departs Fondamente Nove every 30 minutes; for Torcello change to the Line 9 shuttle boat from Burano, timed to match arrivals from Venice. The islands are small and easy to navigate, but check the schedule for island-to-island departures and plan your return so that you don't spend most of your day waiting for connections.

Vaporetto line nos. 1, 2, 5.1, 5.2, and LN cross the lagoon to the **Lido** from the San Zaccaria–Danieli stop near San Marco. Note that the Lido becomes chilly, windswept, and utterly deserted from October to April.

MURANO ★★

The island of Murano has long been famous throughout the world for the products of its glass factories. The illuminating **Museo del Vetro** (Museum of Glass), Fondamenta Giustinian 8 (www.museovetro.visitmuve.it; ℰ **041/739586**), charts the history of the island's glassmaking and is definitely worthwhile if you intend to purchase a lot of glassware, providing plenty of background so you know what you're buying in the stores outside. Daily hours are 10am to 6pm (Nov–Mar to 5pm), and admission is 12€ for adults and 9.50€ for children 6 to 14 and students 25 and under.

Dozens of *fornaci* (kilns) offer free shows of mouth-blown glassmaking almost invariably hitched to a hard-sell tour of the factory outlet store. Once you're on the island, you can't miss these places (and they're pretty much of equivalent quality), but **Original Murano Glass** (9:30am–5pm daily; reserve free tours and demonstrations at www.originalmuranoglass. com), at the Ellegi Glass *fornaci,* Fondamenta San Giovanni dei Battuti 4, is a dependable choice (it's a few minutes walk from the Murano Faro *vaporetti* stop). Almost all the shops will ship their goods, but that often doubles the price. On the other hand, these pieces are instant heirlooms.

Murano is also graced by two worthy churches (both free admission): the largely 15th-century **San Pietro Martire** ★ (Mon–Sat 9am–5:30pm, Sun noon–5:30pm), with paintings by Veronese and Giovanni Bellini, and the ancient **Santa Maria e Donato** ★ (Mon–Sat 9am–6pm, Sun 12:30–6pm), with its intricate Byzantine exterior apse, 6th-century pulpit, stunning mosaic of Mary, and a fantastic 12th-century inlaid floor.

BURANO ★★★

Lace is the claim to fame of tiny, historic Burano, a craft kept alive for centuries by the wives of fishermen waiting for their husbands to return from the sea. Sadly, most of the lace sold on the island these days is made by machine elsewhere. The local government continues its attempt to keep Burano's centuries-old lace legacy alive with subsidized classes. It's still worth a trip to stroll the back streets of the island, whose canals are lined with the brightly colored, simple homes of the Buranesi fishermen—quite unlike anything in Venice or Murano. **Butter biscuits,** known as *buranelli,* are another famous island product—expect to be offered them in almost every store.

Colorful fishermen's homes on the island of Burano.

While you're there, visit the **Museo del Merletto (Museum of Lace Making),** Piazza Galuppi 187 (www.museomerletto.visitmuve.it; *℮* **041/ 730034**), to understand why something so exquisite should not be left to fade into extinction. It's open Tuesday to Sunday 10am to 6pm (Nov–Mar to 5pm); admission is 5€ adults, and 3.50€ for children 6 to 14 and students 25 and under.

TORCELLO ★★

Torcello is perhaps the most charming of the islands, though today it consists of little more than one long canal leading from the *vaporetto* landing to a clump of buildings at its center. Hard to imagine this was once a thriving city in its own right, with at least 20,000 inhabitants in the 16th century. Torcello boasts the oldest Venetian monument, the **Basilica di Santa Maria dell'Assunta ★★★**, whose foundation dates from the 7th century (*℮* **041/2702464**). It's famous for its spectacular 11th- to 12th-century Byzantine mosaics—a "Madonna and Child" in the apse and a monumental "Last Judgment" on the west wall—rivaling those of Ravenna's and St. Mark's basilicas. The cathedral is open daily 10:30am to 6pm (Nov–Feb to 5pm), and admission is 5€ (audio guide an extra 2€; the bell tower is another 4€). Also of interest is the adjacent 11th-century **Santa Fosca** (free admission, closes 30 min. before Basilica), a Byzantine brick chapel with a plain interior, and the **Museo di Torcello** (*℮* **041/730761,** 3€, Tues–Sun 10:30am–5:30pm [Nov–Feb 10am–5pm]), showcasing archeological artifacts from the Iron Age to medieval period, many found on the island. Buy tickets at the basilica entrance (all three attractions 12€; museum and cathedral only 8€).

Peaceful Torcello is now uninhabited except for a handful of families and a population of feral cats, and is a favorite picnic spot. You'll have to bring the food from Venice—there are no stores on the island and only a handful of bars/trattorias plus one fabulous destination restaurant, the **Locanda Cipriani** (www.locandacipriani.com; *℮* **041/730150;** Wed–Mon noon–3pm and 7–9pm; closed Jan to mid-Feb), of Hemingway fame (Queen Elizabeth II, Winston Churchill, and Princess Diana all dined here too). Opened in 1935 by Giuseppe Cipriani (it's still owned by the family), this spot is definitely worth a splurge. Once the tour groups have left, the island offers a very special moment of solitude and escape.

THE LIDO

Although a convenient 15-minute *vaporetto* ride away from San Marco (see transport details p. 397), Venice's **Lido beaches** are not much to write home about and certainly no longer a chic destination (the Grand Hotel des Bains of Thomas Mann's *Death in Venice* fame closed in 2010). For swimming and sunbathing there are much better beaches nearby—in **Jesolo,** to the north, for example. But the parade of wealthy Italian and foreign tourists and Venetian families who still frequent the Lido is an interesting sight indeed.

9

Exploring Venice

The Lido has two main beach areas. **Bucintoro** is at the opposite end of Gran Viale Santa Maria Elisabetta (referred to as the Gran Viale) from the *vaporetto* station Santa Elisabetta. It's a 10-minute stroll; walk straight ahead along Gran Viale to reach the beach. **San Nicolò,** about 1.5km (1 mile) away, can be reached by bus B. Loungers and parasols can be rented for 10€–20€ per person (per day) depending on the time of year (it's just 1€ to use the showers and bathrooms). Keep in mind that if you stay at any of the hotels on the Lido, most have some kind of agreement with the different *bagni* (beach establishments). Note that the restored **Ancient Jewish Cemetery** (Antico Cimitero Ebraico) on the Lido (established in 1386), is open to the public but best appreciated on a tour from the Museo Ebraico (90€; p. 423).

Organized Tours

Because of the sheer number of sights to see in Venice, some first-time visitors like to start out with an organized tour. Although few things can really be covered in any depth on these overview tours, they're somewhat useful for getting your bearings. **Avventure Bellissime** (www.tours-italy.com; ℭ **041/970499**) coordinates a plethora of tours (in English), by boat and gondola, though the walking tours are the best value, covering all the main sights around Piazza San Marco in 2 hours for 25€ (discounts to 22€ available online). For something with a little more bite (literally), **Urban Adventures** (www.urbanadventures.com; ℭ **348/9808566**) runs enticing tours that feature snacking on *ciccheti,* Venice's version of tapas (133€ for 2.5 hr. tour; includes food and wine).

For those with more energy, learn to "row like a Venetian" (yes, standing up), at **Row Venice** (www.rowvenice.org; ℭ **347/7250637**), where 1½-hour lessons take place in traditional, hand-built "shrimp-tail" or *batele coda di gambero* boats for 85€ for up to 2 people. Or you could abandon tradition altogether and opt for a **Venice Kayak** tour (www.venicekayak.com; ℭ **346/4771327**), a truly enchanting way to see the city from the water. Despite restrictions imposed on kayaking by Venice authorities in 2018, tours are still available on Sundays and most afternoons (after 3pm)—check the website for the latest situation. **Venice Adventures**

THE film FESTIVAL

The **Venice International Film Festival** ★, in late August and early September, is the most respected celebration of celluloid in Europe after Cannes. Films from all over the world are shown primarily in the **Palazzo del Cinema** and **Palazzo del Casinò** on the Lido. Ticket prices vary, but those for the less-sought-after films are usually modest. Visit www.labiennale.org/en/cinema for details.

carnevale A VENEZIA

Carnevale traditionally was the celebration preceding Lent, the period of penitence and abstinence prior to Easter; its name is derived from the Latin *carnem levare*, meaning "to take meat away." In Venice, the heyday of Carnevale was the 18th century, but it was outlawed in 1797 and was only revived in 1979 to boost winter tourism. Today Carnevale in Venice builds for a whole month until the big blowout, Shrove Tuesday, when fireworks illuminate the Grand Canal and Piazza San Marco becomes a giant open-air ballroom for the masses. The festival is a harlequin patchwork of musical and cultural events, many free of charge, appealing to all ages, tastes, nationalities, and budgets. Musical events are staged in some of the city's dozens of *piazze*—from reggae and zydeco to jazz and baroque. Book your hotel months ahead, especially for the 2 weekends prior to Shrove Tuesday. Check **www.carnevalevenezia.com** for details.

(www.veniceadventures.net; email supinvenice@gmail.com) offers guided SUP ("standup paddleboard") tours in Venice (April–Oct), with 1-hour sessions ranging from 60€ to 80€.

Especially for Kids

It goes without saying that a **gondola ride** (p. 403) will be the thrill of a lifetime for any child (or adult). If that's too expensive, consider the far cheaper alternative: a **ride on the no. 1** *vaporetto* (p. 397).

Judging from the squeals of delight, **feeding the pigeons in Piazza San Marco** could be the high point of your child's visit to Venice, and it's the ultimate photo op. Purchase a bag of corn and you'll be draped in fluttering and flapping pigeons in a nanosecond.

A jaunt to the neighboring **island of Murano** (p. 425) can be as educational as it is recreational—follow the signs to any *fornace* (kiln), where a glassblowing performance of the island's thousand-year-old art is free entertainment. But be ready for the sales pitch that follows.

Take the elevator to the **top of the Campanile di San Marco** (p. 410) for a scintillating view of Venice's rooftops and cupolas, or get up close and personal with the four bronze horses on the facade of the **Basilica San Marco** (p. 405). The view from its outdoor loggia is something you and your children won't forget. Scaling the **Torre dell'Orologio** (p. 413) or the bell tower at **San Giorgio Maggiore** (p. 424) is also lots of fun.

The **winged lion,** said to have been a kind of good luck mascot to St. Mark, patron saint of Venice, was the very symbol of the Serene Republic and to this day appears on everything from cafe napkins to T-shirts. Keep a running tab of who can spot the most flying lions—you'll find them on facades, atop columns, over doorways, as pavement mosaics, on government stamps, and on the local flag.

WHERE TO STAY IN VENICE

Few cities boast as long a high season as that of Venice, which begins with the Easter period. May, June, and September are the best months weather-wise, and therefore the most crowded. July and August are hot (few of the one- and two-star hotels offer air-conditioning; when they do, it usually costs extra). Hotels are more expensive here than in any other Italian city, with no apparent upgrade in amenities. The least special of those below are clean and functional; at best, they're charming and thoroughly enjoyable, with the serenade of a passing gondolier thrown in for good measure. Some may even be your best stay in all of Europe. Try to reserve your lodging as far in advance as possible, even in the off season.

SELF-CATERING APARTMENTS

Anyone looking to get into the local swing of things in Venice should opt for a short-term **rental apartment.** For the same price or less than a hotel room, you could have your own one-bedroom apartment with a washing machine, A/C, and a fridge to keep your Prosecco cold. Properties of all sizes and price ranges are available for stays of 1 night to several weeks.

In terms of **location,** San Marco is the most convenient part of the city, though anywhere near the Grand Canal will give you easy access to the best of Venice. Apartments in the further reaches of Santa Croce, Cannaregio, Giudecca, and Castello may be slightly cheaper and allow a glimpse of residential life in the city, but getting to and from the main sights will take a lot of time.

For those renting apartments, rather than staying in hotels, secure **luggage storage facilities** are available through BAGBNB from 5€ per day (bagbnb.com). BAGBNB coordinates a network of various businesses throughout Venice prepared to look after your bags—look for the most convenient option on the website.

RECOMMENDED AGENCIES

Airbnb (www.airbnb.com), **VRBO.com**, and **Homeaway.com** are now major players in Venice, each with more than 300 properties listed. On Airbnb you can rent a room in someone's home from just 30€ per night. **Couchsurfing** (www.couchsurfing.com) is also popular and generally safe in Venice, though take the usual precautions (for those who don't know the company, it allows locals to offer free rooms to travelers). **Cities Reference** (www.citiesreference.com; ✆ **06/48903612**) is the best traditional rental agency for Venice, with around 50 properties listed. The company's no-surprises property descriptions come with helpful information and lots of photos. **Cross Pollinate** (www.cross-pollinate.com; ✆ **06/99369799**) is a multi-destination agency with a decent roster of personally inspected apartments and B&Bs in Venice, created by the American owners of the Beehive hotel in Rome (p. 137). **Rental in Venice**

(www.rentalinvenice.com; © **041/718981**) has an alluring website—with video clips of the apartments—and the widest selection of midrange and luxury apartments in the prime San Marco zone (there are less expensive ones, too).

It's standard practice for local rental agencies to collect 30 percent of the total rental amount upfront to secure a booking. When you check in, the balance of your rental fee is normally payable in cash only, so make sure you have enough euros in hand. Upon booking, the agency should provide you with detailed check-in procedures. Most apartments provide a list of nearby shops and services; beyond that, you're on your own, which is what makes an apartment stay a great way to do as the Venetians do.

San Marco

EXPENSIVE

Corte Di Gabriela ★★★   This gorgeous boutique hotel, just a short walk from Piazza San Marco, combines contemporary design with classical Venetian style—ceiling murals, marble pillars, and exposed brick blend with designer furniture and appliances (including free use of iPads, strong Wi-Fi, and satellite TV). The fully renovated property dates from 1870, once serving as the home and offices of Venetian lawyers. It's the attention to detail that makes a stay here so memorable. And breakfast is one of the highlights and well worth lingering over: fresh pastries made by the owners the night before, decent espresso, and crepes and omelets cooked on request.

Calle degli Avvocati 3836. www.cortedigabriela.com. © **041/5235077.** 10 units. 250€–410€ double. Rates include breakfast. *Vaporetto:* Sant' Angelo. **Amenities:** Bar; babysitting; concierge; room service (limited hours); Wi-Fi (free).

MODERATE

Locando Fiorita ★★   Hard to imagine a more picturesque location for this little hotel, a charming, quiet, *campiello* draped in vines and blossoms—no wonder it's a favorite of professional photographers. Most of the standard rooms are small (bathrooms are tiny), but all are furnished in an elegant 18th-century style, with wooden floors, shuttered windows, and richly patterned fittings (A/C and satellite TV are included). The helpful staff more than make up for any deficiencies, and breakfast is a real pleasure, especially when taken outside on the *campiello*.

Campiello Novo 3457a. www.locandafiorita.com. © **041/5234754.** 10 units. 95€–178€ double. Rates include breakfast. *Vaporetto:* Sant'Angelo (walk to the tall brick building and go around it, turning right into Ramo Narisi; at small bridge turn left and walk along Calle del Pestrin to small piazza on your right, Campiello Novo). **Amenities:** Babysitting; concierge; room service; Wi-Fi (free).

Violino d'Oro ★★   The relatively spacious rooms in this handsome 18th-century building have been adorned in a neoclassical Venetian style with exposed wooden beams, crystal chandeliers, and heaps of character.

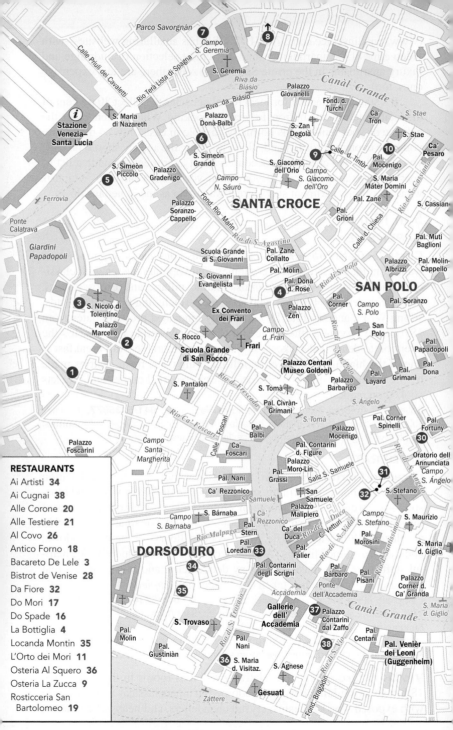

RESTAURANTS

Venice Hotels & Restaurants

Information ⓘ

CANNAREGIO

Pal. Giovanelli
S. Felice
Pal. Fontana
Ca' d'Oro
Pal. Sagredo
S. Sofia
Ss. Apóstoli
Pal. Widman
Pal. Brandolin
Pescaria
Pal. Mangilli
S. Canciano
Pal. Grifalconi
Ca' da Mosto
Rio di S.G. Crisostomo
Pal. Falier
S. Maria d. Miracoli
C. larga G. Gallina
Ospedale Civile
S. Maria d. Pianto
Fàbbriche Nuove
S. Giovanni Crisostomo
Pal. Soranzo-Van Axel
Ss. Giovanni e Paolo (S. Zanipolo)
Teatro Málibran
Pal. Pisani
Palazzo Dieci Savi
Fondaco d. Tedeschi
Pal. Cavazza-Foscari
Campo S. Marina
Rio di S. Marina
Pal. Morosini
Pal. Muazzo
. Aponàl
Rialto
Riva del Vin
S. Bartolomeo
C. Staglieri
S. Lio
Pal. Donà
Pal. Cavignis
Palazzo Cappello
S. Silvestro
Palazzo Dolfin-Manin
S. Maria della Fava
Palazzo Ruzzini
Campo S. Maria Formosa
Pal. Donà
S. Lorenzo
S. Silvestro
Riva del Carbon
Pal. Bembo
M. S. Salvador
Pal. Tasca Papafáva
S. Maria Formosa
Ruga Giuffa
Questura
CASTELLO
Palazzo Grimani
Ca' Farsetti
S. Salvador
C. Guerra
Pal. Querini Stampalia
Pal. Priuli
Pal. Zorzi
S. Luca
C. del Teatro
S. Zulián
Palazzo Soranzo
S. Giovanni Novo
S. Giorgio dei Greci
Cinema Rossini
Campo Manin
C. Fiubera
C. Spadaria
Merc. Orologio
C. Canonica
Palazzo Trevisan-Cappello
S. Zaccaria
Palazzo Contarini d. Bovolo
C. Goldoni
Fabbri
S. Gallo
Torre d. Orologio
Basilica di San Marco
Convento
La Pietà
Ateneo Véneto
Pisc. di Frozzaria
Palazzo Ducale (Doge's Palace)
Pal. d. Prigioni
Teatro La Fenice
S. Fantin
Campanile
Piazza San Marco
Riva d. Schiavoni
S. Moisè
S.S. Moise
Museo Corrèr
Piazzetta
Ponte d. Sospiri (Bridge of Sighs)
S. Zaccaria
SAN MARCO
C. Larga XXII Marzo
C. Vallaresso
Giardini ex Reali
Molo
Palazzo Tiépolo
Capo di Porto
S. Marco
Palazzi Contarini
Palazzo Treves d. Bonfili
Bacino di San Marco
Pal. Gritti
Salute
Pal. Genovese
Dogana da Mar
Punta d. Dogana
S. Maria d. Salute
Seminario Patriarcale
Ex Ospizio

HOTELS	
Ai Tagliapietra 24	Casa Verardo 23
Ai Due Fanali 6	Corte Di Gabriela 30
Al Piave 22	Falier 2
Al Ponte Antico 13	Galleria 37
Al Ponte Mocenigo 10	Locanda Fiorita 31
Antiche Figure 5	Metropole 27
Arcadia 8	Moresco 1
B&B San Marco 25	Pensione Accademia 33
Bernardi 12	Pensione Guerrato 14
Ca' Barba B&B 15	San Geremia 7
	Violino d'Oro 29

433

Most rooms overlook the romantic San Moisè canal, and Piazza San Marco is just a 5-minute stroll. At this price point (with incredible deals in low season), it's reassuring to know you get A/C, satellite TV, and an elevator. Breakfast is an event, a vast spread of homemade cakes and muffins paired with one of the best cappuccinos in the city.

Calle Larga XXII Marzo 2091. www.violinodoro.com. ℂ **041/2770841**. 26 units. 60€–241€ double. Rates include breakfast. *Vaporetto:* San Marco–Vallaresso (walk up Calle di Ca' Vallaresso, turn left on Salizada San Moisè and cross footbridge; hotel is across the *campiello* on the left). **Amenities:** Bar; concierge; room service; Wi-Fi (free).

Castello
EXPENSIVE

Metropole ★★★   This behemoth with a waterfront location is part luxury hotel, part eclectic art museum, with antiques, Asian artworks, and tapestries dotted throughout. But it's no dusty grand dame; on the contrary, it's a chic boutique hotel with rooms opulently furnished in white, red, and gold color schemes. For many guests, however, the main reason to stay here is the building's inspiring history: It began life in the Middle Ages as the Ospedale della Pietà, a charitable institution for orphans and abandoned girls, and later became the music school where Vivaldi taught violin in the early 1700s. After it was converted into a hotel in 1895, Sigmund Freud was an early guest, along with Thomas Mann, who allegedly wrote parts of *Death in Venice* here.

Riva degli Schiavoni 4149. www.hotelmetropole.com. ℂ **041/5205044**. 67 units. 202€–660€ double. Rates include breakfast. *Vaporetto:* San Zaccaria (walk along Riva degli Schiavoni to right; hotel is next to La Pietà church). **Amenities:** Restaurant; bar; babysitting; concierge; room service; Wi-Fi (free).

MODERATE

Al Piave ★★   Al Piave is a cozy, old-fashioned family-run hotel just 5 minutes from Piazza San Marco. Rooms are simply but attractively furnished with richly woven rugs, marble floors, and some of the original wood beams exposed (some come with a terrace, while the family suites are a good value for groups). Bathrooms are relatively big, and the A/C is a welcome bonus in the summer, but there are no elevators, so be prepared if you get a higher floor. Outside of peak months (July, September), Piave is an exceptionally good value, given its proximity to the *piazza*.

Ruga Giuffa 4838. www.hotelalpiave.com. ℂ **041/5285174**. 20 units. 120€–250€ double. Rates include breakfast. Closed Jan 7 to Carnevale. *Vaporetto:* San Zaccaria (find Calle delle Rasse beyond Palazzo Danieli; walk to end of street; turn left and then immediately right; continue to Ponte Storto, cross and continue to Ruga Giuffa—hotel is on left). **Amenities:** Babysitting; concierge; Wi-Fi (free).

Casa Verardo ★★★   Tucked away across a small bridge in the warren of central Castello, this enchanting property occupies a 16th-century *palazzo,* converted to a hotel in 1911. Rooms sport an old-fashioned Venetian style, with Florentine furniture, hand-painted beds, and colorful textiles (antiques and paintings are scattered throughout), but updated with A/C and satellite TV. Some rooms have a view over a canal, others over the shady courtyard and the city. A panoramic terrace on the top floor is a pleasant spot for an aperitif. They'll also take you to Murano for free, but you have to find your own way back.

Calle Drio La Chiesa 4765. www.casaverardo.it. ✆ **041/5286138.** 25 units. 157€–225€ double. Rates include breakfast. *Vaporetto:* San Zaccaria (walk straight on Calle delle Rasse to Campo SS. Filippo e Giacomo; cross *campo* to Calle della Sacrestia, then Calle Drio La Chiesa to Ponte Storto; look for hotel on left). **Amenities:** Bar; babysitting; concierge; room service; Wi-Fi (free).

INEXPENSIVE

Ai Tagliapietra ★★★   This cozy B&B is run by the amicable Lorenzo, who works hard to make guests' stay a memorable one. It's a real bargain in this part of town. Rooms are basic, but spotless, modern, and relatively spacious with private bathrooms. The small, shared kitchenette is available for guests' use (with refrigerator and free tea). Lorenzo usually meets guests at San Zaccaria, gives them a map, prints boarding passes, and generally organizes the trip, making this an especially recommended budget option for first-time visitors.

Salizada Zorzi 4943. www.aitagliapietra.com. ✆ **347/3233166.** 3 units. 70€–100€ double. Rates include breakfast. *Vaporetto:* San Zaccaria (walk straight on Calle delle Rasse to Campo SS. Filippo e Giacomo; cross *campo* to Calle della Sacrestia; take 1st left; cross Salita Corte Rotta and continue to Salizada Zorzi). **Amenities:** Wi-Fi (free).

B&B San Marco ★★★   With just three double rooms, this exquisite B&B, in a peaceful, residential neighborhood, fills up fast, so book ahead. It's a comfortable, charming, yet convenient option, the kind of place that makes you feel like a local, but not too far from the main sights. Your hosts are the bubbly Marco and Alice Scurati, who live in the attic upstairs, and are always happy to provide help and advice. Rooms overlook the Scuola di San Giorgio degli Schiavoni and offer wonderful views of the canal and streetscapes nearby. They're furnished with antiques. Two rooms share a bathroom; the third has private facilities. Breakfast is self-service in the shared kitchen; yogurts, pastries, espresso, cappuccino, juice, and tea.

Fondamenta San Giorgio dei Schiavoni 3385. www.realvenice.it. ✆ **041/5227589.** 3 units. 70€–135€ double. Rates include breakfast. Closed Aug and Jan 7–Carnevale. *Vaporetto:* San Zaccaria (walk on Calle delle Rasse to Campo SS. Filippo e Giacomo; cross *campo* to Calle della Sacrestia, cross canal; turn left at Campo S Provolo on Fondamenta Osmarin; turn left where canal ends, walk to bridge that connects to Calle Lion; at street's end turn left along the canal onto Fondamenta San Giorgio dei Schiavoni). **Amenities:** Wi-Fi (free).

Dorsoduro

EXPENSIVE

Moresco ★★★   An incredibly attentive staff, a decadent breakfast that includes Prosecco (to mix with orange juice, ahem), and lavish 19th-century Venetian decor away from the tourist hubbub make this a popular choice. Rooms seamlessly blend Venetian style with modern design. Some have a terrace (with canal or garden views), while others have spa bathtubs; all have flatscreen TVs. If the weather cooperates, take breakfast in the courtyard garden to really soak up the ambience. The hotel is a 5- to 10-minute walk from Piazzale Roma and the train station, but you'll have a number of bridges and stairs to negotiate along the way.

Fondamenta del Rio Novo 3499, Dorsoduro. www.hotelmorescovenice.com. 🕿 **041/ 2440202.** 23 units. 135€–371€ double. Rates include breakfast. *Vaporetto:* Ferrovia/ Piazzale Roma (from train station walk SW along Fondamenta Santa Lucia, cross Ponte della Costituzione and turn left onto Fondamenta Santa Chiara; cross Ponte Santa Chiara and turn right onto Fondamenta Papadopoli, continue across Campiello Lavadori then along Fondamenta del Rio Novo). **Amenities:** Bar; concierge; free trips to Murano; room service; Wi-Fi (free).

MODERATE

Galleria ★★   Just around the corner from the Accademia, right on the Grand Canal, this hotel occupies a 19th-century *palazzo* in one of the city's most inviting locations. It's been a hotel since the 1800s, hosted poet Robert Browning in 1878, and maintains an 18th-century theme in the rooms, with wood furniture and rococo decor. Hosts Luciano and Stefano serve a simple breakfast in your room. The smallest rooms here really are tiny, and there is no A/C (rooms are supplied with fans when it gets hot), but the fridge of free water and sodas is a lifesaver in summer.

Dorsoduro 878a. www.hotelgalleria.it. 🕿 **041/5232489.** 9 units, 6 w/bath. 80€–290€ double. Rates include breakfast. *Vaporetto:* Accademia (with Accademia Bridge behind you, hotel is just to your left). **Amenities:** Babysitting; concierge; room service; Wi-Fi (free in public areas).

Pensione Accademia ★★   This spellbinding hotel with a tranquil blossom-filled garden has a fascinating history. The Gothic-style Villa Maravege was built in the 17th century as a family residence, but served as the Russian Embassy between World Wars I and II before becoming a hotel in 1950. If that's not enticing enough, rooms are outfitted with Venetian-style antique reproductions, wood furnishings, handsome tapestries, and A/C, with views over the Rio San Trovaso or the garden. Breakfast is served in your room, in the dining hall, or on the patio.

Fondamenta Bollani 1058. www.pensioneaccademia.it. 🕿 **041/5210188.** 27 units. 100€–330€ double. Rates include breakfast. *Vaporetto:* Accademia (turn right down Calle Gambara, which becomes Calle Corfu, which ends at a side canal; walk left over bridge, then turn right back toward Grand Canal to the hotel). **Amenities:** Bar; babysitting; concierge; room service; Wi-Fi (free).

The flower-filled garden of the Pensione Accademia.

San Polo

MODERATE

Ca' Barba B&B ★★ What you'll remember most about Ca' Barba may well be the host, Alessandro, who usually meets guests at the Rialto *vaporetto* stop; inspires daily wanderings with tips, maps, and books, and provides fresh breads and pastries from the local bakery for breakfast. Of the four rooms (reservations are essential, with the best rates on www. airbnb.com), no. 201 is the largest and brightest, with a Jacuzzi tub (no. 202 also has one). All rooms have antique furniture, 19th-century paintings, wood-beamed ceilings, LCD TVs, A/C, and strong Wi-Fi.

Calle Campanile Castello 1825. www.cabarba.com. © **041/5242816.** 4 units. 70€– 334€ double. Rates include breakfast. *Vaporetto:* Rialto (walk back along Grand Canal, turn left at Calle Campanile Castello). **Amenities:** Concierge; Wi-Fi (free).

Pensione Guerrato ★★★ Dating, incredibly, from 1227, this is definitely one of the city's most historic places to stay. The building's long history—it was once the "Inn of the Monkey," run by nuns, with the original structure mostly destroyed by fire in 1513—is worth delving into (the owners have all the details). Rooms are simply but classically furnished, with wood floors, exposed beams, A/C, and private baths—many with original frescos that may date from the medieval inn. Note that some rooms are on the seventh floor—and there's no elevator.

Calle Drio La Scimia 240a (near the Rialto Market). www.hotelguerrato.com. © **041/ 5227131.** 19 units. 120€–150€ double. Rates include breakfast. Closed Dec 22–26 and Jan 8–early Feb. *Vaporetto:* Rialto (from north side of Ponte Rialto, walk through market to corner with UniCredit Banca; go 1 more short block and turn right onto Calle Drio La Scimia). **Amenities:** Babysitting; concierge; Wi-Fi (free).

Santa Croce
EXPENSIVE
Antiche Figure ★★★ The most convenient luxury hotel in Venice lies directly across the Grand Canal from the train station, a captivating 15th-century *palazzo* adjacent to an ancient gondola workshop. History aside, this is a very plush choice, with rooms decorated in neoclassical Venetian style, with gold leaf, antique furniture, red carpets, silk tapestries, and Murano glass and chandeliers, but also LCD satellite TVs and decent Wi-Fi. With the soothing nighttime views across the water it's certainly a romantic choice, and the staff is worth singling out—friendly and very helpful. There is an elevator, just in case you were wondering.

Fondamenta San Simeone Piccolo 687. www.hotelantichefigure.it. © **041/2759486.** 22 units. 112€–305€ double. Rates include breakfast. *Vaporetto:* Ferrovia (from train station cross Scalzi Bridge on left and take a right). **Amenities:** Restaurant; bar; babysitting; concierge; room service; Wi-Fi (free).

MODERATE
Ai Due Fanali ★★ Originally a wooden oratory frequented by fishermen and farmers (later rebuilt), this beguiling hotel features small but artsy rooms, even for Venice: Headboards have been hand-painted by a local artist, exposed wood beams crisscross the ceiling, vintage drapes add a cozy feel, and work by 16th-century Mannerist painter Jacopo Palma the Younger adorns the public areas. Bathrooms are embellished with terra-cotta tiles and Carrera marble. The location is close to the train station, and the roof terrace is the best place to soak up a city panorama (breakfast is served here). It's incredibly popular—book months ahead.

Campo San Simeon Profeta 946. www.aiduefanali.com. © **041/718490.** 16 units. 100€–205€ double. Rates include breakfast. Closed most of Jan. *Vaporetto:* Ferrovia (cross Scalzi Bridge over Grand Canal; continue straight, take 2nd left to Campo San Simeon Profeta). **Amenities:** Bar; concierge; room service; Wi-Fi (free).

Al Ponte Mocenigo ★★★ This gem of a hotel shows it is possible to live that Golden Age Venetian fantasy without breaking the bank (rates are a real bargain in the low season). The especially spacious rooms here are pure 18th-century Venice with big beds; Murano glass chandeliers; and varnished furniture in pastel greens, creams, and golds. Traditional ceiling beams (in the second floor rooms) and original Venetian wood and stone floors complete the effect. Breakfasts—served in an enchanting interior courtyard when weather allows—are substantial, with bacon, scrambled eggs, and sausage in addition to all the usual cheeses, fruits, and cold cuts. Another huge plus: it's steps away from the Stan Stae *vaporetto* stop, meaning easy transfers to/from the airport and elsewhere along the Grand Canal. Advanced reservations highly recommended. Note that there is usually a discount for paying in cash.

Fondamenta Mocenigo 2063. alpontemocenigo.com. © **041/5244797.** 10 units. 65€–370€ double. Rates include breakfast. *Vaporetto:* San Stae. **Amenities:** Bar; babysitting; concierge (24hr); Wi-Fi (free).

INEXPENSIVE

Falier ★ This tranquil budget hotel is in a quiet neighborhood, next to the Frari Church and just a 10-minute walk from the train station. Rooms are fairly compact (potentially cramped for some) but on par for this price point in Venice, and all are air-conditioned. The elegant garden is a swell place for the breakfast (you can also have it in the dining room), featuring warm croissants, cheese, a selection of yogurts and cereals, plus teas, coffee, and fruit juices. The hotel automatically provides free entrance to the Venice casino and a free tour of a Murano glass factory, but the friendly English-speaking staff will also set you up with all manner of other tour options, so just ask if you're interested.

Salizada San Pantalon 130. www.hotelfalier.com. © **041/710882.** 19 units. 110€–155€ double. Rates include breakfast. *Vaporetto:* Ferrovia (from train station, cross Scalzi Bridge, turn right along Grand Canal and walk to 1st footbridge; turn left before crossing and follow smaller canal to Fondamenta Minotti; turn left and the street becomes Salizada San Pantalon.) **Amenities:** Concierge; Wi-Fi (free).

Cannaregio
EXPENSIVE

Al Ponte Antico ★★★ Yes it's expensive, but this is one of the most exclusive hotels in Venice, steps from the Rialto Bridge, with a private wharf on the Grand Canal—to indulge your James Bond fantasy, look no further. Part of the attraction is its relatively small size; with just seven rooms, it feels far more intimate than most hotels in this price range, and service is always superior. Rococo wallpaper, rare tapestries, elegant beds, and Louis XV–style furnishings make this place seem like Versailles on the water. The building was originally a 16th-century *palazzo;* one of the many highlights is the charming balcony where breakfast is served, and where Bellinis are offered in the evenings.

Calle dell'Aseo 5768. www.alponteantico.com. © **041/2411944.** 7 units. 240€–510€ double. Rates include breakfast. *Vaporetto:* Rialto (walk up Calle Large Mazzini, take 2nd left and cross Campo San Bartolomeo; walk north along Salizada S.G. Grisostomo to Calle dell'Aseo on left). **Amenities:** Bar; concierge; room service; Wi-Fi (free).

MODERATE

Arcadia ★★★   This sensational boutique hotel set in a 17th-century *palazzo* has an appealing blend of old and new: The theme is Byzantium east-meets-west, a mix of Venetian and Asian style, but rooms are full of cool modern touches: rainfall showers, A/C, flatscreen TVs, bathrobes, and posh toiletries, with a lobby crowned with a Murano glass chandelier. It's a 5-minute walk from the train station.

Rio Terà San Leonardo 1333, Cannaregio. www.hotelarcadia.net. ✆ **041/717355.** 17 units. 85€–290€ double. Rates include breakfast. *Vaporetto:* Guglie (turn left into Rio Terà San Leonardo; Arcadia is just 30m [98 ft.] on the left). **Amenities:** Bar; concierge; room service; Wi-Fi (free).

INEXPENSIVE

Bernardi ★★   An excellent deal, this hotel offers small, basic, but spotless rooms in a 16th-century *palazzo* (the superior rooms are bigger), owned and managed by the congenial Leonardo and his wife, Teresa. Most rooms come with one or two classical Venetian touches: Murano chandeliers, hand-painted furniture, exposed wood beams, or tapestries. The shared showers are kept very clean (11 rooms have private baths), and fans are provided in the hot summer months for the cheaper rooms with no A/C. Breakfast is very basic, however, and note that the more spacious annex rooms, which have air-conditioning (nearby the main building) don't get the best Wi-Fi coverage.

Calle de l'Oca 4366. www.hotelbernardi.com. ✆ **041/5227257.** 18 units, 11 w/bath. 88€–138€ double. Rates include breakfast. *Vaporetto:* Ca' d'Oro (walk to Strada Nova, turn right to Campo SS. Apostoli, turn left and take 1st left onto Calle de l'Oca). **Amenities:** Concierge; room service; Wi-Fi (free).

San Geremia ★   At this excellent budget option just 10 minutes from the train station, rooms are simple but adequate, with most featuring A/C and views across the canal or *campo*. Note that there is no elevator (some rooms are up three flights of stairs), and breakfast is not provided (but you get 50% off breakfast next door). The rooms have no TVs but Wi-Fi signals are strong. The dorm rooms are a good deal at just 21€ to 25€ per night (for guests under 35 only).

Campo San Geremia 283. www.hotelsangeremia.com. ✆ **041/715562.** 20 units, 14 with private bathroom. 51€–130€ double. Closed Christmas week. *Vaporetto:* Ferrovia (exit train station, turn left onto Lista di Spagna, and continue to Campo San Geremia). **Amenities:** Babysitting; concierge; room service; Wi-Fi (free).

WHERE TO EAT IN VENICE

Eating cheaply in Venice is not easy, though it's by no means impossible. The city's reputation for mass-produced menus, poor service, and overpriced food is, sadly, well warranted, and if you've been traveling in other parts of the country, you may be a little disappointed here. Having said

BÀCARI & CICCHETTI

One of the essential culinary experiences of Venice is trawling the countless neighborhood bars known as ***bàcari,*** where you can stand or sit with *tramezzini* (small, triangular white-bread half-sandwiches filled with everything from thinly sliced meats and tuna salad to cheeses and vegetables), and ***cicchetti*** (tapas-like finger foods, such as calamari rings, fried olives, potato croquettes, or grilled polenta squares), traditionally washed down with an *ombra* or small glass of wine, Veneto Prosecco, or a spritz (a cocktail of Prosecco and orange-flavored Aperol). All of the above will cost approximately 1.50€ to 6€ if you stand at the bar, as much as double when seated. Bar food usually sells out by late afternoon, so while it can make a great lunch, don't rely on it for dinner. A concentration of popular, well-stocked bars can be found along the **Mercerie** shopping strip that connects Piazza San Marco with the Rialto Bridge, the always lively **Campo San Luca** (look for Bar Torino, Bar Black Jack, or the character-filled Leon Bianco wine bar), and **Campo Santa Margherita.**

that, everything is relative—this is still Italy, after all—and you'll find plenty of excellent dining options in Venice. As a basic rule, value for money tends to increase the farther you travel away from Piazza San Marco, and anything described as a *menù turistico,* while cheaper than a la carte, is rarely any good in Venice (exceptions noted below). Note also that compared with Rome and other points south, Venice is a city of early meals: You should be seated by 7:30 to 8:30pm. Most kitchens close at 10 or 10:30pm, even though the restaurant may stay open later.

San Marco

EXPENSIVE

Bistrot de Venise ★★★ VENETIAN It may look a bit like a wood-paneled French bistro, but the menu here is old-school Venetian, specializing in rare wines and historical recipes from the 14th to 18th centuries. It's gimmicky but it works; think fennel soup, homemade pasta with goose sauce and pine nuts, and almond-crusted sturgeon in a black grape sauce, with a yellow garlic and almond pudding. The "historical" tasting menu is a splurge, but we recommend it as the best introduction. Whatever you opt for, expect top-notch service.

4685 Calle dei Fabbri. www.bistrotdevenise.com. ✆ **041/5236651.** Entrees 28€–42€; 4-course tasting menu 74€; historical 5-course menu 110€. Daily noon–3pm and 7pm–midnight (bar 10am–midnight). *Vaporetto:* Rialto (turn right along canal, cross small footbridge over Rio San Salvador, turn left onto Calle Bembo, which becomes Calle dei Fabbri; Bistrot is about 5 blocks ahead).

Da Fiore ★★ TRATTORIA/VENETIAN At this classy yet laid-back Venetian trattoria (not to be confused with the posher *osteria* with the same name), the menu features typical Venetian dishes like squid-ink pasta, but the specials here are the most fun, with *moeche* (local soft-shell crab) a particular treat (the two main seasons are Mar–Apr and Oct–Nov). Desserts are another specialty, with all sorts of sugary *golosessi* on offer, from *buranelli* to *zaletti* (cornmeal cookies, typically eaten dipped in sweet wine or chocolate), and an exceptional *sgroppino al limone* (lemon sherbet). Make sure you visit the bar and *cicchetteria* next door, the **Bacaro di Fiore** (Wed–Mon 9am–10pm), which has been around since 1871, serving cheap wine (spritz 3€) and finger foodlike fried sardines and squid, fried vegetables, and crostini with creamed cod.

Calle delle Botteghe 3461, off Campo Santo Stefano. ℰ **041/5235310.** Entrees 16€–30€. Wed–Mon noon–3pm and 7–10pm. Closed 2 wks Jan and 2 wks Aug. *Vaporetto:* Accademia (cross bridge to *San* Marco side and walk to Campo Santo Stefano; at *campo's* north end, turn left onto Calle delle Botteghe); also close to Sant'Angelo *vaporetto* stop).

MODERATE

Rosticceria San Bartolomeo ★★ DELI/VENETIAN   Also known as Rosticceria Gislon, this no-frills spot is incredibly popular with locals, with a handful of small tables and bar stools, plus bigger tables in the upstairs dining room (which tends to be more expensive). Don't be fooled by appearances. The food here is excellent, with a range of grilled fish and cheap seafood pastas on offer, and a tasty "mozzarella in carrozza" (fried cheese sandwich; 2€). Note that the food displayed on the countertop is reheated to order, but still tastes good. Otherwise just sit at the counter and soak up the animated scene, as the cooks chop, customers chat, and people come and go. Order the roast chicken, salt cod, or polenta—typical Venetian fare without all those extra charges.

Calle della Bissa 5424. ℰ **041/5223569.** Entrees 9€–25€ (pasta downstairs 7€–9€, cicchetti 1.50€–2€). Daily 9am–9:30pm. *Vaporetto:* Rialto (with bridge at your back on San Marco side of canal, walk straight to Campo San Bartolomeo; take underpass slightly to your left marked sottoportego della bissa; *rosticceria* is at 1st corner on your right; look for gislon above the entrance).

Castello

EXPENSIVE

Al Covo ★★ SEAFOOD/VENETIAN   For years, this high-quality Venetian restaurant from Diane and Cesare Benelli has been deservedly popular with American food writers (and TV chefs such as Anthony Bourdain). It features two cozy dining rooms adorned with art (plus some outdoor seating in summer), but it's the food that takes center stage here: fresh fish from the lagoon or the Adriatic, fruits and vegetables from local farms, and meat sourced from esteemed Franco Cazzamali Butchers. The pasta, desserts, and sauces are all homemade. Begin with Venetian *saor,* sweet and sour fish and shellfish, or fried zucchini flowers, followed by fresh monkfish with pancetta on a celeriac fondue, or deep-fried scampi,

An artful presentation at the gourmet favorite restaurant Al Covo.

calamari, and baby sole. Diane's desserts might include rustic pear and prune cake with a grappa-cinnamon sauce or green apple sorbet with Calvados.

Campiello della Pescheria 3968. www.ristorantealcovo.com. ℂ **041/5223812.** Reservations required. Entrees 26€–31€. Fri–Tues 12:45–3:30pm (kitchen closes 2pm) and 7:30pm–midnight (kitchen closes 10pm). Closed usually Jan and 10 days in Aug. *Vaporetto:* Piazza San Marco (walk along Riva degli Schiavoni toward Arsenale and take 3rd narrow street on left, Calle della Pescaria, after Hotel Metropole).

Alle Corone ★★★ SEAFOOD/VENETIAN   This is one of Venice's finest restaurants, an elegant 19th-century dining room inside the Hotel Ai Reali and overlooking the canal. Start with a selection of classic Venetian *cicchetti* (28€) before moving on to risotto with Sicilian red prawns and pistachios (22€) or main courses such as fillets of sea bass with artichokes, small squid and olives, or beef sirloin with mashed potatoes, burrata cheese, baby carrots and hazelnuts. To finish, the homemade tiramisu is spectacular. Reservations recommended.

Campo della Fava 5527 (Hotel Ai Reali). www.hotelaireali.com. ℂ **041/2410253.** Entrees 19€–31€; 6-course tasting menu 85€. Daily noon–2:30pm and 7–10:30pm. *Vaporetto:* Rialto (walk east along Calle Larga Mazzini, turn left on Merceria then right on Calle Stella to the hotel).

Alle Testiere ★★★ ITALIAN/VENETIAN   This tiny restaurant (with only nine tables) is the connoisseur's choice (and an alleged favorite of Meryl Streep, Emily Blunt, and Stanley Tucci) for fresh fish and seafood, with a menu that changes daily and a shrewd selection of wines. Dinner is served at two seatings (reservations are essential), where you choose from appetizers such as swordfish carpaccio or clams that seem to have been literally plucked straight from the sea. The fresh fish fillets with aromatic herbs are always an exceptional main choice, but the pastas—like smoked ravioli with prawns and curry, or spaghetti with clams—are superb. Top things off with homemade peach pie or chestnut pudding. In peak season, make reservations at least 1 month in advance, and note that you'll have a less-rushed experience in the second seating.

Calle del Mondo Novo 5801. www.osterialletestiere.it. ℂ **041/5227220.** Entrees 27€–29€; many types of fish sold by weight. Tues–Sat noon–3pm and 2 seatings at 7 and 9:30pm. *Vaporetto:* Rialto or San Marco. Look for Salizada San Lio (west of Campo Santa Maria Formosa), and from there ask for Calle del Mondo Novo.

Dorsoduro
EXPENSIVE

Ai Artisti ★★★ VENETIAN   This unpretentious, family-owned *osteria* and *enoteca* is one of the best dining experiences in Venice, with a menu that changes daily according to market offerings (because the fish market is closed on Monday, no fish is served that day). Grab a table by the canal and feast on octopus salad, swordfish steak, and an amazing buttery beef cheek with corn polenta, or opt for one of the wonderful pastas (such as fettuccine with spider crab). The tiramisu and chocolate torte are standouts for dessert. What's likely to stay with you in addition to the food is the impeccable service; servers are happy to guide you through the menu, and offer brilliant suggestions for wine pairing. It's a tiny place, so reservations are recommended.

Fondamenta della Toletta 1169A. www.enotecaartisti.com. ℂ **041/5238944.** Entrees 24€–28€. Tues–Sat 12:45–2:30pm and 2 seatings at 7–9pm and 9–11pm. *Vaporetto:* Accademia (walk around Accademia and turn right on Calle Gambara to end at Rio di San Trovaso, turn left on Fondamenta Priuli; take 1st bridge onto road leading into Fondamenta della Toletta).

Locanda Montin ★★ VENETIAN   Montin was the famous ex-hangout of Peggy Guggenheim in the 1950s, and has been frequented by Jimmy Carter, Robert De Niro, and Brad Pitt, among many other celebs. Is the food still any good? Well, yes. Grab a table in the wonderfully serene back garden (completely covered by an arching trellis), itself a good reason to visit, and sample Venetian classics like sardines in *saor* (a local marinade of vinegar, wine, onion, and raisins), and an exquisite *seppie in nero* (cuttlefish cooked in its ink). For a main course, it's hard to beat the crispy sea bass *(branzino)* or legendary monkfish, while the lemon sorbet with vodka is a perfect tart conclusion to any meal.

Fondamenta di Borgo 1147. www.locandamontin.com. ⓒ **041/5227151.** Entrees 18€–27€. Daily 12:15–2:30pm and 7:15–10pm (closed on Wed Nov–Apr). *Vaporetto:* Ca'Rezzonico (walk straight along Calle Lunga San Barnaba, then turn left along Fondamenta di Borgo).

MODERATE

Ai Cugnai ★★ VENETIAN The name of this small trattoria means "at the in-laws," and in that spirit the kitchen knocks out solid home-cooked Venetian food, beautifully prepared and popular with locals and hungry gondoliers. The *spaghetti vongole* here is crammed with sea-fresh mussels and clams, the *caprese* and baby octopus salad are perfectly balanced appetizers, and the house red wine is a top value. Our favorite is the sublime spaghetti with scallops, a slippery, salty delight. There are just two small tables outside, so get here early if you want to eat alfresco.

Calle Nuova Sant'Agnese (Piscina Forner) 857. ⓒ **041/5289238.** Entrees 14€–20€. Mon and Wed–Sun noon–3pm and 6–10pm. *Vaporetto:* Accademia (head east of bridge and Accademia in direction of Guggenheim Collection; restaurant is on your right, on street connecting the 2 museums).

INEXPENSIVE

Osteria Al Squero ★★★ WINE BAR/VENETIAN This enticing *osteria* with perhaps the most beguiling view in Venice is opposite the Squero di San Trovaso (p. 421). Sip coffee or wine and nibble *cicchetti* while observing the activity at the medieval gondola boatyard and workshop, on the other side of the Rio di San Trovaso (drinks served in glasses inside, but in plastic cups if you want to stand outside). It's essentially a place for a light lunch or *aperitivi* rather than a full meal. Snack on delights such as Carnia smoked sausage, *baccalà* (cod) crostini, anchovies, blue cheese, tuna, and sardines in *saor* for a total of around 16€ to 18€ per person. Spritz from 2.50€.

Fondamenta Nani 943–944. ⓒ **335/6007513.** *Cicchetti* 1.40–2.80€ per piece. Thu–Tues 11am–8:30pm. *Vaporetto:* Zattere (walk west along water to Rio di San Trovaso and turn right up Fondamenta Nani).

San Polo

MODERATE

Antico Forno ★★★ ITALIAN/PIZZA Venice is not known for pizza, partly because fire codes restrict the use of traditional wood-burning ovens, but the big, fluffy-crusted pies here are the best in the city. Little more than a hole-in-the-wall (take-out only), Antico Forno has been selling pizza by the slice since 2001, both thick- and thin-crust. Its "La

Pizzaccia-style" pizza is a soft focaccia topped with fresh chopped tomatoes, *mozzarella fior di latte* (from Treviso farms), and everything from Trevisan sausage to gorgonzola and mushrooms.

Ruga Rialto 973. www.anticofornovenezia.it. © **041/5204110.** Pizza slices from 4€. Daily 11:30am–9:30pm. *Vaporetto:* Rialto Mercato (walk into Campo de la Pescaria, follow Ruga Vecchia San Giovanni for around 300m, just beyond Calle del Paradiso).

Do Spade ★ VENETIAN   It's tough to find dining this authentic so close to the Rialto Bridge these days, but Do Spade has been around since 1415 (Casanova ate here). Most locals come for the *cicchetti,* small plates such as fried calamari, meatballs, mozzarella, and salted cod (1.50–3.50€) and decent Italian wines (3€ a glass); you can sit on benches outside if it's too crowded indoors. The more formal restaurant section is also worth a try, with seafood highlights including a delicately prepared monkfish, scallops served with fresh zucchini, and rich seafood lasagna. The seasonal pumpkin ravioli is one of the best dishes in the city.

Calle de le Do Spade 860. www.cantinadospade.com. © **041/5210574.** Entrees 12€–25€. Daily 10am–3pm and 6–10pm. *Vaporetto:* Rialto Mercato (with your back to Grand Canal, walk up Ruga Vecchia San Giovanni, turn right on Ruga dei Spezieri; at end turn left on Calle de le Beccarie O Panataria, then take 2nd right onto covered Sottoportego do Spade).

INEXPENSIVE

Do Mori ★★★ WINE BAR/VENETIAN   Serving good wine and *cicchetti* since 1462, Do Mori is above all a fun place to have a genuine Venetian experience, a small, dimly lit *bàcari* that can barely accommodate 10 people standing up. Sample the baby octopus and ham on mango, lard-smothered *crostini,* and pickled onions speared with salty anchovies, or opt for the *tramezzini* (tiny sandwiches). Local TV (and BBC) star Francesco Da Mosto is a regular, but note that this institution is very much on the well-trodden tourist trail—plenty of *cicchetti* tours stop by in the early evening. Local wine runs 3€ to 5€ per glass.

Calle Do Mori 429 (also Calle Galeazza 401). © **041/5225401.** *Tramezzini* and *cicchetti* 1.80€–3.50€ per piece. Mon–Fri 8am–7:30pm, Sat 8am–5pm (June–Aug closed daily 2–4:30pm). *Vaporetto:* Rialto Mercato (with your back to Grand Canal, walk straight up Ruga Vecchia San Giovanni and turn right on Calle Galeazza).

La Bottiglia ★★ WINE BAR/VENETIAN   This more contemporary *bàcari* (it opened in 2015) features wonderful cheese and meat boards, a well-curated wine list (exceptional Amarone red wine is served here), and excellent panini sandwiches stuffed with prosciutto and cheeses. As you might expect, it's a tiny place, with a few tables outside near the Rio San Stin and just five bar stools inside (most visitors stand).

Campo San Stin (Calle de la Chiesa) 2537. © **041/4762426.** Sandwiches from 6€. Mon–Fri 7am–10pm, Sat–Sun 10am–10:30pm. *Vaporetto:* Ferrovia or San Toma.

EATING cheaply IN VENICE

You don't have to eat in a fancy restaurant to enjoy good food in Venice. Prepare a picnic, and while you eat alfresco, you can observe the life in the city's *campi* or the aquatic parade on its main thoroughfare, the Grand Canal.

Mercato Rialto Venice's principal open-air market has two parts, beginning with the **produce section,** whose many stalls unfold north on the San Polo side of the Rialto Bridge. Vendors are here Monday to Saturday 7am to 1pm (some stay later). Behind these stalls a few permanent food stores sell cheese, cold cuts, and bread. At the market's farthest point, the covered **fish market** is still redolent of the days when it was one of the Mediterranean's great fish bazaars. The fish merchants take Monday off and work mornings only.

Campo Santa Margherita

Every Tuesday through Saturday from 8:30am to 1pm, a number of open-air stalls set up shop on this spacious Dorsoduro *campo*, selling fresh fruit and vegetables. A conventional supermarket, **Punto Simply** (Mon–Sat 8:30am–8pm, Sun 9am–2pm), is just off the *campo* in the direction of nearby Campo San Barnaba, at no. 3019.

San Barnaba This is where you'll find Venice's heavily photographed **floating market** (mostly fruit and vegetables) operating from a boat moored just off San Barnaba at the Ponte dei Pugni in Dorsoduro. This market is open daily from 8am to 1pm and 3:30 to 7:30pm, except Wednesday afternoon and Sunday.

The Best Picnic Spots Given its aquatic roots, you won't find much in the way of green space in Venice (if you are desperate for green, walk 30 minutes past San Marco along the water, or take a *vaporetto* to the **Giardini Pubblici,** Venice's only green park). A much more enjoyable alternative is to find one of the larger *campi* that have park benches, such as **Campo San Giacomo dell'Orio,** in the quiet *sestiere* of Santa Croce. The two most central: **Campo Santa Margherita** (*sestiere* of Dorsoduro) and **Campo San Polo** (*sestiere* of San Polo).

The **Punta della Dogana (Customs House)** near La Salute Church in Dorsoduro is a prime viewing site at the mouth of the Grand Canal. Pull up on the embankment here and watch the flutter of water activity against a canvaslike backdrop deserving of the Accademia Museum. In this same area, another superb spot, **Campo San Vio** (near the Guggenheim), is directly on the Grand Canal and even boasts two benches and the chance to sit on an untrafficked small bridge.

A bit farther afield, you can take the *vaporetto* out to Burano and then no. 9 for the 5-minute ride to the near-deserted island of **Torcello.** If you bring a basketful of bread, cheese, and wine you can do your best to reenact the romantic scene between Katharine Hepburn and Rossano Brazzi from the 1955 film *Summertime.*

Santa Croce
MODERATE
Osteria La Zucca ★★ ITALIAN/VEGETARIAN   Not specifically a vegetarian restaurant, but the romantic, canal-side dining room of *La Zucca* (aka "the pumpkin") does offer a huge range of high-quality

vegetable dishes, from the signature pumpkin-and-ricotta flan and potato cakes to zucchini-and-almond lasagna. The seasonal menu (Italian only, but the staff speak English) also includes plenty of meat dishes, such as succulent rabbit with white wine and lamb with spices. End with one of the homemade cakes—pear cake with ginger or the "spices tart" with red wine and raspberry.

Calle dello Spezier 1762. lazucca.it © **041/5241570.** Reservations recommended. Entrees 10€–20€. Mon–Sat 12:30–2:30pm and 7pm–10:30pm. *Vaporetto:* San Stae (walk straight down Salizada San Stae, turning right on Calle del Tentor; turn left when you hit Calle Del Meglio and follow it as it turns right).

INEXPENSIVE

Bacareto Da Lele ★★★ WINE BAR/VENETIAN   This tiny hole-in-the-wall *bacaro* is worth seeking out for its cheap, fresh snacks, sandwiches, and *cicchetti*. Tiny glasses or *ombras* of wine and Prosecco are just 0.70€–1.50€)—there are no seats, so do as the locals do and grab a space by the canal while you sip and nibble. Opt for a tiny porchetta or bacon and artichoke panini (around 2.50€), antipasti plates (cheese and salami) or a freshly-baked crostini for 1€–2€. Expect long lines here in peak season—the secret is definitely out.

Campo dei Tolentini 183. No phone. *Cicchetti* 1€–2.50€ per piece. Mon–Fri 6am–8pm, Sat 6am–2pm. *Vaporetto:* Piazzale Roma (walk left along Grand Canal, past Ponte della Costituzione, into Giardino Papadopoli; turn right on Fonadmenta Papadopoli then left. Cross park at 1st bridge; next canal is Rio del Tolentini, with the campo across the bridge and Da Lele on southwest corner).

Cannaregio

EXPENSIVE

L'Orto dei Mori ★★ VENETIAN   Traditional Venetian cuisine is cooked up by a young Sicilian chef, so expect some differences to the usual flavors and dishes. Everything on the fairly small menu is exceptional—the *baccalà* (salted cod) especially so—and the setting next to a canal is enhanced by candlelight at night. The place can get very busy—the waiters are normally friendly, but expect brusque treatment if you turn up late (or early) for a reservation. Dinner is usually served in two seatings, one early (7–9pm) and one late, so waiters will be reluctant to serve those who arrive early for the second sitting—even if a table is available, you'll be given water and just told to wait.

Campo dei Mori 3386. www.osteriaortodeimori.com. © **041/5243677.** Entrees 21€–28€. Wed–Mon 12:30–3:30pm and 7pm–midnight, usually in 2 seatings (July–Aug closed for lunch Mon–Fri). *Vaporetto:* Madonna dell'Orto (walk through *campo* to canal and turn right; take 1st bridge on left, walk down street and turn left at canal onto Fondamenta dei Mori; go straight until you hit Campo dei Mori).

Gelato

Is the gelato any good in Venice? Italians might demur, but by international standards, the answer is most definitely yes. As always, gelato parlors aimed exclusively at tourists are notorious for poor quality and extortionate prices. Avoid places near Piazza San Marco altogether. Below are two of our favorite spots in the city.

Il Doge ★★ GELATO   Contender for best gelato in Venice, Il Doge has a convenient location at the southern end of Campo Santa Margherita. These guys use only natural, homemade flavors and ingredients, from an exceptional spicy chocolate to the house specialty, Crema de Doge, a rich mix of eggs, cream, and oranges. Try a refreshing *granita* in summer.

Campo Santa Margherita 3058, Dorsoduro. www.gelateriaildoge.com. ℂ **041/ 5234607.** Cones & cups 1.80€–5.80€. Daily 11am–10pm. *Vaporetto:* Ca'Rezzonico.

La Mela Verde ★★ GELATO   The popular rival to Il Doge for best scoop in the city, with sharp flavors and all the classics done sensationally well: pistachio, chocolate, *nocciola,* and the mind-blowing lemon and basil. The overall champions: *mela verde* (green apple), like creamy, frozen fruit served in a cup, and the addictive tiramisu.

Fondamenta de L'Osmarin 4977, Castello. www.gelaterialamelaverde.it. ℂ **349/ 1957924.** Cones or cups from 2€. Daily 11am–11pm. Usually closed mid-Nov–mid-Feb. *Vaporetto:* Zaccaria.

VENICE SHOPPING

In a city that for centuries has thrived almost exclusively on tourism, remember this: **Where you buy cheap, you get cheap.** Venetians, centuries-old merchants, aren't known for bargaining. You'll stand a better chance of getting a good deal if you pay in cash or buy more than one item. In our limited space below, we've listed some of the more reputable places to stock up on classic Venetian items.

Shopping Streets & Markets

A mix of low-end trinket stores and middle-market-to-upscale boutiques line the narrow zigzagging **Mercerie** running north between Piazza San Marco and the Rialto Bridge. More expensive boutiques make for great window-shopping on **Calle Larga XXII Marzo,** the wide street that begins west of Piazza San Marco and wends its way to the expansive Campo Santo Stefano near the Accademia. The narrow **Frezzaria,** just west of Piazza San Marco and running north-south, offers a grab bag of bars, souvenir shops, and tony clothing stores like Louis Vuitton and Versace. The non-produce part of the **Rialto Market** is as good as it gets for basic souvenirs, where you'll find cheap T-shirts, glow-in-the-dark plastic gondolas, and tawdry glass trinkets.

The **Mercatino dei Miracoli** (ℂ **041/2710022**), held only six times a year in Campo Santa Maria Nova (Cannaregio), is a fabulous flea market with all sorts of bric-a-brac and antiques sold by ordinary Venetians— haggling, for once, is acceptable. It usually takes place on the second Saturday or Sunday of March, April, May, September, October, and December, from 8:30am to 8pm. The **Mercatino dell'Antiquariato** (www.mercati-nocamposanmaurizio.it) is a professional antiques market in Campo San Maurizio, San Marco; it takes place 4 to 5 times a year (usually Mar–Apr, May, Sept, Oct, and Dec; check the website for dates).

Arts & Crafts

Venice is famous for local crafts that have been produced here for centuries and are hard to get elsewhere: the **glassware** from Murano, the **delicate lace** from Burano, and the *cartapesta* (papier-mâché) **Carnevale masks** you'll find in endless *botteghe* (shops), where you can watch artisans paint amid their wares.

Glassblower making a vase in Murano.

Now here's the bad news: There's such an overwhelming sea of cheap glass gewgaws that buying Venetian glass can become something of a turnoff (shipping and insurance costs make most things unaffordable; the alternative is to hand-carry anything fragile). Plus, there are so few women left on Burano willing to spend countless hours keeping alive the art of lace-making that any pieces not produced by machine in China are sold at stratospheric prices; ditto the truly high-quality glass (although trinkets can be cheap and fun). The best place to buy glass is Murano itself—the **"Vetro Artistico Murano"** trademark guarantees its origin, but expect to pay as much as 60€ for just a wineglass.

Atelier Segalin di Daniela Ghezzo ★★ Founded in 1932 by master cobbler Antonio Segalin and his son Rolando, this old leather shoe store is now run by Daniela Ghezzo (the star apprentice of Rolando), maker of exuberant handmade shoes and boots, from basic flats to crazy footwear designed for Carnevale (shoes from 650€–1,800€). Calle dei Fuseri 4365, San Marco. www.danielaghezzo.it. © **041/5222115.** Mon–Fri 10am–1pm and 3–7pm. Sat 10am–1pm. Vaporetto: San Marco.

Il Canovaccio ★ Remember the creepy orgy scenes in Stanley Kubrick's film *Eyes Wide Shut?* The ornate masks used in the movie were made by the owners of this vaunted store. All manner of traditional, feathered, and animal masks are knocked out of their on-site workshop. Calle delle Bande 5369 (near Campo Santa Maria Formosa), Castello. © **041/5210393.** Daily 10am–7:30pm. Vaporetto: San Zaccaria.

Il Grifone ★★★ Toni Peressin's handmade leather briefcases, bound notebooks, belts, and soft-leather purses have garnered quite a following, and justly so—his craftsmanship is magnificent (he makes everything in the workshop out back). Items start at around 25€. Fondamenta del Gaffaro 3516, Dorsoduro. www.ilgrifonevenezia.it. © **041/5229452.** Tues and Fri 10am–6pm; Wed, Thurs, Sat 10am–1pm and 4–7pm. Vaporetto: Piazzale Roma.

La Bottega dei Mascareri ★★ High-quality, creative masks—some based on Tiepolo paintings—have been crafted by brothers Sergio and Massimo Boldrin since 1984. Basic masks start at around 20€, but you'll pay over 75€ for a more innovative piece. The smaller, original branch lies at the foot of the Rialto Bridge (San Polo 80; © **041/5223857**). Calle dei Saoneri 2720, San Polo. www.mascarer.com. © **041/5242887.** Both locations daily 9am–6pm. Vaporetto: Rialto.

Marco Polo International ★ This vast showroom, just west of the Piazza San Marco, displays quality glass direct from Murano (although it's more expensive than if you buy on the island yourself), including plenty of easy-to-carry items such as paperweights and small dishes. Frezzaria 1644, San Marco. www.marcopolointernational.it. © **041/5229295.** Daily 10am–7pm. Vaporetto: San Marco.

Venini ★ Convenient, classy, but incredibly expensive, Venini has been selling quality glass art since 1921, supplying the likes of Versace and many other designer brands. Its **workshop** on Murano is at Fondamenta Vetrai 50 (© **041/2737211**). Piazzetta Leoncini 314, San Marco. www.venini.it. © **041/5224045.** Both locations Mon–Sat 9:30am–5:30pm. Vaporetto: San Marco.

ENTERTAINMENT & NIGHTLIFE

If you're looking for serious nocturnal action, you're in the wrong town—Verona and Padua are far livelier. Your best bet is to sit in moonlit Piazza San Marco and listen to the cafes' outdoor orchestras, with the floodlit basilica before you—the perfect opera set—though this pleasure comes with a hefty price tag. Other popular spots include **Campo San Bartolomeo,** at the foot of the Rialto Bridge (a zoo in high season), and **Campo San Luca.** For low prices and low pretension, the absolute best place to go is **Campo Santa Margherita,** a huge open *campo* between the train station and the Accademia Bridge.

Visit one of the tourist information centers for current English-language schedules of the month's special events. The monthly *Ospite di Venezia* is distributed free or online at **www.unospitedivenezia.it** and is extremely helpful but usually available only in the more expensive hotels.

Performing Arts & Live Music

Venice has a long and rich tradition of classical music; this was, after all, the home of Vivaldi. People dressed in period costumes stand around in

Interior of Teatro La Fenice.

heavily trafficked spots near San Marco and Rialto passing out brochures advertising classical music concerts, so you'll have no trouble finding up-to-date information.

Santa Maria della Pietà ★★   The so-called "Vivaldi Church," built between 1745 and 1760, holds concerts throughout the year, mostly performed by lauded ensemble **I Virtuosi Italiani;** check the website for specific dates. Tickets are usually 28€–30€. Riva degli Schiavoni 3701, Castello. www.chiesavivaldi.it. ☏ **041/5221120.** Vaporetto: San Zaccaria.

Teatro La Fenice ★★★   The opera season runs late November through June, but there are also classical concerts and ballet. Tickets are expensive for the major productions (80€–200€ for the gallery and 145€–350€ for a decent seat); budget travelers can opt for obstructed-view seats (from 25€) or listening-only seats (from 15€). Campo San Fantin 1965, San Marco. www. teatrolafenice.it. ☏ **041/2424.** Vaporetto: Giglio.

Cafes

For tourists and locals alike, Venetian nightlife mainly centers on the many cafes in one of the world's most beautiful public squares: Piazza San Marco. It is also a most expensive and touristed place to linger over a spritz (the Venetian classic cocktail of Prosecco and orange-flavored Aperol), but it's a splurge that should not be dismissed too readily.

Caffè dei Frari ★★★   Established in 1870, this inviting bar and cafe overlooking the Frari church has walls still adorned with the original Art Nouveau murals, an antique wooden bar, and cozy upstairs. The whole place morphs into **Il Mercante Cocktail Bar** in the evenings (Sun & Tues–Thu 6pm–1am; Fri 6pm–2am). Fondamenta dei Frari 2564, San Polo. ℭ **041/5241877.** Tues–Sat 9am–10pm, Sun–Mon 9am–4pm. Vaporetto: San Tomà.

Caffè Florian ★★   Occupying prime *piazza* real estate since 1720, this is one of the world's oldest coffee shops, with a florid interior of 18th-century mirrors, frescoes, and statuary. Sitting at a table, expect to pay 10€ for a cappuccino, 20€ for a Bellini (Prosecco and fresh peach nectar in season), and 14€ for a spritz—add another 6€ if the orchestra plays (Mar–Nov). Standing at the bar is much cheaper (5€ for a cappuccino, 10€ for a Bellini and so on). Piazza San Marco 57. www.caffeflorian.com. ℭ **041/5205641.** Mon–Thurs 10am–9pm, Fri–Sat 9am–11pm, Sun 9am–9pm. Vaporetto: San Marco.

Il Caffè (aka Caffè Rosso) ★★★   Established in the late 19th century, Il Caffè has a history almost as colorful as its clientele—a mix of students, aging regulars, and lost tourists. This old-fashioned, no-nonsense cafe/bar has reasonably priced drinks and sandwiches, and lots of seating on the *campo* (plus a small seating area inside). Campo Santa Margherita 2963, Dorsoduro. www.cafferosso.it. ℭ **041/5287998.** Mon–Sat 7am–1am. Vaporetto: Ca'Rezzonico.

Pasticceria Tonolo ★   This tiny bakery has enjoyed a cult following since 1886 thanks to its deep-fried sweet treats (*frittelle*, Italian-style doughnuts, plus a vast range of sumptuous cakes and cookies; *frittelle* 1.10€–1.30€). Coffee is served in charming, antique blue German porcelain cups (standing room only). Calle San Pantalon 3764, Dorsoduro. ℭ **041/5237209.** Tues–Sat 7:30am–8pm, Sun 7:30am–1pm. Vaporetto: San Tomà.

Birreria, Wine & Cocktail Bars

Venice has never been a late-night clubbing hotspot. Evenings are better spent lingering over a late dinner, having a pint in a *birreria,* or nursing a glass of Prosecco in one of the pricey outdoor bars and cafes in Piazza San Marco or Campo Santa Margherita.

Al Prosecco ★★   Get acquainted with all things bubbly at this smart *enoteca,* a specialist, as you'd expect, in Veneto Prosecco. It features tasty *cichetti* and plenty of outdoor tables from which to observe the laid-back Campo San Giacomo da l'Orio. Most drinks run 3€ to 5€. Campo San Giacomo da l'Orio 1503, Santa Croce. www.alprosecco.com. ℭ **041/5240222.** Mon–Sat 10am–10:30pm (closes 8pm in winter; closed Aug and Jan). Vaporetto: San Stae.

Bar Dandolo ★★   Doge Dandolo built his glorious Venetian Gothic palace three doors down from the Palazzo Ducale in the 14th century, and current occupier Hotel Danieli has been one of the most sumptuous hotels in Venice since 1822. Nestled amid marble columns on the ground floor of the palazzo, this classic Venice bar serves everything from velvet-capped cappuccinos and a traditional afternoon tea (daily 3–6pm; 42€ per person) to a decadent Vesper Martini cocktail. You can also opt for an al fresco drink on the rooftop **Bar Terrazza Danieli** (May–Sept) in the same hotel. Riva degli Schiavoni 4196, Castello. www.terrazzadanieli.com/en/bar-dandolo. ✆ **041/5226480.** Daily 9:30am–1am (pianist plays daily 7pm–12:30am). Vaporetto: San Zaccaria.

Bar Longhi ★★★   The Gritti Palace Hotel really was the 16th-century palace of Doge Andrea Gritti, whose portrait graces one of the antiques-filled lounges (it remains the city's most expensive hotel since opening in 1895). Bar Longhi is the quintessential Venetian watering hole, with lavish décor (hand-sculptured mirrors, Murano glass appliqués, and a marble bar counter) plus paintings belonging to the school of the celebrated 18th-century Venetian artist Pietro Longhi. Afternoon tea, cocktails and champagne are served. Campo Santa Maria del Giglio 2467 (Gritti Palace Hotel), San Marco. www.marriott.com. ✆ **041/794611.** Daily 11am–1am. Vaporetto: Santa Maria del Giglio.

Harry's Bar ★   Possibly the most famous bar in Venice (and now a global chain), Harry's was established in 1931 by Giuseppe Cipriani and frequented by the likes of Ernest Hemingway and Charlie Chaplin. The Bellini was invented here in 1948 (along with *carpaccio* 2 years later); you can sip the signature concoction of freshly-squeezed peach juice and Prosecco for a mere 22€. Go for the history but don't expect a five-star experience—most first-timers are surprised just how ordinary it looks inside (though the bow-tied wait staff still look the part). It's more a restaurant than a bar these days, serving very expensive food (main courses 40–45€), but just stick to the drinks. Calle Vallaresso 1323, San Marco. www.cipriani.com. ✆ **041/5285777.** Daily 10:30am–11pm. Vaporetto: Vallaresso.

Il Santo Bevitore ★★   Beer aficionados will be pleased to learn that Italy has a growing craft beer scene, with this local spot showcasing the best brews from all over the country (many on tap). Sample Milan's Birrificio Lambrate and Birrificio Extraomnes, Parma's Birra Toccalmatto, Udine's Borderline Brewery, and Veneto's very own Mesh Brewery. The small bar overlooks the Rio de Servi just off the main drag (Strada Nova), with a few benches outside for warmer weather. Fondamenta Diedo 2393, Cannaregio. www.ilsantobevitorepub.com. ✆ **335/8415771.** Mon–Fri 4pm–2am, Sat 4pm–midnight, Sun noon–2am. Vaporetto: San Marcuola

DAY TRIPS FROM VENICE

If you only have 3 days or so, you will probably want to spend them in the center of Venice. However, if you are here for a week—or on your second visit to the city—head over to the mainland to see some of the old towns that lie within the historic Veneto region.

Padua ★★★

40km (25 miles) W of Venice

Tucked away within the ancient heart of Padua lies one of the greatest artistic treasures in all Italy, the precious Giotto frescoes of the **Cappella degli Scrovegni.** Although the city itself is not especially attractive (it was largely rebuilt after bombing during World War II), don't be put off by the urban sprawl that now surrounds it; central Padua is refreshingly bereft of tourist crowds, a workaday Veneto town with a large student population and a small but intriguing ensemble of historic sights.

ESSENTIALS

ARRIVING The most efficient way to reach Padua is to take the **train** from Santa Lucia station. Trains depart every 10 to 20 minutes, and take 26 to 50 minutes depending on the class (4.35€–18€ one-way). Padua ("Padova" in Italian) station is a short walk north up Corso del Popolo from the Cappella degli Scrovegni and the old city.

VISITOR INFORMATION The **tourist office** at the train station is usually open Monday to Saturday 9am to 7pm and Sunday 10am to 4pm (www. turismopadova.it; ✆ **049/2010080**). The office in the old city at Vicolo Pedrocchi (same telephone) is open the same hours.

EXPLORING PADUA

The one unmissable sight in Padua is the **Cappella degli Scrovegni ★★★** (www.cappelladegliscrovegni.it; ✆ **049/2010020;** daily 9am–7pm; check website for 7–10pm openings) at Piazza Eremitani, an outwardly unassuming chapel commissioned in 1303 by Enrico Scrovegni, a wealthy banker. Inside, however, the chapel is gloriously decorated with a cycle of frescoes by Florentine genius **Giotto,** depicting the lives of the Virgin Mary and Jesus and culminating in the Ascension and Last Judgment. Seeing Giotto's work in the flesh is spine-tingling; this is where he makes the decisive break with Byzantine art toward the realism and humanism that would define the Italian Renaissance.

Entrance to the chapel is limited, involving groups of 25 visitors spending 15 minutes in a climate-controlled airlock, used to stabilize the temperature, before going inside for another 15 minutes. To visit the chapel you must **make a reservation at least 24 hours in advance.** You must arrive 45 minutes before the time on your ticket. Tickets cost 13€ (6€ for kids ages 6–17 and students under 27).

A tranquil scene in Padua.

If you have time, try and take in Padua's other historic highlights. The vast **Palazzo della Ragione** on Piazza del Erbe (6€; Tues–Sun 9am–7pm, closes 6pm Nov–Jan) is an architectural marvel, the cavernous town hall completed in 1219 and decorated by frescoes by Nicola Miretto in the 15th century. Pay a visit also to the **Basilica di Sant'Antonio** (www.sant antonio.org; ℂ **049/8225652;** admission free; daily 6:20am–7:45pm, closes 6:45pm Nov–Mar) on the Piazza del Santo, the stately resting place of **St. Anthony of Padua,** the Portuguese Franciscan best known as the patron saint of finding things or lost people. The exterior of the church is a bizarre mix of Byzantine, Romanesque, and Gothic styles, while the interior is richly adorned with statuary and murals. Don't miss **Donatello**'s stupendous equestrian statue of the Venetian *condottiere* **Gattamelata** (Erasmo da Narni) in the piazza outside, the first large bronze sculpture of the Renaissance.

WHERE TO EAT

Padua offers plenty of places to eat and drink (Aperol was created here in 1919), and you'll especially appreciate the overall drop in prices compared to Venice. It's hard to match the location of **Bar Nazionale ★★**, Piazza del Erbe 40 (Mon and Sat 7am–10:30pm, Tue, Thurs, Fri 7am–11:30am, Wed 7am–midnight, and Sun 9am–9:30pm), on the steps leading up to Palazzo della Ragione, but it's best for drinks and snacks (excellent *tramezzini* from 2€, panini from 4€, spritz 3€, and glasses of wine just 2.50€) rather than a full meal. For that, make for **Osteria dei Fabbri ★**, Via dei Fabbri 13, just off Piazza del Erbe (www.osteriadeifabbri.it; ✆ **049/650336;** Mon–Fri noon–2:30pm and 7–10:30pm, Sat noon–3pm and 7–11pm, Sun noon–3pm), which cooks up cheap, tasty pasta dishes for under 15€.

Verona ★★
115km (71 miles) W of Venice

The affluent city of Verona, with its handsome red and peach-colored medieval buildings and Roman ruins, is one of Italy's major tourist draws, though its appeal owes more to William Shakespeare than real history. He immortalized the city in his (totally fictional) *Romeo and Juliet, The Two Gentlemen of Verona,* and partly, *The Taming of the Shrew.* In spite of its popularity with visitors, Verona is not Venice; it's a booming commercial center with vibrant science and technology sectors.

ESSENTIALS

ARRIVING The best way to reach Verona from Venice is by **train.** Direct services depart every 30 minutes and take anywhere from 1 hour and 10 minutes to 2 hours and 20 minutes, depending on the type of train you catch (tickets range from 9.25€ to 21.90€ one-way). From Verona station (Verona Porta Nuova), it's a 15-minute walk to the historic center.

VISITOR INFORMATION The **tourist office** at Via Degli Alpini 9 (www.veronatouristoffice.it; ✆ **045/8068680;** Mon–Sat 9am–6pm, Sun 10am–5pm) has maps and tour information.

EXPLORING VERONA

"Two households, both alike in dignity, in fair Verona . . ." So go the immortal opening lines of *Romeo and Juliet,* ensuring that the city has been a target for lovesick romantics

Statue of Juliet with love notes, Casa di Giulietta.

City of Verona.

ever since. Though Verona is crammed with genuine historic goodies, one of the most popular sites is the ersatz **Casa di Giulietta,** Via Cappello 23 (6€; Mon 1:30–7:30pm, Tues–Sun 8:30am–7:30pm), a 14th-century house (with balcony, naturally), said to be the Capulets' home. In the courtyard, the chest of a bronze statue of Juliet has been polished to a gleaming sheen, thanks to a legend claiming that stroking her right breast brings good fortune. **Juliet's Wall,** at the entrance, is quite a spectacle, covered with the scribbles of star-crossed lovers; love letters placed here are taken down and, along with 5,000 letters annually, answered by the Club di Giulietta (locally based volunteers). There's not much to see inside the house, though plenty of visitors line up for a chance of a selfie on the balcony.

Once you've made the obligatory Juliet pilgrimage, focus on actual historic sights. The 1st-century **Arena di Verona** ★ (10€; Mon 1:30–7:30pm and Tues–Sun 8:30am–7:30pm), in the spacious Piazza Bra, is the third largest classical arena in Italy after Rome's Colosseum and the arena at Capua—it could seat some 25,000 spectators and still hosts performances today (see www.arena.it).

To the northwest on Piazza San Zeno, the **Basilica di San Zeno Maggiore** ★★ (www.basilicasanzeno.it; 3€, includes audioguide;

Verona

Information ⓘ

Rome

Verona

Via Giusti
Muro Pardi
Via Carducci
Via S. Chiara
Via S. Paolo
Via Mazza
Via Campofiore
Lungre Teodorico
Ponte Nuovo
Lungadige B. Rubele
Via Filippini
Lungre Capuleti
Via Sottoriva
Ponte Navi
Ponte Aleardi
Via Arche Scaligeri
Via Cappello
Ponte Pietra
Via Pigna
Via Forti
Sant'Anastasia
Via Stella
Via del Pontiere
Piazza del Duomo
Via Rosa
Piazza dei Signori
Piazza delle Erbe
L. Teuzinco
Stradone S. Fermo
Via Garibaldi
Via Mazzini
Via Pallone
Via Alpini
Via del Lanciere
Via E. Corso
P. Bosari
Arena
Piazza Brà
Via Montanari
Ponte Garibaldi
Adige
Via Battisti
Via G. Marconi
To Stazione So. P.ta Nuova / Train Station
Lungre Matteotti
Corso Cavour
Ponte Vittoria
Museo di Castelvecchio
Via Marin
Via Valverde
Corso So. P.ta Nuova
Via IV Novembre
Via dei Mille
Piazza Vittorio Veneto
Via della Repubblica
Ponte Scaligero
Stradone Porta Palio
Via C. Scalzi
Via della Casa
Via Farinata
Via Risorgimento
Via Arsenale
Piazza Arsenale
Regaste San Zeno
Via S. Bernardino
Via Saffi
Zoological Garden
Ponte Catena
Ponte Pontida
Ponte Risorgimento
Via Rosmini
Stradone Porta A. Provolo
Porta Palio
San Zeno Maggiore
Piazza S. Zeno
Cir. ne Maroncelli
Via da Vico
Corso Milano
Via San Marco

1/4 mi
250 m

459

Mar–Oct Mon–Sat 8:30am–6pm, Sun 12:30–6pm; Nov–Feb Tues–Sat 10am–1pm and 1:30–5pm, Sun 12:30–5pm; www.basilicasanzeno.it) is the greatest Romanesque church in northern Italy. The present structure was completed around 1135 over the 4th-century shrine to Verona's patron saint, St. Zeno (who died in 380). Its massive rose window represents the Wheel of Fortune, while the lintels above the portal represent the months of the year. The highlight of the interior is "Madonna and Saints" above the altar, by Mantegna.

WHERE TO EAT

Even in chic Verona, you'll spend less on a meal than in Venice. The most authentic budget restaurant is **Osteria Sottoriva,** Via Sottoriva 9 (*(C)* **045/8014323;** Thurs–Tues 11am–11pm), one of the most popular places in town for lunch or dinner; try the *trippa alla parmigiana* (braised tripe) or the hopelessly rich gorgonzola melted over polenta (main courses 9.50€–15€). **Caffè Monte Baldo,** Via Rosa 12 (www.osteriamontebaldo.com; *(C)* **045/8030579;** noon–11pm daily), is an old-fashioned cafe transformed into a trendy *osteria,* serving classic pastas and scrumptious *crostini* with wine in the evenings.

Treviso ★★

30km (19 miles) N of Venice

Long overshadowed by Venice, **Treviso** is a small, prosperous city of narrow medieval streets, Gothic churches, and an enchanting network of canals, replete with weeping willows and waterwheels (it's known as "piccola Venezia" or "little Venice"). Giotto's follower **Tomaso da Modena** (1326–79), one of northern Italy's lesser-known artistic geniuses, frescoed many of its churches, and its maze of back streets makes for pleasant, often tourist-free exploring. Fashion giant Benetton was founded here in 1965; the city also claims to have invented tiramisu.

ESSENTIALS

ARRIVING The fastest way to reach Treviso is to by **train** from Santa Lucia station. Trains run two to four times an hour from Venice (30–40 min.). Tickets start at 3.55€ one-way. From Treviso Centrale station it's an easy 10- to 15-minute walk to Piazza dei Signori, north across the River Sile (follow signs to "Centro"). Note also that most Ryanair budget flights to Venice actually arrive at Treviso airport (p. 460).

VISITOR INFORMATION The **tourist office** at Via Fiumicelli 30 (www.visittreviso.it; *(C)* **0422/547-632**) is open Monday from 10am to 1pm, Tuesday to Saturday 10am to 5pm, and Sunday 10am to 4pm.

EXPLORING TREVISO

The **Piazza dei Signori ★** is the historic heart of Treviso. The square is anchored by the **Palazzo del Podestà,** rebuilt in the 1870s with a tall clock tower, and the **Palazzo dei Trecento,** the 13th-century town council hall, now home to chic Bar Beltrame beneath the arches. Just beyond the square, on adjacent Piazza San Vito, sits a handsome pair of medieval churches: **Santa Lucia** ★ (www.santaluciatreviso.it; ✆ **0422/5457200**), with a superb Tomaso da Modena fresco of the "Madonna del Pavegio" in the first shrine on the right, and **San Vito** ★ , with its Byzantine-style frescoes from the 13th century. Both are open daily 8am–noon; admission is free. Historic **Via Calmaggiore,** lined with posh boutiques, runs northwest from Piazza dei Signori towards the cathedral. The rela-tively dull neoclassical facade of

Treviso's Buranelli Canal.

the **Duomo** ★ (admission free; Mon–Sat 7:30am–noon and 3:30–7pm; Sun 8am–1pm and 3:30–8pm) is from 1836, but it's flanked by Roman-esque lions that, along with its seven Venetian-Byzantine style green cop-per domes, are remnants of the cathedral's 12th-century origins. The crypt is the most compelling part of the interior, with the tombs of the city's bishops amid a forest of columns and fragments of 14th-century frescoes and mosaics. The highlight in the main body of the cathedral is a fine altarpiece, the "Malchiostro Annunciation" by Titian, from 1520.

A short stroll southwest from the Duomo, the massive brick 13th- to 14th-century Italian Gothic church of **San Nicolò** ★ (admission free; daily 8am–noon and 3:30–6pm) houses some intriguing Gothic frescoes. Tomaso da Modena and his school decorated the huge round columns with a series of saints, notably St. Jerome, St. Agnes, and St. Romuald. Antonio da Treviso painted the absolutely gargantuan St. Christopher—his .9m-long (3-ft.) feet strolling over biting fish—in 1410.

East of Piazza dei Signori, across the **Buranelli,** the most attractive of Treviso's canals, lies the wide Canale Cagnan Grande, whose island hosts a **pescheria** (fish market) Monday to Saturday.

Farther east on Piazzetta Mario Botter is a deconsecrated church that's now an enjoyable museum. The highlight of **Museo di Santa Caterina** (www.museicivicitreviso.it; ✆ **0422/658442;** 6€, or 15€ for special exhibitions; Tues–Sun 9am–12:30pm and 2:30–6pm) is another fresco cycle by Tomaso da Modena, the "Story of the Life of Saint Ursula" (detached from a now-destroyed church and preserved here). There's also a cache of local archaeological finds plus minor works by Titian, Lorenzo Lotto, and Francesco Guardi.

To the south, the 15th-century church of **Santa Maria Maggiore** (admission free; daily 8am–noon and 3:30–6pm) houses a venerated image of Mary (the "Madonna Granda"), a frescoed "Madonna and Child" originally painted in Byzantine style (probably pre–9th century), and later touched up by Tomaso and members of his school.

WHERE TO EAT

Treviso has some excellent restaurants, but its real claim to fame is as the home of **tiramisu**. Legend has it that the addictive dessert was created at restaurant **Le Beccherie,** Piazza Ancilotto 9 (www.lebeccherie.it; ✆ **0422/540871;** daily noon–2:15pm and 7–10:15pm), in the 1960s. The claim has been disputed over the years, but the restaurant is still open and still knocks out an exceptional tiramisu (the "classico" is 6€). In fact, just about every menu in town features tiramisu, as well as Treviso's other culinary specialty, **radicchio** (bitter red lettuce).

The bars and cafés around the **pescheria,** particularly along Via Palestro, are always buzzing, and perfect for sampling good-value local cuisine. For atmosphere it's hard to beat the **Hosteria Dai Naneti** ★★, Vicolo Broli 2 (www.dainaneti.it. ✆ **3403/783158;** Mon–Fri 9am–2:30pm and 5:30–9pm, Sat 9:30am–2pm and 5:30–9pm, Sun 11am–2pm and 5–8pm; May–Sept closed Sun), a cozy tavern, deli, and cheese shop where you can grab a delicious baguette and glass of wine, or just snack at the bar for around 5€ (standing room only).

For a full meal in the center, reserve a table at **Trattoria All'Antico Portico** ★★, overlooking the church at Piazza Santa Maria Maggiore 18 (www.anticoportico.it; ✆ **0422/545259;** Mon 9am–4pm, Wed–Sun 9am–11pm), which serves local specialties such as radicchio risotto and *baccalà alla veneziana* (salt cod); main courses are 16€ to 18€.

MILAN, PIEDMONT & THE LAKES

By Michelle Schoenung

10

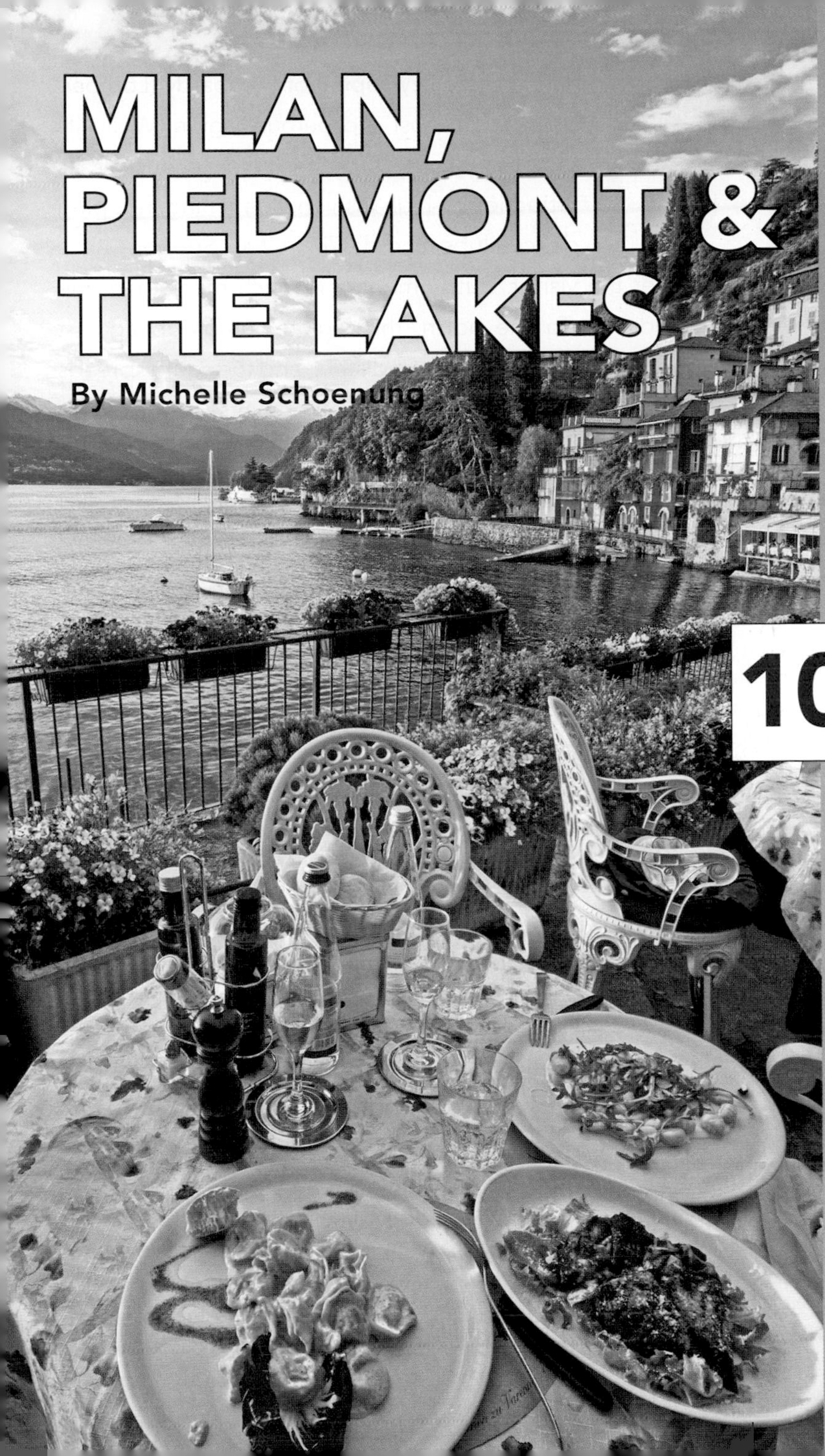

Milan is the glitzy capital of Lombardy (Lombardia), Italy's most prosperous region. While its factories largely fuel the Italian economy, its attractions—high fashion, fine dining, hopping dance clubs, and da Vinci's *Last Supper*—have much to offer the visitor. But Lombardy is much more than one sophisticated city. To the north, the region bumps up against craggy mountains in a romantic lake district, and the south spreads into fertile farmlands fed by the Po and other rivers.

Lombardy feels different from the rest of Italy. The *Lombardi* descended from one of the Germanic tribes that overran the Roman empire, and have over the centuries been ruled by feudal dynasties from Spain, Austria, and France, so they tend to be a bit more Continental than their neighbors to the south—fast-talking, faster-paced, and more business-oriented. They even dine differently, with butter replacing olive oil, and polenta and risotto as common as pasta, though, these days, the Milanese are equally as enamored of sushi and other ethnic foods as they are their traditional dishes.

Backed by the Alps and ringed by lush gardens and verdant forests, the Italian lakes have entranced writers from Catullus to Ernest Hemingway. While each lake has its own distinct charm, they are all ideal for short retreats: Lake Maggiore and Lake Como are both less than an hour from Milan, and Lake Garda is tantalizingly close to Venice.

DON'T LEAVE MILAN & THE LAKE DISTRICT WITHOUT . . .

Paying homage to Michelangelo & da Vinci. You'll find *The Last Supper* in Santa Maria delle Grazie (p. 479) and the *Pieta,* Michelangelo's first work, inside the medieval Castello Sforzesco (p. 469).

Climbing to the roof of Milan's Gothic Duomo. Wander amid the buttresses and statue-topped spires for a citywide panorama. See p. 472.

Taking a window-shopping spin. Browse the high-end boutiques in Milan's Golden Rectangle, then go on a budget-shopping spree through the stock shops and outlets of Corso Buenos Aires. See p. 489.

Ferrying among Lake Maggiore's Borromean Islands. You can tour the palaces of one of Lombardy's last remaining Renaissance-era noble families, and watch the peacocks wander their exotic gardens. See p. 508.

Visiting Lake Garda's picturesque Sirmione. Despite the crowds of summer tourists, this historic town—which has attracted visitors since the

PREVIOUS PAGE: **Elegant resort towns line the shores of Lake Como.**

Romans discovered hot springs here—hasn't lost its charm. Make your way through the picture-postcard *centro storico* to the beach and castle. See p. 513.

MILAN (MILANO) ★★★

552km (342 miles) NW of Rome, 288km (179 miles) NW of Florence, 257km (159 miles) W of Venice) 140km (87 miles) NE of Turin, 142km (88 miles) N of Genoa

Milan—or Milano, as the Italians say it—is elegant, chaotic, and utterly beguiling. Traffic chokes the streets, and it can be bitterly cold in winter and stiflingly hot in summer, but it more than compensates with majestic architecture and robust Northern Italian cuisine. It's a world-class stop on the international fashion stage, the banking capital of Italy, and a wealthy city of glamorous people and stylish shopping streets. Milan also is rich in history, from its Roman ruins and soaring Duomo to a host of ancient churches, medieval castles, and Renaissance palaces.

Massive changes were made to the city in preparation for 2015's World's Fair, known as **Expo Milano.** The city still continues to undergo somewhat of an urban and cultural renaissance. A whole new skyline boasts innovative towers by international starchitects, the already efficient public transportation system continues to expand, new museums continue to crop up, and the city has an overall sense of renewed vitality.

Essentials

ARRIVING

BY PLANE **Milan Malpensa,** 45km (28 miles) northwest of the city, is Milan's major international airport. The **Malpensa Express** train (www.malpensaexpress.it; ✆ **02-7249-4949**), costs 13€ one way (or 20€ roundtrip) and now leaves from both Terminal 1 and Terminal 2 with a 30-minute run half-hourly to Cadorna train station, or hourly to Stazione Centrale (45 min.). Buses run directly to Stazione Centrale, a 50-minute journey, with five trips per hour, for 10€ one-way or 16€ round-trip; they're operated by **Malpensa Shuttle** (www.malpensashuttle.it; ✆ **02-5858-3185)** or **Autostradale** (www.autostradale.it; ✆ **02-3008-9000**). By taxi, the trip into town costs a wallet-stripping 100€ and takes the same amount of time as the bus—50 minutes. We don't recommend it, but it's the only option after midnight. Keep in mind that the two terminals are several miles apart; a shuttle bus between them runs 24 hours a day and takes about 15 minutes. Terminal 1 is the larger, newer terminal, and most travelers will leave in and out of here. Older, smaller Terminal 2 mainly serves low-cost airline EasyJet for flights within Europe.

Milan Linate, 7km (4.5 miles) east of the center, handles European and domestic flights. **Air Bus** (www.atm-mi.it; ✆ **02/48-607-607**) makes the 25-minute trip by bus every 30 minutes between 6am and midnight to

Stazione Centrale for 5€. A roundtrip ticket costs 9€. City bus no. 73 leaves every 10 minutes for the San Babila Metro stop downtown and takes 25 minutes. The express no. X73 is faster and departs every 20 minutes between 7am and 8pm. Tickets for both are 2€. A trip into town by taxi costs roughly 20€.

Malpensa Shuttle buses also connect Malpensa and Linate airports with five daily runs between 9:30am and 6:20pm. The trip takes 90 minutes and costs 13€ (roundtrip 26€).

BY TRAIN   Milan is one of Europe's busiest rail hubs. Trains travel every half-hour to Bergamo (1 hr.), Mantua (2 hr.), and Turin (1 hr. by the AV high-speed train). **Stazione Centrale** is a half-hour walk northeast of the center, with easy connections to Piazza del Duomo by Metro, tram, and bus. The Metro stop is called Centrale F.S. To buy train tickets, use the multilingual automatic ticket machines, which accept cash, credit cards, and ATM cards (they even have a reader for contactless cards). Keep in mind that the credit-card and ATM functions are sometimes out of order; however, there are typically attendants to help (look for official attendants wearing a vest with the Trenitalia logo, and don't let "volunteers" help you—they will often badger you for a tip at the end of the transaction). You may need to validate your ticket in the machines at the beginning of the track as you get on your train, especially if you don't have an e-ticket.

While Stazione Centrale is Milan's major station, trains also serve **Cadorna** (Como and Malpensa airport), and **Porta Garibaldi** (Lecco and the north). All these stations are on the green Metro Linea 2; Cadorna is also on the red Metro Linea 1.

BY BUS   Long-distance buses are useful for reaching the ski resorts in Valle d'Aosta. Most bus services depart from Lampugnano bus terminal (metro Lampugnano) although some originate in Piazza Castello (metro Cairoli). **Autostradale** (www.autostradale.it; © **02-5858-7304**) operates most of the bus lines and has ticket offices in front of Castello Sforzesco on Piazza Castello, open daily 9am to 6pm, and in front of the Duomo in Passageway 2 next to the TIM mobile phone store, open weekdays 8:30am to 6pm and weekends 9am to 4pm. **Savda** (www.savda.it; **0165/367-011**) runs five daily buses (more in the winter) between Milan Lampugnano and Aosta (2½ hr.; 17€) or Courmayeur (3½ hr.; 19.50€).

BY CAR   The **A1 autostrada** links Milan with Florence (3 hr.) and Rome (6 hr.), while the A4 connects Milan with Verona (2 hr.) and Venice (2½ hr.) to the east and Turin (1 hr.) to the west. All this being said, we don't recommend trying to drive around Milan. It's a huge hassle. See p. 467 for more.

GETTING AROUND

BY TRAIN   Milan's most famous sights are within walking distance of each other, but the public transport system, an integrated system of **Metro, trams,** and **buses,** run by **ATM** (www.atm.it; © **02-48-607-607**), is a cheap and effective alternative to walking. The Metro closes at midnight (Sat at 1am), but buses and trams run all night. Metro stations are well signposted; trains are speedy, safe, and frequent—they run every couple of minutes during the day and about every 5 minutes after 9pm. Tickets for 90 minutes of travel on Metro, trams, or buses cost 2€. A 24-hour unlimited travel ticket is a decent value at 7€. Tickets are available at newsstands and Metro stations (all machines have English-language options; the 24-hr. ticket option is listed under "Urban"). Stamp your ticket when you board a bus or tram—there is a 35€ fine (more if not paid on the spot) if you don't.

Lines 1 (red, with stops at Cairoli for Castello Sforzesco and Duomo for Galleria Vittorio Emanuele II and the Duomo) and **3** (yellow, with a stop at Via Montenapoleone) are the most useful for sightseeing.

BY CAR   Driving and parking in Milan are not experiences to relish. First of all, you'll have to pay the Area C congestion charge of 5€ to enter the *centro storico* Monday to Friday 7:30am to 7:30pm. On top of that, the one-way system is complicated, some streets are reserved for public transport only, and there are many pedestrianized areas. Hotels will make parking arrangements for guests—take advantage of that.

BY TAXI   While you can't hail a taxi on the street, taxi stands can be found in major *piazze* and by major Metro stops. There is a taxi stand in Piazza del Duomo and outside Castello Sforzesco; a journey between the two will cost around 7€. Hotel reception staff can call a taxi for you; otherwise, a reliable company is **Taxiblu** at ✆ **02-4040.** Meters start at 3.30€ and prices increase by 1.09€ per kilometer. Expect surcharges for waiting time, luggage, late-night travel, and Sunday journeys. At press time, Uber was still operating legally in Milan.

BY BIKE   With the streets of the *centro storico* largely pedestrianized, Milan is a good city for cycling, with a handy bike-sharing program, **BikeMi,** which is so popular you can't always find bikes at some stations. The tariff for the pass is very convoluted: For 4.50€ a day or 9€ a week, you can buy a pass that allows 30 minutes of free travel between one station and the next. If you keep the bike longer, you are charged at .50€ per 30 minutes (or part of it) up until 2 hours; thereafter your time is charged at 2€ per hour or part of the hour. Once you return a bike, you have to wait 5 minutes before you can start another rental. Bike racks are located outside Castello Sforzesco and the Duomo as well as at tram, bus, and metro

10

MILAN, PIEDMONT & THE LAKES

Milan (Milano)

stops. Buy your pass online (www.bikemi.com), by phone (✆ **02-48-607-607**), or at the **ATM Points** at Centrale, Cadorna, Garibaldi, and Duomo stations (7:45am–8pm Monday to Saturday).

ON FOOT   The attractions of the *centro storico* are all accessible on foot. From Piazza del Duomo, Via Montenapoleone is a 10-minute walk through Piazza della Scala and along Via Manzoni, and it is a 10-minute walk to Castello Sforzesco. Santa Maria delle Grazie and "The Last Supper" are a 30-minute stroll from Piazza del Duomo.

VISITOR INFORMATION

The main **tourist office** (called **IAT,** for Informazione e Accoglienza Turistica) is in Galleria Vittorio Emanuele on the corner of Piazza della Scala (www.visitamilano.it; ✆ **02-8845-5555**). It's open Monday to Friday 9am to 7pm, Saturday 9am to 6pm, and Sunday 10am to 6pm.

CITY LAYOUT

Milan developed as a series of circles radiating out from the central hub, Piazza del Duomo. Within the inner circle are most of the churches, museums, and shops of the *centro storico*. **Parco Sempione** and Leonardo's "The Last Supper" are to the west in a posh neighborhood. The slightly grungy yet hip cafe-filled districts of **Porta Ticinese** and **Navigli** lie directly south, with genteel **Brera** and its classy stores, galleries, and restaurants slightly to the north. The mecca of Milanese fashion, the **Quadrilatero d'Oro** (Golden Quadrilateral), is northeast of the Duomo. North of the center, there's a burgeoning **financial district** between Porta Garibaldi and Centrale stations, while the modern towers of the **CityLife** development rise northwest of Castello Sforesca.

[FastFACTS] MILAN

ATMs/Banks   Banks with multilingual ATMs are all over the city center. Bank hours are roughly Mon–Fri 8:30am–1:30pm and 3–4pm; major branches open Saturday morning for a couple of hours.

Business Hours   Most stores in central Milan are open Tues–Sat 9:30am–7:30pm, with a half-day Monday (3:30–7:30pm). Most shops close on Sundays and some still close for lunch between 12:30pm and 3:30pm.

Doctors/Dentists   The **Centro Medico Santagostino** has several reasonably priced clinics throughout the city and a team of doctors and dentists with many different specialties. Call or make an appointment online; the website lists prices for most types of visits. (www.cmsantagostino.it/en; ✆ **02/8970-1701**) You can also reserve via Whatsapp by sending a message to 344/100-3172.

Drugstores   Pharmacies rotate 24-hour shifts. Signs in most pharmacies post the schedule. The **Farmacia Stazione Centrale** (✆ **02/669-0735**) in Stazione Centrale is open 24 hours daily and the staff speaks English.

Emergencies   All emergency numbers are free. Call ✆ **112** for **police, medical, or fire emergencies.**

Hospitals The **Ospedale Maggiore Policlinico** (📞 **02/55-031**) is a 5-minute walk southeast of the Duomo at Via Francesco Sforza 35 (metro Duomo or Missori). Some of the medical personnel speak English.

Internet The free **Open Wi-Fi Milano** network has hundreds of hotspots all over the city. In addition, many hotels, bars, and cafes offer free Wi-Fi. Throughout the city, branches of the **Arnold Coffee** (www.arnoldcoffee.it) American-style coffee bars offer free Wi-Fi.

Police For police emergencies, dial 📞 **112.** There is a police station in Stazione Centrale but the **Questura** is at the main station, just west of the Giardini Pubblici at Via Fatebenefratelli 11 (📞 **02/62-261;** metro Turati).

Post Office The main post office, **Poste e Telecommunicazioni,** is at Via Cordusio 4 (📞 **02/7248-2508;** metro Cordusio). It's open Mon–Fri 8:20am–7:05pm and Sat 8:30am–12:35pm. The post office in Stazione Centrale is open Mon–Sat 8:20am–7:05pm. Other branches are open Mon–Sat 8:30am–1:30pm.

Safety Milan is generally safe, although public parks and the area around Stazione Centrale are best avoided at night.

Exploring Milan

Dress modestly when visiting Milan's churches: no short shorts for either sex, women must have their shoulders covered, and skirts must be below the knee. The dress code at the Duomo is particularly strict.

Castello Sforzesco ★ MUSEUM   Although it has lived many lives under several different occupiers and been restored many times, this fortified castle is the masterpiece of Milan's two most powerful medieval and Renaissance dynasties, the Visconti and the Sforza. The Visconti built the castle (as well as the Duomo) in the 14th century; after the Sforzas married into the Visconti clan and eclipsed their power, they took the castle in the 1450s, transforming it into one of the most gracious palaces of the Renaissance. Sforza *capo* Ludovico il Moro and his wife, Beatrice d'Este, helped make Milan one of Italy's Renaissance centers by commissioning works by Bramante and Leonardo.

The castle's most recent extensive restoration was by architect Luca Beltrami at the end of the 19th century, though restoration is always ongoing. It opened as a museum in 1905; today it contains a dozen museums, known collectively as the Musei del Castello Sforzesco. Many Sforza treasures are on view in the castle's labyrinthine courtyards and corridors, including a *pinacoteca* (painting gallery) with works by Bellini and Correggio plus Mannerists Ribera and Ricci. For a few years now, the area of the castle known as the Spanish Castle (it was once used as an infirmary by the castle's Spanish garrison in the late 1500s) has been renovated to house the final work of the 89-year-old Michelangelo, his evocative, unfinished "Pietà Rondanini", which was discovered in his Roman workshop at the time of his death in 1564. (rondanini.milanocastello.it; 📞 **02/8846-3703**).
Piazza Castello. www.milanocastello.it. 📞 **02/8846-3700.** Castle courtyards: Free. Daily 7am–7:30pm. Musei del Castello Sforzesco: 5€ (free Tues 2–5:30pm; Wed–Sun 4:30–5:30pm). Tues–Sun 9am–5:30pm (last entry 30 min. before closing). Metro: Cairoli.

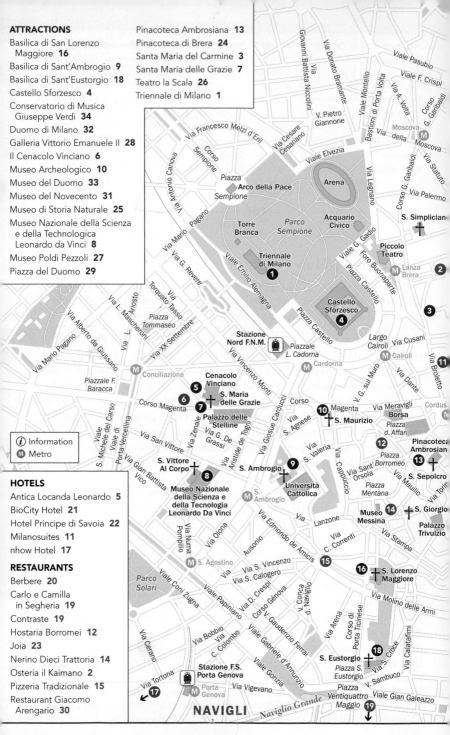

ATTRACTIONS

Basilica di San Lorenzo
  Maggiore **16**
Basilica di Sant'Ambrogio **9**
Basilica di Sant'Eustorgio **18**
Castello Sforzesco **4**
Conservatorio di Musica
  Giuseppe Verdi **34**
Duomo di Milano **32**
Galleria Vittorio Emanuele II **28**
Il Cenacolo Vinciano **6**
Museo Archeologico **10**
Museo del Duomo **33**
Museo del Novecento **31**
Museo di Storia Naturale **25**
Museo Nazionale della Scienza
  e della Technologica
  Leonardo da Vinci **8**
Museo Poldi Pezzoli **27**
Piazza del Duomo **29**

Pinacoteca Ambrosiana **13**
Pinacoteca di Brera **24**
Santa Maria del Carmine **3**
Santa Maria delle Grazie **7**
Teatro la Scala **26**
Triennale di Milano **1**

HOTELS

Antica Locanda Leonardo **5**
BioCity Hotel **21**
Hotel Principe di Savoia **22**
Milanosuites **11**
nhow Hotel **17**

RESTAURANTS

Berbere **20**
Carlo e Camilla
  in Segheria **19**
Contraste **19**
Hostaria Borromei **12**
Joia **23**
Nerino Dieci Trattoria **14**
Osteria il Kaimano **2**
Pizzeria Tradizionale **15**
Restaurant Giacomo
  Arengario **30**

470

Milan

Via de Cristoforis
Corso Como
Via della Liberazione
20
Via Melchiorre Gioia
Via M. Polo
Piazza S. Giochino
21
Via Vittor Pisani
Stazione Centrale
(i)
Via Vitruvio
Piazza S. Camillo de Lellis
Via Benedetto Marcello
Via Boscovich
Via Ruggero
Via Plinio

Bastioni di Porta Nuova
Via C. Galilei
Via Castelfidardo
Piazzale Principessa Clotilde
22
Piazza della Repubblica
M Repubblica
Viale Tunisia
Piazza Cincinnato
Via F. Casati
Via Tadino
Via S. Gregorio
Via G. Aires
Via G. Giorgio
Francesco Redi
Piazzale Lavater

Via Solferino
Via S. Marco
Corso di Porta Nuova
Via A. Appiani
Viale Vittorio Veneto
Via Antonio Zarotto
Via Lodovici Settala
Corso Buenos Aires
Via S. Francesco Romana
Piazza

Via Montebello
Via della Moscova
Via Filippo Turati
Turati M
23
Via Lecco
Via Alessandro Tadino
Via Omboni
Piazza Otto Novembre

Pinacoteca di Brera
Via Fatebenefratelli
Via Principe Amedeo
Bastioni di Porta Venezia
Giardini Pubblici
Planetario
Piazza Guglielmo
Via Metro
Via Giuseppe Sirtori
Piazzale Rosolino Pilo
Via Nino Bixio

BRERA
24
Museo del Risorgimento
Via dei Giardini
Via Daniele Marin
Palazzo Dugnani
Via Palestro
Museo di Storia Naturale
25
Galleria d'Arte Moderna
Via Borghetto

Orto Botanico
Via Monte di Pietà
Via Alessandro Manzoni
Via Senato
Via della Spiga
Via Marina
Corso Venezia
Via Cappuccini
Viale Luigi Majno
Piazza Fratelli Bandiera

Via Brera
Monte Napoleone M
27
Monte Napoleone
Museo Bagatti Valsecchi
QUAD D'ORO
Palazzo Senato
Via Carlo Goldoni

Teatro alla Scala
26
Museo di Milano
Palazzo Serbelloni
Prefettura
Via Vivaio
Corso Concordia
Piazza Risorgimento

Municipio
Piazza F. L. Meda
Via San Damiano
M S. Babila
Corso Monforte
Via Macedonio Melloni
Via P. Sottocomo

28
Galleria Vittorio Emanuele II
Piazza S. Babila
Via Pietro Mascagni
Viale Bianca Maria
Viale Premuda
Via Archimede

(i)
Via Vittorio Emanuele
Via Durini
Via Cerva
Via Passione
34
Via Gaetano Donizetti
Via Marcona

29
Piazza Duomo
Duomo
32
Corso Europa
Via Uberto Visconti di Modrone
Via Filippo Corridori
Piazza Cinque Giornate
Corso Ventidue Marzo

Duomo M
31
Palazzo Arcivescovile
33
Largo Augusto
Piazza S. Pietro in Gessate
Corso Porta Vittoria
Via Fontana

30
Palazzo Reale
S. Stefano
Palazzo di Giustizia
Via Podgora
Via Augusto Anfossi

Piazza G. Missori
Via Larga
Università degli Studi
Via d. Guastalla
Via S. Barnaba
Rotonda della Besana
Via Spartaco

Missori M
Torre Velasca
Largo F. Richini
Via Francesco Sforza
Via Pace
Viale Regina Margherita
Via Monte Nero
Via Fogazzaro

Corso Italia
Corso di Porta Romana
S. Nazaro
Via d. Commenda
Via Manfredo Fanti
Viale Emilio Caldara
Via A. Maffei
Milan **Venice**

S. Eufemia
Via S. Sofia
Via Alfonso Lamarmora
Rome

Crocetta M
Piazza A. Ferrari
Via G. Mercalli
Corso di Porta Romana
Corso di Porta Vigentina
Via Orti
Via Monte Nero
Via Carlo Botta
Via Giorgio Vasari

Via Quadronno

0 ___ 1/4 mi
0 ___ 250 m
Porta Romana
Viale A. Filippetti
M

MILAN FROM on high

Take the trip up to the roof of the Duomo (www.duomomilano.it) for spine-tingling views across the rooftops of Milan and, on a clear day, to the Alps beyond. Atop the Duomo, surrounded by Gothic pinnacles, saintly statues, and flying buttresses, you even get a close-up view of the spire-top gold statue of **"La Madonnina"** (the little Madonna), the city's beloved good-luck charm. You can either ascend by elevator (14€); go to the church's northeast corner, almost to the back of the Duomo) or climb the stairs (10€); stairs are on the church's north flank). A pass combining a roof-top visit with entrance to the cathedral and the Museo del Duomo (see p. 475) costs 13€ if you take the stairs, 17€ if you opt for the elevator. The pass is good for 72 hours and there are discounts for children and seniors. The elevator is open daily 9am to 6:30pm (last ticket sold at 6pm).

Other sneaky viewpoints over the Duomo include the food market on the top floor of department store **La** **Rinascente** (see p. 490) and the posh **Restaurant Giacomo Arengario** (p. 487) at the **Museo del Novecento** (p. 476).

Duomo di Milano ★★★ CHURCH   Although there has been a church here since at least A.D. 355, building began on Milan's magnificent Duomo–the last of Italy's great Gothic structures—in 1368 during the rein of the Visconti family. It took 5 centuries to complete (its mammoth cast-bronze doors were finally finished in 1965). Today it is the fourth largest church in the world (after St. Peter's in Rome, Seville's cathedral, and a relatively new one in Ivory Coast), with 135 marble spires, a stunning triangular facade, and 3,400-some statues flanking the massive yet surprisingly airy, fanciful exterior, which dominates the vast, traffic-free **Piazza del Duomo** (see p. 477).

The cathedral's cavernous interior, lit by brilliant stained glass windows, seats 40,000 but is usually quite serene, divided into five aisles by a forest of 52 columns. The poet Shelley used to sit and read Dante amid monuments that include a gruesomely graphic statue of **St. Bartholomew** (who was flayed alive). Another British visitor, Alfred, Lord Tennyson, rhapsodized about the view from the roof. In the crypt, the **Battistero di San Giovanni alle Fonti** reveals remains of the octagonal 4th-century foundations of an earlier church that stood here, which is almost certainly where Sant'Ambrogio—patron saint and bishop of Milan in A.D. 374—christened the great missionary St. Augustine. Pride of place in the crypt goes to the ornate **gilded tomb of San Carlo Borromeo,** archbishop of Milan and leader of the Counter-Reformation, who died in 1584. Entrance to the crypt is included in admission to the Museo del Duomo (see p. 475), though opening times may be different.

Piazza del Duomo. www.duomomilano.it. ✆ **02/7202-2656.** 3€. Daily 7am–7pm for worshippers, 8am–6pm for visitors. Metro: Duomo.

The ornate spires of Milan's Duomo, one of the world's great Gothic cathedrals.

Galleria Vittorio Emanuele II ★★ SHOPPING MALL   The best place from which to admire the Duomo façade is from the café at the entrance of the Galleria, Milan's late 19th-century prototype of the modern shopping mall. No modern malls come even close to matching the Galleria for style and flair; this wonderful steel-and-glass covered, cross-shaped arcade is a neoclassical beauty, with ornate marble flooring and a massive octagonal glass dome. Inside, the arcade is lined with grand cafes such as **Biffi** and **Savini,** where the local elite gather to dine after a night at the opera. Designer stores here include Gucci, Versace, Prada, Louis Vuitton, and Swarovski. Its span links the Piazza del Duomo with Piazza della Scala, site of the famous opera house.

Galleria Vittorio Emanuele II was the masterpiece of Bolognese architect Giuseppe Mengoni, who designed it in the 1870s to mark the unification of Italy under King Vittorio Emanuele II; mosaic and fresco decorations incorporate patriotic symbols and coats of arms of various Italian cities. Mengoni never saw his magnus opus flourishing—he died in a fall from scaffolding the day before it opened in 1878. Today giggling crowds gather under the dome to spin around on one heel on the private parts of a little mosaic bull in the floor, a legendary good-luck ritual.
Piazza del Duomo. Open 24 hrs. Metro: Duomo.

been an important center of Christianity since Emperor Constantine sanc-
the faith in A.D. 313. The city has more than 100 churches, and, like the Duomo,
many of them lie on pagan foundations. In these, layer upon layer of history can be
stripped back to their early remains.

Two such churches are on Corso di Porta Ticinese. **The Basilica di San Lorenzo Maggiore** was built in the 4th century, using rubble removed from the amphitheater nearby, at the same time as the 16 Corinthian columns standing outside. The church now has a 16th-century facade, but inside, fragments of the original building survive: The octagonal, white-washed Cappella di Sant'Aquilino retains pieces of the 4th-century gold mosaic that once covered all the walls, and to the right of this, stairs lead down to the foundations of the first basilica.

Down the street, the **Basilica di Sant'Eustorgio** has undergone many face-lifts. The foundations of the original 4th-century church are behind the altar in the basilica, while the present Neo-Romanesque facade dates from 1865. The ornate Cappella Portinari dates from the 15th century, built as a memorial to St. Peter of Verona.

In Piazza Sant'Ambrogio you'll find the sublime Lombard Romanesque **Basilica di Sant'Ambrogio.** Built over a Roman cemetery, the church was extensively remodeled from the 8th to 11th centuries, and it is here that the remains of Milan's patron saint, Ambrogio, are housed. The glittering mosaics in the apse and wall frescoes in the side chapels show scenes from the life of the saint, and a great gold altar constructed in the 9th century holds his remains.

The church of **Santa Maria del Carmine** in Brera was built over the remains of a Romanesque basilica and partly remodeled in 1400; most of its present incarnation dates from 1447. Its baroque presbytery was added in the 17th century and the Gothic-Lombard facade in 1880, making the church a true stylistic mishmash.

Museo Archeologico ★★ MUSEUM Milan's expertly curated archeology museum is set in a series of airy galleries housed among the cloisters, towers, and courtyards of the 8th-century convent of Monastero Maggiore of San Maurizio. As was common at the time, the convent was constructed atop an older structure, so part of the museum is built around the remains of an ancient villa and a section of 4th-century Roman walls, which fortified Milan—then called Mediolanum—in its heyday as capital of the Western Roman Empire. The museum also offers a glimpse inside a third-century defense tower, with traces of medieval frescoes on its rounded walls portraying Jesus showing his stigmata to St. Francis. Most of the treasures on display were excavated locally, including ancient Milanese, Greek, and Etruscan artifacts. Highlights of the collection include a 1st-century B.C. **mosaic pavement** unearthed nearby in 1913; the stunning, gleaming 4th-century **Trivulzio Diattreta Cup,** made of t finest hand-blown glass; and busts of various emperors from Caesar on.

Corso Magenta 15. www.museoarcheologicomilano.it. © **02/8844-5208.** 5€ adults. Free Tues after 2pm. Tues–Sun 9am–5:30pm. Metro: Cadorna.

Museo del Duomo ★★★ MUSEUM   Despite the name, this museum is actually located across the piazza on the ground floor of Palazzo Reale. As you face the palace (with the Duomo to your back), the entrance is to the left. Beguiling treasures from the Duomo are displayed here in an imaginatively constructed exhibition that leads visitors on a chronological journey through the life of both Milan and its cathedral. Highlights among the carved cherubs, angels, and Renaissance Madonnas include a room full of startling gargoyles, ethereal 15th-century stained-glass works, scale wooden models of the cathedral, and the original supporting structure of **"La Madonnina"** (see p. 474), who has adorned the Duomo rooftop since 1774. The standout piece is **"Jesus and the Moneylenders"** by Tintoretto, rediscovered by happy accident in the Duomo sacristy after World War II.

Piazza del Duomo 12. museo.duomomilano.it. © **02/7200-3768.** 7€, 3€ under age 26 and seniors. Ticket also includes admission to cathedral. Tues–Sun 10am–6pm. Metro: Duomo.

Museo del Novecento ★ MUSEUM   Next door to the Palazzo Reale, Milan's museum of 20th-century art begins with a circular passageway, which winds up to the entrance on an upper floor. The undisputed star of the collection is Giuseppe Pellizza da Volpedo's seminal **"The Fourth Estate"** (1901), a symbol-laden painting of a labor strike march, which hangs in the passageway outside the museum, free for all to admire. The collection showcases Italian modern art from the Futurist movement to Arte Povera (art made from "poor" materials), trying to make the case that Italy's contribution to the world of art did not end at the Renaissance. While that claim is only partially successful, you will see some brilliant bursts of genius like the magnificent **"Philosopher's Troubles"** (1926) by Giorgio de Chirico and the moving **"Thirst"** (1934) by sculptor Arturo Martini. One of the best things about this museum? The views of the Duomo and its piazza down below.

Via Marconi 1. www.museodelnovecento.org. © **02/8844-0461.** 10€ adults, 8€ for ages over 65 or 18–25, 5€ ages 13–18. Mon 2:30–7:30pm, Tues–Sun 9:30am–7:30pm (Thurs, Sat until 10:30pm). Metro: Duomo.

Museo Nazionale della Scienza e della Tecnologica Leonardo da Vinci ★★ MUSEUM   The cavernous science museum occupies not only the former Benedictine monastery of San Vittore Olivetan but also three modern additions and outdoor spaces. While recent renovations have made the exhibits more fun and interactive, the floor plan is immensely confusing; pick up a brochure at the entrance so you don't

MILAN, PIEDMONT & THE LAKES

Milan (Milano)

ghlights. If you want to
er side of Leonardo da
genius, check out a clutch
nardo's anatomical drawings
and not-so-batty designs for subma-
rines, helicopters, and other engineering marvels, a definite highlight
of this science museum, one of
the world's leading collections of
mechanical and scientific wizardry.
The monastery and its beautiful
cloister are also filled with planes,
trains, carriages, sewing machines,
typewriters, optical devices, and
other exhibits. There's even a mini-
submarine to visit (tickets cost an
extra 8€ and can be purchased at the
museum or online at www.museo
scienza.org/toti). The museum often
holds interactive science workshops

Models of Leonardo DaVinci's inventions are displayed at the Museo Nazionale della Scienza e della Tecnologica.

and has a tinkering zone and maker space for kids, but keep in mind that most activities will be in Italian.

Via San Vittore 21. www.museoscienza.org. ✆ **02/485-551.** 10€ adults, 7.50€ under 25, 5€ seniors. 1-hr guided tour in English 65€. Tues–Fri 9:30am–5pm, Sat–Sun 9:30am–6:30pm. Metro: Sant'Ambrogio.

Museo Poldi Pezzoli ★★ ART GALLERY   This wonderfully eclectic art collection was the life's work of aristocrat Gian Giacomo Poldi Pezzoli, who donated his cache of art and decorative arts to the city in 1879. It is now elegantly displayed in his luxurious 17th-century *palazzo*. The ornate rooms of the ground floor feature Oriental rugs, ancient armor, and rare books. Up the carved marble stairs the riches continue, through extravagant rooms adorned with family portraits, Murano glass, and Limoges china. Scenes from *The Divine Comedy* are featured in stained glass, and gilded pistols sit side by side with precious jewelry. Highlights include the **Armillary Sphere,** crafted by Flemish clockmaker Gualterus Arsenius in 1568 to illustrate contemporary theories of planetary movement, and **Renaissance paintings** by Botticelli and Piero della Francesca in the Golden Room. The clock room boasts 150 watches and clocks from the Renaissance to the late 1800s.

Via Manzoni 12. www.museopoldipezzoli.it. ✆ **02/794-889.** 10€ adults; 7€ seniors and students 11–18; free under 10. Audio guides 5€. Wed–Mon 10am–6pm, closed Tues. Metro: Montenapoleone.

Piazza del Duomo ★★ PIAZZA   The Piazza del Duomo has been the beating heart of Milan since the city was taken over by the Romans in

222 B.C. and known as Mediolanum. This vast traffic-free piazza sees local life passing to and fro daily, added to by the bustle of tourists peering up at the majestic Duomo while dodging pigeons and street sellers pushing cheap souvenirs. From here a tangle of narrow streets branch off in all directions through the city's *centro storico* (historic center). The square took on its present form following the Unification of Italy in 1861, when the medieval buildings were replaced by splendid neoclassical buildings designed by Giuseppe Mengoni (1829–1877), also architect of the **Galleria Vittorio Emanuele II** (see p. 473). Located around the piazza are the superb **Museo del Duomo** (see p. 475), temporary art exhibitions in the **Palazzo Reale** (www.palazzorealemilano.it; ✆ 02/0202), and 20th-century Italian art in the **Museo del Novecento** (see p. 476).

Metro: Duomo.

Pinacoteca Ambrosiana ★★ ART GALLERY   Founded in 1609 to display the collections of the pious Cardinal of Milan Federico Borromeo, this gallery is housed in Europe's second-oldest public library (after the Bodleian in Oxford). The gallery, which mostly features Italian art from the 15th to 20th centuries, has a confusing layout—a maze of courtyards, passageways, stairwells, and any number of tiny exhibition rooms—but it's worth persisting to find four outstanding artworks: the cartoon for **"The School of Athens"** by Raphael (1510); Caravaggio's charming **"Basket with Fruit,"** from around 1599; and Titian's **"Adoration of the Magi"** (ca. 1550). The fourth, the haunting **"Portrait of a Musician,"** has been attributed to Leonardo da Vinci (1490), although many scholars question that provenance. If it is indeed a da Vinci, however, it's his only painting hanging in any Italian museum.

Leonardo's original **"Codex Atlanticus"** is in the Biblioteca Ambrosiana next door along with other rare manuscripts. Drawings from the "Codex", which consists of 1,750 drawings and jottings the master did between 1478 and 1519, can be seen in the Sacristy of Bramante in Santa Maria della Grazie. Leonardo's entire life as an artist and scientist can be found in this extraordinary collection.

Piazza Pio XI. www.ambrosiana.eu. ✆ **02/806-921.** Pinacoteca and Leonardo's Codex Atlanticus 15€ adults, 10€ ages under 18 and over 65, free for kids 14 and under. Pinacoteca only 10€. Tues–Sun 10am–6pm. Metro: Duomo or Cordusio.

Pinacoteca di Brera ★★★ ART GALLERY   Milan's, and indeed Lombardy's, premier art collection resides in a 17th-century Jesuit college, wrapped around a two-story arcaded courtyard. This peerless collection leads the visitor on a circular tour through Italian art from medieval to Surrealism in 38 roughly chronological rooms. Along the way are splendid Renaissance altarpieces, Venetian School and baroque paintings, gloomy Mannerist works, and the odd piece by Carlo Carrà and Umberto Boccioni.

Navigli Grande canal in Milan.

Although the collection is not immense, it is of exquisite quality; just some of the highlights include Piero della Francesca's sublime **Montefeltro Altarpiece** (1474); the ethereal **"Dead Christ"** by Andrea Mantegna (1480); Caravaggio's superb, mournful **"Supper at Emmaus"** (1601); and Raphael's **"Marriage of the Virgin"** (1504), which was expertly restored in the glass-walled, temperature-controlled restoration rooms here, which are open to the public. More modern standouts include Francesco Hayez's **"The Kiss"** (1859) and artist Giovanni Fattori's pastoral scenes, which paved the way for the late 19th-century Macchiaioli School of Italian Impressionists. Moving the collection up to the present day are works by the Italian playboy artist Amedeo Modigliani and sculptor Marino Marini.

Via Brera 28. pinacotecabrera.org. ⓒ **02/722-632-64.** 12€ adults, 8€ seniors, 2€ EU citizens ages 18–25. Free for kids under 18. Audio guide 5€. Tues–Wed and Sat–Sun 8:30am–7:15pm, Thurs 8:30am–10:15pm. Free every 1st Sun of month. Metro: Lanza.

Santa Maria delle Grazie ★★ CHURCH   The delightful Lombard Renaissance church of Santa Maria delle Grazie is often ignored in the mad scramble to see Leonardo da Vinci's world-renowned "Last Supper" (see p. 479) in the *cenacolo* (refectory) of the Dominican convent attached to the church. Started in 1465–1482 by Guiniforte Solari (ca. 1429–1481), the church was subsequently enlarged when the Sforza duke Ludovico il

Moro (see p. 469) decided to make it his family mausoleum. He commissioned Leonardo da Vinci to paint the "Last Supper," and asked Donato Bramante, the leading architect of the Lombard Renaissance—who also helped design St. Peter's in Rome—to add the terracotta-and-cream-colored choir in 1492. Inside the church itself, note the clash of styles between Solari's frescoed Gothic nave and Bramante's airy, somber apse.

Piazza Santa Maria delle Grazie. www.grazieop.it. ℂ **02/467-6111.** Free. Mon–Sat 7am–noon, 3–7:30pm (4–7:30pm summer); Sun 7:30am–12:30pm, 4pm–9pm. Metro: Cadorna or Conciliazione.

Santa Maria delle Grazie, Il Cenacolo Vinciano (The Last Supper) ★★★ CHURCH

Milan's greatest art treasure is also one of the most famous on earth, in part thanks to Dan Brown's blockbuster novel *The Da Vinci Code*. Painted for Ludovico il Moro by Leonardo da Vinci between 1495 and 1497, "The Last Supper" adorns the back wall of the refectory in the Dominican convent attached to Santa Maria delle Grazie. Leonardo's masterpiece depicts Christ revealing that one of his disciples will soon betray him; horror and disbelief are etched into every face, while Jesus remains calm and resigned. As we look at the fresco, Judas sits to the left of Jesus, leaning away from him with the bag of silver clearly visible in his right hand. Is that Mary Magdalene sitting between him and Jesus? (Most historians think it's actually St. John, who was typically depicted as a particularly beautiful youth.) Wherever you stand on the issue, there is no doubt that "The Last Supper" is one of the world's most poignant works of art.

In experimenting with his painting technique, Leonardo applied tempera straight on to the walls of the refectory. As a result, his work began to deteriorate virtually on completion. It suffered several ham-fisted restoration attempts in the 18th and 19th centuries and survived target practice by Napoleon's troops, not to mention a period exposed to the open air

cruising THE CANALS

Milan's **Navigli** area (*navigli* means canals) is the perfect spot for a relaxed drink, people-watching, and a late-night supper. (To get there, take Metro Line 2 to Porta Genova.) Crowded and full of life, its streets are refreshingly casual in ambience after the dressy obsession of the city center. It's one of the few places in Milan where you will see punks, hippies, and Goths, and where you will find vintage-clothing stores.

Building of the canals started in the late 13th century, initially to transport marble slabs from quarries along Lake Maggiore (see p. 507) to build the Duomo. The Naviglio Grande was Europe's first major canal and remains an engineering marvel of the medieval era. Used to import food, commodities, and trade goods, the canals were crucial to Milan's infrastructure until the 1970s, when road transport won out. Take a boat tour of the canals to peek into Milan's industrial heritage; **Navigli Lombardi** (www.naviglilombardi.it; ℂ **02/667-9131**) runs frequent tours.

Seeing "The Last Supper"

Unsurprisingly, Leonardo's "The Last Supper" is on almost every tourist's itinerary of Milan. And with only 30 people allowed in to the Cenacolo Vinciano at a time, it is a challenge to get a ticket if you don't book well in advance. Try the official website first, www.cenacolovinciano.net, or call ✆ **02/9280-0360** (tickets are 10€ from the website, plus a 2€ booking fee; children under 18 enter free but still pay the 2€ fee) **3 months** or more before you are due to visit. If you have purchased your tickets online (up to a maximum of 5 tickets per person), go to the booking office outside the Cenacolo in Piazza Santa Maria delle Grazie at least 20 minutes before your allotted time slot. You will need to show identification that matches the name of the reservation. And remember that the Cenacolo is not in the church of Santa Maria delle Grazie itself, but in the refectory behind it, with a separate entrance of its own.

If you've missed the opportunity to snag a ticket in advance, many tour companies guarantee admission to "The Last Supper" as part of their guided tours of the city, which range from 40€ to 70€ (see "Organized Tours," p. 481).

Don't miss **Leonardo's Vineyard Museum** across the street in the Casa degli Atellani, where da Vinci lived while he was painting "The Last Supper." It is said that he would go back to the house at the end of the day and, given he came from a family of winemakers, tend to his vines in the garden to unwind (www.vignadileonardo.com; ✆ **02/481-6150**). The small vineyard has been revived today, and visitors can tour it and the noble palazzo. Tickets are 10€ for adults and 8€ for those aged 6 to 18.

after Allied bombing in WWII. The latest cleanup of the fresco was completed in 1999, and while the colors are muted, they are thought to resemble Leonardo's original. The famous fresco is now climate-controlled for preservation, and groups of only 30 at a time are allowed in to view it, in preallocated periods of 15 minutes.

Piazza Santa Maria delle Grazie 2. www.cenacolovinciano.net. ✆ **02/9280-0360.** 10€ adults, children under 18 free; 2€ booking fee for all tickets. Tues–Sun 8:15am–7pm. Metro: Cadorna or Conciliazione.

Triennale di Milano ★★★ MUSEUM   Located at the north end of Parco Sempione by the Torre Branca, this sleek temple of contemporary design features on-trend temporary exhibitions of modern craftsmanship, fashion, theater, and photography. An internal bridge on an upper floor, designed out of bamboo planks by Michele de Lucchi, leads from the main exhibition spaces into the permanent collections, focusing on works by iconic names in Italian design like Ettore Sottsass, Gio Ponti, and Piero Fornasetti. The cafe/pizzeria on the main floor is the venue of choice for smart Milanese and their immaculately turned-out offspring. The Terrazza Triennale on the top floor of the museum is an upscale *osteria* serving modern Italian cuisine and craft cocktails; here you'll get great views of the park and Milan's ever-changing skyline

Viale Alemagna 6. www.triennale.org. ✆ **02/724-341.** 18€ adults, 14€ seniors, students, and ages 25 and under; kids under 16 free. Tues–Sun 10:30am–8:30pm. Metro: Cadorna or Cairoli.

Organized Tours

Among the scores of companies offering guided tours of Milan and Lombardy, here are a few of the best. **Zani Viaggi** (www.zaniviaggi.it; © 02/867-131) leads specialist tours to the revered turf of San Siro Stadium (see below) and the shopping outlets of northern Lombardy, while **Local Milan Tours** (www.localmilantours.com; U.S. © 866/663-7017) can organize trips around La Scala (see p. 491) and day trips as far afield as Venice. **Opera d'Arte** (www.operadartemilano.it; © 02/4548-7400) offers guided tours of exhibitions, museums, and historic sites, including a special tour of the Castello Sforzesco with access to the battlements and underground areas of the castle that typically are not open to the public.

Outdoor Activities

Milan is a densely populated urban sprawl where green space is rare and precious. The largest park is the 47-hectare (116-acre) expanse of **Parco Sempione** behind Castello Sforzesco. It is one of the "green lungs" of the city, a favorite place for well-heeled Milanese to walk their dogs along shady pathways sheltered by giant chestnuts; it is here that lovers come to moon around the ornamental lakes. The **Giardini Pubblici** at Porta Venezia is another haven, a firm favorite with families at the weekend for its little fair. Joggers circuit the park, and in winter there's ice-skating on the ornamental ponds. **Parco Solari** and **Gardaland Waterpark** (p. 482) have swimming pools, and **Idroscalo** (p. 483) near Linate offers every outdoor activity from sailing and swimming to climbing or tennis. For sports fanatics, San Siro Stadium (www.sansiro.net; © 02/4879-8201) and **Monza F1 racetrack** (see p. 483) are open for tours.

Especially for Kids

Despite being world-renowned as a hub of high finance, fashion, and design, Milan is after all an Italian city—and all Italians dote on children. The city's rather formal facade belies its many family-friendly attractions, museums, *gelaterie,* and play parks, and everywhere you go, your *bambini* will be worshipped, hugged, and multilaterally adored.

Where to start? Chief among attractions that all kids will love is the ride up to the **Duomo rooftop** (see p. 472) for views across the red rooftops of the city and the new skyscraper district, all the way to the Alps. The **Museo Nazionale della Scienza e della Tecnologica Leonardo da Vinci** (see p. 476) is stuffed full of fun interactive activities for kids. Children ages 4 to 11 can enjoy workshops (usually in Italian) at the Sforzinda children's area in the 14th-century dungeons of **Castello Sforzesco** (see p. 469) while parents explore the decorative arts upstairs. A picnic lunch and a run in the adjoining **Parco Sempione** is a welcome respite from cultural overload.

The **Museo dei Bambini** (Via Enrico Besana 12; www.muba.it; © 02/4398-0402) doesn't have a permanent collection, but offers creative and educational workshops for children ages 2 and up. Opening times and cost of workshops vary, but tend to run around 10 euros.

Another great green public space is the **Giardini Pubblici Indro Montanelli** (see p. 491). Here there are playgrounds, roundabouts, and a little electric train that chugs around the park. The Corso Venezia side of the park is home to the **Museo di Storia Naturale** (www.comune.milano. it/museostorianaturale; *©* **02/8846-3337;** Tues–Sun 9am–5:30pm; admission 5€, children under 18 free), where you can take the kids to see dinosaur skeletons and the carcasses of massive bugs. The **Bagni Misteriosi** (www.bagnimisteriosi.com; *©* **02/ 8973-1800;** Via Carlo Botta 18) near Porta Romana is an outdoor swimming pool from the 1930s that was abandoned for decades and has recently been brought back to life. It is a great place to beat the heat in the torrid summer months, but make sure to arrive early to get a chair or a spot in the grass. Whatever you do, bring a swim cap (this is standard practice in most pools in Italy) or you will be charged 8€ for one.

The newly restored **Darsena,** the historic port of the canal network in the Navigli area, offers plenty of stimulation for the little ones. It's a great

FUN IN THE theme parks

Italy's version of Disneyland, **Gardaland,** is located a couple of hours from Milan in Castlenuovo del Garda (see p. 514), but plenty of other options lie closer to the city. If you are looking to beat the heat in the summertime, the **Acquatica** waterpark (Via Gaetano Airaghi 61; www.acquaticapark.it; *©* **02/4820-0134**) on the far western outskirts of town has splashy water slides, rides, and picnic areas. It opens at the end of May and closes the end of August. To get there, take the subway's lilac line (also called MM5) to the San Siro stop, then either bus 80 (toward Quinto Romano) or the 423 bus (toward Settimo Milanese), both of which stop directly in front of the water park. The park is open daily 10am to 7pm. An all-day ticket costs 19€ adults, 13€ for children under 12 (on Sunday, adult tickets are 23€). Children under 100cm tall enter for free. Enter after 2:30pm for slightly reduced tickets. Pools are 11€ on the weekend, and parking is 2€.

About 30 minutes northeast of Milan in the direction of Bergamo, the **Leolandia** amusement park (Via Vittorio Veneto 52, Capriate San Gervasio; www.leolandia.it) has rides and games for kids of all ages, as well as the delightful Mini-talia, a replica of the major cities and monuments in Italy. More compact and manageable than Gardaland, it may be better suited to smaller children, with features such as Peppa Pig World and Thomas the Tank Engine. Tickets purchased at the park cost 39.50€, but can be half that online. Children up to 89cm (about 3 ft.) enter free. Leolandia opens in late March and stays open through Halloween. In early spring and fall, it's open only weekends; in June and July it's open Wednesday to Sunday; and in August it's open daily. The Z301 bus from Milan to Bergamo, managed by **Nord Est Trasporti** (www.nordesttrasporti.it; *©* **800/905-150**), stops near Leolandia, at Capriate San Gervasio.

place to sit down with a picnic or gelato and watch the boats go by, either in one of the seating areas or at the cafes along the water.

Near the Linate airport, just east of the city center, the **Idroscalo** park (Via Circonvallazione Idroscalo 29, Segrate; www.idroscalo.info; no phone) features a manmade lake that was originally created for seaplanes to land. This area has now been turned into a park and is open daily (summer 7am–9pm; winter 7am–5pm).

Most restaurants will happily rustle up a child's portion of pasta and tomato sauce, and if all else fails, it's usually easy to bribe any child with a visit to one of Milan's delicious ice cream shops; try **Biancolatte** (Via Turati 30; ☎ 02/6208-6177) for baked goods and ice-cream cakes, and **Rinomata Gelateria** (Ripa di Porta Ticinese 1; ☎ 02/5811-3877) in the Navigli area for one of the most traditional ice-cream cones in town.

Outlying Attractions

Autodromo Nazionale Monza ★★ RACING CIRCUIT   Located along the River Lambro, 15km (10¼ miles) northeast of Milan, Monza is an appealing city with a photogenic central core and a sprawling park that is famous throughout Europe. Sadly, the *centro storico* is usually bypassed in favor of this 10km (6.2-mile) Formula One racetrack, the epicenter of car-mad Italy's hopes and dreams. The home of the Italian Grand Prix since 1922, Monza track is now open to any and all who fancy being a racing driver for the day. Race-training sessions are held daily, with half-hour slots available for would-be champions to try out their skills on the track. Rallies, races, and special events take place all year round. Check the website for tickets and event details.

Via Vedano 5, Monza. www.monzanet.it. ☎ **039/24-821.** Trains to Monza take about 15 min. from Centrale or Garibaldi station; park is a 15-min walk from the town center.

Certosa di Pavia ★★★ CHURCH   Located a few miles north of the town of Pavia, this awe-inspiring Carthusian monastery was originally commissioned in 1396 as a mausoleum for Milan's ruling Visconti family (see p. 472). After their dynastic downfall, the Sforza family took over, refurbishing per their exorbitant tastes. The highly intricate Renaissance façade is the swan song of master 15th-century architect Giovanni Antonio Amadeo, who also worked on the **Basilica di Santa Maria Maggiore in Bergamo** (see p. 491). The monastery contains the ornate tomb (but not the bodies) of Ludovico del Moro and his wife, Beatrice, who together shaped the Milanese Renaissance. A tour takes in the peaceful cloisters, monks' cells, and refectory, but the highlight is the decorative church, its swaths of frescoes, the *pietra dura* altar, and the massive **mausoleum** of Gian Galeazzo Visconti.

Via Del Monumento 4, Certosa di Pavia. www.museo.certosadipavia.beniculturali.it. ☎ **0382/925-613.** Admission and guided tours by donation. Tues–Sun 9–11:30am and 2:30–6pm (closes 5:30pm Apr and Sept, 5pm Mar and Oct, 4pm Nov–Feb. Metro Line 3 to Certosa, then a 10-minute walk.

Where to Stay in Milan

Milan is northern Italy's largest commercial center, big on banking and industry, and for years its hotels have tended to chase expense-account customers, often to the detriment of tourists and families. The winds of change are blowing, however. A recent wave of cozy, independent *locandas* and *albergos,* as well as design-conscious boutique hotels, have come along to complement the grand old institutions.

Note that prices are often higher during the week than on the weekend, and room rates really soar when the fashion and design crowd hits town (late Feb, mid-May, and late Sept).

SELF-CATERING ROOMS AND APARTMENTS

If you want to live like a real Milanese, self-catering rooms and apartments can be a great option, allowing you to shop at local markets, try your hand cooking the local cuisine, or at least have a refrigerator where you can keep water, wine, and cheese. Some properties even have washing machines (don't expect dryers—due to the high costs of electricity, most Italians hang their clothes to dry). On **www.airbnb.com**, a one-bedroom apartment tends to run around 120€ per night. The local agency **Milan Maison** (www.milan.maison.com) offers everything from lofts with fully stocked kitchens to studios and one bedrooms with smaller kitchenettes (studios start at 48€ per night; lofts start at 110€ per night but can get as expensive as 497€ per night).

EXPENSIVE

Hotel Principe di Savoia ★★   Every conceivable guest whim is addressed at this grand Beaux Arts institution which is part of the Dorchester Collection of famous hotels. A stay here is truly a luxurious respite from the bustling city outside; guests have access to serene gardens, a soothing top-floor spa, a quality restaurant, an elegant bar, and opulent rooms and suites. The presidential suite even has its own private indoor swimming pool. This luxury comes at a price, but for a bit of old-fashioned glamour, there's nowhere else like it. It's strategically located near both Stazione Centrale and the modern Piazza Gae Aulenti, representing the new face of the city. To reach tony Corso Como, stroll along the landscaped walkways of Piazza Lina Bo Bardi, Milan's version of New York's High Line.

Piazza Della Repubblica 17. www.dorchestercollection.com/en/milan/hotel-principe-di-savoia. ℗ **02/623-01.** 301 units. 220€–510€ double; 325€–4,700€ suite. Metro: Repubblica. **Amenities:** Restaurant; bar; concierge; room service; babysitting; spa; gym; indoor pool; Wi-Fi (free).

Milanosuites ★★★   After a thorough facelift, the former Antica Locanda dei Mercanti has re-emerged as the elegant, light-filled Milanosuites on a cobblestoned street between the Duomo and the castle. Set in a charming 18th-century townhouse (not well marked outside), the one- and two-bedroom suites have parquet floors and sleek white furnishings that add a note of glamour; all have separate living rooms and some have kitchenettes. The property also has a lounge and communal breakfast area, though breakfast usually costs an extra 10€ or so.

Via San Tomaso 6. www.milanosuites.it. © 02/8909-6849. 5 units. 216€–395€ suite. Metro: Cordusio or Cairoli. **Amenities:** Concierge; room service; Wi-Fi (free).

nhow Milan ★★   This boutique hotel is popular with the fashion and design set, who descend on it during Milan's fashion weeks and the Salone del Mobile furniture fair. A sleek reception area sets the scene with an orange color scheme straight from the 1960s. nhow seeks to wow with what it calls "unconventional spaces"—colorful corners for having a drink or admiring the temporary art exhibitions. Glass elevators whiz up to rooms decorated in white and bright solid colors; standard rooms are compact, however, with walk-in showers. Chic loft-style suites with views over Milan's Zona Tortona fashion district have their own upper floor. It's all very trendy, but a little soulless (hence the two- rather than three-star ranking). If you aren't an early riser, no worries: breakfast is served until 3pm and you can request it in your room, except on the day you check out.

Via Tortona 35. www.nhow-milan.com. © 02/489-8861. 246 units. 150€–289€ double; 419€–2,200€ suite. Rates include breakfast. Metro: Porto Genova. **Amenities:** Restaurant; bar; spa; gym; Wi-Fi (free).

MODERATE

Antica Locanda Leonardo ★★★   Located steps from where "The Last Supper" hangs in Santa Maria delle Grazie church, this lovely *albergo* in a 19th-century building overlooks a surprisingly tranquil courtyard garden. It's like stepping into a family home; the rooms have been extensively revamped but retain a wonderfully traditional feel, with heavy antique headboards and dressers, gilt mirrors, and elegant draperies. Like any historic home, it has its quirks—in colder months, it can get a bit drafty, and there are no sleek key cards here (guests are given a room, safe, and front-gate key to carry around). Fortunately, bathrooms have been brought into the 21st century. The cozy lounge and breakfast room remain delightfully of a former age but with modern touches here and there. The more expensive courtyard-facing rooms, many with tiny wrought-iron balconies, are buffered from the late-night noise on Corso Magenta. Piazza del Duomo is about a 20-minute walk from here. Check the website for the most competitive rates.

Corso Magenta 78. www.anticalocandaleonardo.com. © 02/4801-4197. 16 units. 120€–340€ double. Rates include breakfast. Metro: Concilliazione, Cadorna. **Amenities:** Concierge; Wi-Fi (free).

INEXPENSIVE

BioCity Hotel ★★★   This fab little "organic city hotel" housed in a brightly colored villa from the 1920s offers great value and is only a few minutes' walk from Stazione Centrale (as in all Italian cities, the train station is not somewhere you'd want to linger too long at night). It is all a budget hotel should be: small and pristine, with a miniscule bar and breakfast room (serving a basic continental breakfast of cheeses, cold cuts, pastries, and yogurt) and a tiny terrace out back— *and* it's eco-friendly. Guest rooms are stylish with big bathrooms almost fit for a four-star hotel. The minimal reception area manages to squeeze in a little lounge furnished with funky pieces. This gem of a hotel is close to both metro line 2 and metro line 3, both of which zip straight into the *centro storico.*

Via Edolo 18. www.biocityhotel.it. **© 02/6670-3595.** 17 units. 85€–199€ double. Rates include breakfast. Metro: Sondrio. **Amenities:** Bar; Wi-Fi (free).

Where to Eat in Milan

Milan has thousands of eateries, from pizzerias to grand old cafes, Michelin-starred restaurants in highfalutin surroundings to corner bars with a great selection of *aperitivo*-time tapas, *gelaterie,* and traditional *osterie.* Avoid the obvious tourist traps: any place that has a menu showing photos of the dishes.

Cocktail hour starts at around 6:30pm. Around that time, a tapas-like spread of olives, crudités, cold pasta dishes, rice, salads, salamis, and breads make its appearance in every city bar worth its salt. This is when the Milanese appear, as if by magic, from shopping or work, to meet up for cocktails, a bitter Campari, or a glass of Prosecco. By the time *aperitivo* hour is over, thoughts turn towards supper and the restaurants start to fill up. This phenomenon takes place all over Milan.

If you find yourself tiring of Italian cuisine, there's quite a variety of ethnic restaurants in Milan now; sushi and Chinese food are especially popular, especially the dim sum restaurants around Via Paolo Sarpi.

EXPENSIVE

Carlo e Camilla in Segheria ★★ MODERN ITALIAN It may be slightly off the beaten path, but celebrated chef Carlo Cracco's innovative bar and restaurant located in an old sawmill outside the *centro storico* is a favorite with foodies and hipsters. The restaurant has a bare yet warm post-industrial feel with large chandeliers and one long communal table for up to 65 people. Come for a truly unique cocktail (some say these are the best drinks in town) or stay for dinner with modern Italian food that is clean, fresh, and doesn't take itself too seriously. The menu changes with the seasons, but clean flavors and theatrical flair remain constants. Try dishes like ravioli filled with Neapolitan-style meat ragout and served with a tomato-and-saffron sauce, or the playful *uova o provala?* (egg or cheese?), a smoked poached egg in a provola-cheese sauce, served with lime-infused mashed potatoes. Come for the experience, but keep in mind that some of the courses are on the small side—don't expect to leave as full as if you'd been to a local pizzeria.

Via G. Meda 24. www.carloecamillainsegheria.it. **© 02/837-3963.** Entrees 15€–25€. Daily 6pm–2am. Metro: Romolo. Tram 3 from the Duomo goes directly past the front door.

Restaurant Giacomo Arengario ★★★ MODERN ITALIAN
Deserving three stars just for its Duomo views, this centrally located restaurant is a top choice among well-heeled Milanese for business lunches. It is on the top floor of the Fascist-era Palazzo dell'Arengario, which also houses the Museo del Novecento (Museum of the 20th Century) There's a smart little bar for early-evening *aperitivos,* but the real point here is to get a table near those plate-glass windows to gawk at the Duomo. The menu offers a selection of Milanese classics like veal cutlet—risotto in particular is prepared to perfection here—but there are also gourmet takes on dishes like Pasta alla Norma (a Sicilian dish featuring tomato, grilled eggplant, and ricotta), as well as delicacies like oysters, foie gras, and truffles. If you aren't in the mood for a full meal, come for coffee and dessert after a visit to the museum or the Duomo.
Via Guglielmo Marconi 1. www.giacomoarengario.com. Ⓒ **02/72-093-814.** Entrees 18€–50€. Daily noon-midnight. Metro: Duomo

Contraste ★★★ ITALIAN FUSION   The surprises start at Contraste as soon as you arrive, outside what seems to be a residential gate between a local coffee bar and neighborhood pub—the only indication that there's a restaurant here is a small gold sign on the wall. Once you're inside, this Michelin-starred restaurant offers "wow factor" for both the eyes and the taste buds, serving innovative, playful dishes in an intimate, all-white space. Various tasting menus offer intriguing specialties such as a "donut" alla Bolognese (actually a circular lasagna with a hole), crème brûlée with foie gras, and gnocchi with smoked eel and burrata cheese. One of the many "contrasts" here is that, much as at a neighborhood *trattoria,* you can tell the wait staff what you're in the mood for, and the kitchen may just make it for you, fully in line with the restaurant's "less menu" motto.
Via G. Meda 2. www.contrastemilano.it. Ⓒ **02/4953-6597.** Entrees 20€–50€. Mon and Wed–Sat 7–11pm, Sun 12:30–3pm. Closed Tues. Tram 3 from the Duomo (7 stops) stops right outside.

Joia ★★★ VEGETARIAN   Milan is not all bone-marrow risotto and *osso buco,* and this fine-dining vegetarian restaurant (the first in Europe to earn a coveted Michelin star) has become a local institution. The décor, with light wood-paneled walls, is a bit generic, but the real draw is the food. Swiss chef Pietro Leemann is known for his creative vegan and vegetarian dishes, as well as his whimsical and philosophical presentation: Buckwheat rolls filled with cauliflower and harissa are mysteriously named "Inner Landscape," while "Oh My Dear Planet" is a vegan take on *foie gras.* Many items on the menu are also naturally gluten-free. If you prefer something more casual and less pricey, the Joia Kitchen bistro, tucked into a corner of the main restaurant (with a kitchen view!) is open for lunch and dinner Monday to Friday, with vegetarian and vegan main courses starting at 12€. Reservations are recommended for both the main restaurant and the bistro.
Via P. Castaldi 18. www.joia.it. Ⓒ **02/2952-2124.** Entrees 27€–40€. Mon–Sat noon–2:30pm and 7:30–11pm. Closed Sun. Metro: Repubblica

MODERATE

Hostaria Borromei ★★ LOMBARDY   This Milanese stalwart not far from the Duomo is known for its down-home vibe and hearty Lombardian fare (with some southern Italian dishes thrown into the mix), offering a winning experience in lively environs in a 15th-century *palazzo* once owned by the aristocratic Borromeo family. The menu features polenta, saffron risotto, the famed veal *osso bucco,* homemade pastas (such as "mamma's" tagliatelle with tomato sauce, meatballs, and peas), and plenty of seafood, all of which is presented with surprising flair. Cheeses and traditional desserts such as *tiramisu* and *panna cotta*—as well as a refreshing citrus or green-apple sorbet—round out the fare. Book in advance for weekend dining, especially for a seat in the vineyard courtyard in summer.

Via Borromei 4. www.hostariaborromei.com. ℂ **02/8645-3760.** Entrees 13€–44€. Mon–Fri 12:30–2:45pm and 7:30–10:45pm; Sat 7:30–10:45pm. Metro: Cordusio or Duomo.

Nerino Dieci Trattoria ★★ MEDITERRANEAN   You will want to call at least a month in advance for dinner reservations at this popular trattoria offering solid Italian fare at reasonable prices, especially considering its proximity to the Duomo and rest of the *centro storico.* Aside from the trendy open kitchen and neon lettering on the wall, it's laid out with plenty of cozy little corners, well suited for a romantic meal. Service is attentive. The seasonal menu changes frequently—seafood is a specialty—with creative twists on traditional dishes, such as tagliatelle pasta with red shrimp, lime, and pistachio pesto, or amberjack fillet with a side of country-style artichokes. The lunch menu, including main course, dessert, and beverage, is a steal at 9€.

Via Nerino 10. www.nerinodieci.it. ℂ **02/3983-1019.** Entrees 9€–15€. Mon–Fri noon–2:30pm and 7:30–11pm; Sat 7:30–11pm. Closed Sun. Metro: Lanza Brera.

Osteria il Kaimano ★★ NORTHERN ITALIAN   This casual, pleasantly chaotic *osteria* is a reliable pick in the artsy, cobblestoned Brera district. Strong choices include zucchini flowers stuffed with ricotta, ravioli with smoked ham and radicchio, or the Neapolitan-style pizzas that continually slide out of the wood-burning oven. Given the translated menu posted outside, it might look like a tourist trap, but the food (and abundance of locals who frequent the place) tells another story. **Nabucco** (Via Fiori Chiari 10; www.nabucco.it; ℂ **02/860-663**) is another good Brera option with a somewhat similar menu, but Kaimano wins out for its cozy atmosphere and warm service.

Via Fiori Chiari 20. ℂ **02/8050-2733.** Entrees 15€–40€. Daily noon–2:30pm and 6–11:30pm. Metro: Lanza Brera.

Pizzeria Tradizionale ★★ PIZZERIA   A solid pizzeria in the Navigli neighborhood, Pizzeria Tradizionale is a simple canalside affair with checked tablecloths, but it's always crammed and buzzing so you may want to reserve ahead of time. Happy patrons devour enormous crispy pizzas piled high with local salamis and mozzarella, as well as vast bowls of garlic-infused spaghetti alle *vongole* (clams). Though it bills itself as a pizzeria, the menu offers Neapolitan-style fish dishes as well. Service is usually fast and friendly, but not all of the wait staff speaks English. The location on the canals is great, and you can eat outside when weather permits, but the noise ratchets up as the night goes on.

Ripa di Porta Ticinese 7. www.pizzeriatradizionale.com © **02/839-5133.** Entrees 8.50€–18€. Daily noon–2:30pm and 7pm–1am (no lunch Wed). Metro: Porta Genova.

INEXPENSIVE

Berbere ★★ PIZZERIA   Traditionally, Milan has not been a pizza town—Milanese pies are typically simple, flat, and crispy—but a wave of Neapolitan-style pizzerias is changing all that, thanks to top-notch ingredients and dough that is allowed to rise overnight. One of the best new pizzerias in town, Berbere serves "artisanal pizzas" in a light and bright space in the funky Isola neighborhood (there's a second location in the Navigli district as well). Start your meal with *cicchetti* (small appetizers like pureed roasted potatoes with sautéed kale and olives) and then move on to the pizzas made from stone-ground, semi-whole-wheat flour, though there are other dough options to choose from as well. Not too thick or too thin, each pizza is perfectly chewy and airy, with interesting seasonal toppings—many of them organic—like beets, Salina capers, spicy Calabrian 'nduja sausage, *mozzarella di bufala,* or *fiordilatte mozzarella.* Round out your meal with a craft beer or organic wine.

Via Sebenico 24. www.berberepizza.it. © **02/3670-7820.** Entrees 6€–12€. Mon–Fri 7–11:30pm, Sat–Sun 12:30–2:30pm and 7–11:30pm. Metro: Isola.

Milan Shopping

Milan is known the world over as one of the temples of high fashion, with the hallowed streets **Montenapoleone** and **Spiga** in the **Quadrilatero d'Oro** being the most popular places of wallet-stripping worship. Here D&G, Prada, Gucci, Hermès, Louis Vuitton, Armani, Ralph Lauren, Versace, and Cavalli all jostle for Milan's minted fashionistas. The area around Porta Nuova (at the top of Corso Como) is also starting to become a luxury-shopping district. More reasonable shopping areas include **Via Torino** and **Corso Buenos Aires,** where midrange international brands proliferate; if you're clever you can also pick up a designer bargain at outlet store **Il Salvagente** (Via Fratelli Bronzetti 16; © **02/7611-0328**).

Fashion is one Milanese obsession, food is another, and the *centro storico* has many superb delis from which to purchase the purest of olive oils and the finest cheeses. **Peck** (Via Spadari 9; © **02/802-3161**) is still the number-one gourmet spot, although competition is keen from the **Eataly** megastore in Piazza XXV Aprile (www.eataly.it) for all Italian

Upscale shopping in Milan.

comestibles. The **top floor of the La Rinascente department store** in Piazza del Duomo (see p. 477) is another haven for foodies, with its Obika mozzarella bar and fine selection of packaged Italian goods (as an added bonus, you get a close-up view of the Duomo). Opened in 2015, the **Mercato del Duomo** (www.ilmercatodelduomo.it; © **02/8633-1924**) in Piazza del Duomo aims to be a "gourmet cathedral" directly across from the actual cathedral. It has a food market (a good place to grab focaccia or a quick lunch on the run) and various coffee bars, wine bars, aperitif spots, and a high-end restaurant.

English-language books are sold at **Feltrinelli Librerie** (corner of Piazza del Duomo and Via Ugo Foscolo 1/3), **Mondadori Megastore** (Piazza del Duomo 1), **Rizzoli** (inside the Galleria Vittorio Emanuele II, see p. 473), and the Feltrinelli Express inside Stazione Centrale. English-language newspapers can be found on most major newsstands around the *centro storico*.

MILANO MARKETS

Everybody loves a bargain, and there's no better place to find one than at the colorful, chaotic **Viale Papiniano market** (Metro: Sant'Agostino). Its sea of stalls is open Tuesday and Saturday; some flog designer seconds, others leather basics. **Flea markets** spring up on Saturdays along the

Alzaia Naviglio Grande and Fiera di Sinigaglia (metro Porta Genovafor both), and on Sundays at San Donato Metro stop. During the Christmas season, **holiday markets** (complete with ice skating) pop up in different parts of the city, from Piazza Gae Aulenti (metro Garibaldi) to the Castello Sforzesco (metro Cairoli) to the area behind the Museum of Natural History (metro Palestro) in the Giardini Pubblici Indro Montanelli. A large **food market** at the Piazza Wagner Metro is open every morning except Sunday.

Nightlife & Entertainment

Unless you're heading for the Ticinese and Navigli, Milan is a dressy city and generally looks askance at scruffy jeans and sneakers after dark. When many people don't dine until well after 10pm, it's not surprising that clubs and bars stay open until the very wee hours.

Milan has its share of glitzy clubs and cocktail bars, but most explode on the scene and disappear just as quickly. A few spots that appear to be in for the long haul include the vine-covered cocktail terrace at **10 Corso Como** (www.10corsocomo.com; ✆ 02/2901-3581), the evergreen dance club **Hollywood** (www.discotecahollywood.it; ✆ 02/6555-318), and megaclub **Plastic** at Via Gargano 15 (✆ 02/5410-0161—typically open weekends only). A newer kid on the block, **Ceresio 7 Pools & Restaurant** (www.ceresio7.com; ✆ 02/310-392-21) offers a novel setup: a chic, sleek rooftop lounge with two pools where one can enjoy a cocktail while enjoying amazing views of the city.

A venerable Milan institution, the **Conservatorio di Musica Giuseppe Verdi** has two stages for classical concerts, at Via Conservatorio 12 (www.consmilano.it; ✆ 02/762-110). And Milan is forever associated with the grand old dame of opera, **Teatro Alla Scala,** perhaps the world's favorite opera house. La Scala is decked out with sumptuous red seats, boxes adorned with gilt, and chandeliers dripping crystal. Tickets are hard to come by, so book well in advance of the opera season, which runs from December to November, with a break from late July until early September. Book online at www.teatroallascala.org, pay by phone with a credit card (✆ 02/860-77), or buy your tickets direct from La Scala's booking office in the Galleria del Sagrato, Piazza del Duomo, open daily noon to 6pm (closed Aug). The ticket office at the opera house (Via Filodrammatici 2) releases **discounted last-minute tickets** for that evening's performance 2½ hours before the curtain goes up; only one ticket can be purchased per customer.

BERGAMO ★★

47km (29 miles) northeast of Milan.

Bergamo is a city of two distinct characters. The ancient **Città Alta** is a beautiful medieval and Renaissance town perched on a green hill. **Città**

Bassa, mostly built in the 19th and 20th centuries, sits at the feet of the upper town and concerns itself with 21st-century life. Visitors tend to focus on the historic upper town, a place for wandering, soaking in the rarified atmosphere, and enjoying the lovely vistas from its belvederes.

Essentials

ARRIVING   **Trains** arrive from and depart for Milan Stazione Centrale hourly (50 min.; 5.50€). If you are **driving,** Bergamo is linked to Milan via the A4. The trip takes under an hour if traffic is good. *Note:* It's difficult to park in the largely pedestrianized Città Alta—park instead in Città Bassa and take the **funicular** (see below) up to the historic area.

VISITOR INFORMATION   The **Città Bassa tourist office** is close to the train and bus stations at Viale Papa Giovanni XXIII 57 (✆ **035/210-204**); it's open daily 9am to 12:30pm and 2 to 5:30pm. The **Città Alta office** is at Via Gombito, 13 (✆ **035/242-226**), right off Via Colleoni, and is open daily 9am to 5:30pm.

CITY LAYOUT   Piazza Vecchia, the Colleoni Chapel, and most major sights are in the **Città Alta,** which is dissected by **Via Colleoni.** To reach **Piazza Vecchia** from the funicular station at **Piazza Mercato delle Scarpi,** it's a 5-minute stroll along **Via Gombito.** The Accademia Carrara is in the Città Bassa.

GETTING AROUND   Bergamo has an efficient **bus system** that runs throughout the Città Bassa and to points around the Città Alta; tickets are 1.30€ for 75 minutes of travel and are available from the machines at the bus stops outside the train station or at the bus station opposite.

To reach the Città Alta from the train station, take bus no. 1 or 1A (clearly marked Città Alta on the front) and make the free transfer to the **Funicolare Bergamo Alta,** run by ATB Bergamo (Largo Porta Nuova; www.atb.bergamo.it), connecting the upper and lower cities. It typically runs every 7 minutes from 7am to 1:20am.

Exploring the Città Bassa

Most visitors scurry through Bergamo's lower, newer town on their way to the Città Alta, but you may want to pause long enough to explore its main thoroughfare, **Corso Sentierone,** with its mishmash of architectural styles (16th-century porticos, the Mussolini-era Palazzo di Giustizia, and two mock Doric temples); it's a pleasant place to linger over espresso at a sidewalk cafe. The **Accademia Carrara** (Piazza Giacomo Carrara 82, www.lacarrara.it; ✆ **035/234-396**) is worth a peek for its fine collection of Raphaels, Bellinis, Botticellis, and Canalettos. Città Bassa's 19th-century **Teatro Gaetano Donizetti** (Piazza Cavour 15) is the hub of Bergamo's lively cultural scene, with a fall opera season and a winter-to-spring season of dramatic performances; for details, contact the theater at ✆ **035/416-0611** (www.teatrodonizetti.it).

Lombardy & the Lake District

SWITZERLAND

TRENTINO–ALTO ADIGE

VENETO

LOMBARDY

PIEDMONT

EMILIA–ROMAGNA

Adige

Mincio

Po

Oglio

Serio

Adda

Tieino

Po

Sesia

Cervo

L. Maggiore

L. Lugana

L. Como

L. d'Iseo

Lake Garda

Largo d'Isola

Schio
Valdagno
Verona
Ostiglia
San Benedetto Po
To Modera & Bologna
Guastalla
Mantua (Mantova)
To Parma
Asola
Casalmaggiore
Arco
Riva del Garda
Limone sul Garda
Rocca Scaligera
Sirmione
Gardone Riviera
Salò
Desenzano del Garda
Darfo Boario Terme
Brescia
Leno
Verolanuova
Cremona
Darfo
Rovato
Chiari
Soresina
Piacenza
Seriate
Palazzolo
Crema
Codogno
Broni
Sondrio
Bergamo
Treviglio
Lodi
Pavia
Voghera
Chiavenna
Bellano
Varenna
Bellagio
Lecco
Erba
Certosa di Pavia
Tremezzo
Lenno
Cernobbio
Como
Cantù
Saronno
Seregno
Monza
Melegnano
To tona
Loca°no
Lugano
Luinc
Sta. Caterna del Sasso Baliaro
Sasso del Fero
Varese
Legnano
Pho
Milan (Milano)
Abbiategrasso
Vigevano
Verbania
Stresa
Isole Borromee
Arona
Gallarate
Busto Arsizio
Mortara
Novara
Alessandria
Domodossola
Biella
Vercelli
To Turin
Casale Monferrato
Asti

SS46
A4
SR10
A22
SS434
A22
SS62
SS45
SS236
SS420
A21
SS235
SS10
SS415
A1
SS42
A4
SS42
SS233
SS38
SS36
A9
A4
SS596
A7
SS221
A21
A26
SS299
A26
SS142
E62

Milan
Venice
Rome

20 mi
20 km

Exploring the Città Alta

Crammed with *palazzi,* monuments, and churches, the Città Alta centers on two hauntingly beautiful adjoining squares, **the piazzas Vecchia** and **del Duomo.** Bergamasco strongman Bartolomeo Colleoni (below) gave his name to the Città Alta's delightful main street, cobblestoned and so narrow you can almost touch the buildings on either side in places. It's lined with swank shoe shops, posh delis, and classy confectioners.

The **Piazza Vecchia** looks like a set for one of local son Gaetano Donizetti's operas. This hauntingly beautiful square was the hub of Bergamo's political and civic life from medieval times. The 12th-century **Palazzo della Ragione** (Court of Justice) was built by the Venetians; its graceful arcades are embellished with the Lion of Saint Mark, symbol of the Venetian Republic, visible above the tiny 16th-century balcony and reached by a covered staircase to the right of the palace. Across the piazza is the **Biblioteca Civica (Public Library).**

Walk through the archways of the Palazzo della Ragione to reach **Piazza del Duomo** and the **Basilica di Santa Maria Maggiore ★★** (www.fondazionemia.it; ✆ 035/223-327). The basilica itself is entered through an ornate portico supported by Venetian lions; the interior is a masterpiece of baroque giltwork hung with Renaissance tapestries. Bergamo native Gaetano Donizetti, the popular composer, is entombed here in a marble sarcophagus that's as excessive as the rest of the church. The oft-forgotten Tempietto of Santa Croce, tucked to the left of the basilica entrance, is worth seeking out for its endearing fresco fragments of "The Last Supper." The basilica is open Tuesday to Saturday 9am to 12:30pm and 2:30 to 6pm (it closes at 5pm November through March); from April through October it's also open Sunday 9am to 1pm and 3 to 6pm. Mass is held at 10am during the week and 11am on weekends. Admission is free.

Most impressive, however, is the **Cappella Colleoni ★★★** (Piazza del Duomo; ✆ **035/210-061;** free admission), to the right of the basilica doors and entered through a highly elaborate pink-and-white marble facade. Bartolomeo Colleoni was a Bergamasco *condottiero* (mercenary) who fought for the Venetians. As a reward for his loyalty, he was given Bergamo as his own private fiefdom in 1455. His elaborate funerary chapel was designed by Giovanni Antonio Amadeo, who created the Certosa di Pavia (see p. 483). Colleoni lies beneath a ceiling frescoed by Tiepolo and surrounded by statuary. Cappella Colleoni is open March to October daily 9am to 12:30pm and 2 to 6:30pm; and November to February Tuesday to Sunday 9am to 12:30pm and 2 to 4:30pm.

Where to Stay & Eat in Bergamo

The charms of Bergamo's Città Alta are no secret, and hotel rooms are in great demand over the summer, so make reservations well in advance. If you're staying in Milan, the city is an easy hour's journey from Stazione Centrale, making it a perfect day trip.

Al Donizetti ★ CAFE   This *enoteca* (wine bar) and restaurant in the heart of Bergamo Alta was previously a historic pastry shop, as evidenced by the faded Pasticceria Donizetti lettering on the wall above the door. These days, you are more likely to find polenta or a *passito* (raisin wine) on the menu, but Al Donizetti is still a draw for locals and tourists alike for an *aperitivo,* a simple meal of wine with a charcuterie platter, or heartier fare like pumpkin gnocchi in cheese sauce or the Donizetti-style "maxi hamburger." They are incredibly knowledgeable about wine here, but if budget is a concern, make sure to ask about prices before agreeing to a recommended bottle so as to avoid sticker shock. Sit inside and enjoy rustic elegance or opt for the romantic atmosphere outside under the large porticos, perfect for watching people stroll by on the main drag.
Via Gombito 17a. ℂ **035/242-661.** Entrees 12€–30€. Open Wed–Mon 11am–11pm.

Caffè del Tasso ★ CAFE   This charming spot on Città Alta's atmospheric main piazza has been in business since 1476, making it one of the oldest establishments of its kind in Italy. Today it has the rather cozy air of a 1950s teashop, but service is smart, and they're generous with the *aperitivo* snacks. Come for a meal (the eggplant parmesan and polenta with porcini mushrooms are popular) or stop in for coffee or tea and pastries. An early evening drink at one of the outdoor tables on the square on a warm night is truly heavenly, and if you're in the mood for a cold treat, the gelateria next door does a brisk trade in summer.
Piazza Vecchia 3. ℂ **035/237-966.** Entrees 12€–18€. Open daily 8am–midnight.

Hotel Piazza Vecchio ★★   Just steps from the Piazza Vecchio in the historic Città Alta, this ancient townhouse features stone walls and beamed ceilings. Rooms are all simply furnished, but each has brightly colored details and a sleek new bathroom. Quieter rooms at the back of the hotel overlook a labyrinth of alleyways and rooftops. The charming breakfast room has colorful walls and the same traditional beamed ceilings as in some guest rooms. In addition to homemade cakes and croissants, breakfast foods also include cheeses and other farm-to-table products from a local *agriturismo.*
Via Colleoni 3. www.hotelpiazzavecchia.it. ℂ **035/253-179.** 13 units. 150€–310€ double. Rates include breakfast. **Amenities:** Wi-Fi (free).

MANTUA (MANTOVA) ★★★

158km (98 miles) E of Milan, 62km (38 miles) N of Parma, 150km (93 miles) SW of Venice

One of Lombardy's best-kept secrets, Mantua is in the eastern reaches of the region, making it a fairly easy side trip from Milan. Like its neighboring cities in Emilia-Romagna, Mantua owes its handsome Renaissance monuments to one family, in this case the Gonzagas, who conquered the city in 1328 and ruled benevolently until 1707. Avid collectors of art, the

Gonzagas ruled through the greatest centuries of Italian art, and today you can encounter their treasures in the **Palazzo Ducale;** in their summer retreat, the **Palazzo Te;** and in the churches and piazzas that grew up around their court.

Essentials

ARRIVING   Six direct **trains** depart daily from Milan Stazione Centrale (1 hr. 50 min.; 11.50€). There are nine daily trains from Verona (30–40 min.; 4.20€).

The speediest **highway** connections from Milan are via the A4 autostrada to Verona, then the A22 from Verona to Mantua (about 2 hrs.).

VISITOR INFORMATION   The **tourist office** at Piazza Mantegna 6 (www.turismo.mantova.it; 🕻 **0376/432-432**) is open on weekends from 9am to 5pm; during the week, hours are 9am to 1:30pm and 2:30 to 5pm (until 6pm in spring and summer). It's just to the right of the basilica of Sant'Andrea.

CITY LAYOUT   Mantua is tucked onto a fat finger of land surrounded on three sides by the **Mincio River,** which widens into a series of lakes, prosaically named **Lago Superiore, Lago di Mezzo,** and **Lago Inferiore.** Most sights are within an easy walk of one another in the compact center, which is a 15-minute walk northwards from the lakeside train station.

Exploring Mantua

Mantua is a place for wandering along arcaded streets and through cobbled squares with handsomely proportioned churches and *palazzi.*

The southernmost of these squares is **Piazza delle Erbe** (Square of the Herbs) ★, so named for its produce-and-food market. Mantua's civic might is clustered here in a series of late-medieval and early Renaissance structures that include the **Palazzo della Ragione** (Courts of Justice) and **Palazzo del Podestà** (Mayor's Palace) from the 12th and 13th centuries, and the **Torre dell'Orologio,** topped with a 14th-century astrological clock. Also on this square is Mantua's earliest religious structure, the **Rotonda di San Lorenzo,** a miniature round church from the 11th century. The city's Renaissance masterpiece, **Basilica di Sant'Andrea** (see p. 497), is off to one side on Piazza Mantegna.

To the north, Piazza delle Erbe transforms into **Piazza Broletto** through a series of arcades; here a statue honors the poet Virgil, who was born in Mantua in 70 B.C. The next square, **Piazza Sordello,** is vast, cobbled, rectangular, and lined with medieval *palazzi* and the 13th-century Duomo. Most notable is the massive hulk of the **Palazzo Ducale** (see p. 412), which forms the eastern wall of the piazza. To enjoy Mantua's lakeside views and walks, follow Via San Giorgio from the **Piazza Sordello** and turn right on to Lungolago dei Gonzaga, which leads back into the town center.

Tip: If you're spending more than a few hours in Mantua, you may want to consider getting the **Mantova Sabbioneta Card** (home.mantova-card.it) which allows discounted or free access to 17 city museums plus several others in outlying Sabbioneta, as well as free bus transportation and bike sharing. Valid for 72 hours, it costs 20€ (8€ for ages 12 to 18). Just about all of the museums listed in this guide honor the card.

Basilica di Sant'Andrea ★★ CHURCH A graceful Renaissance facade fronts this 15th-century church by architect Leon Battista Alberti. The grandest church in Mantua, it is topped by a dome added by Filippo Juvarra in the 18th century. Inside, the vast classically proportioned space is centered on the church's single aisle. Light pours in through the dome, highlighting the carefully crafted *trompe l'oeil* painting of the coffered ceiling. The Gonzagas' court painter Andrea Mantegna—creator of the Camera degli Sposi in the **Palazzo Ducale** (see below)—is buried in the first chapel on the left. The crypt houses a reliquary containing the blood of Christ, which was allegedly brought here by Longinus, the Roman soldier who thrust his spear into Jesus's side; this is processed through town on March 18, the feast of Mantua's patron, Sant'Anselmo.

Piazza Mantegna. www.santandreainmantova.it. Free. Daily 8am–noon and 3–7pm.

Museo di Palazzo Ducale ★★ PALACE The massive power base of the Gonzaga dynasty spreads over the northeast corner of Mantua, incorporating Piazza Sordello, the Duomo, Castello San Giorgio, and the Palazzo Ducale. Together they form a private city connected by corridors, courtyards, and staircases filled with Renaissance frescoes and ancient Roman sculptures. Within the walls of this fortress-cum-family-palace lies the history of Mantua's most powerful family and what remains of the treasure trove they amassed over the centuries. Between their skills as warriors and a knack for marrying into wealthier houses, the Gonzagas acquired power, money, and the services of some of the top artists of the time, including Pisanello, Titian, and Mantegna.

The most fortunate of many opportunistic unions was in 1490, between Francesco II Gonzaga and aristocratic Isabella d'Este from Ferrara. She commissioned many of the complex's art-filled apartments.

The Palazzo Ducale offers up a glorious maze of gilded, frescoed, marbled rooms, passageways, secret gardens, follies, and elaborate *intaglio* furniture. Standouts include the Arthurian legends adorning **the Sala del Pisanello,** painted by Pisanello between 1436 and 1444; the **Sale degli Arazzi** (Tapestry Rooms) hung with copies of Raphael's tapestries in the Vatican; the **Galleria degli Specchi** (Hall of Mirrors); **Appartamento dei Nani** (Apartments of the Dwarfs), with its miniature replica of the Holy Staircase in the Vatican; and the **Galleria dei Mesi** (Hall of the Months). In the north tower of the Castello San Giorgio, don't miss the incomparable **Camera degli Sposi,** the masterpiece of Andrea Mantegna, who took 9 years to complete it. Commissioned by Ludovico III Gonzaga, it features portraits of members of his family, providing an intriguing glimpse into late 15th-century court life. (*Tip:* Admission to the Camera degli Sposi is limited, so **reserve a time slot for visiting it when you buy your tickets.**)

Piazza Sordello, 40. www.mantovaducale.beniculturali.it. ℂ **0376/224-832.** 13€ for the Castello San Giorgio, Corte Vecchia, and Freddi Collection; 7.50€ for the Corte Vecchia and apartment of Isabella d'Este. All free on 1st Sun every month. Tues–Sun 8:15am–7:15pm. Last entry 6:20pm.

Palazzo Te ★★ PALACE   A 20-minute walk from the historic center along Via Principe Amedeo, this glorious Renaissance summer palace, designed by Giulio Romano between 1525 and 1535, was built for Federico II Gonzaga, the sybaritic son of Isabella d'Este. As his retreat from court life, it was designed to indulge his obsessions. A series of lavishly adorned apartments, decorated by the best artists of the day, reveal Gonzaga's enthusiasms for love and sex, astrology, and horses, from the almost 3-D effect in the **Hall of the Horses** to erotic frescoes by Romano in the elaborate **Chamber of Amor and Psyche.** The greatest room in the palace, however, is a metaphor for Gonzaga power: In the **Sala dei Giganti** (Room of the Giants), Titan is overthrown by the gods in a dizzying display of *trompe l'oeil* painting that surrounds the viewer on all sides

Frescoed ceilings in Mantua's Palazzo Te.

(and overhead!). The Palazzo Te is also home to the **Museo Civico,** whose collections include the Gonzaga family's coins, medallions, 20th-century portraits by Armando Spadini, and a few Egyptian artifacts.

Viale Te 13. www.palazzote.it. ℃ **0376/323-266.** 12€ adults, 8€ seniors, 4€ ages 12–18 and students, free for ages 11 and under. Mon 1–6:30pm; Tues–Sun 9am–6:30pm (hours may be extended in summer).

MORE MANTUA MUSEUMS

En route from the center of town to Palazzo Te, you'll pass **Casa del Mantegna ★,** the house and studio of Andrea Mantegna, now an art gallery (Via Acerbi 47, ℃ **0376/360-506;** admission free; Tues–Sun 10am–1pm, Tues–Wed and Sat–Sun 3–6pm). Close by, in the stark white Palazzo Sebastiano, the **Museo della Città ★** (Largo XXIV Maggio 12; www.museodellacitta.mn.it; ℃ **0376/367-087;** admission 12€; Mon 1–6pm, Tues–Sun 9am–6pm) gallops through the history of Mantua. Among its many architectural fragments is an impressive bust of Francesco Gonzaga, who commissioned the palace in 1507.

Just to the left of the Palazzo Ducale's main entrance, in the old market hall at the corner of Piazza Sordello, the **Museo Archeologico Nazionale di Mantova** houses in one giant space all sorts of local discoveries of Bronze Age, Greek, Etruscan, and Roman pottery, glassware, and utensils (www.museoarcheologicomantova.beniculturali.it; ℃ **0376/320-003;** admission 4€, ages 17 and under free; Apr–Oct Tues, Thurs, Sat 2–7pm, Wed, Fri, Sun 8:30am–1:30pm; Nov–Mar Tues–Sun 8:30am–1:30pm).

The lovely baroque interior of the **Teatro Bibiena ★★** is also worth a peek for its rows of luxurious theater boxes. Find it at Via Accademia 47 (℃ **0376/327-653;** admission 2€, 17 and under free; Tues–Sun 10am–1pm and 3–6pm, plus Sat–Sun 10am–6pm mid-Mar to mid-Nov).

For a change of pace, the **Galleria Storica dei Vigili del Fuoco** (Fire Engine Museum) **★** at Largo Vigili del Fuoco 1 (www.museovigilidelfuoco.it; ℃ **0376/227-71;** admission free) has plenty of historic engines on display. Call beforehand to check open hours, which are usually on weekends.

Where to Stay in Mantua

Like Milan, Mantua sees many expense-account business travelers during the week, with families and tourists flocking in for the weekends and over summer, so book rooms in the town center well ahead of time.

Casa Poli ★★★   Hidden behind the facade of a 19th-century mansion, this bijou boutique hotel is packed nightly with both business and leisure travelers. It's easy to see why. Spotless guest rooms have a chic minimalist style, with parquet floors, funky lights, and equally cool bathrooms. Superior rooms are slightly larger, and there are triple rooms available. The hotel aims to offer the "comfort of a home and the elegance of a hotel" and so the lounge is full of arty books, and the summer courtyard is a great spot for an evening *aperitivo*. But it's the staff that really makes this place shine; they're chatty and informal, and willing to go the extra mile to please guests. It is located about 15 minutes from the center on foot on a well-trafficked street that leads out of town.

Corso Garibaldi 32. www.hotelcasapoli.it. © **0376/288-170.** 27 units. 115€–170€ double. Rates include breakfast. **Amenities:** Bar; concierge; Wi-Fi (free).

Residenza Bibiena ★★   Located on a pretty corner of Mantua's *centro storico* 5 minutes from the Palazzo Ducale, this cozy B&B in a traditional terracotta townhouse has a pleasing old-school charm. Warm color schemes and pretty linens enliven simple rooms with wooden furniture and tile floors. Sizeable family rooms are available, boasting especially large bathrooms for Italian standards. There are four additional rooms at the Residenza Bibiena Deluxe (featuring slightly more modern accommodations) a few doors down toward the lake at Piazza Arche 8. Some of the rooms in these two properties have terraces and even lake views. Keep in mind that the properties are located at one of the main streets leading into the city so traffic noise may be an issue.

Piazza Arche, 5. www.residenzabibiena.it. © **331/508-0876.** 8 units (incl. both properties). 80€ double. Rates include breakfast. **Amenities:** Wi-Fi (free).

Where to Eat in Mantua

Caffè Modi ★ ITALIAN   Named for the artist Amedeo Modigliani, whose moody portrait dominates the restaurant, Modi is a friendly stop on the tourist circuit around Piazza Sordello and the San Giorgio castle. Chill music, gramophones, and threadbare armchairs lend a bohemian charm to the place. The menu offers the usual lineup of local pasta dishes (like pumpkin tortellini in a butter sage sauce) along with *insalatone* (big salads), but it's all well-presented and tasty. Concerts and recitals are held here from time to time. In warm weather, grab a table outside where you can even glimpse views of the water. If you aren't in the mood for a big meal, you can snack on sandwiches, *piadine* (flatbread sandwiches), and *pizzette* (mini pizzas).

Via San Giorgio 4. © **0376/181-0111.** Entrees 10€–17€. Wed–Mon noon–midnight, sometimes later on weekends.

Lo Scalco Grasso ★★ MODERN ITALIAN   This contemporary bistro with minimalist decor likes to push boundaries. It's a sophisticated choice, offering beautifully crafted dishes featuring vegetables—local pasta stuffed with squash, delicate risotto, or perhaps a superb chickpea soup flavored with squid—alongside menu items like a savory "tiramisu" with codfish, or polenta served with stewed donkey or beef cheeks. The tasting menu, 45€, includes a welcome glass of spumante, an appetizer, a first course (like a pasta or risotto), and a second course (meat or fish). Lovely wines are available by the glass or bottle, and little bites of specialties are happily produced for guests to sample before ordering. It's a small space, so reservations are recommended. The restaurant is about a 10-minute walk from the very center of town.

Via Trieste 55. ℂ **349/374-7958.** Entrees 15€–20€. Tues–Sat noon–2pm and 7:30–10pm; Sun noon–2pm; Mon 7:30–10pm (later on weekends).

Osteria dell'Oca ★★★ LOMBARDY   The restaurant "of the goose" is crammed nightly with locals enjoying vibrant cooking at excellent prices. This is a rustic family-run Italian *osteria* at its very best: noisy, happy, and joyous. Some of the best dishes on the menu involve sharing plates of *peccati di gola* ("delectable delights"), local salamis and pancetta with a wedge of creamy polenta, lard, and beetroot salsa. If you are looking for true local specialties, try the pumpkin pasta with butter and sage; "drunken" risotto with lambrusco wine and toasted pancetta; or *tagliatelle alla baffo*, pasta with beans and sausage, based on a family recipe. Only three wines are served, in thick carafes. Opt for the white from local vineyards rather than the *lambrusco,* which is quite sweet. This generous outpouring of food ends with complimentary coffees and a thick hazelnut *digestivo della casa* liqueur. Book ahead for a weekend table. The restaurant is about a 10-minute walk from the center along a busy road that leads out of town. Call ahead for reservations or you may not find a table or will be forced to dine on the late side.

Via Trieste 10. www.osteriadelloca.it. ℂ **0376/327-171.** Entrees 12€–17€. Wed–Sat and Mon 12:15–2:30pm and 7:15–11:30pm; Sun 12:15–2:30pm.

Mantua Shopping & Entertainment

The favored shopping streets in Mantua radiate off Piazza delle Erbe, a delightful cluster of cobbled and arcaded streets sheltering delis stuffed with local cheeses, hams, fresh pasta, and olive oils. **Corso Umberto, Via Verdi,** and **Via Oberdan** are lined with posh boutiques, smart shoe shops, and bookstores. There's a **farmers' market** on Lungorio IV di Novembre on Saturday, perfect fodder for a picnic in the lakeside gardens along Lungolago dei Gonzaga.

Mantua is a cultured city with ample theater and classical concerts; there are regular recitals at cute little 'Teatro Biblena (see p. 499) and a full program of films and concerts at **Mantova Teatro** in the Piazza Cavallotti (www.teatrosocialemantova.it). A chamber-music festival is held every May, and the **Festivaletteratura** literature festival is a popular draw in September.

LAKE COMO ★★★

Como (town): 65km (40 miles) NE of Milan; Menaggio: 35km (22 miles) NE of Como and 85km (53 miles) N of Milan; Varenna: 50km (31 miles) NE of Como and 80km (50 miles) NE of Milan

Life is slower around the northern Italian lakes than in fast-paced Milan. The city of Como is an ideal base for drawing breath and kicking back.

Sitting on the southwestern tip of Lake Como, the city is essentially a center of commerce with a miniscule medieval quarter and a pretty waterfront. Tourists flock to Como for its ancient heritage, fine churches, and lake views. From here, frequent ferry service hops around the lake, visiting its many romantic lakeshore villas and villages.

Essentials

ARRIVING   Trains run from Milan's Stazione Central and Porta Garibaldi half-hourly to Como San Giovanni; the trip takes 1 hour and costs 4.80€. One-hour trains from Milan Cadorna arrive at Como Nord Lago (just off the lakefront promenade, near the ferry point) and cost 4.80€.

VISITOR INFORMATION   The **regional tourist office** at Piazza Cavour 17 (www.lakecomo.com; *②* **031/269-712**) has info on hotels, restaurants, and campgrounds around the lake. The office is open Monday to Saturday 9am to 1pm and 2 to 5pm. You'll also find tourist offices open in summer in several of the small towns around the lake; in **Tremezzo** at Via Regina 3 (*②* **0344/40-493**); in **Varenna** at Via IV Novembre 7 (www.varenna turismo.com; *②* **0341/830-367**); and in **Bellaggio** at Piazza Mazzini (www.bellagiolakecomo.com; *②* **0341/950-204**).

Getting Around   Como is the jumping-off point for most adventures on Lake Como, which is criss-crossed by regular **ferry routes:** It takes 4 hours to travel from one end to the other, with many stops along the way. The most popular are **Tremezzo, Menaggio, Bellagio,** and timeless **Varenna**. Single fares from Como are 10.40€ to Bellagio; a day pass costs 23.30€. Tickets cannot be purchased online. The ferry terminal, run by **Navigazione Lago di Como,** is on the esplanade at Via per Cernobbio 18 (www.navigazionelaghi.it; *②* **800/551-801**).

Exploring Como ★★

Como's tiny *centro storico* is dominated by the flamboyant **Duomo ★★** (Piazza Duomo; www.cattedraledicomo.it; *②* **031/331-2275**), which combines Gothic and Renaissance architecture for two very different facades; long, narrow windows and a Gothic stained-glass rose window mark the western end, with an apse and baroque dome added in 1744 by architect Filippo Juvarra at the eastern end. The Duomo is free, and open daily 7:30am to 7:30pm (Sunday until 9:30pm).

Two blocks south of the Duomo, the 12th-century **San Fedele ★** basilica (www.parrocchiasanfedelecomo.it; free admission; daily 8am–noon, 3:30–7pm) stands above a charming square of the same name. Parts of the five-sided church, including the altar, date from the 6th century, and there are some fine frescoes along the right-hand side aisle.

Como's main street, **Corso Vittorio Emanuele II,** cuts through the medieval quarter and has plenty of upmarket boutiques and classy delis. If you have time, take the 10-minute **funicular ride** from Lungo Lario

Trieste up to hilltop **Brunate ★★,** which has a cluster of excellent restaurants and bars. The funicular runs up a steep cliffside, with glorious views of Lake Como glinting below; at the top are wooded hiking trails that lead north to Bellagio. The funicular ticket office is at Piazza de Gasperi 4 (www.funicolarecomo.it; ✆ **031/303-608;** daily 6am–10:30pm; funicular runs until midnight on Sat and in summer). Tickets are 3€ adults, 2€ for kids under 12 (children under 110cm in height travel free). Trains depart from both ends of the line every 30 minutes.

Exploring Around Lake Como

The romantic waterfront villages of Lake Como, with their cute clusters of yellow and pink houses, majestic *palazzos,* and lush lakeside gardens, are easily explored by ferry (see p. 502) or by car. Here are a few of the highlights, going clockwise round the lake from Como.

LENNO ★★★   For centuries Lake Como was the playground of privileged Lombardian aristocrats, and quite honestly, not much has changed. **Villa del Balbianello** at Lenno (Via Comoedia 5; www.visitfai.it/villadel-balbianello; ✆ **0344/56-110**) is one of the best-known of their fabulous villas, with ornate landscaped gardens and a 16th-century palace sitting high on a peninsula over the lake. (You may recognize it from its recent brush with fame in the Bond movie *Casino Royale.*) The interior is full of priceless French furniture complemented by eclectic artwork from the travels of its former owner, explorer Guido Monzino, who died in 1988 and left the villa to the Italian National Trust. Garden entrance is 10€ adults, 5€ children 4 to 12; garden and villa (with compulsory 60-minute tour) is 20€ adults, 10€ children 4 to 12. It's open mid-March to mid-November 10am to 6pm (closed Mon and Wed). It is a bit of a walk to reach the villa from the center of Lenno, so if you'd like to take a taxi boat from Lenno and be let out right at the villa's dock, the fare is about 8€ roundtrip.

TREMEZZO ★★   On the western side of Lake Como, Tremezzo was the 19th-century retreat of the Italian aristocracy; today it is lorded over by the exceptionally expensive **Grand Hotel Tremezzo** (www.grandhotel-tremezzo.com; ✆ **0344/42-491**) and its wonderfully stylish beach. The plush gardens, museum, and rich art collections of the ornate 17th-century **Villa Carlotta** are open to the public (Via Regina 2; www.villacarlotta.it; ✆ **0344/404-05**). Admission is 10€ adults, 8€ seniors, 5€ students; it's open late March to mid-October 9am–7:30pm (last entry 6pm); late October to mid-March 10am–6pm (last entry 5pm), though hours can vary over holiday weekends.

BELLANO ★   Most people stop in Bellano on the eastern shore of Lake Como to visit the **Orrido** (✆ **334/377-4966;** 4€ adults, 3.50€ seniors and children 6 to 12, children under 6 free), a deep gorge cut out of the cliffs by the River Pioverna as it tears down the hillside. A nighttime trip down the floodlit gorge is a rare and eerie treat, and one that appears to be under threat from hydroelectric plans expected to reduce the flow of the torrent. Opening times vary seasonally but are roughly April to June and September 10am to 1pm and 2:30 to 7pm; and July to August 10am to 7pm and 8:45 to 10pm.

VARENNA ★★★ Adorable Varenna gives Bellagio a run for its money as the prettiest village on Lake Como, with a tumble of pink and terracotta houses in a labyrinth of narrow, cobbled streets, and smart villas clustered around the shoreline. Its winding lakeside path hangs over the water, with bars, shops, and art galleries looking over the lake. Linger a while over a glass of Prosecco and watch the sun go down over the glittering water.

BELLAGIO ★★★ Photogenic Bellagio is the most popular destination around Lake Como yet has so far avoided becoming too overtly touristic. The shady lakefront promenade is lined with chic hotels, bars, and cafes. Pretty medieval alleyways ascend from the lake in steep steps and are lined with souvenir stores selling pricey handmade leather accessories. Regardless of the multitude of tourists, this is still a lovely place to linger for lunch overlooking the lake.

Where to Stay & Eat Around Lake Como

For such a popular destination, Como town suffers from a shortage of decent moderately priced hotels, although there are still plenty of options around the lake. If you're looking for a splurge, Cernobbio is home to one of Italy's most exclusive and expensive hotels, the **Villa d'Este** (see p. 506). The local cuisine draws heavily on the lake, and polenta is as popular here as pasta.

Varenna, one of Lake Como's charming villages.

Hotel du Lac ★★ With one entrance on Varenna's charming waterfront and the other hidden away in its equally photogenic tangle of alleyways, the Hotel du Lac is housed in an elegant 19th-century villa offering prized views across Lake Como. The inside of the property has been renovated in a romantic fashion, with marble pillars and wrought-iron staircases. Each of the 16 rooms has been individually decorated, but they all follow a common theme and are quite spacious (for Europe), with modern bathrooms. Enjoy creative Italian cuisine on the outdoor terrace—chef Alessandro changes the menu weekly based on what is fresh.

Via del Prestino 11, Varenna. www.albergodulac.com. ℂ **0341/830-238.** 16 units. Doubles 185€–285€. Rates include breakfast. Closed mid-Nov–Feb. **Amenities:** Restaurant (lunch only); bar; Wi-Fi (free).

Hotel Paradiso sul Lago ★★★

This great family-run property is powered by solar panels, making it one of the first eco-hotels around Lake Como. Located in a little *piazza* at the top of the village of Brunate above Como town, it offers amazing hilltop views from the breakfast room and a panoramic terrace with swimming pool and

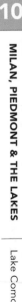

The colorful streets of Bellagio.

Jacuzzi. Some of the simple, clean, functional guest rooms also have great lake views, and there are triple and quadruple family rooms for larger groups traveling together. The drive up the hill on the narrow road is a bit tricky, but you can always take the cable car. Check out the **Mama Gina** café and bistro for a full meal or a sunset cocktail and snacks.

Via Scalini 7, Brunate. www.hotelparadisocomo.com. ℂ **031/364-099.** 12 units. 120€–169€ double, Rates include breakfast. **Amenities:** Restaurant; cafe; bar; outdoor pool; shuttle service; Wi-Fi (free).

Locanda Barbarasso ★★★ MEDITERRANEAN/PIZZERIA

This cozy *locanda* tucked away on a side street off of medieval Piazza San Fedele in the *centro storico* serves artfully presented seafood dishes and regional specialties—including typical dishes from the nearby mountains—as well as crispy pizzas. From outside, it may not look like much, but inside is light and bright with graceful arches and gray stone walls. Try the red-white-and-green risotto with cherry tomatoes, stracciatella cheese, and pesto. Reservations are recommended.

Via Odescalchi 10/12, Como. www.locandabarbarossa.it. ℂ **031/275-3421.** Entrees 8€–20€. Tues–Sun 12:30–2:30pm and 7–11:30pm; closed Mon.

Nest on the Lake ★★

This cute little B&B on the shores of Lake Como is in Lezzeno, a tranquil town just down the road from Bellagio. Bedrooms are in shades of calming pastels, some with four-poster beds, and all have wrought-iron balconies. Continental breakfast is served in a delightful room on the ground floor with stone walls, and owners Raffa and Costantino are always at the ready to recommend restaurants and organize activities. The location midway up the lake makes it a great base for hiking, waterskiing, and wakeboarding. In summer there's a 3-night minimum stay. A self-catering apartment for up to four people is also available.

Via Sostra 17/19, Lezzeno. www.nestonthelake.com. © **031/914-372.** 5 units. 100–110€ double, 120€–140€ apartment. Rates include breakfast. **Amenities:** Solarium; Wi-Fi (free).

La Polenteria ★★★ REGIONAL ITALIAN   While most people associate polenta with hearty winter fare, La Polenteria aims to highlight whatever is season, such as chestnuts and porcini mushrooms in the fall or snails and fresh fish from the lake in spring. There are also a few pasta dishes on the menu. Vegetarians, however, may have a hard time here beyond the polenta, an occasional soup, or pasta with tomato sauce. All desserts are homemade. Only open on weekends, this off-the-beaten-path restaurant is often full, so reserve in advance before you trek up here. The funicular from Como takes you up to Brunate and then you either have to walk or take the bus in the direction of the Faro Voltiano lighthouse.

Via Scalini, 66, Brunate. www.lapolenteria.it. © **031/336-5105.** Entrees 10€–30€. Fri 7:15–10:30pm, Sat–Sun 12:15pm–2:30pm, 7:30–10:30pm.

Splendide Ristorante ★★★ REGIONAL ITALIAN   You would be hard pressed to find a prettier spot on the whole of Lake Como than the geranium-filled terrace of the Hotel Excelsior Splendide in Bellagio as boats pull into the port. Perched over the shimmering waters of the lake, the restaurant concentrates on good local dishes, from polentas and pasta to prawns sizzled in garlic, and fresh lake trout. If you are looking for a quick meal, coffee, or gelato, you can also stop in at the hotel's lounges, which have the same wonderful views from the panoramic veranda.

Via Lungo Lario Manzoni 28, Bellagio. www.hsplendide.com. © **031/950-225.** Entrees 10€–40€. Mar–Nov noon–2:30pm.

Villa d'Este ★★   This Renaissance *palazzo* dating from 1568 was once home to aristocrats and saw princes, princesses, and sultans pass through its gates. Today, a constant procession of major celebs and minor royalty arrive by speedboat or helicopter to luxuriate in what this resort has to offer. Villa d'Este is quintessential Lake Como, overlooking the water amid verdant parklands. It boasts an array of sports facilities, a selection of fine-dining options (guests are expected to dress elegantly for dinner), and refined rooms furnished with priceless antiques. As befits one of the most exclusive hotels in the world, two private villas guarantee complete seclusion from the masses.

Via Regina 40, Cernobbio. www.villadeste.com. © **031/3481.** 152 units. 500€–760€ double; 880€–990€ jr suite. Rates include breakfast. Closed mid-Nov–mid-Mar. **Amenities:** 3 restaurants; 3 bars; nightclub; indoor and outdoor pools; spa; concierge; Wi-Fi (free).

LAKE MAGGIORE ★★

Stresa: 90km (56 miles) NW of Milan

Maggiore lies west of Como, a long, thin wisp of a lake protected by mountains and fed by the River Ticino, which flows on to Milan. Roughly a quarter of the northern section of the lake stands in Switzerland, including the city of Locarno and its delightful satellite resort of Ascona. **Stresa** is the largest town on the Italian side, a timeless resort on the western shoreline, famed for its setting opposite the **Isole Borromee** islands (see p. 508). Regular **ferries** span Maggiore, with frequent stops on the way from **Arona,** south of Stresa; two of the most popular stops are at **Luino,** known for its massive street market every Wednesday, and **Laveno,** which offers cable-car rides up to mountain peaks.

Essentials

ARRIVING   Stresa is linked with Milan Stazione Centrale and Porta Garibaldi by 20 **trains** a day. Journeys take about an hour and cost 8.60€. **Boats** arrive at and depart from Piazza Marconi, Stresa. Many lakeside spots can be reached from Stresa, with most boats on the lake operated by

Isola Bella, Lake Maggiore.

Navigazione Laghi (www.navlaghi.it; ✆ **800/551-801**). The main ferry office, however, is at the lake's southern tip in Arona, at Viale Baracca 1; from there, ferries to Stresa take 40 minutes and cost 6.20€.

By **car,** take the A8 west from Milan to Sesto Calende, near the south end of the lake; from there, follow Route SS33 up the western shore to Stresa. The trip takes just over an hour, but much longer in summer traffic.

VISITOR INFORMATION   Stresa's **tourist office,** at the ferry dock on Piazza Marconi (www.stresaturismo.it; ✆ **0323/-301-50**), is open daily 10am to 12:30pm and 3 to 6:30pm (mid-Oct to mid-Mar closed Sat afternoons and Sun).

Exploring Stresa & the Islands

The biggest town on the Italian side of Maggiore, elegant Stresa is the springboard to the Isole Borromee (Borromean Islands), the tiny baroque jewels of the lake. Now a genteel tourist town, Stresa captured the hearts of 19th-century aristocracy, who settled in grandiose villas strung along the promenade. Just back into the tangle of medieval streets, **Piazza Cadorna** is a mass of restaurants that spill out into the center of the square in summer. There's a food and craft market on summer Thursday afternoons on the promenade, and a lido and beach club on the lakefront.

The three **Isole Borromee** (www.isoleborromee.it) are named for the aristocratic Borromeo family (see box p. 509), who've owned them since the 12th century. Public **ferries** leave for the islands every half-hour from Stresa's Piazza Marconi.

ISOLA DEI PESCATORI ★★   Pescatori is stuck in a medieval time warp, with ancient fishermen's houses clustered together on every inch of the tiny island. As you wander the cobbled streets, you'll discover tiny churches, art galleries, souvenir shops, pizza and pasta restaurants, and, at every turn, a glimpse of the lake beyond. It's an entrancing place to explore, but be warned: The prices are extortionate and the crowds frustrating.

ISOLA BELLA ★★★   The minute islet of Bella is dominated by the massive baroque **Palazzo Borromeo** with its formal Italianate gardens. It makes for an absorbing tour, with conspicuous displays of wealth evident in the rich decor and exquisite furnishings. The terraced gardens are dotted with follies and have spectacular views across Maggiore. Of special interest are the ornate grottoes where the Borromeos went to stay cool, or the painting gallery, hung with 130 of the most important works the Borromeos collected over the centuries. Admission is 17€ adults and 9€ ages 6 to 15, which includes admission to the gardens and the painting gallery. It's open mid-March to mid-October 9am to 5:30pm.

A massive 17th-century bronze statue of San Carlo Borromeo stands in Arona.

ISOLA MADRE ★★ The largest and most peaceful of the islands is Isola Madre (30 min. from Stresa), overspread with exquisite flora in the 3.2-hectare (8-acre) **Orto Botanico.** Pick up a map at the ticket office to identify all the rhododendrons, camellias, and ancient wisteria. Many a peacock and fancy pheasant stalk across the lawns of another 16th-century **Borromeo palazzo,** which is filled with family memorabilia and some interesting old puppet-show stages. Admission to the garden and palace is 13.50€ adults and 7€ ages 6 to 15. It's open March to October 9am to 5:30pm.

Exploring Around Lake Maggiore

Beyond Stresa, Maggiore offers natural beauty and architectural wonders as well as lively towns, markets, and cable car rides up into the mountains.

Arona ★★ As well as having the lake's main ferry office (see p. 508), this sophisticated town at the southern end of Lake Maggiore is a shopping magnet, with its charming **Via Cavour** lined with elegant boutiques and expensive delicatessens. The giant bronze **statue of Carlo Borromeo** (see above), who was born in Arona in 1538, is located just outside of town. It's so huge, you can even climb inside and gaze out at the lake through Carlo's eyes (www.statuasancarlo.it; ✆ **0322/249-669;** admission 6€; mid-Mar–Oct Mon–Sat 9am–noon and 2–6pm, Sun 9am–6pm).

Italy's Medieval Oligarchs

The all-powerful Borromeo family were Lombardian aristocrats who loomed large in Milanese politics and religion for 200 years. They regarded the vast tracts of land around the southern end of Lake Maggiore as their personal fiefdom, where they built castles, monuments, and palaces. The family spawned several archbishops of Milan, including Federico (1564–1631) and Carlo (1538–1584), a singularly wily individual who was canonized in 1610 for his support of the Counter-Reformation against papal infallibility. A great bronze statue of Carlo stands in Arona, looking out across the lake to his former family home, **Rocca Borromeo** at Angera (www.isole borromeo.it), an imposing fortress which now offers visitors a medieval garden, a toy and doll museum, and exhibits of contemporary art. Like the other Borromeo properties, it's open mid-March through mid-October.

Luino ★★   On the western shore of Lake Maggiore just a few miles from the Swiss border, Luino is home to one of northern Italy's most popular **street markets,** with more than 350 stalls taking over the town every Wednesday. Here you'll find spices, piles of salami, grappas, and olive oils, as well as the hand-tooled leather belts and bags for which the region is famous. Extra ferries (www.navlaghi.it) serve the town every Wednesday, and many shoppers visit Luino directly by train from Milan's Stazione Centrale or Stazione Porta Garibaldi (2 hrs; 7.90€).

Sasso del Fero ★★★   East of Laveno, make for Laveno Mombello, and take the 16-minute **cable-car** trip (www.funiviedellagomaggiore.it; ✆ **0332/668-012;** 10€ roundtrip) up the lush Val Cuvia to the Poggia Sant'Elsa viewpoint atop **Sasso del Ferro,** towering 1,062m (3,484 ft.) over Lake Maggiore. You'll find truly breathtaking panoramas, looking west to the snow-capped Alps or south over the lakes Varese, Monate, and Comabbio. If the conditions are right, there'll be plenty of paragliders, and the hills are traversed with hiking trails. Leave time to relax over a Prosecco in the **Ristorante Albergo Funivia** (see p. 510). Times vary according to the weather, but the cable car generally runs April to October (Mon–Fri 11am–6:30pm; Sat–Sun 11am–10:30pm).

Santa Caterina del Sasso Ballaro ★★★   Just south of Reno on the southeastern leg of Maggiore, beneath an inconspicuous car park in Piazza Cascine del Quiquio, an elevator descends to the magical hermitage of **Santa Caterina del Sasso Ballaro** (Via Santa Caterina 13, Leggiuno; www.santacaterinadelsasso.com; ✆ **0332/647-172**). Founded in the 13th century, this Dominican monastery sits photogenically against a sheer rock face, clinging to an escarpment 15m (49 ft.) above the lake. The serene complex of soft pink stone is embellished with Renaissance arches and pretty cobbled courtyards. Don't miss the 14th-century frescoes of biblical scenes in the chapel, which were hidden under lime during the Italian suppression of the monasteries in the 1770s and only rediscovered in 2003. The gift shop sells honey, candles, and soaps made by the monks. Admission is free, but donations are accepted (open Apr–Oct 9am–noon and 2:30–6pm, Nov–Mar Sat–Sun 9am–noon and 2–5pm).

Where to Stay & Eat Around Lake Maggiore

There are many hotels scattered around Maggiore eager to grab the tourist dollar: some good, some bad, many indifferent. The two listed here are exceptional, at opposite ends of the price spectrum. Just like the hotels in the area, food quality varies wildly; pick your restaurants in touristy Stresa with care.

Albergo Funivia ★★   This basic hotel located on the Poggia Sant'Elsa belvedere is only accessible by the Sasso del Ferro cable car (see p. 510). What the hotel lacks in charm, it makes up for in beautiful views over

Lake Maggiore towards the Alps from the balconies in every room (where you can also choose to take breakfast). Rooms are a bit dated, but they are clean. Summer is the best time here, with good weather almost guaranteed. There's a restaurant offering a simple local menu, but the real draw is the terrace, which is always packed on sunny days; at night, it's a delight to sit here watching the lights around the lake glittering in the distance. The rooms closest to the cable car can be a bit loud.

Via Tinelli, 15, Località Poggio Sant Elsa, Laveno Mombello. www.funiviedellago maggiore.it. ℗ **0332/610-303.** 14 units. Doubles 100–120€. Rates include breakfast. **Amenities:** Bar; restaurant; Wi-Fi (free).

Grand Hotel des Iles Borromee ★★★

The tagline of this majestic old hotel—a vast, over-the-top example of Belle Epoque architecture, in Stresa—is "where everything is perfect." As you arrive, the exquisitely manicured and landscaped gardens would certainly give that impression. The interior lives up to the exterior's beauty; all is tastefully ornate and gilded, like a mini-Versailles. Doubles with garden views are decorated in a (relatively) discreet manner, with bathrooms luxuriously outfitted in marble. The fabulously glitzy Hemingway Suite (the famous writer actually stayed there twice, once right after WWII and again in 1948) includes three bedrooms, a living room, four bathrooms, and a terrace overlooking the lake. There's a blissful spa and a gourmet restaurant with a lakeview terrace.

Corso Umberto I 67, Stresa. www.borromees.it. ℗ **0323/938-938.** 172 units. 185€–410€ double; 400€–3,300€ suite. Rates include breakfast. **Amenities:** Restaurant; bar; concierge; spa; sauna; indoor pool; 2 outdoor pools; personal trainer; gym; helicopter pad; Wi-Fi (free).

Ristorante Piemontese ★★ NORTHERN ITALIAN

Stresa's town center is full of anonymous pizza/pasta places, but this fine-dining restaurant is certainly a cut above, as evidenced by the fact that it is frequented by Italian locals. Its owners, the Bellossi family, are serious about food and wine, especially Piedmontese ingredients and wine (hence the restaurant's name). Dishes such as porcini risotto, tagliolini pasta with black truffle, and duck confit star on the menu, with fish and game options changing according to the season. You can dine either in the elegant wood-paneled main restaurant or, in warmer months, outside in a courtyard shaded by trellis vines.

Via Mazzini 25, Stresa. www.ristorantepiemontese.com. ℗ **0323/302-35.** Entrees 13€–30€. Tues–Sun 7:30–10:30pm. Closed Dec–Jan.

Ristorante Verbano ★★ SEAFOOD

While many restaurants on the Isole Borromee are overpriced and underwhelming, Verbano is worth the splurge. Its position on the Isola Pescatori is sublime, with breathtaking views of Isola Bella's Palazzo Borromeo (see p. 508) and lake waters lapping around the terrace. Even if you aren't staying at the hotel, you can zip there and back via taxi boat for a luxurious meal; contact the restaurant for details. Service is exemplary, with courteous, well-informed waitstaff. Chef Patrick Merletti puts the focus on traditional Italian dishes while adapting them to modern cooking techniques. Lake fish is heavily featured on the menu, along with lobster linguine and a selection of risottos. Desserts are a delight for the eyes as well as the palate. The restaurant is popular for wedding receptions and special events, so call ahead to find out about availability.

Via Ugo Ara 2, Isola Pescatori. www.hotelverbano.it. ✆ **0323/304-08.** Entrees 15€–35€. Daily noon–2:30pm and 7–10pm (winter closed Wed). Closed Jan.

LAKE GARDA (LAGO DI GARDA) ★★

Sirmione: 130km (81 miles) E of Milan, 150km (93 miles) W of Venice; Riva del Garda: 170km (105 miles) NE of Milan, 199km (123 miles) NW of Venice

Lake Garda is the largest and easternmost of the northern Italian lakes, with its western flanks lapping against the flat plains of Lombardy and its southern extremes in the Veneto. In the north, its deep waters are backed by Alpine peaks. Garda's shores are green and fragrant with flowery gardens, groves of olives and lemons, and forests of pines and cypress.

Lake Garda and the Sarca River.

Essentials

ARRIVING Regular **trains** run from Milan Stazione Centrale and stops at Desenzano del Garda (fares start at 9.20€). From here it's a 20-minute bus ride to Sirmione; buses make the trip every half-hour for 2€).

Hydrofoils and ferries operated by **Navigazione Laghi** (www. navlaghi.it; ✆ **800/551-801**) ply the waters of the lake. One to two hourly ferries connect Sirmione with Desenzano del Garda in season (20 min. by ferry, 3€); less frequently October to April.

Sirmione is just off the A4 between Milan and Venice. From Venice the trip takes about 1½ hours, and from Milan a little over an hour. There's ample parking in Piazzale Monte Baldo, but then it is about a 15-minute walk into the heart of town.

VISITOR INFORMATION **Sirmione**'s tourist office is at Viale Marconi 8 (www.comune.sirmione.bs.it; ✆ **030/374-8721**). There is also a tourism kiosk at Viale Marconi 2 just before the bridge into the old part of town.

GETAWAY TO gardone RIVIERA

Halfway up the western shore of Lake Garda, this little resort—easily accessible by ferry or bus from Desenzano del Garda—offers visitors a gorgeous backdrop for a little relaxation. Oleanders dot the paved promenade, and the charming *centro storico* (Gardone Sopra) is filled with enticing bars and restaurants.

Uphill from the Gardone Riviera lakefront, the **Heller Garden** (Via Roma 2; www.hellergarden.com; © 0336/410-877) is a tropical paradise founded by Arthur Hruska, a botanist who was also dentist to the ill-fated Tsar Nicholas II of Russia. Hruska planted this botanical haven in the 1900s, and 8,000 rare palms, orchids, and tree ferns now thrive here, thanks to the town's mild, sheltered climate. Today the gardens are curated by Austrian artist André Heller, whose sculptures can be found scattered among the water features, cacti, and bamboo copses. The garden is open March to October daily from 9am to 7pm; admission is 12€, 5€ for ages 6 to 11.

Gardone Riviera's other highlight is the **Vittoriale degli Italiani** (Via Vittoriale 12; www.vittoriale.it; © 0365/296-511), the wildly ostentatious and bizarrely decorated villa home of Gabriele d'Annunzio, Italy's most notorious poet and sometime war hero. He bought this hillside estate in 1921 and died here in 1936; a visit pays tribute to d'Annunzio's hedonistic lifestyle rather than his fairly awful poetry. The claustrophobic rooms of this madcap mansion are stuffed with bric-a-brac and artifacts from his colorful life, including mementos of his long affair with actress Eleonora Duse. The patrol boat D'Annunzio commanded in World War I, a museum containing his biplane and photos, and the poet's hilltop mausoleum are all found in the formal gardens that cascade down the hillside. The villa is open daily—in summer from 9am to 8pm and winter from 9am to 5pm. Admission ranges from 10€ to 16€, depending on which parts you visit. Children 6 and under enter for free, while there are special prices for those aged 7 to 18 and over 65.

In **Riva del Garda,** the tourist office is on the lakefront at Largo Medaglie d'Oro 5 (www.gardatrentino.it/en; © 0464/554-444). There's also a tourist office in **Gardone Riviera** at Corso Repubblica 8 (© 030/3748-736). For all, hours vary depending on the season.

Sirmione

Perched on a promontory swathed in cypress and olive groves on the southernmost edge of Lake Garda, photogenic Sirmione has been a popular spot since the Romans first discovered hot springs here. Despite the onslaught of summer visitors, this historic town manages to retain its charm. Sirmione has lakeside promenades and pleasant beaches and is small enough for everything to be accessible on foot. It is chiefly famous for its thermal springs, castle, and northern Italy's largest Roman ruins.

The moated, fortified **Rocca Scaligera ★★★** (© 030/916-468) was built on the peninsula's narrowest point and today dominates the *centro storico*. Built in the late 13th century by the Della Scala family, who ruled Verona and many of the lands surrounding the lake, the castle is worth a visit for its sweeping courtyards, turreted towers, dungeons, and views across Lake Garda. It's open Tuesday to Saturday 8:30am to 7:30pm, and from 8:30am to 2pm on Sundays; admission is 6€, ages 18 to 25 3€.

From the castle, it's a 15-minute walk (or take the open-air tram from Piazza Piatti) along Via Vittorio Emanuele from the town center to the tip of Sirmione's peninsula and the **Grotte di Catullo ★★** (© **030/916-157**), romantically placed ruins with views across the lake. Built around A.D. 150, the remains are thought to represent two sizeable aristocratic villas. A small museum of Roman artifacts from the site includes jewelry and

Rocca Scaligera castle in Sirmione.

mosaic fragments (Piazzale Orti Manara 4; 8€ adults, 4€ 18–25; free first Sun of month; opening times generally Tues–Sat 8:30am–7:30pm, Sun 9:30am–6:30pm, with shorter hours Mar–Oct).

The massive amusement park **Gardaland** (www.gardaland.it; © **045/6449-777**) is half an hour's drive east of Sirmione at Castelnuovo del Garda. This huge resort includes several hotels and an aquarium and is generally thronged during school vacation periods, but if Disneyland-type places are your thing, you may want to check it out.

Riva del Garda

The northernmost settlement on Lake Garda is a thriving Italian town with medieval towers, Renaissance churches and *palazzi,* and narrow cobblestone streets where everyday business proceeds in its alluring way. Note that Riva del Garda becomes a cultural mecca in October, when the town hosts the international **Lago di Garda Musica Festival** (www.mrf-musicfestivals.com). If you want to see amateur choirs and orchestras perform classical music in magnificent villas and palazzos, with the lake as a breathtaking backdrop, make hotel reservations well in advance. Riva del Garda's **Old Town** is pleasant, although it has only two notable historic attractions. The 13th-century **Torre d'Apponale** (2€, ages 16 and under free) in Piazza III Novembre is open in summer for visitors to climb its 165 steps for views across the lake. The town's moated lakeside castle, **La Rocca,** now houses an unassuming civic museum (www.museoaltogarda. it; © **0464/573-869;** 5€ adults, 2.50€ ages 15–26 and over 65, ages 14 and under free; open Tues–Sun 10am–6pm, typically closes Dec–Jan and sometimes Feb).

Where to Stay & Eat Around Lake Garda

Sirmione and Riva del Garda have a choice of pleasant, moderately priced hotels, all of which book up quickly in July and August, when rates go up. The local cuisine features fish from the lake and lots of pasta.

Hotel du Lac et du Parc ★★★   This massive, family-friendly resort at the top of Lake Garda is surrounded by lush gardens and has swimming pools, spas, and every conceivable luxury. The grounds lead down to a little lakefront beach where you can windsurf, paddle board, take sailing lessons, or take part in many other water sports at the Sailing Du Lac Sailing School. There are different options for accommodations—bungalows, luxurious suites in the villas, or rooms in the hotel in the heart of the resort. Despite the size of the property, the service still feels personal, and attention to detail can be seen everywhere. The gym, spas, and pools are spotless, hotel rooms are cheery and tasteful—ask for one overlooking the park's palm trees and rare plants—and the breakfast buffet is top notch. If you don't want to eat in one of the resorts three restaurants (with two upscale options and a more casual bistro and lounge), there are plenty of dining options in Riva del Garda itself, just a 15-minute walk away.

Via Rovereto 44, Riva del Garda. www.dulacetduparc.com. © **0464/566-600.** 159 units in main hotel. 150€–229€ double; 170€–655€ suites. Rates include breakfast. Closed Dec–April. **Amenities:** 3 restaurants; 3 bars; 2 outdoor pools; indoor pool; gym; spa; sauna; babysitting; kids' club; water sports; concierge; room service; Wi-Fi (free).

out and about **ON LAKE GARDA**

Riva Del Garda's main attraction is the lake, lined with plush hotels and a waterside promenade that stretches for several miles past parks and pebbly beaches. The water is warm enough for swimming May to October, and air currents fanned by the mountains make Riva and neighboring Torbole the windsurfing capitals of Europe. Kitesurfing, kayaking, and sailing are all popular pastimes.

A convenient point of embarkation for a lake outing is the beach next to **La Rocca** castle, where from March through October you can rent rowboats or pedal boats for about 10€ per hour; the concession is open daily 8am to 8pm.

Check out the sailing and windsurfing at **Sailing du Lac** at the luxurious **Hotel du Lac et du Parc** (see p. 515), where windsurf equipment can be rented for 55€ per day or 25€ for an hour. Lessons start at 72€ for 3 hours. A catamaran for 2 to 4 people can be rented for 55€ per hour, but you will need to leave a deposit of 200 euros and you must show identification such as a passport. Catamaran lessons start at 80€ per 2-hour session. The school is open mid-April to mid-October from 8:30am to 6:30pm.

Lake Garda is also renowned for mountain biking; there are more than 80 routes around the lake and up into the Alpine foothills. At **Happy Bike,** Viale Rovereto 72 (www.happy-bike.it; © **347/943-1208,** open daily 9am to 7pm), you can rent a mountain bike for 16€ per day.

Hotel Eden ★   Once home to American poet Ezra Pound, today this pink-stucco palazzo on the lake is a modernized "design hotel" in the heart of Sirmione's *centro storico*. Common areas are bright and feature vivid wallpaper and touches. A breakfast room leads to a shady terrace overlooking the lake, and a swimming pier juts out over the water. The focus on design continues in the guest rooms, where splashy touches here and there liven up simple furnishings. Ask for a lakeview room, as it can be somewhat noisy at night at the back of the hotel.

Piazza Carducci 19, Sirmione. www.hoteledensirmione.it. ℭ **030/916-481.** 30 units. 105€–190€ double. Rates include breakfast. Closed Nov–Mar. **Amenities:** Restaurant; bar; concierge; room service; Wi-Fi (free).

Osteria Al Torcol ★★ ITALIAN   Though it is hard to miss on a quiet side street, Torcol is consistently regarded as *the* standout restaurant in Sirmione and among the best on Lake Garda. This restaurant serves up flavorful and artfully prepared Italian dishes. The food can tend toward nouvelle cuisine (*foie gras* with chocolate dust and vanilla salt, for example), but the decor is rustic and old-world. The wood-beamed interior is packed with bottles of local wines (many available by the glass). Signature dishes include fresh *tagliolini* with pistachio and shrimp as well as selection of fresh fish, such as trout, turbot, or pike. If you have your heart set on views of the lake, this isn't the restaurant for you, but the courtyard is quite an oasis. Make sure to book in advance.

Via San Salvatore 30, Sirmione. ℭ **030/990-4605.** Entrees 13€–30€. Open May–Sept daily 12:30–3pm and 7:30–10:30pm; Oct–Jan Sat–Sun 12:30–3pm and 7:30–10:30pm; Feb–Apr Sat–Sun 7:30–10:30pm.

Trattoria Riolet ★ ITALIAN   If you make the uphill trek (about 20 minutes from the center of Gardone Riviera on foot) to the Trattoria Riolet, you will be rewarded with unsurpassed views over Lake Garda. This hilltop spot is as popular with locals as it is with summer visitors. The cuisine might be basic and rustic—think pasta al pesto, cheesy baked vegetables, lots of grilled fish, or chicken kebabs cooked over an open fire and served with polenta—but everything is fresh and as tasty as could be. There's not always a set menu and options can be limited, so follow your waiter's advice in ordering—and be sure to enjoy a carafe or two of local wine. Call ahead to reserve a table; it can get crowded, especially when the weather is nice.

Via Fasano Sopra 47, Gardone Riviera. ℭ **0365/205-45.** Thurs–Tues 7–10:30pm. Entrees 8€–25€.

TURIN (TORINO) ★★★

669km (415 miles) NW of Rome, 140km (87 miles) E of Milan

It's often said that Turin is the most French city in Italy. The reason is partly historical and partly architectural. From the late 13th century until

Turin

Piazza della
Repubblica

Via del Carmine

Piazza
Savoia

Corte d'Appello

Via della

Pza. San
Giovanni

V. 4 Marzo

Giardino
Reali

Turin

Rome

Pza. XVIII Dicembre
Autostazione
Terminal Bus

Piazza
Arbarello

Via Garibaldi

Stazione di
Porta Susa

Corso Inghilterra

Corso Bolzano

Via Cernaia

Via Pietro Micca

Pza.
Castello

Viale

Via Vinzaglio

Via G. Ferraris

Corso Giacomo Matteotti

Piazza
Solferino

Via S. Teresa

Pza.
San Carlo

Via Maria

Via Giuseppe Verdi

Via Po

Via Rossini

San Maurizio

Via Princ. Amedeo

Corso Duca d. Abruzzi

Largo
Vitt.
Eman. II

Via Roma

Via Carlo Alberto

Via Giovanni Giolitti

Pza. Carlo
Emanuele II

Via Giulia di Barolo

Via Vanchiglia

Corso Stati Uniti

Corso Re Umberto

Corso

Pza.
Carlo
Felice

Pza.
Bodoni

Via dell'Accademia
Albertina

Pza.
Cavour

Vittoria

Pza.
Vittorio
Veneto

Corso Trieste

Vittorio

Emanuele II

Stazione di
Porta Nuova

Aiuola
Balbo

Via Frat Calandra

Corso Cairoli

Ponte Vitt.
Eman. I

Gran
Madre
di Dio

Po

0   1/4 mi
0   0.25 km

Via Sacchi

Via Nizza

Via Berthollet

Corso Guglielmo Marconi

Via Madama Cristina

Via Virgilio

Parco del
Valentino

Ponte
Umberto I

Museo d.
Montagna

Via Caluso

Corso Raffaello

Via Massimo d'Azeglio

Castello del
Valentino

Corso Moncalieri

Pza.
Nizza

Corso
del
Valentino

Parco
del
Valentino

Torino
Esposizioni

ATTRACTIONS

Duomo di San Giovanni
Battista **4**

Mole Antonelliana **11**

Museo Egizio **9**

Museo Nazionale
dell'Automobile
(MAUTO) **16**

Museo Nazionale del
Risorgimento Italiano **10**

Museo della Sindone **1**

Palazzo Madama **8**

Palazzo Reale **3**

HOTELS

Le Petit Hotel **5**

Townhouse 70 **7**

VitaminaM **15**

RESTAURANTS

Cannavacciuolo
Bistrot **13**

Costardi Bros. at EDIT **12**

Officine Bohemien **6**

Trattoria Coco's **14**

Trattoria Santo Spirito **2**

Italy's unification in 1861, Turin was the capital of the **House of Savoy.**
These wealthy aristocrats were as French as they were Italian, with estates
that extended into the present-day French regions of Savoy and the Côte
d'Azur. Under the Savoys, Francophile 17th- and 18th-century architects
razed much of the city and its Roman foundations, replacing them with
broad avenues and grandiose buildings. As a result, Turin is one of
Europe's great baroque cities, befitting a one-time capital of the nation.
These days, thanks in part to the 2006 Winter Olympics and another
makeover in 2011 for the 150th anniversary of Italian unification, Turin
has transformed itself from an industrial power into a vibrant city of

museums, enticing cafes, beautiful squares, and designer shops. This sophisticated city is deservedly gaining a reputation as a go-to destination in northeast Italy.

Essentials

ARRIVING   Domestic and international **flights** land at **Turin Airport** (www.aeroportoditorino.it; ✆ **011/567-6361**), about 13km (8 miles) northwest of Turin. Direct **trains** (www.gtt.to.it; ✆ **011/57-641**) run from the airport to GTT Dora Railway Station every 30 minutes between 5am and 11pm; the 3€ trip takes 19 minutes. **SADEM buses** (www.sadem.it) serve the airport and the main train stations, Porta Nuova and Porta Susa (40 min.; 6.50€ from the ticket office, 7.50€ on board). **Taxis** into town take about 30 minutes and cost 30€ to 50€, depending on the time of day.

Turin's main **train** station is **Stazione di Porta Nuova** on Piazza Carlo Felice. There is regular daily **Trenitalia** (www.trenitalia.com; ✆ **892-021**) service from Milan. The fastest trains take 1 hour, with fares averaging 29€ (though advance-purchase fares can be as low as 9€). Slower trains take up to 2 hours, with fares of 12€ to 17€. **Stazione di Porta Susa** connects Turin with local Piedmont towns and is the terminus for the **TGV service to Paris;** four trains a day make that trip in under 6 hours for around 98€, but there are often specials for as low as 29€ each way.

Turin's main **bus terminal** is **Autostazione Bus,** Corso Vittorio Emanuele II 131 (www.autostazionetorino.it). Buses connect Turin to Courmayeur, Aosta, Milan, and many small towns in Piedmont. A 2-hour **SADEM** (www.sadem.it) bus service to Milan Malpensa Airport costs 22€ each way.

Turin is at the hub of the autostrade grid. The A4 connects Turin with Milan in 90 minutes. Journey time on the A5 to Aosta is around 90 minutes.

GETTING AROUND   All the main sights of Turin are well within walking distance of each other. There's also a vast network of GTT trams and buses as well as one metro line (www.gtt.to.it; ✆ **011/57-641**). The historic Linea 7 tourist tram trundles around a circular route from Piazza Castello. Tickets on public transportation are available at newsstands for 1.50€ and are valid for 90 minutes. All-day tickets are 5€ and last 24 hours. There is no need to drive in the city center.

You can find taxis at stands in front of the train stations and around Piazza San Carlo and Piazza Castello. To call a taxi, you can dial **Pronto** at ✆ **011/5737,** but all hotel reception desks will order a taxi for you. Meters start at 3.50€ and increase by 1.44€ per km up to 8€, after which the per-km rate decreases based on how long you travel; there are surcharges for waiting, luggage, late-night travel, and Sunday journeys.

The **tourist office** on the corner of Via Garibaldi and Piazza Castello (www.turismotorino.org; © **011/535-181**) is open daily 9am to 6pm. There is also a branch across from **Stazione Porta Nuova** in Piazza Carlo Felice (same phone; same hours).

> ### See Turin's Top Sights and Save
>
> If you're planning to visit three or more attractions, you can save money by buying the **Torino+Piemonte Card** (www.turismo torino.org/card), which grants access to over 180 museums, monuments, castles, and royal palazzos, as well as offering discounts on public transportation. All of the attractions covered below are included. A variety of passes are available; a 48-hour pass valid for one adult and one child up to age 12 costs 35€, with discounts of up to 20 percent available off-season if you book online. Passes can be bought at the Piazza Castello tourist office or Stazione Porta Nuova.

CITY LAYOUT With the Alps as a backdrop to the north and the River Po winding through the city center, Turin has as its glamorous backbone the arcaded **Via Roma,** lined with designer shops and grand cafes. Via Roma runs northwards through a series of ever-lovelier baroque squares until it reaches **Piazza Castello** and the palaces of the Savoy nobility.

From here, a walk west leads to the **Area Romano,** a mellow jumble of narrow streets that's the oldest part of the city. Its edge is marked by Via Garibaldi. Or turn east from Piazza Castello along Via Po to one of Italy's largest squares, the **Piazza Vittorio Veneto** and, at the end of this elegant expanse, the River Po and **Parco del Valentino.**

Exploring Turin

The stately arcades of **Via Roma,** Turin's premier shopping street, were designed in 1714 by Filippo Juvarra. This chic thoroughfare runs from the circular **Piazza Carlo Felice,** ringed with outdoor cafes and constructed around formal gardens, north into **Piazza San Carlo,** quite possibly Italy's most beautiful square. In summer Piazza San Carlo is Turin's harmonious outdoor *salone,* its arcaded sidewalks lined with big-name fashion stores and elegant cafes, including the genteel **Caffé Torino** (www.caffe-torino. it; © **011/545-118**). In the center of the piazza prances a 19th-century equestrian statue of Duke Emanuele Filiberto of Savoy. Two 17th-century churches**, San Carlo** and **Santa Cristina,** face each other like bookends at the southern entrance to the square.

At the far north end of Via Roma, the **Piazza Castello** is dominated by **Palazzo Madama** (see p. 524), named for its 17th-century inhabitant, Christine Marie of France, who married into the Savoy dynasty in 1619. Farther north still stands the massive complex of the **Palazzo Reale** (see p. 525), residence of the Savoy dukes from 1646 to 1865.

10

MILAN, PIEDMONT & THE LAKES

Turin (Torino)

Palazzo Reale, Turin.

Duomo di San Giovanni Battista ★ CHURCH   One of the few pieces of Renaissance architecture in baroque-dominated Turin, this otherwise uninspiring 15th-century cathedral is famous as the resting place of the **Shroud of Turin** (see box p. 521). The linen cloth is preserved in an aluminum casket in the temperature-controlled, air-conditioned **Cappella della Sacra Sindone** and closed off from human contamination (and public view) with bulletproof glass. The casket is adorned with a crown of thorns; the faithful come in droves to worship at the chapel, which is the last one in the left-hand aisle. To learn about the history of the shroud, head for the **Museo della Sindone** (see p. 524).

Piazza San Giovanni. www.duomoditorino.it. 𝒞 **011/436-1540.** Free. Mon–Fri 7am–12:30pm and 3–7pm; Sat–Sun 8am–12:30pm and 3–7pm. Bus: 11, 12, 51, 55, 56, 61, 68. Trams: 4, 13, 15, 18.

Mole Antonelliana & Museo Nazionale del Cinema ★★★ MUSEUM   Turin's most peculiar building, dominating the skyline from all directions, was once the tallest in Europe. Building started in 1863 on what was originally meant to be a synagogue; later, city fathers decided to make it a monument to Italian unification (at the time, Italy was ruled by the House of Savoy from its power base in Turin). Set on a squat brick

HISTORY OF THE shroud of turin

The Shroud of Turin is said to be the piece of fabric in which Christ was wrapped when he was taken from the cross—and to which his image was miraculously affixed. The image on the cloth is of a bearded face—remarkably similar to the depiction of Christ in Byzantine icons—and a body marked with bloodstains consistent with a crown of thorns, a spear slash in the rib cage, nail holes in the wrists and ankles, and scourge marks on the back from flagellation.

Carbon dating results are confusing; some suggest that the shroud was manufactured around the 13th or 14th centuries, while other tests imply that those results were affected by a fire that all but destroyed the shroud in December 1532. But the mystery remains, at least in part because no one can explain how the haunting image appeared on the cloth.

Debunkers have attempted to create replicas using lemon juice and the sun, mineral pigments, even aloe and myrrh (the last because of funerary traditions of the time). A 2015 study of DNA in the shroud's dust particles further confused the picture: it was shown to contain genetic material from plants across the globe.

base, the Mole rises through layers of windows and pseudo-Greek columns to a huge ribbed cupola and needlelike spire, all of it looming 167m (548 ft.) above the streets. It is now home to Italy's National Film Museum.

Over the years, the film museum's exhibits have been updated with interactive displays and hands-on activities to keep kids happy. The first galleries track the intriguing development of moving pictures, from shadow puppets to risqué peep shows and flickering images of galloping horses filmed by Edward Muybridge in 1878. Displays use clips, stills, posters, and props to illustrate aspects of movie production, such as the creepy steady-cam work in *The Shining*. There is also a section of movie memorabilia, such as jewels and shoes worn by Marilyn Monroe and Darth Vader's mask from *The Empire Strikes Back*.

A major highlight of a visit includes a panoramic elevator ride through the roof of the museum's vast atrium and up 85m (279 ft.) inside the tower to the 360-degree observation platform at the top. The view of Turin and the surrounding countryside, backed by the Alps, is stunning. **Note:** You can choose to bypass the museum and only do the panoramic elevator for a cost of 8€ (5€ if you have the Torino+Piemonte card, see p. 519). Lines form on weekends, so try to come early.

Via Montebello 20. www.museocinema.it. ℭ **011/8138-561.** Museum and panoramic elevator: 15€, 12€ seniors and students up to age 26, 8€ ages 6–18, free under 5. Museum only: 11€, 9€ seniors and students up to age 26, 3.50€ ages 6–18, free under 5. Elevator only: 8€; 5€ students, seniors, ages 6–18. Open Wed–Mon 9am–8pm, Sat 9am–11pm. Multilingual guided tours by advance booking. Bus: 18, 55, 56, 61, 68. Tram: 13, 15, 16.

Turin (Torino)

Museo Egizio (Egyptian Museum) ★★ MUSEUM

People come from all around Italy and beyond to visit Turin's magnificent Egyptian collection. It is one of the world's largest—no surprise, considering it was also the world's *first* Egyptian museum, thanks to the Savoy kings and their explorers Bernardino Drovetti and Ernesto Schiaparelli, who voraciously hoarded Egyptian ephemera until the early 1900s, when attitudes about cultural plundering changed. Some say this is the most important collection of Egyptian artifacts outside of Cairo, so it's definitely a must-visit when in Turin. After a massive renovation that doubled the exhibition space, there is now an innovative system of escalators leading visitors seemingly on a path along the Nile over three levels of displays. Not only have Egyptian cultural and funereal elements been reconstructed down to the smallest details, the museum also tells the history of the archeological expeditions. There are artifacts from all eras of ancient Egypt, including a papyrus "Book of the Dead." One of the most captivating exhibits is the exquisitely painted wooden sarcophagi and mummies of Kha and Merit, an aristocratic couple whose tomb was discovered in 1906. To beat the lines and crowds, reserve your visit ahead of time online, choosing from among various itineraries. Bags larger than a purse are not allowed in the museum and will have to be left in the coat check on floor -1.

Via Accademia delle Scienze 6. www.museoegizio.it. 🕿 **011/440-6903.** 13€ adults, 9€ ages 15–18, 1€ ages 6–14, free for children 5 and under. Mon 9am–2pm, Tues–Sun 8:30am–7:30pm. Bus: 55, 56. Tram: 13.

Museo Nazionale dell'Automobile (MAUTO) ★★★ MUSEUM

It is only fitting that the car is king at MAUTO, an innovative museum located south of the Parco del Valentino, in the city that spawned Fiat. One enters into a *piazza,* a futuristic covered courtyard that leads into the venue; a café and bookshop are off to the left as you come in. Alfa Romeos and lots of bright-red Ferraris feature heavily among the displays, which start with vintage cars from the days when road travel was only for the very wealthy. The exhibition then progresses through to factory-line mass production. Exhibits also highlight the social, financial, and environmental impact that combustion engines have had on the planet. The different areas of the museum include "Automobiles and the 20th century," "Automobiles and Man," and "Automobiles and Design." Finally, the "Open Garage" section of the museum gives a sneak peek of cars that are part of the museum's collection as they are being restored, but it can only be visited by making an appointment. You don't need to be a car buff to appreciate the lovely lines of a Maserati, and this is the perfect place to bring kids who've traipsed around one too many baroque *palazzo.*

Corso Unità d'Italia 40. www.museoauto.it. 🕿 **011/677-666.** 12€ adults, 8€ ages 6–18 and seniors, free for kids under 6. Mon 10am–2pm; Tues 2–7pm; Wed–Thurs, Sun 10am–7pm; Fri–Sat 10am–9pm. Metro: Lingotto.

Vintage cars at the Museo Nazionale dell'Automobile.

Museo Nazionale del Risorgimento Italiano (National Museum of the Risorgimento) ★★★ MUSEUM Located on Piazza Carignano—one of the most majestic in a city full of splendid corners—the equally handsome red-brick *palazzo* of the same name acquired huge national importance as the occasional home of Italy's first king after the country's unification in 1861. Originally built between 1679 and 1685 by baroque maestro Guarino Guarini, the palace now houses the Museo del Risorgimento (meaning "resurgence" or "revival"): At its heart is the ornate circular chamber where Italy's first parliament met. A visit to the museum may be like stepping into the past, but the fascinating way it presents its displays is quite innovative for an Italian museum, with multilingual signage and labeling, audio guides, video guides, and interactive touchscreens. A cinema room shows films that illustrate the importance of this building and of Turin at this time in history. More than 30 richly rooms detail the military campaigns that led to unification; even non-Italians can easily appreciate the stirring drama of these years. Uniforms, paintings, weapons, maps, and correspondence testify to feats of great bravado, tracing a course through the Italy of the 19th century from Napoleon to Garibaldi.

Via Accademia delle Scienze 5. www.museorisorgimentotorino.it. © **011/562-1147.** 10€ adults, 8€ seniors, 5€ students, 2.50€ primary schoolers, free ages 6 and under; free with the Torino Card. Tues–Sun 10am–6pm. Bus: 11, 12, 27, 51, 51, 55, 56, 57. Tram: 13, 15.

Museo della Sindone (Holy Shroud Museum) ★★ MUSEUM

Despite the fact that the shroud isn't actually kept here and there are no special effects, this endearing little museum is still a hit, fully representing the Shroud of Turin's status as one of the world's most famous religious relics. A visit starts with a 15-minute film (offered in five languages) about the shroud, its provenance, and the various theories and mysteries surrounding it. Visitors then wander through a series of rooms chronicling the shroud's history, from its first mention in 1204, to the fire that nearly destroyed it in Chambéry in 1532, to its arrival in Turin with the House of Savoy in 1578, to modern-day carbon-testing efforts. The last stop is the richly ornamented chapel of Santo Sudario—a private place of worship for the Savoy dukes—where a copy of the shroud is displayed over the gleaming, gilded altar.

The shroud itself is kept in the royal chapel of the Duomo, usually out of public view (see p. 521). It is, however, typically taken out for public viewing every few years, most recently in 2015; the decision to do so is usually made by the reigning pope. Log on to www.sindone.org to find out when the shroud will next be taken out and displayed; advance reservations are required to see the shroud during these brief public displays.

Via San Domenico 28. www.sindone.it. © **011/436-5832.** 8€ adults, 7€ seniors, students, and ages 12 and under. Daily 9am–noon and 3–7pm.

Palazzo Madama—Museo Civico di Arte Antica (Civic Museum of Ancient Art) ★ MUSEUM

Looking like a mash-up of two architectural styles, Palazzo Madama dominates Piazza Castello; its medieval façade faces eastward, while the westward façade is its baroque addition created by architect Filippo Juvarra in the 18th century. Walk around this massive structure and you'll see that it also incorporates a medieval castle, a Roman gate, and several Renaisssance additions. Just as the building has multiple styles, the museum within it—the Museo Civico di Arte Antica—displays collections of art from several past eras, covering four mammoth floors (stop to admire the monumental marble staircase, another Juvarra touch). Works from the medieval and Renaissance periods show off well against the building's austere, stony interior; on the top floor you'll also find one of Italy's largest collections of ceramics. Still, it's all rather disorganized—you'll have to hunt for the star of the show, Antonello da Messina's sublime "Portrait of a Man," which is hidden away in the Treasure Tower at the back of the building. Audio guides, available for 4€, offer more in-depth information for about 100 works. If you need a break, the Caffè Madama offers modern-day treats as well as hot chocolate and pastries inspired by the royal period of the city.

Piazza Castello. www.palazzomadamatorino.it. © **011/443-3501.** 10€ adults, 8€ student and seniors, free under 18. Mon, Wed–Fri 10am–6pm; Sat 11am–7pm; Sun 10am–7pm. Closed Tues. Free admission 1st Wed of month (excluding holidays). Bus: 11, 12, 51, 55, 56, 61, 68; Trams: 4, 13, 15, 18.

Palazzo Reale (Royal Palace) & Armeria Reale (Royal Armory) ★

PALACE Overshadowing the north side of the Piazza Castello, the residence of the House of Savoy was begun in 1646; the family lived here up until 1865. Designed by the architect Amedeo di Castellamonte, the palace reflects the ornate tastes of European ruling families of the time, while its sheer size offers some indication of the wealth of these oligarchs. This Savoy palace gives the flamboyant frippery of Versailles a run for its money, with throne rooms, ballrooms, and apartments hung with priceless Gobelins tapestries and lavishly adorned with silk walls, sparkling chandeliers, ornate wooden floors, and gilded furniture.

The east wing of the *palazzo* houses the **Armeria Reale,** one of the most important arms and armor collections in Europe, especially of weapons from the 16th and 17th centuries. It also has a unique collection of stuffed horses, which look ready to leap into battle at any moment.

Behind the palace are the formal **Giardini Reali (Royal Gardens),** laid out in part by André Le Nôtre, who designed the Tuileries in Paris and the gardens at Versailles.

The Savoy royal family had an even keener eye for paintings than for baroque decor, amassing a collection of 8,000 works of art. The collection's highlights are on display in the **Galleria Sabauda** in the Palazzo Reale's New Wing. (This is a few minutes' walk from the main *palazzo*.) The exhibition kicks off with early Piedmont and Dutch religious works, plus a moody Rembrandt self-portrait and two massive paintings by van Dyck: "The Children of Charles I" (1637) and a magnificent equestrian portrait of Prince Thomas of Savoy (ca. 1634).

Now permanently housed in the basement beneath the Galleria Sabauda, the **Museo Archeologico**'s thoughtfully designed exhibition tells the story of Turin's development from Roman through medieval times. Incorporated into the museum are a section of Roman wall, remnants from the theater nearby, and a mosaic only discovered in 1993.

A Glimpse into Roman Turin

Close to Turin's Duomo (see p. 520) and partly incorporated into the Museo Archeologico (see p. 474) stand two landmarks of Roman Turin: the remains of a theater and fragments of wall, as well as the **Porta Palatina,** a Roman-era city gate, flanked by twin 16-sided towers on Piazza San Giovanni Battista. The **Area Romana** west of the Piazza Castello is the oldest part of the city, a charming web of streets occupied since ancient times.

The **Biblioteca Reale** (Royal Library) is also part of the Palazzo Reale complex; it's free to enter and you'll find it on the right of the main entrance. Founded in 1831, it houses 200,000 rare volumes as well as ancient maps and prints. On the opposite side of the gates is the fine **church of San Lorenzo,** designed by master architect Guarino Guarini in 1666. Its plain facade belies a lacy dome and frothy interior.

Warning: Security rules prohibit visitors from bringing in large bags (backpacks, duffel bags, and luggage) and the palazzo currently offers no place to check these items for safekeeping.

Piazzetta Reale 1. www.ilpalazzorealeditorino.it. © **011/436-1455.** Palazzo and all exhibitions: 12€ adults, 6€ ages 18–25, free for children and seniors. Free admission 1st Sun of month. Tues–Sun 9am–7pm; last admission 6pm. Museo Archeologico closed Sun morning. Bus: 11,51, 55, 56, 68; Trams: 4, 13, 15, 18.

Outlying Attractions

Basilica di Superga ★★ CHURCH Half the fun of a visit to this lovely basilica is the 6.5km (4-mile) journey northeast of the city center on a narrow-gauge railway through the lush countryside of the Parco Naturale della Collina di Superga. The church was built as thanksgiving to the Virgin Mary for Turin's deliverance from the French siege of 1706. Prince Vittorio Amedeo II commissioned Filippo Juvarra, the Sicilian architect who designed much of Turin's elegant center, to build the magical baroque confection on a hill high above the city. The eye-catching exterior, with its beautiful colonnaded portico, elaborate dome, and twin bell towers, is actually more appealing than the ornate but gloomy interior, a circular chamber ringed by six chapels. Many scions of the House of Savoy are buried here in the Crypt of Kings beneath the main chapel.

Strada della Basilica di Superga, 73, www.basilicadisuperga.com. © **011/899-7456.** Basilica admission free; 5€ to visit Royal Tombs or Royal Apartment, 9€ to visit both; 3€ to climb dome. Open Mon–Fri 9am–noon and 3–6pm, Sat–Sun 9am–noon and 3–7pm (closes 1 hr earlier in winter). Tram: Tranvia a Dentiera from Stazione Sassi (6€ roundtrip) to Superga stop. Bus: 61 from side of Ponte Vittorio Emanuele I opposite Piazza Vittorio Veneto.

Palazzina di Caccia di Stupinigi ★ PALACE Yet another Savoy family home is found at Stupinigi, just a few miles southwest from Turin. More great work commissioned in 1729 from the architect Filippo Juvarra resulted in a sumptuous hunting lodge surrounded by royal forests. Built on a humungous scale, the palace's wings fan out from the main house, topped by a domed pavilion. Every bit as lavish as the apartments in the Savoys' city residence, Palazzo Reale (see p. 525), the interior is stuffed with furniture, paintings, and bric-à-brac assembled from their myriad residences, forming the **Museo dell'Arte e Ammobiliamento** (Museum of Art and Furniture). Wander through the acres of apartments to understand why Napoleon chose this for his brief sojourn in Piedmont in 1805 while on his way to Milan to be crowned emperor. Outstanding among the many, many frescoes are the scenes of a deer hunt in the King's Apartment and the triumph of Diana in the grand salon. The elegant gardens and surrounding forests provide lovely terrain for a jaunt. One quirky thing about this palace is that you may find the ticket office closed for lunch between 1 and 2pm.

Piazza Principe Amedeo 7, Stupingi, Nichelino (8.5km (5¼ mi) SW of city center). www.ordinemauriziano.it/palazzina-di-caccia-stupinigi. © **011/620-0634.** 12€, seniors and ages 6–18 8€, kids under 6 free. Tues–Fri 10am–5:30pm; Sat 10am–6:30pm.

Reggia di Venaria Reale ★★★ PALACE   Completing the triumvirate of glitzy Savoy households around Turin, the Venaria was constructed in the mid-17th century to a design by Amedeo di Castellamonte, but sure enough Filippo Juvarra also had a hand in it. This massive complex, its stables, and the awesome formal gardens are now a UNESCO World Heritage Site. Venaria offers a great family-oriented day out with loads of outdoor summer activities as well as a glimpse into the extraordinarily privileged lives of the Savoy family. The Fountain of the Stag dances to music in the lake outside the *palazzo;* on the grounds are follies aplenty and the mock-Roman Fountain of Hercules. Exhibitions in the house include the "Peopling the Palaces" light show conceived by film director Peter Greenaway, who also had a hand in the exhibitions at the Museum of Cinema (see below) in Turin.

Piazza della Repubblica 4, Venaria Reale (10km/6¼ mi NW of city center). www.lavenaria.it. ✆ **011/499-2333.** Price options range from 25€ for palace, gardens & activities to 5€ for gardens only. Tues–Fri 9am–5pm; Sat–Sun 9:30am–6:30pm (last admission 1 hr. before closing). Bus: 11 from Piazza Repubblica. A Venaria Express bus runs Tues–Sun (40 min.), with stops at Stazione Porta Nuova, on Via XX Settembre, and at Stazione Porta Susa.

Organized Tours

The nonprofit organization **Free Tour Turin** (www.freetourturin.com) offers a free 2.5-hour guided tour of the city center (in English and Italian) Thursday through Monday at 10:30am. Tour groups meet outside the Porta Nuova metro station in Piazza Carlo Felice near the Sambuy Garden (look for the guide holding a sign).

Especially for Kids

There's plenty for kids to do in Turin. The **Parco del Valentino** (see p. 531) has lots of open spaces to run around in, plus free admission to the open-air **Borgo Medievale,** a mock-Piedmontese village built for the Italian General Exposition in 1884 (Viale Virgilio 107; www.borgomedioevale torino.it; ✆ **011/4431-701;** open 9am–7pm [8pm in summer]). Most youngsters will be intrigued by the **Museum of Cinema** at the Mole Antonelliana (see p. 520), or at least the trip up the Mole's tower to see the city lying far below. The **Museo Nazionale dell'Automobile** (p. 522) provides an antidote to Turin's baroque attractions. **Zoom Torino** (www. zoomtorino.it) is an immersive zoo—no bars or cages—located about 35 minutes southwest of the city center by car in the town of Cumiana. You can also get there by train, getting out at the Piscina di Pinerolo station and taking the free Zoom shuttle.

If all else fails, pop into **Caffè Fiorio** (Via Po 8; ✆ **011/8173-225**) for some delicious gelato or, in cooler months, Turin's famous hot chocolate.

10

MILAN, PIEDMONT & THE LAKES

Turin (Torino)

Where to Stay in Turin

In recent years, Turin has seen an influx of boutique hotels, giving travelers an alternative to the faceless frumpery of many of the city's older hotels.

SELF-CATERING ROOMS AND APARTMENTS

If VitaminaM (see p. 529) is booked up, try the lower-priced **Spazio Madama Residence** (Via Madama Christina 52; spaziomadamaresidence. cosigeniale.it; ☎ **345/842-3380),** which offers self-catering studio apartments in a modern building in the historic San Salvario neighborhood, 2 blocks from Parco Valentino. These studios look more dormlike than residential, with white walls, blond-wood built-ins, leather chairs, and hardwood floors, but there is an elevator, and it's right by a tram stop. All units have kitchenettes, and some have balconies overlooking the rooftops of Turin and the mountains. Apartments start at around 65€ per night; parking is available for 10€ per day, and Wi-Fi is free.

Le Petit Hotel ★★   Its central location makes the Petit Hotel a great budget option for those who want to be in the center of things— it is 10 minutes' walk from both the Porta Nuova and Porta Susa train stations, and very close to Palazzo Madama and the Egyptian museum. You won't find luxury here, but the rooms are simple with spotless, functional bathrooms. A colorfully furnished breakfast room offers a morning buffet of breads, cheeses, fruit, and pastries, while the hotel restaurant/pizzeria, Marechiaro, serves Italian staples. There are plenty of dining options in the vicinity, but in warm weather it's a pleasant place to sit outside and enjoy people-watching along with a drink or meal. The hotel also has some slightly more modern self-catering apartments, in both standard and deluxe versions.

Via San Francesco d'Assisi 21. www.lepetithotel.it. ☎ **011/561-2626.** 79 units. 89€–129€ doubles; 150€–220€ apartments. Rates include breakfast. **Amenities:** Restaurant; Wi-Fi (free).

Townhouse 70 ★★★   Discreetly located (with very little signage outside) mere steps from Piazza Castello and the Palazzo Reale, the Townhouse could not be better located for sightseers. As part of a small Milan-based chain of luxury hotels, this is a smooth, urbane property with a tiny *aperitivo* bar tucked in one corner of the lobby. There's a breakfast room with a single massive table, where smart businesspeople and families all sit down together. Rooms, which are spacious for a city-center hotel, feature soothing dark colors; bathrooms have massive showers. Quieter bedrooms look over an internal courtyard (where you can grab a cocktail in warmer weather), but keep in mind that privacy may be a concern when your shutters are open.

Via XX Settembre 70. 70.townhousehotels.com. ☎ **011/1970-0003.** 48 units. 135€–170€ doubles. Rates include breakfast. **Amenities:** Bar; concierge; room service (7–10am); Wi-Fi (free).

VitaminaM ★★★ With just two rooms, this B&B is more like staying in a short-term apartment rental, albeit a particularly special one. The funky interiors make it feel like the sophisticated city home of a modern art lover, with light-flooded rooms in silver and red color schemes; the bathrooms are surprisingly luxurious. A library full of books is available to guests, and musical instruments are available as well upon request. Expect little touches like chocolates on your pillow and homemade jams at breakfast. The neighborhood is quite bustling, and this is good news for travelers who want to be surrounded by shops and restaurants, but it also means it is hard to find parking if you come by car, and it can be quite loud on weekend nights. The B&B is four floors up with no elevator, though someone is usually always available to help with your bags. Book well ahead; this is one of the hottest tickets in town.

Via Belfiore 18. www.vitaminam.com. ✆ 347/1526-130. 2 units. 100€–120€ double; additional bed 30€. Rates include breakfast. **Amenities:** Wi-Fi (free).

Where to Eat in Turin

Turin's gourmet reputation outshines other Italian cities renowned for their gastronomy. Many restaurants are strong advocates of the Slow Food movement, and a glance at a menu will tell you whether ingredients are local; look for porcini mushrooms and truffles in season. Wine lists feature Barolo, Barbera, and Barbaresco reds and sparkling Asti whites. Turin is also home to the world's largest food and wine fair, the **Salone del Gusto** (www.salonedelgusto.com), which runs every 2 years in September or October.

Cannavacciuolo Bistrot ★★ ITALIAN REGIONAL Despite the casual-sounding bistro name, this is one of the hottest fine-dining experiences in town, just across the Po River. Italian celebrity chef Antonio Cannavacciuolo's elegant yet minimalist space sets the stage for lighter Piedmontese dishes with influences from southern Italy (Cannavacciuolo is from Campania). Fassona beef tartare comes with a hazelnut mayonnaise, black truffle, and parmesan; tagliatelle with shrimp and orange is more of a nod to the Mediterranean, while Genoese spaghetti with sausage from the town of Bra is a mix of land and sea. There are a variety of tasting menus (75€-95€) for those wanting to try a bit of everything.

Via Umberto Cosmo 6. www.cannavacciuolobistrot.it/torino. ✆ 011/839-9893. Entrees 20€–40€. Mon–Sat 12:30–3pm and 7–11pm; closed Sun.

EDIT Restaurant ★★ REGIONAL Turin has gotten in on the food-hall trend with EDIT (an acronym for Eat Drink Innovate Together), a massive two-level space in what was once a cable factory, located in a gentrifying area just north of the city center. Here, there's a bakery/cafe, pub, cocktail bar, brewery, and a trendy restaurant featuring cuisine by young resident chef Matteo Monti. The post-industrial space with an open kitchen (sit at the bar for a multi-course "chef's table" experience that costs 65€ without wine pairings, 98€ with wine pairings) has exposed brick walls and fancy light fixtures, making for a Milan-meets-Brooklyn feel. The cuisine is creative modern Italian—fassona beef tartare with coconut and curried artichokes, or carnaroli rice risotto with scallops and pumpkin. Grab a drink at Edit's innovative cocktail bar before or after dinner. EDIT is a bit off the beaten path, so map out your transportation options carefully—the nearest train station is Stazione Dora, which is about a 10-minute walk.

Via Cigna 96/15. www.edit-to.com. ✆ **011/1932-9700.** Entrees 16€–28€. Daily 7:30–11:30pm. Bus: 10, 11.

Officine Bohemien ★★ PIEDMONT This offbeat restaurant down a side street in the center of town is casual and slightly edgy. The atmosphere here is laidback, with vintage décor, and a more intimate, romantic feel at night. Lunch sees staples like *pasta al pomodoro* or big salads at a really good price, while dinner is more sophisticated and interesting with dishes like blueberry-infused tagliolini pasta in a gorgonzola cheese-and-pear sauce or beef carpaccio served with fennel marinated with lime and soy sauce. There are also platters of grilled and smoked meats, regional cheeses, and fruits and vegetables, which are all sourced locally. Bread is made fresh daily. The bar sells Piedmont wines, French or Belgian beers, and cocktails, while jazz plays in the background; frequent live music events are held here.

Via San Camillo de Lellis (formerly Via Mercanti) 19. www.officinebohemien.it. ✆ **011/764-0368.** Entrees 8€–12€. Mon noon–3pm, Tues–Fri noon–3pm and 7:30–10:30pm8; Sat 7:30–10:30pm; closed Sun.

Trattoria Coco's ★★ ITALIAN Locals flock here for the down-home cooking and not necessarily for the atmosphere. With its wood-paneled walls and vintage sports photos on the wall, time seems to have stood still at this quintessential *trattoria* and bar in the heart of the San Salvario neighborhood, about a 5-minute walk from Porta Nuova station. While so many Italian restaurants now offer up fusion interpretations of the country's cuisine, Coco's is still making things the way *nonna* used to for Sunday lunch, with Italian comfort food staples like *pasta e fagioli*, Milanese cutlet, *vitello tonnato* (veal in a creamy tuna sauce), and risotto with saffron and toma cheese, all at incredibly reasonable prices. Unfortunately, you can't reserve ahead of time.

Via Bernardino Galliari 28. ✆ **340/251-0393.** Entrees 6€–10€. Mon–Wed 7am–8pm, Thurs–Sat 7am–midnight, closed Sun.

Trattoria Santo Spirito ★★ SEAFOOD Thanks to its prime location in a quaint piazza not far from Palazzo Reale, in the heart of the Area Romana, this trattoria could be mistaken for a tourist trap. But Santo Spirito is well loved by locals for the seafood and the fast, friendly service. Since the mid-1970s, this restaurant has been serving up vast platters of mussels, tuna carpaccio, simply grilled fish, and delicious fettucine served with lobster. Portions are huge—and the prices do reflect that to some extent—so don't be tempted to over-order. This may not be haute cuisine, but it is great home cooking, with fresh ingredients and strong flavors (try the smoked-fish appetizer, the porcini mushroom ravioli, or linguine with squid ink). In summer, tables spread onto the piazza; in winter a cozy fire blazes inside and heaters warm the enclosed patio. Space can be tight, so call ahead for a reservation.

Largo IV Marzo 11. © **011/4360-877.** Entrees 9€–25€, tasting menus 40€. Daily 12:30–3:30pm, 7:30pm–midnight.

> ### Shaken, not Stirred
>
> Turin gave the world the aperitif vermouth, which was invented in 1786 by Antonio Benedetto Carpano; the brands Martini and Cinzano are still made in the Piedmont region. Order a glass at the gorgeous **Art Nouveau Caffè Mulassano** at Piazza Castello 15 (www.caffemulassano.com; © **011/547-990**), or come early to enjoy coffee and tempting cannoli or dainty fruit tarts at the ornate marble counter.

Outdoor Activities

Turin's beautiful playground is **Parco del Valentino,** which cradles the left bank of the River Po between the Ponte Umberto I and the Ponte

Rowers on the River Po, flowing through Turin.

Isabella. Its first incarnation was in 1630, when it was the private garden of the Savoy dukes, but the park was much extended in the 1860s and opened to the public. It's a romantic place to stroll among the botanical gardens, flowerbeds, and manicured lawns. The park's massive **Castello del Valentino,** built in 1660, was once the pleasure palace of Christine Marie of France (see p. 519); it is closed to the public. The castle forms an incongruous backdrop to the **Borgo Medievale** (see p. 527), a riverside replica of a 15th-century Piedmontese village. It's a pleasant walk to the city center along Corso Emanuele Vittorio II, or you can hop Tram 9.

Rowing on the Po is a popular pastime in Turin, with half a dozen rowing clubs, the oldest being Reale Società Canottieri Cerea. You can watch them plying the water as you follow **jogging** and **cycling** routes along the riverside pathways. The city of Turin manages the TOBike (www.tobike.it) bike-sharing platform, with 140 bike stations throughout the city. You have to register on the site, but there are various plans, such as 4YOUflat, which gives you 4 hours of bike time over 24 hours and costs 8€. The official mobile app for the service can be downloaded at www.bicincitta.com.

Shopping & Nightlife

Turin's high-end shopping area is quite simply one of the most beautiful in the world. The arcaded **Via Roma** does full justice to the exquisite fashions of Gucci, Armani, Ferragamo, Max Mara, and so on. At the end of Via Roma, the glass-roofed **Galleria Subalpina** (Piazza Castello 27), which links Piazza Castello with Piazza Carlo, competes with Milan's Galleria Vittorio Emanuele II for sheer opulence in its three levels of art galleries, antiquarian bookstores, and cafes. For those whose pockets may not be quite so deep, **Via Garibaldi, Corso XX Settembre,** and the surrounding streets together offer midrange international brands at reasonable prices.

The windows of Italian food shops are always a thing of joy, and the specialist delis and confectioners of Turin are no exceptions. **Confetteria Stratta** (Piazza San Carlo 191; ℂ **011/547-920**) and **Pasticceria Gerla** (Corso Vittorio Emanuele II 86) are known for their extravagant pastries, cakes, and *gianduiotti* (chocolate with hazelnuts). Turin is famous for its quality confectionery—the city produces 40 percent of Italy's **chocolate.** Turin has two branches of **Eataly** (see p. 489), the current mecca for gourmet Italian fare, one in the center in Via Lagrange 3 and another one in the Lingotto area at Via Nizza 230.

Most newsagents in Turin have English-language newspapers, and the two branches of **Feltrinelli** (Piazza Castello 19, ℂ **011/541-627** or Stazione Porta Nuova ℂ **011/563-981**) sell multilingual books.

Nightlife in the city that invented the vermouth *aperitivo* is sophisticated, and, as in Milan, it starts in the cafes and bars and finishes very, very late. Squeeze in with the Torinese at **Caffè Platti** (Corso Vittorio

The Markets of Turin

The **produce market** in and around Porta Palazzo takes over the gigantic Piazza della Repubblica Monday to Friday 7am to 2pm and Saturday until 7:30pm. A bustling **flea market** takes place in the warren of streets behind the Porta Palazzo every Saturday, among the antique shops on Via Borgo Dora. The second Sunday of every month, the same spot is the scene of an **antiques market,** the continuously expanding **Gran Balon** (www.balon.it), with more than 250 dealers from across northern Italy. There's also a smaller version known only as Balon every Saturday. Come December, a **Christmas market** sets out its stalls in Via Borgo Dora. Turin has many stores specializing in rare books and old prints, and these also sell their wares from stalls along the Via Po.

Emanuele II 72; ☎ **011/454-6151**) for a vermouth, and pick from the plates of enticing little pizzas made on the premises. Choose a Slow Food restaurant for dinner, and then join models and footballers to dance at **Kogin's** (Corso Sicilia 6; ☎ **011/661-0546**).

Dance, opera, theater, and musical performances (mostly classical) are on the agenda all year long—check www.visitatorino.com—but September is the month to really enjoy classical music in Turin, when more than 60 classical concerts are staged around the city during the month-long **Settembre Musica** festival (www.mitosettembremusica.it), which is hosted jointly with the city of Milan. Beyond the festivals you'll find classical concerts at **Auditorium della RAI,** Via Rossini 15 (www.orchestra sinfonica.rai.it; ☎ **011/810-4653**) and dance performances and operas staged at the city's venerable **Teatro Regio** (www.teatroregio.torino.it; ☎ **011/8815-557**).

THE PIEDMONT WINE COUNTRY ★★

South of Turin, the Po valley rises into the rolling hills of Langhe and Roero, flanked by orchards and vineyards. You'll recognize the region's place names from the labels of its first-rate wines, among them **Asti Spumanti, Barbaresco,** and **Barolo.** And vines are not all that flourish in this fertile soil—truffles top the list of the region's gastronomic delights, along with rabbit and game plus excellent cheeses.

Asti ★★★

Asti: 60km (37 miles) SE of Turin, 127km (79 miles) SW of Milan

The Asti of sparkling-wine fame is a bustling working city, but it has many treasures to uncover in its history-drenched *centro storico*—medieval towers (there were about 120 at one time), Renaissance palaces, and piazzas provide the perfect setting in which to sample the town's most famous product, which flows readily in the local *enoteche* and cantinas.

ESSENTIALS

ARRIVING Up to four **trains** per hour link Asti with **Turin Porta Nuova** (35 min; 5.25€) via **Trenitalia** (www.trenitalia.com; ℰ **892-021**). **Arfea** (www.arfea.it; ℰ **0131/225-810**) runs **buses** from Turin Autostazione to Asti; the trip takes 1 hour. By car, Asti can be reached in less than an hour from Turin via Autostrada 21.

VISITOR INFORMATION The **APT tourist office** is near the train station at Piazza Alfieri 34 (ℰ **0141/530-357**). It's open Monday to Saturday 9am to 1pm and 2:30 to 6:30pm; Sunday 9am to 1pm and 1:30pm to 5:30pm.

EXPLORING ASTI

Asti's historic heart is centered on three adjoining squares: **Piazza Libertá,** the vast **Campo del Palio,** and the grand arcaded **Piazza Alfieri.** Each year on the third Sunday of September, the area is mobbed for the **Palio,** Asti's annual horse race (www.palio.asti.it; ℰ **0141/399-482**), now held in Piazza Alfieri (originally it was in Campo del Palio). Like the similar race in the Tuscan city of Siena (see p. 232), Asti's Palio begins with a colorful medieval pageant through the town and ends with a wild bareback ride around the triangular piazza. First staged around 1273, the race coincides with Asti's other great festival, the **Douja d'Or** (www.doujador.it), a weeklong bacchanal celebrating the grape harvest.

Behind Piazza Alfieri stands the Romanesque-Gothic redbrick **Collegiata di San Secondo** (www.comune.asti.it; ℰ **0141/530-066;** daily 7:30am–7pm). This church has two distinctions: it houses the Palio Astigiano, the prestigious banner awarded to the winning jockey at the Palio, and it also contains the tomb of St. Secondo, patron saint of both the race and the town. A Roman officer who converted to Christianity in A.D. 119, Secondo was martyred for his faith, beheaded in roughly the spot where his tomb now stands.

From Piazza Alfieri, the charming and largely pedestrianized **Corso Alfieri** bisects the old town and is lined with Renaissance *palazzi.* At the eastern end is the church of **San Pietro in Consavia** (ℰ **0141/399-489;** Tues–Sun 10am–1pm and 3–6pm, until 7pm in summer) with a 10th-century Romanesque baptistery that was once a place of worship for the Knights of the Order of St. John. The archeology located inside San Pietro in

Precious white truffles from Alba.

Piedmont & Valle d'Aosta

Consavia has recently been renovated. At the western extreme of Corso Alfieri, you'll find the rotund **church of Santa Caterina,** abutting the medieval red-and-white brick-topped **Torre Rossa.**

Asti's 15th-century **Cattedrale di Santa Maria Assunta** (© **0141/ 592-924;** daily 8:30am–noon and 3–5:30pm) is also at the western end of town in Piazza Cattedrale. Its austere exterior hides the gaudy excesses of the interior; every inch of the church is festooned with frescoes by late-15th-century artists, including Gandolfino d'Asti.

Being the agricultural and gourmet hotspot that it is, Asti is blessed with two **food markets.** The larger is held in the Campo del Palio on

PIEDMONT'S REGIONAL wines

The wines of Piedmont are of exceptional quality and distinctive taste. They're usually made with grapes unique to the region, and grown on tiny family plots—making the countryside a lovely patchwork of vineyards and small farms.

Often called "the king of reds," **Barolo** is considered one of Italy's top wines, on par with Tuscany's Brunello and the Veneto's Amarone. It is the richest and heartiest of the Piedmont wines, and the one most likely to accompany game or meat. **Barbaresco,** like Barolo, is made solely from the red Nebbiolo grape, although it is less tannic. **Barbera d'Alba** is a smooth, rich red wine, the product of the delightful villages south of Alba (see p. 536). **Dolcetto** is dry, fruity, mellow, and not sweet, as its name may imply. **Nebbiolo d'Alba** is rich, full, and dry.

As far as white wines go, Spumanti DOCGs are the sparkling wines that put Asti on the map. **Moscato d'Asti** is a delicious floral dessert wine, and the fiery local Piedmont **grappas** are none too shabby either.

Wednesdays and Saturdays, as part of a day-long street market with all kinds of wares; the food stands, however, are only there from 7:30am–1pm. The market spills over into neighboring piazzas, with stalls selling cheeses, herbs, flowers, oils, and wines. The covered **Mercato Coperto** on Piazza della Libertà is open daily except Sunday (Mon–Wed and Fri 8am–1pm and 3:30–7:30pm; Thurs 8:30am–1pm; Sat 8am–7:30pm). Look for white truffles, *bagna cauda* (a fondue-like dip served warm and made with ingredients like olive, oil, butter, garlic, and anchovies), *robiola* cheeses, *amaretti* biscuits, and *nocciolata* (hazelnut and chocolate spread). The region's famous Asti Spumante DOCG sparkling wines can be bought from *cantinas* and *enoteche* in the town center and direct from some vineyards—a list is available from the **tourist office** at Piazza Alfieri 34 (see p. 534).

The Piedmont Wine Villages

Gastro-destination **Alba** ★★ (60km/37 miles south of Turin) is the jumping-off point for visiting the many vineyards of the Barolo wine-producing region. While it's a pleasure to walk along the Via Vittorio Emanuele and the narrow streets of the old town center, wine and food are what Alba's all about. Wherever you go, you'll end up peering into store windows to admire displays of wines, truffles, and the calorific but exquisite *nocciolata* cake made of hazelnuts and chocolate. The streets are crammed with enough enticing restaurants to make gourmands very happy indeed (see p. 538).

Just to the south of Alba lie some of the Piedmont's most enchanting wine villages, sitting on hilltops among orderly rows of vines. The best way to see these villages is to drive; hire cars in Turin from **Avis,** Via

Lessona Michele 30 (www.avisautonoleggio.it; © **011/774-1962**) or **Hertz,** at Corso Turati 37 (www.hertz.it; © **011/502-080**). Before you head out on the small country roads, provide yourself with a list of vineyards from the tourist office in Asti (see p. 534). A detailed map is also a good idea, in case you lose the satellite signal for your GPS.

The main road through the wine region is the SS231, which runs between Alba and Asti. It is, however, a fast, busy, and unattractive highway; you'll want to turn off it to explore Piedmont's rustic backwaters among hazelnut groves and vineyards.

One such enchanting drive heads south from Alba to the wine villages of the **Langhe hills** (follow signs out of town for Barolo on the SP3). After 8km (5 miles), take the right turn for **Grinzane Cavour,** a hilltop village built around a castle harboring the **Enoteca Regionale Piemontese Cavour** (www.castellogrinzane.com; © **0173/262-159**), which is open daily from 9:30am to 7pm (until 6pm Nov–Mar). Here you can sample local wines from over 300 labels; the fine restaurant is perfect for lunch.

Return to the main road, turn left, and after 4km (2½ miles) south, take the right fork to **La Morra,** perched among vineyards with panoramic views over the rolling, vine-clad countryside. La Morra has several cafes and restaurants in which to taste the local vintages. The **Cantina**

The village of Barolo surrounded by vineyards.

Comunale di La Morra at Via Alberto 2 (www.lamorraturismo.it; ✆ **0173/509-204**) represents local growers, selling Barolo, Nebbiolo, Barbera, and Dolcetto. It's open daily (except Tues) 10am to 12:30pm and 2:30 to 6:30pm. La Morra's tourist office (Piazza Martiri 1; www.lamorra turismo.it; ✆ **0173/500-344**) is open on Monday and Tuesday 9:30am to 1:30 p.m. and Thursday through Sunday 10am to 6pm.

Barolo is a handsome little village dominated by two ancient castles; it's 5km (3 miles) along the SP58 from La Morra. Here, too, you'll find a choice of restaurants and shops selling world-renowned red wines from local vineyards. Among these is **Castello Falletti** (www.enoteca delbarolo.it; ✆ **0173/56-277;** Thurs–Tues 10am–5pm), with a wine bar and an *enoteca* offering tastings in its cavernous cellars. They even offer Barolo and chocolate pairings.

WHERE TO STAY & EAT IN THE PIEDMONT WINE COUNTRY

As well as a few decent urban hotels, the Barolo region is the land of the *agriturismo,* with options to stay on wine estates in the hills of Langhe. You can find properties on www.agriturismo.it; search on the Piedmont region or search for specific town names. As for restaurants, they don't come much classier than the best of the Piedmont.

La Cascina del Monastero ★★★ Perfectly situated for exploring the Barolo wine region, this beautiful 16th-century family-run estate is part rustic B&B and part winery, all just minutes away from La Morra. Converted from an outbuilding of soft stone and arcading, the suites and apartments are beautifully furnished with Italian antiques and brass beds. Exposed stone walls (like in the unique Autunno Suite), beams, wooden floors, and homey personal touches add to the ambience, while bathrooms feature modern conveniences. Guest facilities include a large pool, and the unusual spa has a sauna in what appears to be a massive wine barrel. Don't miss out on a chance to taste the estate's wines at some point during your stay. An abundant farm-to-table breakfast is served, allowing you to fuel up before setting out to discover the area. A camping zone is available near the main house, boasting the same lovely scenery.
Cascina Luciani 112A, Frazione Annunziata, La Morra. www.cascinadelmonastero.it. ✆ **0173/509-245.** 10 units. 130€–145€ double; 135€–150€ apartment. Rates include breakfast. Closed Jan and sometimes Feb. **Amenities:** Playground; spa; outdoor pool; room service; sauna; Wi-Fi (free).

Hotel Castello d'Asti ★★ Don't be put off by the unremarkable street; this hotel is a find. Tucked into a lush courtyard garden northwest of Asti's *centro storico,* it's a historic brick townhouse with updated interiors. The spacious rooms are decorated in soft shades of cream, brown, and beige, with sleek marble bathrooms. The suites overlooking the rooftops of Asti are especially large (some even have small kitchens) and all have their own balconies overlooking the gardens or the courtyard. Downstairs there's a lively bar, along with the intimate **Cambiocavallo** restaurant, which serves artfully presented cuisine influenced by the Piedmont and Liguria regions, with specialties from land and sea like Barolo-braised meats or chopped tuna in a sauce made from Ribera oranges and mint.

Via G Testa 47, Asti. www.hotelcastelloasti.com. ℭ **0141/351-094.** 11 units. 105€–155€ double; 155€–235€ suite. Rates include breakfast. Closed Jan. **Amenities:** Restaurant; bar; room service; Wi-Fi (free).

Palazzo Finati ★★   Just around the corner from Alba's main square, Piazza del Duomo, and the town's best shops and gourmet restaurants, this historic *palazzo* offers a taste of old-fashioned luxury. The Finati has a selection of individually designed rooms; some have romantic touches, frescoed ceilings, and terraces overlooking the inner courtyard. Rooms can be connected for larger groups or families. The breakfast buffet includes fresh pastries, fruit, local cheeses, and cured meats, all served in an elegant brick-ceilinged, barrel-vaulted dining room. Parking can be an issue so, if you are coming by car, make sure to request access to the enclosed parking area ahead of time.

Via Vernazza 8, Alba. www.palazzofinati.it. ℭ **0173/366-324.** 9 units. 150€–180€ double, 170€–250€ suite. Rates include breakfast. **Amenities:** Wi-Fi (free).

Ristorante al Castello di Marc Lanteri ★★★ GOURMET   Housed in the fairy-tale castle at Grinzane Cavour along with an *enoteca* selling the best of the region's wines, this elegant restaurant showcases the food of Michelin-starred chef Marc Lanteri. A French chef who grew up on the Italian border, Lanteri offers Franco-Piedmont cuisine, with some influences from nearby Liguria. To truly get into the Piedmontese spirit, try the fassona beef rump steak served with Ratte potatoes (a tuber that originally came from France and was later cultivated in Piedmont) and tarragon-infused carrots; other creative dishes might include spinach farfalle pasta served with cuttlefish, broccoli, and taggiasche olives. The chef's American wife, Amy, is the restaurant's sommelier.

Via Castello 5, Grinzane Cavour. www.castellogrinzane.com. ℭ **338/700-1914.** Entrees 22€–35€. Tasting menus from 55€ w/o wine pairings or 90€ w/ wine pairings. Mon 12:30–2:30pm, Wed–Sun 12:30–2:30pm and 7:30–10pm. Closed Jan.

AOSTA ★★ & VALLE D'AOSTA ★★★

Aosta: 113km (70 miles) N of Turin, 184km (114 miles) NW of Milan; Courmayeur-Entrèves: 35km (22 miles) W of Aosta, 148km (92 miles) NW of Turin

Tucked up against the French and Swiss borders in northwest Italy, the Aosta Valley is a land of harsh, snow-capped peaks, lush pastures, thick forests, waterfalls cascading into mountain streams, and romantic castles clinging to wooded hillsides. A year-round stream of skiers, hikers, cyclists, and nature lovers flock to this tiny Alpine region north of Turin for the scenery, outdoor adventure, and rustic gastronomy.

Aosta

ESSENTIALS

ARRIVING   Aosta is served by 20 **trains** a day to and from **Turin** (2 hr., change in Ivrea or Chivasso; tickets 9.45€) aboard **Trenitalia** (www.tren italia.com; ℰ **892-021**). **Bus service** to Aosta is much less handy: Only a few buses travel from Turin Porta Nuova per day (most change in Ivrea), and even the direct trip takes 2 hours, the indirect route more than 3. However, a SAVDA bus conveniently connects Aosta hourly to **Courmayeur** (1 hr., 3.50€) and other popular spots in the valley.

Autostrada A5 from Turin shoots up the length of Valle d'Aosta en route to France and Switzerland via the Mont Blanc tunnel; there are numerous exits in the valley. The trip from Turin to Aosta normally takes about 90 minutes, but traffic can be heavy on weekends in the ski season.

VISITOR INFORMATION   The **tourist office** in Aosta (Piazza Porta Praetoria 3; www.lovevda.it; ℰ **0165/236-627**) dispenses a wealth of information on hiking trails, ski lifts and passes, bike rentals, and rafting trips. It's open daily 9am to 7pm.

EXPLORING AOSTA

An appealing mountain town with an ancient heart, Aosta—nicknamed "the Rome of the Alps"—is surrounded by snowcapped peaks and steeped in a history that goes back to Roman times. Although you're not going to find much pristine Alpine quaintness here in the Valle d'Aosta's busy tourist center, you will find Roman ruins, medieval bell towers, and chic shops. Aosta's **weekly market** day is Tuesday, when stalls selling food, clothes, and crafts fill the Piazza Cavalieri di Vittorio Veneto.

Well-preserved city walls date from the days when Aosta was one of Rome's most important trading and military outposts. A **Roman bridge** spans the River Buthier, and two Roman gates arch gracefully across the Via San Anselmo. The **Porta Pretoria** forms the western entrance to the Roman town and the

Summer hiking in Courmayeur.

Arco di Augusto the eastern entrance. The **Teatro Romano** and the ruins of the **amphitheater** are north of the Porta Pretoria; the ruins of the **forum** are in an adjacent park. The theater and forum are open generally from 9am to 6pm (typically closed for a few hours in the afternoon in the winter), and admission is free. Architectural fragments from these monuments that were found during excavations are displayed in Aosta's **Archaeological Museum** at Piazza Roncas 12 (✆ **0165/275-902;** open summer daily 9am–7pm, fall and winter Tues–Sun 10am–1pm and 2–5pm). The 7€ ticket is valid for a year and allows for visiting 4 other sites of archeological importance in the region.

The Valle d'Aosta

Most visitors to the Valle d'Aosta come here for the outdoor activities rather than to sightsee; the region has some of Italy's best hiking trails. In summer, climbers, cyclists, and ramblers head for the untamed **Parco Nazionale del Gran Paradiso** (see "Italian Wilderness," p. 541). In winter, the meadows and alpine forests around **Cogne** boast some of the region's best cross-country skiing. There's an **ice rink** in Aosta called **Art on Ice** at Corso Lancieri di Aosta 17 (www.artoniceaosta.it; ✆ **0165/415-66**), and if you're after something a bit different, consider **dog sledding** (www.dogsledman.com) near Courmayeur.

Most visitors, however, come for the **downhill skiing** and **snowboarding** destinations of **Courmayeur, Breuil-Cervinia,** and the **Monte Rose** ski area around the resort towns of Champoluc and Gressoney. There are trails for all levels, from gentle nursery slopes to black diamond runs and mogul fields. Expert skiers are best off at high-altitude **La Thuile** for excellent off-trail powder and heli-skiing. Depending on conditions, the ski season kicks off in early November and runs through April. Altogether there are 800km (500 miles) of ski runs available under the **Valle**

UP AND OVER mont blanc

Riding high over Mont Blanc—Europe's tallest mountain at 4,811m (15,784 ft.)—has to be one of the most awe-inspiring experiences in the Italian Alps. It's an enchanted journey passing over glaciers and steep ravines, mountain lakes, and snowy peaks on the Italian side of the Vallée Blanche.

For years, this epic trek involved three changes of cable car, starting from the little ski village of **La Palud** (3km/1.75 miles above Courmayeur) and ascending through **Le Pavillon** and **Rifugio Torino** to the viewing terrace at **Punta Helbronner** (3,462m/11,358 ft.), in the heart of the Mont Blanc Massif. From here it was possible to take the cable car down to **Aiguille de Midi** on the French side of Mont Blanc, and then the Panoramic Mont-Blanc Gondola on into the party-loving resort of **Chamonix**.

But all that changed in 2015 when a new, vastly improved cable-car service, **Skyway Monte Bianco** (www.montebianco.com), launched. Run by Funivie del Monte Bianco, the system has sleek rotating gondolas departing from a swish new station at **Pontal d'Entrèves** (near the entrance to the Mont Blanc tunnel) on a high-speed connection up to Punta Helbronner for a bird's-eye view of

Monte Bianco and the surrounding peaks of Gran Paradiso and Monte Cervinia (Matterhorn). This service offers breathtaking views, but be prepared to pay for them. A roundtrip ticket from Pontal (Courmayeur) to Punta Helbronner is 52€ for adults (free for children 7 and under) and 39€ one-way, while roundtrip from Pontal to Pavillon du Mont-Fréty—the midway point, which has a restaurant and shopping area—costs 28€ and 21€ one-way. Stopping at the midway point is an option for those who want to enjoy the views but may suffer from altitude sickness at the very top at Punta Helbronner.

If you do venture all the way to Chamonix in your travels, you can make your way back to Courmayeur via the **SAVDA/SAT bus service** through the Mont Blanc tunnel. Six buses run each way, and the journey takes 45 minutes (www.savda.it; tickets 15€, discounts available for children under age 12).

d'Aosta ski pass; multi-day passes cost from 143€ for 3 days up to 502€ for 2 weeks in low season, and from 152€ for 3 days up to 538€ in high season. One child under age 8 skis free with each adult who buys the pass. More details are available at www.skilife.ski.

WHERE TO STAY & EAT IN THE VALLE D'AOSTA

In the ski season, many hotels in Valle d'Aosta expect guests to eat on the premises and stay 3 nights or more, but they are more flexible outside busy tourist times.

The Valle d'Aosta is the land of mountain food—hams and salamis, creamy polenta—and buttery Fontina is the cheese of choice.

Hostellerie du Cheval Blanc ★★ If family comforts and town-center convenience are what you are after, the modern design of the Cheval Blanc (meaning "white horse") fits the bill. Despite its contemporary

The Skyway Monte Bianco ascends Mont Blanc.

style, you will still get Alpine views and a bit of greenery. The hotel is designed around a massive atrium with stylish leather sofas and has two restaurants: the fairly expensive **Le Petit** and the more casual **Brasserie,** which is well-suited to early dinners with kids. The rooms are conventionally decorated in neutral shades, but the bathrooms come in highly ornate marble, most with baths as well as showers. Skiers will appreciate a winter shuttle to the cable car up to Pila, and the pool and sauna provide perfect après-ski relaxation before a night of fun in the bars of Aosta. Guests have access to a gym and wellness center with indoor pool, Jacuzzi, and two saunas.

Rue Clavalité 20, Aosta. www.chevalblanc.it. © **0165/239-140.** 55 units. 130€ doubles; 180€–200€ suite. Rates include breakfast. **Amenities:** 2 restaurants; bar; children's playroom; indoor pool; gym; sauna; spa; room service; Wi-Fi (free).

Osteria da Nando ★★ FONDUE   This cheery *osteria* with terracotta-colored walls and rustic touches is a true family affair, run by the Scarpa family since 1957. Over the years, it has become one of Aosta's most popular restaurants for its hearty yet somewhat sophisticated fare. Try different types of fondue, from *bourguignonne* served with tender beef filet to *raclette* served with creamy Fontina cheese and chunks of chewy bread, alongside the classic Piedmontese *bagna cauda* (anchovy fondue). Other menu items also rely on local ingredients, such as polenta served a variety of ways, tagliatelle with porcini mushrooms, and a zucchini tartlet served over a pumpkin cream. Desserts are playfully presented (like panna cotta with licorice and cinnamon), and the wine selection is impressively local.

Via Sant'Anselmo 99. Aosta. www.osterianando.com. ℂ **0165/44-455.** Entrees 12€–27€. Weds–Mon noon–2pm and 7:30–10pm. Closed 2 wks late Jun–early July.

Ristorante La Palud ★★ PIZZA/SEAFOOD This perpetually packed pizzeria/restaurant has the look of a sophisticated mountain chalet and offers impressive Monte Bianco and glacier views. Thanks to its proximity to the tunnel into France, it is a popular stop-off point, and the crowds keep coming back for enormous pizzas, creamy polenta dishes, and fresh fish brought up from the Ligurian coast on Fridays. In summer, sit outside on the flower-filled terrace; in winter, huddle around the open fire and admire the drifts of snow piled up outside.

Strada la Palud 17, Courmayeur. www.lapalud.it. ℂ **0165/89-169.** Entrees 12€–25€. Daily noon–3:30pm and 7:30–10:30pm.

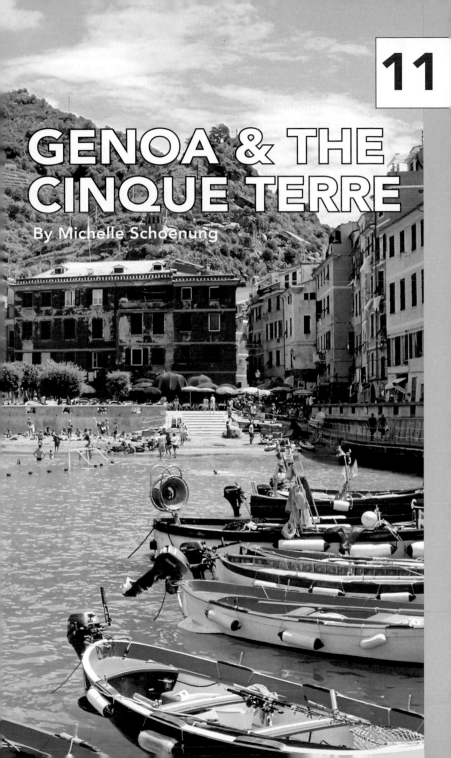

GENOA & THE CINQUE TERRE

By Michelle Schoenung

ugging the Mediterranean coastline from the French border to the tip of Tuscany lies a crescent-shaped strip of land that makes up the region of Liguria. The pleasures of this region are no secret. Since the 19th century, world-weary travelers have been heading for Liguria's resorts, such as San Remo and Porto-fino, to enjoy balmy weather and a sapphire-blue sea. Beyond the beach, the stones and tiles of fishing villages, small resort towns, and proud old port cities bake in the sun, and hillsides are fragrant with the scent of bougainvillea and pines.

Liguria is really two coasts. First, the "white sand" stretch west of Genoa known as the **Riviera di Ponente (Setting Sun)** is studded with fashionable resorts, many of which, like San Remo, have seen their heydays fade but continue to entice visitors with palm-fringed promenades and a gentle way of life. The rockier, more rugged, but also more colorful fishing-village-filled stretch to the southeast of Genoa, known as the **Riviera di Levante (Rising Sun),** extends past the posh harbor of Portofino to the ever-popular villages of the Cinque Terre.

The province's capital, Genoa, is Italy's busiest port, an ancient center of commerce, and one of history's great maritime powers. Despite its rough exterior, it is an underrated gem filled with architectural delights, Italy's largest historic center, and a sense of "real Italy" that has become hard to come by in many of the country's more popular cities. The tragic collapse of the historic Ponte Morandi viaduct on the A10 motorway in August 2018 killed 43 people and left the city reeling. Italians have rallied around the city, calling for visitors to flock here and show their support, but watch for detours if you are traveling into Genoa from the west or headed out toward the Riviera di Ponente (toward San Remo) from town.

DON'T LEAVE GENOA AND THE CINQUE TERRE WITHOUT . . .

Getting Lost in Genoa. It's been 160 years since Charles Dickens enthused on the wonders of losing yourself in the labyrinth of Europe's largest preserved medieval city, but it's still enthralling.

Toasting the Setting Sun. The Riviera di Levante is famous for its sunsets, and justifiably so. Its sheer cliffs afford huge, humbling views of this blazing show. Raise a glass of the region's golden sciacchetrà wine in tribute.

PREVIOUS PAGE: **The colorful fishing harbor at Vernazza, one of the five coastal villages of Liguria's famed Cinque Terre.**

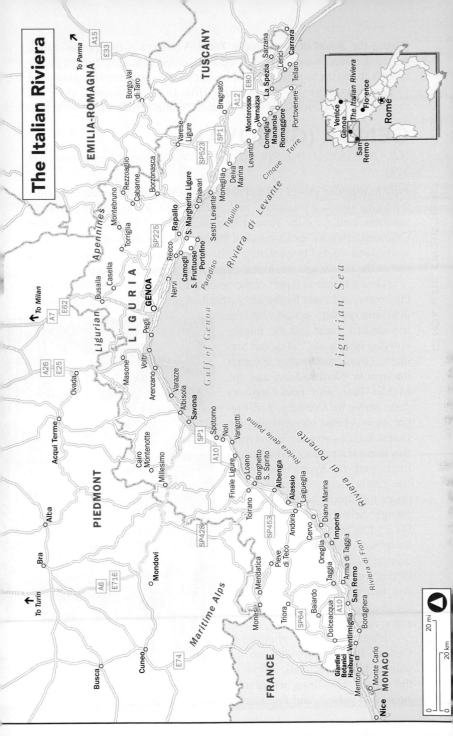

The Italian Riviera

To Parma

A15
E33

EMILIA-ROMAGNA

TUSCANY

Borgo Val
di Taro

Brugnato

Carrara
Sarzana
Lerici
La Spezia
Tellaro
Portovenere

Monterosso
Vernazza
Corniglia
Manarola
Riomaggiore

E80

A12

SP1

Varese
Ligure

SP523

Levanto

Deiva
Marina

Moneglia

Cinque
Terre

Rezzoaglio

Cabanne

Borzonasca

Chiavari

Sestri Levante

Riviera di Levante

Apennines

Montebruno

Torriglia

SP225

Rapallo

S. Margherita Ligure

Recco

Camogli

S. Fruttuoso

Portofino

Paradiso

Tigullio

LIGURIA

Busalla

Casella

Nervi

GENOA

Ligurian

To Milan

A7

E62

Pegli

Voltri

Masone

Arenzano

Gulf of Genoa

Ligurian Sea

A26

E25

Ovada

Varazze

Albisola

Savona

Acqui Terme

PIEDMONT

Cairo
Montenotte

Millesimo

Spotorno

Noli

Varigotti

SP1

A10

Finale Ligure

Loano

Borghetto
S. Spirito

Albenga

Riviera delle palme

Alba

Bra

Mondovì

Toirano

Alassio

Laigueglia

Andora

Diano Marina

Cervo

Imperia

Riviera di ponente

SP428

Pieve
di Teco

Onegia

Taggia

Arma di Taggia

SP453

Mendatica

San Remo

Riviera dei Fiori

Maritime Alps

To Turin

A6

E716

Monesi

Triora

Baiardo

Dolceacqua

SP64

A10

Ventimiglia

Bordighera

Busca

Cuneo

E74

Giardini
Botanici
Hanbury

Mentone

Monte Carlo

MONACO

Nice

FRANCE

Venice

Genoa

The Italian Riviera

Florence

Rome

San
Remo

20 mi

20 km

Seeing the Jewel of the Cinque Terre. Vernazza is the quintessential, postcard-perfect seaside village, with tall, colorful houses (known as *terratetti*) clustering around a natural harbor where you can swim among the fishing boats. Best way to get there? Hike from Monterosso, along the most scenic, if arduous, leg of the famed Cinque Terre trail.

GENOA (GENOVA) ★★

142km (88 miles) S of Milan, 501km (311 miles) NW of Rome, 194km (120 miles) E of Nice

With its dizzying mix of old and new, **Genoa** is as multilayered as the hills it which it clings. It was and is, first and foremost, a port city: an important maritime center for the Roman Empire, boyhood home of Christopher Columbus (whose much-restored house still stands near the medieval walls), and, fueled by seafaring trade that stretched to the Middle East, one of the largest and wealthiest cities of Renaissance Europe.

Genoa began as a port of the ancient Ligurian people at least by the 6th century B.C., and by the early Middle Ages had become a formidable maritime power, conquering the surrounding coast and the mighty outlying islands of Corsica and Sardinia. Genoa established colonies throughout North Africa and the Middle East, and made massive gains during the Crusades. With bigger success came bigger rivals, and Genoa locked commercial and military horns with Venice, which eventually took the upper hand in the late 1300s. Genoa increasingly fell under the control of outsiders, and though self-government returned for a while in the 16th century, sea trade was shifting to Spain and eventually to its American colonies. Genoa's most famous son, Columbus, had to travel to Spain to find the financial backing for his exploration across the Atlantic.

It's easy to capture glimpses of Genoa's former glory days on the narrow lanes and dank alleys of the portside Old Town, where treasure-filled palaces and fine marble

Genoa's Old Town is a maze of streets, historic palaces, and churches.

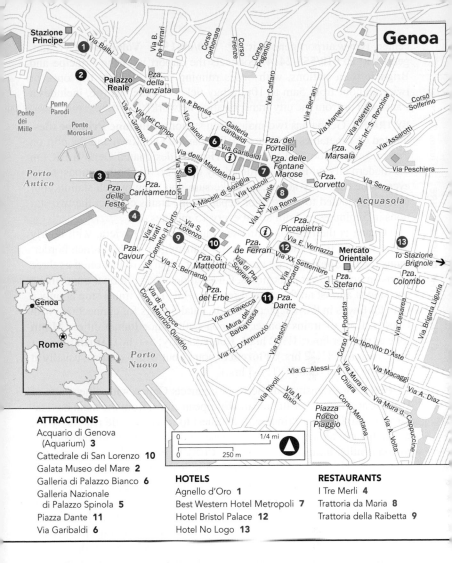

Genoa

ATTRACTIONS
Acquario di Genova
(Aquarium) **3**
Cattedrale di San Lorenzo **10**
Galata Museo del Mare **2**
Galleria di Palazzo Bianco **6**
Galleria Nazionale
di Palazzo Spinola **5**
Piazza Dante **11**
Via Garibaldi **6**

HOTELS
Agnello d'Oro **1**
Best Western Hotel Metropoli **7**
Hotel Bristol Palace **12**
Hotel No Logo **13**

RESTAURANTS
I Tre Merli **4**
Trattoria da Maria **8**
Trattoria della Raibetta **9**

churches stand next to laundry-draped tenements and brothels. The other
Genoa, the modern city that stretches for miles along the coast and climbs
the hills, is a city of international business, peaceful parks, and breezy
belvederes from which you can enjoy fine views of this colorful metropolis and the sea.

Essentials
ARRIVING

BY PLANE Flights to and from most European capitals serve **Cristoforo
Colombo International Airport,** just 6.5km (4 miles) west of the city

center (www.airport.genova.it; ✆ **010/60-151**). **Volabus** (www.amt. genova.it; ✆ **010/558-2414**) connects the airport with the Principe and Brignole train stations, with buses running the 30-minute trip once or twice an hour from 5am to 10pm; buy tickets on the bus (6€, includes a transfer to or from the city transportation network).

BY TRAIN   Genoa has two major train stations: **Stazione Principe** (designated on timetables as Genova P.P.) near the Old Town and the port on Piazza Acquaverde, and **Stazione Brignole** (designated Genova BR.) in the modern city on Piazza Verdi. Many trains service both stations; however, some stop only at one, so make sure you know which station your train is scheduled to arrive at or depart from. Trains connect the two stations in 5 minutes and run about every 15 minutes.

Genoa is the hub for trains serving the Italian Riviera, with hourly trains arriving from and departing for **Ventimiglia** on the French border; trains for **La Spezia,** at the eastern edge of Liguria, run as often as three trains an hour during peak times. Check timetables: regional trains make one stop at almost all the coastal resorts, while faster trains stop at only a few (for towns in this chapter, see individual listings for connections with Genoa). Lots of trains connect Genoa with major Italian cities: **Milan** (one or two per hour; 1½–2 hrs.), **Rome** (hourly; 5–6 hr.), **Turin** (one per hour; regional: 1¾–2 hrs.), **Florence** (hourly but with a change, usually at Pisa; 3 hr.), **Pisa** (hourly; 1½–3 hrs.).

BY BUS   An extensive bus network connects Genoa with other parts of Liguria, and with other Italian and European cities, from the main bus station next to Stazione Principe. It's easiest to reach seaside resorts by the trains that run along the coast, but buses link to many small towns in the region's hilly hinterlands. Contact **PESCI,** Piazza della Vittoria 94r (www.pesciviaggi.it; ✆ 010/564-936), for tickets and information.

BY CAR   Genoa is linked to other parts of Italy and to France by a convenient network of highways. Genoa has lots of parking around the port and the edges of the Old Town, so you can usually find a spot easily. It can be pricey (1.50€–2.50€ an hour), though in some lots you don't pay for the overnight hours. Due to the closure of the Ponte Morandi bridge on the A10 highway, you may run into detours if you enter the city from the west or are traveling out toward the Riviera di Ponente (in the direction of San Remo and France) from Genoa. Until a new bridge is built, you will most likely be rerouted to other highways, but the coastal road may be your best (and most scenic) bet despite the traffic.

BY FERRY   Genoa connects by ferry to several other major Mediterranean ports, including Barcelona, Sardinia, and Sicily (www.traghettitalia. it). Most boats leave and depart from the Stazione Marittima (✆ **010/089-8300**), which is on a waterfront roadway, Via Marina D'Italia, about a 5-minute walk south of Stazione Principe. For service to and from the **Riviera Levante,** check with **Tigullio** (www.traghettiportofino.it; ☎ **0185/284-670**) or Golfo Paradiso (www.golfoparadiso.it; ☎ **0185/ 772091**); there's almost hourly service from 9am to 5pm daily in July and August.

VISITOR INFORMATION

The **main tourist office** is on **Via Garibaldi 12r** across from the beautiful city hall (www.visitgenoa.it; ☎ **010/557-2903**), open daily 9am to 6:20pm. There are also branches near the Porto Antico in **Via al Porto Antico 2,** open daily from about 9am to 6pm with longer hours in the summer months; and **Cristoforo Colombo airport,** open daily 9am to 1pm and 1:30 to 5:30pm.

GETTING AROUND

Given Genoa's labyrinth of small streets (many of which cannot be negotiated by car or bus), the only way to traverse much of the city is on foot—and you'll need a good map. The tourist office gives out terrific maps, but you can also buy an audio guide with map that really helps you navigate the small *vicoli* or alleyways. Genovese are usually happy to direct visitors, but given the geography with which they are dealing, their instructions can be complicated.

BY BUS   Bus tickets (1.50€) are available at newsstands and at ticket booths, *tabacchi* (tobacconists, marked by a brown and white t sign), and at the train stations; look for the symbol **AMT** (www.amt.genova.it; ☎ **010/558-2414**). Otherwise, tickets cost 2.50€ on board on nights and weekends. You must stamp your ticket when you board. Bus tickets can also be used on the funiculars and public elevators that climb the steep hills surrounding the ancient core of the town. Tickets good for 24 hours cost 4.50€, or 9€ for four people (two people travel for free).

> ### Genoa Takes to the Sea
>
> Every June, an ancient tradition continues when Genoa takes to the sea in the **Regata delle Antiche Repubbliche Marinare,** rowing against crews from its ancient maritime rivals, Amalfi, Pisa, and Venice (each city takes turns hosting the event). Another spectacular—though more modern—regatta takes place every April: the **Millevele,** or Thousand Sails, when Genoa's bay is carpeted with the mainsails and spinnakers of nautical enthusiasts from around the world.

BY TAXI   A metered taxi, which you can find at cabstands, is your best bet for getting around Genoa at night. For instance, you may well want to consider taking one from a restaurant in the Old Town to your hotel or to one of the train stations (especially Stazione Brignole, which is a bit farther out). Cabstands at Piazza della Nunziata, Piazza Fontane Marose, and Piazza de Ferrari are especially convenient to the Old Town, or call **Radiotaxi** at ☎ **010/5966.** The meter starts at 5€ and adds .90€ every kilometer (or every minute if the taxi is traveling less than 30 kph). Additional fees are added at night or if one needs to leave city limits.

BY SUBWAY   The city's nascent subway system is a work in progress, with only eight stops on a single line between the new Brignole station and a suburb to the northwest called Certosa (there are convenient stops in between at Stazione Principe and at Dinegro close to the ferry port). The tickets are the same as those used for the bus.

CITY LAYOUT

Genoa extends for miles along the coast, with neighborhoods and suburbs tucked into valleys and climbing the city's many hills. Most sights of interest are in the **Old Town,** a fascinating jumble of old *palazzi,* shabby tenements, cramped squares, and tiny lanes and alleyways clustered on the eastern side of the old port. **Via Garibaldi,** lined with a succession of majestic *palazzi,* forms the northern flank of the Old Town and is the best place to begin your explorations. Many of the city's most important museums and monuments are on and around this street, and from here you can descend into the warren of little lanes, known as ***caruggi,*** that lead through the heart of the city and down to the port. *Note:* These very small alleyways of the Old Town can be sketchy at night; wait for other pedestrians, preferably locals, before entering them.

The city's two train stations are located on either side of the Old Town; wherever you are in the Old Town, you are only a short walk or bus or taxi ride from one of these two stations. **Stazione Principe** is the closest, just to the west; from Piazza Acquaverde, in front of the station, follow **Via Balbi** through **Piazza della Nunziata** and **Via Bensa** to **Via Cairoli,** which runs into Via Garibaldi (the walk will take about 15 min.). From **Stazione Brignole,** walk straight across the broad, open space to Piazza della Vittoria/Via Luigi Cadorna and turn right to follow broad **Via**

A Market Cornucopia

The sprawling **Mercato Orientale,** Genoa's boisterous indoor food market, evokes the days when ships brought back spices and other commodities from the ends of the earth. An excellent place to stock up on olives, herbs, fresh fruit, and other Ligurian products, it is held Monday through Wednesday 7:30am to 1pm and 3:30 to 7:30pm and Thursday through Saturday from 7:30am to 7:30pm with entrances on Via XX

Settembre and Via Galata (about halfway between Piazza de Ferrari at the edge of the Old Town and Stazione Brignole). The district just north of the market (especially Via San Vincenzo and Via Colombo) is a gourmand's dream, with many bakeries, *pasticcerie* (pastry shops), and stores selling pasta and cheese, wine, olive oil, and other foodstuffs.

XX Settembre, one of the city's major shopping avenues, due west for about 15 or 20 minutes to **Piazza de Ferrari,** on the eastern edge of the Old Town. From here, **Via San Lorenzo** will lead you past Genoa's cathedral and to the port, or follow **Via XXV Aprile** north to Piazza delle Fontane Marose, the eastern end of Via Garibaldi.

Exploring Genoa

Acquario di Genova (Aquarium of Genoa) ★★★ AQUARIUM

It isn't hard to see that Genoa's biggest draw is undoubtedly its aquarium, with lines forming along the waterfront even before it opens. The largest aquarium in Europe, it presides over a pier in the Old Port like a huge freight ship. After entering the Blue Planet room, which offers an overview of marine life from all bodies of water, you can wander past more than 50 aquatic displays. There are huge tanks re-creating Red Sea coral reefs, pools in the tropical rainforests of the Amazon River basin, and other marine ecosystems that provide a home for sharks, seals, dolphins, penguins, piranhas, and just about every other kind of water creature. The pier where the aquarium is located is about a 15-minute walk from Stazione Principe and 10 minutes from Via Garibaldi. You could easily spend a day around the old harbor by also visiting the nearby **Galata Museo del Mare** (see p. 554), flying high over the harbor on the **Bigo Panoramic**

Lift, and walking through endangered tropical forests in the great glass globe of the **Biosphere.** A combined ticket called the Aquarium Village Pass allows you to visit them all (54€ adults, 37.50€ children ages 4–12; online discounts available).

Ponte Spinola (at the port). www.acquario digenova.it. ✆ **010/23451.** 26€ adults, 23€ seniors 65 and over, 18€ children 4–12. Mon–Fri 9am–6pm, Sat–Sun 8:30am–7pm (July–Aug daily until 10:30pm). Bus: 1-8 and 12-15. Metro: Darsena.

Cattedrale di San Lorenzo ★

CATHEDRAL Genoa's main cathedral has its own austere dignity, its black-and-white-striped 12th-century facade enlivened by fanciful French Gothic carvings over the main doorway, and a pair of stone lions guarding the steps. A later addition is the bell tower,

's Gothic Cattedrale di San Lorenzo.

completed in the 16th century. In the frescoed interior, chapels house two of Genoa's most notable curiosities: Beyond the first pilaster on the right is a still-unexploded shell fired through the roof from a British ship during World War II; and in the Cappella di San Giovanni (left aisle), a 13th-century crypt contains what crusaders returning from the Holy Land claimed to be relics of John the Baptist. The adjoining treasury (Museo del Tesoro) seems to specialize in sacred tableware of doubtful provenance: the plate upon which Saint John's head was supposedly served to Salome, a bowl allegedly used at the Last Supper, and a bowl thought at one time to be the Holy Grail. Less storied but nonetheless magnificent gold and bejeweled objects reflect Genoa's medieval prominence as a maritime power. You can visit the treasury only by a half-hour guided tour in Italian, but it's still worth seeing what is inside, even if the extent of your Italian is *gelato* and *pizza*.

Piazza San Lorenzo. *©* **010/254-1250.** Cathedral free; treasury 6€ adults, 5€ seniors and students (included in Card Musei cumulative ticket, see p. 555). Mon–Sat 9am–noon and 3–6pm. Bus: 1, 7, 8, 17, 18, 19, 20.

Galata Museo del Mare (Museum of the Seas) ★★ MUSEUM

Located on "museum row" on the port, the Galata bills itself as the largest and most innovative maritime museum in Europe. Visiting the museum is like embarking on a voyage. Despite its modern appearance, the building itself is the oldest surviving construction of the dockyard from the old Republic, where Genovese galleys were built during the 17th century. You enter into the gallery dedicated to the old port with paintings and artifacts of the period, and then it's on to the full-scale reproduction of a Genovese "attack ship," with fun artifacts and props that will engage all ages. There is also an interesting section of the museum on Italians and the places they've immigrated to over the centuries, as well as the more recent phenomenon of immigrants from other countries arriving on Italy's shores.

Ponte Parodi (at the port). www.galatamuseodelmare.it. *©* **010/234-5655.** 13€ adults, 10€ seniors 65 and over, 8€ children 4–12. Mar–Oct daily 10am–7:30pm; Nov–Feb Tues–Fri 10am–6pm, Sat–Sun 10am–7:30pm (last entry 1 hr. before closing). Bus: 1-8 and 12-15. Metro: Darsena.

Galleria di Palazzo Bianco (White Palace) ★★ MUSEUM   The

White Palace can be considered the oldest and, at the same time, the most recent of the magnificent *palazzi* along ritzy Via Garibaldi, also known as the Strada Nuova (and a UNESCO World Heritage site). Although it was built during the mid-16th century by Luca Grimaldi, a scion of one of the most important Genovese families, the gorgeous white facade one sees today was reconstructed in the 18th century. Maria Durazzo Brignole-Sale de Ferrari donated the palace and her art collection to the city in 1884 to create Genoa's first public gallery. The collection is heavy on painters of the Spanish and Flemish schools, including Van Dyck, Rubens, Filippino Lippi, Veronese, and Caravaggio. One of the museum's most notable holdings is the "Portrait of a Lady" by Lucas Cranach the Elder.

Via Garibaldi 11. www.museidigenova.it/it/content/palazzo-bianco (C) **010/557 2193.** 9€ adults; includes entrance to Palazzo Rosso and Palazzo Tursi; included in Card Musei cumulative ticket (see below). Mar 28–Oct 8 Tues–Fri 9am–7pm; Sat–Sun 10am–7:30pm; Oct 11–Mar 26 Tues–Fri 9am–6:30pm; Sat–Sun 9:30am–6:30pm. Bus: 18, 20, 35, 37, 39, 40, 41, 42.

Galleria Nazionale di Palazzo Spinola ★ MUSEUM Another prominent Genovese family, the Spinolas, donated their palace and magnificent art collection to the city in 1958. Not only is the art collection something to behold, the centuries-old home (its lower floors luckily escaped damage during World War II though the two upper floors had to be completely reconstructed) in historic Piazza Pellicceria is a wonderful example of how Genovese aristocrats really lived, among frescos and mirrored galleries. As in Genoa's other art collections, you will find masterworks that range from native artists like Strozzi, da Messina, Reni, Giordano, and De Ferrari, to van Dyck and other painters of the Dutch and Flemish schools, whose commissioned portraits were once such a status symbol among Genoa's wealthy.

Piazza Pellicceria 1. www.palazzospinola.beniculturali.it. (C) **010/270-5300.** 6€ adults, 3€ ages 18–25, free for kids under 18 and seniors, included in Card Musei cumulative ticket (see below). Tues–Sat 8:30am–7:30pm; Sun 1:30–7:30pm. Bus: 1, 18, 20, 34.

Piazza Dante ★ Though most of this square just south of Piazza de Ferrari is made up of 1930s-era office buildings, one end is bounded by the reconstructed **Porta Soprana** ★★, a twin-towered town gate built in 1155. The main draw, though, is the small **house** (rebuilt in the 18th century), standing a bit incongruously in a tidy little park below the gate, said to have belonged to **Christopher Columbus's father,** who was a weaver and gatekeeper (whether young Christopher lived here is open to debate). Bus: 14, 35, 42, 44.

A Cumulative Ticket

Admission to Genoa's major **palaces and art galleries** is grouped together on the **Card Musei** (12€ for 1 day, 20€ for 2 days; or 15€ and 25€ including unlimited use of Genoa public transport). The card includes entrance to the principal palaces, the cathedral treasury of San Lorenzo, the Galleria di Palazzo Bianco, the Galleria Nazionale di Palazzo Spinola, and a handful of other museums around town, plus discounts to the aquarium, the Galata museum, and movie theaters. Pick it up at any city museum, the airport tourist office, or in one of several bookstores downtown (www.visitgenoa.it).

Via XX Settembre is one of Genoa's major shopping avenues.

Via Garibaldi ★★   Many of Genoa's museums and other sights are clustered on and around this street, also known as Strada Nuova, one of the most beautiful in Italy. Here Genoa's wealthy families built palaces in the 16th and 17th centuries that were the envy of all of Europe. Besides the **Galleria di Palazzo Bianco** (see p. 554), the **Palazzo Podesta,** at no. 7, hides a beautiful fountain in its courtyard, and the **Palazzo Tursi** (no. 9), which houses municipal offices, displays artifacts of famous locals: letters written by Columbus and a violin of Nicolo Paganini (still played on special occasions).

Palazzo Tursi entrance included in admission to Galleria di Palazzo Bianco; open same hours as Palazzo Bianco. Bus: 20, 32, 33, 35, 36, 41, 42.

Where to Stay in Genoa

Despite the draw of the aquarium and its intriguing Old Town, Genoa is still geared more to business travelers or conference-goers. A pleasant boom of new quality accommodations has sprouted up, however, as the city starts to become more tourist-friendly. Keep in mind, Genoa books up solid during its annual boat show, the world's largest, in October. During the boat show, hotel prices can jump as much as 25 percent.

SELF-CATERING ROOMS AND APARTMENTS

If you want to feel like more of a local, self-catering apartments are defi-nitely a great option. For example, **Virginia's Rooms** (which can be reserved via Booking.com for an average price of 60€ per night for a two-person deluxe room) are private rooms in a residential area not far from the center. This property not only offers convenient parking for those trav-eling by car but also features flat-screen televisions and swish modern bathrooms along with colorful bedrooms with traditional furnishings. Of course, there are also plenty of apartment options on **www.airbnb.com**, with an average nightly price of 77€ in the city of Genoa.

EXPENSIVE

Hotel Bristol Palace ★   This 19th-century *palazzo* has maintained its opulent oval staircase and exquisite stained-glass dome, making it one of Genoa's most regal hotels. A recent renovation aimed to maintain the hotel's elegance while offering modern amenities like stronger Wi-Fi. Located in the middle of the city's shopping district and mere steps from Genoa's most famous museums and historic palazzos, it is surprisingly quiet and perfectly located for exploring the sights. Given the hotel's proximity to the Teatro Carlo Felice, where opera performances are held, it offers special packages for a weekend immersed in everything opera, including two tickets to a performance. The **Ristorante Giotto** serves sophisticated local cuisine at lunch and dinner most days of the week. An outdoor dining terrace adds even more appeal to this oasis-like lodging in the city center.

Via XX Settembre 35. www.hotelbristolpalace.com. ℰ **010/592-541.** 133 rooms and 5 suites. 130€–470€ double; 249€–699€ jr suite. Rates include breakfast. **Amenities:** Restaurant; bar; babysitting; bikes; concierge; room service; Wi-Fi (free).

MODERATE

Best Western Hotel Metropoli ★★   The location of this hotel right in the center of the action may be its best selling point, and keeping that in mind, if you are looking for peace and quiet, this may not be the property for you. On the corner of a lovely square and a pedestrian-only street in the historic center amid *palazzos* from the 16th century, Hotel Metropoli offers very good lodging with modern amenities, a robust breakfast buffet, and helpful service. Guest rooms are soundproofed, clean, and comfortable, with refurbished bathrooms. Family rooms have bunk beds and game consoles, while upgraded "women's rooms" have a L'Occitane beauty kit and professional-grade hair dryers and flat irons. Come here if location is key but you are not necessarily seeking old-world charm.

Piazza delle Fontane Marose. www.hotelmetropoli.it. ℰ **010/246-8888.** 48 units. 97€–246€ double; 99€–260€ triple. Rates include breakfast. **Amenities:** Bar; room service; Wi-Fi (free).

INEXPENSIVE

Agnello d'Oro ★   This former convent is now a low-cost *locanda* just a few blocks from Stazione Principe and on the edge of the Old Town, which can be seen from the hotel terrace. Guest rooms tend to be very basic, but some still retain the building's original 16th-century character, with high ceilings (rooms numbered in the teens) or vaulted ones (rooms numbered under 10). Some top-floor rooms come with the added charm of balconies and views over the Old Town and harbor (best from no. 56). There's an apartment (3 bedrooms, 2 bathrooms) that sleeps six, perfect for families or larger groups. The friendly owner can be very helpful with sightseeing tips and offers the occasional *aperitivo* on the house. Ferry and cruise-ship terminals are within easy walking distance.

Via Monachette 6, off Via Balbi. www.hotelagnellodoro.it. ℰ **010/246-2084.** 17 units. 70€–100€ double; 160€ for 4 people in 3-bedroom apt. **Amenities:** Bar; concierge; room service; Wi-Fi (free).

Hotel No Logo ★★   No Logo is modern property but low on frills, offering basic services with a lot of personality in one of the liveliest areas of town where "music is in the air." The music theme carries over to guest rooms (room names include "Rock," "Pop," "Reggae," and "Blues"); family rooms are big enough for up to six people. No Logo is conveniently located near Brignole train station in a bustling neighborhood full of bars, restaurants, and nearby shopping on Via XX Settembre. Breakfast, which includes coffee or tea along with orange juice and a selection of baked

---

FAST . . . AND OH, SO good

All over Genoa you'll find shops selling **focaccia,** Liguria's answer to pizza, a thick flatbread often stuffed or topped with cheese, herbs, olives, onions, vegetables, or prosciutto. Many of these *focaccerie* also sell *farinata,* a chickpea fritter that usually emerges from the oven in the shape of a big round pizza. Just point and make a hand gesture to show how much you want. Prices are by weight, and in most cases a piece of either will cost about 1.50€ to 3€. Most focaccia (especially the ones with cheese) and all *farinata* are better warm, so if the piece you are getting looks like it has been there awhile, ask them to warm it up (or, in Italian, "scaldarla").

A favorite spot for both snacks, near Stazione Principe, is **La Focacceria di Teobaldo** ★, Via Balbi 115r (daily 8am–8pm). In the heart of the Old Town, **Focacceria di Via Lomellini** ★, Via Lomellini 57/59 (Mon–Sat 8am–7:30pm), has great *focaccia di Recco* (also called *focaccia al formaggio*), a super-thin focaccia filled with cheese and the specialty of the nearby town of Recco.

Follow up with something sweet at **Fratelli Klainguti** (Piazza Macelli di Soziglia 98; ℰ **010/860-2628**). At Porto Antico, get your focaccia fix (you *will* be addicted after your first taste) at **Il Localino,** Via Turati 8r (Tues–Mon 8am–8pm; closed Wed). You can also get pretty good focaccia at the **Eataly** on the old port near the aquarium.

goods, fruit, and yogurt, is available for 4.50€ per person, though there are also plenty of coffee bars near by if a hotel breakfast isn't your thing.

Via Sauli 5. www.hotelnologo.it. © **010/089-8060.** 56 units. 52€–86€ double; 78€ triple; 104€ quadruple. **Amenities:** Bar; Wi-Fi (free).

Where to Eat in Genoa

I Tre Merli ★★ This stylish restaurant overlooking the action on the *porto antico* is all high ceilings, black-and-white columns, and exposed stone walls, nicely in line with the local architecture. Local seafood stars in dishes such as *fritua* (fried fish, squid, and shrimp with crisp vegetables and fried sage). Cheese *focaccia* comes with artichokes or arugula and Parma ham. On nice days, enjoy the terrace with sea views. There is a 3-euro cover charge per person for service and bread, and considering it is slightly higher than the euro or two that many restaurants ask, you are also paying for the location, but, as throughout Italy, it is not necessary to tip. I Tre Merli also operates a small wine bar and *"affittacamere"* (rooms for rent) in Camogli (see p. 564).

Calata Cattaneo 17. www.itremerli.it. © **010/246-4416.** Entrees 16€–20€. Daily noon–3pm and 7:30–11pm.

Trattoria da Maria ★★ LIGURIAN Located in a nondescript alleyway, this simple trattoria might not look like one of Genoa's most famous eateries, but it is. Unfortunately, Maria has hung up her apron and is no longer in the kitchen, but this spot continues to offer flavorful, no-nonsense dishes such as the near-perfect pesto, stuffed anchovies, and fish sautéed in white wine. Here, you dine side-by-side with lawyers, construction workers, students, and tourists. Pay no mind to the lack of decor, and concentrate on the great dishes this Genovese institution has to offer, with a handwritten menu that changes daily. This is such an authentic spot that wait staff may not be accustomed to speaking English—you will certainly get a chance to practice your Italian here.

Vico Testadoro 14r (just off Via XXV Aprile). © **010/581-080.** Entrees 5€–9€. Fixed-price menu 10€; add 2.50€ for dessert. Mon–Sat noon–3pm and 7–9:15pm.

Trattoria della Raibetta ★ In the alleyways not far from the port, this cozy and historic trattoria—one of the oldest restaurants in the city—serves up Genovese favorites like pasta al pesto, *pansotti* (a homemade ricotta-filled pasta) in walnut sauce, and sea bream with potatoes. The wine list is equally impressive, with hundreds of labels, many of which are local to the area, with a focus on the area's popular names like *vermentino, pigato, sciacchetrà, colli di luni,* and *colline di levanto.* If you've stuffed yourself with pasta and are looking for a simple local dessert, try the *canestrelli* shortbread cookies. Reservations aren't necessary, but it doesn't hurt to book ahead.

Vico Caprettari 12r. www.trattoriadellaraibetta.it. © **010/246-8877.** Entrees 8€–17€. Tues–Sun noon–2:30pm; 7:30–10:30pm.

Entertainment & Nightlife

The Old Town, some parts of which are sketchy in broad daylight, is even more risky after dark. This is an area where petty crimes take place at night and pickpockets linger in the shadows. Confine late-hour prowls in this area to the well-trafficked streets such as Via San Lorenzo and Via Garibaldi. On the edges of the Old Town, good places to walk at night are around the waterfront, Piazza Fontane Marose, Piazza de Ferrari, and Piazza delle Erbe, where many bars and clubs are located.

Genoa has two major venues for culture: the restored **Teatro Carlo Felice,** Piazza de Ferrari (www.carlofelice.it; ✆ **010/589-329**), home to Genoa's opera company, and the modern **Teatro Stabile di Genova** (www.teatrostabilegenova.it; ✆ **010/53-421**), on Piazza Borgo Pila near Stazione Brignole, which hosts concerts, dance, and other programs.

THE RIVIERA DI PONENTE: SAN REMO

140km (87 miles) W of Genoa, 56km (35 miles) E of Nice

Gone are the days when Tchaikovsky and the Russian empress Maria Alexandrovna joined a well-heeled mix of *nobili* strolling along San Remo's palm-lined avenues. They left behind an onion-domed Orthodox church, a few grand hotels, and a casino, but **San Remo** is a different sort of town these days. It's still the most cosmopolitan stop on the Riviera di Ponente, as the stretch of coast west of Genoa is called, catering mostly to sun-seeking Italian families in the summer and, in winter, Milanese who come down to escape the fog and chilly temperatures of their city.

If you've got a few extra days, base yourself in San Remo and explore farther along the coast, all the way to the French border. Train connections are good, and the coastal SS1 road links several charming towns. Highlights include the quiet resort town of **Bordighera** (12km/7.5 miles west of San Remo); one of Europe's finest gardens, **Giardini Hanbury** (28km/20 miles west of San Remo, just past Ventimiglia); and the inland village of **Dolceacqua** (23km/14 miles northwest of San Remo), with its well-preserved medieval core and abandoned castle.

Essentials

ARRIVING **Trains** run hourly between San Remo and Genoa (about 2 hr.). If you're arriving by train, note that San Remo's newer rail station is a bit of a hike from the center of town and the old port. Trains from Genoa continue west for another 20 minutes to Ventimiglia on the French border. Some trains continue on into France; at Ventimiglia you can change onto one of the twice-hourly trains across the border to **Nice,** 50 minutes west.

The fastest **driving route** in and out of San Remo is Autostrada A10, which follows the coast from Genoa (about 45 min. away) to the French

A Day at the Beach

The pebbly beach below the **Passeggiata dell'Imperatrice** is lined with beach stations, where many visitors choose to spend their days: It's easy to linger here, because most provide showers, snack bars, beach chairs, lounges, and umbrellas. Expect to spend up to 15€ for a basic lounge, but more like 20€ for a more elaborate sun-bed arrangement with umbrella. **Note:** As is standard at most European resort towns without "public" sections of beach (which are usually not very nice anyway), you cannot go onto the beach in the main part of town without paying for at least a lounge chair in high season.

border (20 min. away). The slower coast road, SS1, cuts right through the center of town.

FESTIVALS   Since the 1950s, the **Sanremo Festival** (mid- to late February; www.sanremo.rai.it) has been Italy's premier music fest, sort of an Italian Grammy Awards. It's spread out over several days with live performances by Italian pop stars, international headliners, and plenty of up-and-comers. Hotels up and down the coast (and into France) get booked up months in advance. Call the tourist office to try to score tickets.

The seaside resort town of San Remo.

Exploring San Remo

San Remo's two main thoroughfares are **Via Roma** and **Corso Matteotti.** Corso Matteotti runs between **Piazza Colombo,** with its flower market, and the **casino** (see below), passing through the heart of the bustling, pedestrian-only business district. Here you can shop, sit in cafes, and do a bit of Italian people-watching. Midway along Corso Matteotti, turn north on **Via Feraldi** to reach the charming older precincts of town. From **Piazza Mercato,** Via Montà leads into the medieval quarter, **La Pigna,** set on a hill shaped like a pinecone (*la pigna* in Italian). Aside from a few restaurants, La Pigna is a residential quarter, with tall old houses overshadowing narrow lanes that twist and turn up the hillside, with the park-enclosed ruins of a **castle** at the top.

VISITING THE CASINO

San Remo's white palace of a **casino** (www.casinosanremo.it; ⓒ **0184/ 5951**) is the hub of the local nightlife scene, set intimidatingly atop a long flight of steps across from the old train station and enclosed on three sides by Corso degli Inglesi. You can't set foot inside without being properly attired (jacket for gents Oct–June; in general, avoid track suits, shorts, T-shirts, and flip-flops for the entire casino). You must show your passport to enter, and you must be 18 or older. Poker tables start at 2€ games, but the more serious tables attract high rollers from the length of the Riviera. Gaming rooms are open daily 2:30pm to 2:30am (Fri and Sat nights 3pm–3:30am). Things are more relaxed in the rooms set aside for slot machines, where there is no real dress code. It's open Sunday to Thursday 10am to 2:30am and Friday and Saturday 10am to 3:30am.

Where to Stay & Eat in San Remo

Most restaurants and hotels in the "City of Flowers" are concentrated either along the promenade leading into town or in the streets and alleyways in and around the famous Ariston Theater, where the Sanremo Music Festival is held every year. Seafood specialties are a focus in local restaurants; two local favorites featuring specialties specific to San Remo include Paolo & Barbara (Via Roma 47) and Osteria dei Tre Scalini (in Piazza Sardi).

Hotel Villa Maria ★★ Villa Maria offers comfort and quality in a lovely residential setting. Located on the hillside just above the casino, and not far from the beach, it is also a stone's throw from the Empress's Promenade and a biking and walking path. Originally three separate villas, the spacious, almost regal hotel and its many salons recall the golden eras of the 1920s, '30s, and '40s; several public rooms open to a nicely planted terrace. Many of the guest rooms are somewhat outdated (some are being updated), but the hotel's reasonable rates and the setting more than make up for this. Room sizes and styles can vary, so ask what's available when booking or ask to see a few upon arrival. Some rooms have balconies facing the sea.

Corso Nuvoloni 30. www.villamariahotel.it. © **0184/531-422.** 38 units, 36 with private bathroom. 60€–170€ double. Rates include breakfast. **Amenities:** Restaurant; concierge; room service; Wi Fi (free in common areas).

Ristorante L'Airone ★ LIGURIAN/PIZZA Located in a quaint piazza, this cute restaurant in the center of town (exactly halfway between the Ariston Theater and the casino) serves consistently good food at decent prices, which is why it is almost always busy. The menu focuses on traditional Ligurian dishes, such as *spaghetti alla vongole* (with clams), *pasta al pesto,* and *orecchiete pasta* with arugula, pachino tomatoes, and ricotta cheese, along with an excellent thin-crust pizza (unfortunately only served at lunch on Tuesdays and Saturdays). Tables can be a bit close together inside, but in nice weather, you can also dine in the small garden in the back or in the piazza in front. There are several menus just for children. Reservations are recommended, especially for dinner.

Piazza Eroi Sanremesi 12. www.ristorantelairone.it. © **0184/541-055.** Entrees 7.50€–17€. Fri 7:30–11:30pm, Sat–Wed noon–2:30pm and 7:30–11:30pm.

Royal Hotel ★★★ This sprawling seafront resort on the edge of Old Town mixes old-world charm and luxury. Its gardens and seawater pool are spectacular, offering some reprieve from the heat during the scorching summer months. Most rooms have sea views and are tastefully decorated. Along with the 5-star luxury designation, however, come jaw-dropping prices, even in the off-season. The website offers various package deals throughout the year to make this "kingdom of luxury" slightly more affordable. Families traveling in the high season will appreciate the kids' club, where children can play while parents relax or take advantage of the many activities offered. The main restaurant serves up creative, seasonal cuisine that takes inspiration not just from the Mediterranean Sea but from the various regions of Italy as well. The buffet breakfast is particularly abundant.

Corso Imperatrice 80. www.royalhotelsanremo.com. © **0184/5391.** 126 units. 248€–665€ double. Rates include breakfast. **Amenities:** 3 restaurants; bar; 24-hour room service; babysitting; kid's club; concierge; room service; Wi-Fi (free).

THE RIVIERA DI LEVANTE: CAMOGLI, SANTA MARGHERITA LIGURE & PORTOFINO ★★

Camogli: 26km (16 miles) E of Genoa; Santa Margherita Ligure: 31km (19 miles) E of Genoa; Portofino: 38km (24 miles) E of Genoa; Rapallo: 37km (23 miles) E of Genoa

Hugged by mountains that plunge into the sapphire-colored sea, the coast east of Genoa, the **Riviera di Levante** (Shore of the Rising Sun), is more ruggedly beautiful and less developed than the Riviera Ponente. Three of the coast's most appealing towns are within a few kilometers of one another, clinging to the shores of the Monte Portofino Promontory east of Genoa: **Camogli, Santa Margherita Ligure,** and little **Portofino.**

Essentials

ARRIVING   One to three **trains** per hour ply the coastline, connecting Genoa with Santa Margherita (25–30 min.) and Camogli (30–45 min.); the trip between Camogli and Santa Margherita takes 5 minutes by train. To get to **Portofino,** take the train to Santa Margherita and then take a taxi or bus 82 (www.atpesercizio.it; ✆ **0185/373-303**), a 25-minute ride via a beautiful coastal road (bus service every 30 min. to 1 hr.; 1.80€).

In summer, **boats** operated by Golfo Paradiso (www.golfoparadiso. it; ✆ **0185/772-091;** roundtrip tickets 4€–35€ depending on route) run from Camogli to Portofino and Genoa. **Tigullio ferries** (www.traghetti-portofino.it; ✆ **0185/284-670**) make hourly trips from Santa Margherita to Portofino (15 min; 12€ roundtrip). In summer, a boat runs several days a week to the Cinque Terre (30€–40€). Hours of service vary considerably with the season; schedules are posted on the docks at Piazza Martiri della Libertà.

The fastest **car** route into the region is Autostrada A12 from Genoa (exit at Recco for Camogli), which takes about 40 minutes to either Camogli or Santa Margherita. Route SS1 along the coast from Genoa is much slower but more scenic. *Note:* Parking is a challenge in Camogli and Portofino in the summer, and traffic quickly gets clogged on the tiny road between Santa Margherita and Portofino. If you're coming by car, park it in Santa Margherita and take the bus or boat to Portofino.

VISITOR INFORMATION   **Camogli**'s tourist office is across from the train station at Via XX Settembre 33 (www.camogliturismo.it; ✆ **0185/771-066**). In **Santa Margherita**, the tourist office is in Piazza Vittorio Veneto (www.smlturismo.it; ✆ **0185/287-485**). The **Portofino** tourist office is at Via Roma 35 (www.turismoinliguria.it; ✆ **0185/269-024**). All are open daily in summer (Portofino's office is closed Mon); expect shorter hours in winter, and a lunchtime closure between noon and 3pm.

Camogli ★

Camogli remains delightfully unspoiled, an authentic Ligurian fishing port with tall houses in pastel colors facing the harbor and a nice swath of beach. Given also its excellent accommodations and eateries, Camogli is a lovely place to base yourself while you explore the Riviera Levante. It's also a restful retreat from which you can visit Genoa, which is only 30 minutes away. Some say Camogli's name is derived from *"Ca de Mogge,"* or "House of the Wives" in the local dialect, so-named for the women who held down the fort while their husbands went to sea. Another possibility is

Camogli bay.

that it comes from *"Ca a Muggi,"* or "clustered houses," particularly apt when you are out swimming in the sea and turn to look up at the town's wonderful mass of colorful buildings.

EXPLORING CAMOGLI

Camogli is clustered around its delightful waterfront, from which the town ascends via steep, staircased lanes to Via XX Settembre, one of the few streets in the town proper to accommodate cars (this is where the train station, tourist office, and many shops and other businesses are located). Adding to the charm of this setting is the fact that the oldest part of Camogli juts into the harbor on a picturesque little point (once an island). Here ancient houses cling to the little **Castel Dragone** and the **Basilica di Santa Maria Assunta** (© **0185/770-130**), originally built in the 12th century but much altered through the ages; its overwhelming baroque interior is open daily 7:30am to noon and 3:30 to 7pm.

Most visitors, though, are drawn to the pleasant **seaside promenade ★** that runs the length of the town. You can swim from the pebbly beach below, and you can rent a lounge chair from one of the few beach stations for about 15€—highly recommended in the summer months, when finding even a small piece of pebbly sand is nearly impossible.

Getting Festive in Camogli

Camogli throws a well-attended annual party, the **Sagra del Pesce** ★★, on the second Sunday of May, when the town fries up thousands of sardines in a 3.6m-diameter (12-ft.) pan and passes them around for free—a practice accompanied by an annual outcry in the press about health concerns and even accusations that frozen fish is used.

The first Sunday of August, Camogli stages the lovely **Festa della Stella Maris** ★, during which a procession of boats sails to Punta Chiappa, a spot of land about 1.5km (1 mile) down the coast, and releases 10,000 burning candles. Meanwhile, the same number of candles is set afloat from the Camogli beach. If currents are favorable, the burning candles will come together at sea, signifying a year of unity for couples who watch the spectacle.

WHERE TO STAY & EAT IN CAMOGLI

Bar Primula ★ CAFE/LIGHT FARE   Its prime position along the *lungomare* (promenade) has made this spot a Camogli institution for decades. Inside, the tables are a bit close together, so, if weather permits, try to sit outside to enjoy the people-watching. Patrons spill from the front terrace day and night. Pasta and main courses are served at lunch and dinner, but Primula is best for simple foods like paninis, salads, gelato, and the classic *aperitivo*.

Via Garibaldi 140. ✆ **0185/770-351.** Pizzas/entrees 12€–22€. Daily 8am–1am.

La Camogliese ★★   If location and keeping costs down are your main priorities, this family-run hotel is a good option. La Camogliese may be basic, but it's affordable and perfectly positioned at the entrance of the old village, with easy access to the beach and to the bus and train stations. The large, bright rooms have simple furniture and comfortable beds; a few have balconies that require a slight twist of the head to get a sea view (the best views are from rooms 3 and 16B). Bathrooms are small even by Italian standards, but they are adequate. Keep in mind that this hotel fills up fast, especially on weekends and in the summer, so make sure to book early.

Via Garibaldi 55. www.lacamogliese.it. ✆ **0185/771-402.** 21 units. 50€–130€ double. Rates include breakfast. 2- to 4-night required minimum stay. **Amenities:** Babysitting; concierge; exercise room; outdoor pool; room service; Wi-Fi (free).

Hotel Cenobio dei Dogi ★★   The amazing position of this resort, combined with the beautifully manicured grounds and old-world charm of the main building, make this Camogli's most popular (and most expensive) hotel. The fact that it sits perched over the Gulf of Camogli doesn't hurt either. Rooms come in various shapes and sizes (there's a big difference in size and style between "standard" and "classic" rooms) and, for the most part, are tastefully decorated in a mix of tradition and Mediterranean flair. The large pool area and private beach—one part terraced stone, one part pebbles, which is typical of the area—are gorgeous and inviting. The intimate Doge Beauty Spa offers manicures, pedicures, face treatments, and various types of massages. This property is popular with honeymooners.

Via Cuneo 34. www.cenobio.it. (C) **0185/7241.** 108 units. 129€–480€ double. Rates include breakfast and beach facilities. Free parking. **Amenities:** 2 restaurants, 2 bars; babysitting; concierge; outdoor saltwater pool; tennis courts; watersports rentals, Wi-Fi (free).

Locanda I Tre Merli ★   This tiny wine bar right on Camogli's charming harbor also has five cozy, brightly colored guest rooms to let, each of which has views over the water. Breakfast (make sure to reserve the night before) includes warm, fresh focaccia along with yogurt and other sweet and savory options; in warm weather, it's served outside—a slice of true Italian seaside life, with boats coming and going, fishermen unloading their catch, and families and small children playing along the walkway. Ferry boats for Portofino, Genoa, and the Cinque Terre depart from right outside. Be patient with the small staff, and focus on what brought you here—the beautiful setting and ambience. A small wellness area with a hot tub offers a wonderful view of the port, but be aware that the large window also allows those on the outside to peer in (awkward!). If you come by car, parking is available at the top of a very big hill in a tiny lot that can be a tight squeeze.

Via Scalo 5. www.locandaitremerli.com. (C) **0185/770-592.** 5 units. 95€–210€ double; 150€–250€ triple. Rates include breakfast. **Amenities:** Bar; Wi-Fi (free).

Vento Ariel ★★ SEAFOOD   We love the old port setting of this popular restaurant almost as much we love its food. Seafood is done right here; succulent dishes include *patè di seppie* (cuttlefish mousse), "sea-to-table" *acchiuge agrodolce* (anchovies in a sweet-and-sour sauce), and oven-baked fresh fish from the gulf blanketed in salt (the salt is removed before serving, obviously). The wine list is extensive and contains some local, hard-to-find bottles of Vermentino and Pigato, plus the wonderful whites of Liguria. If you can, grab a table outside to drink in the local ambience as well. Reservations are highly recommended. To get here, walk from the

---

Focaccia by the Seaside

It might be the perfect seaside setting, or perhaps there is something in the water, but no matter the reason, Camogli has some of the best focaccia in all of Liguria. Along Via Garibaldi, the promenade above the beach, are many *focaccerie* to choose from, and though it's hard to go wrong with any of them,

Revello, at no. 183 (closest to the church), stands out. There, Tino carries on the tradition passed down by his uncle, who first began pulling focaccia out of the oven here in 1964. Revello is open daily from 10am to 6pm (later in the summer months). You can enjoy your loot on one of the few benches outside.

main part of the promenade, weaving your way down to the medieval archways connecting the *lungomare* to the old port; you'll find the rustic-looking restaurant nestled in the corner facing the *gozzi* (fishing boats of the old harbor).

Calata Porticciolo 1. www.ventoariel.it. ℂ **0185/771-080.** Entrees 12€–25€. Daily noon–2:30pm and 8–11pm.

Santa Margherita Ligure ★

Santa Margherita had one brief moment in the spotlight at the beginning of the 20th century, when it was an internationally renowned resort. Fortunately, the seaside town didn't let fame spoil its charm, and now that it's no longer as well known as its glitzy neighbor Portofino, it could be the Mediterranean retreat of your dreams. A palm-lined harbor, a decent beach, and a friendly ambience make Santa Margherita a fine place to settle down for a few days of sun and relaxation.

EXPLORING SANTA MARGHERITA

Life in Santa Margherita centers on its palm-fringed **waterfront,** a pleasant string of marinas, docks for pleasure and fishing boats, and pebbly beaches, in some spots with imported sand of passable quality. Landlubbers congregate in the cafes that spill out into the town's two seaside squares, Piazza Martiri della Libertà and Piazza Vittorio Veneto.

The train station is above the waterfront, and a staircase in front of the entrance will lead you down into the heart of town. Santa Margherita's landmark of note is its namesake **Basilica di Santa Margherita** (open daily 7:30am–noon and 3–6:30pm), on Piazza Caprera. It's well worth a visit to view the church's extravagant, gilded, chandeliered interior.

One of the more interesting daily spectacles in town is the **fish market** on Lungomare Marconi from 8am to 12:30pm. On Friday, Corso Matteotti, Santa Margherita's major street for food shopping, becomes an open-air **food market.**

WHERE TO EAT & STAY IN SANTA MARGHERITA LIGURE

Grand Hotel Miramare ★★★ This once private villa, an impressive example of Art Nouveau architecture, is pure Riviera elegance. Just a 10-minute walk from the town center along the heavily-trafficked road to Portofino, the Grand Hotel Miramare is all sleek class, featuring carefully restored antique furniture and crystal chandeliers while still having a somewhat contemporary feel. The guest rooms are large, and most have parquet floors, antique rugs, and charming stucco decorations on the walls and ceilings. Fifth-floor suites are larger, a bit more modern, and have balconies overlooking the Gulf of Tigullio. A lovely (but steep) park rises behind the hotel, from which you can take a pleasant hiking trail to Portofino and enjoy fantastic views of land and sea. You can also relax at the small, private pebble beach across the busy road. The **e'SPAce** wellness center offers a variety of massages and other treatments. If you come by car, parking can be a tight squeeze and costs 30€ a day. The hotel often closes from January through March

Via Milite Ignoto 30. www.grandhotelmiramare.it. © **0185/287-013.** 84 units. 220€–600€ double. Rates include breakfast. **Amenities:** Restaurant, 3 bars; babysitting; concierge; outdoor saltwater pool; room service; spa services; watersports rentals, Wi-Fi (free).

Hotel Metropole ★★   This popular family-run hotel is just above the port and a 5-minute stroll from the town center. Some accommodations are in the modern main building, while others are in the more appealing Villa Porticciolo, a dusty red manor house right on the beach; rooms in the villa are smaller, but they're graced with 19th-century stuccoes, and the sea practically laps up against the building. All rooms have large terraces or balconies. Several rooms can be joined to make family suites, and there's a kids' play area and kiddie club at the beach. There is a small

AN excursion **TO SAN FRUTTUOSO**

Much of the **Monte Portofino Promontory** can be approached only on foot or by boat (see below), making it a prime destination for hikers. If you want to combine excellent exercise with magnificent glimpses of the sea through a lush forest, arm yourself with a map from the tourist offices in Camogli, Santa Margherita Ligure, Portofino, or Rapallo, and set out. You can explore the upper reaches of the promontory or aim for the **Abbazia di San Fruttuoso** (© **0185/772-703**), a medieval abbey surrounded by a tiny six-house hamlet and two beaches. It is about a 90-minute hike from Portofino.

Once you reach San Fruttuoso, you may well want to relax on the pebbly beach and enjoy a beverage or meal at one of the seaside bars. You can tour the stark interior of the abbey for 5€ (open June to mid-Sept daily 10am–5:45pm; May Tues–Sun 10am–5:45pm; Mar–Apr and Oct Tues–Sun 10am–3:30pm; and Nov–Feb Sat–Sun 10am–3:45pm). Despite these official hours, the abbey tends to close whenever the last boat leaves. Should you have your scuba or snorkeling gear along, you can take the plunge to visit **Christ of the Depths,** a statue of Jesus erected 15m (49 ft.) beneath the surface to honor sailors lost at sea.

You can also visit San Fruttuoso with one of the **boats** that run almost every hour during the summer months from Camogli. A round-trip costs 13€ (9€ one-way if you then plan to head southward from the abbey) and takes about 30 minutes. For more information, contact **Golfo Paradiso** (www.golfoparadiso.it; © **0185/772-091**). Hourly (in summer) **Tigullio boats** (www.traghettiportofino.it; © **0185/284-670**) run to San Fruttuoso from Portofino (20 min.; 8.50€–13€ roundtrip), Santa Margherita (35 min.; 11€–17€ roundtrip), and Rapallo (50 min.; 12€–18€ roundtrip). Bear in mind that the seas are often too choppy to take passengers to San Fruttuoso, because docking there can be tricky. In that case, there are private boats you can take—smaller, rubber crafts capable of bad-weather landings—though these are expensive. From Portofino, you will likely be charged 100€ for up to 12 people.

private beach, a sunbathing terrace, and a private boat launch. The hotel prides itself on being especially pet-friendly and there are VIP packages for dogs and cats. At the time of writing, a new indoor swimming pool and spa were under construction.

Via Pagana 2. www.metropole.it. *©* **0185/286-134.** 57 units. 120€–360€ double. Rates include breakfast. **Amenities:** 2 restaurants; bar; babysitting; exercise room; swimming pool; sauna; watersports rentals, Wi-Fi (free).

La Paranza ★★ GENOVESE/LIGURIAN The ambience here is nothing special (though some tables do have sea views through the all-glass front), but one visit to this family-run trattoria is enough to understand why many locals claim it's the best restaurant in town. The menu is filled with delicious, innovative dishes, from the *bianchetti fritti* (fried baby sardines) to grilled-to-perfection fresh fish. Ligurian classics, such as fresh *trofie* pasta served with pesto, green beans, and potatoes, are also on the menu. There is also a raw-fish menu. A lot of the desserts are based on seasonal fruit, but the tiramisu is a sure bet all year round.

Via Jacopo Ruffini 46. www.laparanzasantamargherita.it *©* **0185/283-686.** Entrees 14€–30€. Sun–Sat 12:30–2:20pm and 7:30–10:30pm. Closed Nov.

Portofino ★★★

Portofino is almost too beautiful for its own good. In almost any season, you'll be rubbing elbows on Portofino's harborside quays with day-tripping mobs, as well as Italian industrialists, international celebrities, and a lot of rich-but-not-so-famous folks who consider this little town to be the epicenter of the good life. But if you make an appearance in the late afternoon when the crowds have thinned out a bit, you are sure to experience what remains so appealing about this enchanting place—its indelible beauty.

EXPLORING PORTOFINO

The one thing that won't break the bank in Portofino is the spectacular scenery. Begin with a stroll around the stunning **harbor,** lined with expensive boutiques, eateries, and colorful houses set along the quay with steep green hills rising behind them. One of the most scenic walks takes you uphill for about 10 minutes along a well-signposted path from the west side of town just behind the harbor to the **Chiesa di San Giorgio** (*©* **0185/ 269-337**), built on the site of a sanctuary Roman soldiers dedicated to the Persian god Mithras. It's open daily 9am to 7pm.

From there, continue uphill for a few minutes more to Portofino's 15th-century **Castello Brown** (www.castellobrown.com; *©* **010/251-8125**), which has a lush garden and great views of the town and harbor below. It costs 5€ and is open daily 10am to 6pm in the spring and fall (often open until 7pm in summer), and the rest of the year on Saturday and Sunday from 10am to 5pm.

Colorful, exclusive Portofino.

For more lovely views on this stretch of coast and plenty of open sea, go even higher up through lovely pine forests to the *faro* (lighthouse).

From Portofino, you can also set out for a longer hike on the paths that cross the **Monte Portofino Promontory** to the Abbazia di San Fruttuoso (see "An Excursion to San Fruttuoso," p. 569). The tourist office provides maps.

WHERE TO STAY & EAT IN PORTOFINO

Portofino's charms come at a price. Its few hotels are expensive enough to put them in the "trip of a lifetime" category, and the harborside restaurants can take a serious chunk out of a vacation budget as well. A smart alternative strategy is to enjoy a light snack at a bar or one of the many shops selling focaccia, and wait to dine in Santa Margherita or one of the other nearby towns.

Belmond Hotel Splendido ★★★ The Splendido, now a Belmond property, has been the Italian Riviera's #1 resort for more than 100 years. Over the years, it has hosted Bogart and Bacall, Taylor and Burton, and many more members of the rich and famous club. The former monastery turned 5-star luxury hotel sits in the heart of Portofino, surrounded by verdant gardens; the structure and grounds are spectacular. Nearly all of the guest rooms, including 35 suites, have balconies with scintillating views across the picturesque harbor. The **La Terrazza** restaurant not only boasts high-end Italian regional cuisine, it has a vine-covered terrace with breathtaking views of the water. The Splendido's sister hotel—the **Belmond Hotel Mare**—is closer to the water, and is more intimate; it has 14 rooms, some of which offer views of the harbor and famous piazzetta, and 2 magnificent suites. Be warned: the hotel's room rates may make your heart stop momentarily.

Salita Baratta 16. www.hotelsplendido.com. ℂ **0185/267-801.** 67 units. 500€–4,500€ double. Rates include breakfast. Closed mid-Dec to Mar or Apr. **Amenities:** 3 restaurants; piano bar; concierge; room service; wellness center; saltwater infinity pool; tennis court; access to hotel's motorboat; Wi-Fi (free).

Hotel Nazionale ★★ There are two reasons to choose this family-run hotel for your stay in Portofino: location (it sits on the most famous square and town) and price. Rooms are fairly basic with not much in the way of decoration, but you are right on the harbor and paying about one-third of what you would at any other hotel in the village. Several of the rooms are lofted suites with bedrooms upstairs; we highly recommend splurging for one of the five junior suites, as they are a bit more colorful and offer harbor views. Though the hotel has no elevator, luggage service is provided. The hotel's restaurant, **Da Nicola,** offers delightful views of the piazzetta and water, and serves up typical Ligurian cuisine and pizza. Via Roma 8. www.nazionaleportofino.com. ✆ **0185/269-575.** 12 units. 190€–375€ double. Rates include breakfast. Closed mid-Dec–Mar. **Amenities:** Restaurant; bar; concierge; room service, Wi-Fi (free).

Ristorante Puny ★★ LIGURIAN Located on the *piazzetta* in front of the harbor, this colorful restaurant is smack in the middle of it all, so book well in advance. Although the famously gregarious "Puny" (owner Luigi Miroli) has since passed away, his son Andrea has taken over the reins of this family-run waterfront establishment. It is well known for the freshness of its seafood, with a lengthy menu of tasty local dishes including *pappardelle al portofino* (large flat noodles with a mix of tomato and pesto sauce; note that you can even ask for the sauce over gluten-free pasta), the heavenly *pesce al forno* baked in bay leaves, or the famed *orata alla genovese* (sea bream served Genovese-style with potatoes). This has been a favorite haunt of well-heeled locals and tourists for decades, but it maintains a welcoming, cozy feel that keeps people coming back. Be prepared to pay for the location, view, food, and being part of the scene. Piazza Martiri dell'Olivetta 5. ✆ **0185/269-037.** Entrees 20€–30€. Mon–Wed and Fri–Sun 12:30–3:30pm and 7:30–11pm. Closed Jan–Feb.

THE CINQUE TERRE ★★★

Monterosso, the northernmost town of the Cinque Terre: 93km (58 miles) E of Genoa

Rocky coves, dramatic cliffs, and Apennine ridges are the spectacular backdrop to the Cinque Terre (Five Lands), a region that consists of five fishing and wine-making villages dramatically perched along an 11-mile stretch of Italy's Ligurian coast. Terraced vineyards and olive groves climb slopes that are largely inaccessible by road, but have become a hiker's haven stretching southeast from Monterosso al Mare to Vernazza, Corniglia, Manarola, and Riomaggiore.

Not too surprisingly, these charms have not gone unnoticed, and tourists have been coming here in increasing numbers. From May to October (weekends are worst), you are likely to find yourself in a long procession of like-minded, non-Italian speaking trekkers making their way down the coast, or elbow-to-elbow with day-trippers from cruise ships. It's gotten

RIVIERA runners-up

While Portofino and the Cinque Terre get their accolades, it would be a shame to overlook some other lovely seaside destinations that also make a great base for exploring the area. When the Cinque Terre is drowning in tourists (a common occurrence May–Sept), these alternatives offer as much beauty, a bit more breathing room, and more options in terms of accommodations—some better in fact!

Set on opposites sides of the stunning Gulf of Poets lie the picturesque seaside medieval villages of **Portovenere** (tourist info: ✆ **0187/790-691**) and **Lerici** (tourist info: ✆ **0187/969-164**). Once archrivals—Portovenere belonged to Genoa and Lerici to Pisa—both built imposing fortresses to protect themselves from the enemy (and pirates). These incredible edifices still remain along with charming, colorful homes backing up to olive tree-covered hills. The beautiful harbors hold local fishing boats and yachts alike. One can easily take the spectacular ferry ride up to the Cinque Terre in less than an hour.

To the north of the Cinque Terre and only a 5-minute train ride from Monterosso is the sunny seaside town of **Levanto** (tourist info: www.levanto.com; ✆ **0187/808-125**) with its large sand beach, lovely historic center, and lodging options ranging from campsites to 4-star hotels.

A few train stops more, you arrive at **Bonassola, Moneglia,** and **Sestri Levanto** (tourist info: www.sestri-levante. net; ✆ **0185/478-530**) with its breathtaking "Bay of Silence"; any of these towns offer nice beaches and colorful town centers.

so bad that for the past few years Italy has been outlining plans to limit the number of daily visitors to this UNESCO World Heritage site; if that were enacted, hikers wanting to access the Cinque Terre trails might be required to buy tickets ahead of time.

So yes, it's beautiful, especially in the off-season months. But are its good looks blotted out by crowds? Some think so.

Essentials

ARRIVING Cinque Terre towns are served only by local **train** runs. Coming from Florence or Rome, you will likely have to change trains in nearby La Spezia, which has one or two local trains per hour (6–8 min. to the smaller towns). From Pisa, there are about six daily trains to La Spezia (1¼ hr.); from Genoa, there are one or two direct trains per hour to La Spezia, stopping in Monterosso (1 hr., 40 min. from Genoa) and sometimes Riomaggiore (15 min. farther south).

The fastest **driving** route is via Autostrada A12 from Genoa. Coming from the center of Genoa, your route will not be affected by road closures due to the collapse of the Morandi Bridge northwest of the city. Get off at the Corrodano exit for Monterosso. The drive from Genoa to Corrodano takes less than an hour, while the much shorter 15km (9¼-mile) trip from

Corrodano to Monterosso (via Levanto) follows a narrow road and can take half an hour. Coming from the south or Florence, get off Autostrada A12 at La Spezia and follow cinque terre signs.

Navigazione Golfo dei Poeti (www.navigazionegolfodeipoeti.it; © **0187/732-987**) runs a **ferry service** from the Riviera Levante towns, April to November, though these tend to be day cruises stopping for anywhere from 1 to 3 hours in Vernazza before returning.

GETTING AROUND   The best way to see the Cinque Terre is to devote a whole day and hoof it along the trails. See "Exploring the Cinque Terre," p. 575, for details.

Local **trains** make frequent runs (two or three per hr.) between the five towns; some stop only in Monterosso and Riomaggiore, so check the posted *partenze* schedule at the station first to be sure you're catching a local. One-way tickets (around 2€) between any two towns are available—or you can buy a day ticket good for unlimited trips for 13€, meaning you can use it to town-hop. You'd have to use the day ticket five to six times in one day to make it worth your while, so evaluate whether it makes more sense to buy individual tickets.

From the port in Monterosso, **Navigazione Golfo dei Poeti** (www. navigazionegolfodeipoeti.it; © **0187/732-987**) makes eight to ten **boat** trips a day between Monterosso and Riomaggiore (25-min. trip), all stopping in Vernazza and half of them stopping in Manarola as well. A daily ticket for all of the Cinque Terre is 27€, so that you can take as many boats as you like over the day. One-way tickets tend to cost around 6€ and roundtrip tickets for the different villages cost 8€. Children 6 to 11 get a bit of a discount depending on the type of ticket.

A narrow, one-lane coast road hugs the mountainside above the towns, but all the towns' centers are closed to cars. Parking is difficult and, where available, expensive. Some people park along the side of the road, and there are areas where parking is free for a few hours (you will need to have a "parking disk" to show the time you arrived), but if you overstay your time, you risk a hefty fine. Riomaggiore and Manarola both have small **public parking facilities** just above their towns and minibuses to carry you and your luggage down. In Monterosso, try to find parking in the so-called "Loreto" garage, where Strada Provinciale 38 meets Via Roma just before the beginning of the pedestrian zone (there is another lot in an area of town called Fegina, but it's farther away); the price is 2.50€ per hour or 25€ per day, though prices go down for longer stays and are somewhat cheaper in the off-season between November and March.

VISITOR INFORMATION   The Cinque Terre **tourist office** is underneath the train station of Monterosso, Via Fegina 38 (www.prolocomonterosso. it; © **0187/817-506**). It's open Easter through September daily 9am to 5pm; hours are reduced the rest of the year. Even when it's closed, you will usually find a display of phone numbers and other information, from hotels to ferries, posted outside the office.

Additional useful websites for the region include **www.cinqueterre. it** and **www.parconazionale5terre.it**.

Exploring the Cinque Terre

Aside from swimming and soaking in the atmosphere of unspoiled fishing villages, the most popular activity in the Cinque Terre is **hiking from one village to the next** ★★★ along centuries-old goat paths, which are now maintained as a national park (see "The Cinque Terre Card," p. 576). Trails plunge through vineyards and groves of olive and lemon trees, hugging seaside cliffs and affording heart-stopping views of the coast and romantic little villages in the distance. The well-signposted walks from village to village range in difficulty and length, but as a loose rule, they get longer and steeper—and more rewarding—the farther north you go.

Depending on your pace, and not including eventual stops for focaccia and *sciacchetrà,* the local sweet wine, you can make the trip between **Monterosso,** at the northern end of the Cinque Terre, and **Riomaggiore,** at the southern end, in about 4½ hours. You should decide whether you want to walk north to south or south to north. Walking south means

Walking path above Manarola in the Cinque Terre.

The Cinque Terre Card

To access the trails of the Cinque Terre national park, you will need to buy a **Cinque Terre Card,** available at park welcome centers in each town. There are two versions of this card. The **Cinque Terre Trekking Card** (7.50€ adults, 4.50€ children under 12) offers 1-day access to the trails, along with free use of pay bathrooms along the trails, bus service between towns, reduced-price admission to local museums, and use of Wi-Fi at public hotspots. The **Cinque Terre Treno Card** (16€ adults, 10€ children under 12) offers all of the above in addition to unlimited second-class train travel between towns. Considering how cheap train travel is between towns (from 1.80€ to 2.20€ each way depending on which of the five towns you are traveling to), the Treno card is only worth the extra money if you plan to use the train 4 or 5 times during your day of hiking. There are also 2-day cards, family cards, and senior discount cards, as well as a cheaper low-season Treno card (13€ adults, 7.30€ children) valid November through February. Check www. parconazionale5terre.it/cinque-terre-card.php for updated info.

tackling the hardest trail first, which you may prefer, because you'll get it out of the way and things will get easier as the day goes on. Heading north, the trail gets progressively harder between towns—a route you might prefer if you want to walk just until you tire and then hop on the train.

The walk from **Monterosso to Vernazza** is the most arduous and takes 1½ hours, on a trail that makes several steep ascents and descents (on the portion outside Monterosso, you'll pass beneath funicular-like cars that transport grapes down the steep hillsides). The leg from **Vernazza to Corniglia** is also demanding and takes another 1½ hours, plunging into some dense forests and involving some lengthy ascents, but is probably the prettiest and most rewarding stretch. Part of the path between **Corniglia** and **Manarola,** about 45 minutes apart, follows a level grade above a long stretch of beach, tempting you to break stride and take a dip. From **Manarola** to **Riomaggiore,** it's easy going for about half an hour along a partially paved path known as the Via dell'Amore, so named for its romantic vistas (great at sunset).

Because all the villages are linked by rail, you can hike as many portions of the itinerary as you wish and take the train to your next destination. Trails also cut through the forested, hilly terrain inland from the coast, much of which is protected as a nature preserve. The tourist office in Monterosso can provide maps.

MONTEROSSO ★★★

The Cinque Terre's largest village seems incredibly busy compared to its sleepier neighbors, but it's not without its charms. Monterosso is actually two towns—a bustling, character-filled Old Town built behind the harbor,

The beach at Monterosso.

and a relaxed resort that stretches along the Cinque Terre's **only sand beach.** This is where you'll find the train station and the tiny regional tourist office (upon exiting the station, turn left and head through the tunnel for the Old Town; turn right for the newer town).

The region's most famous art treasure is here, housed in the **Convento dei Cappuccini,** perched on a hillock in the center of the Old Town: a "Crucifixion" by Anthony van Dyck, the Flemish master who worked for a time in nearby Genoa (convent open daily 9am–noon and 4–7pm). You will find the most modern conveniences in Monterosso, but you'll have a more "rustic" experience if you stay in one of the other four villages.

VERNAZZA ★★★

Vernazza may just be the quintessential, postcard-perfect seaside village. Tall, colorful houses (known as *terratetti*) cluster around a natural harbor, where you can swim among the fishing boats; above them a **castle** stands high atop a rocky promontory that juts into the sea (the castle, which is nothing special, is open Mar–Oct daily 10am–6:30pm; admission 1.50€). The center of town is waterside **Piazza Marconi,** itself a sea of cafe

Vernazza surrounds a natural harbor.

tables. The only Vernazza drawback is that too much good press has turned it into the Cinque Terre's mecca for American tourists.

CORNIGLIA ★

The quietest village in the Cinque Terre is isolated by its position midway down the coast, its hilltop location high above the open sea, and its hard-to-access harbor. Whether you arrive by boat, train, or the trail from the south, you'll have to climb some 300 steps to reach the village proper (arriving by trail from the north is the only way to avoid these stairs), an enticing maze of little walkways shadowed by tall houses.

Once there, though, the views over the surrounding vineyards and up and down the coastline are stupendous—for the best outlook, walk to the end of the narrow main street to a belvedere that is perched between the sea and sky. Corniglia is the village most likely to offer a glimpse into life in the Cinque Terre the way it was decades ago.

MANAROLA ★

Manarola is a near-vertical cluster of tall houses that seem to rise piggy-back up the hills on either side of the harbor. In fact, in a region with no shortage of heart-stopping views, one of the most amazing sights is the descent into the town of Manarola on the path from Corniglia: From this perspective, the hill-climbing houses seem to merge into one another to form a row of skyscrapers. Despite these urban associations, Manarola is a delightfully rural village where fishing and winemaking are big business. The region's major **wine cooperative,** Cooperativa Agricoltura di Riomaggiore, Manarola, Corniglia, Vernazza e Monterosso, made up of 300 local producers, is here; check www.cantinacinqueterre.com or call ℂ **0187/920-435** for information about tours of its modern (established 1982) facilities. Try to reserve at least 3 days before your visit.

RIOMAGGIORE ★

Riomaggiore clings to the rustic ways of the Cinque Terre while making some (unfortunate) concessions to the modern world. The old fishing quarter has expanded in recent years, and Riomaggiore now has some sections of new houses and apartment blocks. This blend of old and new is a bit of a shame. The village center still looks like something from 50 years ago, bustling and prosperous in a charming setting, while the "new side" of town feels like a half-effort at maintaining the old mostly in color. A credit to both sides is that many of the lanes end in seaside belvederes.

From the parking garage, follow the main street down; from the train station, exit and turn right to head through the tunnel for the central part of town (or, from the station, take off left up the brick stairs to walk the Via dell'Amore to Manarola). That tunnel and the main drag meet at the base of an elevated terrace that holds the train tracks; from there, a staircase leads down to a tiny fishing harbor. At the left of the harbor, a rambling path leads to a pleasant little **beach** of large pebbles.

Where to Stay in the Cinque Terre
SELF-CATERING ROOMS AND APARTMENTS

There have always been quite a few *affittacamere* (room rentals) in the various Cinque Terre towns, but getting information on them meant having local contacts and relying on word of mouth. Now that local room and apartment owners have gotten more Internet savvy, finding rentals online has become much easier, even aside from **www.airbnb.com**, which does have many listings in each of the five towns. For a room with private bathroom for two people, expect to pay anywhere from 70€ to 150€ per night depending on the season and the amenities offered. **L'Ancora** (www.lancoracinqueterre.net) in Riomaggiore has three rooms (with private bath) in an ancient Ligurian building, with traditional elements like wood beams and exposed bricks, but very modern bathrooms. The room on the top floor has a small kitchenette (the owners specify that it be used for making breakfast only). In the heart of Vernazza, **Memo Rooms** (www.memorooms.com) are three simple yet elegant rooms with private bath.

MANAROLA

La Torretta ★★★ Located in an ancient tower in the center of Manarola, this charming lodge is one of the few retreats in the Cinque Terre with a bit of chic flair (the other one is **La Mala** in Vernazza). The property has a range of lovely rooms and suites that mix contemporary and traditional furnishings, along with quirky details. Several rooms have sea views and balconies, and all have nice in-room amenities, such as Nespresso machines and luxurious toiletries. Our favorite rooms are the Design Suite in the main building and the Panoramic Suite in the annex, just a short walk from the main building. Despite the fairly steep prices (and position on the hill), rooms go quickly here in high season, so book way ahead of time. Fortunately, a luggage transfer service means guests don't have to lug their own bags up the hill from the train station.

Vico Volto 20, Manarola. www.torrettas.com. ℰ **0187/920-327.** 11 units. 250€–300€ double. 450€–1,00€ suites. Rates include breakfast. Closed Nov. **Amenities:** Solarium; Wi-Fi (free).

Ostello Cinque Terre ★ Don't expect luxury here, but a good clean bed and bath at more than reasonable prices make this hostel sell out weeks before the high season. Located in the center of town near the church, it's a rare budget alternative in the Cinque Terre. Linens and blankets are included in your stay, but towels must be rented for 2€. Wi-Fi can be spotty outside of the small reception area, and guests are expected to be out of the rooms from 10am to 1pm so they can be cleaned. You can check in from 4pm to 8pm; if you plan to arrive outside of those hours, communicate with the hostel. *Note:* A sister property of the same name in nearby Portovenere—considered one of the "gateway towns" to the Cinque Terre—is open all year. The website is a little buggy: When you make your reservations, confirm which property you are reserving for.

Via Riccobaldi 21, Manarola. www.hostel5terre.com. ℰ **0187/920-039.** 21€–28€ beds in 6-bed dorm rooms; 55€–70€ room with 2 single beds w/private bath; 132€–162€ 6-bed family room w/private bath. 2-night minimum stay. Closed mid-Nov–mid-Mar. **Amenities:** Kayak, bike, and snorkel rental; pay laundry; Wi-Fi (free).

MONTEROSSO

Il Giardino Incantato ★★ A tranquil and relaxing refuge (its name means "Enchanted Garden) in the Cinque Terre's most bustling town, this charming family-run B&B is in a converted 16th-century villa just off Via Roma in Monterosso's old village, a stone's throw from the town beach and the boat pier. Guest rooms have been lovingly decorated with terracotta tiles, wood-beamed ceilings, and wrought-iron beds. The villa sits next to a lovely garden with lemon trees, lavender, and colorful flowers, and this is where breakfast (including Ligurian favorites like focaccia along with typical breakfast staples like cereal and eggs prepared various ways) is served in nice weather. One caveat: The house is full of antiques and other precious objects, so if you are traveling with children, this B&B isn't for you.

Via Mazzini 18, Monterosso al Mare (SP). www.ilgiardinoincantato.net. © **0187/818-315.** 4 units. 180€–200€ double. Rates include breakfast. Closed early Nov–Apr. **Amenities:** Garden.

Hotel Porto Roca ★★   This 4-star hotel is the Cinque Terre's one real resort, spectacularly positioned upon a cliffside overlooking the village, cemetery, and blue sea below. Most guest rooms are in need of an update (and some of the common areas are also a bit "vintage"), but once you step out onto your private balcony suspended above the Mediterranean, it's easy to forget such shortcomings. The restaurant serves typical Ligurian dishes, and in nice weather the cliffside patio offers the best seat in town. Prices are high even for a room in the back without views of the sea; we suggest splurging on a better room in order to enjoy the full experience. If you tire of the infinity pool, there's a section of beach for hotel guests, with free umbrellas and deck chairs. A small wellness area helps you unwind after a day of hiking. Because the hotel is located in a pedestrian-only area, only taxis can enter, so if you aren't up for the walk from the train or closest parking lot, the hotel will send a taxi for you (price included in the cost of your room).

Via Corone 1, Monterosso al Mare (SP). www.portoroca.it. © **0187/817-502.** 43 units. 240€–695€ double; 430€–510€ family room. Rates include breakfast. Closed Nov–Mar. **Amenities:** Restaurant; bar; concierge; spa; pool; room service; Wi-Fi (free).

VERNAZZA

Gianni Franzi ★★   The owner of a trattoria in town also offers 23 rooms to rent in two different buildings; some come with a bathroom, others with excellent coastal views. Keep in mind that most rooms require a steep climb, but luggage service is offered (starting at 2€ per bag). When you arrive in town, stop by the trattoria's harborside bar (even on a Wednesday when the trattoria is closed, there's usually somebody there in the afternoon to take care of new arrivals) or call the numbers listed below. Breakfast is served on a rooftop deck designed like the bow of an ocean liner, offering wonderful views of the sea.

Restaurant address: Piazza G. Marconi 5, Vernazza (SP). www.giannifranzi.it. Restaurant © **0187/821-003;** to book a room, call © **393/900-8155.** 23 units. 70€–160€ double (some w/shared bath). Rates include breakfast. Closed early Jan–mid-Mar. **Amenities:** Restaurant; bar; garden/terrace; Wi-Fi (free).

La Mala ★★★   This stylish four-room *locanda* has a chic yet beachy feel. The rooms are not large but they are well appointed and sunny, boasting gorgeous views of the sea, village, or harbor; bathrooms are clean and modern. Room 26 has a small living area that can accommodate a third bed, making it ideal for families. Room 31 is especially large and bright, seemingly suspended in air between sea and sky. Though it's centrally located, La Mala is far enough removed from the town's center to really feel like a retreat, though you will hear bells chiming from a nearby church. The communal seaside terrace is the perfect spot for a relaxing sunset *aperitivo*. There is no reception area—just call (or find) the owner, Gian Battista, when you arrive in town, and someone will meet you to help with your bags. There's no breakfast area, though rooms have a machine for making coffee and tea, and you'll be provided vouchers for a simple Italian breakfast (such as a cappuccino and brioche) at a local coffee bar.

Via San Giovanni Battista, Vernazza. www.lamala.it. ✆ 334/287-5718. 4 units. 110€–220€ double. Closed Jan 10–Mar. **Amenities:** Wi-Fi (free).

Where to Eat in the Cinque Terre

CORNIGLIA

Osteria a Cantina de Mananan ★★ LIGURIAN   Locals and tourists alike seek out this tiny eatery carved out of an old wine cellar in an ancient stone house. This unique and lively restaurant has very few tables—you may even be asked to share a table with other diners—and there's often only one seating per meal, so be sure to call ahead (and bring cash; credit cards are not accepted). The restaurant follows a "slow-food" philosophy, sourcing vegetables from nearby terraced gardens and seafood from the town's fishermen. Some of the standouts on the simple yet tasty menu include pansotti pasta (a sort of Ligurian ravioli usually stuffed with herbs and cheese) in walnut sauce, anchovies three ways (with lemon, salt, and pickled), or the house specialty, *coniglio* (rabbit) roasted in a white wine sauce. Seasonal specialties will be listed on the big board on the wall.

Via Fieschi 117, Corniglia. ✆ 0187/821-166. Entrees 10€–20€. Wed–Mon 12:30–2:30pm and 7:30–9:30pm; closed Tues. Closed Mon–Fri in Dec, and part of Jan–Feb.

MONTEROSSO

Ristorante Miky ★ SEAFOOD   This family-run restaurant in Monterosso is considered one of the best—and most expensive—in the Cinque Terre. In addition to the friendly service and beautifully presented food, you can dine in a lovely garden with the smell of lemon and rosemary in the air. House specialties include an excellent seafood sampler platter, monkfish ravioli, and *pesce al sale*, fresh fish covered in coarse salt and slowly cooked in a wood-burning oven. Many pasta and rice dishes are served in large terracotta plates that give them a truly unique flavor. An extensive wine list focuses on local producers, and homemade *limoncello* is offered at the end of your meal. You can even buy jars of the family's homemade pesto or marmalade to take with you. Miky certainly isn't cheap, but the food, ambience, and overall experience make it worthwhile. Reservations are highly recommended.

Via Fegina 104, Monterosso al Mare. www.ristorantemiky.it. ℂ **0187/817-608.** Entrees 15€–30€. Daily noon–3pm and 7:30pm–late. Closed Nov–Mar.

VERNAZZA

Ristorante Belforte ★★★ LIGURIAN Perched on a medieval watchtower overlooking the Mediterranean, this upscale restaurant boasts a unique and fantastic setting. Traditional Ligurian cuisine is featured, such as local anchovies served a variety of ways. Other notable dishes include *antipasto misto di pesce,* a selection of five or six small bites of seafood (hot and cold delicacies); and homemade *tagliolini* pasta with squid ink, shrimp, and seaweed. One of the most interesting dishes on the menu is *riso al curry con scampi* (curried rice with scampi); there is a 2-person minimum to order it. There's often a wait, even if you've reserved ahead of time, but it's worth it—if you are able to nab the single table on a small balcony at sunset, you are in for a romantic treat!

Via Guidoni 42, Vernazza. www.ristorantebelforte.it. ℂ**0187/812-222.** Entrees 16€–30€. Wed–Mon noon–3:30pm and 7–10pm. Closed Nov–mid-Mar.

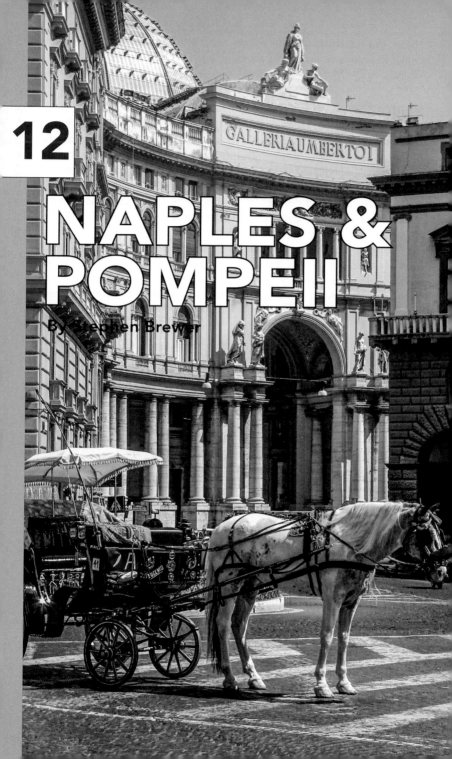

NAPLES & POMPEII

By Stephen Brewer

**B**ienvenuti al sud—welcome to the south. Your first encounter with southern Italy, for better or worse, will probably be Naples. If you've enjoyed the grandeur of Venice, the elegance of Florence, and the awesomeness of monumental Rome, be prepared for a bit of a shock. Naples lives up to its reputation for dirt and grime, delights with its energy and good cheer, and surprises with the sophistication of its monuments and museums. It can be overwhelming, but that's part of the city's allure. And Naples is just the beginning.

There's so much more right around Naples—some of the most extensive remains of the ancient world in Herculaneum and Pompeii, and the natural ominous wonders of Mt. Vesuvius and the Campo Flegeri. You might want to think of the Naples area as Italy on overdrive. Hang on and enjoy the ride.

DON'T LEAVE NAPLES & POMPEII WITHOUT . . .

Prowling Around the Attic of Antiquity. Among the prizes in the National Archaeology Museum, you'll find touchingly human statues of gods and goddesses, frescoes and mosaics from Pompeii and Herculaneum, even some titter-inducing pornography.

Plunging into Neapolitan Street Life. Lively Via Tribunali provides a good taste of the city's color and clamor, from the magnificent church of San Lorenzo Maggiore to the pizzas emerging from the ovens at Sorbillo.

Soaking in Soothing Views. Hit the airy heights by riding the funicular up to the Certosa di San Martino. Admire the vista of Mt. Vesuvius looming over the bay from Castel dell'Ovo or the gardens of the Villa Communale.

Stepping Back into Ancient Times in Herculaneum and Pompeii. It's eerily easy to imagine everyday life as it was 2,000 years ago along the streets of these accidentally preserved seaside towns.

Sampling Naples' Greatest Contribution to World Cuisine. You haven't eaten pizza until you've eaten it in Naples, the city where pizza was born. Follow our recommendations to find the best.

NAPLES ★★

219km (136 miles) SE of Rome

In Naples, Mt. Vesuvius looms to the east, the fumaroles of the Campo Flegrei hiss and steam to the west, and the isle of Capri (see p. 679) floats phantomlike across the gleaming waters of the bay. For all the splendor and drama of this natural setting, one of Italy's most intense urban concoctions is the real show. Naples shoots out so many sensations that it takes a while for visitors to know what's hit them.

Everything seems a bit more intense in Italy's third-largest city, the capital of the south. Dark brooding lanes open to palm-fringed piazzas. Laundry-strewn tenements stand cheek by jowl with grand palaces. Medieval churches and castles rise above the grid of streets laid out by ancient Greeks. No denying it, parts of the city are squalid, yet the museums are packed with riches.

It seems that most of life here transpires on the streets, so you'll witness a lot. The pace can be leisurely in that southern way, and amazingly hectic. When you partake—in a meal, in a *passegiata,* or just in a simple transaction—you'll notice the warmth, general good nature, and a sense of fun. You get the idea—but you won't really, until you experience this fascinating, perplexing, and beguiling city for yourself.

Essentials

ARRIVING Naples is on the main southern rail corridor and is served by frequent and fast **train service** from most Italian and European cities. The trip between Rome and Naples on high-speed (AltaVelocità, or AV) express trains takes only 87 minutes, making this by far the best way to travel between the two cities. Rail Europe and Eurail pass holders should note that AV trains require a reservation and an extra fee (10€). Contact **Trenitalia** (www.trenitalia.it; ⓒ **892-021**) for information, reservations, and fares. High-speed **Italo** trains travel the route, too (www.italotreno.it; ⓒ **060708;** see p. 817). The city has two main rail terminals: **Stazione Centrale,** at Piazza Garibaldi, and **Stazione Mergellina,** at Piazza Piedigrotta. Most travelers will arrive at Stazione Centrale.

Although driving *in* Naples can be hair-raising, **driving** *to* Naples is easy. The city is linked by autostrada A2 to Rome and A3 to Reggio di Calabria, in the far south.

There are no nonstop flights from the U.S. directly into Naples's **Aeroporto Capodichino** (www.aeroportodinapoli.it; ⓒ **081/789-6111**), but many carriers, including low-cost Ryanair and EasyJet, fly into Naples from Italian and European cities, plus a few intercontinental flights. From the airport, which is only 7km (4 miles) from the city center, you can take a taxi into town (make sure it is an official white taxi with the Naples municipal logo); the flat rate for the 15-minute trip to the train station is

16€. **Alibus** bus service to the port (Piazza Municipio) and the train station (Piazza Garibaldi) is run by **ANM** (www.anm.it; ✆ **800/639-525;** 5€ one-way; buy tickets on board or at bars and tobacco shops in the airport). The bus runs every 30 minutes from the airport (6.30am–11.50pm) and from the port (6am–midnight).

Ferries between Naples and Palermo sail once or twice nightly and are operated by **Tirrenia Lines** (www.tirrenia.it; ✆ **089-2123**) and **Grandi Navi Veloci, GNV** (www.gnv.it; ✆ **010/209-4591**). You can buy tickets at travel agencies or at ferry offices in the port area: Tirrenia at Capannone Juta, Calata Porta di Massa; GNV in Piazzale Immacolatella. Accommodations for the 11-hour trip are in business-class-style reclining seats or cabins.

GETTING AROUND   Public transport in Naples comes under the auspices of **Azienda Napolitano Mobilta,** usually referred to simply as **ANM** (www.anm.it; ✆ **800/639-525**); the excellent website, with English translations, is a helpful resource for planning your travels around the city. The **Metropolitana (subway)** has two lines. Line 1 connects the train station in Piazza Garibaldi with such central locations as the archaeological museum (Museo stop), Piazza Municipo, Piazza Dante, and Via Toledo; line 2 runs from Pozzuoli in the western suburbs through the city, with stops that include Mergelina, Piazza Amadeo, Montesanto, the archaeological museum (Museo stop), and Piazza Garibaldi. Several new stations have opened in recent years, with more underway, including a planned expansion of line 1 to the airport. As you ride the system, you'll notice many stations decorated with art installations. Mosaic tiles and lights in the Toledo station are in shades of blue that become deeper and more intense as you descend; psychedelic colors and shapes in the Università station are intended to immerse you in the digital age.

There are also two urban railway networks that can be handy for getting to major attractions. The **Circumvesuviana train** leaves from a station adjacent to the main train station in Piazza Garibaldi and runs southeast around the Bay of Naples to Oplontis, Pompeii and Herculaneum (see p. 624), and Sorrento (p. 638). The **Ferrovia Cumana** runs from Piazza Montesanto to Pozzouli and other towns in the Campi Flegrei (p. 620).

Handy **bus** routes include the R lines (R1, R2, R3, R4), with frequent stops at major tourist attractions (the R4, for example, connects the archaeological museum and Catacombs of San Gennaro), and the electric minibuses (marked e) that skirt the historic district.

Four **funiculars** take passengers up and down the steep hills of Naples. The **Funicolare Centrale,** one of the world's longest (about a mile) and busiest funiculars, connects the central city to Vomero. Daily departures (6:30am–12:30am) are from Piazzetta Duca d'Aosta just off Via Toledo.

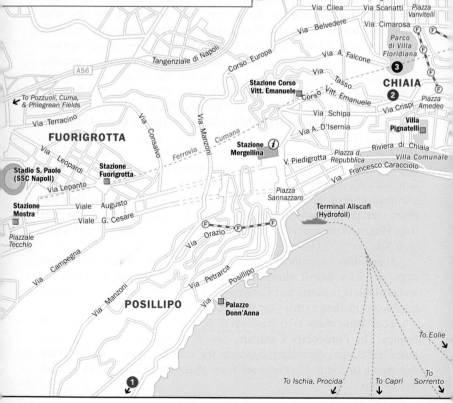

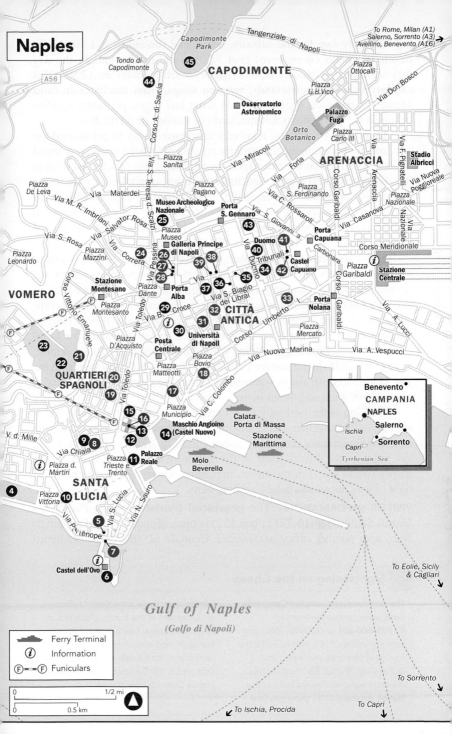

Naples

One-way fare for the subway, buses, and funiculars is 1.10€; daily tickets (Biglietto Giornaliero) cost 3.50€, valid until midnight the day they are validated; weekly tickets (Biglietto Settimanale) are 12.50€. You can buy tickets at newsstands, tobacco shops, from machines in most Metro and funicular stations, and at some bus stops; you must validate tickets in the electronic ticket machines in stations or on the bus.

Taxis are an excellent, relatively inexpensive way to get around the city, and are very reliable and strictly regulated. Official taxis are painted white and marked comune di napoli. Inside a sign lists official flat rates to the seaports, central hotels, and top attractions; don't fret if your driver doesn't use the meter—*not* using the meter is legal for all rides with established flat rates. Taxis don't cruise for street hails, but can be found at many taxi stands around town; for an extra 1€ surcharge, you can request a taxi by phone (© **081/444-444** or **081/555-5555**).

As for **driving** around Naples, we have one word: *Don't.* If you're tempted, take a look at the cars on the street. In the rest of Italy, even the simplest models are kept in pristine condition; here, cars look like they've been used in demolition derbies. Car theft is common—some rental companies won't even extend theft protection coverage if you'll be driving in Naples. If you do bring a car into the city, a convenient place for long-term parking is **Parcheggio Brin,** Via Volta and Via Volta (www.anm.it; © **081/763-2855**) at the eastern edge of the center, easily reached from the Via Marina exit off the A3 autrostrada. Parking costs 2€ for the first 4 hours, 0.50€ each additional hour.

Walking is the best way to get around the city center, where sights are fairly close together, but remember: For Neapolitan drivers, red lights are mere suggestions; cross busy streets carefully. Always look both ways, too, since many drivers scoff at the notion of a one-way street. Zebra stripes (white lines) in the street, indicating where pedestrians have the right of way, mean absolutely nothing here.

VISITOR INFORMATION The **provincial tourist office** at Piazza dei Martiri 58 (© **081/410-7211;** bus 152) is open Monday to Friday 9am to 2pm, with another office at Stazione Centrale (© **081/268-779;** metro

Sightseeing on the Cheap

The confoundingly complex **Campania Card** (www.campaniartecard.it; © **800/600-601** or 06/3996–7650) can save you money if you plan to make the rounds of churches, museums, and archaeological sites. For most visitors, the most basic version will suffice: the **Napoli Artecard** (21€) gives you free admission to three attractions, a discount of 50 percent at the fourth, discounts at other attractions, free use of public transport, and discounts to shops and restaurants. It's for sale at participating sites and at the Campania Card stand at Napoli Centrale train station.

Piazza Garibaldi; Mon–Sat 9am–7pm). The municipality (www.inaples. it) maintains two excellent **tourist information points:** Via San Carlo 9 (✆ **081/402-394**) and Piazza del Gesù (✆ **081/551-2701**), both open daily (Mon–Sat 9:30am–6:30pm; Sun 9:30am–2pm). Any of these offices can give you a free map, an essential piece of gear when navigating Naples.

Exploring Naples

Large as Naples is, it's easy to get to the sights you want to see on foot, letting you experience one of the city's greatest allures—its street life. From Piazza Trieste e Trento, with the magnificent **Teatro San Carlo** and

Galleria Umberto I, Via Toledo leads north. To the left is the Quartieri Spagnoli, a neighborhood of tightly packed narrow lanes, while to the right, just beyond Piazza Dante, is the atmospheric historical center of the city, where many of the churches you want to see face airy piazzas. At the northern end of Via Toledo, about a 10-minute walk beyond Piazza Dante, is Naples' celebrated archaeological museum. You'll probably be safe just about anywhere you wander along the well-worn tourist trail; the crime rate in Naples, despite a bad rap, is a lot lower than it is in many American cities. It's best to avoid the darker corners of the Spagnoli neighborhood at night, however. Pickpockets and purse-and-jewelry snatchers can be a menace, especially around the train station; on Via San Gregorio Armeno, people gawking at shop windows filled with nativity scenes are known to be easy targets.

Naples' atmospheric streets.

SANTA LUCIA AND THE SEAFRONT

Not surprisingly, some of the city's most magnificent squares and public monuments are clustered near the seafront. **Piazza del Plebiscito ★★,** the most beautiful square in Naples, is surrounded by an elegant assemblage of neoclassical landmarks. Among them is the **Palazzo Reale ★** (Royal Palace), with 30 grandiose yet strangely vacuous rooms where Neapolitan royalty ruled and entertained in the 18th and 19th centuries

Getting to Know Napoli

A good way to get to know the city is on a free walking tour with **Napoli That's Amore** (www.napolithatsamore.org). Local professionals lead various highly informative and personalized walks: through the Old Town from Piazza Dante; around the seafront on a Royal Naples route from Piazza Municipo; and a Best of Naples circuit beginning at Piazza Municipo. Go to the website to book; tour times vary throughout the year. There's no fee, but tips are appreciated and well-deserved.

(www.polomusealecampania.beniculturali.it; © **081/580-8255**; palace 6€, courtyard and gardens free; Thurs–Tues 9am–8pm; bus R2 or R3). In the piazza, two Neapolitan kings survey the cobblestones on horseback: the forward-thinking Carlo III (1716–1788) and the treacherous Ferdinando I (1423–1494). It's said you will be blessed with good fortune if you face the Palazzo Reale, close your eyes, and walk backwards across the square between the two kings (much harder to do than you might think—local lore has it that condemned prisoners were once blindfolded and made to perform this feat, and few succeeded).

A short walk up the seafront, the airy **Piazza Municipo** is the best place to view the towers and crenellations of **Castel Nuovo ★** (New Castle), with the white-marble Triumphal Arch of Alfonso I of Aragona

The Castel dell'Ovo and Borgo Morinaro.

squeezed between two of its turrets. You can forgo a visit to the castle's fairly uninspired staterooms and art collection, and simply admire this medieval sea-girt beauty from the outside. (If you do want to step inside, the salons and galleries are open Mon–Sat 8:30am–6:30pm; admission free). Gazing at the castle, you might consider the plight of its former prisoners, who shared their dungeons with crocodiles imported from Egypt for the express purpose of snacking on the doomed souls. In Piazza Municipo you'll also see the water-spouting lions and sea monsters of the **Fontana del Nettuno** ★★, a 17th-century marble showpiece originally installed in front of the Palazzo Reale and carted around the city to several locations since then. It was partly the work of Pietro Bernini, whose greatest creation is the Fontana della Barcaccia at the bottom of the Spanish Steps in Rome (his more famous son, Lorenzo, designed the Fontana dei Quattro Fiumi in Rome's Piazza Navona).

Head south along the seafront to see the city's outrageously picturesque **Castel dell'Ovo** ★★ (Castle of the Egg), on Borgo Marinari (off Via Partenope). As every Neapolitan knows, the ancient Roman poet Virgil placed an egg under the foundations of the castle; when it breaks, a great disaster will befall the city. Considering earthquakes, eruptions of nearby Mt. Vesuvius, plague outbreaks, and wars, it's probably safe to assume the egg is no longer intact. The castle is enchanting even without such legends, squeezed onto a tiny island the Greeks first settled almost 3 millennia ago and a royal residence from the 13th through 20th centuries (✆ **081/795-6180;** free admission; Mon–Sat 9am–6:30pm; Sun 9am–2pm). The little lanes beneath the thick walls are lined with the fishermens' houses of Borgo Marinaro, now occupied by bars and pizzerias. For Neapolitans, a walk across the stout bridge onto the island is a favorite Sunday afternoon outing.

Galleria Umberto I ★★ SHOPPING MALL Shopping malls have only gone downhill since elegant glass-and-iron landmarks like this were all the rage in the late 19th century. The café- and shop-lined gallery modeled after Milan's Galleria Vittorio Emanuele II (p. 473) saw its best days in the years before World War I, but Neapolitans are once again waking up to the pleasures of shopping beneath the glass dome and vaulted wings. If the place works its magic on you, as it

The airy atrium of the Galleria Umberto I shopping arcade.

EVERY DAY IS christmas

Among the many delights of Naples are the *presepi*, nativity scenes that you can find everywhere, any time of the year, although they really come out in force around Christmas. St. Francis of Assisi is said to have commissioned the first *presepe* in the 13th century, but it was here in Naples that the scenes became elevated to high art, bolstered by the patronage of King Charles III in the 18th century. City craftsmen still go all out, carving figures in wood, firing them in ceramics, even fitting them with tailored clothing. Besides mainstays like Mary, Joseph, and the baby Jesus, the Neapolitan cast of characters often includes soccer stars and other celebrities, and settings can be a lot more elaborate than a humble manger: medieval town squares, rusticated villages with thatched cottages, elaborate caves that look like some troglodyte fantasy. On **Via San Gregorio Armeno,** dozens of shops sell figures beginning at about 15€. You can buy a complete scene for anywhere from 100€ to well into five digits, or have one made with figures of your own family and favorite celebrities (as many Neapolitans do). Be aware that pickpockets flock to the street like sheep to a Bethlehem hillside to prey on distracted window-shoppers. Among the most reputable shops are **Gambardella Pastori,** Via San Gregorio Armeno 40 (www.gambardellapastori.com; *C* **081/5517107**); **Giuseppe e Marco Ferrigno,** Via San Gregorio Armeno 10 (www.arteferrigno.com; *C* **081/5523148**); and **Petrucciani Luigi,** Via San Gregorio Armeno 51 (*C* **081/551-2496**).

is sure to do, dip into *The Gallery,* a poignant 1947 novel by John Horne Burnes about American GIs in Naples after World War II. Much of the action transpires in the Galleria.

Entrances off Via Toledo, Via Giuseppe Verdi, Via Santa Brigida, and Via San Carlo. Bus: R2 or R3 to Piazza Trieste e Trento.

Villa Communale ★★ PARK/GARDEN Time was the public was only allowed into the seaside gardens of the royal family once a year, on September 8, the Fiesta di Piedigrotta. That changed with the proletarian sentiments that swept in with the unification of Italy in 1869, and a good thing, too. Following the paths through greenery and past statues and fountains for a km (1/2 mile) or so from Piazza Vittoria on the east to Piazza della Repubblica on the west is one of the city's great delights. The Bay of Naples shimmers to the south, and many of its denizens—octopi, squid, and sea urchins—now reside in tanks at the **Anton Dohrn Zoological Station,** currently open only to researchers. A popular **antiques market** takes over a corner of Villa Communale on the 3rd and 4th weekends of each month from 8:30am to 1pm; contact the tourist office (p. 590) for info.

Piazza Vittoria. Daily 7am–midnight. Bus: C82 or R2.

CENTRO STORICO/SPACCANAPOLI

This warren of tight lanes, a few avenues, and some boisterous piazzas is also known as Spaccanapoli (literally, "Naples Splitter," the street that runs straight through the center of the neighborhood, as it has ever since the Greeks established a colony here). Roughly, the heart of Naples extends north from seaside Castel Nuovo to the Museo Archeologico Nazionale, and east from Via Toledo to the Porta Nolona Fish Market. West of Via Toledo, the even more densely packed Quartueri Spagnoli is a maze of laundry-strung lanes named for the Spanish troops once garrisoned here to keep the rebellious population in line.

Cappella di Sansevero ★★ MUSEUM Only in Naples would a room as colorful, fanciful, mysterious, beautiful, and macabre as this exist. Prince Raimondo di Sangro of Sansevero remodeled his family's funerary chapel in the 18th century, combining the then-fashionable baroque style with his own love of complex symbolism and intellectual quests. Neapolitan sculptor Giuseppe Sanmartino crafted "Christ Veiled Under a Shroud," in which a thin transparent covering seems to make Christ's flesh look even more tormented. (Antonio Canova, the Venetian sculptor, came to Naples a century later and said he would give 10 years of his life to have created something so beautiful.) The prince's father lies beneath a statue of "Despair on Disillusion," in which a man disentangling himself from a marble net suggests a troubled soul seeking relief—provided by the winged boy who represents intellect. Prince Raimondo's mother, who died at age 20, lies beneath a statue of "Veiled Truth," in which a woman holds a broken tablet, symbol of an interrupted life. Raimondo himself is surrounded by colorful floor tiles arranged in a complex maze, symbol of the quest to unravel the secrets of life. Downstairs are the skeletal forms of a man and a woman in which the circulatory systems and musculature are brightly colored, allegedly with the injection of a substance the prince devised. Despite legend, the figures are not the prince's unwilling servants, scarified in the interest of science—they were fashioned from human skeletons and beeswax.

Via Francesco De Sanctis 19 (near Piazza San Domenico Maggiore). www.museo sansevero.it. © **081/551-8470.** 8€, 5€ ages 10–25. Wed–Mon 9am–7pm. Closed May 1 and Easter Monday. Metro: Dante.

Il Cattedrale di Santa Maria Assunta ★★ CATHEDRAL Three times a year—the first Saturday in May, September 19, and December 16—all of Naples squeezes into the great cathedral that King Carlo I d'Angio dedicated to San Gennaro in the 13th century. On these dates the dried blood of the city's patron saint liquefies, or sometimes doesn't. Not doing so foretells terrible events for Naples, such as an outbreak of the plague in 1528 or the earthquake in 1980 that killed 2,000 residents. The rest of the year the blood is kept in a vault inside an altar in the **Canella di San Gunnar,** where a reliquary houses the head that soldiers of the Emperor Diocletian severed from the rest of the bishop's body around 305. Within the cathedral are Naples' two oldest places of worship: The **Capella di Santa Restituta**, the city's 4th-century basilica, supported by a forest of columns from a Greek temple; and the **Capella di San Giovanni in Fonte,** a 5th-century baptistery; if you crane your neck and squint (binoculars or a telescopic lens come in handy) you can make out some endearingly rendered frescoes in the dome.

Via del Duomo 147. © **081/449-097.** Cathedral free; archaeological zone 3€. Mon–Sat 8am–12:30pm and 4:30–7pm; Sun 8am–1:30pm and 5–7:30pm. Bus R1. Metro: Cavour or Museo.

Chiesa del Gesù Nuovo ★ CHURCH The princes of Salerno built what was once their palace in 1470, requesting that the facade be done in *bugnato a punta di diamante,* with stone blocks elaborately cut to create a pattern of projecting points, like cut diamonds. The princes lost the palace a century later thanks to their political shenanigans, and the Jesuit order bought the property and converted its stately salons into a church. In due time they, too, were evicted, but not before enlivening the interior with opulent frescoes and marble work. Above the doorway inside is a dramatic fresco by Francesco Solimena (1657–1747), a mediocre Baroque painter who compensated for his lack of genius with flamboyance—his "Expulsion of Heliodorus from the Temple" is a colorful swirl of flowing draperies and churning robes. The altar of the chapel of the Visitation is the final resting place of Naples' most popular modern saint, Giuseppe Moscatti (1880–1927), a devout physician and biochemist famous for his ability to heal impossible cases. The so-called Holy Physician of Naples is believed to still be working miracles: His shrine is often thronged with the ill and injured seeking his help, and it's said that many have been cured on the spot.

Piazza del Gesù. www.gesunuovo.it. © **081/557-8111.** Free. Daily 7am–1pm and 4–8pm. Bus: R1, R2, R3, or R4. Metro: Dante.

Chiesa di San Gregorio Armeno ★★ CHURCH When nuns fleeing persecution in Asia Minor came to Naples in the 8th century, they brought with them the relics of St. Gregory, an Armenian bishop. Over the centuries they built suitable surroundings for the saint, who now rests in a sumptuous baroque church bursting at the seams with gold leaf and elaborate marble carvings. Stepping into the church, described as "a room of paradise on earth," is like walking into one of the elaborate nativity scenes, *presepi,* that vendors sell up and down the street outside. Neapolitan master Luca Giordano tells the story of the nuns' flight with their precious cargo in a series of dramatic frescoes, "The Embarkation, Journey and Arrival of the Armenia Nuns with the Relics of St Gregory" (1671–84). Gregory, however, is upstaged by one of the nuns, Santa Patrizia, whose dried blood is said to liquefy every Tuesday. The cloisters, on the other hand, are an oasis of tranquility.

Via San Gregorio Armeno 44. ✆ **081/552-0186.** Free. Daily 9am–noon (until 1pm on Sun); cloister daily 9.30–noon. Metro: Cavour.

Galleria Borbonica (Bourbon Tunnel) ★★ HISTORIC SITE Architects for mid-19th-century Bourbon royals engineered this meandering tunnel as an escape route from the Palazzo Reale to military barracks on the harbor, involving some complex maneuvering over, under, and around ancient waterworks (the tunnel is part of an extensive network of subterranean caverns beneath the city; see **Napoli Sotteranea,** p. 599). The Bourbons were ousted before the tunnel was finished and over the years the galleries were used as World War II air raid shelters and as an underground garage for impounded cars. A lot of fascinating detritus has been left behind, adding to the eeriness of being down here in a silent world beneath Naples' raucous streets. Aside from a standard 1-hour walking tour you can also opt to be rafted part of the way through ancient aqueducts (this tour is in Italian only).

Vico del Grottone 4 (or enter through parking garage at Via Morelli 61). www.galleria borbonica.com. ✆ **366/248-4151.** Guided tour 10€; 5€ ages 10–13, under 10 free. Fri–Sun 10am, noon, 3pm, and 5pm. See website for other tour times and prices. Bus C6. Metro: Municipio.

Monastero di Santa Chiara ★★ CHURCH/GARDEN It's not a good sign in a marriage when a wife's only desire is to become a nun, but that's what Queen Sancha wanted, so Robert of Anjou founded Santa Chiara as a place for his wife to retreat. Their granddaughter, Joan, was crowned queen here in 1343, launching an enlightened reign nonetheless marred with plotting, intrigue, the murder of a husband, and her own demise at age 56, when she was smothered with pillows. Her body was thrown into a deep well on the grounds, and once retrieved, buried in an unmarked grave beneath the church floor. During World War II Allied bombers laid waste to most of the church's frescoes, but a few fragments

BAD BOY WITH A brush

The painter Caravaggio arrived in Naples in 1606, fleeing authorities in Rome after he killed a man in a fight over a debt. With his taste for gambling, prostitutes, young boys, rowdiness, and drunkenness, the tempestuous artist must have felt right at home in Naples. The city was then the second largest in Europe after Paris, with 350,000 inhabitants, more than a few of whom shared Caravaggio's reckless disposition. His sumptuous canvases, with their realistic human figures and dramatic use of light, have become emblematic of the city's emotion-filled baroque style.

Three major Caravaggio works are in Naples. The dark, moody, and chaotic "Seven Acts of Mercy" altarpiece is in the chapel of the **Pio Monte della Misericordia,** Via Tribunali 253 (© 081/ 446-944; metro Dante), a fraternity founded by nobles in 1601 to loan money to the poor. Try to identify the various acts of mercy—St. Martin in the foreground giving his cloak to the beggar is easy (clothing the naked)—you'll probably only detect six. But look again at the scene of the old man sucking at the breast of the young woman: That counts as two, visiting prisoners and feeding the hungry. (Classicists identify the pair as the Roman Cimon, who was sentenced to death by starvation, and his daughter, Pero, who secretly suckled him, an act of family honor that won him his release.) While you're here, look at the painting gallery upstairs: It features works by the so-called Cabal of Naples, a notorious trio of painters—Belisario Corenzio, Jusepe de Ribera, and Batistello Caraciollo—who were known to harass or even poison their competitors, destroying the works of rivals who won commissions they thought were rightfully theirs. Admission to the chapel and gallery is 7€ (open Mon–Sat 9am–6pm, Sun 9am–2:30pm).

In the **Capodimonte gallery** (p. 603), Caravaggio's "Flagellation of Christ" depicts two brutish tormentors whipping a nearly naked Christ; a third one in the foreground is preparing his scourge to join in the action. Lighting emphasizes the flailing arms and Christ's twisted, suffering body; it's a visceral depiction of cruelty in action, and one of two flagellation scenes Caravaggio painted while in Naples.

The "Martyrdom of St. Ursula" hangs in the **Palazzo Zevallos Stigliano** (Via Toledo 185; www.gallerieditalia.com; © 800/454-229; metro Montesanto), the lavish headquarters of the Banco Intesa Sanpaolo. Ursula appears unfazed as the king of the Huns—whose marriage proposal she has just refused—shoots an arrow into her breast at point-blank range. (As legend has it, the 11,000 virginal handmaidens accompanying Ursula had just been beheaded, so she couldn't have been too surprised at her jilted suitor's reaction). Caravaggio himself looks on from the background. This was his last painting and the last image we have of him—he died of fever while returning to Rome a couple of months later. Admission to the palazzo is 5€ (open Tues–Fri 10am–6pm, Sat–Sun 10am–8pm).

remain, including biblical scenes by Giotto. Other frescoes line the walls of the delightful lemon-scented cloisters, where columns and benches are covered in colorful Mallorca tiles depicting landscapes, hunting parties, dancers, and other snippets of the good life in 18th-century Naples—surprisingly worldly and frivolous, considering that for 200 years or so the cloisters were enjoyed only by cloistered nuns. This is one of the most refreshing corners of Naples, and well worth the admission fee if you've been walking around the city and need a little peace and quiet.

Via Santa Chiara 49, ℂ **081/797-1235.** Church free, cloisters 5€. Church open Mon and Wed–Sat 7:30am–1pm and 4:30–8pm; cloisters Mon and Wed–Sat 9:30am–5:30pm, Sun 10am–2:30pm. Metro: Dante.

Museo d'Arte Contemporanea Donna Regina (MADRE) ★

ART MUSEUM   It's not New York's Guggenheim or London's Tate Modern, but the **Palazzo Regina** in the middle of medieval and baroque Naples provides a dramatic counterpoint for works by contemporary artists such as Anish Kapoor and Richard Serra. Painter Francesco Clemente, who was born in Naples, decorated two rooms in colorful tile floors and frescoes replicating ancient symbols of the city. Conceptual sculptor Kapoor transformed a room into a white cube with rich blue pigments on the floor that seem to draw you into the bowels of the earth; he also designed the entrance to the Monte S. Angelo subway station to resemble Dante's entrance to the underworld (perhaps sympathizing with riders that commuting can be hell). Across town, the **Palazzo delle Arti Napoli (PAN)** (Via dei Mille 60; ℂ **081/795-8604**) houses rotating exhibits of contemporary art.

Via Settembrini 79. www.madrenapoli.it. ℂ **081/1931-3016.** 8€, free 1st Sun of month. Mon and Wed–Sat 10am–7:30pm; Sun 10am–8pm. Bus: E1. Metro: Cavour.

Napoli Sotterranea ★★ ARCHAEOLOGICAL SITE   These guided

tours of the city's ancient water works are wildly popular and a surefire hit with kids. Some 2,000 years ago, Romans dug huge cisterns beneath the city and connected them with a system of tunnels. Neapolitans used the ancient water supply well into the 19th century, when cholera outbreaks necessitated purer sources. Parts of the cistern network came in handy as quarries and as WWII bomb shelters (some wartime furnishings and graffiti remain). Adding to the mix is a Roman theater that's been unearthed amid the subterranean network. Tours last about 60 minutes and include English commentary. Exit points vary, but usually you climb out of the dark up a long staircase and emerge into the courtyard of an ordinary-looking apartment house—a good illustration of this city's age-spanning layers. Aside from climbing stairs, you'll also be asked to squeeze through a very tight passage (not recommended for the claustrophobic or the overweight). Don't confuse this with tours of the archaeological excavations beneath the church of San Lorenzo Maggiore (see p. 601) or with the Galleria Borbonica (see p. 597).

Vico S. Anna di Palazzo 52. www.lanapolisotterranea.it. ℂ **081/400-256.** 10€, 8€ children under 10. Tours (usually in English): Mon–Fri 10am, noon, and 6:30pm (also 9pm on Fri); Sat 10am, noon, 4:30pm, and 6pm; Sun 10am, 11am, noon, 4:30pm, and 6pm. Tours usually leave from the Gran Caffè Gambrinus on Piazza Trieste e Trento.

National Archaeological Museum (Museo Archeologico Nazionale) ★★★ MUSEUM The echoey, dusty, gloomy galleries of the rundown Palazzo degli Studi provide one of the world's great time-travel experiences, from grimy modern Naples back to the ancient world. Two treasure troves in particular should not be missed. The superb **Farnese Collection** of Roman sculpture shows off the pieces snapped up by the enormously wealthy Roman Cardinal Alessandro Farnese, later Pope Paul III (1543–1549), who was at the top of the Renaissance game of antiquity hunting. His remarkable collection was inherited by Elisabetta Farnese, who married Philip V of Spain and whose son and grandson became kings of Naples and brought the collection here in the 18th century. Among Cardinal Farnese's great prizes was the **Ercole Farnese,** a huge statue of Hercules unearthed at the Baths of Caracalla in Rome. The superhero son of Zeus looks tuckered out, leaning on his club after completing his eleventh labor, and who can blame him? After slaying monsters and subduing beasts, he's just learned he has to go

The Ercole (Hercules) Farnese.

back into the fray, descend into Hell, and bring back Cerberus, the three-headed canine guardian. It's a magnificent piece, powerful and wonderfully human. Carved out of one piece of marble, the colossal **Toro Farnese,** 4m (13-ft.) high, is the world's largest-known sculpture from antiquity and was also unearthed at the Baths of Caracalla. Cardinal Farnese hired a team of Renaissance masters, Michelangelo among them, to restore it. The intricate and delicate work depicts one of mythology's greatest acts of satisfying revenge, when the twin brothers Amphion and Zethus tied Dirce—who had imprisoned and mistreated their mother, Antiope—to the horns of a bull that will drag her to her death.

On the mezzanine and upper floors are mosaics, frescoes, and bronzes excavated from Pompeii and Herculaneum. Seeing these everyday objects from villas and shops hauntingly brings the ruined cities to life. Some, such as baking equipment and signage, are quite mundane, touchingly so;

many, such as the bronze statues of the "Dancing Faun" (on the mezzanine), the "Drunken Faun" (top floor), and five life-size female bronzes known as "Dancers" (top floor) show off sophisticated artistry. Most of the mosaics, on the mezzanine, are from the House of Faun, one of the largest residences in Pompeii. The million-plus-piece floor mosaic, "Alexander Fighting the Persians," depicts the wavy-haired king of Macedonia astride Bucephalos, the most famous steed in antiquity, sweeping into battle against King Darius III of Persia, who's looking a bit concerned in his chariot. The **Gabinetto Segretto** (Secret Room; also on the mezzanine) displays some of the erotica that was commonplace in Pompeii. Some works are from brothels, among them frescoes that show acts lively yet predictable and some bestial, and others include phallus-shaped oil lamps and huge phalluses placed at doorways to bring fertility and good fortune. We might titter at the bulges under togas, but they weren't necessarily intended to be pornography and rather suggest the libertine attitudes of the time.

Piazza Museo 19. www.museoarcheologiconapoli.it. © **081/442-2149.** 15€, under 18 free. Wed–Mon 9am–7:30pm. Metro: Museo or Cavour.

San Lorenzo Maggiore ★★ CHURCH   The most beautiful of Naples's medieval churches seems to inspire great literature. Petrarch, the medieval master of Italian verse, lived in the adjoining convent in 1345, and it was here on Holy Saturday 1338 that Boccaccio (author of *The Decameron*) supposedly first laid eyes on his muse, Maria d'Aquino. The daughter of a count but rumored to have been the illegitimate daughter of Robert of Anjou, king of Naples, Maria was married but preferred refuge in a convent to life with her debauched husband. For Boccaccio, it was love at first sight; he nicknamed her La Fiametta (Little Flame), wooed her with his romantic epic "Filocoppo," and eventually won her over and convinced her to become his mistress (she jilted him for another man a few years later). You can ponder 14th-century romance as you stroll the delightful cloisters, then descend a staircase to witness more of the city's multilayered history: Excavations have unearthed streets from the Greco-Roman city Neapolis, lined with bakeries and shops, an entire covered market, and an early Christian basilica.

Piazza San Gaetano, Via Tribunali 316. www.laneapolissotterrata.it. © **081/211-0860.** Church free. Mon–Sat 8am–noon and 5–7pm. Excavations: 9€, over 65 7€, under 18 6€. Daily guided tours in English at 10:40am, 12:30pm, 2:30pm, 4pm, and 5:30pm. Metro: Cavour.

VOMERO

Life in Naples never really becomes *too* gentrified, but it calms down quite a bit in the hilltop enclave of the Napoli *bene* (the city's middle and upper classes). The trip up here from the center is on the Centrale and Montesanto funiculars.

Certosa e Museo di San Martino (Carthusian Monastery) ★★

The Carthusian monks who took up residence high atop the Vomero hill in 1368 obviously knew something of the good life. Their view is still the best in Naples, across the city and the bay to Mt. Vesuvius. Over the centuries they hired the city's best artists to embellish their environs. Foremost among them, the fractious architect and sculptor Cosimo Fanzago (1591–1678) created the pièce de la resistance, an enormous central courtyard/cloisters that is a masterpiece of the baroque, a grand assemblage of statue-lined porticoes facing a broad lawn. Lest the monks got too comfortable in their earthly surroundings, a gallery of skulls reminded them of their inevitable fate. As if to reinforce the point, in surrounding chapels the Spanish painter Jusepe de Ribera (1591–1652) executed ghoulish scenes of martyrdom and suffering, so realistically portrayed with wounds, wrinkles, and writhing agony that he's been said to partake in "the poetry of the repulsive." As you wander the vast monastery, now housing

An elaborately decorated ceiling at the Certosa di San Martino, once a monastery, now a museum.

the **Museo Nazionale di San Martino ★★**, it's easy to see why royal administrators were so appalled by the monks' lavish lifestyle that they threatened to cut off state subsidies.

The museum is a repository of all things Neapolitan: paintings, prints, sculpture, artifacts, and the *presepi* (Nativity scenes) for which the city has an undying affection (see p. 594). None outshine the 750-piece Cuciniello Presepe, equipped with a lighting system that simulates the cycle of a day from dusk to nightfall. Even larger is the full-size model of the Great Barge used by King Charles of Bourbon in the 1700s, housed amid models and artifacts that honor the city's role as a maritime power. The Gothic cellars are filled with sculpture, including an astonishing St. Francis of Assisi by Giuseppe Sanmartino, who so artfully crafted "Christ Veiled Under A Shroud" in the Cappella di Sansevero (p. 595).

Largo San Martino 8. ✆ **081/578-1769.** 6€. Thurs–Tues 8:30am–7:30pm; ticket booth closes 1 hr. earlier. Closed Jan 1 and Dec 25. Metro: Vanvitelli and then bus V1 to Piazzale San Martino. Bus: C28, C31, or C36 to Piazza Vanvitelli. Funicular: Centrale to Piazza Fuga or Montesanto to Morghen.

Villa La Floridiana & Museo Nazionale della Ceramica Duca di Martina ★★ MUSEUM When King Ferdinand I returned to Naples in 1815 after 10 years of exile, he brought with him a Italian/Spanish wife, Lucia Migliaccio, the duchess of Floridia. Their wedding, just months after the death of Ferdinand's first wife, Queen Marina Carolina of Austria, created an international scandal. The duchess did not care for court life or for Naples, and Neapolitans didn't care for her, so Ferdinand bought her this magnificent retreat on the Vomero hill with gardens and views that would make anyone surrender to the city's charms. The villa now houses the 6,000-plus ceramics collection of another noble Neapolitan, Placido de Sangro, the duke of Martina. Items of interest include King Ferdinand's walking stick, with a glass top that contains a portrait of Lucia; it was said this was the only way the queen would ever appear in court. Admission to the gardens is free, and though a bit ramshackle these days, they're green and luxuriant and you can follow a path through them from the villa to a viewpoint overlooking the city.

Via Cimarosa 77. ⓒ **081/578-8418.** Museum 4€, gardens free. Wed–Mon 8:30am–5pm. Bus: C28, C32, or C36. Funicular: Chiaia to Cimarosa. Metro: Vanvitelli.

FARTHER AFIELD

Catacombs of San Gennaro (St. Januarius) ★ RELIGIOUS SITE
Naples's popular patron San Gennaro was once buried here, forever lending his name to this two-story underground cemetery, used from the 2nd through 11th centuries. Some of the city's earliest frescoes include one depicting a haloed San Gennaro with Mt. Vesuvius on his shoulders, and a charming 2nd-century scene with Adam and Eve. Guides (most speak English) will lead you past the frescoed burial niches and early basilicas carved from the *tufa* rock, providing fascinating insights into the city's long past—with a special nod to Sant'Agrippino, a 3rd-century bishop once interred here, who is almost as popular among Neapolitans as San Gennaro. As you emerge from the lower level of this city of the dead you'll be in the lively Rione Sanità quarter, very much a world of the living. In the 16th and 17th centuries, Neapolitans who became ill were banished to this neighborhood to protect the health (*sanità*) of those living within the city walls. Later it was home to early-18th-century architect Ferdinando San Felice, who built an elegant palazzo at Via Sanità 127; step inside the courtyard for a look at his magnificent double staircase.

Via Capodimonte 13. www.catacombedinapoli.it. ⓒ **081/744-3714.** 9€, 6€ students and over 65, 5€ under 18. Tours (in English) Mon–Sat on the hour 10am–5pm; Sun 10am–2pm. Bus: 24 or R4.

National Museum & Gallery of the Capodimonte (Museo e Gallerie Nazionale di Capodimonte) ★ MUSEUM Italy has many better art collections, but there's plenty to lure you out to this former hunting preserve of the Bourbon kings—the *bosco reale* (royal woods) is one of the few parks in Naples, and sharing the greenery with picnicking

families can be refreshing. The core of the collection is from Elisabetta Farnese, duchess of Parma, who handed down the family's paintings to her children and grandchildren after she became Queen of Spain; they in turn brought them back to Italy when they became kings of Naples. By the time the works got here, however, many of the best had found their way into other collections; what's left tends to be secondary works by a roster of Italian and Northern masters. In fact, the museum's two standout pieces have nothing to do with the Farneses: Caravaggio's dramatic "Flagellation of Christ" (see p. 598), which was brought here in the 1970s, and in the contemporary galleries, Andy Warhol's "Mount Vesuvius," a comic-book-like depiction of an eruption in gaudy modern colors. Upstairs, in the Royal Apartments, there's enough Sèvres and Meissen china to serve a royal feast of epic proportions. Capodimonte ceramics were fired right here on the grounds throughout the 18th century.

Palazzo Capodimonte, Via Miano 1; also through the park from Via Capodimonte. www.museocapodimonte.beniculturali.it. *(C)* **081/749-9111.** 12€. Thurs–Tues 8:30am–7:30pm; last entrance 6:30pm. Bus: R4 (from the Archaeological Museum), 168, 178, C63. Shuttle bus from Piazza Trieste e Trento runs Thurs–Tues hourly; 16€ round-trip fare includes museum admission, 8€ round-trip without museum admission (www.city-sightseeing.it; *(C)* **335/780-3812**).

Where to Stay in Naples

Where you stay in Naples makes a difference. You want a safe neighborhood close to the sights, and our suggestions below meet that criterion. Some good business-oriented hotels have opened near the train station, but this area is not all that convenient or, for that matter, particularly savory after dark. Naples hotels often post special rates on their websites, especially in summer, which is low season in the city.

EXPENSIVE

Grand Hotel Parker's ★★   Naples' oldest grand hotel has been welcoming guests since 1870, when Prince Grifeo decided to transform his palace into a posh stopover where travelers on the Grand Tour could enjoy a bit of Neapolitan luxury. The name comes from British naturalist George Bidder Parker, who bought the enterprise in 1899 while working on the gardens in the Villa Communale (see p. 595). Through wars, earthquakes, and other ups and downs the tradition continues, and this lovely old place on a hillside above the bay is still all about quiet refinement. Lounges are floored with rich marble and hung with a museum-worthy art collection, while the stylish guest rooms all open to balconies and are soothingly done with both traditional and contemporary touches. Choicest rooms overlook the bay, but all guests can enjoy the views from an airy top-floor lounge and dining area and an expansive roof terrace.

Corso Vittorio Emanuele 135. www.grandhotelparkers.it. *(C)* **081/761–2474.** 82 units. 230€–280€ double. Rates include breakfast. Garage parking 25€. Bus: 128. Metro: Amedeo. Montesanto or Centrale funiculars to Corso Vittorio Emanuele. **Amenities:** Restaurant; 2 bars; room service; spa; roof terrace; Wi-Fi (free).

Grand Hotel Vesuvio ★★   Old-world glamour holds sway in this famed waterfront hostelry that pampers the rich and famous with a Grand Tour–worthy experience, plus all the 21st-century amenities, including a spiffy spa. Expanses of shiny parquet, handsome old prints, fine linens on firm beds, and classic furnishings give the large, very comfortable rooms sophisticated-yet-understated polish. The big perk, though, is the view of the bay, the Castel dell'Ovo, and Mt. Vesuvius outside glass doors that open to balconies off many rooms. You'll get the same eyeful from the rooftop restaurant and the bright salon where a lavish breakfast buffet is served. High-season prices are geared to the budgets of celebrities and dignitaries, though seasonal rates and occasional specials bring the experience of a stay here within reach of the rest of us.

Via Partenope 45 (off Via Santa Lucia by Castel dell'Ovo). www.vesuvio.it. ℂ **081/764-0044.** 160 units. 190€–320€ double. Most rates include breakfast. Bus: 152, 140, or C25. **Amenities:** 2 restaurants; bar; fitness center; indoor pool (for a fee); room service; spa; Wi-Fi (free).

MODERATE

Art Resort Gallery Umberto ★   The location is already dramatic enough, but this upper floor of accommodations in the city's 1890s Art Nouveau–style glass shopping arcade (see p. 593) adds over-the-top plush interiors. Painted headboards, swag draperies, gilded furniture—it's not for minimalists, but it's hard to beat for theatricality or location. Many of the rooms face the interior of the *galleria* (but just below the glass roof, so quite bright) while others look out over an adjoining piazzetta; a choice few have little balconies. All guests can enjoy the large interior terrace high above the tile-floored arcades.

Galleria Umberto 1. www.artresortgalleriaumberto.com. ℂ **081/497-6224.** 16 units. 130€–170€ double. Rates include breakfast. Bus: R2. **Amenities:** Bar; concierge; Wi-Fi (free in lobby and some rooms).

Chiaia Hotel de Charme ★   With its bright shops and bars, spiffy, pedestrian-only Via Chiaia may be the city's friendliest address, and this warmly decorated inn in an old noble residence does the location justice. Some smaller rooms face interior courtyards and have snug, shower-only bathrooms, while many of the larger ones on the street side (with double panes to keep the noise down) have large bathrooms with Jacuzzi tubs. Decor throughout is sufficiently traditional and regal to suggest the *palazzo's* aristocratic provenance, and services are more wholesome than they were when the place was an upscale brothel. Pastries and snacks are laid out in the sitting room in the afternoon and evening, the buffet breakfast is generous, and the staff is good at recommending restaurants and providing directions.

Via Chiaia 216. www.chiaiahotel.com. ℂ **081/415-555.** 33 units. 85€–165€ double. Rates include breakfast. Bus: R2. **Amenities:** Bar; concierge; Wi-Fi (free in lobby and some rooms).

Costantinopoli 104 ★★   This 19th-century Art Nouveau palace is set in a palm-shaded courtyard that's mere steps from the archaeological museum but a world away from the noisy city—it even has a small swimming pool for a refreshing dip. Contemporary art and some stunning stained glass grace a series of salons; some rooms are traditionally done with rich fabrics and dark wood furnishings, others are breezily contemporary. The choicest rooms are on the top floor and open onto a sprawling roof terrace—a magical retreat above the rooftops and definitely what you should ask for when booking.

Via Santa Maria di Costantinopoli 104 (off Piazza Bellini). www.costantinopoli104.it. ✆ **081/557-1035.** 19 units. Doubles from 140€. Rates include breakfast. Metro: Museo. **Amenities:** Pool; room service; Wi-Fi (free).

Decumani Hotel de Charme ★★   The heart-of-Naples neighborhood outside the huge portals can be gritty, but these are sprucely regal lodgings, on the piano nobile of the *palazzo* of the last bishop of the Bourbon kingdom, Cardinal Sisto Riario Sforza. Guest rooms surround a vast, frescoed ballroom-cum-breakfast room; all have plush draperies and fabrics and a few antiques complementing hardwood floors and timbered ceilings. Larger rooms include sitting areas and face the quiet courtyard, while many of the smaller, street-facing doubles share small terraces.

Via San Giovanni Maggiore Pignatelli 15 (off Via Benedetto Croce, btw. vias Santa Chiara and Mezzocannone). www.decumani.com. ✆ **081/551-8188.** 22 units. 85€–170€ double. Rates include breakfast. Metro: Dante. **Amenities:** Wi-Fi (free).

Hotel Piazza Bellini ★★   The archaeological museum and lively Piazza Bellini are just outside the door of this centuries-old palace, but a cool contemporary redo softens the edges of city life. An outdoor living room fills the cobbled courtyard, and the rooms, which range across several floors, are minimalist chic with hardwood floors, neutral tones and warm-hued accents, sleek surfaces, and plenty of space for storage, plus Philippe Starck chairs and crisp white linens. Some of the rooms have terraces and balconies, a few are bi-level, and some with limited views are set aside as "economy"—but rates for any room in the house are reasonable and make this mellow haven an especially good value.

Via Costantinipoli 101. www.hotelpiazzabellini.com. ✆ **081/451-732.** 48 units. 90€–140€ double. Rates include breakfast. Metro: Dante or Cavour. **Amenities:** Bar; concierge; Wi-Fi (free).

San Francesco al Monte ★★   This ex-Franciscan convent just above the Spanish quarter and halfway up the San Martino hill makes the monastic life seem pretty appealing. The friars left behind a chapel, a refectory, secret stairways, and lots of atmospheric nooks and crannies, while their cells have been turned into large tiled guest rooms and sprawling suites. Views from all rooms and several airy lounges sweep across the city to the bay. The hillside location is a handy refuge above the fray but an easy walk or funicular ride away from the sights. In the contemplative garden, shaded walkways are carved out of the cliff side; a swimming pool and outdoor bar on the heights above are welcome perks in summer.

Corso Vittorio Emanuele 328. www.sanfrancescoalmonte.it. © **081/423-9111.** 45 units 140€–170€ double. Rates include breakfast. Metro: Amedeo. Montesanto or Centrale funiculars to Corso Vittorio Emanuele. **Amenities:** Restaurant; bar; pool; room service; Wi-Fi (free).

INEXPENSIVE

BnB Naples ★★★ Native Neapolitan Elia has gone into the hospitality business with flair, converting law offices on two upper floors of an old palace near the port into a welcoming little inn. His seven rooms are large and bright, with high ceilings, huge windows opening to balconies in some, and plenty of fine old woodwork and finishes; contemporary furnishings are sparse but comfortable and geared to convenience, with good work spaces, ample lighting, and plenty of room to spread out and lounge. Bathrooms are crisp and up to date. The location, just off Piazza Municipo, is prime for seeing the city, since the port, the historic center, and Santa Lucia seafront are all an easy walk away, and Elia is pleased to suggest ways to go about taking it all in. Modern conveniences aside, an old Neapolitan institution remains—the cage elevator operates on .10€ coins, so arrive with some change in your pocket.

Via Medina 17. www.bnbnaples.com. © **081/551-9978.** 7 units. 60€–100€ double. Rates include breakfast at a nearby bar. Metro: Municipo. **Amenities:** Wi-Fi (free).

Correra 241 ★★ Follow a narrow side street, enter the rear courtyard of an old palazzo, and walk up a ramp into a former factory tucked into a tufa cliff. The old workrooms and storage lofts have been converted into cheerful lodgings furnished with contemporary flair. The yellow concrete floors, rock walls, colorful artwork, even an Etruscan-Greco aqueduct leading off the lobby befit a city that's legendary for its quirky pockets. There's no such thing as standard accommodations here: Some rooms are lit by skylights only, others by windows high up on double-height walls, and still others are two-story—ask about your room's distinct features when you book. Wherever you settle, you'll be only steps from the archaeological museum, but, with that rear courtyard setting, enjoying a rare amenity in Naples: quiet.

Via Correra 241. correra241.hotelinnapoli.com. © **081/1956-2842.** 21 units. 80€–130€ double. Rates include breakfast. Parking 20€. Metro: Dante. **Amenities:** Bar; Wi-Fi (free).

Hotel Il Convento ★ If you want to experience a slice of Neapolitan life—as in laundry flapping outside your window—this is the place for you. While the narrow Spagnoli streets outside teem with neighborhood color and bustle, a 17th-century former convent provides all sorts of cozy ambience, with lots of wood beams, brick arches, and terracotta floors. Two rooms have their own planted rooftop terraces, and two others spread over two levels. Main artery Via Toledo is just 2 short blocks away, taking the edge off comings and goings at night. An eager staff will steer you to neighborhood restaurants and shops.

Via Speranzella 137/a. www.hotelilconvento.com. 𝄞 **081/403-977.** 14 units. 90€–130€. Rates include breakfast. Metro: Toledo or Municipio. Small pets allowed. **Amenities:** Bar; fitness room and sauna; room service; Wi-Fi (free).

Robby's House Bed & Breakfast ★   This is definitely not a place for everyone, or for that matter, for anyone looking for a private bath, a sense of style, any hint of luxury, or TVs or other standard amenities. But the good-size, very frugally furnished rooms in a rambling apartment are ridiculously inexpensive and an excellent value for the basic comfort they offer in a prime city-center location. They're safe and spotlessly clean and an easy walk from the train station and many sights. All have little balconies overlooking one of those narrow, laundry-hung Neapolitan streets. Guests share two antiseptic bathrooms. The attentive host, Robby, likes to advise on what to see in his native Naples—if only he would ditch the harsh overhead lights and invest in some reading lamps. The website photos give a candid assessment of what to expect in terms of decor and style. Payment is cash only, due upon arrival.

Via S. Nicola dei Caserti 5 (off Via Tribunali). www.robbyshouse.com. 𝄞 **081/454-546.** 5 units. Doubles from 35€. Rates include breakfast. Metro: Piazza Garibaldi or Dante. **Amenities:** Laundry service (fee); Wi-Fi (free).

Where to Eat in Naples

Neapolitans love to eat, and you'll love dining here, too. What's not to like about a cuisine in which pizza is a staple? Other dishes to look for include *mozzarella in carrozza* (fried mozzarella in a "carriage"), in which mozzarella is fried between two pieces of bread and topped with a sauce of the chef's design, often with tomatoes and capers; *gnocchi alla sorrentina,* little pockets of potato pasta filled with mozzarella and topped with tomato sauce; *ragu,* a meat sauce cooked for hours and served atop pasta; *parmigiana di melanzane* (eggplant parmesan)—the ubiquitous dish of fried eggplant, tomato sauce, mozzarella, parmigiano, and basil originated here—*crocchè di patate* (fried potatoes), mashed with herbs, cheese, sometimes salami, lightly coated in breadcrumbs and fried; and *pasta e fagioli,* beans and pasta—nothing could be more Neapolitan. Think, too, of seafood, especially *cozze,* mussels, often served *alla marinara* (simmered in tomato sauce), and *polpette,* succulent little meatballs.

EXPENSIVE

Rosiello ★★★ NEAPOLITAN/SEAFOOD   It's a cab ride or long bus trip out to this retreat, on a hilltop above the sea in swanky and leafy Posillipo, but the trek is worth it. Ask your hotel to make reservations and help arrange transport, because a meal on the terrace here is one of the city's great treats. Everything comes from the seas at your feet or the restaurant's

Campania is famous for its pizza.

extensive vegetable plots on the hillside; even the cheese is local. These ingredients find their way into seafood feasts that might include risotto *alla pescatora* (with seafood) and *pezzogna all'acquapazza* (fish in a light tomato broth), but even a simple pasta here, such as *scialatielli con melanzane e provola* (fresh pasta with local cheese and eggplant), is elegant and simply delicious.

Via Santo Strato 10. www.ristoranterosiello.it. ℂ **081/574-2341.** Entrees 10€–25€. Thurs–Tues 12:30–4pm and 7:30pm–midnight (May–Sept open daily). Closed 2 wks Jan and Aug. Bus: C3 to Mergellina (end of line), and then 140.

La Stanza del Gusto ★★ CREATIVE NEAPOLITAN   Chef Mario Avallone prepares some of the most innovative food in town, and he offers it two ways: In a casual, ground-floor cheese bar/*osteria* (**Squistezze**) and in a simple-but-stylish upstairs restaurant. Downstairs, daily offerings are written on blackboards and include the best lunch deal in town—a main course, dessert, wine, water, and coffee for 13€. You can pair cheese and *salumi* (cured meats) with carefully chosen wines or what is probably the city's largest selection of craft beers, or tuck into salads and unusual specialties, such as *arancino di mare,* a fresh take on classic fried rice balls, in this case concealing a core of seafood. Upstairs, locally sourced ingredients find their way into tasting menus that start at 35€; don't miss the *variazione di baccalà,* an amazing presentation of salt cod prepared in several different ways.

Via Santa Maria di Costantinopoli 100. www.lastanzadelgusto.com. © **081/401-578.** Entrees (upstairs restaurant) 14€–20€. Mon–Thurs 11am–11:30pm; Fri–Sat 11am–midnight. Closed 3 wks in Aug. Metro: Dante or Museo.

MODERATE

Europeo di Mattozzi ★★ NEAPOLITAN/PIZZA/SEAFOOD Just about every Neapolitan ranks this attractive center-of-town eatery as a favorite. Walls covered with copper pots, framed photos, and oil paintings suggest that dining here is serious business. Even connoisseurs claim the pizzas here are some of the best in town, and if one of the large pies doesn't suffice as a starter, choose from *zuppa di cannellini e cozze* (bean and mussel soup) or *pasta e patate con provola* (pasta and potatoes with melted local cheese). Seafood *secondi* are the house specialties and include *ricciola all' acquapazza* (a local species in a light tomato and herb broth) and *stoccafisso alla pizzaiola* (dried codfish in a tomato, garlic, and oregano sauce). Reservations are a must on weekends.

Via Marchese Campodisola 4. © **081/552-1323.** Entrees 12€–18€. Daily 12:30–3:30pm and 7:30–11:30pm. Closed 2 wks Aug. Bus: R2 or R3 to Piazza Trieste e Trento.

Tandem ★ NEAPOLITAN Take a seat in the simple room or on the pleasant little terrace on the lane outside and linger over the house specialty, ragu. A lot of locals stop by this friendly, almost-funky little spot for their fix of the city staple, which comes with meat (three or four kinds, slow-cooked) or vegetarian, which is a bit of a desecration. It's served over a choice of pastas, or by itself with thick slices of bread for dunking, along with carafes of the house wine.

Via Paladino 51. © **081/1900-2468.** Entrees 10€–18€. Daily 12:30–11:30pm. Metro: Dante.

Zi Teresa ★★ NEAPOLITAN/SEAFOOD Neapolitans know the Borgo Marinaro tourist traps to avoid, but they flock to this bright room in the shadow of Castel dell'Ovo to soak in the sea views while enjoying excellent fish. This 125-year-old institution is wildly popular for family gatherings, when the kitchen sends out huge platters of seafood grills and *frittura mista.* The decor has a nautical

The Wines of Campania

The wines produced in the harsh, hot landscapes of Campania seem stronger, rougher, and, in many cases, more powerful than those grown in gentler climes. Ones to try are *Lacryma Christi* (Tears of Christ), from a white grape that grows in the volcanic soil near Naples, Herculaneum, and Pompeii; *Taurasi,* a potent, full-bodied red also known as *Aglianico;* and *Greco di Tufo,* a pungent white laden with the odors of apricots and apples. *Falanghina,* one of the most popular white wine varieties, is produced from the famed Falernian grapes favored by the ancient Romans. Another varietal of special interest is fruity *Piedirosso,* a dark red grape that is famously grown on the slopes of Vesuvius and the isle of Capri.

twist, and if that doesn't make the point, the fleet of boats bobbing by the huge terrace will.

Via Borgo Marinaro 1. www.ziteresa.it. ℰ **081/764-2565.** Entrees 9€–20€. Tues–Sun 10am–midnight. Bus: 152, C25, 140, E5 to Via Santa Lucia.

INEXPENSIVE

L'Antica Pizzeria Da Michele ★★★ PIZZA   According to about half the residents of Naples, this no-frills, zero-ambience place serves the best pizza in town—the other half would vote for Sorbillo (see p. 612). Take a number at the door and prepare to wait for a table—the place is always packed. But you won't have to wait long for one of the enormous and simply delicious pizzas that come in just two varieties, *margherita* or *marinara* (toppings are for snobs, say the guys behind the counter): They emerge from the oven in a mere 20 seconds, an act of wizardry that keeps the tables turning quickly. No credit cards accepted.

Via Sersale 1. www.damichele.net. ℰ **081/553-9204.** Pizza 5€–7€. Mon–Sat 11am–11pm. Metro: Piazza Garibaldi.

I Buongustai ★★ NEAPOLITAN/PIZZA   To get away from the crowds on Via Tribunali, walk towards its eastern end, where a neighborhood vibe takes over. This local, no-frills favorite is always busy, with a takeaway counter out front and a small dining room in the rear. A huge selection of pizzas, including one that can be made with your choice of toppings, is served alongside *fritturina* (fried vegetables and other bits), *bruschetti,* and choices from a *tavola calda* (hot table), with grilled sausages, meatballs, and whatever else the chef is making that day.

Via Tribunali 201. ℰ **081/446-768.** Pizzas and entrees 4€–8€. Daily noon–3pm and 7–11pm.

La Campagnola ★ NEAPOLITAN   Students, professors, and neighborhood regulars eat at this plain, homey wine shop/trattoria almost every day, or at least stop by for a glass of the house wine and a plate of fried artichokes or other appetizer. The chalkboard menu changes daily and ranges through Neapolitan home-style favorites like *parmigiano di melanzane* and *vitello limone*. The pizzas are perfect starters, and a meal usually ends with a plate of *zeppole* (fried donuts), courtesy of the house.

Via Tribunale 47. ℰ **081/457-663.** Entrees 7€–10€. Tues–Sun 11:30am–3:30pm and 7:30–11pm. Metro: Dante.

Da Nenella ★ NEAPOLITAN   The guys at this Spagnoli favorite will make you feel like one of the regulars as you crowd into the covered terrace or plain white dining room for satisfying home cooking. Stick to the specials, listed on a board and recited by the busy waiters—*pasta e patate* (pasta and potatoes), maybe some fried fish or roasted pork, and salads of fresh greens. Even with wine, a meal here won't cost more than 12€ or 15€ a head.

Vico Lungo Teatro 103–105. www.trattoriadanennella.it. ℰ **081/414-338.** Entrees 6€–8€. Mon–Sat noon–3pm and 7–11:30pm. Metro: Toledo.

Go Off Your Diet

To truly eat like a Neapolitan, you just may have to set healthy habits aside. Clam-shaped *sfogliatelle*, filled with ricotta cream, is the city's unofficial pastry, available at bars and bakeries all over the city. *Il baba* are little cakes soaked in rum or limoncello syrup and often filled with cream; *delizia al limone* is sponge cake soaked with lemon or limoncello syrup, filled with lemon pastry cream, and iced with lemon-flavored whipped cream. Dark, flourless *torta* Caprese, topped with powdered sugar, is the chocolate cake of choice. For the classic coffee-and-a-pastry experience, try **Scaturchio,** Piazza San Domenico Maggiore 19 (www.scaturchio.it; *C* 081/551-7031); **Sfogliatella Mary** in the Galleria Umberto I (*C* 081/402-218); and **Il Vero Bar del Professore** at Piazza Trieste e Trento 46 (www.ilverobardelprofessore.com; *C* 081/403-041).

For some of Italy's best gelato, **Gelateria della Scimmia,** Piazza della Carità 4 (www.gelateriadellascimmia.it;

C 081/5520272) is a mandatory stop. Naples' elegant temple of chocolate, **Gay-Odin** (www.gay-odin.it) sells chocolate *cozze* (mussels) and chocolate-wrapped coffee beans at shops throughout the city; a convenient central location is at Via Benedetto Croce 61 (*C* 081/551-0794).

Friggatorie shops focus on delicious deep-fried snacks, like *panzarotti* (potato croquettes), *arancini* (fried rice balls), and *pizza fritte* (fried pizza dough topped with sauce and cheese). Top stops are **Friggitoria Vomero,** in the Vomero neighborhood near the funicular stop at Via Domenico Cimarosa 44 (*C* 081/578-3130), and **1947 Pizza Fritta,** in the historic center at Via Pietro Colletta 16 (www.1947pizzafritta-napoli.it; *C* 333/400-8562). **Di Matteo,** a venerable pizzeria in the historic center at Via Tribunali 94 (www.pizzeriadimatteo.com; *C* 081/455-262), also sells fried food from a street-side counter.

Pizzeria Gino e Toto Sorbillo ★★★ PIZZA   Don't let the crowds out front put you off, and don't let one of the other pizza places on Via Tribunali lure you in (some are also confusingly called Sorbillo, run by other family members). Just make your way through the crowd, give your name to the friendly woman with the clipboard, and enjoy the partylike atmosphere on the street as you wait for a table. (The wait is never as long as you think it might be.) Once inside you'll be ushered to a vast upstairs dining room where a long menu of pizzas is accompanied by a palatable house wine. This attractive place is the Ritz compared to rival Michele (see p. 611)—it even allows toppings, as in the Quattro Stagione (Four Seasons) pizza with quadrants of mushrooms, salami, prosciutto, and cheese.

Via Tribunali 32. www.sorbillo.it. *C* **081/446-643.** Pizza 5€–7€. Daily noon–3:30 and 7pm–midnight. Metro: Dante.

Naples Shopping

Via Toledo and **Galleria Umberto I** hold their own as mainstays of Naples shopping, though the clothing and accessories shops in **Chiaia** tend to be

Souvenir shop in Naples.

a little more elegant these days. There, big Italian fashion names have outlets along the Riviera di Chiaia, Via Calabritto, Via dei Mille, Via Filangeri, Via Poerio, and Piazza dei Martiri.

Naples is the home of hand-made **Marinella ties,** a symbol of luxurious quality for more than a century and worn by the likes of Bill Clinton and Aristotle Onassis. The main store and workshop is at Via Riviera di Chaia 287 (www. emarinella.com; ℂ **081/764-3265**). The city is justly famous for other handcrafted goods as well. Heading the list are *presepi,* the nativity scenes crafted and sold along **Via San Gregorio Armeno** (see box p. 594). Another shop selling hand-crafted figurines is **La Scarabatto,** in the historic center at Via die Tribunali 50 (www.lascarabattola.it; ℂ **081/291-735**), where the output includes traditional folk figures and contemporary ceramics.

The lively **Mercato di Porta Nolano** food market stretches around Piazza Nolano, south of the train station. Stalls burst with seafood and local produce and all manner of other foodstuffs; they operate daily until 6pm Monday to Saturday and 2pm on Sunday (pickpockets have a field day here, so watch your effects). Every third Saturday and Sunday of each month from 8am to 2pm (except in Aug), a *fiera antiquaria* (**antiques fair**) is held in the Villa Comunale di Napoli on Viale Dohrn.

Opening hours for stores in Naples are generally Monday to Saturday from 10:30am to 1pm and from 4 to 7:30pm.

Entertainment & Nightlife

Neapolitans make the best of balmy evenings by passing the time on cafe terraces. Top choice is the oldest cafe in Naples, with a Liberty-style interior from the 1860s, the elegant **Gran Caffè Gambrinus,** Via Chiaia 1, in Piazza Trieste e Trento (℃ **081/417-582**). Jean-Paul Sartre and Ernest Hemingway are among the luminaries who have lingered over coffee and drinks here, and the café observes the city's long-standing Suspended Coffee tradition—patrons who buy a coffee may pay for another and leave the receipt in an antique coffee pot so someone less fortunate can retrieve it and enjoy a cup, too.

OPERA & CLASSICAL MUSIC The great Naples-born tenor Enrico Caruso (1873–1921) appeared only once at his hometown's sumptuous opera house, in 1901—he was booed off the stage and vowed never to return. The venerable **Teatro San Carlo,** Via San Carlo 98 (www.teatrosancarlo.it; ℂ **081/797-2412** or 081/797-2331), has been kinder to other performers and composers. The world's oldest opera house, inaugurated on November 4, 1737, has welcomed Rossini, Bellini, Verdi, Puccini, and a veritable who's who of opera greats. The house still stages world-class opera, along with dance and orchestral works, Tuesday through Sunday, December through June. Tickets cost between 30€ and 100€. Guided tours (7€) are available daily at 10:30am, 11:30am, 12:30pm, 2:30pm, 3:30pm, and 4:30pm.

The **Centro di Musica Antica Pietà dei Turchini** music conservatory, Via Santa Caterina da Siena 38, at the base of the Vomero hill near the Vittorio Emanuele funicular stop (www.turchini.it; ℂ **081/402-395**), is well known for concerts of early music, though the repertoire extends to other music as well. Concerts are held in the church of Pietà dei Turchini, beneath paintings by some of Naples' great baroque masters, and in a hall that was once an orphanage where young charges were instructed in singing and musical composition. Star pupils included Alessandro Scarlatti (1660–1725) and Giovanni Pergolesi (1710–1736).

Another great venue is the **Associazione Alessandro Scarlatti,** Piazza dei Martiri 58 (www.associazionescarlatti.it; ℂ **081/406-011**), which stages chamber music concerts at Castel Sant'Elmo and other venues; tickets prices range from 15€ to 25€.

Trianon Viviani, near the Piazza Garibaldi train station at Piazza Vincenzo Calenda 9 (www.teatrotrianon.it; ℂ **081/225-8285**) focuses on traditional Neapolitan song and theater; the concert season usually starts in April, with performances Thursday through Sunday.

BARS & CLUBS This is a port, a cosmopolitan city, and a university town all rolled into one, so the Neapolitan nighttime scene is eclectic and lively. **Piazza Bellini,** near the university at the edge of the historical center, is an especially lively destination. Lined with books and old photos, the cozy rooms of the deservedly popular **Intra Moenia,** Piazza Bellini 7 (www.intramoenia.it; ℂ **081/290–988;** daily from morning to late), are a gathering spot for coffee, light meals, and drinks. **Cammarota Spritz,** Vico Lungo Teatro Nuovo 31, might be Naples' most popular bar, where a mob assembles outside (actually, there's no inside at this street stall) for ridiculously inexpensive drinks served in plastic cups. **Archeobar,** Via Mezzocannone 101/Bis (ℂ **081/1917-8862**), is friendly to students and sightseers alike, with a lively downstairs room and a quieter, book-lined room upstairs where patrons chat quietly and, gasp, even read. **Kestè,** near the university at Largo San Giovanni Maggiore 26 (www.keste.it; ℭ **081/551-3984**), is a dance club and bar with a huge terrace where the youth of Naples peacock around.

Enoteche, or wine bars, provide wines by the glass and the bottle, along with some food and often a relaxed atmosphere. The best are **Enoteca Belledonne,** Vico Belledonne a Chiaia 18 (www.enotecabelledonne.it; ℭ **081/403-162;** closed Sun), with a local vibe; **Barril,** Via Giuseppe Fiorelli 11 (www.barril.it; ℭ **081/4362**), serving wine in chic rooms and a garden; and **Trip,** Via Giuseppe Martucci 64 (www.tripnapoli.com; ℭ **081/1956-8994**).

AROUND NAPLES

To the west of Naples are the weird volcanic landscapes and evocative ancient ruins of the **Campo Flegrei,** the Phelgraean Fields. To the east are two of the world's most famous and well-preserved ancient cities, **Herculaneum** and **Pompeii,** and the volcano that doomed them, **Vesuvius.** You can visit any of these fabled places easily on a day trip and be back in Naples in time for a *passeggiata* and dinner.

Campo Flegrei (The Phlegraean Fields) ★★

On this seaside peninsula just west of Naples, volcanic vents steam and hiss, and ruined villas testify to ancient hedonism. Our alphabet was invented here, when the Latin language officially adopted the characters used for written communication in Cuma. Nero murdered his mother, Agrippina, outside Baiae, the Palm Beach of the ancient world; here Caesar relaxed and Hadrian breathed his last. Away from Pozzuoli and other busy seaside towns, moonlike landscapes are interspersed with lush hillsides carpeted in olive groves and orange and lemon orchards, adding an eerie beauty to the mix.

ARRIVING & GETTING AROUND

A day exploring this strange, mythic landscape begins in seaside **Pozzuoli,** reached from Naples by Line 2 of the Metropolitana (subway) or via the **Cumana Railroad** (www.unicocampania.it; ℭ **800/053-939**), starting from Piazza Montesanto. The Metropolitana station in Pozzuoli is above the main town, near the Anfiteatro Flavio; the Cumana Railroad station is near the seafront and town center, just around the corner from the Serapeo ruins. From Pozzuoli, **SEPSA buses** (www.sepsa.it; ℭ **081/735-4965**) run to the Solfatara. The Cumana Railroad and bus connections will get you to Baia (make a bus connection at Lucrina), Lago d'Averno, and Cuma (change to a bus in Torregaveta). Getting around the Campo Flegrei requires some logistics, but you can get a good sense of the Campo Flegrei in just a day at Pozzuoli. *Tip:* If you plan to see several of the area's sights, for just 8€ you can get a combined ticket, valid for 2 days, which includes the Anfiteatro Flavio, Serapeo, Castello di Baia, Zona Archeologica in Baia, and Scavi di Cuma. Admission to any one of these costs 4€, so if you visit more than two of them, it'll save you money.

POZZUOLI ★★

23km (14 miles) W of Naples

Screen legend Sophia Loren was born in this seaside town in 1934, contributing a bit of color to a place already steeped in lore. The Greek colony of Dicearchia, founded in 530 B.C., became the Roman Puteoli in 194 B.C. You will soon sniff out the origin of the name—from the Latin *putere,* "to stink," from the sulfurous springs surrounding the town. Or possibly, and a little more kindly, the name comes from the Greek *pyteolos,* or "little well." Roman emperors preferred this harbor to the one at Partenope (Naples). Among them was Caligula, who performed his famous stunt at Puteoli: He rode his horse across a floating bridge of boats to Baia, defying the soothsayer who said he had "no more chance of becoming Emperor than of riding a horse across the Gulf of Baiae."

Puteoli was also a busy hub for cargo ships from all over the Roman world, and dockworkers unloaded grain from Egypt, Sicily, and other outposts of the empire and reloaded them with marble, mosaics, and other exports. Among the voyagers who disembarked here was St. Paul,

An underground passageway at the Flavian Amphitheater in Pozzuoli.

sometime around A.D. 60. He'd sailed across the Mediterranean from Caesarea, in present-day Israel, where he'd been imprisoned. From Puteoli he traveled up the Appian Way to Rome to stand trial for alleged crimes in Asia Minor and was later freed.

The town also became famous for *pozzolana,* volcanic ash that reacts with water to form a substance like concrete that allowed engineers to build the huge dome of Rome's Pantheon.

The barbarian Alaric destroyed the Roman town in A.D. 410, but the acropolis, on a tufa-stone promontory pushing into the sea, continued to be inhabited throughout the Dark Ages. A modern town grew up around and on top of the hill in the following centuries. With its storied past, ancient monuments, volcanic landscapes, and sweeping views over the sea and the islands of Ischia and Procida, Pozzuoli is a lot more interesting and appealing than an otherwise scrappy suburban town has any right to be.

Anfiteatro Flavio (Flavian Amphitheater) ★★ RUINS

More than 20,000 spectators could squeeze into the many rows of seats in this late-1st-century theater, the third-largest arena in the Roman world. So much remains that it seems like a crowd is about to mill in for the next gladiatorial show. The theater's engineers, who also built the Colosseum in Rome, devised sophisticated subterranean staging areas with "mechanics" that hoisted wild beasts up to the field of slaughter and pumped in water to flood the arena for mock naval battles. Among the unfortunate victims of the spectacles staged here was Januarius, or San Gennaro, the patron saint of Naples. A painting by Artemisia Gentileschi (1593–1656), a surprisingly successful female artist of the Neapolitan baroque, shows the bishop calmly withstanding the attacks of a ferocious boar. (You can see Gentileschi's painting in the Museo Nazionale di Capodimonte in Naples, p. 603). According to legend, however, the beasts released to devour him fell submissively at his feet. Alas, Gennaro was later beheaded on the crater floor of the nearby Solfatara volcano.

Via Nicola Terracciano 75. www.coopculture.it. © **081/526-6007.** 4€ (or 8€ combined ticket, see p. 615). Hours vary but generally summer daily 9am–8pm, other times 9am–5pm or 6pm.

Rione Terra ★★ ARCHAEOLOGICAL SITE

The Greek city that the Romans renamed Puteoli sits on a promontory above the sea. Built up over millennia, the area was inhabited until the 1980s, when "bradyseism," a settling and rising of unstable volcanic ground, rendered living in the district unsafe, especially after sewer lines burst, creating a public health issue. Excavations beneath crumbling houses from the 16th and 17th centuries has revealed the ancient town, and visitors can now walk down gridlike Roman streets past the foundations of shops, taverns, houses, and slave quarters. It's easy to envision day-to-day life in ancient Puteoli: Grooves in the pavement in front of doorways are tracks on which wooden screens were pulled shut at night; the remnants of lead pipes are from a sophisticated water system fed by aqueducts. The showpiece is a magnificent Greek/Roman temple, incorporated into the baroque Duomo. Columns and marble walls have been uncovered, and the ancient structure now houses a glass-fronted chapel that reveals the many layers of its past. Access from Via Duomo. www.comune.pozzuoli.na.it. ℭ **081/1993-6286.** By guided tour only, often in English, 5€. Weekends 9am–6pm.

Serapeo ★★ RUINS   The 18th-century discovery of a statue of the Greco-Egyptian god Serapis led to centuries of confusion. Serapis was a popular cult figure in the ancient world, a master of abundance and resurrection, and a Serapeum, or temple to the god, was a fixture of many Greco-Roman cities—but not in Puteoli. Here, the statue stood in a niche of a magnificent marketplace where shops ringed a marble-floored arcaded courtyard; in the middle rose a *tholos,* a raised meeting hall decorated with sea creatures. Another mystery arose when 19th-century antiquarians noticed that columns in the marketplace were riddled with holes drilled by mollusks, as if they'd once been underwater. Subsequent investigations revealed that the culprit was bradyseism, where unstable ground slowly settled under the sea level for periods of time, then rose above sea level again, shifting as much as 6 feet in a decade—making living in Pozzuoli a fairly shaky business. In fact, a series of uplifts in the 1980s forced the evacuation of much of the town, damaged 8,000 buildings, and raised the seabed to the point that the harbor can no longer accommodate large craft. As you wander around the site, look for the telltale little holes in the marble columns once submerged in water. Pozzuoli center. From Cumana railway station, turn right and walk 1 block to ruins. www.archeoflegrei.it. ℭ **081/526-6007.** 4€ (or 8€ combined ticket, see p. 615). Wed–Mon 9am–1 hr. before sunset.

Solfatara ★★ PARK   The ancients called this dormant volcano just 1km (½ mile) above the Anfiteatro Flavio "Forum Vulcani" and believed it to be the residence and workshop of the god Vulcan and an entrance to Hades. It's easy to see why: Lunar landscapes hiss, steam, bubble, and spew sulfurous clouds, and the ground beneath your feet can feel as hot as, well, hell. Despite the bubbling, steaming, and heavy stench of sulfur, the volcano has not erupted since 1198. It's quite safe to walk around the caldera floor on the well-marked paths, observing steaming fumaroles, breathing in the vapors, and taking in the ancient mysteries. For sheer drama, look up the slopes to the Bocca Grande, or Big Mouth, where fumaroles continually release steam at temperatures that reach 160°C (320°F). Meanwhile, in the middle of the crater, lakes of gassy mud sizzle at 250°C (482°F). Via Solfatara 161. From Pozzouli stop of Metropolitano line 2, follow Via Oriana to Via Solfatara and turn right; from Cumana railway station, follow Via Rossini to Via Solfatara. www.solfatara.it. ℭ **081/526-2341.** 8€. Apr–Oct daily 8:30am–7pm, Nov–Mar daily 8:30am–4:30pm. Closes at times of increased volcanic activity, so check website ahead of visit. Bus: P9 from Anfiteatro Flavio entrance.

BAIA ★
6km (4 miles) SW of Pozzuoli

Many of the villas and thermal baths of this ancient spa town are now underwater, though enough remains on terra firma to suggest the grandeur of **Ancient Baiae** (the modern town dropped the last "e"). Julius Caesar, Nero, and others of the Roman elite once relaxed and debauched in Baiae's large villas, equipped with swimming pools and other luxuries. Seneca the Younger, the 1st-century philosopher and man of letters, called the place a "vortex of luxury." The poet Ovid said it was "a favorable place for love-making," while Horace chimed in, "No bay on Earth outshines pleasing Baiae." The town takes its name from Baio, the navigator of Odysseus, who is said to be buried somewhere in Baia.

Ancient Baiae was more luxurious than Herculaneum or Capri, other nearby retreats where wealthy Romans escaped the summer heat. (Only Stabia, east across the Bay of Naples, outshone it—see box p. 623). Under Augustus (reigned 27 B.C.–A.D. 14), Baiae became even more exclusive, as imperial property. The town was also famed for its thermal baths, fed by sulfur springs believed to have medicinal properties. Baiae had its share of salacious moments as well. According to legend, this is where the emperor Nero tried to kill his mother, the ambitious and villainous Agrippina, by contriving to have a ceiling crash down on her bed. When that didn't work, he arranged to have her boat rammed at sea, but she swam ashore. The thwarted emperor finally sent a henchman to Baiae to stab the doomed woman. Poster girl for the town's debauchery may have been Messalina, third wife of the emperor Claudius, who was said to be sexually insatiable—gossip claimed she snuck out of her Baiae villa in disguise at night to work at the town's brothel under the name She Wolf.

Ruins of temples, villas, and bathing establishments litter three grassy terraces above the bay. The ruins are not especially well marked nor well preserved. It's believed that a pile of stones near the top may have been the villa of Julius Caesar, who popped from here up to Rome for a meeting of the senate on the Ides of March 44 B.C. (the rest is history). His houseguest at the time was Cleopatra. Enough remains of the Terme di Baiae to show just how elaborate the bathing complexes were. Admission is free weekdays; on weekends 4€ (or 8€ combined ticket, see p. 615). It's open Tuesday to Sunday 9am till 1 hour before sunset.

Much of the ancient town is underwater, preserved as the **Parco Archeologico Sommerso di Baiae ★★** (Underwater Archaeological Park of Baiae). Mosaic flooring, statuary, fishponds, and other ruins litter the seabed amid bubbling geysers and flourishing flora. You can view this undersea world on dives, by snorkeling, or on trips on glass-bottom boats. Dive centers and boat tours operate out of the port and Via Lucullo in Baia; expect to pay about 10€ for a boat trip, 20€ for a snorkeling tour, and 35€ for a guided dive. The office of the **Area Protteta di Baia** (© 081/

523-2739) can provide more info and a list of tour operators; it's at Via Lucullo 94.

Via Sella di Baia 22, Bacoli. www.parcoarcheologicosommersodibaia.it. © **848/800-228.**

Castello di Baia ★★ HISTORIC SITE/MUSEUM   One of the most impressive landmarks in a town steeped in legend is the work of the Aragonese kings of Naples of the 16th century. Their massive complex of thick walls and defensive moats rises from a wave-buffeted headland that was once topped with a villa of Emperor Nero. The sea-facing battlements that Neapolitan royalty built were meant to deter Barbary pirates from North Africa, who would pillage coastal towns and take captives to sell into the Ottoman slave market. More important, the unassailable stronghold with its sweeping views of the bay also ensured protection against the French navy, whose ships didn't stand a chance of sailing past the lookouts to invade Naples. Some of the vast rooms now house the **Museo Archeologico dei Campi Flegrei ★**, showing off statuary and other artifacts from Baia and the surrounding region. Most enchanting are the two nymphaeums, delightful, statue-lined porches that were once equipped with lavish fountains; one is said to have been from the villa of Emperor Claudius and rescued from the sea floor.

Via Castello 39. www.coopculture.it. © **081/523-3797** or 848/800-288. 4€ (or 8€ combined ticket, see p. 615). Tues–Sun 9am–2:30pm

CUMA ★

7km (4½ miles) NW of Lago d'Averno

The Greeks founded their first colony on mainland Italy at Cuma in the 8th century B.C., and Cuma grew into an important center of Greek farming operations in Campania. The settlers soon discovered they had a helpful neighbor: the Cumaean Sibyl, who, according to legend, passed on messages from Apollo. The god told the Sibyl he would grant her one wish. She took a handful of sand and said she wanted to live as many years as the number of grains she held. Then came the catch: Apollo wanted her virginity in return. Sibyl refused, so Apollo gave her long life but not eternal youth. Over the centuries she withered away, eventually becoming so small she could be kept in a jar, then only her voice remained—handy for uttering a last request, "I want to die." The **Sibyl's chamber**—a big draw for advice-seekers from around the ancient world—sits at the end of a long, narrow tunnel cut through volcanic stone, 131.5m (432 ft.) long, some 5m (16.5 ft.) high, and as wide as 2.4m (8 ft.) across. That impressive entrance most likely assured supplicants they were about to hear something gravely important; it can still send chills down the spine.

The Sibyl is said to have ferried Aeneas, son of Aphrodite, across nearby **Lago d'Averno,** where he discovered the River Styx, the gateway to Hades. Legend claims that the lake's waters were once so vaporously lethal (possibly from gas-emitting underwater vents) that it was named after a Greek word meaning "without birds," because winged creatures flying over the waters would plunge to their deaths. In the 1st century B.C., Emperor Agrippa had a canal dug to connect the lake with the sea, providing safe harbor for Roman ships. He also ordered construction of the Grotta di Cocceio (Cocceio's Cave), a straight tunnel between the lake and Cuma, 1km (1/2 mile) long and wide enough for a chariot to pass. The tunnel was passable for almost 2,000 years, until World War II bombs caused a section to collapse.

Via Montecuma. www.coopculture.it. © **081/854-3060.** 4€ (or 8€ combined ticket, see p. 615). Daily 9am to 1 hr. before sunset.

WHERE TO EAT AROUND CAMPO FLEGREI

Sileno ★ SEAFOOD/PIZZA You deserve a good meal after trudging through antiquities and volcanic landscapes, and it should center on fish or seafood, since Pozzuoli is a major port for fishing boats. Part of the catch comes direct to kitchens like the one at this modest place down the street from the Serapeo. It shows up in *linguine alle vongole* (with clams) and other straightforward but delicious pasta and risotto dishes, as well as platters heaped high with *fritto misto di pesce,* a fish fry.

Via Sacchini, 27/A, Pozzuoli. © **081/526–2757.** Entrees 8€–14€. Wed–Mon 12:30–3:30pm and 7:30–11:30pm.

Vesuvius ★★

Towering, pitch-black Mount Vesuvius looms menacingly over the Bay of Naples. The volcano has erupted periodically since A.D. 79, when it buried Pompeii and Herculaneum in eruptions that released 100,000 times the thermal energy of the Hiroshima bomb. Less violent eruptions occurred in 1631, in 1906, and 1944. Mount Vesuvius is the only active volcano on mainland Europe, though another formidable volcanic summit, taller and more active Mount Etna, is only 560km (335 miles) away, on the east coast of Sicily (see p. 771).

The mountain still puffs steam every once in awhile, just to keep everybody on their toes. Volcanologists and geologists say that, given the historic record, a major eruption is likely in the relatively near future. That is, it's a question of *when* rather than *if* the mountain will blow its top again, putting many of the 3 million people who live around the Bay of Naples at considerable risk. That makes Vesuvius one of the most potentially deadly volcanoes in the world.

ARRIVING The most convenient way to visit Vesuvius by public transportation from Naples or Sorrento is on the Circumvesuviana **train** (www.eavsrl.it; © **800/211388** toll-free within Italy) to the Ercolano Scavi. There you can catch **Vesuvio Express** (www.vesuvioexpress.info) vans to the parking lot below the summit. Fares are 10€ round-trip, plus you'll pay another 10€ for admission to the park. Vans run every 45 minutes daily from 9:30am; the last bus makes the run up 2 hours before the park closes. You can also take the **Busvia del Vesuvio** (www.busviadelvesuvio. com; © **340/935-2616**) for a ride on a bumpy back road up the mountain from Pompeii in a 4x4 vehicle that drops you at the summit parking lot; round-trip fare is 22€, including park admission, and the service runs April to October daily 9am to 3pm (sometimes later in July and Aug). Buy tickets at a booth just to the right as you exit the Pompei Scavi train station.

By **car,** take the Torre del Greco exit from the A3 autostrada and follow the signs to Vesuvio. The road ends in the parking lot below the summit, where you'll pay 2.50€ to park. A taxi from Naples costs a flat rate of 90€ round-trip, including a 2-hour wait.

VISITOR INFORMATION The **Parco Nazionale del Vesuvio** (www. parconazionaledelvesuvio.it; © **081/865-3911**) maintains trails and other visitor facilities. All transportation gets you only as far as the park entrance at 1,017m (3,337 ft.) in altitude. You'll pay 10€ to continue on a fairly steep trail to the summit or explore the mountainside on other trails, none of which are wheelchair accessible. The entrance fee also includes admission to the observatory, at 608m (1,994 ft.), the oldest such seismological/volcanological institution in the world, dating from 1841. The park opens daily at 9am, closing at 6pm July–August, 5pm April–June and September, 4pm March and October, and 3pm November through February. The trail to the crater closes in extreme weather.

> ### Funiculì, Funiculà
>
> One way you won't be making the ascent up the mountain is on the Mt. Vesuvius Funicular, which once climbed to the summit from Pugliano, near Ercolano. It opened to great fanfare in 1880, when the song "Funiculì, Funiculà" was written to celebrate the event. Everyone from Connie Francis and the Grateful Dead to Luciano Pavarotti recorded the jaunty tune. The eruption of 1944 wiped out the tracks and sealed its fate; the ascent by road was by then more practical.

EXPLORING VESUVIUS

It might sound like a dubious invitation, but it's possible to visit the rim of the crater's mouth. As you look down into its smoldering core, you might recall that, a century before the A.D. 79 eruption that buried Pompeii, the escaped slave Spartacus, who boldly led an uprising against his Roman captors, hid in the hollow of the crater, which was then covered with vines. The menacing mountain is the centerpiece of 8,482-hectare (20,959-acre) **Parco Nazionale del Vesuvio ★★★** (Vesuvius National Park). The park has laid out nine summit trails, each of them highlighting

Keeping Up with the Pompeiians

All around the shores of the Bay of Naples, various towns reveal the good life wealthy Romans once enjoyed here. **Oplontis,** a swanky seafront suburb of Pompeii (the very name means "opulence"), was also wiped out in Vesuvius's eruption and subsequently buried beneath the highways, apartment blocks, and factories of grimy Torre Annunziata. You can still visit Oplontis' showplace, **Villa Poppea,** a huge spread that was the retreat of Poppea Sabina, second wife of the Emperor Nero. Here she bathed in a milk-filled pool beneath a fresco of Hercules and entertained in mosaic-floored rooms, sea-view gardens, and a massive swimming pool. Poppea's slaves, meanwhile, labored in a primitive kitchen and slept in little cubicles in an adjacent wing, providing a look at life below stairs, Roman-style. The lady of the house, an infamous schemer and plotter, allegedly met a gruesome end when her husband jumped on her stomach in a fit of rage and caused her to miscarry. (Nero repented by finding a beautiful youth who looked just like his wife, having him castrated, and renaming him Poppea.) Entrance to the villa is at Via Seplocri 12, Torre Annunziata

(pompeiisites.org, ✆ 081/857-5347); admission is 5.50€ (or an 18€ ticket that combines Pompeii and Oplontis). The villa is open April through October daily, 9:30am to 7:30pm, and November through March daily, 9:30am to 5pm. It's a short walk from the Circumvesuviana station.

Stabia was another beautiful seafront enclave, long buried beneath **Castellamare del Stabia,** an industrial suburb known for its shipyards. Some of the few excavations there include lavish **Villa di Arianna,** currently closed for restoration, and **Villa San Marco,** where you can view frescoed halls and atria, a massive swimming pool, a long colonnade, and a dining hall that could seat 125 guests. Entrance is off SS14; admission is free and the villa is open daily, April through October 9:30am to 7:30pm, November through March 9:30am to 5pm. Take the Circumvesuviana train to Castellammare di Stabia and get a taxi for the trip out to the villa. A visit to Castellammare comes with a perk: From the station a funivia (funicular) climbs the 1,100m (3,609-ft) summit of Monte Faito, for sensational views across the Bay of Naples.

the lava flows and other geology underfoot. Placards along the way explain the unique micro-environment of the volcanic summit, including many species of orchids and other amazingly tenacious vegetation. The ticket office hands out maps of the routes (short versions are also on the website), which range from easy 1-hour strolls to strenuous 8-hour hikes. The number 5 trail, **Gran Cono,** is the classic ascent to the top. A moderately difficult uphill walk of about half a mile leads from the parking area and ticket office to the 230-m (754-ft)-deep crater. The walk takes about 20 minutes, but forego any notions of being alone in empty volcanic landscapes—cafes and souvenir stands line the route. A guide will lead you around the rim, 650m (2,132 ft.) in diameter. Make sure the guide who approaches you is a bona fide ranger and not a shill looking for a tip; guide service is free with the price of admission and mandatory. Wear sneakers—the lava underfoot can be hard on the feet—and bring a sweater or jacket, because it can be windy and surprisingly chilly on the heights. Once at the top, the view across Naples and the bay to the islands is so mesmerizing you might just forget how menacing Vesuvius really is. As a reminder, consider that before the A.D. 79 eruption, the mountain was more than twice as tall as its current 1,282m (4,206 ft.).

POMPEII & HERCULANEUM ★★★

On that fateful day, August 24, A.D. 79, the people of Pompeii, a prosperous fishing town, and Herculaneum, a resort just down the coast, watched Mount Vesuvius hurl a churning column of gas and ash high into the sky. It was only a matter of time before flows of superheated molten rock coursed through the streets of Herculaneum and ash and pumice buried Pompeii. In Herculaneum, volcanic debris quickly hardened into a layer of rock that fossilized everything—furniture, wooden beams, clothing, skeletons, graffiti, mosaics; in Pompeii, ash and rock fragments buried structures under a layer as deep as 12 meters (20 feet), preserving everything beneath it through the centuries.

Terrifying indeed for the ill-fated townsfolk, but lucky for us, the layers of ooze and ash preserved Pompeii and Herculaneum as time capsules. Pompeii is much more extensive than Herculaneum, with more to see, while Herculaneum provides an easier-to-manage, less crowded experience. With its gridlike streets, Pompeii provides an overview of a large Roman town, while Herculaneum, with its better-preserved houses and artifacts, gives an evocative glimpse into day-to-day life. You could see both in 1 day, and you might consider doing so if your time in the region is limited. However, get a good rest the night before, because seeing the sights involves lots of walking and possible sensory overload—you'll be taking in an enormous amount of information in a short amount of time. If you have to choose between the two, Pompeii provides the more sensational experience.

Essentials

ARRIVING   **Circumvesuviana** trains (www.eavsrl.it; ⓒ **800/211-388** toll-free in Italy) run between Naples Piazza Garibaldi and Sorrento every half-hour, with stops in Herculaneum and Pompeii. For Herculaneum, get off at Ercolano/Scavi (*scavi* means "archaeological excavation"). Herculaneum is 20 minutes from Naples and 50 minutes from Sorrento; the entrance is about 10 blocks from the station. For Pompeii, exit the train at Pompei-Scavi (note that the modern spelling drops the last "I" of the ancient name). The entrance is about 45m (150 ft.) from the station. Pompeii is about 40 minutes from Naples and 30 minutes from Sorrento. The **Campania Express,** which runs between Naples Piazza Garibaldi and Sorrento 4 times a day from mid-March to mid-October, offers express service to the excavations; the trip from Naples to Herculaneum is only 10 minutes and the trip to Pompeii to 30 minutes.

To reach either by **car** from Naples, follow the *autostrada* A3 toward Salerno. If you're coming from Sorrento, head east on SS 145, where you can connect with A3 (marked napoli). Then take the signposted turnoffs for Pompeii and Herculaneum.

LOGISTICS The Herculaneum excavations are open daily 8:30am to 7:30pm (they close earlier, at 5pm, November through March). The Pompeii excavations are open Monday to Friday 9am to 7:30pm, Saturday and Sunday 8:30am to 7:30pm (they also close at 5pm November through March). Last admission at both is 90 minutes before closing. Admission is 13€ for Herculaneum, 15€ for Pompeii. Both sites can be crowded in the mornings, especially when tours arrive in force in July and August. Crowds thin out by early afternoon.

Ticket offices at both sites provide free maps and good, detailed booklets to guide you through the sites. Inside the entrances at both you'll find **bookstores,** where you can purchase additional guidebooks to the ruins (available in English). Audio guides are good accompaniments to your visits. You can rent them at either site for 8€, 6.50€ for 2 people (but sharing is not a particularly good idea), with a kids' version for 5€. Pompeii has a **cafeteria** inside the archaeological zone that's handy for sandwiches and drinks. At Herculaneum a good **cafe/cafeteria** is just outside the entrance. You can store your luggage at both sites (also at the train station in Pompeii), making it possible to work in a visit if you're en route between Naples and Sorrento or the Amalfi Coast.

If you're visiting the sites on a sunny day, wear sunscreen and bring a bottle of water. For more information about Herculaneum, visit ercolano. beniculturali.it, or call ✆ **081/777-7008;** for Pompeii, visit www.pompeii sites.org or call ✆ **081/857-5111.**

Herculaneum (Ercalano)

10km (6 miles) SE of Naples

Excavations began at Herculaneum in the early 18th century and continue to this day, with the fairly recent discovery of a beached boat full of desperate souls trying to make an escape by sea. Another 300 skeletons were found in vaulted stone boathouses on what would have been the town's beach; they were huddled in the shelters waiting to board boats and sail to safety when they were killed instantly by the poisonous vapors of a wall of heated gas and rock sweeping through the town at 100mph. Although many questions about Herculaneum remain unanswered, it's known for certain that this glitzy seaside resort for elite Romans was about a third the size of Pompeii, with a population of about 4,000. Herculaneum had little commerce or industry, and its streets were lined mostly with elegant villas, along with a few apartment blocks for poor laborers and fishermen.

EXPLORING HERCULANEUM'S
ARCHAEOLOGICAL AREA ★★★

The ruins of Herculaneum give the unsettling impression of a ghost town from which residents have only recently walked away. Many of the houses retain their second floors, making them seem more like residences than ruins. The volcanic mud that covered Herculaneum during the eruption of Vesuvius in A.D. 79 quickly hardened to a rocklike material. While making excavations difficult, this semi-rock protected the structures underneath, and rather remarkably preserved wooden beams and floors along with furnishings, clothing, and other household objects. The ruins provide a wealth of rich and intriguing detail about building techniques, architecture, and domestic decoration in Roman times, and, of course, about daily life. The charred wood, staircases, and double-height houses here instill the sense of being in a real town, unlike the remote detachment you might experience in Pompeii and other ancient ruins.

The excavations stretch from the town's main street, Via IV Novembre, to what was once the shoreline (now a kilometer to the west); the rest of the Roman town remains inaccessible beneath the buildings of modern Ercolano. From the Ercolano-Scavi station, follow the signs for Scavi di Ercolano for about 10 blocks down Via IV Novembre; the entrance is about a 10-minute walk from the station. Plan to spend at least 2 hours.

The ruins of Herculaneum, once a seaside resort for the Roman elite.

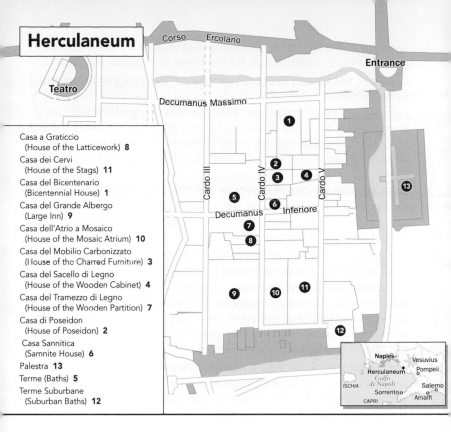

DECUMANUS MAXIMUS Decumanus Maximus is a street lined with shops, some of them still sporting advertisements and price lists. One of the discoveries along this street was a crucifix, proof that Christianity had already come to Herculaneum by the time of the eruption.

TERME DEL FORO (FORUM BATHS) Elegant mosaics of fish, dolphins, and other sea creatures decorate the town's largest and grandest bath complex, with several entrances that include, of course, separate ones for men and women. Enough of the men's section, the **Terme Maschili,** remains to show the range of facilities: a latrine, a changing room lined with benches and shelves for stashing personal effects, and an exercise room. You can still make out the *frigidarium* (cold bath), to the left, and the *tepadarium* (tepid bath), to the right. Once patrons had gone through these ablutions they could settle into the *caldarium* (hot bath) for a long, soothing soak. In the smaller but similarly elaborate **Terme Feminili,** a mosaic of a naked Triton decorates the floor of the changing rooms.

SEDES DEGLI AUGUSTALI (HALL OF THE AUGUSTALS) The Augustals were priests of a cult to Augustus, founder and first emperor of the Roman empire. These rooms with marble floors and elaborate wall paintings did justice to their elite status. Their custodian died in his sleep, in a small room that's still furnished with the bed where his skeleton was found.

CASA DEL TRAMEZZO DI LEGNO (HOUSE OF THE WOODEN PARTITION)
Behind a perfect facade is a rarity in Roman houses, a double atrium. It probably just means that at some point the owner scraped together enough money to buy adjoining houses and merge them. He obviously worked hard: The house is named for a well-preserved wooden screen that separated part of the atrium from the *tablium,* a little room that served as an office.

CASA DEL BELLA CORTILE (HOUSE OF THE BEAUTIFUL COURTYARD)
The namesake courtyard seems almost medieval, with a wide stone staircase ascending to a landing on the second floor. Three skeletons that have been placed here are presumed to be those of a mother, father, and daughter trapped on the beach as they tried to flee.

CASA DEL MOSAICO DI NETTUNO E ANFITRITE (HOUSE OF THE NEPTUNE AND ANFITRITIS MOSAIC) A bright blue mosaic of the sea god and his nymph is just one of many decorations in this house, whose owner likely operated the well-preserved shop next door. Carbonized wooden racks hold amphorae and masonry jars that were found on the counter, still filled with broad beans and chickpeas when they were unearthed.

CASA A GRATICCIO (HOUSE OF THE LATTICEWORK) This is one of the very few examples of working-class housing that has survived from antiquity; the namesake lattices, though cheaply made of interwoven cane and plaster, are remarkably well preserved.

CASA DEI CERVI (HOUSE OF THE STAGS) One of the most elegant houses in town had terraces and porticos overlooking the sea. Decorations say much about its fun-loving inhabitants: Frescoes depict playful cherubs, while courtyards held statues of drunken satyrs and an inebriated, peeing Hercules. The house is named for a statue of dogs attacking a pair of innocent, noble-looking deer, perhaps a commentary on the cutthroat politics and hard-edged social echelons of the Roman era.

VILLA DEI PAPIRI One of the grander seaside villas housed a huge library of 1,000-odd papyrus scrolls, badly charred but intact when they were uncovered during excavations (they're now in the library of the Palazzo Reale in Naples). The onetime home of Julius Caesar's father-in-law, consul Lucius Calpurnius Piso Caesoninus (100 B.C.–43 B.C.), has also yielded a treasure trove of nearly 90 magnificent bronze and marble sculptures, Roman copies of Greek originals that are now housed in the Archaeological Museum in Naples (p. 600). Most famous among them is a sculpture of Pan, the half-man, half-goat god, caught in marble having sex with a nanny goat. The oddly humane scene was unearthed in the 18th century but was thought to be so licentious that it was locked away in the cellars of a royal palace. Fortunately, since the early 19th century randy Pan has been one of the Archaeological Museum's most cherished prizes.

TERME SUBURBANE (SUBURBAN BATHS)　Another bath complex shows off state-of-the art sophistication, with marble floors and benches and an elaborate under-floor heating system in which heat generated by wood fires circulated through a maze of conduits. In the *caldarium* (hot bath) a few stucco friezes still look down on visitors as they did on bathers.

Pompeii

19km (11 miles) SE of Herculaneum, 30km (18 miles) SE of Naples

Italy's most famous archaeological site is the Disneyland of the ancient world. Not that there's anything shallow or ersatz about the extensive excavations of this town on the Bay of Naples, where life stopped so abruptly on August 24, A.D. 79. It's just that no other ancient town has been brought to light so completely, providing an opportunity to step into a world locked in an ancient time. The 4m to 6m (13–20 ft.) of volcanic ash with which Vesuvius buried the city preserved 44 hectares (109 acres) of shops, civic buildings, and private houses. Ever since 1748 archaeologists have worked to painstakingly uncover the town, and the ruins provide the vicarious thrill of sharing space with residents of a lively, ancient Roman port.

The ruins of Pompeii, overlooked by the deadly nearby volcano, Mount Vesuvius.

How many people were living in Pompeii at the time of the eruption is not known. The city had been rocked by a major earthquake in A.D. 62 that, along with fires caused by toppled oil lamps, destroyed temples, houses, and public works. Repairs were still underway in A.D. 79, though many of the city's 11,000 recorded inhabitants had probably resettled elsewhere. The unfortunate Pompeians who remained behind are the most haunting presence at the site. The decaying bodies often left a mold inside the ash and lava that buried them. Excavators filled these empty spaces with plaster, and the eerie, lifelike casts lie in the Garden of the Fugitives and other places around town where the victims fell.

The entrance to the site is almost directly across from the train station. Allow at least 4 hours for even a superficial visit.

EXPLORING POMPEII'S ARCHAEOLOGICAL AREA ★★★

Pompeii was a workaday town, and what stands out amid the ruins is a remarkable evocation of everyday life—streets, shops, bakeries, brothels, baths. The first thing you'll notice is the typical Roman plan of gridlike streets, on which stepping stones appear at every intersection. These were laid down to allow residents to cross the pavement even when the streets were being flushed with water, as they were at least once a day. Stones are spaced in just such a way to allow chariot wheels to roll past them. Raised sidewalks conceal water and sewage pipes, while glittering bits of marble mixed in with the volcanic pavement reflected light to make walking a little easier at night.

Unlike Herculaneum, with its seafront district of lavish villas, in Pompeii the wealthy usually lived among the working classes. Houses are interspersed with shops (which were often combined with dwellings) all over town. Also here are the remains of 25 street fountains, fed by a system of aqueducts and cisterns that fed lead pipes to keep baths, businesses, and homes supplied with fresh water.

PORTA MARINA The site's main entrance is as busy now as it was back in the day, when this impressive gate, one of seven portals in the walls that surrounded the ancient city, opened to the seafront. Pompeii's docks did a brisk business importing and exporting goods that were often transported to and from Rome on the nearby Appian Way. The shimmering sea that once lapped the shoreline in front of the gate is nowhere to be seen: the sprawl of modern Pompei (one "I" in the modern spelling) now stands between the excavations and the sea, which has receded by about 1/2 km (1/4 mile) over the centuries. The **Tempio de Venere** (Temple of Venus), to the right of the entrance, has not fared as well as the gate; a lone column is all that attests to its onetime grandeur.

FORO (FORUM) Pompeii's marketplace, damaged in an earthquake 16 years before the eruption of Vesuvius, had not been repaired when the final destruction rained down. Columns still line the portico that

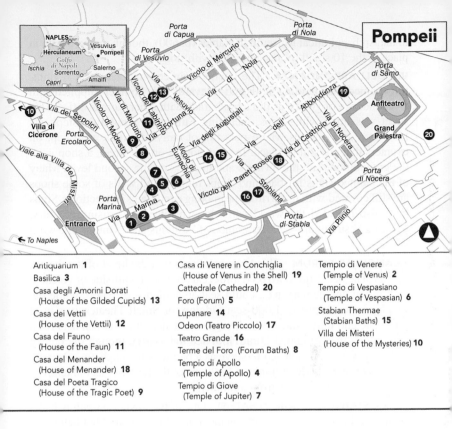

Pompeii

NAPLES
Herculaneum
Ischia
Golfo
di Napoli
Sorrento
Capri
Amalfi
Vesuvius
Pompeii
Salerno

Porta
di Capua
Porta
di Nola
Porta
di Vesuvio
Porta
di Samo

Via dei Sepolcri
Villa di
Cicerone
Porta
Ercolano
Viale alla Villa dei Misteri

Vicolo di Mercurio
Via di Mercurio
Vicolo di Modesto
Via del Labirinto
Vesuvio
Via di Fortuna
Vicolo del Lupanare
Vicolo di Eumachia
Via degli Augustali
Via di Nola
Vicolo di Mercurio

Anfiteatro
Grand
Palestra

Via della Abbondanza
Via Stabiana
Via di Nocera
Via di Castricio
Vicolo dei Pareti Rosse

Porta
di Nocera
Porta
di Stabia

Porta
Marina
Via Marina
Vicolo dell' Stabiana

Entrance
Via Marina

To Naples

Via Plinio

Antiquarium **1**

Basilica **3**

Casa degli Amorini Dorati
(House of the Gilded Cupids) **13**

Casa dei Vettii
(House of the Vettii) **12**

Casa del Fauno
(House of the Faun) **11**

Casa del Menander
(House of Menander) **18**

Casa del Poeta Tragico
(House of the Tragic Poet) **9**

Casa di Venere in Conchiglia
(House of Venus in the Shell) **19**

Cattedrale (Cathedral) **20**

Foro (Forum) **5**

Lupanare **14**

Odeon (Teatro Piccolo) **17**

Teatro Grande **16**

Terme del Foro (Forum Baths) **8**

Tempio di Apollo
(Temple of Apollo) **4**

Tempio di Giove
(Temple of Jupiter) **7**

Tempio di Venere
(Temple of Venus) **2**

Tempio di Vespasiano
(Temple of Vespasian) **6**

Stabian Thermae
(Stabian Baths) **15**

Villa dei Misteri
(House of the Mysteries) **10**

surrounded a large, rectangular open space on three sides and opened to a covered meat and fish market, the **Macellum.** Facing the Forum are the **Basilica** (the city's largest single structure), a law court, exchange, and civic hall. The **Temple of Apollo** (Tempio di Apollo), with its columned portico, was the city's most important religious building. The **Granai del Foro** (Forum Granary) is now the repository for many of the plaster casts of victims made by 19th-century excavators.

LUPANARE GRANDE (LARGE BROTHEL)   Pompeii's most titter-inducing sight and prime photo op is a two-story brothel, just northeast of the forum off Via degli Augustali. Graphic wall paintings reveal what certainly appears to be a libertine attitude toward sex. It's easy to see why, correctly or not, the city is often associated with easy virtue. In the nearby Basilica, where many travelers stopped on a visit to Pompeii, a bit of graffiti loosely read, "If anyone is looking for some tender love in this town, keep in mind that here all the girls are very friendly." A list of prices is inscribed on the wall near the brothel. It's believed that Pompeii may have had dozens of these establishments. Many of the graphic works that once covered the walls of this one, the city's grandest pleasure palace, have been carted off to the Archaeological Museum in Naples (p. 600), though many remain in place in the 10 small rooms equipped with stone beds.

VIA DELL'ABBONDANZA The town's main commercial street is rightfully named: surrounding fields and vineyards kept Pompeii supplied with an abundance of goods, as did a brisk trade with other Roman cities. This street was lined with shops, including **Fullonica Stephani** (Stephen's Laundry), and eateries where pots full of daily offerings were kept on counters that are still in place. In most houses on the street, a shop is on the ground floor and the owner's apartment is on the second level. Many of the painted signs for bars and shops remain, and walls of some shops are still covered with red writing promoting candidates in elections. Signs have also revealed the world's first known bit of advertising punditry, hawking Vesuvinum—a clever combo of Vesuvius and "vinum," the word for wine.

TRIANGULAR FORUM This large open area was the heart of the theater district. The beautiful **Teatro Grande,** carved out of a hillside of volcanic rock in the 2nd century B.C., could seat an audience of 5,000, while the smaller 1st-century-B.C. 1,000-seat **Odeion,** or Small Theater, was used for music and mime shows. Audiences could step out between acts for a stroll along the columned **Quadriportico dei Teatri,** though the breezy walkway was later enclosed to serve as a barracks for gladiators. Nearby is the **Tempio di Iside** (Temple of Isis), one of the best-conserved temples to this goddess to survive from antiquity.

TERME STABIANE (STABIAN BATHS) One of the town's six public baths shows off the floor plan and arrangement of cold, tepid, and hot baths that were typical of these places, a mainstay of all Roman towns to provide a cleanse, relaxation, and socialization. The vaulted *apodyterium* (changing room) was the showpiece here, with fanciful wall paintings of playful nymphs. Looking at them might have brightened the day of the slaves who accompanied their masters to the baths and waited for them in the vast chamber, with orders to keep an eye on their belongings.

CASA DI LOREIUS TIBURTINUS Election placards painted on the facade gave this large house its name: "Vote for Loreius" and "Vote for Tiburntinus." The name doesn't do justice to the owner, the well-off Octavius Quartio. He entertained his guests in a gardenlike *triclinium,* or dining room, where a delightful fresco depicts Pyramis and Thisbe. This lovely maiden and handsome youth of myth belonged to feuding families; centuries later their doomed love inspired *Romeo and Juliet.*

GRANDE PALESTRA Sports events were held on this track and on the surrounding sports fields, while onlookers could escape the sun in the shade of an impressively long portico. A grandiose swimming pool was surrounded by plane trees (you can see the plaster casts of the stumps).

ANFITEATRO (AMPHITHEATRE) The oldest Roman amphitheater in the world (built in 80 B.C.), Pompeii's arena could seat 1,000 people. The first Roman amphitheater to be built of stone, it set a standard for architectural quality surpassed only by the Colosseum in Rome, a century later. Especially enlightened were the entrances designed for crowd control, and the state-of-the-art latrines. The theater became known around the region for its gladiatorial contests, and the ancient counterparts of soccer hooligans packed in for events. Games were banned for 10 years after an A.D. 59 brawl between Pompeians and visitors from nearby Nuceria that left 10 dead—the action on the field obviously just wasn't gory enough for the bloodthirsty fans.

TERME SUBURBANE The city's four bathhouses are among the finest to survive from antiquity. This one is unusual in that men and women shared the facilities. Vividly colored frescoes in the changing rooms depict graphic sex acts and are the subject of ongoing controversy: Were they meant to advertise sexual services available on the upper floors or were they simply amusing decorations? These scenes and other so-called pornography from Pompeii shocked Francis I, king of the Two Sicilies. Coming across erotic artifacts on an 1819 visit to Archaeological Museum in Naples with his wife and daughter, he ordered many of them to be locked

A street and a public fountain, Pompeii.

12

NAPLES & POMPEII

Pompeii & Herculaneum

away in the museum's Gabinetto Segreto (Secret Cabinet) open only to "people of mature ages and respected morals."

CASA DEI VETTII (HOUSE OF THE VETTII)   Pompeii's most elegant patrician villa was the ultimate bachelor pad, the home of wealthy merchants, the Vettii brothers. The huge phallus resting on a pair of scales at the entrance was not intended as a come-hither for female guests but a sign of good fortune—which the black-and-red Pompeian dining room with its frescoes of delicate cupids and colonnaded garden show the brothers had plenty of. Strongboxes embedded in the floor suggest that they might have made at least part of their fortune as money lenders.

CASA DEL FAUNO (HOUSE OF THE FAUN)   The sumptuous decor here is ancient proof that money and good taste can go together. Two of the great treasures of the Archeological Museum in Naples (p. 600) come from this huge spread, covering an entire city block, the biggest house in town. A bronze statue of a dancing faun decorated the *impluvium,* rain tank, used to collect water for the household. A much-celebrated "Battle of Alexander the Great" battle scene is one of many mosaics that decorated the lavish rooms.

VILLA DEI MISTERI (HOUSE OF THE MYSTERIES)   A layer of ash ensured that this 90-room villa near the Porto Ercolano, just outside the walls (go along Viale alla Villa dei Misteri), retained its remarkable frescoes, the best still in place in Pompeii. Set against a background of a deep hue that's come to be known as Pompeian red, figures in the so-called Dionysiac Frieze are shown going through elaborate rituals that, scholars say, may be preparations for a wedding or initiation into a sect of Dionysus (Bacchus), one of many cults that flourished in Roman times.

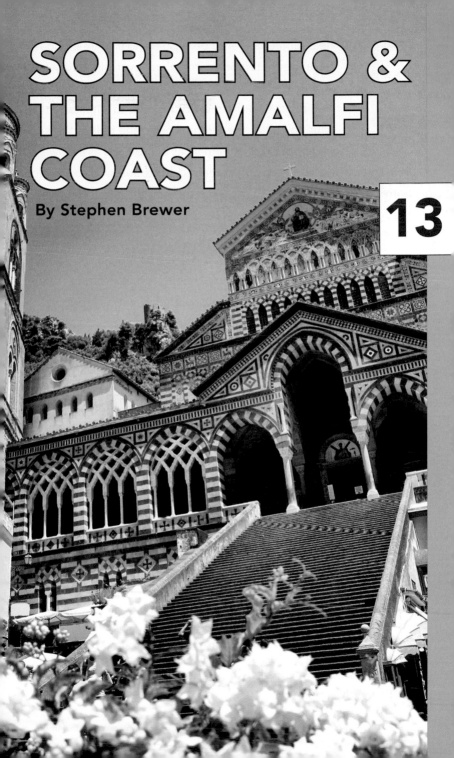

SORRENTO & THE AMALFI COAST

By Stephen Brewer

The beautiful Sorrento peninsula and the Amalfi Coast have been tempting travelers ever since Ulysses sailed by. He filled the ears of his sailors with wax and tied himself to the mast of his ship to withstand the alluring call of the Sirens. Today, the pull of the sea and imposing rock-bound coast remain as compelling as they were in Homer's day. Even though besieged by tourists, graceful old Sorrento is a lovely place, perched high atop a cliff gazing across the sea toward the isle of Capri. The spectacular but nerve-racking Amalfi Drive heads vertiginously east, clinging to cliffs and rounding one bend after another until it comes to Positano, a tile-domed village hugging a near-vertical rock, then to Amalfi, a little seaside town that was once the center of a powerful maritime republic.

With transporting green hillsides, azure seas, and the enticing scent of lemon and frangipani, the charms of Sorrento and the Amalfi Coast are no secret. You'll do yourself a favor if you schedule a visit for the early spring or fall, before and after the summer crowds, and even then accept the fact that you will not have this slice of paradise to yourself.

DON'T LEAVE SORRENTO & THE AMALFI COAST WITHOUT . . .

Floating Between Heaven and Earth in the Belvedere Cimbrone. In the gardens of Ravello's Villa Cimbrone, this coastal panorama of the shimmering Mediterranean meeting the blue sky just may be the most beautiful view in the world.

Strolling Along Capri's Via Tragara. With the sea twinkling far below, a warm breeze rustling the pines, and the legendary Faraglioni rock formations rising from the waves, you'll think you've found heaven on earth.

Taking a Bus Down the Famed Amalfi Drive. Transport by public bus may not seem as glamorous as handling the hairpin curves in an Alfa Romeo, but the views are just as spectacular and you won't have to worry about keeping your eyes on the road.

Soaking on Ischia. Hot, mineral-rich waters bubble up everywhere on this beautiful island—on beaches, into the sea, and most hedonistically, in pleasure-geared thermal parks where luxuriant gardens are laced with soothing pools.

PREVIOUS PAGE: **Amalfi's richly decorated cathedral, one of many showpieces along the Amalfi Coast.**

Campania & the Amalfi Coast

SORRENTO ★★★

50km (31 miles) S of Naples

How does that old song, "Come Back to Sorrento," go? "*Vir 'o mare quant'è bello*"…or "See the sea how beautiful it is." You'll be humming a few bars, because the sea, scented gardens, and sun-drenched vistas that have been luring visitors to this cliff-top town for millennia really are exquisite. Monuments are few and far between, but views from the town center Piazza Tasso or a trek down to Marina Grande, a fisherman's port, show off its irrepressible appeal. Sorrento provides easy access to Naples as well as such fabled places as Capri, Positano, Amalfi, and the ruins at Pompeii, and is usually thronged with happy holidaymakers who, at their best, provide pleasant company.

Essentials

ARRIVING

BY TRAIN   Sorrento is connected to Naples' Stazione Centrale by the **Circumvesuviana** railway (www.eavsrl.it; ℂ **800/211-388,** toll-free in Italy); the ride takes a little over an hour and trains run about every half hour. Their **Campania Express** trains run about 8 times a day from mid-March to mid-October, cutting the trip between Naples and Sorrento to less than 50 minutes.

BY BUS   **Curreri Viaggi** (www.curreriviaggi.it; ℂ **081/801-5420**) offers frequent bus service between Naples airport and Sorrento, with at least 8 trips in each direction every day; one-way fare is 10€. Once on the coast, the best way to get around is on SITA Sud buses (see box below.)

BY BOAT   In summer, ferries and hydrofoils operated by **NLG-Navigazione Libera del Golfo** (www.navlib.it; ℂ **081/807-1812**) and **Linee**

Leave the Driving to SITA Sud

SITA Sud buses (www.sitasudtrasporti.it) connect Sorrento, Amalfi, and other towns along the coast, with departures about every half hour between 6:30am and 7pm; buses also travel between Amalfi and Salerno and the towns in between, with approximately the same frequency. Fares vary depending on destination, but expect to pay about 2€ for the trip between Sorrento and Positano and 3€ to get from Positano to Amalfi. The 24-hour **CostieraSita** pass gets you unlimited rides on SITA buses between all the towns along the Amalfi Coast, from Meta di Sorrento to Salerno, for 10€. You can buy tickets and passes at tobacco shops, newsstands, and bars, as well as at SITA ticket offices at the train stations. During busy summer months, agents sell tickets outside the bus in Amalfi. At these times, buses fill to standing-room-only capacity—you're wise to get early and late buses to avoid daytime waits of an hour or even more. An easy-to-use source for travel info along the Amalfi Coast is **www.positano.com.**

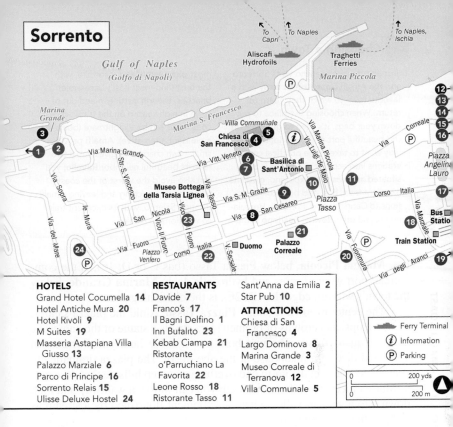

Sorrento

Gulf of Naples
(Golfo di Napoli)

Marina Grande

To Capri
To Naples
To Naples, Ischia

Aliscafi Hydrofoils
Traghetti Ferries

Marina Piccola

Marina S. Francesco
Villa Communale

Chiesa di San Francesco

Via Marina Grande

Via Vitt. Veneto

Basilica di Sant'Antonio

Museo Bottega della Tarsia Lignea

Via S. M. Grazie

Via San Cesareo

Piazza Tasso

Piazza Angelina Lauro

Corso Italia

Bus Station

Train Station

Via degli Aranci

Duomo
Palazzo Correale

Piazza Veniero

HOTELS
Grand Hotel Cocumella **14**
Hotel Antiche Mura **20**
Hotel Rivoli **9**
M Suites **19**
Masseria Astapiana Villa Giusso **13**
Palazzo Marziale **6**
Parco di Principe **16**
Sorrento Relais **15**
Ulisse Deluxe Hostel **24**

RESTAURANTS
Davide **7**
Franco's **17**
Il Bagni Delfino **1**
Inn Bufalito **23**
Kebab Ciampa **21**
Ristorante o'Parruchiano La Favorita **22**
Leone Rosso **18**
Ristorante Tasso **11**

Sant'Anna da Emilia **2**
Star Pub **10**

ATTRACTIONS
Chiesa di San Francesco **4**
Largo Dominova **8**
Marina Grande **3**
Museo Correale di Terranova **12**
Villa Communale **5**

Ferry Terminal
Information
Parking

0   200 yds
0   200 m

Lauro (www.alilauro.it; ✆ **081/497-2222**) make daily runs to and from Sorrento, Naples, Ischia, Capri, Positano, and Amalfi, with limited service between Sorrento and Naples off-season. Boats not only provide a scenic ride, traveling by sea is also a welcome alternative to the traffic-choked coastal roads in high season. The trip between Naples and Sorrento takes only 40 minutes, faster than on the train.

BY CAR Taxis offer a flat rate of 100€ to Sorrento from Naples. By car from Naples, take the A3, and exit at Castellammare di Stabia for the SS145 to Sorrento. Allow about 1 hour and 10 minutes for the drive.

VISITOR INFORMATION Sorrento's **tourist office** is at Via Luigi de Maio 35, off Piazza Tasso (www.sorrentotourism.com; ✆ **081/807-4033;** Mon–Fri 9am–4:15pm and Sat morning in summer). There's also an **information office** in a green caboose outside the train station (daily 10am–1pm and 3–7pm).

Exploring Sorrento

Sorrento is long and narrow, strung out along the top of seaside cliffs. Just about everything you want to see is an easy walk from the train station, with the exception of the two ports, which many residents opt to reach by

Choosing a Town

Just about everyone who visits Sorrento and the Amalfi Coast comes away with a favorite town to which they yearn to return. When choosing the place to put down your bags, it's hard to go wrong in this beautiful part of the world, but you may want to take some practical considerations into account. **Sorrento** is best situated as a base for exploring, given its excellent train, bus, and boat connections to Capri, Naples, Pompeii, Herculaneum, and other towns. **Positano** is the most picturesque and resortlike, with the best (and most easily accessible) beaches, though getting in and out of town in high season on the traffic-choked coast road can be a nightmare (boats are a pleasant alternative). **Amalfi** provides small-town charm and gives you a two-fer—its beautiful neighbor **Ravello;** you can also avoid the worst of the coast traffic by approaching and leaving Amalfi through Salerno, with its excellent train connections to Naples.

bus. **Marina Piccola,** below Piazza Tasso (bus C or D, 1€), is the commercial port where ferries and hydrofoils dock; **Marina Grande,** below the town's western edge (bus D, 2€), is the old fishing port.

The center of town is sunny **Piazza Tasso.** Amid the piazza's cafes, glossy shops, and crowds of promenaders stands a statue of the namesake poet, Tarquato Tasso, who was born into a noble family in Sorrento in 1544 and died in a madhouse at the age of 51. The piazza dramatically spans a deep gorge; the north end overhangs a steep hillside that descends to Marina Piccola, while to the south you can follow a walkway and look down into a verdant valley where a settlement flourished by a stream as early as the 5th century B.C.

The old town spreads out to the west, bisected by busy **Corso Italia** (closed to car traffic evenings in summer and weekend evenings in winter). Along the Corso a few blocks west of the square, at Via Santa Maria

della Pieta, is Sorrento's **cathedral** (www.cattedralesorrento.it; ✆ **081/ 878-2248;** admission free; open daily 7:30am–noon and 3–7pm). Frequent rebuilding has rendered the facade rather bland, except for an intriguing arcaded three-story campanile with embedded Roman columns; inside are doors inlaid with scenes of Sorrento life, a map of the town, and an enormous *presepe* (nativity scene), set on the streets of Naples with Mt. Vesuvius looming behind the manger. North of here are the quieter precincts around the gardens of the **Villa Communale.**

Piazza Tasso lies at the heart of Sorrento town.

Chiesa di San Francisco ★ CHURCH Top choice for the most charming spot in Sorrento goes to the 14th-century Moorish cloisters of this church and convent, where an old pepper tree shades tufa-rock arches interspersed with elaborately capped columns. Inside the church, Francis is shown above the altar in a transcendent moment when, after weeks of fasting and praying, wounds opened on his hands, sides, and feet, bringing him close to the suffering Christ in body as well as in spirit.

Piazza Francesco Saverio Gargiulo. © **081/878-1269.** Free. Daily 8am–1:30pm and 3:30–8pm.

Largo Dominova ★★ SQUARE For Sorrentines, this little square tucked away in the old quarter at the intersections of Via San Cesareo and Via P. R. Giuliani is the real heart of town. At one time that was truly the case: The town council used to meet in the 16th-century Sedile Dominova, an arched loggia with a green-tile cupola. The richly frescoed interior of trompe l'oeil columns and scenes of aristocratic life is now a gathering spot for retired workers. The old gents are used to visitors popping in for a look at their opulent surroundings, so don't be shy.

Marina Grande ★★ NEIGHBORHOOD Walking past a row of narrow houses squeezed along the quays between the steep hillside and the sea, you'll get a sense of Sorrento as an old-time fishing port. Even so, you'll have to contend with shills trying to lure you into restaurants with multi-language menus (a few restaurants here are excellent; see p. 646). It's a nice walk from Sorrento down to the port; just follow the well-marked road from Piazza Vittoria, which eventually becomes a staircase and passes beneath a Greek gate—a reminder that Marina Grande was once a separate town that was vulnerable to pirate raids, a much riskier place to live than fortified Sorrento. You can take a dip here, but the small,

Colorful Marina Grande.

pebbly beach is less than inviting (for better options, see below). The scene is quite romantic in the evening, with moonlight illuminating a harbor full of bobbing boats. Should you have one *limoncello* too many while taking in the spectacle, hop on the D bus to get back up the hill.

Museo Correale di Terranova ★ MUSEUM   Counts Alfredo and Pompeo Correale donated the collection their family had amassed since 1500; the randomness of the assortment is its charm. Neapolitan paintings from the 17th through 19th centuries capture the scenic Sorrento views that have been inspiring travelers since the days of the Grand Tour. Inlaid intarsia furniture is from studios right here in Sorrento, and much of the porcelain was fired in kilns on the grounds of the Capodimonte palace in Naples (some especially delicate-looking pieces are from China and Japan, reflecting the 19th-century aristocratic craze for Far East arts). It's all housed in the salons of an elegant 18th-century villa, with a lovely palm-shaded garden that affords stunning views up and down the coast.
Via Correale 50. www.museocorreale.it. ℭ **081/878-1846.** 8€, free for children 10 and under. Tues–Sat 8am–6:30pm, Sun 9:30am–1:30pm.

Villa Communale ★★ PARK/GARDEN   Views from one side of this delightful, palm-studded patch of greenery take in the port far below and a broad sweep of the bay of Naples. From the far side of the gardens you can take an **elevator** down to Marina Piccola (1€) or follow a well-marked lane and stairway down. A statue of St. Francis stands amid the cliffside gardens, looking contented to be in such pleasant surroundings.

Beaches

You can swim from a pebbly patch at Marina Grande or rent a beach chair at one of the beach clubs there, but for real sand, take the A bus from

Villa Communale is a lovely green place to stroll and drink in sweeping bay views.

Sail Along the Coast

You can spend a pleasant day exploring the coast on cruises with **Marine Club** (www. marineclub.it; ✆ **081/878-2385**), which run from Marina Piccola daily and usually include stops in Positano and Amalfi as well as Capri. It's an excellent way to see the coast in high season without contending with traffic, supplying an affordable taste of *la dolce vita* along the coast (from 50€ per person). Round-trips take a full day.

Piazza Tasso east to **Meta,** where the beach is often jammed with Neapolitans out for a day in the sun. An even more appealing option is west of town, also reachable on the A bus from Piazza Tasso: **Bagno della Regina Giovanna** (Queen Giovanna's Bath) at Punta del Capo, the northwestern tip of the Sorrento Peninsula. Here a small rock-sheltered cove of clear water, reached on a path through citrus and olive groves, was once the private harbor of the ancient Roman Villa of Pollio Felice. Step through the ruins at the top of the cliff, where cultured man of letters Pollio Felice once entertained guests with readings of Virgil and Horace. Just beyond, also reached by the A bus, is **Marina di Puolo,** a little fishing port where you can swim from a sandy beach.

Where to Stay in Sorrento
EXPENSIVE

Grand Hotel Cocumella ★★★   Of all Sorrento's grand hotels, this magically converted monastery is the most serene, set amid lush gardens above the sea in elegant Sant'Agnello, a residential enclave at the eastern end of town. Rooms created from combined monk's cells are chic and sophisticated, mixing antiques with nice contemporary touches, offset with gleaming white tile floors. Some have sea-view terraces while others hang over orange-scented gardens, where a pool is tucked into the greenery. An elevator descends to the sea and a swimming platform.

Via Cocumella 7, Sant'Agnello. www.cocumella.com. ✆ **081/878-2933.** 48 units. 250€–450€ double. Rates include breakfast. **Amenities:** Restaurant; bar; concierge; pool; beach; Wi-Fi (free).

Hotel Antiche Mura ★★   An elegant Art Nouveau–style palazzo built on top of the town's former defensive walls reveals many surprises, including a huge garden filled with lemon trees surrounding a pool, as well as precipitous views from many rooms into the deep gorge that runs through Sorrento. Attractive public lounges flow over a couple of floors and include a conservatory-like breakfast room. Guest quarters are bright and cheerful, with colorful Vietri tile floors; many have balconies facing the gorge or town, while some are tucked into the garden. Service is as gracious and welcoming as the surroundings.

Via Fuorimura 7 (entrance on Piazza Tasso). www.hotelantichemura.com. ✆ **081/807-3523.** 46 units. Doubles from 250€. Rates include breakfast. **Amenities:** Bar; concierge; garage; pool; Wi-Fi (free).

13

SORRENTO & THE AMALFI COAST

Sorrento

Parco di Principe ★★   You'll be stepping into some colorful history when you walk onto these verdant grounds on a sea cliff at the edge of town. Jesuit friars once grew aphrodisiac plants here. In the early 19th century, Prince Leopold, Count of Syracuse, commissioned a villa where he could lead a life wholeheartedly devoted to pleasure away from his fanatically religious wife. Tsar Nicholas II of Russia didn't make it in time to see the *dacha* built on the grounds for his visit a century later. In the 1960s, architect Gio Ponti (designer of Milan's Pirelli Tower) created what is an artistic statement as well as a stunning hotel, all about blue: blue sky and blue sea beyond the terraces and huge windows, blue tiles covering the floors—even the upholstery on the impeccable Modernist chairs and couches is a blue that Ponti calibrated. As a result, these distinctive surroundings are supremely restful, making you feel, as Ponti intended, as if you're floating between sea and sky.

Via Rota 44, Sant'Angello. www.royalgroup.it/parcodeiprincipi. ℭ **081/878-4644.** 96 units. 170€–375€ double. Rates include breakfast. **Amenities:** 2 restaurants; bar; pool; beach; spa; gym; Wi-Fi (free).

MODERATE

Hotel Rivoli ★   Convenience comes with high style at this strikingly revamped convent right in the center of town. A dramatic glass staircase floats up to airy, smartly decorated guest rooms and a rooftop breakfast room and terrace. Cozy, antiques-filled reading nooks open off the landings (there's also an elevator). You'll trade a pool and sea views for a center-of-town location—the pedestrian-only old town lanes are just outside the soundproofed windows, and the train station, port, and bus stops are nearby, making this a very handy base for exploring the coast.

Via Santa Maria delle Grazie 16. www.sorrentorivoli.com. ℭ **081/365-4089.** 8 units. 80€–160€ double. Rates include breakfast. Discounts for longer stays. **Amenities:** Wi-Fi (free).

M Suites ★★★   You might be tempted to settle in for the whole season in these fashionable apartments carved out of a private villa on a hillside atop town. Each of the commodious one-bedroom units sleeps four and has a kitchen, terrace, and large bathroom with Jacuzzi tub. Antiques, Vietri tile floors, and paintings create rich surroundings inside, while extensive gardens and terraces are pillowed in flowers and lush foliage. Views extend across the peninsula to the sea. Guests have use of the pool and facilities at the Hotel Mediterraneo, down the hill in seaside Sant'Agnello.

Via Rubinacci 5. www.msuitesorrento.com. ℭ **081/350-9956.** 3 units. Doubles from 125€; longer stay rates available; minimum stays sometimes required. **Amenities:** 2 restaurants, 2 bars, pool at nearby Hotel Mediterraneo; Wi-Fi (free).

Palazzo Marziale ★★★   You can't help but feel a bit privileged in this character-filled old *palazzo* in the heart of town, as if you're visiting aristocratic relatives. In fact, this is the ancestral home of the proprietors, who've turned a stone-arched entrance court into a glassed-in lounge and furnished the huge guest rooms with old family prints and antiques, adding designer touches with deep color schemes and rich fabrics. All have queen- or king-size beds, sofas that double as extra beds, and enormous marble bathrooms. The cloisters of San Francesco and Villa Communale gardens are just across the street, as is an elevator to whisk you down to the port.

Piazza Francesco Saverio Gargiulo 2. www.palazzomarziale.com. 7 units. © **081/807-4406.** Doubles from 200€. Rates include breakfast. **Amenities:** Restaurant; bar; parking (18€); Wi–fi (free).

INEXPENSIVE

Masseria Astapiana Villa Giusso ★★   An ancient monastery turned noble residence in the hills outside Vico Equense is surrounded by parkland, olive groves, and vineyards, all set on 14 hectares (35 acres) overlooking the sea and the coast. Monks' quarters in the atmospheric old house are charmingly and comfortably done with plump armchairs, antiques, and wrought-iron beds, with a smattering of original frescoes and arched ceilings throughout. Breakfast is served in a vast tiled kitchen, and the grounds are laced with woodland paths, sunny terraces, and other quiet hideaways. Sorrento is 10km (6 miles) west.

Via Camaldoli 51. www.astapiana.com. © **081/802-4392.** 10 units. 90€–120€ double. Rates include breakfast. Discounts for longer stays. **Amenities:** Wi-Fi (free).

Sorrento Relais ★★   No sea views, no balconies, no grand hotel atmosphere—but this small, comfortable inn on the lower levels of an apartment house across the street from the Museo Correale di Terranova is appealing and an extremely good value. Compact, contemporary-style rooms are equipped with excellent beds and good lighting (a rarity in lower-priced Italian hotels) and artfully decorated with striped fabrics, bright colors, and quirky wall coverings. Mood lighting in the showers changes with the touch of a remote control and adds a little extra splash to the spiffy bathrooms. Rooms on the ground floor are bright despite the lack of views—those in the rear are blissfully quiet—though some decidedly less desirable accommodations are in the basement, where a decent breakfast is served in a large, convivial space.

Via Bernardino Rota 5. www.sorrentorelais.com. © **081/1892-0834.** 7 units. 60€–120€ double. Rates include breakfast. **Amenities:** Lounge; Wi-Fi (free).

Ulisse Deluxe Hostel ★★   Hostel life takes on a glossy sheen in these chic, sprawling lounges and large, handsomely furnished guest rooms. A few quadruples remain true to the dormlike hostel image, but for the most part the emphasis is on quiet, hotel-standard comfort. Rooms lack a few thrills—no balconies or sweeping sea views—but white-tile floors shine, wood furnishings are polished to a high gloss, beds are firm (many are king-size), and extras include minibars and a luxury spa with steam room, sauna, and a large pool. The hillside perch is nicely located on the road down to Marina Grande, just west of the historic center.

Via del Mar 22. www.ulissedeluxe.com. ℰ **081/877-4753.** 50 units. 80€–130€ double. Rates include breakfast. Discounts for longer stays. **Amenities:** Bar; spa; pool; Wi-Fi (free).

Where to Eat in Sorrento

For a quick meal and a meat fix, try the veal or chicken kebabs at **Kebab Ciampa,** Via Pieta 23 (www.kebabsorrento.com; ℰ **081/807-4595**), which also serves falafel and meatballs. **Star Pub,** Via Luigi de Maio 17 (ℰ **081/877-3618**), satisfies a hamburger craving, and also makes excellent salads that are meals in themselves, washed down with a well-curated selection of wines and beers. **Franco's,** Corso Italia 265 (ℰ **081/877–2066**), is a local institution, open daily 8am–2am and always crowded, making calzones, *piadine* (stuffed sandwiches), and pizzas in many varieties, served at communal tables.

The best gelato in town is at **Davide,** Via Padre Reginaldo Giuliani 39 (ℰ **081/807-2092;** closed Wed in winter), where the 60 flavors include deliciously creamy *noci di Sorrento* (Sorrento walnuts), rich *cioccolato con canditi* (dark chocolate cream studded with candied oranges), and *delizia al limone* (a delectable lemon cream).

MODERATE

Il Bagni Delfino ★★ SORRENTINE   A meal here comes with a perk, the chance to swim off the adjoining pier. That's a good incentive to eat lightly from the snack food menu, though the heaping platters of fresh seafood pastas are tempting—and a popular Sunday afternoon lunch choice, when locals come down to take in the sun and indulge in excellent cooking and polished service.

Western end of port off Via Marina Grande. ℰ **081/878-2038.** Entrees 12€–24€. Daily noon–2:30pm and 6:30–9:30pm. Closed Nov–Mar.

Inn Bufalito ★ SORRENTINE   The approach here is to use only local products, especially buffalo meats and cheeses (buffalo-milk mozzarella is one of the region's most prized specialties). The brown-toned room gives off a rustic vibe, even though the menu and service are decidedly urbane. Enjoy buffalo steaks or pasta with a heavy sauce of buffalo *ragu,* while a platter of cheeses and salamis is a nice light meal.

Vico I Foro 21. www.innbufalito.com. ℰ **081/365-6975.** Entrees 12€–24€. Tues–Sun noon–3:30pm and 6:30–11pm. Closed Nov–Feb.

Ristorante 'o Parrucchiano La Favorita ★★ SORRENTINE   This old-time Sorrento landmark dates back to 1868, when a former priest decided to get into the restaurant business (the name means "Priest's Place"). The vast, multilevel, greenhouse-like space opens to a vine-covered garden planted with potted citrus trees—guaranteed to give the grumpiest customer a festive dining experience. Tour groups pour in, but there's room for everybody, and the food is consistently good. Some dishes, such as baked pasta crêpes stuffed with ricotta, mozzarella, and minced beef, have been on the menu since the start; recent innovations include some wonderful seafood pastas, like shrimp ravioli in clam sauce. Corso Italia 71. www.parrucchiano.com. ✆ **081/878-1321.** Entrees 10€–25€. Thurs–Tues noon–3pm and 7–11:30pm.

Ristorante Tasso ★★ SORRENTINE　Sorrento prides itself on fresh seafood, and the catch is the focus in this casually elegant room that resembles a garden pavilion (and also has a large garden for alfresco dining). The choices change daily, with two reasonably priced set menus, though you can also dine a la carte. Surprisingly (given the classy surroundings), pizza is a specialty, one that many regulars say is the best this side of Naples.
Via Correale 11d. www.ristorantetasso.com. ✆ **081/878-5809.** Entrees 12€–24€. Daily 10am–11:30pm.

INEXPENSIVE

La Cantinaccia del Popolo ★★★ SORRENTINE　The hams hanging over your head and deli cases next to your table give you a good idea of what to expect at this town favorite on a back lane—a bounty of house-cured meats and local cheeses paired with garden-fresh vegetables, fresh fish, pasta served right from the pan, and expertly grilled steaks. A front garden and homey, rattan-paneled decor adds to a sense that you've walked into a friend's barbecue party, and the house-made wine and limoncello will only enhance the feeling.
Vico Terzo Rota. ✆ **366/101-5497.** Entrees 7€–10€. Tues–Sun noon–3:30pm and 7:30–11pm.

Leone Rosso ★ SORRENTINE/PIZZA　Sorrentines and their visitors crowd the terrace and rambling, bright rooms for simple, straightforward seafood dishes, offered in so many variations that you should put down the huge menu and simply ask one of the friendly, English-speaking waiters to recite the daily specials. That will likely include all sorts of fresh catch, expertly grilled, and heaping platters of *risotto alla pescatore* (seafood risotto) and *spaghetti alla vongole* (spaghetti with clams). Non-pescatarians can enjoy *gnocchi alla Sorrentina,* little pockets of potato pasta filled with mozzarella and topped with tomato sauce, and a big choice of other land-based Sorrento classics. A meal usually ends with a complimentary *limoncello.*
Via Marziale 25. www.illeonerosso.it. ✆ **081/807-3089.** Entrees 7€–12€. Daily noon–11:30pm.

Trattoria da Emilia ★ SORRENTINE　The simple pleasures of this old boat shed in Marina Grande are well-known, so getting a table during the summer rush may require a long wait. Patience pays off with old-time classics such as *gnocchi alla Sorrentina* (Sorrento-style potato dumplings

Lunch and dinner in Sorrento and on the Amalfi Coast often ends with a *limoncello*, usually homemade and often complimentary. Almost every family in Campania has its own recipe, passed on for generations, for this potent and sweet liqueur. True *limoncello* is made from *sfusato di Amalfi*, a particular lemon that has obtained D.O.P. recognition (the stamp of controlled origin for produce, similar to D.O.C. for wine). The Amalfi lemon is large and light in color, with a sweet and very flavorful aroma and taste, almost no seeds, and a very thick skin.

with cheese and tomato sauce) and *fritto misto* (deep-fried calamari and little fish). The best tables, of course, are on the pier outside. No credit cards are accepted.

Via Marina Grande 62. www.daemilia.it. ✆ **081/807-2720.** Entrees 9€–14€. Daily noon–3:30pm and 7:30–11:30pm (closed Tues in winter). Closed Nov–Feb.

Shopping

On a walk along *palazzo*-lined **Via San Cesareo**, you can easily stock up on all sorts of things you don't need, mostly emblazoned with the town's signature lemons. For a bottle of the town's ubiquitous *limoncello* liqueur, head out to the touristic-yet-charming **Giardini di Cataldo,** just off Corso Italia near the train station (www.igiardinidicataldo.it; ✆ **081/878-1888**); in a fragrant lemon and orange grove you can taste and buy *limoncello*, marmalade, and other products made on the premises.

For centuries, Sorrento craftspeople have been known for producing the beautiful inlaid wood designs known as intarsia. You can see fine examples at the **Museobottega della Tarsialignea,** Via San Nicola 28 (www.museomuta.it; ✆ **081/877-1942**), and can order a custom-made piece of furniture if you're tempted. The 19th-century prints of old Sorrento are equally enticing. **Gargiulo & Jannuzzi,** Piazza Tasso 1 (www.gargiulo-jannuzzi.it; ✆ **081/878-1041**), sells fine intarsia, and you can visit the workshops for a demonstration.

Libreria Tasso, Via San Caesaro 96 (www.libreriatasso.it; ✆ **081/807-1639**), stocks a good selection of English-language titles, from the latest thrillers to guidebooks.

Limoncello tasting in Sorrento.

Nightlife

Epicenter of nightlife in Sorrento is the lively terrace of the **Fauno Bar,** Piazza Tasso 13 (www.faunobar.it; © **081/878-1135**), popular for an *aperitivo* and people-watching throughout the day until late into the evening. The adjoining nightclub caters to a mature crowd willing to fork over the 25€ cover charge. Some popular casual bars, usually packed with an international crowd, are **Chantecler,** Via Santa Maria della Pietà 38 (www.chanteclers.com; © **081/807-5868**), and the **English Inn,** Corso Italia 55 (www.englishinn.it; © **333/1599307**).

The **cloister of San Francesco,** Piazza Francesco Saverio Gargiulo, is the evocative setting for summertime concerts. Contact the tourist office (p. 639) for a schedule of events, including others staged at many restaurants and taverns in town. *Sorrento Musical* is a perennially popular revue of Neapolitan songs hosted by **Teatro Tasso,** Piazza Sant'Antonino (www.teatrotasso.it; © **081/807-5525;** tickets cost about 25€ depending on the show, 50€ including dinner).

THE SORRENTO PENINSULA

When Sorrento seems a little too crowded, it's easy to get away. For terrain that's a little wilder and more peaceful, you only need to travel south to the southwestern stretches of the Sorrento peninsula, where the ruggedly beautiful landscapes come with soul-soothing sea views.

Essentials

ARRIVING   By **car,** SS145 leads west from Sorrento, then south for access to the peninsula. **SITA Sud buses** (see p. 638) serve towns on the Sorrento Peninsula. *Tip:* To get the best views on the dramatic coastal drive from Sorrento east along the coast, get a seat on the right-hand side of the bus.

VISITOR INFORMATION   The **tourist office** in Sorrento (see p. 639) has information on towns and activities, including hiking, on the Sorrento Peninsula. Another source for local information is the small tourist office in **Massa Lubrenese,** Viale Filangeri 11 (© **081/533-9021**).

Sant'Agata sui Due Golfi ★★

7km (4½ miles) S of Sorrento

It won't take you too long to figure out where this hilltop village (at 300m, or 990 ft., you could almost say mountaintop) got the "two gulfs" part of its name. Look to the south, and you'll see the Gulf of Sorrento; turn your head to the north, and there's the Gulf of Naples. It's also easy to see why the town was already famous in the days of the Roman Empire as the junction of trading routes across the peninsula. Artisans working on the 17th-century church of **Santa Maria delle Grazie** decided to try to outdo these views and created a ridiculously sumptuous altar with lots of marble, mother of pearl, and lapis lazuli (open 9am–1pm and 4pm–7pm).

Nuns desiring less ostentatious surroundings settled in the **Monastero di San Paolo,** on a hillside 1km (half a mile) outside town; follow Corso Sant'Agata from the center to the pine-shaded drive. You'll only rarely be invited inside the formidable convent, but you're not missing much—the attraction is the **view** from the terrace atop a long staircase: You'll be able to see all the way to Ischia in the northwest and down the coast to Paestum in the east. In the 19th century, especially before the road to Positano and Amalfi opened in the late 1830s, this was a major stop on the Grand Tour, as far along the coast as view-seekers could get. The terrace is generally open April through September daily 8am to noon and 5 to 7pm; and October through March daily 10am to noon and 3 to 5pm.

Marina del Cantone ★★

5km (3 miles) S of Sant'Agata Sui Due Golfi

This cove cut into the cliffs was known to the ancient Greeks as Hyeros Anthos, meaning "Sacred Flower." From Sant'Agata, follow the road down through Metrano then on to Nerano-Marina del Cantone. The beach (mostly pebbles) is the longest for miles around, backed by houses and a few cafes and shops. You'll be part of a crowd here, especially on summer weekends when festive sun-seekers come from as far away as Naples. Looming just offshore are Li Galli, an archipelago of tiny islets once owned by dancer Rudolf Nureyev. They're also known as the Isole Sirenuse—home, legend has it, of the Sirens of *Odyssey* fame whose song lured sailors to their deaths.

Massa Lubrense ★★

5km (3 miles) W of Sant'Agata Sui Due Golfi

Quiet hillside Massa Lubrense was once a powerful rival to Sorrento for dominance over this coast. These days a position off the beaten track and firmly out of the limelight, along with considerable natural beauty, is the town's great asset. You'll want to pause long enough on Largo Vescovado to take in the dead-on view of the shimmering profile of Capri, just across the bay at this point, then step into the church of **Santa Maria delle Grazie** for a look at its colorful majolica floor; it's open daily 8am to noon and 4 to 8pm.

The bell tower of the Santa Maria delle Grazie church rises over quiet Massa Lubrense.

Punta Campanella ★★

9km (6 miles) S of Massa Lubrense

Lands End on the Sorrento Peninsula is this rocky point where a lighthouse guides ships through the treacherous Capri Narrows, the 3km (2 miles) of swift-moving waters between the peninsula and the famous island. Punta Campanella takes its name from the bell on **Torre Minerva,** a 14th-century watchtower that once warned of pirate incursions (*campanella* means "small bell"). It was built next to the ruins of a temple dedicated to Athena (called Minerva by the Romans). With some luck and divine guidance from the goddess of wisdom, ancient sailors could possibly make it through the rock-strewn narrows. Athena might have been kindly disposed to mortals, who surrounded her temple with olive groves to supply the oil they presented as offerings.

Hiking Around the Sorrento Peninsula

The peninsula is traversed by a network of 22 well-maintained **hiking** paths that crisscross valleys, meander atop seaside cliffs, and descend hillsides to secret coves for a total length of 110km (68 miles). The tourist office in Sorrento (see p. 639) can provide you with maps.

One of the most scenic walks is from the village of **Torca** (2km/1 miles southeast of Sant'Agata sui Due Golfi), where Via Pedara becomes a dirt path that descends a cliff face past the ruins of the 12th-century abbey of San Pietro to a delightful cove. Just offshore are the Li Galli islets, the very rocks where it's said the Sirens lured innocent mariners to their deaths.

Another walk descends from the village of **Termini** (5km/3 miles southwest of Sant'Agata sui Due Golfi) into the Vallone della Cala di Mitigliano, carpeted with olive groves and *macchia mediterranea,* typical Mediterranean vegetation that includes the beautifully scented *mirto.* The trail then crosses a plateau with large boulders and the ruins of Torre di Namonte, a medieval watchtower, before beginning a steep descent toward the sea, with the profile of Capri looming ahead.

On the southwestern side of the peninsula, the seashore and offshore waters are protected as a marine park, **Area Marina Protetta di Punta Campanella** (www.puntacampanella.org; ✆ **081/808-9877**). The most scenic way to see the unspoiled coast is to rent a **boat,** hugging the rocky shoreline as you pass hidden coves and stopping now and then for a swim. Marina del Cantone (see p. 650) is the port of departure. Skipper Peppe takes day sailors out on his beautiful boat, *La Granseola* (www.lagranseola. com; ✆ **081/808-1027**). Other seaworthy providers are **Cooperativa S. Antonio** (www.coopsantonio.com; ✆ **081/808-1638**) and **Masticiello Boat Service** (www.masticiello.com; ✆ **081/808-1443**).

13

SORRENTO & THE AMALFI COAST

The Sorrento Peninsula

Where to Eat Around the Sorrento Peninsula

Don Alfonso 1890 ★★★ CREATIVE SORRENTINE   The Iaccarino family has elevated their charming dining rooms and poolside terrace to international fame, and the secret to their success soon becomes clear. A team of excellent chefs makes the most of local produce, with breads and pasta made in house and almost everything else coming from the family garden or a network of local suppliers. Owner and former chef Alfonso Iaccarino grows the vegetables, shops, and orders; his wife, Livia, oversees the dining room. Even the tomatoes here seem like exotic fruits, infusing simple-yet-transporting dishes such as a bouillabaisse with freshly caught fish, or ravioli filled with farmhouse cheese and served with tomato sauce and basil. If you wish to prolong the experience, **Don Alfonso 1890 Relais** houses guests in nine elegant rooms, many with a glimpse of the sea and furnished with antiques (from 400€).

Corso Sant'Agata 11, Sant'Agata sui Due Golfi. www.donalfonso.com. (C) **081/878-0026.** Entrees 35€–45€; tasting menu from 140€. Wed–Sun 12:30–2:30pm and 8–10:30pm (June–Sept also open Tues). Closed Nov–Mar.

Maria Grazia ★★ SORRENTINE/SEAFOOD   Diners have relished the sea views and simple dishes at this waterfront institution for more than 50 years. The bare-bones room right across from boats moored along the pebbly beach lets you know what you can expect—fresh grilled octopus and just-caught fish, along with basic pastas that include the house specialty, *pasta con i cucuzzielli,* spaghetti in a light tomato sauce with baby eggplant, basil, and *caciocavallo* cheese. It's all delicious, washed down with the house white wine, and followed up with a homemade *digestivo* liqueur.

Marina del Cantone. www.ristorantemariagrazia.com. (C) **081/808-1011.** Entrees 10€–18€. Daily noon–4pm and 7–10:30pm. Closed Jan–Feb.

POSITANO ★★

16km (10 miles) E of Sorrento

Hugging a semi-vertical rock formation, Positano—the first town of any size on the Amalfi Drive heading east from Sorrento—is the very essence of picturesque, an enticing collection of pastel-colored houses and majolica domes that spill down a ravine to the sea. Novelist John Steinbeck, after a visit in 1953, described it in words that still ring true: "It is a dream place that isn't quite real when you are there and becomes beckoningly real after you have gone...." It's not surprising that Positano was the retreat for *la dolce vita* set in the 1960s and '70s. In midsummer, its throngs of admirers can seem like an invading horde, much like those that attacked the little kingdom back in the 9th to 11th centuries, when it was part of the powerful Republic of the Amalfis, rival to Venice as a sea power.

Positano's idyllic cityscape and shoreline.

ARRIVING   If you're driving down from Naples, take the A3 and exit at Castellammare di Stabia for the SS145 to Sorrento. The SS163 branches off the SS145 before you get to Sorrento and heads over the peninsula to Positano; drive time from Naples is about 2 hours. **SITA Sud** buses (see box p. 638) connect Positano with other towns along the coast. In summer, ferries and hydrofoils operated by **NLG-Navigazione Libera del Golfo** (www.navlib.it; ℰ **081/807-1812**) and **Linee Lauro** (www.alilauro. it; ℰ **081/497-2222**) make daily runs to and from Sorrento, Naples, Ischia, Capri, Positano, and Amalfi.

VISITOR INFORMATION   The **tourist office** is at Via Regina Giovanna 13 (www.aziendaturismopositano.it; ℰ **089/875-067**), open Monday to Saturday 8:30am–2pm, and also from 3:30–8pm in July and August.

Exploring Positano

Whether you arrive by boat or bus, you're in for an uphill or downhill climb along narrow lanes and steep lanes (wear comfortable walking shoes). At some point you'll want to stay put, probably along the sea at **Marina Grande,** where the town's few fishermen still haul up their boats and ferries arrive and depart. Most of the pebbly shoreline is taken up with a beach, backed by restaurants and bars in what were once shipyards and storehouses when Positano was a naval power. From Marina Grande, **Via Positanesi d'America,** a cliff-side pedestrian promenade, stretches along the shore past the cape of **Torre Trasita** and a 13th-century lookout to the smaller and slightly more relaxing beach of **Fornillo.**

If you wander up the steps from Marina Grande you'll soon find yourself amid a souklike sprawl of shops shaded by bougainvillea-laced trellises. The majolica-domed **Collegiata di Santa Maria Assunta ★★,** Piazza Flavio Gioia (✆ **089/875480;** open daily 8am–noon and 4–8pm), is Positano's main church, founded as a Benedictine monastery in the 13th century. The "Madonna Nera" (Black Madonna), a Byzantine-style icon above the altar, allegedly gave the town its name when a 12th-century pirate ship carrying the icon sailed into a violent storm. Sailors heard the Madonna on the icon saying "Posa, Posa" ("Put me down") and they took their ship to safety in what would become the harbor of Positano. A relief on the campanile outside shows a wolf nursing seven fish, a clue to how the town once made its living. If you're waiting for a bus at the western bus stop (on the Sorrento side of town), step into the small **Chiesa di Nuova,** Via Chiesa Nuova, for a look at its colorful majolica tile floor.

BEACHES & BOATING

Positano has two beaches, **Spiaggia Grande** and the slightly quieter **Fornillo.** You can swim for free at either, or rent a lounger and umbrella for about 10€. Both are backed by open-air beach bars and casual eateries. To reach more idyllic settings, board any of the tour boats that set off from Spiaggia Grande for stops at coves along the coast, or rent a rowboat and poke along the rocky shoreline at your own pace. Boats can be rented from **Lucibello** (www.lucibello.it; ✆ **089/875-032**) for 35€ and 60€ per hour, without skipper, depending on the kind of boat and the duration of the rental.

Many day sailors set their sights on **Li Galli (The Roosters) ★★,** the four small islands visible to the west of Marina Grande. According to Homer, the Sirens lived on the rocky outcroppings and lured mariners to their deaths on the rocky shoals with their enchanting songs. Sirens themselves were less than enchanting in the flesh, birdlike creatures (hence the name, Li Galli, "The Roosters") with human faces

Positano's cathedral is crowned with an exquisite majolica dome.

and the bodies of fish. If the light is right and you've had some wine on the voyage, it's easy to see how the rooster-shaped islets might have appeared to be Sirens rising out of the sea mist. The island to head for is **Gallo Lungo,** where a medieval watchtower rises above a little beach. This is where Russian dancer Rudolph Nureyev settled a few years before his death of AIDS in 1993, transforming a villa built for another Russian ballet star, Léonide Messine (1896–1979), into an Aladdin's cave filled with rich mosaics and kilims. The public is not allowed to step ashore but may swim in the surrounding waters.

HIKING

The 8km-long (5-mile) **Il Sentiero degli Dei** (Path of the Gods) clings to a hillside above Positano, descending from Bomerano, part of the community of Agerola, to Nocelle. The relatively easy, well-signposted trail meanders through cultivated terraces and citrus groves and follows view-filled, vertigo-inducing heights for much of the way. To avoid the strenuous ascent from the coast, take the Sita Sud bus to Amalfi and switch there for a bus to Bomerano. From the village square there, it should take about 3 hours to make the gradual descent.

Where to Stay in Positano

Small, guesthouse-style rooms offer a way to beat Positano's sky-high lodging prices. The tourist office (see p. 653) has a full list of bed-and-breakfasts, home stays, and other moderately priced accommodations.

EXPENSIVE

Hotel Buca di Bacco ★   This former fisherman's hut, much expanded and glorified over the years, is right on Marina Grande. The beachfront perch puts you in the center of the action, so convenience comes with a bit of noise, along with endless sea views from colorfully tiled balconies and terraces. Even rooms with partial or no sea views are a bit of a treat, with handsome antiques and comfy upholstered pieces set on tile floors to create a casual, gracious elegance that's typical of the Amalfi Coast. Three generations of the Rispoli family look after guests with care that extends to excellent meals in a sea-facing dining room and an informal snack bar just off the beach below, a good stop for non-guests as well.

Via Rampa Teglia 4. www.bucadibacco.it. ⓒ **089/875-699.** 46 units. 245€–450€ double. Rates include breakfast. Closed Nov–mid-Mar. **Amenities:** Restaurant; bar; beach (public); babysitting; concierge; room service; Wi-Fi (free).

Palazzo Murat ★★   Gioacchino Murat, Napoleon's brother-in-law and king of Naples, built this enticing and vaguely exotic 18th-century baroque palace near Positano's small port as a summer getaway. It's still a retreat of royal magnitude, set amid a vast garden and orchard swathed in flowering vines and scented with lemons and jasmine. Five especially large rooms, filled with handsome antiques, are in the original palace, and others are in a new but extremely tasteful addition, where tile floors and traditional furnishings adhere to the historical ambience. Most rooms have balconies, some with sea views; others overlook the surrounding greenery, the tile-domed church of Santa Maria Assunta, or the town. Buffet breakfast is served in the garden in good weather.

Via dei Mulini 23. www.palazzomurat.it. © **089/875-177.** 31 units. 250€–650€ double. Rates include breakfast. Closed Jan to week before Easter. **Amenities:** Restaurant; concierge; pool; room service; Wi-Fi (free).

San Pietro ★★★   One of the world's most fabled getaways, this luxurious and enchanting retreat perches on its own promontory above the sea, inviting royalty, movie stars, and just plain folks who want the vacation experience of a lifetime. Opulently tiled terraces cascade down the cliff face, laced with shaded nooks and crannies, perfectly poised for hours of relaxation (and the best setting in Positano for a cocktail, expensive but memorable). Facing the sea through huge windows and private terraces, the large accommodations are a gracious mix of antiques, stylishly informal pieces, and elaborate tiles and artwork. The pièce de résistance is the private beach, reached by an elevator that descends through the cliff. For those who want to venture farther, the hotel's private yacht takes guests on complimentary coast cruises, and a free shuttle plies the 2km (1 mile) to town. Many guests, however, choose to stay put in such hedonistic surroundings, relying on the glorious, view-filled terrace of **Il San Pietro** restaurant for exceptional sustenance.

Via Laurito 2. www.ilsanpietro.it. © **089/812-080.** 60 units. Doubles from 600€. Rates include breakfast. 3-night minimum stay in high season. Closed Nov–Mar. **Amenities:** Restaurants; bar; concierge; health club; pool; room service; sauna; spa; tennis court; Wi-Fi (free).

MODERATE

La Fenice ★★★   All the charm and beauty of Positano comes to the fore in this little parcel of heaven clinging to a cliff on the outskirts of town. A stay requires a bit of walking and climbing, to and from the town center (about a 10-minute stroll) and on the gorgeous property itself, along shaded walkways and stone stairways through gardens and groves to the pool and private beach below—an amenity that's the pride of only a few other much more expensive retreats along the coast. Charming and simple whitewashed rooms, most with tiled terraces overlooking the sea, are tucked into a couple of villas and several cottages that descend the hillside amid lemon groves and grape vines. Owner Constantino Marino and his family live on the property and make guests feel at home, and that includes carting bags up and down the stairs and serving informal meals made with produce from the garden (meals served on request).

Via Giuglielmo Marconi 4. lafenicepositano.com. © **089/875-513.** 14 units. 140€–160€. Rates include breakfast. Closed Dec–Feb. Cash only. **Amenities:** Pool; beach; Wi-Fi (free).

Hotel Dormira Fornillo ★★   It's hard to imagine a more dreamlike spot than this promontory several hundred feet above the same-named beach. The simple decor and basic comforts don't match the grandeur of the setting, but rooms are large and airy and cheerfully decked out with bright tiles. Many guests will be happy to forgo luxuries and amenities in a perch like this, with sweeping views over town and the sea—a perk from all the rooms, opening to patios and the pine-shaded, edge-of-the-cliff garden beyond. Reaching this spot requires some maneuvering steps and narrow lanes, so notify the staff before your arrival to work out the logistics and get help carrying your bags.

Via Fornillo 27. www.hoteldimorafornillo.it. ⓒ **089/811-422.** 7 units. 120€–170€. Rates include breakfast. Closed Nov–Mar. **Amenities:** Garden; Wi-Fi (free).

Hotel Savoia ★★   You won't find a lot of luxurious amenities, but this hotel's great location right in the heart of Positano, steps from the beach and easy to reach by car and with bags, is coupled with pleasant decor—bright tile floors, comfortable beds, and attractive traditional furnishings. Some rooms have sea views, and others take in the sweep of the old town climbing the hillside. The old-fashioned ambience comes with a provenance: The D'Aiello family has been running this place since 1936, when Positano was a getaway for a select few, and that's how they treat their guests still.

Via Cristoforo Colombo 73. www.savoiapositano.it. ⓒ **089/875-003.** 39 units. 180€–240€ double. Rates include breakfast. **Amenities:** Bar; babysitting; concierge; room service; Wi-Fi (free).

La Rosa dei Venti ★★   Each of the humbly furnished, tile-floored rooms in this house high on a hillside in a quieter part of Positano comes with a big perk: a large planted terrace with a sea view. It's tempting to settle in here and stay put, but moving around town and the coast is easy to do; the beach at Fornillo is at the bottom of many flights of steps, shops and restaurants are nearby, and it's an easy climb up to the bus stop or along lanes into the heart of town and the harbor.

Via Fornillo 40. www.larosadeiventi.net. ⓒ **089/875-252.** 130€–190€ double. Rates include breakfast. **Amenities:** Wi-Fi (free).

Where to Eat in Positano
EXPENSIVE

Next 2 ★★ AMALFITAN   Step through the iron gates into one of Positano's most sophisticated lairs. A softly lit courtyard with knockout sea views and a contemporary room of dazzling white linens and bright cushions are the settings for refined takes on local favorites, made with fresh ingredients, many from the restaurant garden. Fried ravioli stuffed with ricotta and mozzarella is set on a bed of tomatoes plucked from the vine minutes before, while *fiori di zucchini* (zucchini flowers) are filled with ricotta, mozzarella, and basil and served with pesto sauce. Fresh fish is a specialty, paired with the same homegrown ingredients.

Via Pasitea 242. www.next2.it. © **089/812-3516.** Reservations recommended. Entrees 16€–25€. Daily 6:30–11:30pm. Closed Nov–Mar; closed Mon off-season.

MODERATE

Da Adolfo ★ AMALFITAN/SEAFOOD   One of Positano's old-time favorites, tucked away in a secluded cove east of town, is part beach club and part restaurant. The kitchen focuses on local specialties, such as mozzarella *alla brace* (grilled on fresh lemon leaves), followed by a beautifully seasoned *zuppa di cozze* (mussel stew). Come for lunch and spend the afternoon, making use of the adjacent changing rooms, showers, and chair-and-umbrella rentals. Sooner or later, though, you'll have to face the 450 rugged steps up the hillside to the road—better yet, take the free water-shuttle service back to town.

Via Spiaggia di Laurito 40. www.daadolfo.com. © **089/875-022.** Entrees 10€–18€. Daily 1–4pm. Closed mid-Oct–early May.

Il Ritrovo ★★ AMALFITAN/PIZZA   Just being in this mountainside village above Positano is a treat, far removed from the crowds and frenzy 450m (1,500 ft.) below. The airy terrace makes the most of the sea and mountain views, and the menu is inspired by both. *Grigliata mista* (grilled meat medley) and the chicken roasted with mountain herbs are hearty and excellent, as are the excellent pastas laden with fresh seafood. Chef Salvatore might come out and insist you follow up a meal with one of his homemade liqueurs. He shares his considerable skills in year-round cooking classes. You can take the SITA bus up from town, or the restaurant will send a car down for a free pickup.

Via Montepertuso 77, Montepertuso. www.ilritrovo.com. © **089/812-005.** Entrees 10€–20€; fixed-price menu 30€–40€. Thurs–Tues noon–3:30pm and 7pm–11:30pm; open daily Apr–mid-Oct. Closed Jan and sometimes other winter months.

INEXPENSIVE

Pupetto Cafe ★ AMALFITAN/PIZZA   The Pupetto hotel operates this bar on a shady deck just above the sand and rocks on Fornillo beach, serving sandwiches, salads, snacks, and drinks throughout the day. Service is top-notch and attentive, but the crowd is casual (no one frowns at beachwear and bare feet) and tends to hang around a long time, shuttling back and forth between the tables and the beach loungers below. Climb the stairs to the hotel's lemon-scented terrace for a more substantial lunch or dinner of grilled fresh fish, seafood pasta, or pizza.

Via Fornillo 37. www.hotelpupetto.it. © **089/875-087.** Cafe: sandwiches and salads from 5€; May–Oct daily 9am–sunset. Restaurant: entrees 12€–22€; pizza 7€–10€; daily 12:30–3pm and 7:30–10pm. Closed Nov–Mar.

Shopping

Though Positano appears to have sold its soul to the devils of commerce, with a few exceptions the endless rows of shops are curiously unenticing. If you can't resist, consider loungewear, a throwback to the '70s when Moda Positano was all the rage. The excellent **Sartoria Maria Lampo,** Viale Pasitea 12 (www.marialampo.it; ℂ **089-875-021**), is a holdover from those days. The town is also famous for handcrafted sandals, often made while you wait. Top shoemakers are **La Botteguccia,** Via Regina Giovanna 19 (www.labottegucciapositano.it; ℂ **089/811-824**) and **Safari,** Via della Taratana 2 (www.safari positano.com).

Positano is famous for handcrafted sandals.

BETWEEN POSITANO & AMALFI ★

East of Positano, the famed Amalfi Drive swings into full gear, twisting and turning past a number of charming small coastal towns. Anytime outside of winter, however, you can really only explore them if you're traveling by bus, since parking for nonresidents is close to impossible.

With a generous profusion of porticos and domes, medieval **Praiano** and its adjacent twin, **Vettica Maggiore** (6km/4 miles east of Positano), sit 120m (394 ft.) above sea level on the slopes of Monte Sant'Angelo as they drape seaward over the promontory known as Capo Sottile. It's said that "Whoever wants to live a healthy life spends the morning in Vettica and the evening in Praiano," which is probably just supposed to mean that this is a good place to spend an entire day, wandering up and down staired alleyways and relaxing on the little beaches. The towns were the preferred summer residence of the Amalfi doges, who loved the beautiful views over Positano, Amalfi, and the Faraglioni of Capri. The settlements eventually merge into a sea-facing, majolica-paved piazza in front of the church of San Gennaro, which seems more like the deck of a ship than a shelf of terra firma. Twin towns, twin harbors: East of Praiano is tiny, picturesque **Marina di Praia,** set at the bottom of a deep chasm with a small pebbly beach and clear waters; the stout 13th-century Torre a Mare stands on a promontory above. To the west is a tiny slip of pebbles at **Gavitella,** tucked into a cove beneath olive groves (follow the signs for "Spiaggia").

Residents of gravity-defying **Furore,** 18km (11 miles) southeast of Positano, might have the strongest legs in Italy, since it's a climb of more than 500m (1,600 ft.) from one end of the town to the other, from the sea to a sky-high perch above. Down at sea level, where you'll probably want to spend your time, is the fjord of Furore, a deep cleft in the cliffs that provides a natural harbor. (It's 944 steps down from the bus stop, next to the bridge that spans the fjord, to the strip of pebbles along the harbor.) When water roars though the fjord with a fury, it's easy to see how the town got its name. You can sit in one of the little bars above the fjord and consider the perils of coastal life as you sip delicious wines from the

Steps lead down to the picturesque mouth of the fjord in Furore.

town's highly acclaimed winery, **Cantine Marisa Cuomo,** Via Lama 14 (www.marisacuomo.com; ✆ **089/830348**).

Rambling little **Conca dei Marini,** 2km (1 mile) east of Furore, is really just a hamlet of houses perched hillside along the coast road. It's hard to believe that the little harbor beneath Capo di Conca once bustled with boatbuilding and provided moorage for 27 galleons, making the town richer than Amalfi. More recently, Conca's views and out-of-the way quiet have lured a long line of privacy-seeking celebs, among them Jackie O, Carlo Ponti, Princess Margaret of England, and the Queen of Holland.

Today Conca is best known as the jumping-off point for the touristy **Grotta dello Smeraldo** (Emerald Grotto). Stalactites and stalagmites in the town's famous sea cave, discovered in 1932, produce transcendent light effects, and an otherworldly blue-green aura envelops the grotto when the sun is high and the sea is calm (it's open daily 9:30am–4pm, but best between noon and 3pm). You can reach the cave via an elevator from the Amalfi Drive (SS 163), or a long series of steps; after which you climb into a rowboat for an all-too-short glide through the spectacle. You can also take a boat from Amalfi, just 5km (3 miles) down the coast (trips usually 15€, including admission to the grotto). Admission is 5€, including the rowboat ride.

While you're in Conca, take time to try Sfogliatella di Santa Rosa, a delicious pastry invented by 17th-century nuns at the local **Convento di Santa Rosa.** The enterprising sisters replaced the traditional ricotta-cheese filling of the popular Neapolitan *sfogliatella* with cream and a dash of *amarene,* candied sour cherries in syrup. And mamma mia!—the creation was a hit that you can still taste in pastry shops all along the coast.

AMALFI ★★

19km (12 miles) E of Positano

From the 9th to the 11th century, the seafaring Republic of Amalfi rivaled the great maritime powers of Genoa and Venice. Nowadays, its capital, Amalfi, is prominent mostly as an alluring resort town. Set among lemon groves and olive trees on the slopes of the Lattari Mountains and the Bay of Salerno, Amalfi is a town of medieval streets and sunny squares, its imposing harbor now filled with sailboats and yachts. Despite its popularity, Amalfi doesn't seem crushed by tourism as Positano does—at least not in the early morning and evening hours before and after the tour buses and boats descend. To the delight of beach lovers, the town is within easy reach of some the best stretches of sand and pebbles on the coast.

ARRIVING   If you're coming to Amalfi from Positano by land, you'll follow the famous Amalfi Drive (SS 163) by car or take a **SITA Sud bus** (see box p. 638). If you're driving directly to Amalfi from Naples, take *autostrada* A3 to Vietre sul Mar, then head west on SS 163 from there; total

Evening stroll along Via Amalfi.

travel time from Naples is about 1½ hours. **Taxis** offer a flat rate of 130€ to Amalfi from Naples Airport. By public transport, take the high-speed **train** to Salerno from Naples (see p. 669) and from there head west up the coast on the SITA Sud bus (that's about 1½ hours faster than taking the Circumvesuviana train from Naples to Sorrento and the bus down the coast from there). There's also a SITA Sud express bus between Naples and Amalfi, but its schedules are geared to locals: They operate mornings and late afternoons on some days, but the return bus to Naples from Amalfi travels in the wee hours of the morning.

In summer, **ferries** and **hydrofoils** operated by **NLG-Navigazione Libera del Golfo** (www.navlib.it; ✆ **081/807-1812**) and **Linee Lauro** (www.alilauro.it; ✆ **081/497-2222**) make daily runs to and from Sorrento, Naples, Ischia, Capri, Positano, and Amalfi.

VISITOR INFORMATION   The **tourist office** (www.amalfitouristoffice.it; ✆ **089/872-239**) is on the waterfront in Palazzo di Città, Corso delle Repubbliche Marinare 19. It's open Monday to Friday 9am to 1pm and 2 to 6pm, Saturday 9am to noon (open only in the mornings in winter). They hand out some useful booklets on walks in and around town, which you can also download from the website.

Exploring Amalfi

Right by the ferry pier in the center of town, **Piazza Flavio Gioia** opens onto the harbor. The square commemorates the local navigator who some say invented the compass around 1300 (a dubious claim, since sailors used rudimentary compasses, likely introduced by Arab navigators, long before). Let's just say he might have perfected the compass for marine use. It is fact that Amalfi sailors provided material for some of the first nautical charts of the Middle Ages and also developed a maritime code, the **Tavole Amalfitane,** which was followed in the Mediterranean for centuries, with guidelines for everything from terms for haulage to conditions for the crew. This document is on view in the **Arsenale della Repubblica** (see below).

Amalfi's former role as one of the most important ports and maritime powers in the world is illustrated in a pair of tile panels created by artist Renato Rossi in the 1950s; they're embedded in a wall along the harbor front by the **Porta della Marina.** To the east, on **Corso delle Repubbliche Marinare** near the tourist office, a 1970s-era ceramic piece tells more of Amalfi's history, from its founding by Romans to the arrival of St. Andrew's body from Constantinople.

The medieval heart of Amalfi, a maze of covered walks and narrow streets, stretches from **Piazza Duomo,** a lively cathedral square near the seafront, into an increasingly narrow ravine. You can walk the length of town in 10 minutes or so, along Via Amalfi from Piazza Duomo up to the **Paper Museum** (see p. 664). For much of the town's history, Via Amalfi was a rushing stream; you can still hear water gurgling beneath the pavement. To navigate the town as medieval residents once did, walk up the **Ruga Nova Mercatorum,** a tunnel-like alleyway east of Via Amalfi that ends in Piazza Santa Spirito. A fountain in the square, Capo di Ciuccio (Donkey's Head), is so called because the hard-working beasts could pause here and dip their muzzles into the cool water. A local family has decorated every inch of the rocky wall behind the basin with a year-round nativity scene.

Arsenale della Repubblica ★ HISTORIC SITE   The Republic of Amalfi's power in the Mediterranean was maintained in this medieval shipyard, where galleys up to 40m (131 ft.) long were built, to be powered by 120 oarsmen. The stone-vaulted boatsheds now house the solid-looking gold coins *(tari)* that Amalfi once minted and the documents with which the republic wielded its considerable legal clout. The spotlight here is on the 66-chapter **Tavole Amalfitane,** a maritime code that more or less established the laws of the high seas from the 13th to 16th centuries. Storms have erased much of the complex, but 10 of 22 piers retain some semblance of their former appearance.

Largo Cesareo Console 3. 2€. Easter–Sept daily 11am–8pm.

Duomo ★★ CHURCH   This monument to Amalfi's rich past, covered in black-and-white marble and rich mosaics, sits atop a monumental staircase just inland from the sea. The **Chiostro del Paradiso** (Cloister of Paradise) is decidedly Moorish, with a whitewashed quadrangle of interlaced arches and brightly colored geometric mosaics. Amalfi's medieval nobles are entombed in sarcophagi set around this exotic enclosure. The **Crypt** houses the remains of St. Andrew, Amalfi's protector saint. It was important for Amalfi to have a famous patron, just as Venice had St. Mark, so soldiers brought the remains of Andrew back from Constantinople at the end of the 4th Crusade, in 1206. Legend has it that Andrew has been working miracles ever since. After the pirate Ariadeno Barbarossa attacked Amalfi in 1544, his fleet suddenly sank in a giant sea surge. Andrew's other miraculous presence is in the form of a thick ooze, reverentially called "manna," that appears on this tomb every once in a while. An 18th-century baroque restoration of the interior added lots of marble and mundane frescoes, but it's a disappointment after that wonderfully fanciful facade and cloisters. An austere medieval basilica next door holds a museum of gold chalices and other treasures.

Piazza del Duomo. museodiocesanoamalfi.it. Duomo: ☏ **089/871-059.** Free. Museum and cloister: ☏ **089/871-324.** 3€. Both: July–Sept daily 9am–7:45pm; Oct–Feb daily 10am–1pm and 2:30–4:3pm; Mar–June 9am–6:45pm.

Museo della Carta (Museum of Paper) ★ HISTORIC SITE Among the many goods Amalfi's sailors and merchants brought back from their voyages was paper, a popular commodity throughout the Middle East that Arab traders had come across in China. From the 13th through the mid-19th centuries, Amalfi was one of Europe's largest exporters of paper, produced in factories whose ruins dot the Valle dei Mulini (Valley of the Mills) at the end of town. Water wheels once powered machines that beat linen, cotton, and hemp into fine parchment. In the remains of one of the once-thriving mills a guide shows off vintage machinery and the paper that is still sold in Amalfi shops. A path through the valley (see "Hiking" below) takes you past several evocative factory ruins.

Palazzo Pagliara, Via delle Cartiere 24. www.museodellacarta.it. ☏ **089/830-4561.** 4€. Mar–Oct daily 10am–6:30pm; Nov–Jan Tues–Sun 10am–4pm.

BEACHES & BOATING

Amalfi's **beaches** are two pebbly strips on either side of the harbor. The tiny town of **Minori,** however, surrounded by citrus groves at the mouth of a small stream, 3km (2 miles) east of Amalfi, has an asset that's the envy of almost every town on the Amalfi Coast, a long, sandy beach. **Maiori,** separated from Minori by a rocky headland, has an even longer beach, backed by a palm-lined promenade. **Pasticceria Napoli,** Corso Regina 64 (www.pasticcerianapoli.it; ☏ **089/853-182**) serves ricotta-filled *sfogliatelle* and other pastries to savor on the beach. SITA Sud buses (see box p. 638) serve both towns.

From the harbor at Amalfi's **Marina Grande** you can rent **boats**—with or without a skipper—to explore the coast. **Cooperativa Sant'Andrea** (www.coopsantandrea.it; ℂ **089/873-190**) offers regular service to the beaches of Duoglio and Santa Croce, only a few minutes away; in summer, boats leave every 30 minutes between 9am and 5pm.

HIKING

A popular **hike** from Amalfi is the easy walk along **Valle dei Mulini** (Valley of the Mills). Follow Via Amalfi through town until it turns into a well-signposted trail through lush countryside to the **Mulino Rovinato** (Ruined Mill), about 1 hour away. Flour mills once thrived here, as did the paper mills. If you continue to climb the hill, you'll come to the **Vallone delle Ferriere,** where now-ruined *ferriere* (iron mills) operated into the 19th century. At the top of the valley is a waterfall; allow 2 hours to reach the falls from Amalfi. If you're really ambitious and have another 2 hours, continue from here up to Ravello (see p. 669).

Where to Stay in Amalfi

EXPENSIVE

Hotel Luna Convento ★★ St. Francis himself founded this seaside monastery in 1222. The beautiful cloisters and transformed monks' cells and chapel also have a history of hospitality, as one of the first grand hotels on the Amalfi Coast, receiving guests since 1822. Among the famous guests were Norwegian playwright Henrik Ibsen, who wrote *A Doll's House* here in 1879. American playwright Tennessee Williams also spent time here, as did heads of state Otto von Bismarck and Benito Mussolini. Adding even more luster to the atmospheric surroundings are a 15th-century Saracen watchtower, now housing a bar and standing guard over a little private beach and a large seawater pool. Most of the plain-yet-chic guest rooms, many carved out of former monks' cells, have sea views and some have terraces; all are embellished with nice art and antiques to enhance the historic provenance. Lounging in the sunny gardens that once supplied the monks' kitchens is yet another experience to savor at this unusual retreat.

Via Pantaleone Comite 33. www.lunahotel.it. ℂ **089/871-002.** 48 units. Doubles from 280€. Rates include breakfast. **Amenities:** 2 restaurants; bar; babysitting; concierge; outdoor pool; room service; Wi-Fi (free).

Hotel Santa Caterina ★★★ One of the world's fabled getaways not only delivers the stay of a lifetime, it also makes guests feel right at home. Rooms and suites are luxurious yet unpretentious, set in gardens and citrus groves hovering above the water. Colorful Vietri tiles and handsome antiques add notes of elegance, while balconies and terraces make the most of a cliffside location with the sea twinkling below. A glass elevator and winding garden path descend to a private beach and saltwater swimming pool, and memorable meals are served in a vine-covered, glassed-in dining room or on a seaside terrace. Several private bungalows with private pools tucked into citrus groves provide the ultimate hideaways.

Via Nazionale 9. www.hotelsantacaterina. it. ℂ **089/871-012.** 66 units. Doubles from 280€. Rates include breakfast. Closed Nov–Mar. **Amenities:** 2 restaurants; 2 bars; beach; concierge; gym; pool; room service; spa; Wi-Fi (free).

MODERATE

Hotel Lidomare ★ One of Amalfi's few bargains is set on a small square just beyond the main street, providing pleasant, old-fashioned ambience in a 13th-century *palazzo.* You might find the enormous, high-ceilinged, tile-floored guest rooms either charmingly old-fashioned or a bit ramshackle, but

The sandy beach at Atrani, just east of Amalfi.

many have sea views, and all are furnished with antiques and comfy old furnishings. Amalfi's beach is just steps away.

Largo Piccolomini 9. www.lidomare.it. ℂ **089/871-332.** 15 units. 103€–145€ double. Rates include breakfast. **Amenities:** Wi-Fi (free).

Residenza Luce ★★★ These attractive and comfortable rooms near the town center top the list for an affordable stay in Amalfi. Half of the handsomely decorated, tile-floored units are bi-level, with sleeping lofts tucked above living areas; many have balconies and all have large windows opening onto medieval lanes and squares. A sunny rooftop breakfast room overlooks the surrounding hills, while the beach and port are just steps away.

Via Fra Gerardo Sasso. www.residenzaluce.it. ℂ **089/871-537.** 10 units. Doubles from 125€. Rates include breakfast. **Amenities:** Wi-Fi (free).

INEXPENSIVE

Albergo Sant'Andrea ★★ One of the most authentic ways to experience old Amalfi is from these tidy rooms smack dab in the center of town, right across from the Duomo. Views of that magnificent facade are the focal point of some of the guest rooms, while others look out to sea (and others into alleyways). The old-fashioned rooms are well maintained and a good size, but decidedly bare-bones—for guests not looking for luxury, the location, warm hospitality, immaculate surroundings, and some of the lowest rates on the Amalfi Coast might compensate.

Piazza Duomo. www.albergosantandrea.it. ℂ **089/871-145.** 8 units. 80€–100€ double. Rates include breakfast. **Amenities:** Wi-Fi (free).

Where to Eat in Amalfi

Amalfi is well suited to cafe sitting. On Piazza Duomo, the elegant **Bar Francese** (℃ **089/871-049**) serves excellent pastries. Another sweet stop on the piazza is **Pasticceria Pansa** (℃ **089/871-065;** closed Tues), concocting delicious pastries since 1830; try their *torta caprese* or sticky, lemon-flavored *delizia al limone*. **Gelateria Porto Salvo,** Piazza Duomo 22 (℃ **089/871-636;** closed Jan–Mar), is one of the best *gelaterie* on this part of the coast—try the *mandorla candita* (candied almond) flavor. **Gran Caffè di Amalfi,** Corso Repubbliche Marinare (℃ **089/871-047**), overlooks the sea, making it a prime spot for an *aperitivo*.

EXPENSIVE

La Caravella ★★★ MODERN AMALFITAN   You'll leave today's world behind when you step into this 12th-century palazzo in medieval Amalfi. In romantic dining rooms, candlelight plays off stucco walls adorned with patches of colorful frescoes—a stage-like setting for some of the best food on the coast. It was the first restaurant in Italy to earn a Michelin star, way back in 1967, and ever since then the *dolce vita* set has made a beeline to these linen-covered tables for Amalfi classics as simple as *scialatelli alla caravella* (handmade pasta in a tomato-seafood sauce) or *pezzogna* (fresh local fish), enlivened with local lemons and mountain herbs. Reservations are a good idea, especially in summer. Refined as the food and the setting are, smart informal attire is acceptable; after all, this place is playful enough to embellish its tables with ceramic donkeys.
Via Matteo Camera 12. www.ristorantelacaravella.it. ℃ **089/871-029.** Entrees 25€–35€; tasting menus from 50€ (lunch) or from 90€ (dinner). Wed–Mon noon–2:30pm and 7–11pm. Closed Nov and Jan.

Da Gemma ★ SEAFOOD/AMALFITAN   Amalfi's old-time classic, in warm-hued rooms tucked behind the cathedral and in the hands of the Grimaldi family for several generations, holds high standards for the seafood it serves to a loyal and discerning clientele. The house *zuppa di pesce* is a meal in itself, prepared only for two. Equally memorable is the special pasta *paccheri all'acquapazza,* with shrimp and monkfish. The dessert of choice is *crostata* (pie with jam), made with pine nuts and homemade marmalades of lemon, orange, and tangerine. Reservations, especially on weekends, are a must.
Via Frà Gerardo Sasso 11. www.trattoriadagemma.com. ℃ **089/871-345.** Entrees 16€–26€. Daily noon–2:30pm and 7–10:30pm (closed Fri Nov–mid-Apr). Closed 6 wks Jan–early Mar.

Ristorante Al Mare ★ PIZZA/AMALFITAN   The bamboo-roofed, alfresco dining terrace just above the beach at the Hotel Santa Caterina (see p. 665) is an alluring spot for a seaside lunch. The menu offers a nice choice of pizzas, grilled fish, and pastas that include the hotel specialty, *tagilolini limone*, homemade noodles with a lemon cream sauce. Prices aren't exactly in the beach-shack category, but it's hard to beat the magnificent surroundings for a dash of informal glamour.

Via Nazionale 9. www.hotelsantacaterina.it. ✆ **089-871-012.** Entrees 20€–35€, pizzas from 20€. May–Oct daily 12:30–3:30pm.

MODERATE

L'Abside ★★ SEAFOOD/AMALFITAN   If this charming small place were more formal you could call it a temple of gastronomy—after all, it occupies part of a former church. As it is, the delightful whitewashed and arched room adds casual charm to a delicious meal (also served on a terrace out front in good weather). Seafood and vegetables are so fresh that even a simple bruschetta with anchovies is memorable, as are the homemade pastas and garden-fresh salads.

Piazza dei Dogi. www.ristorantelabside.it. ✆ **089/873-586.** Entrees 9€–20€. Mon–Sat noon–10 :30pm.

'a Paranza ★★ SEAFOOD/AMALFITAN   The walk between Amalfi and Atrani (see below) is an excellent way to begin and end a meal, especially when the feast is as memorable as those served in this old-fashioned room off Atrani's main piazza. Any meal should include the antipasti, from heavenly slices of fresh tuna to stewed octopus to grilled razor clams. Seafood reigns here, but other local favorites include *sarchiapone,* a long gourd stuffed with meat, or *melanzane con la cioccolata*—yes, that's right, eggplant with chocolate, deep fried and topped with walnuts and dried fruit.

Via Dragone 1–2, Atrani. www.ristoranteparanza.com. ✆ **089/871-840.** Entrees 12€–23€. Wed–Mon 12:30–3pm and 7–11pm.

Il Tari ★ AMALFITAN/PIZZA   The name (after the coin used in the days of the Amalfi Republic) and the setting (an old stable that's been chicly redone with white walls and colorful artwork) harken back to older times in Amalfi, as does the simple menu of traditional favorites. *Scialatielli* (long, fettuccine-like noodles) comes laden with mussels and other seafood (a trio of pastas with various sauces is served as a starter), and the fish soup with pasta and beans is an old Amalfi recipe. Excellent pizza is served at lunch and dinner, and set menus are a very good value.

Via P. Capuano 9. www.amalfiristorantetari.it. ✆ **089/871-832.** Entrees 8€–19€. Wed–Mon noon–3pm and 7–10pm.

Around Amalfi: Atrani ★★

Pretty little Atrani is just 1km (half a mile) east along the coast, an easy 15-minute stroll. Leaving town, follow the sidewalk along the main road until you come to a staircase (signposted for Atrani) up to a path that's really a series of alleyways between hillside houses; it soon drops down to

the sea again. From the beach, a maze of vaulted alleys and stepped streets leads through a labyrinth of white houses to **Piazza Umberto I,** where more than a few window boxes put the final flourishes on the charming tableau. M.C. Escher (1898–1972), the Dutch artist who depicted scenes filled with intricate geometric patterns and complex perspective, loved Atrani and sketched the town; looking at the layer upon layer of connected whitewashed houses, it's easy to see Atrani's influence on his work.

By the 12th century, Atrani had bounced back from Vesuvius eruptions and barbarian invasions to become the preferred residence of Amalfi aristocrats. In fact, Amalfi

Lemon tree terraces descend to the sea at the clifftop Hotel Santa Caterina.

doges were crowned and buried in the 10th-century **church of San Salvatore de Bireto.** Inside, beyond the bronze doors pillaged from Constantinople, a plaque shows off two peacocks, signs of vanity and pride, something the rich little town once had aplenty.

RAVELLO ★★★

7km (4 miles) N of Amalfi

Clinging to a mountainside high above Amalfi, Ravello can seem like a world removed from the clamor along the Amalfi Drive. This sense of escape, along with views and some of the world's most splendid gardens, has long made this aerie 1,000 feet above the coast a refuge for the rich and famous. Its eclectic group of admirers has included composer Richard Wagner, writers D.H. Lawrence and Gore Vidal, and actress Greta Garbo. Like they did, you'll come here to do not much else but stroll in the gardens, gaze at the coastline, and maybe relax for a few days in one of many villas converted into luxury hotels. Ravello is simply a beautiful, beautiful place, maybe more so than any other town in Italy.

ARRIVING The most convenient way up to Ravello from Amalfi is the **SITA Sud bus** (see box p. 638). If you're going directly to Ravello from Naples, the quickest route is via high-speed train to Salerno (as quick as half an hour) and then the **SITA Sud** bus up the coast. If you're driving from Naples, take the A3 to a well-marked exit near Angri, then climb over the mountains from the north on SP2b and SP1 before dropping into Ravello on the Valico di Chiunsi; total drive time is about 2½ hours. *Note:* When arriving by car, park as you approach town in a large public parking lot at Piazza Duomo, where you'll pay 1.50€ an hour.

VISITOR INFORMATION Ravello's **tourist office,** Via Roma 18 (www. ravellotime.it; ℂ **089/857-096**), is open daily 9am to 7pm (to 6pm Nov–May). The town is largely **pedestrian,** with steep, narrow lanes and many stairs.

Exploring Ravello

The heart of town is **Piazza del Vescovado,** a terrace overlooking the valley of the Dragone, and the adjacent **Piazza del Duomo.** Climb up steep Via Richard Wagner (behind the tourist office) to reach **Via San Giovanni del Toro,** lined with some of Ravello's grandest medieval palaces, built as hilltop retreats for wealthy families of the Amalfi Republic and now housing some of Italy's most distinguished hotels. Two pockets of welcoming greenery open off the street—the public gardens of the Commune, or Town Hall, and the Giardini Princiepessa di Piemonte, opening to sweeping views on one side.

Auditorium Niemeyer ★★ LANDMARK Ravello's most controversial landmark was inaugurated in 2010 to critical architectural acclaim but the disdain of many residents and visitors. Naysayers find the sweeping, dazzling-white canopied white roof of Brazilian architect Oscar Niemeyer's auditorium sorely out of keeping with Ravello's medieval ambience. It's hard, though, not to admire the way the sinuous curves tuck so naturally into the hillside. And no one can complain about the pleasure of enjoying a concert while viewing the spectacle of sea and sky through the huge eye-shaped window.
Via della Repubblica 12. ℂ **089/858-360.** Open for concerts and film screenings (check tourist office for schedules).

Duomo ★★★ CHURCH All the glories of Ravello's past seem to come to the fore in the beautiful cathedral that Orso Papiro, first bishop of Ravello, founded in 1086. The 54 embossed panels of the 12th-century bronze doors, cast in Constantinople, were intended to delight the faithful with stories of Christ's miracles and other familiar Bible stories. Another piece of scripture comes to life in the beautiful mosaics of the **Ambone dell'Epistola** ★★★, a pulpit dating from 1130, which depict the story of Jonah being swallowed by the whale. Opposite is another pulpit resting atop twisting columns that in turn rise out of the backs of two regal-looking lions, with a mighty eagle perched atop the whole affair. Add to that a wonderful collection of Roman sarcophagi and columns, bits of medieval frescoes, and a titled floor that tilts gently toward the entrance, an artful attempt to enhance the perspective and visually enlarge the space. The cathedral's patron is honored in the **Cappella di San Pantaleone.** The physician saint was beheaded in Nicomedia (in present-day Turkey) on July 27, 305, and the blood housed in his reliquary is said to liquefy and come to a boil every year on the anniversary of his death.

Piazza del Vescovado. *©* **089/85831.** Duomo: Free. Daily 9am–noon and 5:30–7pm. Museum: 2€. Summer daily 9am–7pm; winter daily 9am–6pm. Guided tours available.

Museo del Corallo ★ MUSEUM/SHOP   For centuries, craftspeople around the Bay of Naples carved precious cameos and other objects out of coral and shell. In fact, the earliest object in this stunning private collection is a 3rd-century-A.D. Roman amphora with a coral formation inside it. The 600 pieces here are the possessions of cameo craftsman Giorgio Filocamo, whose Camo workshops are attached to the museum. That he still toils is a tribute to his love for the art, since his antique pieces, such as a 17th-century coral Christ on the Cross, are coveted by museums around the world. Filocamo has carved cameos for Hilary Clinton, Pope John Paul II, and Princess Caroline of Monaco, and you can pick up one of his creations for yourself in the adjoining shop.

Piazza Duomo 9. www.museodelcorallo.com. *©* **089/857-461.** Free. Mon–Sat 9:30am–noon and 3–5:30pm.

Villa Cimbrone ★★★ GARDEN   Englishman Lord Grimthorpe— dilettante, gardener, and erstwhile banker—created this grand villa in 1904, embellishing a crumbling 14th-century farmhouse with towers, turrets, and exotic Arabesque details (the villa is now a hotel). The lavish salons and gardens soon became associated with the 20th-century elite, few more elusive than Swedish actress Greta Garbo, who hid out here in 1937—not to be alone, but to be with her lover, the conductor Leopold Stokowski. The high point of the lavish gardens, quite literally, is the **Belvedere Cimbrone,** where you'll have the dizzying sensation of being suspended between sea and sky. The writer and long-time Ravello resident Gore Vidal, who never really had anything very nice to say about anything or anybody, called the outlook "the most beautiful view in the world."

Via Santa Chiara 26. *©* **089/857-459.** Gardens 7€ adults, 4€ children. Daily 9am– sunset. Last admission 30 min before close.

Villa Rufolo ★★ GARDEN   The 14th-century poet Boccaccio was so moved by this onetime residence of 13th-century merchant prince Landolfo Rufolo that he included it as background in one of his tales. In the mid-19th century, Scotsman Sir Francis Reid transformed the house into an exotic fantasy, with Moorish cloisters surrounded in part by interlacing arcs. The most famous visitor to the palace was Richard Wagner, who composed an act of *Parsifal* here in 1880 and used the surroundings for his Garden of Klingsor, home of the Flower Maidens; the Norman tower was renamed Klingsor's Tower in his honor. Paths wind through beds of rare plantings to lookout points high above the coastline, where the surreal scene of sea meeting sky in a wash of blue is as transporting as the house and gardens. The lower garden, known as the Wagner Terrace, is the setting for the **Concerti Wagneriani** during the summertime Ravello festival.

Piazza Duomo. www.villarufolo.it. © **089/ 857-621.** 7€, 5€ children 5–12, under 5 free. Summer daily 9am–8pm, winter daily 9am–sunset (tower, 10am–6:30pm). Last admission 15 min. earlier.

HIKING

Hikers can take heart in the fact that from Ravello it's all downhill—or mostly, since a popular hike is up to the **Monastery of Saint Nicholas** at an altitude of 486m (1,594 ft.). From the center of Ravello, take the road to Sambuco for 1km (half a mile) and from there the trail up to the monastery. Plan on 2 hours for

A sweeping view from the Villa Rufolo garden.

the 9km (6-mile) round-trip. Now, the downhill stretch: From the town center, take another footpath—actually, a series of steps and hidden alleys—that descends all the way down to seaside **Minori** (see p. 664). Start from the alley to the left of Villa Rufolo, next to the small fountain. It will take you past the 13th-century Annunziata church, then the church of San Pietro, before you reach the hamlet of Torello. From there the path descends through olive trees to Minori. The hike down takes half an hour, the return trip at least double that, though the hamstrung-challenged may opt to take the bus back up.

Where to Stay in Ravello
EXPENSIVE

Palazzo Avino ★★★ A 12th-century patrician palace strikes just the right balance between comfort and opulence, with enough antiques, Vietri ceramic floors, and fine linens to satisfy the most discerning guests. Views extending for miles up and down the coast make the most of Ravello's aerie-like position. They're enjoyed through huge windows in just about every room, on the rooftop terrace with two Jacuzzis, from the sumptuous gardens and pool that cascade partway down the cliff, and from the hotel's double-Michelin-starred, dinner-only **Rossellinis** (see p. 674). A free shuttle takes guests to the **Clubhouse by the Sea** (open May–Sept), the hotel's beach club, with a small outdoor pool, a waterside terrace with lounge chairs and umbrellas, and a casual restaurant.

Via San Giovanni del Toro 28. www.palazzoavino.com. ℂ **089/818-181.** 43 units. Doubles from 350€. Rates include breakfast. Closed late-Oct–Mar. **Amenities:** 2 restaurants; bar; concierge; gym; pool; room service; spa; Wi-Fi (free).

Hotel Palumbo ★★★ This popular stop on the 19th-century Grand Tour circuit (and a favorite of many 20th- and 21st-century celebs) only seems to get better with age, holding its own against much glitzier competitors as a mainstay of old-world refinement. Beyond the bougainvillea-covered entryway is an exotic and rarefied world of columns, arches, exquisitely tiled floors, and finely upholstered, highly buffed furnishings. The ambience extends throughout the 12th-century palazzo and an adjacent annex, and many of the antiques-filled guest rooms open to terraces overlooking the coastline and the hotel's gardens and lemon groves. This isn't a place to pad around in your beach togs, but the nooks and crannies and citrus-scented walkways are such a romantic throwback you'll be happy to dress for the part.

Via San Giovanni del Toro 16. www.hotelpalumbo.it. ℂ **089/857-244.** 21 units. Doubles from 350€. Rates include breakfast. Closed Jan–Feb. **Amenities:** Restaurant; bar; Wi-Fi (free).

MODERATE

Hotel Parsifal ★★ A monastery-turned-holiday-getaway is hardly a rarity on the Amalfi Coast, but few offer good-value accommodations like these in such charming architectural surroundings. The cloisters, tiled hallways, fishpond, and flower-filled patios still exude a peaceful, contemplative air, just as the original 13th-century residents intended. White-washed rooms fashioned from the former monks' cells are plain and frugal enough to suit their former inhabitants, and the slightly rickety, old-fashioned ambiance is embellished with colorful tile floors and, from some rooms, sensational sea views. Meals in the friendly sea-view dining room may well remind you of the days when rooms came with board, an experience you may or may not care to relive.

Via Gioacchino D'Anna. www.hotelparsifal.com. ℂ **089/857-144.** 17 units. 165€–210€ double. Rates include breakfast. **Amenities:** Restaurant; bar; concierge; Wi-Fi (free).

Hotel Rufolo ★★ Your postcards home might be a little more florid while staying at this ages-old villa in the heart of town, converted to a *pensione* for an arty set more than a century ago. American writer Gore Vidal lived in an adjacent villa at the end of the garden path, and D.H. Lawrence hid away in room 423 while writing *Lady Chatterley's Lover*, leading a monklike life despite the scenes erupting on his pages. It's hard to live here like a monk these days: Rooms and suites are filled with fine old furnishings set on gleaming Vietri tile floors, a large pool sparkles in the verdant garden, and a hedonistic spa pampers guests. Then, too, of course, there are all those glorious views.

Via San Francesco 1. www.hotelrufolo.com. © **089/857-133.** 34 units. 170€–340€ double. Rates include breakfast. **Amenities:** Restaurant; bar; pool; spa; Wi-Fi (free).

INEXPENSIVE

Cecco Rooms★   With Ravello's most lavish pleasure palace hotels as neighbors, these simple, lower-level rooms may seem a bit humble. Then again, they place you in the best part of town at a fraction of the price of the luxury lodgings that line the street, and the prime real estate comes with views over the town and surrounding valleys. Gardens and the town center are just steps away, and the pleasant, low-key accommodations open to outdoor space.

Viale Giocchino d'Anna 6. ceccorooms.com. © **389/545-8477.** 5 units. From 95€ double. Rates include breakfast. **Amenities:** Kitchen, high-speed Internet access.

Where to Eat in Ravello

The name **Babel Wine Bar, Deli, and Art,** Via Santissima Trinità 13 (www.babelravello.com; © **089/858-6215**) says it all about this delightful little space where ceramics and paintings by Amalfi artists are a backdrop for a selection of local wines and delicious snacks, including bruschetta with creamy locally made *burrata* cheese. The garden-bar of the **Hotel Rufolo** (see p. 673) is a choice spot to sit back, relax, and soak in Ravello's getaway ambiance.

EXPENSIVE

Rossellinis ★★★ CREATIVE AMALFITAN   Meals in this elegant dining room and view-filled terrace come with credentials—two Michelin stars and a reputation as one of Italy's best. What might come as a surprise is an ambiance that's not informal but far from stuffy—a sense that with food this good and prices this high, no one needs to be anything other than comfortable. Service is impeccable; the staff will gladly lead diners through chef Mario Deleo's creative takes on local cuisine, infused with extra passion since he's from the region. Even the bread, with ham baked into it, is exceptional, as are such sublime creations as ravioli stuffed with squid or cod in an olive crust. Meals are paired with local wines and followed with mountain cheeses and sweets that, like everything else, are satisfying without being overwhelming.

Via San Giovanni del Toro 28 (in the Palazzo Avino, p. 672). www.palazzoavino.com. © **089/818-181.** Entrees 28€–32€; tasting menus from 120€. Daily 7:30–11pm. Closed Nov–Mar.

MODERATE

Cumpa' Cosimo ★★ AMALFITAN   Netta Bottone runs the restaurant her family started back in 1929, serving generous portions of pastas (including an extravaganza with seven types of noodles topped with seven different sauces) and big platters of *frittura di pesce* (fish fry) and some very well-done lamb and veal dishes (Netta also runs the butcher shop next door). Artichokes and other vegetables are right out of nearby garden plots. Whatever you order, Netta herself may well serve it with a flourish and a kiss on the cheek.

Via Roma 44. © **089/857-156.** Entrees 11€–18€; pizza 6€–10€. Daily 12:30–3pm and 7:30–11pm. Closed Mon Nov–Feb.

INEXPENSIVE

Pizzeria Vaccaro ★★ AMALFITAN/PIZZA   Lemon groves and vineyards have long occupied residents of **Tramonti,** about 12km (8 miles) inland from Ravello, and in their spare time they invented a quick bite called pizza (a claim supported by many others, for sure). The pizzas here, once baked in communal bread ovens, are undeniably delicious and make the little village quite a culinary outpost. Local nuns added to the offerings when they came up with *concierto,* a bitter-sweet digestive liquor concocted from nine different mountain herbs and spices. Try these local specialties at what many fans claim is the best pizzeria on the Amalfi Coast. Delectable crusts are topped with ingredients from local farms: salami and mozzarella are homemade, vegetables are homegrown, olive oil is from local groves, and the bread is oven-fresh.

Via Vaccaro, Tramonti. © **089/876-140.** Entrees 8€–15€; pizza from 7€. Daily noon–3:30pm and 5:30–midnight.

Pizzeria Vittoria ★★ PIZZA/AMALFITAN   It's refreshing to know that life in Ravello can come down to earth, too, as it does in this friendly pizzeria near the Duomo. Thin-crust pies with a huge variety of toppings are the draw; even the classic Margherita seems like perfection, given that everything is fresh—tomatoes and basil from the garden, mozzarella from nearby farms, herbs from the mountains. Some simple pasta dishes are similarly delicious. The tile-floored rooms can be packed, even at lunch, so plan on eating early or late.

Via dei Rufolo 3. www.ristorantepizzeriavittoria.it. © **089/857-947.** Entrees 10€–15€. Mon–Sat 12:15–3pm and 7:15–11pm, Sun 7:15–11pm. Closed Nov–Mar.

Shopping

In addition to the cameo handiwork that might tempt you at the **Camo** workshops at the Museo del Corallo (see p. 671), you'll encounter some beautiful ceramics at **Ceramiche d'Arte Carmella,** Via die Rufolo 16 (www.ceramichedartecarmela.com; © **089/857-303**). **Profumi della**

Costiera, Via Trinita 37 (www.profumidellacostiera.it; *②* **089/858-167**), carries a remarkable selection of limoncello and other sweet liqueurs, while the in-town outlet of 150-year-old **Episcopio Winery,** operated by the Palumbo family, is adjacent to their Hotel Palumbo (see p. 673).

Nightlife

Ravello's otherwise staid entertainment scene ramps up considerably in the summer, when the town hosts the internationally famous **Festival di Ravello** (www.ravellofestival.com; *②* **089/858-422**) from July through September. The focus is on classical music and includes concerts of Wagnerian works in the garden of **Villa Rufolo ★★** (p. 671). Tickets run from 15€ to 130€.

Beautiful ceramics in Ravello.

THE RUINS OF PAESTUM ★★★
35km (22 miles) S of Salerno; 100km (62 miles) SE of Naples

South of Salerno, soaring seaside cliffs and forested mountains give way to a wide, flat agricultural plain. Rising from the grassy landscapes is an amazingly dramatic sight: three honey-colored temples, some of the best-preserved remains of the ancient world. The scene is especially picturesque in spring and early summer, when poppies and wildflowers surround the ruins. Adding to a sense of timelessness are huge, sluggish Italian water buffalo, who have grazed the low-lying grasslands for the past 1,000 years or so, producing the milk that yields the region's deliciously creamy *mozzarella di bufala.*

Essentials

ARRIVING **Trains** stop at two stations near the ruins: **Capaccio-Roccadaspide** and **Paestum,** only 5 minutes from each other. Either station is only about a 10- to 15-minute walk from the archaeological area, with Paestum being the more convenient. Via Porta Sirena leads from Paestum train station to Via Magna Grecia, which cuts through the middle of the archaeological site. The trip to either is about 30 minutes from Salerno and 90 minutes from Naples, though you can shorten the journey from Naples by taking the high-speed train to Salerno and connecting to the local train there. Contact **Trenitalia** (www.trenitalia.it; ℭ **892021** in Italy) for fares and information.

Paestum is well connected to Salerno by bus, via **BusItalia Campania** (www.fsbusitaliacampania.it; ℭ **089/252-228** or 800/016-659, toll-free within Italy) with regular service to Paestum from Naples and Salerno (both line 34). **SITA Sud** buses (www.sitasudtrasporti.it) also run from Salerno to Paestum. **Autolinee Giuliano Bus** (www.giulianobus.com; ℭ **0974/836-185**) has several lines between Naples, Salerno, and Paestum.

By **car,** take autostrada A3, exit at Battipaglia onto SS 18, and follow the brown signs for Paestum.

VISITOR INFORMATION   You'll find a **tourist office** (www.infopaestum. it; ℭ **0828/811-016**) at Via Magna Grecia 151, by the Archaeological Museum, near the entrance to the temples (daily 9am–1pm and 2–4pm).

Exploring the Ruins

While the forum and other parts of the town have been reduced to rubble, Paestum's three magnificent **temples,** excavated around 1750, are remarkably intact. So are parts of the circuit of massive defensive **walls,** 5m (16½ ft.) thick on average, 15m (50 ft.) high, and 4,750m (15,584 ft.) in length, with 24 square and round towers along their length. At the monumental western gate, **Porta Marina,** you can climb the walls and walk on the patrol paths, enjoying excellent views over the ruins and coast. Wear comfortable shoes and bring a hat and water. Allow at least an hour to see the temples and another hour for the museum (see below).

Archaeological Area of Paestum ★★★   The enclosed site contains the three temples (all built facing east) and a number of other ruins that were part of the sacred area at the center of the ancient Greek town. The **Via Sacra (Sacred Street)** runs arrow-straight through the length of the site, connecting all three temples, its Roman pavement laid over the original Greek road. When it was built, the road continued for about 12km (7½ miles) to connect the Greek town of Poseidonia with the Sanctuary of Hera, on the river Sele about 9km (5 miles) up the coast.

Tempio di Hera (Temple of Hera) ★★★   The oldest of Paestum's temples was built in 550 B.C. with a massive portico that's still supported by 50 columns. Worshippers attended rites in front, gathering around a sacrificial altar (now partially ruined) and a square *bothros,* a sacrificial well where the remains were thrown. The temple is believed to have been part of a huge complex dedicated to Hera, wife and sister of Zeus and the goddess of fertility and maternity.

Tempio di Nettuno (Temple of Neptune) ★★★ The world's best example of a Doric temple dates from around 450 B.C. and is lined in travertine stone that glows a magical gold hue when struck by the sun's rays. Perfect proportions lend a slender elegance, while thick, closely spaced columns give the temple a sturdy, almost forceful presence. This is the best preserved of Paestum's temples: only the roof and internal walls are missing. In front are two sacrificial altars; the smaller one is a Roman addition from the 3rd century B.C.

Tempio di Cerere (Temple of Ceres) ★★ The smallest of the three temples, at the northern end of the site, was built at the end of the 6th century B.C., probably in honor of the goddess Athena. Under the Romans it was dedicated to Ceres, their goddess of agriculture and fertility; Christian tombs in the portico suggest later use as a church.

Main entrance Via Magna Grecia 917; secondary entrance Porta della Giustizia (Justice Gate) off Via Nettuno, for ticket holders only. www.infopaestum.it. *©* **0828/721-113.** Mar–Nov 9€, Dec–Feb 6€, under 18 free, includes admission to museum. Daily 8:30am–7:30pm (last entry 40 min earlier).

National Archaeological Museum of Paestum ★★ MUSEUM

Across from the entrance to the temples, this modern museum displays a wealth of artifacts from centuries of excavations. Star of the show is the fresco of a young man taking a swan dive into a rushing stream, from the so-called Tomb of the Diver, probably dating to around 470 B.C. The meaning of the simple, powerful image has long been debated, though a good guess is that the diver is gracefully making the transition from earth into the other world. The young man was clearly an athletic sort—flasks filled with the oil he used to prepare himself for wrestling matches were found next to a skeleton assumed to be his. Four other frescoes from the same tomb complex depict scenes of a symposium—more or less a drinking bash—probably to give the deceased a good send-off. These images are unique, the only tomb frescoes from the ancient period that depict human figures.

A frieze from the nearby Sanctuary of Hera includes some mythological scenes that would have delighted a 6th-century-B.C. audience, such as the comical story of Hercules and the Kerkopes. As legend has it, the hero had fallen asleep when these two scamps snuck up and stole his weapons. Hercules awoke, captured the miscreants, and tied them upside down to a pole that he carried over his shoulder. The Kerkopes started laughing and Hercules demanded to know why. They told him they were laughing at his hairy backside, so he started laughing, and set the boys free (Zeus was less amused by their antics and later turned them into monkeys). Another delightful scene depicts two lithe and gleeful maidens running, their finely sculpted robes flowing around them—the joy of these images suggests just how light-hearted ancient Greek religion could be.

Via Magna Grecia 918. *©* **0828/811023.** 9€, includes admission to temples. Tues–Sun 8:30am–7:30pm (last entry 40 min earlier).

CAPRI ★★★

5km (3 miles) W off the tip of the Sorrentine peninsula

Rugged, mountainous Capri (pronounced *Cap*-ry, not Ca-*pree*), just off the tip of the Sorrentine Peninsula, is one of the most glamorous and

beautiful islands in the world. The legend-steeped, gossip-soaked outcropping of limestone, a mere 4 square miles in size, has beguiled a long list of admirers. Emperor Tiberius ruled the Roman Empire from these pine- and rosemary-scented cliffs, and Russian novelist Maxim Gorky exiled himself to the island from 1906 to 1913. British music-hall star Gracie Fields used to belt out tunes for the likes of Maria Callas and Liz Taylor at her seaside hideaway on Marina Piccola. Poets Pablo Neruda and Rainer Maria Rilke took inspiration from the magical landscapes. The island is still a magnet for the rich, the famous, artists, eccentrics, and just plain folks. All delight in the same pleasures: stark-white villas, garden walls dripping with bougainvillea and hibiscus, azure seas lapping rugged coasts, a chorus of birdsong, and a heady taste of the good

Beachgoers by Marina Grande, Capri.

life. The emperor Augustus was onto something when he called the island Apragopolis, or "City of Sweet Idleness."

AVOIDING THE CROWDS

Whether or not Capri's beauty will transcend the tourist crowds for you depends on your tolerance levels and when you come. Avoid summer weekends especially, when Neapolitans visit for the day and bronzed sun worshippers arrive from as far away as Rome. To enjoy the island at its best, you might want to forgo summertime altogether and visit in spring or early fall. Note that the island shuts down almost entirely from November to May.

Essentials

ARRIVING   You can easily reach Capri from either Naples or Sorrento, and in summer there's also regular ferry service from Amalfi and Positano.

Don't let the profusion of companies confuse you: At tourist offices, docks, and most hotels on the islands and along the Amalfi Coast you'll find simplified listings of ferry schedules. From Naples's Molo Beverello dock (take bus or taxi from the train station), the **hydrofoil** *(aliscafo)* takes just 45 minutes and departs several times daily (some stop at Sorrento). Regular **ferry** *(traghetto)* service departing from Porta di Massa is cheaper but takes longer (about 1½ hr. each way). Many companies operate in the Bay of Naples, all of similar quality; the main thing is to figure out which boat is going where you want to go, when it's departing, and how long the trip will take. **Alilauro** (www.alilauro.it; ⓒ 081/497-2222) connects Capri and Salerno, Positano, Amalfi, and Ischia; **NLG-Navigazione Libera del Golfo** (www.navlib.it; ⓒ 081/552-0763) runs to Capri from Naples, Sorrento, and Castellammare di Stabia. **Caremar** (www.caremar.it; ⓒ 081/189–66690) runs ferries to Capri from Naples and Sorrento; **SNAV** (www.snav.it; ⓒ 081/878-1430) runs hydrofoils and catamarans to Capri from Mergellina and Naples (Molo Beverello) as well as to Ischia. In summer, Amalfi-based **Cooperativa Sant'Andrea** (www.coopsantandrea.it; ⓒ 089/873190) offers scheduled service from Amalfi, Capri, Minori, Salerno, and Sorrento; Positano-based **Lucibello** (www.lucibello.it; ⓒ 089/875-032) also makes runs to and from Capri.

From the harbor, you can take a **taxi, bus,** or the **funicular** up to Capri Town and bus or taxi to Anacapri (see "Getting Around," below). Porters will approach you at the dock, and if you're taking a bus or funicular, *don't be in a hurry to shoo them away.* Turn over your bags and they will soon appear in your hotel lobby, saving you the trouble of lugging them onto tightly packed conveyances or dragging them along the island's pedestrian-only lanes. These fellows are trustworthy, and the charge is well worth the 6€ to 8€ per piece of luggage (depending on size). Many hotels will send a car to meet your boat, so ask when booking.

GETTING AROUND   The island is served by funiculars, taxis, and buses. From the ferry dock in Marina Grande, take the funicular or a bus to **Capri Town** (2€ for either, buy tickets at the office near the funicular terminal, from newsstands or tobacco shops; if you buy tickets on board the bus, they will cost 2.50€). Buses also run between Capri and **Anacapri** about every 15 minutes throughout the day. If you wish to explore further, there's a chair lift from Anacapri to the top of Monte Solaro (see p. 688).

The **funicolare** (ⓒ 081/837-0420) is the picturesque means of transportation between Marina Grande—where the ferries and hydrofoils land—and the town of Capri. They depart every 15 minutes; the ride takes 5 minutes, arriving in the heart of town, off Piazza Umberto I.

The public **bus** system is excellent, but in high season, a ride in one of these diminutive vehicles can feel like being in the proverbial sardine can. Buses run between Marina Grande, Capri, Marina Piccola, Anacapri, the Faro (Lighthouse) at the far southwestern tip of the island, and the Grotta Azzurra on the northwestern coast.

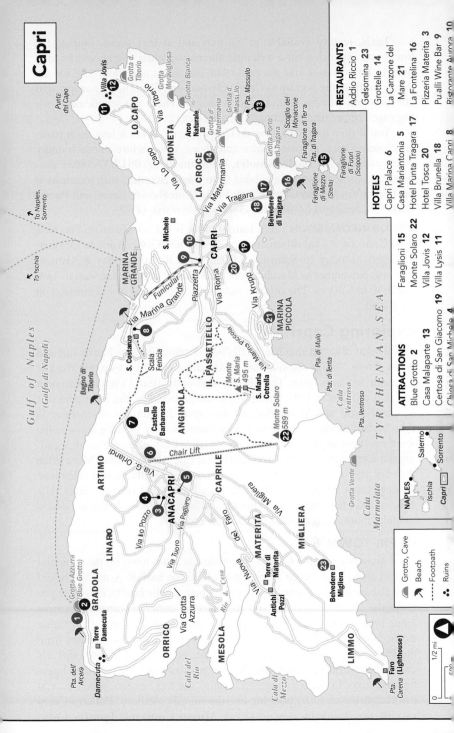

Capri

To Naples, Sorrento
To Ischia

Gulf of Naples
(Golfo di Napoli)

NAPLES
Ischia
Capri — Sorrento
Salerno

TYRRHENIAN SEA

Punta del Capo
Villa Jovis
Grotta d. Tiberio
Grotta Meravigliosa
Grotta Bianca
LO CAPO
Via Tiberio
MONETA
Arco Naturale
Grotta di Matermania
Grotta d. Massullo
Pta. Massullo
Scoglio del Monacone
LA CROCE
Via Matermania
Via Lo Capo
Grotta Porto di Tragara
Faraglione di Terra
Via Tragara
Via Tragara
Belvedere di Tragara
Faraglione di Mezzo (Stella)
Faraglione di Fuori (Scopolo)
Pta. di Tragara

S. Michele
Bagno di Tiberio
MARINA GRANDE
Funicular
Via Marina Grande
Piazzetta
CAPRI
Via Roma
Via Krupp
MARINA PICCOLA
Pta. di Mulo
Pta. di Terta

S. Costanzo
Scala Fenicia
Via Marina Piccola
IL PASSETIELLO
Monte S. Maria 495 m
S. Maria Cetrella
▲ Monte Solaro 589 m
Cala Ventroso
Pta. Ventroso

Castello Barbarossa
ANGINOLA
Chair Lift

ARTIMO
Via G. Orlandi
ANACAPRI
Via lo Pozzo
Via Pagliaro
Via Tuoro
LINARO
Via del Faro
CAPRILE
Via Migliera
MATERITA
Via Nuova
Torre di Materita
Rio d. Cesa
Antichi Pozzi
MESOLA
MIGLIERA
Belvedere Migliera
Cala Marmolata
Grotta Verde
Cala del Rio
Cala di Mezzo
LIMMO
Pta. Carena
Faro (Lighthouse)

ORRICO
Pta. dell' Arcera
Grotta Azzurra (Blue Grotto)
Torre Damecuta
GRADOLA
Via Grotta Azzurra
Damecuta

Grotto, Cave
Beach
Footpath
Ruins

0   1/2 mi
0   500

ATTRACTIONS
Blue Grotto **2**
Casa Malaparte **13**
Certosa di San Giacomo **19**
Chiesa di San Michele **4**
Faraglioni **15**
Monte Solaro **22**
Villa Jovis **12**
Villa Lysis **11**

HOTELS
Capri Palace **6**
Casa Mariantonia **5**
Hotel Punta Tragara **17**
Hotel Tosca **20**
Villa Brunella **18**
Villa Marina Capri **8**

RESTAURANTS
Addio Riccio **1**
Gelsomina **23**
Grottelle **14**
La Canzone del Mare **21**
La Fontelina **16**
Pizzeria Materita **3**
Pu alli Wine Bar **9**
Ristorante Aurora **10**

Taxis, readily available at the port and at taxi stands outside the towns, are expensive but a welcome alternative when you encounter long lines to board buses and the funicular. Taxi fares are about 15€ for the short ride from the port up to Capri; 15€ between Capri and Anacapri; and 20€ between Marina Grande and Anacapri. There are supplements for baggage (2€ per piece) and nighttime services.

You'll do a lot of walking on Capri, where all but a few main roads are closed to cars, so wear comfortable shoes. You can hire an eco-friendly electric scooter at **Charlie Scooter,** Via Roma 70 (𝒸 081/837-5863); gas-powered scooters also are available from **Capri Scooter,** with locations at the port at Via Marina Grande 280; Via le Botteghe 16, Capri; and Piazza Barile 26, Anacapri (𝒸 **081/837-3888** and 081/362–0082).

VISITOR INFORMATION   The **tourist office** is in Capri Town on Piazzetta Italo Cerio (www.capritourism.com; 𝒸 **081/8375308**). April to October, it's open Monday to Saturday 8:30am to 8:30pm, Sunday 8:30am to 2:30pm; November to March, hours are Monday to Saturday 9am to 1pm and 3:30 to 6:30pm. The office's website is a goldmine of information on the island.

Exploring Capri

You'll soon discover that life on the island, quite literally, has its ups and down. From Marina Grande, the main harbor, you'll go up, via road or funicular, to Capri Town. The white houses of the island's main settlement rise and dip across hilly terrain on a saddle between the twin peaks of Monte Tiberio and Monte Solaro. Anacapri, the island's other town, is even higher, tucked onto the slopes of Monte Solaro. Getting down to the sea from these towns, and elsewhere on the island, often means descending the formidable, grotto-laced cliffs that ring the shoreline. More often than not you do so via paths and steps, hundreds of them, that often lead to viewpoints where you can catch your breath and take in views. The easiest, and often only, way to get around is on foot, and it would be hard to find a more inviting place on the planet to walk.

CAPRI TOWN ★★

Most visitors approach Capri's mountainside main town on the funicular railway that climbs steep slopes just behind the harbor. A traffic-choked road also makes the ascent, as does a footpath for the hearty. However you make the climb, as soon as you step into the enticing warren of narrow lanes lined with walled villa gardens you'll realize you're in a rather exotic place that's lofty in more ways than one. Town life radiates from the **Piazzetta,** a small square that at times is so full of visitors that it's called the "world's living room." While the crowd of Gucci-dressed beauties and suave Lotharios suggest a certain "see and be seen" glamour, you can escape the scene by popping into the sturdily medieval **Palazzo Cerio** to visit the decidedly down-to-earth **Museo Caprense Ignazio Cerio**

Dining alfresco in Capri Town.

(www.centrocaprense.org; ℭ 081/837–6681; 3€; open Mon–Fri 10am–1pm), with its archaeology and natural history exhibits. Overlooking the square is the pleasantly plain **Torre dell'Orologio,** rising above the old city gateway, and tucked next to it is the homey **church of Santo Stefano.**

If the square's collection of celebrities, jetsetters, obscure royals, and many pretenders starts to get on your nerves, remember that the island has attracted a jaded set for centuries. Early-20th-century novelist D.H. Lawrence grumpily referred to Capri as "a gossipy, villa-stricken, two-humped chunk of limestone, a microcosm that does heaven much credit, but mankind none at all." You might also want to remember that not too many centuries ago the hilly uplands that cradle the pretty white town were grazing land for the goats, *caprerae,* which gave the island its name.

It's easy to escape the fray, even in busy Capri Town. From the Piazzetta the old town's narrow streets lead west past glittering shops along vista-filled, pine-scented walkways to the more sedate **Certosa di San Giacomo** (see p. 684). Just beyond are the **Giardini di Augusto ★★,** terraced public gardens that overlook the sea with panoramic views toward Monte Solaro, the Faraglioni, and Marina Piccola. German steel manufacturer and longtime visitor Friedrich Alfred Krupp (1854–1902) laid out the gardens to show off the island's rich flora. An unexpected presence amid the flowerbeds and viewpoints is a statue of Vladimir Lenin (1870–1924), the first leader of the Soviet Union. In 1908 the great revolutionary stayed on Capri as a guest of Russian writer Maxim Gorky, who lived here from 1906 to 1913. Gorky, a novelist and political activist, began his *Encyclopedia of Russian History* on the island and was living in the villa opposite the gardens, now the Villa Krupp hotel.

Certosa di San Giacomo ★ RELIGIOUS SITE The island's most imposing architectural landmark is this former monastery built by Count Giacomo Arcucci in the 14th century as a place to retire from the world. Arcucci's former employer, Queen Joanna I of Naples, provided the prime parcel of land and the funds. Having managed to remain on the good side of the queen, who was adept at political intrigue (her husbands and lovers had a way of meeting grisly ends), Arcucci became a Carthusian monk, ending his days in solitary contemplation. The monks were not popular with the islanders, however; after confiscating residents' hunting and grazing lands, the community added insult to injury by taxing them for ongoing improvements to the monastery. Things came to a nasty head when the brothers locked out islanders who showed up at their gates seeking refuge from the plague of 1653. The suffering populace retaliated by throwing plague victims' corpses over the monastery walls.

Ironically, the complex, perched poetically above the sea, is quite community-oriented these days, housing the island's public library and a high school. Its cloisters make an evocative setting for concerts, and the garden that looks out into azure infinity is a favorite spot for romantic tête-à-têtes. Also on the premises is the quirky **Museo Diefenbach,** which shows the works of painter Karl Wilhelm Diefenbach, an advocate of peace, free love, and nudism who lived on Capri from 1900 to 1913. He was a bit of an attraction himself, walking the paths barefoot in a white robe, his long gray hair flowing behind him.

Via Certosa. www.polomusealecampania.beniculturali.it. ℗ **081/837-6218.** 6€. Open Tues–Sun, June–Aug 10am–7pm, May 10am–6pm, Apr and Sept–Oct 10am–5pm, Nov–Mar 9am–2pm.

Villa Jovis ★★ ARCHAEOLOGICAL SITE From Capri Town, a comfortable 45-minute stroll of about 2.4km (1½ miles) ends with a steep climb to the northeastern tip of the island and the most sumptuous and best-preserved of the 12 villas the Roman emperor Tiberius (ruled 14–37 A.D.) built on Capri. The emperor spent the final 10 years of his reign on the island, partly because he was fond of the scenery and the views, but also because the sheer waterside cliffs and few closely guarded harbors made the island unassailable to assassins—an antidote to his increasing paranoia. Even then, the emperor had his bread imported from Positano, afraid the islanders would poison him. He installed elaborate baths, forcing his architects to adapt to the mountaintop location by devising an ingenious way to collect rainwater. Eight levels of walls and many stair-cases remain to suggest the size of the villa, probably covering about 1½ acres, with vast terraces and floors of reception halls and living quarters clinging to the craggy summit of Monte Tiberio. The covered Loggia Imperiale follows the cliff edge to the Salto di Tiberio, a 330m-high (1,083-ft.) precipice from which it was said Tiberius would hurl lovers who'd fallen out of favor with him. Whether or not you believe this—many historians consider it nothing more than grisly gossip—you can enjoy the views across the island and over the straits to the Sorrento Peninsula.

Via Tiberio. www.capritourism.com. © **081/837-0381.** 6€. Open Tues–Sun, June–Sept 10am–7pm, Apr–May and Oct 10am–6pm, Nov–Dec and Mar 10am–4pm.

Villa Lysis ★ ARCHITECTURAL SITE Of the many eccentric for-eigners who have sought refuge on Capri, Baron Jacques d'Adelsward-Fersen (1880–1923) might be the most colorful character of all. When a scandal involving French schoolboys (and a subsequent prison stint) forced the dissolute baron to leave France in 1905, he came to Capri with his lover, the famous young Roman model of erotic photographers, Nino Cesarini. The house Fersen built on the heights just below Villa Jovis (see above) is a neoclassic fantasy of marble, columns, tile work, and gilt mosaics, with a motto etched in stone above the entrance proclaiming the premises to be a "shrine to love and sorrow." (The name Lysis, from the Socratic dialogues, is a reference to homosexual love.) The furnishings have long since been removed, but the blue-and-white majolica-tile lounge, the huge bedroom with three windows facing the Bay of Naples and three facing Monte Tiberio, and the many terraces all suggest that Fersen drowned his sorrows in the good life. And more than that: In the Chinese room in the basement, specially built for smoking opium, he suc-cumbed to an overdose of cocaine while sipping Champagne.

Via Lo Capo. www.capritourism.com. © **081/838-6111.** 2€. Open Thurs–Tues, June–Aug 10am–7pm, late Mar–May and Sept–Oct 10am–6pm, Nov–Jan 10am–4pm.

MARINA PICCOLA ★★

The island's largest beach, on the southern shore, is nothing much, just a pebbly strip tucked picturesquely amid the rocky shorelines, but the water is clean and crystal clear. The pretty cove has been a focus of island life since the Romans harbored their boats here. In recent centuries fishermen have been sharing the space with visiting glitterati, who frequent the many little bathing establishments perched on the rocks to swim and lounge in the sun, but mostly just to be part of the island's social scene. Even the most jaded beachgoers can't help but admire the views of the famous **Faraglioni,** three rock stacks jutting out of the sea nearby (see below). It's said that the outcropping that divides Marina Piccola neatly into halves is the very rock from which the Sirens tried to lure Ulysses and his crew onto the shoals and wreck their ships. That's a lot of mumbo-jumbo, of course, but the story adds even more romance to an already idyllic setting.

While buses make frequent runs between Capri Town and Marina Piccola, the classic approach is on Via Krupp, a steep path that descends the cliffs in a series of giddy switchbacks from the Gardens of Augustus at the edge of Capri Town. Friedrich Alfred Krupp had the walkway built at the turn of the 20th century so he could easily travel between his two yachts at Marina Piccola and his suite at the Quisisana Hotel in Capri Town. When word leaked out that Krupp also used the path to access the notorious Grotta di Fra Felice, a cave at the base of the cliff where gentlemen enjoyed the sexual favors of island youth, he was eventually forced to leave Italy, and he committed suicide soon after. *Note:* Falling rocks can render passage unsafe and the path is often closed for repairs.

Faraglioni ★★★ NATURAL WONDER   Among Italy's most famous natural sights are these three rock stacks rising as high as 100m (330 ft.) from the sea off the island's southeastern coast. The outermost rock is home to a type of bright blue lizard, the *Podarcis sicula coerulea,* found nowhere else on the planet. It's believed that the blue color serves as camouflage that allows the little reptiles to blend in with the surrounding sky and water. Records suggest that ancient Roman aristocrats imported the colorful creatures from Greece to brighten up their island gardens. The middle stack, Faraglione di Mezzo, is punctured with a poetic little archway where waves have worn away part of the base. It's a popular game for anyone at the helm of a boat to navigate the opening. A shale ledge connects the rock closest to shore, Stella, to the island, and the base shelters two famous beaches with bathing establishments, **La Fontelina** (p. 695) and **Da Luigi.** Boats ferry customers back and forth to Marina Piccola, but a far more sporting way to reach the base of the rocks is on the hundreds of steps that descend from Punta Tragara.

PUNTA TRAGARA ★★★

Just 10 minutes beyond the Piazzetta, on pine-shaded paths, is a world far removed from the clamor and bling. The island's most dazzling walks are along this stretch of coastline on Via Tragara and its eastward continuation, Via Pizzolungo, skirting lush vegetation on the top of the cliffs and affording glimpses of spectacular seascapes through the trees. The enchanting paths intersect at the Punta Tragara lookout, a perch high above the sea and the Faraglioni. Among those who admired the views was poet-in-exile Pablo Neruda, who in 1953 stayed in a villa on Via Tragara as a guest of Edwin Cerio (see Museo Caprense Ignazio Cerio, p. 682). Steps leading down to the Faraglioni from the viewpoint are informally known as the Neruda path; a plaque honors the poet at the top.

Isolated beyond Via Tragara atop Punta Massullo is **Casa Malaparte,** a boxlike villa that seems to grow out of the rock, with steps in the shape of an inverted pyramid leading to a rooftop terrace. It's the creation of freethinking, outspoken Curzio Malaparte, who curried favor with Fascists, communists, and even Italy's Allied liberators during the 1930s and WWII years. The house, still vilified by islanders for its harsh intrusion on protected lands, is the star of Jean-Luc Goddard's 1963 film *Contempt*. Its cold, vast spaces and vertigo-inducing perch high above the sea reflect the estrangement and sense of looming disaster between the couple, played by Brigitte Bardot and Michele Piccoli. The film might afford your only look at the interior; the house is now owned by the Ronchi Foundation and is open only occasionally for cultural events.

BLUE GROTTO (GROTTA AZZURRA) ★★★

Italy's tourist-trap extraordinaire can be beguiling, despite all the hassle a visit entails—the frenzy of climbing off a motorboat into a small rowboat, waiting for your turn to be rowed in, lying back, squeezing through a narrow opening, and being rowed out again just as you are beginning to enjoy the experience. The magical colors of the water and walls of this huge grotto are extraordinary, even more so than they appear in countless photographs. Little wonder that postcard writers have rhapsodized about the cave since it became part of the tourist circuit in the 19th century. (Actually, a small, ancient Roman dock and some statues retrieved from the sea floor suggest this outlet of a vast system of shoreline caverns was known long before then.) It's open daily 9am to 5pm (www.capri.com). In summer, boats leave frequently from the harbor at Marina Grande, transporting passengers to the grotto's entrance for 17€ round-trip (that includes the fee for the rowboat that takes you inside). If you get to the entrance to the Blue Grotto under your own steam (via bus from Anacapri), you'll still pay 15€ to be rowed in. The boat trip out from Marina Grande is well worth a couple extra euros, delivering sea-level views of the island's spectacular cliffs and rugged shoreline.

ANACAPRI ★★★

Capri's second town, perched on heights surrounded by vineyards, is a pleasant place where, once away from the main square, life transpires like you might have hoped it would on a small island in the Mediterranean.

Your first impression, as you arrive at the main squares, Piazza Della Pace and Piazza Vittoria, might be otherwise. This is where crowds gather to board buses down to the Blue Grotto, get onto the chairlift to be whisked up Monte Solaro, and make the short walk out to Villa San Michele (see p. 689). And you might already be a bit shell-shocked by your ride up here in the noisy little orange bus that zips along the island's narrow main road from Capri Town, grinding around switchbacks in first gear. You may well wonder where all those glamorous habitués of the Piazzetta cafes have gone, as elderly housewives jab you with sharp elbows and knock you around with huge bags full of mysterious foodstuffs. Time was, the only way to get between Capri's two towns was on the **Scala Fenicia** (Phoenician Staircase), a steep path (with no authenticated connection to the ancient peoples of its name) of 881 steps—and many superb views.

But wander off the square onto Via Orlandini and you'll soon be passing tailor shops and shoemakers. Villagers sit on benches in front of the **church of Santa Sofia,** and from there you can meander along narrow lanes lined with vineyards, lemon groves, and flower-filled gardens. An easy 20-minute walk along Via Migliara takes you to **Philosophers Park ★,** a parcel of hillside carpeted in scrub and broom, where winding paths are lined with 60 ceramic plaques bearing inscriptions from the great philosophers (www.philosophicalpark.org; free admission; dawn–dusk). Just beyond the garden, the **Belvedere Migliara** overlooks the southern coast. Or follow Str. Faro di Carena out to Punta Carena, about 2km (1 mile) beyond Anacapri at the southwestern tip of the island, with its landmark **Faro** (lighthouse). A coastal path, the **Sentiero die Forini,** or Path of the Forts, makes for some good hiking out here (see Hiking, p. 690), and the little cove beneath the Faro is one of the nicest places on the island for a swim. From there, a bus takes you back to Anacapri.

Chiesa di San Michele ★★ CHURCH The 18th-century builders of this octagonal church made a wise decision when they decided to install a delightful **majolica floor,** now one of the island's most colorful manmade sights. Francesco Solimena (1657–1747), the undisputed master of Neapolitan baroque painting, did the design, full of his typical flamboyance, and Naples' finest ceramics master, Leonardo Chiaiese, executed the hand-painted tile work. Their minutely detailed assemblage re-creates the drama-filled moment when Adam and Eve are expelled from the Garden of Eden, as a unicorn, a goat, and other unlikely creatures look on. The final effect of the piece is so pleasing that no one's ever felt comfortable treading on the floor, creating some logistical problems. Pews were never installed, and worshippers and visitors are relegated to a wooden walkway around the perimeter. Those in the know head up the spiral staircase for a bird's-eye view of the multicolor scene.

Piazza San Nicola. © **081/837-2396.** 3€. Apr–Sept daily 9am–7pm, Oct 10am–5:30pm, Nov–Mar 10am–2pm; closed 2 wks late Nov–early Dec.

Monte Solaro ★★★ NATURAL WONDER Capri's highest peak soars to 590m (1,932 ft.), a magnet for view seekers who "ooh" and "ahh" at the island and the Bay of Naples unfolding at their feet. You can hike up along fairly easy paths in about an hour (the easiest is the well-marked route that begins next to Villa San Michele). The chairlift **Seggiovia Monte Solaro** (capriseggiovia.it; © **081/837-1428**) departs from Anacapri's Piazza Vittoria and whisks you to the top in just 12 minutes. Tickets cost 9€ one-way, 12€ round-trip, free for children 8 and under; hours are daily May through October 9:30am–5pm; March and April 9:30am–4pm; November through February 9:30am–3:30pm. Emperor Augustus greets you at the top, his right arm outstretched as if he's claiming everything in the name of the Roman Empire.

Villa San Michele ★★★ HISTORIC HOUSE   Swedish doctor and writer Axel Munthe built this remarkable and gracious house in the 19th century on the ruins of one of Tiberius's villas. He had the funds and inspiration to fulfill his wish that "My home shall be open for the sun and the wind and the voices of the sea—like a Greek temple—and light, light, light everywhere!" Perched on a ledge at the top of the Scala Fenicia entrance to Anacapri (see p. 688), the spacious, airy rooms are filled with Munthe's art and antiques. An arbor-lined path leads to panoramic views across the bay. A sphinx looks out to sea—touching its well-worn hindquarters is said to bring good luck.

Munthe preferred San Michele to his residences in England and Sweden, though a devastating eye condition forced him to forgo the bright light of Capri for a time in the 1920s. In his absence he rented San Michele to the eccentric heiress Luisa Casati (1881–1957). The socialite famously said "I want to be a living work of art" and shocked islanders by doing so—walking around the island with leashed cheetahs and wearing live snakes as jewelry. Her lavish lifestyle at Villa San Michele and elsewhere left her $25 million in debt; she lived out her days in relative poverty in London. After successful eye surgery, Munthe returned to Capri, living many happy years here before returning to Stockholm during World War II as a guest of the royal family.

Viale Axel Munthe 34. www.villasanmichele.eu. © **081/837-1401.** 8€. May–Sept 9am–6pm; Apr and Oct 9am–5pm; Mar 9am–4:30pm; Nov–Feb 9am–3:30pm.

Beaches

Inviting as Capri's crystalline waters are, getting into them can be bit of a challenge. The most convenient place to get wet is **Marina Piccola,** where the pebbly beaches are accessible by bus from Capri Town. Also near Capri Town is **Bagni di Tiberio,** a nice, sandy stretch on the north side of the island about 1km (a half-mile) east of Marina Grande. Getting down from the cliff path and, especially, back up, requires a bit of a climb, though you can also get there and back in one of the little boats from Marina Grande for about 3€ each way. Other beaches are **next to the Blue Grotto** (Via Grotta Azzurra), accessible by bus from Anacapri; below the Faro (lighthouse) at **Punta Carena,** at the southwestern tip of the island, also reached by bus from Anacapri; and at the base of the **Faraglioni,** reached by hundreds of steps from the Via Tragara or by boat from Marina Piccola. You can bring a towel and lounge on the beach and rocks at any of these places. Most are lined with beach clubs *(stabilimenti balneari)* that usually open mid-March to mid-November 9am to sunset, and charge about 20€ a day for use of a changing room, chair or lounge, and towels; you'll find snack bars at most, excellent restaurants at some (see "Where to Eat," p. 693), and pools at a few.

Hiking

Capri is heaven for walkers. The island is laced with paths that beckon anyone with a good pair of walking shoes, a sun hat, and a bottle of water. Paths are indicated on most maps of the island, including those from the tourist office; you can also download them from the office's website, www.capritourism.com. Some especially enticing routes just outside Capri Town take you across handsome, view-filled landscapes around Punta Tragara and to some of the island's most famous sights, including the Faraglioni and Villa Jovis. A less-traveled but no less exhilarating route is on the western side of the island, the **Sentiero die Forini (Path of the Forts).** This 5km (3-mile) walk between the Blue Grotto and Faro (lighthouse) at Punta Carena passes four small coastal fortresses erected over the centuries to keep pirates and foreign powers at bay. However busy the island might be, here you'll find yourself amid Mediterranean countryside and an almost inexhaustible supply of sparkling sea views.

You may opt to take the chairlift to the summit of Monte Solaro (see p. 688) and hike down back to Anacapri through wooded countryside into the **valley of Cetrella.** You'll be following paths once used by the Carthusian monks of the Certosa di San Giacomo (see p. 684) who came out here to check on their herds. The route passes the aptly named **Villa Solitaria,** the former home of British novelist Compton Mackenzie (1883–1972). Mackenzie and his wife, Faith, lived on Capri from 1913 to 1920 and intermittently thereafter. The island's famous tolerance of homosexual foreigners, along with Faith's affair with the classical pianist Renata Borgatti, inspired Mackenzie's lesbian-themed 1928 *Extraordinary Women.* A less secular landmark is just down the path, where the little **hermitage of Cetrella** and its **church of Santa Maria** nestle in a verdant copse. The church is not often open, so check with the tourist office before setting out if a look inside at the double nave is on your list of must-sees.

Where to Stay on Capri
EXPENSIVE

Capri Palace ★★★ At this delightful getaway in Anacapri on the slopes of Monte Solaro, everything is geared to soothing relaxation. An expanse of green lawn surrounds the swimming pool, chic lounges are quiet and welcoming, and guest rooms are done in restful creams with rose-colored tile floors and white linens. Some suites have private pools, and some rooms look across the sea all the way to Vesuvius, but even the outlooks from rear rooms over the green flanks of Monte Solaro are relaxing. A shuttle bus runs to the port, Capri Town, and a delightful beach club with platforms that make it easy to dip into the Mediterranean.

Via Capodimonte 2, Anacapri. www.capri-palace.com. © **081/978-0111.** 79 units. Doubles from 330€. Rates include breakfast. Closed mid-Oct–mid-Apr. No children under 10 June–Aug. **Amenities:** 2 restaurants; bar; beach club; pool; room service; spa; Wi-Fi (free).

Hotel Punta Tragara ★★ French architect le Corbusier designed this multilevel villa in the 1920s, and Winston Churchill and Dwight Eisenhower are among those who have enjoyed falling asleep to the sound of waves lapping on the shore far below. Each of the stylish quarters is different, some strikingly contemporary, others comfortingly traditional, though all are luxurious without being pretentious. All also open onto terraces, and most offer views of the Faraglioni. You can make the descent to the sea on the hundreds of steps outside the gate, or enjoy a swim in the two pools tucked into gardens.

Via Tragara 57, Capri Town. www.hoteltragara.com. © **081/837-0844.** 45 units. 450€–650€ double. Rates include breakfast. Closed mid-Oct–mid-Apr. **Amenities:** Restaurant; bar; concierge; gym; 2 pools; room service; spa; Wi-Fi (free).

Villa Marina Capri ★★ On its view-filled perch above Marina Grande, this late-19th-century villa has been converted into a romantic island getaway, set amid lush gardens and sunny terraces. Rooms are quietly glamorous and named for the artists and bohemians who have landed on Capri over the years—but decor is firmly geared to soothing contemporary comfort. Most rooms open to the outdoors and sea views. Among

Views of the Marina Grande from the pool terrace at Villa Marina Capri.

the pampering amenities are a spa, restaurant, and notably attentive service, as well as free shuttle service to the port and to Capri Town.

Via Prov, Marina Grande 191, Capri. www.villamarinacapri.com. ✆ **081/837-6630.** 21 units. Doubles from 250€. Rates include breakfast. Closed late-Oct–Apr. **Amenities:** Restaurant; bar; pool; spa; free shuttle; Wi-Fi (free).

MODERATE

Casa Mariantonia ★★ A gracious old villa near the Church of San Michele commands some of the best real estate in Anacapri—a shady lemon grove, lawns, gardens, and a big swimming pool all right in the center of town. Four generations have been welcoming guests to the family home, which mixes traditional island architecture with contemporary touches for a relaxed but luxurious ambience. The family claims that great-grandmother Mariantonia invented *limoncello,* which may be a bit of a stretch. Even so, sipping the homemade elixir on a terrace next to the trees from whence it comes is a great Capri experience.

Via Guiseppe Orlandi 180, Anacapri. www.casamariantonia.com. ✆ **081/837-2923.** 10 units. 140€–190€ double. Rates include breakfast. Closed Jan–Mar. **Amenities:** Bar; pool; Wi-Fi (free).

Villa Brunella ★★ Flower-filled terraces spilling down the hillside from Via Tragara seem to pull you right into the magic of Capri, with eye-popping sea views from each of the airy, tile-floored guest rooms. Ambience hovers between cozy old-fashioned Italian hospitality and romantic getaway, with some nice antiques and overstuffed armchairs in the bright rooms and plenty of bougainvillea-filled nooks and crannies on the pine-shaded grounds. A pool sparkles on a welcoming patio, and guests have access to a beach club at Marina Piccola. The **Terrazza Brunella** provides excellent food in elegant surroundings for those occasions when even the short walk into town seems like an effort.

Via Tragara 24, Capri Town. www.villabrunella.it. ✆ **081/837-0122.** 20 units. 190€– 270€ double. Rates include breakfast. Closed Nov–Apr. **Amenities:** Restaurant; bar; pool; room service; Wi-Fi (free).

INEXPENSIVE

Hotel Tosca ★ You don't have to break the bank to stay on the island or even sacrifice style at this pretty little retreat on the quiet side of Capri Town, near the Gardens of Augustus. Many of the bright, whitewashed rooms have sea views, some have terraces, and all look out over lush gardens. Arches, vaulted ceilings, and tile floors help create the ambience of a simple-yet-tasteful island house. Breakfast is served on a breezy sea-view terrace.

Via Dalmazio Birago 5, Capri Town. www.latoscahotel.com. ✆ **081/837-0989.** 11 units. 75€–165€ double. Rates include breakfast. **Amenities:** Wi-Fi (free).

Where to Eat on Capri

EXPENSIVE

Grottelle ★ CAPRESE   A trek along the southern side of the island is rewarded with a stop at this out-of-the way lair tucked onto a ledge above the Arco Naturale. A cave etched out of limestone cliffs and a panoramic terrace provide plenty of ambiance, perhaps more memorable than the meal itself, though simple dishes like *zuppa di fagioli* (bean soup) and *spaghetti con pomodoro e basilica* (with fresh tomatoes and basil) are perfectly fine accompaniments to the views that extend across the sea to the Amalfi Coast. To find this delightful spot, wander east from Punta Tragara; it's about a 20-minute walk from the Piazzetta.

Via Arco Naturale 13, Capri Town. ✆ **081/837-5719**. Entrees 15€–30€. Fri–Wed noon–3pm and 7–11pm. Closed Nov–Mar.

Ristorante Aurora ★★ CAPRESE   You'll get a taste of Capri's high life at the island's oldest eatery, where photos of celebrities hang above the white banquettes. A few may also be sitting around you in the minimalist main dining room or on the terrace facing Capri Town's main thoroughfare. Despite all the glitz, the third generation of the D'Alessio family sticks to the basics, serving island classics like the trademark thin-crust *pizza all'acqua*, with mozzarella and hot peppers, *sformatino alla Franco* (rice pie in prawn sauce), and spaghetti *alle vongole* (clams).

Via Fuorlovado 18, Capri Town. ✆ **081/837-0181**. Entrees 12€–22€. Apr–Dec daily noon–3:30pm and 7:30–11pm.

MODERATE

Gelsomina ★ CAPRESE   The sparkling swimming pool is a tempting draw on a warm summer day at this countryside retreat outside Anacapri. Come for the day, to swim, have lunch, and maybe walk to the Belvedere della Migliera viewpoint just down the road. It's also a popular evening spot. Dining is on a terrace overlooking the sea, and the food is a perfect complement to the low-key setting, with many ingredients plucked straight from the surrounding gardens. Homemade *ravioli di caprese* is light as a feather and stuffed with delicious ricotta from a local producer. Anacapri is about 15 minutes away on foot, on lanes that slice through vineyards and gardens. A free shuttle is available. Five modest **guest rooms** (115€–190€) are above the restaurant, under the same management as the pleasant, reasonably priced **Villa Ceselle** hotel (www.villa ceselle.com) near the center of Anacapri.

Via Migliara 72, Anacapri. www.dagelsomina.com. ✆ **081/837-1499**. Entrees 10€– 18€. Daily 12:30pm–3:30pm and 7–11pm (no dinner mid-Oct–mid-May). Closed mid-Nov–Mar.

Pulalli Wine Bar ★★ CAPRESE   To find a hideaway in the jam-packed Piazzetta, just look up to this little terrace next to the clock tower.

The bird's-eye view from this lofty perch comes with wine, a selection of cheeses, or a full meal—the *risotto al limone* (lemon-flavored risotto) is especially transporting in this magical setting, all the more so since it's served in a hollowed-out lemon. To secure one of the seven tables in this coveted spot, it's best to reserve ahead.

Piazza Umberto I 4, Capri Town. 𝄐 **081/837-4108.** Entrees 10€–25€. Wed–Mon noon–3pm and 7pm–midnight. Closed Nov–Easter.

Inexpensive

Pizzeria Materita ★ PIZZERIA/CAPRESE   All the warmth of little Anacapri comes to the fore in this busy local favorite on an animated square overlooking the church of Santa Sofia. Pizzas from the wood-fired oven and the palatable house wine are crowd pleasers, though the simple pastas are solidly tasty, too. Busy waiters often come around with fresh fish that soon reappear perfectly grilled with island herbs.

Via Giuseppe Orlandi 140, Anacapri. 𝄐 **081/837-3375.** Entrees 8€–18€. Daily noon–3:30pm and 6:30–11pm.

Beach Clubs

Some of Capri's most beloved institutions are the *stabilmenti balneari,* beach clubs, where you can eat well and begin or end a meal with a swim and some lounging. A day at one of these charming places is, like so much else about Capri, a simple pleasure with a glamorous twist.

Addio Riccio ★★★ SEAFOOD   The cliffside pavilion that serves as the informal beach bistro of the Capri Palace hotel (see p. 690) is done in soothing shades of blue and crisp white and hangs just above the Grotto Azzurra, bathed in the same mesmerizing light. The setting is so delightful that you won't want to leave after feasting on a fish lunch, and you don't have to—the top level is a sunning platform, filled with lounges and umbrellas, while, better yet, stairs and a path descend to wave-washed swimming platforms below. Lunch draws crowds even from the mainland, and dinner is also served in summer months, making this the prime spot on the island for a romantic evening. The kitchen transforms what's said to be the freshest seafood on Capri into such creations as turbot baked in a salt crust, and a spaghetti with urchin roe that's so good, you'll wonder why you've been missing out on this treat all your life. Buses from Anacapri to the Grotta Azzurra stop just outside the door, as do shuttles from the Capri Palace.

Via Gradola 4, Grotta Azzurra. www.capripalace.com. 𝄐 **081/837-1380.** Entrees 20€–40€. Daily 12:30–3:30pm and 8–11pm. No dinner mid-Oct–mid-May; closed Nov–mid-Apr.

La Canzone del Mare ★ SEAFOOD/CAPRESE   The British music-hall star Gracie Fields came to Capri in the 1930s and decided she would be the happiest woman on earth if "one small blade of grass on this wonderful, gentle place could belong to me." She eventually bought Il Fortino, a house fashioned out of a ruined fort at Marina Piccola. Over the years she carved bathing platforms out of the rocks, installed a salt-water pool shaped like the island, and built terraces and lounges that would accommodate a restaurant, an American bar, and a few guest rooms, as well as living quarters that served as an informal retreat from life at her villa in Anacapri. Fields died of pneumonia after performing on the Royal Yacht anchored offshore, but her bathing establishment and restaurant still flourish. A meal of fresh vegetables and seafood pastas is a lot more expensive than you might expect from the simple surroundings, but the atmosphere is fun and eccentric, and Fields is still a presence. Five rooms named after famous former guests (like Elizabeth Taylor) provide sleeping quarters about as close to the sea as you'll find on Capri.

Via Marina Piccola 93. www.lacanzonedelmare.com. ℰ **081/837-0104.** Entrees 20€–40€. Daily 12:30–3:30pm and 8–11pm. Closed Nov–Apr.

La Fontelina ★★ CAPRESE/SEAFOOD   Many travelers spend the winter months dreaming of a summertime lunch on the rocks at the base of the Faraglioni, where a meal comes with a swim in one of Europe's most legendary seaside settings. A fruit-loaded Sangria is the house drink, the Caprese salad—with *mozzarella di bufala* and just-off-the-vine tomatoes—is legendary, and the fish is so fresh you might think it jumped right out of the sea and onto your plate. Lunch is the only meal served, and it's necessary to reserve for one of the two seatings, at 1 and 3pm. Most guests come early and hang around long after a meal to lounge on the rocks and dip into the crystalline waters. You can reach this spot by following the Punta Tragara paths from Capri Town (see p. 682) or take a launch from and to Marina Piccola, for 6€ a person each way.

Via Faraglioni. www.fontelina-capri.com. ℰ **081/837-0845.** Entrees 20€–40€. Daily noon–7pm. Closed mid-Oct–late April.

ISCHIA ★★

30km (18 miles) NW of Capri; 42km (26 miles) SW of Naples; 20km (13 miles) W of Pozzuoli

While Capri is swathed in glamor and sophistication, Ischia (pronounced EES-kee-a) is scented with sulfur, rising off hundreds of hot springs. These wellsprings have been the island's calling card ever since ancient Romans stepped ashore and discovered the pleasures of a long, soothing soak. **Monte Epomeo,** the island's 788m-high (2,585-ft.) dormant volcano, still has enough life in it to feed the mineral hot springs, producing therapeutic muds that are the stock in trade for the island's 150 spas. As a result, Ischia is often called the "island of eternal youth," a moniker that more aptly describes the young Neapolitans who peacock around cafes and bronze themselves on the many beaches. Ischia is also known as the Isola Verde (Green Island), not, as some assume, for its verdant slopes, but for the green-tinged karst (limestone) that underlies much of the landscape. Even so, Ischia *is* refreshingly green with forests, orchards, and vineyards, and the towns along its 37km (23 miles) of shoreline are laidback, pleasant places that might lack the sophistication of Capri but for many admirers are all the better for it.

Essentials

ARRIVING Ischia's three main harbors—**Ischia Porto** (the largest), **Forio,** and **Casamicciola**—are well connected to the mainland, with most ferries leaving from Pozzuoli and Naples's two harbors (Mergellina Terminal Aliscafi and Stazione Marittima). Both **ferry** and **hydrofoil** *(aliscafi)* services are frequent in summer but slow down during the winter, when the hydrofoil is sometimes suspended because of rough seas. **Caremar** (www.caremar.it; 🕿 081/189–66690), **Medmar** (www.medmar group.it; 🕿 081/333-4411), and **SNAV** (www.snav.it; 🕿 081/878-1430) offer ferry service from Naples, Pozzuoli, Capri, and Procida to Ischia Porto and Casamicciola. **Alilauro** (www.alilauro.it; 🕿 081/497-2222) runs hydrofoils from Naples (Mergellina and Molo Beverello) to Ischia Porto and to Forio. *Note:* In high season, car access to the island is restricted and car slots are limited; if you plan to bring your car, make your reservations well in advance.

GETTING AROUND Public transportation on Ischia is excellent, with a well-organized **bus** system with **EAV** (🕿 800/0539-309 toll-free in Italy). One line circles the island in a clockwise direction (*circolare destra* marked cd), and the other counterclockwise (*circolare sinistra,* marked cs). A number of other lines crisscross the island. Tickets cost 1.50€ from a bar, tobacco shop, or news kiosk 2€ on the bus (daily pass 4.50€). The tourist office (see below) can provide a printout of the bus schedule, or you can usually find the latest one online at **www.ischia.it**.

Taxis wait at stands strategically located around the island, including Piazza degli Eroi (🕿 081/992-550) and Piazzetta San Girolamo (🕿 081/993-720) in Ischia Porto; Piazza Bagni (🕿 081/900-881) in Casamicciola; and Piazza Girardi in Lacco Ameno (🕿 081/995-113).

You can **rent motor scooters, bicycles,** and **cars** on the island from a number of agencies, including **Autonoleggio In Scooter** in Forio (www.autonoleggioinscooter.it; 🕿 081/998-513 or 320/421-8039) and **Island Center,** Via V. Di Meglio 161 in Barano (www.islandcenterischia.it; 🕿 081/902-525).

VISITOR INFORMATION The main **tourist office** (www.infoischia procida.it; 🕿 081/507-4231) is at Via Sogliuzzo 72, Ischia Porto, where you'll find free maps as well as information and brochures. In summer an information booth operates at Piazza Antica Reggia 11, Ischia Porto.

Exploring Ischia

Ischia is large as far as its neighbors in the Bay of Naples go, about 46 sq. km (18 sq. miles). Most of its main settlements—Ischia Porto,

Massive Castello Aragonese dominates Isola Ponte, a tiny island attached by causeway to Ischia.

Casamicciola, and Lacco Ameno—are on the north shore, with Forio on the west coast.

Boats call at **Ischia Porto,** with the island's one great historic landmark, the **Castello Aragonese,** in adjoining Isola Ponte. The busy harbor of Ischia Porto is a volcanic crater that was landlocked until 1854, when Bourbon King Ferdinand II had a channel cut to the sea. He created one of the most thrilling sea entrances anywhere, as ferries and yachts navigate the impossibly narrow cut and emerge into a becalmed lake surrounded by colorful waterside cafes and green hillsides carpeted with the island's distinctive white, flat-roofed houses.

Casamicciola is a famous spa town that's been devoted to the healing arts since the 17th century. Among the arthritic, gouty, and otherwise ailing travelers who found their way here, Norwegian playwright Henrik Ibsen came for a cure in the 1860s, with time off from treatments to read the works of philosopher Soren Kierkegaard and write his famous verse drama *Peer Gynt.* He's honored with a plaque in Piazza Marina, near a statue of King Vittorio Emanuele II.

Lacco Ameno is the island's most sophisticated resort. Looming just offshore is the **Fungo,** a mushroom-shaped lump of wave-sculpted tufa that is as iconic to Ischia as the Faraglioni are to Capri. The arrival of Richard Burton and Elizabeth Taylor in 1963 to shoot the barge scenes from the blockbuster film *Cleopatra* ensured the town's celebrity. The quiet little backwater became a jet-set hotspot when newspapers around the world ran paparazzi photos of the adulterous lovers yachting and swimming offshore.

Forio holds down the west coast and compensates for its lack of beauty with spectacular stretches of sand, a lively resort scene, and some extremely palatable wines from the surrounding vineyards.

Wherever you settle, you won't be too far from the sights. A road follows the coast around the island, and buses make it easy to get from one town to the other.

Castello Aragonese (Aragonese Castle) ★★★ HISTORIC SITE Greeks settled this rocky islet as early as the 5th century B.C., building watchtowers to keep an eye on enemy fleets. The fortifications atop 91m (300-ft.) cliffs have been a plum for invaders ever since, from ancient Neapolitans and Romans to Goths to Normans. King of Naples Alfonso I gave the walled complex its present form in the mid-15th century as a defense against pirate raids, shoring up watchtowers and walls and installing churches, terraces, and squares that give the walled compound a village-like air. At one time some 17,000 people sheltered within the walls, among them nuns, monks, and soldiers. The British shelled the compound during the Napoleonic Wars, and did a pretty good job of it, though enough remains to give an idea of the onetime might of the citadel. Many churches still stand, in various states of repair. The frescoed crypt is about all that remains of the **Cattedrale dell'Assunta,** while the **Chiesa dell'Immaculata** and hexagonal **San Pietro a Pantaniello** are fairly intact. A somber if not downright macabre presence is the small **Cimitero delle Monache Clarisse,** attached to the island's convent. When the inhabitants breathed their last, they were left sitting on stone chairs as a reminder of what becomes of our earthly presence—the spooky-looking seating arrangement is still in place, minus the bones.

You can ponder all this as your make a circuit of the breezy ramparts, a vertigo-inducing lookout hundreds of feet above the crashing waves. An elevator whisks visitors up to the castle entrance, though the climb up the stairs and ramps provides a more authentic experience.

Piazzale Aragonese, Ischia Ponte. www.castelloaragoneseischia.com. ✆ **081/992-834.** 10€ adults, 6€ youth 10–14; free for children 9 and under. Daily 9am–sunset.

Villa La Mortella ★★ GARDEN Sir William Walton (1902–1983), one of the greatest English composers of the 20th century, and his Argentine wife Susana Walton (1926–2010) settled on Ischia in 1949. Walton found the peace and light conducive to composition, and Susana became enchanted with the idea of creating a garden at their home, La Mortella (the Myrtles) on the west side of the Monte Vico promontory outside

Forio. She worked with the great landscape designer Russell Page to landscape the Valley Garden, filling it with rare Mediterranean and South American species, great sweeps of orchids and other flowers, and fountains, ponds, and brooks. Walton could control the valves from his study and turned off the jets when the gurgling disturbed him. Lady Walton designed the sunny, view-filled Hill Garden as a tribute to her husband, working in the soil herself well into her later years. The exotic romance of the gardens are an apt tribute to the Waltons, who married just a few months after meeting in Buenos Aires; in a fit of spite, the bride's father spent his daughter's entire dowry on the Champagne served at the wedding reception. It's customary on a walk along the garden paths to wave at the palms, following Lady Walton's belief that "You have to wave at them when you go by because they think you haven't paid attention."

Via Francesco Calise 39. www.lamortella.it. ℂ **081/986-220.** 12€ adults, 10€ seniors and ages 12–18, 6€ children 5–11. Apr–Oct Tues, Thurs, and Sat–Sun 9am–7pm.

Beaches

Ischia has a commodity that's the envy of Capri and towns along the Amalfi Coast: long stretches of sand. Beach-going is especially pleasant in May and September, but in the dog days of summer the sands are jam-packed with a mixed crowd of islanders, day-tripping Neapolitans, and Germans and Russians drawn to Ischia by the combined allure of thermal baths and beaches. If you're staying on the east coast in or near Ischia Porto or Ischia Ponte, your best bet is **Spiaggia dei Pescatori ★,** where local fishermen beach their boats; it's just west of the Aragonese Castle. On the north coast, the scenic beach on the bay of **San Montano ★★** is tucked onto the flanks of the promontory of Monte Vico near Laco Ammeno. On the west coast, south of Forio, **Spiaggia Citara ★★** has hot mineral springs that flow out to sea at its southern edge. On the south coast, the island's most beautiful beach is 2km/1¼ mile-long **Spiaggia dei Maronti ★★★.** Also on the south coast, just east of the little village of Sant'Angelo, is so-called **Fumarole beach,** where hot underground vapors heat the sand to such high temperatures that islanders come to bury chicken and fish in aluminum foil, splashing around a bit as they wait for their food to cook. The sands also provide welcome relief to arthritis sufferers, who plonk down and let the heat penetrate their aching joints. Just offshore, geysers bubble up to create natural hot-tub-like pools. A flotilla of little boats ferry passengers from the town marina to this otherworldly seascape, about 5€ each way; the pools are also easy to reach on a seaside path.

Spas & Thermo-Mineral Baths

Ischia's *terme,* or thermal baths, have been popular ever since ancient Greeks soaked their weary bones in the natural hot springs. Elaborate thermal parks are top among the island's many attractions. Most facilities offer slightly lower rates after midafternoon, so opt for a late entrance and a sunset soak. They also offer multi-day passes, for those who want to spend most of their time on Ischia quite literally in hot water.

Parco Termale Castiglione ★★

Low-key is not quite the right word for a place that splashes out with 10 pools, but they're tucked into tastefully designed seaside terraces laced with all sorts of quiet nooks and crannies. If the pool temperatures get to be a bit too relaxing—they range from 82° to 104°F (28°–40°C)—a stone jetty is poised for a dip in the sea. The absence of a beach, and the serious mud and thermal treatments, makes the park more popular with a sedate crowd than it is with families, so screaming kids aren't likely to disturb the peace.

Ischia has long been known for its thermal baths, such as this garden pool at Parco Termale Negombo.

Shore road between Ischia Porto and Casamicciola. www.termecastiglione.it. ✆ **081/982-551.** 28€ a day, 24€ after 1pm, 9€ children 2–12; 2€ more in Aug. Mid-Apr–Oct 9am–7pm.

Parco Termale Giardini Poseidon ★

Everything about Ischia's largest spa is over the top, with 22 pools, a large private beach, tropical gardens, and several restaurants. The kitsch runs high, including toga-bedecked statues, yet it's hard not to feel like a figure of ancient legend in the complex's nicest feature, an eons-old natural thermal cave etched out of a cliff. It's a toss-up who enjoys these surroundings more, Germans and their *kinder* or Italian families, so be prepared for a crowd.

Via Giovanni Mazzella, Citara Beach, near Forio. www.giardiniposeidon.it. ✆ **081/908-7111.** 33€ a day (35€ July–Aug), 28€ after 1pm (30€ July–Aug), 16.50€ children 4–11 (17.50€ July–Aug). Mid-Apr–Oct, daily 9am–7pm.

Parco Termale Negombo ★★★

If you have time and/or inclination to visit only one thermal establishment on Ischia, make it this delightful spot on the island's most picturesque cove, San Montano. Gorgeous gardens, laid out by botanist Duke Luigi Camerini, surround 12 pools and facilities that include saunas, steam rooms, and massage cabins. While waterfalls and luxuriant plantings provide a transporting getaway atmosphere, just as alluring is the beach of fine sand. You could happily spend a day traipsing back and forth between the warm pools and the refreshing sea, with some naptime in the shade next to one of the garden's beautiful, albeit ersatz, waterfalls.

San Montano beach, on the promontory of Monte Vico near Lacco Ameno. www.negombo.it. ℂ **081/986-152.** 33€, 26€ after 1:30pm, 22€ after 3:30pm; children less than 4½ ft. and more than 3¼ ft. tall, 22€, 20€ after 12:30pm, 18€ after 3pm. Late Apr–mid-Oct, daily 8:30am–7pm.

Where to Stay & Eat on Ischia

Albergo Il Monastero ★★ The labyrinth of stone-walled, arched passageways, courtyards, and arbor-shaded seaside terraces of this former monastery are enticing in themselves, all the more so since the old premises are set within Ischia's spectacular **Castello Aragonese** (p. 697). Whitewashed guest rooms carved out of former monks' cells are spacious and soberly stylish, with handsome furnishings and knockout sea views from most. A huge panoramic terrace atop the castle walls is the setting for breakfast and delicious dinners, fed by produce from the hotel's garden. *Note:* The hotel is only accessible by foot, and accommodations are reached by what can seem like endless staircases.

Castello Aragonese. www.albergoilmonastero.it. ℂ **081/992-435.** 20 units. 105€–145€ double. Rates include breakfast. Closed mid-Oct–mid-Apr. **Amenities:** Restaurant; Wi-Fi (free).

La Brocca ★★ SEAFOOD Lacco Ameno might be the toniest town on the island, but simple old-time ways still hold sway at this no-frills spot facing the sea and Il Fungo. The friendly family could be the town's goodwill ambassadors as they rush between the dining room and terrace to serve straightforward and delicious preparations of fresh-off-the boat seafood. Any of the pastas *alla pescatora* (with seafood), washed down with a chilled carafe of the house white, deliver a memorable feast.

Via Roma 24, Lacco Ameno. ℂ **081/900-051.** Entrees 8€–15€. Daily noon–2:30pm and 7:30–9:30pm.

Da Ciccio ★★ SEAFOOD A seat on the little terrace in front of a half-century-old island favorite comes with killer views of the Aragonese Castle (p. 698). That's about as showy as it gets at this little hole in the wall, where Ciccio and son Bruno focus on fresh seafood in memorably delicious preparations: thick mussel soup is steeped with mountain herbs and topped with fried bread; squid is stuffed with bread crumbs, raisins, and chopped fish; and linguine is laden with clams.

Via Luigi Mazzella 32, Ischia Ponte. ℂ **081/991-686.** Entrees 10€–15€. Wed–Mon noon–2:30pm and 7–11pm.

Hotel della Baia ★★ At this delightful little getaway tucked onto the myrtle-clad hillside above San Montano Bay, a lounge is shaded by lime trees, and all the simple-chic rooms open to bougainvillea-filled terraces. Just down the road are two of the island's best places to swim and lounge, a sandy beach in a beautiful cove and **Negombo,** the nicest of Ischia's thermal parks (p. 699).

San Montano beach, on the Monte Vico promontory, near Lacco Ameno. hoteldellabaia.negombo.it. © **081/986-150.** 16 units. 100€–125€ double. Rates include breakfast. **Amenities:** Bar; pool; beach; Wi-Fi (free).

Mezzatorre Resort & Spa ★★★ A former fortress at the end of a rocky promontory provides a sense of privileged escape. Survey the sea and 17 acres of pine-scented gardens from beautifully appointed rooms in the dark-red 15th-century watchtower. All of the airy, view-filled accommodations are spectacular, including spacious quarters in modern annexes scattered among the gardens, stylishly done in bright Mediterranean color schemes and a chic mix of antiques and contemporary pieces. Thermal pools tucked onto seaside terraces, a hot springs and spa, and a private beach ensure you can partake of a wellness regimen without ever leaving the property.

Via Mezzatorre, Forio. www.mezzatorre.it. © **081/986-111.** 60 units. 220€–550€ double. Rates include breakfast. Free parking. Closed Nov–Apr. **Amenities:** 2 restaurants; bar; babysitting; concierge; health club; 3 pools; room service; spa; outdoor tennis courts; Wi-Fi (free).

14

BASILICATA
& PUGLIA

By Stephen Brewer

S outh of Naples, the Mezzogiorno begins in earnest. The name, which literally means "midday," evokes rugged, sun-baked landscapes. But that doesn't begin to describe the riches you'll discover in the instep and heel of the Italian boot, or, officially, Basilicata and Puglia. Some of Italy's great architectural marvels are here, from the *sassi* cave dwellings in Matera to the fantastical cone-shaped *trulli* in Alberobello, not to mention the honey-colored baroque churches and palaces of Lecce.

Outside these towns and cities, the landscapes are a sweep of groves, orchards, vineyards, and fields, often edged by beaches. It's estimated that more than 6 million olive trees carpet the southeast, yielding almost half the country's oil production, and almost any view is likely to take in gnarled trunks growing out of red earth. Where there's good olive oil, there's good wine and good food. The region's simple but delicious *cucina povera* (peasant cooking) will nicely fuel your explorations—and you'll never think of a fava bean with indifference again.

DON'T LEAVE BASILICATA & PUGLIA WITHOUT . . .

Climbing Through Matera. One of the oldest continually inhabited places on earth, Matera is a vertical maze of lanes and staircases connecting hill-clinging neighborhoods of *sassi* cave dwellings.

Gawking At The *Trulli*. Hundreds of these round, conical roofed houses line winding lanes in Alberobello, creating a fantasy-like townscape.

Being Dazzled by the White Cities. In the beautiful Valle d'Itria, the hill towns of Cisternino Locrotondo, Martina Franca, Ostuni, and Ceglie Messapica are so glaringly bright you'll need sunglasses while wandering through their labyrinthine streets.

Going For Baroque In Lecce. The city is a showplace of extravagance from the 17th-century, when craftsmen carved saints and sinners, gods and goddesses, and entire scenes into limestone as if it were butter.

MATERA ★★

254km (158 miles) SE of Naples, 73km (44 miles) S of Bari, 136km (82 miles) NE of Brindisi

In Matera, it's all about caves: A vast honeycomb of thousands of caverns riddling the chalk cliffs above the gorge of the Gravina River. It's

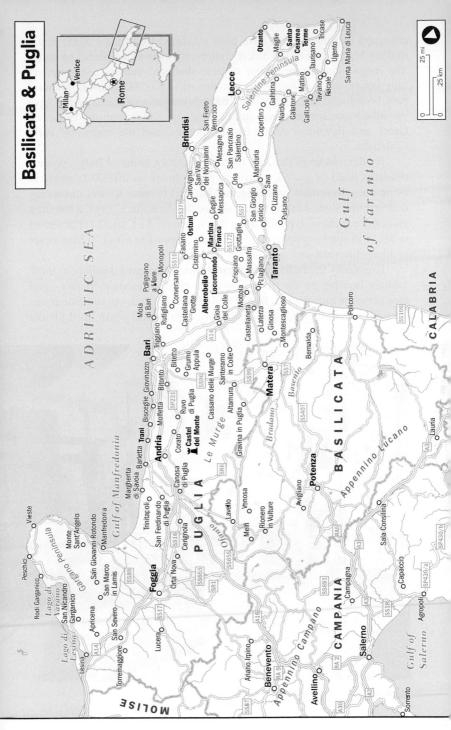

Basilicata & Puglia

Milan
Venice
Rome

ADRIATIC SEA

Gulf of Manfredonia

Gulf of Taranto

Gulf of Salerno

MOLISE

CAMPANIA

PUGLIA

BASILICATA

CALABRIA

Appennino Lucano

Appennino Campano

Le Murge

Gargano Peninsula

Salentine Peninsula

Lago di Varano
Lago di Lesina

Ofanto
Bradano
Basento

Peschici
Vieste
Rodi Garganico
San Nicandro Garganico
Apricena
San Marco in Lamis
San Giovanni Rotondo
Monte Sant'Angelo
Manfredonia
Lesina
Torremaggiore
San Severo
Lucera
Foggia
Orta Nova
Cerignola
Trinitapoli
San Ferdinando di Puglia
Margherita di Savoia
Barletta
Trani
Andria
Canosa di Puglia
Corato
Castel del Monte
Ruvo di Puglia
Molfetta
Bisceglie
Giovinazzo
Bitonto
Bari
Triggiano
Mola di Bari
Polignano a Mare
Monopoli
Conversano
Castellana Grotte
Rutigliano
Bitetto
Grumo Appula
Cassano delle Murge
Santeramo in Colle
Altamura
Gravina in Puglia
Gioia del Colle
Castellaneta
Laterza
Ginosa
Montescaglioso
Matera
Bernalda
Policoro
Pisticci
Pomarico
Ferrandina
Potenza
Avigliano
Venosa
Lavello
Melfi
Rionero in Vulture
Lauria
Sala Consilina
Capaccio
Agropoli
Sorrento
Salerno
Avellino
Benevento
Ariano Irpino
Campagna
Cisternino
Ostuni
Fasano
Alberobello
Locorotondo
Martina Franca
Ceglie Messapica
Grottaglie
San Giorgio Ionico
Crispiano
Massafra
Mottola
Pelagano
Taranto
Pulsano
Lizzano
Sava
Manduria
Oria
San Pancrazio Salentino
Mesagne
San Vito dei Normanni
Carovigno
Brindisi
San Pietro Vernotico
San Pietro
Oria
Squinzano
Copertino
Nardò
Galatone
Galatina
Gallipoli
Sannicola
Santa Maria di Leuca
Ugento
Racale
Taviano
Matino
Tricase
Tiricase
Casarano
Maglie
Otranto
Santa Cesarea Terme
Lecce

25 mi
25 km

A14
A16
A3
SS16
SS89
SS17
SS655
SS665
SR1
SS407
SS658
SS96
SS99
SS172
SS7
SR6
RA5
SS106
SS407
SS91
SS18
SP430/b
SP430/a
RA2
RA9
A30
SS87
SS379
SP231

estimated that these caves have been inhabited for at least 9,000 years, making Matera one of the oldest continuously inhabited places on earth. The rugged landscapes appear to have sheltered hunters and gatherers long before then, as well—the remains of a 150,000-year-old hominid have been found in a nearby cave. Excavations around the cathedral have unearthed successive waves of occupation: 3,000-year-old ceramics, Greek and Byzantine coins, Roman houses, and the coffins of early Christians.

By the middle of the 20th century, however, some of Italy's poorest residents lived in Matera's caves, with as many as 20,000 troglodytes eking out a miserable existence in what had become a vast, unsanitary underground slum. Man and beast shared the dank, dark caves, a breeding ground for malaria, typhoid, and other diseases. As Carlo Levi observed in his 1945 autobiographical novel *Christ Stopped at Eboli,* "I have never in all my life seen such a picture of poverty."

Eventually the Italian government moved the cave dwellers to more sanitary housing on the ridge above the cliffs in modern Matera—and then came the turn-around. By the mid-1980s, the rock-cut settlement was attracting attention for its unique beauty, a delightful warm-hued jumble

Interior of a traditional cave house in Matera.

of steep "streets" and meandering staircases running right over the rooftops of underlying houses. Matera is so richly evocative of ancient Mediterranean civilization that it's been the location for many biblical films, most famously Pier Paolo Passolini's *The Gospel According to St. Matthew* (1964) and Mel Gibson's *The Passion of the Christ* (2004).

Many restaurants have opened in the caves (one even offers Pasta Mel Gibson, a variation of the town's peasant classic with chili peppers and fried breadcrumbs). Other rock dwellings have been converted to hotels, where guests can enjoy the thrill of sleeping in a cave without having to share quarters with a donkey. This unique cave city is now a UNESCO World Heritage site, and last year Matera was in the spotlight as a European Capital of Culture. You can get a good sense of Matera and see the main sights in a full day, and the city makes a good overnight on the circuit south from Naples and the Amalfi Coast into Puglia.

Essentials

ARRIVING If you're arriving in the region by **air,** the closest airports are in Bari and Brindisi (information for both can be found at www.aeroporti dipuglia.it). **Pugliairbus** (www.aeroportidipuglia.it) makes hourly trips between Bari airport and Matera throughout the day, and **SITA Sud** (www.sitasudtrasporti.it; *✆* **080/790-111**) buses make 6 trips a day; travel time is 75 minutes. Matera is 73km (44 miles) south of Bari via SP236; from Brindisi, it's 136km (82 miles) northeast via E90 and SS7.

Trains from Rome and other major Italian cities stop at Bari; to continue to Matera, switch to the narrow-gauge train operated by **Ferrovie Appulo Lucane** (**FAL**; ferrovieappulolucane.it), which runs every 1 to 2 hours (no service Sun) and takes about 1½ hours. Trains arrive at Matera Centrale station, with buses running down to the *sassi* from there.

If you're traveling to Matera from Naples, the easiest way is **by car,** following the A3 south, then the E847 east through Potenza; the drive takes a little more than 2 hours. **Bus** service between Naples and Matera, run by Marino (www.marinobus.it; *✆* **080/3112335**), takes 4½ hours, with six buses a day. About a dozen **trains** (www.trenitalia.com) make the 3- to 4-hour run daily between Naples and the nearby town of Ferrandina, where you can catch a bus to Matera (fare around 3€).

GETTING AROUND The only easy way to get around Matera is **on foot,** and be prepared for a lot of climbing. Most of the *sassi* district is closed to car traffic; if you're arriving by car, make arrangements in advance with your hotel for arrival and parking. Most hotels have agreements with lots and garages in the modern town where you can park for a slight discount of about 12€ a day, and garages will usually drop you off and pick up at a point close to your hotel for about 5€. It's possible to drive to the bottom of Sasso Barisano and continue along Via Madonna delle Virtù into the bottom of Sasso Caveoso, though this is encouraged only to drop off bags, plus your hotel must supply your license plate number to the police in advance; even at that it's best to avoid this hair-raising trip and leave the car above. The dispatch number for **Matera taxi** is ✆ **334348.**

VISITOR INFORMATION Matera has no government-run tourist office. Private agencies abound, but these are in business to sell you expensive walking tours of the *sassi* rather than provide information. Your hotel will most likely provide you with a map. A good online resource is **www. sassiweb.it.** For excellent background on Matera, step into **Casa Noha,** Recinto Cavone 9 (www.fondoambiente.it/luoghi/casa-noha; ✆ **0835/335-452**), where visual projections onto cave walls and a good soundtrack trace the city's history and its unique social and architectural heritage; the staff can also set you up with a free walking-tour app. It's open April through October 9am to 7pm, 10am to 6pm the rest of the year (closed late January and February); admission is 6€, 2€ ages 6–18.

Exploring Matera

Matera is essentially divided into three districts. At the top of the ridge is the center of the modern town, or **Civita,** where the Duomo stands amid squares and palaces. Below spread the *sassi* (literally, "stones"), the cliff-hugging districts of cave dwellings. **Sasso Barisano** is to the north and **Sasso Caveoso** to the south, though the lanes and alleyways of one meander into the lanes and alleyways of the other.

The best way to appreciate the *sassi* is to plunge in and wander, following one of the well-marked stone staircases off Via Duomo in the Civita. At the foot of the cliff in each *sasso* is one street with a cluster of shops and cafes—in Sasso Barisano it's **Via dei Fiorentino,** in Sasso Caveoso, **Via Bruno Buozzi.** No need to rush down to these, though. Along the way are wonky staircases, blind alleys, crumbling stone court-yards with a profusion of greenery, and many remarkable vistas.

Trying to find a specific address in the *sassi* can be challenging, but a few sights are worth seeking out. The **Casa-Grotta di Vico Solitario ★,** off Via Bruno Buozzi in Sasso Caveoso (www.casagrotta.it; ✆ **0835/310118**), re-creates a dwelling from the 1950s, when the government cleared out the *sassi* and moved residents up to modern Matera. The crude authentic furnishings include a ridiculously high bed that kept occupants well off the frigid stone floor and provided storage space beneath. It's not as filthy as it must have been when residents shared the space with pigs and donkeys, but accompanying film footage conveys the district's former squalor. The house is usually open daily 9:30am to 9pm; admission is 3€. Also in Sasso Caveoso is another relic of the district's past: the ancient underground passages of **La Racolte delle Acque ★** (www.laraccoltadelle

Overlooking the Civita, or medieval heart of Matera.

acquematera.it; © **328/209-9219;** enter at Via Purgatorio Vecchio), which carried the city's often-unhealthy water supply, channeling rainwater collected from streets and roofs into deep cisterns. They're open daily April through October, 10am to 1pm and 2 to 7pm; November through March, they're open Saturday and Sunday only, 10am to 1pm and 4 to 8pm. Admission is 3€.

One of Matera's best-preserved rock church complexes, **Santa Luccia alle Malve ★★,** in Sasso Caveoso, © **327/9800–3776**) provided refuge for monks fleeing 8th-century persecution in the Middle East; it later became a convent for Benedictine nuns, who in the 13th century frescoed the caves in colorful scenes that include a breastfeeding Madonna. The church is open daily, 10am to 7pm; admission is 3€. **Madonna delle Virtù e San Nicola dei Greci ★★,** in Sasso Barisano on Via Madonna delle Virtù (© **0835/319-825**), is a maze of 10th- and 11th-century frescoed chapels and living quarters that held a community of nuns on one level and monks on another; at one point the low-slung caverns open to an almost majestic apse with a domed ceiling. The complex is open daily, June through September 10am to 8pm; October, April, and May 10am to

1:30pm and 3 to 6pm; and November through March 10am to 1:30pm; admission is 5€.

Some of the best views of the *sassi* are from the **Parco della Murgia Materana** ★ (www.parco murgia.it), along the gorge of the Gravina River just below town. High ground affords sweeping views, while the ravines are riddled with caves that have been used as churches, stables, and shepherds' shelters. Enter the park off Via Madonna delle Virtù.

Duomo ★ CHURCH The residents of the *sassi* are never out of sight of the city's soaring cathedral, completed in 1270 on high ground at the side of the cliff just above them. A wealth of carvings on the facade deliver a morality lesson to the faithful: A mermaid warns of the passions likely to steer us off a path of righteousness; an eagle is poised to devour meeker animals, just as we are always prey to sin;

Exterior of a house carved in tufa stone in Matera's *sassi* district.

the Archangel Michael battles the dragon (representing the forces of evil) before an audience of the town's medieval elite. Similarly moralistic frescoes once covered the interior; most were destroyed in many renovations, but a terrifying 13th-century *Last Judgment* remains, to the right of the entrance. Archangel Michael is here too, wielding his sword in hell, where serpents attack the damned—among them popes, monks, and kings, proof that no one escapes the final judgment. An antidote is the utterly charming 16th-century nativity scene in a side chapel, where shepherds and their flocks are set against a re-creation of Matera, looking just like it does today—just the sort of place where Christ would be born.

Piazza del Duomo. Free (audioguide 2€). Daily 9am–7pm.

Where to Stay in Matera

Many Materani have converted caves into rentals, and many of them are available through Airbnb (www.airbnb.com). Typical of the unique Sassi accommodations available is the view-filled double room with a balcony that Marghertia Albanese rents near her delightful jewelry shop, **Arterego**, at Via Rosario 48 (www.arterego.it; © **338/295-5845**).

Alle Malve Bed & Breakfast ★ No one says a cave dwelling can't have a crisp, chipper vibe, and this ancient house that's partly dug into the hillside at the foot of Sassi Caveoso is downright cheerful. Contemporary touches in the bright lounge and guest rooms include a floating staircase, a sunken sitting area in front of a crackling fire, and large, state-of-the-art bathrooms. Papevero is an especially appealing room, with high wooden ceilings and a large terrace.

Via Bruno Buozzi 102. www.allemalve.com. ℂ **0835/312-816.** 5 units. Doubles from 65€. Rates include breakfast. **Amenities:** Wi-Fi (free).

Sextantio le Grotto della Civica ★★ If the Flintstones had hired a big-name decorator, they might have been treated to a design-magazine-worthy abode like these luxurious cave sanctuaries overlooking the Gravina River gorge at the edge of Matera. Furnishings are rustic chic, with authentically old pieces scattered around cavernous spaces where soft light flickers off stone walls. Luxuries include freestanding tubs, fireplaces, and (in many rooms) terraces overlooking the sweep of green, rock-studded countryside. The attempt to re-create the look of a primitive cave dwelling without sacrificing creature comforts can seem a bit forced, but it's hard to quibble with the luxury of stepping out of bed onto a cave floor heated from beneath. Breakfast, drinks, and some meals are served in an ancient church hewn out of the rock.

Via Civita 28. legrottedellacivita.sextantio.it. ℂ **0835/332-744.** 20 units. 150€–350€ double. Rates include breakfast. **Amenities:** Bar; cafe; Wi-Fi (free).

Fra I Sassi Residence ★★★ Of the many cave hotels in Matera, this beautiful enclave at the bottom of Sasso Barisano is one of the most welcoming. These are caves with a view, where well-designed and comfortably furnished rooms (some with sunken tubs) open onto a bright terrace—a

---

Cave Art

The Palazzo Pomarici is a wonder in itself, a 16th-century palace with frescoed salons and—since it sits in the middle of the *sassi*—many cave rooms. Today it's the evocative setting of the **Museum of Contemporary Sculpture Matera (MUSMA),** displaying works by an international roster of artists. The museum is in Sasso Caveoso on Via San Giacomo (www.musma.it; ℂ **0835/330-582;** admission 5€; open daily Apr–Sept 10am–8pm; Oct–Mar 10am–6pm). Meanwhile, in the Civita on Piazzetta Giovanni Pascoli, the **Museo Nazionale d'Arte Medievale e Moderna della Basilicata** (www.visitmatera.it/palazzo-lanfranchi. html; ℂ **0835/256-2540)** displays, among various paintings and religious objects, colorful paintings by artist and political activist Carlo Levi (1902–1975), who was exiled to this region in the 1930s for his anti-fascist activities. Levi's autobiographical novel, *Christ Stopped at Eboli,* brought the region's poverty and squalid living conditions to world attention, and his hard-hitting paintings here capture the hardships of peasant life in the *sassi.* The museum is open daily 9am to 8pm (Wed 11am–8pm); admission is 3€.

front-row seat for a spectacular vista of dwellings clinging to the surrounding hillsides. Welcoming outdoor spaces are well supplied with loungers, the perfect perch for a drink, a nap, or just soaking in the views. The breakfast room does double duty as a bar/cafe.

Via D'Addozio 102. www.fraisassiresidence.com. 𝄞 **0835/336-020.** 9 units, plus 8-bed hostel. 125€–140€ double; hostel rates on request. Rates include breakfast. **Amenities:** Bar; Wi-Fi (free).

San Giorgio Hotel ★★   You will feel like a bona fide troglodyte—albeit a high-living one—in one of these well-equipped dwellings scattered throughout Sassi Barisano. Most have one or two bedrooms, and many are multilevel and, given their unusual settings, rich in arches, vaults, and other architectural details, including fireplaces and terraces in some. An accommodating staff serves breakfast in a pleasant room in the main house.

Via Fiorentini 259. www.sangiorgio.matera.it. 𝄞 **0835/334-583.** 11 units. 120€–210€. **Amenities:** Wi-Fi (free).

Where to Eat in Matera

Panifico Perone il Forno di Gennaro, Via Nazionale 52 (www.ilfornodi gennaro.com; 𝄞 **0835/385-656**) is a long-standing Matera institution; it moved out of the Sassi into the new town 60 years ago but still bakes its delicious bread and focaccia in wood-fired ovens. **Pasticceria Schuma,** near the Duomo at Via XX Settembre 10 (www.pasticceriaschiuma.com; 𝄞 **0835/331-862**) is another venerable favorite, serving snacks and sandwiches alongside an irresistible selection of cakes and pastries.

La Talpa ★★ BASILICATESE   Matera's caves don't get any more inviting than these snug, white-walled rooms hung with old cooking implements and filled with cozy, gingham-topped tables. The homey setting is suited for such local dishes as *purea di fave con cicorielle di campo* (broad bean puree with chicory) or *cavatelli* with chickpea puree, arugula, porcini mushrooms, and tomatoes. Lamb and veal are grilled to perfection, and pizzas emerge from a wood oven at the back of the cave.

Via dei Fiorentini 167. www.latalparistorante.it. 𝄞 **0835/335-086.** Entrees 9€–18€. Wed–Mon 7:30pm–midnight, Sun also noon–4pm.

Le Botteghe ★★ PUGLIAN   Partly dug out of a cave and opening to a bright square in Sasso Barisano, this restaurant is a refined setting for cooking that whole-heartedly presents the best of local cuisine. You will be encouraged to have a full meal, and it would be a shame not to do so. Try the *orecchiette al Tegamino,* ear-shaped pasta baked with ham, cheese, and tomatoes, or any of the local pastas, then move on to the house specialty, expertly grilled meat. The house-baked bread is delicious.

Piazza San Pietro Barisano. www.lebotteghematera.it. 𝄞 **0835/344-072.** Entrees 10€–22€. Sat–Mon 1–2:30pm and 8–11pm, Tues–Fri 8–11pm.

Oi Mari ★ BASILICATESE/NEAPOLITAN   This convivial spot in Sasso Barisano took its name from a famous Neapolitan serenade—and that's not the only way in which this cheery candlelit cave takes its inspiration from Naples. The pizzas are the best in town, filling the cavernous space nightly with eager enthusiasts. No need to settle for pizza alone, though. You can nicely stretch out a meal with heaping platters of *antipasto di mare,* with octopus, squid, and *baccala,* or choose from a wide array of seafood pastas and meat dishes.

Via dei Fiorentini 66. www.oimari.it. ℰ **0835/346-121.** Entrees 8€–18€. Mon–Tues and Thurs–Fri 7:30pm–midnight; Sat–Sun 12:30–3pm and 7:30pm–midnight.

Trattoria Caveosa ★ BASILICATESE   Bold contemporary art decorates this convivial multilevel cave in the same-named *sasso* neighborhood, but when it comes to food, it's all about old-fashioned cuisine—wholesome, straightforward preparations that don't pretend to be anything other than *cucina povera,* poor man's grub. Fresh local produce shows up in dishes like *strascinate con rape mollica fritta,* pasta topped with broccoli, chili peppers, and breadcrumbs, or lamb fried with onions, tomatoes, mushrooms, and wild onions.

Via Bruno Buozzi 21. www.ristorantedelcaveoso.it. ℰ **0835/312-374.** Entrees 6€–12€. Thurs–Tues 12:30–3pm and 7:30–11pm.

TRANI ★★

85km (51 miles) N of Matera

This little seaside city would bring a smile to the face of the most hardened traveler. A once-thriving medieval seaport, Trani has twisting lanes and airy piazzas lined with palaces and churches, all hewn from golden limestone that glows with just a tinge of pink when the sun hits it. Sooner or later the maze untangles alongside the shimmering blue waters of the Adriatic, where, from certain angles, one of the most dramatic cathedrals in Italy seems to rise right out of the waves. Trani is also a jumping-off point for Frederick II's remarkable **Castel del Monte** to the west and the beautiful **Gargano peninsula** to the north.

Essentials

ARRIVING   Trani is just off the A14 autostrada, which follows the Adriatic coast between Bari and Rimini. If you're driving from Matera, head north to Altamura, then follow signs through Corato to Trani from there. Trani is anywhere from 4½ to 8 hours by **train** from Rome, depending on routing and changes; for schedules and tickets, go to www.trenitalia.com.

The closest airports are in Bari and Brindisi; information for both can be found at www.aeroportidipuglia.it.

GETTING AROUND   You'll want to stash the car as soon as possible and navigate the old city on foot. Head toward the seafront, where you'll find park-and-display parking next to the Duomo and Castello Svevo.

VISITOR INFORMATION   Visit **www.viaggiareinpuglia.it** for information about the region. Trani has a **tourist office** at Piazza Trieste 10 (✆ **0883/ 588-830**). On the Gargano peninsula, you'll find tourist offices at Vieste (Piazza J.F. Kennedy, ✆ **0884/708-806**) and Peschici (Via Magenta 3, ✆ **0884/915-362**).

Exploring Trani

For most of Trani's history, travelers approached the city by sea. Today you'll likely come into town through the scruffy outskirts sprawling across the flat Puglian plain, but you'll still want to head to the port. The enormous 13th-century Castello Svevo along the shoreline is proof of Trani's onetime power, street names like Via Synagoga are reminders of a large medieval Jewish population, and Via Cambio (Street of the Moneychangers) testifies to Trani's role as a major Mediterranean trading center. During the Crusades, Trani was an embarkation port for Christian forces heading to the Middle East; soldiers of the elite Knights Templar order received blessings in the courtyard of the church of Ogisanti, on Via Ogisanti—walk past to see its splendidly medieval exterior.

Duomo ★★   For your first glimpse of this gleaming Romanesque-style masterwork, head for the east side of Trani harbor: You'll see the **campanile** (bell tower) stretching 59m-high (194-ft.) toward the sky, while the church's sheer limestone walls seem to be rooted not in the ground but in the sea. This dramatic union of sea and sky lifts the spirit—an effect no doubt intended by the architects and craftsmen who began work in 1097. Their singular mission was to outdo Bari, their neighbor just down the coast, which had just snatched the relics of St. Nicholas (see box p. 716) and was building a basilica to house them, sure to draw crowds of pilgrims. Trani had a new saint of its own to promote, San Nicola Pellegrino (St. Nicholas the Pilgrim), an extremely pious Greek shepherd boy who, after a long sea voyage, collapsed and died from exhaustion in front of the 7th-century church of Santa Maria, which formerly occupied this site. (Nicola reputedly spent all his waking hours continually reciting the phrase "Kyrie Eleison"—"Lord, have mercy"—a habit that may have annoyed his companions but nevertheless won him almost instant sainthood). The foundations of the Santa Maria church are still in the crypt, where the saint's tomb rests among a forest of columns. The main church above is a soaring display of arches, columns, and vaults, all luminously fashioned from golden limestone. The heavy bronze doors were created by Barisano da Trani, whose most famous work is the doors in Monreale outside Palermo (see p. 761). The intricate panels depict familiar biblical figures as well as dragons, lions, archers, and jugglers—look for the panel where the artist portrays himself, humbly at the feet of San Nicola.

Piazza Duomo 9. www.cattedraletrani.it. ✆ **0883/500-293.** Free. Daily 9:30–12:30pm and 3:30–7pm (closes at 6pm Nov–Mar), Sun 4–8:30pm (closes 8pm Nov–Mar).

One of the eight octagonal towers in Castel del Monte, Trani.

AROUND TRANI

Castel del Monte ★★ HISTORIC SITE   Topping a small mount above the fertile Puglian plains, this majestic castle comes into sight from miles away, just as the enlightened Frederick II, Holy Roman Emperor and King of Sicily, intended when he ordered it built in 1237. The distinctive octagonal shape may look familiar—it's reproduced on every 1-cent euro printed in Italy. What's not clear, however, is what this castle was built for. It has no moat or circuit of walls, so it wouldn't have been practical for defense, despite the strategic hilltop position (certainly no enemy could approach without being spotted). Frederick's passion for science and mathematics is reflected in the precision of the octagonal shape with eight octagonal towers, which blend Islamic and Gothic influences. Large trapezoidal rooms on two floors are warmed by fireplaces, implying a certain degree of luxury—was the castle meant for entertaining or as a hunting lodge? A few fragments of mosaics, frescoes, and marble work remain, and it's known that an ingenious plumbing system fed by rainwater supplied baths and latrines. Frederick's successors converted the castle to a prison, where poor souls languished in cold chambers. To visit Castel del Monte from Trani, head southwest for 12km (7 miles) on SP130 to

Bari: A Visit to Santa Claus

A 4th-century bishop of Myra, Turkey, St. Nicholas—whose gift-giving habits gave rise to the Santa Claus tradition—lay at peace in his hometown until 1076, when pirates stole his bones and brought them to Bari, now the largest city in Puglia. Nicholas was a big prize, a top draw for pilgrims from all over Christendom, and Bari zealously built the almost fortress-like twin-towered **basilica of San Nicola** to house him. St. Nick's feast day, December 6, is a big event in Bari, especially the ceremony in which a flask is lowered into the crypt to extract a miraculous liquid said to be emitted by the saint's remains (they even sell it in little bottles). The basilica, on Largo Abate Elia (✆ **080/5737111**) is open Monday through Saturday 7am to 8:30pm and Sunday 7am to 10pm, and admission is free. Around the basilica, you can explore the little lanes and squares of **Bari Vecchia,** an intriguing old quarter that juts into the sea. Café-lined Piazza del Ferrarese is the liveliest corner; along atmospheric Arco Basso and Arco Alto, women sell homemade *orecchiette* and other goods from tables in front of their doors. Modern Bari, laid out in a grid around the historic quarter and a massive 12th-century castle (now government offices), is quite pleasant, inspiring the saying "if Paris had the sea, it would be a little Bari." Bari is easy to reach from anywhere in the region, via Autostrada A14.

Andria, then south another 18km (11 miles) in the direction of Spinazzola. From Matera, head to Altamura, then to Gravina, and follow signs to Spinazzola.

18km (11 mi) south of Andria. www.casteldelmonte.org. ✆ **0883/569997.** 5€, 2.50€ ages 18–25. Mar–Sept daily 10:15am–7:45pm; Oct–Feb daily 9am–6:45pm.

Promontorio del Gargano ★★★ NATURAL WONDER   The spur of the Italian boot is this thumb-shaped promontory northwest of Trani, mostly now protected as the **Parco Nazionale del Gargano.** Much of the peninsula's mountainous interior is carpeted with the ancient oak and beech forest known as the Foresta Umbra, which once covered much of Central Europe, while the coast is a magical seascape of cliffs, rock formations, caves, islets, and sandy beaches. Come August, Italian families head in droves to low-key summertime-only resorts around the white-washed towns of **Vieste** and **Peschici.** In centuries past, both towns continually fended off pirates and other invaders—in Viestre in 1554 the Turks beheaded more than 5,000 men, women, and children.

Still a popular pilgrimage site, the **cave of St. Michael the Archangel** in Monte Sant'Angelo (www.santuariosanmichele.it) is the oldest shrine in Western Europe, founded in the 7th century (the archangel is believed to have appeared there three times). Admission to the chapels and rock-hewn sanctuary is free. It's open Monday–Saturday 7am–1pm and 2:30–8pm (closes at 7pm Nov–Mar), Sunday 7:30am–12:30pm and 2:30pm–7pm; in July and September it stays open all day with no midday break. Even more popular is the sanctuary of **Padre Pio** (www.conventosantuariopadrepio.it)

Rock outcroppings protect the golden sands of Vieste, on the Gargano peninsula.

in San Giovanni Rotondo, where the beloved saint (canonized in 2002) and mystic served as a priest from 1916 to 1968. Padre Pio's shrine includes a stunning church, Chiesa San Pio Da Pietrelcina, by modern architect Renzo Piano; it's the second-most-visited Catholic pilgrimage site in the world, after Mexico City's Our Lady of Guadalupe, with 7 million pilgrims per year. The Pietrelcina church is open daily 6am to 7:30pm.

From Trani, the closest Gargano gateway city is Manfredonia, about 80km (50 miles) northwest via SS16 and SP77. Once there, SS89 skirts the peninsula; expect at least half a day of slow driving to make the circuit.

Park headquarters in Monte Sant'Angelo, 90km (55 mi) NW of Trani. www.parks.it/parco.nazionale.gargano.

Where to Stay & Eat in Trani

B&B Palazzo Paciotti ★★   A restored palace in the old quarter near the cathedral oozes with Trani's long history, but beyond the rich stone facade the large, high-ceiling spaces on the third floor (with elevator) are spruce and modern. Low-slung chairs are upholstered in white, beds framed in white steel are a sharp take on the four-poster, and modern bathrooms gleam with sparkling mosaic tiles. Breakfast is served in an upper-floor sunroom with terrace, shared with the slightly snazzier, slightly more luxurious Le Dimore del Re on another floor of the palace (for information, go to www.ledimoredeire.it).

Via della Giudea 41. www.palazzopaciotti.it. ✆ **340/238-8121.** 5 units. 80€–90€ double. Rates include breakfast. **Amenities:** Wi-Fi (free).

Corte in Fiore ★★★ SEAFOOD   Cast aside any notions of an old fisherman's haunt serving the region's famous *cucina povera* in this luxurious contemporary space. A few outdoor rooms meander through the courtyard of an old palace near the port, covered in winter, and always full of greenery offsetting chic white furnishings. The short, simple menu is a fish fancier's delight, with antipastos of fresh sashimi and sushi or a cooked selection of the chef's choice, depending on what's fresh; follow-ups are a few grilled choices and perfectly prepared seafood pastas and risottos.

Via Ognissanti 18. www.corteinfiore.it. ✆ **0883/508-402.** Entrees 12€–25€. Mon 9am–5pm, Tues–Sat 1–2:15pm and 8–10:15pm, Sun 1–2:15pm.

THE VALLE D'ITRIA: *TRULLO* COUNTRY ★★

The Valle d'Itria can seem like a magical place, where cone-shaped stone *trulli* houses poke above olive groves. *Trulli* are sprinkled over farms and fields throughout this part of Puglia, and in Alberobello, a little town at the heart of the Valle d'Itria, more than 1,600 of these beehive houses line the hilly, winding lanes. The scene, which looks like something out of a children's storybook, has earned UNESCO World Heritage Site status. And Alberobello is just the beginning: The road winds south through the Valle d'Itria to a string of hilltop towns built of gleaming white stone.

Alberobello ★★

Alberobello has 1,620 *trulli,* and the effect is whimsical, even a bit weird. Walking through the narrow streets you can't help but feel you've stepped into the pages of a fairy tale, or a scene from *The Hobbit.* You'll be forgiven for making a crack or two, like "These are *trulli* charming." Just don't think you're being clever, because the residents of Alberobello have heard it all.

   Most of the *trulli* of Alberobello date from the mid-16th century to the 19th century, when they most likely proliferated for two reasons: They were easy to build, with stones put in place without mortar, and their design was flexible. At first the conical-roofed stone huts were sheds and shelters for farmers in the fields, but in Alberobello the *trullo* (from the Greek *troulos,* "dome") became the standard house type. Local lore has it that the technique became popular because when tax inspectors came around, residents could dismantle their *trulli* and erase any evidence of

The *trulli* district in Alberobello looks like a fairy-tale stage set.

them; more likely is that since no mortar was used, the structures didn't qualify for full taxation. With thick stone walls supporting a conical roof, *trulli* could only be single-room structures—each rooftop you'll see around town corresponds with a single room below, though many *trulli* are clustered together to create multi-room residences.

ESSENTIALS

ARRIVING　From Bari by **car,** head south on S100 and then east (sign-posted) on S172. To find the *trulli,* follow Via Mazzini, which turns into Via Garibaldi, until you reach Piazza del Popolo. Turn left on Largo Martellotta, which will take you to the edge of the popular tourist area; the *trulli* are well signposted once you get to town. A parking lot off Largo Martellotta charges about 2€ an hour; a machine dispenses a ticket to place on your dashboard. From Bari by **train,** service on Ferrovia del Sud Est (FSE; www.fseonline.it) runs hourly (every 2 hrs. Sun), taking about 1¾ hours.

EXPLORING ALBEROBELLO

You need an hour or two to tour the *trulli,* starting from **Largo Martel-lotta.** This airy pedestrianized square separates the *centro storico*'s two *trulli* zones: Rione Monti, to the south, and Rione Aia Piccola, to the northeast. **Rione Monti** is the larger and busier of the two, and many of its *trulli* are now coffee bars and, of course, gift shops. It's hard to resist leaving Alberobello without a small-scale replica of a *trullo,* crafted in the same type of stone that the town's builders used.

Once you've adjusted to the whimsy, cross the square and walk up the hill into quiet, residential **Rione Aia Piccola,** which seems much more like a quaint village. Here you can get away from the crowds and appreciate the surreal aspect of the ancient *trulli.* From Aia Piccola's hillside, you'll get a great view across the valley to the spectacle of Monti's hundreds upon hundreds of densely packed *trulli.*

The most monumental house in town is the **Trullo Sovrano (Sovereign Trullo).** It's not in Aia Piccola or Monti but on the far northern edge of modern Alberobello at Piazza Sacramento 10 (www.trullosovrano.eu; ✆ **080/432-6030**). From Largo Martellotta, walk north into Piazza del Popolo and then follow Via Vittorio Emanuele north to Piazza Sacramento. This rare two-story *trullo* comprises 16 separate, joined structures surrounding a central *trullo* with a cupola. A prominent family built the compound, complete with stables, barns, and a farm court, in the late 18th century. It later became headquarters for a religious confraternity and today shows off *trulli* domestic life, with a bread-baking oven and some quaintly furnished rooms. It's open daily 10am to 1:15pm and 3:30 to 6:30pm. Admission is 1.50€.

As you walk around town, notice the sculpted pinnacles, or finials, atop many *trulli.* These probably had no function other than to advertise which *trullaro* (*trulli* craftsman) built the house. Some *trulli* have artwork on the sides of their roofs, often traditional pagan, Jewish, and Christian symbols—look for a radiant orb, representing the sun and Christ, or a heart with an arrow through it, depicting the heartache of the Virgin Mary.

WHERE TO STAY & EAT IN ALBEROBELLO

While it's easy to see the appeal of staying in a setting as unique as the *trulli* zone, remember that you will essentially be stepping onto a Disney-like stage set, with thousands of selfie-taking gawkers trooping up and down the narrow streets. On the other hand, once the day-trippers leave, having the strange townscape almost to yourself is a magical experience.

La Cantina ★★ PUGLIESE   The Lippolis family has been satisfying local appetites since 1958. Their homey, stone-walled eatery just outside the *trulli* district is such an institution that the street out front is named for them. Offerings are *cucina povera* (simple, "poor" food) with some nice twists, prepared in an open kitchen overseen by owner-chef Francesco. He usually sends out some delicious *bruschetta,* on thick local bread with rich olive oil and fresh tomatoes and mozzarella, perhaps followed by local *salumi* and *burrata.* The pork from nearby Martina Franca is grilled to perfection. La Cantina has only seven tables, so booking is essential, even in the winter.

Vico Lippolis 8. www.ilristorantelacantina.it. ✆ **080/432-3473.** Entrees 9€–15€. Wed–Mon noon–3pm and 8–11pm. Closed 2 wks in Feb and 2 wks in July.

The whitewashed interior of a beehive-shaped *trulli* house.

La Fontana 1914 ★ PUGLIESE   For a quick bite on the main square, step into a butcher shop that also grills meat to order, serving platters and sandwiches in an informal, old-fashioned room off to the side. Chicken and chips is the top choice of the local kids who crowd in for a snack; another favorite is the *bombette,* pork shoulder wrapped around melted cheese and spiced with herbs. Salads are made with farm-fresh vegetables, and decent house wine is served by the glass or carafe.
Largo Martellotta 55. ℭ **380/369-6969.** Entrees 5€–9€. Daily 8am–11pm.

Masseria Torre Coccaro ★★★ You can jump from one architectural experience to another with a 45-minute drive northeast from Alberobello over to the coast, where this centuries-old *masseria,* a fortified farm compound, offers an experience as transporting as the *trulli.* Accommodations are tucked into haylofts, towers, and in the case of the cavernous Orange Garden suite, carved out of a rocky hillside. All surround citrus-scented gardens and a lake-like swimming pool. Dining is in an elegantly transformed stable block; cooking lessons are available.
Contrada Coccaro 8, Savelletri di Fasano. www.masseriatorrecoccaro.com. ℭ **080/ 482-9310.** 39 units. 305€–485€ double. Rates include breakfast. **Amenities:** Restaurant; bar; babysitting; bikes; exercise room; outdoor pool; room service; spa; Wi-Fi (free).

Trulli e Puglia B&B ★   We can't resist: These accommodations in the heart of the Monti quarter are *trulli* unique, with a cluster of well-restored *trulli* showing off the stonework and conical, beehive ceilings that make these dwellings so distinctive. Several are two stories, with sleeping lofts atop spiral staircases, and all sport rustic furnishings and wood finishes for a cozy atmosphere. All units have fridges and a few have kitchenettes, plus such modern conveniences as air-conditioning (not really necessary, given the thick walls and stone roofs) and surprisingly spacious, nicely appointed bathrooms. Innkeeper Mimmo and his staff provide a welcome that's as memorable as the architecture.

Via Monte San Michele 58. www.trulliepuglia.com. © **080/432-4376** or © 347/553-8539. 6 units. 60€–90€ double. Rates include breakfast. **Amenities:** Bar; Wi-Fi (free).

A SIDE TRIP TO THE GROTTE DI CASTELLANA

The **Grotte di Castellana** is a vast network of caves, 3,350m (11,050 ft.) long and 125m (412 ft.) deep, carved out over centuries by water streaming through the limestone that underlies this part of Puglia. The caves are 17km (11 miles) north of Alberobello via SS172 and SS237.

An enormous tunnel leads into the **Grave,** a huge chamber lit by a skylight through which sunbeams and moonlight enter to flicker across the walls and floor. The vastness and eerie light have given rise to all sorts of legends of demons and lost souls floating through the depths. From the Grave, a series of paths winds through other underground rooms with names like **Corridoio del Serpent** and **Corridoio del Deserto,** filled with stalagmites and stalactites. At the end of the network of corridors is the majestic **Grotta Bianca,** where walls gleam with white alabaster and the rock formations are translucent. Visits are only by guided tours. Tours in Italian, English, French, and German run roughly every hour (and half-hour in summer) on a complex timetable that offers short (1 hr.) and long (2 hrs.) tours from 9am to noon in winter and 9am to 7pm in summer, with hours varying by the month (www.grottedicastellana.it; © **080/4998221**). From November to February, the caves are open by reservation only. Admission is 16€ for the long tour (13€ ages 6–14, free for 5 and under), 12€ for the short tour (10€ ages 6–14, free for 5 and under); the short tour does not include the Grotta Bianca. Bring an extra layer: It's 15°C (59°F) in the caves year-round.

The White Cities

South of Alberobello and its cone-roofed *trulli* are a string of hill towns hewn out of light-colored stone, so glaringly bright in the sun that they're collectively known as the "white cities." It's easiest to reach them **by car,** heading south through the Valle d'Itria along SS172 to Locorotondo and Martina Franca, with short detours to Cisternino, Ostuni, and Ceglie Messapica; the towns are all well signposted. You can also easily reach 4 of them **by train,** with 15 to 20 connections a day from Bari and Brindisi.

Ostuni is on the state railway's Adriatic line (www.trenitalia.com), while Cisternino, Locorotondo, and Martina Franca are served by Ferrovie del Sud Est (www.fseonline.it). Marozzi (www.marozzivt.it) operates buses that connect all the towns with each other and with Bari. If you're traveling by car you can make a fairly leisurely ramble through the five towns in a couple of days; they're close enough to one another that any of them would make a convenient base for exploring the region in more depth.

LOCOROTONDO ★★★

8km (5 miles) SE of Alberobello on SP172

As you approach this unabashedly cheerful little town you might think you're seeing a mirage: a ring of bright white houses with pointed gable roofs (called *cummerse*) crown the top of a hill. From a distance the scene looks a little like a rimrock canyon from the American West, or a Hanseatic port on the Baltic Sea—except, of course, for the baroque church domes rising above the rooftops. Locorotondo means "round place," and once inside the gates you'll see why: Streets of light-colored stone are flanked by white houses that hug the contours of the hilltop in near-perfect concentric circles. Surrounding them are the old protective walls, skirted by a ring road from which you can see far across the plains below—a view that earns Locorotondo the nickname "balcony of the Valle d'Itria." Locorotondo is famous for its white wine, which you can sample in any of the restaurants and bars in town, or from the **Cantina Sociale del Locorotondo**, near the railway station below town at Via Madonna della Catena 99 (www.locorotondodoc.com; ✆ **080/431-1644**).

   The town's **tourist office** is at Piazza Vittorio Emanuele 27 (✆ **080/431-3099**) and is usually open daily 9am–1pm and 4–7pm.

MARTINA FRANCA ★★

6km (4 miles) S of Locorotondo on SP172, 14km (9 miles) S of Alberobello

This lively hill town with its baroque finery and whitewashed back alleys was founded in the 10th century by coastal residents fleeing Saracen attacks along the Adriatic and Ionian coasts. The *centro storico* is an intriguing tangle of medieval lanes that lead from one piazza to another— a layout deliberately planned to confuse plunderers.

   The **tourist office** in Piazza Roma (✆ **080/480-5702**) is usually open Monday through Saturday 9am to 1pm, plus 4–7pm on Tuesday and Thursday. You can't drive in Martina Franca's *centro storico* but you can park a few blocks away on Via Giuseppe Aprile, Via Gabriele d'Annunzio, Piazza Francesco Crispi, Piazza Umberto, or Via Verdi.

   At the center of town are two adjoining squares, Piazza Plebiscito and Piazza Immacolata. Rising above **Piazza Plebiscito** is the **Basilica di San Martino** ★★ (✆ **080/4306536**; free; daily 8am–12:30pm and 4:30–8pm), its facade richly adorned with baroque relief sculptures depicting episodes from the life of St. Martin. The most famous scene shows the

Piazza Plebiscito and the Basilica di San Martino, Martina Franca.

saint, a Hungarian soldier in the Roman legions, meeting a poor beggar on a chilly November night and cutting his military cloak in half with his sword to keep the beggar warm. Martin's feast day on November 11th coincides with the grape harvest, earning him the honor of patron saint of wine. Also in the square is the **municipal clock tower,** erected in 1734, with a *meridiana* (sundial) inscribed on an eye-level plaque. In pretty **Piazza Immacolata,** the landmark is century-old **Caffè Tripoli** (Via Garibaldi 25; © **080/480-5260**), where the specialty is *granita di caffè* (espresso with whipped cream). **Via Cavour,** leading south from Piazza Immacolata, is the main street of the Lama, the old quarter. Lining the handsome street are baroque *palazzi,* with fanciful arches and balconies, often crawling with stone cherubs. On and off Via Cavour (and also north of the two piazzas) is a tangle of whitewashed back streets, impossibly narrow passageways, and blind alleys. Some of the defense walls and towers still exist around the old city's perimeter, and the streets just below offer terrific views over the Valle d'Itria.

The town's culinary specialty is *capocollo di Martina Franca* (cured pork), cut from the top of the neck where it meets the shoulder, and cured with local wine, herbs, and wood smoke. Butcher/deli **Romanelli,** just off Piazza XX Settembre at Via Valle d'Itria 8–12 (© **080/480-5385**), will let you sample its *capocollo* for free (along with *taralli* and red wine in paper cups, depending on the time of day), and you can buy sliced *capocollo* by the *etto* (100 grams).

CISTERNINO★★

10km/6¼ miles E of Locorotondo on SP134, 12km/7 miles NE of Martina Franca on SP61 and SP13

Like its near neighbor Locorotondo, this sunny whitewashed hilltop town is smaller and quainter than busy Martina Franca and Ostuni, with their modern outskirts. Before plunging into the labyrinth of medieval lanes that converge in central Piazza Vittorio, stop to enjoy the views over the Valle d'Itria from the base of the **Torre Normano Sveva,** at the edge of the ridge on which the town is built.

Cisternino is famous for its Fornelli Pronti—literally, ready ovens, holdovers from the times when butchers operated communal ovens where meat was grilled upon purchase. Shops all over town still do the honors, grilling *bombetti*—veal crusted in breadcrumbs and Parmigiano and rolled around caciocavallo cheese—and serving them, alongside other grilled meats and carafes of local red wine, at outside tables. One popular spot is **Zio Pietro,** Via Duca d'Aosta 3 (www.ziopietro.it; ✆ **080/444-8300**).

OSTUNI ★★

16km/10 miles E of Martina Franca on SP17

Other nearby towns may bill themselves as "white cities," but they're positively beige compared to gleamingly white Ostuni. Practically blinding in summer, perched atop a commanding hill 8km (5 miles) above the Adriatic

coast, Ostuni makes it clear you're close to Greece. Ancient Greeks, in fact, are among the dozens of invaders and occupiers who came and went over the past 2,500 years, though the town's mazelike streets and arched steps tumbling down hillsides are mostly medieval. Especially beneficent to Ostuni over the ages were two female rulers, Isabella of Aragon and her daughter, Bona Sforza, who in the 16th century made the city a cultured outpost and added walls and lookout towers along the coast, where beacon fires were lit to warn of approaching pirates.

In **Piazza della Libertà,** at the foot of the hill where the oldest part

The whitewashed facades of Ostuni.

of town clings, look for the statue of Sant'Oronzo perching more than 60 feet atop La Colonna di Sant'Oronzo. The patron saint of nearby Lecce, Oronzo is honored here for allegedly saving Ostuni from the plague twice, in 1657 and 1771. Below the saint, on a warm weekend night everyone from miles around gathers in the piazza to chat, stroll, and sit in one of the cafes. From Piazza della Libertà, **Via Cattedrale** winds up through *la città Bianca* to the hilltop Gothic **Duomo,** with its marble facade swooping into a gracious curve on one side; it's open daily 9am to 1pm and 3 to 7pm (admission 1€). Above a doorway to the left of the main entrance, Oronzo appears again, this time cradling Ostuni in his protective arms.

The **tourist office** at Corso Mazzini 6 (www.comune.ostuni.br.it; © **083/339627**) is generally open Monday to Saturday 10am to 1pm and 3:30 to 5:30pm, though hours vary.

CEGLIE MESSAPICA ★★
13km/8 miles SW of Ostuni on SP22

A bit farther afield, this quiet town is even older than the other White Cities, having been founded by seafaring Greeks in the 7th century B.C. The town flourished again in the 16th century under the kingdom of Naples, and a large hilltop castle, **Castello Ducale,** was enlarged. Today the Cegliese are surrounded by miles of rich farmlands, vineyards, and olive groves, and the town is a prosperous-looking assemblage of elegant squares and narrow lanes lined with cubical white-washed houses that lend a Moorish appearance. Unlike Ostuni or Martini Franca, with their booming modern outskirts, Ceglie Massapica doesn't extend much beyond the fragments of its original town walls, its whiteness offset by the greenery of the Puglian hills.

WHERE TO STAY & EAT IN THE WHITE CITIES

La Sommità Relais ★★★   A 16th-century fortified palazzo on a lane behind Ostuni's Duomo is full of hidden charms within thick stucco walls. On the ground floor, stylish lounges and an elegant restaurant are fashioned out of a maze of high arched rooms that open to a walled garden; upstairs a seaview terrace, a perfect perch for cocktails, is tucked onto the ramparts. Sleek contemporary-styled guest rooms are full of perks; some have terraces facing the plain and seashore below, others surround cool interior courtyards and have deep soaking tubs and other luxuries (one even has a fireplace).

Via Scipione Petrarolo 7, Ostuni. www.lasommita.it. © **0831/305925.** Doubles from 110€. Rates include breakfast. **Amenities:** Bar; restaurant; spa; Wi-Fi (free).

La Tavernetta ★ PUGLIESE   Step down off the busy street into this white- walled and arched cellar and you're transported to old Puglia, where waiters who've been here for decades dispense one traditional Pugliese classic after another, at decidedly old-fashioned prices. House specialties include *fave e cicoria* (pureed fava beans with sautéed chicory), *orecchiette al ragu* (handmade ear-shaped semolina pasta with a robust sauce), and *braciole* (sliced veal stuffed with parsley, cheese, and garlic and simmered in tomato sauce).

Via Vittorio Emanuele 30, Martina Franca. ℰ **080/430-6323.** Entrees 5.50€–15€ Tues–Sun 12:30–2:45pm and 7:30pm–midnight.

Osteria del Tempo Perso ★★ PUGLIESE   Even in its former guise as a bakery, the *osteria* "of lost time" must have been charming, its rough-hewn walls carved out of a cave. Today the linen-topped tables spread into an atmospheric adjoining room, hung with old farm implements dangling among beautiful local ceramics. In these colorful surrounds, just around the corner from the Duomo, the food sticks close to local tradition, with lots of Adriatic seafood. Try the house special casserole, *tegamino di funghi,* with bread, mushrooms, and zucchini flowers.

Via G. Tanzarella Vitale 47, Ostuni. www.osteriadeltempoperso.com. ℰ **0831/ 304819.** Entrees 7€–16€. Daily noon–11pm.

Masseria Salinola ★★★   A centuries-old walled olive estate welcomes guests into stylish rooms and suites fashioned from an old salt warehouse; they're full of arches, stonework, and old beams, enhanced with luxurious beds and well-curated family pieces. A former stable is now a character-filled, hearth-warmed lounge and dining room that spills onto a terrace in warmer months; a pool shimmers amid luxuriant gardens and palm-shaded nooks. Though Ostuni is just a short drive away, a family-style dinner of local favorites made with garden-fresh ingredients, served most evenings, may tempt you to stay put in such relaxing surroundings.

3km (2 mi) S of Ostuni off SP 29. www.masseriasalinola.it. ℰ **0831/308330.** Doubles from 130€. Rates include breakfast. **Amenities:** Bar; restaurant; pool; Wi-Fi (free).

Pizzeria Casa Pinto ★★ PIZZERIA   It's probably not much of an exaggeration to say that on weekend nights most of Locorotondo crowds into these tiny rooms, one of them taken up by a huge pizza oven. Tables are tucked into an almost cavelike vaulted cellar, and the pizzas are almost as distinctive, made with organic products. Some are topped so lightly with olive oil and cheese that they seem more like savory baked bread than pizza. Other toppings are more traditional, but any choice should be washed down with the town's signature white wine.

Via Aprile 23, Locorotondo. www.pizzeriacasapinto.it. ℰ **346/274-9859.** Pizzas 6€–8€. Daily noon–5pm and 7pm–midnight.

Sotto le Cummerse ★★★   In welcoming Locorotondo, visitors can live like a native in these 13 distinctive lodgings tucked into houses around the old town. All are different, ranging from simple ground-floor studios to multilevel suites; all are nicely furnished in traditional style and make the most of stone walls, fireplaces, and other vintage details. Many have terraces, as well as up-to-date bathrooms, some equipped with Jacuzzis.

Breakfast is served in a welcoming room near the reception, where the accommodating staff is on hand well into the evening hours.

Via Vittorio Emanuele 138, Locorotondo. www.sottolecummerse.it. © **080/431-3298.** 90€–240€ double. Rates include breakfast. **Amenities:** Wi-Fi (free).

A Side Trip to the Seacoast

Just to the east of the Valle d'Itria, the Adriatic washes up onto a long stretch of appealing beaches. One of the most picturesque seaside towns anywhere is **Poligano sul Mare,** 30km (18 mi) north of Alberobello, where waves crash into coves hemmed in by rock faces topped by tall white houses. The intriguing old town provides a pleasant diversion from sunning and swimming. **Parco Naturale Regionale Dune Costiere** (www.parcodunecostiere.org) follows the coast for 8km (5 mi) just below Ostuni, with sandy beaches backed by dunes and centuries-old olive groves; San Leonardo, at the southern edge of the park, is 11km (7 mi) northeast of Ostuni on SP19. The nature preserve of **Torre Guaceto** (www.riservaditorreguaceto.it), 24km (13 mi) southeast of Ostuni, has miles of pristine sands backed by dunes and marshes, and its offshore coral formations are a lure for snorkelers.

LECCE ★★

113km (68 miles) SE of Alberobello, 40km (25 miles) SE of Brindisi, 408km (245 miles) SE of Naples

Sophisticated Lecce combines baroque architecture and urbane elegance with typically southern Italian radiance. The handsome old city center is clad almost entirely in irresistibly warm golden limestone, amplified by *il barocco leccese*—a particularly ebullient version of 17th-century Italy's fondness for baroque architectural decoration. Because the local limestone is fairly soft and easy to chisel, sculptors covered church facades and civic palaces with saints, angels, and intricate details as if they were drawing on paper. While it's easy to describe the limestone as "buttery," "milky" might be more apt—milk was applied to the final work, to seep into the pores of the stone and harden it.

Founded by Greeks more than 2,200 years ago, Lecce also has a Roman theater and amphitheater and the bastions of the 16th-century Castello Carlo V (Castle of Charles V, the Habsburg Holy Roman Emperor). Lecce is often promoted as the "Florence of the South," but the city's identity is southern Italian through and through, devoted to agriculture—especially olive oil and wine—more than tourism. Lecce is a pleasant base for day trips around the rest of the Salento peninsula.

Essentials

ARRIVING High-speed Frecciargento **trains,** usually with a change in Foggia or Ancona, connect Lecce with Rome in 5½ hours. Lecce is also connected to Bari and Brindisi by frequent train service. The journey from

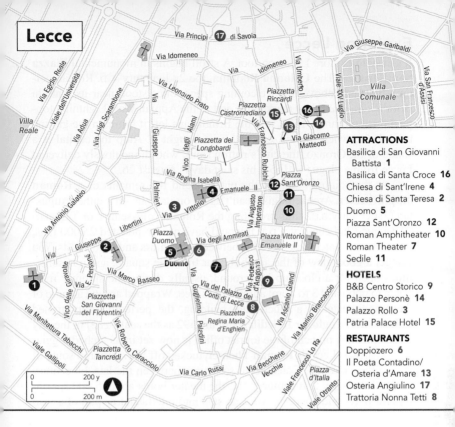

Lecce

Via Principi **17** di Savoia
Via Idomeneo
Via Giuseppe Garibaldi
Via Egidio Reale
Viale dell'Università
Via Luigi Scarambone
Via Leonardo Prato
Via Idomeneo
Via Umberto I
Viale XXV Luglio
Villa Comunale
Via San Francesco d'Assisi
Villa Reale
Via Adua
Via Giuseppe
Via degli Alami
Piazzetta Riccardi
Piazzetta Castromediano **15**
16
Via Francesco Rubichi
13
14
Piazzetta dei Longobardi
Via Giacomo Matteotti
Via Regina Isabella
Palmieri
Via Antonio Galateo
Libertini
Via Vittorio Emanuele II
4
3
Via Augusto Imperatore
Piazza Sant'Oronzo
12
11
10
Via Giuseppe
Via E. Personè
Piazza Duomo
2
Via Marco Basseo
5 Duomo **6**
Via degli Ammirati
7
Piazza Vittorio Emanuele II
Vico delle Giravolte
1
Piazzetta San Giovanni dei Fiorentini
Via Roberto Caracciolo
Via del Palazzo dei Conti di Lecce
Via Guglielmo Paladini
Via Federico d'Aragona
9
8
Piazzetta Regina Maria d'Enghien
Via Ascanio Grandi
Via Marino Brancaccio
Via Manifattura Tabacchi
Viale Gallipoli
Piazzetta Tancredi
Via Carlo Russi
Via Beccherie Vecchie
Viale Francesco Lo Re
Piazza d'Italia
Viale Otranto

0   200 y
0   200 m

ATTRACTIONS
Basilica di San Giovanni Battista **1**
Basilica di Santa Croce **16**
Chiesa di Sant'Irene **4**
Chiesa di Santa Teresa **2**
Duomo **5**
Piazza Sant'Oronzo **12**
Roman Amphitheater **10**
Roman Theater **7**
Sedile **11**

HOTELS
B&B Centro Storico **9**
Palazzo Personè **14**
Palazzo Rollo **3**
Patria Palace Hotel **15**

RESTAURANTS
Doppiozero **6**
Il Poeta Contadino/ Osteria d'Amare **13**
Osteria Angiulino **17**
Trattoria Nonna Tetti **8**

Bari takes about 1½ hours; from Brindisi it's a half-hour trip. Visit www.trenitalia.com for schedules and information. Note that Lecce's train station is about 2km (1¼ miles) from the center of the old quarter; from the train station, buses 11, 12, and 14 run to Porta Napoli at the edge of the *centro storico*. The fare is 1.30€ and you can purchase tickets at newsstands; for more information, go to www.sgmlecce.it.

If you have a **car** and are arriving from the north, follow signs to Brindisi, then take state highway SS613 south to Lecce (38km/24 miles, or about a half-hour). Most of the center is closed to car traffic and parking is extremely limited; it's best to leave your car in one of the large lots in Piazza Muratore, Piazza Giuseppe Libertini, or elsewhere on the perimeter of the *centro storico*. You can most likely make parking arrangements with your hotel for one of these lots in advance of arrival.

VISITOR INFORMATION   A **tourist office** is near the Duomo at Corso Vittorio Emanuele 16a (www.infolecce.it; ℂ **0832/521877**); it's open Monday through Friday 9:30am–1:30pm and 3:30–7:30pm, weekends 10am–1:30pm and 3:30–7pm. The office also operates an **info-point** in the Sedile, on Piazza Sant'Oronzo, open the same hours.

It's easy to explore Lecce on foot. A stroll begins in monumental **Piazza Sant'Oronzo.** The **Colonna Romana,** the 2nd-century-A.D. Roman column that rises above this welcoming space, once stood near its mate in Brindisi; together they marked the end of the Appian Way. Lightning toppled this column in 1528, and the Brindisians left it lying on the ground until 1661, when the citizens of Lecce bought it. Atop the capital is a statue of St. Oronzo, the city's patron saint, who miraculously delivered Lecce from a plague in 1658; his saint day is August 26.

At the southern side of the piazza stand the remains of a **Roman amphitheater.** Archaeologists can't agree on its date—it's either Augustan (1st century B.C., thus predating the Roman Colosseum), or Trajanic-Hadrianic (2nd century A.D.). It would have accommodated 25,000 fans, who came to watch bloody fights between gladiators and wild beasts. You can get a good view of the amphitheater from the square, and it is sometimes open for a close-up look round, usually during the summer from 10am to noon and 3 to 7pm; admission is free. Wrapped around a curve of the amphitheater is a much later building, the perfectly proportioned **Palazzo del Seggio,** or **Il Sedile,** built in 1592 as the seat *(sede)* of the city government. A branch of the tourist office is now set in its arched loggia.

Nearby is Lecce's **Roman Theater,** tucked off Via Ammirati south of Piazza Sant'Oronzo. Constructed sometime between the late 1st century B.C. and the early 2nd century A.D., the theater holds about 5,000 spectators for plays and concerts. You can step into the theater as part of a visit

Piazza Sant'Oronzo, Lecce's principal square.

to the adjacent **Museo del Teatro Romano** (www.infolecce.it; ✆ **0832/279-196;** Mon–Sat 9:30am–1pm, admission 3€).

To the west of Piazza Sant'Oronzo is a string of extravagantly baroque churches. To get an eyeful of their facades, follow Via Vittorio Emanuele and its continuation, Via Giuseppe Libertini, past the Duomo to the 18th-century Porta Rudiae. The **Chiesa di Sant'Irene,** the first church you come to on Via Vittorio Emanuele, was built in 1591. Priest-architect Francesco Grimaldi designed it with the same flair he showed with his baroque landmarks in Naples and Rome, adorning the facade with columns, niches, statues, and a wolf from the town's coat of arms. St. Irene, who stands above the portal, was Lecce's patron saint before Oronzo. Lecce's first telegraph station was installed in the tower in the mid-19th century, while the nave became a community meeting hall during the unification of Italy. The 17th-century **Chiesa di Santa Teresa,** farther up on Via Libertini (✆ **0832/33269**), has also served multiple humble purposes, as a police barracks, a school, and a tobacco warehouse, despite its fanciful facade by master sculptor Giuseppe Zimbalo (see the Duomo and Santa Croce, below). Though the facade was never finished, it still features an exuberance of columns and statuary, among them the two Saint Johns, the Baptist and the Evangelist. Inside is what might be the town's most macabre work of art, a lifelike statue of a bloodied, emaciated Christ lying in a coffinlike glass box. By comparison, the **Basilica di San Giovanni Battista,** a few steps up Via Libertini (✆ **0832/308540**) is a joyful place, where cherubs float through the light-filled interior. Admission to most of Lecce's churches is free, and they're generally open daily from 7am to noon and 3:30 to 7pm.

Basilica di Santa Croce ★★ CHURCH   The *barocco leccese* hits fever pitch at Santa Croce (Holy Cross) basilica, where sculptors crammed the facade with lions, angels, sea creatures, Turks, goddesses—hundreds of figures in all, crowding the columned tiers. Most significant might be those turbaned Turks, whose forces menaced Lecce and the rest of southern Europe for centuries before being defeated at the Battle of Lepanto in 1571. The victory ensured the dominance of Christianity in Europe, and in many ways, this expanse of masonry celebrates Christian values. Even those strange-looking beasts and figures on the lower tiers represent the Christian forces that conquered the Turks (the griffon stands for the Republic of Genoa; Hercules represents the dukes of Tuscany). It's okay if you don't understand much of the iconography—just stand in Via Umberto I out front and soak in the spectacle. (The façade may still be under a tarp for restoration; it's scheduled to be completed by 2020.) The facade is the work of three generations of local masons; most notable is master Giuseppe Zimbalo (1620–1710), also known as Lo Zingarello, the "Tiny Gypsy." His son, Francesco, did the portals and some of the most beautiful work in the interior, with its forest of carved columns. Look for his richly carved tomb of local saint Francesco di Paolo, an animal-loving hermit friar much like St. Francis of Assisi; you'll see scenes of his most acclaimed miracles, include restoring life to a roasted lamb and a fried trout. He was also the envy of boatmen—he could hoist up his robes to catch a breeze and sail across the sea.

Via Umberto I. www.viaggiareinpuglia.it. ☏ **0832/241-957.** Free. 9am–noon and 5–8pm.

Duomo ★ CHURCH Lecce's cathedral stands in an almost completely enclosed square, a setting that is both dramatic and practical: In times of siege, residents would take refuge in the huge piazza, with its narrow entrances that could be completely closed off. Despite doing double duty as a fortress, the square is remarkably playful. Giuseppe Zimbalo, one of the creators of Santa Croce (above), also reworked the chiseled facade of the 12th-century Duomo, embellishing it with sculpted saints and other figures. High above the entrance is Lecce's patron St. Oronzo. Zimbalo also designed the adjacent **campanile** that towers 64m (210 ft.) above the piazza, ascending in tiers like a wedding cake. The **seminary,** across the square, has a chiseled facade that could have been squirted out of a pastry tube, the work of Giuseppe Cino, a student of Zimbalo. The exuberant **Bishop's Palace (Palazzo Vescovile),** with its arches and saint-filled niches, is still home to Lecce's archbishops. The extravagance continues north up **Via Palmieri,** past a long line of sculpted palace facades to the triumphal arch of **Porta Napoli,** the main city gate, built in 1548 to honor a state visit from Holy Roman Emperor Charles V.

St. Oronzo, Lecce's patron saint, presides over the Duomo's ornate façade.

Piazza del Duomo. Via Vittorio Emanuele. www.cattedraledilecce.it. ☏ **0832/308-557.** Free. Daily 7am–noon and 4–7pm.

Where to Stay in Lecce

B&B Centro Storico ★★★ Every inch of this beautifully restored lodging, on one floor of a baroque palace, is carefully tended by the two proprietor brothers, who extend the same attention to their guests. Centuries-old stone window frames were sculpted to capture maximum sunlight; expertly restored baroque ceilings form *volte a stella,* star-shaped vaults; sleeping lofts are tucked above gleaming wood floors in former salons turned suites. A mix of antiques and modern pieces add to the appeal of these character-filled and extremely comfortable spaces.

Above is a rambling roof deck with a hot tub and a cottage-like guest room with its own private terrace. Breakfast is served in a nearby cafe.

Via A. Vignes 2. www.centrostoricolecce.it. ✆ **0832/242-727.** 6 units. 60€–100€. Rates include breakfast. **Amenities:** Roof terrace; hot tub; Wi-Fi (free).

Palazzo Persone ★★★ These wonderful rooms surrounding the courtyard of a palazzo in the heart of the old quarter display a mix of centuries-old details—fireplaces, absurdly high beamed ceilings, gently time-worn wood and tile, midcentury furniture, and contemporary touches. The welcome from the daughter-mother-father owners is as warm as the city's honey-colored stone. Breakfast is served in a pleasant cafe facing the lane out front, while a dining room incorporates part of a 16th-century synagogue and *mikveh* (ritual bath).

Viale Umberto I 5. www.palazzopersone.it. ✆ **0832/279-968.** 6 units. 70€–90€ double. Rates include breakfast. **Amenities:** Bar; café; Wi-Fi (free).

Palazzo Rollo ★★ Stepping into the vine-covered courtyard of this 17th-century palace is like entering a world unto itself, the private domain of the Rollo clan for more than 200 years. In its current guise the old surroundings house guests in a magical warren of suites that are more homey than luxurious, with tile floors, old-fashioned furnishings, and almost endless nooks and crannies. Four ground-floor apartments off the courtyard have been fashioned out of stone-vaulted old storerooms. A luxuriant roof garden offers plenty of shady spots from which to take in the view over the bell tower next door and the *centro storico* rooftops.

Via Vittorio Emanuele II 14. www.palazzorollo.it. ✆ **0832/3017152.** 4 suites, 4 apartments. Doubles from 70€. Rates include breakfast. **Amenities:** Wi-Fi (free).

Patria Palace Hotel ★★ Lecce's bastion of luxury has been pampering guests since 1797, and these days does so in richly upholstered and carpeted rooms, where traditional furniture creates a clublike lair that's especially popular with traveling business folk. The old *palazzo* would be almost stodgy if it weren't for its neighbor, the flamboyant Santa Croce basilica. A few rooms have private terraces, while a roof garden is a perfect spot to enjoy a bottle of wine while admiring the baroque surroundings.

Piazzetta Riccardi 13. http://patriapalace.com. ✆ **0832/245111.** 67 units. 99€–139€ double. Rates include breakfast. **Amenities:** Restaurant; bar; concierge; room service; Wi-Fi (free).

Where to Eat in Lecce

An almost mandatory stop in Lecce is **Natale,** at Via Trinchese 7A (www.natalepasticceria.it), for the best gelato and pastry in town. **Mamma Elvira Enoteca,** Via Umberto I 19 (www.mammaelvira.com; ✆ **0832/0169-2011**), an especially welcoming bar/shop, is the place to introduce yourself to wines of the southeast.

Doppiozero ★ PUGLIESE Lecce shows off its most hip, urbane side in a cafe and deli where repurposed bottles light long communal tables and bottles of the local vintage are stacked to the high ceilings. Alongside them are big wheels of cheese, hams, long salamis, and vats of olive oil. These and other market-fresh ingredients, also available for takeaway purchases, find their way into sandwiches and deli boards, along with crostini, salads, soups, and a few daily pastas. The light fare is a hit with a youthful crowd that doesn't seem to mind the pleasant but rushed service.

Via Paladini 2. © **0832/521-052.** Entrees 8€–12€. Daily 8am–midnight (closes at 4:30pm Mon in winter).

Il Poeta Contadino/Osteria d'Amare ★ PUGLIESE/SEAFOOD

You'll be reminded that Lecce is almost on the Adriatic in this comfy little room with big glass windows facing Piazza Sant'Oronzo, where the freshest seafood shows up in a few well-done preparations each day, from sandwiches generously filled with fillets of swordfish and fresh vegetables to basic pastas along the lines of *spaghetti alla vongole* (with clams). From the *"poeta contadino"* (poet farmer) side of the menu comes a nice selection of meat-and-vegetable-topped *bruschetti,* pastas with fresh vegetables, and other land-based, simple fare, all accompanied by good local wines by the glass.

Piazzetta Castromediano 8. © **392/540-2344.** Entrees 8€–16€. Mon–Sat 12:30–3pm and 7–10pm and Sun 11:30am–midnight.

Osteria Angiulino ★★ PUGLIESE

These brightly tiled, vaulted rooms are Lecce's favorite outpost for *cucina povera,* and that really translates as the region's authentic cuisine. Many of the dishes are vegetarian, including an appetizer of green beans and fava beans, parboiled to perfect crunchiness. The *melanzane alla parmigiana* is a perfect meatless main-course follow-up. On the carnivorous side of the menu is horsemeat prepared in every way imaginable—as meatballs, chopped, filleted, and topped with a green sauce, or in a savory stew. The house wine is as hearty and affordable as the cuisine.

Via Principe di Savoia 4. © **0832/245146.** Entrees 5€–8€. Mon–Sat 12:45–3pm and 7:45–11pm.

Trattoria Nonna Tetti ★★ PUGLIESE

Warm and inviting, with lots of tile and stone, this is another outpost for local cooking. The big menu also expands into the rest of Italy, but the standouts are strictly Leccese, like *ricciareddhe* pasta with cherry tomatoes, garlic, and cheese, or wild chicory with a purée of boiled fava beans.

Piazzetta Regina Maria 17. © **0832/246036.** Entrees 8€–12€. Mon–Sat noon–3pm and 7–midnight.

Lecce Shopping

For a selection of local crafts, including *cartapesta* (papier-mâché), ceramics, and terracotta, step into **Mostra Permanente dell'Artigianato,** Via Francesco Rubichi 21 (© **0832/246758**). Works of dozens of local artists are on display in the cavernous space, from nativity figures to abstract sculpture to embroidered clothing. **Cartoleria Pantheon Lecce,** Via Giuseppe Libertini 69 (www.pantheon-lecce.com; © **0832/521312**), whisks you off to Florence, so enticing are the creamy leather goods, from iPhone cases and leather-bound diaries to briefcases and bags.

Lecce Beaches

The most popular beach for the Leccese is San Cataldo, 15km (9 miles) east on SP364, a long stretch of sand backed by low cliffs. South of this popular summer town, the beach is backed by the protected San Cataldo reserve (www.pugliaandculture.com), where land that was once malaria-infested swamp is now green pine and eucalyptus forest. Another 8km (5 miles) south on SP366 is the Cesine nature preserve (www.riservale cesine.it), with trails that lead across wetlands and through forests to remote beaches. The bay at **Torre Dell'Orso** (Bear Tower), 28km (17 miles) southeast of Lecce on SP1 and SP3, is edged with white sand; off-shore, the Due Sorelle (Two Sisters) rock formations rise out of the turquoise water. Behind the beach stands the ruined 16th-century Torre dell'Orso that gives this stretch of coast its name.

Side Trips to Otranto and Gallipoli

OTRANTO ★★

45km (28 miles) SE of Lecce

It's said if you look hard enough on a clear day you can see all the way to Albania from **Otranto,** the easternmost town in Italy. Two colors

Turquoise seas and gleaming white houses at Otranto.

dominate here: the electric turquoise of the sea and the gleaming white of the old quarter. You can get here by **car** (45 min. southeast of Lecce via SS16) or by **train** (**Ferovia Sud Est FSE;** www.fseonline.it; travel time a little over an hour, change in Maglie). The **tourist office** is at Piazza Castello 8 (✆ **0836/801436;** daily 9am–noon and 3–6pm).

Castello Aragonese ★ FORTRESS Otranto's 15th-century sea-facing fortress, surrounded in part by a moat filled with fearsome green water, looks mighty enough. However, the thick fortifications failed to thwart the invading fleet of Mehmet the Conqueror, who in 1480 took the city in just 2 weeks. Most of the garrison and townsfolk fled as the Turkish ships approached; those who took refuge in the fortress poured boiling water over the ramparts, but to little avail. When the castle and town were overrun, more than 800 captives chose to die rather than renounce Christianity. (Tailor Antonio Primaldi proclaimed, "since the Lord died on the cross for us, it is fitting that we should die for him.") The skulls of the so-called Martyrs of Otranto are stacked in the Duomo (see below). Don't come here hoping to see the setting of Horace Walpole's gothic novel, *The Castle of Otranto*—the fortress looks nothing like its fictional self.
Piazza Castello. ✆ **0836/210094.** 5€. Daily 10am–8pm (hours vary in winter).

Cattedrale di Otranto ★★★ CHURCH Otranto's formidable 11th-century cathedral was built atop various remains of the town's previous inhabitants—a village founded by the Messappi tribe in the 8th century B.C.; a Roman villa; and an early Christian church. Inside, you can't miss the remarkable **Tree of Life floor mosaic,** created in the 1160s under the direction of monk-artist Pantaleone. Laid out on the floor like a genealogy tree, its trunk and branches cover much of the church, telling a medieval version of the history of civilization. Some figures are easy to identify— Adam and Eve, Noah, the goddess Diana, King Arthur, Alexander the Great—while others are mysterious (horse heads, mermaids, couples riding fish). It even refers to Islam, then prevalent in southern Italy. The *beati martiri,* the skulls of citizens beheaded after the 1480 Ottoman sack of the Castello (above), are preserved in a side chapel.
Piazza Basilica. ✆ **0836/87111.** Free. Daily 7am–noon and 3–5pm (till 7pm summer).

BEYOND OTRANTO

Head south from Otranto on coastal SP87 for 17km (10 miles) to **Santa Cesarea Terme**, a spa town for over 500 years, thanks to the stinky sulfuric waters emerging from its underlying rock, alleged to cure all kinds of maladies. Take a soak in the thermal pools at the **Terme di Santa Cesarea** spa facility, Via Roma 40 (www.termesantacesarea.it; ✆ **0836/-944070;** admission 4€–5€; open 9am–7pm, shorter hours in winter).

At the southern tip of the peninsula, **Santa Maria di Leuca** (58km/35 miles south of Otranto), you can climb up to the lighthouse and adjacent

basilica, called **Santa Maria de Finibus Terrae** (End of the World; www.basilicaleuca.it), for a bracing, almost 360-degree panorama of the Adriatic and Ionian Seas. Swing another 12km (7 miles) around the tip to **Pescolus** to enjoy its long beach, nicknamed the "Maldives of Puglia" for its fine white sands and azure waters. From here it's 55km (33 miles) back to Otranto, or continue up the peninsula's east coast on SS274 to Gallipoli.

GALLIPOLI ★★★

52km (32 miles) east of Otranto, 30km (18 miles) southeast of Lecce on SS101

The wave-washed old town of Gallipoli is a photogenic concoction of white houses and churches crammed onto a small island, connected by a

The medieval Tree of Life mosaic on the floor of Otranto Cathedral.

single bridge to the tidy new town on the mainland. Greeks founded the once thriving port, and Normans left behind a fortress that rises out of the sea on the islet's eastern edge. The old town's meandering lanes open into squares presided over by baroque palaces and churches, then emerge into seaside promenades. On the northern side of the old town, a sandy beach stretches beneath 14th-century seawalls. For many visitors the real attractions are the beautiful beaches that flank Gallipoli. To the south, along pristine **Baia Verde,** lie several beaches, the least crowded of which is **Punta della Suina,** part of the **Punta Piazza nature preserve** (take SS274 and SS239 south 10km/6 miles from Gallipoli). Another long stretch of dune- and pine-backed white sands surround **Punta Prosciutto** (Ham Point), 43km (26 miles) north of Gallipoli on SP112 and SP359.

SICILY

By Stephen Brewer

15

Sicily has been conquered, settled, and abandoned by dozens of civilizations, from the Phoenicians, Greeks, and Carthaginians in antiquity to the Arabs, Berbers, Moors, and Normans in the Middle Ages, to the Spanish and Bourbons in the Renaissance, and finally (at least nominally), modern Italy. It's an intricate and violent story that nonetheless left a fascinating legacy. Touring the relics of Sicily's tumultuous past can sometimes make you feel that you're visiting several different countries at once.

Though separated from the mainland only by the 5km-wide (3 miles) Stretto di Messina (Strait of Messina), the 25,708 sq. km. (9,926 sq. mile) island, the largest in the Mediterranean, has a palpable, captivating sense of otherness. Some Sicilians will refer to a trip to the mainland as "going to Italy." The island offers the full package of Italian travel experiences: evocative towns, compelling art, impressive architecture, ancient ruins, and a robust culinary heritage. Alongside the jewels of Sicily's glorious ancient past (Agrigento, Siracusa, Segesta, Piazza Armerina) you'll see baroque cities rebuilt after devastating earthquakes (Noto and Ragusa)— and some hideous postwar concrete monsters. The island's geographic palette goes from the arid, chalky southeast to the brooding slopes of Mt. Etna to the brawny headlands of Palermo and the gentle agricultural landscapes of the east, all surrounded by cobalt seas and beaches where you can swim from May to October.

Then, of course, there are the Sicilians themselves. The descendants of Greek, Carthaginian, Roman Vandal, Arab, Norman, and Spanish conquerors, they can be welcoming yet suspicious, taciturn yet garrulous, reverent of tradition yet determined not to be shackled by the past. True to stereotype, Sicilians are a passionate people, and their warmth can make even everyday transactions memorable.

In Goethe's words, "The key to it all is here."

DON'T LEAVE SICILY WITHOUT . . .

Wandering Through a Palermo Market. The local bounty, from fresh tomatoes to huge slabs of tuna, is staggering, but the real treat is watching the shills and hagglers in action.

Gazing Skyward in Monreale's Cathedral. Biblical characters, saints, angels, and the heavenly pantheon look down from a sea of colorful mosaics.

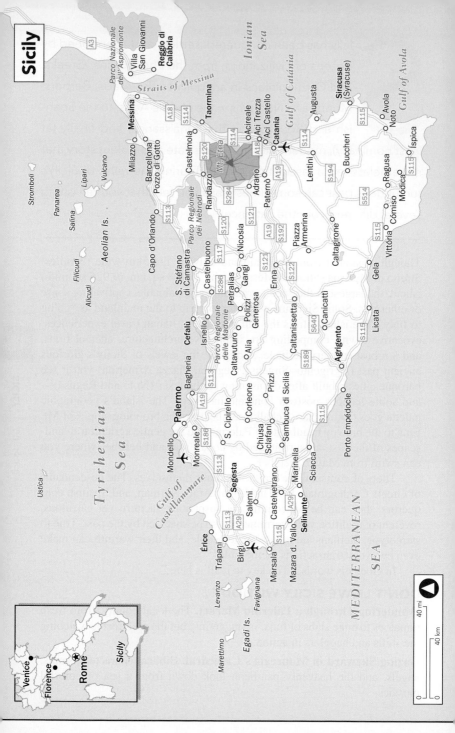

Sicily

Inset map
Venice
Florence
Rome ⊛
Sicily

Main map labels

Ustica

Tyrrhenian Sea

Stromboli
Panarea
Salina
Lipari
Vulcano
Filicudi
Alicudi
Aeolian Is.

A3
Parco Nazionale dell'Aspromonte
Villa San Giovanni
Reggio di Calàbria

Straits of Messina

Ionian Sea

Messina
Milazzo
Barcellona
Pozzo di Gotto
A18
S114
Taormina
Acireale
Aci Trezza
Aci Castello
Gulf of Catània
A18
Catania
Augusta

Castelmola
S120
Castelbuono
Randazzo
S284
Mt. Etna
S114
S114

Capo d'Orlando
S113
Parco Regionale dei Nebrodi
S. Stéfano di Camastra
S120
Nicosia
S121
Adrano
Paternò
A19
Lentini
S194
Bucchéri
Siracusa (Syracuse)

S117
Castelbuono
S286
Petralias
Gangi
Polizzi Generosa
Enna
S121
Piazza Armerina
S122
Caltagirone
Gulf of Avola
S115
Avola
Noto
Ispica
S115

Cefalù
Isnello
Parco Regionale delle Madonie
Alia
Caltavuturo
Canicattì
S640
Gela
Ragusa
S514
Módica
Cómiso
Vittória
S115

Bagheria
A19
S113
Corleone
Prizzi
Chiusa Sclafani
Sambuca di Sicilia
Caltanissetta
S189
Agrigento
Licata
S115

Palermo
Mondello
Monreale
S186
S. Cipirello
Porto Empédocle
Porto Empédocle

Segesta
S. Ciprello
Sciacca
S115

Gulf of Castellammare
Salemi
Castelvetrano
A29
Marinella
Selinunte

Érice
Trápani
Birgi
Marsala
Mazara d. Vallo
S115
S113
A29

Levanzo
Favignana
Egadi Is.
Maréttimo

MEDITERRANEAN SEA

0 40 mi
0 40 km

740

Communing with the Ancient World. It's easy to do on an island so richly endowed with remnants of the Greek and Roman past. Top stops are the theaters in Taormina and Siracusa, the temples at Agrigento, Segesta, and Selinunte, and the mosaics in Piazza Armerina.

Hitting the Heights. Take in the panoramic views from elegant, mountainside Taormina and aerie-like, medieval Erice. Highest and most dramatic of all: The summit of Mt. Etna.

Going for Baroque. Swaths of Noto, Ragusa, Siracusa, and other towns in the southeast are stage sets of honey-colored limestone fashioned into curvaceous facades and curling staircases.

PALERMO ★★★

233km (145 miles) W of Messina, 721km (447 miles) S of Naples, 934km (579 miles) S of Rome

In Palermo, street markets evoke Middle Eastern souks, and famous monuments bear the exotic artistic signature of the Arab-Norman 12th century, when the city was one of Europe's greatest cultural and intellectual centers. Palermo is Sicily's largest port, its capital, and a jumble of contradictions. Parts of some neighborhoods remain bombed out and not yet rebuilt from World War II; unemployment, poverty, traffic, crime, and crowding are rampant. Yet Palermo boasts some of the greatest sights and museums in Italy, and looming over it all is crown-shaped Monte Pellegrino, what Goethe called "the most beautiful headland on earth."

Even the mix of monuments can be baffling: Byzantine mosaics, rococo stuccoes, Islamic red domes, Catalonian-Gothic arches. Yet there is magic in its madness, and those who embrace the city's chaotic charm discover artistic gems and memorable vignettes of street life. You won't love every inch of this alluring yet hectic place, but you'll be swept away by much of the city, and you may come away with the travel experience of a lifetime.

Essentials

ARRIVING

BY AIR   Palermo's dramatically situated **Falcone-Borsellino Airport** (a.k.a. Punta Raisi; www.gesap.it; ✆ **091/702-0273**) is on the sea among tall headlands 25km (16 miles) northwest of the city center. Palermo is well served by flights from all over Italy and many European cities, though not by nonstop flights from the U.S. All the major rental car companies have operations here, although if you drive into Palermo with a rental car, get clear directions and parking information from your hotel. An easier way to reach the center from the airport is with the **shuttle bus** run by **Prestia e Comandè** (www.prestiaecomande.it; ✆ **091/580457**). The buses depart every half-hour from 5am to 12:30am (service from

Palermo begins at 4am and ends at 10:30pm); the trip takes 45 minutes and costs 6.30€ one-way, 11€ round trip. In central Palermo, buses stop at several points along Via Libertà, Teatro Politeama, the main train station, and Via Emerico Amari (port). A **train service,** the **Trinacria Express,** connects the airport with the main train station, but the "express" part is a bit of hyperbole: Service is slow at the best of times, often more than an hour, and the line is often nonoperational. Scheduled service from Palermo begins at 4:45am and ends just after 8pm, and from the airport service runs from 5:54am to 10:05pm; fare is 5.50€ each way. You can purchase tickets at desks in the station and airport or from machines near the platform. **Taxis** are plentiful; expect to pay about 50€ from the airport to town, but be sure to settle on a price before you set off. You can share a cab for about 7€—drivers will cor-

Palermo's Duomo is a mishmash of architectural styles, befitting Sicily's rich cultural stew.

ral you as you exit the terminal. This is a safe and reliable option, though you will have to slip the driver a little extra to take you to your destination rather than dropping you at an intersection nearby.

BY TRAIN   It is possible to get to Palermo from mainland Italy by train, coming down through Calabria and across the Strait of Messina on ferries equipped with railroad tracks on the cargo deck. It's a novel way to arrive in Sicily, but takes some time (the trip from Rome to Palermo is at least 11 hours, from Naples to Palermo 9–10 hours). Night trains between Palermo and Rome and other mainland cities usually have sleeping accommodations. All trains come into **Palermo Stazione Centrale,** at the edge of the historic center. Passenger rail service around the island is generally spotty and slow, but there's decent service on routes between Palermo and Messina, Catania, and Agrigento. For more information, go to www.tren italia.com; ✆ **89/2021.**

BY BUS   **Buses** from elsewhere in Sicily arrive at a depot adjacent to the train station. Bus travel in Sicily is excellent, with good connections between most cities. Coaches are clean and modern, with comfortable, upholstered seats, A/C, and smooth suspensions. The main bus companies

RESTAURANTS
Antica Focacceria
  San Francesco **11**
Arte e Tradizione **21**
Casa del Brodo **6**
Ferro di Cavallo **5**
La Cambusa **13**
Nini Franco U'
  Vastiddaru **12**
Osteria dei Vespiri **25**
Ottava Nota **18**
Palazzo Sambuca **20**
Pani câ Meusa **7**
Panineria Friggitoria
  Chiluzzo **22**

Palermo

Villa Trabia

Giardino Inglese

Milan • Venice
Florence
Rome ★ • Naples
Sardinia
Palermo
Sicily

Via Giacomo Cusmano
Via Sammartino
Via Principe di Villafranca
Via XX Settembre
Via della Libertà

Via Archimede

Borgo Vecchio

Corso Scina

Via **Dante**

Piazza Castelnuovo

Teatro Politeama

Piazza Sturzo

Via Emerico Amari

Piazza S. Oliva

Via Principe di Belmonte
Pza. Florio

Via Ruggero Settimo

❶ *Via Mariano Stabile*

Via Francesco Crispi
Via del Mare

C. Finocchiaro
Via Goethe
Via P. Aragona

NEW CITY

Via Sammuzzo

←**35** *Via Marco Polo*
Via Pietro Ranzano

Piazza di Giustizia

Via Volturno
Teatro Massimo
Piazza Verdi

Via **❷** *Cavour*

Via Squarciatupo
Via Flippo Patti

Amedeo
Via Gaetano Mosca

Via Sant' **Capo Market**

Agostino
Via S. Basilio
Via S. Bandiera

❸

❹ **Chiesa di S. Domenico**

Piazza S. Domenico

La Cala

Via del Celso

Via **Maqueda**

Duomo **31** **OLD CENTER**

29 30 *Quattro Canti*

Vittorio

5

Vucciria Market

6

7

Alberto

←**34** Corso

Pal. dei Normanni

32

Villa Bonanno

Piazza Indipendenza

Cappella Palatina

Corso Pisani

28

Via Porta di Castro

Piazza della Vittoria

Via

Emanuele

San Francesco d'Assisi

9

8

❿
12
13
11
14

Piazza Marina

Foro Italico

Via Roma

26

25

24

15

16

17

20

19 18

Alloro

33

Via Antonio Mongitore
Via Alberghiera

Ballarò Market

27

Via del Bosco

Via *Divisi*

Via Schiavuzzo

Piazza Rivoluzione

23

22

Santa Teresa

21

LA KALSA

Corso Re Ruggero
Via dei Bene detini

Corso Tukory

Piazza G. Cesare

Via *Garibaldi*

Via Lincoln

Piazza

Stazione Centrale

0 — 1/4 mi
0 — 250 m

ATTRACTIONS
Catacombe dei Cappuccini **34**
Chiesa della Martorana/San Cataldo **8**
Duomo **31**
Galleria d'Arte Moderna **26**
Galleria Regionale della Sicilia/
  Palazzo Abatellis **19**
Il Castello della Zisa **35**
Museo Archeologico Regionale
  Antonino Salinas **2**
Oratorio del Rosario di San Domenico **4**
Oratorio del Rosario di Santa Cita **3**

Oratorio di San Lorenzo **10**
Palazzo Chiaromonte Steri/
  Museo dell'Inquizione **15**
Palazzo dei Normanni
  and Cappella Palatina **32**
Palazzo Mirto **14**
Polo Museo d'Arte
  Contemporanea della
  Sicilia **29**
San Giovanni degli
  Eremiti **33**
Stanza al Genio **23**

HOTELS
Al Giardino dell'Alloro **24**
Ariston Hotel **1**
Butera 28 **17**
Eurostars Centrale Palace **30**
Grand Hotel Piazza Borsa **9**
Hotel Porta Felice **16**
Il Giardino di Ballarò **28**
Palazzo Brunaccini **27**

in Sicily are **Interbus** (www.interbus.it; © **091/616-7919**; also known as **Etna Trasporti, Segesta,** and **Sicilbus,** depending on which part of Sicily you're in), and **Cuffaro** (www.cuffaro.info; © **091/616-1510**), which operates buses between Palermo and Agrigento.

BY CAR   The northeastern tip of Sicily is separated from mainland Italy by the 5km- (3-mile) wide Stretto di Messina (Strait of Messina), which is crossed by regular car ferries between the Calabrian port of Villa San Giovanni (just north of Reggio Calabria, essentially the "toe" of the Italian peninsula's boot) and the Sicilian city of Messina. From Messina, which lies on the well-maintained A20 and A18 *autostrade,* it's a straight shot west to Palermo (233km/145 miles; about 2 hrs.). If you're planning to drive down from Naples or Rome, prepare yourself for a long ride: 721km (448 miles) south from Naples or 934km (580 miles) south from Rome.

BY SEA   Palermo's large port is served by passenger ferries from the Italian mainland cities of Naples, Civitavecchia (near Rome), Livorno, and Genoa, and from the Sardinian city of Cagliari. Nearly all are nighttime crossings, departing between 7pm and 9pm and arriving the next morning between 6am and 8am. Some of these ferries are tricked out like miniature cruise ships, with swimming pools, beauty salons, discos, and cabins in various configurations, from four-bunk dorms to private rooms. Ferries from Naples are the most numerous, operating daily year-round. The Naples–Palermo route is run by **SNAV** (www.snav.it; © **081/428-5555**), **Tirrenia Lines** (www.tirrenia.it; © **800/804-020**), and **Grandi Navi Veloci** (GNV; www.gnv.it; © **010/209-4591**). The ferry trip takes 11 hours. **GNV** also operates overnight ferries to Palermo from Civitavecchia (the cruise ship port for Rome) and from Genoa. Schedules vary depending on weather conditions, so always call on the day of departure even if you've already confirmed your reservation.

GETTING AROUND PALERMO

Walking is the best way to get around Palermo—distances are never great within the historic center. Buses run by **AMAT** (amat.pa.it; © **091/350-111**) charge 1.40€ per ride and 3.50€) for an all-day ticket. Bus tickets are sold at *tabacchi* and some newsstands; if you buy them on board, you will pay 1.80€. Four tram lines, with the same fares, service outlying districts.

VISITOR INFORMATION

Municipal **tourist information offices** (www.palermotourism.com) are located at the airport (© **091/591-698;** Mon–Sat 8:30am–7:30pm) and in the city center at Piazza Castelnuovo 35 (© **091/6058351;** Mon–Fri 8:30am–2pm and 2:30–6:30pm). Other city-run tourist offices are in Piazza Bellini (turismo.comune.palermo.it; © **091/740-5908;** Mon–Fri 8:30am–6:30pm and Sat 9:30am–6:30pm), and elsewhere around the city, including the port. The **Micro-Tourist Information Centre Palermo** at

Via Torremuzza 15 in the Kalsa district (www.visitpalermo.it; © **091/783-8185**) is a for-fee service where you can rent bikes or arrange kayaking and hiking excursions. The office also arranges some offbeat tours, such as a tour of sites in Palermo where anti-Mafia activity has centered and a visit to artisan studios in the Kalsa district.

SAFETY

Palermo is home to some of the most skilled pickpockets on the continent. Police squads operate mobile centers throughout the town to help combat street crime, but **your best defense is common sense.** Don't flaunt expensive jewelry, cameras, or wads of bills, and be especially careful in crowded street markets and on buses; routes to Monreale and Mondello, popular sightseeing destinations, are fertile ground for pickpockets. Thieves on scooters are adept at snatching jewelry and handbags. Do not carry a wallet anywhere accessible, even in an inside jacket pocket, where someone (or a pair, as is often the case) brushing against you can easily get to it. When traveling around Sicily, don't leave documents, cash, credit cards, expensive electronics, and other valuables in an unattended car, even out of sight in the trunk. Stash them safely at your hotel or, if you're on the move and stopping at an attraction en route, carry them with you.

Neighborhoods in Brief

Palermo is divided into four historical districts, or *mandamenti,* that spread out from **Quattro Canti,** or Four Corners. (Time was, and not too long ago, that it was unthinkable for Palermitani from one of these districts to marry someone from another.) The actual name of the square is Piazza Vigliena, after the viceroy who commissioned it; it marks the intersection of north-south **Via Maqueda** and east-west **Corso Vittorio Emanuele.** The square is also known as Theater of the Sun, because at any given time of day, the sun is shining on one of its four corners. Each corner of the square is decorated with a three-tiered niche: The first tier of each holds a fountain and a statue representing one of the four seasons; the second tier displays a statue of one of the Spanish Habsburg kings; and the third tier has a statue of the patron saint of whichever neighborhood adjoins the niche.

ALBERGHERIA   Southwest of the Quattro Canti, this is the oldest of the four *mandamenti,* also known as the mandamento Palazzo Reale because the royal palace was set here, in the highest part of the city. The Albergheria is filled with narrow, dimly lit alleyways and decaying buildings. Still, there are some exquisite corners—especially the splendid **Piazza Bologni,** with its noble palaces and statue of Charles V, and the historic market **Il Ballarò** extending from Piazza Bologni to Corso Tukory.

IL CAPO   The northwestern neighborhood, enclosed within Via Maqueda, Corso Vittorio Emanuele, Via Papireto, and Via Volturno, is a warren of

Palermo's four historic districts meet at Quattro Canti, where statues in niches identify each district's character.

tiny winding streets and alleyways spread out behind the Teatro Massimo. At its heart is the largest of Palermo's markets, **Il Capo** (see p. 745), once the headquarters of the secret society of the Beati Paoli, who robbed from the rich and gave to the poor. Pickpockets still adhere to this age-old principle, so watch your wallet.

CASTELLAMMARE Owing its name to the castle that once overlooked the sea, this northeastern quadrant is bordered by Corso Vittorio Emanuele, Via Cavour, Via Roma, and Via Crispi. Though heavily bombed in World War II, the neighborhood still has some spectacular palazzi and churches, such as the **Oratorio del Rosario di Santa Cita** and the **Oratorio di San Lorenzo** (p. 751). The centuries-old market **La Vucciria,** once the beating heart of Palermo, is here (see p. 760), with a few remaining butcher shops, fishmongers, and hole-in-the-wall eateries—and, more recently, a nightlife scene.

LA KALSA Settled a thousand years ago by Arabs, this southeast quadrant, bounded by Via Lincoln, Via Roma, Corso Vittorio Emanuele, and the Foro Italico, still has an exotic aura. Some patches were never rebuilt after 1943 air raids; the never-completed church **Santa Maria dello Spasimo** (Via dello Spasimo; © 091/616-1486) is a skeleton of broken Gothic vaults. Even 10 years ago, walking down La Kalsa's narrow lanes was risky business (it's still wise to avoid empty areas after dark), but a rash of hip restaurants and bars have recently opened in old *palazzi*. The excellent **Galleria Regionale della Sicilia** (p. 749) is here, as is a delightful shady park in the middle of Piazza Marina, cooled by breezes off the nearby sea.

NEW CITY The monumental **Teatro Massimo** at Piazza Verdi roughly marks the division between the Old City and the New City. Head north along Via Maqueda, which becomes Via Ruggero Séttimo, to the massive double squares at Piazza Politeama, site of the **Teatro Politeama Garibaldi.** North of the square, swanky **Viale della Libertà** runs up to the Giardino Inglese (the English Gardens). This is Palermo's Art Nouveau quarter, though many streamlined beauties were torn down to make way for ugly cement behemoths, marring the neighborhood/s elegance.

Exploring Palermo

Most of everything you want to see is within walking distance of the Quattro Canti, where Via Maqueda meets Via Vittorio Emanuele.

Il Castello della Zisa ★ PALACE   Few places in Palermo evoke the Arab past as evocatively as this pleasure palace of pleasure-loving Norman king William I. Arriving in Palermo, the 12th-century ruler went gloriously native, hiring craftsmen to create his summer retreat—Zisa translates as "splendid"—in Moorish style. Arches, niches, fountains, towers, and ingenious cooling systems (contrived from breezes flowing over pools and through interior vents) were all geared to creating an exotic retreat. Just enough remains of the palace, derelict until a recent restoration effort, to suggest its onetime glory.

Piazza Gugliemo il Buono (near Piazza Camporeale at end of Via Dante). ℭ **091/652-0269.** 6€. Mon 9am–1:45pm, Tues–Sat 9am–7pm. Bus: 106, 124, or 134.

Catacombe dei Cappuccini (Catacombs of the Capuchins) ★ CEMETERY   In 1599, the occupants of the adjoining Capuchin monastery discovered that the bodies of the brothers they placed in their catacombs soon became naturally mummified (albeit with the aid of chemical infusions), and Sicilians began demanding to be buried along with them. In these chambers, the corpses of some 8,000 people in various stages of preservation now hang from walls and recline in open caskets. It would be easy to write the spectacle off as eerie (which it certainly is), but for the loved ones the deceased left behind, a spot here provided a bit of comforting immortality. Wearing their Sunday best, the dead are grouped according to sex and rank—men, women, virgins, priests, nobles, professors (possibly including the painter Velasquez), and children. This last grouping includes the most recent resident, 2-year-old Rosalia Lombardo, who died in 1920 and whom locals have dubbed "Sleeping Beauty." Giuseppe Tommasi, prince of Lampedusa and author of *The Leopard* one of the best-known works of Sicilian literature, was buried in the cemetery next to the catacombs in 1957. His great-grandmother, the model for the Princess in the novel, is in the catacombs.

Piazza Cappuccini 1. www.palermocatacombs.com. ☎ **091/212-117.** 3€. Daily 9am–1pm and 3–6pm. Closed Sun afternoons late Oct–late Mar. Bus: 327 from Piazza Indipendenza.

Chiesa della Martorana/San Cataldo ★★ CHURCH

These two Norman churches stand side by side, separated by a little tropical garden. George of Antioch—Sicilian king Roger II's Greek admiral—founded Santa Maria dell'Ammiraglio in 1141; the church was later renamed **Chiesa della Martorana** for Eloisa Martorana, who founded a nearby Benedictine convent. The nuns gained the everlasting appreciation of Palermitans when they invented marzipan, and *frutta di Martorana*—in which marzipan is fashioned into the shape of little fruits—has outlived the order. George of Antioch, for his part, loved Byzantine mosaics and hired the North African craftsmen who'd just completed work on the Cappella Palatina (p. 752) to cover this church's walls, pillars, and floors with stunning mosaics. Christ crowns Roger II, George appears in a Byzantine robe, and Christ appears again in the dome, circled by angels. The Arab geographer/traveler Ibn Jubayr visited Palermo in 1166 and called the church "the most beautiful monument in the world." In 1266 Sicilian nobles met here and agreed to offer the crown to Peter of Aragon, ending a bloody uprising against French rule known as the Sicilian Vespers. A baroque redo has rendered the interior a little less transporting than it was then, but it's still beautiful.

Maio of Bari, chancellor to William I, began the tiny **Chiesa di San Cataldo** next door in 1154; after he died in 1160, the church was left unfinished. The red domes and the lacy crenellation around the tops of the walls are decidedly Moorish, while the stone interior, with three little cupolas over the nave, evoke the Middle Ages.

Piazza Bellini 2, adjacent to Piazza Pretoria. ☎ **091/616-1692.** La Martorana: Free. Mon–Sat 9am–1pm and 3:30–5pm; Sun 8:30am–1pm. San Cataldo: 2€. Tues–Fri 9am–5pm; Sat–Sun 9am–1pm. Bus: 101 or 102.

The Fountain of Shame

Adjoining Chiesa della Martorana in Piazza Pretoria, naked nymphs, gods, and goddesses romp over the 16th-century **Fontana Pretoria,** created by Florentine sculptor Francesco Camilliani for the garden of a Tuscan villa; it was sold to Palermo as a centerpiece of the city's new waterworks. Palermitans call the nude-encrusted fountain the "Fountain of Shame"; nuns from a nearby convent went so far as to lop the noses off the naked males (you can still see some clumsy reattachments)—the sisters could not bring themselves to touch the members that really offended them.

Colorful mosaics in della Martorana church in Palermo.

Duomo ★ CATHEDRAL   All those who came, saw, and conquered in Palermo left their mark on this cathedral, an architectural pastiche that lies somewhere between exquisite and eyesore. It is, however, noble enough as befits the final resting place of Roger II, the first king of Sicily, who died in 1154, and other Norman–Swabian royalty. Neapolitan architect Ferdinando Fuga began a restoration in 1771 in an all-encompassing neo-classical style, adding a cupola that sticks out like a sore thumb on the original Norman design. You can still pick out some of the original elements: four impressive bell towers from the 14th century; the middle portal from the 15th century; and the south and north porticos from the 15th and 16th centuries.

Piazza Cattedrale. ✆ **091/334-373.** Duomo free; crypt and treasury 1€ each. Church: Mon–Sat 7am–7pm, Sun 8am–1pm and 4–7pm. Crypt and Treasury: Mon–Fri 9am–2pm, Sat 9am–5:30pm, and Sun 9am–1pm. Bus: 101, 104, 105, 107, 139.

Galleria Regionale della Sicilia/Palazzo Abatellis ★★★ MUSEUM   Competing for attention with this fine collection is the late-15th-century *palazzo* that houses it, built around two courtyards and beautifully restored in the 1950s. On display is an array of the arts in Sicily from the 13th to the 18th centuries, though it's hard to get beyond the gallery's most celebrated work, the **"Trionfo della Morte"** ★ ("Triumph of Death"). Dating from 1449 and of uncertain attribution, this huge study in black and gray is prominently displayed in a two-story ground-floor gallery (climb the stairs to the balcony for an overview). Death has never looked worse—a fearsome skeletal demon astride an undernourished steed, brandishing a scythe as he leaps over his victims (allegedly members of Palermo aristocracy, who were none too pleased with the portrayal). The painter is believed to have depicted himself in the fresco, seen with an apprentice praying in vain for release from the horrors of Death; the poor and hungry looking on have escaped such a gruesome fate for the time being. The precision of this astonishing work, including details of the horse's nostrils and the men and women in the full flush of their youth, juxtaposed against such darkness, suggests the Surrealism movement that came to the fore 400 years later.

The second masterpiece of the gallery, in room 4, is a refreshing antidote, and also quite modern-looking: the white-marble, slanted-eyed bust of **Eleonora di Aragona** ★ by Francesco Laurana, who captured this likeness of Eleanor, daughter of King Ferdinand I of Naples, shortly before she married Ercole d'Este in 1468 and became the duchess of Ferrara. In room 11, Antonello da Messina's **"Annunciation"** is probably the artist's most famous work, completed in 1476 in Venice. He depicts the Virgin as an adolescent girl, sitting at a desk with a devotional book in front of her, clasping her cloak modestly to her chest. She raises her hand, seemingly to us viewers but probably to Gabriel, who has just delivered the news that she is to be the mother of the son of God. Considering that news, her expression is remarkably serene. It's one of the most lovely and calming works anywhere.

Via Alloro 4, Palazzo Abatellis. www.regione.sicilia.it/beniculturali/palazzoabatellis. 𝓒 **091/623-0011.** 8€ adults, 4€ children; 10€ combined ticket with Palazzo Mirto (p. 753) and Oratorio dei Bianchi. Tues–Fri 9am–6:30pm and Sat–Sun 9am–1pm. Bus: 103, 105, 139.

Museo Archeologico Regionale Antonino Salinas (Regional Archaeological Museum) ★★★ MUSEUM

A head-spinning repository of artifacts from Sicily's many inhabitants and invaders—Phoenicians, Greeks, Saracens, Romans—are set in the former convent of the Filippini. The most important treasures are metopes (temple friezes) from Selinunte (see p. 806)—sumptuous detailed marbles depicting Perseus slaying Medusa, the Rape of Europa by Zeus, Actaeon being transformed into a stag, and other scenes that bring these myths vividly to life. Among the other artifacts—anchors from Punic warships and mirrors used by the Etruscans—is a rare Egyptian find: The **Pietra di Palermo** (Palermo Stone), a black stone slab dating from 2700 B.C. that is known as the Rosetta stone of Sicily. Discovered in Egypt in the 19th century, it was in transit for the British Museum in London when it was shuffled off to the corners of a Palermo dock. The hieroglyphics reveal the inscriber's

THE oratories OF GIACOMO SERPOTTA

Some of Palermo's most delightful places of worship are oratories, private chapels funded by societies and guilds and usually connected to a larger church. Giacomo Serpotta, a native master of sculpting in stucco, decorated several oratorios in the early 18th century. Hours vary, but most are open Monday through Saturday 9am to 6pm. Admission to one oratory usually includes admission to a second one.

Serpotta was a member of the Society of the Holy Rosary, and he decorated the society's **Oratorio del Rosario di San Domenico** (Via dei Bambinai; ☏ **091/332-779; 6€**) with delightfully expressive putti (cherubs), who are locked forever in a playground of happy antics. His 3-D reliefs depict everything from the Allegories of the Virtues to the Apocalypse of St. John to a writhing "Devil Falling from Heaven." Anthony van Dyck, the Dutch master who spent time in Palermo in the 1620s, did the "Madonna of the Rosary" over the high altar.

Serpotta also worked between 1698 and 1710 on the **Oratorio di San Lorenzo** (Via dell'Immacolatella; ☏ **091/332-779; 3€**), creating panels relating the lives of St. Francis and St. Lawrence to create what critics have admiringly called "a cave of white coral."

Some of the most expressive of the stuccoes depict the martyrdom of Lawrence, who was roasted to death and nonchalantly informed his tormentors, "I'm well done. Turn me over." Caravaggio's last large painting, a Nativity, once hung over the altar, but it was stolen in 1969 and never recovered.

The all-white **Oratorio del Rosario di Santa Cita** (Via Valverde 3; ☏ **091/332-779; 6€**) houses Serpotta's crowning achievement: a detailed relief of the 1571 Battle of Lepanto, in which a coalition of European states defeated the Turks, more or less preventing the expansion of the Ottoman Empire into Western Europe and so defending Christianity against Islam. Serpotta's cherubs, oblivious to international affairs, romp up and down the walls and climb onto window frames.

attention to detail: a list of pharaohs, details of the delivery of 40 shiploads of cedarwood to Snefru, and flood levels of the Nile.
Piazza Olivella 24. www.regione.sicilia.it. ☏ **091/611-6805.** 3€. Tues–Sat 9am–6pm, Sun 9am–1:30pm. Bus: 101, 102, 103, 104, 107.

Palazzo Chiaramonte Steri/Museo dell'Inquisizione ★ PALACE/
MUSEUM   The Inquisition was put in force in Sicily from about 1600 to 1780 as a means for the Roman Catholic church to stifle the aristocracy and control the populace. Accused were held in this palace, built in 1307 for the powerful Chiaramonte family, when it was headquarters of the Aragonese/Spanish viceroys of Sicily. The lower floors housed prisoners from all levels of society in miniscule cagelike cells that were left untouched through the centuries, preserving a wealth of graffiti: hearts, caricatures, maps, initials, and verse inscribed by the hapless souls who were left here to rot or, worse, tortured and hung. An antidote to all this misery is a bright gallery that houses the exuberant *Le Vucciria,* a scene of the nearby market saturated with color and realism, by Palermitano

painter Renato Guttuso (1912–1987). Even more refreshing are views of the sea and the old city from the top-floor **Sala Magna,** with an elaborately painted ceiling that depicts scenes from the Bible and mythology. You can only visit on guided tours, offered in English.

Piazza Marina 61. www.musei.unipa.it. *©* **091/607-5306.** 8€, 5€ 65 and over and children 10–17. Tues–Sun 10am–7pm.

Palazzo dei Normanni ★★ and Cappella Palatina ★★★ PALACE

The cultural influences of Sicily collide in this palace dating back to the 8th century B.C., when Punic administrators set up an outpost in the highest part of the city. In the 9th century A.D. the Arabs built a stronghold on the spot for their emirs and their harems, and in the 12th century the Normans turned what was essentially a fortress into a sumptuous royal residence. Here Frederick II presided over the early 13th-century court of minstrels and literati that founded the Scuola Poetica Siciliana, marking the birth of Italian literature. Spanish viceroys took up residence in 1555, and today most of the vast maze of rooms and grand halls houses the seat of Sicily's regional government.

Entrance to the Cappella Palatina, Palazzo dei Normanni.

Arab–Norman cultural influences intersect most spectacularly in the **Cappella Palatina,** a chapel covered in glittering Byzantine mosaics from 1130 to 1140. Work was finished in time for the coronation of Roger II, who proved to be not only the most powerful of European kings but also the most enlightened. High in the cupola at the end of the apse is Christ Pantocrator (holding the New Testament in his left hand and making the blessing with his right hand), surrounded by biblical characters, some interpreted a little less piously than usual—an unremorseful Adam and Eve happily munch on the forbidden fruit and greedily reach for a second piece. Shame prevails in the next scene, when God steps in reproachfully and the naked couple cover themselves. The mosaics are vibrant in the soft light, an effect especially powerful in scenes depicting water—in the flood and the Baptism of Christ, the water actually appears to be shimmering.

Scenes on the wooden ceiling were done in a 3-D technique using small sections of carved wood, known in Arabic as *muqarnas.* A team of Egyptian carpenters and painters created the playfully secular scenarios of dancers, musicians, hunters, drinkers, and banqueters in a harem. They're best seen with binoculars or a telephoto lens.

The **Royal Apartments** are open to the public when the Sicilian parliament is not in session. Tuesdays through Thursdays, legislators meet in the **Salone d'Ercole,** named for its mammoth 19th-century frescoes depicting the twelve labours of Hercules (perhaps an apt emblem for legislators wading through government bureaucracy). Rooms from the years of Spanish rule are fairly pompous, but earlier eras are also represented, as in the **Sala dei Presidenti,** a stark medieval chamber hidden in the bowels of the palace for centuries, completely unknown until it was exposed by a 2002 earthquake. The **Torre Gioaria** (Tower of the Wind) provided a 12th-century version of air-conditioning: A fountain in the middle of the tower (since removed) spouted water that cooled the breezes coming from the four hallways. Much less hospitable are the **Segrete,** or dungeons, where the cold stone walls are etched with primitive scenes of Norman warships. The otherwise enlightened Frederick II allegedly took his interest in science to perverse lengths in these chambers, shutting prisoners in casks to see if their souls could be observed escaping through a small hole at the moment of death. Frederick was also fascinated by the stars and brought many astronomers and astrologers to his court. His Bourbon successors shared the interest and in 1790 added an astronomical observatory, still functioning, at the top of the **Torre Pisana.** From these heights in 1801 the priest Fra Giuseppe Piazza discovered Ceres, the first asteroid known to mankind.

Piazza del Parlamento. www.ars.sicilia.it. © **091/626-833.** Cappella Palatina and Royal Apartments 12€, 10€ seniors and ages 14–17; Cappella Palatina only 10€, 8€ seniors and ages 14–17. Mon–Sat 8:15am–5:40pm; Sun 8:15am–1pm. Bus: 104, 105, 108, 109, 110, 118, 304, 309.

Palazzo Mirto ★★ HISTORIC SITE   The streets of old Palermo are lined with palaces; though some are decrepit and/or abandoned, many are still the homes of artistocratic families. Few are as beautifully maintained as the home of the princes of Lanza Filangieri, one of Sicily's oldest families. The last of the princes bequeathed his 17th-century home to the city in the 1980s, leaving behind the copious trappings of his aristocratic lifestyle: furnishings, statues, rococo fountains that splash on hidden patios, and elaborate tableware (including plates given away as party favors, decorated with images of the costumed nobs who once danced the night away in the over-the-top ballroom). It's hard to imagine that life in the grandiose, tapestry-hung salons could have been very comfortable or relaxed, especially for the fashionable 20th-century princes and princesses whose photos appear casually on ornate side tables. Then again, it would have been transporting to while away an evening in the smoking room decorated in painted-silk scenes of everyday life in China as a 19th-century artisan imagined it to be. As it is, the remarkably well-preserved palace affords a voyeuristic glimpse into long-vanished eras.

Via Merlo 2. ☎ **091/616-7541.** 6€. Tues–Sat 9am–6pm, Sun 9am–1pm. Bus: 103, 105, 139.

San Giovanni degli Eremiti ★ CHURCH   Palermo's most romantic landmark is a simple affair, part Arab, part Norman, with five red domes atop a portico, a single nave, two small apses, and a squat tower. As befits the humble Spanish recluse it honors, St. John of the Hermits, the church is almost devoid of decoration, though the surrounding citrus blossoms and flowers imbue the modest structure with an otherworldly aura. Adding to the charm of the spot is a Norman cloister, part of a Benedictine monastery that once stood here.

Via dei Benedettini 3. ☎ **091/707-1425.** 6€ adults; 3€ students, seniors, and children. Tues–Sat 9am–7pm; Sun–Mon 9am–1:30pm. Bus: 109 or 318.

Where to Stay in Palermo

Palermo has some excellent hotels, with rates much lower than they are in Rome or Florence. For convenience and atmosphere, don't stay too far beyond the neighborhoods in the old center (see p. 745).

EXPENSIVE

Eurostars Centrale Palace ★★   A wonderful location steps from the Quattro Canti puts this much-redone yet still grand *palazzo* within easy reach of most sights. Public rooms, including a vast frescoed salon where breakfast is served, evoke the 1890s Belle Epoque when the 17th-century *palazzo* was first converted to a hotel. The good-size guest rooms are comfortably functional, with luxe touches like rich fabrics and mosaic-tiled bathrooms; double-pane windows in the front rooms keep the street noise at bay. A rooftop terrace with an airy dining room is a retreat from the city below, with views extending to Monte Pellegrino. It's a great spot for cocktails on a warm summer night.

Via Vittorio Emanuele 327 (at Via Maqueda).www.eurostarshotels.co.uk. ☎ **091/ 8539.** 104 units. 75€–220€ double. Breakfast included in most rates. Bus: 103, 104, 105. **Amenities:** 2 restaurants; bar; exercise room; sauna; room service; babysitting; Wi-Fi (free).

Hotel Porta Felice ★ It's a sign that the old Kalsa district is on the upswing that this elegant and subdued retreat has risen amid a once derelict block of buildings just off the seafront. Marble-floored public areas are coolly soothing, while guest rooms are sleekly contemporary, with just enough antique pieces and expanses of hardwood to suggest traditional comfort. A rooftop bar and terrace is a welcome refuge, while the downstairs health spa is geared to ultimate relaxation.

Via Butera 35. www.hotelportafelice.it. ☎ **091/617-5678.** 33 units. 130€–240€ double. Rates include breakfast. Bus: 103, 104, 105, 118, 225. **Amenities:** Bar; spa; Wi-Fi (free).

MODERATE

Butera 28 ★★★ The 17th-century Lanza Tomasi Palace, facing the seafront, is the home of Duke Gioacchino Lanza Tomasi, the adopted son of Prince Giuseppe Tomasi di Lampedusa, author of one of the greatest works of modern Italian literature, *The Leopard.* The gracious duke and his charming wife, Nicoletta, have converted 12 apartments of their *palazzo* to short-stay apartments, filling them with family pieces and all the modern conveniences, including full kitchens and, a traveler's dream come true, washing machines. Apartments have one or two bedrooms; some have sea views and terraces, some are multilevel, and all have beautiful hardwood or tile floors and other detailing. The duchess also offers cooking classes, and she, the duke, and their hospitable assistants are on hand to provide a wealth of advice to help you get the most out of their beloved Palermo.

Via Butera 28. www.butera28.it. ☎ **333/316-5432.** 12 units. Doubles from 85€. Bus: 103, 104, 105, 118, 225. **Amenities:** Kitchens; Wi–Fi (free).

House of Tiles

One of Palermo's delightful hidden treasures is the **Stanza al Genio ★,** a collection of 2,300 historic tiles of Neapolitan and Sicilian manufacture. They cover every inch of a private apartment on the *piano nobile* of an old palace in the Kalsa district. An informative guide will walk you through the kitchen, dining room, and living room, explaining the glorious ceramics carpeting the walls and floors. The museum is at Via Garibaldi 11 (www. stanzealgenio.it; ☎ **340/097-1561);** Tuesday–Sunday tours in English are at 10am and 3pm, in Italian at 11am and 4pm. Admission is 9€.

Grand Hotel Piazza Borsa ★★ This conglomeration of three historic buildings seems to take in a bit of every part of Palermo's past—the banking floor and grand offices of the old stock exchange, a monastery, and a centuries-old *palazzo*. These elements come together atmospherically in surroundings that include a cloister, open-roofed atrium, paneled dining rooms, and frescoed salons. Guest rooms are a bit more businesslike, though large and plushly comfortable, with hardwood floors and furnishings that cross tradition with contemporary flair; the best have balconies overlooking the surrounding churches and palaces. A spa and exercise area includes a sauna and steam room.

Via dei Cartari 18. www.piazzaborsa.com. ✆ **091/320075.** 103 units. 120€–200€ double. Rates include breakfast. Bus: 103, 104, 105, 118, 225. **Amenities:** Restaurant; bar; babysitting; concierge; spa; Wi-Fi (free).

Palazzo Brunaccini ★★ Princess Lucrezia Brunaccini probably wouldn't recognize the home from which she reigned over 18th-century Palermo society, but her dignified old *palazzo* still commands a beautiful and tranquil piazza just steps from the madness of the Ballarò market. Salons and the airy guest rooms are a pleasant mix of traditional grandeur and clean-lined contemporary touches, with oil paintings, wall hangings, and antiques thrown into the mix. Many of the high-ceilinged rooms overlook the piazza and surrounding neighborhood from small terraces.

Piazza Lucrezia Brunaccini. www.palazzobrunaccini.it. ✆ **091/586904.** 18 units. 125€–145€ double (discounts for stays of 3 or more nights). Rates include breakfast. Bus: 104, 105, 108, 109, 110, 118. **Amenities:** Restaurant; bar; Wi-Fi (free).

INEXPENSIVE

Al Giardino dell'Alloro ★★ This pleasant city-center getaway is tucked away from the fray of the surrounding Kalsa quarter, with brightly colored, nattily furnished rooms around a garden at the end of a little alley. Resident felines are as friendly as owner/manager Donatella, who's on hand with a wealth of advice. The flower-filled patio seems like the most becoming place on earth after a day of exploring Palermo.

Vicolo San Carlo 8. www.giardinodellalloro.it. ✆ **091/617-6904.** 5 units. 70€–85€ double. Rates include breakfast. Bus: 103, 105, 139. **Amenities:** Wi-Fi (free).

Ariston Hotel ★ The sixth floor of an apartment building near Teatro Massimo houses bright, airy rooms spread along a corridor off a comfortable lounge. Furnishings are of the basic wood-veneer modular variety and luxuries don't extend much beyond free coffee and tea, but the premises are spotless, owner/manager Giuseppe is a welcoming host, and a smattering of modern art hits just the right tasteful notes—all making this terribly pleasant place an excellent value.

Via Mariano Stabile 139. www.aristonpalermo.it. ✆ **091/332-2434.** 8 units. 60€–75€ double. Bus: 101. **Amenities:** Wi-Fi (free).

Il Giardino di Ballarò ★★★ The stables of the Palazzo Conte Federico were converted to a bakery more than a century ago, and now they've been revamped in the style of a casually luxurious country house, steps from the Ballarò market. In the downstairs lounges, plump couches surround a fireplace against a backdrop of old brick, arches, and columns, while a breakfast lounge and several guest rooms face a rear garden filled with banana trees and other exotic plantings. Two rooms are tucked under the eaves beneath huge skylights, and large family rooms have two bathrooms. The distinctive decor is enhanced with splashes of color, kilims, and contemporary art, all reflecting the refined taste of proprietor Annalise Correnti, whose two daughters are gracious and capable hosts.

Via Porta di Castro 75/77. www.ilgiardinodiballaro.it. ⓒ **091/212215.** 7 units. 85€– 115€. Rates include breakfast. Bus: 104, 105, 108, 109, 110, 118. **Amenities:** Bar; garden; Jacuzzi (use by arrangement); Wi-Fi (free).

Where to Eat in Palermo

The opulent **Antico Caffè Spinnato** (Via Principe di Belmonte 115; ⓒ **091/583231**), established in 1860, is the place to linger over a pastry and coffee. In the Kalsa quarter, **Ciccolateria Lorenzo** (Via Quattro Aprile 7; ⓒ **091/840846;** closed Mon.) has a wonderful selection of cakes and the best hot chocolate in Palermo. For a huge selection of elaborate pastries, head to the corner of Via Lincoln and Via Nicolo Cervello, across from the Villa Giulia botanical gardens, where neighboring **Bar Touring,** 38 Via Lincoln, ⓒ **091/616-7242,** and **Bar Rosanero,** Piazzetta Porta

---

Fast Food Palermo Style

Palermitani can put Americans to shame when it comes to a fondness for fast food, though the *cucina povera* (literally "poor man's cuisine") that street vendors and simple eateries sell here is a delicacy in itself. One favorite is *arancine* ("little oranges"), saffron-flavored rice balls, usually filled with meat ragu or ham and mozzarella, rolled in bread crumbs, and fried. Other fried favorites are *cazzilli* (potato croquettes) and *panelle* (chickpea fritters). Commanding a side of Piazza Kalsa, **Panineria Friggitoria Chiluzzo,** Piazza della Kalsa 10, is Palermo's go-to spot for street food. Even in the heat of summer, a big vat of oil boils away to turn out *panelle* and *pane e panelle,* in which the fritter is tucked between heavenly pieces of sesame

bread. You'll enjoy your meal, served daily from 8am to 5pm, at shared tables overlooking the palm-studded square and the wonderfully Arabesque 16th-century Greek Gate. **Nini Franco U' Vastiddaru,** Via Vittorio Emanuele 21 (ⓒ **091/325-987**) masters the art of deep frying and also serves *panino con la milza* (bread roll stuffed with slices of boiled spleen and melted cheese) from a takeout window or in a bare-bones room and a terrace overlooking Piazza Marina; the buzzing spot is open long hours, daily from 9am to midnight. Another popular spleen-stop is **Pani ca Meusa Porta Carbone,** facing the marina at Via Cala 62 (ⓒ **091/323-433**) and open Monday through Saturday, 7:30am to 10pm.

Reale 6, ☎ **091/616 4229,** outdo each other with their displays of home-made sweets. The Riso di Paradise, a concoction of chocolate, rice, and whipped cream at **Antica Gelateria Patricola** (on the waterfront at Foro Umberto 1; ☎ **091/851223;** closed in winter) will bring you back daily.

EXPENSIVE

Osteria dei Vespiri ★ SICILIAN   In a quiet corner of the Kalsa, this restaurant is set in several small, simple rooms on the lower floor of the beautiful Palazzo Valguarnera-Gangi (film buffs take note: The ballroom scene in The Leopard was filmed upstairs). The menu changes from osteria offerings in winter to fanciful variations on fresh seasonal ingredients in summer, when the main dining scene moves to a terrace out front. Reasonably priced winter set menus feature such well-prepared basics as pasta alla Norma (with eggplant) and grilled meats, while summertime tasting menus are a bit fussier and more expensive, offering such Sicilian classics as softly roasted tuna and pasta with sea urchins.

Piazza Croce dei Vespiri. www.osteriadeivespri.it. ☎ **091/617-1631.** Winter menus from 25€, summer menus from 30€. Mon–Sat 12:30–2:30pm and 7:30–10:30pm. Bus: 103, 104, 105, 118, 225.

Ottava Nota ★★ SICILIAN   "New Sicilian" is in full force at the most exciting of the restaurants that have opened in the once-derelict Kalsa district in recent years. Ottava Nota's sleek, black-on-gray decor is the setting for creative takes on Sicilian classics. Tuna tartare is served with avocado, risotto is laced with leeks and tuna caviar, and eggplant meatballs are topped with tomato cream. Duck, beef, and fish are market fresh and beautifully prepared, but you may not want to go beyond the pastas with fresh seafood—linguine with scallops, risotto with shrimp, tagliatelle with sea urchins. Despite the chic vibe, the friendly, attentive service is strictly old-school, and a meal begins with a complimentary glass of Prosecco.

Via Butera 55. www.ristoranteottavanota.it. ☎ **091/616-8601.** Entrees 10€–20€. Mon 8–11pm; Tues–Sat 1–3pm and 8–11pm, Sun 1–3pm. Bus: 103, 104, 105, 118, 225.

Palazzo Sambuca ★★ SEAFOOD/SICILIAN   While the beautifully restored Palazzo Sambuca in the Kalsa quarter is one of Palermo's great baroque landmarks, this ground floor namesake is white and chicly contemporary, with a couple of small, intimate dining rooms. A mother and son team oversees the kitchen while father and daughter tend to guests, serving Sicilian classics on a daily-changing menu. Fish and seafood are the focus—lightly fried baby squid, seafood risottos, simply grilled and baked fresh fish—but land-based classics, including perfectly grilled steak, are given the same reverence; all are part of a warm and elegant experience.

Via Alloro 26. ☎ **091/507-6794.** Entrees 12€–24€. Mon–Sat noon–3pm and 7–11pm. Bus: 103, 104, 105, 118, 225.

MODERATE

La Cambusa ★ SICILIAN/SEAFOOD   Palermitani have been coming to this Kalsa outpost to enjoy Sicilian favorites for decades, in good weather enjoying the beautiful Piazza Marina from the terrace out front and at other times dining in one of two plain dining rooms warmly decorated with paintings by local artists. The city's ties with the sea come to the fore in such classics as *zuppe di cozze* (mussels soup) and *bucatino fresco con le sarde* (homemade buccatini with fresh sardines), though land-based dishes include some excellent vegetarian choices, such as a memorable *ravioli ricotta e pistachi,* ricotta and pumpkin ravioli, served in a mushroom sauce.

Piazza Marina. www.lacambusa.it. © **091/584574.** Entrees 9€–18€. Tues–Sat 6–11pm, Sun 12:30–3pm and 7:30–11pm. Bus: 103, 104, 105, 118, 225.

Casa del Brodo ★★ SICILIAN   With a setting in two plain rooms on the edge of the now sadly diminished Vucciria market, this century-old institution serves old Sicilian specialties that you might not encounter outside of home kitchens. *Fritelle di fava* (fava beans) are fried with vegetables and cheese; *carni bollite* is a tantalizing assortment of tender, herb-flavored boiled meats; and the *macco di fave* (meatballs and tripe) is a carnivore's delight. The namesake *brodo* (broth) is served several ways, best as tortellini in brodo, with housemade pasta. To sample Sicilian home cooking at its best, order one of the good-value fixed-price menus.

Corso Vittorio Emanuele 175. www.casadelbrodo.it. © **091/321-655.** Entrees 8€–16€; fixed-price menus from 20€. Wed–Mon 12:30–3pm and 7:30–11pm (closed Sun June–Sept). Bus: 103, 104, 105, 118, 225.

Ferro di Cavallo ★ SICILIAN   Bright red walls seem to rev up the energy to high levels in this ever-busy favorite, but the buzz is really about the good, simple food served at very reasonable prices. A decent *antipasti* platter offers a nice sampling of *panelle* (fried chickpea fritters) and other street food, but go with the daily specials to get the full flavor of the kitchen. The preference is for beans and celery, broad beans and vegetables, meatballs in tomato sauce, boiled veal, and other classics. Service hovers between nonchalant and brusque, but the jovial atmosphere compensates, and you'll pay very little for your homey meal.

Via Venezia 20. www.ferrodicavallopalermo.it. © **091/331835.** Entrees 7€. Mon–Tues noon–3pm, Wed–Sat noon–3pm and 7:30–10:30pm. Bus: 103, 104, 105, 118, 225.

INEXPENSIVE

Antica Focacceria San Francesco ★ SICILIAN/SNACKS   Palermo street fare is good anywhere you have it, but it's especially savory in this atmospheric, marble-floored institution founded in 1834. If you've shied away from buying a *panino con la milza* (bread roll stuffed with slices of boiled spleen and melted cheese) from a street vendor, you might want to jump in and try the delicious specialty here. You can also snack or

15

SICILY | Palermo

lunch on *panelle* (deep-fried chickpea fritters), *arancini di riso* (rice balls stuffed with tomatoes and peas or mozzarella), *focaccia farcita* (flat pizza with fillings), or other sandwiches, curtly dispensed from a busy counter. Via A. Paternostro 58. www.afsf.it. ℂ **091/320264.** Sandwiches 3€–5€. Daily 11am–11pm (closed Tues Oct–Mar). Bus: 103, 105, 225.

Arte e Tradizione PIZZA   One of the city's favorite pizza parlors and probably the liveliest spot in the Kalsa quarter is always jam-packed. In the large, bright room, and on the terrace facing a scrappy patch of greenery, you're likely to be rubbing elbows with students and long tables occupied by extended families. Aside from some appetizers, you won't find much but pizza, with choices running to the dozens and including some decadent dessert concoctions. The kitchen and staff can barely keep up with the crowds, so you might wait a bit for your pizza and service can be hurried. Reservations are essential on weekends, when you're unlikely to get a table without one. Via Santa Teresa 2. ℂ **091/252-4451.** Pizzas from 6€. Tues–Sun 6pm–midnight. Bus: 107, 224.

Palermo Entertainment & Nightlife

Palermo is a cultural center of some note, with an opera and ballet season running from November to July. The principal performance venue is the restored **Teatro Massimo** ★★, Piazza G. Verdi (www.teatromassimo.it; ℂ **091/605-3111**), which boasts the third largest indoor stage in Europe. Francis Ford Coppola shot the climactic opera scene here for *The Godfather: Part III*. Built between 1875 and 1897 in a neoclassical style, the theater was restored in 1997 to celebrate its 100th birthday. Tickets range from 10€ to 125€. The box office is open Tuesday to Sunday 10am to 3pm. Guided tours in English are given Tuesday through Saturday from 9:30am to 6pm and cost 8€, 5€ for under 25 (bus 101-104, 107, 122, or 225).

Do Some Market Research

You can't do justice to Palermo without swinging through one of its street markets. Nowhere is Palermo's multicultural pedigree more evident than at the stalls of the **Ballarò** (in Piazza Ballarò), **Capo** (from Via Porta Carini south toward the cathedral), and even the sadly declining **La Vucciria** (on Via Argenteria, north of Via Vittorio Emanuele and east of Via Roma). These open-air souks go on for blocks, hawking everything from spices to seafood to handicrafts to electronics. Delve even deeper into Palermo's market culture at the neighborhood **Borgo Vecchio** market (along Via Ettore Ximenes to Via Principe di Scordia) in the newer part of the city, northwest of Piazza Politeama. Antiques vendors with many unusual buys congregate at the **Mercato delle Pulci** (Flea Market) along the Piazza Peranni, off Corso Vittorio Emanuele.

The old **Vucciria market,** no longer the lively shopping souk it once was, is remerging as a nightlife scene. **Via Chiavettieri,** leading into the neighborhood off Via Vittorio Emanuele, is lined with bars where your aperitivo comes with free *cicchetti* (snacks). The decrepit old market square and lanes surrounding it are also lined with street-food outlets and bars, and the square fills up with tables on weekends—and during soccer matches, broadcast on a huge outdoor screen. Some of the most sophisticated watering holes are in the **New City.** Few are more generous than **Graal,** several blocks beyond Teatro Massimo at Via Sant'Oliva 10 (✆ **091/333-533**), where cocktails come with a cornucopia of appetizers: pasta, seafood, pizza, so much food you probably won't need dinner afterward.

Side Trips from Palermo

For many Palermitans, a warm summer day means one thing—a trip to **Mondello Lido,** 12km (7½ miles) west of Palermo, where Belle Epoque Europeans once came to winter. Their Art Nouveau villas face a sandy beach that stretches for about 2km (1¼ miles), though there's little or no elbow room in July and August. Bus no. 806 makes the 30-minute trip from a stop on Via Libertà next to the Giardino Inglese.

Should you wish to do more than lie on a beach, many other sights are within easy reach of Palermo.

MONREALE ★★★
10km (6 miles) S of Palermo

On Monte Caputo overlooking the Conca d'Oro (the Golden Valley), this hilltop village would be just another of the many that dot this fertile area south of Palermo if it weren't for its majestic Duomo, one of Italy's greatest medieval treasures, sheathed in shimmering mosaics. The locals even have a saying, "To come to Palermo without having seen Monreale is like coming in like a donkey and leaving like an ass."

ARRIVING   **AMAT buses** (www.amat.pa.it; ✆ **091/350-111**) leave approximately every 1 hour and 15 minutes throughout the day from a stop near Palazzo dei Normanni, on Piazza Indipendenza (2€ one-way). If you are **driving** (it's about a 30-min. drive), leave your vehicle at the car park at Via Ignazio Florio. From there take a cab or walk up the 99 steps that lead to the cathedral.

Exploring the Duomo
Duomo ★★★ CATHEDRAL   Legend has it that the idea for this cathedral came to William II in a dream when, during a hunting expedition, he fell asleep under a carob tree. In his slumber, the Virgin Mary appeared to him, indicating where a treasure chest was located—and with this loot he was to build a church in her honor. Legends aside, William's ambition to leave his mark was the force behind the last—and the

Interior of the Cathedral of Monreale.

greatest—of Sicily's Arab-Norman cathedrals with Byzantine interiors. Best of all, the cathedral in Monreale never underwent any of the "improvements" that were applied to the cathedral of Palermo, so its original beauty was preserved.

For the most part, the exterior of the building is nothing remarkable. But inside, mosaics comprise 130 individual scenes depicting biblical and religious events, covering some 6,400 sq. m (68,889 sq. ft.), and utilizing some 2,200 kg (4,850 lb.) of gold. The shop in the arcade outside the entrance sells a plan of the mosaics with a legend detailing what's what, a mandatory aid to enjoying the spectacle; binoculars are also handy.

Episodes from the Old Testament are in the central nave (a particularly charming scene shows Noah's Ark riding the waves) while the side aisles illustrate scenes from the New Testament. Christ Pantocrator, the Great Ruler, looks over it all from the central apse; actually, he gazes off to one side, toward scenes from his life. Just below is a mosaic of the Teokotos (Mother of God) with the Christ child on her lap, bathed in light from the window above the main entrance. Among the angels and saints flanking Teokotos is Thomas à Becket, Archbishop of Canterbury, who was murdered on the orders of William's father-in-law, Henry II (he is the second from the right). William II is buried here and honored with a mosaic showing him being crowned by Christ. The heart of St. Louis, or

Louis IX, a 13th-century king of France, rests in the urn in which it was placed when the king died during a crusade in Tunisia; the urn was transported to Sicily, at the time ruled by Louis's younger brother, Charles of Anjou.

The cloisters adjacent to the cathedral are an Arabesque fantasy, surrounded by 228 columns topped with capitals carved with scenes from Sicily's Norman history. A splendid fountain in the shape of a palm tree adds to the romance of the place.

Piazza Guglielmo il Buono. ℰ **091/640-4413.** 4€; 2€ north transept and treasury; 2€ roof. Mon–Sat 8:30am–12:30pm and 2:30–5pm (closes 4:30pm Nov–Mar), Sun 8–9:30am and 2:30–5pm (4:30pm Nov–Mar). Cloisters daily 9am–7pm.

CEFALÙ ★★
81km (50 miles) E of Palermo

If you saw the Oscar-winning film *Cinema Paradiso,* you've already been charmed by the former fishing village of Cefalù, now a popular resort. The filmmakers wisely left out the hordes of white-fleshed northern Europeans who roast themselves on the crescent-shaped **beach,** one of the best along the northern coast, which stretches beneath the tall white houses of the old town. Towering 278m (912 ft.) above the beach and town is **La Rocca,** a massive and much-photographed crag. The Greeks thought it evoked a head, so they named the village Kephalos, which in time became Cefalù. It's a long, hot, sweaty climb up to the top, but once there, the view is panoramic, extending all the way to the skyline of Palermo in the west or to Capo d'Orlando in the east.

ARRIVING From Palermo, some three dozen **trains** (www.trenitalia.com; ℰ **892-021**) head east to Cefalù (trip time: 1 hr.). By **car,** follow Route 113 east from Palermo to Cefalù; count on at least 1½ hours of driving time. Once in Cefalù, park along either side of Via Roma for free, or pay 1€ per hour for a spot within one of the two lots signposted from the main street; both are within an easy walk of the town's medieval core.

VISITOR INFORMATION The **Cefalù Tourist Office,** Corso Ruggero 77 (ℰ **0921/421-050**), is open Monday to Saturday 8am to 7:30pm, Sunday 9am to 1pm. It's closed on Sunday in winter.

Exploring Cefalù
Getting around Cefalù on foot is easy—no cars are allowed in the historic core. The city's main street is **Corso Ruggero,** which starts at Piazza Garibaldi, one of four historic gateways to the town. Well-marked off Via Vittorio Emanuele in the town center is a reminder of everyday life for centuries: the river Cefalino flows through a series of large basins in the communal laundry, with a channel carrying the dirty rinse water into the sea just below.

Duomo ★★★ CHURCH Anchored on a wide square at the foot of towering La Rocca, the twin-towered facade of Cefalù's Duomo forms a

Duomo di Cefalù.

landmark visible for miles around. Legend has it that Roger II ordered the construction of this mighty church in the 12th century after his life was spared in a violent storm off the coast. In reality, he probably built it to flex his muscle with the papacy and show the extent of his power in Sicily. Inside are more mosaics, and even if you've become inured to the charms of these shimmering scenes in Palermo and Monreale, you're in for a bit of a surprise: This being a Norman church, Christ is depicted as a blond, not a brunette. In his hand is a Bible, a standard fixture in these images of Christ the Pantocrator (the Ruler), with the verse, "I am the light of the world; he who follows me shall not walk in darkness." Columns in the nave are said to be from the much-ruined Temple of Diana halfway up La Rocca (to inspect the rest of the stony remains, climb to the top of La Rocca).

Piazza del Duomo. cattedraledicefalu.com. ℰ **0921/922-021.** Duomo free; cloisters 3€. Church open Apr–Oct daily 8:30am–6:30; Nov–Mar Mon–Sat 8:30am–1pm and 3:30–5pm, Sun 3:30–5pm. Cloisters open Apr–Oct daily 10am–1pm and 3–6pm, Nov–Mar Mon–Fri 10am–1pm.

Museo Mandralisca ★ MUSEUM   There is only one reason to step into this small museum, and it's a compelling one: "Ritratto di un Uomo Ignoto" ("Portrait of an Unknown Man"), a 1470 work by the Sicilian painter Antonello da Messina. Seeing this young man with a sly smile and twinkling eyes—some say he was a pirate from the island of Lipari—is an experience akin to seeing the "Mona Lisa," and you won't have to fight your way through camera-wielding crowds to do so.

Via Mandralisca 13. www.fondazionemandralisca.it. ✆ **0921/421-547.** 6€, ages 11–15 4€, ages 6–10 2€. Daily 9am–7pm.

Where to Eat in Cefalù

For cakes and cookies, stop by **Pasticceria Serio Pietro,** V. G. Giglio 29 (✆ **0921-422293**), which also sells more than a dozen flavors of the most delicious gelato in town.

Osteria del Duomo ★★ SICILIAN/SEAFOOD   A prime spot across from the Duomo with great views of the Rocca makes this a worthy stop, and the fresh seafood does justice to the locale. Seafood salads are a perfect choice for lunch on a summer's day, and piscivores will love the *carpaccio de pesce* (raw, thinly sliced fish). Carnivores can tuck into the similarly excellent carpaccio of beef. Reserve on weekends.

Via Seminario 3. ✆ **0921/421-838.** Entrees 8€–16€. Daily noon–midnight. Closed mid-Nov–mid-Dec.

SEGESTA ★★★

75km (47 miles) SW of Palermo

The **Tempio di Segesta,** one of the best-preserved ancient Doric temples in Italy, proves yet again that the Greeks had a remarkable eye for where to build. Part of the ruined ancient city of Segesta, for millennia this beautiful structure in a lonely field overlooking the countryside has been delighting those lucky enough to gaze upon it. The temple was especially popular with 18th-century artists traveling in Sicily, whose paintings usually included flocks of sheep and herds of cattle surrounding the temple.

ARRIVING   From Palermo, three **trains** a day make the 1¾- to 2-hour journey to Segesta. The station is about 1km (½ mile) from the park entrance. It's more convenient to reach Segesta **by bus; Tarantola** (www.tarantolabus.com; ✆ **0924/31020**) operates three buses daily, departing from Viale Lazio next to Palermo's central train station (trip time: 1¾ hr.). By **car,** take the autostrada (A29) running between Palermo and Trapani. The exit at Segesta is clearly marked. The journey takes a little under an hour from Palermo.

Exploring the Parco Archaeologico (Archaeological Park)

The archaeological site, which is outside the modern town of Calatafimi, is still the subject of study by archaeologists from around the world. There's a small, canopied eating area opposite the only cafe, where visitors can unwind or rest during their visit.

Area Archeologico Segesta ★★★ RUINS   The **Tempio di Segesta (Temple of Segesta)** stands on a 304m (997-ft.) hill, on the edge of a deep

The Greek Temple of Segesta.

ravine carved by the Pispisa River. Built in the 5th century B.C., the temple was never finished, its columns left unfluted and its roof missing. It's been suggested that the temple was actually a ruse, begun to impress diplomats from Athens who, it was thought, would see the project as a sign of the city's wealth and therefore ally with Segesta against Selinunte. Construc-

Red-Hot Lava & Sparkling Seas: Aeolian Island Escapes

The **Aeolian Islands** can seem like exotic getaways, even as close as they are to Sicily's civilized north coast (they're reached by fer- ries and hydrofoils from the port of Milazzo). The seven islands share sparkling waters and lava-etched landscapes, and each has its own devotees. Especially popular are **Vul- cano,** a stomping ground for summertime partiers and known for black-sand beaches and thermal baths, and **Stromboli,** whose volcano sends red-hot lava tumbling down its slopes to meet the sea with a loud hiss.

tion halted as soon as the dele- gation left town. Segesta's other great sight is the perfectly pre- served **Teatro (Theater),** hewn out of rock at the top of 431m (1,414 ft.) Mount Barbaro (accessible by a hike of 4km [2½ miles] or by buses that run every half-hour; 1.50€). The *cavea* of 20 semicircular rows could seat 4,000 spectators, who enjoyed views across the surrounding farmland to the Gulf of Castellamare. Those stunning views surely competed with any performance—and still do, during summertime stagings of operas, concerts, and plays.

Parco Archaelogico Segesta. ℂ **0924/952-356.** 6€ adults, 3€ ages 18–25. Apr–Sept daily 9am–7:30pm; Mar 9am–6:30pm; Oct–Feb 9am–5pm. Ticket office closes 1 hr. before park closes.

TAORMINA ★★★

53km (33 miles) N of Catania, 53km (33 miles) S of Messina, 250km (155 miles) E of Palermo

Guy de Maupassant, the 19th-century French short-story writer, played the tourist shill and wrote, "Should you only have 1 day to spend in Sicily and you ask me 'what is there to see?' I would reply 'Taormina' without any hesitation. It is only a landscape but one in which you can find everything that seems to have been created to seduce the eyes, the mind and the imagination." Lots of visitors have felt the same way. The Roman poet Ovid loved Taormina, and 18th-century German man of letters Wolfgang Goethe put the town on the Grand Tour circuit when he extolled its virtues in his widely published diaries. Oscar Wilde was one of the gentlemen who made Taormina, as writer and dilettante Harold Acton put it, "a polite synonym for Sodom," and Greta Garbo is one of many film legends who have sought a bit of privacy here.

With its beauty and sophistication, Taormina has a surfeit of star quality itself. The town seems more international than Sicilian, and visitors often outnumber locals. Then again, perched precariously on a cliff between the sinister slopes of Mount Etna and the glittering Ionian Sea, its captivating alleyways lined with churches and *palazzi,* Taormina is almost over-the-top beautiful, and what is more Sicilian than that?

Essentials

ARRIVING   If you plan to arrive by **air,** the most convenient airport for Taormina is Catania's **Fontanarossa** airport (aeroporto.catania.it), which has numerous connections to mainland Italy and major European cities. Nine daily buses operated by Etna Transporti (www.etnatrasporti. it) run up the coast from there to Taormina, stopping in downtown Catania (trip time: about 1½ hours; tickets about 5€ one-way).

Shopping on Taormina's Corso Umberto I.

767

If you're arriving by **car**, the A18 highway connects with Messina from the north (45 min.; take Taormina exit) and Catania from the south (50 min.; exit at Giardini Naxos and follow signs up hill to Taormina). If your hotel offers parking, get very clear instructions about how to arrive—Taormina is a mind-boggling maze of tiny one-way streets and hairpin turns. Otherwise, take advantage of the large public parking garages just outside the old town, both clearly signposted with blue "P"s on all roads that approach Taormina. On the north side of town, **Parking Lumbi** (✆ **0942/24345**) charges 14€ per day (16€ per day in Aug) and has a free shuttle from the garage to the Porta Messina gate of Taormina proper. On the south end of town, the multilevel garage **Parking Porta Catania** (✆ **0942/620-196;** 15€ per day/17€ in Aug) has the advantage of being practically in town, just 100m/328 ft. from the Porta Catania city gate. Down by the beach at Mazzarò, in the vicinity of the lower cable-car station, is **Parking Mazzarò** (14€ per day, 16€ in Aug).

Taormina is well served by **buses** from the rest of Sicily, usually connecting through Catania (visit www.etnatrasporti.it for schedules). Taormina's bus station is on Via Pirandello, near Porta Messina, on the north end of town. **Trains** to Taormina run on a line between Messina and Catania, each between 40 minutes and 1½ hours away, depending on the speed of your train. See www.trenitalia.com; ✆ **89/2021** for schedules; service on Sundays is infrequent. Taormina's train station is shared with the seaside town of Giardini-Naxos, so it's 1.6km (1 mile) away from town—you'll have to take a bus up the hill to Taormina (infrequently from 9am–9pm; 2€ one-way), or a taxi (about 15€).

VISITOR INFORMATION   The **tourist office** is in Palazzo Corvaja, Piazza Santa Caterina (✆ **0942/23243** or 0942/24941; Mon–Thurs 8:30am–2pm and 4–7pm; Fri 8:30am–2pm). Here you can get a free map, hotel listings, bus and rail timetables, and a schedule of summer cultural events staged at the **Teatro Greco** (Greek Theater; see below).

Exploring Taormina

Just about everything to see in Taormina unfolds from the main drag, **Corso Umberto I,** which slices through town from Porta Messina, in the north, to Porta Catania, in the south. It only takes 15 minutes to walk the length of the Corso. Taormina is also a handy base for trips to Mount Etna—the high-altitude visitor areas are only about 1 hour away by car.

Teatro Greco (Teatro Antico) ★★★ RUINS   With their penchant for building in beautiful settings, the Greeks perched the second-largest ancient theater in Sicily (after Siracusa's, see p. 781), on the rocky flanks of Mount Tauro. The backdrop of smoldering Mount Etna and the sea crashing far below certainly provided as much drama as any theatrical production. Romans rebuilt much of the theater, adding the finishing touches on what we see today in the 2nd century A.D., and put the arena to

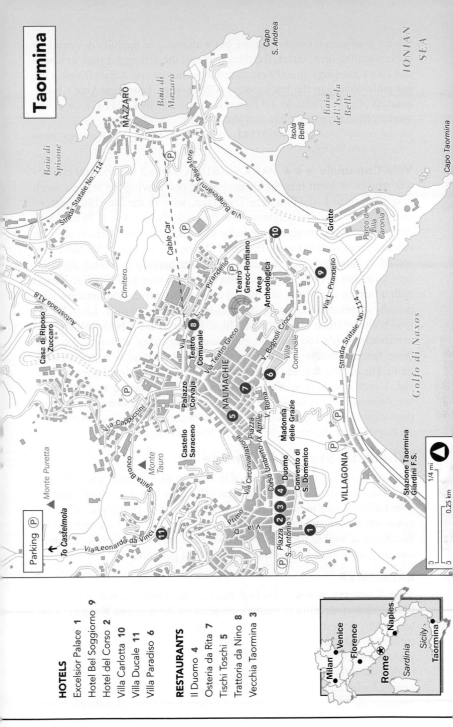

Taormina

IONIAN SEA

Capo S. Andrea

MAZZARÒ

Baia di Mazzarò

Baia di Spisone

Baia dell'Isola Bella

Isola Bella

Capo Taormina

Strada Statale No. 114

Cable Car

Cimitero

Via Bonifazio/Via Pescatore

Via Pirandello

Casa di Riposo Zuccaro

Autostrada A18

Via Cappuccini

Teatro Greco-Romano
Area Archeologica

Via L. Pirandello

Grotte

Parco di Villa Caronia

Via Teatro Greco

Teatro Comunale

Palazzo Corvaja

NAUMACHIE

V. Bagnoli Croce

Villa Comunale

Strada Statale No. 114

Golfo di Naxos

Via Circonvallazione

Salita Branco

Monte Tauro

Castello Saraceno

Piazza IX Aprile

Corso Umberto I

Madonna delle Grazie

V. Roma

Convento di S. Domenico

Duomo

Via D. Primo

Piazza S. Antonio

Via Leonardo da Vinci

▲ Monte Puretta

← *To Castelmola*

VILLAGONIA

Stazione Taormina
Giardini F.S.

◀ N

0   1/4 mi
0   0.25 km

Parking Ⓟ

HOTELS

Excelsior Palace **1**
Hotel Bel Soggiorno **9**
Hotel del Corso **2**
Villa Carlotta **10**
Villa Ducale **11**
Villa Paradiso **6**

RESTAURANTS

Il Duomo **4**
Osteria da Rita **7**
Tischi Toschi **5**
Trattoria da Nino **8**
Vecchia Taormina **3**

Milan
Venice
Florence
Naples
Rome ✳
Sardinia
Sicily
Taormina

use for gladiatorial events. In ruin, but with much of the hillside *cavea,* or curved seating area, intact, the theater is still the setting for performances and film screenings, greatly enhanced by columns and arches framing the sea and volcano in the background. Check with **TaorminaArte**'s headquarters, Corso Umberto 19 (www.taoarte.it; ℂ **0942/21142**), or at the tourist office for exact dates and show times.

Via del Teatro Greco. ℂ **0942/21142.** 10€, audio guide 5€. Daily Apr–Sept 9am–7pm; Oct–Mar 9am–4pm.

Villa Comunale ★★★ PARK/GARDEN   Of all the colorful characters who have spent time in Taormina, the one leaving the biggest mark may have been Lady Florence Trevelyan, who in the late 19th century created these beautiful gardens, now the park also known as Parco Duca di Cesarò. Lady Trevelyan allegedly was asked to leave Britain after an entanglement with Edward, Prince of Wales, son of Queen Victoria. She settled in Taormina, married, and lived quite happily in the lovely, adjacent villa that is now the hotel **Villa Paradiso** (see p. 773). Her liaison with a farmer, much of it conducted amid these groves and terraces, supposedly inspired D.H. Lawrence's *Lady Chatterley's Lover.* Lady Trevelyan built the stone and brick pavilions in the park for birdwatching and entertaining—it's too bad the gates are swung shut at sunset, because these fanciful follies would be perfect for whiling away a hot summer night. During the day, the 3 hectares (7½ acres) of groomed terraces provide a nice respite from the busy town, filled as they are with luxuriant vegetation, cobblestone walkways, picturesque stone stairways, and a sinuous path lining the park's eastern rim with superb views over the sea.

Via Bagnoli Croce. No phone. Free. Daily 8:30am–7pm (6pm in winter).

Where to Stay in Taormina

The hotels in Taormina are some of the best in Sicily. Quite a few close in the winter, but those that remain open offer rates at a fraction of summertime tariffs. If you're driving to a hotel at the top of Taormina, call ahead to see what arrangements can be made for your car. Ask for exact driving directions as well as instructions on where to park—the narrow, winding, one-way streets can be bewildering once you get here.

EXPENSIVE

Villa Carlotta ★★★   Tucked away at the edge of town, this castellated 1920s stone villa is another creation of Andrea and Rosaria Quartucci, who work their magic at **Villa Ducale** (below). A wall of Byzantine catacombs adds an air of mystery, but what wins you over is the classic-yet-contemporary style and wonderful sense of privacy and comfort. Most of the warm-hued, stylish rooms have terraces and sea views, and many overlook the luxuriant rear gardens, with a swimming pool amid the greenery. Service is personalized and attentive, and there's a shuttle bus to

MEET mighty MOUNT ETNA

Warning: Always get the latest report from the tourist office before setting out for a trip to Mount Etna. Adventurers have been killed by a surprise "belch" (volcanic explosion). Mount Etna remains one of the world's most active volcanoes, with sporadic gas, steam, lava, and ash emissions from its summit.

Looming menacingly over the coast of eastern Sicily, Mount Etna is the highest and largest active volcano in Europe. The peak changes in size over the years but it currently soars 3,324m (10,906 ft.). Etna has been active in modern times: In 1928, the little village of Mascali was buried under lava, and powerful eruptions in 1971, 1992, 2001, and 2003 caused extensive damage to facilities nearby. Throughout the year, episodes of spectacular but usually harmless lava fountains, some hundreds of meters high, are not uncommon, providing a dramatic show for viewers in Taormina.

Etna has figured in history and in Greek mythology. Empedocles, the 5th-century-B.C. Greek philosopher, is said to have jumped into its crater in the belief that he would be delivered directly to Mt. Olympus to take his seat among the gods. It was under Etna that Zeus crushed the multiheaded dragon Typhoeus, thereby securing domination over Olympus. Hephaestus, god of fire, made his headquarters in Etna, aided by the single-eyed Cyclops. The Greeks warned that when Typhoeus tried to break out of his prison, lava erupted and earthquakes cracked the land. That must mean that the monster nearly escaped on March 11, 1669, one of the most violent eruptions ever—it destroyed Catania, about 27km (17 miles) away.

Etna is easy to reach by car from Taormina. The fastest way is to take the E45 autostrada south to the Acireale exit. From here, follow the brown etna signs west to Nicolosi, passing through several smaller towns along the way. From Nicolosi, keep following the etna signs up the hill toward **Rifugio Sapienza** (1,923m/6,307 ft.), the starting point for all expeditions to the crater. The faux-Alpine hamlet here has tourist services and cheap and ample parking, and is the base station of the **Funivia del Etna** cable car (www.funiviaetna.com; ✆ **095-914-141;** daily 9am–4:15pm/3:45 in winter), which takes you to the **Torre del Filosofo** (Philosopher's Tower) station at 2,900m (9,514 ft.). You can also hike up to the station, but it's a strenuous climb and takes about 5 hours. The final ascent to the authorized crater areas at about 3,000m (9,843 ft., as close to the summit as visitors are allowed) is via *Star Wars*-ish off-road vehicles over a scrabbly terrain of ash and dead ladybugs (dead ladybugs are everywhere on Mount Etna). Conditions at the crater zone are thrilling, but the high winds, exposure, and potential sense of vertigo are not for the faint of heart.

The round-trip cost of getting to the top of Etna, including the cable car ride, the off-road vans, and the requisite authorized guide at the crater zone, is about 55€. Etna is not a complicated excursion to do on your own, but if you'd prefer to go with a tour, Taormina is chock-full of agencies that organize Etna day trips.

the beach. Villa Carlotta also operates the **Taormina Luxury Apartments** (www.taorminaluxuryapartments.com) up the street.

Via Pirandello 81. www.hotelvillacarlottataormina.com. ✆ **0942/626-058.** 23 units. 180€–350€ double. Rates include breakfast. Parking 10€. Closed Jan–early Mar. **Amenities:** Restaurant; concierge; health club; pool; Wi-Fi (free).

Villa Ducale ★★★　Andrea and Rosaria Quartucci have fashioned a family villa into a warm and stylish getaway perched high on a hillside above the town, with flower-planted terraces, Mediterranenan gardens, and extraordinary eagle's-nest views that extend as far as Calabria. Distinctive rooms and suites, in the villa and a house across the road, are done in Sicilian chic, with extremely comfortable furnishings set against warm hues that play off terracotta floors; they are enlivened with beams, arches, and other stylish architectural details, equipped with luxurious baths, and fitted out with fine linens and works by local artists. Service is exceedingly warm and personal, and a lavish buffet breakfast and complimentary sunset cocktails, accompanied by a spread of Sicilian appetizers, are served on a living-room-like terrace; lunch and dinner are available on request. The hotel has no pool, but there's a Jacuzzi, and a shuttle makes a run to a private beach (and also to town).

Via Leonardo da Vinci 60. www.villaducale.com. ℭ **0942/28153.** 15 units. 120€–400€ double. Rates include buffet breakfast. Parking 10€. Closed Jan–early Mar. **Amenities:** Jacuzzi; room service; Wi-Fi (free).

MODERATE

Excelsior Palace ★　The word "palace" in the name is a bit misleading—this sprawling pink hotel, just off Corso Umberto behind the Duomo, dates only to the early 20th century. Rooms have not been upgraded since a time when burnt-orange bathroom tiles and floral carpets were all the rage, but they're well maintained, and every one has a view—many of Mt. Etna and the coastline—and many have little balconies with just enough room for two chairs. Though the place is often filled with groups, service is attentive and old-world, with waiters in ties and jackets serving cocktails in frumpy lounges full of overstuffed couches and armchairs. The magnificent garden is the best amenity, draped over a promontory above the town and sea and the setting for a magnificently perched swimming pool—making this a top summertime choice.

Via Toselli 8. www.excelsiorpalacetaormina.it. ℭ **0942/23975.** 85 units. 75€–240€ double. Rates include breakfast. Amenities: Restaurant; bar; concierge; pool; Wi-Fi in public areas (free).

Hotel Bel Soggiorno ★★　You could be nowhere but Sicily in this rather grand old villa surrounded by lush gardens that tumble down a hillside, filled with lemon and orange trees, exotic flowers, and sweeping coastal vistas. Tile-floored guest rooms are plain but comfortable, with handsome iron bedsteads and simple wooden furniture. All open through French doors to balconies and, in many cases, huge terraces. A friendly staff serves breakfast, with some cooked choices, in a beautiful orangerie and on an adjoining patio. As bucolic as the surroundings are, the center of town is an easy 10-minute walk away.

Via Luigi Pirandello 60. www.belsoggiorno.com. ℭ **0942/23342.** Doubles from 90€. Rates include breakfast. **Amenities:** Bar; gardens; Wi-Fi (free).

Villa Paradiso ★   Lady Florence Trevelyan, who created the beautiful gardens that are now the Villa Communale (see p. 595), lived in this villa until her death in 1907. The elegant house then passed to the Martorana family, three generations of whom have proven to be outstanding hoteliers and avid renovators, adding entire floors to the original house. Family antiques, comfy armchairs and couches, and paintings (many presented by guests over the years) fill lounges and bright, handsomely decorated guest rooms, where balconies and sun-drenched sitting alcoves face the sea. Breakfast and dinners are served in a top-floor, glassed-in restaurant, **Settimo Cielo** (Seventh Heaven), which it really seems to be. Between June and October, the hotel offers free shuttle service and free entrance to the Paradise Beach Club, about 6km (4 miles) to the east, in the seaside resort of Letojanni.

Via Roma 2. www.hotelvillaparadisotaormina.com. ℂ **0942/23921.** 37 units. 90€–240€ double. **Amenities:** Restaurant; bar; room service; Wi-Fi (fee).

INEXPENSIVE

Hotel del Corso ★   You'll forgo spas, pools, and other chic luxuries in these basic lodgings right in the heart of town, on Corso Umberto near the Duomo, but you won't give up views of the sea and Mt. Etna. They fill the windows of many of the rooms and spread out below the top floor lounge, breakfast room, and sun terrace; some rooms have less dramatic but pleasing views of the town. Black-and-white terrazzo floors, iron bed-steads, and soothing neutral colors add a lot of spark to the comfortable guest rooms, a few of which have small balconies. Book well in advance, especially on weekends, when this good-value property fills up fast.

Corso Umberto 328. www.hoteldelcorsotaormina.com. ℂ **0942/628-698.** 15 units. 80€–110€ double. Rates include breakfast. **Amenities:** Wi-Fi (free).

Where to Eat in Taormina

The ultimate Sicilian summer refreshment, the sorbet-like *granita,* is perfect at **Bam Bar,** not far from the Grand Hotel Timeo at Via di Giovanni 45 (ℂ **0942/24355**). Specialties are the almond *(mandorla)* or white fig *(fico bianco),* but there are usually a dozen or more flavors to choose from.

MODERATE

Il Duomo ★★ SICILIAN   The decor leaves something to be desired, with harsh lighting and a green-and-orange color scheme—to avoid it, choose a table near the large window overlooking the Duomo, or better yet in good weather, on the side terrace. Fortunately, the food takes no such liberties in taste, sticking to traditional Sicilian recipes, with some well-conceived modern twists. This is the best place in town to try pasta con sarde (with sardines and breadcrumbs); the fish is fresh and nicely enlivened with capers, tomatoes, and olives.

Vico Ebrei (at Piazza Duomo). www.ristorantealduomotaormina.com. ℂ **0942/625-656.** Entrees 10€–16€. Daily noon–3pm and 7–11pm.

Tischi Toschi ★★★ SICILIAN/SEAFOOD   A warm-hued yellow room facing a little piazza and decorated with old ceramics is the setting for creative takes on old Sicilian classics. Even *pasta alla Norma* (with eggplant and ricotta) seems like a work of art here, and is topped with a grilled eggplant. Venture further into some dishes you might not find in many other places, such as *insalata di pesce stocco,* a salad made from dried cod, raw fennel, and tomato dressed with olive oil and parsley, and *sarde a beccafico,* sardines stuffed with pine nuts and fennel and served with lemon and orange. Don't miss the delicious fried artichokes, and end a meal with the heavenly, refreshing lemon jelly.

Via F. Paladini 3 (off Corso Umberto). www.tischitoschitaormina.com. © **339/364-2088.** Entrees 10€–18€. Daily noon–3pm and 6:30–11pm.

Vecchia Taormina ★★ SICILIAN/PIZZA   One of Taormina's long-time favorites keeps a steady stream of regulars happy with what are reputed to be the best pizzas around. The *pizza alla Norma,* the ingredients of the classic eggplant-laden pasta on a flaky crust, makes good on the claim. The kitchen also does nice versions of spaghetti con vongole (with clams), or topped with fresh sardines and breadcrumbs, as well as other classics, serving them in two cozy rooms and a delightful outside terrace.

Vicolo degli Ebrei 3. © **0942/625-589.** Entrees 10€–15€. Daily noon–11:30pm.

INEXPENSIVE

Osteria da Rita ★★ SICILIAN/PIZZA   Taormina needs more easy-going eateries like this pleasant little place tucked away between the Corso and Villa Communale. Pizzas, sandwiches, salads, omelets, and a few pasta dishes—including heaping platters of spaghetti carbonara and *pasta alla Norma*—are served in a small, plain room and on a picture-perfect piazzetta out front. Service is friendly and prices are reasonable.

Via Calapitrulli 3. © **0942/681-051.** Entrees 7€–13€. Daily noon–3pm and 7:30–10:30pm (sometimes closed for lunch).

Trattoria da Nino ★ SICILIAN   Good, no-nonsense Sicilian *cucina casalinga* (home cooking) is the recipe for success in this unpretentious, brightly lit room (with an airy terrace in warm weather) across from the upper station of the cable car. Pastas are housemade (deliciously delicate gnocchi, little potato dumplings, are served *alla Norma,* with eggplant and ricotta), and the fish is fresh and served simply grilled. Nino's is a local institution, a 50-year veteran of the Taormina dining scene, and it's always packed; they don't take reservations for groups of fewer than six.

Via Pirandello 37. www.trattoriadaninotaormina.com. © **0942/21265.** Entrees 8€–18€. Daily noon–3pm and 6–11pm.

Beaches Near Taormina

To reach Taormina's best and most popular beach, **Lido Mazzarò,** you have to go south of town via a cable car (© **0942/23605**) that in theory but often not practice leaves from Via Pirandello every 15 minutes (3€ each way, 10€ day ticket, 50€ weekly ticket for nonresidents, spring and summer only) between 8am and 8pm (from 9am on Monday). The soft, finely pebbled beach is one of the best equipped in Sicily, with bars, restaurants, and hotels. You can rent beach chairs, umbrellas, and watersports equipment at kiosks from April to October. To the right of Lido Mazzarò, past the Capo Sant'Andrea headland, is the region's prettiest cove, where twin crescents of beach sweep out to the minuscule **Isola Bella** islet.

North of Mazzarò, the long, wide beaches of **Spisone** and **Letojanni** are more developed but less crowded than **Giardini,** the large resort beach south of Isola Bella. A local bus leaves Taormina for Mazzarò, Spisone, and Letojanni; another heads down the coast to Giardini.

Taormina Shopping

Shopping is all too easy in Taormina—just walk along **Corso Umberto I.** Ceramics are one of Sicily's most notable handicrafts, and Taormina's shops are among the best places to buy them on the island, as the selection is excellent. **Di Blasi Ceramiche,** Corso Umberto I 103 (✆ **0942/24671**), has a nice range of designs and specializes in the highly valued "white pottery" from Caltagirone. Mixing the new and the old, **Carlo Panarello Antichità,** Corso Umberto I 122 (✆ **0942/23910**) offers Sicilian ceramics (from pots to tables) and also deals in eclectic antique furnishings, paintings, and engravings.

Side Trips from Taormina
CASTELMOLA ★★

Taormina gets high praise for its gorgeous views, but for connoisseurs of scenic outlooks, the real show takes place in the village of Castelmola, an eagle's nest 3km (2 miles) northwest of Taormina, and about 300m (1,000 ft.) feet higher. The Ionian Sea seems to stretch to the ends of the earth from up here, and you'll be staring right into the northern flanks of Mt. Etna. For the full experience, make the trip up on foot, following routes that begin at Porta Catania and Porta Messina (the tourist office or any hotel desk can give you directions); the Porta Messina trail passes a section of the Roman aqueduct and the Convento dei Cappuccini, where you can pause for a breather. Either route involves an hour or so of fairly strenuous walking, but once at the top, stop at Castelmola's **Bar Turrisi** (Piazza Duomo 19; ✆ **0942/28181;** daily 10am–midnight, until 2am weekends) for a glass of *vino alla mandorla* (almond wine) and a look at its peculiar art collection. If that's more walking than you care to do, you can also drive up to Castelmola (park below the village and walk in) or take an orange bus that runs more or less hourly from Porta Messina (2.20€ round-trip).

GOLE DELL'ALCANTARA ★★

In a series of narrow gorges on the Alcantara (Al-*cahn*-ta-rah) river, rushing ice-cold water fed by snow melt on Mt. Etna darts and dashes over fantastically twisted volcanic rock, creating a scenic spectacle that's especially refreshing on a hot day. The basalt rock formations were sculpted into these wild shapes thousands of years ago by cool water flowing over molten debris during eruptions on Etna. The gorge is now protected as **Parco Fluviale dell'Alcanta** (www.parcoalcantara.it; ✆ **0942/985010**), though ticket booths, turnstiles, and elevators into the gorge lend an amusement-park aura. Get away from the crowds with a hike along the riverbed, stopping now and then to lounge on flat riverside rocks and wade and even swim in the chilly water. From October to April, only the upper area of the park, with an overlook trail above the gorge, is open. It costs 8€ to enter the park (open daily 7am–7:30pm). Amenities include a gift shop, cafeteria, picnic areas, and toilets. You can reach the Gole dell'Alcantara by car from Taormina in 35 minutes or you can take **Interbus** (www.interbus.it; ✆ **0942/625301**) for the 1-hour trip, with several daily runs from Taormina (5€ roundtrip). Organized excursions (from 25€) to the gorges are also offered by tour operators in Taormina, often in conjunction with a visit to Mount Etna.

SIRACUSA ★★

This small, out-of-the-way southern city packs a one-two punch. Siracusa was one of the most important cities of Magna Graecia (Greater Greece), rivaling even Athens in power and influence. The still-functioning Teatro Greco, where Aeschylus debuted his plays, is one of many landmarks of this ancient metropolis. Ortigia, the quaint historical center spreading over its own island, belongs to a much later time, when palaces and churches were built in baroque style after the earthquake that destroyed much of the southeast in 1693.

Siracusa might seem far removed from most of Europe, but in making the trip to the southeast coast you'll be following in the illustrious footsteps of the scientist Archimedes, statesman Cicero, evangelist St. Paul, martyr St. Lucy, painter Caravaggio, and naval hero Admiral Lord Horatio Nelson, all of whom left a mark on this rather remarkable place. According to myth, Leto stopped here to give birth to Artemis, one of the twins she conceived with Zeus; she continued on her way and delivered Apollo on the Greek island of Delos.

Essentials

ARRIVING   If you plan to arrive by **air**, the most convenient airport for Siracusa is Catania's **Fontanarossa** airport (aeroporto.catania.it), which has numerous connections to mainland Italy and many European cities.

Interbus buses (www.etnatrasporti.it) run almost hourly between Siracusa and Catania. Siracusa is 45 minutes south of the airport via E45 and SS114; it's 1½ hours south of Taormina on the A18, and about 2 hours south from Messina. Driving time to Palermo or Agrigento is about 3 hours. Siracusa is well connected with the rest of Sicily by bus (www.etnatrasporti.it) and train (www.trenitalia.com; © **89/2021**); bus service tends to be more efficient and frequent. Both trains and buses arrive in Siracusa at the station on Via Francesco Crispi, between the Parco Archeologico (Archaeological Park) and Ortigia Island. Bus 20 and small shuttle buses run between the station and Ortigia, a fairly easy 15-minute walk.

GETTING AROUND   You won't need a car, just your own two feet and perhaps a few bus or cab rides to see the best of Siracusa proper. If you're traveling by car, ask your hotel before arriving about the best place to park. Ortigia Island is ringed with public lots, including the large **Talete** complex at the northern end, near the bridge to the mainland. Parking is .60€ to 1€ an hour, payable in machines. These lots use a computerized camera system in which you enter your license number when leaving and pay the appropriate amount. Much of Ortigia, with the exemption of the circumference road and a few main thoroughfares, is off-limits to nonresidents and monitored with cameras, so pay close attention to signs.

VISITOR INFORMATION   The **tourist office,** at Via San Sebastiano 43 (© **0931/481232**), is open Monday to Friday 8:30am to 1:30pm and 3 to 6pm, Saturday 8:30am to 1:30pm. There's another office in the historic center at Via della Maestranza 33 (© **0931/65201**); it's open Monday to Friday 8:15am to 2pm and 2:30 to 5:30pm, Saturday 8:15am to 2pm.

Exploring Siracusa

Ortigia Island is Siracusa's *centro storico,* a mostly pedestrian zone where narrow alleys lined with romantic 18th-century *palazzi* spill onto Piazza del Duomo. The ancient ruins are a good half-hour walk north of Ortigia along Corso Gelone.

ORTIGIA ISLAND ★★★

The historic center of Siracusa is an island only about 1 sq. km (¾ sq. mile), with breezy, palm-shaded seaside promenades fringing its shores. Although Ortigia was settled in ancient times, most of the island today is baroque, with grandiose palaces and churches lining narrow lanes and flamboyant piazzas.

The first landmark you'll come to after you cross Ponte Umbertino from the mainland is the **Temple of Apollo,** the oldest Doric temple in Sicily. The Apollion would have measured 58m × 24m (190 ft. × 79 ft.) when it was built in the 6th century B.C. It later served as a Byzantine church, then a mosque, then a church again under the Normans; it's now

Siracusa's Ortigia Island.

an evocative ruin, with the temple platform, a fragmentary colonnade, and an inner wall rising in the middle of Piazza Pancali.

The **Piazza del Duomo,** certainly one of the most beautiful squares in Sicily, is all about theatrics—a sea of white marble softened by pink oleander and surrounded by flamboyant palaces with elaborate stone fili-gree work and wrought-iron balconies. Similarly fanciful are the frothily baroque **Duomo** and the pretty church of **Santa Lucia alla Badia,** its tall, marble baroque facade embellished with twisted columns, pediments, and a wrought-iron balcony. Also on Piazza del Duomo is an entrance to the **Hypogeum** (no phone; 3€; Tues–Sun 9am–1pm and 4–8pm), a network of underground chambers and corridors dug as air-raid shelters in World War II.

Head south from Piazza del Duomo to the waterfront, where you'll come to **Fonte Aretusa,** a basin where papyrus grows in a shallow pool that supplied Siracusa with fresh water for millennia. Classical myth, however, tells a different story: The nymph Aretusa was bathing in a river in Greece when the river god Alpheus took a liking to her. She asked the goddess Artemis, protectress of young women, for help in avoiding his advances; Artemis turned Aretusa into a river that emerged here. Not to be thwarted, Alpheus followed suit, and the two of them bubble forth for eternity.

Chiesa di Santa Lucia alla Badia ★★ CHURCH Sicracusans get a spring in their step when passing the fanciful facade of the city's favorite church, crossed with a wrought-iron balcony from which cloistered nuns once watched goings on in Piazza Duomo. St. Lucia, a plucky 4th century Siracusan virgin, is the city's patron. Born of wealth, from an early age she adopted Christian principles and decided to give her worldly goods to the poor. Her piety and generosity annoyed the young man to whom she'd been betrothed, and out of spite for seeing Lucia's sizable dowry squandered, he denounced her to Roman authorities. Lucia was condemned to prostitution, but refused to be dragged off to a brothel. Authorities tied her to a pillar and lit a fire beneath her; she proved to be flame-resistant. Finally, a soldier plunged a sword into her throat. You'll see depictions of this gruesome act throughout Siracusa and the rest of Sicily, where the saint is very popular (tamer versions show her holding the sword that killed her). The church's prize is Caravaggio's **"Burial of St. Lucia,"** commissioned in 1608 when the artist had just escaped from a prison in Malta and fled to Siracusa. Note how, with his characteristic lighting, the artist highlights the muscular gravediggers, showing their brute strength, while the mourners seem small and meek in the background. A shaft of light falls on Lucia's face and neck, highlighting the stab wound that killed her; she is a study in serenity, having entered the heavenly kingdom.

Piazza Duomo. ✆ **0931/65328.** Free. Tues–Sun 11am–4pm.

Duomo ★★ CHURCH Don't be deceived by the frothy baroque look of Siracusa's main church—its roots are much more ancient than that playful exterior suggests. The two tiers of Doric columns that define the facade were once part of the 5th-century-B.C. Temple of Athena, one of the best-known sights of the ancient world, built to mark a Greek victory over the Carthaginians. Cicero, the Roman orator and traveler, reported that the temple was filled with gold, the doors were made of gold and ivory, and a statue of Athena atop the pediment was visible for miles out to sea. Romans made off with much of the gold, alas, and 9th-century Arab marauders took the rest. The church was first fashioned from the temple around the 7th century; a statue of the Virgin now stands atop the pediment as Athena once did. Other ancient columns line the aisle in the church's strikingly simple interior, while a silver statue in a side chapel protects an important Christian relic—an arm of Santa Lucia, Siracusa's patron saint (see above).

Piazza Duomo. ✆ **389/550-3267.** 2€. Daily 8am–noon and 4–7pm.

Galleria Regionale Palazzo Bellomo ★ MUSEUM This elegant 13th-century palace houses Sicilian works from the Middle Ages through the 20th century, including Antonello da Messina's **"Annunciation"** (1474). The artist's remarkable attention to detail is evident: Tall windows, beams, columns, the Virgin's bed, and a blue-and-white vase compose an intricately rendered interior, with bright light infusing the spaces. The scene is typical of the Flemish paintings that were popular in Naples, where Messina studied after leaving his native Sicily as a teenager. Via Capodieci 16. ✆ **0931/69511.** 8€. Tues–Sat 9am–7pm, Sun 2–7:30pm.

THE ANCIENT RUINS ★★★

Of all the Greek cities of antiquity that flourished in Sicily, Siracusa was the most important, a formidable competitor of Athens. In its heyday, the city dared take on Carthage and even Rome. Sprawling Greek and Roman ruins are these days surrounded by an unremarkable section of the modern city. To reach the ruins, walk north along Corso Gelone (or better yet, take bus no. 1, 3, or 12, or a cab from Ortigia's Piazza Pancali) or take buses 11, 25, or 26 from the front of Siracusa's central train station.

Castello Euríalo ★ RUINS   Part of a massive, 27km- (16-mile) long defense system, this 4th-century-B.C. fortress is surrounded by three trenches, connected by underground tunnels. These supposedly impregnable defenses were never put to the test: Siracusa fell to the Romans in 212 B.C. without a fight, because the entire garrison was celebrating the feast of Aphrodite. It was here, legend has it, that the Greek mathematician Archimedes famously cried "Eureka!" having discovered the law of water displacement while taking a bath. The evocative ruin overlooking the Siracusan plain is the best-preserved Greek castle in the Mediterranean. The defenses are at the far end of the archaeological zone, about 5km (3 miles) outside the city center near a village called Belvedere; buses 25 and 26 pass the entrance. Piazza Euríalo 1, off Viale Epipoli. ✆ **0931/481-111.** 4€. Daily 9am–5:30pm.

Catacombe di San Giovanni ★★ RUINS   Spooky subterranean chambers, installed in underground aqueducts that had been abandoned by the Greeks, contain some 20,000 ancient Christian tombs. They are entered through the Church of San Giovanni, now in ruin but holy ground for centuries; this was the city's cathedral until the church was more or less leveled by an earthquake in 1693. St. Paul allegedly preached here when he stopped in Siracusa around A.D. 59, and a church was erected in the 6th century to commemorate the event. The Cripta di San Marciano (Crypt of St. Marcian) honors a popular Siracusan martyr, a 1st-century-A.D. bishop who was tied to a pillar and flogged to death on this spot.

Piazza San Giovanni, at end of Viale San Giovanni. © **0931/64694.** 8€ adult, 5€ seniors and under age 16. Daily 9:30am–12:30pm and 2:30–5:30pm (Nov–Mar until 4:30pm, July–Aug until 6pm). Closed Jan.

Museo Archeologico Regionale Paolo Orsi ★★★ MUSEUM

One of Italy's finest archaeological collections shows off artifacts from southern Sicily's prehistoric inhabitants through the Romans, showcasing pieces in stunning modern surrounds. Amid prehistoric tools and sculptures are the skeletons of a pair of dwarf elephants, as intriguing to us as they were to the ancients: It's believed that the large central hole in these skeletons' faces—actually a nasal passage—inspired the myth of the one-eyed Cyclops. Look for the often-reproduced grinning terra-cotta Gorgon, originally part of the frieze of the Greek temple of Athena (see Duomo, p. 779), where it was placed to ward off evil. You'll also see votive cult statuettes devoted to Demeter and Persephone—mother and daughter goddesses linked to fertility and the harvest. Legend had it that Hades, god of the underworld, abducted Persephone in Sicily and carried her down to his realm; her angry mother Demeter fought for her return, and the gods struck a deal—Persephone could return to Earth every spring and summer, making nature bloom, but she had to resume her duties as queen of the underworld in fall and winter, causing the lands above to wither and die. The museum's most celebrated piece is the **Landolina Venus,** a Roman copy of an original by the great classical Greek sculptor Praxiteles. The graceful and modest goddess, now headless, rises out of marble waves; French writer Guy de Maupassant called her "the perfect expression of exuberant beauty."

In the gardens of the Villa Landolina in Akradina, Viale Teocrito 66. www.siracusa turismo.net. © **0931/464-022.** 8€ or 13.50€ combined ticket with Parco Archeologico della Neapolis. Tues–Sat 9am–6pm; Sun 9am–1pm.

Parco Archeologico della Neapolis ★★★ RUINS   Many of Siracusa's ancient ruins are clustered in this archaeological park at the western edge of town, immediately north of Stazione Centrale.

The **Teatro Greco ★★★** (Greek Theater) was hewn out of bedrock in the 5th century B.C., with 67 rows that could seat 16,000 spectators. It was reconstructed in the 3rd century B.C., appears now much as it did then, and is still the setting for ancient drama in the spring and early summer.

Only the ancient theaters in Rome and Verona are larger than the **Anfiteatro Romano,** created around 20 B.C. Gladiators sparred here, and a square hole in the center of the arena suggests that machinery was used to lift wild beasts from below. Historical evidence suggests that the arena could be flooded for mock sea battles called *naumachiae;* pumps could also have flooded and drained a reservoir in which crocodiles are said to have fed on the corpses of victims killed in the games. The Spanish carted off much of the stonework to rebuild city fortifications when they conquered Siracusa in the 16th century, but some seats remain—the first rows would have been reserved for Roman citizens, those right above for wealthy Siracusans, and the last rows for the hoi polloi.

What is now a lush grove of lemon and orange trees, the **Latomia del Paradiso** (Quarry of Paradise) was at one time a fearsome place, vast, dark, and subterranean—until the cavern's roof collapsed in the great earthquake of 1693. Originally prisoners were worked to death here to quarry the stones used in the construction of ancient Siracusa. What is certainly the most storied attraction in the park is here: the **Orecchio di Dionisio** (Ear of Dionysius), a tall and vaguely ear-shaped cave dug into the cliff by the Greeks to expand the limestone quarry for water storage. Something about this huge cavern always inspired more dramatic accounts, such as the legend (completely unfounded) that the cave was once a prison for Athenians captured by Dionysus' mercenaries in the Peloponnesian Wars; supposedly he liked how the cave's acoustics amplified their screams as they were tortured. Almost as fascinating is the well-documented purpose of the **Ara di Ierone** (Altar of Heron): 5th-century B.C. Greeks built the altar, 196m (636 ft.) long and 23m (75 ft.) wide and approached by gigantic ramps, to sacrifice 450 bulls at one time.

Via Del Teatro (off intersection of Corso Gelone and Viale Teocrito), Viale Paradiso. www.siracusaturismo.net. ✆**0931/66206.** 10€, or 13.50€ with Museo Archaeologico. Daily Apr–Sept 9am–7:30pm (until 4:30pm on performance evenings in summer); Oct–Feb 9am–4:30pm; Mar 9am–6pm. For performance tickets (30€–70€) contact **INDA,** Corso Matteotti 29, Siracusa (www.indafondazione.org; ✆**0931/487200**).

Where to Stay in Siracusa

The choice place to stay in Siracusa is Ortigia, with enough character, charm, and comfortable accommodations to keep the most discerning traveler happy. A good agency for apartments in Ortigia is **Case Sicilia** (www.casesicilia.com; ✆ **339/298-3507**). For villas, **The Thinking Traveler** (www.thethinkingtraveller.com) has a carefully edited list of well-equipped properties in and around Siracusa.

Algilà Ortigia Charme Hotel ★ A slightly exotic air pervades this old stone palace at the edge of the sea. Interiors surrounding a peaceful inner courtyard with a splashing fountain are accented with carefully restored stone work and wooden beams, offset by beautiful multicolor tiles and other rich details. Rooms combine conventional luxury with all the modern amenities, plus a surfeit of four-poster beds, antiques, and tribal kilims; many have sea views. The in-house restaurant serves Sicilian classics and seafood beneath a beautiful wooden ceiling.

Via Vittorio Veneto 93. www.algila.it. ⓒ **0931/465-186.** 30 units. 170€–400€ double. Rates include breakfast. **Amenities:** Restaurant; room service; Wi-Fi (free).

Approdo delle Sirene ★★   This bright, stylish little inn occupies two floors of a seaside apartment house, beautifully refashioned as light-filled quarters with a slightly nautical flair, as befits the sparkling blue water just beyond the tall windows. In the contemporary guest rooms, polished wood floors offset handsome furnishings, striped fabrics, and bold colors. Several rooms have French doors opening to small balconies, though some rooms are sky-lit only—flooded with light but without views. The sunny breakfast room/lounge and terrace provide plenty of panoramas, however. The hosts, mother and son Fiora and Friedrich, are a hospitable on-the-scene presence and can arrange all kinds of tours and excursions. They also have free bikes available for guests' use.

Riva Garibaldi 15. www.apprododellesirene.com. ⓒ **0931/24857.** 8 units. 95€–130€ double. 2-night minimum stay June–Aug. Rates include breakfast. **Amenities:** Bikes; Wi-Fi (free).

Domus Mariae Benessere Guest House ★   The Ursiline sisters who still occupy a wing of this seaside convent have found their calling as innkeepers. The large, bright rooms border on vaguely luxurious, with plush headboards on extremely comfortable beds, attractive rugs on tile floors, and lots of counter and storage space in the large bathrooms. Some rooms have sea views, while others face an atrium-like courtyard. Surprising indulgences, given the surroundings, include a lovely roof terrace and a lower-level spa, with a small pool and Jacuzzi. An in-house restaurant serves a rather monastic buffet breakfast as well as a well-prepared dinner of healthful Mediterranean fare.

Via Veneto 89. www.domusmariaebenessere.com. ⓒ **0931/60087.** 21 units. Doubles from 60€. Rates include breakfast. **Amenities:** Bikes; pool; spa; Wi-Fi (free).

Henry's House ★★★   The namesake Henry was a now-departed friend of the owners, and he could not have a nicer legacy than this distinctive seaside palazzo at the southern edge of Ortigia. Several terraces, including a few private spaces off some of the rooms, look over the sea, while salons filled with antiques and artifacts are homily atmospheric. Guest quarters are tucked away on several floors and have beams, tile floors, and character-filled furnishings that further enhance the sense that you're staying with a cultured Sicilian uncle.

Via del Castello Maniace 68. www.hotelhenryshouse.com. ⓒ **0931/21361.** 14 units. 140€–160€. Rates include breakfast. **Amenities:** Bar; room service; Wi-Fi (free).

Hotel Gutkowski ★★　Two old houses facing the sea at the edge of Ortigia are warm, hospitable, and capture the essence of southern Italy—Sicilian hues on the walls, colorful floor tiles, and views of the blue water or sun-baked roofs of the old city. Each room is different, some with balconies, some with terraces; furnishings are functional but chosen to provide restful simplicity—old Sicilian and vintage mid-century pieces offset by contemporary tables and bedsteads. A rooftop terrace serves as an outdoor living room for much of the year, and the bar serves regional wines and one or two well-prepared dishes in the evenings.

Lungomare Vittorini 26. www.guthotel.it. ⓒ **0931/465861.** 25 units. Doubles from 85€. Most rates include breakfast. 2-night (or more) minimum stay required at some times. **Amenities:** Bar; restaurant; Wi-Fi (free).

Where to Eat in Siracusa

Caseificio Borderi, tucked in among piles of fresh fish in Ortigia's morning market at 6 Via die Benedictis (www.caseificioborderi.eu; ⓒ **329/985-2500**), is a required stop on the food circuit for its huge selection of house-made cheeses, cured meats, olives, and wine; the staff hands out samples and makes delicious sandwiches (4€), paired with excellent wines by the glass. Another market stop is **Fratelli Burgio,** Piazza Cesare Battista 4 (www.fratelliburgio.com; ⓒ **0931/60069**), where a *tagliere* (platter of cheeses and other antipasti) is a meal in itself.

Archimede ★★　SEAFOOD/PIZZA　This Siracusa institution has been serving meals since 1938, and in these whitewashed, vaulted dining rooms since 1978; over the decades the elegant, arched rooms have remained a favorite for a night out, even back when the surrounding neighborhood was moldering in neglect. Specialties veer toward Sicilian classics: spaghetti with *ricci* (sea urchin), tagliolini al *nero di seppie* (pasta with cuttlefish ink), and *pesce all'acqua pazza* (fish cooked with garlic, tomatoes, capers, and olives). Many fans claim that no one in Sicily makes them better. The kitchen is also equipped with a wood-fired oven that turns out what many Siracusans consider to be the best pizza in town, available in different sizes, including one that's a perfect starter.

Via Gemmallaro 8. www.trattoriaarchimede.it. ⓒ **0931/69701.** Entrees 12€–24€. Mon–Sat 12:30–3:30pm and 7:30–11:30pm.

Darsena da Ianuzzo ★★　SEAFOOD　"Darsena" means dock, and the town piers line the harbor just across the street from this brightly lit room with a terrace out front. Several generations of Siracusans have counted on Darsena for the freshest fish in town, displayed on ice in cases near the entrance. A waiter will bring some of the just-caught offerings around for your inspection, then take it back to the kitchen to be grilled or roasted to your preference. *Riccio,* sea urchin, and other local specialties are served raw and in a long, long list of deftly prepared seafood pastas.

Riva Giuseppe Garibaldi. www.ristorantedarsena.it. ⓒ **0931/61522.** Entrees 9€–18€. Tues–Sun noon–3pm and 7–11pm.

Don Camillo ★★ SIRACUSAN/SEAFOOD   Another long-time Siracusa favorite, Don Camillo is slightly more formal than Archimede (see above), with lots of polished antiques offsetting the handsomely tiled floors, rows of vintage wines, and vintage photos of Ortigia. House specialties, like spaghetti *delle Sirene* (with sea urchin and shrimp in butter) and *tagliata al tonno* (with sliced tuna), have been drawing loyal regulars for years; on weekend evenings the vaulted rooms fill with Siracusan families out for a special meal.

Via Maestranza 96. www.ristorantedoncamillosiracusa.it. © **0931/67133.** Entrees 14€–24€. Mon–Sat noon–2:30pm and 8–10:30pm.

L'Osteria da Seby ★ SIRACUSAN/SEAFOOD   Oil paintings, linen tablecloths, and exposed stone create a setting that, while warm and hinting at rusticity, is a bit more formal than the food warrants. What's best about this friendly place, a favorite of guests from hotels on the nearby waterfront, is the straightforward *osteria* fare: seafood pastas and risottos, mixed grills, and well-done standards such as scallopini in lemon sauce.

Via Mirabella 21. www.losteriadaseby.it. © **0931/181-5619.** Entrees 9€–18€. Tues–Sun noon–3pm and 7–11pm.

Taberna Sveva ★ SIRACUSAN/SEAFOOD   Escape the crowds with a walk out toward the Castello Maniace at the tip of Ortigia, where a breeze-cooled terrace facing a cobbled square is the perfect setting for a summer meal of classic vegetable and seafood pastas and fresh fish. In cooler weather, the hospitality retreats to a rich-hued bare-bones room that sets the stage for perfectly grilled steaks. Indoors or out, land-based or from the sea, meals are served at rough-hewn tables on hand-painted ceramics, lending just the right homey touch to this honest cooking.

Piazza Federico di Svevia. © **0931/24663.** Entrees 8€–15€. Daily 11:30–3pm and 6:30–10:30pm.

Beaches Near Siracusa

Some of the best, most unspoiled shoreline in all of Italy is on Sicily's southeastern coast. **Fontane Bianche** is the closest beach to Siracusa, 15 minutes away. It's an almost-square bay with laidback beach clubs and luxurious deep sand. **Lido di Noto,** 15 minutes from the baroque hill town of Noto (see p. 786), is a lively beach strip with great waterfront restaurants. Half the beach is private beach clubs (where you pay around 10€ for day use of a lounge chair, umbrella, and shower facilities), and half is free public access.

Between Noto and Pachino, the beautiful **Vendicari Nature Reserve,** 11km (7 miles) south of Noto on SP19, is set amid miles of fragrant citrus groves growing behind beaches backed by wetlands, a refuge for many exotic migratory birds. Vendicari's most popular beach is **Calamosche,** on an intimate cove framed by rock cliffs and sea caves; from the Calamosche parking area it's about a 15-minute walk along a path to the beach.

Isola delle Correnti ★★, a little over an hour south of Siracusa at Sicily's southeastern tip, is one of the best beaches on Sicily, though it's a bit more windswept and wavy than the other spots. On a clear day, you can see Malta, just 100km (60 miles) to the south.

Side Trip to Noto ★★★

31km (19 miles) SW of Siracusa

Dubbed the "Stone Garden" for its sheer beauty, this little town is like a baroque stage set, with rich-looking buildings of golden stone lining its main street, Corso Vittorio Emanuele. Noto sits on a high plateau surrounded by olive groves and almond trees, and the town heights provide splendid vistas of the Asinaro Valley.

ESSENTIALS

ARRIVING Take the A18 south from Siracusa for 27km (17 miles), then exit and head north up a hill,

Calamosche Beach, south of Siracusa.

following blue signs toward Noto. Near town, follow yellow signs to Noto's *"centro storico"* (brown "Noto Antica" signs lead to the ruins of the old city, outside town.) It's about a 35-minute drive. It's also easy to reach Noto by bus (55 min.; 6€ round-trip), with either **AST** (www.azienda sicilianatrasporti.it) or **Interbus** (www.interbus.it); a dozen buses per day run from Ortigia or Siracusa train station. Buses arrive at Piazzale Marconi, a 5-minute walk from the *centro storico*.

VISITOR INFORMATION The **tourist office,** Via Gioberti 13 (*©* **0931/ 836-503**), is open May to September daily 9am to 1pm and 3:30 to 6:30pm; and October to April Monday to Friday 8am to 2pm and 3:30 to 6:30pm.

EXPLORING NOTO

This hill town on the flanks of Mount Alviria was a flourishing place in the late 17th century, having outgrown its medieval core and expanded into streets lined with palaces and convents. On January 11, 1693, all came tumbling down when the strongest earthquake in Italian history leveled Noto and much of southeastern Sicily. The ruins of that old city can be seen at the **Noto Antica** archaeological site outside town.

The good to come out of such a devastating tragedy is that Noto was rebuilt—not on the same site but on the banks of the River Asinaro, and not haphazardly but in splendid, unified baroque style. Noto is a stage set of honey-colored limestone, with curvaceous facades, curling staircases, and wrought-iron balconies. You will be surrounded by all this theatricality on a walk down **Corso Vittorio Emanuele.** In addition to baroque fantasies, this street is also the setting, at number 125, of the **Caffe Sicilia,** a richly atmospheric old-fashioned place that many aficionados claim makes the best *granita* and *gelato* on the island (© **0931/835013**). Things hit an architectural high note on a side street, **Via Nicolaci,** with the beautiful elliptical facade of the **Chiesa di Montevirgine,** and the playful **Palazzo Villadorata,** where expressive maidens, dwarves, lions, and horses support the balconies.

Work on the 18th-century landmarks is ongoing, while much of the rest of the town seems to languish in disrepair—suggesting that in Noto the attitude is, "If it ain't baroque, don't fix it."

Freshly picked almonds in Noto.

Side Trip to Ragusa ★

79km (49 miles) SW of Syracuse.

Like Noto (see above), Ragusa was all but obliterated by the powerful earthquake of 1693; like Noto, it began immediately to be rebuilt as a planned city in exuberant baroque style. In Ragusa, however, most of the wary residents decided instead to relocate to an adjacent ridge, separated by a deep ravine, the Valle dei Ponti. Today, Ragusa Superiore is the modern center of the sprawling, bifurcated town, while baroque Ragusa Ibla is a place to wander on quiet lanes and through big piazzas overlooked by flamboyant 18th-century churches. Some topnotch dining and lodging options (see below) make Ragusa worth more than a hurried day trip.

ESSENTIALS

ARRIVING   Three **trains** a day make the 2-hour trip to Ragusa from Siracusa. **AST buses** (www.aziendasiciliatrasporti.it; © **0932/681-818**) make the 3-hour run seven times daily. The train and bus stations are in Ragusa Superiore on Piazza del Popolo and adjoining Piazza Gramsci.

By **car** from Siracusa, the quickest route takes you through Noto (p. 786) then southwest along Route 115 to the town of Ispica, at which point the highway swings northwest toward Ragusa.

Ragusa Ibla, a baroque set piece.

The **tourist office,** Via Capitano Bocchieri 33 (℄ **0932/221-511**), is open Monday to Friday 9am to 1:30pm; on Tuesday and Thursday it's also open 4 to 6pm.

EXPLORING RAGUSA IBLA

The most scenic way to reach historic Ragusa Ibla from modern Ragusa Superiore is by taking the 242 steps of the Salita Commendatore down the hillside. (Otherwise, take city bus no. 3 from Piazza del Popolo.) You can take a breather along the way on a landing in front of **Santa Maria delle Scale** (St. Mary of the Steps), enjoying views of the ochre-colored houses of Ragusa Ibla spreading out at your feet. The path eventually winds down and around to **Piazza del Duomo,** where a dramatically curved staircase leads to the sumptuous facade of **Cattedrale di San Giorgio ★★** (℄ **0932/ 220-085**), open daily 9am to noon and 4 to 7pm. Its three tiers of columns and balconies are the piéce de resistance of architect Rosario Gagliardi, the master of the Sicilian baroque. Gagliardi's second-best work is just east, **Chiesa di San Giuseppe ★,** Via Torre Nuova 19 (℄ **0932/621-779;** open daily 9am to noon and 4 to 6pm), with its tall, convex three-tiered facade embellished with columns and statues of saints. Inside, above a striking floor of black asphalt interspersed with majolica tiles, is one of Ragusa's most beloved paintings, the so-called **"Our Lady of the Cherries."** In an altarpiece portraying the Holy Family, Mary holds cherries in her apron, offering them to passersby.

Just down the street are Ragusa's beautiful public gardens, **Giardino Ibleo ★★.** Long avenues lined with palms are idyllic places to stroll, with stone benches tucked into shady alcoves. At the edge of the gardens, a terrace opens to views across the Valley of Irminio. The gardens are free and open daily 8am to 8pm.

EXPLORING MARINA DI RAGUSA ★

Ragusa's seaside getaway, 25km (15 miles) southwest, is a pleasant collection of houses facing a sandy beach and marina. Smaller, quieter, and more famous these days is adjacent **Punta Secca,** fictional home to Inspector Montalbano of the popular TV series; fans will recognize his house near the lighthouse. The series is also filmed on location in Ragusa, Modica, Scicli, and other towns in this corner of the southeast.

WHERE TO STAY & EAT IN RAGUSA

Ragusa Ibla is where you will want to stay and probably eat, and options are improving all the time. A sign of a new wave of gentrification sweeping over town is **I Banchi,** Via Orfanotrofio 39, a stylish bakery, food shop, wine bar, and casual eatery that would seem trendy even in Rome (www.ibanchiragusa.it; ℄ **0932/655-000;** open daily 8:30am to 11pm).

La Bettola ★ SICILIAN   The 1940s-era decor suggests simpler times, and Sicilian classic dishes keep that throwback ambience going strong,

15

SICILY

Siracusa

arriving at tables bedecked with red-checked tablecloths in the homey dining room and large front terrace. Daily offerings are listed on a chalkboard: homemade caponata, octopus salad, platters of spaghetti a la Norma, or simple grilled pork cutlets topped with fresh herbs.

Largo Camerina 7. www.trattorialabettola.it. ℂ **0932/653-394.** Entrees 10€–15€. Mon–Sat 12:30–2:30pm and 7:30–11:30pm, Sun 12:30–2:30pm.

Ciccio Sultano Duomo ★★★ NEW SICILIAN/SEAFOOD   If the baroque extravagance of this part of Sicily sweeps you away, you'll find the culinary complement at this famed spot, the creation of Chef Ciccio Sultano. The fussy parlorlike dining rooms, all dark polished wood and red velvet, suggest an extravagant experience, and nothing that emerges from the kitchen dispels the notion. Regional ingredients and age-old Sicilian traditions form the foundation for dishes that combine homemade pastas, local seafood, and fresh garden produce in remarkably innovative ways, such as a *cannolo* of creme fraiche, raw shrimp, and caviar, or in relatively down-to-earth preparations, like fresh pasta with bottarga (fish roe). Leave financial concerns at the door: The best way to indulge in the extravagance is with one of the tasting menus. Reserve well in advance.

Via Capitano Bocchieri 31, Ibla. ℂ **0932/651-265.** Entrees from 40€; tasting menus from 130€. Mon 7:30–11:30pm, Tues–Sat 12:30–2pm and 7:30–10:30pm.

Hotel Antico Convento ★★   The Capuchin monks who settled this convent in the 16th century had a good eye for location at the edge of town atop the Irminio valley, and the setting was enhanced even more in recent centuries with the addition of the town's beautiful public gardens, the Giardino Ibleo, which now surround the stone walls. The small monks' cells, converted to guest rooms, remain simple though not austere, with bright stone floors and handsome wooden built-ins, and they overlook a peaceful cloister, the gardens, or the valley below. A bar and restaurant spills into the cloister in warmer months.

Giardino Ibleo. Via Margherita 41. www.anticoconventoibla.it. ℂ **347/147-2915.** 24 units. Doubles from 80€. Rates include breakfast. **Amenities:** Restaurant; bar; Wi-Fi (free).

Locanda Don Serafino ★★   Accommodations in two adjoining medieval palazzi on a narrow lane above Piazza Duomo are reached by a gloriously primitive rock-hewn staircase, and the wonderful quirks continue from there, in poshly outfitted cave rooms and dramatic two-floor vaulted suites. For many guests the character-filled surroundings amply compensate for the lack of spa and other luxe amenities, even an elevator. Many come to enjoy dining in the locanda's offsite **restaurant** (on Via Avvocato Giovanni Ottaviano, ℂ **0932/248-778;** Wed–Mon 1–2:30pm and 8–10:30pm; no lunch July–Aug), one of the finest in Sicily, serving memorable meals (entrees 30€–35€) in a maze of stone-vaulted rooms and caves at the edge of town. The food is innovative yet more traditional and down-to-earth than the striking decor might suggest, relying on a bounty of fresh local ingredients that come to the fore in such signature dishes as *zuppa di pesce don Serafino* (a rich fish soup).

Via Via XI Febbraio 15.www.locandadonserafino.it. © **0932/220-06,** 11 units. Doubles from 90€. Rates include breakfast. **Amenities:** Restaurant, Wi-Fi (free).

PIAZZA ARMERINA ★★★

134km (83) miles NW of Siracusa, 158km (98 miles) SE of Palermo

Travelers make a big effort to get to this dusty, sunbaked hilltown in the center of Sicily to see the richest collection of Roman mosaics in the world, at the **Villa del Casale,** in the countryside 5km (3 miles) outside of town. From elevated walkways you'll gaze down upon wild beasts, superheroes, and the monsters of myth, depicted in glorious and colorful mosaic tableaux. The masterful ancient artistry is in a near-miraculous state of preservation, providing a fascinating window into 4th-century-A.D. preoccupations. These brilliant mosaic scenes are as entertaining as a good film, one in glorious Technicolor. Mosaics aside, Piazza Armerina is a friendly, handsome town that rolls up and down hilly terrain, well worth walking around from the hilltop Duomo through the 13th-century center.

Intricate mosaics at the Villa Romana del Casale in Piazza Armerina.

Essentials

ARRIVING From Taormina, Siracusa, or anywhere in the east, take the A19 west from Catania, exit at Dittaino, and head south following blue signs for Piazza Armerina. From Palermo, take the A19 east and south, exit at Caltanissetta, then immediately look for signs for Piazza Armerina. (The route is SS626 south to SS122 east to SS117bis.) You can reach Piazza Armerina by **SAIS bus** (www.sais autolinee.it; © **800/211-020**); from Palermo (a 2-hr. trip) there are 5 buses a day, 3 on weekends; coming from Siracusa or other east coast towns, take a bus from Enna (40 min; 4 buses a day). Once in Piazza Armerina, take local bus B to the site (15 min; runs daily 9am–noon and 3–6pm); taxis also eagerly await visitors.

Exploring Villa Romana del Casale

Built between 310 and 340, this enormous villa of a rich and powerful landowner was the center of a vast agricultural estate. The villa was almost completely covered by a landslide in the 12th century, but this natural disaster turned out to be a blessing, because the mud preserved almost 38,000 square feet of mosaic flooring. Rediscovered in the 19th century, the villa was excavated and restored starting in the early 20th century.

The place must have been magnificent, more a palace than a mere villa, with 40 rooms, many of them clad in marble, frescoed, and equipped with fountains and pools. Heating the villa were *terme,* or steam baths (Rooms 1–7), with steam circulating through cavities in the floors and walls. The villa was built to impress, and the ostentation reached its zenith in mosaics of mythology, flora and fauna, and domestic scenes that carpeted most of the floors. Given the style and craftsmanship, they were likely the work of master artists from North Africa.

The villa's 40 rooms are arranged around a garden courtyard, or peristyle. Take time as you wander through the rooms simply to enjoy the mosaics, noticing the expressions, colors, and playfulness of many of these scenes. Remember, the scenes were intended to delight visitors.

Corridors of the **peristyle** (Room 13) contain the splendid Peristyle mosaic, a bestiary of birds, plants, wild animals, and more domesticated creatures such as horses. Mosaics in the adjoining **Palestra** (exercise area, Room 15) depict a chariot race at Rome's Circus Maximus. Along the north side of the peristyle is the **Sala degli Eroti Pescatori ★** (Room of the Fishing Cupids, Room 24), probably a bedroom. The occupant would have drifted off to a scene of four boatloads of winged cupids harpooning, netting, and trapping various fish and sea creatures. Just past these rooms is the **Sala della Piccola Caccia** (*piccola caccia* meaning "small hunt," Room 25), where hunters in togas go after deer, wild boar, birds, and other small game as Diana, goddess of the hunt, looks on. In one scene the hunters roast their kill under a canopy.

The long hall to the east is the **Corridoio della Grande Caccia ★★★,** or Corridor of the Great Hunt (Room 28), measuring 65m (197 ft.) in length. The mosaics depict men capturing panthers, leopards, and other exotic animals, loading them onto wagons for transport, and finally onto a ship. They're obviously bound for Rome, where they will be part of the games in the Colosseum. A cluster of three rooms east of the north (right-hand side) end of the Grande Caccia corridor includes the **Vestibolo di Ulisse e Polifemo** (Vestibule of Ulysses and Polyphemus, Room 47), where the Homeric hero proffers a *krater* of wine to the Cyclops (here with three eyes instead of one, and a disemboweled ram draped casually over his lap) in hopes of getting him drunk. In the adjacent **Cubicolo con Scena Erotica** (Bedroom with Erotic Scene, Room 46), a seductress with a side gaze and a nicely contoured rear end embraces a young man. Off the southwest side of the Grande Caccia corridor is one of the most amusing rooms of all, the **Sala delle Palestrite,** Room of the Gym Girls (Room 30). According to ancient literary sources, their skimpy strapless bikinis, which would fit right in on any 21st century beach, were standard workout apparel 1,700 years ago—the bandeau top was called the *strophium,* and the bikini bottom the *subligar.* The girls are engaged in various exercises—curling dumbbells, tossing a ball, and running.

South of the central block of the villa and peristyle, the **Triclinium** (Room 33) is a large dining room with a magnificent rendition of the Labors of Hercules. In the central apse, mosaics depict the Gigantomachy (Battle of the Giants), in which five mammoth creatures are in their death throes after being pierced by Hercules' poison arrows.

Villa Romana, Strada Provinciale 15. www.villaromanadelcasale.it. © **0935/680-036.** 10€. Daily 9am–7pm (until 5pm Nov–Mar).

AGRIGENTO & THE VALLEY OF THE TEMPLES ★★★

129km (80 miles) SE of Palermo

The evocative skeletons of seven temples of honey-colored stone, arranged on a long ridge with commanding views of the sea, comprise one of the most memorable sights of the ancient world—the embodiment of classical dignity. Colonists from Crete or Rhodes established Akragas in the 7th century B.C., and by the 5th century B.C. the city was one of the great Mediterranean powers, with close to 200,000 residents. The Greek poet Pindar described Akragas as the most beautiful city "inhabited by mortals" but commented that its citizens "feasted as if there were no tomorrow." The city poured part of its enormous wealth into temples erected along a ridge overlooking the sea, their bright pediments becoming well-known landmarks along southern sea routes. Carthage and Rome fought over the city for centuries until Akragas became part of the Roman Empire in 210 B.C. Tumbled by earthquakes, plundered for marble, and overgrown from neglect, today the temples are proud remnants of ancient grandeur.

Essentials

ARRIVING Agrigento is about 2½ hours by **car** from either Palermo or Siracusa. From Palermo, cut southeast on the SS121, which becomes SS189 before it finally reaches Agrigento. From Siracusa, take the A18 autostrada north to Catania and the A19 west toward Enna; just past Enna, exit the A19 and follow signs south through Caltanissetta and down to Agrigento. (The "coastal route" from Siracusa—taking the SS115 all the way—may look more direct on the map but is much more time-consuming, up to 5 hours on an often very curvy two-lane road.) **Parking** is below the temples, near the entrances to the western section (Zeus) and eastern section

(Collina dei Templi). A well-marked path leads along the ridge past the temples. A shuttle bus (3€ each way) connects the parking areas with the top of the site, though the walk is not terribly strenuous.

Bus connections between Palermo and Agrigento are fairly convenient: **Cuffaro** (www.cuffaro.info; © **0922/403-150**) runs nine buses per day and drops you right in front of the entrance to the archaeological site; the 2-hour trip costs 9€ one-way, 14€ round-trip. There's also bus service from Siracusa, but it's at least 4 hours each way.

A **train** from Palermo takes 2 hours; there are 12 trains daily. From Siracusa, trains take 6 hours, with a change in Catania. For information, visit www.trenitalia.it; © **89/2021.** Agrigento's rail station, **Stazione Centrale,** is at Piazza Marconi; from there, take a cab or local bus (lines 1, 2, or 3) to the temples, 10 minutes away.

VISITOR INFORMATION The **tourist office,** in the modern town at Piazzale Aldo Moro 7 (© **0922/20454**), is open Sunday through Friday 8am to 1pm and 3 to 8pm, Saturday 8am to 1pm. Another tourist office is at Via Empedocle 73 (© **0922/20391**), open Monday to Friday 8am to 2:30pm and Wednesday 3:30 to 7pm.

Exploring the Ruins

As you enter the valley surrounded by hills planted with olive and almond trees, you'll see that "valley of the temples" is a misnomer, as the temples are perched along a ridge. The park is divided into eastern and western zones, with entrances at each.

Parco Valle dei Templi ★★★ RUINS   In the eastern zone are Agrigento's three best-preserved temples. **The Temple of Hercules (Tempio di Ercole)** is the oldest, dating from the 6th century B.C. At one time the temple sheltered a celebrated statue of Hercules, long since plundered. Gaius Verres, the notoriously corrupt 1st-century-B.C. governor of Sicily, had his eye on the statue as he looted temples across the island, though there is no record of Verres getting this prize. Eight of 36 columns have been resurrected, while the others lie rather romantically scattered in the tall grass and wildflowers; they still bear black sears from fires set by Carthaginian invaders. The **Tempio della Concordia (Temple of Concord),** surrounded by 34 columns, has survived almost intact since its completion in 430 B.C. It was shored up as a Christian basilica in the 6th century, so was never plundered, and its foundations rest upon soft soil that absorbs the shock of earthquakes. The **Temple of Juno** had no such structural resiliency and was partly destroyed in an earthquake, though 30 columns and sections of the colonnade have been restored. A long altar was used for wedding ceremonies and sacrificial offerings.

The western zone would have been the setting of the largest temple in the Greek world, if the **Temple of Jove/Zeus (Tempio di Giove)** had ever

The Tempio della Concordia, Valley of the Temples, Agrigento.

been completed—and if what was built had not been toppled in earthquakes. A copy of an 8m- (26-ft.) tall telamon (sculpted figure of a man with arms raised) lies on its back amid the rubble; the original is the pride of the site's Museo Archeologico. Several such figures were used as columnlike supports on the temple; the German writer Goethe, who was much impressed with the massive 20m- (66 ft.) high columns, took home with him a painting of one of the temple carytids, a female figure similarly used for support. The nearby **Temple of Castor and Pollux (Tempio di Dioscuri** or **Tempio di Castore e Polluce),** with four Doric columns intact, honors Castor and Pollux, the twins who were patrons of seafarers; Demeter, goddess of marriage and the fertile earth; and Persephone, the daughter of Zeus and the symbol of spring.

For more detailed explanations, in both Italian and English, of the many artifacts unearthed here, stop by the **Museo Archeologico** (Via dei Templi; ✆ **0922/40111;** Mon 9am–1:30pm, Tues–Sat 9am–7:30pm), between the ruins and Agrigento town. However, after a long and dusty outing at the ruins, this isn't a mandatory stop.

Parco Valle dei Templi. www.lavalledeitempli.it. ✆ **0922/621-611.** 10€ temples only, 6€ museum only, 13.50€ combined ticket. Daily 8:30am–7pm. Separate admission 13.50€ for evening hours: July–Aug Mon–Fri 7–11pm and Sat–Sun 7–midnight.

Where to Stay & Eat in Agrigento

Hotel Villa Athena ★   An 18th-century villa set in gardens within the Valley of the Temples might be the best-located perch in all of Italy. Looking at the Temple of Concord, illuminated at night, is one of Sicily's great travel experiences and can be enjoyed from the balconies and even the beds of many of the rooms, done with smart traditional furnishings and handsome fabrics. The beautiful garden, surrounding a pool, is also a prime spot to enjoy the view while enjoying a glass of wine.

Via Passeggiata Archeologica 33. www.hotelvillaathena.it. ⟨ **0922/596-288.** 27 units. 170€–330€ double. Rates include breakfast. Bus: 2. **Amenities:** Dining room; 2 bars; outdoor pool; room service; Wi-Fi (free).

L'Ambasciata di Sicilia ★ SICILIAN   One of the few reasons to venture into modern Agrigento is a chance to enjoy a hearty meal at this old-fashioned favorite, a city institution since 1919. True to its name, the kitchen makes it a point to act as Sicilian ambassadors and introduce diners to the island's finest cuisine, with delicious preparations of fresh fish, along with *linguine al'Ambasciata* (prepared with meat sauce, bacon, calamari, and zucchini). Meals are served in a small dining room crammed to the ceiling with marionettes and other colorful artifacts; there's also a breezy terrace overlooking the surrounding rooftops.

Via Gianbertoni 2, off Via Atenea. www.ristorantelambasciatadisicilia.it. ⟨ **0922/20526.** Entrees 7€–12€. Wed–Mon 9am–9pm. Closed 2 wks Nov.

SICILY'S WEST COAST ★★

On the west coast of Sicily, you'll find the storied port towns of Trapani and Marsala, while a winding uphill half-hour drive (or a funicular ride from Trapani), will take you to medieval, mountaintop Erice. The coast between Trapani and Marsala is lined with dazzling white salt pans, protected as a nature reserve and populated by migratory birds. At the southern end of the coast is the vast archeological park of Selinunte, littered with Greek temples and other evocative ruins. Though you can get from place to place by bus, you'll find it a lot more convenient and rewarding to explore this part of the island by car.

Arriving

BY PLANE   **Vincenzo Florio Airport** at Birgi, 15km (9 miles) from the center of Trapani (www.airgest.it; ⟨ **0923/610-111**), is the island's third-largest and the main Ryanair hub for Sicily from the U.K. From here, **AST** (www.aziendasicilianatrasporti.it; ⟨ **091/620-8111**) **buses** run hourly into Trapani (fare 5€).

BY CAR   From Palermo, the A29 autostrada is the fastest route southwest into Trapani, about a 1½-hour drive. Marsala is another 45 minutes south on Route 115; the drive from Trapani up to Erice takes about half an hour.

Selinunte is 2 hours' drive from Palermo via A29 and E90 (exit at Castelvetrano); the drive between Trapani and Selinunte takes a little over an hour.

BY TRAIN There's frequent daily train service (www.trenitalia.it; *℃* **89/ 2021**) between Palermo, Trapani, and Marsala. The journey from Palermo to Trapani takes 2½ hours; it's another 30 minutes on to Marsala. Trapani's main station at Piazza Stazione offers luggage storage. For Selinunte, take the train to Castelvetrano, 23km (14 miles) from the ruins, where you can board a **Salemi** bus (www.autoservizisalemi.it; *℃* **0923/981-120**) for the final 20-minute lap of the journey.

BY BUS From Palermo, **Salemi** (www.autoservizisalemi.it; *℃* **0923-981-120**) runs long-distance bus service to Trapani airport (1½ hrs.), Marsala (1¾ hours), and Selinunte (1¾ hr.; change buses at Castelvetrano for another 20 min. trip to ruins). **AST Buses** (www.aziendasicilianatrasporti. it; *℃* **0923/21021**) run between Marsala and Trapani (Piazza Montalto) three times a day, a 35-minute journey, and also go from Trapani's Piazza Montalto up to historic Erice (daily 6:40am–7:30pm, fare 2.40€), a winding, uphill 50-minute trip.

BY BOAT Trapani is a major embarkation point for **ferries** and **hydrofoils.** Most depart for the Egadi Islands of Marettimo, Levanzo, and Favignana. Service is also available to the islands of Ustica and Pantelleria, and to the mainland ports of Civitavecchia near Rome and Tunisia in North Africa. Ferries depart from the docks near Piazza Garibaldi. Service is offered by **Liberty Lines** (www.libertylines.it; *℃* **0923/873-813**) or **Grimaldi** (www.grimaldi-lines.com; *℃* **081/496-444**).

Trapani ★★

100km (62 miles) SW of Palermo, 14km (8⅔ miles) SW of Erice, 31km (19 miles) N of Marsala

Wedged between two especially scenic stretches of shoreline, Trapani spreads along the coastal plain below Mount Erice. The historic center, on a sea-girt promontory, is an atmospheric maze of medieval streets and squares. To the northeast is the dramatic headland at San Vito Lo Capo, with fine beaches and the Zingaro nature reserve. Stretching south of Trapani are coastal salt pans that have been harvested since antiquity.

VISITOR INFORMATION **Trapani Infopoint,** Via Torrearsa 69 (www. trapanistruzioniperluso.com; *℃* **0923-23190**) provides maps and info about exploring Trapani and other places on the west coast and is open daily 8am to 7pm.

EXPLORING TRAPANI

The old town extends westward out to sea, with a typical North African feel to the labyrinth of narrow streets that wind toward the **Torre di Ligny,** built in 1671 on the tip of the peninsula. Many elegant baroque buildings

Trapani's main street, Corso Vittorio Emanuele, and Palazzo Senatorio.

line **Corso Vittorio Emanuele,** sometimes called Rua Grande, as it extends west from the **Palazzo Senatorio,** the 17th-century, pink-marble town hall. Adjacent 18th-century **Via Garibaldi** (also known as Rua Nova, or "New Road") is flanked with palaces and churches. One of them, the 17th-century baroque **Chiesa del Purgatorio,** houses the single greatest treasure in Trapani: The *Misteri,* 20 life-size wooden figures from the 18th century depicting Christ's Passion. Every year they are carried through town for Good Friday's **Processione dei Misteri** (Procession of the Mysteries). The church is open daily 8:30am to 12:30pm and 4 to 8pm but is often closed. **Via Torrearsa** leads down to a bustling *pescheria* (fish market) where tuna is traded; the valuable commodity is caught in nearby waters and traded with buyers from as far off as Japan. **Villa Margherita,** public gardens stretching between old and new Trapani, is an inviting oasis with fountains, banyan trees, and palms rustling in the sea breeze.

Santuario dell'Annunziata/Museo Regionale Pepoli ★ CHURCH/ MUSEUM   The cloisters of a 14th-century convent enclose a collection of archaeological finds and art, many of it salvaged by a local aristocrat, Count Pepoli. With his fine eye, the count found the best examples of coral carving, a popular Trapani tradition that local craftspeople pursued up until the early 20th century, when nearby coral beds were depleted. Many of the works, in which coral is often intermingled with silver filigree, are by local artisans Andrea and Alberto Tipa. Among their creations is a spectacularly elaborate *presepe* (nativity scene). Before leaving the premises, step into the convent's **Cappella della Madonna** to see a graceful, sculpted scene of the Virgin and Child, attributed to the 14th-century Tuscan master Nino Pisano.

Via Conte Agostino Pepoli 200. © **0923/553-269.** 6€. Tues–Sat 9am–5:30pm, Sun 9am–12:30pm.

Erice ★★★

96km (60 miles) SW of Palermo, 14km (8⅔ miles) NE of Trapani, 45km (28 miles) NW of Marsala

Medieval Erice, high atop Mount Erice (743m/2,438 ft.), is all about views. On a clear summer's day, you can see west to the Egadi Islands, east to Mount Etna, and south to Africa, but the town puts on a good show even in the mists and fogs that frequently roll in, with towers and craggy rocks poking through a hazy blanket of gray. Erice is an atmospheric place, where you'll stop to admire an arch, a door, or a bell tower as you wander its steep cobblestone streets, flanked by churches and stone houses with elaborate baroque balconies packed with cascading geraniums. The city is famous throughout Sicily for its pastries, so be sure to sample such delights as tangy *dolci di Badia* cakes, made from almond paste and citron juice.

From Trapani, you can either take an AST bus (see p. 797), or choose a more adventurous option: the **funivia** (cableway; www.funiviaerice.it; © **0923/560023**). From the cable-car station on Via Capua in lower Erice, it whisks you to the top in about 10 minutes at a cost of 9€ round-trip, 5.50€ one way (wheelchair accessibility available). To get to the funicular, take **ATM Trapani** bus no. 21 from Trapani's Piazza Giovanni Paolo II, leaving every 30 minutes (www.atmtrapani.it; © **0923/559575;** fare 1.20€). *Note:* The cableway closes Monday mornings for general maintenance, does not operate in inclement weather, and often isn't running when you want it to; check before going, but generally the service operates Monday 1 to 8pm, Tuesday to Friday 8:30am to 8pm, and Saturday and Sunday 9:30am to 8:30pm.

EXPLORING ERICE

Whether you come up to Erice by road or cable car, you will arrive at **Porta Trapani,** one of three entrance gates of the city (the other two are Porta Spada and Porta Spagnola, farther north). The 12th-century Porta Trapani is imbedded in the Elymian-Punic walls, an extensive defense barrier laid out by the Elymians (the ancient inhabitants of western Sicily) around 1200 B.C. and later fortified by the Carthaginians from North Africa to guard the city from attackers coming from the west.

15

SICILY

Sicily's West Coast

Approaching Erice's 12th-century Castle of Venus.

Steep, cobblestone **Via Vittorio Emanuele** leads past churches and monasteries to the town's high point and central square **Piazza Umberto I.** From there, Via Guarnotti leads through Piazza San Giuliano to the beautiful **Giardino del Balio,** surrounding the Norman-era **Castello di Venere.** A cliffside promenade beneath the castle affords the most spectacular views in western Sicily, all the way to Tunisia, a distance of 170km (106 miles), on a clear day. The gardens are always open.

Castello di Venere (Castle of Venus) ★ RUIN   The Normans who conquered Sicily in the 12th century built a massive mountaintop castle, a majestic show of might, on the site of an ancient temple to Venus, goddess of love. Medieval towers and the ruins of walls still surround the compound, and through defensive slits and other openings you can look out over the plains of Trapani and the Egadi Islands, showing off the site's defensive advantage. Still visible are the foundations of the temple and precincts that housed a cult whose young female devotees serviced male worshippers sexually. This was deemed such an honorable profession that when the women ended their duties at age 21, they were considered especially desirable brides.

East end of Giardano del Balio. www.fondazioneericearte.org. © **366/671-2832.** 4€, 2€ ages 11–16, free for children 10 and under. July–Sept daily 10am–7pm (Aug until 8pm); Apr–June and Oct 10am–6pm. Closed Nov–Mar.

Chiesa Matrice (Royal Duomo of Erice) ★ CHURCH   Erice's 14th-century Duomo was constructed with stones from the ancient Temple of Venus, and the campanile (bell tower) that rises 28m (92 ft.) next to the church also has an ancient past, built in the late 15th century atop a watchtower from the 2nd century B.C. Frederick of Aragon, who eventually lost Sicily to the Spanish, built the campanile so his sentries could watch for invading troops in the sea lanes far below. The church's porch, dubbed the "Gibbena" (from the Latin *agi bene,* meaning "act well"), is a later addition, built to accommodate penitents who weren't allowed to partake in the Mass. They missed out on worshipping under a vaulted, arabesque ceiling in front of the enormous altarpiece of Carrara marble, depicting the life of Christ.

Piazza Umberto I. ℂ **0923/869-123.** 2€, free for children 12 and under. Mon–Fri 9:30am–12:30pm and 3:30–5:30pm; Sat–Sun 9:30am–1pm and 3:30–6pm.

Along the West Coast

Moving along the coastline, from just above Trapani down to Marsala, the stunning natural beauty of western Sicily is on full display.

RISERVA NATURALE DELLO ZINGARO & SAN VITO LO CAPO ★★

The tiny town of **Scopello,** 35km (21 miles) directly east of Trapani, is the beginning of the most beautiful stretch of coastline in Sicily, running north for 12km/7½ miles up to the dramatic bluffs of San Vito Lo Capo. Beaches here can be impossibly crowded in summer, but they're paradisiacal, alternating sand and pebble strands washed by waters as clear and warm as the Caribbean. At the edge of Scopello, the **Tonnara di Scopello**—an abandoned 13th-century tuna-processing plant—is an especially idyllic spot to swim, a sparkling cove surrounded by wind-sculpted rocks. Much of the land is set aside as the **Riserva Naturale dello Zingaro** (www.riservazingaro.it; ℂ **0924/35108**), the first designated wildlife area in Sicily, covering nearly 1,600 hectares (3,954 acres) of Mediterranean maquis and coastline. Within the reserve, the **Grotta dell'Uzzo,** a cave that served as a dwelling in Paleolithic times, is now a refuge for six different types

---

Sicily's Pastry Capital

Erice is renowned throughout Sicily for its pastries, refined by cloistered nuns from the 14th to the 18th century. Maria Grammatico, raised in the nearby San Carlo convent, became famous in Italy when she wrote her autobiography, *Bitter Almonds.* Her crunchy almond cookies, rum- or orange-filled marzipan balls, and confections fashioned from chocolate-covered almond paste at **Pasticceria Grammatico** (Via Vittorio Emanuele 14; www.mariagrammatico.it; ℂ **0923/869-390**) are a modern legend. **Pasticceria San Carlo** (Via S. Domenico 18, ℂ **0923/869-586**) does not enjoy the same celebrity status, but the offerings are also beautiful and tempting. Both can supply you with a mixed assortment of cookies and other treats to fortify a walk around town.

San Vito Lo Capo and the scenic coastline near Trapani.

of bats (off-limits to all but sanctioned naturalists). Motorized vehicles are prohibited within the reserve—the only transport is by mule.

THE SALT MARSHES ★★★

Stretching from Trapani to Marsala along route SP21, the salt pans skirting the coast have been harvested since antiquity. For millennia, salt was used as a preservative for perishable food and for the Romans as payment for mercenaries (the word "salary" is from the Latin *salaries* meaning "soldier's allowance for the purchase of salt"). The area is now protected as the **Riserva Naturale Orientata Saline di Trapani e Paceco** (www.wwfsa lineditrapani.it; ✆ **0923/867-700**), covering 1,000 hectares (2,471 acres). The horizon is broken by red-and-white stone windmills, and in the late afternoon migrating birds perform spectacular in-flight choreographies.

MOZIA ★★★

A mere kilometer offshore from the northern outskirts of Marsala, the tiny island of **San Pantaleo** lies in the Stagnone, a lagoon and nature reserve. Owned by the prominent Marsala winemaking family the Whitakers (www.fondazionewhitaker.it), the islet is a wonderful place to observe pink flamingoes, curlews, and egrets; in summer the sparse landscape is abloom with white sea daffodil and sea lavender. Footpaths meander among the scattered ruins of the ancient city of Motya (today's **Mozia**), a 6th-century B.C. Phoenician stronghold. At its height, the island settlement was surrounded by nearly 2.5km (11-2 miles) of defensive walls. In 397 B.C., Dionysius the Elder of Syracuse mounted a massive attack on the inhabitants, who retreated to Lilybaeum (now Marsala). Today, little is left but crumbling low walls here and there. Most intact are the **Casa dei Mosaici** (House of Mosaics), with scenes of animal life dating to the 4th to 3rd century B.C., and the **Tophet,** a Phoenician burial ground for victims of child sacrifice, with intricately carved gravestones *(stele).* The small on-site museum displays a number of excavated artifacts, including a sensual marble statue of a young man in a wet tunic, the **Giovane di Mozia** (Young Man of Mozia), dating to around 440 B.C. Admission to the museum is 9€ (5€ students and children); it's open daily 9:30am to 6:30pm (Nov–Mar 9am–3pm).

Arini and Pugliese ferries (www.arinipugliese.com; ✆ **347/779-0218**) run daily year-round to Mozia from Marsala (Contrada Spagnola). A round trip costs 5€ (2.50€ students and seniors). Be sure to pick up a free island map at the boat landing—it's essential for making sense of the littered ruins and remains.

THE EGADI ISLANDS

This archipelago of three islands (Favignana, Levanzo, and Marettimo) forms the westernmost point of Sicily and, served by ferry and hydrofoil from Trapani and Marsala, is a place to get away from it all. The islands are popular summertime retreats for swimming and scuba diving, but the rest of the year their 4,600 inhabitants are left to live from the fruits of the sea, as they have done for centuries. Home to the largest tuna fishery in Sicily, the islands are famous for the annual *mattanza,* an age-old method of culling tuna by forcing them to swim into a long corridor of nets known as *camera della morte,* or chamber of death.

Salt of the Earth

When the Carthaginians first landed in the area from North Africa they saw the potential for salt production and created basins from which to harvest the valuable commodity. The process exploits the high level of salinity in the seawater and the wind and sun that contribute to the evaporation process. In mid- to late winter, water is pumped into the pans through a canal. Over the next few months the water is left to evaporate, when it assumes a reddish color dense with mineral pigment. Around July, just as the water reaches a sluggish consistency, the salt is raked, harvested, and brought onto dry land to complete the exsiccation process. What look like little salt huts line the road, covered in protective terracotta tiles. Once completely dry, the salt is cleansed of debris and packaged.

Marsala ★

124km (77 miles) SW of Palermo, 31km (19 miles) S of Trapani, 48.5km (30 miles) SW of Erice

This thriving little port on Cape Boéo, the westernmost tip of Sicily over-looking the Egadi Islands and Tunisia, is where the world-famous Marsala sweet wine is produced. You can sample some amber yellow Marsala in one of the town's quaint wine shops, or head through the hills along roads lined with prickly-pear cacti to a vineyard nearby. Townspeople sip the dark, vintage Marsala as a dessert wine with hard piquant cheese, fruit, or pastries. Famous product aside, Marsala is an elegant town with baroque palaces and churches, Roman ruins, a lively fish market, and a long sandy coastline stretching to the north and south.

VISITOR INFORMATION The **tourist office,** at Via 11 Maggio 100 (ⓒ **0923/714097**), is open Monday to Saturday 8am to 1:45pm and 2 to 8pm and Sunday 9am to noon.

EXPLORING MARSALA

Enter the city from the **Porta Garibaldi,** a massive arched gateway from the 1600s crowned by an eagle. Garibaldi is honored because it was at Marsala that the 19th-century freedom fighter and his red-shirted volunteers overthrew the Bourbon regime, paving the way for the independence of southern Italy. The road from the gate leads to **Via Garibaldi,** where it ends at the busy **Piazza della Repubblica,** the heart of the city. The square's 18th-century **Palazzo Senatorio,** now the Town Hall, is nicknamed "Loggia" for its flank of elegant arcades. Leading north from Piazza Repubblica is the main thoroughfare, **Via 11 Maggio,** flanked by the town's most splendid baroque palaces. To the northwest, facing the sea on the **Lungomare Boéo,** the archaeological museum (see p. 805) stands amid old *bagli,* Marsala wine warehouses.

Chiesa Madre ★ CHURCH It's only fitting that Marsala's most imposing church is dedicated to Britain's St. Thomas à Becket, given the English connections that brought the city such wealth over the centuries (see box p. 805). Legend has it that a ship headed for England, carrying materials to build a church dedicated to Becket, was forced by a storm to seek haven at Marsala, and the crew simply built the church here instead. It's more likely that the cultlike popularity of the saint, murdered in Canterbury cathedral in 1170, had spread as far as Sicily by the 13th century, when the church was founded. The most impressive decorative pieces in the three-aisle interior are also by outsiders—the Gaginis, a 15th-century family of Swiss sculptors who worked their way down the Italian boot until they reached Sicily, undertaking commissions in Palermo and elsewhere around the island. Their best work here, by Domenico Gagini, is lovely *Madonna del Popolo* in the right transept.

Piazza della Repubblica. ⓒ **0923/716295.** Free. Daily 7:30am–7pm.

Museo Archeologico Nave Punica–Baglio Anselmi ★★ MUSEUM
A former wine warehouse *(baglio)* houses gold jewelry from ancient Mozia (see p. 802), as well as the museum's showpiece, a relatively well-preserved **Punic ship** (Punic being the Latin name for Carthage, the ancient kingdom in what is today's Tunisia). It's believed the ship, discovered in shallow waters in 1971, was constructed for the Battle of the Egadi Islands during the First Punic Wars between the Romans and Carthaginians in 241 B.C. and sank on its maiden voyage; some scholars argue that the vessel was not a warship but was used to carry cargo. Measuring 35m (115 ft.) long, the ship was manned by 68 oarsmen. Large sections remain, enough to suggest the sleekness and power of the wooden shell covered with sheets of lead fixed with bronze nails. They are on display along with bowls, plates, animal bones, cannabis leaves, and other material carried on board. Behind the museum (included with admission) are the excavations of ancient Lilybaeum, as Marsala was known in Roman times. Among the relics are the remains of a villa with a steam room and still-glittering mosaics.

Lungomare Boéo. *C* **0923/952535.** 4€ adults, 2€ ages 17 and under. Tues–Sat 9am–7pm, Sun 9am–1:30pm.

Museo degli Arazzi (Tapestry Museum) ★★ MUSEUM Eight Flemish tapestries, made in Brussels between 1530 and 1550, are the legacy of a bishop of Messina, who donated them to his hometown of Marsala. Tucked away for centuries, and at one point almost auctioned off, the exquisite silk and wool pieces once hung in the royal palace in Madrid. They depict scenes from the Roman wars against the Jews from A.D. 66 to

---

The Wine that Put Marsala on the Map

On a dark and stormy night in 1770, English trader John Woodhouse was forced to anchor in Marsala. He headed for a tavern, downed some local wine, discovered it tasted similar to the Portuguese "Porto," and realized the commercial potential. Woodhouse began to mass-produce and export the wine. He got a big break when the famed Admiral Horatio Nelson developed a taste for Marsala and decided that the British Navy should allot sailors a glass per day. Around the same time, Joseph Whitaker, another English entrepreneur, inherited a vast vineyard in Marsala and further expanded the wine's reputation by exporting it to the United States. He also bought the island of Mozia (p. 802), where he founded an archaeological museum and published important studies of Tunisian birds. One more enterprising businessman entered the scene when Vincenzo Florio, from Palermo, purchased the Woodhouse wine empire in the mid-19th century and refined Marsala grapes. The Florios, who also exported tuna, were one of Sicily's most prominent families well into the 20th century. Sample Marsala at **Enoteca La Ruota** on Lungomare Boéo near the archaeological museum (number 36-A, *C* **0923/715-241**), while admiring the Stagnone lagoon lying in front of you.

A.D. 67, when troops of Flavius Vespasian occupied Jerusalem. The tapestries are kept in darkened rooms to avoid damage.

Via Garraffa 57. © **0923/711-327.** 4€. Tues–Sat 9:30am–1pm, Sun 9:30am–12:30pm.

Selinunte ★★★

122km (76 miles) SW of Palermo, 55km (34 miles) SE of Marsala, 73km (45 miles) SW of Trapani

On Sicily's southwestern coast, this Greek colony was once one of the most powerful cities in the world, home to 100,000 inhabitants. Then the great Carthaginian general Hannibal virtually destroyed the city in 409 B.C. He spared only the temples—not out of respect for the deities, but to preserve the loot they housed. Even in the context of those brutal times the wrath of the Carthaginians was abhorrent. An army of 100,000 men descended on the city with battering rams, and in an orgy of destruction raped, looted, plundered, and butchered, killing most of the inhabitants and enslaving the rest. Today the vast archaeological park comprises 270 hectares (670 acres), making it Europe's largest archaeological site. Selinunte is not just large, it's also a bucolic spot where you can walk amid the ruins, gaze out to sea, and ponder what life was like millennia ago. As you walk amid the wildflowers and smell the wild herbs, remember that the town name comes from the Greek word *selinon,* meaning parsley.

Tip: Selinunte is entirely do-able as a day trip from Palermo—it's about a 2-hour drive via the A29/E90 autostrada (exit at Castelvetrano)—but it's a good idea to leave early in the morning. You'll need at least 4 hours to explore the ruins, and you don't want to do that in the full heat of mid-day. You'll have a more leisurely visit if you base yourself in one of the other towns on the west coast.

VISITOR INFORMATION The **tourist office** at Via Giovanni Caboto (© **0924/46251**), near the archaeological park, is open Monday to Saturday 8am to 2pm and 3 to 8pm and Sunday 9am to noon and 3 to 6pm. You can enter the park at two points, with ample parking near each: from Via Selinunte in the village of Marinella di Selinunte and from Via Mediterraneo in the village of Triscina di Selinunte.

EXPLORING THE ARCHAEOLOGICAL PARK

Given the enormity of the area, allow yourself at least 3 hours to visit, preferably in the early morning. Bring drinks for your visit, as it can get hot under the sun. If you're not up to extensive walking, you can hop on an electric train that makes a circuit through the ruins; tickets cost 6€.

Parco Archeologico Selinunte ★★★ RUINS   The archaeological grounds have three designated zones: The East Hill and temples, the Acropolis and ancient city, and the Sanctuary of Demeter Malophorus. You will likely start your visit from the East Hill, adjacent to the main entrance. Archaeologists are still trying to determine which deity each of

Acropolis of Selinunte.

the Doric temples was dedicated to—for now, they are simply denoted by letters of the alphabet. The **East Hill** was the sacred district of the city, with three temples surrounded by an enclosure. Temple E, which was in all probability dedicated to Hera (Juno), was built between 490 and 480 b.c and has a staggering 68 columns. The Metopes, reliefs that are the pride and joy of the archaeological museum in Palermo, are from this temple. Temple F is the oldest of the trio, built between 560 and 540 B.C.; in its original state, the temple had a double row of six columns at the eastern entrance and 14 columns on either side. Temple G, now an impressive heap of rubble except for a lone standing column, was destined to be of colossal proportions if it had been completed in 480 B.C.

The **Acropolis,** a district of gridlike streets surrounded by defensive walls, was the center of social and political life. Here atop a plateau stood most of Selinunte's important public and religious buildings, as well as the residences of the town's aristocrats. Temple C, the earliest surviving temple of ancient Selinus, was built here in the 6th century B.C. and is still surrounded by 14 of its resurrected 17 columns. From the Acropolis, you cross the now-dry Modione River to the **Sanctuary of Demeter Malophorus,** the ruins of several shrines to Demeter, goddess of fertility. The custom was for worshipers to place stone figurines in the shrines to honor Demeter; as many as 12,000 such figurines have been unearthed.

www.visitselinunte.com. © **0924/46540.** Admission 6€. Daily 9am to 7pm.

Where to Stay & Eat on Sicily's West Coast
ERICE

Il Carmine ★★ This refurbished 15th-century convent in Erice still shows traces of monastic living in simple, no-frills rooms and shower-only bathrooms. Yet the spartan surroundings are loaded with character, and views into the gardens are as soothing as they were intended to be. A separate entrance ensures you won't disturb convent life.

Piazza del Carmine, Erice. www.ilcarmine.com. © **0923/869-069.** 6 units. 55€–85€ double. Rates include breakfast. **Amenities:** Restaurant; Wi-Fi (free).

Hotel Elimo ★ A 400-year-old palazzo in the heart of Erice's historic core welcomes guests in stone-walled lounges where, in the chilly months, a fire blazes in a hearth beneath beamed ceilings. Guest quarters are a bit more conventional, though comfortable, and some have views over the plains below, as do the restaurant and terrace.

Via Vittorio Emanuele 75, Erice. www.hotelelimo.it. © **0923/869377.** 22 units. 70€– 120€ double; 160€ suite. **Amenities:** Restaurant; bar; Wi-Fi (free).

Hotel Moderno ★★ The "moderno" dates to the conversion of a 19th-century Erice house just after World War II, though old-fashioned charm prevails. Antiques, brass, and wicker pieces lend a homey touch, and about a dozen rooms open onto private balconies or terraces. The view from the terrace, where breakfast can be taken in warm weather, is stunning, and the restaurant is excellent.

Via Vittorio Emanuele 67, Erice. www.hotelmodernoerice.it. © **0923/869-300.** 40 units. 80€–110€ double. Rates include breakfast. **Amenities:** Restaurant; bar; Wi-Fi (free).

Monte San Giuliano ★★★ SICILIAN You'll navigate some steps and stone alleyways to reach this garden hideaway, where a table on the terrace or in the rustic dining room seems, like much of medieval Erice, far away from the modern world. The menu shows off Arab influences in the flavorful seafood couscous, with many nods to such local favorites as lamb with a pistachio crust; pasta is served with *sarde* (sardines) or *pesto alla Trapanese,* with garlic, basil, fresh tomatoes, and almonds.

Vicolo San Rocco 7, Erice. www.montesangiuliano.it. © **0923/869-595.** Entrees 8€–15€. Tues–Sun 12:15–3pm and 7:30–9:30pm. Closed part of Jan.

MARSALA

Grand Hotel Palace ★ The 19th-century estate of an English wine importer in Marsala has been redone, but the premises retain a luxurious, old-world aura, so hushed and quiet you feel that even the statues might doze off and topple over. The most character-filled rooms are in the old house, but those in the new annex are fine, too. All are spacious and outfitted with traditional furnishings; many have sea views. In the surrounding gardens, stately trees are a backdrop for the swimming pool.

Lungomare Mediterraneo 57, Marsala. www.grandhotelpalace.eu. (C) **0923/719-492.** 56 units. 90€–130€ double. Rates include breakfast. **Amenities:** Restaurant; bar; outdoor pool; room service; babysitting; Wi-Fi (free).

Trattoria Garibaldi ★ SICILIAN/SEAFOOD   At this 50-year-old institution near Marsala's cathedral, four arched, colorful dining rooms serve local favorites with a well-deserved reputation for freshness. Seafood, simply grilled with spices or served atop couscous, has a decidedly North African flair, while the homemade local pasta *busiati* with fresh fish is a specialty you probably won't find beyond the west coast.

Piazza dell'Addolorata 35, Marsala. (C) **0923/953-006.** Entrees 7€–13€. Mon–Sat 12:30–2:45pm and 7:45–10pm; Sun 12:30–2:45pm.

Villa Favorita ★★   An early-19th-century hunting lodge is a rather exotic retreat, tucked into lush gardens at the edge of historic Marsala. The fanciest guest rooms and suites are on the upper floors of an elegant villa, with wide-oak and tile floors and arched loggias opening onto a courtyard. Others are garden bungalows that resemble stone igloos— they're unusual but attractive, sort of an Italian take on glamping, divided into small sitting rooms and bedrooms with a cramped bathroom and scattered among greenery and shaded lanes surrounding a beautiful swimming pool. The atmosphere is casual and the grounds are full of many shady corners for relaxing. A pizza oven is fired up in the summer, and the restaurant serves well-done Sicilian dishes. From the center of Marsala, take SS115 north toward Trapani; the hotel is signposted.

Via Favorita 23, Marsala. www.villafavorita.com. (C) **0923/989-100.** 29 bungalows, 13 units in main building. 85€–110€ double. Rates include breakfast. **Amenities:** 2 restaurants; bar; outdoor pool; tennis court; Wi-Fi (free).

TRAPANI

Trapani is a good place to try what's considered to be the oldest handmade pasta in the world, *busiati.* The curly, eggless pasta has a firm texture and mealy taste, and is good eaten with pesto sauce made Trapanese-style with cherry tomatoes. For the past 70 years, the favorite stop in town for quick bite has been **Pizzeria dal 1946,** Via Nunzio Nasi, with slices and pies to take out or eat in, in several atmospheric, always crowded rooms (Wed–Mon 11am–late; (C) **0923/21464**).

Ai Lumi Tavernetta ★ SICILIAN   The narrow, arched ground floor of a palazzo, filled with heavy rustic tables and chairs, is a cool retreat in which to enjoy Trapanese classics. Seafood is plentiful, as are such meat specialties as roast lamb in a citrus sauce and *busiati,* the thick local pasta that seems like perfection itself when topped with *pesto trapanese,* made of tomato, basil, pecorino, and almonds. The terrace in front is one of the nicest places in Trapani to spend a summer evening. Upstairs are 12 pleasant, well-furnished rooms, some with kitchenettes, with doubles starting at 70€.

Corso Vittorio Emanuele 75, Trapani. www.ailumi.it. © **0923/872-418.** Entrees 8€–18€. Sept–July Mon–Sat 7:30–11pm; Aug daily 7:30–11pm.

Ligny Bed and Breakfast ★★ Right at the edge of the sea at the end of Trapani's historic town, an old palazzo offers high-ceilinged rooms, each with a panoramic terrace that takes in sweeping views of the gulf and Erice rising above the shores. Beaches, the port, and the town sights are within an easy walk. Iron bedsteads and some old family pieces add a homey touch to the rooms, up two flights of stairs; bathrooms are shower-only, and some are not en suite. Credit cards are not accepted.

Via Torre Ligny 114, Trapani. www.ligny.it. © **0923/194-1515.** 5 units. 40€–70€ double. Rates include breakfast. **Amenities:** Wi-Fi (free).

Osteria La Bettolaccia ★★ SICILIAN Trapani's longtime favorite never disappoints, drawing big crowds (reserve if you can) to a couple of rambling, tile-floored rooms near the seafront. The kitchen prepares what many regulars claim is the best seafood couscous in Sicily, laden with calamari and a spicy sauce. Another favorite is spaghetti with swordfish, tuna, tomatoes, herbs, and breadcrumbs.

25 Via Enrico Fardella, Trapani. www.labettolaccia.it. © **0923/21695.** Entrees 8€–15€. Mon–Fri 12 :45–3pm and 8–11pm, Sat–Sun 8–11pm.

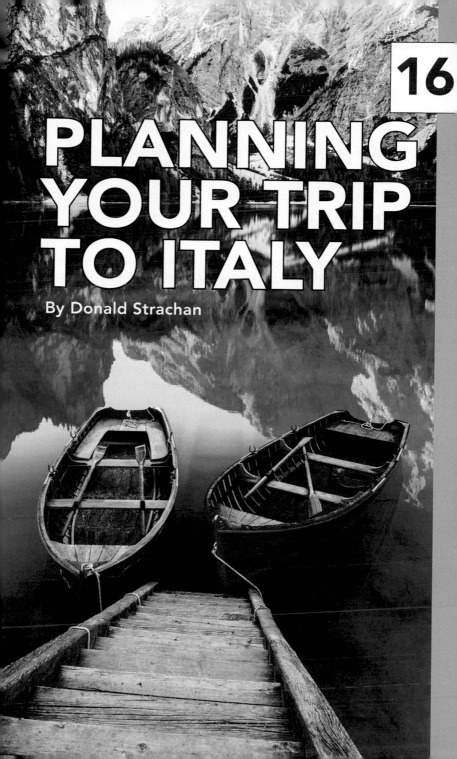

PLANNING YOUR TRIP TO ITALY

By Donald Strachan

This chapter has lots of planning tools, including information on how to get to Italy, how to get around, and the inside track on local resources you can tap. If you do your homework on festivals and events, pick the right place for the right season, and pack for the climate, preparing for a trip to Italy should be pleasant and uncomplicated. See also "When to Go," p. 35.

ARRIVING
By Plane

If you're flying across an ocean, you'll likely land at Rome's **Leonardo da Vinci–Fiumicino Airport** (FCO; www.adr.it/fiumicino), 40km (25 miles) from the center, or **Milan Malpensa** (MXP; www.milanomalpensa-airport. com), 45km (28 miles) northwest of central Milan. These are Italy's major intercontinental hubs, and it is almost always cheapest to fly long-haul to one or the other. Rome's much smaller **Ciampino Airport** (CIA; www. adr.it/ciampino) and Milan's **Linate Airport** (LIN; www.milanolinate-airport.com) serve low-cost airlines connecting to European cities and other destinations in Italy. For information on getting to central Rome from its airports, see p. 63; for Milan, see p. 394. From 2019, travelers can board a direct high-speed train from Rome's Fiumicino Airport to Florence or Venice **without** going via central Rome.

FLYING DIRECTLY TO VENICE, BOLOGNA, PISA, NAPLES, OR PALERMO

If you are arriving in Italy from somewhere else in Europe, it's often cheaper to fly direct on a budget carrier to one of several smaller Italian cities. Among the most convenient are Venice's **Marco Polo Airport** (VCE; www.veniceairport.it), Bologna's **Marconi Airport** (BLQ; www.bologna-airport.it), Pisa's **Galileo Galilei Airport** (PSA; www.pisa-airport.com), **Naples International Airport** (NAP; www.aeroportodinapoli.it), or Palermo's **Punta Raisi Airport** (PMO; www.gesap.it). For information on getting into central Venice from the airport, see p. 394; for reaching Florence from Pisa Airport or Bologna airport, see p. 169; for reaching central Naples from the airport, see p. 586. For information on arriving in Sicily via Palermo's airport, see p. 741.

By Train

Italy's major cities are well connected to Europe's rail hubs. You can arrive in Milan on direct trains from **France** (Paris, Lyon) by **TGV**

TURNING TO THE internet or apps FOR A HOTEL DISCOUNT

It's not impossible to get a good deal by calling a hotel, but you're more likely to snag a discount online or with an app. Here are some strategies:

1. Browse extreme discounts on sites where you reserve or **bid for lodgings** without knowing which hotel you'll get. You'll find these on **Priceline.com** and **Hotwire.com**, and they can be money-savers, particularly when booking within a week of travel (when hotels can get nervous and resort to deep discounts). These feature mostly major chains, so you are very unlikely to end up in a dump.

2. Review discounts on the **hotel's website**. Hotels often give the lowest rate to travelers who book through their site, rather than via a third party or agent. But you'll only find truly deep discounts in the **loyalty** section of the sites—so join the club.

3. Use the right **hotel search engine.** They're not all equal, as we at Frommers.com learned by putting the top 20 sites to the test in 20 destinations around the globe. We discovered **Booking.com** listed the lowest rates for hotels in the city center, and in the under $200 range, 16 out of 20 times—the best record, by far, of all the sites we tested. And Booking.com includes all taxes and fees in its initial results (not all do, which can make for a frustrating shopping experience). For top-end properties, again in the city center, both Priceline.com and HotelsCombined.com came up with the best rates, tying at 14 wins each.

(en.oui.sncf/en/tgv) or from **Switzerland** (www.sbb.ch/en). Connect at Milan to Venice, Florence, or Rome (see "Getting Around," p. 466). TGV services also connect France with Turin. Several routes connect **Vienna** with Italy via a comfortable overnight Austrian sleeper train. These **Nightjet** (www.nightjet.com) services visit Verona, Bologna, Milan, Florence, Rome, and Venice, among other places. Prices start from 29€ per person if you book ahead (up to 180 days is permitted); specially configured family couchette cabins *(Liegewagen)* start from 199€ for 1 to 3 adults and up to 4 children ages 14 and under (6 people max.). Other Nightjet services connect Munich, Germany, with Venice, Florence/Bologna/Rome or Verona/Milan.

Thello (www.thello.com) also operates an overnight service connecting Paris with Milan and Venice. After crossing the Alps in the dead of night, the train calls at Milan, Brescia, Verona, Vicenza, and Padua, before arriving in Venice around 9:30am. For Florence, Rome, and points south, alight at Milan (around 6am) and switch to Italy's national high-speed rail lines; see p. 817. Accommodation on the Thello train is in sleeping cars, as well as in six- and four-berth couchettes. Prices range from 29€ per person for the cheapest advance "Smart fare" in a six-berth couchette to 290€ for sole occupancy of a better-quality sleeping car (these can take one, two, or three passengers). It's worth paying extra for these accommodations if you can.

Book your rail travel in Italy; online at **Loco2** (www.loco2.com) or **Rail Europe** (www.raileurope.com); or use an agent such as **International Rail** (www.internationalrail.com; ✆ **+44 871/231-0790**).

GETTING AROUND
By Car

Much of Italy is accessible by public transportation, but to explore vineyards, countryside, and smaller towns, you need a car. You'll get the **best rate** if you book your car far ahead of arrival. Try the website **AutoSlash. com,** which applies any coupons on the market to your rental and then monitors your booking. If the price drops, they'll make you a new reservation. We have found AutoSlash.com to be the best search engine for rentals by far, although it is a bit clunky to use: You must wait for an email back before you can see the options, but thankfully that email usually comes within minutes of your request. Car rental search companies usually report the lowest rates available between 6 and 8 weeks ahead of arrival. Rent the smallest car possible and request a diesel rather than a gasoline engine, to minimize fuel costs. You must be 25 or older to rent from many agencies (although some accept ages 21 and up, at a premium price).

You also must have nerves of steel, a sense of humor, a valid domestic driver's license, and strictly speaking (for non-EU citizens), an **International Driving Permit** (see below). Insurance on all vehicles is compulsory.

Note: If you're planning to rent a car in Italy during high season, you should **book farther in advance.** It's not unheard of to arrive at an airport in July to find every agent all out of cars, perhaps for the whole week.

It can sometimes be tricky to get to the *autostrada* (fast highway) from the city center or airport, so consider renting or bringing a GPS-enabled device, or installing an offline sat-nav app on your phone. In bigger cities you will first have to get to the *tangenziale,* or beltway, which will eventually lead to your highway of choice. The beltway in Rome is known as the Grande Raccordo Anulare, or "Big Ring Road."

The going can be slow almost anywhere, especially on Friday afternoons leaving the cities and Sunday nights on the way back into town, and rush hour around any city can be epic. Driving long-distance for a day or so on either side of the busy *Ferragosto* (August 15) holiday is to be avoided *at all costs.* See **www.autostrade.it** for live traffic updates and a road-toll calculator.

Autostrada tolls can get expensive, costing approximately 1€ for every 15km (10 miles), which means it would cost about 18€ for a trip from Rome to Florence. Although European fuel prices have fallen slightly in recent years, gas remains around 1.50€ *per liter* at time of writing, and has been climbing. (Diesel is usually around .10€ cheaper.) The

PrezziBenzina app or website (www.prezzibenzina.it) is handy for finding the lowest-priced local gas station. Still, add in the price of car rental, and it's often cheaper to travel by train, even for two people.

Before leaving home, you can apply for an **International Driving Permit** from the American Automobile Association (AAA; www.aaa. com; ✆ **800/622-7070** or 650/294-7400). You should apply at least a month before travel; the license costs $20. In Canada, the permit is available from the Canadian Automobile Association (CAA; www.caa.ca; ✆ **800/222-4357**). Technically, you need this permit and your actual driver's license to drive in Italy, though at a rental desk, your license alone often suffices. But why risk it? Traffic police can fine you for driving without an IDP. Visitors from within the E.U. need only carry a domestic driver's license.

Italy's equivalent of AAA, the **Automobile Club d'Italia** (ACI; www.aci.it), will respond if you place an emergency call to ✆ **803-116** for road breakdowns (✆ **800-116-800** from an overseas cellphone). You'll be charged for this service if you're not a member.

DRIVING RULES Italian drivers aren't all maniacs; most of them only appear to be. Spend any time on a highway and you will have the experience of somebody driving up from behind insanely close, headlights flashing. Take a deep breath and don't panic: This is the aggressive signal for you to move to the right so he (invariably, it's a "he") can pass, and until you do he will stay mind-bogglingly close. On a two-lane road, the idiot who swerved into your lane to pass someone in the opposing traffic expects you to veer obligingly over toward the shoulder so three lanes of traffic can fit. He would do the same for you. Probably. Many Italians seem to think blinkers are optional, so be aware a car in front could be ready to turn at any moment. It is compulsory to keep your headlights illuminated—set to dip—even during the day.

Autostrade are toll highways, denoted by green signs and prefaced with an *A,* like the A1 from Milan to Florence, Rome, and Naples. A few fast highways aren't numbered and are simply called a *raccordo,* a connecting road between two cities (such as Florence–Siena and Florence–Pisa).

Strade statali (singular: *strada statale*) are state roads, sometimes without a center divider and two lanes wide (although sometimes they can be a divided four-way highway), indicated by blue signs. Their route numbers are prefaced with an *SS,* as in the SS11 from Milan to Venice. On signs, however, these official route numbers are used infrequently. Usually, you'll just see blue signs listing destinations by name with arrows pointing in the appropriate directions. It's impossible to predict which of all the towns that lie along a road will be selected to list on a particular sign. Sometimes a sign gives only the first minuscule village past the turnoff. At other times it lists the first major town down that road. Some signs mention only the major city the road eventually leads to, even if it's hundreds of kilometers away. It pays to study the map before coming to an intersection, to carry a GPS device, or to download an offline GPS app for your smartphone. The *strade statali* can be frustratingly slow thanks to traffic, traffic lights, and the fact they bisect countless towns: If you're in a hurry to get where you're going, pay for the autostrada.

The **speed limit** on roads in built-up areas around towns and cities is 50 kmph (31 mph). On two-lane roads it's 90 kmph (56 mph), and on the highway it's 130 kmph (81 mph). Italians have an astounding disregard for these limits. However, police can ticket you and collect any fine on the spot. The blood-alcohol limit in Italy is .05%, generally achieved with just two regular-size drinks; driving above the limit can result in a fine of up to 6,000€, a driving ban, or jail. The blood-alcohol limit is zero for commercial drivers and for anyone who has held a driver's license for less than 3 years.

Safety belts are obligatory in both the front and back seats; ditto child seats or special restraints for minors under 1.5m (5 ft.) in height, although this latter regulation is often ignored. Drivers may not use a handheld cellphone while driving—yet another law locals seem to treat as optional.

PARKING   On streets, **white lines** indicate free public spaces, **blue lines** are pay public spaces, and **yellow lines** mean only residents are allowed to park. Meters don't line the sidewalk; rather, there's usually one machine on the block where you punch in coins corresponding to how long you want to park. The machine spits out a ticket that you leave on your dashboard.

If you park in an area marked *parcheggio disco orario,* root around in your rental car's glove compartment for a cardboard parking disc. With this device, you dial up the hour of your arrival and display it on your dashboard. You're allowed *un'ora* (1 hr.), *due ore* (2 hr.), or whatever the sign advises. If you do not have a disk, write your arrival time clearly on a sheet of paper and leave it on the dash.

Parking lots have ticket dispensers, but exit booths are not usually manned. When you return to the lot to depart, first visit the office or automated payment machine to exchange your ticket for a paid receipt or exit token, which you will then use to pass the exit barrier.

ROAD SIGNS   A **speed limit** sign is a black number in a red circle on a white background. The **end of a speed zone** is just black and white, with a black slash through the number. A red circle on white, a black arrow pointing down, and a red arrow pointing up means **yield to oncoming traffic,** while a red-and-white triangle pointing down means **yield ahead.**

Many city centers are closed to traffic, and a simple white circle with a red border, or the words *zona pedonale* or *zona traffico limitato,* denotes a **pedestrian zone** (you can often prearrange to drop off baggage at your hotel); a white arrow on a blue background is used for Italy's many **one-way streets;** a mostly red circle with a horizontal white slash means **Do Not Enter.** Any image in black on a white background surrounded by a red circle means that image is **not allowed** (for instance, if the image is two cars next to each other, it means no passing; a motorcycle means no

Harleys permitted; and so on). A circular sign in blue with a red circle-slash means **no parking.**

Gasoline (gas or petrol), *benzina,* can be found in gas stations along major roads and on the outskirts of town, as well as in 24-hour stations along the autostrada. Almost all stations are closed for the *riposo* and on Sundays (except for those on the autostrada), but most have machines that accept cash. All gas is unleaded. Diesel is *gasolio* (or simply *diesel*).

By Train

Italy, especially its northern half, has one of the best train systems in Europe with most destinations connected by rail. Consequently, the train is an excellent option if you're looking to visit the major sites without the hassle of driving. The vast majority of lines are run by the state-owned **Ferrovie dello Stato,** or FS (www.trenitalia.com; ✆ **892021**). A private operator, **Italo** (www.italotreno.it; ✆ **060708** or 892020) operates on the Turin–Milan–Florence–Rome–Naples–Salerno high-speed line; on two branches north from Bologna, to Ferrara-Padua-Venice or Verona-Trento-Bolzano; and between Turin and Venice via Milan and Verona.

Travel durations and ticket prices vary considerably depending on what type of train you are traveling on. The country's principal north–south high-speed line links Turin and Milan to Bologna, Florence, Rome, Naples, and Salerno. Milan to Rome, for example, takes under 3 hours on the quick train, and costs 99€–107€ in standard class—though you can find tickets as low as 20€ if you buy way ahead and travel in off-peak hours. Rome to Naples takes 70 minutes and costs 48€ (walk-up fare) on the fast train, or you can spend 13€ for a trip on a slower train that takes over twice as long. To bag the cheapest fares on high-speed trains, try to **book around 100 to 120 days before your travel dates.** The **Italo news-letter** (and homepage) regularly advertises limited-time promo code discounts of up to 50 percent off advance fares, making them crazy cheap.

TYPES OF TRAIN　The speed, cleanliness, and overall quality of Italian trains vary widely. The high-speed **Frecciarossa,** along with **Italo**'s rival high-speed service, is the fastest of the fast. These trains mostly operate

Travel Times Between the Major Cities

CITIES	DISTANCE	(FASTEST) TRAIN TRAVEL TIME	DRIVING TIME
Florence to Venice	281km/174 miles	2 hr.	3 hr.
Florence to Milan	298km/185 miles	1 hr., 40 min.	3½ hr.
Milan to Venice	267km/166 miles	2 hr.	3¼ hr.
Milan to Rome	572km/355 miles	2 hr., 55 min.	5½ hr.
Rome to Florence	277km/172 miles	1½ hr.	3 hr.
Rome to Naples	219km/136 miles	1 hr., 10 min.	2½ hr.
Rome to Turin	669km/415 miles	3 hr., 50 min.	6½ hr.
Rome to Venice	528km/327 miles	3hr., 25 min.	5½ hr.

on the Turin–Milan–Florence–Rome–Naples–Salerno line, and run up to 300 kmph (186 mph); new FS equipment (Frecciarossa 1000) has a potential top speed of 400 kmph (249 mph). Frecciarossa services also run down Italy's east coast (Milan–Rimini–Ancona–Bari–Lecce) and connect Milan with Venice (with stops in Verona and Vicenza). The cheapest class on both operators is perfectly comfortable, even on long journeys (although Business class on the Frecciarossa is well worth paying a little extra for, especially if you can find a cheap advance fare). These are Italy's premium rail services.

The **Frecciargento** uses similar, slightly downgraded hardware, and travels a little slower; it links Naples, Rome, Florence, Verona, and Venice at speeds of up to 250 kmph (155 mph). There are also Rome–Bari–Lecce, Rome–Mantua, Rome–Bolzano, Rome–Naples–Reggio Calabria, and Rome–Genoa Frecciargento services. Frecciargento trains have the usual two classes, First and Second. The less frequent **Frecciabianca** service isn't a genuine high-speed service, merely an upgraded train running on standard track. Useful routes include regular Rome–Pisa trains and links between Milan and the Adriatic Sea coast.

Speed and cleanliness come at a price, with tickets for high-speed trains usually costing around three times the slower "regional" train. With *Le Frecce* you **must make a seat reservation** when you buy a ticket. If you are traveling with a rail pass (see p. 819), you must pay a 10€ supplementary fee to ride them and reserve a seat. Passes are not accepted (for now) on Italo trains.

Intercity (IC) trains are another step down, in both speed and comfort; as with *Le Frecce,* seat reservations are compulsory on IC trains. The slower *Regionale* (R) and *Regionale Veloce* (RV) make many stops and can sometimes be on the grimy side, but they are also very cheap: A Venice–Verona second-class ticket will put you back only 9€, compared with 27€ on the high-speed service. There is no advantage in booking R or RV services ahead of travel; just turn up, get a ticket, and ride. Old *Regionale* rolling stock is slowly being replaced, and comfort is improving. However, overcrowding is sometimes a problem on these standard services on Friday evenings, weekends, and holidays, especially in and out of big cities, or just after a strike. In summer, the crowding escalates, and many trains going toward a beach in August bulge like an overstuffed sausage.

TRAIN TRAVEL TIPS If you don't have a ticket with a reservation for a particular seat on a specific train, then you must **validate your ticket by stamping it in the little yellow box** on the platform before boarding the train. If you board a train without a ticket, or without having validated your ticket, you'll have to pay a hefty fine on top of the ticket or supplement, which the conductor will sell you. If you board a train without a ticket or realize once onboard that you have the wrong type of ticket, your best bet is to search out the conductor, who is likely to be more forgiving because you found her and made it clear you weren't trying to ride for free.

Schedules for all trains leaving a given station are printed on yellow posters tacked up on the station wall (a similar white poster lists all the arrivals). These are good for getting general guidance, but keep your eye on the electronic boards and screens that update with delays and track (*binario*) changes. You can also get official schedules (and more train information, also in English) and buy tickets at www.trenitalia.com or www.italotreno.it, or at an online agent such as **Loco2** (www.loco2.com).

In big cities (especially Milan and Rome) and tourist destinations (above all Venice and Florence), ticketing lines can be dreadfully long. Don't be scared of the **automatic ticket machines.** They are easy to navigate, allow you to follow instructions in English, accept cash and credit cards, and save you the stress of waiting in an interminably slow line. (Note that you can't buy international tickets at automatic machines.) Better still, rail **apps** for both Italo and Trenitalia offer paperless ticketing, and easy payment via credit card or PayPal. You can also just show a copy (paper or electronic) of your booking confirmation, which has a unique PNR code.

SPECIAL PASSES & DISCOUNTS   To buy the **Eurail Italy Pass,** available only outside Europe and priced in U.S. dollars, contact **Rail Europe** (www.raileurope.com). You have 1 month in which to use the train for a set number of days (the base number of days is 3, and you can add up to 5 more). For adults, the first-class pass costs $250, second-class is $199. Each additional day costs $40 to $45 more for first class, around $35 for second class. Up to two children ages 2 to 11 travel free with any adult pass-holder. For youth travelers (27 and under), a 3-day second-class pass is $167 and additional days about $30 each.

Buying your rail pass early in the year is sometimes rewarded with an extra day's travel at no additional cost (such as pay for 3 days, get 4) or seasonal discounts (we have seen up to 35% off some Eurail passes). Saver passes are available for groups of two to five people traveling together at all times, and amount to a savings of about 15% on individual passes. There are also Italy–Austria, Italy–Greece, Italy–Spain, Italy–France, and Italy–Switzerland rail pass combinations.

Note: Booking every rail journey online ahead of arrival will usually beat a rail pass on price, especially if you factor in the cost of making compulsory seat reservations on Italy's high-speed trains. However, because the cheapest online fares are nonrefundable, you gain flexibility with a pass.

Children 14 and under ride half-price on Italian trains, while kids under 4 don't pay, although they also do not have the right to their own seat. State railways also sometimes offer free tickets for children 14 and under traveling with an adult; ask about "Bimbi gratis" fares when buying (ticket machines will offer this option automatically, if it's available). The **Italo Family** fare, available at the station and online, includes free travel for up to three kids ages 14 and under accompanying an adult paying full fare (in Smart class only, Monday–Saturday).

By Bus

Although trains are quicker and easier, you can get just about anywhere in Italy on a network of local, provincial, and regional bus lines. Keep in mind that in smaller towns, buses exist mainly to shuttle workers and schoolchildren, so the most runs are on weekdays, early in the morning, and usually again in midafternoon.

In a big city, the **bus station** for intercity trips is usually near the main train station. A small town's **bus stop** is usually either in the main square, on the edge of town, or just outside the main town gate. You should always try to find the local ticket vendor—if there's no office, it is invariably the nearest newsstand or *tabacchi* (signaled by a sign with a white t), or occasionally a bar—but you can usually also buy tickets on the bus. You can sometimes flag down a bus as it passes on a country road, but try to find an official stop (a small sign, sometimes tacked onto a tree or pole). Tell the driver where you're going and ask courteously if he'll let you know when to get off. When he says, *"È la prossima fermata,"* that means yours is the next stop. *"Posso scendere a…?"* (*Poh*-so *shen*-dair-ay ah…?) is "Can I get off at…?"

For details on urban bus transportation, see individual chapters. Perhaps the only longer-distance bus you will want to take in Italy is the efficient **Florence–Siena** service; see "Siena," p. 232. However, if you are traveling on a tight budget, check **FlixBus** (www.flixbus.it) intercity fares, which often significantly undercut train prices. A long-distance bus is *un pullman.*

By Plane

These days, the only internal air connection you will likely make is to the island of **Sicily.** From Milan, **easyJet** (www.easyjet.com), **Air Italy** (www.airitaly.com), and **Ryanair** (www.ryanair.com) connect Malpensa Airport with both Palermo and Catania. Ryanair also links Bergamo, Bologna, and Pisa with Palermo and Trapani. Direct Rome–Sicily routes are flown by **Alitalia** (www.alitalia.com), **Vueling** (www.vueling.com), and Ryanair. Alitalia also operates direct Venice–Catania, Milan (Linate)–Catania, and Bologna–Catania flights. **Volotea** (www.volotea.com) flies to Palermo from Venice, Verona, Turin, Ancona, Naples, Bari, and Genoa, and to Catania from all of those cities except Turin.

[FastFACTS] ITALY

Area Codes The **country code** for Italy is **39. City codes** (for example, Florence 055, Venice 041, Milan 02, Rome 06) are incorporated into the numbers themselves. Therefore, you must dial the entire number, **including the initial zero,** when calling from *anywhere* outside or inside Italy and even within the same town. For example, to call Milan from the United States, you must dial

011-39-02, then the rest of the phone number. Phone numbers in Italy can range anywhere from 6 to 12 digits in length.

ATMs The easiest and best way to get cash is from an ATM, referred to in Italy as *un bancomat.* ATMs are easy to find in Italian cities; smaller towns usually have one, but it's good practice to fuel up on cash in urban centers before heading to villages or rural areas.

Before traveling, confirm with your bank that your card is valid for international withdrawals and that you have a four-digit PIN. (Some ATMs in Italy will not accept any other number of digits.) Also, be sure you know your daily withdrawal limit before you depart. *Note:* Many banks impose a fee when you use a card at another bank's ATM, and that fee can be higher for international transactions (up to $5 or more) than for domestic ones. In addition, the bank from which you withdraw cash may charge its own fee, although this is not common practice in Italy.

If at the ATM you get an on-screen message saying your card isn't valid for international transactions, don't panic: It's most likely the bank just can't make an electronic connection to check it (occasionally this can be a citywide epidemic). Try another ATM or another town.

Business Hours **Banks** tend to be open Monday–Friday 8:30am–1:30pm and 2:45–4:15pm. General opening hours for **stores, offices,** and **churches** are from 9:30am to noon or 1pm, and again from 3 or 3:30pm to 7:30 or 8pm. The early afternoon shutdown is the *riposo*, the Italian siesta (in downtown areas of large cities, stores don't usually close for the *riposo*). Most stores close all day Sunday and some also on Monday (morning only or all day). Some public services and business offices are open only in the morning.

Traditionally, **state museums** are closed Mondays. Most large museums stay open all day long otherwise, although some smaller places close for *riposo* or are only open in the morning (9am–2pm is popular).

Credit Cards The evolution of international computerized banking has led to the triumph of plastic throughout Italy. It's still a good idea to carry some cash—small businesses may accept only cash or may claim their credit card machine is broken to avoid paying card fees. **Visa** and **Mastercard** are almost universally accepted, and some businesses, typically at the luxe end, take **American Express. Diners Club** tends not to be accepted in Italy. Be sure to let your bank know you'll be traveling abroad to avoid having your card blocked after a few days of big purchases far from home. *Note:* Many banks assess a 1 percent to 3 percent "transaction fee" on **all** charges you incur abroad, whether you're using the local currency or your native currency. *Tip:* If a store clerk offers you the choice, **make payment in local currency** (Euros), not your home currency. Their system's exchange rates will invariably be poor compared to your bank or card provider.

Customs Foreign visitors can bring into the country most items for personal use duty-free, including merchandise valued up to 450€. Returning to the United States, U.S. citizens can bring with them up to $800 of goods, including one liter of alcohol, but no meats or fresh fruits and vegetables. Vinegars, oils, jams, chocolates, and certain cheeses are permissible (vacuum-packed cheeses yes; raw milk cheese no).

Disabled Travelers Most of the top museums and churches have installed ramps at their entrances, and several hotels have converted first-floor rooms into accessible units. Other than that, you may find many charming parts of Italy tricky to tackle. Builders in the Middle Ages and the Renaissance didn't have wheelchairs in mind when they built narrow doorways and spiral staircases, and preservation laws prevent Italians from doing much about this in some areas.

Public transportation is improving, however, with generally better access for passengers in wheelchairs, particularly on modern local buses and new transit developments like Florence's tram. There are usually dedicated seats or areas for those with disabilities, and Italians are quick to give up their place for somebody who appears to need it. **Trenitalia** has a special number for disabled travelers to call for assistance on the rail network: ☎ **02/323232. Italo** has dedicated wheelchair spaces on every train: Call ☎ **060708** for any station assistance you need.

Drinking Laws People of any age can legally consume alcohol in Italy, but a person must be 16 years old to be served alcohol in a restaurant or bar. Bars generally close by 2am, though alcohol is often served in clubs after that. Supermarkets carry beer, wine, and liquor.

Electricity Italy operates on a 220-volt AC (50 cycles) system, as opposed to the U.S. 110-volt AC (60 cycles) system. You'll need a simple adapter plug to make the American flat pegs fit the Italian round holes, and, unless your appliance is dual-voltage (as some hair dryers, travel irons, and almost all gadgets are), an electrical currency converter. You can pick up the hardware at electronics stores, travel specialty stores, luggage shops, and airports.

Embassies & Consulates The **Australian Embassy** is in Rome at Via Antonio Bosio 5 (www.italy.embassy.gov.au; ☎ **06/852-721**). The **Australian Consulate-General** is in Milan at Via Borgogna 2 (☎ **02/7767-4200**).

The **Canadian** Embassy is in Rome at Via Zara 30 (www.italy.gc.ca; ☎ **06/85444-2911**). The **Canadian Consulate** is in Milan at Piazza Cavour 3 (☎ **02/6269-4238**).

The **New Zealand Embassy** (www.nzembassy.com/italy; ☎ **06/853-7501**) is in Rome at Via Clitunno 44.

The **U.K. Embassy** (www.gov.uk/government/world/italy; ☎ **06/4220-0001**) is in Rome at Via XX Settembre 80a. The **British Consulate-General** is in Milan at Via San Paolo 7 (☎ **02/723001**).

The **U.S. Embassy** is in Rome at Via Vittorio Veneto 121 (it.usembassy.gov; ☎ **06/46741**). There are also **U.S. Consulates General** in **Florence,** at Lungarno Vespucci 38 (☎ **055/266-951**); in **Milan,** at Via Principe Amedeo 2/10 (☎ **02/290-351**); and in **Naples,** in Piazza della Repubblica (☎ **081/583-8111**).

Emergencies The best number to call in Italy with a **general emergency** is ☎ **112,** which connects you to the *Carabinieri* who will transfer your call as needed. For the **police,** dial ☎ **113;** for a **medical emergency** and to call an **ambulance,** the number is ☎ **118;** for the **fire department,** call ☎ **115.** If your car breaks down, dial ☎ **116** for **roadside aid** courtesy of the Automotive Club of Italy. All are free calls, but roadside assistance is a paid service for nonmembers.

Family Travel Italy is a family-oriented society. A

crying baby at a dinner table is greeted with a knowing smile, rather than a stern look. Children can almost always request discounted smaller portions, and sometimes even get a special treat from the waiter, but the availability of such accoutrements as child seats for cars and dinner tables is more the exception than the norm. (The former, however, is a legal requirement: Be sure to ask your rental car company to provide one.) There are plenty of parks, offbeat museums, markets, ice-cream parlors, and vibrant street-life scenes to amuse even the youngest children. Child discounts apply on public transportation, and at public and private museums.

Health You won't encounter any special health risks by visiting Italy. The country's public health care system is generally well regarded. The richer north tends to have better **hospitals** than the south.

Italy offers universal health care to its citizens and those of other European Union countries (U.K. nationals should remember to carry an EHIC: See **www.nhs.uk/ehic**). Others should be prepared to pay medical bills upfront. Before leaving home, find out what medical services your **health insurance** covers. *Note:* Even if you don't have insurance, you will be treated in an emergency.

Insurance Italy may be one of the safer places you can travel in the world, but accidents and setbacks can and do happen, from lost luggage to car crashes. We recommend looking at the following online marketplaces for insurance: **SquareMouth.com**, **Insure-MyTrip.com** and **TripInsurance.com**. All three allow users to quickly and easily compare policies from different, vetted travel insurance companies. We find the user interface at SquareMouth to be the more intuitive, but all three are excellent resources.

Internet Access   You will find Wi-Fi in almost every hotel, but if it is essential for your stay, make sure you ask before booking. Don't always expect to find a connection in a rural *agriturismo*—digital detox is sometimes part of their appeal. In a pinch, hostels, local libraries, and some cafes and bars have Web access. Several spots around Venice, Florence, Rome, and other big cities are covered with free Wi-Fi access provided by the local administration, but at these and any other Wi-Fi spots around Italy, antiterrorism laws make it obligatory to register before you can log on. Take your passport or other photo ID if you go looking for an Internet point. **High-speed trains** often have free Wi-Fi (but throttle Skype, video streaming, file sharing, and similar data-hungry services).

LGBT Travelers   Italy as a whole, northern Italy in particular, is gay-friendly. Homosexuality is legal, and the age of consent is 16.

Same-sex civil unions became legal in 2016. Italians are generally more affectionate and physical than North Americans in all their friendships, and even straight men occasionally walk down the street with their arms around each other—however, kissing anywhere other than on the cheeks at greetings and goodbyes may draw attention. As you might expect, smaller towns tend to be less permissive than cities and beach resorts.

Italy's national associations and support networks for gays and lesbians are **ArciGay** (www.arcigay.it) and **ArciLesbica** (www.arcilesbica.it). Most cities have a local office. See **www.arcigay.it/sedi** for a map directory of local affiliates.

Mail & Postage   Sending a postcard or letter up to 20 grams, or a little less than an ounce, costs 1.15€ to European countries, 2.40€ to North America, and a whopping 3.10€ to Australia and New Zealand. Full details on Italy's postal services are available at **www.poste.it** (some of it in English).

Mobile Phones   **GSM** (Global System for Mobile Communications) cellphone technology is used by most of the world's countries; you can turn on a phone with a contract based in Australia, Ireland, the U.K., Pakistan, or almost every other corner of the world and have it work in Italy without missing a beat. In the U.S., service

providers like Sprint and Verizon use a different technology—CDMA—and phones on those networks need GSM and/or 4G/LTE compatibility to work in Italy. (Most current high-end models have it; older phones may not work.) If you are coming from the U.S. or Canada, you may need a multiband "world" phone.

All travelers should activate "international roaming" on their account—contact your service provider before leaving. But—and it's a *big* but—using roaming can be very expensive, especially if you access the Internet on your phone. It's usually much cheaper, once you arrive, to buy an Italian SIM card (the fingernail-size removable plastic card found in all GSM phones). This is an especially good idea if you will be in Italy for more than a week. You can **buy a SIM card** at cellphone shops in every city: The main service providers are **TIM** (www.tim.it), **Vodafone** (www.vodafone.it), **Wind** (www.wind.it), and **3** (www.tre.it). With an Italian SIM card in your phone, local and national calls may be as low as .10€ per minute, and incoming calls are free. Value prepaid data packages are available—usually with LTE/4G data inclusive—as are prepaid data bundles for iPads and other tablets. Not every network allows **tethering**—ask if you need it. **Note:** U.S. contract cellphones are

often "locked" and will only work with a SIM card from your home service provider, so check whether you have an unlocked phone before buying an Italian SIM card.

Buying a phone is another option, and you shouldn't have any trouble finding one for about 20€. Use it, then recycle it or eBay it when you get home. It will save you a fortune versus alternatives such as roaming or using hotel telephones, as will Wi-Fi and a VoIP calling service like Skype or Apple's FaceTime.

THE VALUE OF THE EURO VS. OTHER POPULAR CURRENCIES

€	Aus$	Can$	NZ$	UK£	US$
1	1.60	1.51	1.70	0.86	1.12

Money & Costs From-

mer's lists exact prices in the local currency. The currency conversions quoted below were correct at press time. However, rates fluctuate, so before departing, consult a currency exchange website, such as **www.oanda.com/ currency/converter**, to check up-to-the-minute rates.

Like many European countries, Italy uses the **euro** as its currency. Euro coins are issued in denominations of .01€, .02€, .05€, .10€, .20€, and .50€, as well as 1€ and 2€; bills come in denominations of 5€, 10€, 20€, 50€, 100€, 200€, and 500€. You'll get the best rate if you **exchange money** at a bank or one of its ATMs. The rates at "Cambio/ change" exchange booths are invariably less favorable but still better than what you'd get exchanging money at a hotel or shop (a last-resort tactic only).

Traveler's checks have gone the way of the Stegosaurus.

Newspapers & Maga-

zines *The New York Times International Edition* and *USA Today* are available at most newsstands in the big cities, and sometimes even in smaller towns. At larger kiosks in the bigger cities you can find the *Wall Street Journal Europe, The Economist,* and most major European newspapers and magazines.

Pharmacies Italian

pharmacies offer essentially the same range of generic drugs available in North America and internationally. Pharmacies are ubiquitous (look for the green cross) and serve almost like miniclinics, where pharmacists diagnose and treat minor ailments with over-thecounter drugs. Carry the generic name of any prescription medicines, in case a local pharmacist is unfamiliar with your overseas brand name. Pharmacies in cities take turns doing the night shift.

Police For emergencies,

call *℗* **112** or *℗* **113.** The *Carabinieri* (*℗* **112;** www. carabinieri.it) normally only concern themselves with

serious crimes, but point you in the right direction. The *Polizia* (*℗* **113;** www. poliziadistato.it), whose city headquarters is called the *questura,* is the place to go for help with lost and stolen property or petty crimes.

Safety Italy is a remark-

ably safe country. The worst threats you'll likely face are pickpockets who sometimes frequent touristy areas and public buses; keep your hands on your camera at all times and your valuables in an inside zip-pocket. Don't leave anything valuable in a rental car overnight, and leave nothing visible in it at any time. If you are robbed, you can fill out paperwork at the nearest police station (*questura*), but this is mostly for insurance purposes or to get a new passport issued— don't expect them to hunt down the perpetrator. In general, avoid public parks at night. Areas around rail stations are often unsavory, but rarely worse than that.

Senior Travel Seniors

and older people are treated with deference in

Bus ticket (from/to anywhere in the city)	1.50€
Double room at Capo d'Africa (very expensive)	155.00€–325.00€
Double room at Lancelot (moderate)	140.00€–200.00€
Double room at Mimosa (inexpensive)	89.00€–150.00€
Continental breakfast (cappuccino and croissant standing at a bar)	2.50€–4.00€
Dinner for one, with wine, at Glass (very expensive)	60.00€–150.00€
Dinner for one, with wine, at La Barrique (moderate)	30.00€
Dinner for one, with wine, at Li Rioni (inexpensive)	15.00€
Small gelato at Fatamorgana	2.50€–3.50€
Glass of wine at a bar	3.00€–8.00€
Coca-Cola (standing/sitting in a bar)	2.50€/5.00€
Cup of espresso (standing/sitting in a bar)	1.00€/2.50€
Admission to the Colosseum and Forum	12.00€/14.00€ online

Italy, but few specific programs exist. The one exception is at museums and sights, where those aged 60 or 65 and older will often pay a reduced admission. There are also special train passes and reductions on bus tickets (see "Getting Around," p. 814). As a senior in Italy, you're *un anziano,* or if you're a woman, *un'anziana,* "elderly"—it's a term of respect. Let people know you're one if you think a discount may be in order.

Smoking   Smoking has been eradicated from inside restaurants, bars, and most hotels, so smokers tend to take outside tables at bars and restaurants. If you're keen for an alfresco table, you are essentially choosing a seat in the smoking section; requesting that your neighbor not smoke may not be politely received.

Student Travelers   An **International Student Identity Card (ISIC)** qualifies students for savings on travel tickets, entrance fees, and more. The card is valid for 1 year. You can apply for the card online at **www. myIsic.com** or in person at **STA Travel** (www.statravel. com; *☎* **800/781-4040** in North America). If you're not a student but are aged 30 and under, you can get an **International Youth Travel Card (IYTC)** or an **International Teacher Identity Card (ITIC)** from the same agency, either of which entitles you to some discounts. Students will also find that many university cities offer ample student discounts and inexpensive youth hostels.

Taxes   No sales tax is added onto purchases in Italy, but a 22 percent value-added tax (in Italy: **IVA**) is automatically included in just about everything, except some foods and a few specific goods and services, where rates of 4 percent and 10 percent apply. Local transportation, hotels, and dining are among a group of goods taxed at 10 percent. For large purchases, non–E.U. residents can get IVA refunded. Several city governments have also introduced an **accommodation tax.** For example, in Florence, you will be charged 2€ per person per night for a 1-star hotel plus .80€–1€ per night per additional government-star rating of the hotel, up to a maximum of 7 nights. So, in a 3-star joint, the tax is 4€ per person per night. Children 11 and under are exempt. Venice, Rome, and many other popular localities also levy their own taxes. This tax is not usually included in a published room rate.

Tipping

In **hotels,** service is usually included in your bill. In family-run operations, additional tips are unnecessary and sometimes considered rude. In fancier places with a hired staff, however, you may want to leave a .50€ daily tip for the maid and pay the bellhop or porter 1€ per bag. In **restaurants,** a 1€ to 3€ per person "cover charge" is automatically added to the bill, and in some tourist areas, especially Venice, another 10 percent to 15 percent is tacked on (except in the most unscrupulous of places, this will be noted on the menu somewhere; if unsure you should ask, è incluso il servizio?). It is not necessary to leave any extra money on the table, though it is not uncommon to leave up to 5€, especially for good service. Locals often leave nothing. At **bars and cafes,** you can leave something very small on the counter for the barman (maybe 1€ if you have had several drinks), although it is not expected; there is no need to leave anything extra if you sit at a table, as they are likely already charging you double or triple the price you'd have paid to stand at the bar. It is not necessary to tip **taxi** drivers, though it is common to round up the bill to the nearest euro or two.

Toilets

Aside from train stations, where they cost about .50€ to use, and gas/petrol stations, where they are free (with perhaps a basket seeking gratuities for the cleaners), public toilets are few and far between. In an emergency, standard procedure is to enter a cafe, make sure the bathroom is not *fuori servizio* (out of order), and then order a cup of coffee before bolting to the facilities. It is advisable to always make use of the facilities in a hotel, restaurant, or museum before a long walk around town. Public toilets—and often those in bars, too—can be dirty, with no seat or toilet paper. It's best to carry a pack of tissues with you, especially if you're traveling with children or teens who are easily grossed out.

Websites

Following are some of our favorite sites to help you plan your trip: **www.italia.it/en** is the official English-language tourism portal for visiting Italy; **www.arttrav.com** is excellent for cultural travel, exhibitions, and openings, especially in Florence and Tuscany; **www.summerin italy.com/traveltips/ transport-strikes-in-italy** provides updates on the latest rail, road, and airline strikes; **www.prezzi benzina.it** finds the cheapest fuel close to your accommodations or destination (they also have a smartphone app); **www. ansa.it** and www.thelocal.it supply you with Italian news in English; and naturally, **www.frommers.com/ destinations/Italy** offers more expert advice on the country.

Index

A

Abbazia di Monte Oliveto
Maggiore, 261
Abbazia di Sant'Antimo, 261–262
Abbey of San Galgano, 250
Accessibility, 821–822
Accommodations. *See also*
Accommodations index
most charming, 5
tipping, 826
websites for discounts, 813
Acquario di Genova, 6, 553
Acquatica waterpark, 482
Acropoli pass, 234
Active adventures
best of, 11–12
in Cogne, 541
on Lake Garda, 515
Mont Blanc, 542
in Turin, 531–532
Addresses
in Florence, 172
in Venice, 400
Aeolian Islands, 766
Agrigento, 793–796
Ai Tre Scalini, 160
Air travel
to Bologna, 347–348
to Florence, 169
to Genoa, 549–550
to Italy, 812
in Italy, 820
to Milan, 465–466
to Naples, 586
to Palermo, 741–742
to Perugia, 308
to Rome, 63–64
to Siracusa, 776
to Taormina, 767
to Venice, 394–397
to west coast of Sicily, 796
Al Prosecco, 453
Alabaster, 285
Albergheria (Palermo), 745
Alberobello, 718–722
Alexanderplatz Jazz Club, 158
Amalfi, 640, 661–669
accommodations, 665–666
arrival information, 661–662
Atrani, 668–669
attractions, 663–665
restaurants, 667–668
visitor information, 662
Amalfi Coast, 635–702
Amalfi, 661–669
Amalfi Drive, 659–661
best in 2 weeks itinerary, 45
Capri, 679–695
choosing towns, 640
Ischia, 695–702
memorable experiences, 636
Positano, 652–659
Ravello, 669–676
ruins of Paestum, 676–678
sailing along, 643
Sorrento, 638–652

Amalfi Drive, 659–661
Anacapri, 687–689
Ancient Rome, 66–67
accommodations, 129–131
attractions, 88–100
restaurants, 141–142
Ancient ruins itinerary, 57–60
Anfiteatro Flavio, 617
Aosta, 540–541
Apartment rentals. *See* self-
catering apartments
Arch of Constantine, 88
Archaeological Area of
Paestum, 677–678
Architectural landmarks, best
of, 10
Archivio di Stato, 237
Area Archeologico Segesta,
765–767
Area codes, 820–821
Arena di Verona Opera
Festival, 38
Arezzo, 264–269
Arona, 509
Arsenale della Repubblica, 663
Artisans, Florence, 222–223
Assisi, 321–328
accommodations, 326–327
arrival information, 321–322
attractions, 322–326
restaurants, 327–328
visitor information, 322
Asti, 533–536
Atelier Segalin di Daniela
Ghezzo, 450
ATMs, 468, 821
Atrani, 668–669
Attractions
Agrigento, 794–795
Alberobello, 719–720
Amalfi, 663–665
Aosta, 540–541
Arezzo, 265–267
Assisi, 322–326
Asti, 534–536
Atrani, 668–669
Bologna, 350–358
Camogli, 565–566
Campo Flegrei (The Phlegraean
Fields), 616–621
Capri, 682–690
Cefalù, 763–765
Chianti region, 247–249
Cinque Terre, 575–579
Città Alta, 494
Città Bassa, 492
Como, 502–503
Cortona, 270–272
Erice, 799–801
Ferrara, 370–373
Florence, 176–206
Gallipoli, 737
Genoa, 553–556
Gubbio, 317–318
Ischia, 696–701
Lake Como, 503–504

Lake Garda, 513–514
Lake Maggiore, 509–510
Lecce, 730–732
Lucca, 288–291
Mantua, 496–499
Marsala, 804–806
Matera, 708–710
Milan, 469–483
Modena, 367–368
Monreale, 761–763
Montalcino, 259–262
Montepulciano, 252–254
Naples, 591–604
Noto, 786–787
Orvieto, 338–341
Ostia Antica, 162–163
Otranto, 735–736
Padua, 455–456
Palermo, 747–754
Parma, 386–388
Perugia, 308–312
Piazza Armerina, 792–793
Pienza, 256–258
Pisa, 297–301
Portofino, 570–571
Positano, 653–655
Ragusa, 789
Ravello, 670–672
Ravenna, 378–382
Rome, 72–126
ruins of Paestum, 677–678
San Gimignano, 276–278
San Remo, 562
Santa Margherita Ligure, 568
Segesta, 765–767
Selinunte, 806–808
Siena, 235–241
Siracusa, 777–782
Sorrento, 639–643
Sorrento Peninsula, 649–651
Spello, 328–329
Spoleto, 332–334
Stresa & Isole Borromee, 508–509
Taormina, 768–770
Tivoli & the Villas, 164–166
Trani, 714–717
Trapani, 797–799
Treviso, 460–462
Turin, 519–527
Urbino, 319–320
Venice, 405–429
Verona, 457–460
Vesuvius, 622–624
Volterra, 282–284
west coast of Sicily, 801–803
Auditorium Niemeyer, 670
Auditorium–Parco della Musica,
158–159
Authentic experiences, best of,
3–4
Autodromo Nazionale
Monza, 483

B

Bàcari, 441
Bacaro di Fiore, 442

838

PHOTO CREDITS